THE EAGER DEAD

THE EAGER DEAD

A Study in Haunting

Archie E. Roy

Book Guild Publishing
Sussex, England

First published in Great Britain in 2008 by
The Book Guild Ltd
Pavilion View
19 New Road
BN1 1UF

Typesetting in Times by
Keyboard Services, Luton, Bedfordshire

Printed and bound in Great Britain by
Athenaeum Press Ltd, Gateshead

A catalogue record for this book is available from
The British Library

ISBN 978 1 84624 183 3

To Jean, Countess of Balfour,
who knew the people and kept the records,
this book is respectfully and gratefully dedicated.

Where are the dead – those who have loved us and whom we have loved; and those to whom we have done some irreparable injury? Are they gone from us for ever, or do they return?

Lord Halifax's *Ghost Book*

Contents

Foreword

Even before he had written a word, the author of this book could be in no doubt that he was going to produce a classic of paranormal literature. For he was aware that he was about to complete one of the most fascinating unfinished stories in the history of psychical research: that of the Cross Correspondences.

As everyone in the field knows, these were a series of scripts, apparently authored by several deceased founders of the Society for Psychical Research, including Frederic Myers, Edmund Gurney and Professor Henry Sidgwick, whose purpose was to provide irrefutable evidence of the reality of life after death.

Their purpose is neatly summarised by G.N.M. Tyrrell in *The Personality of Man*: 'These communicators gave clearly and candidly the reason for the cross-correspondences which they claimed to be producing. They said that they were doing it because a single theme distributed between various automatists [i.e. automatic script writers], none of whom knew what the others were writing, would prove that a single independent mind ... was at the back of the whole phenomenon.' It might be compared to distributing parts of a jigsaw puzzle among a group of strangers, whose connection would only become obvious when they all got together round a table.

The final result of this attempt was stunningly impressive, but also highly complicated and relentlessly highbrow. For example, one set of messages referred to tombs of two members of the Medici family in the church of San Lorenzo, in Florence, which Myers knew well, and to the Michelangelo sculptures on them. There are obscure bits of Medici family history, and the messages included bits in Greek, Latin and Italian. As a proof of life after death it is quite overwhelming, but – it must be admitted – far too elaborate to convince anybody who does not have time to study the thousands of pages that constitute the Cross Correspondences. So the work that was intended to convince the human race of the reality of life after death now gathers dust on library shelves

Hence, I would argue, the immense importance of this book *The Eager Dead*. Professor Archie Roy has set out to tell his extraordinary story in a style that should reach the widest possible audience. For it not only reveals that a great love story lies behind the Cross Correspondences, but that it is also a mystery story that invites endless speculation.

The love story I am referring to is that of a remarkable woman called Winifred Coombe-Tennant. When she died in 1956, her *Times* obituary listed her many achievements: work in the suffrage movement, chairman of the War Pensions Commission, work as a JP and in prisons, delegate to the League of Nations. What it did not mention was that she was also 'Mrs Willett', one of the most gifted spirit mediums of the twentieth century, and a central figure in the story of the Cross Correspondences. This was all kept secret until her Willett identity was finally revealed in the *Journal of the Society for Psychical Research*. What was also kept secret, and is now revealed for the first time, is a story that would have created an unprecedented scandal: a story of an adultery not only condoned by the 'spirits' behind the Cross Correspondences, but apparently arranged by them with the highest possible motives.

Winifred was born in 1874, and at the age of 21 married a country landowner who was 43. It seems doubtful that she loved him. Her first child Christopher was born two years later, in 1897, and a daughter, Daphne, in 1907. Tragically, Daphne died when she was less than 18 months old, and her mother was so shattered that she became for a long period unsocial and introspective. But it also had the effect of renewing her interest in spiritualism, which she had allowed to lapse during her years as a busy housewife, and in the Society for Psychical Research.

This had been formed in 1882 by, among others, her brother-in-law Frederic Myers, and since his death the Society had been investigating the series of automatic writings that purported to come from the founders of the SPR, notably from Myers, who had died in 1901. One of the ladies who were engaged in automatic writing was Mrs Verrall, who lectured on classics at Newnham, and was married to the Cambridge scholar A.W. Verrall. Winifred Coombe-

Tennant wrote to her, describing her desolation at her daughter's death, and was delighted to receive from Mrs Verrall the assurance that Daphne was not lost forever, and that moreover, her death had been part of a scheme, since it was referred to in the Cross Correspondences even before her birth. Never one to sit on the sidelines, Winifred was soon training herself to do automatic writing. In due course, she would become one of the greatest mediums of the century.

Understandably, though, she preferred to keep it a secret, and became known thereafter as Mrs Willett.

Now comes the truly extraordinary part. As she became more involved in mediumship, the 'communicators' made it known that they had in mind an interesting plan that involved Winifred. This was nothing less than that she should bear a child, a kind of 'designer baby', whose paternity should be, in effect, divided among the Cross Correspondence group, in particular Edmund Gurney, a distinguished founder member of the SPR, who had died tragically (probably of asthma) in 1888 at the age of 41. Through his communications, Gurney had already told her that he loved her.

Her reaction was at first negative, but it seems the idea slowly grew upon her. After all, she was only in her mid-thirties. But how was it to be brought about? By some kind of virgin birth?

Apparently not. It seemed the spirits had another plan. The actual father would be Gerald Balfour, the younger brother of the politician Arthur J. Balfour, an enthusiastic student of psychical research, whose sister had been married to Professor Henry Sidgwick. And so – to cut short a story whose details can be found in this volume – Winifred and Gerald Balfour found they were passionately attracted to one another, and became lovers. The result was the birth of a son Augustus, who was always known by his second name Henry. The plan was, it seems, for Henry to become some kind of Messiah, an instrument of the spirits behind the Cross-Correspondences, and who was destined to bring peace to the warring human race.

It was a bold and breathtaking scheme, an attempt by a group of spirits who could foresee the conflicts of the coming century, to bring a golden age. But it seems that even spirits are not omniscient, and the attempt would fail. Why it failed is one of the fascinating mysteries associated with this book. Archie Roy addresses it in the final section.

Obviously, many answers are possible, ranging from the sympathetic to the cynical. The cynical view would be that a remarkable man and woman, brought together by an extraordinary investigation, decided to have an affair, and so became the parents of a young man of considerable charm and intellect. Yet he never felt called upon to try and exert a major influence on his fellow man, and ended by becoming a Catholic priest, and virtually a monk.

A less cynical view would be that the spirits were aiming a little too high, and that, human nature being what it is, they failed to grasp that most human achievement involves conflict and self-doubt – not to mention that most difficult of all concepts, free-will. One of the participants in this story felt that Henry was a little too angelic and lacking in inner conflict. That is certainly my own impression.

Even after his mother's death, Henry still had an important role to play. In 1957, the year after her death, an Irish medium named Geraldine Cummins received a letter from W.H. Salter, Honorary Secretary of the SPR, telling her that a member who had lost his mother would like the opportunity to make contact. All she was told was that the man was called Major Henry Tennant. Five days later Miss Cummins received the first of many scripts. They were eventually published under the title *Swan on a Black Sea*, and its editor, Signe Toksvig, remarked that parts of the script had been cut out because it was 'too correct about private affairs to be published'. The major – who, oddly enough, was a sceptic about spiritualism – was totally convinced by it, as was Professor C.D. Broad, who wrote an introduction.

So, altogether, a deeply puzzling affair, whose embers will be stirred back into life by this panoramic and immensely readable book. For there can be no doubt that, whether one approaches it as a believer or not, Archie Roy has done a magnificent job.

Colin Wilson

Introduction

Great expectations. If Charles Dickens had not forestalled me with respect to the title of his book I would have been sorely tempted to use it. Nevertheless, although the relevance of that title will become abundantly clear, the title I finally did choose is decidedly more appropriate.

This is a true story. With one or two exceptions, all the people involved in it are real, their actions, and in many cases even their thoughts, fully documented. Yet at the time of writing this foreword, the number of living people who know all of the story, or even part of the story, can still be counted on the fingers of one hand. It is probable, moreover, that at any particular time in the past, even after most of the events embodied in the story had taken place, there has never been as many as a dozen people who have known the story in its main outline. Indeed for many decades all that a larger number of people knew was that there was some secret, the exact nature of which could not be pinned down. It slipped away on any attempt at closer scrutiny, in a sense recalling St Augustine's complaint about the nature of time: 'When I don't think about it I understand it very well but when I do think about it I find I don't understand it at all.' In fact, ignorance of some key elements of identity, dates and events made it quite impossible for them to have gone beyond more than a vague suspicion that there was something odd behind the scenes. Only as late as 1960 did a part of the mystery become clear and then little more than a hint. The major part of the story still remained 'classified'.

Yet many of the people involved in the unfolding events of this remarkable story were prominent men and women. They included a British Prime Minister, Arthur James Balfour, 1st Earl of Balfour, later Foreign Secretary, involved in the creation of the post-First World War League of Nations, creator of the Balfour Declaration that promised a Near East home for the Jewish people. His brother Gerald William Balfour, the statesman and philosopher and 2nd Earl, also played a major part in the story, as did their sister Eleanor Mildred Balfour, mathematician and one-time Principal of Newnham College, University of Cambridge. She became the wife of Professor Henry Sidgwick, who held the chair of Moral Philosophy in Cambridge University. He, too, was a major player.

Winifred Coombe-Tennant of Cadoxton Lodge, Wales, was likewise deeply involved. Appointed by the British Government to be first woman delegate to the League of Nations, later in her life a magistrate, a prison visitor, a member of the Eisteddfod, highly respected in the arts in Wales, broadcaster for the BBC, throughout her long life she successfully hid her other identity from the world behind her prominent professional activities. Only a very small band of people who also knew that identity, and resolutely kept the secret, could read the long obituary that appeared on September 1, 1956 in *The Times* after her death, and note with satisfaction that what it did not include showed that they had been successful.

One of her sons, Major Augustus Henry Coombe-Tennant, MC, Croix de Guerre, was paradoxically a key player but for a good part of his life did not know it, at best holding at times suspicions little stronger than those held by some of the curious on the fringes of the secret. A brilliant Cambridge University graduate, a Second World War hero, a post-war MI6 secret agent, and later a Benedictine monk and parish priest, only in the last part of his life did he learn the secret, although it is still debatable if he ever knew it in its entirety. In a real sense this story is in large part the story of Henry Coombe-Tennant, his life and the hopes a number of the key players held for him.

There were other important participants in the inner circle but we will meet them later.

The chain of events in the story is stretched over many years, over a century at least, from 1875 to 1989. Many of the events in the story, known to a few of the public, would have remained kaleidoscopic and essentially short of meaning to even a moderately knowledgeable person who had no access to the Kremer Archive. Careful study of the documents it contains – letters, papers, memoranda, hitherto kept from the public domain, reveals the full story. They were collected by Jean, Countess of Balfour, daughter-in-law of Gerald, 2nd Earl of Balfour. She had been made the official custodian of the secret in 1930 by those in the know and had devoted a large part of her life to the collection of any relevant material passing among the players. A woman of extreme discretion, dedication, high intelligence, sensitivity and perception, she had continued her task until her death in 1981. By that time all but two of the major players had passed on.

It was her daughter, Lady Alison Kremer, who contacted me and invited me to consider writing the story. In doing so, she gave me permission to make a preliminary study of the Kremer Archive. My first study of the archive convinced me that I *had* to accept Lady Kremer's invitation, though I was conscious of my fear that I would not be adequate to the task, which would be a long one involving a prodigious amount of additional research. In passing, it is worth noting that the author of *Ben Hur*, General Lew Wallace, said that it took him seven years to write his book, and research and investigation consumed most of the appropriated time. Nevertheless I accepted Lady Kremer's invitation principally because of my worry that the extraordinary story that the archive told might never see the light of day or that its contents might in some accident such as a fire be destroyed and forever lost. I also knew that it gave, on a number of levels, an important insight into the reasons that made a small number of highly intelligent and well-educated people devote a considerable part of their lives to a continuing study of the story and its promises, and continually sustained their hopes that these promises might be fulfilled in due course of time.

Many of the people involved in the story began their lives in the Victorian era. They were therefore educated and conditioned by the ethos of the times and experienced the unparalleled changes that took place throughout that age in the mapping of the Earth, the exploration of the heavens and above all, the inexorable advance of science and technology which seemed to many intelligent people to sweep away the certainties of orthodox religion, leaving human beings without any support in a cold and immense universe totally indifferent to their existence. From being the chosen though errant sons and daughters of God, certain, at the least, even when they transgressed, that He was aware of their existence and cared for them, each and every one, they were faced, particularly in the educated West, with the possibility that they simply belonged to that animal species that grew a big brain and had employed it to fabricate religious myths to be used as comfort blankets against the horrors of the darkness of an unpredictable environment and the deeper, final darkness of death. In the midst of the pervasive ever onwards, ever upwards optimism of the Victorian age, therefore, there were many who accepted the seemingly irrefutable and bleak teachings of science in astronomy, in geology, in Darwinism, anthropology and anatomy and who stoically embraced a materialist philosophy. The mind was the brain in action; the personality was the product of nature and nurture and likewise housed in the brain. Use science and technology to make the best of this life for yourself and your fellow humans for after you die there is nothing. You no longer exist. But there were others who rejected this philosophy of despair and, acknowledging the power of the scientific method, attempted to use it to seek a more hopeful outcome by a careful, patient, rational study of a second extraordinary product of the Victorian age. Some of them are players in this story and to understand their actions, it is necessary to begin with a short account of that formidable and foundation-shattering Victorian age.

There are still many of the older members of the present population who have at least a vague knowledge of that era, though in this philistine age of dumbing-down, even more people, in their lack of an adequate and systematic education in history, might be excused, in their ignorance, for confusing Victoria with the first Elizabeth and, if asked, hazard a guess that her major war was fought against Hitler. The recent ceremonies commemorating the events and sacrifices of the First and Second World Wars have highlighted this appalling lack of knowledge and misunderstanding, especially among the younger generation. As Simon Heffer put it, 'When one sees the level of knowledge of our past enjoyed by even semi-educated people in the nineteenth century, which enabled them to engage in the debate about the rights and wrongs of the Civil Wars, one appreciates the full extent of modern ignorance.' No doubt films, television programmes and books have given us glimpses, often hopelessly distorted, of a Victorian era that, although it is but little more than a century removed from us in time, is essentially as remote from us as the age of that first Elizabeth. For so quickly has our society been changed by two world wars, the juggernaut progress of science and technology, and an ever-available frothy, frenetic fairground of frivolous, intelligence-free TV, that our standards of living, our morals, our ability to acquire information from all parts of the world, our slavery to trivial pursuits, to fool's gold word-bites, to facile, faulty and superficial media pronouncements, and our vacuous idolisation of people famous for merely being famous, have turned the Victorians into incomprehensible strangers, almost into an alien society.

Most of our players were British. Since it is absolutely essential to understand the environment that nurtured their motivations and beliefs, we will concentrate mainly on the Victorian age in its homeland although its influence pervaded Europe and the United States. Even given its tragic imperfections, it was an age of such stupendous achievements that in studying it we can well begin to understand the rather inchoate call for a return to Victorian values that in recent years has been heard in the land.

Acknowledgements

A book of this nature inevitably goes through a number of successive drafts, the process being somewhat similar to changes in a species due to evolutionary factors. Hopefully it is not a process that leads to the extinction of the species! One of these factors is the effect on the author of the considered reactions and criticisms of those people he has persuaded to read a particular draft. I have been fortunate in the number of my friends and colleagues who have unstintingly helped me in this way and I am deeply indebted to them. Having read the draft or revised draft I gave them, they have by their written response or by their patience in discussing its shortcomings with me, undoubtedly helped me to produce a much improved version of the book.

Among those who read earlier drafts are Dr David Clarke and Dr Robin Green of the Department of Physics and Astronomy, Glasgow University, and Professor Bonnie A. Steves, Associate Dean of Research and Knowledge Transfer, of the School of Computing and Mathematical Sciences, Glasgow Caledonian University. Professor Bernard Carr, of the Physics and Astronomy Department of Queen Mary College, University of London (a past President of the Society for Psychical Research (SPR)), Ms Mary Rose Barrington, Mr David Rousseau and Mrs Julie Rousseau, members of Council of the SPR, have also significantly helped me by their opinions. I am also indebted to Ms Tricia J. Robertson, President of the Scottish Society for Psychical Research and Mr Nick Kyle, Vice-president of the SSPR for their help in this way. To Dr Lorn Macintyre I also tender my sincere thanks.

I am particularly indebted to my late friend and colleague Mr Montague Keen, an acknowledged authority on psychical research, who throughout the project from its inception in 1999 until his death early in 2004 took a deep interest in it, receiving successive chapters and subsequent variations on them from me. His perceptive comments and generous suggestions helped me immeasurably in producing better drafts. The table he produced assessing the accuracy of the Geraldine Cummins script data is but one instance of his skill and dedication in this difficult and complicated field.

My debt to Dr Alan Gauld, of the Department of Psychology, Nottingham University, and a former President of the Society for Psychical Research (SPR), is equally great. As well as being a leading authority on psychical research, he has also an unparalleled knowledge of the history of psychical research from before and after the creation of the SPR. He also knew personally a number of the major players in this story such as Henry and Alexander Coombe-Tennant, Professor C.D. Broad and W.H. Salter. Dr Gauld's generous and thoughtful study of a later version of the book resulted in him sending me a most valuable multi-page document containing many suggestions for improvement. Most of these I have been happy to incorporate.

It was Lady Alison Kremer who invited me to write a book based on the contents of what I have called the Kremer Archive, a collection of documents, letters, memoranda, manuscripts, photographs, etc. collected and safeguarded by her mother Jean, Countess of Balfour, from 1930 until her death in 1981. These documents, most of them hitherto unpublished, were the work of noted psychical researchers such as Gerald, 2nd Earl of Balfour, J.G. Piddington, Professor Sir Oliver Lodge, Mrs Sidgwick, Mrs Verrall, W.H. Salter and Alice Johnson. Throughout the project from its inception, when I accepted Lady Kremer's invitation, she has provided me with much helpful advice and encouragement. Discussions with her husband Tom have also been decidedly useful.

I am also very grateful for the generous help given to me by Dom Philip Jebb, the archivist of Downside Abbey, when I visited the abbey in June 2004 to obtain certain information about Henry Coombe-Tennant's life there. Documents he gave me copies of and his reminiscences of Henry were invaluable.

My deep thanks also go to Colin Wilson who read the final version of the book and generously decided that it showed merit and who provided the foreword.

In a book of this nature, where references to activities and events, and reports of these, are often dated to the last half of the nineteenth century, as well as to many other additional more recent publications are concerned, it has become apparent to me that where I have wished to take extracts from published works I have found it necessary in many cases to embark on something like a reverse exercise in genealogy. Unlike the more common procedure, where one works from the present generation backwards, in the present exercise one has to begin at the earliest generation of publisher and try to establish their 'family tree' to the present date – if they in any way still exist for sadly mortality can strike author and/or publisher without leaving any subsequent generation to make contact with. Two books, for example, that were invaluable in providing information concerning Henry Coombe-Tennant's Second World War record and the record of the Welsh Guards in that war, *Return Journey* by Major A.S.B. Arkwright and *Welsh Guards at War* by Major L.F. Ellis, seem to fall into that category of mortality for I was unable despite a number of enquiries to make contact with author or publisher. Consulting *The Writer's Handbook* has been of decided value in following out the family trees of most of the publishers from whose works I wished to make extracts and I thank those from whom I have received permission to make these extracts.

In particular, I would like to thank the Society for Psychical Research for permission to take a not inconsiderable number of extracts from the society's *Proceedings* and *Journal*.

Likewise I am grateful to Mr Tony Ortzen of Psychic Press for permission to take numerous extracts from one of my previous books on the paranormal, *The Archives of the Mind*.

I am deeply indebted to the Mary Evans Picture Library for providing the pictures within the text of the book.

My sincere thanks likewise go to the Book Guild team for their skill in making the production stages of the book such a painless process.

Nevertheless, in spite of all the help I have been given, nothing in this life being perfect, there may well still be 'sins of omission and commission' in the text. For these I am wholly responsible.

The Shears of Atropos

According to mythology, the destiny of every human being is determined by the three Fates, the daughters of Zeus and Themis. Clotho spins the thread of life, Lachesis measures its length, and Atropos cuts it when the span of life is ended.

Buckingham Palace, 1857

In the quiet room the plump matronly woman dipped the nib of her pen into the inkwell, thought for a moment and wrote: 'he told us some certainly extraordinary things.'

She paused and recalled her beloved Albert's face as they had sat listening to what the Emperor and his Empress had revealed to them. If what Napoleon and Eugénie had told them was true – and there was no reason to doubt their words – then Mr Home was undoubtedly a most remarkable man and surely worthy of serious study. Albert was also impressed, she thought. She would question him further about his reactions; she valued his keen interest in all things scientific and all innovative matters of technology. Indeed after the prominent part he had played in creating the Great Exhibition in 1851, no one now could doubt his intellect and concern for the country he had adopted. And now he was her Consort.

And we must try it again for ourselves, she resolved. A smile touched her lips. Dear Albert. In her mind she recalled so many incidents where Albert, so much more serious than she was, would be shocked by her opinions or actions and solemnly reprove her in his sober Saxe-Coburg-Gotha manner. But it works both ways.

1

She had on occasion rebuked him for his harshness to others, pointing out to him that if they had not been well brought up and taken care of, they might also have gone astray.

In the years to come during her long reign, she would retain an ever-increasing interest in the subject they had talked about. Even in those dark, despairing, immediate years of her widowhood when life and every vestige of happiness seemed ended, those years when she withdrew from society to Osborne House and some of her subjects believed that she was dead, or mad, her mind returned again and again to the possibility that the dead still walked among the living.

The Court learned to live with the outward expressions of, some said, her love of death. As the years passed, the small, ever-stouter figure, dressed by day in funereal black widow's weeds, still at night slept with the dead Albert's nightshirt in her bed, still frequently prayed at his mausoleum at Frogmore, still kept, on the headboard of every bed she slept in, the photograph of Albert on his deathbed. When she too departed this life in the arms of her grandson Willy, the German Kaiser, her extended family gathered round her, that photograph still hung on her deathbed.

Advisers and politicians learned to live with her disturbing habit of gazing at Albert's portrait and asking his advice before coming to a decision regarding important affairs of state. Lord Clarendon wrote: 'She acts as if he was in the next room, indeed it is difficult not to think that he is so for everything is set out on his table, the blotting book open, pen upon it, even his watch going.'

In the John Brown years, some even believed that the real reason for the extraordinary influence of the brusque, often drunken, imperious Scottish Highland servant was not the earthy one assumed by many of those who surreptitiously referred to her as 'Mrs Brown' but that she believed he was her contact to Albert.

In the first years of her reign as a teenager queen, Lord Melbourne, her father-figure prime minister, had often entertained her with his ghost stories. Gladstone, later on, interested her greatly with his accounts of the mediums, genuine and fraudulent, he had investigated. She knew of the investigations into the genuineness of Daniel Dunglas Home carried out by the eminent scientist William Crookes, who later received a knighthood from her for his services to science.

But now, on this evening in 1857, still early in her long reign, Victoria felt that something strange had been introduced into the busy happy circle of her home life with her children and the husband who gave her 'such feelings of heavenly love and happiness she could never have hoped to have felt when she came to the throne.'

Victoria, with a sigh of content, dipped her pen once more into the inkwell and continued her journal entry.

Hagley Hall, Stourbridge, March 21st, 1875

The young woman, in her delirium, drifted in and out of consciousness and in and out of time. After three weeks of typhus fever, which even her youth and ardent desire to live could not throw off, the sudden collapse now had finally destroyed any hope in those who nursed her that she would live. Her sister Lavinia, sitting by her bedside in the shaded room, watched over a travesty of the vibrant attractive woman May had been, her features and body now ravaged by the disease. Even her glorious dark hair had been cut off in a futile effort to relieve the pain in her head. There seemed nothing left now of the abundant love and sympathy and keen interest in life she had shown that had made her so attractive to all those who met her.

In one of these delirious outbursts May was obviously at the pre-Christmas Ball at the Gladstones' house at Hawarden where she first met Arthur. But now the fevered brain telescoped that first meeting with others into a confused collage of memories. 'Oh, he does interest me more and more ... I do wish he had a little more backbone – perhaps it will come with age... He has so many good qualities but also such peculiarity... Oh to see him in a ballroom is a sight in itself...!' The stubbled head moved and the ghost of a smile, tender, momentary, appeared.

Now, Lavinia thought bleakly, she's in the Long Room at 4 Carlton Gardens. She thinks it's one of our musical evenings. She recalled how May, a gifted pianist, delighted in accompanying those who sang Handel's oratorio songs or lighter pieces. How happy she was when Arthur Balfour was there and participated.

The dying girl's voice struggled on as if it alone was hanging on to life. 'I love this exhibition ... the people, the crowds, the pictures, even the worst of them... But I love everything now for I saw him at Latimer... I know – I know – his feelings towards me.' A look of bewilderment on the ravaged face. 'But still he does not speak.'

Her sister remembered the exhibition of Old Masters they had seen at Burlington House just a few weeks before. She remembered May's happy face, remembered her own sudden irritation at Arthur's hesitancy. It's so abundantly clear his whole heart is May's. And when he does finally get around to proposing, I know she'll return his love. For they really are meant for each other. But now...? Her sister's fragmentary words echoed her thoughts and she knew with utter and bitter certainty that she was right. At the point of death, Mary Catherine Lyttelton was now fully aware of her love for Arthur and also knew what death was snatching away.

She died on the morning of Palm Sunday, March 21st, the beginning of spring. She was twenty-four years of age.

September, 1876

Extract from Frederic Myers' mother's letter to her son concerning the death of Annie Marshall.

I had been very anxious – we all had – at the fixed stony look in her face. She grew silent towards me, after having been quite frank and loving – & I could not with all my entreaties get her to speak of what was in her mind, after she had once said that she saw that she had been quite wrong in everything – in this last step for W. [Walter Marshall] (the certif.) & all together about religion – in rejecting Xtianity –. I hoped she wd. pass through this crisis – & get a fuller happier faith – she was continually praying and getting me to read T. a Kempis to her – We came together on Monday & she brightened up during the drive & talked more like herself. I left her at O. Ch. at 7 p.m. thinking the children would cheer her. Next morning she was missing – a shawl by the lake – and in deep water she was found.

Annie Marshall had left the house that September night in utter despair, completely shattered by the vortex of family and other troubles that had burdened and tormented her for years, troubles without end or solution that must have made her, in her utter nervous exhaustion, embrace the idea of death, the only possibility she could see of achieving peace. Her attempt to cut her throat with a pair of scissors failed to inflict a fatal wound. She finally achieved her goal by drowning herself in Ullswater.

The Aiguille Blanche, the Swiss Alps, Wednesday morning, July 19, 1882

A wonderful morning, a wonderfully satisfying climb. Time now to make the descent. Johan is ready. We're still roped together.

To climb in life. To have a goal: to know that things go well, to know that one is fit and prepared for the climb beckoning before you. It's a good analogy. Here on the mountain we are well equipped with suitable clothing, ice axes, ropes, boots and spikes, well prepared. And for fifteen years I've worked and studied to fit myself equally well for my chosen career... No: it chose me! Even as far back as the fishing boat at Dunbar with Burgoyne helping me to catch fish and crabs to dissect... Getting the microscope from Professor Huxley ... how difficult it is at first to learn to keep both eyes open and ignore input to the eye not looking into the microscope... And my accursed cough. How I struggled with it to keep it quiet in the lecture room. How many I must have irritated with it!

How satisfying it is to place each foot just right, to hear it crunch on the next step on the mountain. Slowly and steadily, that's the way. And to choose with equal care the next step on the path of research. The Naples Stazione Zoologica – that was good. I learned so much there... The fish – so many of them... That wonderful development of the dorsal fins of the Elasmobranch fishes. The gradual progress towards the origin of the vertebrate limbs – what a glorious vista of creation, and evolution! What a multitude of secrets still remain to be discovered.

How rhythmic one's breathing is on a climb. The steady drawing of the keen, cold air into the lungs, followed by the expulsion of the breath. How taut one's fists are ... like having a very tight pair of gloves on – the enhanced circulation in them, of course. Up here one is so conscious of the body's processes, especially when they go well, especially after that nasty bout of typhus.

The glacier below has quite a layer of snow on it. Like so many other things, one's eyesight seems so much better up here. Maybe it is. Even one's thinking. On such a climb as this – on holiday – I shouldn't be dwelling on work ... if you can call it work. I shouldn't even be thinking of Cambridge and embryology and the next steps to take. But everything is going so well and it is absolutely fascinating. It'll be so good when Gerald joins me and we can go climbing together again.

The exact circumstances of the accident remain unknown. When their bodies were found on the glacier some days later they were still roped together. Both the guide, Johan Petrus, and his companion, Francis Maitland Balfour, must have died instantly in the fall.

It is not known which of them slipped on the rocks and dragged the other down. Certainly it was a difficult climb they were on, attempting to scale the unconquered Aiguille Blanche of Mont Blanc, but Petrus was a professional guide and Francis Balfour was no novice. He excelled in mountain climbing. In 1880 and 1881 he and his elder brother Gerald had climbed near Zermatt and in the Chamonix district. When the bodies were examined it was found that the heel nail of one of Francis's boots had been completely torn off, but no firm deduction could be made from that.

Professor Francis Maitland Balfour's body was buried in the Balfour family burial ground at Whittingehame, not far from Edinburgh. There is a little wood of beech trees near his grave. He was just thirty years of age when he died but he had already been recognised as the foremost embryologist in Great Britain. In his short and brilliant career he had founded a school for the study of animal morphology in Cambridge University and was the first professor of his subject, the chair having been specially created for him. In taking that chair he had had to turn down invitations to succeed the brilliant biologists George Rolleston at Oxford and Sir Charles Wyville Thomson at Edinburgh. At the time of his death in the Alps he had held the Cambridge chair for only a few months.

In my dream I woke and found myself looking at the following scene. Three figures, which somehow I took to be three women of a goddess-y description, were grouped together, and on the ground in front of them were lying things on which there was writing.

I say 'things' because I don't know whether they were paper or engraved wood or stones – all I know is that there were many and each had writing on them. Suddenly a lot of figures appeared and began looking at these written-upon 'things' and to pick them up. One of the things was apparently being guarded by one of the three women (?) because I saw several figures try and pick it up but were not allowed to. The figures gradually picked up all the written-upon things except the one just mentioned. Then I suddenly saw a tall majestic figure coming toward it; it was glowing with rays of yellow light and all the figures (except the three women) bowed down before it and seemed to be doing homage to it.

It came along to where the one remaining 'thing' was and then picked it up and the woman (?) took it (the Majestic Figure) to the two others. The next thing I remember is that the Majestic Figure came towards me and took my face between its hands and gazed into my very soul and I into its soul. (I don't know whether it was a man or woman.)

I can't describe what follows because it was all 'feelings' and escapes definition. But I felt just worship, then amazement, then joy – and the figure seemed to feel no amazement but great tenderness, and it said these words: 'You have not chosen me but I have chosen you' and then the word 'Mother' is the next I remember. I knew it was speaking to me and I only remember that the last words *meant* … that when I next saw it it would be in the likeness of a human Babe and that what was written on the thing picked up was a destiny that it should come into the world through me. I felt the light becoming stronger and stronger and all became confused—

… And the next thing I remember was that I found myself walking along a country road and saw some people far away walking to me. When they got near I saw that they were men with a child in front. Suddenly I recognised Daphne. She was running and carrying a tall Madonna Lily in her hand – taller than herself.

7

The men were Frederic Myers, Edmund Gurney, and Henry Sidgwick... They were walking together. They looked at me earnestly and I found a letter in my hand which I opened. The paper was blue or bluey-grey and the ink white, there was one sentence only, printed in large letters. I only remember: 'If you believe... Vision ... cease motoring at once.'

The next thing I remember is that I found myself sitting up in bed feeling that I was smothering and could not breathe ... every *line* of Frederic Myers' face stamped on my memory... every vein and wrinkle... his hair whiter than I had remembered in life... the whole Dream came back to me, like a series of magic lantern pictures ... as if I were re-seeing it again ... the three Women ... the glowing radiant Figure ... the written upon 'things' ... the road... Daphne.

I got up and turned on my electric light but I felt so unnerved and *frightened* (very stupid of me but so it was) that I could not bear to be alone so I went along to my Mother's room and woke her. I got into her bed and told her about my dream ... and soon I felt better but very bewildered.

Winifred Coombe-Tennant

April 9, 1913

The day of Babe's birth was a very long and strenuous one. I was in touch with Edmund Gurney, who urged me not to try for definite communications but as he said to 'conserve your vitality'... The birth stretched over the time from 2.30 a.m. to 11.45 p.m. Owing to the size of the child and his position very high up with me, he got caught on some bones and made no progress in descending in spite of labour pains being present. The Doctor decided about 9.45 p.m. to use instruments. Just before I went off under chloroform I asked E.G. who was with me. He said that in addition to himself there were Henry Sidgwick, Frederic Myers and Daphne. I was *surprised* at bringing Daphne to such a scene. I then was given chloroform and went dead off.

What I now proceed to relate I did not know until several weeks later. When I was completely unconscious, the Doctor on further examination told the nurse that the child could not be born alive. He repeated this from time to time and the nurse was dreadfully upset and said the Doctor (who is really a friend as well as a medical attendant) was very anxious and upset too. However, contrary to expectation, it was possible to bring the child into the world and when the Doctor had carefully examined him and moved his limbs he called out to the Nurse that he was perfect. He did not cry at once from the result of being partly stupefied by chloroform...

When I came to at first I remembered nothing, nor where I was nor who I was. Then I got a sense of noise, then I heard squeals and wondered what they were, then I recognised it was a child crying, then I got nearer to understanding what happened, then I heard rattling of objects in a basin, then I heard a man's voice, then I suppose I moved a little, for the Doctor came over to me and said 'Yes, it is a boy.' I asked if he were perfectly all right. He said he was an exceptionally fine child. I said his name was Augustus.

I had to undergo about half an hour's intense pain to expel the afterbirth, and when that was over I was too exhausted for them to attempt to move me, so blankets were piled on me and I was left in peace, my Mother sitting some distance away, and both the Nurse, Doctor and Babe out of the room.

Then comes the following point, difficult to relate but Mrs Sidgwick wanted me to attempt to make some sort of record about it.

I can best describe by saying I had two brains working at the same time.

One brain only wanted to think about the release from pain, the joy of Babe's being there and safe and *a man child*, and also of 'them' and the excitement and wonder of it all. The other brain wanted to shut out the first brain, and Brain No. 2 was obsessed by one thought which simply overflowed and succeeded in drowning Brain No.1. The thought was 'the dark young man.'

To explain this I must go back to Mrs Sidgwick's house in Cambridge in – I believe it was on my first visit on January 19th, 1912, that I got a strong impression about a photograph hanging in her dining-room in a not very conspicuous position, and which I could only see by turning my head well round, as it was rather at the back of me as I sat at meals and I was only in the room at meal-times. It shows a rather dark, I think carbon or platenotype print of the head and shoulders of a young man. He looks down, one sees the outline of a nose and cheek, it is I believe a 3/4 face position. I somehow felt it was extraordinarily familiar to me and I got interested in it and felt rather oddly about it. I told Mrs Sidgwick that it was the only thing in the house I got any impression about. I had looked forward to being in the house because I felt I should like to be where Henry Sidgwick's things were, but I got no impression of any kind except from this photograph. I think it was on the next occasion of my being in the house (May 1912) that I talked to her again about the picture as we were having some meal, Mr Balfour being present. I said I felt rather uncomfortable about it, not being able to account for my feeling. I knew somehow the face – and feeling I might be getting rather nervy and silly. I was then told that it was possible there was something supernormal about the impression. I was also told that the man was dead.

I thought no more about it as far as I know until Brain No. 2 simply drowned me in the feeling of his presence, so close to me that if I had put out my hand I felt I should have touched him. I felt he was stationed there, beside me, and that no anxiety or worry was possible for me while he kept watch.

I tried to think about Edmund Gurney – but he seemed to have vanished. I 'saw' only the dark young man and it would not be accurate to imply that I even mentally saw a man and nothing more. The sense I had was of being in close touch with a mind and personality which somehow I knew and who knew me. It was very queer, but I was too weak then to try to analyse it, so I simply lay feeling as if I was taken charge of and needn't bother about anything.

The impression of his nearness lasted many hours, quite 12, towards the end of which I was able to get outside it at moments, enough to as it were to analyse what I was feeling. I came to the conclusion that it would be an interesting point from an S.P.R. point of view on the effect of anaesthetics on the brain. I had heard that people recovering from unconsciousness suffered from odd tricks of the brain, remembering some trivial event of long ago, or getting some *idée fixé* of a quite paltry and unreasonable description. I never attached any meaning to it (when I say I, I mean when my 2 Brains had as it were come together) until I was told that the experience might not be so totally idiotic as I had imagined by Mr Balfour or Mrs Sidgwick (I forget which) at Fishers Hill on June 13 when I spoke of it to them. I told Mrs Sidgwick

10

not to tell me anything about my dark young man, as I wanted to keep him as I knew him with me in such a crisis of my life and did not want my impression blurred by being told anything about him. I felt that nothing anybody could tell me would add to my complete apprehension of a nature and personality, though I do not know who he is, when he lived or when he died, nor did I speak to him, nor did he speak to me.

(signed) Daphne's Mother

Fishers Hill, Woking, March, 1930

On the evening of the 10 March, 1930, I was sitting with E.M.S.* in A.J.B.'s† bedroom, while the nurse was playing the records of Handel's *Messiah* on the gramophone just outside the door.

A.J.B. had been a little better the last two days and was, I felt, when I glanced at his attentive face, deeply contented and absorbed in listening to the music he loved with his whole heart. The nurse, having fixed in the records, had gone downstairs.

I had, at first, simply an odd sort of feeling of expectancy, as though anything might happen, and presently I became aware with a sensation of a mighty rushing wind (which was entirely subjective, as nothing around me was even stirred), that the room was full of a radiant, dazzling light. This I felt rather than saw, as a blind person might do, and I started trembling. Now it seemed to me that there were people there too; they had no concern with me, they were invisible; but I knew that they were clustered about A.J.B.'s bed, and that their whole attention was concentrated on him. They seemed to me to be most terribly eager, and very loving and strong; and I recollect feeling a good deal of apprehension because I felt they were there for some purpose, though I did not know what it could be.

I could not stop the trembling, so I was wondering if I ought to go out of the room into the passage for a little while, when it seemed to me that something like a voice within me said, 'You are not to go away,' and I looked at E.M.S. sitting in the armchair to see if she was aware of anything unusual, but she did not appear

---

*E.M.S. = Eleanor Mildred Sidgwick.

† A.J.B. = Arthur James Balfour.

11

to be. The music came to the passage where the words occur: 'And in my flesh shall I see God.' At that moment my eyes were *compelled* to look at A.J.B. His face, transfigured with satisfaction and beauty, seemed to express all the glorious vision which both music and words conveyed; and I stared, fully expecting him to die at that moment, and to pass straight into the Heaven that awaited him on all sides. But his face changed, and then he was shaken with the seizure that marked the last phase of his illness, and I was filled with terror and distress. Perhaps my shock was the greater for having just been upon such spiritual heights; and the extraordinary thing was that I was vividly aware that the feeling in the room had *not* changed, that the radiant joy and light still thrilled around him, and that the agonising spectacle of the poor body's affliction caused no dismay to those unseen ones who watched, but that *it was what they had wanted* to happen. That was what seemed to me so incredible as I fled for the Nurse; and as I ran immediately afterwards to telephone for the Doctor, I was saying over and over to myself, '*It* was *intended* – *it* was *intended.*'

The idea seemed positively to be burnt into my mind: I had the strange sensation of being two persons, one still lingering in A.J.B.'s room aghast at the callousness of those beings who had appeared so loving, the other doing what was required in the urgency of the moment. Everyone was afterwards so surprised at my promptness: I could hardly say, which was the case, that I had been in a sense prepared! But finally when I returned to normality I found myself with the profound conviction that all was well.

Thinking it over afterwards I began to realise that though to my bodily view it was terrible, to those who see the spirit it may have been simply a fierce effort to cast off the body and set free a soul already with them; and since a merciful unconsciousness accompanies the onset of a stroke we do not know, and never will know, into what peace and joy his soul may have receded in that little space. But the physical constitution was too strong to be thus easily thrown aside, and then he was found to have lost the power of speech, a deprivation of human intercourse which must have been to him a great sadness. During the next ten days he gradually weakened, and died on the morning of the 19 March, 1930.

Jean Balfour

Dear Henry,

I do not expect the occasion will ever arise when you will need to know, and that I shall ever tell you, the things which I now write you: these things which intimately concern you fill my mind and need utterance really for the sake of my own peace.

You first came to Whittingehame on 1st September 1930, for a week... Your mother brought you... There were two objects in this visit: one was that Ral and I should meet you, and you meet us: and the other was that 'script' might be obtained through your mother, while she was staying here... This was a secret from most people including yourself, for at this time you did not know that your mother was a sensitive.

Now you must know that ever since I entered this House, I have been aware of what a very extraordinary house it is: I mean that it is full of invisible people, and has an inner life of its own... When AJB was ill, I got to know a certain atmosphere in his room at Fishers Hill, where I distinguished a group of radiant powerful beings. When we entered Whittingehame to live there, I recognised that same feeling again, and now he is among them. I know who most of them are, but there are many more who press around, and have no part in the family history. They belong to the inner life of the House, and move about, watching us, with invisible feet. My impression is that there are great numbers of these mysterious dead, and that this house is like a window through which they strain gratefully, and wait their chance. What it all means I can't imagine: but I am not a visionary, nor unbalanced; I just know the House has another house within its walls which is full of the dead, who simply wait, and watch the world from here.

Well, before you and your mother came here, it seemed to me that the inner life of the House was stirred: it seemed to be gathered together as if excited. I was excited too: we both fully expected that your mother would be the means of expression for all sorts of psychic phenomena. Then you can imagine my astonishment, and my intense disappointment, when, upon her arrival, the unseen people of the House withdrew, and there seemed to be no point of contact. It was the most extraordinary thing: not even Nunkie did I once feel, and the whole house was empty and ordinary to the last degree. It was a shock to me to realise how conscious I had been of the life of the dead, now that it had receded; I thought it might be my own imagination because I did not like your mother, but my own disappointment was really too genuine for that. What was interesting was that she felt the same sense of barren-ness, and knew herself that there was nothing here which it was in her power to tap... She also implied that *we* had already changed the atmosphere of the House from what it was in AJB's days: which amused me, because my own impressions are that AJB comes where *we* are and that the unseen people press round about our life with eagerness, and I could no more guess why they had withdrawn than she could. The thought did cross my mind, however, that perhaps it was all done on purpose, and that they have finished with her and that they await another. And that brings me on to another very extraordinary thing, which is you yourself.

From the moment Ral and I set eyes on you we loved you: we just knew that you were *one of us*, and that we should always be friends with you and always love you. It wasn't only that you were one of our own generation: it was that we both felt that *you belonged here*, and that the House wanted you. For the dead loved *you* when you were with us, going upstairs, on the Boat at sea, anywhere in the House, there were the eager dead watching – oh, it was too extraordinary the feeling it gave one! But when your mother joined us they retired. Once, when you came into the study to ask me for a book..., they crowded in from every side, so close that I could hardly bear it. I almost wished that you would go away! And you looked up with a very slightly puzzled look, and afterwards I wondered what had been in your mind. For the atmosphere was charged to breaking point and I trembled all over when you'd gone. Ral came in, and said to me: 'I can't think why I like Henry so much, for I used to hate him as a child and now I've absolutely fallen for him.' I said: 'The dead are frightfully pleased with him: I think he excites them somehow.'

Jean Balfour

Oflag VIB, Germany, August, 1942

In the POW camp the escape committee agreed that Tennant would join Arkwright and Fuller as a third man in their escape team. The original choice was now too ill with rheumatism to take part. It

14

had been argued that the two man team probably stood a better chance of success even with a last minute substitute with three in the escape team than only two.

In the hut, Captain Augustus Henry Coombe-Tennant of the Welsh Guards was playing the old but still serviceable piano. As usual there was a number of POWs forming an inpromptu glee club singing choruses and songs everyone knew by heart, so often had they heard them. Occasionally they would fall silent as Tennant broke into a jazz medley. He had enormous talent, an excellent memory and possessed an extensive repertoire of all the pre- and early wartime jazz. It had been a real stroke of luck finding that the Oflag had a piano. Often he would give a concert lasting two hours, with no repetitions, containing all kinds of music, classical and lightweight, lifting the minds of his fellow prisoners from the spartan drabness of their surroundings and uncertainty of their future.

During his captivity he had entertained his fellow prisoners in this way so often that, like many pianists and actors, he could think quite clearly about other things while he was performing. And tonight he had much to think about. The prospect of a sudden sharp change in the controlled life he had been leading for the past two years reminded him of Dr Johnston's famous dictum: 'the prospect of a man being hanged in the morning wonderfully concentrates his thoughts', or something like that. Breaking out with the other two men in a hazardous enterprise with no certainty of success had certainly stirred up all manner of thoughts. He wondered if he might, after two years shut away from the world, have become conditioned to camp-life so strongly that it would be a tremendous effort to even leave the camp. Still, others had done it. He tried to dismiss the thought of how small the percentage of those who had attempted to escape had actually succeeded.

He found his mind turning to the debacle in Holland and then France in 1940, the effortless – even contemptuous – way the Germans had swept back the Belgians, Dutch, French and British forces, splitting them with their 'sickle-cut' plan. My God, he thought, we hadn't the foggiest idea then how to fight them or how fast their blitzkrieg would roll us up. The Dutch had surrendered five days after the offensive began on May 10th. By May 18th, the Belgian Army had capitulated; by May 20–21, the German advance of 150 miles had brought it to the Channel coast. By May

26th, the British War Office was frantically organising the evacuation of the British Expeditionary Force. There had followed the Dunkirk miracle when about 340,000 British and French were carried to safety by the Navy and an armada of small boats.

Into his mind flashed the contrast to that masterful blitzkrieg of his first wartime visit to Holland. It was the morning of May 10th, a Friday when he was ordered to proceed to Tunbridge Wells. The Irish and Welsh Guards had been on twelve hours notice to move. They had been training at Oldean Camp, Camberley but because it was the Whitsun weekend about two-thirds of the officers had been absent on leave. He remembered that the small sub-post office at Oldean had been overwhelmed with the task of dispatching telegrams recalling them. When he reached Tunbridge Wells he found that the Irish Guards had been given their orders to go abroad at once. To make up the Battalion to its proper complement they had drawn on some of the Welsh Guards. He had been among the chosen.

They left that evening on a special train and were carried across the Channel by two Channel steamers painted grey, arriving at the Hook of Holland early on Monday morning. They were landed on the beach with their equipment and expected to be met by Dutch mechanised transport, which was to have taken them up to the Hague where their function was to assist the Government to organise the campaign. They were also supposed to resist and round up the fifth columnists who were there in strength. When they arrived they found no transport and decided to dig in on the beach.

The morning was spent disposing the Battalion, fixing Headquarters, digging in and arranging for Company Headquarters. He had been Second in Command. He remembered the assistance given to him by some Dutchmen, some in the uniforms of the Dutch Army, to help him decide on the locations of the various headquarters. They were finally fixed in some coastguards' cottages which at least had strong concrete sides.

It was not until eleven a.m. that the first German reconnaissance aircraft appeared. German bombers arrived about two p.m. He watched them fly over the harbour where they scored a direct hit on a destroyer which was in dock. The bomb exploded in the engine room but the ship, which gave off enormous clouds of black smoke, did not sink. Soon afterwards a number of 500 lbs. bombs were dropped on the Battalion. One hit Battalion Headquarters.

Another fell near men in a trench causing a few casualties. Henry formed the idea that the tactics adopted by the aircraft suggested that the Germans had an exact knowledge of the disposition of the British force. He had to accept that those Dutchmen who had assisted him in making the decisions he took must either have been fifth columnists themselves or had been in touch with enemy agents.

Soon after the raid a soldier arrived and told Henry that there was a horse in a field near the beach which appeared to be unable to get up. Henry went up to the place and found that the horse had broken its leg. He was preparing to shoot the animal when a Dutchman arrived in a great state of excitement. He implored Henry not to kill the animal, for he had arranged for a slaughterer to come and kill the horse. Henry asked if it was certain that the slaughterer would come and if so how long he would be. The Dutchman replied that he expected the slaughterer in an hour and that he hoped he would come. Eventually Henry and the Dutchman walked up to the Hook to see the slaughterer. Henry saw that the town had suffered heavily from aerial bombing. A number of houses had been destroyed and there were several people on stretchers in the streets, which were carpetted with broken glass. They eventually saw the slaughterer who was most unwilling to come and despatch the horse particularly as at that moment they could hear the sounds of distant sirens wailing another air raid warning. However the slaughterer was finally coerced by Henry's determination and, taking a humane killer, they made their way back to the meadow beside the sea where the horse was put out of its suffering.

In the prisoner of war camp Henry found himself shaking his head as he marvelled yet again at how long he had spent making sure that horse had been put out of its misery while the German armoured divisions and infantry swept onwards through France and Belgium. It was positively surrealistic the Battalion sitting there waiting – for what? – while catastrophe was well in progress elsewhere.

During the late afternoon heavy gunfire was heard inland. It continued for many hours.There were some Royal Engineers and Marines about and they reported that a group of Dutch howitzers were shelling a wood which was supposedly occupied by fifth columnists and Germans. Late that evening more aircraft came over but no bombs were dropped. The ensuing night was fairly quiet. In the early hours a British marine arrived saying that he had a message from the Commander in Chief of the Dutch forces to the Officer commanding the British Expeditionary Force. Henry found that it stated that the British were expected to take all steps necessary to their security. Henry immediately reported this to the C.O. and heard that arrangements were being made to take the force off in destroyers at once. They heard that the navy ships could only venture into the harbour for a very short time owing to the risk of aerial bombing. Accordingly they destroyed their ammunition and food and marched over to the harbour with as much kit as they could carry. When they got there they heard that it would be impossible to return the one and a half miles to get the rest so Henry's valise, marked Captain A.H.S. Coombe-Tennant, Welsh Guards, and much other equipment, was left on the beach. Henry wondered yet again what had happened to his valise.

He embarked on the second destroyer which managed to get safely out of the harbour into the Channel. Suddenly they heard an aircraft engine and a German plane dived through a cloud. It loosed a trail of bombs that exploded with vicious violence round the ship. At the same time the plane machine-gunned the ship killing a number of men and wounding others. The aircraft disappeared as quickly as it had appeared. Some time later the ship had to stop while various floating and magnetic mines on their course were exploded with pom-pom guns.

They reached Dover in the afternoon, thankful to see the familiar white cliffs Henry for one had not expected to see again quite so soon.

It had been his baptism of enemy fire. I don't suppose you ever forget that first time even if you are in the thick of it at other times. The impression made on him by the explosion of a bomb near at hand was not so much that of noise but of a blast that approximated to a terrific earthquake. The walls seemed to shake violently backwards and forwards, the windows being blown out across the room. He had been in Company headquarters when a heavy bomb had dropped on Regimental headquarters nearby. The latter was fortunately not full at the time and the casualties were not heavy. Altogether some 12 men were killed in the abortive expedition and a further 30 wounded, 12 of whom died soon after their return.

Later that disastrous month he had his second encounter with the Germans. The Welsh Guards were not expected to turn back the enemy but to buy time to help ensure the successful evacuation of the B.E.F. By May 30th their determined efforts came to an end when they were finally cornered in Boulogne. With no further ships available, running out of ammunition and suffering heavy casualties, they were forced to surrender.

There were so many prisoners taken in the course of the disaster that in many areas the Germans didn't really have the manpower to spare to control them closely. Sometimes he had tried to analyse why he had made no attempts to escape in that time of confusion and emotional numbness but he had been unable to come to any firm conclusion.

In the early days in the prison camp his chief worry was how soon his Mother would learn that he was safe and well. With the constant memory of the son Christopher she had lost in the slaughter of the first war, it must have been absolute hell for her when war broke out again and another of her sons went on active service, also in the Welsh Guards. After she learned he was a prisoner his concern had turned to making the best of his situation. Her letters and those from friends at home had helped and in his infrequent ones he had tried to give a relatively reassuring picture of his life in the Oflag. He grinned. The changing weather had been a useful topic – 'which, after many weeks of bitter cold has today given us something like an English April morning – very cold here now: thirty-four degrees of frost on parade this morning. We have enough coal to keep the stove in all day. I have enough food, clothes and tobacco... Music takes up a good deal of my time.' Nevertheless the arrival of Red Cross parcels had been more than welcome.

Now, after two years, he was to chance the unknown once more. He told himself that it was the total inability to even guess what was ahead of them in the near future – certainly not the foreseeable future – that caused the tightening in his stomach, the sharpening of his nerves.

He ceased his piano-playing with a fine flourish and stood up.

'All right, gentlemen,' he smiled. 'Concert's over.'

The Ardennes, France, 1944

Even muffled up it was bitterly cold in the modified bomber. Outside the aircraft the night reigned, an impenetrable black void. The steady drone of the engines were of little reassurance.

19

Hope my shivering is not put down to fear. But I'm not the only one. We're all afraid. I'm sure even the pilot is tense, even if he's done this trip many times. Probably has engraved on his mind the pitcher going to the well once too often. The hymn-writer didn't know how truly he wrote: 'When danger calls or battle, be never *wanting* there!' One time when the modern meaning is more appropriate than the older! So many uncertainties. Not to know if we'll be shot down, or if the parachute will open or if I'll hit the right place or drop *'in another part of the forest'* – after all it is the Ardennes! – or if the maquis will meet me or if a reception committee from the Germans will be there with their nasty little ways. Somehow not even a double first at Cambridge in Moral Sciences nor a training in philosophy seems the best preparation for this caper.

What a change from forty-two and the Oflag. And what a change from the debacle in France in forty. Now with Uncle Joe pushing ever closer to the Reich, we do know that we will win eventually. But what will we win? What does winning mean in a modern war? Europe will end up a total disaster area. If the first casualty of war is truth, the second is morality and the third is civilisation. He thought again of the deliberate descent of Germany under the Nazis into organised barbarism. Sometimes, he thought, you learn things in Intelligence you'd perhaps be better off not knowing. The quicker this war is finished off the better.

For some reason he remembered the day in May 1940 he had spent with his brother between that first abortive expedition to Holland and the second visit when he had been taken prisoner at Boulogne with his men. It was Sunday, May 19th. He'd travelled from Oldean to the Ministry of Economic Warfare. Queenie had been with him. When he was told he could go up, he found someone to look after the dog in the 'Porters'. Alexander was in his office. He was introduced to Cahan and Berry. A large scale map of Holland was pinned up on the wall. They looked particularly at the Hook and the country around it and discussed how far the Dutch resistance had been successful and how much German material had been destroyed in the campaign. They had also discussed the extent of the Fifth Column in Holland.

Alexander had then introduced him to Scanlan, head of the Italian and Scandinavian Sub-section of Black List. Scanlan had fought in Flanders in the first war and, after it, had worked in the Public

Records Office and in the British Museum. Now he was doing his bit again for the war effort. After a while he took Alexander and himself to see Wingate, the head of Black List Section. They all went to look at another map, this time of Northern France. He remembered that they had discussed the strategical implications of the 'Break Through' in the neighbourhood of Rethel. None of them, he recalled, had been very optimistic. In the aircraft he found himself grimacing. Really, none of them had any idea then that the information he could give them was already ancient history, so swiftly were events marching in the Nazi blitzkrieg. They might as well have been discussing Caesar's Gallic War.

He and Alexander finally took their leave and went downstairs, collected Queenie from the 'Porters' and left the building. They went out round the sandbag obstruction in the doorway of Berkeley Square House into the warm, bright sunshine.

They walked to the Athenaeum and left Queenie in the Porters' Lodge. They had lunch at an open window, which looked on to irises and rhododendrons in flower in the garden to the south of the Club. After a leisurely lunch, followed by excellent coffee in big cups, they rescued Queenie from her confined space and walked past St James's Palace into the Green Park. It was a day of cloudless sunshine and a strong wind was blowing. They walked up the slight hill towards Piccadilly, past pink may flower trees in blossom. It seemed the right thing to do to sit down on two chairs and watch the trees and the vividly green grass stirred by the passing breeze.

They talked of many things. He asked Alexander about himself and his plans for the future. He remembered how Alexander had shrugged and he realised that in the total uncertainty of the situation it was just not possible for any sensible answer to be given. They had agreed that it was good to think of Mother safe at Didlington. Much of the time had been spent in silence but silences can speak. He thought again of the understanding that had flowered so wonderfully in the same way as their surroundings after the late winter, a unity of spirit and communion that had grown between them, so that, some weeks before, on Wimbledon Common, they had opened to each other and talked of the significance of each other to their innermost lives that he believed no circumstances could touch. Time passed. It was time to walk back to Piccadilly. He had to rejoin Ralph Pilcher and Twining who was motoring him back to Oldean. As he and Queenie climbed the steps of the bus to its upper level he looked back and saw Alexander watching them. He waved and received a wave in return before they were carried away into the distance.

The noise of the aircraft's engines was still unchanged and there was no indication as yet that they were nearing the drop zone.

It was obvious to him that he was recalling these memories to take his mind, as far as they could, off what lay ahead. At least, he thought, their formidable mother had no idea where he was at that moment. As far as she knew, he was safe in England, on essential and important war work. Mrs Winifred Coombe-Tennant of Cadoxton Lodge, Wales, was no doubt still giving her ungrateful servants hell and complaining about the dreadful vicissitudes in her life caused by wartime conditions.

He smiled. I wonder if I shall ever see her again, or Alexander, or the Balfours? In surprisingly sharp, clear images, he recalled his visit with his mother in September 1930 to Whittinghame. How welcome they made me – Gerald, Ral, Jean. Yet it was strange. The house itself had a distinct atmosphere of welcome. But that's fanciful. But for some reason, Mother was not satisfied. She seemed somehow disappointed. At that time he had not got to the age when he could question her. Though even now she could clam up and simply refuse to discuss a topic if she had no intention of being drawn on it. And make you feel guilty that you had even thought of questioning her. She would have done well in Intelligence, he thought. She really operated on a 'need to know' basis. What was it that she was hiding? He remembered that he had once been visited at Eton by a friend of his Mother, Dame Edith Lyttelton. She had hinted that there was something to do with his Mother – and himself – that very few people knew about. But he had made nothing of it at the time and now, he had other things to think about. He must ask Alexander about it when – if – he got back.

Almost as if the pilot had been waiting for him to get to this point in his thoughts he heard him announce: 'Five minutes to the drop zone.' Somehow the drone of the engines seemed louder. From then on the final check and a final rehearsal of mission data dominated his thoughts.

PART 1

LIFTING THE DARKNESS

1

Let There Be Light

Sit down before fact as a little child, be prepared to give up every preconceived notion, follow humbly wherever and to whatever abysses nature leads, or you shall learn nothing.

Thomas Henry Huxley

The night of November 30th–December 1st, 1936.

In the darkness the great building burned furiously. Its situation on Sydenham Hill made the wind-fanned flames of the conflagration visible from most of the vast sprawl of London. By the early morning it was evident to the exhausted firefighters and the onlookers that it was beyond saving. All that remained amid the smouldering twisted wreckage were the towers. In 1941 they themselves were demolished because they were considered to be a conspicuous and convenient landmark for the bombers of Hitler's Luftwaffe. Many elderly Londoners, even in the midst of the murderous London Blitz, had time to spare to feel sadness that one of their last ties with the Victorian age had been finally broken.

After eighty-five years, the last remnants of the Crystal Palace were no more.

It was in October 1849 that the plan to hold an exhibition of 'the works of industry of all nations' was announced. Prince Albert, as President of the Royal Society of Arts, offered himself to the public as a leader of the enterprise. That he did not intend to be merely a figurehead quickly became evident. On a call for funds to enable the project to go ahead, Queen Victoria set an example by heading the list of subscribers. The necessary funding was quickly forthcoming: the contract with Messrs Fox and Henderson

25

for £79,800 was subsequently increased and would amount to £150,000 if the building housing the exhibition was to be a permanent feature and not a temporary construction. If we accept a factor of 1000 as a reasonable devaluation in the buying power of money, then in modern terms the cost of the larger figure should be £150 million, a sum that is in startling contrast to the £800 million poured into the creation and subsequent support of the Millennium Dome, that upturned wok built in Greenwich one and a half centuries later in which inadequacy and hubris were cooked to perfection.

The Great Exhibition was formally opened by the Queen on May 1st, 1851 and it remained open until October 11th of the same year. During its five and a half months of existence the exhibition attracted more than six million visitors, with almost half a million people visiting it during its last week. Final accounting showed that the enterprise had made a substantial profit. Indeed money from the profits helped to fund what became the South Kensington complex of colleges and museums.

The building in Hyde Park was entirely novel in concept. The design of Mr George Paxton, who was subsequently knighted for its success, arose from his previous experience of constructing giant conservatories for the Duke of Devonshire at Chatsworth, in particular one in 1840, and the lily house in 1850 for the Duke's rare *Victoria regia*. Constructed of prefabricated sections of sheet glass and ironwork, the building's size and extent created problems of construction that Paxton and the Victorian engineers triumphantly overcame. The pleasingly graceful effect of the giant building constructed of a network of slender iron rods framing the sheets of glass quickly suggested to a journalist the name of the Crystal Palace.

And it was huge. It occupied an area of some 21 acres, four times the area of St Peter's in Rome. Its length was 1851 feet, its maximum width being about one quarter of this figure. A transept intersected the building and was 108 feet in height so that fully mature trees could be incorporated. Upon being asked by the Queen what could be done about the nuisance of the birds therein, the Duke of Wellington replied gruffly, 'Sparrowhawks, ma'am, sparrowhawks.' There were three tiers of elevation, the central one being of height 64 feet, the middle being 44 feet in height while the outermost was 24 feet high. On the ground floor and galleries there were more than 8 miles of display tables.

If the architecture was awesome in its size and artistic style, the contents of the Crystal Palace fully matched it in magnitude and magnificence. The exhibition committee, under the guidance of Prince Albert, had issued an invitation to the world, believing that the British contribution could not be outclassed by anything produced elsewhere; they also believed that in a time of unparalleled progress by humanity – the Victorian belief of ever onwards, ever upwards – such a timely exhibition would not only be celebratory but educative and inspiring. The invitation was taken up. Nearly half of the 14,000 exhibitors were non-British. There were 1760 French exhibits; the United States sent 560. Nevertheless, it was Britain's contribution that stood at the helm. In 1851, Britain was still truly the workshop of the world and in the Crystal Palace, Britons and visitors to Great Britain could see the triumphs of British technology and engineering prowess for themselves. Not only that, they could absorb it all in an atmosphere of artistic opulence and view cultural advances displayed to their advantage in the imposing glass palace. The Crystal Palace even contained a majestic pipe organ constructed by 'Father' Willis. It was indeed a building fulfilling its line of descent from giant greenhouses for it must have been to all who visited it a hothouse of impressions, in its artistic and intellectual heat forcing attitudes of respect for science, technology and the arts and inspiring many of the visitors to compare the triumphs of reason and the scientific method to the increasingly bankrupt dogmas of the orthodox church.

Looking back at Prince Albert's vision of universal progress from a viewpoint on the other side of the monstrous, murderous and failure-bestrewn twentieth century, it would be easy to dub it naive and accuse him and others of neglecting the essential and seemingly eternal flaws in human nature. But Prince Albert and other intelligent and well-educated people of his time were well aware of the propensity of a large section of the human race to choose self-interest and try to get away with whatever they could with no more regard for others than a shark has for the prey it devours. After all, it was only twenty-five years since Parliament had passed the Slavery Abolition Act and fifteen years would pass before slavery was abolished in the United States after the American Civil War. They had only to look at the poor and destitute of Britain's cities or the hordes of human beings labouring slavishly in its mines and sweatshops to see the evil side of the human being at work. Nevertheless educated people had good reason by the middle of the nineteenth century to believe that science, technology, the arts and education could civilise humanity and lead to a better future for everyone.

From the publication of Newton's *The Principia* in 1687, science and technology had progressed at ever-increasing speed. And in the years since Wellington and Blücher defeated Napoleon at Waterloo in 1815, not a year had passed without some dark area of nature being illuminated by the light of the scientific method. Newtonian dynamics and celestial mechanics had largely given up their secrets to European scientists before the even more perplexing phenomena of heat, light, sound, electricity and magnetism followed suit. The educated Briton was doubtless familiar with the scientific attainments of his fellow countrymen reported in the serious press. He knew that Michael Faraday had laid the foundations for the understanding of electricity and magnetism by his brilliant experimental techniques and his concept of lines of force. He might well have laughed with rueful appreciation at the anecdote of Faraday and the politician: 'Tell me, Mr Faraday,' said the politician, 'what possible use can this ever have?' 'Well,' Faraday replied, 'if a practical use is ever found for it, you will doubtless find a way of taxing it.'

In the first half of the nineteenth century, Sadi Carnot and James Joule had been among those scientists arriving at a reliable understanding of the nature of heat. By the second half of the nineteenth century the Scottish scientist James Clerk Maxwell had found the relationship between electromagnetism and the velocity of light. It is noteworthy that much of this research was pursued out of sheer curiosity and with little care whether or not discoveries would ever be 'useful'. 'One thing of which you can be absolutely certain,' commented Lord Rutherford of his early experiments in atom-smashing, 'this will have no practical use whatsoever.'

However, by the middle of the century it was an everyday experience to see the applications of science in operation. The Victorian engineers, spurred on by the entrepreneurial spirit of the age, were planning and constructing the web of railways that in time would cover the British Isles and become the successful rival to the canal system. Steamships were taking the place of sailing ships. Tunnels and bridges of astonishing audacity and design were being created. Perhaps the two engineers and inventors that epitomise this civil and marine engineering revolution were father and son Sir Marc Isambard Brunel and Isambard Kingdom Brunel. The father (1769–1849), an émigré engineer and inventor from France, had been chief engineer of New York City where he had perfected a method of mass-producing ships' pulleys by mechanical means. In 1799, on the invitation of the British government, he installed his machines in Portsmouth harbour. Never at rest, he produced a stream of inventions and also acted as a civil engineer. In the latter capacity he designed the suspension bridge on the island of Réunion and the floating landing piers at Liverpool. He also saw through to completion the tunnel under the Thames between Rotherhithe and Wapping for which he patented the tunnelling shield. He was knighted in 1841. His son (1806–1859) was, if anything, a more original and versatile civil and marine engineer than his father. Bridges, tunnels, docks, railways and ships were designed and created by him, including the Clifton suspension bridge over the Avon Gorge in Bristol and the Maidenhead Bridge, which had the flattest brick arch in the world. In his railway work – comprising more than a thousand miles of track in the West Country, the Midlands, South Wales and Ireland – he built the famous Box Tunnel and introduced to the Great Western Railway (known affectionately as 'God's Wonderful Railway') the broad gauge of rails seven feet apart.

In his marine engineering career Brunel built three ships, each at the time of construction the largest in the world – the *Great Western* (1837), the *Great Britain* (1843), and the *Great Eastern* (1858). The third was used to lay the first successful transatlantic cable in 1866. During the Crimean War (1854–6), Brunel designed a floating armoured barge which was used in the attack on Kronstadt in 1854. The following year his prefabricated hospital was shipped to the Crimea and assembled there.

The Victorian engineers built to last. Many people alive today will remember the extraordinary television programme which showed the hulk of Brunel's great ship, the *Great Britain*, on its return from the Falklands, brought up the river to pass under Brunel's Clifton Suspension bridge, finally to enter Brunel's Dock in which it had been built not far from the terminus of Brunel's Great Western Railway. The modern idea of building in 'obsolescence' to their work would have had to be very carefully explained to them.

The Victorians were also addressing the terrible and tragic problem of disease and the high death rate, though progress was painfully slow. Cholera and typhus epidemics were part of life – and death. Medical science was making some advances but it was becoming clear to the far-sighted that the greatest contribution towards a healthy population would be the provision of clean air, clean water and an efficient sewage system. With the Victorians' enormous and inevitable dependence on coal for power and heating, and the miasmic output from a forest of factory chimneys, there was little that could be done to provide clean air and it was not until well into the twentieth century that the killing of thousands of people by a single London fog forced politicians to act. As far as the other two goals are concerned, to a large extent we are still reaping the benefits of the Victorian civil engineers' colossal creation of reservoirs and sewage systems for London and the other fast-growing cities of Great Britain. Nevertheless, the benefits of their achievements did not come immediately. As any visitor to a Victorian cemetery will discover, it is awesome to see on so many family gravestones the long lists of children who died in infancy.

The Great Exhibition also took place at a time when the world was being opened up by explorers whose exploits, discoveries and triumphs fired the imagination and pride of their fellow countrymen. Among them was the Scotsman David Livingstone (1813–73). He became famous not only for his African explorations but also for his dedicated efforts in his childhood and youth to educate himself while working in a cotton mill on the banks of the River Clyde. His strong Calvinistic faith spurred him on to study Greek, theology and medicine for two years in Glasgow while still working part-time at the mill so that he could fit himself to be a medical missionary. In 1840 he set sail for South Africa. In his first fifteen years there, his work as an explorer, missionary and strong opponent of slavery brought him recognition from the Royal Geographical Society. In his subsequent explorations, the Society supported him and kept his astonishing achievements before the public in Great Britain. His own lecture tour throughout the British Isles describing the strange and terrible conditions in Africa, the dangers he had faced, the need for greater efforts to spread Christianity and civilisation through the Dark Continent, and his opposition to the barbarity of slavery, fired many of his listeners to follow him. In later years, when he seemed lost and probably dead somewhere in

Africa, the nation was riveted when Henry M. Stanley, the journalist sent to search for him, returned and gave his account of finding him, sick and failing, and supplying him with the medicine and food without which he would almost certainly have died. The phrase 'Dr Livingstone, I presume,' spoken by Stanley when he met him, passed into the language.

It was not only the exploration of the world. Discoveries were being made about the universe outside the Earth. Just five years prior to the opening of the Great Exhibition the size of the Solar System had been almost doubled by the discovery of a new planet, subsequently named Neptune. To many it had seemed to be the culminating triumph of Newtonian gravitation and celestial mechanics for the discovery had been made in a way entirely different from that in which Sir William Herschel had found the planet Uranus in 1781. In his survey of the heavens Herschel had discovered a fuzzy comet-like object that only after further observation was realised to be a hitherto unknown planet. Since 1824, however, the planet had been steadily departing from its predicted orbit. The possibility that there was yet another planet further out from the Sun that was perturbing Uranus's orbit was a natural and exciting supposition but it was also thought by many authorities that its discovery would be a matter of chance. Two young men thought otherwise and independently set out to calculate where the new planet should lie in the Solar System, beginning from the discrepancies between predicted and actual orbital positions.

John Couch Adams (1819–92) was still an undergraduate at Cambridge University when he noted in his diary his determination to carry out the necessary calculations. Urbain J.J. Le Verrier (1811–77), a young French astronomer, likewise formed the intention of finding the new planet. The train of events that followed became a cause célèbre between Great Britain and France, inflaming chauvinistic passions on both sides of the Channel. When Adams had completed his calculations, he sent a copy of his papers to the Astronomer Royal, Sir George Airy, who looked at them and did not take them very seriously. In the meantime Le Verrier had communicated with Johann Gotffried Galle in Berlin and had sent him the direction in which he should turn his telescope. Dr Galle and his assistant did so. The new planet was found very close to the position Le Verrier had calculated for it. It was also close to Adams' position for it.

Once the cross-Channel chauvinistic hullabaloo about priority had died away, the real triumph was appreciated. Without looking through a telescope but employing sophisticated mathematics and Newton's law of gravitation, the existence and direction of an unknown planet sunk in the depths of space could be predicted by the effects its spectral gravitational 'fingers' produced on another planet's orbit. It was a further revelation of the power of reason and science. The Professor of Astronomy at Glasgow University, John Nichol, a tireless popularist of astronomy in the nineteenth century, of the 'The heavens declare the glory of God' school of writing, wrote a special book about the achievement.

Other notable astronomical achievements had occurred prior to the Great Exhibition. A year after the discovery of Neptune, William Parsons, the 3rd Earl of Rosse, completed the construction of the 'Leviathan', the largest telescope of the nineteenth century. With it the 3rd Earl discovered the spiral shapes of a number of the celestial objects known as nebulae, now recognised as galaxies, island universes each containing on average one hundred thousand million stars. Among the nebulae he studied and drew so carefully were the Orion Nebula, near the middle star in the sword of Orion, and the Crab Nebula, a name suggested to him by its curious shape.

But perhaps the most thought-provoking event in astronomy had occurred a year after Victoria came to the throne. From the time of the great Danish astronomer Tycho Brahe in the second half of the seventeenth century, attempts had been made by astronomers to measure the distance to a star. If the Earth travelled about the Sun, then surely the nearest stars would be seen to wobble back and forth against the background of the more distant stars in the same way that people standing nearest to a roundabout at a fairground would be seen by a rider to apparently oscillate back and forth against the more distant onlookers. This parallactic shift was not detected until 1838, when the German astronomer Friedrich Wilhelm Bessel measured it for the first time with respect to the rather faint star 61 Cygni. Bessell's success gave the distance of 61 Cygni to be about 11 light years, where a light year is the distance travelled by light in one year. Since light takes about eight minutes to travel from the Sun to the Earth, this meant that even one of the nearest stars was some million times further from the Earth than the Sun. At least some educated people began to wonder whether, in a universe built on such a vast scale, the human race, inhabiting a tiny speck in that

Young Mr Darwin

The evolutionist

The pillar of
the scientific
establishment

Charles Darwin

boundless immensity, could be really of any importance in the scheme of things. Indeed was there a scheme of things at all?

There were other explorers in the Victorian era even more influential in their discoveries than Livingstone and Stanley. Their discoveries were not only in territorial realms but also in the realm of living and extinct species, arrived at by reading the battered incomplete fossil record and by studying the implications of the strata in cliffs and mountains. Of these the three most outstanding and influential were Charles Darwin, Alfred Russel Wallace and Thomas Henry Huxley. Their legacy was destined to be an earthquake high on the cultural and religious Richter scale, one that shattered many of the strongest and oldest Western belief structures. In its aftermath it created fear and despair, hatred and enmity, yet for many it was embraced eagerly for its liberating effects from outmoded dogma that insulted anyone of rational and open mind. Many people today, with the discoveries being made from genomic research, would agree that the original legacy of Darwin, Huxley and Wallace's discoveries is still being added to on an almost daily basis. A considerable proportion of the human race, however, still exists that simply cannot swallow the medicine and indeed choke in the process, an example of the old adage that some drink of the waters of the fountain of knowledge, others merely gargle.

Darwin was the man who prepared the case and presented it for the world's judgement. It seems certain, however, that if he had not lived, Wallace would have done so himself. Whoever in fact had done it would have received the enthusiastic support of Huxley.

Both Darwin and Wallace in the early part of their careers spent a considerable time abroad, travelling and studying the lives of plants, animals and peoples in remote parts of the world. It is not a coincidence that in their lifetimes each of them was interested in and studied a variety of subjects. None of them was the type of scientist who becomes a world expert on some tiny corner in nature but on almost everything else has no opinion of value to offer.

Charles Darwin (1809–82) set sail on HMS *Beagle* in December 1831 as the unpaid naturalist. He was just twenty-three years of age. Fit, tireless and insatiably curious, he lost no opportunity on the voyage to spend long periods of time ashore on the South American continent studying plants, animals and the strange peoples he encountered. In the Galapagos Islands he studied the differences among the different kinds of birds and tortoises living there. Darwin's talents lay partly in his skills as an observer and recorder of everything he encountered, partly in his supreme ability to theorise productively about his findings. His five years on the *Beagle* provided him with the best conditions in which his genius and skills could flourish.

He came home already a scientific celebrity. In 1836 he was made a fellow of the Geological Society. Two years later he was elected to the Athenaeum and the following year to the Royal Society. His books on geology, zoology and natural history added substantially to his reputation as one of the most productive scientists of the age. But behind the scenes, his continuing studies concerning 'the species problem' were filling notebook after notebook, producing in him not only a growing sense that his researches would justify his theory of organic evolution and the survival of the fittest but also a deepening dismay regarding its conclusions with respect to the human race. In 1858, however, his hand was forced when Alfred Russel Wallace sent him a paper which, to Darwin's consternation, showed that Wallace had also arrived at the theory of evolution. A number of Darwin's friends, including Thomas Henry Huxley, saved the day by arranging for a joint paper by Darwin and Wallace to be read to the Linnean Society on July 1st, 1858.

Alfred Russel Wallace (1823–1913) had pursued a career as a naturalist, working in Brazil for a number of years in the Amazon region. His papers and books brought him funding from the Royal Geographical Society, enabling him to travel to the Malay Archipelago where he spent eight years collecting biological specimens and studying them. His work included the publication of many scientific articles, and it was one of these that he sent to Darwin. In it was

Wallace's theory that new species arise by the progression and continued divergence of varieties that outlive the parent species in the struggle for existence. In all its essentials it was the theory of evolution.

In his later life, although he was acknowledged as one of the foremost naturalists in the world, Wallace had to depend upon his writings for a living. It was only in 1881, by the efforts of Darwin and Huxley, that he was added to the Civil List. Several of his books became standard texts, and he received a number of awards from the Royal Society, the Linnean Society and the Royal Geographical Society. He was also elected to the Royal Society. To the end of his long life he remained interested in a wide variety of social and political causes, always ready to stand up for any movement he deemed worthy and unfairly treated.

The cat of evolution theory was now out of the bag. Darwin's text *On the Origin of Species by Means of Natural Selection* was published in 1859. It was a best-seller, the first edition selling out immediately. Most of the scientific world welcomed and embraced the theory. Its reception by the public was more varied and there was savage opposition to it by many of the clergy. Almost anyone who could think it through could see that, just as Newton's mechanical world had no need for divine intervention, so Darwin's living world was also subject to immutable mindless laws. The most terrifying thing to many, however, was that they could see no reason now to believe that the human race was anything more than the end result of innumerable random events.

Darwin had now outed himself and had to face not only the plaudits but also the vitriolic attacks on him. It is an age-old technique of debate that if you cannot fault a man's work, try to show him to be an enemy of the people, a corrupter of the young and so on. Darwin suffered both physically and mentally in the face of condemnatory sermons, indignant newspaper articles and the polemical cut-and-thrust lectures of those biologists who could not accept his ideas. Nevertheless, he continued to work at a wide variety of botanical and biological subjects and also experimented in his garden at Down House in Kent. There was little trace now of the adventurous young Mr Darwin of HMS *Beagle*. Darwin would remain a semi-invalid for much of the rest of his life, and it is possible that much of his ill-health was psychosomatic in origin, a scourge fashioned for his self-blame. Yet he by no means completely shut himself away from the world to wrap himself defensively in his research. He attended many scientific meetings and participated fully in the village life of Downe. He also had the good fortune to be married with many children, a number of whom became noted scientists. In his life at Down House he had the opportunity of breaking off his scientific work to play with them and study them, even comparing their early development with that of the first young apes that had just reached London Zoo.

Darwin married his first cousin Emma, the granddaughter of Josiah Wedgwood, founder of the Staffordshire pottery dynasty. For a time Emma hesitated about marrying Charles, worried as she was about his 'honest and conscientious doubts about the Christian Revelation'. She believed without reservation Christ's promise of salvation through faith and throughout their long marriage, the widening gulf between them was a source of deep sadness to both of them. They did agree, however, on bringing up their children in a liberal way that was unusual for those times. When they bought Down House in 1842 they filled it with expensive furniture, asking themselves the question: 'Shall we make the furniture a bugbear to the children or shall we let them use it in their plays?' Many years later Emma recalled that they agreed on the latter course, 'so chairs and other furniture used to get piled up for railways and coaches, just as the fancy took them. I believe we have all been much the happier as a consequence.'

A sombre backcloth, however, particularly for Darwin was the death in 1851 of his oldest and favourite daughter, Anne, at the age of ten. For the rest of his life his thinking was deeply affected by this tragedy which seemed to him an agonising example of the survival of the fittest. He even wondered if interbreeding between first cousins might be the cause though it seems more likely to have been childhood tuberculosis. Shortly after Annie's death, Darwin wrote: '... she held herself upright, and often threw her head a little backwards, as if she defied the world in her joyousness.' Darwin's love for his daughter Annie, his home life and its effect on the development of his theory of evolution is given in the wonderful book by his great-great-grandson Randal Keynes entitled *Annie's Box*. The box of the title is her writing case, still in existence, containing goose-feather quills, sealing wax, ribbons, paper and envelopes. It also contains Darwin's notes on Annie's health throughout the last months of her short life.

T.H. Huxley – the scientific crusader   T.H. Huxley – Darwin's Bulldog

When Darwin published his book on the origin of species in 1859 he found that much of the pressure was taken off him by the magnificent support he got from his scientific colleagues, particularly the biologist Thomas Henry Huxley (1825–95), one of the giants of the Victorian age and a staunch friend of Darwin. It was the following year at the meeting of the British Association for the Advancement of Science that Huxley trounced 'Soapy Sam' Wilberforce, the bishop of Oxford. In the famous encounter, Wilberforce mockingly asked Huxley whether the apes were on his grandmother's or grandfather's side. Huxley replied that he would rather have an ape as his ancestor than a wealthy bishop who prostituted his gifts of eloquence in the service of falsehoods. In the following years Huxley never missed an opportunity to defend Darwin's work, believing with heart and soul that it would be through science that the secrets of nature would be revealed and human condition ameliorated. He was never at rest. He had a number of nicknames – 'Pope Huxley', for the messianic fervour with which he professed his belief in science as the hope of mankind; 'Darwin's Bulldog', for his continued defence of Darwin and 'The General', a name given to him by the students of South Kensington when he used Royal Engineers as invigilators for the Department of Science and Arts' public exams. His children often addressed him as 'The Lodger', because he was so often away from home!

Huxley was also a member of the X Club. This private London dining club, which lasted from 1864 to 1892, had only nine members but it was one of the most powerful and influential clubs in the British Isles. The other eight members were George Busk, a retired surgeon, comparative anatomist and microscopist; Edward Frankland, a well-known chemist; T.A. Hirst, a mathematician; Joseph Dalton Hooker, the eminent botanist; John Lubbock, a banker, ethnologist

37

and entomologist; Herbert Spencer, a sociologist and philosopher of evolution; William Spottiswoode, Queen's Printer and amateur mathematician; and John Tyndall, the famous experimental physicist. All were brilliant, hard-working, far-seeing men and all were utterly convinced that science, technology and the power of rational thought were the hope of mankind and that these disciplines should be sold to the nation by example and by, in a well-known modern-day phrase, education, education, education. Their continuing careers as scientists, popular lecturers, essayists and writers of influential textbooks ensured that the public were kept informed of the latest advances, while they skilfully used their reputations to promote their ideas to the British government. It is fair to say that the influence of this small number of gifted, dedicated, far-sighted men in Victorian Britain was out of all proportion to the efforts of any political party of the time.

Facing them, however, were the entrenched forces of privilege, stupidity, greed, prejudice, indifference and violence, indeed all the negative elements of human nature that have brought down every civilisation history has ever recorded. Only a year before the Great Exhibition, the disastrous Irish Potato Famine, exacerbated by the inadequate efforts of the British government, had helped bring about the deaths of at least one million men, women and children. As many emigrated. A large number of organisations raised money to alleviate the suffering but for all their efforts the problem was simply too big for them.

There had also been the Crimean War in which Great Britain, France and Ottoman Turkey opposed Russia in a struggle that cost the lives of a quarter of a million men, the majority of them succumbing to disease. It is best remembered for the disastrous charge of the Light Brigade, immortalised by Lord Tennyson's poem, and the heroic efforts of Florence Nightingale, who fought to establish a competent nursing service in the face of doctors' hostility, inadequate supplies and gross overcrowding in the filthy wards that for most patients were simply miserable waiting rooms for death. It is also remembered for the hard-hitting dispatches sent by William Russell, war correspondent for The Times, revealing to an appalled British public the unbelievably squalid conditions their troops were condemned to endure because of the total ineptitude of the military management.

In the following decade came the American Civil War (1861–65), the first recognisably modern war, using primitive submarines, railroads, iron-clad warships, aerial reconnaissance by balloon, the first war to be truly covered by journalists and by photography. Mathew Brady's pictures of the war's battlefields and the dead were marvelled at by the American public. In the *New York Times* in 1862 appeared the comment:

> Mr Brady has done something to bring home to us the terrible reality and earnestness of war. If he has not brought bodies and laid them on our dooryards and along the streets, he has done something very like it ... the same sun that looked down on the faces of the slain blistering them, blotting out from the bodies all semblance to humanity, and hastening corruption, [by photography has] caught their features upon canvas, and given them perpetuity for ever...

By the end of the war, modern improved methods of killing the enemy had slain almost two-thirds of a million men, mutilated countless others and almost destroyed a civilisation. Among the American exhibits in the Great Exhibition of 1851 had been artificial legs and Colt's repeating pistol. The Civil War made each a growth industry.

In the aftermath of the Civil War, a group of young intellectuals in Cambridge, Massachusetts, founded The Metaphysical Club. Convened in 1872, it lasted a much shorter time than the British X Club, but was nonetheless brilliantly effective in countering the slide into nihilism that threatened to poison the United States inheritance. Among the club's members were the philosopher John Dewey, Oliver Wendell Holmes, who became the Supreme Court Justice; the mathematician and philosopher Charles Pierce; and the psychologist William James. In hammering out their philosophical creed of 'pragmatism', these talented and disillusioned men condemned the old beliefs as demonstrably and irretrievably flawed, turned their backs on certainty, and embraced Darwinism, applying it not only to the living world but also to the realm of ideas. Their philosophical legacy, like the first shoots of growth after the destruction of a forest by conflagration, spread throughout the stricken American mind, contributing significantly to its recovery and to the American nation's spectacular growth in the post-Civil War decades.

In the nineteenth century on the other side of the globe, the Chinese fought and lost two wars (1839–42) and (1856–60) against the drug-runners who were pouring so much opium into China that the rocketing number of addicts was seriously damaging the social structure of the country, creating misery for millions. The demand for the drug brought immense financial returns to the drug-runners, enabling them to buy Chinese luxury goods such as tea, silk and porcelain which they shipped to the West. The British fought the first Opium War and were joined by the French during the second for it was their nationals who were the drug-runners and surely had to be supported in the entirely laudable interests of opening up China to trade with the West.

After a closing ceremony held on October 15th, 1851, the Crystal Palace was dismantled and re-erected, with significant alterations and improvements, on Sydenham Hill, overlooking London from the south, on an estate bought by the Crystal Palace Company in 1852. A special branch of the railway was built to connect it to the London and Brighton Railway. The terminus station was at one end of a glass-and-iron colonnade 720 feet long, 17 feet wide and 18 feet high that led to the great palace. For many years, the Crystal Palace would be the location for exhibitions, concerts and even football matches. Its well-planned gardens, sculptures and monumental waterworks – designed and constructed by Sir Joseph Paxton – attracted Londoners and others from further afield to enjoy the later triumphs of the Victorian age. And so it remained until the disastrous fire in 1936. But it was in its first incarnation in Hyde Park in the year 1851 that it made its major impact on humanity, for it was then that Prince Albert and his team of Victorians, embracing the spirit of the age, met the right challenges, recognised the right architectural concept and succeeded in creating in the Crystal Palace their statement that the continued goal of lifting the darkness from the human situation lay in fostering science and its handmaiden technology, and supporting international commerce.

2

A Woman Called Victoria

*We all feel a bit motherless today, mysterious little Victoria
is dead and fat vulgar Edward is King.*

Henry James

By the end of the nineteenth century Great Britain possessed the
most powerful and widespread empire the world had ever seen.
Almost a quarter of the human race lived within it. Truly it was
an empire on which the sun never set.

At the head of this vast and awesome conglomerate of nations
a small, stout widow presided as Queen and Empress, Defender
of the Faith, revered, feared, loved, epitomising the stability and
confidence of an age many people would look back on with awe
and reverence. The Queen had had a long reign: to many of her
subjects she must have appeared to be immortal but, although she
had appreciated her Golden and Diamond Jubilees, by the turn of
the century she was a frail, weary old lady troubled by sciatica
and failing sight, given to brooding on the vast number of her
friends and loved ones who had preceded her to the grave. She
doggedly saw in the New Year of 1901 before succumbing on
January 22nd to her final illness. Surrounded by children and
grandchildren she died in the arms of her grandson Willy, the
German Kaiser. At the foot of the bed stood Bertie, the Prince of
Wales, thereafter King Edward VII. The Victorian age was over.

She had come to the throne in 1837 as a teenager. Her life prior
to becoming Queen had contained little happiness. Her parents, the
Duke and Duchess of Kent, were the poor relations of the Royal
Family. She was still a baby when her father died. Edward, Duke

41

of Kent, on his deathbed, appointed the Duchess as guardian of his infant daughter. From then on it was a continual financial and political struggle for the Duchess, in spite of the help and advice of her brother Prince Leopold, later the King of Belgium. In later years she came under the strong influence of Sir John Conroy, who had been the Duke of Kent's equerry. As she grew up, Princess Victoria came to dislike him intensely for the way he, as Comptroller of the Household of the Duchess of Kent, influenced and indeed ruled the Duchess, Svengali-like, as he sought to obtain extreme power. In her turn the Duchess genuinely feared for Victoria's life because of tales fed her by Conroy, that some of those at Court wanted her daughter out of the way to further their own ambitions.

For these reasons Victoria was kept away from the Court as much as possible; she slept in her mother's bed and was hardly ever allowed to be alone. She was never without guards. Matters became a shade easier when William IV came to the throne but by then the young Victoria had created for herself an impassive, controlled façade that troubled and perplexed some of those who came into contact with her. When she came to the throne, she lost no time in distancing herself from her mother, Sir John Conroy and anyone else who had tried to influence and control her. Only one person, her governess, Louise Lehzen, was close to her and could do no wrong. Even she went after Victoria's marriage to Albert for he and Lehzen never got on. The impassive, controlled Victoria, however, could explode with rage on occasion.

Prince Albert was understandably more than a little apprehensive when he made his first visit to Windsor to meet Victoria. He wrote:

[She] is said to be incredibly stubborn and her extreme obstinacy to be constantly at war with her good nature; she delights in Court ceremonies, etiquette and trivial formalities... She is said not to take the slightest pleasure in nature and to enjoy sitting up at night and sleeping late into the day.

However, all went well. In her journal the Queen wrote: '... it was with some emotion that I beheld Albert – who is beautiful.' She wrote further: 'Albert really is quite charming and so excessively handsome, such beautiful blue eyes, exquisite nose, a beautiful figure, broad in the shoulders and a fine waist.' She proposed; he accepted, much to the satisfaction of their uncle Leopold. They were first cousins and he had played a part in engineering their meeting. The wedding took place on February 10th, 1840 in the Chapel Royal, St James's Palace. Some idea of her happiness is obtained from her own words about their first evening together:

> My dearest dearest dear Albert sat on a footstool by my side, and his excessive love and affection gave me feelings of heavenly love and happiness I never could have hoped to have felt before! To be called by names of tenderness I have never yet heard used to me before – was bliss beyond belief! Oh! this was the happiest day of my life...

From then on throughout her marriage she gloried in private in being Albert's adoring and submissive wife as much as she later lived to the full the role of Great Britain's Victoria, the formidable Queen Empress, the grandmother of many of Europe's crowned heads.

Albert was exactly the right man for her and for the future direction of the monarchy. The Prince von Saxe-Coburg-Gotha was a highly intelligent, well-educated man and was equally at home in the arts and the sciences. He was strong-willed and hyper-conscientious, devoted to Victoria though prepared to oppose her at times when he saw fit. He was a person with whom she could discuss anything; he was the trusted father figure she had never known and, to her great joy, after some years of chauvinistic and totally unjustified resentment towards him from various levels of society, he was successful in winning and enjoying immense popularity in his adopted country. In 1857 he was made Prince Consort and Victoria's dependence on him as husband, father of their children, counsellor, unofficial first minister and hard-working statesman grew still deeper. On at least two occasions, in 1856 with Prussia and in 1861 with the United States, his quiet advice suggesting the rewording of Foreign Office despatches prevented them from being regarded as ultimatums. There is no doubt that his influence on Victoria changed the Queen from a frivolous young girl into the monarch who to the end of her life continued to discuss state matters with her ministers and worked her way through the stream of papers awaiting her perusal and signature.

Victoria and Albert's eminently happy life was marred only by Albert's bouts of ill-health, possibly brought on by his inordinately heavy workload. By the winter of 1860 he was suffering from insomnia and rheumatism. In November 1861 he went down to Cambridge to sort out his son Bertie, later King Edward VII, who was involved with a young woman called Nellie Clifden. Albert caught a chill. Within a short time it had developed into the typhoid fever from which he died some days after.

The Queen was devastated. She collapsed into a complete nervous breakdown, writing to her uncle Leopold: 'My life as a happy one is ended! The world has gone for me.'

In the following years Victoria threw herself into a morbid celebration of Albert's death. She had an enormous mausoleum at Frogmore built for his body, large enough to house her own as well when her time came to be, she fervently believed, reunited with him. She kept with her the keys to the mausoleum gate and on many occasions she went to pray beside his tomb. A frenzy of activity ensued in which memorials to Albert were created everywhere, the most famous of these being the Albert Memorial and the Royal Albert Hall. She neglected affairs of state and was dubbed the Widow of Windsor.

The Blue Room at Windsor, where Albert died, was photographed so that, after cleaning, it could always be put back as before. Often in bed she would clasp in her arms one of Albert's nightshirts; each evening a fresh one was laid on the bed and enough hot water and a clean towel were also provided for the departed Prince Consort.

Two other features of her life after Albert's death became apparent. The Court saw that she never forgave her son Bertie for, as she believed, being the cause of Albert's death. If the Prince Consort, ill as he was, had not had to go to Cambridge to sort out the mess Bertie had got himself into... After his mother's death, however, King Edward was known to say that although she had died in the arms of the Kaiser, her last word had been 'Bertie'.

The Court also saw that as the years went on she behaved as if Albert was still there, as if she felt his presence, as if he could still support, encourage and advise. She told Uncle Leopold how she would pray by Albert's bedside 'to be guided by my darling to do as he would wish.'

It was four years before the 'Widow of Windsor' overcame her deep aversion to public life and resumed her duties. Various reasons have been given for her slow emergence from seclusion. It is said that she did not smile again until one March morning in 1864 she looked out of the window at Osborne and saw, on the path below, the kilted Highland servant John Brown at the head of the pony Lochnagar harnessed to the Queen's pony cart. Brown stood there, looking up at the window. It was a moment that can be said to have begun the most extraordinary and mystifying chapter in the long reign of Queen Victoria.

In her journal the Queen relates how she and Prince Albert at Balmoral were looked after by Highland servants, among them the young man John Brown. On Albert's suggestion Brown became her personal gillie, or attendant. After she gradually emerged from seclusion after Albert's death, John Brown and Queen Victoria would go on long walks and rides together. To its bemusement, the Court saw the Queen becoming more and more dependent upon this strange, dour, proud, fierce, abruptly spoken Highlander, a man disrespectful of authority, sometimes drunken, often openly scornful of the Queen's stated opinions to the Court: 'Wumman! That's the daftest thing I've iver heard!' And in meek and mild tones the Queen would reply, 'Oh John. Do you think so?'

Victoria gave Brown the title of the 'Queen's Highland Servant'. He was answerable to no one but the Queen. He was permanently with her wherever she went, with no thought of taking short or extended leave. In 1876 Brown was given a cottage at Balmoral. By this time his salary was more than satisfactory and the Queen was writing: 'You will see in this the greatest anxiety to show more and more what you are to me and as time goes on this will be more and more seen and known.'

In her eyes, however, Brown was faultless. The Queen wrote: '[He is a] real comfort ... for he is devoted to me, so simple, so intelligent, so unlike an ordinary servant.' Her fulsome praise of him and all his ways continued in many entries: '... how his only object of interest is to be of service to me' ... 'and God knows how much I want to be taken care of...'

John Brown's power and influence over Queen Victoria became all that, so many years before, Sir John Conroy could ever have dreamed of achieving. The other servants at court found themselves having to use Brown as a go-between between themselves and Victoria. He was even known to issue orders himself.

There came a time when the Queen's advisers, not just singly but together, told her that Brown should be sacked. They were appalled by the rumours circulating throughout the nation by word and in print. The gutter press referred to Queen Victoria as 'Mrs Brown'. They poked fun at the Scotsman's dress and drinking habits. In the satirical magazine *Punch*, issued when the Queen was away on tour, a cartoon appeared of an unkempt Brown, in Highland dress, lounging against the empty throne of England, obviously wondering if he should aspire to it. In *Tinsley's Magazine*, an American visitor to England talked of his astonishment when at a high-society dinner the men joked about 'Mrs Brown' and explained to him that 'Mrs Brown' was the Queen:

> I was told that the Queen was not allowed to hold a review in Hyde Park, because Lord Derby and the Duke of Cambridge objected to John Brown's presence; that the Prince of Wales remonstrated with his mother over a cartoon depicting Brown in charge of the crown and the throne; that the Queen was insane and that John Brown was her keeper; that the Queen was a spiritualist and John Brown was her medium – in a word, a hundred stories, each more absurd than the other, and all vouched for by men of considerable station and authority.

The advisers were turned away with a considerably large flea in their ear. Queen Victoria made it very clear to them that she would keep John Brown by her side, that she depended upon him and just as he was devoted to her, so she was devoted to him. One can imagine the stunned, hopeless looks the advisers gave each other as they retreated.

John Brown remained with Queen Victoria until he died in March 1883. He is said to have died of pneumonia following a chill. The Queen herself was ill at the time and there was some delay before anyone could bring himself to break the news to her. Finally her son Prince Leopold, Duke of Albany went to her. As the author Peter Underwood puts it in his *Queen Victoria's Other World*, 'an awful silence came over the Queen, only the tears trickling in rivers down her cheeks betraying that she was not a wax effigy.'

After the Queen recovered somewhat, she threw herself, just as she had done on the death of Prince Albert, into an active and sustained effort to put up memorials to John Brown – in busts, statues and written memoirs. John Brown, she said in letters, had been her best and truest friend – 'as I am his'. The Court Circular contained tributes to him and his services. One impressive statue of John Brown was set up at Balmoral. It was by no means the only one. When Bertie became king he lost no time in personally smashing many of these busts and statues. Photographs were destroyed; at Windsor Castle Brown's apartment was turned into a billiards room.

A year after John Brown's death, Queen Victoria wanted to publish a memoir to her devoted servant. The memoir certainly existed at one time in manuscript but was never published; it was almost certainly destroyed. Nevertheless, in 1884, the Queen did publish *More Leaves from a Journal of Our Life in the Highlands*, in which she relates all manner of episodes involving the faithful Highland servant.

The speculations of most people who have read anything about Queen Victoria's life and her astonishing dependence upon John Brown, or have seen the 1997 movie *Mrs Brown,* have rarely gone beyond reasonably familiar and earthy grounds. The Queen had lost Albert at a comparatively early age. Neither she nor Albert was prudish and it is known that she enjoyed lovemaking with him. Although she could not have known it, almost forty years of widowhood lay before her. In her loss, did she gradually become obsessed with John Brown, the dependable Highlander originally chosen for her by Albert? He was a man almost her own age; by his origins he was apart from the Court, and unlike any other person she knew, he would speak his mind bluntly, fearlessly and honestly. He gained her total confidence. He was the man who talked with her without pomp and ceremony. He carried out simple acts of kindness towards her. Did trust turn to love? Did they become lovers? Did there even exist, as some people have suggested, a behind-the-scenes morganatic marriage?

There is something not quite right about that picture. For this is Victoria, devoted wife of Albert, who impressed everyone by her total belief that he was ever near her in spirit and that they would be reunited at her death, who often went and unlocked the door of the mausoleum at Frogmore so that she could enter and pray by his tomb, who kept his rooms at her palaces exactly as they were when he died, who even kept a photograph of his corpse on its deathbed hung a foot above the pillow on the unoccupied side of every bed she slept in.

There has long been another but little-known scenario around, one that reconciles many of the seemingly conflicting factors in the story and involves other people relevant to the scene. It is by no means irrelevant to the theme of this book.

Robert James Lees, born in 1849, showed ostensible signs of psychic abilities from the age of three when he spoke of a figure who appeared beside his bed. As the years passed, there were other alleged experiences including seeing the ghost of a boy murdered by previous occupants of the house. As a child, Robert began to sit with the Lees family and their friends in a spiritualistic circle when spiritualism became popular in Britain in the mid-1850s. It was during one of these sittings after the Prince Consort's death in 1861 that Robert, in trance, spoke as if an entity was possessing him. The entity wanted a message to be taken to the Palace. At first there was a natural reluctance to do this but, in the event, an account of the seance was written up and a copy was sent to the Palace. A week later two strangers arrived for a sitting. The entity manifested again, claimed to be Prince Albert and identified them correctly by name. They said that they would be glad to take a message if signed by a private pet-name that only he, Prince Albert, and one other person knew. This was done.

The Queen sent for the boy, and after a seance at Windsor she became convinced that the entity was in truth Albert. She wanted to keep the boy Lees as her official resident medium. After some discussion the entity said that that was not necessary, that in fact there was a man who would do just as well and that it was only on special occasions, when the Prince Consort could not communicate through this man, that Lees should be sent for. The man was named as John Brown. Miss Eva Lees, Robert James Lees' daughter, said, 'When we saw a carriage and pair bringing the two gentlemen arrive we knew where he [her father] was going and what he was going for.'

For the rest of the Queen's life this situation continued. She sent for Lees shortly before her death to thank him for his services. In the Arthur Findlay College, Stansted Hall, there is on display a newspaper obituary of Robert James Lees, dated 1931, just after he died. It states that he had last visited Queen Victoria early in 1900. She died, it will be recalled, on January 22nd of the following year. Miss Lees said that the Queen told her father: 'I am going to the Isle of Wight and I shall never come back. I hope God will reward you.'

Robert James Lees lived a long and respected life as a medium, novelist, teacher and editor. At one time he was a member of the Society for Psychical Research. He was a deeply religious man of good reputation and he never publicised an account of his relationship with Queen Victoria. The information about it comes largely from his daughter and, as Peter Underwood has demonstrated, there are a number of discrepancies in the account. But is it totally false or is there a basic truth in it?

There is that account in *Tinsley's Magazine* by the American visitor who related the various gossipy stories he had been told regarding the Queen. '... it is said that the Queen was a spiritualist and John Brown was her medium...'

There can be no doubt that the Queen, even before Albert's death, was aware of the swift spread of spiritualism in all levels of society. In fact, she was surrounded by or met people who had attended seances or investigated alleged psychic phenomena. When the Emperor Napoleon III and Empress Eugénie of France visited Queen Victoria in 1857, Victoria and Albert were fascinated by their guests' accounts of sittings with the famous medium Daniel Dunglas Home, when massive pieces of furniture rocked and tables slithered from one end of the room to the other. Eugénie was quite convinced that she had clasped her dead father's hand. Victoria wrote in her journal: 'he [Napoleon] told us some certainly extraordinary things.'

Even before 1857 the Queen and Albert were experimenting with table-turning, a practice that had become a popular pastime throughout society. In 1853 they tried it at Osborne House with Lady Ely who was reputed to be psychic. That they did so in the face of orthodox disapproval of such matters – after all, Queen Victoria was officially the Defender of the Faith and the Church had thundered against such gross superstitious practices – is probably a result of Victoria's stubbornness and open-mindedness supported by Albert's scientific curiosity about such matters. There seems no doubt that not only did Queen Victoria believe that a spiritual world existed but that under suitable conditions it could be contacted. There is an entry in her journal where she records how Princess Feodora, just before she died, talked about a beloved child who predeceased her. 'Surely,' she goes on, 'at the approach of death the veil is raised and such pure spirits are allowed to see a glimpse of those dear ones waiting for them.'

At least three of Victoria's prime ministers – Lord Melbourne,

Disraeli and Gladstone – were interested in psychic matters, the last two intensely so. Lord Melbourne, her first prime minister, claimed that he often saw ghosts. The Queen met both Gladstone and Disraeli in 1845. In later years she was well aware of their interest in the paranormal. Both Gladstone and Disraeli knew Robert James Lees. It is said that the ailing Disraeli took his last walk leaning on the arm of Lees.

Gladstone attended seances, investigated mediums and was latterly a member of the Society for Psychical Research, saying that its research was the most important being conducted anywhere in the world. Queen Victoria enjoyed hearing Gladstone's accounts of his psychic adventures, though, as she once said, 'he speaks to me as if I was a public meeting.' Gladstone in fact swung in and out of Victoria's favour in contrast to Disraeli who was always the charmer.

Disraeli was certainly aware of the Queen's interest in the paranormal and her belief that we survive death for he was a great friend of Lady Ely who joined Victoria and Albert in table-tilting sessions. If indeed Victoria conducted seances it makes complete sense of his remark on his deathbed. When he was asked if he would like a visit from the Queen, he is reported to have said: 'No, better not. She'll only ask me to take a message to Albert!'

In addition to those members of her Court, her prime ministers and visiting foreign rulers who took more than a passing interest in psychic matters, there were also meetings with Sir William Crookes (who investigated the mediums Daniel Dunglas Home and Florence Cook) and the Revd Stainton Moses, a psychic himself. There is therefore little doubt that Queen Victoria was probably intensely interested in the psychic strand that contributed to the complex tapestry of beliefs, scepticism, rationalism, orthodox religion, science, technology and other sometimes violently conflicting interests in the intellectual life of the Victorian era. Her open-mindedness and stubbornness and refusal on many occasions to listen to her advisers would surely have operated if she believed that there was any possibility of reaching by psychic means her beloved Albert. And there is no doubt whatsoever that John Brown occupied a very special place in her life. It is a great pity that her memoir on Brown was suppressed as it might have shown that Brown was a great deal more than a devoted servant. It has been suggested that what Ponsonby destroyed included records of Brown's sittings with the Queen. In fact, purely coincidentally of course, most of Brown's own papers went missing.

According to the therapist Lionel Logue, who helped Queen Victoria's great-grandson King George VI to cope with his painful and distressing speech defect, the King told him how on one occasion he had come across one of Brown's own diaries describing seances held with the Queen. The King remarked: 'My family is no stranger to spiritualism.' After King Edward VII's death, his widow, Queen Alexandra, sat with the powerful Scottish medium John Campbell Sloan.

Death came to Queen Victoria on January 22nd, 1901. She had been ill for some days and it was obvious that the end was near. Many of her large family of children and grandchildren were present at her bedside. Some forty years earlier, a few weeks before he died, Prince Albert had said to her: 'We do not know in what state we shall meet again, but that we shall recognise each other and be together in eternity I am perfectly certain.' If the important field of psychical research known as the near-death experience is truly a glimpse of a life beyond death, it may be that as her earthly gaze faded, she saw awaiting her the figure of her beloved Albert. And I certainly think it a distinct possibility that during her long, lonely widowhood, she received from time to time great comfort and spiritual strength from sittings with Robert James Lees and that strange, enigmatic Scotsman, John Brown.

3

A Sense of Something Strange

> GLENDOWER: *I can call spirits from the vasty deep.*
> HOTSPUR: *Why, so can I, or so can any man;*
>   *But will they come when you do call for them?*
>
> *Henry IV, Part 1*, William Shakespeare

By the early 1870s it must have seemed to the members of the X Club and their growing network of scientists and educators that although the war against ignorance, vested interests, incompetence and religious beliefs was ongoing and might not be won in their lifetimes, it was going their way. For one thing, orthodox religion was on the defensive, its grip on many educated and rational people slackening. Hell-fire sermons thundered from the pulpit had less and less effect upon congregations.

To many, the application of the scientific method seemed to have largely discovered the rules governing the world and some scientists even thought that they could now pronounce on what was possible in nature and what was not. There surely was no longer any need now to attribute phenomena to gods, spirits, demons, and the like. When the Sun was gradually blotted out in a solar eclipse, it was not because a dragon was swallowing it up or that the sins of the people were causing a deity to deliver a dire warning to repent and change their ways. It was simply because of the gravitational dynamics of the Earth-Moon-Sun system which at predictable times could bring the Moon in between the Sun and the Earth, intercepting the Sun's rays. The illnesses of human beings and animals were not due to spells by witches or invasion by demons. Edward Jenner's pioneering work in inoculation by cowpox had demonstrated – in spite of the opposition of many members of the medical establishment – how the ravages of smallpox could be prevented by a repeatable and understood medical procedure. The brilliant researches by Louis Pasteur in the fields of medicine, agriculture and industry had shown that micro-organisms were responsible for many of the maladies animals, plants, silkworms and human beings suffered from. Like buggy whips on the advent of the motor car, demons, malevolent spirits and witches' spells should have been rendered obsolescent and confined to the attic of outmoded beliefs. Certainly in those classes in the West who kept up with the discoveries of science and medicine, agnosticism – a word invented by Thomas Henry Huxley – would be a better standpoint to take than blind belief unsupported by evidence. By the 1870s, therefore, church-going was for many a social habit; it was also a statement that they believed in supporting morality, that they were good citizens. Perhaps many of them were also subconsciously hedging their bets.

A church-going Victorian business man was once asked by the psychical researcher Frederic Myers the question: 'Sir, tell me, what do you think will happen to you when you die?' The business man quickly changed the subject. But Myers was persistent. 'No, no, sir. Please tell me what you think will happen to you when you die.' The business man's face screwed itself into a grimace as he said rapidly: 'Well, I suppose I shall enter into the joy of my Lord but why talk about such an unpleasant subject?'

Nevertheless, at the same time, millions of citizens still derived spiritual comfort from the Church. Dedicated parish priests, by their perceptive sermons and devoted pastoral care, together with the religious feelings that arise at times in most human beings, still produced an unquestioning belief that there was a spiritual dimension to life. And yet when a loved one died and the family stood round the open grave and the priest intoned the phrase 'in the sure and certain hope of resurrection', a number of them must have wondered numbly at the extraordinary juxtaposition of 'sure and certain' with the word 'hope'.

There was therefore a ready welcome in many quarters to the early reports of phenomena that eventually were brought under the umbrella name of spiritualism. To many, the events described in the reports were contrary to common sense and everyday experience. Yet they were creepy and exciting and somehow in many people's minds they seemed to resonate with age-old belief systems. Although such happenings had been reported since the dawn of history, they had been largely discounted by the intelligent and lumped under ignorant superstition, especially now that science had demonstrated how much of nature's phenomena could be explained. But now a new phase seemed to have begun and to many it was triggered by the experiences of the Fox family in their wooden-framed house at Hydesville, near Rochester, New York State.

The year was 1848, the month March. The Fox family consisted of a father and mother and seven children. Two daughters, Margaret, aged fifteen, and Kate, aged twelve, were involved in the events from the beginning. Later a third older daughter, Leah, who had married and left home, would also become involved. Inexplicable noises began to be heard in the house – raps, bangings and scratching sounds, many of them in the younger girls' bedroom. After the parents had convinced themselves that the girls were not playing tricks, they became alarmed and the neighbours were called in. Questions posed by the people present were answered by means of agreeing upon a simple code of 'one rap for yes' and 'two raps for no'. They also hit on the idea of having a person call out the letters of the alphabet when they had asked a question. Their excitement increased when the answers told of a murder that had been committed in the house. The answers were supposedly given by the spirit of the murdered man and he revealed that his body was buried in the cellar. Naturally an attempt was made to find the body by digging but it was unsuccessful because of the waterlogged nature of the earth in the cellar. In later years it was reported that bones had been found or that when a wall collapsed in the cellar more bones had been revealed.

A new twist to the train of events occurred when the family left the house. Noises occurred in the new house, and it became clear that the phenomena were somehow dependent on the presence of the adolescent girls. Soon committees were being formed to test the genuineness of the phenomena. Were the girls frauds? Most of the members of these committees were initially hostile and sceptical about the case, and they attended meetings in the confident expectation that they would soon discover how the trickery was accomplished. They were by no means gullible people. Some were hardheaded journalists who doubtless would have welcomed an opportunity to expose fraud. The train of committees lengthened. By now, too, the types of phenomena had increased. Furniture moved by itself;

it was reported that heavy tables levitated to the ceiling and veritable drum-rolls of bangs and raps could be heard. Many of the committees were divided in their opinions but a number of influential people such as Horace Greeley, founder of the *New York Tribune*, stated that, whatever the cause of the rappings, the ladies did not make them, indeed *could* not make them.

Like a sudden appearance of foot and mouth disease followed by a lightning spread of cases throughout a region, the Fox phenomena quickly seemed to 'infect' much of the North American continent. Circles of people were being set up to experience the alleged supernatural phenomena that occurred in the presence of people now being called 'mediums', in recognition of the fact that they were presumably the intermediaries to a realm where the spirits of the dead dwelt. Apart from the physical manifestations, the mediums in various ways brought the sitters messages purporting to be from their loved ones. Many of the messages were banal in the extreme, and their descriptions of the next world the epitome of wishful thinking. But even a message as trivial as 'Uncle George is so pleased you have redecorated the front parlour, it badly needed it' could be accepted readily and probably unquestioningly as evidence of survival of Uncle George by a sitter who had just finished that chore and knew that the medium could not have known of it.

More sophisticated and swifter methods of communicating with the spirits were developed by groups of people who perhaps did not have access to a medium. The ouija board and the planchette were created for this purpose. The ouija board was the simpler of the two, and got its name from a combination of the French and German words for 'yes'. Using the smooth top of a table, cards bearing each letter of the alphabet were set out in a circle. Two additional cards had the words 'yes' and 'no' on them. Sometimes an arc of cards bearing numbers was also utilised. In many experiments nothing more than an upturned tumbler was placed in the centre of the circle. The participants each placed one finger on the bottom of the tumbler and awaited developments. Quite often the tumbler would slide to one letter after another, spelling out answers to the questions asked by the sitters. Quite often the speed with which the tumbler indicated the letters was so fast that the member of the circle chosen to record the answer had great difficulty in keeping up with the stream of letters. There is no doubt that meaningful answers can be obtained by this procedure but it is not a practice to be indulged in frivolously. The source of the replies is not by any means guaranteed to be benevolent.

The planchette consisted of a small wooden board on castors or wheels. It was often heart-shaped with a pencil at the apex pointing downwards. Invented in France in the nineteenth century, it was employed to facilitate automatic writing.

An appreciation of the wildfire spread of spiritualism and the first attempts of scientists to grapple with it can be obtained from Brian Inglis's scholarly book *Natural and Supernatural*, acclaimed when it appeared by, among many, Bernard Levin, Arthur Koestler and Colin Wilson and receiving praise in such journals as the *Economist*, *New Scientist* and *Psychology Today*. His second work on the subject, *Science and Parascience*, was a worthy successor, bringing the story up to 1914. But what most nineteenth-century people did not know was that spiritualistic phenomena and mediums were not a modern innovation, nor could one say that the movement had begun in the United States and crossed the Atlantic. The Neoplatonists, Porphyry and Iamblichus, active in the third and early fourth century AD, were keenly interested in the earlier pagan religious sect that practised *theurgy*, a system of magic devoted to getting into contact with the Unseen. By doing this, the theurgists hoped to save their souls and, as a bonus, obtain foreknowledge of the future. The subsequent work of the Neoplatonists resulted in theurgy becoming an intellectual and moral force in ancient Rome.

There is no doubt that the theurgists used mediums. In the important paper by E.R. Dodds, 'Supernormal Phenomena in Classical Antiquity', Dodds states that two terms were used to refer to the person who was capable of entering a trance: *docheus* – the recipient – and *katochos* – the one who is held down. He also adds that the word *meson*, the literal equivalent of the English word 'medium', was suggested but rejected by Iamblichus. If the accounts given by Iamblichus of the phenomena occurring at the sessions are to be trusted, the two words are certainly appropriate and the whole procedure bore a marked resemblance to the modern spiritualistic seance.

In fact, at an era much nearer to the Victorian age than the latter days of the Roman Empire, spiritualism, channelling, mediumistic phenomena and psychical research came together in the form of one remarkable man, Emanuel Swedenborg. His fully documented career is one of the most astonishing in the annals of psychical research and the yet uncharted shores of human personality. He was born on January 29th, 1688, in Stockholm, Sweden. His father, Jesper Svedberg, was raised amongst a farming community based in Dalecarlia noted for their strong independent spirit. Jesper Svedberg studied theology at Lund and Uppsala universities, going on to hold successive positions as Court Chaplain, Dean of Uppsala and Bishop of Skara. Swedenborg's mother, Sara Behm, married Jesper in 1683. In recognition of the family's contributions to society it was ennobled in 1719 and the family name was changed to Swedenborg.

As a young man, Swedenborg lived with his sister and uncle who also exercised an extensive influence on him. Eric Benzelius, Swedenborg's uncle, in turn held the posts of librarian, then Professor of Theology at Uppsala University, progressing to become Bishop of Linköping and later Archbishop of Uppsala. It is not surprising then that Swedenborg's upbringing was strongly influenced by academic and religious circles.

At the age of twenty-one, after graduating from Uppsala University, Swedenborg embarked on a series of travels throughout Europe to widen his education. Highly intelligent, energetic and interested in a remarkably wide range of disciplines, he studied not only mathematics, natural history and astronomy but also watchmaking, engraving and the design and construction of mathematical instruments. These pursuits were in addition to his other academic and theological studies. By 1714, the depth and range of his genius included the creation of numerous mechanical inventions, among them designs for a submarine and flying machine. He also did research on a method of finding terrestrial longitude from the Moon's successive positions against the celestial sphere, a problem that was finally solved later in the century by the creation of accurate chronometers by Thomas Harrison.

By 1715, Swedenborg had begun publishing Sweden's first scientific journal *Daedalus Hyperboreus* ('The Nordic Daedalus'), in which he wrote accounts of his own mathematical discoveries and inventions and also of the work of the Swedish engineer, Christopher Polhem. Swedenborg by now was not only a prolific publisher of scientific papers but was in the process of writing books on his many fields of study. All his life he would remain eager to promulgate his discoveries for what he believed to be the betterment of the human race. He epitomised the complete natural philosopher in the old sense of one who has devoted himself to the study and understanding of all natural phenomena. His achievements were also becoming recognised throughout Europe. Before he was thirty years of age King Charles XII of Sweden appointed him to the post of Extraordinary Assessor of the College of Mines. His ever-growing fields of study embraced not only mathematics and astronomy – including compilations of tables predicting eclipses of the Sun and Moon – but chemistry, metallurgy, navigation, dock embankments and the science of mining. His intellectual pursuits also extended to military engineering and it was his activities in this sphere that helped to turn the fortunes of one of the many campaigns of Charles XII. A more than competent financier and political economist, he anticipated the conclusions of Adam Smith.

In 1718 Swedenborg published the first work on algebra in the Swedish language and in 1721 a work on chemistry and physics. There came a gap in the succeeding ten years but it turned out that in that decade he had obviously been thinking deeply and productively about many topics apart from his duties as a civil servant and mining engineer. In 1733 he began a new European journey and the following year published in Leipzig (in three folio volumes) *Opera Philosophica et Mineralia* ('Philosophical and Logical Works'). His conclusions about many aspects of nature, reached by inductive argument, are strikingly similar to those of modern scientists. He also suggested a process of formation of the Solar System's Sun and planets from nebular material, an idea predating the Kant–Laplace nebular hypothesis.

In 1736, granted a new leave of absence from his office as assessor, this remarkable man was off again on his travels, this time visiting France, Italy and Holland. In Amsterdam he produced a new work in two enormous volumes called *Oeconomia Regni Animalis* ('The Economy of the Animal Kingdom'). By the time this work appeared, Swedenborg had turned fifty years of age. As these volumes show, he had been engaged in prolonged and productive research into human physiology and anatomy. His conclusions concerning the nature of the human brain, mainly drawn from the work of experimentalists and microscopists, led him to the theory that the cortex was the centre for all higher psychical activities and the seat of the human soul.

If at this period of his life Emanuel Swedenborg had died from illness or accident, it seems reasonable to suppose that his reputation now as a responsible, massively prolific, innovative scientist and engineer in many fields would have been accepted without dispute. He did live, of course, and the remaining thirty years of his life astonished and flabbergasted his contemporaries. For Swedenborg, the man of science, engineering and all those other subjects he had mastered and illuminated by his discoveries, was suddenly transformed into a visionary and mystic, who now almost daily reported his travels into various spiritual planes of existence, including heaven and hell. It was a transformation that seems to have taken place in London in April 1744:

> The same night the world of spirits, hell and heaven, were convincingly opened to me, where I found many persons of my acquaintance of all conditions. Thereafter the Lord daily opened the eyes of my spirit to see in perfect wakefulness what was going on in the other world, and to converse, broadawake, with angels and spirits.

In his new state of mind, Swedenborg believed that the spheres he visited were places in which a separation of souls took place: those who were largely selfless and worthy were gathered into the heavenly realm to be guided and helped by angels while those of a selfish, brutal and cruel disposition gravitated into a slumlike hell in which they tormented and deceived each other and in turn were tormented by demons. Angels and demons were not of a different order to human beings but were human beings who had lived on earth and who were either undeveloped souls – the demons – or highly developed souls – the angels. Swedenborg maintained that at will he could now enter these realms and talk to the angels he met there, obtaining advice and information from them that he could not otherwise have known. He now began to produce a voluminous output of books in Latin concerning his life as a spiritual philosopher, describing not only his own spiritual experiences but also what he had learned and observed concerning the nature of the universe beyond the material, and the roles that human beings, both individual and together, were destined to play.

The facile conclusion quickly put forward by many of his contemporaries was that poor old Swedenborg, possibly through overwork, had become mentally disturbed to the point of insanity. As he continued to publish his strange views, couched in a framework of Christian symbolism, he became an outcast from a hostile church. And yet many of his contemporaries noted that he was no babbling fool. To the contrary, Swedenborg remained his old, sober, courteous, kindly self. His friend Cuno, an Amsterdam banker, once remarked, 'When he gazed at me with his smiling blue eyes it was as if truth itself was speaking from them.' He continued to attend Court and dine with friends. But it was noted by more and more people that in his new mode of existence, he would frequently seem to abstract himself from the company he was in, his lips moving as if there were additional unseen members there that he was listening and replying to. It is in some of these well-authenticated accounts that we see that the easy and comforting assumption that Swedenborg had simply lost his head cannot be maintained.

At Court one day, the Queen of Sweden said to him, 'I believe, Count Swedenborg, that you visit heaven and hell?' 'Indeed I do, your Majesty.' 'Ah, then, perhaps you will give my brother my best regards.' Some time later he was back at court. He drew the Queen aside and whispered some words in her ear. Observers saw her face become chalky white. Afterwards she stated: 'Only God and my dead brother knew what Count Swedenborg has just told me.'

In 1759 he was one of sixteen guests at dinner at the Gothenburg Mansion. It was noticed that about six o'clock in the evening he became alarmed. He informed the company that a fire had broken out in Stockholm – about three hundred miles away. At intervals thereafter he told the guests of the progress of the conflagration, commenting on whose house had now been consumed by the fire. Later still in the evening he jumped up: 'God, be praised! It has been put out just a few houses from mine.' Swedenborg also gave a detailed account of the disaster to the Governor two days before messengers arrived with reports relating how the fire had indeed developed exactly according to the 'eye-witness bulletins' Swedenborg had given. The philosopher Immanuel Kant investigated this event, noting that the guests were reliable and credible witnesses, and thereafter admitted that he himself had been much disturbed to find himself unable either to believe or disbelieve in it.

One of the most famous of these authenticated incidents involving Swedenborg occurred in Amsterdam. Again it occurred at a dinner.

The Czar of Russia, Peter III, had been deposed and Catherine the Great had taken his place. A look of shock appeared on Swedenborg's face and, when a member of the company inquired what was wrong, he informed them that the conspirators had just murdered Peter III in a cellar. He asked them to note the date and what he had told them. A few days later his words were confirmed by published accounts in newspapers.

There are many more occasions where it would appear that Swedenborg, in his post-natural philosopher mode, was clairvoyant, clairaudient and even precognitive. He continued to live his strange life, publishing his careful, scientific and detailed descriptions of the new realms, their inhabitants and their moral laws, yet still travelling extensively and demonstrating to his friends that he had lost nothing of his intelligence. In 1761, just eleven years before he died, he received a commendation from Sweden's prime minister on the reports he had prepared on Sweden's financial state.

Indeed his mind remained clear until his death at the age of eighty-four, in London, England – a death whose date he had predicted with complete equanimity. When he learned that the Wesleys, the great evangelists, wished to meet him, but could not do so until April or May, he wrote back that it would be too late by then because he would have passed on. It is on record that Swedenborg only paid his rent up until the end of March. Having thanked his landlady for her services, he retired upstairs to his room, where he died on March 29th, 1772.

Although in life his mystical teachings were largely ignored, within a few years after his death support for them spread and a Swedenborgian movement developed and ultimately became a religion. The first Swedenborgian churches were established in England in 1778 and in America in 1792. When the modern spiritualism movement developed in the mid-nineteenth century, Swedenborg's teachings about the afterlife and the moral laws governing the evolution of human beings in this world and the next were influential in formulating the canon of spiritual teachings that today most spiritualists adhere to.

In sharp contrast to the privileged upbringing and education of Swedenborg is the early life of the influential Victorian 'channeller', Andrew Jackson Davis, the so-called Poughkeepsie Seer. Born in Blooming Grove, Orange County, New York State on August 11th, 1826, Andrew was the sixth child and only son of an often drunken cobbler and his wife, a deeply religious but illiterate woman. Only one of his five sisters survived girlhood. It is perhaps not surprising that being brought up in such a luckless, tragedy-prone family, the boy was frail and of a nervous disposition.

The family drifted from place to place, ending up in Poughkeepsie in 1838. Andrew took a number of unskilled jobs with tradesmen, artisans and farmers but never lasted long at any. The turning point in his life came in December 1843 when a local tailor, William Levingston, a keen amateur mesmerist, managed to entrance him. Travelling mesmerists were popular in that age, some of them claiming not only to demonstrate what we would now term the hypnotic state but also the marvellous abilities bordering on magic that sometimes ostensibly seemed to be awakened by mesmerism. Levingston was fascinated by the new Davis. When hypnotised he claimed he could see through a human body as if it was made of glass. In that state Davis would confidently make diagnoses of the person's health and maladies. Levingston now devoted his time to the 'Poughkeepsie Seer', as Davis came to be known.

In March 1844 Davis experienced a strange, altered state of consciousness during which he wandered many miles from Poughkeepsie into the Catskill Mountains. He claimed after his journey that he had had meetings with Galen, the Greek physician, and Emanuel Swedenborg. Descending the mountain, he fell asleep in a graveyard. When he awoke, he found himself with Galen. Galen talked at length with Davis concerning his, Galen's, healing methods and presented him with his staff. Soon after, Davis saw Swedenborg, who predicted that Davis would 'become a vessel for the perception of wisdom, opening the soul's way to harmony'. Thereafter Davis attempted to climb over the cemetery wall and got caught on a post. He lost his temper and Galen changed his mind about giving him his staff, obviously judging that after his lack of control he was not yet worthy of it. Some time later, Davis regained his normal consciousness and found that he had wandered home.

Davis continued to have visions that convinced him that he had a mission in life. He was to become an oracle, revealing divine truth. It was while healing in Bridgeport, Connecticut that Davis met a herbalist doctor, S. Silas Lyon, and formed the opinion that he had found the right man to mesmerise him and realise his destiny. He therefore dismissed Levingston and went to New York with Lyon, where he continued to heal. Three months later he chose the Universalist minister the Revd William Fishbough to act as his scribe and in November 1845 the three men began to produce and record Davis's channelled book *The Principles of Nature, Her Divine Revelations, and a Voice to Mankind, By and Through Andrew Jackson Davis, the 'Poughkeepsie Seer' and 'Clairvoyant'.* It was published in January 1847.

The way by which this lengthy – 782-page – book was produced is of interest. When a production session was scheduled, Davis, Lyon and Fishbough would gather in the parlour of their New York apartment. Lyon would then proceed to hypnotise Davis. After a few minutes, Davis would shudder convulsively then remain motionless for some five minutes. During this time, blindfolded to protect his eyes from the light, he would enter a cataleptic state, in which he lay rigid and cold, hardly breathing. Finally, though still entranced, he would be restored to some normality and begin to dictate. His utterances came only a phrase or two at a time. Lyon would repeat each phrase to Fishbough, who wrote them down. Each session could last anywhere from forty minutes to four hours, producing about five pages. The sessions were usually witnessed by three people chosen by Davis. The author Edgar Allan Poe, the Fourierist Albert Brisbane and trance poet Thomas Lake Harris were often present. By far the most important, however, was Dr George Bush, Professor of Hebrew at New York University. A great biblical scholar and Swedenborgian, Bush enthusiastically endorsed the authenticity of Davis's trance pronouncements.

The book sold well, going into four editions alone before the end of the year. The enthusiastic, lengthy review of it in the *New York Tribune* by Professor Bush must have helped. Davis's lack of formal education simply increased the awe with which it was received, for both Lyon and Fishbough said that they had made no changes except in grammar and spelling. What it taught about the creation of the world, what it revealed about God and mankind's destiny struck a chord with its readers, especially the American people who felt perhaps at that time more than at any subsequent era that they were in the holy task of carving from the wilderness a new creation, doing God's work. Man was the pinnacle of God's achievements and death was certainly not the end. In his spiritual progress, a human being ultimately united with the Godhead. Numerous pronouncements were made concerning the creation and development of the solar system, and the evolution of the Earth. A history of language, myths, religions, biblical matters, human societies and much more filled the vast tome. Definite opinions regarding the worth or otherwise of a wide variety of human institutions and professions were scattered throughout.

The book was not received without criticism or even accusations of fraud. Some of its critics pointed to parts of it that seemed to have been lifted from current orthodox scientific theory or taken from Swedenborgian doctrine. Was it the undistilled production of the almost uneducated Davis even now barely into his twenties or had other hands fine-tuned it? Nevertheless, Davis's fame as the Poughkeepsie Seer spread. His reputation was not even seriously harmed by his subsequent involvement with Mrs Catherine Dodge, a wealthy married woman twenty years older than Davis. She managed to get the law to dissolve her marriage and in July 1848 Davis and Catherine were married. It was not a marriage made in heaven and lasted only a few years. She died in 1853, leaving her fortune to her husband.

Andrew Jackson Davis's career was a long one, an amalgam of spiritualist, herbalist and healer. He wrote other books on spiritual diagnosis and healing and continued his lectures. At the age of sixty he qualified as an orthodox physician and herbalist and, although he slipped thereafter to some extent from the public eye, he remained a respected figure. In his old age he ran a bookstore in Boston. He died as recently as 1910 at the age of eighty-four.

Sir Arthur Conan Doyle stated that he could not doubt that, as an ignorant youth, Davis had been invaded by some source which provided him with great knowledge; that he, before he had heard of Swedenborg or his teachings, claimed to have met him and learned from him; and that his subsequent extraordinary life, in such contrast to his miserable and unpromising start in life, was a direct consequence of those visionary experiences.

The sudden proliferation of ostensible psychic phenomena and spiritualist circles in the mid-nineteenth century, therefore, was by no means a new phase in human affairs. By 1850 the stage had been set for the entrance of one of the most formidable mediums ever studied by investigators of psychic phenomena – Daniel Dunglas Home. Born in Scotland in 1833, and allegedly related to the famous Home family of the Scottish borders, he was adopted by an aunt living in the United States. At the age of seventeen, he was told in no uncertain terms to leave when in his presence furniture moved of its own accord. More than that, he was able on occasion to tell his aunt when people she was acquainted with would die. Fortunately for him, word of his burgeoning psychic gifts had spread and, one might say, entering into the spirit of the times, he began to give seances. Enthusiastic reports by people who attended these meetings came to the ears of Professor David Wells of Harvard and William Cullen Bryant. Both of them were keen investigators of alleged spiritistic phenomena. Their subsequent experiences with Home led them to state that a wide variety of physical phenomena had occurred; there had been evidence that some type of intelligence had been at work and they had been able to convince themselves that no fraud had been practised.

In the following five years, people of impeccable reputation bore witness to the growing list of paranormal events that occurred in Home's presence. He had levitated; spectral hands had been seen to lift objects; a hand had written on paper with a pencil. There has survived the account of Frank L. Burr, editor of the *Hartford Times*, of events at a seance in Connecticut in August 1852. With respect to Home's levitation, Burr wrote that he was 'taken up into the air... He palpitated from head to foot with the contending emotions of joy and fear ... and the third time he was carried to the ceiling of the apartment, with which his hands and feet came into gentle contact.' Burr also noted how those present saw a hand 'very thin, very pale and remarkably attenuated' writing with a pencil: 'The hand afterwards came and shook hands with each one present. I felt it minutely. It was tolerably well and symmetrically made, though not perfect; and it was soft and slightly warm. IT ENDED AT THE WRIST.'

By the time Home sailed for Great Britain in 1855, he was famous and firmly caught on the revolving wheel of scepticism, demonstration, acclamation, and renewed scepticism. Unless he had supreme confidence in his own abilities, his peripatetic life under the sceptical eyes of the doubters must have been extremely stressful. There is a description of him in his early twenties by the poet Robert Browning, who noted Home as a well-grown young man above average height with a rather handsome and prepossessing face indicative of intelligence. There are photographs confirming

Browning's words. In them Home appears beardless with slightly long hair and a moustache. Later in his life Princess Metternich described him as being fairly tall, slim, well-built, and in his dress suit and white tie looking like a gentleman of the highest social standing. 'His face was attractive,' she wrote, 'in its expression of gentle melancholy.'

It would be tedious and unproductive to describe in detail many of the hundreds of sittings Home gave during the European part of his career. His life was effectively his early American career writ large. The list of well-known people of good reputation who testified that they had witnessed a wide variety of paranormal phenomena under conditions that they believed made fraud impossible would form a substantial book itself. Among them were Lord Adare, Robert Bell, Robert Chambers, William Crookes, Ralph Waldo Emerson, Sir Edwin Landseer, the Master of Lindsay, Henry Wadsworth Longfellow, Lord Lytton, John Ruskin, William Makepeace Thackeray, Alexey Tolstoy, Alfred Russel Wallace, to name but a few. It is important to realise that Home for the most part would demonstrate in rooms that he simply had no chance of preparing like a conjuror or stage magician. It is also important to realise that the events almost always took place in adequately lit rooms so that the sitters at all times were able to see everyone present, including Home.

Home's social standing rapidly rose over the years. It was in 1857 that the Emperor Napoleon III, the Empress Eugénie and Prince Murat saw a table rising off the floor in the presence of the medium. They sat on more than one occasion with Home and had even more startling experiences which they would describe to Queen Victoria and Prince Albert when they visited them in England later that year. The following year in St Petersburg, Home married a god-daughter of Czar Nicholas – Alexandrina de Kroll, sister-in-law of Count Gregoire de Koucheleff-Bresboradka. The best man was Alexandre Dumas; Alexey Tolstoy was one of the groomsmen. Tolstoy was one of the sitters in 1859 when Home returned to England and was persuaded by Mrs Milner-Gibson, the wife of the President of the Board of Trade, to give a series of seances in her house.

It is, however, the two series of sittings with Home carried out in the second half of the 1860s and the first half of the 1870s that have the most importance for the study of Victorian spiritualism.

The first series was organised by Lord Adare. He had no knowledge of spiritualism but was puzzled by the accounts of so many people who had attended sittings with Home. His father, the Earl of Dunraven, on the other hand had studied the subject to some extent and was a trained scientist and observer. He attended as many of the sittings as he could and was kept informed about events at the others by letters from his son. He wrote an introduction to the collected letters when they were privately printed in 1869. The document was published in 1924 as part of the *Proceedings of the Society for Psychical Research*. Among the people who attended was Adare's friend, the Master of Lindsay, who later in life (as the Earl of Crawford) would become a Fellow of the Royal Society and the President of the Royal Astronomical Society. He was present with Adare and Captain Wynne on the occasion when they claimed they had seen Home levitate and, while horizontal, float out of a window on the third storey of Adare's London house and return through another window. Sceptics have tried to discredit the testimony by quoting discrepancies in the witnesses' accounts, but so far no acceptable rational explanation has been put forward to explain the phenomenon.

Among the people present at other sittings in the series were the journalist H.T. Humphries, the barrister H.D. Jencken and Mr and Mrs Hall, in whose house Mr Humphries saw Home elongate his body:

> Mr Home was seen by all of us to increase in height to the extent of some eight or ten inches, and then sank to some six or eight inches below his normal stature. Having returned to his usual height, he took Lord Adare and the Master of Lindsay, and placing one beside each post of the folding doors, lay down on the floor, touching the feet of one with his head and the feet of the other with his feet. He was then again elongated, and pushed both Lord Adare and the Master of Lindsay backward along the floor with his head and feet as he was stretched out, his arms and hands remaining motionless by his side.

Mr Hall made some measurements and said that the two men had been pushed by Home more than seven feet apart.

One of the most spectacular paranormal phenomena demonstrated by Home was his seeming ability to avoid being burned in circumstances that would have had any normal person shrieking in agony. Even more spectacular was Home's power to convey this incombustibility to another. In 1869, in a letter to Lord Dunraven, Mrs Hall related how:

> Mr Home stirred the fire, which was like a red-hot furnace, so as to increase the heat ... and finally drew out of the fire with his hand a huge lump of live, burning coal, so large that he held it in both hands as he came from the fire place ... Mr Hall was seated nearly opposite to where I sat; and I saw Mr Home, after standing for about half a minute at the back of Mr Hall's chair, deliberately place the lump of burning coal on his head ... I had perfect faith that he would not be injured. Someone said, 'Is it not hot?' Mr Hall answered, 'Warm, but not hot'. Mr Home had moved a little away, but returned, still in a trance; he smiled, and seemed quite pleased; and then proceeded to draw up Mr Hall's white hair over the red coal; Mr Home drew the hair into a sort of pyramid, the coal, still red, showing beneath the hair.

Evidently Home then handed the coal to Mrs Hall, who did find it warm to her hand but when she bent down to examine it more closely, the heat was so intense that she had quickly to draw her face away.

In the December 1889 *Proceedings of the Society for Psychical Research* there is a paper by William Crookes, a Fellow of the Royal Society. Crookes gives, after an introduction, the original notes of eleven of his sittings with Home between May 9th, 1871 and April 21st, 1872. The sittings took place in three houses: Miss Douglas's house at 81 South Audley Street; Mr Crookes' house at 20 Mornington Road; and his brother Mr Walter Crookes' house at 24 Motcombe Street. The total number of people who took part was twenty-seven, not including Home. Crookes was present at all eleven sittings, Mrs Crookes for ten. Mrs Humphrey and Mrs Walter Crookes attended on seven occasions; Mr Walter Crookes on six; Miss Douglas was present on four occasions, and Mr Serjeant Cox and Miss A. Crookes were present on three occasions. Most of the others, like Mr Alfred Russel Wallace, were present on only one occasion.

Sir William Crookes

Sir William Crookes (1832–1919) was one of Victorian Britain's outstanding scientists. He was elected to the Royal Society in 1863 and was by no means ignorant of the spiritualistic movement. In 1867 Philip, his youngest brother, died. William and his wife were persuaded by Cromwell Varley, an electrical engineer, to attend a number of seances. Crookes' experiences at these seances determined him to investigate in a serious scientific manner the anomalous phenomena he and so many other sitters seemed to have encountered. His intention to do so, signalled in the *Quarterly Journal of Science*, which he edited, was widely welcomed. A *Times* leader of December 26th, 1872 could still chide the scientific establishment in the following words:

> That in a generation that boasts itself to be one of exact science and plain matter-of-fact a belief should have been so long-lived, and should have grown even to such large proportions that Mr William Howitt, one of its chief fanatics, can number its adherents at 'twenty millions', and that it should have attained to such an age and vitality without its falsity having been demonstrated to the satisfaction of all but the very ignorant is very strange indeed. It is evident either that the subject is surrounded by unusual difficulties or that in this matter our scientific men have signally failed to do their duty by the public... We believe the latter to be the case.

In January 1874 Crookes did publish an article describing some of his experiences at the eleven sittings between May 1871 and April 1872 he had had with D.D. Home. To put it mildly, the article was not well received since it made it plain that Crookes believed he and others had indeed witnessed *under scientific conditions* a large range of paranormal phenomena, including movements and levitations of a table and other objects, the ability to handle red-hot coals, the materialisation of hands and the playing of an accordion.

In his introduction to his paper in the December 1889 *Proceedings of the Society for Psychical Research*, Crookes stated that he had had every intention of incorporating into a book his printed and unprinted observations into the phenomena called 'spiritual', but that pressure of his scientific work had so far prevented this. However, on the invitation of the Society for Psychical Research, he had agreed to contribute some of his notes on seances with D.D. Home. 'Their publication will show that I have not changed my mind... I find nothing to retract or to alter. I have discovered no flaw in the experiments then made, or in the reasoning I based upon them.' With regard to the question of possible deceit he goes on to say: 'I was on my guard even in D.D. Home's case, although I am bound to say that with him I never detected any trickery or deceit whatever, nor heard any first-hand evidence of such from other persons.' Discussing conjuring and the fact that many other exposures of fraudulent mediumship had since taken place, he adds, '[that they have], I think, ... made more clear that certain of Home's phenomena fall quite outside the category of marvels producible by sleight of hand or prepared apparatus.' Crookes ended his introduction with a remarkably prophetic caution:

Those who assume ... that we are now acquainted with all, or nearly all, or even with any assignable proportion, of the forces at work in the universe, show a limitation of conception which ought to be impossible in an age when the widening of the circle of our definite knowledge does but reveal the proportionately widening circle of our blank, absolute, indubitable ignorance.'

Of the meeting in Miss Douglas's home on the evening of May 9th, 1871, Mr William Crookes reported:

Mr Home sank back in his chair... He then rose up in a trance and made signs for his eyes to be blindfolded. This was done... He went to the candle on a side table (close to the large table) and passed his fingers backwards and forwards through the flame so slowly that they must have been severely burnt under ordinary circumstances. He then held his fingers

70

up, smiled and nodded as if pleased, took up a fine cambric handkerchief belonging to Miss Douglas, folded it up in his right hand and went to the fire. Here he threw off the bandage from his eyes and by means of the tongs lifted a piece of red hot charcoal from the centre and deposited it on the folded cambric; bringing it across the room, he told us to put out the candle which was on the table, knelt down close to Mrs W.F. and spoke to her about it in a low voice. Occasionally he fanned the coal to a white heat with his breath. Coming a little further round the room, he spoke to Miss Douglas saying, 'We shall have to burn a very small hole in the handkerchief. We have a reason for this which you do not see.' Presently he took the coal back to the fire and handed the handkerchief to Miss Douglas. A small hole about half an inch in diameter was burnt in the centre, and there were two small points near it, but it was not even singed anywhere else. (I took the handkerchief away with me and on testing it in my laboratory, found that it had not undergone the slightest chemical preparation which could have rendered it fireproof.)

Mr Home again went to the fire, and after stirring the hot coal about with his hand, took out a red-hot piece nearly as big as an orange, and putting it on his right hand, covered it over with his left hand so as to almost completely enclose it, and then blew into the small furnace thus extemporised until the lump of charcoal was nearly white-hot, and then drew my attention to the lambent flame which was flickering over the coal and licking round his fingers; he fell on his knees, looked up in a reverent manner, held up the coal in front and said: 'Is not God good? Are not His laws wonderful?'

Going again to the fire, he took out another hot coal with his hand and holding it up said to me, 'Is not that a beautiful large bit, William? We want to bring that to you. Pay no attention at present.' The coal, however, was not brought. Mr Home said: 'The power is going,' and soon came back to his chair and woke up.

There was a circular table present at the sittings at Miss Douglas's home, of height three feet and diameter three feet, with one central pillar on three legs, round which the people present sat. It weighed 32 pounds. On a number of occasions it tilted:

... and kept inclined sufficiently long for those who wished to look under with a candle and examine how the hands of Mr Home and the others present were touching it. Sometimes it stood on two legs, and sometimes it was balanced on one. I, who had brought a spring balance in my pocket, was now invited by Mr Home to try an experiment in the alteration of weight.

In a number of such experiments, Crookes satisfied himself that when requested, the table would become grossly lighter or heavier, the table's weight being measured by the balance. On some of these occasions the hands of the sitters rested lightly on top of the table. In one of the events,

as soon as the words 'Be heavy' were spoken, the table creaked, shuddered, and appeared to settle itself firmly into the floor. The effect was as if the power of a gigantic electro-magnet had been suddenly turned on, the table constituting the armature. All hands were, as before, very lightly touching the upper surface of the table with their fingers. A force of 36 lb. was now required to raise the foot of the table from the floor. I lifted it up and down four or five times, and the index of the balance kept pretty constant at 36 lb., not varying more than 1/2 lb... Mr Home once lifted his hands for a moment quite off the table. His feet were tucked back under his chair the whole time.

The second time the 'increased weight' was called for, the reading on the spring balance reached 45 pounds. On that occasion, 'the ends of the fingers [of the sitters were] underneath the table top, the palms being upwards and the thumbs visible, so that, if any force were unconsciously exerted, it should tend to diminish the weight'.

On a number of these evenings there were movements of furniture, on one occasion the sitters witnessing a small table moving when no one was near it; people's clothes were tugged without anything being seen, trains of raps were heard, Home was seen to levitate, and a hand was seen by some of the sitters. A wooden lath:

lifted itself up on its edge, then reared itself upon one end and fell down. It then floated up four inches above the table, and moved quite round the circle, pointing to Mrs Wm. Crookes. It then rose up and passed over our heads outside the circle!

Later on:

The lath, which on its last excursion had settled in front of the further window, quite away from the circle, now moved along the floor four or five times very noisily. It then came up to Mr T., and passed into the circle over his shoulder... The lath then went to the water bottle and pushed it several times nearly over, to move it away from the opening in the table. The lath then went endways down the opening. 'The tumbler moved about a little. The lath moved up through the opening in the table and answered 'Yes' and 'No' to questions, by bobbing up and down three times or once.

During eight of the reported sittings an accordion played music in a manner that seemed impossible for Home to have managed in any normal manner. Apart from Home's levitation feats and his incombustibility, the experiments with the accordion that Crookes carried out are among the best known. Home would hold the instrument with one hand, letting the keyed end hang downwards. His hand and the accordion would be under the table, his other hand resting on the tabletop. While the musical instrument was playing, the gentlemen in the group looked under the table to see what was going on. The keyed end would be seen to be rising and falling vigorously, the keys moving as the music required. No hand, strings, wires or anything else could be seen touching that end. Crookes' reports make it clear that the music was played skilfully and beautifully. During the second seance when Alfred Russel Wallace was present and the accordion was again played, Wallace, looking under the table, said that he saw a hand distinctly moving the instrument up and down and playing on the keys. Crookes notes that on two occasions a man's rich voice accompanied the music from a corner of the room and on one of these occasions a bird was heard whistling and chirping.

In order to investigate the phenomenon, Crookes and his associates fashioned a wire cage through which electricity could be passed at will. A door in the cage enabled an accordion belonging to

Crookes himself to be placed inside where it could be seen through the wire mesh, the door now being securely fastened. Home raised his hand up and down above the cage; the observers saw the accordion moving up and down and heard it play music. Crookes switched on the electric current. Again the accordion played and as well as before.

Crookes and his colleagues then went on to study the mediumship of a young woman called Florence Cook. She had been recommended to Crookes by Home himself. This carried some weight, as Home was scathing about fraudulent mediums. Again, Crookes reported that he became convinced over the course of the sittings that the phenomena he and his group witnessed with Florence Cook were paranormal. They included the materialisation of a woman who walked about the seance room in Crookes' house, talked with the sitters and seemed to be in all respects indistinguishable from a real human being. Photographs of the alleged materialised spirit still exist, although their value as evidence is debatable. Again the sceptics of the time poured scorn on Crookes and his colleagues, even passing it around that Crookes was having an affair with Florence and had helped her to fake the phenomena.

Crookes' first report was therefore eagerly awaited. It appeared in 1871 and described the experiments with the accordion and the wire cage, also an experiment concerning the ability of Home to move paranormally a board attached to a spring balance. William Huggins, the astronomer and pioneer spectroscopist, and Serjeant Cox, a barrister, were present.

If Crookes thought that his careful report would be treated seriously he was mistaken. In an anonymous article in the *Quarterly Review* the following argument was taken. The phenomena could not happen in nature therefore Home had deluded Crookes, Huggins and Cox. For them to have been so easily taken in by this fraudulent medium, they really could not be considered to be investigators of any capability. An utterly scurrilous attack on their scientific and professional skills then followed, the writer stating that the qualifications they had – both Crookes and Huggins were Fellows of the Royal Society – had been conferred upon them with considerable hesitation. There were a number of other completely false libels in the article. The anonymous author was subsequently identified to be Dr Carpenter, one of Crookes' most persistent opponents, also a Fellow of the Royal Society and the Registrar at London University. The revealing sequel to Crookes and his colleagues was that Carpenter, instead of suffering a well-deserved rebuke from the scientific establishment for his cowardly and dishonest attack, got off scot-free. In later years, he continued openly to oppose research into psychical phenomena and was joined enthusiastically by one of the members of the X Club, John Tyndall. In Tyndall's lectures, in seemingly irrefutable terms, he gave reasons why the phenomena of spiritualism simply could not exist in the material world. 'Surely,' he added, 'no baser delusion has ever obtained dominance over the weak mind of man.'

Charles Darwin was much more ambivalent. He knew Crookes' calibre as a scientist, yet in his own scientific studies he had long held the conviction that the universe operated according to cold lifeless laws; there was absolutely no evidence for belief in human survival after bodily death. When his beloved daughter Annie died, her lovable personality, her happy and trusting nature, ceased to exist. This bleak conclusion he had stoically accepted. All that remained of her were some of her physical possessions like her writing box and those memories of her that existed in the minds of people who had known her. And they too would cease to exist. Certainly, like many, he had been intrigued with the astonishing spread of the spiritualistic movement in North America and Europe, but he had also noted that few, if any, scientists had undertaken a scientific study of the field. Now Crookes and his colleagues had had the courage to do so, and their findings triggered painful trains of thought in his mind. Did there exist in some way a realm inhabited by the spirits of the dead from which they could struggle to convince those left behind of their continued existence? Did Annie in some way still exist? Had he let her down – and thousands of other living people – in nailing the flag of agnosticism to his mast?

Darwin could not turn away from the problem.

In due course a seance was set up in the house of one of Darwin's brothers, Erasmus. Thomas Huxley's brother George was present as was Francis Galton, the anthropologist and eugenicist together with the philologist Hensleigh Wedgwood. George Lewes, a versatile writer and thinker in many fields but a sceptic in spiritualistic matters, also attended, along with George Eliot (Mary Ann Evans) the novelist. Charles Darwin was there but went upstairs before the main phenomena occurred. When he came downstairs again he found that all the chairs were standing on the table; they had been lifted over the heads of those present round the table. The medium was Charles Williams and, although the room had been in darkness, two of the sitters had held the medium's hands and feet all the time.

Darwin, even more disturbed and perplexed by now, wrote an account of the seance to Thomas Huxley. That member of the X Club, unlike the staunch materialist Tyndall, agreed to attend a seance, even although he had turned down an invitation by Alfred Russel Wallace some years before. On that previous occasion he had said that he was just not interested and in a letter wrote astringently:

> If anyone could endow me with the faculty of listening to the chatter of old women and curates in the nearest cathedral town, I should decline the privilege, having better things to do ... the only good that I can see in a demonstration of the truth of 'spiritualism' is to furnish an additional argument against suicide. Better live a crossing-sweeper than die and be made to talk twaddle by a 'medium' hired at a guinea a seance.

Now Huxley reluctantly agreed to attend a seance where Williams was again the medium. In the darkness, with the Huxley brothers on either side of the medium, each holding one of his hands, nothing happened. When Wedgwood replaced George Huxley, however, a variety of phenomena were experienced by the sitters. When an armchair approached Wedgwood's leg and managed to find its way onto the table, Thomas Huxley gave it as his opinion that it proved nothing. Williams could somehow have managed to release a foot and hooked the armchair to the table, and then used a hand (Wedgwood admitted that he had momentarily lost contact with the medium's hand) to lift the chair onto the table. It did not seem to have occurred to Huxley that even if that was the explanation, it fell far short of an adequate explanation for the event at the previous seance when Darwin had come downstairs to find that *all* the chairs were standing on the table. How long would that have taken to achieve? But then Huxley was in a sceptical frame of mind and so he felt that he was justified in not wasting any more of his time trying to do research in this hideously elusive, crepuscular and morally dubious environment, so different from the clear fields of study he had previously and productively worked in. Darwin, in any case, was rather relieved by Huxley's negative pronouncement. He did make one more attempt to set up a seance at which Huxley would be one of the sitters and Home would be the medium but it came to nothing. Perhaps Darwin had felt a measure of self-contempt at the way in which his continued grief over Annie's death seemed to be driving him into assessing the truth of spiritualism. There is no record that he continued to attend further seances.

From then on it was downhill as far as scientific research into spiritualism. In other European countries there were, like Crookes, individual scientists who persevered in their research such as Johann Zollner, Professor of Physics and Astronomy at the University of Leipzig (working with the controversial psychic Dr Slade), Alexander von Boutlerow, Professor of Chemistry at the University of St Petersburg (working with Home) and William Barrett, Professor of Physics at the Royal College of Science, Dublin. However, for the most part, the scientific establishment tended to look upon such figures as mavericks who substituted emotion and gullibility for rational thought whenever they ventured into spiritualism.

It is probable that apart from the unpleasant profusion of fake mediums battening on to the bereaved, there were two other factors that made scientists reluctant to involve themselves. Many of them sincerely believed that widespread involvement in spiritualism would lead to a return to the horrendous Dark Ages from which rationalism and science had rescued the human race. For in the centuries before Newton's appearance on the scene, Europe had experienced a witchcraft holocaust. It is estimated that during the witchcraft centuries between 100,000 and 250,000 human beings, most of them women, were accused of witchcraft, tortured hideously until they confessed and in their agony named others as accomplices, condemned to death and burned at the stake. The second factor that put most scientists off was the non-intellectual nature of most of the phenomena. Although some sort of intelligence of a primitive, impulsive and immature nature sometimes seemed to be behind the phenomena, given to promising portentously that great things would be produced if the sitters were patient, over many years there did not seem to be any real progress. It gave some participants a decidedly uneasy feeling that they were being played with. And by what?

4

Along the Lonely Shore

I shall not commit the fashionable stupidity of regarding everything I cannot explain as fraud.

Carl Gustav Jung

Sometime in the closing weeks of 1881, Edmund Dawson Rogers, a respected journalist and spiritualist, invited Professor William Barrett to his house – Rose Villa, in Hendon Lane, Finchley, London. Barrett stayed the night. During their discussions, Rogers 'suggested that a society should be started on lines which would be likely to attract some of the best minds which had hitherto held aloof from the pursuit of the inquiry.' That inquiry was to be a careful, rational research into the alleged phenomena of spiritualism. Barrett, also a spiritualist, agreed. Barrett approached Frederic Myers and possibly Edmund Gurney but according to Alan Gauld, 'Myers and Gurney were not hopeful about the prospects of such a Society, and made their support conditional upon Professor Henry Sidgwick accepting the Presidency.' In the event, Sidgwick consented though with no more optimism that such a society would succeed than Myers and Gurney. Their pessimism was probably due to the fact that a number of other societies of a similar kind had been formed in the past but had not survived. In addition, they were well aware of the generally unfavourable reception given by the educated to the aims of such societies and to the beliefs of spiritualists.

Barrett called a conference of people who might be interested in such a society. It was held on January 5th–6th, 1882, at 38 Great Russell Street, London, a spiritualists' meeting house. The creation of a society was proposed and a steering committee formed which met at Hensleigh Wedgwood's house on the 7th and 9th January. On February 20th, the conference was reconvened and the Society for Psychical Research (SPR) was formally constituted. As already mentioned, Henry Sidgwick agreed reluctantly to be President.

Barrett must therefore be admitted to be one of the founding fathers of the society, though it is probable that Edmund Dawson Rogers suggested the idea to him. Barrett was also involved in the creation of a society with similar aims in the United States in January 1885. During a tour there in 1884 he had aroused the interest of a number of educated people and the American Society for Psychical Research was founded, with the astronomer Simon Newcomb as President. William James, arguably the best psychologist the United States has ever produced, became its leading light.

In his 1972 paper on the founders of the SPR, Fraser Nicol shows how the myth arose that the society was 'founded by a group of scholars and scientists'. In point of fact the composition of the first SPR Council was 68-per-cent spiritualist; with spiritualists elected as honorary secretary and honorary treasurer. It is of interest to look at the make-up of that first Council, as Nicol does, dividing them into spiritualist and non-spiritualist.

Spiritualists	*Non-spiritualists*
W.F. Barrett, physicist	Walter R. Browne, civil engineer
E.T. Bennett, hotel keeper	Edmund Gurney, scholar
Mrs George Boole, author	F.W.H. Myers, scholar and poet
Alexander Calder, businessman	Frank Podmore, civil servant
Walter H. Coffin, scientist	J. Lockhart Robertson, alienist
D.G. Fitzgerald, telegraphy expert	Henry Sidgwick, philosopher
C.C. Massey, barrister	
Revd W. Stainton Moses, schoolmaster	
F.W. Percival, scholar	
Edmund Dawson Rogers, journalist	
Morrell Theobald, accountant	
Hensleigh Wedgwood, philologist	
George Wyld, physician	

Mrs George Boole was the widow of the well-known mathematician. She resigned from Council in September 1882, uncomfortable with the fact that she was the only woman. The other members classified as spiritualists were all educated men, many of them following professions. The Revd W. Stainton Moses was not only a schoolmaster but was himself a noted psychic. On the non-spiritualist list were four Fellows or former Fellows of Trinity College, Cambridge – Browne, Gurney, Myers and Sidgwick.

Six committees were set up by the first Council to investigate thought-reading, mesmerism, Reichenbach phenomena, apparitions and haunted houses, spontaneous experiences and physical mediumship. The honorary secretaries of four of them were professed spiritualists.

By any standards, the SPR's work in psychical research during the next thirty years was astonishingly prodigious, both in quality and quantity. Several major investigations resulted in publications that have withstood the test of time. The *Proceedings of the Society for Psychical Research* in those years contain thousands of pages of papers of a very high order. Nicol points out that the effective workers in the SPR were all young or early middle-aged. When the SPR was formed, the oldest was Sidgwick, aged 43. The ages of the others were: Barrett 38, Gurney 34, Hodgson 26, Myers 39, Pease (a friend of Podmore who took part in investigations) 24, Podmore 26, Mrs Henry Sidgwick 36. Oliver Lodge joined the Society at the age of 32. The average age was 33. As Nicol puts it: 'Youth was indeed at the prow and the wisdom of Sidgwick at the helm. They had zest, imagination and drive. Never again in the Society's history have so many young people been in the forefront of leadership.'

In the early years of the SPR, many of the spiritualists in the society and on its council resigned, increasingly dissatisfied and irritated by what seemed to them to be excessive caution displayed by the investigators when drawing conclusions from their work. The proportion of spiritualists fell to a minority and the opinions of the members of Council and indeed most of the SPR's membership became increasingly sympathetic to the professed 'mission statement': *The purpose of the Society for Psychical Research ... is to examine without prejudice or prepossession and in a scientific spirit those faculties of man, real or supposed, which appear to be inexplicable on any generally recognised hypothesis.*

Throughout its existence to the present date, the SPR has enjoyed the allegiance and expertise of some of the most gifted scientists, psychologists, physicians, philosophers and statesmen. As Brian

Inglis, in his foreword to Alan Gauld's book *Mediumship and Survival*, puts it:

There can be few organisations that have attracted so distinguished a membership. Among physicists have been Sir William Crookes, Sir John Joseph Thomson, Sir Oliver Lodge, Sir William Barrett and two Lord Rayleighs – the third and fourth Barons. Among the philosophers: Sidgwick himself, Henri Bergson, Ferdinand Schiller, L.P. Jacks, Hans Driesch and C.D. Broad; among the psychologists: William James, William McDougall, Sigmund Freud, Walter Franklin Prince, Carl Jung and Gardner Murphy. And along with these have been many eminent figures in various fields: Charles Richet, a Nobel prizewinner in physiology; the Earl of Balfour, Prime Minister from 1902 to 1906, and his brother Gerald, Chief Secretary for Ireland in 1895–6; Andrew Lang, polymath; Gilbert Murray, Regius Professor of Greek at Oxford and drafter of the first Covenant of the League of Nations; his successor at Oxford, E.R. Dodds; Mrs Henry Sidgwick, Principal of Newnham College, Cambridge; Marie Curie; the Hon Mrs Alfred Lyttelton, Delegate to the League of Nations Assembly; Camille Flammarion, the astronomer, and F.J.M. Stratton, president of the Royal Astronomical Society; and Sir Alister Hardy, Professor of Zoology at Oxford.

Such a list, as Arthur Koestler pointed out … ought to be sufficient to demonstrate that ESP research 'is not a playground for superstitious cranks'. On the contrary, the standards of research have in general been rigorous – far more rigorous, as psychologists have on occasion had to admit, than those of psychology.

To put it another way: in the first century of the SPR's existence, among the 51 presidents of the society there were 19 professors, 10 fellows of the Royal Society, 5 fellows of the British Academy, 4 holders of the Order of Merit and one Nobel prizewinner.

Membership of the SPR rose rapidly from 150 at the beginning of 1883 to 946 in January 1900. Henry Sidgwick, the first President, was precisely the right person to hold that role in that first phase of the society's existence. The Professor of Moral Philosophy at Cambridge University, he was very widely respected in the academic world for his character, intelligence and learning. He steered the society through the shoals of disagreements between spiritualists and agnostics and his careful and searching criticisms of the investigators' reports added much to their value. He had also a talent for discerning who among his colleagues would be best suited to carry out particular investigations.

By the time of his death in 1900, much of the control of the society's work had passed into the hands of what had became known as the Sidgwick Group – including Sidgwick, Gurney, Myers, Hodgson, Mrs Eleanor Sidgwick, Lodge, Podmore and Piddington. Two distinguished members of the Balfour family could also be linked to the group – Arthur James Balfour and Gerald William Balfour, both brothers of Mrs Sidgwick. A further sister, Evelyn Balfour, was married to Lord Rayleigh.

In its first twenty years, among the major investigations published by the SPR were *Phantasms of the Living* and the 'Report on the Census of Hallucinations', a study of William Eglinton (the slate-writer); the Davey-Hodgson study of 'mal-observation', Madam Blavatsky, Eusapia Palladino (the physical medium), Mrs Piper (the mental medium); and studies of the stages of hypnotic trance and telepathic hypnotism. There were also numerous reports on the investigations of ostensibly haunted houses such as the so-called Cheltenham Haunting.

Phantasms of the Living, published in 1886, was a two-volume work of more than 1,300 pages. Edmund Gurney wrote most of it, while Frederic Myers contributed a long introduction. Cases were collected and exhaustively studied in which people claimed to have had the experience of seeing someone who they afterwards realised could not possibly have been present. Just over 700 cases were found and included. A brief summary of the work involved does not even begin to do justice to its importance or to convey an adequate impression of the astounding amount of work involved in assessing the validity of the individual cases: from interviewing those involved to doing research in record offices. Gurney was the principal interviewer, travelling extensively throughout the United Kingdom, covering thousands of miles, interviewing hundreds of people, either percipients or witnesses. Podmore and Sidgwick did less of this type of work. Other investigators such as Myers, Mrs Sidgwick, Hodgson, Wedgwood and a number of others participated to a lesser degree. As Alan Gauld remarks in his *Founders of Psychical Research* (1968): 'When one remembers that during those three years Gurney also carried out some arduous experimental and theoretical work on hypnotism, as well as his duties as the SPR's Hon. Secretary and editor, his industry and application become staggering.'

The publication received favourable reviews as well as a number of criticisms, which the investigators tried to address in their next major work. The 'Report on the Census of Hallucinations' was begun in connection with the International Congress of Psychology held in Paris in 1889. It was in fact a policy within the SPR to link up the society's research with studies conducted in more acceptable fields of study such as psychology, and a number of the active members of the SPR played a prominent part in the 1889 congress as well as subsequent congresses. An ambitious census throughout the United Kingdom was carried out with the aid of 410 volunteer collectors, mostly members of the SPR or their friends. The collectors asked people to answer the question: 'Have you ever, while believing yourself to be completely awake, had a vivid impression of seeing or being touched by a living being or inanimate object, or of hearing a voice; which impression, so far as you could discover, was not due to any external physical cause?'

Seventeen thousand people answered the question, of whom over two thousand answered in the affirmative. It was a formidable achievement when we remember that even in modern times, professional pollsters often content themselves with polls of one thousand people. The amount of work that followed the SPR census was immense, largely carried out by Professor and Mrs Sidgwick, Miss Alice Johnson, Frank Podmore and Dr A.T. Myers. Doubtful cases were ruthlessly discarded. There remained a statistically significant number of strong cases in which there was independent testimony that the recipient of the experience had told one or more people of experiencing an apparition of a person before he or she could possibly have learned of that person's death.

Taken in conjunction with the material in *Phantasms of the Living*, the SPR studies set up (and still do) a strong challenge to the critic or sceptic who dismissed (or dismisses) a priori the hundreds of accounts by people of good reputation of apparitions they had seen. Apart from any other consideration, these studies provided a strong case for the existence of the faculty of telepathy – a word coined by F.W.H. Myers himself. More recent studies of a similar nature carried out in a number of countries simply strengthen the earlier work of the SPR.

Perhaps the best approach for the person new to psychical research who wishes to learn in more detail why these two monumental pieces of work are still treated as important studies by the vast majority of psychical researchers is to read G.N.M. Tyrrell's monograph *Apparitions*, published in 1953. In it he gives examples of the types of cases studied by the investigators, together with Gurney's concise, logical arguments why the body of evidence should be taken seriously. One of the most thought-provoking collective properties of the cases, obtained from people scattered over the British Isles who had no experience of any previous surveys of this sort – indeed, there had been none – is that hundreds of the cases fell neatly into only four categories: (1) experimental, (2) crisis, (3) post-mortem and (4) haunts. The first category contained a number of cases in which a person had deliberately tried to make an apparition of himself – or of someone else – appear unexpectedly to a friend in a distant place, and succeeded. In the second category the apparition of a person in danger of dying by illness or accident appeared within a few hours of the crisis to friends or relatives, in some cases thousands of miles away. In the third category the apparition of a person was seen a considerable interval of time, perhaps a number of years, after the death of that person. Finally, there were a number of cases of the good old-fashioned haunting type. People, many of whom had no expectation of seeing an apparition or had any knowledge that the place they were in had a reputation of being haunted, had an experience that sometimes resembled a real traumatic, emotional event that had occurred there. In one-third of the cases, where the apparition occurred in the presence of more than one person, all present saw it.

Richard Hodgson's first major piece of research began in 1884 when the SPR's committee appointed to investigate the alleged miraculous powers of Madame Blavatsky and her Theosophical Society chose Hodgson as their investigator. He was sent out to India in November 1884 to look into the phenomena supposed to have occurred there. Various people had claimed that her occult powers were false and that the so-called Tibetan Mahatmas with whom she worked did not exist. The outcome of Hodgson's thorough investigation persuaded him that an enormous and fraudulent system had been set up by Madame Blavatsky and her confederates including the fabrication of the Koot Hoomi letters, supposedly written by one of the mysterious Mahatmas but really written by Blavatsky herself in a disguised hand. In the course of this visit to India, Hodgson greatly increased his knowledge of a wide variety of conjuring tricks that helped him on many subsequent occasions in the necessary work of exposing trickery. As a consequence he acquired a well-deserved reputation as a hard, sceptical unmasker of deception: he became the SPR's 'Rottweiler', set on people the officers of the society suspected of fraudulent practices. It is, however, fair to add that almost a century later, Dr Vernon Harrison claimed that Hodgson's scathing exposures were seriously flawed.

The idea that spirits of the dead could not only speak through mediums but also manipulate material objects in some mysterious way to convey messages or answer questions has, of course, existed in modern Western spiritualism from the days of the Fox family's experiences in their house in Hydesville in 1848. Bangs from the headboards of beds, table-tilting, the use of the ouija board and the planchette, the inexplicable fall of pictures from walls or the wanderings of furniture were supplemented with slate-writing, paintings paranormally created and psychic photographs displaying 'extras' – images of deceased people not present when the photographic plate was exposed. As electrical and electronic apparatus such as telephones, static and mobile, tape recorders, radio and television sets and desktop computers became part and parcel of many households' possessions, they too have been reported as being used paranormally by poltergeists or by the spirits of the dead.

The SPR investigators did not make the mistake of believing that if fake coins were in circulation, all coins must be counterfeit. Nevertheless, the dismayingly large proportion of the mediums they investigated who turned out to be cheats, and the investment of time careful investigation of them entailed, led some of the Sidgwick Group to promulgate the dictum that if a medium was caught cheating *at any time*, that medium should not only be exposed but none of his or her ostensible previous or future phenomena should be taken to be of genuine paranormal origin. One consequence of this harsh protocol was to lead to a further exodus of convinced spiritualists from the society. Another was to cause disagreements between the 'one strike and you're out' group and those investigators who maintained that a genuine medium, perhaps taking part in a study carried out by important psychical researchers, might find her powers temporarily absent and yield to the temptation to fake the phenomena. Indeed, the Italian physical medium Eusapia Palladino on occasion warned investigators that they should control her hands and feet effectively at all times, for when she was in trance, she would try to cheat.

Eusapia Palladino, born January 21st, 1854, was the child of peasants. She was intelligent, shrewd and manipulative. In the history of physical mediumship she is often said to occupy a place second only to that of Daniel Dunglas Home. During her life (she died in 1918), she was studied not only by a number of the SPR investigators but also by the criminologist and psychiatrist Cesare Lombroso and the physiologist, Charles Richet. Other scientists included Giovanni Schiaparelli, the astronomer, and Giuseppe Gerosa, Professor of Physics. A notable series of studies was carried out on Palladino in 1894 by Richet, Frederic Myers, Oliver Lodge and at Richet's summer home on the Île de Roubaud. Later on Professor and Mrs Sidgwick joined them. Their favourable report in the *Proceedings of the Society for Psychical Research* was drastically criticised by Richard Hodgson, who showed at great length that the arrangements on the island left open the possibility for trickery. This harsh criticism was accepted by the Île de Roubaud group. The outcome was to arrange a new series of sittings in Cambridge in 1895. In some of those sittings she impressed, among others, J.J. Thompson and Lord Rayleigh. Hodgson, who was there and participated in controlling Palladino's limbs, in one session deliberately let go of her hand. As she had previously warned she would do, she cheated. The Sidgwicks and Myers supported Hodgson in his contention that this invalidated all the previous ostensible paranormal physical phenomena. No doubt some of the Sidgwick Group, like Galileo after he was forced to admit that the Earth could not move, might have muttered under their breath the psychical research equivalent of *'Eppur si muove!'* ('It moves nonetheless').

The European investigators, however, continued to study Palladino. By now they accepted that the SPR would be of little further help to them since the group's search for perfection in preventing cheating had placed it in a somewhat sterile position. Between 1905 and 1908 Palladino was involved in a careful series of investigations at the Sorbonne in Paris by a group of scientists including Charles Richet, Jean-Baptiste Perrin, Jules Courtier, Professor of Psychology,

Pierre and Marie Curie, and Jacque-Arsène d'Arsonval, Director of the Laboratory of Biological Physics (published by Courtier in 1908). They planned the series with scrupulous care, utilising a wide variety of monitoring and recording instruments in the laboratories they used. It had been suggested on a number of occasions by people that hypnotism of the sitters by a medium was a possibility that might account for sitters' testimony that impossible events had occurred. Certainly the apparatus could not be subject to any hypnotic influence, however powerful it might be, and some of the scientists studying the instruments were stationed in another laboratory where there was no non-paranormal way in which Eusapia could have hypnotised them.

The scientists' reports were overwhelmingly supportive of the view that a wide variety of genuine paranormal physical events had taken place in Palladino's presence. The SPR, now effectively under the direction of Mrs Eleanor Sidgwick since the deaths of her husband in 1900 and Frederic Myers in 1901, realised that the SPR had to undertake another study of Eusapia Palladino. Richard Hodgson had died in 1905 but in 1908 the SPR persuaded three other 'Rottweilers' to undertake a further investigation of Palladino. They were Everard Feilding, Wortley W. Baggally and Hereward Carrington. Feilding, the assistant Honorary Secretary of the SPR, was completely sceptical about physical mediumship. Baggally, a skilled conjuror, claimed that every physical medium he had personally investigated was a fraud. Carrington, an American, had written a book revealing the tricks bogus mediums played. The sceptical trio conducted eleven seances with Palladino in a Naples hotel. After the sixth, Feilding wrote: 'I have seen this extraordinary woman ... held hand and foot ... by my colleagues, immobile, except for the occasional straining of a limb while some entity has over and over again pressed my hand in a position clearly beyond her reach.' Feilding also noted and recorded his colleagues' and his own reactions to the events they observed. 'Tables, we knew, or thought we knew, do not go into the air by themselves; curtains do not bulge out without some mechanical agency; and although we saw them do so, we still refused to believe that they did.' Their detailed and strongly favourable report was published in the *SPR Proceedings* in 1909. It was subsequently reprinted in 1963 in an edited volume of Feilding's collected papers entitled *Sittings with Eusapia Palladino and Other Studies*.

Indeed the question must be asked. Was there never, ever, with Palladino controlled over the course of those years by dozens of scientists – and highly skilled and sceptical people like J.N.Maskelyne and other magicians – and in the Sorbonne series with the furniture and other objects monitored by recording apparatus, and on many occasions in good light, was there never, ever, an occasion when a psychokinetic event occurred? One ventures to suggest that if psychokinesis had been any other frontier scientific study of a less controversial nature such as quantum mechanics, it would have been accepted as proven to occur beyond a reasonable shadow of doubt before the end of the first decade of the 20th century.

No doubt some of the SPR investigators' ultra-sceptical reluctance to accept that physical paranormal events could occur arose from the Hodgson–Davey study, which showed that a large proportion of human beings are, to put it mildly, poor observers. William Eglinton was a medium who achieved an international reputation partly for the ostensible paranormal slate-writing that occurred in his presence: a single slate pressed against a table would subsequently be found to have a relevant message written on it that had not been there when inspected earlier; or two slates pressed or even screwed together would afterwards be found to have a message upon the inner surfaces when subsequently separated. Mrs Sidgwick and Richard Hodgson realised from personal experience that many of the witnesses' accounts of their supposedly unbroken vigilant observation of the medium were decidedly faulty. S.J. Davey, a young man who had had some experience of sitting with Eglinton, resolved to devote much of his time trying to duplicate by conjuring many of Eglinton's slate-writing features. His efforts were ultimately rewarded by his ability, as an amateur 'medium', to reproduce most of Eglinton's phenomena. Moreover, he learned that most sitters were easy to distract, enabling the necessary tricks to be carried out without him being observed. In 1886, with the help of Richard Hodgson, Davey was able to demonstrate how mal-observation on the part of the sitters and skilled conjuring by the 'medium' could account for at least most of the ostensible paranormal phenomena demonstrated by the slate-writers. The Hodgson–Davey papers, published in the *Proceedings of the SPR* in 1887 and 1892, are still worth reading.

To some extent then it is not surprising that the SPR remained in general highly sceptical as far as *physical* phenomena were concerned.

However, the early part of the twentieth century brought a number of so-called *mental* mediums of spectacular talent on to the scene and the SPR investigators found themselves involved in new and totally unexpected researches. By the 1920s, the society's major investigations of mediumship had largely turned away from physical to mental mediumship. The investigators had come to the conclusion that the study of outstanding mental mediums such as Mrs Piper, Mrs Thompson, Mrs Leonard and Mrs Willett, and the output of the group of so-called automatists such as Mrs Verrall, Mrs Holland, Mrs Piper and Mrs Willett, were far richer, more easily controllable and more rewarding fields of psychical research than attempting, often in darkness, to ensure that the ostensible physical phenomena were truly paranormally obtained and were not the products of frauds.

5

Paradise Lost

God's in His heaven, all's right with the world.

Robert Browning

If for the worst and most permanent suffering there were no possible assuagement of hope, if I found in myself and all around me an absolute conviction that the individual existence ceased with the death of the body, and that the present iniquitous distribution of good and evil was therefore final, I should desire ... the immediate extinction of the race.

Edmund Gurney

It has been remarked that a number of societies had been set up prior to the SPR's formation with similar missions to investigate in a rational, scientific manner the whole range of allegedly paranormal phenomena claimed to have been witnessed by a multitude of people. It has also been stated that none of them lasted. Why then did the SPR? What was so special about it? Why was the work it produced between the time of its formation in 1882 and the end of the Victorian era so significant that for the open-minded student it still has relevance in psychical research to the present date? What was so special about the way it was run and the manner in which its investigators carried out their work? What were the elements in their background that made them such skilled psychical researchers?

A suitable point to begin an attempt to answer these questions is to look at the people who effectively controlled the society's work during its earliest decades: Sidgwick, Gurney, Myers, Hodgson, Mrs Eleanor Sidgwick, Lodge, Podmore and Piddington. In addition, two other distinguished members of the Balfour family could be linked to the group – Arthur James Balfour and Gerald William Balfour, both brothers of Mrs Sidgwick and both of whom became presidents of the SPR, the former in 1893 and the latter from 1906 to 1907. A further sister, Evelyn Balfour, was married to Lord Rayleigh, who was President of the society in 1919. Looking at this list, it is remarkable how few of the people were scientists by training or profession. Many of them had been associates a considerable number of years before the SPR was created, while their experience of investigating mediums also often predated the society. Sidgwick's active interest in the paranormal had begun when he was an undergraduate at Cambridge and joined the Cambridge Ghost Club. As early as 1874, Sidgwick, Myers, Gurney and Arthur Balfour were conducting a long series of investigations into both physical and mental mediumship. Myers remembered for the rest of his life the 'starlight walk' he had with Sidgwick in 1869 when he asked Sidgwick 'whether he thought that when Tradition, Intuition, Metaphysics had failed to solve the riddle of the Universe, there was still a chance that from any actual observable phenomena – ghosts, spirits, whatever they might be – some valid knowledge might be drawn as to the World Unseen.' Sidgwick affirmed that there was. While many members of the group had had no formal training in science, their own educations, the professions they followed and their high intelligence prepared them well for their future investigations. They appreciated the methods of science and its many successes and were skilled in examining and assessing evidence put before them, searching it for any weaknesses.

Remarkable, too, is that a number of them had had profoundly tragic experiences in their lives – among them Myers, Arthur Balfour and Gurney – bringing them face to face with the supremely important questions – is death the end and the total destruction of those I have loved? These tragic events had instilled in them a powerful drive to investigate the only body of alleged phenomena that seemed to have relevance to those questions. Nevertheless, their allegiance to truth and their realisation that a cold, cautious and logical approach to their investigations was probably the only mode of procedure that would protect them from the danger of wishful thinking earned some of them the reputations they acquired of never accepting any alleged paranormal phenomena as having been proven beyond a reasonable shadow of doubt. Certainly as far as physical phenomena were concerned, for some of them their verdict-producing machine seemed to many to have become permanently jammed at the third Scottish verdict – 'not proven'.

Fraser Nicol, in his 1972 review of Alan Gauld's seminal book *The Founders of Psychical Research*, gives another important factor in the make-up of the group members and indeed of a number of their associates. He writes:

> Strictly, this is not a history of the society but of persons – of their backgrounds; their developing thoughts and outlooks; their intense activities over a period of twenty years; their successes and their failures. After an opening chapter on 'The Rise of Modern Spiritualism in America' Gauld passes to what he describes as 'The Genesis of Reluctant Doubt'. By this he means the decline of religious belief, a loss which he ascribes to the new intellectual climate represented by the writings of the younger Mill, the Comtists, Darwinism and other influences, all pointing to a purely materialistic view of human life. The impact of these new ideas on intelligent young men brought up in religious households was sometimes shattering; and in this regard it is surely not without significance that so many of the S.P.R.'s early leaders were the sons of clergymen: Barrett, Gurney, Myers, Podmore and Sidgwick. In 1862 Sidgwick confessed, 'I am only a Theist'. In 1880 he wrote, 'I sometimes say to myself that I believe in God; while sometimes again I can say no more than "I hope this belief is true and I must and will act as if it was." ' Myers felt his Christian belief badly shaken. Was death the end? As Gauld says, 'The prospect of annihilation seemed to rob his life of all its point and purpose.'

To a certain extent, then, many of the investigators were people who could be said to have been expelled from paradise. With increasingly stoical resignation, they honestly accepted the evidence that they now wandered within a terrible world shaped by powerful material and organic forces, a world where these forces at any moment could snatch away loved ones, not through any purpose

Professor
Henry Sidgwick

Edmund Gurney

Frederic W.H. Myers

or plan, malignant or benign, but merely because of the random chaotic occurrence of material factors. To them, Browning's affirmation that 'God's in His heaven, all's right with the world' was as bitter as gall, indeed a fatuous, insulting nonsense: their outlook on the human situation was better expressed by Gurney's anguished cry:

> If for the worst and most permanent suffering there were no possible assuagement of hope, if I found in myself and all around me an absolute conviction that the individual existence ceased with the death of the body, and that the present iniquitous distribution of good and evil was therefore final, I should desire ... the immediate extinction of the race.

In their wanderings through this desert of disbelief, they had now got a glimpse of an oasis of evidence in the shape of paranormal phenomena. But was it real or was it a mirage? Was it evidence that paradise in some way did exist? Was it evidence that 'the Universe was friendly'? Or would the oasis on sustained, cold critical examination reveal itself to be at most a product of wild physical forces still roaming outside the ordered farms of scientific knowledge, bizarre psychological phenomena produced by the brains of human beings?

Three of the members of the Sidgwick Group are of particular importance not only because of their intelligence, training and work in psychical research but also because of their personalities. Like the great figures of American presidents carved on the face of Mount Rushmore, they dominated the landscape in which they and their fellow workers laboured and their influence lasted long after their deaths, indeed to the present day. They are Professor Henry Sidgwick, Frederic W.H. Myers and Edmund Gurney.

93

Henry Sidgwick was born on May 31st, 1838, in Skipton, Yorkshire. When he was three, his father, the Revd William Sidgwick, who had been the headmaster of Skipton Grammar School, died and Henry and his three siblings were thereafter brought up by their mother. He was a highly intelligent boy and went to school at Rugby in 1852. Three years later he went up to Trinity College, Cambridge, where he studied mathematics and Classics. He did well, winning a number of university prizes and in 1859 he was Senior Classic, First Chancellor's Medallist and thirty-third Wrangler. He was given a teaching fellowship at Trinity. As the years passed, however, he became increasingly unhappy as his mounting religious agnosticism brought him to the point where he could no longer honestly affirm his status as a *bona fide* member of the Church of England – a condition of his appointment. If he had been able to swallow his doubts or suppress his conscience it is possible that in due course of time his talents might have raised him to one of the highest ecclesiastical offices in England. Sidgwick's deep sense of morality made it impossible for him to do this and in 1869 he resigned. Sidgwick's resignation was not unexpected. As George Eliot later said of him, he was already a man whose friends tacitly expected him to conform to moral standards higher than they themselves cared to maintain. In fact, his resignation encouraged others to follow suit and such high-mindedness would eventually lead Parliament to abolish the University Tests. As a result of Sidgwick's action, Trinity College created a special lectureship for him in moral sciences, and in 1883 he became Knightsbridge Professor of Moral Philosophy, a post he held until the end of his life.

In point of fact it was not just the consequences of Darwinism upon religion that was shaking religious belief. In the middle of the 19th century, German scholars in particular were studying the Bible, employing the same critical methods to it and its sources as they would have employed to any other text. When their work reached England, it was looked upon by many as destructive – even evil – but it influenced the more liberal and thoughtful clergy together with other intelligent people. It was not surprising then that Henry Sidgwick, among others, felt a dismay bordering upon misery at these assaults from all sides upon religious beliefs including his own. In the ten years between his appointment to the teaching fellowship and his resignation, he fought a rearguard action, studying philosophy, Arabic and Hebrew (to get nearer to the minds of the Hebrews), evidence concerning the occurrence or not of biblical miracles, and theology. It is not an exaggeration to say that for years he agonised over the question of his religious beliefs or lack of them. To the end of his life he longed for justification for them. As Gauld puts it: 'Only in terms of the existence of a supreme and supremely moral Being, guiding all things to good ends, could he conceive why his knowledge of Duty should be to him as insistent as his knowledge of the physical world.'

In 1876 Sidgwick married Eleanor Mildred Balfour, a highly intelligent and remarkably well-educated woman who was especially talented in mathematics. In her twenties she had worked with her brother-in-law, Lord Rayleigh, in scientific research. Sidgwick and his wife had met as members of the group that in 1874 had begun a careful investigation of cases of ostensible paranormal phenomena. Apart from these interests, they both were intensely interested in the education of women. Sidgwick himself, as early as 1871, had been highly influential in the establishment of Newnham College at Cambridge as the first women's college. His wife was Treasurer (1876–1919), Vice-principal (1880–92) and Principal (1892–1910) of the college. At the time of their engagement, Sidgwick had written to his mother: 'I feel sure that you will come to love her, she is very quiet and undemonstrative; but so sweet and simple and calm and helpful.' Mrs Sidgwick's strong, logical mind later enabled her to become one of the SPR's most effective assessors of material collected and advanced in the field of psychical research.

By the end of his life Sidgwick had achieved national and international respect for his book *The Methods of Ethics*, first published in 1874. He had become almost a father figure in Cambridge, his long white beard, gentle voice and slight stammer heightening his almost otherworldly, sage-like aura. People with religious doubts and other problems were especially drawn to him, knowing that they would be received with sympathy, even if their arguments were shallow and ill-formed.

In his tribute to Sidgwick, Frederic Myers wrote of how he himself belatedly recognised the sterling qualities of the man, during his famous starlight walk with Sidgwick on December 3rd, 1869. He wrote:

This was, I fear, but a slow and late conversion to the sense, which so many men had already reached, of Sidgwick's penetrating wisdom. When I think of other Trinity men whom I have found worthy of respect ... Montagu Butler, R.C. Jebb, G.O. Trevelyan, Henry Jackson, – of Balfours, Lytteltons, Darwins, – of W.K. Clifford, Lord Rayleigh, F.W. Maitland, Walter Leaf, Henry Butcher, Edmund Gurney, and the rest; – it seems to me as if all these had been prompter than I to appreciate that which in the end I knew so well. Nay, but in the end, perhaps, of all these, only Arthur Balfour and Edmund Gurney fell into quite the same attitude towards Sidgwick as myself: – the attitude as of 'companions of Socrates'.

Sidgwick was precisely the right person to be made President of the newly formed Society for Psychical Research in 1882. Apart from his talents and keen mind, his willingness to join and become President was a boost to the new society's status. Any organisation that Henry Sidgwick took a part in had to be taken seriously. He was president from 1882 to 1884, serving a second term in that office from 1888 to 1892. Frank Podmore in a letter sent to the *Daily Chronicle* wrote:

That he [Sidgwick] gave largely – very largely – of his personal means to help the work of investigation in those earlier years is the least of his benefits. He presided throughout at our councils; he took an active share in the tedious work of experiment, of examining witnesses, of collecting and appraising evidence; the lines on which our work could best be done were laid down by his advice and pursued under his personal direction; all the publications of the society were issued under his immediate supervision. That of late years he has delegated to others many of these functions was due less to any decay of his personal interest in the work of investigation than to the feeling that his immediate supervision of all details was no longer necessary... Whatever position the S.P.R. may hold today, whatever good work it may have done in exposing error or in directing attention to neglected facts in human psychology, its success is due, in the largest measure, to the wisdom, the clear insight ... and, above all, to the pre-eminent justice and veracity of our first president.

Henry Sidgwick's death from cancer in 1900 was a sombre and severe shock to his many colleagues and friends. His attitude to the progress of the illness and to an operation that seemed at first to go well but was subsequently found to be unsuccessful was one of calm courage and acceptance. It was an attitude that reminded many of the death of Socrates. Among the many letters he wrote during these last few months was one to Frederic Myers just prior to his operation. In it he said:

> I have an organic disorder which, the expert said more than a fortnight ago, must soon render an operation necessary... I believe that the chances of the operation are on the whole favourable ... but how long I shall live after it is uncertain...
>
> Life is very strange now: very terrible: but I try to meet it like a man, my beloved wife aiding me. I hold on – or try to hold on – to duty and love; and through love to touch the larger hope.
>
> I wish now that I had told you before, as this may be farewell. Your friendship has had a great place in my life, and as I walk through the Valley of the Shadow of Death, I feel your affection. Pray for me.
>
> This may be farewell, but I hope not.

Henry Sidgwick died on August 28th, 1900 at Terling Place, in Essex, the home of his wife's brother-in-law, Lord Rayleigh. He was succeeded as President of the SPR by Frederic Myers. Myers was by then the only one left alive of the original three – Sidgwick, Gurney and Myers – who had joined the new society and worked so tirelessly to establish the science of psychical research. Edmund Gurney's death in 1888 at the early age of forty-one had been a severe blow to his friends and colleagues and to psychical research because of its total unexpectedness and bizarre nature. It had also robbed the society of one of its most energetic researchers, a man, Myers wrote, 'whose dominant capacity lay in intellectual insight, penetrating criticism, dialectic subtlety.'

Edmond Gurney, Classical scholar, musician, experimental psychologist and psychical researcher, was born on March 23rd, 1847 in Hersham, Surrey. He was the fifth child in a family of eight. His father, John Hampden Gurney, was a clergyman. When he entered Trinity College in 1866 it was to study Classics but this was an interest second to his love for music and his determination to become an outstanding composer and pianist. As Myers put it, 'Called upon to choose between classical and mathematical studies, he chose classics almost at hazard, and worked at them, one may say, in the intervals of his practice on the piano.' Even so, he achieved high distinction and prizes as a Classical scholar and in 1872 he was elected to a Trinity fellowship.

Gurney returned to music, however, studying at Harrow under John Farmer and for a number of years continued his struggle to fulfil his musical ambitions. Finally he accepted the bitter truth that he would never attain concert standard nor indeed achieve first rank as a composer. His first book, *The Power of Sound*, published in 1880, was a result of his years of struggle – a treatise on the philosophy of music. It was well received, but this proved poor consolation for a man as sensitive as Gurney, a man who was increasingly despondent concerning human suffering. Myers wrote:

Edmund Gurney's compassion for his neighbours' suffering was based, not so much on removable, as on irremovable things; on that endless disproportion between man's desire and his attainment which evolution can only intensify; on that sudden snapping of man's deepest affections which evolution can only teach him to feel as a still crueller wound; on that wail of anguish which, though it should arise from one hopeless, helpless creature amid the whole planet's broad content, must still prevent us from regarding with enthusiasm, with worship, a universe in which a single sentient being is born to unmerited and unrequited woe.

Edmund Gurney's own life was ravaged by an appalling tragedy. Towards the end of 1875 three of his sisters were drowned in a boating accident on the Nile. Before that personal tragedy Gurney had shown facets of his personality – wit and a marked sense of humour – that had brought him a wide circle of friends. Francis W. Maitland, who had walked in the Tyrol with him, said of him, 'On a good day it was a joy to hear him laugh.' After the tragedy, his life darkened, a darkness deepened at times to almost unbearable blackness by his compassion for anyone's or indeed any living creature's suffering.

In 1877 he married Kate Sibley, an intelligent, attractive girl.

They had a daughter, Helen May. In the same year he began medical studies at University College, London, and by 1880 had obtained his degree in Medicine. He found, however, that he could not stand the medical horrors he witnessed in St George's Hospital and turned instead to the study of law, only to abandon that, too. It is tempting to speculate what this intelligent, caring, hypersensitive man's later life would have brought if in the 1870s he had not been attracted to psychical research. It is also interesting to realise that Gurney's training at Trinity, his medical studies and his equally thorough study of law produced in him an armoury of skills and knowledge that, coupled to his keen intelligence and energy, transformed him into the tireless, dedicated, innovative psychical researcher he became when he helped to found the SPR in 1882.

In psychical research he found his life's work. Like Sidgwick and Myers and many of the other people who created the society, he had been buffeted by the onslaughts of science upon religion; he, too, had been expelled from paradise and had lost any hope that life was anything else but a meaningless, tragic, chance interplay of physical forces. His motivation for his work in psychical research was not a personal craving for a future life after death but an attempt in some sense to rescue a providential universe. As Myers put it: 'Reason had convinced [Gurney], not that if there were a future life the universe *must* be good, but that if there were a future life the universe *might* be good; and that without such a life the universe could *not* be good in any sense in which a man moved with the sorrows of humanity ought to be called upon to use that word.'

Edmund Gurney had served his apprenticeship in psychical research in the 1870s. Now his unofficial apprenticeship was over and, acknowledging like the others that he had begun a long, often lonely journey on a mapless, treacherous terrain, he became a dogged cartographer of the dark continent of the human mind. The abundant source of energy he had tapped in his previous studies was now turned onto psychical research and in the short six-year spell before his death, his contribution to the subject was vast and productive. All of the work he collaborated on (described in the previous chapter) proved to be of lasting value. His own extensive and innovative projects in experimental hypnosis, carried on until his early death, placed him, according to Myers, in the same league as the great pioneers of hypnosis – Braid, Esdaile and Elliotson.

Here the two major questions he sought to answer in his carefully designed experiments were: 'Is the hypnotic state ever induced by some yet unrecognised agency – some specific influence of operator on subject?' and 'What is the relation of the memory in one hypnotic state to the memory in another hypnotic state, and of both to the normal or waking memory?' His most important papers on hypnotism were published between 1884 and 1888 in the *SPR Proceedings*. Much of his material was also published in the British philosophical journal *Mind*. Gurney's work was taken very seriously by Frederic Myers. In discussing Myers' theory of the Subliminal Self, Alan Gauld states in *The Founders of Psychical Research* (1968):

> These [Gurney's] experiments seemed to show that a subject's memories of successive trances may form a memory-chain which is inaccessible during his waking hours, but can be immediately recaptured when he is again hypnotised. Furthermore, different memory-chains may even be established for states of light and of deep hypnosis.

One wonders how far psychical research would have progressed if Edmund Gurney had been given a few more productive years. But that was not to be. On the night of June 23rd, 1888, he died in a hotel in Brighton. The next day, the door was forced and Gurney's body was found lying in bed, his right hand holding over his nose and mouth a pad of cotton wool on top of which was a sponge bag. A small empty bottle was found on the table. Although a verdict of accidental death was delivered by the coroner, rumours have persisted that Gurney committed suicide. Evidence supporting the verdict of accidental death was given by Gurney's brother Alfred and Myers' brother Arthur, who was a physician. They testified that Gurney had suffered on occasion from insomnia and neuralgia and had been in the habit of using chloroform to dull the pain and put himself to sleep. This explanation is by no means implausible. Gurney was not the only person who had sought relief from pain in this way and not the only person who had underestimated the danger of letting themself be rendered unconscious by chloroform. It was an age in fact where a rather less than cautious attitude to little-understood drugs was prevalent. Fraser Nicol has stated, in his 1972 study of the founders of SPR, how, in the research he carried out into Gurney's life story and into 'the rather awful history of chloroform accidents in the nineteenth century (even in the operating theatre) ... that it would be an act of unreason to doubt the propriety of the jury's verdict'. He goes on to describe how

Cromwell Varley, F.R.S. almost died in similar circumstances. He, too, used chloroform to relieve pain, applying the sponge to his face when alone in bed. Usually, the sponge fell away when he lost consciousness. This time it remained on his face. He afterwards recalled ... 'After a little time I became conscious ....and I saw myself on my back with the sponge to my mouth, but was utterly powerless to cause my body to move.' His wife, feeling something was amiss, hurried to the bedroom 'and immediately removed the sponge, and was greatly alarmed.'

The interpretation of Gurney's death as suicide, typically pushed by Trevor Hall, suggested that Gurney's presence in Brighton was caused by information that his major collaborator in some of his most important experiments in telepathic hypnotism had deceived him. Alan Gauld attaches little value to this hypothesis.

Whatever the truth of Gurney's death might be, it was a dreadful blow to his friends. It was also a blow to their work in quantity and quality. Nevertheless they closed ranks and continued their investigations into psychical research, dividing up their friend's work amongst themselves. By now Frank Podmore and Oliver Lodge had joined them. Myers and Podmore, one of the society's most active members, succeeded Gurney as joint secretaries.

It is time now to consider the third member of the trio of men who played such important roles in the creation of the SPR and its impact upon psychical research. In assessing Frederic Myers and his monumental contribution to the subject, it is staggering to realise how unknown he is today outside the circle of psychical researchers who have studied his papers and his two volume book *Human Personality and its Survival of Bodily Death* (1903). The present author can well remember the frisson of surprise that ran round a recent International Conference of the SPR at Northampton University when a young parapsychologist referred to him vaguely as 'Some guy called Myers'. It was as if a young speaker at a contemporary physics conference had used the phrase: 'Some guy called Einstein.'

Frederic ('Freddy') William Henry Myers was born on February 6th, 1843, in Keswick, Cumberland. He was the eldest son of the Revd and Mrs Frederic Myers, his two brothers Earnest James and Arthur Thomas being born respectively in 1844 and 1851, the year of his father's death. Susan Myers, his mother, was the daughter of John Marshall, a rich local landowner. A diary or journal kept by Susan while her husband was alive gives us a picture of a happy, loving family in which Frederic Myers senior's teaching was reinforced by his wife's unquestioning religious faith. She was an intelligent, loving woman of good sense and her journal is invaluable in providing much information about Myers' early years.

From his earliest years Freddy was highly intelligent but hypersensitive, and accepted with absolute conviction what his mother told him about God, heaven, hell, goodness and evil. Questions that he asked – remarkably perceptive for his years – stemmed not from doubts but from attempts to obtain a greater understanding of the intriguing mysteries his mother was revealing to him. Susan relates an incident that occurred to him when he was just over four years of age:

> One day he came to me after his walk scarcely able to refrain from tears, telling me he had seen 'such a sad thing! a little mole that a cart had gone over & killed.' Then his face cleared up & he said very earnestly 'But Mamma I *do* think that little mole's soul is gone to heaven – don't you?' 'No my child – that mole had not a soul at all you know –' and 'Oh Mamma' – & then he could not refrain from a burst of tears, when his comfort was taken from him.

The horror of this incident haunted Myers for years. Forty-five years later in his autobiography, *Fragments of Inner Life*, he wrote: 'To this day I remember my rush of tears at the thought of that furry innocent creature, crushed by a danger that I fancied it too blind to see, and losing all joy forever by that unmerited stroke. The pity of it! The pity of it! and the first horror of a death without resurrection rose in my bursting heart.'

This extreme sensitivity, coupled with high intelligence, a remarkable memory and a strong desire to embrace and understand the nature of everything he encountered in life remained with him throughout his life. From an early age he showed considerable talent as a poet. As a fourteen-year-old schoolboy at Cheltenham College, he entered three poems for the college's English verse prize. The poems were placed first, second and fourth. At the age of sixteen, he sent a poem to a national competition to celebrate the centenary of the birth of Robert Burns and was given second place. At Trinity College, Cambridge, which he entered in 1860 to study Classical literature, he continued to compose much acclaimed verse. Later in life he largely gave up producing these competition works. Much of his later pieces of poetry were the products of a breaking heart.

Myers' time at Trinity was by no means a smooth and eventless period. His temperament, intelligence, seemingly easy ability to achieve anything he put his mind to, his over-the-top enthusiasm for anything he professed an interest in, however trivial, seemed to many of his contemporaries to be the output of a highly intelligent and competent but limelight-seeking actor. Most of those who did not know him well disliked him, even loathed him. Those who did come to know him saw behind the façade a pilgrim tirelessly and sincerely searching for a hidden spiritual dimension. He was a classical scholar of outstanding ability and fervid dedication to all that was admired and respected in the Classical world of the Greeks and Romans. That dedication had begun, not in Trinity but in school.

In the early 1890s when he was working at his autobiography *Fragments of Inner Life*, he wrote: 'That early burst of admiration for Virgil ... was followed by a growing passion for one after another of the Greek and Latin poets. From ten to sixteen I lived much in the inward reciting of Homer, Aeschylus, Lucretius, Horace and Ovid. The reading of Plato's Georgics at fourteen was a great event; but the study of the Phaedo at sixteen effected upon me a kind of conversion. At that time, too, I returned to my worship of Virgil, whom Homer had for some years thrust into the background. I gradually wrote out Bucolics, Georgics, Aeneid from memory; and felt, as I have felt ever since, that of all minds known to me it is Virgil's of which I am the most intimate and adoring disciple... The discovery at seventeen, in an old school book, of the poems of Sappho, whom till then I had known only by name, brought an access of intoxicating joy. Later on, the solitary decipherment of Pindar made another epoch of the same kind.'

He graduated from Trinity in 1864, becoming a lecturer in Classics, and was made a fellow of Trinity the following year. In

1869 he resigned his fellowship to devote a major part of his time to the education of women. Three years later he obtained a post as a school inspector.

In the 1860s he was greatly influenced by Mrs Josephine Butler, the wife of George Butler, Vice-principal of Cheltenham College and later Principal of Liverpool College. She was a very attractive woman, still young, and not averse to using her feminine charms in her crusades in support of Christianity. Her work among prostitutes and her campaigns against the Contagious Diseases Acts later in her life brought her fame. As Gauld drily remarks in *The Founders of Psychical Research*:

> At this time however [the time of her Christianity crusade] she was chiefly engaged in what might be described as the spiritual seduction of promising young men. Her religion was emotional rather than dogmatic, and her methods of conversion were simple. Having aroused her quarry by her exciting concern for his welfare, she would flatter him with an earnest account of her own inner trials and victories – an account delivered perhaps at twilight while she lay with her slim form stretched out upon a sofa – and at last capture him by a well-staged denouement. She might, for instance, call him into her room to find her kneeling in pale beauty before her mirror, devoutly praying for his salvation. Only men with the coolest heads could resist such an appeal; and Myers was not one of them.

I have before me a copy of *Saint Paul*, one of the two long religious poems Myers wrote under Butler's influence. The dedication, dated September, 1867, is to J.E.B. The poem was enthusiastically received and was reprinted several times. The second poem, *St John the Baptist*, published in 1868, was somewhat less successful.

For some years, then, Myers was clearly reconciled to Christianity, and there is no doubt that he was much happier during these years, exhibiting something of a missionary spirit to his fellows. However, by the end of the 1860s the spell was lifting. There was a steady loss of faith, doubt encroached on his mind and in 1869 he realised, when he was ill with pneumonia, that he was no longer a Christian. In his autobiography he attributed his disillusionment to 'increased knowledge of history and of science, from a wider outlook on the world. Sad it was, and slow; a recognition of insufficiency of evidence, fraught with growing pain.'

Although Myers had been a student of Henry Sidgwick at Trinity, their close friendship did not really develop until the late 1860s. Sidgwick had been impressed by Myers as an undergraduate and had hoped that he would not lose touch with him. Myers does not seem to have been drawn towards Sidgwick until they discovered their mutual interest in investigating ostensible paranormal phenomena. Myers on his part came to depend upon Sidgwick's calm and totally reasoning nature to prevent him from going overboard and allowing reason and logical process to be swamped by enthusiasm.

Through his mother, Susan, Myers was related to the wealthy Marshall family. She was the aunt of Walter James Marshall, who in 1866 married Annie Eliza Hill. At the time of the wedding, Annie was twenty-one; Marshall was some eight years her senior. Although the marriage produced five children, there were troubles for them in plenty, troubles that multiplied and intensified over the years. Walter seemed to be manic-depressive, his increasingly fluctuating moods disturbing and alarming Annie; she herself was by no means robust. Two of Annie's sisters died insane and John, Walter's brother, had his own difficulties. Myers knew them well, his cousin Walter since childhood, Annie since her marriage to Walter.

Susan Myers was a confidante for Annie who derived support and comfort from the older woman. In 1871 Myers himself learned something about Annie's dire situation when he spent a few days with Walter and Annie at Vevey, in Switzerland. They met again in January 1873. Two months later she spent some time with Susan at Cheltenham. As Myers attempted as best he could to alleviate in some small way her sadness, a change gradually took place in his feelings for her; he fell completely in love with her with all the strength his ardent temperament could muster. As he came to know her better in the talks they had, the belief grew in him that in her he had found his soulmate. In such a situation it was perhaps inevitable that she also fell in love with him, though it was a love encircled by her duty to her husband and children.

In his autobiography, Myers alluded to the profound effect his and Annie's platonic love had on him. It obviously enhanced his image of Annie. By the time they acknowledged their mutual love

105

for each other, Myers was increasingly caught up in his investigations into the phenomena of spiritualism. He was beginning to hope that his ardent love for Annie, the qualities he found in her, and perhaps some element of truth in spiritualism would combine to restore his belief in the reality of a transendental spiritual realm:

> ... so soon as I began to have hope of a future life I began to conceive earth's culminant passion... I felt that if anything still recognisable in me had preceded earth-life, it was this one profound affinity; if anything was destined to survive, it must be into the maintenance of this one affinity that my central effort must be thrown. I was like a half-drunken man suddenly sobered by the announcement that he has come into a fortune... From that hour the moral victory was won; – achieved with steadfastness, though not yet with more than steadfastness; with no inward felicity in such obedience to the highest law...
>
> ... To me it seemed as though I then saw Virtue clear. An effect was wrought upon me which neither Mrs Butler's heroic Christianity nor Henry Sidgwick's rightness and reasonableness had ever produced. And although in my own heart I still felt the recurrent conflict between the savage and the sage, – between the half-human instinct and the deliberate choice of upright man; – yet in this one matter the impulse which prompted me to virtue became like the impulse of self-preservation itself. I knew in the deep of the heart that Virtue alone was safe, and only Virtue lasting, and only Virtue blest; and Phyllis [Myers' name for Annie] became to me as the very promise and earnest of triumphant Virtue.

Over the period from 1873 to 1876 Walter Marshall's mental problems intensified. His illness developed to the point where his behaviour became more and more irrational, irresponsible and frighteningly unpredictable. The strain upon his wife became unbearable. A family conference was called and expert advice was taken. The result was that in May 1876 the sadly troubled man was committed to an asylum at Ticehurst. The prognosis was not favourable.

Throughout these years Frederic Myers and his mother had tried their best to help Annie. Myers wrote to her; he saw her on a number of occasions and sometimes helped by taking Walter away with him to give her some relief. Annie stayed with Susan Myers in April 1876 at Cheltenham. At the beginning of August, Myers and his brother Arthur sailed to Norway and it was while Myers was abroad that the tragedy culminated. Annie, still desperately anxious to do the right thing, found that her worries were not alleviated but increased by Walter's committal to an asylum. Late in August a second family conference agreed that decisions should be made by a council of five persons. Walter should be transferred and put under the care of a Dr Hall of Brighton. The conference was held at Keswick. Myers' mother and Annie drove from Keswick to Old Church. Some days later Susan Myers wrote to her son, still in Norway:

I had been very anxious – we all had – at the fixed stony look in her face. She grew silent towards me, after having been quite frank and loving – & I could not with all my entreaties get her to speak of what was in her mind, after she had once said that she saw that she had been quite wrong in everything – in this last step for W. (the certif.) & all together about religion – in rejecting Xtianity –. I hoped she wd. pass through this crisis – & get a fuller happier faith – she was continually praying and getting me to read T. a Kempis to her – We came together on Monday & she brightened up during the drive & talked more like herself. I left her at O. Ch. at 7 p.m. thinking the children would cheer her. Next morning she was missing – a shawl by the lake – and in deep water she was found.

Annie Marshall had left the house in utter despair, completely shattered by the vortex of troubles that had tormented her for years, troubles without end or solution that must have made her, in her utter nervous exhaustion, embrace the idea of death as the only possibility she could see of achieving peace. Her initial attempt to commit suicide by cutting her throat with a pair of scissors failed to inflict a fatal wound. She finally achieved her goal by drowning herself in Lake Ullswater.

The effect of her death – and the manner of it – had a profound effect upon Myers. In the poems and prose in his autobiography, published privately as a booklet of forty-three pages under the title *Fragments of Inner Life*, he writes:

107

And amid these ponderings another inward illumination rose upon my way. In 1873 there dawned upon me a new knowledge of what divineness can lodge in a woman's soul. My poem on *Teneriffe* reflects the first intoxication of that opening glory; the buoyancy which lifts beyond the clutch of fate; the sheer exultation that in the Universe such a creature could breathe and live. Then as love grew, – 'love that never found his earthly close', – that early triumph became a more imperious yearning. The poem entitled *Honour* breathes the sadness of a passion accepting moral barriers, and with no celestial hope. Then after that the poems in which alone this story can be told reveal that loved one as identified more and more with whatever in me I learnt to be imperishable, with all that was striving upwards into life divine.

Chapter 6, headed *Mourning* contains the following passage:

Some of the serenest hours of those mourning years were spent in that valley in the grounds of Hallsteads, on Ullswater, which has been the setting of much of my inward life. Outside it lie the wilder beauties of Cumberland; within are a grandeur and solitude which foster without overwhelming the heart. There are tower and spire of cedar and cypress, high walls of flowering laurel, and rhododendrons massed amid the shade. There for many a twilight hour I have paced alone, and shaken from the thick syringas their load of scent and rain. The childhood of Phyllis also had been spent in a scene resembling this; she had been nurtured amid antique simplicity, and in an ancestral moorland home...

When I think of that valley I understand the hauntings of the earthward-hovering soul. For I haunt it now; even now, when I would think steadfastly of myself, my image comes to me as pacing that glade of silence, between the ramparts of impenetrable green. I feel a twilight that deepens into darkness, a calm where winds are laid, and in my own heart a grave intentness, as of one who strives to lift into an immortal security the yearning passion of his love.

In Chapter 8, entitled *The Final Faith*, Myers summarises his spiritual development through Hellenism, Agnosticism and Christianity, to a belief in immortality.

The poem entitled *Honour* comes from the agnostic period of my life, and its tone is one of almost intolerable strain. Then, as it happened, during that period of ardent passion, I received my first assurance of things unseen. The later poems in Chapter V show the nature of the change induced. The painful effort of self-restraint merges at last in a solemn exultation. For, in fact, as soon as I began to have hope of a future life I began to conceive earth's culminant passion *sub specie aeternitatis.* I felt that if anything still recognisable in me had preceded earth-life, it was this one profound affinity; if anything were destined to survive, it must be into the maintenance of this one affinity that my central effort must be thrown. I was like a half-drunken man suddenly sobered by the announcement that he has suddenly come into a fortune. The first impulse was the mere resolve that nothing here on earth should prejudice that chance of happiness to be...

From that hour the moral victory was won; – achieved with steadfastness, though not yet with more than steadfastness; with no inward felicity in such obedience to the highest law.

But a further step was to come. I knew her to be an immortal creature; I discerned in her as it were the visible sign of her immortality; I felt with Plato that Love is an inlet into the spiritual world; that it is out of proportion to earthly existence; that more than the mere delight of the terrene comradeship must be the hidden motive of that extreme emprize; – that the desire, as Plato has it, 'for the *eternal* possession of the Beautiful' must have its root in some august remembrance of a remote pre-natal day.

Among the pure Ideas which men in some dim fashion discern on earth, 'Wisdom', says Plato, 'we cannot see, or terrible had been the love she had inspired.' To me it seemed as though I then saw Virtue clear...

In the sonorous prose and poetry of his autobiography there does not seem to me any grounds for doubting the total sincerity of Myers' love for Annie. His ardent and sensitive nature, his search for perfection, his Classical education, his position in the Victorian world, all contrived to mould his response to her. In truth, he was not the first man, nor was he the last, to fall in love, to go overboard, to succumb so completely to the enchantment of the beloved's presence that he invests her with every perfect attribute. Perhaps in our modern world we are more realistic – certainly it is easier for the beloved to live without such a burden of perfection – but perhaps in our modern acceptance of imperfection we have in a real way lost our innocence.

Myers' involvement in psychical research after Annie's death was far removed from his earlier investigations into the paranormal in company with Sidgwick and his other companions. His previous work in that field had indeed been serious and sustained and by no means a dilettante occupation, but now, to the end of his life, his dedication to the subject was total. It was a dedication braced by the resolution that only a complete acceptance of truth, no matter what the truth might be, was the way forward. As the years passed, he began to see that it was in mental mediumship rather than physical mediumship that fruitful research lay. And it was finally through his sittings with two mediums, Mrs Piper and Mrs Thompson, that he believed he had obtained reliable evidence that Annie had succeeded in getting through to him the fact of her survival. 'Twelve years after departing,' he recorded in his autobiography, 'a message came. It was repeated; I feel it sure. I rest in the belief that love has surmounted the sundering crisis, and has lived beyond the gulf of death.' Faye Hammill, in her *Times* review of a book by John Beer entitled *Providence and Love: Studies in Wordsworth, Channing, Myers, George Eliot and Ruskin*, published in 2000, sums up Myers' beliefs precisely.

> Myers' experiences – the crisis of faith, the attempt to replace it with an ideal Platonic love, the perception of that love as providential, the response to the death of a beloved, and the exploration of the possibility of a life after death – provide a focus for Beer's discussion of Victorian thinking about providence and love. Of Myers' conversation with George Eliot, in which she pronounced that God was inconceivable, immortality unbelievable, but duty absolute, Beer comments: 'For Myers that desperate sense of the modern predicament could be alleviated only if one could discover some assured evidence of personal immortality, underpinning human affections by restoring the awareness of a divine providence. Without such an assurance, his position could be sustained only by falling back on the tentative Platonic solution he had already formulated.'

110

In March 1880, Frederic Myers married Eveleen Tennant, a young and beautiful member of a wealthy family. The marriage produced three children and was generally a happy one. Eveleen was an intelligent woman, a noted portrait photographer and was devoted to her husband. She took part with him in the Cambridge experiments with Eusapia Palladino but she often found dissatisfaction in her inability to be always first in his thoughts. Too often for her liking, his mind seemed to be in distant places. In one of her letters to him she wrote, 'You can do without me but I *cannot* live without your love – & yet I feel *sometimes* I don't have it and darkness encompasses me your poor Evie.' Undoubtedly she had a tendency to possessiveness and extreme jealousy but in all fairness her mutilation of his autobiography after he died was an act that many women might have been induced to carry out when they read in it evidence of their husband's undying and ardent devotion to a deceased lover.

Myers' health began to deteriorate in 1898. In November 1899 he was diagnosed as having Bright's disease. In the latter part of 1900 he succeeded Henry Sidgwick as President of the SPR and stoically carried on his work. But it was a presidency of short duration. On January 17th, 1901, he died in a clinic in Rome in the presence of his family. In his tribute to Myers in the *Proceedings of the SPR*, Oliver Lodge wrote:

The termination of his life ... was physically painful ... but his bearing under it all was so patient and elevated as to extort admiration from the excellent Italian doctor who attended him ... In the intervals of painful breathing he quoted from one of his own poems (The Renewal of Youth)...
'Ah, welcome then that hour which bids thee lie
In anguish of thy last infirmity!
Welcome the toss for ease, the gasp for air,
The visage drawn, the Hippocratic stare;
Welcome the darkening dream, the lost control,
The sleep, the swoon, the arousal of the soul!'

Lodge's tribute also contains the following passage:

I never knew a man so hopeful concerning his ultimate destiny. He once asked me whether I would barter, if it were possible,

111

my unknown destiny, whatever it might be, for as many aeons of unmitigated and wise terrestrial happiness as might last until the fading of the sun, and then an end... He would not!

Such was his faith: by this he lived and died. Religious men in all ages have had some such faith, perhaps a more restful and less strenuous faith; but to Myers the faith did not come by religion: he would have described himself as one who walked by sight and knowledge rather than by faith, and his eager life-long struggle for knowledge was in order that he might by no chance be mistaken... He [spoke] of himself ... as having 'often a sense of great solitude, and of an effort beyond my strength; "striving" – as Homer says of Odysseus..., "striving to save my own soul and my comrades' homeward way."'

Among the other tributes paid to Myers after his death was one by Professor William James, also published in the *Proceedings of the SPR*. From someone who knew Myers and his work and who was probably the United States' most outstanding psychologist, it shows the extraordinarily high opinion James had of Myers' contribution to psychical research and psychology.

Brought up entirely upon literature and history, and interested at first in poetry and religion chiefly; never by nature a philosopher in the technical sense of a man forced to pursue consistency among concepts for the mere love of the logical occupation; not crammed with science at college, or trained to scientific method by any passage through a laboratory; Myers had it as it were to re-create his personality before he became the wary critic of evidence, the skilful handler of hypothesis, the learned neurologist and omnivorous reader of biological and cosmological matter, with whom in later years we were acquainted. The transformation came about because he needed to be all these things in order to work successfully at the problem that lay near his heart; and the ardour of his will and the richness of his intellect are proved by the success with which he underwent so unusual a transformation.

James, in his long and respectful tribute, contrasts Myers' dedicated approach to psychical research and the phenomena he studied to the closed mind, arrogant attitude of James's own colleagues:

112

his keenness for truth carried him into regions where either intellectual or social squeamishness would have been fatal, so he 'mortified' his *amour propre* ... and became a model of patience, tact and humility wherever investigation required it. Both his example and his body of doctrine will make this temper the only one henceforward scientifically respectable.

James then spends some seven pages of his tribute summarising Myers' major contributions to the understanding of human personality, in particular Myers' concept of the Subliminal Self – 'the enveloping mother-consciousness in each of us, from which the consciousness we wot of is precipitated like a crystal.' James's criticisms of Myers' work are of the same nature one master of a science might use in acknowledgement of an astounding tour-de-force synthesis in that science delivered and developed by another master. He ends his tribute to Myers with the following passage:

Behind the minute anatomists and the physiologists, with their metallic instruments, there have always stood the out-door naturalists with their eyes and love of concrete nature. The former call the latter superficial, but there is something wrong about your laboratory-biologist who has no sympathy with living animals. In psychology there is a similar distinction. Some psychologists are fascinated by the varieties of mind in living action, others by the dissecting out, whether by logical analysis or by brass instruments, of whatever elementary living processes may be there. Myers must decidedly be placed in the former class, though his powerful use of analogy enabled him also to do work after the fashion of the latter. He loved human nature as Cuvier and Agassiz loved animal nature; in his view, as in their view, the subject formed a vast living picture. Whether his name will have in psychology as honourable a place as their names have gained in the sister science, will depend upon whether future inquirers shall adopt or reject his theories; and the rapidity with which their decision shapes itself will depend largely on the vigour with which this Society continues its labours in his absence. It is at any rate a possibility, and I am disposed to think it a probability, that Frederic Myers will always be remembered in psychology as the pioneer who staked out a vast tract of mental wilderness and planted the flag of genuine science upon it. He was an enormous collector. He introduced for the first time comparison, classification, and serial order into the peculiar kind of fact which he collected. He was a genius at perceiving analogies; he was fertile in hypotheses; and as far as conditions allowed it in this meteoric region, he relied on verification. Such advantages are of no avail, however, if one has struck into a false road from the onset. But should it turn out that Frederic Myers has really hit the right road by his divining instinct, it is certain that, like the names of others who have been wise, his name will keep an honourable place in scientific history.

There were other tributes, for example from Charles Richet, physiologist and Nobel prizewinner. More recently Alan Gauld, in discussing Myers' theory of the Subliminal Mind and showing how Edmund Gurney's discoveries in experimental hypnotism had influenced Myers, has written:

Myers thinks that what happens in hypnosis is that some part of the subliminal self comes forward in response to an appeal sent, as it were, downwards from the supraliminal [roughly the consciousness] and displaces the supraliminal self, or part of it. Deep hypnosis and light hypnosis may bring forward a different subliminal stream, and the two streams may have quite separate memory-chains.That the subliminal streams of consciousness revealed by hypnosis continue active even when the ordinary workaday stream of consciousness has resumed its rule is shown by a number of recorded observations; and especially by the observation that a post-hypnotic suggestion, completely forgotten by the subject but none the less requiring a calculation for its performance, may be correctly executed without the subject having the least awareness of having carried out any calculation.
    In hysteria, dreams, hypnosis and somnambulism it seems to be the same, or pretty much the same, stratum of the subliminal self which comes forward; a layer characterised by a certain childishness, incoherence and dramatic tendency. Indeed, under hypnosis memories of somnambulistic states or even of dreams, memories lost to the waking consciousness, may be recovered; this proves that the same stream of

consciousness is involved in all three cases. Now amid the childishness that emerges from this layer of the Personality we also find indications of faculties superior to those of the empirical consciousness. There is ore as well as detritus in the subliminal. Dreamers and hypnotic subjects may solve problems refractory to their waking consciousness, may recover forgotten memories or show sensory hyperacuity. A genius is someone in frequent touch with his subliminal, though perhaps with a deeper layer of it than that commonly tapped by dreamers and hypnotic subjects. The inspiration of genius ('subliminal uprushes' as Myers terms them) may seem to him to be quite alien; as dream-scenes may appear to a dreamer. Among many literary samples Myers quotes De Musset's 'On ne travaille pas, on ecoute, c'est comme un inconnu qui vous parle a l'oreille,' and R.L. Stevenson, who could actually dream the adventures which provided the plots for his novels. Musical works would emerge complete and unpremeditated into Mozart's mind. Arithmetical prodigies may find the answers to unsolved problems come into their minds without any conscious processes of ratiocination.

The emergence in dreams, hysteria, hypnosis and somnambulism of a subliminal stream of consciousness may bring with it hints not just of heightened faculties, but of quite novel faculties. Myers adduces a number of cases in which telepathy or clairvoyance or even precognition have seemingly been exercised in a dream, a somnambulic state or an hypnotic trance. Such faculties emerge into view, Myers seems to believe, only or chiefly when the subliminal was being tapped; and so they are essentially subliminal faculties. This suggests that the subliminal consciousness, far from being (as Janet had supposed) a symptom of degeneration and of disintegration, may in fact be evolutive, and may represent the most fundamental part of the Personality.

At his death, Frederic Myers left unfinished a book he had been working on for years. His colleagues Richard Hodgson and Alice Johnson undertook the formidable task of assembling and editing the material and it was published in two volumes in 1903 under the title of *Human Personality and Its Survival of Bodily Death*. Alan Gauld in his book *The Founders of Psychical Research* devotes two chapters to Myers' theory of the Subliminal Self, and though considering it and its applications difficult to follow, qualifies that statement by noting that Myers was still working on it at the time of his death. In commenting upon Gauld's statement that 'as one would perhaps expect, Myers' eyes continually wander from the path at his feet towards the distant and numinous heights which lie before him,' Fraser Nicol (1972) remarks:

> This may indeed create difficulty for our understanding of Myers, but it is not, I suggest, a defect. Great acts of creation are less likely to emerge from rational cogitation, but rather as sudden inspirations that seem at first to have no rational basis whatever. In the history of psychical research no man had been so richly endowed with original ideas as Frederic Myers. He invented the term 'subliminal uprush', and it does not need much reading between the lines to realise that he was a constant recipient of it. In his book, his ideas – often undeveloped – are strewn through the 1300 pages so prodigally that if their author had lived a hundred years he could not have worked them all to fruition. Frederic Myers was the Coleridge of psychical research.

It is a century since *Human Personality* was published. It remains a monument to the genius of Myers; it is still a goldmine of great value to anyone patient enough to read it in its entirety. Poet, Classical scholar, psychologist and psychical researcher, Myers was truly one of the giants of the Victorian age. His turbulent life, his enthusiasm and the tragedy in his life may well have been *his* necessary apprenticeship preparing him for the task he devoted himself to in the last quarter-century of his life. Like a number of the other founders of the SPR he had been a man expelled from paradise and his life had been a tireless and dedicated honest search for the way back, even for evidence that it had ever existed. More than the others, however, work in psychical research had convinced him that it did exist, that there was a way back and that death was the necessary gateway to a new and infinitely better existence.

It has been remarked that it is understandable that Frederic Myers' wife Eveleen attempted to expunge from the record of his life explicit references to Annie. A century before Princess Diana's dark remark that 'there were always three people in that marriage', Eveleen might well have made the same complaint even though one was dead. When *Human Personality* was being prepared for publication, she persuaded the editors to omit the communications Myers had received through the mediums Mrs Piper and Mrs Thompson, communications that he believed had come from Annie and had finally convinced him that there was survival of bodily death, communications that he had intended would be given a prominent place in *Human Personality*. It is likely that she destroyed the material. Again, she 'edited' the short autobiography, *Fragments of Inner Life*, which Myers had written in the early 1890s and had privately printed in 1893. There were only twenty-five numbered copies. Six of these he sent in sealed packets to six close friends, four were reserved for his wife and three children and he directed that the rest should 'remain for the present in my study'. In 1904 Eveleen published a booklet entitled *Fragments of Prose and Poetry* which was essentially *Fragments of an Inner Life* but with every part referring to Annie removed. In so doing, it seems that Eveleen Myers may have unwittingly destroyed one of her husband's most audacious experiments.

On January 27th, 1891, Myers wrote on a sheet of paper the statement:

If I can revisit any earthly scene, I should choose the Valley in the grounds of Hallsteads, Cumberland.

This paper he sealed in an envelope which he gave to Oliver Lodge as a posthumous test for survival. Myers died on January 17th, 1901. Some days later Mrs Verrall, who had been a friend and neighbour of Myers in Cambridge, began her automatic writing again in case Myers, if he had survived death, was able to communicate proof of his survival through her writing. On July 13th, 1904, her script contained the following words:

I have long told you of the contents of the envelope. Myers' sealed envelope left with Lodge. You have not understood. It has in it the words from the Symposium – about Love bridging the chasm.

117

In October 1904 *Fragments of Prose and Poetry* was published.

On December 13th, 1904, Lodge opened the sealed envelope at a meeting of the SPR Council and its contents were read and compared with Mrs Verrall's script. It was agreed that the test had been a failure and this conclusion was published in the *Journal of the Society for Psychical Research* in January 1905.

In October 1958 the distinguished scholar and SPR member W.H. Salter published a paper in the society's *Proceedings* in which he argues that the parts (in prose and poetry) of Myers' autobiography cut out by Eveleen emphasised the platonic nature of his love for Annie, and the importance he attached to Plato's *Symposium*, in which Love is shown as able to bridge the chasm between this world and a transcendental spiritual realm. Salter argues skilfully and cogently that in Myers' reference to his desire to revisit the 'Valley in the grounds of Hallsteads, Cumberland', where he walked and talked with Annie Marshall, is not in conflict or irrelevant to the message in the script writtten automatically by Mrs Verrall.

What is clear is that Myers, Gurney and Sidgwick, in their honest and totally dedicated search for signs that the human situation was not entirely hopeless, had by their work finally raised some hope, not only for themselves but for the human race. Myers himself had posed the ultimate question 'Is the Universe Friendly?' Alan Gauld summed up the result of their work in the following words.

'There had lately been much to suggest to them that the Universe was neither friendly nor yet unfriendly; it was just blankly indifferent. Psychical research seemed to offer a touch of warmth and hope in face of this chilling prospect. It was at least a candle in the darkness which was beginning to loom on every side.'

PART 2

GREAT EXPECTATIONS

6

One White Crow

In order to disprove the theory that all crows are black it is enough to find one white crow.

William James

I can hardly wait to die.

Richard Hodgson

Dr Richard Hodgson died suddenly and unexpectedly on the afternoon of December 20th, 1905 after a strenuous game of handball in the Union Boat Club of Boston. It was a shock to his many friends at the Tavern Club, where he was perhaps the most popular member. Earlier that afternoon a number of the members had seen him, with customary enthusiasm and good-natured tolerance, tease some men present who were hotly denouncing a member for defending an unpopular cause. That evening his lifeless body was carried upstairs. Psychical research had lost one of its most dedicated and redoubtable investigators.

Richard Hodgson was born in Melbourne in Australia in 1855. He had his schooling there and afterwards entered Melbourne University. He intended to follow a career in law but in 1878 his interest in philosophy brought him to England to study the subject further at Cambridge University. There he read for the Moral Sciences tripos and took honours in 1881. While at Cambridge as a student of the Moral Sciences he was naturally brought into contact with Henry Sidgwick and there developed between them a strong friendship and strong respect for each other; it is not surprising

121

Richard Hodgson   Mrs Piper

then that the young Australian's conversations with the quiet-spoken, slightly stuttering academic should have stimulated Hodgson's interest in psychical research. When Sidgwick and his colleagues created the Society for Psychical Research in 1882, Hodgson joined, his name appearing in the SPR's first published list of members.

In 1887 Hodgson went to the United States to take up the position of Secretary of the American Society for Psychical Research (ASPR), which in 1890 became a branch of the SPR. Apart from brief visits to Britain he returned only once in 1897, when he stayed a year, serving as a member of the SPR Council and as editor of the *Proceedings* and *Journal*. Even after his return to the United States, however, he continued to correspond with Frederic Myers and others in Britain. After Myers died, leaving his monumental book *Human Personality* unfinished, it was Hodgson and Miss Alice Johnson who completed and edited that vastly important work.

The task that Richard Hodgson encountered, and which was to occupy his energy, training, intelligence and perception, year after year, was the study of the mediumship of Mrs Leonora Piper. As time passed, Hodgson became ever more convinced that in Mrs Piper a psychic faculty shone forth that, compared with most other mediums' gifts, was like a searchlight compared to glow-worms. His study of the Piper mediumship became his most absorbing work. In fact, the long years of research into the mediumship of Mrs Piper by Hodgson and his fellow psychical researchers began a new phase in psychic studies, one that strengthened their belief that *mental* mediumship was going to be far more productive and enlightening than continuing to stumble along after the deceptive will-o'-the-wisp of *physical* mediumship.

When Hodgson went to America in 1887 he found that a number of SPR members there, especially Professor William James, were already interested in the trance phenomena of Mrs Piper. As often happens in these cases, James had become interested not because he had had sittings with her but because of the experiences with her of people he knew. His mother-in-law, Alice Gibbons, had had a sitting with her and was so impressed that she convinced her daughter, James's sister-in-law, to go. What he heard from them persuaded James to arrange for a sitting with Mrs Piper, though he attended in an attitude of extreme scepticism, his intention being to detect how the trick was done so that he could enlighten his gullible womenfolk. His sitting, however, greatly intrigued him and with a number of his friends he began to study Mrs Piper's mediumship.

When Hodgson subsequently arrived in the United States to take charge of the ASPR, James took the opportunity to pass the study over to him. Within a fortnight of his arrival in Boston, therefore, he became involved in what was to become his life's work. At first he maintained his habitual cool scepticism. As he put it himself, in an SPR report published in its *Proceedings* in 1889:

> I was compelled to assume in the first instance, that Mrs Piper was fraudulent and obtained her information previously by ordinary means such as inquiries by confederates, etc... That I did not obtain a sitting at my first visit might be pointed to as a very suspicious circumstance, and it might well be supposed that, in consequence of my known connection with the Society for Psychical Research, Mrs Piper might have previously 'got up' information about myself and other active workers in the society in the expectation of future use.

But his experiences with her led to a change of mind and to a number of positive reports written by him and by Professor James. The Boston housewife was consequently invited to cross the Atlantic, where she was studied by SPR investigators including Frederic Myers and Oliver Lodge. The carefully controlled sittings added to the weight of evidence demonstrating her startling ability in trance to obtain a wealth of information by paranormal means. A century has passed since these investigations. As far as I know, no one has, in that century, put forward anything like a convincing case that all the knowledge exhibited by Mrs Piper was acquired in any normal way. The big question for psychical researchers regarding that knowledge was how much of it was obtained by telepathy and clairvoyance and how much, if any, came from communication from the dead.

What was the nature of the experiences Hodgson had with Mrs Piper that changed his mind so radically?

As we have seen, Hodgson initially treated the young Boston housewife with caution, testing her capacity for fraud, weighing up her ability to fish for information in the unguarded verbal slips of her sitters. He even had her and her husband and other persons connected with her followed by private detectives for a time.

When Hodgson first met Mrs Piper she would go into trance accompanied by violent and alarming contortions – and talk in a way quite different from her normal manner and voice. Usually she would be 'controlled' by a Dr Phinuit, a distinct personality, irascible and touchy, who claimed to be the spirit of an old French medical man. He would act as a 'master of ceremonies', ostensibly performing as an intermediary between the sitters and the spirits of the deceased, often relatives of the sitters who appeared anxious to convince the sitters that they had survived death. From the beginning of her career, Mrs Piper cooperated fully with the psychical researchers studying her mediumship, often to her own extreme discomfort. Phinuit claimed to have neither the sense of taste nor smell, and he showed not the slightest discomfort when induced by Hodgson to take several inhalations of strong ammonia (though, as Hodgson laconically noted, 'Mrs Piper suffered somewhat after the trance was over'). When a lighted match was held to the left forearm, it was drawn away slowly as if only a vague discomfort was experienced. 'Oui, I feel it,' exclaimed Phinuit. 'Did you feel pain?' 'No, felt cold, cold – I think.' It was almost as if he was someone who, under a local anaesthetic, could remain conscious and comment on his sensations. Hodgson soon realised, however, that it was what the medium communicated that mattered.

For Mrs Piper it had all begun when, worried about her health, she visited a blind medium named J.R. Cocke, who gave medical advice, being ostensibly controlled by a French physician with a name pronounced 'Finny'. On her second visit, Mrs Piper lapsed into unconsciousness. As she did so she was aware of a flood of light and saw strange faces. Further visits seemed to develop her ability and she tried sitting at home with friends and relatives. She acquired various controls who went by the names of 'Chlorine' (an Indian girl!), Johann Sebastian Bach, Mrs Siddons, Longfellow

124

and Commodore Vanderbilt. Dr Phinuit, apparently by agreement among the other controls, subsequently took over and remained her chief control for many years.

The nature of 'controls' is by no means clearly understood even today and has a considerable literature. For the reader new to them we suggest that s/he consults Gauld's book *Mediumship and Survival* (1982) for an introduction to the subject.

Sometimes Phinuit was in top form, describing in accurate terms the deceased relatives of the sitters, relaying their purported statements and a host of relevant facts Mrs Piper could not in any conceivable way have learned. Over the years she would take part in thousands of sittings involving hundreds of sitters, the vast majority of them total strangers who would suddenly present themselves anonymously to Mrs Piper. The proceedings were frequently planned and overseen by cautious and highly competent psychical researchers like Hodgson, James, Lodge and others, so it is understandable to anyone of open mind why these researchers ultimately abandoned the fraud theory and accepted that in Mrs Piper they had a psychic of superstar quality. As Lodge put it in 1889:

By introducing anonymous strangers, and by catechising her myself in various ways, I have satisfied myself that much of the information she possesses in the trance state is not acquired by ordinary commonplace methods, but that she has some unusual means of acquiring information. The facts on which she discourses are usually within the knowledge of some person present, though they are often entirely out of his conscious thought at the time. Occasionally facts have been narrated which have only been verified afterwards, and which are in good faith asserted never to have been known; meaning thereby that they have left no trace on the conscious memory of any person present or in the neighbourhood.

By now Hodgson, too, fully subscribed to that opinion. With respect to 'first sittings', in which a person Mrs Piper had never met before was put before her, he wrote in an 1897 report for the *Proceedings*:

Now, although for the purpose of establishing that Mrs Piper possesses some supernormal faculty, the records of 'first sittings', where precautions have been taken to prevent Mrs Piper's acquiring knowledge beforehand as to the sitter, are especially valuable, they cannot lead us very far in the direction of complete explanation. They may add largely to the proof that Mrs Piper's trance-personality shows knowledge of particular facts about the sitter which Mrs Piper cannot intelligently be supposed to have acquired by normal means, that private facts known only to the sitter are frequently communicated, and that occasionally a knowledge is manifested of events entirely unknown to the sitter and afterwards verified. Further, accompanying this exhibition of supernormal knowledge there may be a more or less personal element characteristic of some deceased friend of the sitter, and leading the sitter to the conclusion that he is in direct and actual communication with this departed friend, it is, nevertheless, difficult to suppose that however remarkable such first sittings may be, they could form a satisfactory basis for the 'spiritistic' theory. They might indeed be profoundly suggestive of such a theory, and in the minds of many might raise a presumption in its favour, but they would still be apt to remain, for the probing investigator, inadequate; they would still be apt to appear as comparatively isolated groups of facts, bound together, as it were, only by the plastic and mysterious, but persistent personality known as Phinuit.

Nevertheless, 'Dr Phinuit' could fall down and did so on numerous occasions. The investigators recognised that he could employ tricks, fishing at times to obtain information from the sitters. Hodgson remarked that he had 'been at sittings where Phinuit has displayed such pattering and equivocation, and such a lack of lucidity, that I believe had these been my only experiences with him I should have without any hesitation have condemned Mrs Piper as an imposter.' Phinuit himself confessed: 'Sometimes when I come here, do you know, actually it is hard work for me to get control of the medium. Sometimes I think I am almost like the medium, and sometimes not at all. Then [when the control is incomplete] I am weak and confused.'

Hodgson also noticed that when Phinuit was having difficulty in getting names or other data a sitter or sitters had in the forefront of their mind, he would change the subject and often be successful when the sitter was no longer thinking consciously about the data but had allowed it to 'sink' below the threshold.

Hodgson, and others, puzzled long over Phinuit's true nature and 'his' abilities. On one occasion the father of 'Mr M.N.' died suddenly and unexpectedly of heart failure after an attack of bronchitis in London. Dr Phinuit had six weeks previously told Mr M.N.'s wife that Mr M.N.'s father would die in a few weeks. He was ill for the last three days of his life and Dr Phinuit told Mr M.N. that he, Phinuit, would try to discuss with his father certain matters in connection with his will before he died. When Mr M.N. did arrive in London, his sister, who was at her father's bedside for the last three days of his life, told him how their father had repeatedly complained of the presence of an old man at the foot of the bed, who annoyed him by discussing his private affairs!

A visit by Mrs Piper to England in 1889 produced fresh evidence of her ability in trance to acquire in a paranormal fashion obscure pieces of information. Both Oliver Lodge and Frederic Myers, the former at his Liverpool home, the latter in Cambridge, carried out a series of investigations of her powers using the most elaborate precautions to make sure she was cut off from any putative confederates. Both became totally convinced that her powers were genuine. Lodge brought more than forty people to her, all strangers to her. The information that she, or rather her control Dr Phinuit provided, in many cases was shown on subsequent inquiry to be correct, even when the sitter had no conscious recollection at the time that it was.

One morning, Lodge received unexpectedly a gold watch from one of his uncles. He handed it to Mrs Piper when she was in trance. Dr Phinuit told him that the watch had belonged to another of Lodge's uncles. He then described episodes and adventures of the uncles when they were boys. Lodge could neither confirm nor deny these alleged events. When he consulted his uncle he found that he had forgotten most of the details. Only when they got in touch with yet another uncle were the stories confirmed.

If we leave aside Dr Phinuit's claim that he obtained his information from the surviving spirit of the dead uncle, we are faced with the rather breath-taking proposition that Dr Phinuit, whatever he may or may not have been, could find and fetch, sometimes with some difficulty, information that was not even in the minds of the sitters but resided in the conscious or subconscious minds of people scattered around the world. It is largely as a result of such studies that the 'super-telepathy' or 'super-ESP' theory was advanced. If one goes even further and accepts the materialistic proposition that the mind is merely the brain in action, then additional difficulties for the super-ESP theory arise. The medium's active brain must have the ability to know in which living brains around the planet appropriate pieces of information have been stored and by some means retrieve, compare and dramatise this information to produce a convincing communicator.

Hodgson formed the opinion that some open-minded sitters were better than others more sceptical. When the former sat, the conditions were more conducive to the reception of meaningful items; the latter type of sitter inhibited the medium. Hodgson also noted from his close and long-term acquaintance with Mrs Piper that her health played a part. In March 1893, Mrs Piper underwent a serious surgical operation for the removal of a tumour which had been a source of trouble for some years and had interfered a great deal with her sittings. It is a curious fact that two days before the operation, the surgeon who operated, Dr Lena V. Ingraham, with two other doctors, had a conversation with Dr Phinuit! The operation was performed at Dr Cushing's Sanitarium in Brookline, Massachusetts. Hodgson remained at the sanitarium while the operation was being performed in case his assistance was required if any unusual event occurred. He reported:

After the operation and while Mrs Piper, who had been taken to her room, was still under the influence of the ether, and apparently unconscious of any person present, Dr Ingraham requested me to enter the room, as Mrs Piper was calling for me. I went in and spoke to her, but she seemed to be quite unaware of my presence, although she moaned occasionally, and several times called out spasmodically 'Mr Hodgson'. During this interval of unconsciousness her attention became fixed as upon an object of interest, and she exclaimed: 'Who is that old man? Take him away.' Then came a pause, as if she was listening, and she then added, 'Oh, no. He's a nice old man. He can stay.' This naturally caused me to think of Phinuit.

The first sittings Mrs Piper gave after her operation were two in the early part of September to a previous sitter, and were largely personal. I was present taking notes... At the first sitting, September 7th, 1893, Phinuit said, with reference to the operation: 'I saw the medium on a long table and helped her out. I saw Hodgson too, and tried to make the medium see me.'

After she had recovered from the operation, Mrs Piper was able to give sittings with much greater regularity than before and appeared to be much less exhausted by them. By 1896 her health improved so substantially that Hodgson judged her thereafter to be a thoroughly healthy woman.

By 1896, Hodgson had also witnessed another remarkable development in Mrs Piper's mediumship. On March 12, 1892, a sitter had taken to Mrs Piper several test articles, among them a ring that had belonged to an 'Annie D—'.

> Phinuit made references to this lady, giving the name Annie, and just before the close of the sitting Mrs Piper's right hand moved slowly up until it was over the top of her head. The arm seemed to become rigidly fixed in its position, as though spasmodically contracted, but the hand trembled very rapidly. Phinuit exclaimed several times: 'She's taken my hand away', and added, 'she wants to write'. I put a pencil between the fingers, and placed a block-book on the head under the pencil. No writing came until, obeying Phinuit's order to 'hold the hand', I grasped the hand very firmly at its junction with the wrist and so stopped its trembling or vibrating. It then wrote: 'I am Annie D— [surname correctly given] ... I am not dead... I am not dead but living... I am not dead ... world ... goodbye... I am Annie D—'. The hold on the pencil then relaxed, and Phinuit began to murmur 'Give me my hand back, give me my hand back.' The arm, however, remained in its contracted position for a short time, but finally, as though with much difficulty, and slowly, it moved down to the side, and Phinuit appeared to regain control over it.

This strange new automatic writing facility developed rapidly. On April 29th, 1892, Hodgson provided a table for Mrs Piper's right arm to rest upon and, after some intervening difficulties were overcome, the automatic writing was customarily produced on a block-book placed on the table. During many sittings thereafter, writing was used to communicate an entity's messages, or to carry on a conversation with a sitter.

129

But it became much more than that. The writing by the hand did not necessarily silence Phinuit. On many occasions, while Phinuit would be conversing audibly with one sitter, the hand would be writing answers to questions by another sitter, so that by this means two entirely different discourses would be proceeding independently of one another involving two ostensibly different entities and two sitters.

It was early in 1892 that a series of events had begun that led Dr Hodgson to take a further crucial step away from his original stance of cool disbelief. He knew many people in Boston, and among them a young lawyer, George Pellew, an associate of the ASPR who, far from believing in survival after death, maintained that it was not only incredible but inconceivable. At the end of one long discussion with Hodgson on the survival question, Pellew vowed that if he died before Hodgson and found himself 'still existing', he would 'make things lively' in the effort to prove that he had survived death.

Pellew had been living in New York for three years when in February 1892, at the age of thirty-two, he was killed in an accidental fall. Richard Hodgson learned of its occurrence within a day or two. In the following few weeks, Hodgson was present at a number of sittings with Mrs Piper. It was on March 22nd, 1892, between four and five weeks after Pellew's death, at a sitting Hodgson went to with Mr John Hart, an old friend of Pellew's, that something significant happened. At first, Phinuit, acting as intermediary as usual, gave information about a George Hart, a deceased uncle of John Hart. Phinuit then said: 'There is another George who wants to speak to you. How many Georges are about you any way?'

From then on, with Phinuit continuing to act as intermediary, a communicator claiming to be George Pellew dominated the sitting. His name was given correctly as well as the names, both first and last, of several of Pellew's most intimate friends, including that of Mr Hart. In addition, incidents were referred to which were then unknown to both the sitter and Hodgson. In his 1897–8 report Hodgson recalled how 'One of the pair of studs that John Hart was wearing was given to Phinuit' and the conversation that followed:

J.H.: 'Who gave them to me?'
G.P.: 'That's mine. I gave you that part of it. I sent that to you.'

J.H.:	'When?'

J.H.: 'When?'

G.P.: 'Before I came here. That's mine. Mother gave you that.'

J.H.: 'No.'

G.P.: 'Well, father then, father and mother together. You got those after I passed out. Mother took them. Gave them to father, and father gave them to you. I want you to keep them. I will them to you.'

The report continues:

Mr Hart notes: 'The studs were sent to me by Mr Pellew as a remembrance of his son. I knew at the time that they had been taken from George's body, and afterwards ascertained that his stepmother had taken them from the body and suggested that they would do to send to me, I having previously written to ask that some little memento be sent to me.'

James and Mary [Mr and Mrs] Howard were mentioned with strongly personal specific references, and in connection with Mrs Howard came the name Katherine. 'Tell her she'll know. I will solve the problems, Katherine.' Mr Hart notes: 'This had no special significance at the time, though I was aware that Katherine, the daughter of Jim Howard, was known to George, who used to live with the Howards.' On the day following the sitting I gave Mr Howard a detailed account of the sitting. These words 'I will solve the problems, Katherine,' impressed him more than anything else, and at the close of my account he related that George, when he had last stayed with them, had talked frequently with Katherine (a girl of fifteen years of age) upon such subjects as Time, Space, God, Eternity, and pointed out to her how unsatisfactory the commonly accepted solutions were. He added that some time he would solve the problems, and let her know, using almost the very words of the communication made at the sitting. Mr Hart added that he was entirely unaware of these circumstances. I was myself unaware of them, and was not at that time acquainted with the Howards, and in fact nearly every statement made at the sitting, during which I was the note-taker, concerned matters of which I was absolutely ignorant.

That sitting of March 22nd, 1892 was just the beginning of it. Within a few weeks, the George Pellew entity was being 'allowed' by Phinuit to use the voice. At a sitting on April 11th, 1892, the first sitting given to the Howards (who were of course unintroduced), the entity made a long series of statements which were so intimately personal and totally characteristic of George Pellew that the Howards, who had not hitherto had the slightest interest in psychical research, found themselves deeply impressed with the feeling that they were indeed holding a conversation with their friend whom they had known so many years. Every reference to persons made by the entity was correct:

G.P.: Jim, is that you? Speak to me quick. I am not dead. Don't think me dead. I'm awfully glad to see you. Can't you see me? Don't you hear me? Give my love to my father and tell him I want to see him. I am happy here, and more so since I find I can communicate with you ... I want you to know I think of you still. I spoke to John about some letters. I left things terribly mixed, my books and my papers; you will forgive me for this, won't you?...
(What do you do, George, where you are?)
I am scarcely able to do anything yet; I am just awakened to the reality of life after death. It was like darkness, I could not distinguish anything at first. Darkest hours just before dawn, you know that, Jim. I was puzzled, confused. Shall have an occupation soon. Now I can see you, my friends. I can hear you speak. Your voice, Jim, I can distinguish with your accent and articulation, but it sounds like a big bass drum. Mine would sound to you like the faintest whisper.
(Our conversation then is something like telephoning?)
Yes.
(By long distance telephone.)
[G.P. laughs.]
(Were you not surprised to find yourself living?)
Perfectly so. Greatly surprised. I did not believe in a future life. It was beyond my reasoning powers. Now it is as clear to me as daylight. We have an astral facsimile of the material body... Jim, what are you writing now?
[G.P. when living would probably have jeered at the associations of the word 'astral'. – R.H.]

(Nothing of any importance.)

Why don't you write about this?

(I should like to, but the expression of my opinions would be nothing. I must have facts.)

These I will give to you and to Hodgson if he is still interested in these things.

(Will people know about this possibility of communication?)

They are sure to in the end. It is only a question of time when people in the material body will know all about it, and everyone will be able to communicate... I want all the fellows to know about me... What is Rogers writing?

(A novel.)

No, not that. Is he not writing something about me?

(Yes, he is preparing a memorial about you.)

That is nice; it is pleasant to be remembered. It is very kind of him. He was always kind to me when I was alive. Martha Rogers [Roger's deceased daughter] is here. I have talked with her several times. She reflects too much on her last illness, on being fed with a tube. We tell her she ought to forget it, and she has done so in good measure, but she was ill a long time... She is a beautiful little soul. She sends her love to her father... Berwick, how is he? Give him my love. He is a good fellow... How is Orenberg? He has some of my letters. Give him my warmest love. He was always very fond of me, though he understood me least of all my friends. We fellows who are eccentric are always misunderstood in life. I used to have fits of depression. I have none now. I am happy now. I want my father to know about this. We used to talk about spiritual things, but he will be hard to convince. My mother will be easier...

From then on the Pellew communicator rapidly developed its ability to participate at sittings, often describing the difficulties involved in doing so. Hodgson, from his long study of Mrs Piper's mediumship, had been persuaded that even if the entities were truly the spirits of the dead, they had almost to enter a trance or sleeping state themselves to use the medium. In one moment of flippancy, he remarked that for spirit to talk to sitter, and vice versa, it was as if both had to communicate using a dead-drunk messenger. Now, it seemed as if the Pellew entity was mastering better than most communicators the difficult task. No matter what other

133

communications 'Pellew' wanted to make, he always was able to recognise any friend of George Pellew who happened to attend a sitting. He never failed to announce himself and, with the appropriate emotional and intellectual responses, recognise, among a stream of sitters brought before him by Hodgson, those known to George Pellew, giving their names. All except one, an exception Hodgson felt to be as significant as any recognition that had been made.

A Miss Warner had a first sitting on January 6th, 1897. 'Pellew' seemed to have only a vague recollection of the sitter although Phinuit and others gave her a good deal of correct information about her family and friends. At a sitting the following day, 'Pellew' wrote for some time and Miss Warner finally remarked that she remembered George Pellew but that he knew her mother better. 'Pellew' asked who she was. Hodgson said that her mother was a special friend of Mrs Howard. The conversation continued:

'Pellew': I do not think I ever knew you very well.
Miss W.: Very little. You used to come and see my mother.
'Pellew': I heard of you, I suppose.
Miss W.: I saw you several times. You used to come with Mr Rogers.
'Pellew': Yes, I remembered about Mr Rogers when I saw you before.
Miss W.: Yes, you spoke of him.
'Pellew': Yes, but I cannot seem to place you. I long to place all of my friends, and could do so before I had been gone so long. You see I am further away. I do not recall your face. You must have changed...
Hodgson: Do you remember Mrs Warner?
[Excitement was shown by the hand.]
'Pellew': Of course, oh, very well. For pity sake are you her little daughter?
Miss W.: Yes.
'Pellew': By Jove, how you have grown ... I thought so much of your mother, a charming woman.
Miss W.: She always enjoyed seeing you, I know.
'Pellew': Our tastes were similar.
Miss W.: About writing?
'Pellew': Yes. Do you know Marte at all?
Miss W.: I've met him once or twice.

134

'Pellew': Your mother knows. Ask her if she remembers the book I gave her to read.

Miss W.: I will.

'Pellew': And ask her if she still remembers me and the long talks we used to have at the home evenings.

Miss W.: I know she does.

'Pellew': I wish I could have known you better, it would have been so nice to have recalled the past.

Miss W.: I was a little girl.

Hodgson's comments on this sitting are significant as a measure of his changing opinion. He wrote in his 1897–8 report:

Now it should be remembered that these sittings were held five years after the death of G.P.; and that G.P. had not seen Miss Warner for at least three or four years before his death, that she was only a little girl when he had last seen her, that she had not been, so to say, a special friend of his, and that she had, indeed, changed very much in the intervening eight or nine years.

This non-recognition, then, by G.P. is a perfectly natural circumstance, and when we compare the details given by Phinuit of Miss Warner's family, and the incidents mentioned by Hart, through G.P. writing in connection with her brother ... incidents, moreover, which were unknown to the sitters, – and when we remember also that both Miss Warner and myself were fully aware of her name and of the fact that she had known G.P., the very non-recognition seems to me to afford an argument in favour of the independent existence of G.P., as contrasted with the conception of some secondary personality depending for its knowledge upon the minds of living persons.

'George Pellew' communicated regularly in the five years following Pellew's death. His control of the medium was outstanding. Out of at least 150 people who had sittings with Mrs Piper in that time, he recognised at least 30 correctly who had been known to Pellew. Alan Gauld (in a private communication):

Hodgson only prints a few of the relevant recognitions. Insofar as one can work out where the recognitions are likely to be found and can thus turn up the original scripts, it becomes apparent that what should and what should not be counted as a recognition is far from clear-cut. Hodgson says nothing about what (if any) criteria of recognition he may have adopted.

At one of his early communications, 'Pellew' reminded Hodgson of the promise Pellew had made two years or more before his death that, if he found himself still existing, he would devote himself to proving this fact. Hodgson, after five years of 'Pellew's' endeavours, had to admit that he had succeeded. In spite of all the difficulties in communication, he had converted Hodgson, the former arch-sceptic, to a belief in survival.

Towards the end of Hodgson's 1897–8 report in the *Proceedings*, we find him affirming this belief in the following words:

> at the present time I cannot profess to have any doubt but that the chief 'communicators' to whom I have referred in the foregoing pages, are veritably the personalities that they claim to be, that they have survived the change we call death, and that they have directly communicated with us whom we call living, through Mrs Piper's entranced organism.

In the last few years of his life, nothing in his continued study of the Piper phenomena caused him to change his mind. Untiringly he strove to form from the mountain of evidence a reasonable hypothesis concerning the nature of the 'spirit world'. Many of his conversations with a number of the controls such as Phinuit and the entity known as 'Imperator' shaped the philosophy and belief he expressed in a letter to a friend written in 1901:

> I went through toils and turmoils and perplexities in '97 and '98 about the significance of the whole Imperator regime, but I have seemed to get on a rock after that, – I seem to understand clearly the reasons for incoherence and obscurity, etc., and I think that if for the rest of my life from now I should never see another trance or have another word from Imperator or his group, it would make no difference to my knowledge that all is well, that Imperator, etc., are all that they claim to be and are indeed messengers that we may call divine.

Dr Richard Hodgson died suddenly and unexpectedly on December 20th, 1905. On December 28th, through the entranced Mrs Piper, a message purporting to be from him was delivered. Hodgson during his lifetime had often laughingly said that if he passed over and Mrs Piper was still officiating here below, he was so thoroughly familiar with the difficulties on this side that he would control her better than she had ever yet been controlled. The implication was that if he could do so, he would provide, as he believed George Pellew had done, convincing evidence of his survival.

After this first indication of December 28th, 'Hodgson' communicated regularly for some years. Professor William James, Sir Oliver Lodge, Mrs H. Sidgwick and Mr J.G. Piddington were among the sitters at these sessions, and accounts of these sittings, together with their evaluations of the evidence provided by 'Hodgson', were reported in Volume 23 of the *Proceedings* in 1909. In addition, after Frederic Myers died, 'Hodgson' and 'Myers' both communicated together through Mrs Piper, each communicator being aware of the other's participation in the session. That 'Hodgson', who displayed many of the mannerisms, characteristics and turns of phrase of Richard Hodgson living, provided a large amount of information Mrs Piper could not have known normally is certain. Even making due allowance for the information about him, his life and his friends Mrs Piper must have acquired in her many years of dealing with him, there still remained much that could only have been paranormally provided.

At a sitting on January 30th, 'Hodgson' suddenly said to the sitter: 'Do you remember a story I told you and how you laughed, about the man and woman praying?' The sitter replied: 'Oh, and the devil was in it. Of course I do.' 'Hodgson': 'Yes, the devil, they told him it was the Lord who sent it if the devil brought it ... about the food that was given to them ... I want you to know who is speaking.' The story referred to an episode in Hodgson's life. The American branch of the SPR had never fully paid its expenses, and although the Secretary's salary had always been very small, Hodgson had, after the first years, been reluctant to have any part of it charged to the mother country. The result had occasionally been pecuniary embarrassment on his part. During his last visit to England, shortly after Myers' death, this embarrassment had been extreme; but an American friend, divining it in the nick of time, rescued him by an impulsive and wholly unexpected remittance. To this remittance he replied by a letter which contained some banter and, among other things, cited the story of a starving couple who were overheard praying to God for food by an atheist who was passing the house. The atheist climbed on to the roof and dropped some bread down the chimney, and heard them thank God for the miracle. He then went to the door and revealed himself as its author. The old woman riposted: 'Well, the Lord sent it, even if the devil brought it.' The sitter at that particular seance on January 30th was the generous American friend. It is certain, according to Professor William James, that Mrs Piper had no normal knowledge of this incident and of the correspondence.

Much relevant advice was given by 'Hodgson' concerning the papers and other belongings he had left behind. The 'Hodgson' entity tried with each new sitter to provide evidence that he was indeed Richard Hodgson, striving at least as determinedly as the 'Pellew' communicator had done. On one occasion the entity burst out, almost in exasperation: 'Well, if I am not Hodgson, he never lived!'

Nevertheless, as Professor William James argued, even if it was the surviving personality of Richard Hodgson trying to prove his continued existence, the very fact that it was Hodgson made it an extremely bad case for testing spirit return. He was so well known in psychical research circles, and had been so closely associated with Mrs Piper for so many years, that although the paranormally produced data at the sittings where 'Hodgson' manifested are numerous and impressive, they are equally consistent with the super-ESP theory, the survival theory and the cosmic reservoir theory formulated by James himself. Again, Gauld's book *Mediumship and Survival* gives a good introduction to these theories. In the end, James found that he could not embrace the spirit hypothesis unreservedly, though Oliver Lodge did so. In his 1909 report on 'Mrs Piper's Hodgson Control', James stated cautiously:

if ever our growing familiarity with these phenomena should tend more and more to corroborate the hypothesis that 'spirits' play some part in their production, I shall be quite ready to undeafen my ears... The facts are evidently complicated in the extreme, and we have as yet hardly scratched the surface of them. But methodical exploration has at last seriously begun, and these earlier observations of ours will surely be interpreted one day in the light of future discoveries which it may well take a century to make ... we can therefore well afford to play a waiting game.

The best part of a century has now passed since those words were written and many would say that little progress has been made in understanding the strange but important phenomena that Dr Richard Hodgson dedicated his life to. Down the decades of years the despairing cry of the 'Hodgson' communicator still echoes, challenging us to continue that search for truth: 'Well, if I am not Hodgson, he never lived!'

Mrs Leonora Piper died on July 3rd, 1950 at the age of ninety-one, forty-five years after her faithful student Hodgson quitted this life. Her trance mediumship came to an end in 1911 on the initiative of the Imperator band of controls. After a very deep and prolonged trance from which she recovered with extreme difficulty, they said that it would be unwise, not to say dangerous, for her mediumship to continue in this manner. The control called Imperator therefore closed the 'light'. She continued to practise automatic writing, however, and continued her work as a member of the group of automatists in the so-called 'Cross-Correspondences'. Long years of study of these Cross-Correspondences produced material that convinced many in the ultra-cautious Sidgwick Group that something of quite extraordinary importance was being revealed to them. It was something that would play a dominant part in the rest of their lives.

7

Vignettes and Valedictions

*All records of experiments must depend ultimately on the
probity and intelligence of the persons recording them, and it
is impossible for us, or any other investigators, to demonstrate
to persons who do not know us that we are not idiotically
careless or consciously mendacious. We can only hope that
within the limited circle in which we are known, either alternative
will be regarded as highly improbable.*

Henry Sidgwick, 1883

By 1906 the Sidgwick Group of the SPR had lost by death a
number of its most prominent and active members. Among them
were the founding members Edmund Gurney (died 1888), Professor
Henry Sidgwick (died 1900) and Frederic Myers (died 1901). Dr
Richard Hodgson died in December 1905. The group in particular
and psychical research in general suffered further losses in 1910
when on August 26th, Professor William James died, followed
swiftly on December 29th by the death of Professor Henry Butcher,
Professor of Greek at Edinburgh University. Less than two years
later, Dr Arthur Woolgar Verrall, the noted Classical scholar, died
on June 18th, 1912. By the beginning of the First World War,
therefore, the Sidgwick Group's most prominent and active
investigators and collaborators were reduced to Professor Oliver
Lodge, Miss Alice Johnson, Mrs Verrall, Mr J.G. Piddington, Mrs
Sidgwick and Mr Gerald Balfour.

The eminent physicist and pioneer in radio, Sir Oliver Lodge,
became interested in psychical research because of his friendship
with Edmund Gurney. Gurney at that time was collecting and

tabulating the material for *Phantasms of the Living*. Through Gurney he met Myers and in 1884 he became a member of the Society for Psychical Research. He was subsequently engaged in the study of both physical and mental mediums, including Eusapia Palladino and Mrs Piper. With respect to Eusapia, he could not dismiss as fraud all the ostensible phenomena he had witnessed and this viewpoint was strengthened by the experience of his son, Mr Brodie Lodge, at Charles Richet's house in 1898, when a heavy table was reported by him as having levitated, in broad daylight out of doors.

For many people, Lodge's pioneering scientific work has been obscured by his psychical research. A number of scientists scorned him for 'dabbling in the occult'. Sir James Dewar, the inventor of the vacuum flask, denounced Lodge as 'that arrant humbug who is doing so much harm to British science'. However, most in the scientific community respected his work on the ether and the development of wireless telegraphy.

Lodge became President of the SPR after Frederic Myers' death in 1901. The death of Myers only a few months after Professor Sidgwick's demise had been a severe blow to the SPR. Lodge's acceptance of the presidency just a year after he had been appointed Principal of the newly founded University of Birmingham was therefore much appreciated by those close to the society's work. He was re-elected President for the years 1902 and 1903. In all the years he was associated with the SPR he proved to be a strong supporter and guide of its work. Long before his son Raymond was killed in the First World War his researches forced him to accept that we survive death. He first made that declaration as early as 1902 and it was a belief formed after due comparison of how well the telepathy theory and the survival theory fitted the evidence. In his presidential address of that year, he said:

If any one cares to hear what sort of conviction has been borne in upon my own mind as a scientific man, in some 20 years familiarity of these questions which concern us, I am very willing to reply as frankly as I can. First, then, I am for all present purposes convinced of the persistence of human existence beyond bodily death; and although I am unable to justify that belief in a full and complete manner, yet it is a belief which has been produced by scientific evidence, that is, it is based upon facts and experience, though I might find it

Sir Oliver Lodge

impossible to explain categorically how the facts have produced that conviction.

In personality, Sir Oliver Lodge was a gentle man, with marked gifts of tact, geniality and sympathy. A remarkably vivid picture of Lodge and his environment has been given by Nea Walker, who was one of his secretaries for a number of years. Her experiences working with Lodge largely inspired her two books *The Bridge* (1927) and *Through a Stranger's Hands (1935).*

Sir Oliver chose me during the summer of 1915 to replace another woman secretary who was getting married, and my work was to begin in October of that year. I well remember the, to me, terrifying interview before my appointment, when he asked me whether I 'spoke French, German, Italian, and Spanish?' I could only claim the first two. Then, – 'What about Greek and Latin?' The Greek alphabet and a very shaky acquaintance with Latin, were all I could muster. 'Humph, – well, how about Physics and Mathematics?' These were nil. 'What do you know about psychical research?' I could not possibly say that I had only heard of 'Sir Oliver Lodge and his Spooks'. So there was an embarassed pause. Then, – 'Ever heard of Myers, Gurney, Sidgwick?' I had not. 'Dear, dear, they are household words here. Do you object to psychical research?' I could not say, – I knew nothing about it. (Sigh): – 'Well, let's go and have tea', and I was led from the summerhouse at Mariemont, through the lofty book-lined study, to the dining-room with its long table seating ten or fifteen people comfortably, and fairly regularly. This teatime was to be, for the next five years, a very familiar and pleasant scene: Lady Lodge's chair was at the end of the table. Sir Oliver sat

142

on her left; any guests near them; then as many of 'The Family' as might be in; and near the doors leading to the study and the hall respectively, always room for Mr Briscoe (Sir Oliver's University Secretary) and me... And, though one sat, as it were, 'below the salt', that being conveniently near the door by which one had entered, Sir Oliver had a charming way, if a distinguished guest were present, of remarking, – 'That is Miss Nea Walker, she knows your wife', – or some equivalent description, mostly based upon a very flimsy link. Often one would rather not have been noticed in one's distant corner, but the kindly wish to put at ease was none the less appreciated. And, frequently, the interesting conversation tempted me to linger listening when I ought to have been back at work in my room. Thought for employees did not end with tea, for we all had a glass of hot milk at eleven; and Sir Oliver would often, during the 1914–18 war, ask me if I were 'sure I was getting enough to eat at home?' ...

Very occasionally, if tired or worried, he might answer irritably at tea-time about some trifle, and immediately there would be an expression in his eyes so like that of a St Bernard who has been rude to some smaller friend. I cannot think that he ever let the sun go down on his wrath in things large or small. His attitude towards anything frail was always gentle, and it was an unforgettable picture to see him carry a baby grandchild firmly cradled in the crook of one arm – the baby so obviously feeling comfortable and safe that it did not cry.

Mr Bristoe worked in Sir Oliver's study, but I had a room near the front door to which Sir Oliver came when he had time for what was the lighter part of his work. I often did not see him of a morning; he would come in and dictate for a couple of hours; or, I should find a note on my table after lunch saying, – 'N.W., come to the summerhouse'. These entries and summonses used, for the first six months or so, to cause me to shake at the knees each time: it must have been due to his great height and big voice, for I later found that there was nothing to fear, only much to love.

Of his work with the Society of Psychical Research she wrote:

I had been nervously expecting to take up my work with

Sir Oliver on the first of October 1915, but was alarmed by a telegram asking me to come on the afternoon of September 29th to Mariemont. On arrival I was asked to 'go to the summerhouse with my shorthand notebook', and there, without further preliminaries, Sir Oliver began to dictate. It proved to be a report on his first anonymous sitting with Mrs Leonard which had taken place on the 27th. I was bewildered. I had never done any work like it, and went home wondering whether I had been dreaming or was 'going mad'. The next day I tried to transcribe my notes, and left the effort on Sir Oliver's desk, to find it the following morning on mine, scored and marked and corrected in every direction. I thought, – 'That's the end of this post for me!' and waited for the wrath to come. But, to my amazement, when I shakily apologised for having evidently made a hopeless muddle of it, Sir Oliver said, - 'Oh, but I made the muddle of your typing – it's only that I don't yet know how I want it set out.' So we settled down to work out the method and the rest of that winter went mostly in preparing the book *Raymond*. It was at this time that I learnt always to give prominence to the weaknesses of evidence laboriously gathered, and to record at once every tiny item whether it seemed relevant or not. Also to regard oneself as suspect, and, whenever feasible, to get outside testimony to the truth of one's statements.

Then came the publication of *Raymond*, and the terrific correspondence which resulted, from opponents, from sympathisers, and from people bereaved by the war. All this correspondence fell to my lot, except what Sir Oliver sent on to Mr J. Arthur Hill, after always answering the first letter himself...

Sir Oliver was working hard in all kinds of other directions, at the University, and on research connected with the war; often in summer when I arrived at nine o'clock, he would say proudly that *he* had been 'doing mathematics' in the summerhouse since seven. And I know that his day often ended with reading aloud to The Family for a couple of hours after an eight o'clock dinner. But he always made time to answer, almost by return, the bereaved people who wrote to him. Sometimes he sat in my room, sometimes, even in winter, in the summerhouse, clad in a large fawnish check Inverness coat

with a hood, though he always wore a cap, or a panama hat...
At these times he allowed himself to smoke – always a cigarette
in a long holder. One could never forget his hands with their
long sensitive fingers – rather like the Duerer etching, only
more powerful.

When he had been up to London for SPR meetings he would
immediately after his return dictate a full account to J.A.H.,
or to Lady Lodge, if she were away from home. And sometimes
he would stop and tell me tales of the old days at the SPR,
elucidating a reference which he knew I should not understand.
Thus, quite quickly, Myers, Gurney, Sidgwick, Richet, Mrs
Verrall, Eusapia, Mrs Piper, and many other names became
household words to me also; and now I feel astonishment
when I realise that, as to me in 1915, they still have no
meaning for the many. At these times I learnt how deep was
his affection for Mr Myers; how much he felt Mrs Verrall's
death and admired her courage; and how he regarded, almost
with awe, Professor Sidgwick's 'shining integrity'.

In 1919 came Sir Oliver's retirement from the Principalship
of Birmingham University... I had commitments in Birmingham
then, and could not leave to settle with him in Wiltshire when
he decided to go there... So ... he decided to carry on his
work with me by post ... my work from then on evolved into
dealing with his bereaved correspondents and, while trying to
help them, carrying out experiments which might be useful in
psychical research. This work he generously financed... I often
wonder whether those whom he helped had the faintest idea
of his generosity to them, for he was never a rich man. I
remember being troubled frequently because what I was doing
was not helping *him;* but his answer invariably was: 'If you
are doing psychical research work of any sort, you are doing
my work.' ...

There are memory pictures of him at Normanton too... One
of those closely associated in my mind in the picture of his
declining years is his chauffeur-valet Walker. I have rarely
seen anything as beautiful as the way Sir Oliver depended
upon Walker, and the unobtrusiveness of any necessary help
Walker gave. The friendship, and mutual respect and affection,
were so obvious.

Ms Alice Johnson was a member of a large family well known in Cambridge and entered Newnham College in 1878. She had a distinguished career. She was the first Demonstrator in Animal Morphology in the Balfour Laboratory from 1884 to 1890, and contributed several papers to the *Proceedings of the Royal Society*, including 'On the Development of the Cranial Nerves of the Newt', at a time when few contributions by women were included. It was natural that, being close to Professor and Mrs Sidgwick, she should also have come into contact with psychical research. She took part in a number of the early projects of the SPR. She was a member of the committee which took and presented the *Census of Hallucinations*, one of the recognised classics of psychical research; in 1899 she became editor of the society's *Proceedings*; and in 1903 she was appointed organising secretary. She became Research Officer of the SPR in 1908 and was closely connected with a number of other ongoing investigations, such as the study and interpretation of the Cross-Correspondences.

Alice Johnson's tenure of office began at a difficult time for the SPR, largely arising from the deaths of Professor Sidgwick and Frederic Myers within a year of each other, and she was one of those who helped by their efforts to steer it over this critical period, enabling it to maintain the quantity and quality of its work and keep strictly to the mission statement formulated by its founders. Though invariably polite, Johnson was sharply critical, if the need arose, to protect the evidential standards on which the society had always insisted.

Something of Alice Johnson's meticulous, dogged approach to psychical research is suggested by the reaction of the poet W.B. Yeats, who sometimes visited the SPR's rooms in Hanover Square. On one occasion after a talk with Johnson, 'whose attitude to psychic phenomena was a good deal more critical than his own', Yeats declared: 'It is my belief that if you people had been standing around when the Almighty was creating the world, He couldn't have done it.' The automatic writings of the 'SPR group of automatists', which began shortly after Myers' death, presented entirely new problems of investigation. Nothing could have been made of them without most careful and systematic documentation on the one hand, and on the other, great enterprise as regards interpretation and theory. Subsequent developments have shown how well and truly were laid the foundations of this novel and difficult study, the importance of which was on the increase throughout Alice Johnson's tenure of office. With this study she was from the first intimately associated, and several of her most important papers in the SPR *Proceedings* deal with automatic scripts, particularly Mrs Holland's, and the theory of cross-correspondences.

Isobel Newton, who joined the office staff in 1903, paid tribute to her invaluable work:

In the office her manner was gentle and rather shy. But her rule was absolute. She was exacting to a degree in the manner of accuracy and thoroughness. Her displeasure was expressed by [a] slight but unmistakable coldness of manner...; never by words of blame...

It was obvious that her advent as Secretary the previous March had opened a new era in the routine work. We generally found it difficult to trace references before that time, but with those of a later date it was a simple matter. In a few months she had gathered the loose ends together and had welded them into a system in which there was no confusion and no uncertainty...

Few members of the society knew her as we knew her in the office. Some saw her as a rather austere little figure, with an academic manner which alarmed them. I [saw] her with a firm grip on the affairs and the policy of the society, opposing tooth and nail everything that threatened to weaken its scientific character or lower its scientific prestige. She was a formidable foe, with an indomitable will. She had no vulnerable spots which might have deceived and diverted her. She held herself intact, and subordinate to her incorruptible integrity... The contrast between her weakness and her strength inspired in me a strong partisanship. Even now I am touched by her heroic qualities and frail physique.

Even after her retirement in 1916 through ill-health she retained her keen interest in psychical research and enjoyed being consulted on matters important to the society. She died on January 13th, 1940.

Mrs Margaret Verrall (Margaret de Gaudrion Merrifield) was born in 1859. She entered Newnham College, Cambridge to read Classics

Mrs Margaret Verrall

and was later Classical Lecturer there. She married Dr A.W. Verrall on June 17th, 1882. She joined the SPR in 1889 and took part in crystal-gazing and other experiments. On Mrs Piper's first visit to England, and later, Mrs Verrall sat with her. She was a close friend and neighbour of Frederic Myers and soon after his death began automatic writing to give him the opportunity of communicating if he had survived the death of his body. This marked the beginning of the scripts of the SPR group of automatists. Her daughter Helen Verrall also became one of the group. Mrs Verrall's scripts run from March 5th, 1901 to June 24th, 1916. She reported on her scripts down to January 1905 in the SPR *Proceedings*, reluctantly consenting to Mrs Eveleen Myers' demand that references to communications from Myers should be deleted. Mrs Verrall edited volumes I and II of her own scripts, also volumes I and II of the Willett scripts and the volume of 'Mac' scripts. She also wrote the 'Delta Case', privately printed.

Both Mrs Sidgwick and Mrs Willett testified to her warm, lovable and charming nature. It was a nature with a core of calm courage, exemplified by her letter dated May 17th, 1916 to Mrs Sidgwick:

Posted May 21
Private

5, Selwyn Gardens,
Cambridge.
May 17, 1916

Dear Mrs Sidgwick,

I write to-day, though probably I shall not send this for some days, as the news I have to give must go to Helen first, and if possible I mean to keep it back from her till she and her husband are alone in their own house; she is staying with his parents now.

I learnt a few days before I saw you that no recovery is to be looked for, and that death is not, probably, far distant. Fresh symptoms showed on Monday May 8, & I learnt on May 10 that there is malignant disease & nothing to be done. The doctor talks of '3 or 4 months', but of course all is uncertain, and neither the progress of the disease nor my power to resist can be reckoned on with knowledge. There must be pain but they will give me all the help they can, and at present it can be controlled by sedatives which induce sleep but leave my mind unclouded.

Naturally my friends must hope with me that the release will come before long.

Will you tell Mr Piddington and Mr Balfour, – I don't want it known generally yet till dates are a little more determined – and I leave it to you and them to tell Winifred when you think best.

I hope I am not leaving much work unfinished. I can't manage anything involved or that needs consideration, but if there are any questions which should be answered I will do my best.

As to papers, I think I have made all proper arrangements. There are a lot of 'Willett documents', originals of early W. sets, correspondence and so on, which Helen will send to whatever seems to be the best destination: – probably, as things now are, to Fishers Hill? But she will take instructions from you, of course. There is much of which she knows, and ought to know nothing, but she can be trusted to send the papers, so marked, unread. But if you, or any of you, have other wishes in this matter, I will meet them. Perhaps A.J. [Alice Johnson] if she is well enough, could come and do up parcels for despatch. But I don't want anyone in Cambridge told just yet about my health.

I don't think there is anything else to say. I shall go with strong hope that my work though altered will not be stopped. I have had a full and very happy life, and with Helen's happy marriage my last responsibility ended. Had I kept health and power to work, I was content to wait, but only content, not desirous. And as it is, I try not to count too eagerly on the reunion and the new experiences. For the friendships that have come to me here I am deeply grateful and only those of us

who have been at Newnham know what we feel for you and
Mr Sidgwick. It is beyond all expressing.
  Yours always affectionately,
  Margaret de G. Verrall.
Helen comes to me tomorrow (Monday)

Mrs Verrall died on July 2nd, 1916.

Mr John George Piddington was a man who made the SPR and
its activities his life's work. J.G. Smith, as he was then, joined the
society in 1890, and became a member of Council in 1899. Although
his original surname was Smith (his father's surname) he changed
it to Piddington, his mother's name, to avoid confusion with several
other Smiths then prominent in the SPR. In the same year, on the
proposal of Frederic Myers, he became Honorary Secretary, acting
jointly with Myers until the latter's death, and resigning in 1907.
He became Honorary Secretary in 1899, Honorary Treasurer in
1917 and President in 1924 and 1925. He had sittings with a
number of mediums including Mrs Piper and Mrs Thompson. From
the early days of the influx of automatic scripts he was an important
member of the investigating group and contributed a number of
papers on them to the *Proceedings*. As the quantity of material
grew over the years he played a prominent part in editing a large
number of the volumes comprising the scripts of different automatic
writers. Much of his time was devoted to the study of the Cross-
Correspondences and he lived for more than twenty years at Fishers
Hill, Woking, with Gerald W. Balfour. Indeed for many years the
work of interpreting the scripts was largely shared between him
and Gerald Balfour, but latterly fell upon him alone. He died in
April 1952.
  During his terms of office he was closely concerned in two
events of importance to the society. The first was the creation in
1901 of the Research Endowment Fund, of which he was for many
years the active trustee. The second was the separation, after Richard
Hodgson's death in 1905, of the American branch of the SPR and
its transformation into the American SPR.
  As Honorary Treasurer (from 1917 to 1921) he looked after the
society's finances with special care, nursing the Research Endowment
Fund from very small beginnings, so that in due time it might

produce an income sufficient to pay a salary for a full-time research officer, with qualifications and status equivalent to those of a university research worker in any of the recognised branches of science. The income of the fund did grow, but after the First World War, so fast did the value of money decline, that even fifty years after the fund was started, the society still lacked an endowment sufficient to enable it to make the most of the possibilities for research arising throughout that period.

For some years before the First World War, Piddington had been living as a near neighbour of Gerald Balfour and, by 1920, he had come to reside at Fishers Hill, where both of them lived until after the outbreak of the Second World War. Mrs Sidgwick also made her home there about the same time, remaining there until her death in 1936. So it came about that, for the period between the end of the First World War and the society's jubilee in 1932, three leading members of the Council – Mrs Sidgwick, Gerald Balfour and Piddington – were in close contact with each other, living for most of that period in the same house, and were thus well placed to give the society the strong central direction it needed.

The First World War had brought a large influx of new members, many of whom knew nothing of the past history of the society or its standards of investigation, and many approached some of the society's problems emotionally and uncritically. Attempts were made, and not without influential backing, to force the SPR to work on a 'positive' doctrinal basis, to substitute showmanship for research, and, failing all else, to split the society, but they all broke on the rock of Fishers Hill.

There might be a risk in any organisation that so close a combination of 'elder statesmen' would confine its activities to those in which the elder statesmen had a special interest. Nothing of that sort happened with the Fishers Hill group. At this time their own interest were centred on the 'mental' phenomena – trance-mediumship of the kind practised by Mrs Leonard, automatic writing, 'phantasms', experimental telepathy – and much research on those lines was carried out during the period. But at the same time physical mediumship was being investigated with as much vigour as at any period in the society's history, as is evidenced by the papers published in the SPR's *Proceedings* and *Journal*.

J.G. Piddington retired from the Council in 1932 after more than thirty years membership of it. He continued to be an active member of the Committee of Reference until 1940. Valuable as were his administrative services to the society, it is his part in interpreting the scripts of the SPR group of automatists that calls for special notice. This was the task of a team that included Mrs Sidgwick, Oliver Lodge, Alice Johnson, and G.W. Balfour, but the main work fell on Piddington, and increasingly so as ill-health or advancing years compelled the withdrawal of the others.

As we have seen, Mrs Eleanor Sidgwick was the eldest sister of Gerald William and Arthur James Balfour. She was born in 1845 and spent her early life at the family home, Whittingehame, in Scotland. She kept house till, in 1876, she married Henry Sidgwick. She possessed a very fine, gentle and calm nature and had extraordinary powers of concentration and perspicacity. After her marriage she and her husband lived at Cambridge where they knew the Verralls, the Myers family and other persons connected with the SPR. She was a woman of formidable intelligence, a brilliant mathematician and at one stage in her career worked with the famous physicist Lord Rayleigh who also became President of the SPR. A strong supporter of the cause of education for women, she helped to found Newnham College, becoming second Principal in 1892. Her keen intelligence and logical powers of thought made her invaluable to the SPR. She was President in 1908–9 and again, jointly with Sir Oliver Lodge, in 1932. She remained on the Council of the SPR until the end of her life and died in 1935 at the age of ninety.

For many years before her death she lived at Fishers Hill, the home of her brother Gerald Balfour. She was the author of many important papers published in the SPR *Proceedings* and her tireless exercise of close-knit thought and cool judgement was of great benefit to the SPR as long as she lived.

Gerald William, 2nd Earl of Balfour, was born on April 9th, 1853. The younger brother of Arthur James Balfour, he succeeded him as Earl in 1930. He was a fellow of Trinity College where he numbered among his friends A.W. Verrall and S.H. Butcher. He had a distinguished career in politics, being MP for Leeds from 1885 to 1906 and was Chief Secretary for Ireland after his brother Arthur James Balfour's term of office as Prime Minister. He was President of the Board of Trade from 1900 to 1905. As a young man he used to go mountaineering with his brother Frank Maitland

Balfour but after the latter's death in the Alps in 1882, his grief was so intense he never climbed again. A strong Classical scholar, he had also studied metaphysics and philosophy. In later life he became increasingly devoted to psychical research, particularly to the Cross-Correspondences and the psychological aspects of Mrs Willett's mediumship. It was his sister Eleanor and her husband, Henry Sidgwick, who introduced him to the SPR. He was elected to the Council in 1890 and continued to serve on it until his death. His home, Fishers Hill, was built near Woking in 1902. During the period 1919–40 his colleague and friend J.G. Piddington also lived there. Together they tried to interpret the meanings hinted at in the Cross-Correspondences. Balfour's extensive knowledge of the scripts, together with his calm and critical mind, were admirably suited to the work of interpretation. It was also a work that held an abiding and strong emotional interest for him.

Balfour died in 1945 at Whittingehame at the age of ninety-one. He had been President of the SPR in 1906 and 1907. Among his papers that appeared in the *Proceedings* was 'The Ear of Dionysius', a paper published in 1916 concerning a particular theme in the Cross-Correspondences, a summary of which will be given later. Perhaps his most important work was his 'Study of the Psychological Aspects of Mrs. Willett's Mediumship and the Statements of the Communicators Concerning Process', published in the SPR *Proceedings* in 1935.

Jean, Countess of Balfour, left a memoir, written in 1973, of events at Fishers Hill in the days when Gerald Balfour, J.G. Piddington and Mrs Sidgwick were engaged in the task of studying the Cross-Correspondence scripts. Jean Lily Cooke-Yarborough was born in Romsey, Hampshire, on February 2nd, 1900. She married Robert Arthur Lytton, Gerald Balfour's son, and by 1930, after the death of Arthur James Balfour, was made a confidante of the Fishers Hill group. In fact, by that time she had already read all the major literature connected with the SPR's work, having become a member of the SPR soon after her marriage. It was on the suggestion of Betty Balfour, Gerald's wife, who thought she was both 'thoughtful and discreet', that she became accepted as the group's confidante and later the archivist of much of the material arising from the group's collective or individual activities.

In her memoir, written in April 1973 and intended for release in 1995, Jean Balfour wrote about the main figures engaged in the study of the Cross-Correspondence scripts. She was an intelligent, highly perceptive and observant woman who saw and understood, perhaps rather more clearly than most people, the virtues, foibles and idiosyncracies of the Fishers Hill group. The pictures in her memoir are therefore 'Cromwellian' in style, warts and all, rather than the 'official' portraits that, after the death of a notable person, are often retrieved from the pending obituary file, hurriedly updated if necessary and rushed into print. They are worth quoting at length:

In December, 1972, I succeeded, after some correspondence and a visit in person, in obtaining an assurance from Maclehose & Co. Ltd, of Glasgow, who are expecting to be taken over next year by another firm, that the two Piddington boxes, left to me by J.G.P. [J.G. Piddington] upon his death, which contain the Script volumes and his commentaries upon them, will be safeguarded until 1995: and also that I, and my co-trustees, will be notified if any change of circumstances should arise meanwhile.

I think therefore that a short account of what I remember of the interpreters of the Scripts, from 1925 onwards, might be of some interest to future readers.

The White Study, at Fishers Hill, was a quiet room, overlooking the terrace, to which few strangers, if any, were admitted: and where even B.B. [Betty Balfour] (my mother-in-law and mistress of the house) whenever she crept in with bent head, spoke in a whisper. E.M.S. [Eleanor Sidgwick] ('Aunt Nora') lay always on her sofa, alongside the bookcases that lined the wall: beside her, [on] a small table, covered with papers and books, was always a hand-mirror and a comb, 'to see if her hair was tidy', she used to say! as she was absolutely the least vain of women; it simply enabled her to avoid having to go upstairs to arrange herself when meals were announced.

G.W.B. [Gerald W. Balfour] (my father-in-law) would sit at his large desk in the centre of the room, occasionally we would find him in the big armchair near the fireplace: books were everywhere and must never be disturbed.

The life of the house revolved around B.B. (his wonderful

J.G. Piddington

wife, the beloved friend of all the young) who loved people. She was the most hospitable, warmhearted, irrepressibly gay person imaginable, always interested in something or someone, so that she must talk about it. Her enthusiasms would have carried her anywhere, if her husband, whose sympathies were far more circumscribed, had not, almost continually, put the brake on. But her lovely sense of humour saved her too: she could always laugh at herself. People, family and friends of a wide circle, constantly came and went, always to see and to talk with 'Aunt Betty', as they called her. Around her, always, the ripples of life and of fun, went on, and events happened, and things of human interest took place, while the White Study, and Mr Pidd's Room – those two islands of quiet industry – remained quite unruffled, and immersed (as any future students of their life work upon the Scripts will realise) in a kind of Dreamland.

At meals, the complete household assembled, E.M.S. fairly punctual: J.G.P. would appear from down his staircase while the serving was going on; and G.W.B. arrived late, solemnly, without apology, just as we had all begun.

Upstairs, at the top of the house, J.G.P. had his 'sanctum'. The windows faced south, but he never looked at the magnificent view. The clacking of his typewriter penetrated along the passage; and at the first glance, on entering, the room seemed full of large tables, on which lay scores of books, all open, sometimes on top of one another; these contained his innumerable 'references' which he was always seeking, and piecing together, in his search to find the meaning in the Scripts. There, in this remote fastness, at the top of a staircase, which left behind all the noises of that cheerful and friendly house, he worked and thought, and played on his very fine Grand piano. When he had finished any piece of work, or was on the track of

155

some clue which required another opinion to evaluate it, he would descend, and spend some time in the White Study: here he and G.W.B. would talk; and E.M.S. would listen, and possibly pronounce judgement, for she was deeply interested in the problem of interpretation, although she took no part in it.

J.G.P.'s day was perfectly regular: in the morning he worked: at lunch he appeared in the dining room where he discoursed on the newspapers, topics of the day, or some book he was reading: in the afternoon he walked for about an hour: and in the evening, he very often played for an hour or so on G.W.B.'s Grand piano, which we could hear, as we talked or played table-games in the drawing room: that was his one relaxation; and he played well, with great precision though not, I think, with a great deal of feeling; but later, from pressure of his work, he gave it up. Gradually he gave up everything, even his daily walk until (as Willy Salter says in his book on Scripts, privately printed in 1948) he was forced to ask the group of automatists to stop writing while he laboured on to the final, eighth volume of Notes and Excursuses.

J.G.P. was reddish-haired with blue eyes: his head was very large, his forehead high and his face, when I knew him late in life, was covered with fine wrinkles. Very neat and spare in figure, he walked fast with ease; he liked meeting people though his interest in them was quite superficial, and he was on good terms with members of the family circle: he enormously appreciated B.B. who often made him giggle! During the period when G.W.B. neglected his wonderful wife (1912–19) although neither of them divulged the fact all through those years, somehow the family 'caught on' to what was happening – or at least the older members did – and it was commonly supposed among them that B.B. found consolation for her loneliness in 'Mr Pidd'. Nothing could have been further from the truth. J.G.P. was almost what might be called completely sexless: no one could ever understand – even G.W.B. who knew him so well – why he had got married, years ago. He once said to me that he himself really couldn't imagine why! I think it only lasted a short time, but his daughter Leo was the result. For a few years he and his wife had a house together, but soon after Fishers Hill was built, he took up his abode there, providing his wife with a house in London. For some time, 'Mrs Pidd', who, poor thing, complained a good deal, came for a few days to Fishers Hill. I remember meeting her but she couldn't bear the country, and it was only too obvious that G.W.B. couldn't bear her. The daughter Leo spent half her time with her mother in London and half at Fishers Hill, otherwise at a boarding school, and was devoted – along with so many others – to B.B.

Meanwhile the study of the Scripts, which J.G.P. found utterly fascinating, absorbed more and more of his time and energy. The research alone, both to find, and then to follow up, the references in the writings, was an enormous job, let alone the arduous mental work of compiling numerous papers on the various topics. The majority of these expositions appeared from J.G.P.'s pen, at first in the SPR's Proceedings, and latterly in the volumes of 'Notes and Excursuses', privately printed from 1934 onwards.

When I first came into the Balfour family, only the first and second volumes of 'Notes and Excursuses' had been printed, in 1921 and 1927 respectively; but through my friendship with J.G.P., I read in manuscript the contents of Vol III (eventually printed in 1934) which is almost entirely his own work, though discussed with G.W.B. of course; and he used to talk to me sometimes on the lines of the excellent 'Introduction' to that volume, which explains the peculiar difficulties encountering the investigators of the Scripts. How acceptance of myself as a sympathetic repository for their ideas on interpretation came about is as follows. B.B. remarked to G.W.B. one day that she thought I would be a good person to be let into the secret of the Scripts, because I was both thoughtful and discreet. They considered this very seriously for several minutes, and then 'Aunt Nora' observed that I had been a member of the SPR ever since my marriage in 1925. J.G.P. then said that if I had read all the more important 'Cases for Survival' in the SPR. Proceedings, such as the 'Statius Case', the 'Ear of Dionysius' etc, and also the two volumes of Myers' 'Human Personality', and preferably Podmore's 'Phantasms of the Living', I might be considered as a suitable person. To this I replied, humbly and quietly 'Well, I <u>have</u>, you know.' That settled it.

I was tremendously interested in psychic research then, and always have been. Although I often puzzled over certain points of interpretation, I had neither the erudition nor the temerity to criticize the conclusions to which the investigators had come. They had enormous experience and great learning, and I could never get over their amazing patience and industry – How hard they worked to catch the thought, so often implicit, so seldom clear of the communicators (they who sent the message whoever they were) and how sure they became that there was intelligent design behind and beyond the automatists' writings. J.G.P.'s paper on 'Dido and Sichaeus' in SPR. Proceedings Vol 29, p.30 is a good example I think of just how he worked. The 'cross-correspondences', when studied from the beginning right through the SPR. Proceedings, are the most fascinating and most astonishing phenomenon of our times.

Now to turn to my father-in-law G.W.B. In personal appearance he had a noble-looking presence: he was tall and thin, with beautiful features, so that people said of him that he was like a Greek god. When young his hair was dark, but his skin was very clear and fine, his eyes dark blue, and when I knew him, thick wavy snow-white hair covered his head. He was not interested in people, and I must say that, beyond giving a lovely smile (but only if he liked you!) he was conspicuously lacking in social grace, and never made the least effort to help his wife in putting a guest at ease. But he took a great pleasure in beautiful things, of which the house was full, due to his early travels in Europe, especially in Italy where he had lived for a few years after his marriage. His children all adored their mother, Ral (his son, my husband) did not like his father at all, and greatly preferred his uncle A.J.B. [Arthur J. Balfour] who had a warm and imaginative nature, which children could always detect. His daughter Mary as a child remarked of him 'To tell Father about a trouble or a problem would have been like confiding in a beautiful statue that neither saw nor heard...'

He must have been either a very simple, or a very complicated, character. I think, in my opinion, he was never as interesting a person as his wife, and especially he was cold. I remember realising on one occasion, that he never forgave, or forgot, a wrong that had been done to him: I didn't feel for many years that I had really got to know him until, in old age, when he lived the last four years of his life so close to us at Whittingehame, he was greatly softened and often loveable. So perhaps at bottom he was really rather simple. He was said to have some flair for business and had connections with various companies in the City of London; but of course in his day it was not the fashion for somebody well-born to go into business. Yet it always seemed to fascinate him. If he had a weakness, I suppose it was vanity, as I gradually realised throughout the long history with 'Peco'. This was a singularly unsuccessful venture for manufacturing briquettes out of peatbogs – developed in Denmark and in Ireland. G.W.B.'s great friend – one of the few people he really enjoyed and welcomed, Mr Tertrupp, a Swede, could always, with the aid of a little flattery, persuade him to sink a few more thousands into this firm which it was hoped would eventually restore his riches: but it gradually ruined him.

In the days when G.W.B. became interested in psychic research the SPR. was almost a family affair: Henry and Nora Sidgwick were very much the moving spirits of the work, with of course F.W.H.M. [Frederic Myers] – and both A.J.B. and the brother-in-law John Rayleigh (the scientist who discovered argon) were closely concerned too. After the loss of his favourite brother F.M.B. [Francis Maitland Balfour] who was killed in the Alps in 1888, G.W.B. never climbed again, which had been his greatest pleasure up till then, and having built Fishers Hill in 1902 at his own expense, he retired from active political life and devoted himself to the SPR. He was, I think, naturally indolent, and though he had produced articles in philosophy in Hibbert's Journal, etc., he had not the creative drive of his brother A.J.B.: but of course it must be mentioned that, although he lived to be 90, he was never at all strong. But after he had met Mrs Willett, her mediumship became his life's work and all the subsequent papers upon her in the SPR. Proceedings are written by him. When the first clues to the meaning of a large part of the Scripts were revealed in 1912 through Mrs Willett, he put together the papers on the 'Palm Sunday Case', to be found in Vol I 'Notes and Excursuses'. Vol II 'N.&.E.', which is entirely devoted to the topic of 'The Chosen Child', is also all his work: but, to my mind, the attempt to interpret the symbolism of the rainbow and of the references to music, is too vague to be convincing. But once he was committed to his special relationship with Mrs Willett, the whole of his inner life concentrated itself upon 'Augustus'. There can be no doubt that he was deeply influenced by her profound maternal ambition: but he evidently had an unusual type of ambition of his own – a sort of vanity – which centred on the anticipated fame of his offspring – not for himself.

He was I think a completely pagan person. First, as a lover of Greek art, and then as a student of Greek antiquity, the Greek classics and philosophy were his 'Gospels' – he needed nothing more. He used to say that he had never any sense of sin, and he was so magnificent to look at that this seemed quite natural! In his old age, during the last two years of his life, when I read aloud to him all the Willett volumes, with his own annotations on them, it was quite clear that he still felt sure that he had been led to do the work of the gods...

I must [however] put on record that in the end he came to realise what a beloved and wonderful person his own wife B.B. was, although he did not actually know it until after she had died. He used to say of her 'She was perfect – absolutely perfect...'

E.M.S. was I think a very remarkable person, and I loved her from the first moment I saw her. She always asked after my own family and remembered that I had interests apart from the Balfours, who were, I suppose as I look back, a very arrogant lot! Once Ral (my husband) remarked about people in general that they could be broadly described as first-rate or second-rate people – it had nothing to do with birth, position or achievement but with their character, born in them: Aunt Nora was first rate in every way. Two examples were her beautiful modesty, so that many never guessed how brilliant she was and her manner to servants, which was invariably courteous, considerate and gracious. Besides having extraordinary good brains, she was industrious by nature: once, in course of a family conversation, she said she thought that to solve a mathematical problem was one of the most exciting things she had ever known. She was a little person with small bones and lovely delicate hands; I suppose she was very plain in looks, but she could look quite beautiful, at moments, when intellectually

Mrs Eleanor Sidgwick

fascinated with the talk around the table, when a pink flush crept into her cheeks. Her skin was so fine and clear, her eyes pale green: she had a sort of ageless face and a very high and noble forehead, above a tranquil, thoughtful gaze. One of her nephews asked 'What was she like as a girl?' to which G.W.B. replied 'Exactly the same as she is now.' The nephew remarked 'She must have been the greatest phenomenon of her time.' But deep inside her, I think buried since youth, was a very vivid imagination! When a girl, she had the power of inventing the most fascinating stories for her younger brothers and sisters at bed-time, but these were too exciting and had to be stopped.

She was rather silent, and some people thought she was limited in her outlook – but I discovered she was a warm person, without being at all passionate; on several occasions she was unexpectedly made the recipient of the life stories of people she met in railway trains. She had a surprisingly acute understanding of people in spite of very small personal experience of emotional life. She said of herself in a childish game when everyone was telling of their big moments, 'My life has been a grey one but I like that colour.' ... Yet she really understood Frederic Myers, who was a very emotional and complicated character. (And of course she loved and admired Henry Sidgwick deeply). She must have had true imaginative power to be so understanding, and so much loved by many such very different people. For instance she knew and was very much attached to Miss Radclyffe-Hall and her friend, who wrote the 'Well of Loneliness' – they were SPR members around 1921–24.

The question of what the Scripts really mean is a great puzzle. E.M.S. who was 'in the know' about everything, but did not attempt to interpret them, held a view of the Scripts

161

that was somewhat different to the view of G.W.B. and J.G.P. She accepted their interpretation, however, as far as it went... She regarded the Scripts as a <u>psychic phenomenon in time</u>: it had been able to manifest itself in this the 20th century because, in all probability the time was propitious. That is to say, the necessary conditions were suitable, and there were the three requisite groups – Those who sent the messages, the 'Seven Communicators' among whom F.W.H.M. and certain others were passionately involved, creating a 'drive' from the other world: the mediumistic group, starting with M.V. [Mrs Verrall] and the others, entirely private persons, unknown to the world, and faithfully committed to the automatic writing: and the record-keepers, G.W.B., J.G.P. and Alice Johnson (for early years), who received the communications, found and annotated the references, and attempted to interpret what they meant. The meaning seemed to go beyond the mere evidence of personal survival, and to suggest that the other world had a hand in bringing about certain events of importance to the human race in this world.

As to whether this interpretation was right, E.M.S. was always, I think, open to doubt. She was inclined to think that it was not unlikely that it was impossible to <u>interpret</u> the Scripts at all, in view of our very limited knowledge; in fact she once remarked that she thought the whole thing (the phenomenon of the Scripts) might conceivably recur again, or emerge from the unconscious, in another future age and that perhaps <u>by then</u> we might be more competent to understand what was really the meaning of it all – our knowledge of psychology was possibly inadequate. She was quite prepared for a hundred years to have to pass before the Scripts could be fully understood. I did not realise it then, as I do now, looking back on the past, that E.M.S. was naturally an extraordinarily good psychologist for the time at which she lived. I think she must have gauged the dangers of thought transference, in a way that G.W.B. and J.G.P. never did. The enormous labour she undertook of making the 'List of Scripts', (found at the beginning of Vol I Notes and Excursuses, privately printed 1919) which shows exactly where and when the automatists had actually seen each other's work, is evidence of this: but seeing is not the only danger. In those days we were not aware, as we are nowadays, of the leakage of ideas that can go on beneath the threshold of consciousness: and I think she already suspected it. Although she never entirely said so, her caution in expressing an opinion of her own upon the meaning of the Scripts, suggests to my mind that she was aware of the fluidity of the Unconscious. Perhaps that was why she was apparently so good a 'sitter' – she had such a wonderfully open and yet so wise and well-balanced an attitude of mind...

8

The Enigma Variations

For now we see through a glass darkly, but then face to face.

St Paul, 1 Corinthians 13.12

In the year 1906 the SPR's Research Officer, Miss Alice Johnson, was engaged in collating and studying the output of a number of ladies who were able to produce automatic writing. Originally there were three in the group – Mrs Verrall, her daughter Helen Verrall, and the American medium Mrs Piper. Mrs Piper had been connected to Mrs Verrall and her daughter because of close correspondences between material in their scripts and material produced by Mrs Piper. All three knew each other or knew of each other.

A fourth major automatist was added to the group in 1903. This was 'Mrs Holland', who in fact was Mrs Alice Fleming, the sister of Rudyard Kipling and lived in India with her army officer husband. Because her husband and some members of her own family disliked psychical research, she took the pen name of Mrs Holland. She had a keen interest in literature but had no classical learning. According to W.H. Salter (*An Introduction to the Study of Scripts*, 1948):

> In India [Mrs Holland] read *Human Personality* soon after it was published, and the interest aroused by reading it impelled her to resume the practice of automatic writing which she had for several years discontinued. In June 1903 she wrote to Miss Alice Johnson, then Research Officer of the S.P.R., enclosing a short script. After some correspondence she began to send Miss Johnson scripts from time to time.

On the 7th November 1903 she wrote a long script addressed to *My dear Mrs Verrall, 5 Selwyn Gardens, Cambridge,* which was Mrs Verrall's address. The script purports to come from Myers, and is full of reminiscences of *Human Personality.* Mrs Verrall is mentioned in that book more than once: she is described as being of Newnham College, Cambridge, but her address is not given. It is difficult to suggest any normal explanation of how Mrs Holland, who had no Cambridge associations, could know Mrs Verrall's address, or how, assuming she knew that, she could have known that Mrs Verrall had a greater interest in scripts inspired by Myers than the scores of other persons whose names appear in Myers' book. The day after she received the script Miss Johnson told Mrs Verrall that a lady in India had sent her some automatic writing containing Mrs Verrall's address, but said nothing further about the script.

Mrs Verrall was at this time trying to get in her scripts an answer to a test question put by Mrs Sidgwick, the widow of Henry Sidgwick, as to what text of the Bible had a special meaning for him during the latter part of his life. On the 25th December 1903 Mrs Verrall's script quoted a text which was not the one asked for, but had a similar meaning; the script directed her to ask the question on the *17th January*, the anniversary of Myers' death, an injunction repeated in a script of the 9th January 1904. On *17th January 1904* she wrote, *S is the letter on the envelope and on a seal*, and the script added that the question had been answered and the text given. A script written by Mrs Holland on the same day has the following passage: *The sealed envelope is not to be opened yet – not yet I am unable to make your hand form Greek characters and so I cannot give the text as I wish – only the reference – 1 Cor. 16–13* i.e. 'Watch ye, stand fast in the faith, quit you like men, be strong.' This text had no resemblance to Sidgwick's text, the gist of which had already been given in Mrs Verrall's script, but had a special association for Myers and Mrs Verrall which humanly speaking could not have been known to Mrs Holland. The Greek original of the middle part of the text ('Stand fast in the faith, quit you like men') is carved over the entrance to Selwyn College, Cambridge, which Myers would pass whenever he left his own house to visit

166

the Verralls or the Sidgwicks. There is a small mistake in the Greek text, as carved, which offended Myers' scholarly sense and had more than once been mentioned by him to Mrs Verrall. For evidential reasons Mrs Verrall's scripts during the winter 1903–1904 were being sent to Oliver Lodge, and Mrs Holland's to Miss Johnson. It was not until October 1905 that Miss Johnson told Mrs Verrall of the statement in Mrs Holland's script of *17th January 1904* that the sealed envelope was not to be opened yet, and asked her to look up her script of that date to see if there were any coincidence between it and Mrs Holland's script.

A fifth automatist of importance was Mrs Willett, whose automatic writing subsequently evolved into something much more intriguing. Over the years, she developed a particular faculty that encouraged the sustained study of her mediumship. Oliver Lodge, Gerald Balfour, J.G. Piddington, Alice Johnson, Mrs Sidgwick and Mrs Verrall became the principal investigators of her mediumship. Mrs Willett's gift enabled the investigators to have long direct conversations with the ostensible communicators. The opportunity to test and assess the communicators' statements and responses to questions, together with their personality traits as revealed in these conversations, enabled the investigators to form firm opinions as to the nature of these unseen entities. One of the most important and instructive papers ever published on the subject is 'A Study of the Psychological Aspects of Mrs Willett's Mediumship and the Statements of the Communicators Concerning Process', by Gerald William, Earl of Balfour, published in volume 43 of the *Proceedings of the SPR*, in 1935.

There were a number of other people involved in the automatists' group including two brothers and three sisters, surname Mackinnon, living in Glasgow and referred to as the 'Macs'.

All the automatists were people of good reputation, honest and straightforward. None, with the exception of Mrs Piper, was a professional medium or at first deeply interested in psychical research or spiritualism. They simply found that they had the ability to do automatic writing. The scripts intrigued them and some of them wanted to find out what it all meant.

In Myers' model of human personality, the personality consists of the supraliminal (roughly equated to the conscious personality) and the subliminal (even more roughly equated to the subconscious). Gurney's work in hypnosis indicated that there were levels in the subliminal not normally accessible to the conscious mind in which memory – and active – chains of thought could take place. Myers went further and hypothesised that there were dimensions in the subliminal that ranged from layers characterised by a childishness, incoherence and dramatic tendencies to regions and faculties superior to any displayed by the normal consciousness. Some of these levels seemed to have an urge to express themselves in consciousness and this could happen in dreams, hysteria, hypnosis and somnambulism.

This can also happen when the person is able to produce automatic writing. The automatist, sitting with a block of blank paper and holding a pencil, finds that the hand writes script, the content of which is often a complete surprise to the writer. It invariably purports to come from someone other than the automatist doing the writing. It often includes statements or opinions that would appear to be quite foreign to the normal belief system of the person. The ability to write automatically is not one that necessarily appears suddenly. Often weeks or months of patient sitting have to elapse before the hand holding the pencil will move, perhaps making only a few squiggles on the paper before eventually writing readable script.

There are different opinions concerning the advisability of attempting to write automatically. Some authorities believe that it allows suppressed material or even nascent secondary personalities to 'surface' and influence or even attempt to take over the body. Like using a planchette or ouija board, it can produce material that is at least potentially harmful especially to those who have impressionable minds.

As we have seen, Mrs Verrall had taken up automatic writing again soon after Frederic Myers' death in January 1901 in case, if he survived, he wanted to let his friends know of his continued existence. A study grew of the scripts of other automatists. During 1906–7 it was discovered that the automatic scripts from different automatists bore certain significant resemblances to one another and to the material being produced by Mrs Piper. From then on, efforts were made by the society to keep the automatists in ignorance of each other's output. Geography helped. India, the United Kingdom and the United States were the interested parties' locations. Alice Johnson and Piddington collated and studied the Scripts, helped by people such as Lodge and Gerald Balfour. The investigation went on for many years and demanded not only inexhaustible patience but a great deal of specialised literary and Classical knowledge. Piddington became the most outstanding interpreter and student of the Scripts.

A large proportion of the Scripts purported to come from the deceased founders and members of the SPR. They were often signed. As G.N.M. Tyrrell put it in his study of psychical research *The Personality of Man* (1947):

[The] communicators gave clearly and candidly the reason for the cross-correspondences which they claimed to be producing. They said that they were doing it because a single theme distributed between various automatists, none of whom knew what the others were writing, would prove that a single independent mind, or group of minds, was at the back of the whole phenomenon. Thus, it could not easily be explained by cross-telepathy among the automatists. Also, recondite points in classical literature were introduced to prove the identity of the authors, for Myers, Verrall and Butcher had all been front-rank classical scholars.

At any one time the scripts often contained several themes, interwoven, fragments from them being distributed among the automatists, often in a variety of ways. For example, at the beginning of the Cross-Correspondences in 1907, Mrs Holland, in India, wrote on April 16th: 'Maurice, Morris, Mors. And with that the shadow of death fell upon him and his soul departed out of his limbs.' Mrs Piper, on an extended visit to England, on April 17th spoke the words *Sanatos* and *Tanatos*; on April 23rd the word *Thanatos* and on April 30th the word *Thanatos* three times. On April 29th, also in England, Mrs Verrall, writing automatically, wrote, among other things: 'warmed both hands before the fire of life, it fails and I am ready to depart.' She also wrote 'Come away, come away' and the Latin sentence: 'Pallida mors aequo pede pauperum tabernas regumque turres (put in) pulsat,' – Pale death with equal foot the huts of the poor and the towers of the rich (put in) strikes'. Thus the theme of death was given by Mrs Holland in Latin (*mors*) and English, by Mrs Piper in Greek (*thanatos*) and by Mrs Verrall both allegorically and in Latin.

It was Alice Johnson who recognised the ingenious nature of the communications, their relation to each other and called them 'Cross-Correspondences'. Certainly, when the Cross-Correspondences really got going, they became increasingly labyrinthine in their ingenuity. Sometimes the investigators became baffled and had to ask for clues to the solutions of the current literary and Classical puzzles being teasingly distributed in the scripts. Hints were given by what became known as the 'Script Intelligence', a non-committal term used to refer to whatever was designing and delivering the puzzles to the automatists. It was therefore at times a two-way process between investigators and the Script Intelligence.

Some of the themes or puzzles were delivered over a number of years; at first obscure, it was only possible to realise that they were there when some key element was finally revealed in the scripts that made the investigators restudy the scripts of past years. Indeed, on occasion, the Script Intelligence – almost in the chiding manner of a schoolmaster faced with a surprisingly obtuse class that has not done its homework properly – would ask the investigators to restudy the scripts provided over a particular period of time. As Montague Keen puts it:

> By scattering fragments of these messages, in themselves meaningless, through scripts recorded by different mediums at different times in different places, the ostensible communicators appeared dedicated to the provision of unchallengeable evidence: as and when the disparate pieces were fitted together they would show unmistakeable signs of an organising intelligence. There could be little doubt that this subtle scheme was the deliberate design of Myers' intelligence. As the SPR Proceedings (Vol 21) records on page 382, he instructed Margaret Verrall in unambiguous terms: 'Record the bits, and when fitted together they will make the whole. I will give the words between you neither alone can read, but together they will give the clue of events.

One problem for anyone in the present generation who attempts to assess the worth of the Cross-Correspondences is that in our present age hardly anyone has a literary or Classical education at all comparable with that of Myers, Verrall and Butcher. Of the few scholars who have, it is fair to say that only a small fraction of them have ever heard of the Cross-Correspondences and of those who have, only a small fraction of them have shown any interest in studying them. The very nature of the themes, in many cases spread out in pieces over years among the automatists, and intricately woven into the fabric of the scripts, makes it difficult to dissect out any particular theme for display.

A first step for the interested reader in coming to some appreciation of why the Cross-Correspondences are taken seriously by so many psychical researchers would be to read the section on them in Alan Gauld's book *Mediumship and Survival*, followed by Tyrrell's account of them in *The Personality of Man*. H.F. Saltmarsh's book *Evidence of Personal Survival from Cross-Correspondences* and W.H. Salter's privately printed book *An Introduction to the Study of Scripts* are also worth seeking out. It is unfortunate that *all* four of them are out of print; any remaining copies of them outside the public libraries are probably only to be found in second-hand bookshops.

However, the following account, taken from Tyrrell's excellent book *The Personality of Man*, should give the reader a good first impression of the formidable display of ingenuity and Classical expertise demonstrated in one of the simpler cases – the Ear of Dionysius. Though not strictly a Cross-Correspondence it will also show the inadequacy, not to say fatuousness, of any sceptic's supposed explanation of the Cross-Correspondence material as being simply the result of coincidence – especially when it is appreciated that only two of the group of automatists had any pretensions at all to Classical knowledge.

In the Ear of Dionysius case, the deceased Dr Verrall purports to dictate through Mrs Willett the first script and addresses it to his widow. 'Do you remember you did not know and I complained of your Classical ignorance IGNORANCE.' Then come references to Acoustics, to a Whispering Gallery, to Toil, to Slaves, to a Tyrant, to a One-eared Place, to the Field of Enna, to Syracuse and to the Athenian expedition against it; and the word 'Orecchio' was given with the comment 'That's near'. There is also a reference to Philemon, 'not the Pauline Philemon'. All this clearly referred to the Ear of Dionysius – a grotto hewn out of the rock at Syracuse, Sicily, at the behest of the city's tyrant, Dionysius I *c.*430–367 BC. This grotto had the properties of a whispering gallery and was used by the tyrant to overhear conversations of his prisoners who, confined in the grotto, were compelled to work it as a quarry. Mrs Verrall recalled that she had once asked her husband during his lifetime about this grotto and that he had laughingly rebuked her for her ignorance about it.

The script then went on to refer to the adventures of Ulysses (Odysseus) as given in Homer, and introduced the figure of the one-eyed monster Polyphemus. After that, the story of the lovers, Acis and Galatea, was brought in. The scene of this story was in Sicily and Sicily is throughout much stressed by the scripts. There is a Polyphemus in the Acis and Galatea story, and he figures as the villain of the piece – the 'monster Polyphemus', he is called – who loves Galatea but is rejected by her and in furious jealousy crushes Acis to death with a rock. Polyphemus, Galatea and the jealousy of a rejected lover all form the theme of those scripts.

The investigators became rather puzzled, and thereupon the communicators supplied a hint. Polyphemus, they said, was to be conjoined with Cythera and the Ear-Man and, they added, 'Cyclopean Phylox'. He laboured, they added, in the stone quarries and drew upon the earlier writers for material for his satire, *Jealousy*. Philoxenus of Cythera, the investigators duly note, was a poet of some note in antiquity who had lived in the court of Dionysius at Syracuse, but had been confined by him as a prisoner in the stone quarries (i.e. in the Ear of Dionysius) because he had conceived a passion for Dionysius' beautiful mistress, Galatea. In his confinement he revenged himself by composing a dithyramb entitled either *Kyklops* or *Galatea*, in which he represented himself as Odysseus (Ulysses) who, to take vengeance on Polyphemus (under which name he parodied Dionysius), estranged the affections of the nymph Galatea, of whom Kyklops was enamoured.

All the strands of this Classical soap opera were found to converge in a single narrative contained in a book of a specialist nature entitled *Greek Melic Poets*, the only source in which all the references found in the Cross-Correspondence occur. No one but a specialist in or student of the Classics would be likely to read this book, but Dr Verrall was known to have possessed a copy and to have used it as a textbook in connection with his lectures. Even so it does not contain all the information given in the scripts. Few besides Verrall and Butcher could have worked out these intricately interconnected links leading to a solution contained in a book that only a small group of front-rank scholars were aware of. There is also a good deal of personal characterisation in the manner of the scripts and in the communicators' comments, which was very convincing to those who knew the purported communicators in life. This characterisation, too, has to be dealt with by any theory that attempts to explain the phenomena. Add to this the fact that Mrs Willett, through whom all this particular case came, though well read in general literature, had no deep Classical knowledge.

The suggestion, which itself would involve paranormal activity, that Mrs Verrall, herself a Classical scholar, and anxious to prove the survival of her husband, could have subconsciously concocted this puzzle – and others – and secreted bits and pieces of it in the automatists' subconsciousnesses, has to overcome the fact that the Cross-Correspondences, after her death in 1916, continued just as vigorously and as ingeniously as before. To the more elaborate but related proposition that the puzzles could have all been prepared subconsciously during their originators' lifetimes and, in espionage jargon, 'planted' like 'sleepers' in the automatists' subconsciousnesses to be 'wakened' at some appropriate future date, the following remarks may be made.

First, a number of the Cross-Correspondence cases involved a two-way process, the investigators' efforts at decipherment involving a contemporary reaction on the part of the Script Intelligence when it sees it has to make things easier for the investigators to produce a solution. Second, the increasingly elaborate nature of the above objections, necessarily invoking the operation of some paranormal faculty involving telepathy, clairvoyance and precognition on a massive scale in order to avoid the simple hypothesis that the communicators were who they said they were – shows the power of the Cross-Correspondences in displaying the paranormal in action, challenging anyone studying them to provide an acceptable and parsimonious hypothesis.

The main communicators, ostensibly Frederic Myers, Henry Sidgwick and Edmund Gurney, spoke of their plan to prove their survival of death and described the experiments they were carrying out to try to improve the means of communication. In particular, they were trying, they said, to guide the development of Mrs Willett's mediumship. They did not want another 'Piper'; they wanted her to retain her consciousness and not slip into the trance state with, perhaps, a 'control'. On one occasion, when Oliver

Lodge was sitting with Mrs Willett, the Gurney communicator, through the script, said, 'She is very dazed. Look.'

Lodge: 'Ought I to wake her up?'
Gurney: 'I will. I don't want her to develop into a second Piper.'
Lodge: 'No, I know you consider we have had that, and that now you are arranging something different.'
Gurney: 'New.'

The communicators maintained that the Willett method was better than the trance medium method. That was not to say it was easy. In everyone's mind there is a multitude of associations and a finite vocabulary. Most people, hearing the words 'bread and—?' will usually give the response 'butter' except perhaps if you are a Roman historian, who might reply 'circuses'. A person's finite vocabulary is comprised of words familiar to him. In particular it does not include the technical terms of disciplines he has never come in contact with. All this could cause the communicators a great deal of trouble, they said. It seemed their views had to be transmuted into linguistic modes of expression familiar to Mrs Willett with the ever-present danger that the trains of associations urged into action in Mrs Willett's mind would, like a horse with the bit between its teeth, run uncontrollably away from the desired goal. And if the words were simply not there, the difficulties would be compounded.

An excellent illustration of many of the features of this phase in the mediumship of Mrs Willett is given in the following passage from Balfour's 1935 paper. The sitting was held on May 11th, 1912; in it, Balfour is the sitter G.W.B. Some time before this sitting Balfour had delivered a lecture at Cambridge entitled 'Parallelism and Telepathy'. In the *Hibbert Journal* for April 1910 he had published an article on the same subject. The three philosophical theories on the mind-body problem, Epiphenomenalism, Interactionalism and Parallelism had been discussed in the lecture and the article. Mrs Willett was not interested in philosophy and it is unlikely that she had read the article. The script record has the following passage in it; Mrs Willett is speaking:

'Yes... Oh, how did I get here? It's like Alice in the looking-

174

glass. I see a glass that seems to shut out, and then someone seems to put out a hand and pull me through. Sweet after rain ambrosial showers [A misquotation from Tennyson's *In Memoriam*].

(*Pause*) 'Oh, I'll try. Tennyson. (*Pause*) I'm seeing thoughts but I'm not catching them. What are the three tenable – I don't get that next word and then it goes on – in regard to the phenomenon of consciousness? Somebody asked a question.

'Do you know Henry Sidgwick has sometimes such a quizzical look on his face. He said to me, "Don't make two bites at a cherry but bolt this whole and see what happens".

(*Sighs*) 'Sounds to me very stupid. I've hunted about in my mind and I don't find anything else. What does it mean? It's only words. (*Gesticulating with both hands*) There, just like that is – then there's a word that long – (*motioning with hands*) consciousness.

'I've got it – Oh, it's disappointing when my lips won't say it. L— touched me, and I can say it now. (*L— was a deceased relative of Mrs Willett's who did not communicate but sometimes seemed to help the communications in some way.*)

'Epiphenomenal – that's the last of the three words.

'Oh, Sidgwick said (*waving her hands*) something to do with a room and a lot of people.

'Listen not to the specious lure of the parallelistic phantasy, but nail unto the mast that complicated fragment of truth – nail unto the mast? – the flag of – Oh, I'm so sorry, I'm afraid I've lost it. (Nail unto the mast *was spoken interrogatively, as if the automatist was asking whether she had the right words.*)

'Don't go (*entreatingly*) I'll try again. Oh, how gentle and strong he is.

'He says, Tell him to nail to the mast the flag with one word on it, which is a symbol for a complicated fragment of truth – but he says it's the right line, he says like that – though baffling and perplexing, cleave thou to it. It's because it's only partially apprehended that the timid and the lazy mind slips back from it into the barren and easy and absolutely worthless theory, he says, of a dual (*placing her two hands parallel to each other*) dual, side by side, presumably independent,

175

Oh, he says, the whole thing's full of fallacies, you can't stretch it to that, he says.

'He's telling L— something. It's so odd. L—'s knowing something which I'm not knowing, but I'm knowing that when L— touches me I shall know it too. It's the flag word. (*triumphantly*) I've got it! Oh, but now I've to give it out.

'Oh, I'm all buzzing. (*Waving hands*) I can't think why people talk about such stupid things. Such long stupid words. (*Sighs and stretches herself: then places her hands side by side, saying*) That's gone away now.

'Now it's a thing like this (*drawing with her finger in the air*) [drawing of wriggly line]. It's like a plait – it's woven strands.

'Oh! I see it a hundred ways but I can't get it out.

(*G.W.B.*: 'I understand.')

'Somebody says: 'Don't help her.' '

'Oh, I think I can draw it better. *[Drawing of some lines and underneath is written INT UR AC SHUN.]*

'Edmund makes me laugh. He says, Well think of Ur of the Chaldees. He's making a joke, and they're very angry with him: but the point of it is the terrible effect of disembodiment on one singularly sensitive to shades of sound. He says that Ur would make Fred shudder.

'I must try it you know, it's perfectly ridiculous. (*Here INT UR AC SHUN was added to the foot of the drawing.*)

'Henry says, Thread the maze, but don't lose that strand. There's a lot of confused thinking suggested by that word to many minds. You've all of you only been fingering at the outsides of the theory, but it's there where the gold lies.

'Consciousness (*waving hands*) and matter, mind and matter; and he says, There was a line about the will that felt the fleshly screen. (*Browning*, The Last Ride Together) Oh, oh, there are some very mystical (*word omitted from the record here: perhaps 'meanings'*) wrapped up in those lines of Tennyson's. He says, I have quoted Browning, but the mind of Tennyson playing on the mysteries of consciousness – the phenomena of consciousness – is extraordinarily interesting to anyone studying the mysteries – Oh, what a word in-ter-ac-tion-alism (*pronounced slowly, syllable by syllable*).

'What is the parallelistic theory? (*Expression of great disgust*)

176

To have to come all the way to talk about these things! He says, just to say that. He says that Frank, I and Frank, he says, are a splendid combination in studying the interaction of mind and matter, because you want biological and philosophical knowledge. But, he says, I can't now say what I want to.

I simply cannot go on any longer: that must be all. (*Probably a remark by the automatist on her own account; at least so I thought at the time from the tone in which the words were uttered.*) (*Laughs heartily*) Edmund says, this is really the last bite. The interaction – I'm not sure that word's quite right. It's either action or interaction (*? Int ur ac shun*), though he says that it might be interaction for the interactionalist.

'The light cast upon interaction by the researches into human faculty. It's very odd: do you know they can have machines for telling you the pressure in boilers? Well, there's a machine they've got to find out what's the pressure in me, and all that (*putting her hands to her head*) is too full. It's full to painfulness.

(*G.W.B.*: 'Hadn't you better stop?')

'He says, Just let me throw this, and then that's all. You can't make parallelism square with the conclusions to which recent research points. Pauvres parallelistes! They're like drowning men clinging to spars. But the epiphenomenalistic bosh (*pronouncing with difficulty*) that's simply blown away. It's one of the blind alleys of human thought.

'Oh! I don't want to hear any more: I'm tired.

'And the other and perhaps more specious kind of bosh has got to go too.

(*laughing*) 'Edmund spoke of the philosophic omelettes. He said research is breaking a lot of eggs, and some schools had best get their egg-whisks ready.'

It is evident that whatever the communicators are, whether they are who they say they are, or the products of the Script Intelligence or Mrs Willett's subconscious, they act as if they are intelligent and knowledgeable; they have convincing and consistent personalities, very strongly reminiscent of the people they claim to be. They recognise the people they should. We are told that the humour of the Gurney communicator is typical of the real Gurney: when 'Myers' took over, the script 'changed in a characteristic way and a slow and deliberate writing began'.

To anyone who has open-mindedly and conscientiously studied the literature of mediumship of the calibre demonstrated by Mrs Piper or Mrs Willett, or has had extended experience of sitting with a first-class medium, the glib generalisation by dedicated sceptics that it must all be due to faulty reporting, fraud and wishful thinking is itself palpable wishful thinking, a revealing demonstration of a refusal to acknowledge facts that threaten their model of reality.

It is worth noting that, even if the communicators are who they say they are, it does not follow that in their new state of existence they are omniscient. The Gurney entity, communicating through Mrs Willett, said on one occasion: 'You never seem to realise how little we know. I'm not – sometimes I know and can't get it through, but very often I don't know,' while on another occasion the Frederic Myers entity, communicating through Mrs Holland, wrote, in something like despair:

> The nearest simile I can find to express the difficulties of sending a message – is that I appear to be standing behind a sheet of frosted glass – which blurs sight and deadens sound – dictating feebly – to a reluctant and very obtuse secretary. A feeling of terrible impotence burdens me – I am so powerless to tell what means so much – I cannot get into communication with those who would understand and believe me.

'For now,' said St Paul, 'we see through a glass darkly; but then, face to face.' If some of the communicators are to be believed, the view from the other side is not much clearer.

A final example shows again why the investigators took the Cross-Correspondences very seriously indeed. It is the Lethe Case (reported in Volumes 24 and 25 of the SPR *Proceedings*). Although not strictly part of the Cross-Correspondences, it is worth relating here for several reasons, and not merely because it is one of the classics of psychical research. Not only was it one of the reasons why Mrs Willett was recognised by the investigators as an outstanding medium, but it also exemplified the sort of case that persuaded the investigators to acknowledge the very tenuous basis on which any explanation other than one accepting the active participation of a discarnate intelligence could be advanced. Moreover, it centred on the evidentiality of the discarnate Frederic Myers, whose messages were being channelled, so it was claimed, through two mediums thousands of miles apart, and it represents aspects of Myers' learning and character without plunging the reader into the labyrinth of so many of the Cross-Correspondence puzzles.

In March 1908, George Dorr, a vice-president of the SPR, was conducting a long series of sittings with the medium Mrs Piper. At that time, not only was the 'Hodgson' entity still communicating through her but an entity claiming to be Frederic Myers was also communicating. Sometimes both entities were ostensibly 'present' so that a three-cornered 'conversation' between sitter, 'Myers' and 'Hodgson' would take place. Dorr invited the Myers entity to say through voice or pen what the word 'Lethe' suggested to him. Mrs Piper was ignorant of the Classics, but responded by producing in trance a string of references, almost all of them drawn from Ovid's *Metamorphoses*. When the results, which greatly impressed Dorr, were brought to the attention of Oliver Lodge in London, he decided to pose the same question to Mrs Willett through whom the same personality claimed to be speaking. Lodge took the precaution of putting the question in a sealed envelope, to be opened only when the medium was satisfied that the question could be put to 'Myers(w)' (this is how the interpreters referred to the 'Myers' entity who communicated through Mrs Willett; similarly 'Myers(p)' was used to refer to the 'Myers' entity communicating through Mrs Piper, and so on). The medium received the sealed envelope on September 30th, 1909. When it was opened and the question in it put to Myers(w), the response contained another stream of accurate names and places, but this time all drawn from references appearing in Virgil's *Aeneid*. Lodge had not expected the responses to be identical, if only because it was generally accepted that the medium's mind often had a distorting effect on the words transmitted. He was surprised, however, at the large number of accurate references, nearly all of them drawn from a different Classical source, although there was sufficient overlap with the earlier Piper communication to fortify the belief that the same mind must have been responsible.

The Willett script showed clearly that her communicator was well aware of what had been transmitted by 'Myers' via Piper (referred to as 'Myers(p)') in the USA. Not only did he, or it, get the bemused Mrs Willett to scribble the name 'Dorr' several times, but he inserted a quotation which, he said, was 'nothing of the normal intelligence of my machine' – that is, Mrs Willett. The quotation referred to a 'door to which I found no key, and Haggi

Babba' [Ali Baba]. To ram home the allusion, there followed a reference to 'open sesame'. As for references to Lethe, the name of the river which flows past the fields of Elysium and from which the newly dead, if destined to return to earth, must first wash away their earthly sins and memories by drinking its purifying waters, Myers(w) quoted directly from the Sixth Book of the *Aeneid*: 'The will again to live. The will again to live the River of Forgetfulness.' This quotation is also to be found in Myers' own essay on Virgil (*Classical Essays*), and was incorporated in his poem 'The Passing of Youth'. This could hardly be coincidental because the first response which Myers(p) had earlier given through Piper to the same question was 'Do you refer to one of my poems?'

To ensure that the earthly investigators could not ascribe this to Mrs Willett's subliminal recollection of a Myers poem she might once have read, the Willett script was scattered with arcane but accurate references to the Lethe theme. 'In valle reducta' ('a sheltered vale') is the opening phrase of Virgil's description of the Lethe in the *Aeneid*, and there follow references by Myers(w) to bees and lilies, mainly in the form of Latin quotations. Less direct, but more characteristic of Myers, are his references to the Doves and the Golden Bough amid the Shadows, relating to the branch that Aeneas had to obtain before he could enter the infernal regions in order to arrive at the Lethe.

Subsequent scripts show the Myers(w) source overflowing with allusions to the Lethe theme. Among these was mention of 'Darien, a peak in Darien', a clear reference to Keat's sonnet 'On First Looking into Chapman's Homer' describing stout Cortez's vision of the Pacific Ocean from a peak in Darien. This phrase had been occasionally employed by the SPR founders to signify cases where dying persons seemed to catch glimpses of another world. In the deluge of information showered on the bewildered Mrs Willett by the author of her automatic scripts, no effort is spared to link the Lethe theme with Myers' own works and beliefs. Thus, whereas the Lethe passage in Virgil may readily be taken to indicate that souls prepare themselves for rebirth once all mundane memory had been washed away, Myers(w) qualifies the phrase 'will again to live' by writing 'Not reincarnation: Once only does the soul descend the way that leads to incarnation.'

Ever thorough, the SPR investigators discovered that Mrs Willett's own library contained a popular book entitled *Stories from Virgil*, although it contained no mention of the Lethe. On February 2nd, 1910, however, Lodge devised a further test for Mrs Willett's next spell of automatic writing, wishing to be certain that she could not have known or recalled some of these references for herself. There followed literary parallels linking the story of Ulysses (Odysseus) and his visit to the underworld with that of Aeneas. In the course of this the script refers to one line of Keats' 'Ode to a Nightingale' wherein appear the words 'Lethe-wards had sunk'.

This extended summary may perhaps explain the vigour with which one distinguished scholar, Professor C.J. Ducasse, in his 1972 essay 'What would Constitute Conclusive Evidence of Survival?', looking only at the Piper evidence (and in apparent ignorance of the still more impressive experiment subsequently conducted by Lodge with Mrs Willett's help) posed the rhetorical question:

Is it the least plausible that Mrs Piper – a woman of limited education – not only herself had or had got by ESP the knowledge of the recondite details of Ovid's writings required for the allusions made by the purported Myers – some of which knowledge Dorr did not himself have; but in addition herself had and exercised the capacity which Myers had (but which even Mrs Verrall who was a lecturer in classics at Newnham College, said she herself did not have) so to combine these allusions as to make them say together tacitly about Lethe something which Myers knew, but which was other than any of the other things which, singly, those allusions referred to; and which it took Piddington much study and thought to identify?

In 1917 Mrs Eleanor Sidgwick admitted that the Cross-Correspondences, which were still taking place and would continue to do so for another thirteen years, had convinced her that survival of death took place. In her cool, succinct and intelligent way she wrote of the relationship between a pair of automatists:

We have to seek the designer. It cannot be the supraliminal (i.e. conscious) intelligence of either automatist, since *ex hypothesi*, neither of them is aware of the design until it is completed. Nor, for a similar reason, can it be attributed to

181

some other living person, since, so far as can be ascertained, no other living person had any knowledge of what was going on. It is extremely difficult to suppose that the design is an elaborate plot of the subliminal (i.e. subconscious) intelligence of either or both automatists acting independently and without any knowledge on the part of the supraliminal consciousness; and the only remaining hypothesis seems to be that the designer is an external influence, not in the body.

She concluded: 'I must admit that the general effect of the evidence on my own mind is that there is cooperation with us by friends and former fellow-workers no longer in the body.'

The key word is 'Selection'. Who did the selection of the material given in the communications? Mrs Sidgwick's words are reminiscent of a Myers(w) statement in 1910. On June 5th, Myers(w) emphasises the importance of the evidence for *Selection* in Mrs Willett's script in words almost teasingly addressed to the investigator J.G. Piddington.

Write the word Selection.
Who selects, my friend Piddington?
I address this question to Piddington.
Who selects?

9

The Players on the Other Side

We cannot simply admit the existence of discarnate spirits as inert or subsidiary phenomena; we must expect to have to deal with them as agents on their own account – agents in unexpected ways, and with novel capacities. If they are concerned with us at all, the part which they will play is not likely to be a subordinate one ... the kind of action which now seems likely to be transmitted from one world to the other is of a type which in the natural course of historic evolution has scarcely been likely to show itself until now. For it depends, as I conceive, on the attainment of a certain scientific level by spirits incarnate and excarnate alike.

Human Personality, Frederic Myers

At this point it may be convenient to summarise the overall situation with respect to the Cross-Correspondences and ask some important questions. What were the belief systems of the people involved in studying and trying to interpret the Scripts, and how did they evolve over time? Who or what did they consider the Script Intelligences to be, and what was the evidence for their existence? Did the Script Intelligences have a hidden agenda, perhaps even more than one agenda?

The total mass of the literature concerned with the Cross-Correspondences is enormous. It began with the production of the first script in 1901 and continued for over thirty years. The importance attached to the Scripts by the interpreters was so great that the majority of the scripts were eventually privately printed in volumes which contain annotations to each script. These volumes in total extend over 6,400 pages. The nine volumes of *Notes and Excursuses*, also privately printed, are entirely devoted to analysing and commenting on the scripts and themselves run to 4,400 pages (see Appendix). The SPR *Proceedings* include a number of major papers discussing several of the themes involved in the scripts; another 3,000 pages. The total of 14,000 pages forms a mass of material that must surely cause an understandable hesitation in anyone who is considering a serious study of the Cross-Correspondences. Added to that is the fact that hardly anyone today has the Classical education that the original interpreters had. One recent critic of the importance and significance of the Cross-Correspondences – Christopher Moreman – prepared 'pseudo-scripts' from passages chosen at random from books also chosen at random from a local public library. '[He] had originally wanted to enlist a team of Classics post-grads to ... simulate the original group of investigators but there were none available' and had to make do with a group of English post-graduates instead. *Sic transit gloria classici.*

It seems to be a common assumption that any belief system which a researcher brings to his field of study – whether it be merely a 'hunch' or a strong conviction that some hypothesis must necessarily be true – will cause him to concentrate on any material able to support his hypothesis and ignore or explain away anything in conflict with it. Thus sceptics have sometimes claimed that the belief in survival brought by the interpreters to their studies influenced their interpretations of the Cross-Correspondences. According to such an argument, the interpreters must have industriously grafted onto what was essentially a 'passive' mixture of Classical references and poetical quotations, produced by the random outpourings from the automatists' subconsciousnesses, a web of pseudo-meaningful connections ingeniously spun from their well-stocked minds. This hardline scepticism essentially promotes four different propositions:

(a) that a prejudiced researcher cannot maintain a cautious, non-committal and neutral attitude to his research;

(b) while the ability of one or more industrious people to produce correspondences from a body of randomly acquired data may seem striking, it is without any significance whatsoever because of the method by which the data were derived;

(c) the interpreters of the Cross-Correspondences were *already* believers in survival when they came to study the Cross-Correspondences;

(d) there was no overall directing Script Intelligence.

The first proposition is, of course, nothing new and is a potential danger in any discipline involving research. The research student is, or should be, warned of this danger by their supervisor and, if both are competent, the research should be immune from this selective tendency. With time, most students will build into their minds an automatic check upon their deductions and a concern to include all the data available. The work done for a Ph.D. is not, as one unkind soul once said, merely a shovelling of old bones from one graveyard to another. Sadly, of course, examples have been found in *most* research disciplines (and in other occupations – even politics!) of people who have deliberately massaged or manufactured 'data' to promote their own theories or their careers. Fortunately, there also exists a powerful fraud-safe factor in any research discipline. The nature of research and of peer-review, the necessary publication of papers in learned journals where the author not only states the reasoning s/he followed to arrive at the conclusions s/he came to but also provides the evidence and data used, will enable the unconvinced to repeat the work and check its validity. Sometimes the cheat will get away with it for years but sooner or later they will get their comeuppance.

Everyone of us has a set of what one might call workaday beliefs that we continually use, consciously or unconsciously, to assess our experiences and guide our course of action. 'Common sense tells me...' is a phrase often used in a given situation where 'common sense' is the distilled wisdom drawn from previous experience and the experience of trusted others. Unlikely to be included in a person's 'file' of common sense are highly unusual events that almost no one has experienced. In passing it may be remarked that David Hume's proposition that evidence of miracles – that is, events that violate natural laws – should never justify our setting aside massively evidenced natural laws was answered by St Augustine more than a millennium before Hume was born when the saint said that miracles are not a contradiction of nature's laws but only of what we believe to be nature's laws.

Many of a person's common-sense beliefs, if examined, are found to be held with various degrees of probability but are acted upon as if they were absolutely true. An astronomer, for example, orders his life as if he believes that the Sun will rise tomorrow. But he will also admit that total confidence in the theory of the nature of the Sun's internal constitution may be unjustified in some obscure but disastrous way and as a consequence the Sun might explode tonight. Nevertheless he lives as if this tiny departure from certainty does not exist. Ordinary life indeed would be rendered impossible if this unconscious process did not occur of pushing probable or improbable events respectively to the boundary positions of certain or impossible and we had to compute and compare the exact probabilities of myriad factors in our day-to-day decision-making.

The professional sceptic, however, would have it that the psychical researcher who believes in survival of death *for whatever reason* cannot be trusted to carry out research in an uncommitted way but will always find data and cases to support that belief. This view is tantamount to identifying such a psychical researcher with the fundamentalist believer whose mindset acts as an impregnable rock against which the waves of evidence, however powerful and persuasive, break impotently. It is a view that also demonstrates the sceptic's arrogant contempt for the psychical researcher and disregard for their honesty and professional integrity. He also omits from consideration that the nature of research is such that it is very rare for the psychical researcher to work as a loner, unchecked in the deductions he draws from his work. If, however, we were to adopt this point of view, would it not be logical to suppose it also true that the professional sceptic, likewise possessing a strong conviction amounting to certainty *for whatever reason* that paranormal phenomena do not exist, will never find any and will subconsciously influence the planning of his or her investigations into paranormal phenomena in such a way that they demonstrate that such phenomena do not exist?

The sceptic's second proposition is based on the fact that human beings have been described as pattern-seeking animals. This is certainly true. The built-in desire to find patterns in any body of experience is a valuable survival instinct, and one that is almost impossible to shut down. From the drowsy imagining of patterns of faces and animals in the leaping flames of a fire to the deadly serious search for patterns in the thousands of Enigma-encoded German messages recorded by the British during the Second World War, there are innumerable examples of the use of this faculty. If one has a prior belief that the works of Shakespeare were written by Bacon, it is probable that by studying these works one can find ingenious ways in which Bacon left clues or messages revealing that he was the author. However, as we have already seen, the work performed by the interpreters of the Cross-Correspondences and the nature of the Cross-Correspondences themselves were of an entirely different kind.

We turn now to the third proposition: that the interpreters of the Cross-Correspondences were already believers in survival when they began their attempt to decipher the Scripts. The period in which most of the Scripts were written was the first thirty years of the twentieth century. The main interpreters who studied the Scripts were Mrs Verrall, Miss Alice Johnson, Mrs Sidgwick, Sir Oliver Lodge, Mr J.G. Piddington. and Mr Gerald Balfour. Balfour's brother Arthur Balfour was involved but did not himself study the Scripts. In 1901, the year when the first script was written, it is probable that only Lodge had a firm belief in survival. It will be remembered that it was during his presidential address in 1902 that he declared his belief in survival, forced upon him by twenty years of psychical research. At that time it would seem that the others had no firm scientifically based conviction that survival took place. Montague Keen, in considering this question, writes:

> Although the principal investigators slowly changed their minds about survival, not least as a result of their intensive study of the cross-correspondence evidence, it is certainly not the case that they were at all eager to embrace the concept. Even as late as 1916, Mrs Sidgwick, who played a critically important role in the CC work, set out to demonstrate in her monumental study of the mediumship of Mrs Piper ... that the communications were far more likely to have derived from the medium's own psyche, supplemented by a variety of telepathic messages from the living ... Alice Johnson, whose early work with the mediumistic communications particularly of Mrs Verrall and Mrs Holland was the foundation of the CCs, was no enthusiast.

Nevertheless, by 1916, the year in which Mrs Verrall died, the situation had changed. It is apparent from the letter she wrote to Mrs Sidgwick on May 17th, a few weeks before her death, informing Mrs Sidgwick of her impending demise, that she expected to survive the death of her body and would enter a new experience. A year later Mrs Sidgwick stated her own conviction after sixteen years' study of the Cross-Correspondences that survival of death took place. Arthur Balfour himself had now, by the evidence presented to him, become firmly convinced of survival, as had Gerald and J.G. Piddington. Miss Johnson, at least, was taking the proposition very seriously indeed.

It is therefore clear that the interpreters of the Cross-Correspondences changed their attitude to the question of the survival of death *during* the period 1900 to 1930, when the vast majority of the Cross-Correspondence scripts were being created and studied. It should be noted, however, that among the principal analysts who were privy to Scripts which were not to be publically available for several decades thence, the evidence supporting the case for survival of death was, as we shall see, more persuasive than that in the public domain. Nevertheless, despite their existing or growing conviction of survival, all the interpreters went to great lengths to ascribe evidence to psi – parapsychological phenomena – wherever possible. In 1900, there was an almost unanimous vote among the interpreters (the minority vote being that of Lodge who *did* believe in survival) that conclusive evidence existed that some mediums could paranormally acquire information. By 1917, however, after sixteen years of study of the Cross-Correspondences, the state of play had changed dramatically. Now the investigators were firm believers in survival. As we have seen, before her death in 1916, Mrs Verrall had also 'voted' for that belief.

With respect to the fourth proposition – that there was no overall directing Script Intelligence – we have already shown that this position is logically untenable. One recalls the communicator 'George Pellew' who reasoned with Hodgson and other sitters through Mrs Piper's mediumship, also 'Hodgson' who gave a wealth of relevant information and displayed marked irritation at not being accepted as the surviving spirit of Richard Hodgson. There was also the communicator who claimed to be Myers, who transmitted through Mrs Piper to Mr Dorr a long list of Classical details related to Lethe, then subsequently through Mrs Willett to Sir Oliver Lodge an entity (Myers(w)) gave highly related and relevant information from Virgil concerning Lethe, subsequently transmitting a teasing remark to Piddington to ask himself 'who does the selection, friend Piddington?' One should also keep in mind the involved conversations between Lodge and Balfour on this side and communicators claiming to be their friends Myers, Gurney and Sidgwick, who said they had survived bodily death, were trying to provide convincing evidence that they had done so and were therefore trying something new. These conversations enabled the interpreters to form over time a careful assessment of the degree of intelligence and traits of personality displayed by the communicators. Whether we attach a name to the entity communicating through Mrs Willett who claimed to be Myers, or try to be non-committal and use a catch-all title like the Script Intelligence, we have to accept that, in the true meaning of the word 'communication', a two-way process was taking place.

The Script Intelligence existed, *whatever it was* – secondary personalities, dramatic creations in the subliminals of the automatists and mediums, spirits of the dead, perhaps entities we in our bodily state simply cannot imagine. It and the Cross-Correspondences over the years were able to change drastically the points of view of very cautious interpreters, leading them to accept or to take very seriously indeed the Script Intelligence's first agenda – to demonstrate that their friends had survived death. By 1917, the interpreters had also been brought face to face with and involved in the Script Intelligence's second and third agendas, the 'Story' and the 'Plan', and Myers' prophetic statement given at the beginning of this chapter would seem to them yet another example of his remarkable genius.

At this point it will be useful to reinforce the view that the Cross-Correspondences have to be taken very seriously indeed by giving W.H. Salter's careful consideration of the phenomena and interpretation of the Scripts, which he wrote in 1952 when he was acknowledging the important part that J.G. Piddington played in research into them. Probably more than anyone in his generation, Salter worked to maintain the SPR on the course on which it was originally set by its illustrious founders.

From the end of the First World War until very near the end of his life, Salter devoted the greater part of his time and energy to the honorary service of the SPR. He first became a member of Council, by cooptation, in December 1919. He became Honorary Treasurer on December 9th, 1920, in succession to Piddington, and held that office until September 30th, 1931, when he resigned. In March 1924 he was appointed Honorary Secretary and occupied that post continuously until 1958, and so had seven years in which he combined the offices of Honorary Treasurer and Honorary Secretary. It was not in pursuance of any preconceived theory of his own that he became deeply involved in psychical research, mastered the subject and, in addition to his own work, spent much time and energy helping others to further their own enquiries. Apart from his papers and books, still of great value in helping to form some appreciation of the importance of the Cross-Correspondences in psychical research and the understanding of human personality in all its multifarious ramifications, his meticulous attitude to the subject, never going beyond what, in his considered opinion, the evidence justified, embodied the best traditions of the law and science.

In his paper on the Palm Sunday Case (which we will turn to in the following chapter), published in the SPR *Journal* in 1959–60, Salter wrote:

[With respect to the Scripts] the problem that faced the interpreting group may be shortly stated thus. For about thirty years from 1901 onwards a round dozen of automatists, many but not all of them members of the society, produced well over three thousand 'scripts', a word given for convenience an extended meaning to include not only pieces of automatic or inspirational writing, but also records of trance uttering, inspirational speech, and impressions received in sleep or waking or various states between. At an early stage it was noted that there were connexions between the scripts of various automatists, and also between them and the records of sittings with Mrs Piper, that appeared to be neither fortuitous nor due to normal association between them. These were the simpler 'cross-correspondences'. The connexions were usually made through the recurrence of the same phrase, quotation from the same literary source, or insistence on the same topic.

As the result of wider and closer study it was noted that the cross-correspondences interlocked with each other in such a way as to make a pattern covering a very large portion of the script material. As integral parts of the pattern were found (1) references to verifiable facts which were certainly not within the conscious knowledge of the automatists at the time they were made and had, so far as could be ascertained, never been within his or her normal knowledge, and (2) predictions relating to both public and private matters. Was it possible, by any rational and consistent method of interpretation, to establish what the pattern was, how it came into existence, and whether it contained any particular meaning?

190

This would have been a stiff enough job if the interpreters had been set to work on a final, complete set of scripts, in neatly typed fair copies, with all the quotations traced to their sources in half-a-dozen literatures, all the personal allusions annotated, and everything indexed. But in fact all the searching out of literary sources and all the annotating and indexing had to be done while the scripts were pouring out, and the interpreters had at the same time to frame, with such assistance as they could derive from directions in the scripts, canons for interpretation of a mass of material, disconnected, allusive, and symbolic. Further study made it almost certain that the obscurity was often deliberate and designed to prevent either automatist or interpreter from guessing the drift before what the script-intelligence, to use a non-committal term, considered the appropriate moment. In the Introduction to his paper in Volume XXXIII of *Proceedings* (pp. 439–60) Piddington gave a brief and lucid account of the principles on which he and his fellow-interpreters had worked. The work had been mainly done by him and Balfour in consultation, but no progress could have been made in it without the index, the compilation of which fell almost entirely upon him.

It was a task calling for infinite patience, tireless industry, and scrupulous accuracy in detail, in all of which Piddington was highly gifted. If there was the smallest variation in the form in which a quotation occurred in different scripts, any slight mis-spelling of a name or error as to a date, Piddington was down on it at once. The slip might, so far as the automatist's conscious mind was concerned, be unintentional, but possibly it might be a device of the script-intelligence, as I have called it, to attract special attention to the passage where it occurred. Above all, having fixed his rules of interpretation he was prepared to follow them to their logical conclusions, even if it meant attributing to the script-intelligence intentions of a surprising kind and, as regards details of the pattern, meanings repugnant to his own robust common-sense. For it must be emphasized that he was not at all a cranky or eccentric person. Apart from psychical research, he conformed very closely in manner to the typical Englishman of his age and education. Fortunately, perhaps, although he was well-informed and well-read on many subjects, he had no special leaning towards poetry, so that in tracking down the sources of the many poetic quotations with which the scripts overflow, he had to move from step to step by careful study and had no temptation to jump to conclusions.

What, it may be asked, was the net result of all this labour and ingenuity? To put it at the lowest, the interpreters produced order out of chaos, so that when they had done their work nearly the whole of the enormous mass of scripts fitted into a coherent pattern of which they had no conception when they started their labours – nearly the whole, that is to say, apart from exhortations to the automatists and interpreters and discussions as to experimental methods, which of course lie outside the pattern; and even when these are excluded there remain passages where the interpreters confessed themselves unable to discover a coherent meaning.

It would of course be easy enough for an unscrupulous interpreter to select tit-bits here and there from so large a mass, arrange them arbitrarily, interpret them according to the caprice of the moment, and thereby obtain any pattern he pleased. Those, needless to say, were not the methods of Balfour or Piddington or any of their fellow-workers. That so many pieces of the puzzle fitted neatly into place to produce an elaborate design incorporating many details that, considered by themselves, are extremely odd, seems to me strong evidence that the design really is there, and is not the product of the interpreters' fantastic ingenuity.

Nor can it be assigned to the normal knowledge of each others' scripts acquired by the different automatists, e.g. through reading *Proceedings*, where several scripts were from time to time published, nor yet to rational inference based on such knowledge. Of the principal members of the group 'Mrs Holland' (Mrs Fleming) died without knowing even the main outlines of the pattern; Mrs Stuart Wilson does not know them yet [1952]; Mrs Verrall only learnt them from Piddington after most of her scripts had been written, and was with difficulty persuaded to accept his account; and my wife was equally hard to persuade when informed after her own scripts had ceased.

The choice seems to lie between three hypotheses, all paranormal, separately, or perhaps in some combination of them. To begin with the hypothesis involving the smallest departure from views acceptable to most psychical researchers, it might be argued that some person consciously or subconsciously designed the pattern and contrived to distribute it by telepathy among the members of the group, each of whom reproduced in his scripts the portion allotted to him. Those who incline to this view generally cast Mrs Verrall for the principal part, as she was the earliest of the group, and had the literary knowledge sufficient for producing the pattern as we have it. On the other hand she had no normal knowledge of some of the facts woven into the pattern, and the pattern went on unfolding itself for many years after her death in 1916. It should be noted that even this hypothesis, which may be taken as the minimum worth discussion, postulates telepathy of a kind very different from anything established or suggested by quantitative or qualitative experiment.

This same difficulty attaches to the second hypothesis, which is that the pattern was created by the subconscious minds of the automatists, acting as a group with a collective character that persisted notwithstanding the death or retirement of some of its members and the accession of others. This meets the difficulty as to the development of the pattern after 1916, but raises problems of its own, particularly as regards the implication of collective constructive activity on a very large scale carried on entirely at the subconscious level.

The third hypothesis is that the pattern was devised by some intelligence or group of intelligences external to the group of automatists, and, more specifically, by a group of communicators including Sidgwick, Myers, and Gurney, with each of whom some of the scripts claim to originate. This was the view that after prolonged study all the principal interpreters accepted, although several of them were not lightly persuaded to accept it. Piddington's natural scepticism was reinforced by a personal dislike, which he expressed to me, for the idea of surviving; but this did not prevent his accepting the survivalist view which he maintained in his paper in Volume XXXIII of *Proceedings*.

It may be doubted, however, whether Balfour, Piddington, and the other interpreters would have been willing to devote the immense amount of time and labour that the elucidation of the scripts demanded, if the sole object of the scripts had been to establish the survival and identity of the ostensible communicators. That was only the first stage in the declared purpose of the script-intelligence. The declared ultimate purpose is the creation of a universal and durable order of peace between nations and between classes, in the promotion of which the communicating group is, with many other persons, represented as engaged. This, one need hardly say, is an ideal that has appealed to many people at many times, and occasional references to it might have been expected in the scripts of automatists whose outlook on life was that of the members of 'the S.P.R. group'. When found there, they would have called for no particular notice. What struck the interpreters as significant was the prominence given to this topic in the whole mass of scripts, the persistence with which it is dwelt on from their beginning in 1901, and the peculiar way in which it is woven into a pattern embodying various paranormal features, cross-correspondences, verifiable statements of facts not normally known to the automatist making them, and predictions of public and private events, some of which had in the interpreters' opinion been fulfilled.

All this seemed to warrant their belief that they were in touch with discarnate intelligences having power to influence the actions of living men and women and foresee future events, and using that power to promote an enterprise of immense importance for the welfare of mankind. Holding that belief they were willing to spare neither time nor labour year after year in clearing up every doubtful point connected with the scripts, and to put the result of their labours in an orderly permanent form, so that, if the predictions were fulfilled, it should be beyond dispute exactly what the predictions were, when they were made, and from whom they claimed to come.

'These all died ... not having received the promises.' The interpreters never supposed that they would receive them during their lives. But Piddington, the last survivor of them by several years, told me in the autumn of 1950 that though he was sure that the predictions had been correctly interpreted, the continued deterioration in world affairs had for some time made him wonder whether the communicators and their associates had not undertaken more than they could perform. No precise date is given for fulfilment in the scripts, but the suggestion is certainly made that a beginning at least would take place in the lifetime of persons living at the date of the First War. It seems to me desirable that should be stated now, without waiting for the predictions to be fulfilled by the course of events, or falsified by the lapse of time.

As I have already said, this is not the occasion to attempt a final appraisement of the scripts, and when the occasion does arise the attempt should be made by someone with a fuller knowledge of the whole of the scripts than I can claim. But I have read carefully more than half of them and, so far as concerns the material I have read, I am prepared to accept the interpreters' construction of it as substantially correct, even as regards points where the eccentricity to be expected in any work of complex symbolism might appear to have been given very free scope. But just as in ordinary life two people telling the same story with every desire to be accurate will each tell it from a different angle, so with the automatists of 'the SPR group'. For example, all the scripts claim to be inspired by persons who have survived bodily death, and there is general agreement among the automatists as to who these persons are, but with some of the automatists they are presented in a highly individualised dramatic form, with others the emphasis is on what 'they' say and do, on their collective and, perhaps, inter-personal activity. It has sometimes seemed to me that in this and in other connexions the interpreters have overstressed the personal aspect, and that the cause of this may have been that with both Balfour and Piddington their subtle powers of reasoning were not tempered by psychic faculties, so that, quick as they were to discern what was or was not significant in substance, they were prone to accept too literally the dramatic form with which the substance was clothed. I hesitate, however, to bring even this minor criticism against a piece of work on so great a scale as the interpretation of the scripts, and one carried out with so much toil and skill.

10

The Palm Sunday Story

And if God wills, I shall but love thee better after death.

Elizabeth Barrett Browning.

They say that faint heart never won fair lady; and it is amazing to me how fair ladies are won, so faint are often men's hearts.

The Warden, Anthony Trollope

It is worth recalling that the automatic scripts were scattered among a group of automatists in different countries, from which they were then sent to the offices of the SPR. The scripts were often signed and purported to be from the Founding Fathers of the SPR. Discovering that they had survived the death of their physical bodies, they had concocted a plan to demonstrate that they still existed. When they were still in the body and carrying out psychical research, they had often been faced with the problem of interpreting the information paranormally acquired by mediums. Had it been derived by telepathy and clairvoyance from the minds of sitters or people not even in the same country or could it have come from the spirits of the deceased trying to prove they had survived? A stated intention of the script communicators was to concoct from their knowledge of literature and the Classics themes that would be presented in a manner that strengthened the survival hypothesis and rendered less plausible the super-telepathy and clairvoyance explanation. We have seen that many psychical researchers, initially highly sceptical, such as Mrs Sidgwick, Sir Oliver Lodge, Gerald Balfour and J.G. Piddington, were forced to agree that over the years the ostensible communicators succeeded admirably, convincing the interpreters that the communicators were who they claimed to be.

Frederic Myers had suggested in his book *Human Personality* that perhaps the cooperative actions of a group of discarnate spirits would be a better method to demonstrate survival of bodily death than any effort by a spirit trying to communicate personal details through a medium. Indeed, as the years passed and the study by the investigators of the automatists' scripts painstakingly proceeded, it had become clear to them that the scripts did demonstrate clear evidence of intelligent design, not just of one theme but many. To the investigators it became more and more convincing that the scripts were the result of purpose, intelligence and education far beyond anything that could be assigned to any one automatist. It also became clear that the Script Intelligence interacted with the investigators, dropping helpful, and at times teasing, hints if the themes of the Cross-Correspondences proved too difficult for the investigators to decipher. It was demonstrably a two-way process.

The themes of the Scripts were represented in fragmentary references to Classical subjects or in quotations from relevant poems, or in short phrases, or hinted at in symbols or names of figures in literature and legend. Once the key to the puzzle was recognised, the themes suddenly made sense like the picture on a completed and complicated jigsaw puzzle. It would become clear not only what the theme was, but what the purpose of choosing such a theme had been, for in many cases it referred to particular events in the lives of people both living and dead. Such a theme was exhibited in the strange and poignant Palm Sunday Story, the Cross-Correspondences in this case developing over a period of almost twenty years. Many who have studied this case have accepted that it is a remarkable demonstration of undying love and devotion by people on both sides of that inevitable and inescapable appointment we call death.

The group of seven ostensible communicators involved in the case consisted of Henry Sidgwick, Frederic Myers, Edmund Gurney, Francis Maitland Balfour, Annie Marshall, Laura Lyttelton and Mary Catherine Lyttelton. The first three were of course the principal investigators in the early years of the SPR. None of the other four was involved with psychical research during his or her lifetime. Francis Maitland Balfour, the brother of Arthur James and Gerald

William Balfour, and of Mrs Sidgwick, was the brilliant young biologist who had died tragically young in a climbing accident in the Swiss Alps in 1882. For more than a decade he had worked and studied to fit himself for his chosen career. Just thirty years of age when he died, he had already been recognised as the foremost embryologist in Great Britain. In that short and brilliant career he had founded a school for the study of Animal Morphology in Cambridge University and was the first professor of his subject, the chair having been specially created for him. In taking that chair he had had to turn down invitations to succeed the brilliant biologists George Rolleston at Oxford and Sir Charles Wyville Thomson at Edinburgh. At the time of his death in the Alps he had held the Cambridge chair for only a few months.

Annie Marshall was the woman loved deeply by Frederic Myers, who overwhelmed by her troubles, and in total despair, drowned herself in Lake Ullswater in 1876. Laura Lyttelton was the first wife of Alfred Lyttelton who died in childbirth in 1886. Alfred Lyttelton's sister, Mary Catherine Lyttelton, was the third woman in the group of seven, the so-called 'Palm Maiden' in the Palm Sunday Case.

The investigating group whose members studied the script phenomena and tried to make sense of them consisted of six people, Mrs Margaret Verrall, Sir Oliver Lodge, Ms Alice Johnson, Mr J.G. Piddington, Mrs Sidgwick and Gerald William Balfour. The automatists were Mrs Margaret Verrall, Ms Helen Verrall, Mrs 'Holland', Mrs 'Willett' and Mrs Leonora Piper. It was Margaret Verrall – acting both as automatist and interpreter – who played the central role in the revelation of this extraordinary case.

It was on Palm Sunday, 1875, that a young woman, Mary Catherine Lyttelton, died of typhus. She was almost twenty-five years of age. Though not of exceptional beauty, she had beautiful long dark flowing hair and a singularily vivacious and attractive personality. Dame Edith Lyttelton, her brother's second wife, wrote: 'Love and sympathy streamed out from her. She was one of those people who charge the atmosphere with life when they appear.' She was also a fine pianist and loved to take part in the musical evenings that were so much a feature of Victorian family life in that social circle.

Arthur James Balfour met Mary Lyttelton for the first time at

Christmas in 1871. It was at a ball at Hawarden Castle, William Gladstone's home in Flintshire, Wales. There seems no doubt that Balfour was immediately attracted to her and soon fell in love with her. She had been engaged the previous year to Edward Denison, nephew and heir of the Speaker of the House of Commons, but he, suffering from tuberculosis, had gone to Australia for his health and had died there. Knowing of this tragedy in Mary Lyttelton's life, Arthur Balfour hesitated to intrude upon her grief, but they soon became firm friends, finding that they shared the same interests. The friendship progressed; there were obstacles, however, and it was not until the early part of 1875 that Arthur, by now convinced that more than anything else in life he wanted to marry her, made his feelings clear to her. It must have been obvious to her long before he spoke that he was strongly attracted to her. But even then he did not formally propose: he intended to do so at their next meeting. Her sister Lavinia wrote:

I can recall May's happy face when I met her ... at the Burlington House Exhibition of Old Masters. She had just come from Latimer, where Arthur was, and he had spoken to her, as he afterwards told me, of his feelings for her ... he intended to propose at the next opportunity.

Soon after that meeting, however, she contracted typhus and after a short illness died on Palm Sunday, 1875, just before her twenty-fifth birthday. Lavinia heard her, in her delirium, speak of her last talk with Arthur Balfour and from her words, Lavinia was convinced that Mary Lyttelton now loved Arthur as fully as he loved her.

Arthur was heartbroken by her death. Afterwards he wrote to his friend Edward Talbot:

I used to dream, knowing the sad story of her life, that perhaps with me her wearied heart might have at last found rest ... but God has provided a far more full and perfect calm; and I do feel how selfish are the longings ... for the 'might have been'. In the meantime, I think – I am nearly sure – that she must have grasped the state of my feelings towards her ... and now, perhaps when she watches the course of those she loved who are still struggling on earth, I may not be forgotten.

Some time after Mary Lyttelton's death, Arthur Balfour carried out a certain course of action which he kept secret from everyone except Mary's sister Lavinia. That course of action, and a number of other events, are relevant to the Palm Sunday story. To people of our brash generation it is bewildering, difficult, indeed nearly impossible, to understand how Arthur Balfour, devoted to and deeply in love with Mary Lyttelton, could have allowed three years to pass without asking her to marry him. But things were different in Victorian times. In addition, for part of that period, there had been obstacles and it was characteristic of Balfour that he never did anything precipitously. In the end, however, he waited too long. For him her loss was devastating. He never married. Every year thereafter to the end of his long life, unless prevented by urgent political matters, he kept Palm Sunday as a special day of remembrance, passing it in seclusion with Mary's sister. Though his life was a full one, occupied by intellectual interests, writing and politics – he was Prime Minister from 1902 to 1906 – he remained essentially solitary in disposition.

To give some impression of the nature of the scripts obtained by the automatists and in particular convey the way in which Mrs Willett's psychic gift developed, a sample of a script by her, written on Palm Sunday, March 31st, 1912, is given below. The investigators' interpretations are given as notes at the end of the script.

WILLETT 289 31 March, 1912
(Written on Palm Sunday)

Gurney[1] it is a new strand I want to grasp today – there are many threads – let the thoughts flit idly – remember the mountain spring it bubbles up without effort and its waters are the sweetest.

Effortless meditation, that will help me best, the message is not for you and is not for me: through me it comes but I am only a channel, and you likewise are only a channel.

Begin now – Day – the day it is to which an allusion is wanted – not the date but the day – It moves according to the seasons – according to the Moon – but it is the day, that is full of meaning[2] the Entry – say that – amid the throng[3] who sang, how fickle is the mob – the stainless years – what is the quotation – beneath the sky[4] Momento mori – Pass on

200

– yes, say that Oh memory, cast down thy wreathed shell[5] the graves of long ago. It is an old story yet even new. We watched her breathing as she slept[6] but what is the poem where Rossetti speaks of the death of his sister[7] Is it Xmas Eve? Churches Festivals[8] that has meaning – the Church and the State – that is obscure but go on – Feed my sheep – the Shepherd's crook – there is a link there?[9]

A community of thought links some today, a community of sympathy.[10] But not alone on your side – Other and greater is the flow, here – I believe in the

Communion of Saints

Blessed are the pure in heart –

Be thou faithful unto death –

It is known, faith on both sides

Star bedecked the head – the broidered robe – the stars singing in their spheres.

You have made a mistake about the robe, but never mind – I want a simple sentence known to you and you will not write it. The love that waits beyond Death. Say that – try again – she looked long, gazing, gazing – piercing the distance with eager eyes, that is better[11] the plighted troth – roses for a maiden dead[12] say that try again Gurney – let the pencil move freely – Help – there is one who asks your help – try again.

this is he was great by land as thou by sea – that has a meaning[13]

She is trying to speak – will anyone hear – will anybody hear – not distant – not set in other spheres – but near – nearer than hands and feet – speak for she hears, and spirit with spirit can meet.[14]

The long silence that yet has meant no sundering – the sharpness of the pang has been overlaid with many other things, rolled around with rocks[15] My love involves the love before – I shall not lose thee though I die – say that[16]

You are tired – but there is meaning in what I say – the little bark that puts forth upon the waters – the dark waters of interpretation bearing a message – One waits beside the shore to know its fate.[17]

The Days of Memories, and the Memories of Days – Unbend the bow – You are wandering – enough now – Gurney – say it for me – this – stretch forth thy hand – damsel, I say unto thee arise[18] the spirit broke the bonds – soared and yet hovers – Farewell

E[19]

Notes
(1) Gurney – E.G., in this case Control of Mrs Willett.
(2) i.e. Palm Sunday.
(3) i.e. The Entry into Jerusalem.
(4) Tennyson, *In Memoriam*, LII.
(5) Oscar Wilde, 'The Burden of Itys'.
(6) [Thomas] Hood, 'The Deathbed'.
(7) Rossetti, 'My Sister's Sleep'.
(8) The Rossetti poem suggests Xmas Eve and so leads on to 'Churches Festivals'; Palm Sunday of course is the one wanted.
(9) 'The Shepherd's Crook', or pastoral staff is the symbol of a bishop – here is a reference to Bishop Talbot, brother-in-law of M.L. Mention of the 'Church and State' suggests the Talbots and A.J.B. united in thought on this day.
(10) The friends and relations of M.L. are meant.
(11) Allusions to 'The Blessed Damozel', D.G. Rossetti's poem.
(12) Shelley, 'Remembrance'.
(13) Tennyson's 'Ode to the Duke of Wellington'. The Christian name of Wellington was *Arthur*, and A.J.B. being his godson was called after him: it is an implicit allusion to A.J.B.
(14) Tennyson, 'The Higher Pantheism'.
(15) Wordsworth, 'A Slumber Did My Spirit Seal'.
(16) Tennyson, *In Memoriam*.
(17) M.L. herself waits to know if her message will be understood and reach its destination.
(18) Mark V. 41.
(19) E = Edmund Gurney, who generally controls Mrs Willett's scripts of this date.

On numerous occasions during a session, Mrs Willett, having first produced automatic writing, would then go into her own type of trance in which she could perceive and hear inwardly those she believed to be the communicators from the other side. At the same time, however, she was still conscious of the sitters and could convey their words to the communicators and what the communicators were trying to convey to her. Quite often, however, although the communicators seemed to exhibit an enormous patience at her inability to grasp the meanings of their messages, they would at times lose patience and react in ways characteristic of their earthly personalities.

Given below is a Willett sitting in which script and speech are given. The notes are by Gerald William Balfour (G.W.B.).

WILLETT 291 and 292, 14th April, 1912
(G.W.B. recording)

EXTRACT FROM THE SCRIPT PRECEDING TRANCE

I want to say the scripts had meaning and I want to say more about that, but do not question me –

A for ARTIST   ART[1]

(*Here follows trance. Mrs W speaking*)

Oh, I see – Yes, I will – She's quite young (*laughs*) what amazing fashions! Oh, don't look so sad!

She says, It was for him, it was for him. She says Not for them, it was for him.[2] She isn't speaking to me but I can hear those words, and they belong to her. She is such a curious looking figure – her hair done – she's very attractive – gentle-looking Oh, (*sighs*) Edmund says, the Lily and the Wheel – round and round like fireworks.[3]

Hist! something about the dogs being fed. Hist, said Kate, 'tis only the boy carolling as he gives the hounds their messes![4]

Do you know the dark young man?[5] He says to me, Try Siena.

And he says, A variant of the Wheel, but not a Highland Mary[6]

There was a bridge over the river – oh, something about a very big house and the trees stretching away[7]

He says, there's a poem called The Sisters. He says he doesn't care about the poem, it's the title he wants[8]

The flowers and the grave, was that understood?[9]

G.W.B. (*We believe we understand the scripts*)

(*Mrs Willett then took the block and pencil and drew as follows*):

Pass on[10]

(*Mrs Willett then said*):

She seems to draw something like that – that's the girl in the odd clothes. She looks very pale. It's all very confused. Somebody wants to say something to somebody – Seated upon a (*pause*) Edmund says You donkey! and then they all laughed[11]

203

And Henry said, the day of small things, but Nora will see the point[12]

Henry says he's glad when Nora and the mother are together[13]

What has Petrarch got to do with it?[14]

He says, If Piddington[15] wants a severe mental exercise, let him find out that which connects the ass and the poet[16]

And another poet:

Three Queens, from them rose. A cry which shivered to the tingling stars[17]

She never fully realised until she got here, across the Sands of Dee[18]

All that's bright must fade. Something – although it fade and die that night, it was the plant and child of light[19]

Romance – Then came a wind – Death

(*Mrs Willett sighs*) The sad girl is gone. They tried to comfort her.

G.W.B. (Do you want any message sent anywhere?)

It has been sent – Give it him. Oh, she sees him through her – And that's why she cries, because the picture is so dim[20]
(*Mrs W. Laughs*)

You're a very mysterious person – but I like you, though I don't know who you are – I can feel him touching me all down my arm and on my face – He's so near and never will tell me his name[21]

Gone!

Waking stage

What a lot of books!! (*pause*) I've seen a picture of a very old-fashioned girl – flounces and odd sleeves –

Not a crinoline[22] (*pause*) That's all I can remember

(*long pause*)

I saw someone who was unhappy – she wanted to know something and I couldn't tell her –

Notes

(1) Attempt at the name Arthur? A.J.B.'s younger sister Alice often called him 'Artie'.

(2) The Palm Maiden refers to the message of the last script (Willett 290), meant for A.J.B.

(3) Edmund Gurney gives the symbols of M.L. 'Lily' for Mary and 'Wheel' for Catherine – her two Christian names.

(4) From Browning, 'Pippa Passes'. (Kate = Catherine of Cornaro,

the Queen.) Probably this is an attempt to suggest the name Catherine.

(5) 'the dark young man' = Francis Maitland Balfour.

(6) These sentences are somewhat obscure. The name Catherine is still being aimed at, and there has been a reference to a 'Catherine Wheel' in 'fireworks' (see Note (3)). St Catherine of Alexandria whose symbol is a wheel, perished in early youth. St Catherine of Siena, though her name is the same, died at a great age but by the words 'a variant of the Wheel', the communicator may wish to indicate that he is not confusing the two, for the latter was 'not a Highland Mary' – i.e. did not die young. The old song of 'Highland Mary' is appropriate to M.L.'s case. The verse runs

But O! fell Death's untimely frost,
That nipt my bud sae early!
Now green's the sod and cauld's the clay,
That wrap's my Highland Mary.

(7) Is this Hagley Hall? But there is no 'bridge over the river' – perhaps Whittingehame is meant.

(8) There are two poems by Tennyson called 'The Sisters', but I suspect that what F.M.B. wants is an allusion to 'the sisters', i.e. May Lyttelton and Lavinia Talbot.

(9) These were previous references to M.L.'s grave in Hagley Churchyard, in the scripts of other automatists.

(10) The drawing is meant for an arrow though the tail feathers are out of place. 'Pass on' may mean 'pass on to Arthur' (i.e. A.J.B.?): this is a suggestion by G.W.B.

(11) Reference to Palm Sunday, and the entry into Jerusalem – Christ seated upon an ass.

(12) Henry = Henry Sidgwick. Nora = E.M.S. There is probably intended a pun in 'the day of small things' on the name of Lyttelton.

(13) 'the mother' = the mother of Daphne, Mrs Willett herself.

(14) This may refer to Petrarch's love for Laura, cut off by death at twenty-four years old, immortalized in his Sonnets.

(15) J.G.P. – one of the investigators, and interpreters of the scripts, is meant. He subsequently

(16) discovered that here in note (16) there is a double reference between 'the ass', i.e. upon Palm Sunday and the Entry into Jerusalem ('riding upon an ass'); and the 'Poet', i.e. Petrarch. Now Petrarch first saw Laura on 6 April, 1327, and Palm Sunday in 1327 fell on 5 April. Laura died on 6 April, 1348, twenty-one years later; thus that date (6 April) must have been an important one in the poet's life; and as in 1348 Palm Sunday fell on 13 April, another close date, it is very likely that the Church Feast and the loss of his love were connected in *his* memories.

(17) Tennyson's *Morte d'Arthur*, reference to the death of King Arthur

(implicit allusion to A.J.B.). The Three Queens, from other scripts, appear to represent the three ladies of the group in the Other World; one is Annie Marshall (Phyllis); Laura Lyttelton (M.L.'s sister-in-law seems to be the second; M.L. was the third.

(18) Charles Kingsley, 'Oh Mary, go and call the cattle home across the sands of Dee'.

(19) Ben Jonson, 'It is not growing like a tree.'

(20) M.L. only sees A.J.B. through Mrs Willett, so these words suggest: she has no direct contact with him, nor he with her. Is this a reference to the dream experience Mrs W. had of looking at A.J.B. and of 'seeing through into his soul'? Mrs Willett seems to have had an impression of the inner sadness in M.L.'s personality which others had observed during her lifetime.

(21) The mysterious person is F.M.B. again – 'The dark, or the dim, young man.'

(22) '*Not* a crinoline' distinguishes the Palm Maiden from the Balfours' mother, Blanche Balfour, who was of crinoline date.

We now have to consider the Palm Sunday symbols that appeared in profusion, scattered through the scripts of the automatists in the years from 1901 to 1912. The investigators later came to the conclusion that this had been deliberately done as a necessary preliminary planting of clues almost in the traditional detective-story style, so that the subsequent solution to this cryptic set of symbols would provide hard evidence of post-mortem planning.

From 1901 to 1912 scripts were obtained containing words, phrases, symbols, drawings which were often easily recognised but which produced no understanding of why they should have been inserted in the automatic writing of Mrs Holland (in India) and Mrs Margaret Verrall and Miss Helen Verrall (both in England). There were references to the Palm Maiden, May Blossom, Palm Sunday, the Blessed Damozel, the Pilgrim, Berenice, the hair of Berenice and King Arthur. Candles and candlesticks often appeared in words and in drawings: mention was frequently made of a lock of hair; the Greek sigma sign was drawn in its many variations; something purple was mentioned; a metal box containing a precious thing, a periwinkle, scallop shells and an emerald ring were represented. Additionally there appeared Ariadne's Crown, a mention was made of a casket, and a drawing appeared of an ornamented box with the words 'a small gold box highly ornamented and embossed. The blue flowers are periwinkles.' In the script by Mrs Verrall, March 25th, 1907, there was a hint that in sleep immortal things touch the minds of the living and then it was added 'thus does this mortal put on immortality by keeping hold of the things, the true things seen in sleep.' This was interpreted by the investigators as a reference to the famous passage in 1 Corinthians 15.53, about the mortal putting on immortality.

It was in 1912 that Mrs Willett's script communicator asked insistently that Gerald Balfour should sit with her while she produced new automatic writing. This was done. The resulting script said that the earlier scripts from 1901 to 1912 should be re-examined. In a script dated July 6th, 1912, the communicator says 'look back. Far back I come. Years ago I have been beating at the door. Shall I ever reach him?' Responding to hints in the new scripts, the investigators discovered that for over ten years the continued love of Mary Lyttelton for Arthur Balfour had often been referred to obliquely in these old scripts. Nevertheless there were still many references in symbols and drawings that the investigators failed to make anything of.

In 1916 Mrs Willett continued to produce scripts and by then had fully developed her distinctive style of mediumship in which she could 'see' and 'hear' the communicators while still being able to talk to the investigator sitting with her. The Script Intelligence now implored Arthur Balfour to sit with Mrs Willett. He agreed reluctantly to do so. The resulting script now referred explicitly to Mary Lyttelton and to the hitherto unintelligible fragments and clues scattered through the early scripts of the automatists. It wanted them studied again. For the first time, Arthur told his brother Gerald about the action he had taken after Mary's death so many years before. And quite suddenly and convincingly, all became clear to the investigators.

When Mary Lyttelton died in 1875, Arthur Balfour in his grief visited her stricken family. He brought with him a beautiful emerald ring and asked that the ring, which had belonged to his mother, be placed on Mary's finger and buried with her body. That wish was carried out. On another visit to the family in Oxford, Arthur was shown by Mary's sister Lavinia, as she recorded in her diary, 'a beautiful thick and long strand of Mary's hair with the pretty wave and gold colour in it'. The long tress of hair had been kept by Lavinia when Mary's very lovely thick hair had been cut off to relieve the pain in her head during her last illness. Lavinia also records how Arthur Balfour had a beautiful bronzed silver box made for the lock of hair. It was lined with purple satin. Into the lid of the box were engraved periwinkles and other spring flowers. Also worked into the silver was the great text from 1 Corinthians 15.53–54.

> For this corruptible must put on incorruption and this mortal must put on immortality. But when this corruptible shall have put on incorruption and this mortal shall have put on immortality, then shall come to pass the saying that is written, Death is swallowed up in Victory.

The investigators then saw for the first time the full relevance of the multitude of symbols scattered through the 1901–12 scripts. Mary Lyttelton was the Palm Maiden; she died on Palm Sunday; she was called May by her family and friends hence the May Blossom reference; the 'Blessed Damozel' in D.G. Rossetti's poem of that name 'leaned out, From the gold bar of Heaven', and, yearning for her lover, prayed that he would be reunited with her. 'Berenice's Hair' referred to the lock of hair Arthur had had the silver casket made for. In the legend Berenice sacrificed her beautiful hair to the gods for her husband's safe return from war. In fact, the lock of hair was a frequent symbol in the scripts. The periwinkles were represented among the spring flowers engraved on the casket which was lined with purple velvet. In the scripts a casket was frequently mentioned. And in the script by Mrs Verrall, dated March 25th, 1907, there was the explicit reference to the famous passage in 1 Corinthians about the mortal putting on immortality. This was the passage Arthur Balfour had had engraved on the silver box over thirty years before.

But what about the frequent references to scallop shells, candlesticks, stairs, both in words and drawings, the Greek sigma sign, the Pilgrim and King Arthur?

The way they are mentioned – once the investigators were given the key to the solution – made immediate sense. The Greek sigma sign has various forms in the early Margaret Verrall scripts:

$$\Sigma \; M \; \}\; \in \; (\; \odot \; \rightharpoondown$$

All are recognised variations of sigma. The investigators saw that M could be the capital letter of Mary Catherine Lyttelton's first name, (the half-circle form could represent the beginning of her second name while ₷ is actually referred to as a twisted curl. The candlestick, often mentioned or drawn, is also significant, for one of the few photographs of Mary Lyttelton in existence shows her standing at the foot of a staircase and holding just such a candlestick as depicted in the scripts. As for the scallop shells, the Pilgrim and King Arthur, these too made sense to the investigators. The scallop shells appear in the Lyttelton coat of arms and also are alluded to in the nursery rhyme, 'Mary, Mary quite contrary', perhaps a reference to her first name. Arthur Balfour seemed to be very frequently and appropriately hinted at in the scripts by mention of events in the life of King Arthur; he was also referred to as a pilgrim and faithful knight: there were quotations from Tennyson's 'Ode on the Death of the Duke of Wellington' (who in fact was Arthur's godfather after whom he was named). Incidentally, cockle shells or scallop shells were also carried by pilgrims to the Holy Land. Other links refer to Dante and Beatrice, Petrarch and Laura, and other lovers tragically separated by death.

Now the script written by Mrs Willett on Palm Sunday, March 31st, 1912, seemed to convey a message. It could be interpreted, the investigators realised, as coming from Mary Lyttelton to Arthur Balfour and was an attempt to convey to him that she still existed and loved him and waited to be reunited with him. In the delirium of her last illness she had realised that she loved him and was losing him in death. And for a long time afterwards she had tried to get through to him.

Arthur Balfour was characteristically slow in coming to any conclusion about this interpretation. Perhaps, although he still laid aside Palm Sunday in remembrance of the girl he had loved and lost almost forty years before, he did not want to commit himself or open old wounds which had marked his life and were the ultimate reason he had never married. But when he sat with Mrs Willett in 1916, the script produced claimed to be from Mary – it was signed M. Mrs Willett appeared to be asleep, but her hand wrote steadily; A.J.B. supplied her with fresh paper. It was a long and emotional script.

WILLETT 376
19 June, 1916
in the Long Room, 4 Carlton Gardens
(A.J.B. present)

TRANCE SCRIPT

The *May Flower* – the ship that sailed to the New World. But it is not of a ship but of a person I want it said.

The *May Flower*.

A slender girl with quantities of hair worn in heavy plaits – I see her standing in the glade of a Park – over-arching trees. What has she to do with Coma Berenice?[1] (*Spoken*) A question I can't answer.

A.J.B. (*I understand*)

(*Writing resumed*) And add to that Silvery Sirmio – is that understood?

A.J.B. (*No*)

Row us out from Desenzano – another password. There is a connection between the Poem and the Coma but Gerald (G.W.B.) will explain that. There is a *double* connection Sirmio has a literary connection with a Classical poet, and Coma belongs to the same *poet* – that is Association A. Association B is Ave Frater – is that clear? Assisi[2]

A.J.B. (*Yes.*)

Go back to Berenice. I never could make out whether the threads of that had been identified. It has been said Ariadne and Berenice – two constellations compared.[3] The lock of hair – that is the link – is that clear?

A.J.B. (*Yes.*)

The Classical one. Someone said Ptolemy. a *campaign*. Berenice's vow. She cut the lock from her head. It had been there, the poem says, through the years of the past. The vow – Did she offer other Bulls as well?[4]

All these Classical allusions are scattered about and disguise a reality that touches the Blessed Damozel – is that clear? The stars in *her* hair were seven.

As waters stilled at even.

(*Mrs Willett then spoke aloud*):

A man holds before me letters ... I have never known him but I call him the Dark Young Man.

A.J.B. (*What sort of letters?*)

Big square letters – would you like me to copy what he showed me?

(*written*) OXFORD

(*spoken*) He holds another letter up.

(*written*) Lux mundi

 [*Drawing of a lighted candle in a candlestick.*]

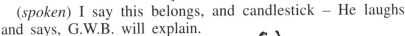

(*spoken*) I say this belongs, and candlestick – He laughs and says, G.W.B. will explain.

(*written*) This – the bearer of this   is here, and tries to give a Salutation

[5]She is standing close to a young man with rather curly hair parted in the middle and small semi-whiskers – can you recognise him?

A.J.B. (*Is it — ? naming another member of the Lyttelton family – a brother.*)

No – Excalibur is the association that makes it clear.[6]

A.J.B. (*Guessing that it must be himself asks: Is it Arthur?*)

Yes, of course.

The May blossom has never ceased to bloom unfading there sweet-scented as in the meadows near her home. She sends the word through a poem REMEMBER[7] and through another sonnet...

 'And if God will
 I shall but love thee better after Death.'[8]

The lock of hair Berenice The symbol.

But oh! behind it lay the beating human heart with all its faithfulness and love, and its passionate belief in the Faithful Knight.

A.J.B. (*I understand – Is there more to tell?*)

Later – and elsewhere – some day at...[9]

Notes

(1) *De Coma Berenices* is the title of Catullus's poem giving the story of Berenice's hair which she cut off and dedicated in a Temple for the safe return of her husband.

(2) 'Silvery Sirmio' and 'Desenzano' are quoted from Tennyson's 'Frater Ave atque Vale', the title of which is taken from the final words of a poem of Catullus, 'Brother, Hail and Farewell'. Is it a greeting from F.M.B.? [The brown *Brother* of St Francis of Assisi's Order.]

G.W.B. noted on the above: ASSOCIATION A – between Tennyson's poem and Catullus's *De Coma Berenice* = the particular brother, F.M.B., and the hair, is clear enough.

ASSOCIATION B seems to refer to the two brothers now associated in this trance, or to F.M.B. and M.L. together on the other side. In the scripts F.M.B. is often represented as helping M.L. to communicate

Mr Shackleton Bailey, a member of the S.P.R., illustrates the connection thus:

Tennyson provides the two associations thus;
A. Sirmio (Catullus)   B. Frater ave atque Vale (Catullus)
Coma (Catullus) = M.L.   Frater = F.M.B.

(3) G.W.B. had asked a question about this.

(4) For 'did she offer bulls as well?' cf Catullus, *De Coma Berenice*, LXVI, 33–4

'Atque ibi me cunctis pro dulci conjuge Divis
Non sine taurino sanguine pollicita es.'

Mr Shackleton Bailey translates:

'And there you promised me to all the gods for your dear husband, not without bull's blood.'

(G.W.B. observed: It seems very unlikely that this detail should have been normally known to Mrs Willett)

(5) Bearer of the two forms of 'Sigma' = M.L.

(6) At first A.J.B. does not recognise that it must be himself. Mrs Willett seems to be seeing a phantasm, as though she was between the two worlds.

(7) Christina Rossetti, 'Remember'.

(8) Elizabeth Barrett Browning, *Sonnets from the Portuguese*.

(9) Note by Jean Balfour, the compiler of this case. In the records blank spaces are left where proper names occur on account of the necessity for privacy. I am sure the word here must be Whittingehame. It was of course assumed by everyone, including I am sure A.J.B. himself, that A.J.B. would die in the ordinary course of events at Whittingehame, his home. But as a matter of fact, he died at Fishers Hill. There follows here the only instance in Willett script of the use of M as signature, and its form is peculiar, suggestive of the Greek 'Sigma' turned over, or even of a W for Whittingehame.

It was after this script that Arthur Balfour, finding the script quite disturbingly meaningful, told his brother Gerald for the first time about the fashioning of the silver box for the lock of Mary's hair.

The scripts continued. In 1926, when Arthur Balfour was old and frail and recovering from pneumonia, he himself wrote Mary a message after a script had been produced begging him to believe in her existence. He said that the message for her should be read to Mrs Willett when she was in the altered state of consciousness in which she wrote her scripts. The message is at the same time austere and moving.

> The message [Mary's message to Balfour] in its essentials is understood by him and is deeply valued... Assuredly he does not require to be told that 'Death is not the end'. Yet there is in her message a note almost of pain which leaves him perplexed. She seems for the first time to find in him a change which although admittedly superficial she dwells on almost with intensity. He knows of none. Half a century and more have now passed. Births and deaths have followed each other in unceasing flow. The hour of reunion cannot be long delayed. During all this period he has had no access to her mind except through the rare intervention of others, no intuition of her presence, although he does not doubt its reality.
>
> Through his complete deficiency in psychic gifts he has no intuition of that 'closeness beyond telling' of which the message speaks with such deep conviction, and which he conceives to be of infinite value. Further messages would greatly help. Of the mysteries of birth he thinks much, but dares say nothing.

Three years later, in October 1929, Arthur Balfour was living with his brother Gerald at Fishers Hill. On the occasion of the general election of that year he visited Bognor to give up his Seals of Office to King George V, thus ending his political career (he had been Lord President of the Council). He was now eighty-one years of age and his health was failing rapidly. Mrs Willett, on a visit to the brothers at Fishers Hill, was sitting quietly in Arthur's room. Present were Arthur and his brother Gerald as well as their sister Mrs Eleanor Sidgwick. Mrs Willett slipped into her disassociated state and had an experience that moved her profoundly. When she came back to normal consciousness she described it as follows:

> Arthur Balfour's sitting-room seemed to be filled with presences – such light, such radiances. In particular there was one figure there – things coming out of that figure – such wonderful things... It was a woman's figure – quite young, dressed in

an old-fashioned dress. Lovely quantities of hair gathered around her head... Impossible to describe all the things that seemed coming from her – the mass of sureness, tenderness and power. It made everything else in the room appear dead while every form of life you can imagine radiated from her. I told G.W.B. (Gerald Balfour) that it seemed as if in a sense Time had vanished.

When you have an experience like that, you know masses that no mere words can describe. If I could only draw – a perfect line can sometimes express what no words can.

WILLETT 420
18 October 1929
at Fishers Hill

This was the last Willett trance.

Mrs Willett agreed to try for script or trance in the sitting-room. A.J.B. was lying on the couch, G.W.B. was prepared to record, and Mrs Willett sat near the couch, with pencil and block before her; but no script was forthcoming, it was all trance-speech this time. The gramophone in the passage outside was playing Bach's Air on a G string. By the time the music ceased Mrs Willett appeared to be asleep; and then began to speak so rapidly, and in such a low voice that G.W.B. had considerable difficulty in recording; and the record, although verbally accurate in the main, may thus be imperfect here and there.

TRANCE SPEECH:

I see people – Oh, I wish I could – there's a message for somebody – (*pause*) There are three people here, and one of them is the dark young man.[1]

He says to me, I'm quite asleep now. And there's another man I don't know, loosely-knit – holding something in the shape of a pear. He says that should identify him – .[2] Then there's the beautiful lady who made me so cold the other night, looking down at somebody in bed.[3]

She's all bright and light, and she says to me, 'How long I have been waiting to send this message!' You know, she's trembling, because she's so eager, and the dark young man

214

explains to her that if the message is to be sent she must control her feelings. And you know she's so full of passionate tenderness that she can't and she keeps on saying 'Oh, my dear, oh, my dear, oh, my dear!'

She says it doesn't make (some words here not taken down) it's only the top of their minds that is blind, but deep down there is something that knows, so it doesn't matter when people cannot stretch out – it's a separate faculty.

She picks up a book, reading aloud, and I hear some of the words – 'We two, we two, will do this together, and I myself will teach him.' Oh, and look here, she says, 'Will you remember and say often to yourself, "Are not two prayers a perfect strength, and shall I be afraid?"'

And in this book that she is reading there is a prayer that she is going to make to Christ, and it ends with the words, 'Together, I and he.'

And she pushed the dark young man away, and poured out such a flood of words that I could never repeat all: and it's all about not to be vexed or troubled, and just to be patient, because everything is so perfectly all right, and she never, never goes away.

And she thinks – well, she had an experience – and then somebody watched beside her until – it was in Spring – and when the time of Hosanna had come, she reached peace – Oh, this is the point about it, for you to remember, that she knows every inch of the road, and there is nothing to mind about it all: Time is nothing.

And she says. 'Oh, my dear, my dear,' and 'that you are never alone.' And she wants you to know that she is absolutely unchanged, and that earth has the broken arc, and heaven the perfect round.

And that's not the future, it's always been. Only she longs to be able to speak, and now she knows you've heard it. Only to know that ... you had great possessions...

(*These last words were imperfectly heard by the recorder.*)

You know, she's so full of peace – she's like a lovely lily. And she says, 'The dark young man is with me, and the lady of the picture in your little room – not in this house.[4] How very different these two people are – the lady of the picture and this peace lady.

215

And she says, 'You'll have to use your imagination to see yourself always with company!' and to try to give as many hours to sleep as possible. She wants you to sleep much more than you do, because when you are asleep you see them and are happy; and always when you wake, you forget. But it doesn't matter, and she knows that you know all about her; and she's not troubling about evidence now – that's done with – It's just companionship. Deep calling unto deep. Such a longing to comfort and help, but underall the absolute certainty of joy.

She's leaning down and stroking. Like that.

(The automatist had taken A.J.B.'s hand and was stroking it.)

and saying – and suddenly she tells me the most important thing she has to say,

'Tell him he gives me Joy'

(Here A.J.B. clutched Mrs Willett's hands fiercely, but she did not seem to feel it in the least.)

How wonderfully happy she is! I've got to go back now. She clings to me; and when I'm asleep she's with me sometimes because her nature is so compassionate and generous.

But the dark young man has a message – not for you, but for Gerald, to say they are satisfied ... they direct, and are satisfied. And the lady with the beautiful eyes says to me – 'You must go back, but I stay here.'

WAKING STAGE

Mrs Willett said, 'I smelt may-blossom' (*long pause*) She then opened her eyes, and addressing A.J.B., whom she was facing, she said, 'For a minute I didn't know you... My head feels full – not uncomfortable but full.'

Notes
(1) Francis Maitland Balfour.
(2) Alfred Lyttelton, M.L.'s brother, the famous cricketer,who died in 1913. He appears in the scripts after 1914, with the emblem of a pear-shaped jewel, or Saxon jewel (such as is associated with the Saxon King Alfred).
(3) This is M.L., and the 'somebody in bed' is of course A.J.B., whom the automatist, in her trance-state, does not recognise.
(4) The lady of the picture – Blanche Balfour, A.J.B.'s mother, whose portrait as a young girl hung in his bedroom at Whittingehame; Mrs Willett had never been into this room.

Arthur Balfour suffered his final illness, a stroke, on March 10th, 1930.

Lady Jean Balfour, the wife of Robert Arthur Lytton, who became the 3rd Earl of Balfour, was present in Arthur Balfour's bedroom when the illness struck. She knew of the love story but not about the tress of hair in the silver box which was still in the keeping of Lavinia Talbot. On the evening of March 10th, she was sitting with Mrs Sidgwick in Arthur Balfour's bedroom as he rested in bed. They were listening to records of Handel's *Messiah*. Lady Jean Balfour wrote an account of her experiences later that month.

Fishers Hill, Woking
March, 1930

On the evening of the 10 March, 1930, I was sitting with E.M.S. in A.J.B.'s bedroom, while the nurse was playing the records of Handel's Messiah on the gramophone just outside the door.

A.J.B. had been a little better the last two days and was, I felt, when I glanced at his attentive face, deeply contented and absorbed in listening to the music he loved with his whole heart. The nurse, having fixed in the records, had gone downstairs.

I had, at first, simply an odd sort of feeling of expectancy, as though anything might happen, and presently I became aware with a sensation of a mighty rushing wind (which was entirely subjective, as nothing around me was even stirred), that the room was full of a radiant, dazzling light. This I felt rather than saw, as a blind person might do, and I started trembling. Now it seemed to me that there were people there too; they had no concern with me, they were invisible; but I knew that they were clustered about A.J.B.'s bed, and that their whole attention was concentrated on him. They seemed to me to be most terribly eager, and very loving and strong; and I recollect feeling a good deal of apprehension because I felt they were there for some purpose, though I did not know what it could be.

I could not stop the trembling, so I was wondering if I ought to go out of the room into the passage for a little while, when it seemed to me that something like a voice within me said, 'You are not to go away,' and I looked at E.M.S. sitting in the armchair to see if she was aware of anything unusual, but she did not appear to be. The music came to the passage where the words occur: 'And in my flesh shall I see God.' At that moment my eyes were compelled to look at A.J.B. His face, transfigured with satisfaction and beauty, seemed to express all the glorious vision which both music and words conveyed; and I stared, fully expecting him to die at that moment, and to pass straight into the Heaven that awaited him on all sides. But his face changed, and then he was shaken with the seizure that marked the last phase of his illness, and I was filled with terror and distress. Perhaps my shock was the greater for having just been upon such spiritual heights; and the extraordinary thing was that I was vividly aware that the feeling in the room had not changed, that the radiant joy and light still thrilled around him, and that the agonising spectacle of the poor body's affliction caused no dismay to those unseen ones who watched, but that it was what they had wanted to happen. That was what seemed to me so incredible as I fled for the Nurse; and as I ran immediately afterwards to telephone for the Doctor, I was saying over and over to myself, 'It was intended – it was intended.'

The idea seemed positively to be burnt into my mind: I had the strange sensation of being two persons, one still lingering in A.J.B.'s room aghast at the callousness of those beings who had appeared so loving, the other doing what was required in the urgency of the moment. Everyone was afterwards so surprised at my promptness: I could hardly say, which was the case, that I had been in a sense prepared! But finally when I returned to normality I found myself with the profound conviction that all was well.

Thinking it over afterwards I began to realise that though to my bodily view it was terrible, to those who see the spirit it may have been simply a fierce effort to cast off the body and set free a soul already with them; and since a merciful unconsciousness accompanies the onset of a stroke we do not know, and never will know, into what peace and joy his soul may have receded in that little space. But the physical constitution was too strong to be thus easily thrown aside, and then he was found to have lost the power of speech, a deprivation of human intercourse which must have been to him a great sadness. During the next ten days he gradually weakened, and died on the morning of the 19 March, 1930.

In her account of the Palm Sunday Case, published thirty years later, Jean Balfour gives her own considered thoughts on a number of aspects of the affair. She wrote:

Certain points arise from the consideration of the 'Palm Sunday' Case as set out in the Willett scripts. One of the things we may observe is that at first sight it appears as if the love between the 'Knight' [A.J.B.] [Arthur Balfour] and the 'Palm Maiden' was stronger on her side than on his. Why else did she make such efforts over so many years to get in touch with him, whereas he never sought for any communication from her.

With regard to A.J.B. we know almost nothing of his own inner thoughts throughout his long life. He was intimate with no one, he was extremely reserved, and he left no private papers beyond a small photograph of M.L. [Mary Lyttelton] in a locked box. What we do know, from his letters to his friend, Edward Talbot, when he was a young man, is that for a period the significance of his loss when M.L. died seemed to grow with the years, and we can have little doubt that her death was the ultimate reason why he never married anybody. We also know that when in middle age he played with the idea of marrying a certain lady for the sake of the family inheritance, he said to E.M.S. [Eleanor Sidgwick], 'But she must understand that I have no heart to offer her – nothing but ashes.' (told to Jean Balfour by Betty Balfour and by E.M.S. herself) So his feelings were evidently exceedingly strong after all those years: and I think that it was largely on account of the strength of those feelings that he was at first an unwilling sitter to Mrs Willett. It was only during his last years that he showed a deep excitement over the scripts which concern this Case as propounded to him by G.W.B. [Gerald Balfour]. Yet there is no record that he ever volunteered any comment, beyond the first incredulity of 1912 upon the various sittings as they occurred which might reveal his true thoughts, and he never sought a sitting of his own wish.

On the other hand, M.L. is represented in the scripts as

being eager, passionate, 'homeless in the heart of Paradise', still hungry for human joys. In judging of this we must remember that all subliminal phenomena are largely influenced by the medium's own mental attitude to these things, and Mrs Willett was a lady of very high emotional sensibility. Many people would find it most distressing to imagine that M.L. might be suffering real grief over what life had never given her. All we know is that she had a warm and ardent temperament, and that at first she found A.J.B. lacking in the usual attributes of masculinity; and we also know that by the time of her death, a very strong and deep feeling had grown up between them both. Her sister's little book of notes certainly bears out the suggestion made in 1912 in WILLETT 292 that she (M.L.) 'never really knew until she got there, across the Sands of Dee', that is to say, across to the other side of death; and perhaps – ? 'that he really loved her as she him' – is what we may legitimately infer was the intended conclusion of that Willett passage. For what the scripts certainly suggest is that she had access to his subliminal mind, and so, presumably, she knew after death, if she did not know before, what had been the true state of his heart; whereas he, on his own testimony, was completely impervious to any intimation which might have invaded his conscious mind from the Other World. What I think is a probable explanation of the language of some of the Willett scripts, notably W.417, is that Mrs Willett, having 'tapped' a poignant memory, not necessarily of M.L.'s own, but it could be from the thought or memory of her family still alive at that date thinking over the events of long ago, magnified the regret by a process of sympathetic distortion, and gave it undue prominence. I think this assumption is legitimate from what we know of the dramatising propensity of the subliminal mind – its effect on Mrs Willett may have caused her to 'harp' on the tragic theme.

There seems to me to be no need to suppose that M.L. was unhappy all those years about a relatively unimportant thing compared with the far bigger and deeper contact which the scripts persistently assert was present between the lovers. As I remarked before, from what we know of M.L.'s disposition it would be more true of her relationship to A.J.B. when Mrs Willett says... 'Tell him he gives me joy', and it is significant that Mrs Willett comments upon this message that 'she (M.L.) tells her that it is the most important thing she has to say'.

Perhaps some people will feel that many questions might have been asked of the 'communicators' through Mrs Willett, and further evidence for this Case obtained. This does not seem to have been done. G.W.B., E.M.S., and J.G.P. were all very old, and the reticence over private affairs which was typical of the generation to which they belonged, seemed to preclude them from making enquiries of A.J.B. about his early memories. Now all are dead.

Yet should we really have gained very much more? Questioning a medium and receiving an answer must always be influenced to a certain extent by the medium's own personal preconceptions, which too frequently confuse and mislead. Also the mere asking of a question opens the door to thought-transference, in which telepathy between the living can never be ruled out. We do not yet know the full extent of subliminal activity, and so it must be admitted that there is nothing in this Case that was not known to somebody somewhere and therefore could not be explained by telepathy from persons still alive who knew, or had once known, the facts.

Whether we regard the 'Palm Sunday' scripts as emanating from personalities in the Other World or not, they do furnish us with a fascinatingly interesting study. Those who devoted years to them certainly felt with increasing conviction that in this phenomena evidence for 'the hand of the Other World' could be found, and that it was evidence of a sort quite unlike anything known hitherto. The scripts also suggest to us a spiritual history of a constant relationship growing with the years on either side of the grave, which, whether we believe in it or not, must set us thinking again on all the spiritual values. From my own point of view, what is valuable to posterity are that the scripts are very nearly our only guides to the profound emotions of A.J.B.'s life. I believe, in spite of the difficulties in interpreting symbolism, that we have here an inward glimpse into the personality of one who but for the scripts might always have been misunderstood.

It is not an easy task to assess the Palm Sunday Case. Many questions may be asked from the viewpoint of psychical research, and an enormous and painstaking amount of research and study must be invested if answers are to be found that are both intellectually and morally satisfying. These questions can be posed on a number of levels.

How much did the automatists, Mrs Willett, Margaret Verrall, Helen Verrall, Mrs Holland and others know, consciously or subconsciously, of the story of Mary Catherine Lyttelton and Arthur James Balfour? Did the group of very intelligent and cautious investigators read far too much into the scripts' contents? What is happening when an automatist is producing automatic writing? Especially what does it mean when someone like Mrs Willett develops as a medium to the point that when she is in an altered state of consciousness she appears to perceive people who are certainly not present in any bodily sense? Can chance coincidence explain the Palm Sunday Case? Can the super-telepathy–clairvoyance theory cover it all? That is, was there a massive, decades-long extrasensory collaboration, indeed a conspiracy between the subliminal minds of honest people, both automatists and participants in the Palm Sunday history? Does the case, with its thirty years of scripts filled by poetic references, symbols, allusions persuade one, if all these other possibilities are found wanting, that the communicators were who they claimed to be? Did Henry Sidgwick, Frederic Myers, Edmund Gurney, Francis Maitland Balfour (the 'Dark Young Man'), Annie Marshall, Laura Lyttelton and Mary Catherine Lyttelton all, on the far side of death, combine to create and transmit the monumental and labyrinthine structures of the Cross-Correspondences to show their continued existence? And did Mary Lyttelton, the Palm Maiden, over the years make strenuous efforts to realise her own agenda to get through to Arthur Balfour and assure him of her continued love? Especially, since she 'never really knew until she got there, across the Sands of Dee' that her love for him was so strong. 'Tell him that he gives me joy' is her message through Mrs Willett, who added, 'she tells me [that is] the most important thing she has to say'.

We are faced, in a way, with the sort of problem encountered in a court of law, for we are dealing with human personality in all its complexity. For myself, after careful study of the case and the scripts I have to dismiss any questions of coincidence or fraud as being wildly improbable. However, with respect to how much the automatists and interpreters knew of the Mary Lyttelton–Arthur Balfour story we can say the following.

Mrs and Miss Verrall and Mrs Holland, who produced the scripts between 1901 and 1912 wherein much of the symbolism, quotations and allusions are entwined, knew nothing of the romance, of the silver box, or of the photo of Mary Lyttelton with the candlestick. Neither did Mrs Willett until she met Gerald Balfour in 1911 and later, in 1915, Dame Edith Lyttelton. Additionally, Gerald and J.G. Piddington deliberately tried to keep Mrs Willett in the dark. As for the interpreters, Gerald Balfour and Mrs Sidgwick knew all the story except the making of the box for the lock of hair. It was only in 1916 that they were told this by their brother Arthur. Piddington knew vaguely that Arthur Balfour in his youth had loved a girl who had died. Alice Johnson knew about Francis Maitland Balfour's tragic death in a climbing accident but there is no reason to believe she knew of the unhappy love affair. Oliver Lodge knew neither of the emerald ring buried with Mary's body nor of the box created for the hair. In fact, only the Lyttelton family, in particular Lavinia, had the whole story.

And it is important to remember that by 1912, the events of the affair lay almost forty years in the past, its memories overlain by a lifetime's fresher memories. It must be remembered, too, that in the crucial Willett script of March 31st, 1912 – incidentally written on Palm Sunday – when the Script Intelligence revealed that Mary was striving to make her continued existence known to Arthur Balfour and asked for the 1901–12 scripts to be re-examined in that light, the investigators, although they now with this help recognised the significance of a multitude of allusions and symbolism, still made nothing of the symbols and allusions referring to the silver box and the lock of hair. Only in 1916 did these become clear when Arthur, as a result of his own sitting with Mrs Willett, told his brother Gerald about the box. I therefore must accept that the most reasonable view is that we are dealing with powerful paranormal activity displayed over decades and involving many minds. Whether all those minds were incarnate or not is another question.

If we are dealing only with incarnate minds – with the results of telepathy and clairvoyance coupled with subliminal dramatisation – then again we have to say that it is on a scale never demonstrated in any parapsychological laboratory. Indeed there is no hard evidence that such a faculty operating in this way even exists. If we dismiss that faculty as the cause, then we must take the survival hypothesis very seriously indeed, though always keeping in mind the thought that the explanation may be totally beyond our finite embodied minds to grasp.

Let this chapter end with a quote from a letter Arthur Balfour wrote to a friend whose son had been killed in the First World War:

> For myself I entertain no doubt whatever about a future life. I deem it at least as certain as any of the hundred and one truths of the framework of the world ... it is no mere theological accretion, which I am prepared to accept in some moods and reject in others. The bitterness lies not in the thought that those I love and have lost are really dead, still less in the thought that I have parted from them forever: for I think neither of these things. The bitterness lies in the thought that until I also die I shall never again see them smile or hear their voices. The pain is indeed hard to bear, too hard it sometimes seems for human strength. Yet, measured on the true scale of things it is but brief: death cannot long cheat us of love.

His last affirmation of faith and conviction is echoed in Elizabeth Barrett Browning's sonnet quoted in the script, according to the Script Intelligence, to get Mary Lyttelton's message through to Arthur Balfour:

> And if God wills, I shall but love thee better after Death.

11

Winifred

We are prisoners on the ship of life, carried on a swift temporal current, signed on for the duration of the voyage. We are conscious of the changing scenes, recording in our memories those that are gone, anticipating, predicting, planning the ship's course, trying to avoid foreseen reefs, attempting to steer for desirable ports yet knowing that the inexorable power of the current we call time will always bear us onwards willy-nilly. We have no anchors strong enough to hold us fast, no engines powerful enough to voyage against the current. Time ... like an ever-rolling stream bears all its sons away.

A Sense of Something Strange, A.E. Roy

During the years of the Palm Sunday Case, 'Mrs Willett' was undoubtedly the most valuable medium of the Sidgwick Group. By 1916 Mrs Piper was still active in the production of automatic writing and Mrs Gladys Leonard had already acquired a justified reputation as a medium of the first rank. 'Mrs Willett', however, was the Sidgwick Group's treasure, prized for her particular form of sensitivity where she could not only write automatically but 'see' and hear the communications while in a semi-trance state. The investigators were understandably concerned to keep her out of the public eye and to study her mediumship in private. It was anonymity that was also welcomed by Mrs Willett herself. She was always a very private person. 'Never give unnecessary information' was a favourite saying of hers. In any case her life and public work as Mrs Winifred Coombe-Tennant would almost certainly have been grossly disturbed and in all probability seriously impaired if the world had learned that she was 'Mrs Willett' the medium.

It is now time to go more closely into Winifred's life, for the circumstances of her 'double life' became such that it deeply affected the lives of those close to her, bringing joy to some and great sadness to others. Even after her death, events occurred that led directly to the vastly important Cummins–Willett scripts, which can be found in the book *Swan on a Black Sea* published by G. Cummins in 1965. Indeed, much of what follows about her life is taken from Professor C.D. Broad's extensive and valuable foreword to that book. (The Cambridge philosopher Professor Broad played an important part in the life of Winifred's youngest son, Henry, being his tutor when he was at Trinity College, Cambridge from 1932 to 1935. He also kept in touch with Henry during the Second World War, even when Henry was a prisoner of war in Germany. Broad was also of course the famous and respected psychical researcher, being the President of the SPR twice in his career, in 1935–6 and in 1958–60.)

Winifred was the daughter of George and Mary Pearce-Serocold, of Derwen Fawr, near Swansea. She was born on November 1st, 1874, and christened Winifred Margaret Pearce-Serocold. Her father led an active and eventful life. Born in 1828, he joined the Royal Navy at the age of thirteen, seeing service in the First Anglo-Chinese War (1839–42). In 1842, as the youngest midshipman in the fleet, he had the honour of carrying on a silver salver the document which on signing would become the Treaty of Nanking. Later in his naval service he was engaged in the suppression of the slave trade. He also spent ten years sheep-farming in Australia. Winifred's mother, Mary, was her father's second wife.

Much of Winifred's education, not unusual in Victorian times for a girl, took place at home. It is fair to say that in some respects it was more than adequate; in others it was decidedly sketchy. Much later in her life she revealed to Jean Balfour that in her teenage years she suffered tremendously from shyness.

On December 12th, 1895, just into her twenty-second year, Winifred married Charles Coombe-Tennant of Cadoxton Lodge, Glamorganshire. The name Cadoxton is derived from the sixth-century Welsh saint and martyr Cadoc, whose name appears in a number of Welsh place names such as Llangattock. Winifred's husband was twenty-two years older than her and was a member of a remarkable family that had been settled at Cadoxton for a number of generations. His father Charles Tennant (1796–1873) was for a part of his life a Member of Parliament, while his mother, Gertrude Barbara Rich Collier (1819–1918) was a descendant of Oliver Cromwell through his daughter Frances. The first twenty-four years of her life were spent in France, where she knew a number of eminent Frenchmen such as Flaubert, Gambetta and Renan. After she married, she held a salon at her house in Richmond Terrace in London for many years. Among the eminent Victorians who visited regularly were Gladstone, Ruskin, Tennyson, Thomas Hardy and George Eliot. Almost up to her death in 1918 at the age of ninety-nine she retained her clarity of mind and her interests.

It was Charles Coombe-Tennant's paternal grandfather, George, who first settled in Glamorganshire. He had abundant energy and a keen head for business. Over the years, he added to the land he owned, and from 1817 to 1824 he constructed the Tennant Canal from Swansea to the Brecon Hills. His grandson, Charles Coombe-Tennant, was therefore a man of property and Jane Austen's dictum that 'It is a truth universally acknowledged, that a single man in possession of a fortune must be in want of a good wife' comes inevitably to mind. Of his three sisters, one, Eveleen, married Frederic Myers in 1880, just two years before he helped to found the SPR, while another sister, Dorothy, married the famous explorer H.M. Stanley. One cannot help wondering what they thought of their brother marrying a woman half his age.

Cadoxton Lodge, Glamorganshire, became Winifred's home after she became Mrs Charles Coombe-Tennant. Her first child, Christopher, was born at Cadoxton Lodge on October 10th, 1897. After her marriage – which seems to have been a happy one – her shyness appears to have largely disappeared. Family records tell of her gaiety as a young wife and the enjoyment of a busy social life. Her husband, so much older than her, gives an impression of having been a kindly, tolerant, peace-loving gentleman. By now, also, she had gained the status of 'lady of the manor', fulfilling the romantic ambitions of many young women of that era. Tragedy struck, however, in 1908.

Although Winifred, as Jean Balfour put it, was a lady who had a very strong predilection for maternity, Christopher's birth had been a difficult one and he was in serious danger of losing his life when born. It was not therefore until 1905 that she found herself longing for another child. This desire persisted until it became a daily thought. She consulted her doctor, whose opinion was that she was now thoroughly strong and healthy and that in the case of a second child he did not think there would be any risk. On January 6th, 1907, at Cadoxton, she gave birth to a daughter, who was named Daphne. The little girl did not live long. She died in Chelsea, London, after five days' illness shortly after midnight on the night of July 20–21, 1908; she was just one year and seven months old. From all accounts, the child, even at that early age, had shown a particularly attractive and loving personality. Indeed Sir Oliver Lodge wrote of her: 'From the testimony of those who knew the infant I judge that nothing less than genius will account for the impression she made.'

Such a tragic and unexpected loss had a shattering effect not only on the mother but also on Christopher, then eleven years of age. Apart from her grief, which was naturally profound, Winifred now became introspective and brooding, and would hardly see anyone. Many years later, her second son, Alexander, told Jean Balfour that, 'whereas as a girl she was very sociable, loved parties and was of a gay, happy nature; after Daphne's death, she shut herself up from all society for a considerable period, she was so completely grief-stricken.' At this time, she started to keep a journal in which she noted her daily thoughts and the events in her life. According to Jean Balfour, 'although I have never read any of it, I know of part of it, and it seems that her whole world had disintegrated with the loss of the child. It was suggested to me by one of her sons that the father was at a loss to understand this profound and long-lasting sorrow, or at least was unable to comfort her.'

It was during this period of grief and retirement from the world that she took up automatic writing and began a correspondence with Mrs Verrall. She also became a member of the SPR. Winifred knew that Mrs Verrall had the ability to write automatically and apparently had received communications from the deceased Frederic Myers. In the letter she sent to Mrs Verrall she told her about the death of her daughter: 'I wanted to tell you at once – so that no allusion might be lost or misunderstood in any communication... If through any channel any word of her comes, you will tell me – for I am her mother... I knew and loved F.W.H.M. [Frederic Myers].' (Mrs Verrall at that time had met Winifred only twice, once at Leckhampton House, Myers' house at Cambridge, some twelve years before, and once at a meeting of the SPR: 'But we had no conversation beyond a word or two. I knew that she had a house in Wales. I also knew that she was the mother of a boy of 10 or 11, but I did not know that she had a younger child, and I had not seen any notice of the child's death.') From this approach, Winifred came to believe that she had received sound evidence through Mrs Verrall and her daughter Helen's automatic writing, not only that Daphne had survived death but also that her short life had been foretold in their scripts. W.H. Salter, in his 1963 paper in the SPR *Proceedings*, 'The Rose of Sharon', made a careful assessment of the value of this evidence, and evidently took it seriously. Winifred's own belief in survival was expressed in her words that death is 'no more than a doorway admitting to a fuller and freer life'. When the First World War broke out and her son Christopher was on leave from Flanders, they agreed that if he died in the war, he was to try to find on the other side his uncle by marriage, Frederic Myers, as well as his sister Daphne. He was always to keep in mind that his mother would believe in his continued existence and that contact would continue.

As with so many of his generation, Christopher Coombe-Tennant died in the trenches on September 3rd, 1917, just before his twentieth birthday. Educated at Winchester, he passed into Sandhurst as a prize cadet. In 1917 he joined the Welsh Guards and crossed to Flanders on August 9th. After his death a memoir, *Christopher*, was compiled by Sir Oliver Lodge with Winifred's cooperation and published by Cassell in 1918. He does seem to have had an extremely fine character. As C.D. Broad puts it: 'His letters, his actions, and the many moving tributes paid to him after his death by persons of all ranks of society, show him to have been ... gentle, sensitive, and highly intelligent, yet courageous and spirited, with a deep appreciation of beauty in nature, in human character, in literature and in art ... The vast majority of the letters in *Christopher* are between him and his mother ... It is plain from them that there was an extremely close link between mother and son. The father is very little in the picture, and one might be inclined to infer ... that he played a somewhat minor role in a predominantly matriarchal household. Lodge states, however, that Charles Coombe-Tennant had much to do with Christopher when the latter was young, and that their relations remained intimate and almost fraternal up to the end. They used to play chess, billiards, and picquet together; and Christopher, who ... had intended to pursue his studies at Trinity College, Cambridge, was initiated into Greek by his father.'

The preparation of Christopher's memoir had an unexpected consequence on the close friendship between Winifred and Gerald Balfour, who had been her principal sitter for so many years. When she asked him to write a foreword to the memoir, he did so but what he wrote was not sufficiently eulogistic to please her. His daughter-in-law Jean Balfour recalled his undisguised astonishment at her response: 'She was utterly unreasonable, she wanted me to depict him as being not only extremely remarkable but almost perfect – he was neither.' Winifred never forgave him although as far as Augustus Henry, her youngest son, was concerned, she continued to write to him, he being his godfather, and to discuss with him every detail of the child's development and schooling.

On September 7th, 1917, the day after news of Christopher's death had arrived, his mother wrote in a letter, 'He is to me as if just out of a severe operation... He will soon get his bearings there and whether he does it happily and easily depends on what telepathic impressions he gets from us – especially from me.' These calm words, expressed with such certainty, exhibited her spiritual development, her present positive attitude to life, its challenges and its vicissitudes and for the last half of her life she exemplified these virtues in her private and public service.

By the time Christopher died, Winifred had had two other children, both boys. Alexander was born on November 20th, 1909 and Augustus Henry on April 9th, 1913. Her husband Charles died on November 5th, 1928, in his seventy-seventh year. By that time Alexander had entered Trinity College, Cambridge, his brother Henry following him four years later. Professor C.D. Broad recalls in the foreword to *Swan on a Black Sea*:

Henry ... read Moral Science (in which he displayed outstanding ability), [and] was my pupil during the whole of his time at Cambridge. We soon became very good friends, and we have kept in touch with each other from that day to this [1965]. While he was up at Trinity I met his mother occasionally when she visited him in Cambridge, and I still possess a collection of Emily Bronte's poems which she gave me. Soon after he went down I met her once or twice at her London home (then in Portland Place), when calling on him. While he was a prisoner of war in Germany I had some correspondence with her about sending books to him... She struck me (if I may say so) as a somewhat formidable lady, and I admired the way in which Henry, ... combined perfect politeness and respect towards her with complete refusal to be dominated by her.

I had not the slightest idea at the time, or indeed until it was made public after her death, that she had mediumistic gifts and had regularly exercised them. Still less did I suspect that she was the famous 'Mrs Willett', whose mediumship had played so important a part in the history of psychical research in the first quarter of this century.

When her youngest son Henry entered Trinity in 1932, Winifred was in her late fifties, and had long been committed to her life of public service. In that continuing life which took up a large part of her time and energies she perhaps inevitably developed the calm, strong, efficient magisterial carapace that seemed increasingly to control and submerge the altered state of personality she formerly had turned into as Mrs Willett.

Not unexpectedly, in the years before the First World War she had been a keen supporter of the votes for women movement. During the war she served on a number of committees and in 1920 became a Justice of the Peace. She was a Visiting Justice at Swansea prison from 1920 to 1931 and was active in politics. In 1922 she stood as Liberal candidate for the Forest of Dean constituency. She was also an enthusiastic Welsh nationalist, not surprising when it is remembered that she was of Welsh descent on the side of her mother, Mary Richardson of Derwen Fawr. When the League of Nations was formed after the war, she was appointed as a delegate by the British Government to its assembly. Not content with these duties, she entered fully into the artistic life of Wales, being honoured on a number of occasions for her services. All in all she was a woman to be respected and was thought by many to possess a high intelligence and a deep practicality about life. A comment by C.D. Broad in this regard is of interest:

she was one of the many conspicuous counter-instances to the silly popular belief that a person with mystical or mediumistic gifts must *eo ipso* be 'moony' and incompetent in practical affairs. Other notable counter-instances, within the circle of the S.P.R., were Mrs Verrall, her daughter Helen … and Dame Edith Lyttelton. And, if we care to go further afield and to look higher, we might mention St. Birgitta of Sweden, St. Teresa of Spain, and Florence Nightingale, as women conspicuous for energy, business ability, and outstanding practical achievement, who would have made a very poor showing on the currently accepted tests for bodily and mental normality and psychological integration.

Jean Balfour gave an assessment of Winifred from a different perspective:

I did not know her very well. I doubt if anyone knew her *well*. She was handsome, on a large scale, and moved with energy and decision. The first time I ever met her, she showed me how to wrap up a baby in the approved Welsh style. My son Gerald was the baby and he strongly disapproved!

She was essentially a primitive person but this is not to say that she did not have a very good brain without being at all 'intellectual' – she was practical, rather, and had, I should say, considerable executive ability without much psychological insight, but then she was not particularly interested in *people*, nor was she a lover of causes. She was a tremendous individualist, being a person of few, though very powerful ideas deeply rooted in the sphere of her emotions. She regarded everything in relation to herself and those she cared for. The people who loved her best were I think those who depended upon her – they would get the best out of her: she was a strong personality and everybody knew it.

Over the years, the changing priorities of Winifred's interests, her work and her worries are evident from her letters. On Sunday June 13th, 1920, she wrote to Gerald Balfour:

I've not written before as I wanted to post in S. whither I have to go on Tuesday, and I wanted your Cambridge visit to be over. No doubt I shall read in the Times of your functions there…

I came home to a great arrear of work – to a quantity of

domestic matters and to many unanswered letters – and to general toil. And I've been steadily going at it from morn till night until now I can say that I am more or less even with it all and should be able to meet each day's special business without finishing early or late. Today I stole a couple of hours in the garden, my first real visit to it – your Delphiniums in great beauty and a wonderful show of white fox-gloves – the roses seem to be doing very badly. W.O. [the Wise One = Henry] disports himself on the lawn like a young lamb. He looks very well and handsome – grown and filled out and I long for you to see him, which – please God – you will soon do. C. [her husband] went up to RT on Thursday for 2 or 3 weeks: this eases my existence... Meanwhile we are in difficulties with our workmen – wages! – and nearer home I have the annoyance of looking for a good Cook-Housekeeper... Also I'm not satisfied with the chauffeur, who is very idle and driving carelessly. It is difficult to keep an idly inclined manservant up to the collar, and C. is no use even were he here. Home-life involves much patience these days. I have 6 servants if you include the chauffeur, at exorbitant wages and am nowise as well served as in the days when I had three at far lower scale. I must go off to bed now and will finish this tomorrow. How thankful I am that poor Ral is over his immediate ordeal – how he has suffered, that boy – it is a pain even to think of it – what must it have been to have gone through!

Tuesday, 9 a.m.

I am adding a few lines before I start [out]. A lovely day, hot and still. I hope you have the same for your ceremonies.

I have good accts. of A. [Alexander] and he is now playing cricket. My days are more or less alike here. Yesterday I chaired a long hot meeting of garrulous women – tomorrow we have Pensions Committee – the Ministry has destroyed our present organisation and dismissed our staff by the end of this month and has completely failed to act ... nor can we do so as any scheme of ours has to be 'approved by the Ministry'. There is evidently chaos up in London – and we are simply carrying on as best we can.

The early years of the Second World War were a time of almost unbearable anxiety to her. She had suffered the death of her eldest son, Christopher, in the First World War. Now, on the outbreak of

233

the Second World War, there was the ever-present possibility of her being also robbed by war of her youngest son, Henry. Like Christopher, he also had joined the Welsh Guards. In the debacle of 1940 he had been taken prisoner at Boulogne with others of the Second Battalion thirty-six hours after the last ship had left. He spent the following two years at an Oflag in Germany. Later, in August 1942, he escaped with two of his fellow prisoners and after a long and hazardous journey through occupied Europe made it back to England. There he became involved in intelligence work, at times in extremely dangerous circumstances. In 1944 he was dropped behind the German lines in France to help the Maquis.

Early in 1945 Jean Balfour sent Winifred Henry's last letter to his godfather, Gerald Balfour, written from Holland when Henry was with General Hodge's forces. Sadly, the letter had arrived two days after Balfour's death. In her covering letter Jean commented on the unique friendship between Henry and his godfather, how happy they were together, the way they used to sit, sometimes talking, sometimes silent for hours together, in perfect companionship, where the difference in age simply did not count. Jean added that she felt uncertain that she and Ral would see Henry often in the future, unless they 'could live far more in London, for it was above all GWB whom Henry came to see and though he was always charming to us, I did not feel he had a great deal in common with us; his interests were, I thought, so much more intellectual than Ral's or mine.' Winifred's reply, Jean noted, was most typical of herself and she remembered saying to Ral, 'She must be almost alarming as a mother and perhaps that is why neither Alexander nor Henry has ever married. I should hate to be her daughter-in-law!' Here is Winifred's reply in full:

N.B. Henry's address: 25/2/45
Major Coombe-Tennant, M.C.,
1st Battalion Welsh Guards,
British Liberation Army.

My dear Jean,
I am so glad to have your letter – and thank you for sending me Henry's of 15th, which just missed his godfather. They had indeed a close community of spirit and great delight in each other's company. But you have got Henry all wrong when

in people: and as a result she resented a lot of people, and had not a great many friends: she was very quick at sensing who liked her.

I visited her in London a few times after GWB's death: she was I think very unhappy. I suppose she had begun to realise that Henry might not have it in him to be all that she had once believed possible. She became rather bitter about him – and on one occasion she broke out to me that he had been *ruined* by the War, by the prison camp, and by his friends in the Army. Before the War he had been 'full of promise' – now he was 'different'.

As far as I could see, the experiences of the War, the prison-camp (where at least he had not been ill-treated, but had had a piano and other ameliorations) and the companionship of his men-friends, had all contributed to Henry's maturity – he had grown up, and perhaps grown away from her, as sons do. But it seemed to me that she could still have retained friendship with him and shared many mental interests. (She was pleased with the fact that every evening she went downstairs to dinner on his arm!) It was on this occasion that I *urged* her to talk to him about psychic subjects, and to tell him about her secret life in it but the idea seemed to upset her, and she wouldn't even consider it. This would have brought mother and son closer together.

As I knew from Henry, he was extremely interested in such things, and tried on several occasions to draw her into talking, but she always put him off, saying that *she* was fully convinced of the reality of the spiritual world, and that he should go and talk to Professor Broad, for Henry had a questioning mind.

The next time I saw her she didn't even want to talk about Henry, but the mention of Alexander's little family brought a gleam of light into her eyes.

4th June, 1945.

My dear Jean,
Your train-writ letter of 28th May came today but you don't give me any address so that I must send this up to Whitt[ingehame] & it will take days to reach you. When Henry's Welsh Guards Battalion got back from Germany to rest and refit he volunteered

again to rejoin his Parachute Allied Service and on May 22, after being kept waiting in a camp near here (in company with Queenie), he was flown to an airfield near Hamburg as Senior of 3 officers. First news of him came 1st June. He is attached to H.Q. 1st French Army & is assisting in the evacuation of Channel Islanders, close to Lake Constance – having motored the whole length of Germany from North to South. He says I cannot write to him as letters would not reach him. He passed through Frankfort and Hanover ... all a mass of ruins. Heidelberg undamaged. They slept each night in small villages – the Germans very 'docile' – but as without any escort I judge it was a risky job as pockets of Nazis remain in semi-hiding. I only wish this trouble with Syria had not arisen – the French so sore now. Fortunately Henry is persona grata to the French military authorities with whom he has served before now, in the Maquis – and he gets on well with them and speaks French well. I have put your letter among a number to show him whenever he gets back. He is set on going to the Far East – so my heart is pretty heavy! But he is a wonderful person and has built up a great reputation in the Army. Alexander still in Athens. Horrible weather here – gales and rain but fine most of Saturday when 4th of June observed. Henry hasn't had any leave for some time. I know how much he would like to get up to Scotland if he could.

I hope your boy Gerald is all right. I saw he had been ill on some journey. Looking out over Europe today it is difficult to see any Peace!

Will you let Mary have Henry's news. As you know he is not a letter writer.

Ever yours,
Winifred Coombe-Tennant

4/12/45

Dear Jean,
I was indeed glad to get your letter ... the vanishing of [indecipherable] summed up under the words 'Fishers Hill' has left a yawning gap in my life, never to be filled. I am desperately tired in mind and body and should much like to

curl myself up and & go to sleep – to wake somewhere *not here!*

Henry. So far away on the Palestine–Lebanon Frontier. He went off in command of P. of Wales Coy. 1st Battalion Welsh Guards at the end of September ... and is now 50 miles from his Battalion in complete contentment with the country, his own life, and its setting. He has freedom and power being i/c of troops of his own. In a later letter he says he's making roads and planting vegetable gardens – expecting to ascend Mount Hermon (white with snow) on donkey-back – was visiting Damascus and in 7 days expected leave preXmas hoping to get a jeep to explore Transjordania and Iraq ... the enclosed letter tells you something of his doings and contentment – I'm thankful but anxious, and of course, hungry for his rare and irreplaceable companionship. Will you send his letter on to Mary with my love, and tell her she is often in my thoughts. I'm afraid she *must* send it back to me, as I've no secretary and not enough time to type it again, being submerged in horrible business affairs of both Alexander & Henry, who have left me with Powers of Attorney!

Henry took dog Queenie with him in the troopship, contrary to all regulations. She is well and happy after an encounter with a water-buffalo in which she got kicked and went lame for 3 days. Henry's Welsh servant adores her & she rules the camp!

Alexander: At Intelligence HQ near Hanover & hoping Foreign Office will release him at the end of January. After nearly 2 years in Egypt and Athens he finds Germany a great change & will be glad to get out of it.

West Domus! ... When you go there will you look and see if my Christopher's memorial in the Chapel is intact – a cheerful Della Robbia bas-relief, & tablet below, very breakable through blast and I'd like to know if still *in situ.*

Myself Yes, I hope to be back in London sometime in January, and will let you know. I should be so glad to see you. I've been cut off from everybody for 6 dark desolating *homeless* years in Norfolk, Monmouthshire, & (suburban) Windsor! I'm to see Helen Salter too ... 10,000 years since we met ... Her mother Oh rara avis! A burning vital soul, well laced with donnish steel and granite – but essentially an *illuminati* – the eagle and the dove.

I feel a return to London will restore to me some of the links I've never ceased to value – and to hunger for. That unique Fishers Hill group. DD Lyttelton will be accessible – Dear Pidd marooned in hated Somerset ... the next generation of Balfouriana inevitably totally unknown to the Ancients. I don't even know how many children you've got ... nor whether any Reithians married – nor what has happened to Carolus & Co ... a vanished world. There is a wonderful passage in Chateaubriand's *Memoirs d'Outre Tombe* in which he speaks of the groups he has known ... assembling ... revolving ... vanishing. Of course life has always been like that!

I can't go back to my house as [it is] blast-damaged ... shall be in a service flat pro tem – I want eventually to find the unattainable ... someone ... to come and lend me a hand with life in general until I reach Journey's End ... I don't know whether I shall go back to my big London house – I see no daughters-in-law in the offing. I should like to spend my remaining years encompassed by liberty and rest!!

As you will see I am of those who cry for the moon.

Fare you well – I will send on your messages to Henry. He writes a weekly letter full of his doings and ruminations.

Ever yours,

W.C.T.

London 1/11/46

Dear Jean,

I have sent on your letter to Henry and am asking Mr Pid to send on to you a copy of the latest news I have from Henry – which I don't want back. I am glad you are to be in Edinburgh through the winter ... better I feel sure. No time for more now. Ever yours, W.C.T.

80 St James's Court
Buckingham Gate
London, S.W.1

27/1/47

Dear Jean,

This is to give you news of Henry. I can't remember whether I wrote and told you that he'd left Palestine, having been given a very good staff appointment as a member of a Military Mission to Saudi Arabia, a job entirely after his own heart. The Mission is led by a Brigadier and consists of 8 officers and 25 Non-Commissioned officers – its base will be in the desert, inland from Mecca & 5000 feet above sea level. They are being flown in at the present moment, to Jedda on the Red Sea. Henry is Deputy Assistant Adjutant and Quartermaster General. They will at times move about on camels and in Arab dress! It is a 3 year appointment and carries high grade, pay, and good leave – so that he hopes to be back on leave next winter. You can imagine I am thankful to have him out of Palestine. He has been in Cairo for the past 2 months, up to his eyes in preparations and expects to be off now within a week – accompanied by Jacko, one of Queenie's six months old sons – said to be 'a grand dog'.

Henry has been learning Arabic ever since he went to Palestine in October 1945 – and he has been much in the desert in Trans-Jordan – & done immense journeys there in T.E. Lawrence's tracks. He loves the desert and its way of life – as indeed I do, though I only know it from brief visits to Morocco, Algeria and Egypt. I enclose an extract from the regimental history of the Welsh Guards (not wanted back of course) which refers to him.

I'm still tied to this flat because, just as I was about to go back to my house, the engine of the oil-burner that supplies hot water & central heating went wrong and had to be sent to the makers for repair – on a waiting list! I shall not be able to move before the end of March, much to my annoyance. It is a frightful business getting in anyway after more than 7 years away from it. I have a good Secretary–Chauffeuse–Housekeeper, an ex-Wren who was Catering Officer and Quarters Officer for some years and who is to run the house for me – she had hoped with a WREN crew – but so far has only a Cook in hand.

I hope all is well with you and yours. The cold here is Arctic and snow falling steadily. I've never been shut up in the U.K. so long before and just pine for sunshine, warmth and foreign parts! Please let me have your news. I see D.D. [Dame Edith Lyttelton] at times – much aged and very ailing.

Farewell. Kind greetings from yours ever,
Winifred Coombe-Tennant.

30 August 1948

Dear Jean,

Henry asked me to send you a copy of the book which gives an account of his escape from Germany in 1942 & which has been written by one of the two men who escaped with him – *Return Journey*.

It gives such a picture of the courage and resource of the Resistance Movement in Denmark, Belgium & France – little understood or appreciated here because we were never 'occupied' by the Germans.

Henry is away on duty pro tem and left in a hurry or would have written himself. The world is so full of conflict that we none of us can feel any security.

I think of you, dear Jean

Ever yours,

Winifred Coombe-Tennant

Winifred was now almost seventy four years of age. As the years passed and they began to take their toll of her health, her public-service duties continued to diminish in number, though she still struggled to carry out some engagements. Her world was contracting; the certainties she had entertained about the future were crumbling. The anxieties she felt concerning her remaining two sons, the seeming deterioration in the world about her and her increasing incapacity coloured her attitude to life, doubtless engendering the feelings of resignation and disappointment pervading her subsequent letters to Jean Balfour. During the last few years of her life she resided at 18 Cottesmore Gardens, Kensington, London.

27. IV. 52

My dear Jean,

I was very glad to get your letter. The main purport of this one is to ask you to remind the Salters that neither Alexander nor Henry have the least idea of who Mrs Willett is.

I agree that it is essential that you and they should add to yourself a small group of trustworthy people of about your own age to increase the actual number of the Guardians of the Scripts, & to allow one or two more people to begin to study the material on the lines laid down by GWB and JGP.

This is the sole way of ensuring Continuity. Whether the unprinted more important documents could be typed & copies deposited outside this country I don't know – but European conditions make their destruction an anticipabable [*sic*] risk. You are right I am sure not to aim now at bringing in what Fishers Hill used to call 'Young Grinders'. None have spare time nor the background qualifying them for such work.

I envy JGP! I have never been more tied in all my life... This is a largish house to run. I have a lot of work of my own and now Henry's correspondence on my hands. I have a resident Secretary-Housekeeper who is no good & very disagreeable to live with. She has been with me a year and is a good typist – essential to me – I pay her £4 a week & long to replace her by someone who would take the housekeeping entirely off my hands, in June, and be a friendly soul pleasant to live with – especially now that I live here alone with 3 maids. If you hear of anyone remember me. I have to go to Wales on May 7 for a week to open an Art exhibition in Swansea, a great effort.

Ever yours, dear Jean.   W.C.T.

At the top of the letter scrawled sideways across it is: 'My greetings to Ral. I hope his new work still enables him to live at home.'

1952–21–X

My dear Jean,

I *was* so glad to hear from you – your letter found me in Wales where I was on the Glamorganshire Coast in a small quiet Hotel almost in the sea looking across to the Devonshire Coast – Parthcawl. I was there a month, my first holiday for over a year. I got back to London on the 13th and found chaos in the house ... my Secretary-Housekeeper down with influenza and Cook almost living at the Dental Hospital – my parlourmaid having walked out without notice 3 days previously ... Life has been full of toil and worries. I've got piles of unanswered letters – I am dog-tired – enough of my woes! Henry was posted for 2 years at the beginning of April into the American Zone of Western Germany (Intelligence) where he lives in a large country house, fed like a fighting

cock, staying in castles with rich complacent Huns …
the whole country bursting with food and amenities! I of
course know nothing of his work but he moves around a lot
and has been up to Berlin once … is working *very* hard I
gather a persona grata to the Americans and to the Huns!
I sent you a copy of a letter I had from him recently which
will amuse you and Ral – he has been back (by air) once
for three days … says nothing of future visits. You can imagine
how I miss him and how dull I find life without him! I
am i/c of his bullterrier. Alexander is now a partner in his
firm (Cazenove) and also an enthusiastic farmer – he has taken
over two farms on his estate in Wales and has Friesian Dairy
cows – pedigree. Some from the Rayleigh-Strutt herd. He goes
down at weekends when he can – has a hardworking Danish
Bailiff.

I live here in a too large house which I can't run under 3
servants – am full of work of one sort or another – if anyone
could be free to attend to it without interruptions. In the
autumn was broadcasting in the Home & Overseas Services
… opening Art Exhibitions in Wales – young painters always
coming and going – my land in S. Rhodesia giving me much
to think about & but a small income – but still solidly there
– & Alexander thinks any paper money may become almost
worthless – he takes a gloomy view of the future of the U.K.
– Taxation & labour troubles – disappearance of the habit of
hard work – inability to live hard and the general international
situation … thank goodness I have not got a long lap to travel
through.

Where is Mary – I thought she was out in Kenya. Eve
[Lady Eve Balfour, founder of the Soil Association] I know
is in scientific agriculture … where do Caroline & K live –
what news of Nellie & the two red-heads?

Do let us meet if and when you come to London.

I wish my sons would marry – no sign of it. I gather Henry
has got a sort of K position & did well in the War Office –
he was there 3 years and lives at home. His address is Park
House, Tannenwald, Frankfurt, Germany.

Give my love to Ral. Even you 'Young Grinders' are getting
older! As for me I am Methusela.

Love from W.C.T. What is big Whittingehame now?

1st February 1954

My dear Jean,

I was so glad to get your letter and have often thought of you, but as I have been making my bed in Hell between work, business and family matters etc., I have had more or less to give up all personal correspondence.

I so much look forward to seeing you and Wednesday the 10th is quite all right for me if later on you find that it suits you. Peaceful tea at time of your choice is what I suggest. You must let me know.

As for Henry, he has just had good promotion. He was second in charge of his Unit in the American Occupied Zone of Germany, and is now 1st in charge of the Unit of his special Service at Headquarters of British Troops in Austria. He has only been there a few weeks but is entirely pleased with his surroundings, companions and status and has the best sort of ski-ing at his door. He has spent one day in Vienna and will shortly be moving into a house of his own, which he looks forward to because he is tired of living in a Mess. There is no chance of his being back in this country until after mid-April and usually he only comes for about three nights, flying both ways.

Of course, I miss him very much, and my one comfort is that he has left his dog with me, a Staffordshire Bull Terrier who brings some sort of life into the house. Alexander is living in a flat of his own nearby and still unmarried to my great regret.

I have to dictate my letters as my right arm and hand troubled by arthritis and I have to save them as much as I can.

I am broadcasting a 15 minute talk on the BBC Welsh Home Service on 9th February from 8.15 to 8.30 p.m.

à bientôt

Ever yours,
Winifred

Many years earlier, before the Second World War, when Winifred had visited Whittingehame after Arthur Balfour's death, she revealed to Jean a great fear of sudden death. She thought it the most

245

terrible thing that could happen to anyone. Jean was surprised at this; she had supposed that a person to whom the other world would be not only very real, but almost familiar, would not have been so much afraid at crossing over. She thought it showed the deep contrast between 'Mrs Willett', who in trance did not always want to come back to this world, and Mrs Coombe-Tennant. It was the latter, she thought, who said to her that she felt 'there should be time to make peace with God and to be prepared for death, if possible, by a long illness.'

Winifred's own case must have come close to what she wanted. Her health was latterly very poor, but her last days brought her the satisfaction of Alexander's marriage and good news of Henry. Characteristically, in a letter to Jean, she had a few complaints to make about what seemed to her the tardiness of her passing, rather in the manner of one who is unaccustomed to waiting in a draughty station for an annoyingly late train.

27 2 55

I am so sorry to have been long in answering your letter ... so full of interesting news. Life rushes on and I find it difficult to keep up with it and the doings of my friends. I've been fearfully ill ... a year ago I got a severe attack of shingles from which I have never completely recovered & learned that people who get it at my age often never do. I wouldn't in the least mind dying and not go on living like this, always feeling ill and good for nothing and getting gradually worse is a tiring and dispiriting business. At the moment I am living chiefly in bed.

Alexander made a most happy marriage in September to a delightful girl – all I could have chosen – and [they] are very happy.

Henry after 2 years in Germany and one in Austria is at the moment posted to the War Office, but no one can say for how long. At the moment he is in Oxford. He is dreadfully overworked and goes to Austria on the 6th for 3 weeks skiing holiday – where then I don't know. I'm sure he'd love to come up for a flying visit and when I see him I'll tell him April would be good for you. Talk was he was to be sent to Sweden but the only thing War Office Intelligence ever reveals is that they know nothing whatever until they suddenly say

'In a fortnight you go to...' He expected Far East as he'd travelled there about 1930 – was very glad to have even a brief spell of the U.K. Is still in the Welsh Guards...

Dear Jean, I think of you and all your family ... & hope I can soon change my world! People live too long! Helen came to see me not long ago ... must have been after a year's interval, I think. Both her children living away from home... Told me no solution of GWB – Pid – [some words illegible here]. I told her of my complete distrust of Chas Strutt. Farewell, my dear. If you come south let me see you.

Ever yours,   Delta's M.

Winifred died peacefully on August 31st, 1956, at her home in London. The following day her obituary appeared in *The Times*. It gave a full account of her long and active life of public service. But it was not until December of the following year that a closely guarded secret of over forty years duration came to light in a further obituary. It was published in the *Journal* of the SPR and revealed for the first time to the members of the society that 'Mrs Willett' had been Mrs Winifred Coombe-Tennant. Even then, however, there remained one more carefully guarded secret that had existed for just as long and would be kept for another half-century.

12

With a Higher Power

Either our concept of what we call the subconscious must be radically altered, so as to include potencies of which we hitherto have had no knowledge, or else some cause operating through but not originating in the subconsciousness of Mrs Curran must be acknowledged.

The Case of Patience Worth, Dr Walter Franklin Prince

There can be few of us who have looked through a magnifying glass and not been intrigued at the new perspective presented to us of familiar objects. The smooth back of the hand becomes rough, porous, even scaly, with hairs magnified to massive spikes like a forest of trees with their branches stripped off in some Lilliputian typhoon. A grain of sand, depending upon the magnifying power of the lens, may be seen as a craggy, sparkling, bejewelled boulder or even a Hubble Space Telescope picture of an asteroid. The great Dutch pioneer microscopist Antony van Leeuwenhoek, with microscopes consisting of single high-quality lenses of very short focal length, was able to enter the world of the tiny, magnify its territory, voyage over it, study the life he found there and make innumerable discoveries of fundamental importance. In the course of the half-century between 1673 and 1723, his observations and deductions drawn from them helped to lay the foundations for the sciences of bacteriology and protozoology.

The historian and biographer may also act as microscopists, observing and studying the events in small yet crucial time intervals in the lives of nations or people, subsequently yielding an understanding of observed purposeful actions on their part. The microscopes of the historian and biographer, however, unlike Leeuwenhoek's single, high-quality lens constructions of increasingly higher powers, are of various kinds, comprising as they usually do written records ranging from important treaties or agreements, carefully composed letters directed not only to their official recipients but also designed to be leaked to others, scribbled notes someone forgot to destroy, memoranda written before and perhaps rewritten after particular events (hindsight is so perfect a science!). Even seemingly trivial and unimportant laundry lists can assume a significance far beyond their mundane purpose. As a historian once remarked with respect to the alleged evil deeds of Richard III, it does seem strange that some of his victims were still sending away their laundry years after he killed them.

In the case of Winifred Coombe-Tennant's mediumship, a more detailed knowledge of the events in her life in the short period 1908 to 1916 provides a similar enlightenment. It enables us to make sense of much of her later life, including her obsessive interest in her youngest son, Henry, her conviction that she and he had a complete and unique spiritual understanding, and her supremely confident belief that he was a man of power, someone of great talent and leadership, guided surely by destiny to achieve in his later life much higher and far more important things than those in his already entirely admirable and indeed quite outstanding war and post-war record.

In 1901 Mrs Coombe-Tennant became an associate member of the SPR but resigned in 1905. She had long admired Myers and his work but her interest in psychical research did not deepen until the tragic loss of her daughter Daphne in July 1908. She knew that Mrs Verrall, a woman she had met in 1896, was an automatic writer whose scripts sometimes claimed to be from Frederic Myers. It was because of her relation to Myers by marriage and her bereavement in 1908 that she contacted Mrs Verrall and asked her to look out for any references to Daphne in her current scripts. Some months later she read about the scripts being produced by 'Mrs Holland' and she decided to see whether she herself could produce automatic writing. She succeeded, but although the scripts ostensibly came from Myers, she was at first unconvinced and destroyed them.

Further scripts produced a better impression upon her and she was finally encouraged by Mrs Verrall to work with Sir Oliver

Lodge who subsequently had many sittings with her. He became convinced of her importance as a channel for the principal communicators, Frederic Myers and Edmund Gurney. He was very much impressed when, in the already-related Lethe Case (see Chapter 8), the Myers(w) communicator in the United Kingdom displayed indisputable knowledge of the response of the Myers(p) communicator's answers in 1908 in the United States to Mr Dorr's challenge as to what 'Lethe' meant to him. Furthermore, the intelligence behind both communicators cleverly chose the replies of Myers(w) to make it very difficult indeed if not downright ridiculous to invoke super-telepathy as the most reasonable paranormal explanation.

As Mrs Coombe-Tennant's mediumship developed, the entities who wrote firstly through Mrs Piper and then through Mrs Coombe-Tennant herself stated in totally unambiguous ways that they were engaged in planning experiments for Mrs Coombe-Tennant, involving her in their endeavours with Professor Henry Sidgwick, first President of the SPR, to prove to the world that they had survived death. They also had two other agendas. One ultimately became known as the Palm Sunday Story, many of the clues to it having been planted in the scripts of other automatists in earlier years. The other agenda was the Plan, which the interpreters came to believe the communicators revealed very explicitly firstly through Mrs Piper and then through Mrs Coombe-Tennant. Like the Story, it also seemed to have been more cryptically revealed through the earlier scripts of a number of the other automatists in the group.

It was the interpreters who gave Winifred Coombe-Tennant the pen-name 'Mrs Willett' she used throughout the years of her mediumship. It is important to keep in mind that only a very few people ever learned in her lifetime that she was Mrs Willett. It was a secret carefully guarded. Even the SPR did not know her identity beyond a few members of Council such as Sir Oliver Lodge, Mrs Sidgwick, Gerald and Arthur Balfour and some others closely involved in the study of her mediumship, such as Mrs Verrall and Alice Johnson. In a true sense 'Mrs Willett' *was* the society's own private medium even although the membership and most of Council did not know *who* she was. In that respect she was totally different from other powerful mediums such as Leonora Piper, Gladys Osborne Leonard, Geraldine Cummins and Eileen Garrett, who not only openly collaborated with and were studied by a wider group of SPR investigators but also led public lives as mediums.

Throughout Winifred's active career as a medium, her contribution to the problem of survival was massive, not just in the many scripts her automatic writing produced but also in the way her mediumship developed, producing the so-called Daylight Impressions (D.I.s). It was a faculty in some respects similar to the American medium Mrs Pearl Curran's ability to 'see' the scenes, 'hear' the voices of the people present, and even 'take' from the market stalls and 'taste' the strange fruit the entity Patience Worth was describing through Mrs Curran's automatic writing (see W.F. Prince, *The Case of Patience Worth*, 1927). By it, it became possible for the investigators of Mrs Willett's mediumship to have long direct conversations with the ostensible communicators and from her words form a clear impression of the 'scenes' and 'people' she was 'seeing' and 'hearing'. The opportunity to test and assess the communicators' intelligence, their statements and responses to questions and to converse with them, together with their personality traits as revealed in these conversations, led the investigators to form firm opinions as to the nature of these unseen entities. In the end, it was the weight of evidence that convinced them that survival of death took place. Moreover, it was a survival that seemed to retain the communicator's intelligence and memories, his idiosyncratic traits of personality, his ability to 'meet' and plan with others on the other side and continue to further his and their interests.

But all this lay in the future. At this point it is of importance to consider Winifred Coombe-Tennant's personality and state of mind when she made her initial approach by letter to Mrs Verrall in 1908. On the night of July 20th–21st, 1908, she had lost a deeply loved little daughter who even at eighteen months had had a singularly attractive and lovable personality. When Winifred plucked up her courage and wrote to Mrs Verrall on July 28th, she was a very vulnerable woman still in her early thirties desperately seeking assurance that in some way there *was* a scheme of things that made her loss understandable and not irrevocable. There was no indication then, in her appearance or manner, of the magistrate, the strong-willed chairwoman of committees and delegations and art exhibitions she would be a quarter of a century later who seemed so formidable a person to Professor C.D. Broad. At this stage in her life she was an upper-class Edwardian lady, always well-dressed; she carried her slightly plump though graceful figure well, she had an intelligent and attractive though not classically beautiful face. Her hair was thick and dark and stylishly well-groomed. Up until July 1908 she had enjoyed a fulfilled, favoured life in the upper echelons of privileged society. And she had now had the heart of her life torn out.

Her ardent desire to get into touch with her dead child or at least justify a belief that in some way she still existed led her to take up automatic writing. Throughout the early stage of her mediumship, her scripts were being studied by Mrs Verrall with increasing interest. She finally brought them and also all the scripts of the other automatists that seemed to refer directly or obliquely to Daphne and the circumstances of her birth, her Welsh home and her early death, to Sir Oliver Lodge's attention. Visiting Sir Oliver and Lady Lodge at Birmingham on March 20th and 21st, 1909, Mrs Verrall left scripts for them to study. Mrs Willett's next script was obtained on March 25th before she had heard anything from Lodge or Mrs Verrall of the result of the latter's visit to Birmingham. The original script was handed in a dated and sealed envelope to Mrs Willett's mother, and a copy was sent shortly afterwards to Lodge. This plan was henceforth adopted, extracts relevant to Mrs Verrall being sent to her from time to time, while complete copies were sent to Lodge within a few hours of their production. These copies were given by him to Mrs Verrall in October 1909. In fact, shortly after Mrs Verrall's visit to Birmingham, Lodge opened up communications with Mrs Willett, his first letter being received by her an hour or two after the production of the script of March 25th. She replied to him on March 26th, 1909, and her next script on March 27th was mainly addressed to him. At first Mrs Willett had been decidedly reluctant to bring Lodge into contact with her. She knew him to be the famous scientist who was the Principal of the University of Birmingham and who had been the President of the SPR a few years before. But finally overcoming her characteristic reluctance to share personal information, she agreed with Mrs Verrall and subsequently had a number of sittings with him. He was very much impressed and she became one of the Sidgwick Group's automatists.

The scripts of March 25th and March 27th are given below. In their style they give clear examples of Willett scripts. In many of the scripts, the surname of the ostensible communicator, especially when Myers(w) is communicating, is repeated at frequent intervals throughout the script. The script is often signed F or E presumably for Frederic (Myers) or Edmund (Gurney). The simple explanation that a frequent repetition of the communicator's name will enable the reader to know who claims to be communicating at that moment may not appear plausible but it is difficult to suggest a more convincing hypothesis unless in some way this procedure of frequently repeating the communicator's name helps the communicator to get the message through.

In addition, the number of well-known words misspelt in the scripts is at first sight surprising considering that, although Mrs Willett in her normal writing of letters sometimes, though not often, misspelled a word – who does not?, both Myers and Gurney were highly literate men. This, however, together with the frequent breakdowns when a failed attempt to write a word is abandoned in scribbles and a new attempt is made, often preceded by the communicator's name, and is successful, may also merely be a symptom of the immense difficulties the communicators (whoever or whatever they are) had in keeping the channel open and getting the message through. For there is no doubt that, in modern parlance, the communicator was using a very noisy transmission system. It was even worse than that: it has already been noted that the communicator's train of thought could be hijacked onto another track by associations stimulated from the medium's memory.

March 25, 1909.   F.W.H.M.

[Note: 'scribbles' can mean 'illegible' but more often refers to an essentially random scribbling.]

Myers yes I wish to write a few words I am absolutely satisfied with progress in every direction am also satisfied with the result of Mrs V. meeting with Lodge absolutely satisfied (scribbles) result exceeding my expectations. I wish now to say something. You are to try for script every other day now as I wish to say several things. Do not imagine you can be fatigued by telepathic work in moderation it is not fatigueing & I wish the habits of scripts to be kept up. Tell Mrs Verall later I appreciate her work very greatly very greatly & I hope

I mark my complete confidence in her by giving her highly important work to do. It is my best means of marking my complete confidence in her. Lodge is on the right track but he must move slowly for he can see the colosal importance of this experiment & he must move with the usual deliberation of science & indeed this deliberation is itself a sign of the grasp he now has of the importance of this experiment. I wish to add one thing a message for him not to go yet it is this. I anticipate that times may arise[2] when this machine may be thrown out of effective action for periods & I wish Lodge to say this to you [i.e. to O.J.L.]. That which I have earnestly asked of you (scribbles) Myers that which I have earnestly asked of you for my work I shall desire you then to give more freely at such times not less but more that is the thought I want to press on you not less in times of apparent uselessness but more for never let it be forgotten the price has been paid the wages are due not for present & future usefulness only but for the past therefore let not the measure of avaible work here be the only gauge of the due reward & the due no (scribbles) & of that which I trust you to supply here no there is another claim which has nothing to do with mere efficiency of phisical condition enabling length of telepathic work. I can do no more than suggest a meaning lying at the back of this message to you my friend not on the surface but at the back. Look beyond the present. I have now no more to say [i.e. to Mrs Willett] but try for a script every other day & do not by self suggestion adopt the often purely autoinvented limitations of automatists who talk of disturbance of new surroundings & of change of habits as if they were some immense power over which they had no control. Control comes with practise & I believe that sensitives can imunise (?)* themselves to a large extent Farewell F

---

*Mrs Verrall wrote: 'Mrs Willett added a note to this script, viz: "Much of this script is ununderstandable to me. Is there such a word as 'imunise'?"'

March 27, 1909   F.W.H.M.

This script, purporting to be from Myers, is mainly addressed to Sir Oliver Lodge.

Myers yes I wish to write now Myers for Lodge this he (scribbles) no now write more quietly he is to retain all the matter refering to the Daphne case nothing is to be returned to you nothing I wish for the present all to be kept by him. Also I wish you to do exactly what he tells you & to answer any questions he may put in the fullest possible manner pause (I did) Yes now continue I have Lodges message message message do try to be passive now & let me say what I want. I have his message & I thank him for it & I desire him to understand the fact that I am well aware of the small amount of time at his disposal & of the right he is not to be hurried but to take his own time. Explain to him that I am not unreasonable it is not quantity I want though that too I could do with God knows but quality & what he can do for my work no one else can this is partly because of the extraordinary raprochement between his nature & yours let him translate this thought into the terms of colour & realise the rays are quite diverse in density (scribbles) but complementary the one to the other this is a veritable Godsend to me & the fact that I have actually established touch through risks and difficulties not aprehended your side is an encouragement to me that is beyond my power to express now to go to another subject Myers cannot Mrs Verrall suggest another group of scripts covering much the same period for you to go slowly over. You must have time because we have to convey by impulse by daylight impressions & generally by telepathic impulses the clues in many instances & these you get better without help. If you get help from your side you will begin to rely on that instead of relying on us & on yourself. I should like you to have some new new to you I mean scripts to work on the placing side by side can then be done when you and Mrs Verrall meet. I want the preliminary spade work to be going on Myers let her reply to me here what she thinks I am not peremptorily desiring her to do it but am asking her in view of the (scribbles) what I have said to think the matter over & to act as she thinks best. It is more important for you to work at scripts than for the result of such work to reach others anyhow just at present therefore I suggest what I do. Myers one more subject D.I. I think you might try definitely for these at a fixed time on the days you do not try for scripts I find

E.G. & you having all sorts of odds & ends of conversations & at last I dont know what he has told you or (?) anyhow it is a constant anxiety to me as to what he is doing because you & he really are on such extraordinarily close terms telepathically that he just converses with you as if you were over here & he wont see that you are part of a plan a cog in a wheel he is always going off onto the human side onto you as an individual this is why he you c well never mind but you I expect find me terribly business like after your interviews with Gurney and Daphne. Yes I took her to see Lodge* she did so but this is not to be mentioned at present or they will think you are romancing. You must be a sensitive and yet not sensitive that is the difficulty could I but isolate high high above leve above the level of daily life my machine whilst yet retaining it in its terestrial [*sic*] environment I could do great things no more F

* Mrs Verrall wrote: 'Mrs Willett notes that before this script, between March 20 and March 25, 1909, she had a D.I. in which Daphne spoke words to the effect that she had seen "that big man wiz a beard you know Zodze he knows 'bout me." (There is an odd mixture of baby language in the D.I.'s in which Daphne speaks.) The remark in the script was not due to any question or thought of Mrs Willett's, who had in fact forgotten the D.I. with Daphne till reminded of it by reading the script.'

There is a definite and interesting suggestion in this script that Myers(w) is worried that Gurney(w) has his own agenda rather different from the one the communicators are engaged in carrying out. Myers(w) is also worried that Gurney(w)'s charm and facility in communicating privately with Mrs Willett will enable him to seduce her into helping him to achieve his agenda. There is no doubt that in the Scripts in general Myers(w) is more diffident and thoughtful, frequently demonstrating episodes reminiscent of the living Myers' ardent and sensitive nature, being indeed more grateful than Gurney(w) for his chance to get through to Lodge. In one long script (April 8th, 1909), Myers(w), amid many matters, has the following passages (the notes are my own):

Lodge my Good friend My dear friend do you remember the carrier pigeon and the beleagered fortress[1] Well I think that fortress is truly where my lot has been cast these last years & your direct address to me as man to man is indeed the pigeon's homeward flight. My great difficulties I cannot explain now in truth I can say but little in this first word of mine in answer to yours. That you should speak to me as man to man is balm to one who has been knocking at many doors knocking insistently & who has seen where the sounds reached that they were universally attributed to the listeners own dissasociated personality...

Myers I will not now write further as on the subjects which are suggested by the rest of your letter I have much to say & I therefore desire to make them the subject of a seperate script. Let me add one word my dear Lodge. No effort to be of use will be spared from this side & if it were possible for me to fully convey to you what emotion and joy glows within me at the sound of your words of welcome I would attempt to express Myers express that which I feel. Let me say only that I believe I have at last succeeded in proving not only survival but identity that I am Myers & that I am in myself though enlarged yet in the main & in the real Ego identical with that Myers which sought to save his own soul & his comrades homeward way[2] Myers farewell...

(1) This refers to Myers' *Fragments of Inner Life*, p. 38.
(2) It will be remembered that Sir Oliver Lodge's tribute to Myers after his death included the following passage. 'He [*spoke*] of himself ... as having "often a sense of great solitude, and of an effort beyond my strength; 'striving' – as Homer says of Odysseus ... 'striving to save my own soul and my comrades' homeward way.' "'

It will also be remembered that Lodge, as a result of a decidedly cautious twenty-year study of psychical phenomena, had been forced to conclude some years before that survival of death took place. It is therefore understandable that, while still employing reservations concerning the origin of the Scripts, he should have been responsive to these purporting to come from his old friend Myers, especially when the communicator's style so resembled that of the Myers he knew so well.

In contrast to this expression of deep gratitude by Myers(w),

257

Gurney(w), in a script and Daylight Impression (D.I.) of January 28th, 1910, responds characteristically during a discussion being held between him and Mrs Verrall (who was sitting with Mrs Willett). The discussion had reached the topic of the possible enlargement of the investigating group, and Mrs Verrall had suggested as possible additions Mr Podmore and William James. Gurney(w) snapped back: 'Podmore is not to be given another opportunity of disbelieving in my existence. William James is to be told... '

This acerbic remark of Gurney(w)'s referred to Frank Podmore's notorious scepticism. A pioneer of psychical research, an early member of the SPR and a member of its first council, he began as a spiritualist and ended up as a professed disbeliever in all paranormal activities except telepathy. Though unable to fault D.D. Home's phenomena, Podmore stated: 'to say that because we cannot understand some of the feats, therefore they must have been due to spirits or psychic force, is merely an opiate for the uneasiness of suspended judgement, a refuge from the trouble of thinking.' This is all very well but does somewhat provoke the image of a threatened octopus of prejudice defended by an inky cloud of verbiage. With respect to reports of physical phenomena, Podmore would concoct elaborate theories as to how the phenomena could in theory have been faked. Where the evidence gathered by the investigator was overwhelmingly in favour of genuine paranormal events, he would proceed to rubbish the investigator, making it abundantly clear that if he himself had been present, his markedly superior investigative talents would have demonstrated the precise manner of fraud. Podmore merits the title of the founding father of the ultra-Sceptical school, still in existence today, though in fairness, unlike the fundamentalist ultra-sceptics who even deny telepathy, Podmore did accept *its* existence.

In the early period of Mrs Willett's script writing, Myers(w) was the dominant communicator. Indeed, up until the end of April 1909, he remained so but from the beginning of May, Gurney(w) began to communicate on more and more occasions. From then on into 1910, they both remained the principal communicators, sometimes communicating in sequence during the same script or D.I. Other communicators transmitting material included Henry Sidgwick(w) and Daphne(w) but their appearances are few, though on a small number of other occasions they participated with either Myers(w) or Gurney(w). Gurney(w)'s influence thereafter grew until he became the principal communicator. His strong-willed personality is evident in his requests (sometimes commands) to the investigators and his, at times, steamroller approach to their suggestions. On occasion he tells them that they should accept that Myers and Sidgwick are in full accordance with his ideas and plans. That he is not always a being of sweetness and light is evident from the material obtained during a D.I. of Mrs Willett, and received by Mrs Verrall during a visit to Mrs Willett on Saturday October 29th, 1910. The italicised comments in parentheses are the *sotto voce* remarks of Mrs Willett as they occurred. The D.I. was preceded by script:

Gurney D.I. at once I have much to say.

(*He looks terrible*) I want Lodge to read this and no part of it is to be shown to others without his consent.

The rush of what I want to say is so tremendous that I may break here and there. I want to protest with my whole soul against the action of Alice Johnson. Make it clear. I believe her motives to be to her own self good. It is a case where the zeal for which she believes to be scientific procedure, has led her into what I call a dishonourable action. (*He's ferocious*). She has taken advantage of the total ignorance of this child in regard to her A.J.'s own wellknown standpoint and what the whole mass of hypotheses which has been necessary for testing purposes but some of which are by the best informed already discarded – still worse she has tampered with Lodge's influence and she has dragged in to her own controversy with Lodge one who is quite unfitted to gauge the merits of it. I cannot believe that Mrs S. or you have been party to this that she should try to throw discredit upon that which we have got through with Piper in the middle of a set of Sittings, the control of which lay in Lodge's hands. It would have been justified only thus (1) that she should have told Lodge exactly what she proposed to say and (2) that she should have made clear that the inferences she drew from these facts which lie outside dispute are nothing more than the expression of her personal opinion and are not ex cathedra statements of the S.P.R.

Lodge will U.D. [understand] that I know what Hell is when I see erroneous conclusions offered as facts when such conclusions strike a vital blow in the mind of one untrained at the whole authenticity of what we have achieved in conveying to her through the P. light [Piper] I conveyed a truth which I desired Lodge to tell you. Long had I laboured towards it, long had I waited. The bewilderment has been followed by at first a trembling and then a joyful acceptance.

Its my life I'm fighting for, its my happiness, its my work.

Tell Lodge for God's sake make clear where facts end and where Johnsonian theories begin and tell him I saw in 2 hours danger that the work of months might be swept away.

I never strained the telepathic pressure to such an extent as I did in suggesting the fallacies of the Johnsonian postulates – some points I got gathered into concrete form – ask her for this. Take to Lodge the paper she addressed to Alice (*He's blazing*) Even Henry [Sidgwick] was with me when I instanced the lengths to which pseudoscientific dogmatism can go as seen in assertions made by her.

(A) upon the (no begin again)

it was at Birmingham slates – this is not evidential, its known to the normal personality – Lodge wrote a question, Miss J. has no more data than his report yet she does not hesitate to assert that the medium by trickery acquainted herself with the contents and (B) splendid instance of making a hypothesis into a fact and observed phenomena as it were a hypothesis when she dogmatises upon physical phenomena of which she has absolutely no 1st hand knowledge. Loads upon the shoulders of an already heavily burdened spirit the responsibility (wait) for preventing muscular action telekinetic [said very slowly] (*how splendid he is*). Tell Lodge that if he will not protect a sensitive whose development is entrusted to him from being dipped into all the refuse water which has accumulated in the course of a long investigation I E.G. will not be responsible for results. Lodge can take care of himself, let him and Alice fight it out, but I'll have no hitting below the belt.

There are 2 theories, both legitimate

(1) that the critical faculty too acutely encouraged – not good word – they'll say my style is not improved – developed – better word – tends to inhibit receptive power

(2) – Johnsonian – (makes him think of Pope's Dogmas of Infallibility)

(2) that a rigorous cultivation of critical faculty will exercise restraining influence upon the subliminal to which she perhaps legitimately attributes so much. Excellent woman but matter in wrong place occasionally. Tell Lodge this.

By God I'll make them realise she is dear to me. I'll take her right out of it, let her work with Lodge only – But that's not what I want really. I'm not alone. To sum up once more. My protest that A.J. should offer to one unable to discriminate her own gratuitous presumption re normal P. knowledge and 2ndly without consultation with the experimenter in charge of sittings whom she knows does not accept her conclusions.

(Here intervened some unrecorded talk on other subjects with M. de G.V. [Mrs Verrall] Then it resumed)

Tell Lodge you, who U.D. the vital importance of preserving – wrong – not weakening in her mind the evidential bearing of what I (E.G.) have said to her through the Piper way, [here I read over at request] can U.D. that Miss J's work must be undone – and forthwith –

[Here I heard Alex's voice and the door was tried]

Don't switch me off

I definitely forbid any other meeting between Miss J. and D's M. [Daphne's mother = Winifred] unless it is to take place in the presence of Lodge himself or after Lodge has become acquainted with the contents of this D.I. and has had an opportunity of speaking with me (E.G.) on the matter.

I'm not attributing evil intentions, but saying that the whole incident is not in accord with my sense of honour, and sensitives should not be used as battledores between experimenters whose standpoints differ.

Tell Lodge her paper largely telepathic
        thank him.
     he's done much

Myers' love for him led long ago to his being chosen to have management of psychical development here.

Saturday, Oct. 29, 1910.

It may be remarked that Gurney(w)'s anger and frustration tend to support the interpretation that this outburst is an example of intelligent intercourse, one which goes far to demolish the 'static' interpretation of post-mortem messages as time-ossified and unidirectional.

A further procedure was initiated in the Willett mediumship when Mrs Willett received a letter on April 7th, 1909 from Lodge, with an enclosure addressed to Myers(w). During a D.I. on the same morning she read both documents to the communicator and was told to expect the answer in script the next day. The script obtained on April 8th, 1909 was the one in which Myers(w) expressed his gratitude to Lodge for talking 'man to man' with him and quoted part of the tribute Lodge had given to Myers after his death in the *Proceedings* of the SPR. Myers(w) does not go into any real detail in his response except to proffer advice on how Lodge should treat Mrs Willett and how the communicators and Lodge should proceed with experiments.

I wish to ask you many questions & some are contained in those scripts from this machine not yet perused by you. Let me set down two to which answer may be made not before you desire & not before you have come to any definite conclusion Let me ask first whether the use of the word Experiment has been fully grasped & admitted by you & secondly if you will admit it as even a M Myers a hypotheses. There is the second question which must be faced & which I have already addressed to you. Do you feel able to give me as Experimenter (scribbles) Myers your moral approval I admit that it is a question upon which I cannot expect unanimity of judgement either your side or this but I feel I Myers feel confident that the weight of your approval would tell here with some.

Read me Lodges letter slowly.

I wish to say that about telepathy I shall write further but I shall embody my remarks in a separate script.

Go on reading.

Stop now I wish to go back to Son behold thy Mother & to ask you again to promise me as far as in you lies to accept that charge with all that it implies not that I can be blind to the paucity of opportunity now. Much more apparent than real though but look beyond the present & remember it is not only as a machine that I wish her to be considered there is another claim & therefore I repeat or rather I will not repeat for you will find what I mean in one of the scripts which has not yet reached you. Do not leave her for too long periods without a friendly hand. If I could tell you something of the difficulties that I have at times with her you would understand this too is where Gurney helps me he understands how to reassure & to encourage her.

Read again

Myers Lodge has it struck you that the steps leading up to descent into generation might be induced by hypnotic pressure upon both Agents (scribbles) & Myers & also whether you have grasped the idea that self projection may be definitely hip (scribbles) hypnotically induced under given conditions Myers I have not got that last part clear but I have a reason for not wishing to do so at present. Let me have answers to those two Myers I will not now write further as on the subjects which are suggested by the rest of your letter I have much to say & I therefore desire to make them the subject of a seperate script. Let me add one word my dear Lodge. No effort to be of use will be spared from this side...

The phrase 'Son behold thy Mother' appears abruptly in the script, curiously and perhaps coincidentally connected to the fact that at this time Winifred was some two months pregnant and would give birth to her second son, Alexander, on November 20th, 1909. However, throughout the pregnancy, which was deliberately kept secret from Mrs Verrall and Helen Verrall to see if anything related to it would appear in their scripts, frequent references to children and pregnancy did appear both in the scripts proper and D.I.s. It also seemed reasonable to deduce that those on the other side now had a particular agenda concerned with the birth of a child, that birth and the child being in some sense 'steered' from the other side.

On April 5th, at 5.45 p.m. Winifred had a D.I. described as a sentence 'dropped in'. It was recorded at the time and given in a sealed envelope to Mrs Willett's mother, whose endorsement is dated April 5th, 1909, 8.10 p.m. The sentence was: 'Sidgwick said he should never know another moment's peace until he saw her with another child in her arms.'

On April 19th, 1909, about 12.30 p.m., Mrs Willett had a D.I. of which she gives the following account (the asterisks and accompanying notes are the author's):

I was resting when suddenly there was E.G. He began 'Well can you hear what I say?' I said 'Yes' and he spoke for some time; he went from one topic to another & then he ended by telling me that the only two points I need record are

1. that I am to try for Sc tomorrow and that the Sc would be about* –
2. That Daphne would 'be taken to see Lodge again'** & would come & tell me the result after she had been there.

* A blank was left here in the copy sent, but a note, separately recorded, shows that the subject was the 'coming child'.
** For a previous visit, see Mrs Willett's of March 27th, 1909, and accompanying note. This visit is described below.

On April 21st, 1909, about 7.45 a.m., Mrs Willett had a D.I. in which Gurney(w) and Daphne(w) were both present. Daphne reported, in baby language, that she had been again to see Sir Oliver Lodge, that she had climbed on to his lap, and that he never saw her, but continued to read 'right through' her.

On the night of April 19th, Mrs Willett had a dream about Henry Sidgwick. She had never dreamed of him before, nor ever had any sense of him being 'near'. She reported:

In my dream he was sitting quite close to me, his wife beside him, I have never seen him, & I have seen her once at a S.P.R. meeting about 1901 or 1902. I should not know her if I saw her to the best of my belief.

What surprised me was that he was looking at me so tenderly, we seemed all to be sitting at a table, I knew he was Henry Sidgwick but I had the sensation of looking at a living man whose face I had only known in a photograph... I got a keen sense of Henry Sidgwick's personality. I noticed especially his eyes, & that his neck was thin, showing the muscles as he turned. Mrs Sidgwick was smiling at me, she looked very happy, & I was astonished when she leaned forward & stroked my cheek, just as one might a child's ... The next part of my dream was where I was driving in a carriage & in a carriage behind me were the Sidgwicks. The road we drove along was broad, stone curbs to the pavements, trees (not old) each side, villa-ish houses on one or both sides. We came to a road that came off at right angles to the left & into this my carriage turned.* As we did so some sort of heavily laden cart drawn by two horses had some sort of accident & my carriage had to pull up so that the Sidgwick's carriage came up with it. My dream went on after this but I can't remember it. I woke up, went over it carefully as far as I could & fell asleep.

* Mrs Verrall writes: 'This description corresponds generally with that of Sidgwick Avenue, from which a road at right angles on the left leads, after another sharp turn, to the Principal's rooms at Newnham College. Mrs Willett had stayed in Cambridge during Mrs Sidgwick's principalship, and must have driven along Sidgwick Avenue, but she had never visited the College. In May, 1911, when Mrs Willett was staying with me, as we were walking up Sidgwick Avenue, she stopped, looked around her, and said "This is the road of my dream, and there" (pointing to the road on the left) "is the road into which we turned."'

On July 27th, 1909, at a time when Mrs Willett was lying down, overwhelmed by 'a sense of physical and spiritual exhaustion', she had a D.I. from Myers in which he said, 'I want to write a script, a few words only.' Accordingly, she fetched paper, and so on, and the following script was obtained.

Script of July 27, 1909   F.W.H.M.

Myers one word only definitely & for good I tell you this the destiny of the coming child is not that of Daphne Myers the destiny of the coming child is to serve on your side on your side not on this not until the normal sum of man's years has been attained. I believe the clear fixing of this in your mind is absolutely essential.

[Then after some answers to questions about Mrs Willett's health & other personal matters:] Myers the essential thing is to avoid friction – Patience and do not give way to depression about the future.

[Here Mrs Willett said that after former experiences (presumably Daphne's death) she was unable to feel security in anything.]

Yes, I understand it *all*.

Yes, yes reread my first words and grave them on your

mind. You will not only distress yourself by any forebodings but you will hinder us from helping you and the child that is coming, for you will cut yourself off in some degree from our telepathic help Myers whereas there is much that we can do if you will trust my word given in solemn Myers token of unchanging love and honour towards you... F

On the same date Winifred received a D.I. from Gurney(w):

Cant you take my word and Fred's written word and believe what we say – you don't realise that this coming child has been the result of immense work here and that its object is to give you something to live for because we want you where you are and we want to reconcile you to staying there...

The entry of September 9th, 1909 was a D.I. received between 2 and 4 a.m. It involved Sidgwick and Gurney. Mrs Willett writes in her report:

Some time in the night (last night), before dawn, I judge about from 2 to 4 a.m., I woke, and the D.I. came with no sense of person until E.G. [Gurney] said, 'You have got what we wanted, go to sleep now – which I did. The impression is quite clear to me ... it is –

H.S. is now intensely interested in 'the effect of maternity on character'.[1] He had not grasped it in its fulness before; he regrets it (!) in one way, because he regrets that it is 'a physical experience' which alone can 'open the door into so rich a spiritual treasure.' He says if he could return he would take 'a class at Newnham and preach' the doctrine of 'the relative unimportance of Non-Maternal work.' He speculates much on 'what the effect of paternity would have been on him' – he thinks he could not have maintained his 'tentative attitude towards life' – he cannot yet understand 'how Clough maintained it', having children of his own. He thinks the effect on him (H.S.) would have been to 'force him to conclusions,' and so perhaps might have had 'a negative effect upon his intellectual life,' but it would have increased his 'executive efficacy' for life.

(1) Note by Mrs Willett. – The words in inverted commas are verbally accurate.

266

In his 1948 book *An Introduction to the Study of Scripts*, W.H. Salter writes:

> The fact of her [Mrs Willett's] pregnancy was carefully concealed from Mrs Verrall and H.V. [Helen Verrall]. The scripts ... written by them between Daphne's death and Alexander's birth strongly reinforce the implications of the 'Daphne' scripts that the communicators were aiming at something more than proving survival and establishing their own identity. They seemed to be claiming an ability to influence the birth of children and the minds and characters of children yet unborn.

On May 21st, 1909, during a D.I. impression about 11.15 a.m., with Mrs Verrall as sitter, and Myers(w) and Gurney(w) taking it in turn to communicate, Mrs Verrall was asked by Myers 'to prepare all as if for publication, to get all corroborated, and then all is to be shown to a group or Sub-Committee. The Committee should consist of Piddington, Lodge, A.J. [Alice Johnson], E.M.S. [Eleanor Mildred Sidgwick], and Gerald Balfour if he would like it. This group must come into touch with this machine.' (More about importance of personal contact, &c., without which the group could not understand the evidence.)

Mrs Verrall wrote as a footnote:

> on May 19, I had suggested that Mrs. Willett should consult the communicators on the question of including Mr. G.W. Balfour in the group of persons investigating the Delta Case.

The question of the make-up of the investigating committee came up again on January 28, 1910 when Gurney(w) dismissed scathingly the suggestion that Frank Podmore should be invited to join. From other evidence it seems that certainly by February, 1910, Mrs Willett had been introduced to the Balfours and had been to Fishers Hill. To meet members of one of the most famous, intelligent and influential families in Britain must have been quite an event, made more so when she learned that Gerald Balfour and Mrs Sidgwick also, like Lodge, held her psychic talent in high regard. Nevertheless they all had great charm and gentleness and quickly put her at her ease, especially when she realised that she was not in any way 'on trial'.

Largely as a result of this meeting, Gerald Balfour became a frequent sitter with her, ultimately becoming her principal sitter. The few years following it would also produce the final development and perfection of her mediumship, the production of the Palm Sunday scripts and D.I.'s, and the explicit exhortations by Gurney(w) to fulfil his extraordinary request and so initiate the Plan.

13

Preaching to the Converted

What can be avoided,
Whose end is purposed by the mighty gods?

Julius Caesar, 1.2, William Shakespeare

When spirits begin to speak with man, he must beware lest
he believe in any thing; for they say almost any thing; things
are fabricated of them, and they lie.

Emanuel Swedenborg

In 1910 and 1911 Mrs Piper came to England and gave a number of sittings. It was arranged that Mrs Willett should sit with her under the supervision of Sir Oliver Lodge. Both Mrs Piper and Mrs Willett were now recognised as powerful mediums by Lodge. When they were thousands of miles apart, they had produced the weighty evidence in the Lethe Case provided by the entities Myers(p) and Myers(w), making it beyond any reasonable shadow of doubt that Myers(w) knew what Myers(p) had provided in answer to the question 'What does the word Lethe mean to you?' Not only that, but the Myers(w) intelligence had characteristically and skilfully designed his answer to make it extremely difficult to introduce super-telepathy between the Atlantic-separated mediums as a plausible paranormal explanation. It was therefore logical that the experiment of one powerful medium sitting in the immediate proximity of another powerful sensitive should be made if the opportunity arose. Unlike many ideas that produce results followed by a rueful regret and drastic reassessment down-

269

wards of their usefulness, the Piper–Willett sittings did produce completely unexpected and astonishing results. The reactions of both Mrs Willett and Lodge indicate their shock, bewilderment and even consternation at the content of the material the sittings produced.

The dates of the sittings with Mrs Piper in 1910 were May 9th, October 12th, October 13th, October 23rd, November 6th, November 9th, December 2nd; in 1911, the dates were February 8th and February 10th. The first was held in the London rooms of the SPR. Thereafter they were held in Birmingham. It was on October 23rd that what became subsequently known as 'Edmund Gurney's request' was first mentioned. The list of dates given above were copied by Mrs Willett from her diary in the presence of Alice Johnson on July 23rd, 1913.

During 1910 and 1911, Mrs Willett was herself producing scripts and D.I.s. There is no doubt that her mediumship, though powerful, was still developing and that the communicators were becoming more skilled as time went on in getting their thoughts and advice through to Mrs Willett or to the sitter. If the sitter was Lodge and it was a D.I. he would scribble down his notes of what Mrs Willett was saying.

Given below is a script taken from a typed copy of an unpublished Willett script of October 11th, 1910. It refers to a dream experience of Mrs Willett on the night of October 10th–11th.

Gurney   yes I want to write   Dont be discouraged   these failures spring from simple causes   Myers is persuaded that Lodge will not let himself be switched off the track indicated by any delay in effecting the initial operation – viz that of inducing trance   there is a great deal of self suggestion at the back of the failure but rest assured that no break with the Imperator group has occured   It is simply a machine that has got out of running   good running condition takes some time to get back into the old grooves   Whatever you do Lodge dont let the thing get switched off Daphne Case work   Yes I want you to write as I tell you I am opposed to introducing other influences & I would rather have Bang right down failures than successes in other directions
Weve got to get those two machines to work together   the Experience last night is veridical & it should be noted   Gurney

270

tell Lodge he's quite wrong in thinking RH [Richard Hodgson?] is out of this job he is not Myers wishes there to be no pause in the efforts to attain the trance state but says that Lodge is to sit alone if it is impossible to have you there Let him keep something to be used psychometrically

Myers is responsable for this advice You need not think it will bring down any vials of wrath on your head

It is a desparately trying business I know – I am so sorry dear Mother of Daphne that it has to be gone through but we need your help & you will not give it at its best by letting yourself be too sensitive to incarnate temperaments I cannot imagine how we do achieve what we do when I see the complexity of the factors we have to take account of Myers will write some Sc later not today Myers will write further Mind you tell Lodge from me to stick to us & to our word & and to remember there is a gold mine if he can get it

Mrs Piper is *not* exhausted her psychic condition has been enfeebled by jugglery but that is past of course we fully realise this will give the occasion for the sceptic to blaspheme You must try to put it out of your mind the idea that there is anything inhibiting in your presence A few failures with other sitters may be quite useful in that way Rector is all right it is simply a hitch at a very awkward moment I admit & how much it means to us only those who know what work it has been to get to this point could realise

We have difficulties enough without any last straws Just make up your mind to be passively hopeful & willing to be patient We are doing our utmost and have all the help here we can get It is bound to work out into something in little time You write very slowly today never mind

Did you feel my presence that evening

Well I came drawn to you by the sadness of that moment of recalled anguish Music has that evocative power I thought Lodge was realising it too I wish I had Lodge in some vast wilderness he is so bunged up with preoccupations of a very terrene though partly celestial type

Gurney Alexander is doing famously

1. Gurney hold tight I am near you you are not going to be discouraged so much centres round you Never think of yourself as divided from that which is kindred to you

271

in spirit   It is only an appearance not a reality that is the law of super terene gravity

Gurney   yes   yes
How priceless your understanding courage is to me the loyalty which I can always turn to amid much that is difficult
Yes   I have difficulties too
Gurney   well better luck tomorrow   Just tell Lodge we are doing our utmost & what we want & intend to get is worth the effort

E

Why do you write gravity when I wish gravitation
      Gurney   Correct it
Gurney

On the evening of November 7th, 1910, before the expected Piper sitting next day, the following original (and to date unprinted) script was received:

Gurney let me write
I want to speak to Lodge tonight
Myers ask me to say that you should ask tomorrow through Piper this question
What is the meaning of the word
   Madonna
Just that and no more
Shew this to Lodge

Mrs Willett, who had been feeling increasingly bewildered and worried by the results of the Piper sittings of October and November 1910, felt compelled to write an account of her reactions not only to them but also to what Sir Oliver Lodge had told her concerning her own recent D.I.s. She therefore prepared the following notes:

By Mrs Willett   Cadoxton. Nov 12. 1910
I have for some days felt an irresistible compelling impulse to record what follows about the Piper Sittings of Oct. & Nov. 1910.

Certain sheets have been withdrawn and certain passages cut out. As I believe reference to these ommitted [*sic*] parts may be made elsewhere I wish to put on record that they concern

1. E.G.'s feeling for me. He stated that he had waited to tell me of it until he could convey it through Piper–Light, as he thought I should believe it then. Sir Oliver having read the Piper Sc. informed me that the same statement has been made through me in D.I. The idea that Edmund Gurney could really love me – in the full sense of the word – is so incredible that at any rate during my lifetime, I do not propose that anyone but Sir Oliver Lodge & Mrs Verrall should know of that part of the Piper Sc in which the statements about it are made.

2. The second point referred to in withdrawn Piper sitting sheets is this. E.G. asked me to bear another child – to be, as he says Alexander is, in some sense his child – & to be 'a playmate' for Alexander. Considerable portions of Piper Sittings were devoted to urging this. My answer so far has been that I will consider it. My normal self has no intention of this sort, as far as I know. My health at such times is so up & down, & the whole thing is such a labour for me that having given birth to three children I thought my task accomplished. There has been up to this date (Nov 12, 1910) no opportunity of any sort for conception & I do not think that the idea of further children has occured to my husband. If I do bear yet another it will only be as a direct result of E.G.'s repeated requests & my love for him. He has stated that he will take care of me all through, that I shall pass through its [illegible] & that the result will be an 'Optimus Opus'. (which expression is unknown to me) Various Sc confirming Mrs Piper Sc have come through my own hand. Sir Oliver has seen the Piper Sc and some of mine upon this subject. I propose to show him what I now write & get his confirmation.

Winifred Coombe-Tennant

E.G. alludes to this subject as his request. He says F.W.H.M. is in complete agreement with him & (in my Sc) that H.S.'s approval will be recorded elsewhere.

The following is an extract from Myers(w) script of November 17th, 1910:

Guyon   you will know more later   Follow our guidance   you will know happiness and peace   Gurney's child that is to come will be a great Incarnation of Divine Efulgence
Devi   <u>Divine</u>
[I here asked if Alexander were not that]
    Differently   A is to be a light   the next a Genius   Refer to H.P. page ninety two
[I here asked if I should do so at once]
    <u>Now</u>
[I thereupon looked it up in my (abridged edition, the only one I ever had) Human Personality. Page 92 begins (from the Chapter III 'Genius') 'and incorporate from earth, air and sun. Still less can we predict or limit the possible variations of the Soul' etc down to 'Even God is divine.' which is the end of the chapter. The paragraph of which 'Still less' etc forms part begins 'We know not in what direction'. I therefore take FWHM to refer to the portion of H.P. beginning with those words down to the end of the Chapter. I knew there was such a chapter but whether at the end or beginning of the Book I did not know. Nor have I opened the book for nearly a year. The appropriateness of the words seems beyond chance – as referring to E.G.'s 'Request' made through Mrs Piper.]
    Myers that is all
    Go forth in confidence & know that this is your destiny
      Have faith

Sir Oliver Lodge, by now thoroughly intrigued and somewhat bewildered by the Gurney request, wrote an account of the Piper and Willett scripts, partly in response to Mrs Willett's wish that he did so, but probably also in an effort to clarify his own thoughts about the sittings, their meanings and their outcome. In what follows, 'delta matter' refers to any material concerning the Daphne Case.

Private statement to be checked and deposited with other
delta matter

Mariemont,
Edgbaston.
1 Dec. 1910
Yesterday, on the 30th November 1910, Mrs Willett asked me

to make a statement concerning what I knew at this date of her relation to Piper Script, & of its connexion with her own, – especially concerning portions which, in accordance with her promised rights as a sitter & in accordance with advice from E.G.(w), she has removed or excised from the records.

I state therefore that there has been close correspondence between the Piper record & some portions of her own scripts, portions which since they came during a dazed or unconscious period of a D.I. in my presence, she was herself (or I believe) not in the least normally aware of. Clearly however there ought to be some contemporary record of every part of the Piper scripts – especially as some of it is in the nature of prediction. Part of them had come in my presence, & it seemed so important that some one should be aware of all that they contained that instructed by E.G.(w), who quite realised and indeed urged the necessity, Mrs W. consented to show me the other portions also. I have now seen all up to date.

The omitted portions have reference to three main points

(a) a Willett point, or ordinary prediction.

(b) an Alexander point, or E.G. fact.

(c) a Daphne Mother point, or E.G. request.

Of these (b) alone has been communicated to Mrs Verrall, & to her alone of the inner group. E.G.(w) permitted this communication, though Mrs W. rather shrank from letting even her friend Mrs Verrall know, because it seemed to her so strange & unlikely a claim. Mrs Verrall had however probably already grasped most of it, through her study of her own & other scripts.

I will summarise the three points as follows (the first was quite briefly dealt with – it only came incidentally – & has only to be recorded, like every other prediction, for what it is worth) –

(a) A prediction of Mr Willett's decease, which it is asserted will occur by an accident, within a period of time not much greater than a year. (I assured Mrs W. that predictions of death are rather common in SPR experience, & that we do not attach much weight to them)

(b) That a strong & remarkable feeling of affection – real love I might say – is felt by E.G. for Mrs W.; (expressions of this feeling 'I love you dearly' etc have been allowed to remain in the original Piper script on condition that they are not reproduced in any copies circulated by me) and that he has been able to exert beneficent psychic influence not only upon her (of which she was to some extent already aware, feeling deeply grateful for his care and guidance under difficult circumstances) but also upon her child Alexander. Some of this is asserted to have been pre-natal influence, and E.G.(w) now claims Alexander is in some special way connected with him by reason of this influence – using such phrases as 'I love him so', 'my boy', etc.

He admits the natural human parenthood to the fullest extent, but says that much of Alexander's psychic development is & will be due to agencies acting across the veil, or from the immaterial region.

(He is also represented, through Piper, as in close and affectionate intimacy with the deceased child Daphne, but no claim to any sort of 'psychic paternity' is made in her case. She is however represented as rather specially under his guardianship.)

(c) The third point is one that has to be kept altogether secret for the present, even from Mrs Verrall and perhaps especially from her, because of anticipated C.C.s. [Cross-Correspondences]

It is a request made by E.G.(p) to Mrs Willett that she will allow him to exercise spiritual control over yet another child – girl or boy not specified – a child by no means yet in contemplation.

If ever another child is born to her he claims beforehand that its birth has long been planned, planned in the highest quarters, to an extent which it is difficult to exaggerate; he anticipates that it will possess a remarkable personality – a genius in fact of high order – & will prove to be the greatest of his psychic works, to which all else has been leading up. E.G.(p) definitely stated that the child on its psychic side would be effectively his.

This request of E.G.(p) has been somewhat of a thunderbolt to Mrs Willett. After the first Piper sitting at which it appeared, she was dumbfounded for the rest of the day. It was within my knowledge that her own script, during dazed D.I., had recently pointed clearly enough in this direction, though her normal consciousness was, I am certain, unaware of the fact, & I had not mentioned it to her, of course, (though I

276

have now) but the Piper script was quite explicit and very emphatic.

It has been stated through Mrs Piper, as well as through Mrs Willett, that Imperator approves of E.G.'s wish, & it has been further stated that E.G. will watch over her to the utmost and make it easier for her than was possible with Alexander. That she is to fear nothing and allow herself to be guided by higher powers.

She assures me that nothing was further from her mind, or Mr Willett's, than to have another child. She had thought & hoped that her duties in this direction were over. Her state of health at such times* is such as to make it a very severe task & one from which she shrinks.

* as shown by the series of envelopes kept by Mrs Willett during the Alexander period & also by some indications in a delta memoir.

A considerable portion of the Piper sittings was devoted to urging the desirability of complying with E.G.'s request, & to overcoming Mrs Willett's reluctance to it.

An earlier part of the Piper scripts had urged her to undertake modified Piperian duties, & to allow herself to be entranced when necessary; but this work she soon expressed herself as willing to perform, if able. As to the other and weightier matter however she wishes it made quite clear that if ever it does happen it will be solely at E.G.'s reiterated request.

I am bound to record the definite Piper Rector Imperator prediction that it will happen, though no date is specified. I rather gather that there is an intention – or Gurney, Myers intentions are – to get this prediction recorded, unconsciously and far less explicitly, elsewhere. They clearly want us to understand their power of planning and arranging things, & in that sense their power of prediction.

Mrs Willett now informs me that as a result of a strong impulse she has herself made a short statement concerning some excised or withdrawn portions of Piper script, & that this statement is contained in a sealed envelope, dated 12 November 1910, which she had already sent me for filing. This envelope I have not opened, & am desired not to open. The date of its receipt [was] endorsed on it by me at the time.

277

I have also received from her a second envelope dated 18 Nov., which I am likewise desired to retain.

I anticipate that these envelopes, or one of them, will be confirmatory of what I have now recorded concerning suppressed Piper matter; so I shall put this statement of mine with them. And I shall add to the packet any other envelopes with which Mrs Willett may in future entrust me.

Oliver Lodge

1 Dec. 1910

An additional note was made by Mrs Willett on December 6th, 1910, concerning omitted portions of Piper Script:

6 Dec. 1910
Hubborn,
Christchurch,
Hants.

In my statement made Nov. 12 1910 on this matter I forgot to say that in addition to the 2 points stated then there is 1 further point – viz: that 'Mr Willett' would not live much more than a year, & would meet with an accident.

Sir Oliver Lodge reassured me by telling me that these sort of predictions are not uncommon & that no one pays attention to them.

I am therefore not worrying about it.

W.

There follows an original script of January 3rd, 1911, the first part of which has never been printed. It is catalogued as W. 229 – in other words, Mrs Willett's 229th script – and headed 'Not for circulation [ended at 11.50 a.m.]'.

For Sir OJL & Mrs V only

Mrs Willett wrote: sudden strong impulse to try for Sc, which I had had no intention of doing. The script begins:

Gurney   Yes I have come to you

Drawn by the Knowledge that you would understand &
know & be with me in the thought that is uppermost now the
thought of the unsatisfied hunger which was the Motive Impulse
of my Life I hungered for what the very conditions of Life
and Human Fate make impossible   I tried for Planetary
Satisfaction & Being[1] Superplanetary in one section of my
Ego I was ever a hungered   Gurney it is only Here that I
found – after long waiting – the food I needed
It is for us a Gargantuan[2] task the reaching back   It is only
to those whose Hearts hold a welcome for us that we can
come with any ease
Beating at shut doors we cannot effect much
How M V has grown grown since early [material missing]
Say   grown accessible   approachable   Yes how she has moved
Gurney   I am thinking especially of my career My career as
I viewed it and as it was
Say Comparison
Some achieved so much and I   to my mind at least   so little
I never did what I wished to do
I only vaguely approximated to what I wished to be I had
bursts of *joie de vivre* in early manhood
But they gave place soon very soon to the sense of effort and
of stress
If I had had one with whom I had been in tune
There was a vision but it was too late & looking back I see
that even that was or would have been a will of the wisp
Put to the **test** the test of my character & of life It would
have been dead sea fruit
Gurney I had planned my life so differently
Maladie de l'Ideale
Even Cinquecento would have left me hungry for the moral
values would have been lacking[3]
Gurney I now I can come & speak here the best Home I ever
had
Do you know what Ruskin said constituted Home for Man
Say the glow-worm's spark & the stars shine overhead & the
Roof-Tree & the makers of Home[4]
Gurney   How my thoughts go back today to earlier days
Gurney   I remember the River & the fields & the Courts   yes
Courts   not of law & the sense of   well go on   generous

vying that is the **sense** between friends & the testing of powers
All comes back to me   I never regretted leaving   leaving my
life   I regretted nothing   I regret nothing now   There were
such irretrievable mistakes in my life
From here I see the <u>necessity</u> of that stage & that is why I
have learnt to acquiesse [*sic*]
Myers was so different in his outlook You never understood
him Gurney He was an optimist by temperament
No s   Gurney let me write   let the pencil run
Gurney   I am turning to you now when the old Welt Schmertz
is upon me
Melancholy   how well I knew it Gurney & say the Roll of
the Organ & the Rings of voices high in the groined (?) roof
Why the (?) Hieratic Call[5]
Yes say that
lifelong ever & ever
We delve to meet[6]
Oh no I cannot say it
Metaphors all wrong[7]
whence cometh he whose garments are dipped in blood
Prophesy with her Good things, tidings of great joy
Rejoice & put on strength Wake the Harp & Tabret   Saying
with him that weepeth arise eat & drink   Put on strength Oh
Zion   Rejoice
Lesbia[8] Perhaps Les (?)
Lethe
Yes I want that   Lethe
Say it again
Lethean streams descend where the harebell trembles in the
breeze of evening & high on the precipice the sun climbing
to the Zenith[9]
One note of melancholy from the Forsaken Dead
Why Forsaken   What is there to forsake & the meaning is
clear
Peristile[10]
No academy they Paced
Ambulatory ambulance no ambul   to solve
And one crowned with Roses &   yes go on   who was it as
they sat and discussed
came a noisc and the flare of the torches

They came in and made merry & one marked them
When they slept   He sat
He still sat
Lucian   Lucullus
Lustia   Lucastia
Lalage   Lalage[11]
I want another scene
Show(?) me one that shall accompany me with garlanded
OXON ~ oxen
Priests slain   the Tomb beneath the walls & the blood of
Bulls[12]
Sartoris
The games & the outpoured juice of the vine   Amphorae the
jars the jars
You are weary & are going slowly
farewell
Not the word I meant
    [sudden break & pause – then very slow *strange* Sc][13]
Myers   He is very weary   weary
He is very weary
Myers
Rest   Not E.G.
Rest   He says that   Always that   <u>Rest</u>

Mrs Willett commented: this last bit of Sc took a very long
time to come & I felt most strange & somehow <u>apalled</u> [*sic*]
as it came.

Certainly it is not surprising that Mrs Willett should have felt
appalled by this script, heavy with emotion, resembling the almost
unconscious drifting regret-laden thoughts of a person on the verge
of sleep.
   Her typed notes on the script of January 3rd, 1911 are given
below:

This script I count one of my 'E.G. Personal Scripts' but as
it tailed off into quotations ect. [*sic*] I sent it for Sir O.J.L.
& Mrs. Verrall to see.
   1 A good deal of hesitation here & I was seized with that
      wretched feeling that I was not getting what was wanted.

2 I think Gargantua was a sort of giant but I know nothing more about him [a reference, of course, to Rabalais's hearty giant].

3 There seems great confusion in all this & it conveys nothing much to me & I have no means of ascertaining whether it is discriptive of E.G. or not.

4 Seems vaguely to remind me of some Ruskin quotation I have read somewhere but I cant get it clear.

5 As these words were written I had a sudden 'flash' that it was the day a service for Mr. B. [Samuel Henry Butcher] was to be held in Cambridge (I had seen it somewhere in some paper) & felt sure Mrs. Verrall was at it. I have read Hieratic Call in an F.W.H.M. book, either *Fragments* or the Abridged H.P. [*Human Personality*] as refering to chanting of Priests I believe.

6 There was a break in the Script here & from <u>here</u> it could be circulated if desired.

7 What follows is all from various parts of the Bible, but I have not thought it necessary to look up as it would take me a very long time to do so.

8 Not known to me.

9 This Lethe reference conveys nothing to me & how can the breezes of evening <u>accompany</u> a <u>climbing</u> sun. How E.G. could say the meaning was clear I can't imagine.

10 A place with columns. I have seen them at Pompei.

11 Conveys nothing to me all this. I have heard the name Lucullus & 'Lalage' was an American girl I once knew.

12 Old Testament?

13 Words fail me to describe the <u>fearfulness</u> of the end of the Script. I literally felt I was <u>dead</u> & on the 'other side' as it came; so close to 'them' they were touching me. It came very slowly, one word at a time. It had no sense of personality with it.

On January 16th, 1911, Sir Oliver Lodge added a note to his previous account about Edmund Gurney's request.

I think it may be worthwhile to add a line to my previous statement about 'E.G.'s request' or rather about his statements concerning Alexander, – which amount for present purpose to much the same.

There appears to be for the present and past few years some talks of 'Virgin Birth' in the air – Miss Bates's books for instance – & I hear rumours of others who have opinions on this subject. I have none, & I derive no support to such an idea from the W. & Piper Scripts. The phrase 'psychic paternity', as they use it, has no such meaning. No claim is for a moment made that the body is provided by other than perfectly normal means. All that they claim is that they influence the psychic development and can do this still better now than they could do with Alexander. That is what they mean, and all that they mean, by psychic paternity. (Incidentally it may be that this idea has a far-reaching application and something like it may explain how it happened that a Virgin Birth legend grew up in connexion with Christianity – for I suppose that Psychic Paternity was extraordinary action in that great historical case.) But returning to delta matters, the sole difficulty in carrying out E.G.'s request seems to me to rest with Mr & Mrs Willett & their domestic arrangements. Much of the private Piper Script was directed towards diminishing normal objection & removing normal difficulties. The P script and Mrs W.'s D.I. Script showed remarkable agreement in this respect.

O.J.L.

Let it be understood (I have probably said it before in the earlier statement deposited with this) that the Willett scripts on this subject have all been D.I. scripts, that is to say scripts written in trance; – for the dazedness of the D.I. had intensified, before these came, into unmistakable though light and easy trance.

The normal supraliminal Mrs W. knew nothing about these matters till she got them through Piper sittings. It was after that, that I told her, that I had had similar information through her own D.I. scripts from E.G.

Yes & I might go further about joint parentage &, referring to the 4th Eclogue & [illegible]

    Cara deum suboles magnum Jovis incrementum

say that substituting the Willetts for deorum(?) & E.G. for Jupiter you get Alexander.

Incrementum may signify psychic paternity. I expect that Virgil and the Sibyl knew all about that.

I am writing this to Mrs Verrall & I shall put this page in with the rest.

O.J.L.   16.1.11

On February 9th, 1911, after the last Piper sitting on February 8th, Lodge prepared a supplementary statement about the suppressed portion of the Piper sitting of December 2nd, 1910:

9 Feb. 1911

I have today been shown a complete copy of all the Piper script which came on Dec 2, & I find it very clearly & connectedly confirmatory of everything that had been indicated before about a Gurney plan or request that the Willetts would provide a brother to Daphne and Alexander. Daphne herself indicated her wish, & E.G. spoke of it as a definite plan whereby he would be able to exercise psychic control or influence more markedly than he had done in the case of Alexander. He spoke of it in the following terms – among others. 'This is going to be the _most_ wonderful production of spirit power that has ever been known.'

I did not gather that any such child was as yet on the way, in fact I understand it to be implied that it is definitely not so at present but I think that I am meant to understand that no human obstacle will be placed in the way of their contribution to Gurney's wish by the Willetts. I record this because it is evidently meant as a sort of prediction, though doubtless a prediction in itself on the physical side of a very ordinary kind.

Yesterday viz 8 Feb 1911 there was another Piper sitting at which Mrs Willett was present, & in this sitting E.G. again referred to the same subject saying

'When my child appears I shall glorify God'.

but still certain references which came to 'time' & 'patience' which occurred at intervals throughout this as well as earlier sittings, lead me to suppose that nothing has as yet been accomplished towards the desired end.

284

This statement was written in my presence at Cadoxton on July 10, 1913, & has remained ever since in my possession. Alice Johnson, July 23, 1913

Augustus July 10, 1913

The following was given by me in outline to Mrs Sidgwick when we met at Fishers Hill, June, 1913, and at her desire I now write it out more in detail.

In 1910 I had some sittings with Mrs Piper at Birmingham under the supervision of Sir OJL in the months of Oct, Nov, Dec and in 1911 in Feb. At the second sitting E.G. said he wanted to talk to me alone and Sir OJL was out of the room during most of the sitting, the latter fact I recorded in my diary.

The gist of E.G.'s communication at this sitting and subsequently alluded to at later sittings was the request from 'them' that I would lend myself to pass another child into the world from & for them.

The gist of my answer was that I could not undertake to do so.

In Nov 1910 I wrote a brief note recording these matters, sealed it up, and sent it to Sir OJL on Nov 12/10. I early made it clear to Sir OJL that I could not allow the Piper records on this particular subject to be copied for circulation (as all the other parts of the sittings were) nor did I wish the passages to remain in the original record. I believe he consulted JGP who said that in other cases matters of a very private nature had been removed by cutting from the original records.

The passages referring to what I shall call the E.G. request were, after having been read by Sir OJL, cut out of the records with his permission & destroyed by me. There as far as I was concerned the matter ended at that date.

I believe that Sir OJL wrote a statement confirming what I have here said as E.G.'s request, & if so this, & certainly my own statement, is at this present moment in his possession.

The Piper scripts were confused & there were certainly many minds in them. My feelings generally were

1. I did not want any more children
2. I had not the courage to face the phisical ordeal it involved, being for me rather unusually heavy.

285

3. No more children were desired by anyone else.

4. I had mixed feelings about the genuineness of EG(p) & the Piper controls generally.

The sittings which took place after the 12 Nov. when I wrote the statement above referred to did not add anything of great interest as far as I can remember. They consisted largely of repetitions, arguments & occasionally rather strained communications between me and E.G.

After Feb. 1911 I had nothing more to do with Mrs Piper & as far as I am concerned her sittings ended there.

This brings me down to Spring 1911.

After that date E.G.(w) frequently returned to the subject & I think E.G.(w) had a more convincing effect on me than E.G.(p) though I expect the effect ought to have been the other way round.

I was much influenced by his telling me of H.S. views on the matter, & I got to the point of considering occasionally whether I would ever change my mind.

I was also influenced by the fact that my decision was not totally unconnected with cowardice over the phisical part of it – that made me suspect that that feeling might be playing a larger part than I was aware of. Of course the recognition of this had a great spur to overcoming it, because one hates to feel we can be beaten by material things like that from doing anything one's mind feels to be fine and wise – & I had got near to the point of seeing it *might* be fine to agree, & work with 'them' in the matter according to their wishes.

It was not until near the autumn of 1911 that I really achieved the point of the spirit being willing though the flesh was weak. *By the autumn I had so rearranged my life that the conception of the child would have been possible* [Author A.E. Roy's emphasis].

On the night of February 1–2, 1912, I had a very vivid dream connected with the whole subject which I recorded and sent to Miss A.J. (See copy affixed herewith)

E.G. from time to time had assured me the child would come. That dream was a prophecy of [illegible] was not fulfilled. I cannot say when I began to call Babe Augustus, but certainly early in 1912.

In the case of Augustus I had no definite supernormal

intimation that conception had taken place. This is different to what occurred in the case of Alexander... The only possible supernormal note is imparted(?) by my sudden unwillingness to start from [illegible] on receiving a telegram from my mother telling me of my father's death and asking me to go to her. It was impossible for me at that date to know definitely that there was any reason for not undertaking a long journey but I felt a sudden conviction that I ought not to go & that conviction was associated in my mind with the thought of a child.

During the months of Augustus's coming the companionship between me and E.G. was really too close and constant to admit of being recorded day by day. There are therefore no 'E.G. envelopes' as there were in the case of Alexander.

E.G. attended to my health, diet, exercise, etc & of course by winter would have been [illegible] coming from an SPR point of view if it had not been for my feeling so closely in touch with 'them'. I also got the impression very clearly though without being able to [illegible] that a larger group of people were working at Augustus than was the case over Alexander – I felt that more than my own group (by which I mean delta & her 3 companions) were surrounding me though I never got a clear impression of who or what it was. Still I felt *surrounded*. I received much help in many matters from the other side. I write this down in a way to show just how it seemed to me, without of course making any claim that it is evidentially important.

[Copy made by A.J. [Alice Johnson] on June 24th, 1913, of contents of an envelope sent to her sealed up by Mrs W. on February 3rd, 1912, & which has been kept ever since, sealed & locked up, by A.J. till, at Mrs W.'s request, she opened it on the morning of June 24th, 1913.]

Night of February 1–2, 1912   Hilvers, Shottermill, Surrey
Account of dream by Mrs Willett

In my dream I woke and found myself looking at the following scene. Three figures, which somehow I took to be three women of a Godess-y description, were grouped together, and on the ground in front of them were lying things on which there was writing.

I say 'things' because I don't know whether they were paper or engraved wood or stones – all I know is that there were many and each had writing on them. Suddenly a lot of figures appeared and began looking at these written upon 'things' and to pick them up. One of the things was apparently being guarded by one of the three women (?) because I saw several figures try and pick it up but not allowed to. The figures gradually picked up all the written upon things except the one just mentioned. Then I suddenly saw a tall majestic figure coming toward it, it was glowing with rays of yellow light and all the figures (except the three women) bowed down before it and seemed to be doing homage to it.

It came along to where the one remaining 'thing' was and then picked it up and the Woman (?) took it (the majestic figure) to the two others. The next thing I remember is that the Majestic Figure came towards me and took my face between its hands and gazed into my very soul and I into its soul. (I don't know whether it was a man or woman.)

I can't describe what follows because it was all 'feelings' and escapes definition. But I felt just worship, then amazement, then joy – and the figure seemed to feel no amazement but great tenderness, and it said these words:

'You have not chosen me but I have chosen you' and then the word 'Mother' is the next I remember. I knew it was speaking to me and I only remember that the last words meant (I don't remember the actual ones) that when I next saw it it would be in the likeness of a human Babe and that what was written on the thing picked up was a destiny that it should come into the world through me. I felt the light becoming stronger and stronger and all became confused —— and the next thing I remember was that I found myself walking along a country road and saw some people far away walking to me. When they got near I saw that they were men with a child in front. Suddenly I recognised Daphne – She was running and carrying a tall Madonna Lily in her hand – taller than herself. The men were F.W.H.M. [Myers], E.G. [Gurney] and H.S. [Sidgwick] ... They were walking together – they looked at me earnestly and I found a letter in my hand which I opened. The paper was blue or bluey-grey and the ink white, there was one sentence only, printed in large letters. I only remember:

If you believe ... Vision ... cease motoring at once.

The next thing I remember is that I found myself sitting up in bed feeling that I was smothering and could not breathe ... every line of F.W.H.M.'s face stamped on my memory ... every vein and wrinkle ... his hair whiter than I had remembered in life ... the whole Dream came back to me, like a series of magic lantern pictures ... as if I were re-seeing it again ... the three Women ... the glowing radiant Figure ... the written upon 'things' ... the road ... Daphne.

I got up and turned on my electric light but I felt so unnerved and frightened (very stupid of me but so it was) that I could not bear to be alone so I went along to my Mother's room and woke her. I got into her bed and told her about my dream ... and soon I felt better but very bewildered.

Winifred Coombe-Tennant

Additional note. It seems to me that the dream, *if* there is anything in it, points to my being on the way of having another child.

Apart from the *possibility* of such a thing there is no phisical reason to lead me to suppose so – & it will be about ten days before the only phisical symptom ever present at an early stage – viz. an irregularity – could be present.

I have therefore absolutely no means of knowing whether the Dream is prophetic or not. But my Mother advises me to forego motoring until I can be sure & I shall do that. Also I record this dream and shall, whether it be false or true, send it eventually to Mrs Sidgwick or Miss Johnson so that a *failure* may be on record as well as successes – such as the Sir O.L. dream & others recorded in delta papers.

P.S. Daphne seemed about 9 years old, about the same size as Alice in Wonderland in the illustrations in that book.

Copy of Mrs Willett's mother's statement by Alice Johnson:

Hilvers, Shottermill, Surrey
Feb. 2nd, 1912

Early this morning soon after 5 a.m. I was lying awake & I heard a knock at my door & Winifred came in. She seemed much upset & dazed & nervous & said she had had such a strange dream & had seen delta. I said 'Get into my bed', which she did, & she told me the dream, which was the same as in the record I have seen. We talked some 20 or 30 minutes & then she went back to her own room & slept.

I have been in close touch with my daughter before the births of all of her children & for the first month or so she has never experienced any physical discomfort.

Now the only symptom which could lead her to have any apprehension as to her condition cannot occur for more than a week from this date.

[Signed – Mrs Willett's Mother]

Account by Mrs Willett of Augustus Henry's birth, April 9th, 1913:

The day of Babe's birth was a very long and strenuous one. I was in touch with E.G., who urged me not to try for definite communications but as he said to 'conserve your vitality'. He assured me that I would not be left alone for one minute. The birth stretched over the time from 2.30 a.m. to 11.45 p.m. Owing to the size of the child and his position very high up with me, he got caught on some bones and made no progress in descending in spite of labour pains being present. The Doctor decided about 9.45 p.m. to use instruments. Just before I went off under chloroform I asked E.G. who was with me. He said that in addition to himself there were H.S., F.W.H.M. and Daphne. I was *surprised* at bringing Daphne to such a scene. I then was given chloroform and went dead off.

What I now proceed to relate I did not know until several weeks later. When I was completely unconscious, the Doctor on further examination told the nurse that the child could not be born alive. He repeated this from time to time and the nurse was dreadfully upset and said the Doctor (who is really a friend as well as a medical attendant) was very anxious and upset too. However, contrary to expectation, it was possible to bring the child into the world and when the Doctor had carefully examined him and moved his limbs he called out to the Nurse that he was perfect. He did not cry at once from the result of being partly stupified by chloroform.

I now return to my own actual experiences. When I came to at first I remembered nothing, nor where I was nor who I was. Then I got a sense of noise, then I heard squeals and wondered what they were, then I recognised it was a child crying, then I got nearer to understanding what happened, then I heard rattling of objects in basin, then I heard a man's voice, then I suppose I moved a little, for the Doctor came over to me and said 'Yes, it is a boy.' I asked if he were perfectly all right. He said he was an exceptionally fine child. I said his name was Augustus.

I had to undergo about half an hour's intense pain to expel the afterbirth, and when that was over I was too exhausted for them to attempt to move me, so blankets were piled on me and I was left in peace, my Mother sitting some distance away, and both the Nurse, Doctor and Babe out of the room.

Then comes the following point, difficult to relate but Mrs Sidgwick wanted me to attempt to make some sort of record about it.

I can best describe by saying I had two brains working at the same time.

One brain only wanted to think about the release from pain, the joy of Babe's being there and safe and *a man child*, and also of 'them' and the excitement and wonder of it all. The other brain wanted to shut out the first brain, and Brain No. 2 was obsessed by one thought which simply overflowed and succeeded in drowning Brain No. 1. The thought was 'the dark young man.'

To explain this I must go back to Mrs Sidgwick's house in Cambridge in – I believe it was on my first visit in January 19th, 1912, that I got a strong impression about a photograph hanging in her dining-room in a not very conspicuous position, and which I could only see by turning my head well round, as it was rather at the back of me as I sat at meals and I was only in the room at meal-times. It shows a rather dark, I think carbon or platenotype print of the head and shoulders of a young man. He looks down, one sees the outline of a nose and cheek, it is I believe a 3/4 face position. I somehow felt it was extraordinarily familiar to me and I got interested in it and felt rather oddly about it. I told Mrs Sidgwick that it was the only thing in the house I got any impression about. I had looked forward to being in the house because I felt I should like to be where H.S's things were, but I got no impression of any kind except from this photograph.

I think it was on the next occasion of my being in the house (May 1912) that I talked to her again about the picture as we were having some meal, Mr Balfour being present. I said I felt rather uncomfortable about it, not being able to account for my feeling. I knew somehow the face – a feeling I might be getting rather nervy and silly. I was then told that it was possible there was something supernormal about the impression. I was also told that the man was dead.

I thought no more about it as far as I know until Brain No. 2 simply drowned me in the feeling of his presence, so close to me that if I had put out my hand I felt I should have touched him. I felt he was stationed there, beside me, and that no anxiety or worry was possible for me while he kept watch.

I tried to think about E.G. – but he seemed to have vanished. I 'saw' only the dark young man and it would not be accurate to imply that I even mentally saw a man and nothing more. The sense I had was of being in close touch with a mind and personality which somehow I knew and who knew me. It was very queer, but I was too weak then to try to analyse it, so I simply lay feeling as if I was taken charge of and needn't bother about anything.

The impression of his nearness lasted many hours, quite 12, towards the end of which I was able to get outside it at moments, enough to as it were to analyse what I was feeling. I came to the conclusion that it would be an interesting point from an SPR point of view on the effect of anaesthetics on the brain. I had heard that people recovering from unconsciousness suffered from odd tricks of the brain, remembering some trivial event of long ago, or getting some *idée fixe* of a quite paltry and unreasonable description. I never attached any meaning to it (when I say I, I mean when my 2 Brains had as it were come together) until I was told that the experience might not be so totally idiotic as I had imagined by Mr Balfour or Mrs Sidgwick (I forget which) at Fishers

Hill in June 13 when I spoke of it to them. I told Mrs Sidgwick not to tell me anything about my dark young man, as I wanted to keep him as I knew him with me in such a crisis of my life and did not want my impression blurred by being told anything about him. I felt that nothing anybody could tell me would add to my complete aprehension of a nature and personality, though I do not know who he is, when he lived or when he died, nor did I speak to him, nor did he speak to me.

[signed] Daphne's Mother.

14

Watching and Waiting

For unto us a Child is born, unto us a Son is given, and the government shall be upon his shoulder: and his name shall be called Wonderful Counsellor, the mighty God, the everlasting Father, the Prince of Peace.

Messiah, G.F. Handel (taken from Isaiah 9.6)

On the day after the birth of Augustus Henry, Mrs Sidgwick wrote her brother Gerald the following letter:

1 Grange Terrace,
Cambridge

April 10/13

Dearest Gerald,

I have told the good news about Mrs T [Coombe-Tennant] to Mrs V [Helen Verrall]. She was greatly astonished and of course pleased. She has not had the slightest suspicion, nor has she had any feeling that the reasons suggested for her not meeting Mrs T. were incomplete and insufficient. She feels sure that Helen does not know of her antartic [sic] script – as sure as she can be without looking up her records. I forget whether it was you or Mr Piddington who asked me to find this out.

The number you are to begin with in Willett Script is 251. I will send copies of the dreams tomorrow. They occurred on the early morning of October 1, 1912 and on the night of October 15–16 respectively. Mrs Willett takes them as belonging to each other...

Mrs Verrall has on reflexion interpreted her recent script about the unseen feet as an M.L. script she told me. It was at any rate not a reference to the coming babe!

Your loving

E.M. Sidgwick.

The Society for Psychical Research.
20, Hanover Square,
London, W

July 17, 1913

Dear Mr Balfour,

I have not got all the H.V. Scrs. here; but I expect the ones you refer to are 'Peace hath her victories' (Augustus is 'no less renowned than' Alexander!) etc. We have now found references back to 1905 & I believe that the second names, John & Henry, were also pre-arranged. The 'Henry' is particularly interesting.

I should much like to see you & show you the points that I think come out. So many Scs. are involved that it would take an enormous time to write them out. I am staying here until next Monday (July 21) & should then be at the S.P.R. rooms on Tuesday & the following days from 11 a.m. onwards. If you were in London any day that week, perhaps you could manage to come. I think we should want an hour or two to do the thing at all thoroughly. The S.P.R. rooms will probably close for the summer holidays at the end of July.

But I fancy there was some idea of your going to stay with Mrs Sidgwick at the beginning of August. I shall probably be in Cambridge then, and you might prefer in that case for us to go over the Scrs. with her. Of course I want to take the first opportunity of talking to her about it.

Yours sincerely,

Alice Johnson.

P.S. Have you observed that Augustus's head is the same shape as Shakespeare's?! It comes out beautifully in one of your photographs.

On October 26th, 1913, at 6.15 p.m., Mrs Verrall penned the following thoughts on her notepaper, the first page of which is headed with her address, 5 Selwyn Gardens, Cambridge, and is black-bordered – presumably from sheets kept after the death of her husband on June 18th, 1912.

Mrs Sidgwick has just shown me the copy of Mrs W's dream on the night of Oct 19–20, 1913. There is no doubt, I think, that the FWHM's 'Latin quotation' (which can hardly be a quotation in any case!) is a comment on the lineage of the Child of the 4th Eclogue. I still feel uncertain of the precise import of 'on both sides'.

But I think there is a connexion between her dream & my sending her Augustus's engraved box. The Latin quotation inside that box is Virg. <u>Aen</u>. <u>vi</u> 791 'Hic vir, hic est, tibi queni promitti saepius audis Augustus'.

There I stopped – quite deliberately, because I did not wish to emphasise the Golden Age wh. Augustus was to bring back. But the 4th Eclogue & this passage from <u>Aen.vi</u> are closely interrelated: see for example Warde Fowler's note on p.83 of the Mayor – Conway – Fowler book, where he begs readers to look at several Virgilian passages which bear on the point that 'Augustus is ever in Virgil's mind ... the son of the divine Julius & the ... regenerator of the world.' Of these, the 'most striking' is 'the famous one in <u>Aen.vi</u> (788 ff)'. See also Conway pp 39–42.

The dates are rather neatly fitted. Mrs W.'s dream was on the night of Oct. 19–20: the box reached me on Monday Oct. 20. I showed it on that date to Mrs Sidgwick who called here about 2.15 p.m.

It is rather interesting that the next words in my quotation refer to the <u>lineage</u> of Augustus: 'Devi genus'.

What 'on both sides' means I cannot guess. Mrs W. thinks it may refer to a sentence in my letter to her. As far as I remember I wrote, speaking of Augustus: 'Love to him and his from me and mine, and you and I know that 'ours' include more than the visible ([illegible] or family or some such thing.)'.

If there is any connexion between Mrs W.'s dream and my motto, it looks as if it were due to something other than

The Balfour
brothers with
Blanche. Sitting
L to R: Eustace,
Blanche, Cecil,
Standing L to R:
AJB, GWB,
FMB.

Whittingehame.

Trinity College,
Cambridge,
1907.

Gerald W. Balfour, aged 17 at Eton.

Francis M. Balfour, aged about 18.

Gerald W. Balfour in 1884.

Francis M. Balfour, the 'Dark young man' of the Scripts.

Mary C. Lyttelton.

Arthur James Balfour as a young man when he fell in love with Mary Lyttelton.

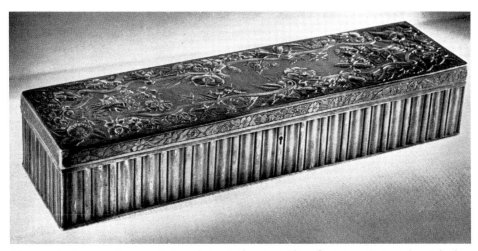

Above: The bronze silver casket made by Arthur J. Balfour for Mary C. Lyttelton's lock of hair.

AJB as a member of parliament.

AJB with King George V.

AJB as prime minister.

Gerald W. Balfour, 1905.

Lady Betty, wife of Gerald W. Balfour.

Gerald W. Balfour with Ruth, his first child.

Jean Cooke-Yarborough, who married Robert Arthur Lytton Balfour (RAL), Gerald W. Balfour's son.

Henry Coombe-Tennant, Welsh Guards, some time before 1940.

Winifred Coombe-Tennant in Edwardian mode and in her thirties.

Winifred Coombe-Tennant with baby Henry.

Jean Cooke-Yarborough, who married
RAL in 1923.

Jean Balfour with her son Gerald.

Jean, Gerald
minor and RAL.

Jean (Countess of Balfour)
in her sixties.

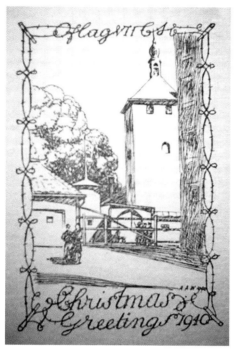

Christmas card from German prison camp, 1940.

Christmas card from German prison camp, 1941.

An impression of the escape from Oflag VIB.

Mlle Andrée de Jongh, celebrated World War Two resistance fighter, who helped Henry Coombe-Tennant and his fellow officers escape to Gibraltar.

telepathy. I thought of the motto as soon as I decided early in September to have a motto at all, but I did not quite decide on the form of the gift till the end of the month of September. But the motto has been on my mind constantly, as I wrote it & had a drawing of it, which I sent back 2 or 3 weeks ago. The arrival on Oct. 20 was quite unexpected: I had given the maker until the end of the month, & did not know when it would be delivered.

M. de G. V.

The Society for Psychical Research.
20, Hanover Square,
London, W.

Feb. 11, 1914

Dear Mr Balfour,

I had a talk with Mrs W. last Friday about her recent script (January 10), & two or three points turned up that I thought you might be interested in hearing about, as they seem to me to have a bearing on her non-recognition of the 'dark young man'

The reason why I discussed the script with her was that I wanted to confirm my own recollections about what parts of my paper that has just come out in the <u>Proc</u>. had been mentioned by me to her, as I think the script shows supernormal knowledge of other parts of the paper. (She already knew that the script contained a veridical message to Mrs Verrall). I began by asking her what meaning she attached to the words 'precipitate' 'dimorphism' 'crystallization'. Afterwards I showed her the Table of Contents of my paper, saying, you remember I told you about so-&-so, & so-&-so – does anything else strike you as familiar? (I have now sent her the paper, having long ago promised to do so.)

I then gave her a copy of her Sc of Jan. 10 (from which all annotations except her own had been removed) & asked her to read it through carefully & tell me what phrases were familiar to her, & in what connection. She read it aloud to me, making remarks as she went on.

When she came to 'who smote the sounding farrows,' she

297

asked 'Isn't that from <u>Ulysses</u>?' I said 'yes, I think it is.' This confirms Sir O.L.'s view that the source of the phrase – but no doubt there may be, as Mrs Verrall suggested, some idea of the <u>Persae</u> behind it.

But the thing that interested me most was connected with 'Diana – Dimorphism.' She did not know what 'Dimorphism' meant. I asked her to think of words formed from the same syllables, & she soon got to 'Di' meaning <u>'two'</u>. Then she suggested that 'morphism' was derived from Morpheus, & that it meant 'twice asleep'. I asked her what 'amorphous' meant, & on the same principle she said perhaps it meant 'sleepless'. We managed to get a little nearer by way of 'anthropomorphic', which she knew the meaning of & finally got to Dimorphism meaning two forms – 'perhaps (she suggested) body & soul.' I left it at that.

This was at the beginning of our talk. In going over this Sc. we came to 'Diana – Dimorphism' & I reminded her that when we had worked over a lot of Scs. together last July, (looking for Augustus refs.) there were refs. to the moon among them. (As far as I can remember, it was she who first started looking for moon refs. as she considered they were Δ [i.e. Daphne] refs. I acquiesced in a general way to her lead in all these things but indicated that I regarded them as birth refs. applying not only to Daphne but to the other children too.

Of course I knew that J.G.P. regarded the Moon as a symbol of M.L. & of course I accept this; but I always believed that that did not exhaust its meaning. In talking to Mrs W. I naturally confined myself to what I believe to be its other meaning).

But – at last I come to the point! – as soon as I mentioned the Moon, she said 'But what has Diana to do with the Moon?' I thought this a very odd question to ask, but I explained. 'Oh,' she said – as if rather disgusted and disappointed – 'I thought she was a real goddess, who hunted.' (Incidentally this confirms Mrs Verrall's interpretation of 'To hunt on the mountain' as a ref. to Hippolytus). 'So she was', I said 'but she was also the Moon.' I went on to remind her of <u>Endymion</u> & various things I knew she was familiar with, but I could not get her to recognise that she knew that Diana was the moon. The more I thought of this afterwards, the queerer it seemed to me, as I feel sure she knows as well as I do that Diana is the moon.

Almost immediately after Diana in the script comes 'Downing'. This is another thing that she knows & always refused to recognise. It comes in one of my published papers & in the Holland script Vol. which she has, & I have mentioned it to her several times, as – in some way that I don't understand – connected with Δ [i.e. Daphne] refs. & therefore of interest to her. (The name Florence = Mrs Maitland – occurs in M.V. 115 B in the Vol. which Mrs W. has)

These instances & 'the dark young man' non-recognition look very much like the negative hallucinations produced by hypnotism. I am coming to believe that whenever she is what you call 'obfuscated', it is produced by an external suggestion, & it is a sign that the topic about which she is obfuscated is of special importance. This certainly seems to be the case in regard to F.M.B., as I believe that the 'Dimorphism of Diana' is intimately connected with our central problem – by which I mean the nature of the connexion between M.L. etc & the children. I think that 'Downing' either comes into this or is one of the things that will throw light on it. It would take much too long to tell you just now all my grounds for thinking this, & you may already think this letter much too long!

But please show it to Mrs Sidgwick & to Mrs Verrall if she cares to see it. I hear they are both staying with you just now.

Yours sincerely,
Alice Johnson.

P.S. Probably you noticed in W. Sc. of Dec. 14, 1913, 'She left lonely the Kings of the Sea' – referring to L.L. This fits in with my idea that Forsaken Merman quotations are applied to her as an instance of someone who left her husband & children.

The Society for Psychical Research.
20, Hanover Square,
London, W.

October 19, 1914

Dear Mr Balfour,

Here is the Holland Sc. that you wanted. I find that I can really manage to do without it for some little time; but please do not keep it indefinitely!

This lot was received by Mrs W. on Apr. 27, 1911 (though she had seen those up to: 239 inclusive on Nov. 12, 1910); but the notes written on this copy were mostly added after she had returned it to me.

I enclose also the note on A.J.B. that I mentioned to you this morning. I see I was wrong in speaking of it as a <u>dream</u>. It was only thoughts of him – so persistent as to be noted in her diary – And it comes <u>after</u> what is, I think, the first mention of you in her Sc – see 112(2). But that hardly seems enough to account for it, so I propose to add it as 121 A, unless I hear from you that you think after all it isn't worthwhile. You will see that the first part of the Holland Sc. (237) with which it coincides is definitely Balfourian.

I am glad to think of her as still in your beautiful garden which I enjoyed so much yesterday. It was altogether a delightful weekend.

Yours very sincerely,
Alice Johnson.

[Attached.]

Note by Mrs W. dated Jan . 16, 1911 on Holland 236
(June 9, 1909).

'Do you think this "A" could be Mr A. Balfour, because I note in my diary on 16th [June, 1909] 'Many thoughts of the Darling & of Arthur Balfour, though why of him? He keeps on coming into my mind.' (I have met him once at a dinner-party at my Mother-in-law's, but don't know him)'

Note by A.J.

The entry in the diary was verified by me. In regard to the 'A', I asked Mrs Holland if she had heard that H.S. stammered & she wrote in reply: 'I have a hazy recollection that some one this year told me he used to stammer. Some one told me a story (I cannot recall what) that made me laugh & said 'Arthur Sidgwick is particularly witty & amusing.' 'Is he related to Professor Sidgwick?' asked I. 'Yes, his brother; but unlike him he does not stammer; the elder man stammered very badly at times.' When I read over the script, 'The Stammarian's Funeral' annoyed me as a vulgar attempt at a pun, & I did not trace the connection.

It seems to follow that 'A' here is A.S. – not A.J.B.

The latter part of the script seems to refer to Daphne.

But see the script of June 16, 1909 – i.e. the one contemporary with Mrs W.'s Note, – much of which is appropriate to A. J. B. while the Alpine refs. are, I think, undoubtedly to F.M.B., because of their connection with similar Holland Alpine refs.

The Society for Psychical Research.
20, Hanover Square,
London, W.

February 21, 1915

Dear Mr Balfour,

I am going to Cadoxton on Monday, March 1, to stay for a week, & I shall take with me copies of two or three points about Daphne which I mean to ask Mrs Tennant's leave to quote in my notes on Holland script. One of these is a statement she wrote for me in Jan. 1911 about how she chose the name of Daphne & when, which I propose to quote, if she does not object in connection with the Daphne and Augustus – civic crown – script which I showed you. You said, when I showed it to you, that you thought I had better not tell her about my interpretation of the script. Of course I will not do so if you are still of the opinion that I had better not. But my impression is that hitherto we have told her all the points we have made out about the children, except those involving the other people, & this seems to me to be a reasonable principle, because – roughly speaking – anything that came about the children in her own scripts could hardly be evidential, & anything she is told about the children in other scripts probably tends to stimulate her own. This Daphne & Augustus point is one that no doubt she would particularly like to know.

At the same time I don't at all want to press for your leave to tell it, if you think it unwise to do so. I am perfectly willing to abide by your decision & of course shall say nothing about it to her <u>unless</u> I hear from you that I may. Do not trouble to write unless to say this.

I was very sorry to miss you when you called at Holy Well on Monday afternoon, but it was nice to have had a little opportunity of scriptic talk with you earlier.

I am much looking forward to seeing the Wise One at his present stage. I hear that both he and his mother approve of the new nurse, which is satisfactory.

Yours very sincerely,
Alice Johnson

For the Sidgwick Group of investigators, the first twenty years of the twentieth century brought a series of fascinating, genuinely exciting, paranormal events into their lives that it was impossible for them to avoid facing and assessing, using every ability they possessed – intelligence, education, analytical skill, caution and natural scepticism. There is no doubt that all of them carefully considered singly and in discussion among themselves every possible theory that might enable them to avoid accepting the growing conviction that the scripts were being produced, designed and dictated over many years to the automatists by a Script Intelligence – for want of a more definitive term – according to a long-term and breathtakingly ambitious plan that had more than one item on its agenda. They had ultimately dismissed any non-paranormal explanation and they continually considered at every stage just how far they could avoid accepting survival of death by putting forward the part played by telepathy among the living as an adequate and satisfactory explanation for psychical phenomena.

It will be remembered that only Sir Oliver Lodge, among the group, accepted the proposition that the most satisfactory theory to account for the phenomena he had studied was that at least some people survived for at least some years after the death of their physical body. Certainly Myers before his death in January 1901 had also become convinced by the evidence he and others had gathered that human personality survived death. It will also be recalled that the first scripts written by Mrs Verrall were motivated by his death to give him a chance – if he had indeed survived death – to communicate.

By 1908, the Daphne case began to make its inroads into their

302

cautious scepticism when Winifred, grief-stricken by the sudden death of her daughter Daphne, wrote to Mrs Verrall and asked her to look in the scripts for any reference to the little girl. In his perceptive summary of the case, sadly unpublished before his death, the psychical researcher Montague Keen shows just how impossible it was for anyone of open mind to avoid coming to the conclusion that massive paranormal activity concerning the circumstances of Daphne's life had been appearing in the scripts of a number of automatists *even before Daphne had been born*. Keen pointed out:

It was only as a result of a retrospective examination of Helen Verrall's earlier scripts, however, that there were discovered unmistakeable references to Daphne both before she was born and during her brief life. None of these clues had conveyed any meaning at the time. Most striking, perhaps, was the name of Llangattock (August 29, 1906); a reference to the Welsh word 'sarn', the name of a lane near Daphne's birthplace; the name of Winifred; a map resembling the outline of the coastal part of Wales visible from Daphne's birthplace; and a description of the church where she was christened. The final reference, which occurred within hours of Daphne's death, relates to the day of the feast with myrrh and frankincense, i.e. Epiphany, the day of Daphne's birth. Included are three references to laurel or bay trees (*Daphne laureola*). In each of Helen's seven scripts from which these references are drawn, Llangattock (the only place thus named in Wales) is accompanied by such other qualifying features as a placename, and appropriate topographical reference or date, or to laurels. In scripts which followed, there was a range of similar concordances. Their cumulative effect was impressive. Several such references appeared before the automatists knew anything of Mrs Willett [Mrs Coombe-Tennant], and long before Daphne's birth. Likewise, a correct description of the view from Cadoxton in Glamorgan. Fragments then appeared in French which seemed to relate to a recent visit Winifred had paid to France. There was a poem 'à ma cousine Angèle' appearing just as Winifred had left a child called Angele. There were also references to the 'Chelsea baby'. Daphne died in Chelsea, London. In the scripts she is almost everywhere referred to as Delta.

Of these messages the most specific and unambiguous was

303

the name of the Welsh village where her home at Cadoxton stands. It was among references all of them associated with clues meaningless to Mrs Verrall and her daughter [Helen], but highly significant to Winifred. Many of the scripts' allusions to Daphne, the circumstances of her birth, the type and colour of the ribbon she wore, and what her pendant looked like, were found to have appeared from as early as 1902 onwards, and even included references to the Coombe-Tennant coat of arms.

Had all these references derived from Mrs Verrall herself, there might have been a lingering suspicion of subliminal contamination, but clues were also appearing in the scripts of Mrs Holland in India, who knew nothing about Winifred. Even Mrs Forbes, another automatist who played a minor role, kept getting an elaborate capital D in her scripts. What particularly impressed Winifred was a drawing closely resembling a pendant which she had presented to the child. On the same day that Daphne died, Helen Verrall had produced a script later seen to contain two fairly unambiguous references to the tragic event. Yet Daphne's very existence was unknown to her.

... On August 8th, 1908 [Daphne died on July 21st, 1908], Helen [Verrall] received a script in the form of a 'poem of great beauty'. A few days later Winifred reported that it appeared to relate closely to the circumstances of Daphne's death and her own subsequent actions and emotions. 'To me,' she wrote, 'they are overwhelmingly descriptive of facts that no-one was aware of.'

Another weighty body of evidence making it difficult for the Sidgwick Group to avoid accepting that some discarnate intelligence was responsible for the phenomena was of course the Lethe Case.

For all their deep involvement with the Cross-Correspondences the Sidgwick Group did not live isolated, academic lives untouched by the succession of tragic events taking place in the second decade of the twentieth century.

Almost a precursor to, and microcosm of, the ghastly tragedy of the First World War, the sinking of the liner *Titanic* on the night of April 14th–15th, 1912, brought to some people for the first time the shocking realisation that man's hubris, coupled with his inability to assess a situation correctly, could lead him into bringing about tragedies of his own making. The liner, the largest ship in the world, the pride of British shipbuilding, widely believed to be unsinkable, sailed on its maiden voyage carrying a representative assembly of people of all classes, from millionaires and their entourage of servants to poor emigrant families seeking a decent life in the New World. On the urging of the Chairman of the White Star Company, who wanted the ship to gain the Blue Riband (given for the fastest transatlantic crossing) on its maiden voyage, the master, Captain Smith, believing in the invincibility of his ship, ignored five warnings about icebergs in the North Atlantic. At 11.40 p.m., the *Titanic*, at full speed, struck an iceberg which ripped the ship's hull below the waterline as easily as a tin-opener rips open a can. A fatal flaw in the design of the supposedly watertight bulkheads, allowed the icy floodwaters to pour into successive sections, sealing the ship's fate. Two hours and forty minutes after the collision with the iceberg, the *Titanic* sank. For most of that time, many of the passengers, so convinced were they that the ship was unsinkable, refused to leave it and this unshakeable refusal to enter the lifeboats undoubtedly increased the dreadful loss of life. By a bitter irony, the dedicated efforts of the engineers who stayed heroically at their posts to keep power and the ship's lights running throughout the liner's slow death probably contributed to the reluctance of the passengers to leave the brightly lit ship. The high proportion of fatalities, however, almost three-quarters of the 2207 people on board, was mainly due to the fact that the liner, deemed by its builders to be unsinkable, carried too few lifeboats, with a capacity for only half of the people on board. Many of those launched were not even full when they were rowed away.

The shockwaves generated by the *Titanic* tragedy – the realisation of the destruction of the indestructible and the consequent awesome loss of life – was totally overshadowed two years later when on August 4th, 1914, Great Britain went to war, joining the cascade of European nations tumbling into the abyss of conflict, and causing Sir Edward Grey to make his prophetic remark on August 3rd that the lamps were going out all over Europe. During the war's long duration, many other nations would be dragged in, the British Dominions and Empire immediately following the United Kingdom's example, the United States in 1917.

In the first few months of the conflict, even with the example of the American Civil War still relatively fresh in thinking people's minds, there were indeed many who believed sincerely that the new conflict would all be over by Christmas. Perhaps some of them took the view that it was just not possible that in their modern, civilised, cultured, scientific and technological world, a world of international congresses, exhibitions and friendships, the leaders of the family of European nations would not quickly realise the appalling potentialities for total disaster in the conflict and speedily devise an acceptable solution that would bring peace. The following four years of the First World War, with a death toll of combatants of over nine million, most of them dying in the killing fields of northern France, demonstrated the completely unrealistic nature of that view. It also demonstrated the total inability of the governing classes to stop the madness even if the majority of them wanted to. Neither the crowned heads of Europe, mostly closely related to each other, nor the politicians, could produce anything offering any chance of a quick, peaceful and rational solution.

In 1916, on the first day of the disastrous Battle of the Somme, the British Army lost 20,000 soldiers, with an additional 40,000 wounded. There were innumerable abortive attempts of this type to break the trench-system deadlock, with thousands of men's lives regularly sacrificed to artillery, machine gun or poison gas to achieve a hundred yards of an advance only for it to be lost subsequently to the enemy's equally expensive counter-attack. In the light of this deadlock the war councils embarked on campaigns of attrition or blockade in the bleak hope that the enemy would ultimately lose so many of its armed forces, or its women and children be so starved, that it would be ground down into surrender before they themselves would come to that pass. The inevitable demonisation of the enemy by the propagandists on both sides and the repeated patriotic exhortations to the populations to support, undoubtedly with God's help, their countries and armed forces against the evil and barbarous enemy, further decreased the possibility that any government trapped in the ever-deepening tarpit of such a war could find a way of ending the bloodshed.

The grit and endurance of millions of ordinary human beings in extraordinarily vile conditions in the trenches, or in surface vessels or submarines, or in primitive warplanes where the average life expectancy was two weeks, the innumerable acts of heroism recognised in a fraction of cases by the Victoria Cross, or the Eiserne Kreuz or the Croix de Guerre or whatever the country's appropriate medal was called, draws from that day to this searing reactions of pride, fury and despair at the outpouring by so many of the finest human attributes of courage and self-sacrifice in a conflict that demonstrated with hideous clarity the utter uselessness of mankind's leaders and organisations to prevent its occurrence and continuation.

Every aspect of the First World War's nightmare landscape has been obsessively researched, dissected, and studied in thousands of books, pamphlets, papers, articles, films and television programmes. For millions of families at the time, however, their more limited perspective and direct agonising crucifixion was the death of a family member – father, uncle, husband, brother, son, nephew. Death did not operate a quota system. For many families, more than one fatality was demanded of them. And for millions of other families whose males did come back to them, they returned shattered by their experiences in spirit, mind and body. Even if ostensibly unwounded in body by the conflict, thousands spent the rest of their lives in torment reliving their wartime experiences. Much of the wartime poets' output was a scream of raw agony at the utter obscenity of it all.

Innumerable other sufferers who did survive the First World War, such as Robert Graves, might seemingly recover after a number of years. Yet, meeting the wartime poets Siegfried Sassoon and Edmund Blunden long after the conflict of the War was over, Graves realised how all three of them were still mentally damaged. He himself, walking down a London street, would see the pavement littered with the bodies of the fallen; he described how shells used to come bursting on his bed at midnight. During the day strangers would assume the faces of friends who had been killed. Episodes from the past would continually invade the present. 'The war was not yet over for us,' he wrote,

I would have a sudden very clear experience of men on the march up the Béthune–la Bassée road... Or it would be a deep dug-out at Cambrin, where I was talking to a signaller; I would look up the shaft and see somebody's muddy legs coming down the steps, and there would be a crash and the tobacco smoke in the dug-out would shake with the concussion and twist about in patterns like the marbling on books.

These persistent flashbacks lasted like a dreadful alternate life imposed on him and he was not released from it until well into 1928.

As the war dragged on and the long lists of casualties continued to appear in the newspapers, the offices of the mainstream churches brought to many who had lost loved ones some measure of comfort. But for a host of other grieving families who had largely given up religious convictions, there was nothing but a numb and desolate blackness of spirit. For many, it was truly the end of their world. Others, having some vague recollection of something they had read or been told about the claims of spiritualism, sought out mediums in a desperate attempt to obtain some evidence or assurance that their deceased menfolk had not been totally annihilated but had in some way survived.

In the agony of the First World War the number of those professing to be mediums rose sharply. Some were genuine; some were much better than others, the spread of ability among mediums being as wide as that among professional and amateur footballers. Many others were unscrupulous frauds, battening greedily on the misery of the bereaved and employing a variety of tricks to convince their victims that they had indeed been given proof that their loved ones had survived death.

One of the genuine mediums, Gladys Osborne Leonard, undoubtedly ranked with Professor William James's one white crow, Mrs Piper. Like many naturally gifted psychics she had experienced, from childhood, paranormal phenomena that she naturally assumed everyone had. Born on May 28th, 1882, her parents, Isobel and William Jocelyn Osborne, were prosperous, churchgoing people, respectable, kind, but ultra-careful to keep all knowledge of the fact of death from their daughter. At the age of eight, however, she was introduced to the inevitability of death in an unexpected manner.

Every Sunday the little girl was taken by her father to visit one of his friends, a cheerful kindly man. But this particular Sunday, something was different. The blinds behind the house windows were drawn and the parlourmaid who opened the door had a tear-stained face. 'The master's gone,' she sobbed. Later, Gladys, puzzled and frightened by the obvious distress she had witnessed, asked her father where his friend had gone. He replied abruptly: 'Don't ask questions, dear.'

Worse was to come. Two days later she saw her father leave their house clad in sombre black. When she asked the housemaid about this, she was told: 'They're burying Mr Underwood ... deep under the earth... Of course he can't get out ... stop asking questions.' 'Will my mother be buried?' 'Of course ... and you and me and everybody.' After this the child found and read the burial service: 'ashes to ashes, dust to dust...'

Even today, jounalistic accounts of funerals often use a revealing choice of phrases as well-worn as a set of tyres long past their legal and safe limits. 'And so, just one week after her passing, the Queen Mother ... took her last journey to the graveyard of ... to be laid to rest beside her husband who had died almost half a century earlier.' Whether or not such phrases are the result of lazy and hackneyed usage or some sincere but hopelessly confused attempt to soften the impact of death and the loss of a loved one, their use actually reinforces the numb belief that in some way the body is the person. Their mutual rejection of such a belief is perhaps the only place where the materialist reductionist and the person who believes in some form of survival can agree. For the materialist, the death of the physical body totally destroys the personality housed in the brain. That person no longer exists. For the survivalist, the personality still exists in some manner but has departed from the body it formerly occupied: *in short, no one who has died has ever been buried in a graveyard or cremated.*

Gladys Leonard published her autobiography, *My Life in Two Worlds*, in 1931. There she records that in her childhood she had waking visions: 'Soon after waking, even while dressing or having my nursery breakfast, I saw visions of most beautiful places ... Walking about were people who seemed radiantly happy ... I remember thinking to myself, "How different they are, how different from down-here people, how full of love and life and peace they are".' Her bewildered father, worried by this manifestation of an unhealthy imagination in his daughter, forbade her ever to tell such stories again.

Gladys experienced again her family's strong disapproval of anything ostensibly 'occult' when, having visited a spiritualist meeting she saw advertised, she rushed home to tell her family all about it. Her horrified mother forbade the teenage girl to ever visit such a vile and wicked place again. Nevertheless, the girl's interest in spiritualism continued throughout the difficult years that followed.

Mrs Leonard

The family lost its money; she trained as a singer but lost her singing voice through diptheria just as she was about to go into opera. From then on she earned a somewhat precarious living with touring theatrical companies.

She continued to attend spiritualist meetings and try to develop any psychic powers she might have. Her acting career continued and she met and married a fellow actor, Frederick Leonard. The marriage was good for both of them and until his death in the mid-1930s their bond grew ever closer. He, too, was interested in psychic matters and gave her devoted support throughout their early poverty-stricken years and the subsequent period in her life when she became a respected professional medium sought after by the bereaved seeking comfort and psychical researchers seeking a more objective truth.

In 1913 when working at the London Palladium, she and two other actresses had the habit of occupying themselves in their dressing room with table-tilting as they waited for 'calls'. As the table tilted and messages were spelt out, various communicators purported to appear, including Gladys's mother. A long, unpronounceable name beginning with the letter F was given. The actresses asked the entity if they could shorten it to 'FEDA'. This was agreed. Thereafter Feda communicated regularly. She claimed to be a young girl who had been a Hindu ancestress of Gladys – in fact Gladys's great-great-grandmother. She said she had been raised by a Scottish family until the age of thirteen and had then married an Englishman, William Hamilton, and died a year later in childbirth in 1800.

The next development occurred one day when Mrs Leonard fell asleep while table-tilting with her friends. On waking, she was told that Feda had spoken through her. From then on Feda became Mrs Leonard's chief control and remained so in the subsequent period you speak of him as an intellectual – pure and simple – having nothing in common with you and Ral – In his highly integrated character there are many mansions. His powers of affection and craving for it are deeply hidden in a reserve few may penetrate. It has been given to me to enter into a unity of spirit with him in the past few years through which much has been revealed to me of the 3 Henrys – Henry as God made him – Henry as moulded by the impact of circumstances and experience – & Henry as a social animal and it is from the standpoint of this knowledge that I know quite surely that his standard about the value of people has nothing whatever to do with their intellectual categories – & that he touches life at a dozen different angles. His war record shows him to be as much a man of action as a man of thought. He has 'horse sense', which, I suspect, underlies his remarkable powers of leadership – he knows and loves the common man, and men who were with him in peacetime soldiering, or active service, in Prisoner of War Camps & wartime service here – or now in the field once more – have written to me of how the common man loved him and found in him a sense of fellowship.

I do know as an actual fact that he is drawn towards Ral & has a very real affection for him – you must not let the future become a Henry-less one but keep touch with him as in days past – if there are indeed days on earth set as his portion.

The latest news of him is a letter in a mudstained envelope, dated February 17th – written in a slit trench. He must be in the thick of this bitter struggle on the Western Front – & my heart is very heavy – but both he and I know, & acknowledge, that our relation, the one to the other, has nothing to do with time and place – and has even now the element of immortality implicit within it.

These long war years have been full of stress & weariness for me, as you will understand – made darker by the fact that I have been homeless – Cadoxton having been requisitioned on the outbreak of war & our London home too big to staff. I was with cousins in Norfolk – that wild unspoiled beloved Breckland, of great heaths and stone pines – & then with them on the top of a mountain in Monmouthshire – till April 1942 when I came here, to an atmosphere so incredible and alien,

in a sense, that I do not even now cease to marvel at it ...
A Trollope world of Clerics, with watertight compartments of
Military Knights, and Court Officials – all looking down their
noses at each other. But I have joys – noble music in Chapel
– Bach, Palestrina, Byrd, Handel – the freedom of two private
libraries – friends at Eton – absolute quiet as the Castle is
closed for the duration – a quick access to London. Since
October 1940 I have been contending with Government
Departments, with the help of a group of M.P.'s, on Prisoner
of War matters and my work is now heavier than ever since
their position in Germany grows more and more precarious.
Added to this I have all Alexander's business affairs on my
hands. He is in the Foreign Office, commissioned as a Major
& lent to the Military – he was sent to Egypt in April last,
and landed in Greece on 'D Day' – where he still is – in all
these riots and disturbances he has been involved. As I see
U.N.R.A. is to take over on 1st April I hope he will be moved.
I hope you have good news of your Gerald. I suppose your
children are all sorts of ages by now, but perhaps like me you
can't see the pattern of the post-war world which will be
theirs.

Tell Ral I spent an hour yesterday in Luxmore's Garden –
gay with spring flowers – swans sailing on the river – Lupton's
Tower chiming out the quarters – a blessed interlude with
spring sunshine flooding down from a cloudless sky. Farewell
my dear, and I hope to see you both in the not distant future.

Ever yours,

Winifred Coombe-Tennant.

After G.W.B.'s death in early 1945 and the end of the Second
World War, Winifred retired more and more from active life. She
had always spent a lot of energy complaining about her many
occupations and activities, which allowed her no peace of mind
and denied her the rest she felt she needed. Yet it was obvious
that, right into old age, she adored 'running' everything and for
many years she was very able. Jean Balfour later described her
state of mind at this period:

She was restless and critical, and I think never very interested

236

of more than forty years in which Mrs Leonard carried on her career as a medium.

It was early in 1914 that Feda told Mrs Leonard, via a planchette and via her sitters, that she should begin her work as a professional medium. 'Something big and terrible is going to happen to the world', Feda insisted, 'and Feda must help many people through you.' It was a difficult decision to make but Mrs Leonard made it. She gave up her acting career and her husband gave up his to help her. At first, it seemed as if they had embarked on a course that doomed them to penury and obloquy. Matters changed after the outbreak of the First World War when the slaughter in the trenches of the Western Front brought a host of the bereaved seeking some word of comfort that their relatives had survived. Among them was a French lady, a widow whose two sons had been killed in action. The comfort Feda provided by the accurate information she gave was so striking that the Frenchwoman told Sir Oliver Lodge's wife. Lodge himself became interested in Mrs Leonard's work and, under the assumed name of Mr Brown, had two sittings with her. The quality of these sittings so impressed him that he thereafter took a strong interest in her, advising her on her financial affairs and warning her against overdoing the number of sittings she gave. Mrs Leonard was by now entirely dedicated to her work: she had even given up smoking and alcohol and had become a strict vegetarian.

It was the publication of Sir Oliver Lodge's book *Raymond, or Life and Death* (1916) that made Mrs Leonard famous. Lodge's son Raymond was killed on September 14th, 1915 near Ypres. His parents got the news by telegram from the War Office on September 17th. Lady Lodge had a sitting on September 27th with the medium A. Vout Peters. A message was received about some photographs, one of which was said to be of Raymond among a group of men. Sir Oliver Lodge had no knowledge of any photograph in which Raymond was in a group. Yet two months later a letter was received by the Lodges containing the following passage: 'My son, who is medical officer to the Second South Lancers has sent us a group of officers taken in August, and I wondered whether you knew of this photo and had a copy. If not, may I send you one, for we have half a dozen and also a key.' The picture was received on December 7th. On December 6th, Lady Lodge found a reference in Raymond's diary (returned from the front) to a photo taken on

August 24th. If he ever saw a print he never mentioned it in any of his letters.

Lodge had a sitting with Mrs Leonard on December 3rd. Feda described the photo in some detail. Lodge, on December 6th, wrote a fellow researcher as follows.

Concerning that photograph that Raymond mentioned through the medium A. Vout Peters (saying this: One where he is in a group of other men. He is particular that I should tell you this. In one you will see his walking stick), he has said some more about it through Mrs Gladys Osborne Leonard. But he is doubtful about the stick. What he says is that there is a considerable number of men in the photograph; that the front row is sitting, and that there is a back row, or some of the people grouped and set up at the back; also that there are a dozen or more people in the photograph and that some of them he hardly knew; that a man whose name begins with B is prominent in the photograph, and that there is also a C; that he himself is sitting down, and that there are people behind him, one of whom either leaned on his shoulder, or tried to. The photograph may come any day now, so I send this off before I get it.

Later he wrote:

The photograph was delivered at Mariemont between three and four p.m. on the afternoon of December 7. Considered as a photograph of Raymond it is bad, but considered as evidence it is good. For on examining the photograph, we found that every peculiarity mentioned by Raymond, unaided by the medium, was strikingly correct. The walking stick is there, but Peters had put the stick under his arm (which is not correct), and in connection with the background, Mrs Leonard's control had, by gesture, emphasized vertical lines. There are six prominent vertical lines on the roof of the shed, but the horizontal lines in the background generally equally conspicuous.

By a 'mixed lot', we understand members of different companies – not all belonging to Raymond's company, but a collection from the several... As to 'prominence', I have asked

312

several people which member of the group seemed to them the most prominent, and except as regards central position, a well-lighted standing figure on the right has usually been pointed to as most prominent. This one is 'B' as stated. There is also an officer whose name began with C. Some of the group are sitting while others are standing behind. Raymond is one of the sitting, and his walking stick or regulation cane is lying across his feet. The background is dark and is conspicuously lined. It is out of doors, close in front of a shed or military hut, pretty much as suggested to me by the statements made in the Leonard sitting – what I called a 'shelter'.

But by far the most striking piece of evidence is the fact that someone sitting behind Raymond is leaning or resting a hand on his shoulder. The photograph fortunately shows the actual occurrence, and almost indicates that Raymond was rather annoyed with it; for his face is a little screwed up, and his head has been slightly bent to one side out of the way of the man's arm. It is the only case in the photograph where one man is leaning or resting his hand on the shoulder of another, and I judge that it is a thing not unlikely to be remembered by the one to whom it occurred.

Through information supplied by Mrs Cheves I obtained prints of all the accessible photographs which had been taken at the same time. I found that the group had been repeated, with slight variations, three times – the officers all in the same relative positions but not in identically the same attitudes. One of them is the same as the one we had seen, with his hand resting on Raymond's shoulder, and Raymond's head leaning a little to one side, as if rather annoyed.

In another the hand had been removed, being supported by a stick, and in that one Raymond's head is upright. This corresponds to his uncertainty as to whether he was actually taken with this man leaning on him or not. In a third variation, however, Captain S.'s leg rests on or touches Raymond's shoulder, and the slant of the head and the slight look of annoyance have returned.

As to the evidential value of the whole communication, it will be observed that there is something of the nature of cross-correspondence, of a simple kind, in the fact that a reference to the photograph was made by one medium, and details given by another in answer to a question which I had asked about it; the communicator showing awareness that previous reference was made through another channel.

And the elimination of ordinary telepathy from the living, except under the far-fetched hypothesis of the unconscious influence of complete strangers,was exceptionally complete; inasmuch as all of the information was recorded before any of us had seen the photograph.

Understandably, in the harrowing circumstances of the First World War, Lodge's book became a best-seller, with eight editions printed in seven months. Mrs Leonard's stream of visitors became a flood.

While she continued to attend to these sitters, she also collaborated with Lodge and other psychical researchers in a series of sittings devoted to the study of her psychic gifts and the light they shone on the nature of human personality. The sittings led to over thirty papers in SPR publications, together with a number of books. Like Mrs Piper, she was at times followed by detectives but in over forty years of study, she was never detected in fraudulent activity. On the contrary, the impression left upon investigators and friends was of a patently honest person totally dedicated to her work, sensitively aware of the burden of sorrow and loss so many of her sitters carried with them.

Among the people who studied her mediumship were Sir Oliver Lodge, Lodge's secretary Miss Nea Walker, Una, Lady Troubridge and Miss Radclyffe Hall, Mr and Mrs W.H. Salter, the Revd Charles Drayton Thomas and Professor C.D. Broad. All were by any standards careful investigators of wide experience. Apart from obtaining evidence of paranormal activity and trying to distinguish whether it originated in some form of super-ESP activity from the living and/or discarnate activity by spirits, they pursued research into the nature of Feda.

Sitters generally got an impression of Feda as a usually happy, childlike girl with a high-pitched voice, and an often mischievous sense of humour, who did her best to help. On occasion she told sitters that she was learning and progressing through controlling Mrs Leonard and helping to link up people on earth with the ones they loved on the other side. She could become uncertain or wary, if she did not quite know what to make of some sitters or communicators and at times could be disapproving of them – even of Mrs Leonard. On one occasion, Mrs Leonard, who usually wrapped a rug round her knees to minimise the loss of body heat a sitting produced, mislaid it and used her almost new fur coat instead. When Feda 'arrived' she sniffed the air and muttered, 'Dead animals; hurt animals. I feel their vibrations all over me. Where are they?' Mrs Leonard's hands felt around, seized the fur coat and tore it apart. She remarked with a certain satisfaction: 'She ought to know better than to wear dead animals all over her.' Over the years, Feda seemed to mature somewhat, though she still retained much of her childlike nature; some of her mispronounciations of words remained, together with grammatical errors and seeming misunderstanding of certain words' meanings.

A curious but highly significant procedure introduced in Mrs Leonard's mediumship – the book test – was suggested by Feda herself. It is well described by Mrs Eleanor Sidgwick who wrote an important paper on such tests for the SPR *Proceedings* in 1921:

> The so-called book tests we have to examine are attempts by Mrs Leonard's control, Feda, to indicate the contents of a particular page of a particular book which Mrs Leonard has not seen with her bodily eyes, and which is not, at the time of the sitting, known to the sitter. For example, Feda might tell the sitter that the communicator wants him to go to the bookcase between the fireplace and the window in his study, and in the third shelf from the bottom to take the seventh book from the left and open it at the forty-eighth page, where, about one-third of the way down, he will find a passage which may be regarded as an appropriate message from the communicator to him. In the most typical cases, the interior of the sitter's residence and sometimes even the sitter's name, is unknown to Mrs Leonard. The sitter himself is unlikely consciously to remember what book occupies the exact place indicated, and even if he has read the book which he often has not, it is practically certain that he does not know what is on the specified page.
>
> A good book test, therefore, would exclude ordinary telepathy from the sitter as an explanation and would make it extremely difficult to suppose that Feda derives her information from any living human being.

There were many successful book tests conducted over the years of Mrs Leonard's mediumship and space allows only one to be given.

Edward Wyndham Tennant (known as 'Bim' to his family and friends), a son of Lord and Lady Glenconner, was killed in the Battle of the Somme in September 1916. Lord Glenconner was intensely interested in forestry: he often gloomily reminded the family on walks through the woods that, although they may have thought the young trees healthy, his expert eye could see signs in the leaves that the trees were being ruined by the beetles. It became a family joke. On occasion young Bim had been known to whisper to his mother when they began such a walk: 'Let's see if we can get through the wood without hearing about the beetle.' When his father was depressed about something, Bim had been known to say to other members of the family: 'I see all the trees have got the beetle today.'

At a sitting with Mrs Leonard on December 17th, 1917, Feda said: 'Bim now wants to send a message to his Father. This book is particularly for his Father; underline that, he says. It is the ninth book on the third shelf counting from left to right in the bookcase on the right of the door in the drawing-room as you enter; take the title, and look at page 37.' Lady Glenconner, in her book *The Earthen Vessel* (1921), states that when the search was made, it was found that the book indicated was *Trees* by J. Harvey Kelman. On page 36, quite at the bottom and leading on to page 37, they read that: 'Sometimes you will see curious marks in the wood; these are caused by a tunnelling beetle, very injurious to the trees.' It may be noted that Mrs Leonard had never been in the house in question.

For some years Winifred Coombe-Tennant had been convinced of the reality of survival of death. The discovery of the convincing evidence in a number of the Cross-Correspondences written even before the birth of her daughter Daphne that the little girl's future existence had been referred to unmistakeably in them, taken in conjunction with Winifred's rapid development of her mediumship, removed any doubt she had. When the First World War broke out and her son was on leave from Flanders, they agreed that if he died in the war, he was to try to find on the other side his uncle by marriage, Frederic Myers, and his sister Daphne. He was always to keep in mind that his mother would believe in his continued existence and that contact would continue.

By the end of the war, important changes had taken place in the Sidgwick Group. Sir Oliver Lodge was no longer a sitter with Mrs Willett. He had, as it were, been eased out, much to his chagrin, by the group which was now a much smaller and closer one made up by Gerald Balfour, J.G. Piddington and Eleanor Sidgwick. Mrs Verrall had died in 1916. In the same year Miss Alice Johnson had retired from the post of Research Officer of the SPR because of ill health. The part she played in the society's work during the years from 1903 to 1908 as Organising Secretary of the society and then as Research Officer to 1916 had been a large and important one. In passing, it may be noted that in her SPR obituary it is mentioned that in the Combined Index for the *Proceedings* and the *Journal*, the entries under her name occupy more than four pages. Within her research work, her involvement with the automatists and their scripts had been invaluable, careful and cautious, no matter that she had been irritably taken to task on occasion by the Gurney communicator.

Arthur Balfour retained a great interest in and respect for Mrs Willett because of the remarkable transformation the Palm Sunday case had produced in him. It had convinced him that Mary Lyttelton had survived death and was waiting for him to pass over to the other side and rejoin her. But he did not have a particularly active interest in psychical research and during the war his time and attention had been fully employed. In Asquith's coalition government he succeeded Winston Churchill in 1915 as First Lord of the Admiralty; from 1916 until the end of the war he was Secretary of State for Foreign Affairs in Lloyd George's government. In 1917 he was persuaded by the Zionist leaders to formulate the Balfour Declaration, pledging British help for their efforts to establish a national home for world Jewry in Palestine. It was a pledge that formed a major impetus in the creation of the state of Israel.

Winifred herself found more and more of her time during the war taken up with her appointments to various committees. At the end of the war she was in addition appointed by Lloyd George as the first woman delegate to the newly created League of Nations.

* * *

317

Throughout the First World War, Winifred remained completely convinced by the Gurney and Myers communicators of the existence of the Plan. Gerald Balfour and J.G. Piddington were likewise convinced. It is probable however that Mrs Sidgwick's conviction was tinged by her inherent scepticism and built-in training to try to test to destruction any other hypothesis that might conceivably account for the phenomena without invoking survival. Nevertheless, two major events had occurred that must have strengthened the Sidgwicks' belief in the Plan.

Firstly, the Gurney and Myers comunicators, particularly Gurney, had urged Winifred to have another child. This spiritually designed and influenced infant would be planned by the workers on the other side, including the scientist Francis Maitland Balfour. The child would grow up singularly gifted, to the extent that in some unspecified way he would be able to achieve the gigantic task of reconciling the nations so that they would cooperate in a lasting peace. This peace, they said, would usher in a golden age of prosperity and happiness. Indeed in 1913, a child had been born to Winifred, though after the birth of Alexander she had had no intention of adding to her family.

Secondly, the communicators had also stated that before the Plan could be brought to fruition there would occur wars. Now the world had indeed experienced a war of such devastating magnitude that in its death toll, mutilation of combatants and spread of worldwide misery, it dwarfed any previous conflict. The First World War certainly fitted the Plan's agenda, exhibiting as it did the total inability of people to prevent its occurrence or to bring it to a speedy end when they viewed with horror its evil propensities for smashing civilised behaviour and instilling rabid chauvinistic hatred among the nations.

It is perhaps understandable therefore, that after the First World War, the Sidgwick Group, still receiving and studying enigmatic scripts from the automatists, should continue to take them seriously and attempt to decipher their gnomic statements. They would also watch for future developments and keep a discreet but close eye on Augustus Henry. In addition they resolved to try to ensure that during his childhood and beyond he would be given every chance of fulfilling the destiny said to be waiting for him. In truth, it could be said that they were a group of people who possessed great expectations.

PART 3

THE SOLITARY TRAVELLER

15

Letter to Henry

Manifestations which occur in haunted houses depend, let us say, on something which has taken place a long time ago. In what way do they depend on that past event? Are they a sequel or only a residue? Is there fresh operation going on, or only fresh perception of something already accomplished? Or can we in such a case draw any real distinction between a continued action and a continued perception of a past action?

Human Personality and its Survival of Bodily Death,
F.W.H. Myers

In 1925 Jean Lily Cooke-Yarborough married Gerald Balfour's son Ral (Robert Arthur Lytton, who became the 3rd Earl of Balfour). Jean became a member of the SPR soon after her marriage and retained a dedicated and productive interest in psychical research all her life. In September 1930 she was staying at Whittingehame when Winifred and her son Henry visited the house, staying for a week. Gerald Balfour was also there at the time. It proved to be a week of revelation for Jean and her husband, a time when the pieces of a jigsaw first came together; indeed the whole year proved to be a remarkable period of illumination for both her and Ral.

On the evening of March 10th, 1930, Jean had the powerful visionary experience at Fishers Hill (related in Chapter 10) when Arthur Balfour suffered the onset of his final illness. Soon after his death on March 14th, Mrs Sidgwick let her into the facts of both the Story and the Plan. The group of interpreters also made her the archivist of the Scripts and most of the material connected with their study and interpretation. By the end of the year she had made a preliminary study of the collected scripts held at Fishers Hill. She was a woman of thirty with a young family. On September 20th she wrote the first part of a letter, which she only completed at Whittingehame in December. The addressee was Henry Coombe-Tennant. It is an important document, in which Jean both attempted to obtain for herself a clear perspective of the meaning of the revelations of that year and strove to carry out her sense of duty towards Henry, who had become suddenly far more significant to her and Ral. Nevertheless, although the letter was addressed to Henry, she came to the conclusion that it should not reach his hands before many years had passed and included with it instructions about its future.

A private letter to Henry Tennant written by Jean Traprain at Whittingehame in December 1930.

To be kept by Ral in the event of my death. Not to be read by Henry for 50 years.

First part   Whittingehame 20th September 1930
I do not expect the occasion will ever arise when you will need to know, and that I shall ever tell you, the things which I now write you: these things which intimately concern you, fill my mind and need utterance really for the sake of my own peace.

You first came to Whittingehame on 1st September, 1930, for a week when you were 17. I say 'first' for I am quite sure that it will not be the only time – rather the first of many times. Your mother brought you, and G.W.B. [Gerald William Balfour] was staying here. There were two objects in this visit: one was that Ral and I should meet you, and you meet us: and the other was that 'script' might be obtained through your mother, while she was staying here, which it was hoped would afford some evidence of A.J.B.'s [Arthur James Balfour] personal survival. This last was a secret from most people, including yourself, for at this time you did not know that your mother was a sensitive.

First I must tell you that Ral and I regarded your coming with no particular enthusiasm: I had never met you, but had been told by Kathleen that you were frightfully clever, very dull, and never wanted to do anything! Ral had last seen you

322

as a child of about 8, and had disliked you. I knew from Ral that his father and your mother were great friends, and that his father took a special interest in you, his god-child: and I knew that Ral and his sisters disliked your mother in some way that seemed rather unjustified, though I did not think about it at all.

The Fishers Hill group of S.P.R. investigators had intimated to me, through B.B. [Betty Balfour], that they wished to hand on to my keeping the interpretation of the 'script' produced privately for them by various automatists during the last 30 years. I understood from B.B. that much of the script material was of a private nature and to do with A.J.B. and M.L. [Mary Lyttelton]; and that another topic of great importance was yourself – that your birth had been foretold, and that your mission in the world was to be somehow a remarkable one, of Messiah-like proportions. I was deeply excited and interested at being allowed to join with these distinguished people in their work and felt (as I had always felt up till then) that my own peculiar gifts are fitted to investigate mental phenomena and in these things lies my passionate interest. It was going to be a very great event to me – the greatest event of my intellectual life.

Then I also knew a story, which B.B. had first told me in 1924, and had once more touched upon several years later; this was the story that once G.W.B. had ceased to love B.B. or to need her, during 8 years, that he had formed a great friendship with another woman during that time; that Kathleen was born during that time; that B.B. had been very unhappy but that now she was happy, because when he came back to her, he valued her so much more than he had ever before: it seemed to her that their relations were so much better, that the unhappiness had been worthwhile. Ral had told me that the other woman was your mother, and that their friendship was largely based on the SPR work which was carried on at that time with your mother's cooperation as a sensitive.

But between the time that B.B. had told me the story, my marriage & my children's coming, and A.J.B.'s end, had intervened, and the thought of her story had grown dim to me.

Now you must also know that ever since I entered this

323

House, I have been aware of what a very extraordinary house it is: I mean that it is full of invisible people, and has an inner life of its own. When I first came, I was so conscious of the personality of 'the mother', Blanche Balfour, that I could not distinguish much beyond her, but soon I discovered many others. When A.J.B. was ill, I got to know a certain atmosphere in his room at Fishers Hill, where I distinguished a group of radiant powerful beings. When we entered Whittingehame to live there, I recognised that same feeling again and now he is among them. I know who most of them are, but there are many more who press around, and have no part in the family history. They belong to the inner life of the House, and move about, watching us, with invisible feet. My impression is that there are great numbers of these mysterious dead, and that this house is like a window through [which] they strain gratefully, and wait their chance. What it all means I can't imagine: but I am not a visionary, nor un-balanced; I just know that the House has another house within its walls which is full of the dead, who simply wait, and watch the world from here.

Well, before you and your mother came here, it seemed to me that the inner life of the House was stirred: it seemed to be gathered together as if excited. I was excited too: we both fully expected that your mother would be the means of expression for all sorts of psychic phenomena. Then you can imagine my astonishment, and intense disappointment, when, upon her arrival, the unseen people of the House withdrew, and there seemed to be no point of contact. It was the most extraordinary thing: not even 'Nunkie' (A.J.B.) did I once feel, and the whole house was empty and ordinary to the last degree. It was a shock to me to realise how conscious I had been of the life of the dead, now that it had receded: I thought it might be my own imagination because I did not like your mother, but my own disappointment was really too genuine for that. What was interesting was that she felt the same sense of barren-ness, and knew herself that there was nothing here which it was in her power to tap. She only had two short scripts in her bedroom, to the effect that 'A.J.B. was with the group and was working' (which anyone could have known would have been the case!). G.W.B. was not dissatisfied with these but your mother told me she was quite at a loss to understand the feeling she had that there was absolutely 'nothing doing' here, and she was very disappointed too. She even tried in the study, without success, and came to the conclusion that it must be because she had been so occupied of late with the affairs of this world (your brother having come of age) that her mind could not get quickly in tune with the affairs of the other. But she also implied that we had already changed the atmosphere of the House from what it was in A.J.B.'s days: which amused me, because our own impressions are that A.J.B. comes where we are, and that the unseen people press round about our life with eagerness, and I could no more guess why they had withdrawn than she could. The thought did cross my mind, however, that perhaps it was all done on purpose, and that they have finished with her and await another. And this brings me to another very extraordinary thing, which is you yourself.

For the moment Ral and I set eyes on you we loved you: we just knew that you were one of us, and that we should always be friends with you and always love you. It wasn't only that you were one of our own generation: it was that we both felt that you belonged here, and that the House wanted you. For the dead loved you when you were with us, going upstairs, on the Boat at sea, anywhere in the house, there were the eager dead watching – oh, it was too extraordinary the feeling it gave one. But when your mother joined us, they retired. Once, when you came into the study to ask me for a book and I showed you the pictures of Nunkie and little Gerald, they crowded in from every side, so close that I could hardly bear it: I almost wished that you would go away! And you looked up with a very slightly puzzled look, and afterwards I wondered what had been in your mind. For the atmosphere was charged to breaking point and I trembled all over when you'd gone. Ral came in and said to me 'I can't think why I like Henry so much, for I used to hate him as a child, and now I've absolutely fallen for him.' I said 'The dead are frightfully pleased with him: I think he excites them somehow.'

Your mother came and sat in the study while I rested, and I thought what a contrast in the feel of the room. She talked

325

to me at length about her own life, which deeply interested me, and made me grow fond of her. She told me she was only 19 when she married a man quite old enough to be her father. I could see she had never loved him, and that her babies had been the great reality of her life. This had had the effect of increasing her idea of motherhood to a passion beyond what most women have. She told me of the loss of Daphne and wept when she did so: I saw most visibly the desolation grief can cause in a strong nature, and I was deeply sorry for her, though I felt that her present tears were less for Daphne than for the picture of the mother bereft. She also told me of her friendship for Mrs Verrall, the early stages of development of her script-writing, and of her first visit to Fishers Hill and its inmates in 1910. There she stopped, and we talked about people until lunch. When she left me I said to myself:– 'You are a very deep woman: you are not nearly as deep as I am: why did you say you wanted to tell me the story of your life and then end it at the place where I know you first began to live.' For I felt that: even from my very slight knowledge of her character, I could gauge perfectly well that she must have experienced something very great, apart from the loss of Daphne, and as she never mentioned you at all, I could not help thinking she had kept something back. She had spoken much of her friendship with G.W.B. and I still thought it was probably a platonic affair, based on his profound interest in her psychic powers – for I thought her so very un-attractive, and then I had almost forgotten my conversation with B.B. so long ago: I fancied that perhaps her psychic experiences had been the bigger reality.

At dinner that night I saw you looking at me, and it came over me anew that you were so very like Ral: I thought 'There is something about Henry, I cannot tell what it is, unless perhaps it is his gentleness that I like enormously. There are things in him which are so like Ral, that he is the only other person I have ever met, besides Ral, that I feel I would be capable of falling in love with.'

That night, when we went to bed, I told Ral what had been in my mind. He said 'I knew you were thinking that, for I suddenly said to myself, "Henry is the sort of person Jean might love."'

I said 'Do you mind that?' and he replied 'No, I am deeply interested.'

I then said 'But what I cannot understand is why he should be so like you: he has characteristics in common with you such as his way of walking to the extent that I have never seen in anyone before: he is also very like your father, more like him than you are, he has got, for instance, the same hands.'

Then Ral said 'I now believe what I have always suspected, that Henry is my father's son.'

This was a very great shock to me. I believed from what B.B. had told me of the scripts and what they were supposed to mean, that Henry was the 'spiritual child' of the whole group of spirit communicators, of whom a very important member was F.M.B. [Francis Maitland Balfour]. I know that his mother was supposed to have been 'influenced' before his birth, and I was not in a way surprised to see some likeness in you to portraits of F.M.B. which I should have put down to spirit influence. But the likeness to one of my own generation was quite un-expected; and nothing can describe the turmoil of feelings I now experienced.

My first reaction was joy, which we both shared, that we had found a brother! No wonder we had loved him straight away. Ral then told me of his father's intense excitement over your birth, which had not escaped the sharp wits of his own children: and of how obvious it always was to him & to his sisters that you were all in all to G.W.B.

I went through a frightful period of jealousy and rage for Ral's sake: why should you, who escaped delicate health & was loved by G.W.B. as well as by your mother, have been the object of such special devotion, and not Ral? Why should you, and not Ral, have been so tenderly excused, and watched over with such interest, by G.W.B. when he had found his eldest son so irritating & disappointing? Ral laughed at me, it was characteristic of him not to consider himself – he felt no resentment, had no blame for his father: delight in having a brother he loved was enough for him: but oh, I did suffer!

And then I was filled with the bitterest resentment for B.B.'s sake. I remembered anew what she had told me long ago, and caught again the loneliness and misery of those 8 years. I could not bear it for her: I loved her too much; it was almost as though it had been done to me. Yet I could not blame G.W.B. – he was not a man who would do such a thing lightly. Ral said 'Poor father, he must have had some bad moments over it.'

Nor could I blame your mother: I remembered how young she had been when she married a man she did not love: and I knew besides that in great passions there is no right and wrong, but necessity for fulfilment or the death of the spirit. I also knew now where the biggest reality of her life had lain, and that you are the particular fulfilment in this case.

But what breaks the heart is the suffering involved: my darling B.B. who never did a selfish thing, feeling herself forsaken: Ral as a child having his birthright withheld and given to another and how much easier his early years would have been if he had known of the existence of this other son (who was the apple of his father's eye) so that there would have been no need for him to suffer so, in feeling that somehow he had always failed to please that father.

But put against these things, your mother's happiness when G.W.B. came into her life: and what she revealed to him, for I've no doubt she loved him more passionately than ever his own wife did, angel though she is: and G.W.B.'s joy, to watch you grow up, and be satisfied that the same literary sense, the same type of mental processes were coming out in you, which were his own, and which Ral failed so disappointingly to give him. And B.B.'s present happiness, which is a fact. And the conviction of G.W.B. and the script-interpreters that you have a work in the world to do, for which you were born, which if it be true, makes everything worthwhile.

This brings me to the last profound emotion which I experienced in connection with the discovery of your parentage – the true interpretation of the scripts. For now an uncomfortable fear tormented me. B.B. had told me that you were supposed to be the 'spiritual son of A.J.B. and M.L.' in a more intimate sense than even as the spiritual son of the whole group of script-communicators. This I had always thought a very odd idea, considering that A.J.B. was living in this world when you were born. However, who was I to question when I had never seen the scripts? But now I knew you to be G.W.B.'s physical son, and surely there was no need to go further than that for spiritual parentage as well. A great love had bred you: quite apart from whether you turned out to be a sort of Messiah or not, you will probably be remarkable. On one side you are the offspring of one of the best brains that ever lived, on the other, of one of the greatest mediums that ever lived. You may always have been open to spirit influence, both before and after you were born. But why should you have to be made out to be A.J.B.'s son, when G.W.B. ought to have rejoiced in having produced you himself? And had the scripts, which claimed to understand so much, and to foretell the coming of a better world, nothing to say about B.B.'s suffering?

Thus I began to feel that if I studied the scripts, I should not be able to agree with the interpretation put upon them by men whom above anyone else I respected & admired: for I felt it was not straightforward: thus my interest in what I had considered was going to be such an invigorating work during the rest of my life, diminished to a suspicion that a gigantic mistake was being made somewhere.

With such tremendous emotions singing in my mind, it was little wonder that I was soon far from well. A letter from B.B. at this time, in which she said that of all things, the thing she would most hate, would be that Kathleen should ever fall in love with you, revealed to us that she knew too whose son you were. I wrote telling her we knew, and that I had gone through a time of agonised rebellion & bitterness for his sake. I had indeed often wept in the night. Her reply startled me in the extreme: dashing off in a panic to save me un-necessary worry, I suppose, she wrote that she had not really suffered, that she connected her happiest moments with that story, that G.W.B. and your mother had had to produce you, in order to make the scripts come true – oh I was angry! Not only is it impossible to produce a child without the medium of physical love, but why turn round and say she had never suffered? when I knew – for I know her well – that she had longed to die for misery.

And what was I to believe, in all this mixture of truth and falsehood? and I would not admit that she was telling me the truth: I was in great distress. One thing alone, there was, that I clung to with joy, and that was the new brother. Whatever

329

the scripts meant, whatever B.B. meant, whatever Ral had been denied, we both loved you and knew that you belonged to the House and to us.

On the day you went away, and your mother left this house, back came the unseen people, and moved to and fro, exactly as usual. That night I talked to Ral; and told him of the distaste I now felt for joining the Fishers Hill group of script-interpreters: I had an odd feeling that the dead wished me to go to Fishers Hill & take over that work, but I did shrink terribly from it. I was very unhappy. Ral said:

'If they have made an advance to you, you can't refuse to go: for fairness' sake, you must have a look at the scripts for what they are worth.'

This decided things for me: I shall go to Fishers Hill and when I return & have read the scripts, I will tell you what I think.

Second part
Whittingehame   16th December 1930
It is a good thing, Henry, that you will never read this letter, for it leaves me free to put down without scruple the contents of my mind.

Not only have I been to Fishers Hill, but also read the major part of the whole scripts material, so that I consider I am in a better position to judge.

The scripts were given into my hands, and I was told the conclusions the interpreters had come to, by themselves; but what stirred me infinitely more was a conversation with B.B. which I had one day in the garden. She had told your mother that we had guessed whose son you were, and begged her leave to tell us the whole story. Your mother was much amazed, and could not sanction the truth to be told us yet. But it had to come: and B.B. suddenly said, as we talked of you in the garden, 'I must tell you – but never let it be known that you knew.'

I said 'You must tell me because I have a feeling that this is one of the things for which my life has been lived to know, besides, I know it already.'

She then told me the following story, which I afterwards roughly noted down in pencil, though her words have so burnt themselves into my mind, that I could have remembered them perfectly well without doing that.

She said that your mother first came to Fishers Hill in February 1910: I asked if G.W.B. and she had seemed interested in each other in any marked way? She said it had not struck her so, she knew they were interested in psychic matters, which concerned her not at all, and she thought that they liked each other quite well: it was when they met again, and your mother had her first trance with G.W.B. in June the same year, that she noticed that the two were becoming very much interested in one another: this she did not in the least resent, but was glad that the study-group should have a new cooperator.

G.W.B. and B.B. went for a motoring tour next summer 1911, and spent some days at Cadoxton with your mother in July, and then went on to other places, including the Lakes, where they were in September and where Kathleen was conceived. By this time G.W.B. had seen your mother several times, but B.B. was not in the least distressed at this, though she did not quite see all that her husband seemed to see in her; but of course in those days she knew nothing at all about his work in psychic investigations – nor was she interested.

So she had a very great shock, when she told G.W.B. that she was convinced they were going to have another child, after 10 years (an event which at first caused her personally intense pleasure), to find he was absolutely horrified, and did not express any pleasure, but dismay, at the prospect. She was astonished, for he had never before re-acted with such horror from such a thing: still more amazed was she when, a few days later, he asked to have his dressing-room bed made up, and told her he thought he would in future sleep away from her. He offered no explanation and she was at first too hurt and stunned to ask for one. For 8 years they slept apart.

At this point B.B. let go and poured out the expression of her feelings which had never been opened to anyone before, and I simply listened with my eyes smarting with tears.

She said that she was so unhappy that she prayed for death. She no longer regarded the coming of her baby with any joy, but only as a possible escape from life for she hoped she would die when it was born. Her joy & interest in life disappeared; in order to keep herself fully occupied she took

331

up activity of all sorts in local charities and women's suffrage but her heart died. She made one or two efforts to get back what she had lost: once she went to him and said 'Won't you sleep with me again tonight? I am so lonely.' and once she said 'I feel so dreadfully ill and tired – won't you be with me just once?' and then she asked one day 'Have I done something to anger you?' but he only looked frightfully uncomfortable and always said No. Once she went to him sobbing, and felt she would die when the baby was born: would he not even kiss her, and come to say goodnight to her that night? But it was as if a spell had been cast over him, he neither saw nor heard.

She told me she had sometimes a strange impression that little Ral, aged about 9 (just before he went to a prep. school) knew she was unhappy, for he was so curiously gentle to her, and used to watch her. She felt dreadfully ill and sick with the baby coming, and as the time went on and it became apparent that it would be a dangerous birth as the child was in a wrong position, she became more certain than ever that at last she would die, and daily looked forward to death.

Meanwhile G.W.B. occasionally saw your mother and was at Cadoxton during part of July 1912, which must have been the time that you were conceived; and was the month in which Kathleen was born. She was the only one of B.B.'s children at whose birth instruments had to be used, and the poor mother did not die: she said to me 'If I had been delicate, I should have died, but I was too strong.'

Her disappointment at having to live was very great and now followed a long and delayed convalescence with much physical discomfort and depression of spirit. She said what surprised her greatly was G.W.B.'s contentment at having yet another daughter. She had thought that he might like her better if she gave him another son, but instead he seemed really rather relieved that it was a daughter, and she had the impression that he had emphatically not wanted it to be a son!

They went to Whittingehame that autumn, and one day, after she had somehow begun to feel that she counted again for something with G.W.B. (it must have been in September 1912) she entered his dressing room one morning when he was still in bed. Sitting on the floor beside his bed, she took his hand and said 'I can't bear it any longer: I promise I will make no demand on you, only you must tell me what has happened to us.': then, as he looked very unhappy, she said 'You must let me know who it is – is it D.M.?' [Daphne's mother] He nodded and burst into tears. She then said, weeping too 'Oh why didn't you tell me long ago? – I only want to share things with you: I don't want to take you away from her, I only want you to trust me to understand everything.'

Of course he was amazed at this spirit, and then he told her, how he had been deeply attracted to D.M. and that she had persuaded him that love like theirs should have its way; that they had both come to the conclusion that the spirit-communicators on the other side had indicated that her children were remarkable in a mysterious way: and that then, his love had given her another child – they could not help it – who would be born in the Spring of 1913. He added that he had wanted to tell B.B. but that D.M. had not thought she could possibly understand: and that now he did not suppose that B.B. would ever have anything to do with him again.

Then this wonderful woman, seeing how much he had suffered himself, set herself to understand & share everything: insisted on a meeting with your mother, in which she embraced her and told her that she knew all and absolutely understood: heard the whole story of the scripts, and was deeply interested in it: and accepted you, Henry, with such generosity & love as she would have shown to her own children.

When I had heard this, I embraced her in silence; I was satisfied now that I knew the whole truth, and my emotion knew no bounds. I said 'But didn't you hate Mrs Tennant?' She replied 'Never, once I was allowed to know and understand – before that, yes: but when I talked to her, I loved her, for I felt that she had adored Gerald: and when I read the scripts, I could almost have worshipped her as a being from another world. She was such a wonderful channel for the unseen things to come through.'

Then I said 'I think it wonderful of you to have loved Henry'. She said 'Of course I loved Henry for he is Gerald's child, and then I share all that Gerald feels about him: there is just one thing, however, that I could not help resenting, about D.M., and that was, the way she always ignored Kathleen.

333

I felt that was rather unfair, for I did show her I was ready to love Henry; but she seemed sometimes positively to dislike Kathleen, which of course made Kathleen hate her!'

Then I told her what an agony of jealousy for Ral's sake I had gone through: she cried 'Oh, I do so understand, for I had that too. It was the one thing that distressed me continually even after Gerald and I had made it up. But one thing comforted me for that and was more and more a compensation as time went on, and that was, that it made Ral Nunkie's son. It was A.J.B. to whom Ral turned far sooner than to his father, as he grew up: those two had a confidence in each other which grew with the years: and A.J.B. knew it,' she said, 'he knew perfectly well that Ral and his father were not happy together, and he himself was Ral's friend': but she had not known, until A.J.B's last years how much he himself loved Ral. 'You know, Jeannie,' she said, 'I realised he adored Ral when I used to watch him greet him on the occasions when Ral came to see him, and he told so many people, DD Lyttelton, Etty Desborough, Lady Wemyss, that he loved him. I remember Alice Salisbury once saying to me – 'How he does love Ral!' And he loved to think that Ral would have Whittingehame and he loved little Gerald so, as well.'

Then she told me how the 8 years of separation came to an end. She said she thought that after you were born, your mother became more and more absorbed in watching you grow up, that the chief thing that bound her and G.W.B. together was the interest they shared in you. Then, near the end of the War, Christopher was killed: and your mother compiled a memoir of him, for which she asked G.W.B. to write a chapter. It was to give a sketch of his character, which G.W.B. accordingly did, to the best of his powers. But she was very angry, and deeply hurt, and refused to include the sketch in the memoir, because G.W.B. had not found it in him to say that Christopher was one of the most remarkable beings that ever lived! G.W.B. was also hurt, and puzzled beyond measure, by what seemed to him unreasonableness on her part (– for even then, I do not believe he had ever discovered how ambitious she was! –) but could bring himself to no other decision.

She then set him free of all ties to her, and told him she

did not wish him to live again with her: the watchful B.B. soon discovered his distress though he was far too loyal a nature to condemn the way he had been treated: and then they were re-united, and entered, as B.B. said, into far greater happiness than could ever have been theirs, without the experiences both had undergone: hers, joy and gratitude that life had restored to her an even greater security and bliss; his, a deeper love, because a deeper appreciation of the unique companion & lover at his side; both together reaping a singularly perfect relationship.

What a satisfactory story; and now with a mind more at peace, I proceeded to peruse the 'Scripts'.

I can't say very much to you upon this because I am as yet upon the very outskirts of an investigation which I have a suspicion may reveal knowledge on the part of the spiritual communicators of things going on in this world of an intimate and startling nature. I entirely fall in with the view of the interpreters that several efforts were made by the other side to produce a child who would be peculiarly open to their influence, which eventually culminated in the production of you: but I do not so far see anything to connect you, intimately or otherwise, with A.J.B. I do see, however, connections between you, as 'Augustus', with the references to 'Aeneas': (I shall elucidate these things in a paper in due course) and it is also my strong impression that the scripts deal with the spiritual history of more persons than simply A.J.B. and yourself. Of course their way of indicating obliquely by means of symbolism the persons or notions to which they intend attention to be drawn, is naturally open to mis-interpretation; but I think by no manner of means can 'Aeneas' be taken to represent A.J.B.: I think he is G.W.B., and that 'Dido' is B.B. This will startle the interpreters, I have no doubt, but I do not make this statement without thought. For there is an amazing history suggested in what looks like a purposeful manner, expressed in a variety of automatists' work during first the period of G.W.B.'s estrangement from his wife and your birth. One could not help reflecting:– 'Surely someone – somewhere – is very unhappy,' and 'Dido' fits in very interestingly. For B.B. to all intents and purposes did die in the spirit. And Aeneas sailed away under the strong will of the gods to do their work, and from him and Lavinia came the glory of the Roman Empire, in due course 'Augustus'. When I read your mother's scripts I discovered a new thing, that the person whom G.W.B. loved was 'Mrs Willett', not the same person at all as Mrs Tennant. Mrs Willett is a creation from another world, a poet, a lover, whose soul is a channel through whose clarity [?] the purposes & extraordinary understanding & spiritual power of the other world is revealed: and now I know what B.B. meant when she said that there were moments when she felt she could worship your mother.

You are the child of 'Mrs Willett' and G.W.B. and I believe the spirit-group wanted the combination for their own purposes. I do not personally see evidence that you will be a Messiah, exactly, but I do think it is indicated that you will do remarkable work for them, and will be a 'bringer of light'. Do you remember your dream of light which you told me on the sands at North Berwick?

My own impression is that you will be a very great medium: physiologically you ought to be, with such parents: and what an inestimable instrument in the hands of the other world, if they had another first rate 'machine' for the purpose of throwing light before the dim gropings of mankind. (For religious teachings upon the state of the dead are gradually failing us, and agnosticism is the death of the spirit, and mankind seeks, as never before, reliable evidence of the powers and character of the unseen.) And I think that sort of thing was their aim ... For this purpose G.W.B. was blinded by love and sent away from B.B. on the work of the gods. And there are, in my opinion, suggestions that only a woman of great spiritual worth could have helped make the whole thing come off to its complete value: surely this is B.B. And now she has gained more than she ever lost; and so the triumph of goodness & love, in which the scripts so enhance one's eager belief, so that to read their language is to be filled with peace, is seen to be an integral part of the great plan.

If I am right, what a glorious thing is here: that the departed, being a step further on than we, watch our spiritual element and influence us for good.

In fact, all the fears that tormented me before I went to Fishers Hill, have vanished into the certainty that the things we so strenuously idolise and desire, are those which prevail in the end; that I have been enabled to fully understand B.B.'s story: and that the material of the scripts is a study upon which I can enter with eager interest, and peculiar assurance: while our affection for you, (yet another of those important events which we share mutually in such a magic way) will keep you in touch with us: for *you belong here*, although you don't know it!

Jean Traprain

16

Growing Pains

The young Winston Churchill to his father: 'Father, how should I live?'
Lord Randolph Churchill, with a shrug: 'Just do the best you can, my son.'

There is a frighteningly wide range of abilities in parents to mould positively or otherwise their offspring's physical and mental development, even when they usually believe sincerely they are doing their best for them. Together with the equally wide range of personal qualities genomes conjure up, and the influence of those other people the child encounters in its early life, the sub-sequent personality, interests and health it displays in maturity are infinitely more difficult to predict even today than a one-year detailed global day-to-day weather forecast. Some broad-brush major scenarios remain the limits of our predictive abilities in these matters.

Indeed the science of chaos theory is based on the proposition that for a complex system, even small changes in the system can through time propagate far-ranging and essentially unpredictable major changes. The well-known 'butterfly in the Brazilian rain forest' example states in a seemingly ridiculous way that a slight change in the position and fluttering of wings of the butterfly can result in consequent and cumulative effects that in time will cause a major storm in the North Atlantic. It is also accepted now that a tiny change in the orbit of an asteroid – perhaps a kilometre or two in its closest pass-by distance from the planet Jupiter could bring about, thousands of years later, a collision with planet Earth resulting in the annihilation of the human race.

It was the great French mathematician Henri Poincaré who at the beginning of the twentieth century pioneered chaos theory, understanding clearly its implications. He also pointed to human affairs as the most familiar and everyday example of chaotic systems, giving as an example the conception of Napoleon. Examples of chaos in action are easy to find. A young man, fresh from school and intending to go to university, is on a walking tour. He enters a café and orders a soft drink to quench his thirst. One of the myriad trivial decisions every person experiences in life faces him when he has finished his orange juice. Does he have a second orange juice or does he resume his walk? He decides to have the second orange juice: he is in no hurry and it is hot outside. While he is drinking it and thinking over his quandary concerning his future studies, an older man enters the café, orders a drink and, the café being quite crowded, joins the young man at his table. They begin to talk. The younger man learns that the older is a biochemist. To the older man it is a fascinating and rewarding career. The younger man, who includes chemistry in his good grades list, is so strongly influenced by the older man's enthusiasm that he decides to make it his principal subject in his university studies.

In due course of time he graduates and proceeds to postgraduate research. Because he is observant, he notices a curious biochemical effect in a discarded dish lying on his laboratory desk. He studies it and makes the discovery of a powerful antibiotic. Brought into production, it saves countless thousands of lives. Among those lives are human beings of every kind, including brilliant and charismatic people, whose subsequent careers bring unpredictible major changes for good or for evil.

All because the young man decided to have a second glass of orange juice?

In 1931 G.W.B. gave Jean Balfour a letter enclosing three photographs of Henry he had received from Mrs Tennant in 1915. At that time the little boy was about two years of age. In one photo the child is by himself; in the other two he is with G.W.B. or A.J.B. The child is handsome, appears intelligent but rather solemn. The accompanying letter is illuminating:

May 26 / 15
Cadoxton Lodge,
Vale of Neath,
South Wales.

These will show you The Wise One as he looks now – except that of course nothing gives you his colouring which is so vividly beautiful that all photographs seem as moonlight not sunlight.

You will be hearing all about him – & of the blessed time just past, so I wont write more. I'm very busy, & very wistful – laying my uphill shoulder to the wheel.

Delta's M.

[Note by Jean Balfour on this letter:] 'Given to Jean by G.W.B. when he knew I was collecting things about Henry in 1931.'

As a child Henry was sensitive, highly intelligent and very observant. He would want to do his best and always be worthy of his marvellous mother. He would want to live up to the portentous, cloaked hints she must, being human, have made from time to time about his special destiny, hints he could at that early age have made little of, but hints his memory would have registered. Later at Eton he was visited by Dame Edith Lyttelton and it is highly likely on occasion she added her own coded remarks to the programming he already carried. Certainly she revealed to him that his mother was a remarkable woman who was involved in important psychic work but at that age it could have made very little sense to him. In addition, of course, he could not have failed to notice the coldness and 'irrconcilable differences' separating his parents and wondered why they were so different to the parents of some of his friends.

In due course of time Henry followed his brother Alexander to Eton. Carefully cosseted as a child, his early years at Eton must have been perplexing in the extreme and often must have included desperately unhappy episodes. He was among large numbers of boys of every kind, from ones whose temperament and intelligence were not dissimilar to his, to those who were enthusiastically serving apprenticeships in brutality. Many of them would serve their country courageously, selflessly giving their lives during the coming war;

others, if Hitler had won and occupied a defeated and demoralised Britain, may well have found congenial places in a British Vichy-type administration.

Among the masters there would also be a wide variety in personality, some of them being found to be much 'softer' in their approach to their charges than others. *Tom Brown's Schooldays*, giving the life at Rugby of Tom Brown, is in some measure probably similar to Henry's Eton experience. In later life, Henry remarked wryly that an education at Eton was a rather good preparation for his experiences in the German prison camp during the war.

The advent of adolescence at a single-sex school raised other problems of the kind experienced by boys whose lives were being upturned by the testosterone storm. Like ships previously sailing on a calm sea but now buffeted by unexpected and frequent assaults of nature, Henry and his schoolmates would be differently equipped mentally to face these storms. Henry had been told nothing about sex by either his mother or her husband. He had to acquire what little information he possessed on the subject from his schoolmates, and much of this information would be wildly unreliable. Marginally more reliable sources of information would come from the infrequent and brusque 'take a cold shower' talks on the subject given by school staff. Even today, eighty years later, in a culture in Britain that prides itself on promoting a wide and reliable distribution of knowledge in sexual matters, the remarkably high numbers of teenage pregnancies and STD cases demonstrates just how imperfect sexual education is. If throughout the course of the centuries navigation had been as badly taught as sexual education is, the number of shipwrecks would have been astronomically higher than the actual recorded number. Perhaps the Lutine Bell at Lloyd's would have been tolled not because a ship was lost at sea but rung when one successfully made port!

It has already been seen in Jean Balfour's letter to Henry, written in 1930, that he made a decidedly favourable impression on both Jean and her husband Ral when, in September 1930, at the age of seventeen, he first came with his mother to visit them at Whittingehame. Both Jean and Ral, wishing to get to know him better and penetrate the barrier of reserve that even then was present, involved him in as many activities as possible, and engaged him in many topics of conversation.

Jean thought it advisable to record the following notes:

Record of dreams and mental experiences of H.A.C.T. told me by himself.

(1) The first time he came to Whittingehame was on Sept. 1st to 8th, 1930. He then told me, during a walk, that he often dreamed of the most beautiful colours: and also related the following dream, which he said was a very pleasant one and which he had had only a few days before he came to Whittingehame:–

He dreamed that he was looking at a pair of dark curtains which were drawn. He saw them as in a picture, as though he looked down a telescope; and the joining of the two curtains was horizontal as it might be the lids of an eye which was closed. As he looked, he saw the right hand and part of the arm of a woman come across the picture, and lift up the upper curtain by its edge, which rolled back, like the opening of an eye: this let in such a flood of sunlight that he was dazzled and awoke.

(2) The second time I saw him was at Fishers Hill, Woking. Nov. 8th to 10th. During a walk, he told me again that he had been dreaming of colours, which were most vivid and beautiful; and that very often when he was going to sleep, he had a curious experience of music. It was a habit with him to go over in his mind, while going to sleep, some piece of music of which he was fond: he would hear it mentally as he followed it note by note: then, just before sleep came, he would become conscious that the music actually existed, and he would hear it externally: this invariably woke him up and he would have to go to sleep all over again...

He said he once had a terrifying dream: he dreamed he was standing on the seashore, and looking at the smooth water before him, when suddenly, from every part of the sky, there came the most brilliant flashes of lightning which hurt his eyes: and at the same moment, there burst over him the most tremendous thunder, with crashes & reports which seemed almost to burst his eardrums: and he covered his ears with his hands, and awoke. I reminded him of the dream of the drawn curtains, and he said 'That was a pleasant dream, but there is a dream I have had several times which is very unpleasant,' and he related it as follows:–

342

First he said that he thought it often came after a day of very strenuous excitement, and that it was not a dream in the ordinary sense of the word, because he was not asleep, but that he was certainly in a sleepy condition, and generally too restless to get off to sleep. The dream experience was that he himself seemed to be three persons: he would rise up from the bed, and look at his three selves, who lay tossing & restless trying to go to sleep. Sometimes he was all three of them, sometimes he was in either of them, but on the whole he thought that he himself was really the person who was looking down at the three on the bed – in fact there seemed to be four of him. Also the bedroom was absolutely full of people – everybody he had ever known, nearly – but it was all very shadowy and dim, and he could not say that he could recognise anyone, he did not trouble to look at them, but only wished they would go away and leave him alone. His impression was that they were trying to make him do something – He thought it might be their overwhelming presence that made him feel himself divided into three – or even four – people and he said it was a horribly unpleasant dream.

The last time it had come, however, which was about 3 weeks ago, he had been very determined, when he realised it was starting; and had sat up in bed and said vehemently to himself:– 'There is nobody in the room besides yourself, and you are not three people, you are yourself and there is only ONE of you.' After this he was able to go to sleep.

I asked if he had ever 'felt' things like ghosts in houses, (for I wanted to know if he had been aware of the 'People of the House' as I call them, at Whitt) but he said No.

The 'horribly unpleasant dream' of the people, people known to him, crowding round him and trying to make him do something, does suggest at least a subconscious nervous awareness that a number of those known to him had great expectations concerning him. If so, it is probable that in their hopes for his future some of them were not entirely successful in concealing them. The fact that he had no indication of what they were expecting of him would also have magnified his discomfort.

Jean Balfour also made written notes about a number of

343

conversations she and Ral had with Henry, again at Whittingehame, the following year. Again both she and her husband did their best to draw him out of his shell and make him feel the genuine warmth of friendship they had for him:

Record of talks with Henry at Whitt April 1931 (Aged 18)

First, he shows himself a remarkably good thought-reader. We tried one day for fun: I thinking, he guessing. I have before been considered a good 'transmitter'; Henry was invariably right. It was less thinking of actual objects than feeling emotions – for instance I imagined myself laughing, on one occasion: Henry at once said 'I get the feeling of merriment.'

He asked me if I had ever noticed that the full moon was conducive of dreaming. I said 'No, why? Ought it to be?' He said he didn't know, but some one had suggested to him that it might be. (Was 'someone' his mother or Nunkie G?)

He said had I ever thought of people as <u>foods</u>, as <u>colours</u> or as <u>keys</u> of music? He often sensed people this way. We had great fun over this: agreed that Nunkie G. was like celery, his mind being very crisp and delicately flavoured, his colour clear light blue, his 'tone' a high treble note.

Auntie colour brown, food a doughnut, sound a groan! etc: etc; with much laughter.

Henry said he often dreamed of exquisite music making a pattern of tones & semitones & octaves etc: in what seemed like a universe: but he could not reproduce it waking.

April 1931

In a talk with Ral, Henry & he somehow got on to the subject of sex and its problems. Henry told Ral he had at that time great need for physical relief, which worried him, as he felt it was stronger than other young men had to contend with. Ral said in his opinion, it was a mistake to regard this as wrong: it was natural at that stage in one's life: it was incidental to growth in body and mind, and above all, not to be worried about. Henry said that his mother had never told him anything about matters of sex: the headmaster of his private school had told him something, not enough: he had picked up what he knew.

344

He was evidently going through the mental questioning & physical restlessness of adolescence: Ral borrowed my 'Paper on Sex,' (which I had written for Gerald to read in the future) & Henry read it. He told Ral he found it fascinatingly interesting. We had many conversations together, on all sorts of subjects, and among other things, he seemed to me to show a great interest, & reverence for, motherhood.

It was evidently an idea that had been presented to him in very early days, with great beauty, and also with mystery. It had therefore more significance for him than it has for the ordinary young man.

Talking with Ral one day, he asked him his views about homo-sexuality: Ral said 'There I can't help you: homo-sexuality only touched me for a very short stage one term at Eton and never really attracted me at all.'

I could not help wondering if his mother had ever failed him by being secretive on subjects when his mind sought for knowledge. It must have been terribly difficult for her to explain relations between men and women in love without giving herself away: and perhaps she never lived with Mr Tennant again after having met G.W.B. Children, I believe, are so quick subconsciously to sense these unexplained complications.

Henry is at the moment too introspective not to be a little boring: he is very indolent, perhaps because his limbs are so long! Also sometimes very rude, with the unconscious rudeness of a Balfour!

J.T.

In April 1931, while Henry was at Whittingehame Jean received the following letter from Winifred Coombe Tennant:

21 / 4/ 31
Cadoxton Lodge,
Vale of Neath,
South Wales.

My dear Jean,
Today brought me your letter – & the first one I have had

345

from Henry since he left here a week ago. Whilst I feel it is very remiss of him not to have sent a word long before this, I don't mistake the cause. A boy (as you will find out when Gerald mi [minor] is at school) doesn't write home when he is quite happy, when the life going on around him absorbs his whole time & interest, when he's not looking before and after but just basking in a satisfactory present! Henry's letter exhales the spirit of supreme contentment – he is indeed <u>very</u> happy – he is (as I knew before) much drawn to Ral, & he is more ready to talk freely with you than anyone else. You are giving him exactly what he needs. He is developing very rapidly and finding Eton a pretty unsatisfactory sort of a place. He goes with the Library next Half and becomes Captain of his House in the following one, & that may improve matters – but he wants more than anything else just now human companionship from young people.

I've not sent him his Reports yet, but in his Tutor's letter comes this paragraph:–

'And now for where you can help him most. In some ways he is too reserved, & the very best thing you can do for him now is, I am sure, to throw him among <u>young</u> people as much as possible, & I would add as many nice people of the opposite sex.'

We have very few neighbours down here, Death Duties having closed at least half a dozen of the larger houses, & the sort of 'Tennis parties' of the summer are very boring. I rejoice to think of Henry with you both, & he loves being with you.

Yours ever,
Winifred Coombe-Tennant

May, 1931.

Henry's mother reported to G.W.B. that his tutor said of him:

'He is the sort of man who <u>might</u> do anything – lead a great cause, stem a revolution: but his inspiration must come <u>from outside</u>: it will never with him come from inside.'

July 1935

D.D. Lyttelton [Dame Edith Lyttelton] told Betty Balfour that she had had a talk with Henry on religion, a month ago: and that he had told her – quite simply – that 'I have always felt that my hand was held in God's.'

D.D. said she often wondered why people thought Henry was clever. B.B. said – 'I agree, for he is no social addition to a party, he never utters: but I suppose that to achieve a double first at Cambridge in one year, especially when he missed one term by travelling in China, shows him to have really remarkable brains.'

D.D. then said: 'His master who went with him to China said of him, "Henry will be one of the world's great leaders."'

B.B. told me (when she reported this conversation) that she often wondered if D.D. had guessed Henry's true parentage: she believed she might have guessed partly because of her knowledge of the Scripts, and partly because she had known G.W.B. as a young man, and would be able to appreciate Henry's striking likeness to him.

J.T.

In July 1944, Jean confided her impressions of Henry to paper after he visited her and Ral. His visit was a short one, lasting only a few days. There is no doubt that his hosts found the experience enjoyable yet somewhat perplexing.

Henry came to visit us in March 1944: and as always Ral and I experienced a slight sense of disappointment at the end of his few days here. So pleased we had been to see him, excited, we are so fond of him: then he comes, he is just as usual. Charming smile, one is astonished again at his good looks and his quiet pleasantness; but one never gets any further, I never feel I know him any better, and that is why there is always afterward this feeling of disappointment, as if something was lacking that should have been there.

But what do we expect?

Is it that he, and we, have after all so very little in common? – his tastes are probably mainly intellectual ones. I do not believe he is in the least fond of us, in spite of coming so

347

regularly and in spite of all our welcome. It is his godfather he comes to see: and with him he seems to be as intimate as he is with anyone in the world. Perhaps we expect him to like us <u>because</u> he is 'one of the family', whereas to him we are merely a little more than acquaintances, so our attitude to him may be a little unreasonable. He treats us quite naturally and makes no effort to get to know <u>us</u>. To Nellie and Mary it is clear that he has always been an object of a good deal of curiosity and I know that they also assume that of course they love him and he must love them: they therefore take special pains to entertain him. But I know that if I were not so interested in him, <u>because</u> I know secret things about him, I should consider him quite a dull young man, and I expect he thinks us a little boring!

G.W.B. [Gerald W. Balfour] thinks Henry is extremely reserved, almost secretive by nature: I said to G.W.B.: 'He is really <u>very</u> fond of you.' G.W.B. said, 'I am sure he is, but you know he was very frequently at Fishers Hill and he knows me well.' And it is clear that G.W.B. has studied him, and made efforts to keep in touch with him, & to win his confidence as he has done with no other young person.

But I wonder how really fond of anyone Henry is? His lack of emotional enthusiasm always strikes me, for so much has been given to him. Very fond though he may be of G.W.B., one can hardly feel passionately about a very old man, even one with whom one has intimate conversations and whose intellectual tastes are similar to one's own: and I find myself wondering if he entertains really <u>warm</u> feelings for anyone?

Lack of inner fire, absence of vitality of emotion, is not a thing one expects to see in one destined to be a Messiah: but perhaps this will presently awaken in him and astonish us all; and perhaps this criterion makes our judgement of him unfair – possibly the next world-saviour will be just a scientist, and only secondarily an idealist. He is now 31 and has never had a love affair, to anyone's knowledge: – what can he know of the deep things of life? Ral reminds me that he is not in the least intimate with us, if with anyone, and that he may be having a love affair with someone whom he could never marry. If so, it must have happened since his escape from Germany, for he then said that he had not missed female companionship in the way some prisoners do: and I somehow think, if it had come to him, he would no longer give me this impression of being so detached from all that is vital and hot-blooded, for these experiences affect the whole personality surely.

The Scripts suggest that 'the experiment' was designed to evolve a <u>new type</u> of being: perhaps Olga Petro (a friend of ours who was staying here last July and met him) hit the nail on the head when she said that he gave her the impression of being 'like an angel' – perhaps his nature will never suffer the emotions and problems connected with sex? What a singleness of purpose he could bring to bear upon the affairs of life, if this were indeed so! And yet he might fail in understanding one of the greatest gifts of gods to men.

I wonder what impression he makes upon his relatives and friends? G.W.B. says he is <u>very</u> attached to D.D. [Dame Edith Lyttelton] and is really intimate with her: but it did not seem to me that he was in the least shaken by the news that poor D.D. is in hospital with shingles, and though he expressed a desire to have her address, he had to be reminded to get it from Mary before he left. I once asked G.W.B. if he thought Henry had any inkling of what the Scripts led us to expect would develop in him? He replied 'Yes, he had little doubt that Henry had a fairly good idea of it: neither D.D. nor his mother (the two people closely in touch with him always) were in the least what one would describe as discreet, and he felt certain they had long ago dropped broad hints.' I very much regret that he should have any knowledge whatever of the possibility that he is fated to play a great part in human affairs, for such a knowledge, if taken seriously, would be bound to set any young man apart from his fellows. In one destined to be a Messiah, of the traditional sort, the passionate conviction of being 'chosen and sent', arises <u>from within</u>. Yet he has some awareness of 'being guided'; in a recent letter from his mother to G.W.B., she notes that Henry was frightfully pleased with his new job (some sort of secret training with the Allied Commandos), that he felt 'it was part of a plan, and that he was satisfied.' This sentence reminded both G.W.B. and me of a late Willett Script, in Vol. <u>vi</u> (the words are almost identical) and we <u>can't</u> be certain, as it was his mother who reported it, whether she more or less put the words in

349

his mouth. Ral thinks, however, that the words can be construed another way as the natural expression of a young man's satisfaction, who, having at first been told that no escaped prisoner would be allowed to volunteer for Commando work, finds circumstances change in the course of a year, and the way open to the fulfilment of his own plans and hopes.

With G.W.B. this time, he had an interesting talk on the subject of survival, in which they discussed the varieties of awareness and guidance, external to their own selves, but not related to any personal source. His considerations are evidently the result of some months of careful thought, for he said that if G.W.B. had asked him that question (i.e. if he ever felt himself guided?) only 3 months ago, he would probably have answered it quite differently. I very much wonder what had happened to change his opinion? But I think almost all young men with ability feel a purpose in life: Gerald once told me that he had certainly believed that the big events of his life were somehow intended and inevitable and Ral feels the same: so we may be in danger of thinking that there is more in Henry's statements than is really the case. On the other hand, we must not be unfair to him and all that is interesting should be carefully recorded. Only time can reveal the truth.

It would interest me very much to know what effect it would have upon Henry to know whose son he is, for he will no doubt have to be told one day. It might make him exceedingly happy to find that he and his godfather, to whom he is so really attached, were after all closely related. G.W.B. asked him if he would welcome communications giving evidence of his survival after his death which must come soon: Henry replied Yes, and said he believed that if a close spiritual bond existed between two persons this should be quite possible & certainly easier: this shows the closeness that exists between him and his godfather...

At the time (July 2nd, 1944) when Jean wrote the above note it was barely a month after D-Day, June 6th, the date of the invasion of Europe by the Allied Armies. Henry's visit had occurred just three months before D-Day and he had by then been a member of British Intelligence for a considerable time after his escape from Germany. It is not unreasonable to suppose that like many others

350

involved in covert operations, he had become conditioned into monitoring every utterance he made, even to close friends. During the War, even the ordinary populace had a conscious knowledge that care had to be taken not to let slip information that could be helpful to the enemy. Countless thousands of posters reinforcing this knowledge had appeared during the war years all over the United Kingdom. Many carried the brilliant cartoonist Fougasse's warning 'Careless talk costs lives'. They usually incorporated a major Axis figure such as Hitler or Goebbels or Mussolini, hidden under the table or concealed nearby in a conveniently large aspidistra, gleefully taking notes about information revealed in conversations between well-meaning citizens or members of the Armed Forces.

Arthur Koestler, in his book, *The Challenge of Chance*, gives a strange example of this vigilance at work. He draws attention to a series of happenings connected with the crosswords in the London *Daily Telegraph* appearing in the month before the Allied invasion of Europe on D-Day. Among the codewords given by the planners to a number of the operations in the invasion were 'Overlord', referring to the invasion plan, and 'Neptune', codename for the naval operations. The artificial harbours to be positioned at the beaches were called 'Mulberry', while the two beaches in Normandy selected for the American landings were named 'Utah' and 'Omaha'. In the *Daily Telegraph* crossword of May 3rd, the word 'Utah' appeared. The May 23rd crossword included 'Omaha', while that of May 31st carried 'Mulberry'. 'Neptune' and 'Overlord' appeared in the same crossword, that of June 2nd. To say that MI5 were understandably concerned is an understatement. The fact that all five words, not the most common in use, had been put in crosswords just before the biggest invasion in history, all five words being top-secret codenames, led to a careful investigation. Koestler states: 'The crosswords had been composed by Mr Leonard Sidney Dawe, a schoolmaster who lived in Leatherhead, Surrey. He had been the Daily Telegraph's senior crossword compiler for more than twenty years. He had not known that the words he used were codewords, and had not the foggiest idea how they had come into his head.'

Henry had been living in this cloak-and-dagger 'only on a need to know' atmosphere for years. His previously reserved nature, perhaps partly inherited from his mother, perhaps strengthened by events in his youth, together with the enhanced caution enforced by intelligence work, could well have produced the man whose cold, reserved and secretive persona was remarked upon by G.W.B. It is really not surprising then that Henry, on top of his previous reserve, would have dismayed others naturally open and affectionate by the stand-offish and reserved barrier they were unable to penetrate.

Jean Balfour continued her July 2nd, 1944, note as follows:

...During June I had several very interesting conversations with G.W.B. on the scripts, especially with reference to Willett 417. He discussed the relations between M.L. [Mary Lyttelton] and A.J.B. [Arthur J. Balfour] at the time of her death, and I have taken careful notes of his views on the references to 'Guinevere' and 'Recantation' in connexion with this subject which are among my private papers, and of which I sent a copy to Mr Pidd. Here I want to put on record his views upon the relations between M.L. and Mrs Willett, the former being on the other, the latter being on this side of death.

As for myself, I still question whether we have enough evidence to assume that A.J.B. and M.L. <u>were</u> the spiritual parents of Augustus?

I have said so to G.W.B. and <u>he</u> is so completely convinced himself that he could only refer me to the whole study of the Scripts in bulk yet again: but <u>I</u> cannot so far read as much as he does into the interpretation of them. The 'Birth' scripts seem to me too vague and I do not trust Mrs Willett's scripts <u>alone</u> because I think, except when she is directly under trance conditions, she is influenced too much by her own personality. In so far as her work is corroborated by the scripts of the other automatists, <u>that</u> is evidence, but I do not think that extends so far as those who interpret the Messianic references would wish to believe.

That Henry was a result of an experiment in incarnation, designed by F.M.B. [Francis Maitland Balfour], assisted by the others of 'the group over there' I have no doubt: but the scripts and trances in which M.L. takes an active part (I mean Willett scripts) seem to me always to be directed into getting into touch with A.J.B. and only very indirectly to refer to the 'birth of Augustus' topic. I certainly believe that Mrs Willett, with her unusual mediumistic powers, and her strong pre-dilection for mother-hood, was a perfect instrument, once she was trained, for the dual purpose of (a) communicating with

A.J.B. for the sake of M.L. and (b) giving physical form and birth to the pre-ordained Child: and <u>here</u> F.M.B.'s influence always undoubtedly predominates.

Why is not F.M.B. the 'spiritual father' of Augustus? – I consider that he is.

After the terrible blow of M.L.'s death, it would appear that A.J.B. fell even more in love with her than he was before he lost her; she became for him the ideal being (like Dante & Beatrice) making it impossible for him to entertain serious thoughts of ever marrying anyone else. The scripts suggest, and I assume rightly, that he was perfectly faithful always – does this mean 'faithful in spirit', or that he never experienced sexual passion? No-one knows, or ever will know: I <u>think</u> the latter. G.W.B. says he was very fond of Mary Elcho, and more intimate with her for many years than with anyone, but <u>he</u> is sure that he was never in love with her.

Now it must be borne in mind that M.L. had a very passionate temperament. G.W.B. seems to think that this in itself makes a point of close contact between her and Mrs Willett. This closeness in the relations between communicator and medium is frequently referred to in scripts: it is one way in which M.L. has contact with A.J.B. – 'She sees him (A.J.B.) through her (Mrs W.) and that is why she cries, because the picture is so dim.'

Then there was the meeting at Fishers Hill when A.J.B. shook hands with Mrs Tennant (cf: the script W. 335 that followed this meeting, April 24, 1914.) 'She (M.L.) put out her hand and touched him' (and he never knew) and 'oh, the whole room was a blaze of light.'

G.W.B. also points out that M.L. profoundly influenced Mrs Willett's subconscious mind and may be said to have dominated her to the extent of possession on certain occasions. That being so, then I can't help questioning why A.J.B. did not fall in love with Mrs Willett when he met her, or at least display some interest in her? (especially on the occasion of the meeting at Fishers Hill referred to above, when the small Augustus Henry, aged one year, was presented to him.) Perhaps I take too earthly a view of what is meant by 'spiritual parentage'? and it is true that the scripts constantly emphasize A.J.B.'s imperviousness to psychic influences.

The answer would seem to be that since A.J.B. was incapable of being stirred to passion, G.W.B. had to play the part for him, and Mrs Willett was the means by which M.L. experienced the earthly love previously denied and have the spiritual son of herself and the Faithful Knight. I should like to know if Mrs Willett was in trance at the time when 'the Child' was conceived: I could not very well have asked such a question! I do not however think that the two conditions are humanly compatible, because sexual passion is primarily bodily and trance is not: but one can say with truth that very strong physical passion may be compared to trance. There is the sense of being beyond the body – the transcendental feeling. (cf: Willett 327. Vol: iv. p.29. 43. With ... 'the afterwash of such liberty.') Mrs Willett perhaps genuinely believed herself inspired and in consequence may have attached undue importance to her own emotions: to this may be added her intensely strong idealisation of mother-hood (for she always thought her previous children were gods in embryo); and also I think it must be recognised that one of her most salient characteristics is ambition of the secret, inverted kind, a thing which all brilliant mediums I ever heard of have in common, and are naively un-aware of.

Thus it was quite natural that both she and G.W.B. should regard this child as something very special, quite apart from the fact that in the scripts it is clear that 'the group on the other side' are exceedingly triumphant once his birth was successfully accomplished. But still I ask. Why attribute the fatherhood to A.J.B.? It seems because he was a very great man, and it is assumed that his gifts shall eventually rest, like the mantle of Elijah, upon Henry.

Certainly Henry has absolutely first rate intellectual powers, and there is something about him that suggests a very fine, rare nature.

Yet the birth of Augustus does not appear to be to M.L. what the interpreters would lead one to expect. One of the most puzzling things in the scripts is the way the subject of the 'unborn children' crops up, after the birth of the 'Messianic Child'. [In] Mrs Willett 417 (dated Feb. 6th, 1926. when Henry was nearly 13 years old) it is clear that M.L. is not satisfied, she still wants those 'little ones, for whom she should have been the gate of life.' Is it the <u>direct</u> line of the family that is of special importance to her, as it certainly was to A.J.B.?

Jean Traprain.

Whittingehame. July 2nd

A year later, just after the end of the Second World War in Europe, Jean wrote a further note concerning her views on Henry and his possible future. By now, with the death of Gerald Balfour at the beginning of 1945, she had acquired more information about Henry, filling her with dismay and providing her with one of those classic 'If I only knew then what I know now' regrets.

Further questions under a slightly different light.

by Jean Balfour.

June 1945

A good deal of time has passed since I first knew Henry & wrote the 'Private Letter' to him – a life time of happenings both to me, to Ral and to him. These last years, with G.W.B. living close to us, I have become infinitely more familiar with the Scripts: and since I wrote that letter, I have got to know Mrs Tennant much better: I have become fond of her, though I never would call her a normal being.

I have watched Henry's development, not very closely because circumstances have prevented him & us from frequent meetings, but with very profound observance, and we are very fond of him. But not until now, five months after G.W.B.'s death, have I ever seen the letters of 1930 and 1931, or known of those extremely important years in Henry's life. Some of these letters have a bearing on the conversation between Ral and Henry recorded in the black folder, dated April 1931, which was the last time Henry ever stayed with us, apart from recent visits to G.W.B., after he had escaped from Germany, these last two years. If <u>only</u> at that time we had known more, or could have kept more closely in touch! I do not know, of course, what transpired during the process of psycho-analysis which Henry underwent: but his mother would not have spared any trouble to get the very best advice. Only personally I have a profound distrust of psycho-analysts, and we could not help thinking

355

that if a close friendship had been allowed to develop between us & him, we might have been able to bridge over his problems <u>with</u> him: but perhaps his mother distrusted us because we knew too much about other things.

I can't help feeling that far too much fuss was made over a propensity which is very usual in adolescence. If any psychic maladjustment really existed in Henry, I should say it was rooted much further back, and to do with his very earliest views of women. Did he ever feel the coldness that existed between Mr and Mrs Tennant, or was the idea of the sacredness of motherhood so much emphasized to him that it inhibited the normal development of interest in mating? I wonder if the Psychologists knew as much as they ought to have known, of the circumstances before he was ever born?

My impression is that after his Mother inveigled him into remaining on at Eton, when his own ardent desire was to leave for a more active life, he never fully trusted her again: and the increasing reserve, which G.W.B. described to me as 'almost secretive', may have dated from this time. A real friendship between the two brothers also dated at this time which can have brought nothing but good.

Last autumn I wrote the paper called 'Questions in 1944.' I wish now to say that I think that a good deal of that paper is a little unfair. I did not then know ... that Henry had ever known such deep unhappiness. But it is true to say that I do not at present feel the 'heavenly promise' in Henry that I did when I wrote the Letter. Is this because I have become cynical and earthly? Or is it that only the young, on the verge of manhood, ever give the impression of incarnate divinity? Is it that as the experience of life comes to them, that transcendant evanescence gets inevitably dulled? – yet because of experience, they should be more <u>understanding</u> men, & isn't that just as important for leadership of mankind?

Henry has had such experience, travel abroad, Army training, a few months of actual war; then the prison-camp in Germany, the stress and strain of the long-drawn-out escape: and since then, Secret Service work of the most thrilling kind, and now he is engaged in a military job of training others for the war in Japan, which exercises so admirably his powers of leadership – what a full life he has had for one of 32!

And yet, in spite of good looks, perfect manners, fine achievement, brilliant brains and lots of experience, he strikes one as a singularly passion-less creature, without any great enthusiasms. Yet he is rare, and good: and there is lots of time still for him to develop in startling ways. Only nothing about him just <u>now</u> gives me the feeling that a mere spark is needed to light up a great blaze in him. But suppose, if he should fall in love? – <u>That</u> might provide the spark. But will he, ever? I think myself it would take some courage to bring home a wife to that wonderful almighty mother of his! A perusal of these letters alone gives one a picture of the especial problems she herself creates in the life of those around her. These letters made me wonder with infinite pity for her son. Whether the possibility of failure of the Great Plan, (a possibility which was always present) has augmented with the years: and whether the Group, having succeeded in producing their new being in the first place, could not extend their influence sufficiently far into this world of flesh, to dominate his growth all the way. If his mother could always have remained 'Mrs Willett', they might have been able to do so much more than could ever have been the case when Mrs Tennant took possession of the field.

We on the earth are so blind, and our sense of the true values of spiritual growth is so overlaid by the considerations of what seems right in the eyes of this world.

These are only thoughts & questions. Time alone can give the answers.

J.B.

17

Henry's War

You are in the power of your enemy. You owe your life to his humanity, and your daily bread to his compassion. You must obey his orders, go where he tells you, stay where you are bid, await his pleasure, pursue your soul in patience.

Ex-PoW Winston Churchill.

Henry Coombe-Tennant left Trinity College, Cambridge, in 1935 having achieved a double first. It was supposed by most people who knew him that he would have a brilliant future academically or perhaps go into politics. His tutor, Professor Broad, was disappointed when instead he took a commission in the Regular Army instead of applying for a fellowship. In fact, he joined the Welsh Guards, following in the footsteps of his older brother Christopher. He was highly observant, trained to assess evidence and events and it seems quite certain that he knew, like many others, that war could not be avoided.

In the ominous days towards the end of the 1930s when the prospect of war grew ever stronger, the 1st Battalion of the Welsh Guards was ordered to Gibraltar to reinforce the garrison there. A second regular Battalion was formed on May 18th, 1939 and when war was declared on September 3rd of that year it was stationed at the Tower of London. During most of the so-called 'phoney war', while Lord Gort's British Expeditionary Force was transferred to France, it remained on duty at the Tower. Henry always remembered the particular rituals of this tour of duty in King William's fortress, rituals greatly increased in number by additional wartime duties and defence measures. He learned with his comrades the stylised drill and discipline required to mount King's Guard, the 2nd Battalion mounting it for the first time on 16th October. It was not in fact until April 1940 that the battalion was relieved of London duties, much to the relief of many of the men, and sent to Oldean Camp, Camberley, for intensive training.

By this time Henry had been commissioned, and it was as a captain that he found himself and his men at Oldean Camp, in company with the 2nd Battalion Irish Guards. Until that time their serious training for active service had barely had time to begin. It had scarcely got underway before the 'phoney war' in western Europe was shattered by the German blitzkrieg, unleashed on May 10th, 1940. The previous month Norway and Denmark had been overrun. Now after severe air raids of key towns and airfields, the Germans began the invasion of Belgium, Holland, Luxembourg and France. By May 20th–21st, the German forces had advanced 150 miles, bringing them to the Channel ports. By May 26, the British War Office was frantically organising the evacuation of the British Expeditionary Force. There had followed the Dunkirk miracle when about 340,000 British and French troops were carried to Great Britain in safety by the Navy and an armada of small boats. In less than four weeks, the German conquest was complete.

In that short time of confusion and disaster, Henry took part in two expeditions to Europe. It was the morning of May 10th, a Friday, when he was ordered to proceed to Tunbridge Wells. The Irish and Welsh Guards had been on twelve hours' notice to move. Although they had been training at Oldean Camp, Camberley, it was the Whitsun weekend and so about two-thirds of the officers had been absent on leave. The small sub-post office at Oldean had been overwhelmed with the task of dispatching telegrams recalling them. When Henry reached Tunbridge Wells he found that the Irish Guards had been given their orders to go abroad at once.

They left that evening on a special train and were carried across the Channel by two Channel steamers painted grey, arriving at the Hook of Holland early on Monday morning. He remembered the smell of the salt water, the sun glinting off the gentle swell, the feeling of almost hypersensitivity he had had during the crossing. They were landed on the beach with their equipment and expected to be met by Dutch mechanised transport to take them up to The Hague where their function was to assist the government in organising the campaign. They were also supposed to round up fifth columnists.

When they arrived they found no transport and decided to dig in on the beach.

The morning was spent disposing the battalion, fixing headquarters, digging in and arranging for company headquarters. Henry had been second in command. Assistance was given to him by some Dutchmen, some in the uniforms of the Dutch army, to help him decide on the locations of the various headquarters. They were finally fixed in some coastguards' cottages, which at least had strong concrete sides.

It was not until 11 a.m. that the first German reconnaissance aircraft appeared. German bombers arrived about 2 p.m. He watched them fly over the harbour where they scored a direct hit on a destroyer which was in dock. The bomb exploded in the engine room but the ship, which gave off enormous clouds of black smoke, did not sink. Soon afterwards a number of 500-lb bombs were dropped on the battalion. One hit battalion headquarters. Another fell near men in a trench causing a few casualties. Henry formed the idea that the tactics adopted by the aircraft suggested that the Germans had an exact knowledge of the disposition of the British force.

Soon after the raid a soldier arrived and told Henry that there was a horse in a field near the beach unable to get up. Henry went up to the field and found that the horse had broken its leg. He was preparing to shoot the animal when a Dutchman arrived in a great state of excitement. He implored Henry not to kill the animal, for he had arranged for a slaughterer to come and kill the horse. Henry asked if it was certain that the slaughterer would come and if so how long he would be. The Dutchman replied that he expected the slaughterer in an hour and that he hoped he would come. Eventually Henry and the Dutchman walked up to the Hook to see the slaughterer. Henry saw that the town had suffered heavily from aerial bombing. A number of houses had been destroyed and there were several people on stretchers in the streets, which were carpeted with broken glass. They eventually saw the slaughterer who was most unwilling to come and despatch the horse, particularly as at that moment the sounds of distant sirens wailing another air-raid warning could be heard. However, the slaughterer was finally coerced by Henry's determination and, taking a humane killer, they made their way back to the meadow beside the sea where the horse was released from its suffering.

Back in England and recalling the events, Henry found himself shaking his head as he marvelled yet again at how much time he had spent making sure that the horse had been put out of its misery while the German armoured divisions and infantry swept onwards through France and Belgium. It was positively surrealistic the battalion sitting there waiting – for what? Into his mind came a graphic picture of the British and French playing what they thought of as a leisurely game of bridge with the Germans when suddenly, without warning, their opponent shouted 'Snap!', slammed down a card on the table and seized every card in play and in their hands.

During the late afternoon, heavy gunfire was heard inland. It continued for many hours. There were some Royal Engineers and Marines about and they reported that a group of Dutch howitzers were shelling a wood that was supposedly occupied by fifth columnists and Germans. Late that evening more aircraft came over but no bombs were dropped. The ensuing night was fairly quiet. In the early hours a British marine arrived in a great hurry saying that he had a message from the Commander in Chief of the Dutch forces to the officer commanding the British Expeditionary Force. It stated that the British were expected to take all steps necessary to their security. Henry immediately reported this to the C.O. and heard that arrangements were being made to take the force off in destroyers at once. By that time the Dutch Queen and her ministers had left Holland. The British Force now heard that the Navy ships could only venture into the harbour for a very short time owing to the risk of aerial bombing. Accordingly they destroyed their ammunition, food and any petrol stores and marched over to the harbour with as much kit as they could carry. When they got there they heard that it would be impossible to return the one and a half miles to get the rest, so Henry's valise, marked Captain A.H.S. Coombe-Tennant, Welsh Guards, and much other equipment, was left on the beach.

He embarked on the second destroyer which managed to get safely out of the harbour into the Channel. Suddenly they heard an aircraft engine and a German plane dived through a cloud. It loosed a trail of bombs that exploded with vicious violence round the ship. At the same time the plane machine-gunned the ship, killing a number of men and wounding others. The aircraft disappeared as quickly as it had appeared. Some time later the ship had to stop while various floating and magnetic mines on their course were exploded with pom-pom guns.

361

They reached Dover in the afternoon, thankful to see the familiar white cliffs Henry for one had not expected to see again quite so soon.

It had been his baptism of enemy fire. The impression made on him by the explosion of a bomb near at hand was not so much that of a blast but a terrific earthquake. The walls seemed to shake violently backwards and forwards, and the windows were blown out across the room. He had been in company headquarters when a heavy bomb had dropped on regimental headquarters nearby. The latter was fortunately not full at the time and the casualties were not heavy. Altogether some twelve men were killed in the abortive expedition and a further thirty wounded, twelve of whom died soon after their return.

On Sunday May 19th, he managed to spend part of the day with his brother in London. In the morning he travelled from Oldean to the Ministry of Economic Warfare. Queenie had been with him. When he was told he could go up, he found someone to look after the dog in the 'Porters' (porter's lodge). Alexander was in his office. A large-scale map of Holland was pinned up on the wall. They looked particularly at the Hook and the country around it and discussed how far the Dutch resistance had been successful and how much German material had been destroyed in the campaign. They had also discussed the extent of the fifth column in Holland.

Alexander had then introduced him to Scanlan, head of the Italian and Scandinavian sub-section of Black List. Scanlan had fought in Flanders in the first war and after it ended had worked in the Public Records Office and in the British Museum. After a while he took Alexander and himself to see Wingate, the head of Black List Section. They had a look at another map, this time of northern France. He remembered that they had discussed the strategical implications of the 'break-through' in the neighbourhood of Rethel. Really, none of them had any idea then that any information he could give them was already ancient history, so swiftly were events marching in the Nazi blitzkrieg. They might as well have been discussing Caesar's Gallic War. He and Alexander finally took their leave and went downstairs, collected Queenie from the 'Porters' and left the building. They went out round the sandbag obstruction in the doorway of Berkeley Square House into the warm, bright sunshine.

They walked to the Athenaeum and left Queenie in the porter's

362

lodge. They had lunch at an open window, which looked on to irises and rhododendrons in flower in the garden to the south of the club. After a leisurely lunch, followed by excellent coffee in big cups, they rescued Queenie from her confined space and walked past St James's Palace into the Green Park. It was a day of cloudless sunshine and a strong wind was blowing. They walked up the slight hill towards Piccadilly, past pink may flower trees in blossom. It seemed the right thing to do to sit down on two chairs and watch the trees and the vividly green grass stirred by the passing breeze.

They talked of many things. He asked Alexander about himself and his plans for the future. He remembered how Alexander had shrugged and he realised that in the total uncertainty of the situation it was just not possible for any sensible answer to be given. They had agreed that it was good to think of Mother safe at Didlington. Much of the time had been spent in silence but silences can speak. He thought again of the understanding that had flowered so wonderfully in the same way as their surroundings after the late winter, a unity of spirit and communion that had grown between them, so that, some weeks before, on Wimbledon Common, they had talked of the significance of each other to their innermost lives that he believed no circumstances could ever touch.

Time passed. It was time to walk back to Piccadilly. He had to rejoin Ralph Pilcher and Twining who was motoring him back to Oldean. As he and Queenie climbed the steps of the bus to its upper level he looked back and saw Alexander watching them. He waved and received a wave in return before they were carried away into the distance.

Later that disastrous month, Henry had his second encounter with the Germans. Back at Camberley, and while out on an exercise on the morning of May 21st – preparing for an 'attack' in the pine-wooded country near the Staff College – the 2nd Battalion of the Welsh Guards was ordered by telephone to proceed overseas again that same afternoon with the 2nd Battalion Irish Guards. May 21st was a beautiful day. As their vehicles drove south-east towards Dover, the pleasant and familiar countryside of Kent and Surrey, peaceful in the spring sunshine, seemed utterly remote from reports of the savage, chaotic fighting, the terrified streams of refugees machine-gunned from the air to maximise the confusion and jam up the roads, the efficient, swift onward progress of the German armoured divisions.

363

When they reached Dover shortly before midnight the Guards were informed that they were to cross the Channel that night to Boulogne. They crossed on a destroyer and two other ships, the S.S. *Biarritz* and *Mona's Queen*. A few miles off Boulogne they got their first glimpse of the shambles of war waiting for them as described by Major L.F. Ellis in *The Welsh Guards at War*:

> We soon saw a burning tanker, obviously bombed. She was an eerie sight in the half light; the flames spread a deep red glow under a big pall of smoke... It seemed to take hours till, after frantic signals from the ... ships stopped outside, the boom was opened to allow us to enter. A small French fishing-boat was coming out at the same time and I wondered what fish they hoped to catch and land.

The quay was filled by large crowds:

> Every kind of soldier and civilian – French, Belgian, Dutch and British. Even some German prisoners of war waiting to be taken off in ships that had brought the Brigade over. In the midst of this very orderly crowd stood three or four men with led horses – the chargers of H.R.H. the Duke of Gloucester and the Commander-in-Chief, Lord Gort. I was sorry for the groom: he was obviously very tired and puzzled as to how he was ever going to get his chargers on board a boat. Later I was told that they were shot on the quayside.

At that moment the Guards did not know that they were not expected to turn back the enemy already threatening the Channel port but to buy time to help ensure the successful evacuation of the troops further north from the Dunkirk pocket. There, some 350,000 British, French and Belgian troops facing the German armour were confined to an ever-shrinking area. It was hoped that a dogged defensive effort by the Guards further south would at least get the attention of some of the panzers and relieve the pressure on the area around Dunkirk. Indeed the brigade's orders at that time were to defend Boulogne 'to the last man and the last round'. Inevitably, the staunch, disciplined defence that followed by men who had been dropped into it as a result of the lack of moral fibre of almost all pre-war politicians recalls Kipling's bitter couplet: 'If any question why we died,/Tell them, because our fathers lied.'

The Welsh and Irish Guards did their best. In the light of vague and almost certainly outdated intelligence, much of it by stragglers coming into the town, the Irish Guards were stationed to the south-west of the harbour and river, the Welsh Guards to the north-east. Without artillery and tanks, they formed their line of defence. In fact, any satisfactory defence of the port would have dictated a line in the surrounding hills far longer than that number of Guards could have manned.

The detailed account of the last stand of the defenders of Boulogne is a story – not at all uncommon in the history of war – of a small, hopelessly outnumbered, outgunned and ill-equipped force achieving by sheer determination, improvisation and outstanding bravery a defence that, even in ultimate defeat, shines like a victory and remains an inspiration to those following them. Arriving in the darkness of the early morning of May 22nd, the Irish and Welsh Guards sought out and prepared their strong-points, retreating under heavy fire when forced to do so to hastily set-up new defensive positions. Ultimately, with the Royal Navy's help, part of their forces were successfully evacuated from the burning port. Those who in the confusion could not get away fought it out to the end.

In fact the Navy ships were closely involved throughout the enagagement:

One after another destroyers had entered and left the harbour, the perils of their task increasing as the enemy's guns got into action from the high ground which surrounded the port and as air bombardment increased. The naval guns were indeed the only effective answer to the enemy's long-range attack, for the army had no artillery to support it. The Navy's heroism … made a deep impression on all the troops at Boulogne. They talk still of the destroyer that was hit and set on fire as she entered the harbour. With her hull damaged and a raging furnace, there was grave risk that she would sink in a position which would block the entrance and put an end to all further use of the basin; yet efforts to deal with the fire were not allowed to slacken for a moment the pace with which her own guns were being served; and eventually she got away, her stern aflame and all her guns still blazing at the enemy.

Towards the end, communications began to fail. Small groups of men were forced to occupy buildings and, believing that the last destroyer had left, tried to break out to the south. Some were captured almost at once; some did get clear of the town and were taken after several days' journeying across country. A larger party of troops held on, still putting up resistance. A diary entry completes their story:

May the 25th. – The men were in great form and we organised quite a decent breakfast and made every man wash and shave and clean his weapons. We replenished ammunition from an abandoned R.A.F. lorry; I found some more for my revolver. The party on the other side of the road shot another German bicyclist and that attracted the heavy tanks. They lumbered incredibly slowly up the road and then with great deliberation started to pump shells into the opposite house. The position was absolutely hopeless.

The cost of the defence was heavy for the Welsh Guards. Over three hundred were finally captured. All the wounded fell into enemy hands. Henry was one of these totally exhausted, starving, stressed yet emotionally numbed men who, in the abnormally intense silence after the cessation of hostilities, found himself a prisoner of war.

The circumstances of Captain Albert Arkwright's capture eloquently describe the initial state of the prisoner captured after prolonged combat:

I and some thirty officers and other ranks of my battalion had lain exhausted on the stone floor of a cart-shed, and the feeling of utter hopelessness and despair, which I am sure must have been common to us all, was completely eclipsed by the state of physical and mental fatigue at which we had arrived. For during the previous ten days and nights we had been almost without sleep and never without anxiety, and the sudden lifting of all responsibility coupled with the knowledge that at last we could sleep brought an end to the tension and a strange feeling of complete relief. I suppose that none of us really cared whether he was alive or dead; certainly we had not grasped the full significance of our ignominious position. We were too tired, too lacking in emotion to realize anything except that at last we could sink into oblivion.

There were so many prisoners taken by the Germans in the course of their Western Europe four-week blitzkrieg that in many areas the Germans didn't really have the manpower to spare to control them closely. Sometimes in the prison camp Henry had tried to analyse why he had made no attempts to escape in that time of confusion and emotional numbness but he had been unable to come to any firm conclusion.

In the early days in the prison camp his prime worry was how soon his mother would learn that he was safe and well. With the constant memory of the son Christopher she had lost in the slaughter of the first war, it must have been absolute hell for her when war broke out again and another of her sons went on active service. After she learned he was a prisoner, his concern turned to making the best of his situation. Her letters and those from friends at home helped and in the infrequent ones he wrote to her he tried to give a relatively reassuring picture of his life in the Oflag. The changing weather was a useful topic – '... after many weeks of bitter cold [the weather] has today given us something like an English April morning ... very cold here now: thirty-four degrees of frost on parade this morning. We have enough coal to keep the stove in all day. I have enough food, clothes and tobacco... Music takes up a good deal of my time.' Nevertheless, arrival of Red Cross parcels was always more than welcome.

In respect of food parcels the prisoners and their relatives had not only been fighting the German authorities but also British bureaucracy at its most intransigent. An excerpt from *The War Behind the Wire* by Patrick Wilson, a book on the PoW situation, is illuminating and details the role that the ever-indefatigable Mrs Coombe-Tennant played in challenging that bureaucracy.

Nevertheless blind bureaucracy got in the way of humanity. As for ensuring that food and medicine sent from home got through to prisoners in the German camps, the DPW's [Directorate of Prisoners of War's] reactions was to shrug off responsibility for that entirely. International convention decreed that it was up to the military authorities in the country holding prisoners to feed and clothe them adequately.

Prisoners' rations were to be equal to those available to a private soldier in that country. The Germans, as signatories of the Geneva Convention, were expected to honour that commitment. Therefore, the mind of officialdom decreed any supplies sent from home were extras, and a matter for the Red Cross. There was an almighty row about this which was never satisfactorily resolved. Relatives were posting parcels of food and clothing to addresses in Germany; nothing was getting through.

The 'Sunday Express' took up the issue, aided by the formidable Mrs Coombe-Tennant, whose son – a captain in the Welsh Guards – was in Oflag VI B. She wrote to Mrs Churchill, mother to mother, telling her that prisoners like her son had been left to 'rot in starvation and in rags'. The government had been giving the job of looking after them to the Red Cross, she said, but it had failed to check if the Red Cross – a voluntary body, after all – was up to the job, which it was not. Mrs Churchill (who also had a son in the army) may have been moved, but her husband was not, and he refused an enquiry. However, the senior civil servant in the War Office had taken note. Sir James Grigg had heard reports about the shortcomings of the Red Cross, 'and if half of what is said is true it looks as if there might be a very considerable scandal brewing', he confided to his colleagues.

Before me are copies of two Christmas Cards, drawn by one of the prisoners, A.A.West, in Oflag VII C and sent in 1940 and 1941. Above the words 'Christmas Greetings', and especially on the 1941 card, are depicted scenes from camp life – opening Red Cross parcels, forming a band, skating, games activities, learning German, sunbathing. The pictures of a number of the prisoners are cleverly drawn to give the impression that they are healthy and active with a good deal of freedom. The overall effect aimed at is that they are in something almost approaching a holiday camp. The reality was somewhat different.

However, for someone of Henry's temperament, education and

training, captivity in Oflag VII C and thereafter in Oflag VI B was not the crushing, destructive experience it was for some other prisoners. He found that he was able to cope successfully with his life in a prisoner-of-war camp. His health was good; the relatively spartan food agreed with him; he became engaged in a number of positive activities – including study and teaching, always an outward sign of a sustained belief that in the end there would be a future of freedom at home – and of course he was able to use his great gifts as a pianist to lift the minds of his fellow prisoners from the bleakness of their captivity and the anguish of defeat. Without a score, without pause and without repetition, he would often play for them a wide range of music from Beethoven to jazz for two hours on end.

Henry was also involved with plans to escape and sat on one of the many 'escape committees' that sprang up inside the POW camps. Such committees' purpose was to assess escape plans, veto the more hare-brained, give their blessing to the more hopeful and do everything in their power to organise all that would be required for a successful attempt. Clothes, food, fake papers, maps, a primitive compass, even some instruction in navigating by the stars, there was a multitude of necessary articles to be fabricated or procured to maximise the escaper's chance of making it back home if he managed to leave the camp behind him. And all these had to be hidden ingeniously from the random searches made from time to time by the guards.

In the usual POW camp, a narrow choice of escape method presented itself. Escape was effected either by going under the wire, through the wire or over the wire. A scheme utilising the second method might of course be such that it provided a chance of getting through a gate. In Oflag VI B, the camp where Henry was held, a careful and continuous assessment of the situation by some of the prisoners began to favour the third choice – namely over the wire

Oflag VI B was roughly rectangular in shape, in area about 35 acres. Within the perimeter the prisoners lived in groups of large wooden huts, about one hundred and fifty men being accommodated in each hut, open ground separating the buildings. At each corner of the camp stood a high watchtower manned by sentries during the hours of daylight, armed by rifles and light automatic weapons. They also had powerful searchlights. In addition, at night, additional sentries patrolled outside the wire fence and yet another force of sentries, known to the prisoners by the cricketing term as the 'deep field', patrolled at least four hundred yards outside the wire.

The term 'wire' is a massive understatement. It consisted of a formidable obstacle of two stout post-and-barbed wire fences eight feet high, built to preclude any apertures larger than one square foot. Between the fences was a mass of twisted and coiled barbed wire four feet high. In addition, the inner fence had a wire apron, leaning inwards, not only giving additional height to the obstacle but also providing yet another predicament for would-be escapers. A line of tall lamp posts outside the perimeter lit up the obstacle at night while inside the perimeter a tripwire, about two feet high, ran parallel to the fence. The perimeter lights, searchlights and warning telephones were all on separate wiring systems with the wires carried at a height of some six feet above the top of the wire fence. The camp lighting system was on yet another circuit.

It might be expected that any plan to get out over these obstacles would have been classified by the escape committee as wildly impractical. There was one small advantage, however. The camp guards were not the flower of the German Wehrmacht. By 1942 it was engaged in fighting the Russians, the British and Commonwealth forces in Africa or guarding the Channel coast. Some of the guards were old while others had obvious physical defects, so it seemed reasonable to assume that their ability to shoot a moving target on a dark night was not high. There still remained that risk of wounding or death, and there still remained the depressing and discouraging statistic that only a small percentage of escapers ever made it home. You could assess these risks, play safe and decide to wait out the war. A very large number of prisoners did not adopt that decision.

The extraordinary plan to get over the wire was based on the ingenuity and electrical expertise of a number of the officers in the Oflag who had discovered a method of extinguishing from inside the camp every light simultaneously, both interior and exterior to the perimeter. On an evening 'rehearsal' in May 1942, they had managed to do so. Buoyed up by their success they worked throughout the summer months perfecting the second part of the plan – the planning and construction of the necessary parts of the wooden ladder-like hinged bridge contraption that they hoped could be carried in the darkness to the wire, thrown up and over and used by the escapers to surmount the formidable obstacle. In addition, of course, there was the usual hard work of providing everything the escapees would need on their journey to the coast. Once the list of escapers had been drawn up, there was also the problem of training them so that the whole operation could, it was hoped, be carried out in less than three minutes.

About the middle of August, the committee in Oflag VI B got something else to think about. The German authorities notified the inmates that the whole camp was to be moved in the near future. The officers would be split into three parties, each going to a different camp. Lists of names were delivered and it was noted with some alarm that a number of the men elected to the escape team were on the list of those officers liable to be moved on in the first party. There was one glimmer of hope. If they followed previous custom, the Germans, three days prior to the move, would order the inmates to hand in their kit. In the event they did so, telling the prisoners that the first party would hand in their kit on August 27th and move from the camp on August 30th. The second and third parties would move on September 1st and 3rd respectively.

The escape attempt when it came utilised four apparatuses and forty-one men. Early in the project, all the chosen teams had been composed of two men. To maximise the chance of success if a team did escape, the members were expected over the weeks beforehand to improve their physical fitness as much as possible. Unfortunately, early in August, the prisoner who had been elected to be Henry's partner had to withdraw. His attacks of rheumatism showed that he was simply not fit enough to take part. It was decided that Henry would join the two-man team composed of Captain Albert S.B. Arkwright, a Scots Fusilier and Captain Rupert J. Fuller, a Yorkshireman.

On the night of the escape the men, hands and faces blackened, kitbags ready, stood waiting in the hut for the signal that the perimeter lights had been put out. Those at the front of their queue were ready to lift the apparatus. One can imagine the racing pulses, the sudden spasms of panic at the realisation of the multitude of things that could go wrong, the gnawing dread that it would end in quick capture even if their apparatus could be manoeuvred in the darkness into position, fully extended and let them crawl over the high, wide obstacle of vicious, twisted barbed wire they so desperately wanted to avoid falling into.

The lights went out. It seemed pitch dark. The fifteen yards between them and the fence were covered, the two leaders hoisted up their end of the ladder and the claws caught on the top strand of wire. Captain Fuller jammed the butt of the ladder on to the ground. Captain Arkwright caught up the decking by the handles, stumbled over the tripwire, recovered and began climbing the ladder. At the top, after a false start where he rammed the end of the decking into the electric wires suspended above the fence, he managed to disengage it and got the end to drop on top of the far side of the obstacle. As he scuttled over the decking on hands and knees and dropped to the ground on the far side the first shot rang out. He ran forward through a field of sugar beet, measured his length over a single strand of barbed wire they had not previously noticed from the camp, disentangled himself with Rupert's help. Henry was with him. They spread out and ran abreast for a further two or three hundred yards. As they did so they heard the shouts of the sentries interspersed by shots that must have been fired at random. They came to a field of corn with the cut harvest already standing in stooks. Now lack of breath from the nervous tension and their exertions took over and they slowed to a rapid pace. Gradually the noises died away behind them and the stillness of the night enfolded them.

In the POW camp they had discussed endlessly the best plan for avoiding recapture. It was essential that during the first night as much distance as possible should be put between them and the camp and so they had avoided burdening themselves with all sorts of things such as extra food and anything else beyond the absolutely essential such as their primitive compass and water bottles made in the camp. They had memorised the main features in a map of the camp's environment and their first night's goal was a heavily wooded area some ten miles further north. In addition they had decided to journey thereafter during darkness and hide and sleep during the days in suitably secluded places. For food and water they meant to rely on the countryside for it was late summer and they should be able to dig up potatoes and get fruit from orchards. With luck it should be possible to cook the potatoes in the ashes of any small, carefully hidden fires of dry wood they might safely light if the place was particularly concealing.

It took some days before they were really able to sleep by day. Usually their sleep was shallow and fitful. They found that even in the early mornings it was often more than chilly and they had to huddle together to conserve warmth. Henry would deploy his macintosh groundsheet, the three escapers would lie down, snuggle together and put the two macintosh coats they also had over themselves. The man in the middle was obviously the best off and they took that place in turn. At midday, their meal might be some Red Cross chocolate, apples from their last source of supply and water. They seldom cooked at that hour. Rarely were they able to have a fire both morning and evening. If so, they would sometimes roast the potatoes by placing them in a scooped out hole, then cover them with earth before lighting the fire above them. They were left among the ashes all day. Before the evening fire was lit they were turned so that the fire cooked their unroasted sides.

During the afternoon, if their hiding place was suitable, they carried out their 'housekeeping', which could include shaving, washing themselves and their socks, mending them and other clothing if required. It was a disciplined activity that not only kept up their morale but greatly helped to maintain their appearance and comfort. Map-reading came next; as they got further from the camp the fine detail of their knowledge was lost. Here, however, Henry, as navigator, was of great help. During the first three nights they moved exclusively across countryside, with Henry navigating by the stars. When these were not visible, he used Rupert's home-made compass.

On a number of occasions they had narrow escapes. Walking along a railway line even at night ran the risk of a signal box, a railwayman's hut or level-crossing keeper's house being occupied with someone still awake late at night. In any event the trio soon became disenchanted with that route. They found that unless there was a footpath running along the permanent way, it was uncomfortable and tiring in the darkness to choose to walk either on the sleepers or on the rough stones between them. You could badly sprain or break an ankle that way when you misjudged the distance. They had one alarm when a level-crossing keeper did emerge from his hut and challenged them. They made a rapid withdrawal. On another occasion, dawn found them still looking for a suitable lying-up place. They had to choose a clump of trees on a hillside from which they could see the railway line down below. They were tired and very hungry. That evening they climbed up to a quarry. Quickly they lit a fire behind one of the sheds in the quarry, cooked potatoes and made tea. They were on the point of enjoying their meal when they saw a German in uniform about ten yards away. Only a few bushes screened them from him. Henry said afterwards that the German looked straight at him and must have seen him. Two things probably saved them. The German must have assumed that they were some of the workmen in the quarry. In addition, a moment later they saw a girl appear. No doubt 'clothed with cursing as with a garment', he led his girlfriend out of sight down a small path. The three British officers beat a hasty retreat in the opposite direction.

On another night towards morning they found themselves in an area where numerous noticeboards warned them that they were on War Department land. The escapees were suffering from thirst and in a fairly thick wood they found a deep cart rut with sufficient water for their needs. They made porridge and tea and boiled enough of the stagnant water to fill their bottles. They spent the day there undetected. It was the beginning of a night of shocks. Half a mile later they heard the sound of German troops singing on the march. The trio lay low for a few hours before making a fresh start about midnight. Soon they came to a village. The three found some figures moving near to them and decided to take a chance. Instead of retreating and arousing suspicion concerning their reasons for being there, they began to walk boldly down the road through the village. It turned out to be a village where German troops were billeted. About the centre of the village a man stepped out of the shadows and shone a torch on them. They strode on, knapsacks on their backs. Once clear of the houses they left the road in case the man sent a bicycle patrol after them.

Still later on that eventful night, depending upon the North Star to guide them, they found a well-defined track leading in the right direction through the marsh and heath and woodlands they had been walking over. They decided to take it. It brought them to a large entrance gate with stone pillars, the gates lying invitingly open. Luckily Henry spotted a noticeboard that told them to slow down to ten kilometres per hour since they were entering a German barracks. By now totally exhausted, as much from nervous shock as from physical expenditure of energy, they struggled on, through what ultimately turned out to be agricultural land. They slaked their thirst at a stream, filled their bottles, and some hundred yards further on, came to an orchard of trees laden with ripe apples. Unlikely as it would have seemed to them some minutes before, they ran riot among the trees, taking a bite here and there, discarding any apple that was not quite to their discerning taste. Finally they filled their haversacks and pockets and went on their way.

In this manner, their dogged, twisting, precarious march across Germany continued night after night, sometimes dangerously eventful, at other times being without alarming incident for several nights. But inevitably all three were becoming more and more exhausted physically and mentally by lack of enough food and the strain of making instant decisions, any one of which could lead to capture. Albert Arkwright remembers his state of mind, in which the incidents experienced in a sequence of days and nights became something of a jumble in his mind.

I remember finding a plum-tree laden with ripe plums and picking handfuls of them. I remember a place where rabbit-holes and rabbit-runs abounded, and my futile efforts to snare one. I remember walking brazenly through quite a large town in the small hours of the morning and an old woman who, for some reason best known to herself, suddenly opened the door of her house, and the gasp of surprise she gave at seeing us pass by her threshold... Then there was the day we lay in the middle of a young wood and watched a glider making successive flights from a neighbouring eminence... There were nights when we were moving not so far from Münster and Osnabrück and searchlights and anti-aircraft fire were visible, and we were glad to think that our enemies were having a taste of their own medicine...

They were now nearing the third week of their trek across Germany and knew that they must be somewhere near the frontier between Germany and Holland. Finding a canal, they followed the towpath for three nights until it became time to make for the part of the frontier they meant to cross. Before that could be attempted they had to cross the River Ems. It took them some time to find a bridge, involving a detour of some three miles downstream. They managed to cross the bridge just before daylight. The prospect of spending their last day in Germany kept all three in a state of considerable excitement, jabbed continually by shards of fear that at this last minute of the first objective, the escape from the enemy country, something would happen to turn their success into failure.

They now had only three or four miles to go but their trials were not yet over. They had a small river, a railway and a road to cross. And a disgustingly wet, soggy, treacherous marsh reminiscent of the Dartmoor bog in *The Hound of the Baskervilles.* Visibility was poor. There was a light mist and no moon. In their first struggles to cross the marsh both Henry and Albert fell one after another into a morass. They came out soaked to their middle and stinking. It was obvious that there was a good chance that they could spend the rest of the night trying to negotiate the marsh and end up in daylight still trapped in it. They decided to withdraw to the higher ground and try to find a way round it. Accordingly, when they reached firm ground once more, they followed the contour as best they could, checking their direction by compass and were glad to find before long that it had changed from north to north-west. Even better, they came across a track running due west. Their luck was in. They soon left the marsh behind, forged westwards ... until, having left the marsh at least three or four miles behind them they realised that unless their calculations and navigation had gone disastrously wrong, they were now in Holland.

Walking on they came to grass, fields and small country houses. They passed a gate with a notice on it. Henry told the others that it was written in Dutch. Their hearts must have leapt with joy and a certain grim satisfaction. A canal further on running east and west confirmed from their memorised maps that they were indeed in Holland. They walked under a road bridge and as they left it behind a crowd of cyclists went over it.

Finally, by the time day was breaking, they had to settle for a lying-up place in a thick hedgerow. Even although they were in Holland, they could not knock at the first door they came to. Behind it might be Nazi or quisling. In a way, their new situation was less certain than before. In Germany they could assume that the vast majority of people would attempt to turn them in. Here, although it seemed reasonable to suppose that almost everybody might want to help escaped British officers, they found it difficult to ask anyone to risk their lives and perhaps the lives of their families at the hands of the Nazis if their helpers were caught aiding POWs to escape. And so, although by now they were getting to the limits of their food, preparations and indeed fitness, they adopted what to many might have seemed a foolish course of action. They would continue their journey and see what turned up.

376

In the hedgerow they tried to sleep. The weather had broken and they huddled together, wet and cold and miserable. That afternoon a small boy leading a pony came along, smiled at them and bade them good day. They felt sure that he at least guessed that they were ex-prisoners. They stayed where they were. As darkness fell, they were loading their kitbags when they saw two men approaching. The trio of officers reasoned that if they were not there to help them and were going to turn them in, they would not have waited for darkness to fall. One man stayed with them while the other went away. After a while they heard a whistle. Their companion gestured to them to follow him and they rejoined the first man at a farm. He led them into the stable, up a ladder into a hayloft. A little later their new friends brought them bread and butter and warm milk and by gestures told them to remain there quietly for the night. Long afterwards, Albert Arkwright tried to give his account of their feelings and admitted that they were impossible to describe.

> In a few short hours we had been transferred as if by magic from a world of enemies to a world of friends, and though we knew that our troubles were by no means over, our whole prospect and outlook on life had changed... We were no longer three individuals groping our way amongst a host of hostile people; rather, we were like three pawns in a game in which eager hands were suddenly stretching out all round the board to push us on to our ultimate goal. We had become complete passengers and no longer had the ability to move under our own steam; from now onwards we had to rely implicitly on the moves they made; if they played badly we should be taken by their opponents; if they were skilful we should reach the other end of the board... These were the thoughts that came to us as we lay buried deep in the dry straw; and gradually warmth and comfort stole into our tired bodies and we slept like logs.

They were now in the hands of the underground movement, composed of people who combined their attempts to live normal lives under enemy occupation with courageous efforts to help escaped prisoners journey home. The dangers in such selfless efforts were manifest – coming to the attention of the occupiers or a collaborator; prisoners in transit by train or car or bus giving themselves away by ignorance of language or custom though the underground had furnished them with money, tickets, fake papers, passports and civilian clothes; or falling victim to a plan of entrapment, if the authorities suspected a family of aiding escapees. Those uncovered and arrested could expect brutal interrogations and severe punishments not only for themselves but for their families. Yet there were many hundreds in the network who helped escapees, well aware of the colossal risks they ran – farmers, doctors, vets, engineers, shopkeepers, labourers, ex-soldiers... In addition there were the women, no less competent and courageous, playing their parts. If there had not been a war, in all probability many of the members of the network might never have suspected that they possessed such deep stores of courage.

In the houses the trio stayed in, they almost felt as if they were long-lost friends of the family. The hospitality in food and drink was quite overwhelming though, knowing how strict rationing was, the trio often felt guilty at the inroads they must be making into their hosts' provisions. Their hosts, particularly the women, were curious about their backgrounds in civvy street. In houses that possessed a piano, Henry was sometimes asked to play. As Albert put it:

> Henry was the most versatile pianist I have ever met. His favourite composer was Beethoven, and although he had never had what might be described as a musical education his playing of Beethoven's sonatas was, to me at any rate, a joy to hear. But Henry did not stop short at the Classics, and he was not too proud or highbrow to find enjoyment and relaxation in modern dance music. I think he played this entirely by ear for he seemed able to play any tune that he had ever heard.

In one of the houses they stayed in, the hostess, having served them breakfast, produced a remarkably dirty pack of cards and proceeded to tell their fortunes. It was quite a performance. Madame's English, though with an American accent, was fast and fluent. As she revealed what the cards told her not only about their future but about their past, hilarity grew. They had all been born under a lucky star – that, they could believe – and just around the corner there was a huge fortune waiting for each of them. She could not say exactly when they would see their own country again – here there was much hesitation, shakings of head and a performance of occult calculations – but it should be within three weeks. She then told them about their past, about their numerous love affairs, how they were incurable lady-killers and for years had been unable to make up their minds which of their unfortunate victims to select for a wife. Being the only bachelor in the trio, Henry came in then for much ribbing on this account.

Their progress southwards continued. By car and train and even by bicycle, often accompanied by one of the network to smooth out their way, they crossed into Belgium, staying in Liège and Brussels for a few days. All three felt utterly inadequate in their heartfelt thanks when it came time to leave each band of helpers. 'Come back and see us after the war' was a frequent response.

In Brussels the extraordinary efficiency of the organisation was again displayed. They were still wearing the suits given to them in the Dutch barn, by now so shabby that their owners could never have been taken to be more than artisans. After lunch their hair was cut and they shaved. A bell rang and an old gentleman and a girl who spoke perfect English appeared. Laden with suitcases and handbags, they set these down, opened them and, like travelling salesmen, spread out every article of men's attire. After half an hour, the British officers were not only completely and stylishly dressed but were given a small attaché case containing razors, soap and towels. They handed over their identity cards to the girl and she left. When she came back some time later, she returned the identity cards together with a permit, with the official stamp of the Nazi occupying authority in Brussels, signed by a German officer, authorising the trio to travel into France on business of a private nature. The next day, they were taken down to the main railway station. Three men met them who were to act as their guides on the journey. They split into three pairs, each made up of an officer and one of the guides. In the train each pair sat in a different compartment of the same carriage. Everything went well until a Nazi officer came down the corridor, questioning people in French and examining their papers. Rupert, whose French was minimal to the point of invisibility, did not satisfy him. He told Rupert that at the frontier he would have to wait. At the little frontier town of Baisieux the train stopped on Belgian soil, everyone got off and the train moved onto French soil. The Nazi led Rupert away out of his fellow officers' sight and they felt leadenly that that was the last they would see of him. Their guides were also in a state of extreme anxiety.

After passing through customs the passengers embarked once more on the train. Just as the train was about to pull out of the station, the carriage door opened and Fuller swung himself into it. He turned, leaned out of the window and waved to someone. Later, he said that he had been in a state of complete despair when he was taken into the Nazis' office. Indeed it was a state of almost total nervous collapse, for the shock of capture after coming so far on his journey from the Oflag was far more shattering than it would have been if he had been recaptured soon after the escape. And that feeling gave him the idea. He began to pretend to be a man of low intelligence, even of mental instability, wandering about the room before the Nazi officers, muttering to himself, even mumbling the name and address that was given on his identity card. One of the men tapped his head, the other shrugged and went so far as to offer Rupert a cigarette. At that, Rupert played his last card. He tapped the Nazi emblem that the official was wearing round his neck and mumbled, 'Qu'est ce que c'est que ca?' That did it. The poor fool's papers were in order so they walked him to the carriage and even assisted him to board.

The rest of the journey to Lille was uneventful. There they caught a train for Paris where they arrived about seven-thirty in the evening. An elderly man and a young woman were waiting for them. The three guides had met them many times before and accompanied them in the Metro to the safe house. The guides would have a meal with them then catch the night train back to Brussels where, Albert mused, they would wait for their next 'cargo'. And so it would go on, until the end of the war came, or they would get caught and be executed.

In the safe house they encountered the usual warm welcome. There were of course papers and other preparations to be made for the next stage of their journey. The also met the elderly man's daughter. Both were Belgians. The young woman, Mlle Andrée de Jongh, was a most remarkable woman. Though quiet and unobtrusive, she was highly intelligent and played a leading part in the organisation's planning and activities in the field. In her clandestine career she was responsible for the safe passage across Belgium and France of scores of prisoners of war of many nationalities.

The trio were now Frenchmen and the following day new identity cards, complete with photographs, were presented to them together with small dark-blue berets to wear. They also found that evening that they were to have as company on the next stage of their travels three others, Andrée and two men they met at the station. One, François, was another member of the organisation. It is possible that one reason for his presence was to make the number of travellers up to six, the number of people required to fill a first-class compartment, so that no strangers would share it with them.

The second man was a young Russian who had escaped from a German POW camp. He spoke no language other than Russian and the trio immediately named him Stalin. The mention of this name at least attracted his attention. 'Stalin' had been an air-gunner and had been shot down in a raid somewhere over Eastern Germany. He had ended up in a POW camp near Berlin. In this camp conditions were so appalling that the inmates were dying like flies of starvation or disease. He knew that if he was there for even a few weeks he would be dead, or so feeble or sick that he would be unable to make any attempt to escape. In fact he succeeded in getting out within three days of his arrival there. By train-hopping he had managed to reach the French frontier where he had been picked up by the organisation. Since they couldn't return him to Russia they had decided that he should go to England.

The British officers' excitement surged to new heights as the south-bound express swept them onwards through France. They had plenty of food and drink They were able to sleep fitfully through part of the night. When daylight came they were still a few miles short of Bordeaux. Their journey continued through the pleasant villages and towns of southern France until the train arrived at St-Jean-de-Luz, close to the sea and the Spanish frontier. At this stop they were met by a little French lady and a swarthy, well-built man. The man was Basque, by name Henri; the woman was addressed by Andrée as '*Ma tante*'. They were fed well at lunch on stewed rabbit and then ordered off to bed since it was clear they had not slept much during their train journey the previous night. When they came downstairs Henry, who had shared a bed with Stalin, confided to the others that the Russian's idea of real comfort was to wind most of the bedclothes around his body until he was almost submerged. They were given canvas shoes with soles made of coarse, woven grass for the following night's journey into Spain over the mountains. Even on smooth rock and patches of ice or snow such shoes gave remarkable footing.

The following morning a new member of the organisation arrived, an Englishman who had been trapped when the Germans overran Belgium and France. He had now taken on the job of guiding escapers who arrived at St Jean de Luz over the mountains into Spain. The trio were advised to eat well and get as much rest as possible for their journey by foot would be about twenty miles and involve several steep climbs. Henry and his companions were a little anxious at the thought of this climb over the mountains in darkness. Apart from that, the frontier was apparently patrolled on the French side by Germans and on the Spanish by Spanish customs officials.

When they set out that evening their first stop was at a farm. After supper, when it was dark, they began the major part of their journey. As a guide, they had a disreputable Basque peasant, Jean, who made a living doing 'this and that'. He stowed all their belongings, not too many by this time, into his capacious rucksack and led the way. Strung out behind him came Andrée, François, Stalin, Rupert, Henry and Albert. Soon they were beginning their climb. There was a full moon to light their way. Near the summit they stopped for a breather and a last look at France. Soon they were descending the other side to a river they had to ford. As they descended, often slipping and dislodging stones in spite of their canvas shoes, the landscape – and themselves – brightly illuminated by the moonlight seemed a situation guaranteed to pick them out by even the most short-sighted patrol. Nevertheless luck, and an experienced smuggler, was on their side and they forded the river which at that point was thigh-deep.

They scrambled up a railway embankment, followed by a steep rise up to a road. They went on, climbing steadily again. After a time they could see due west the twinkling lights of the town of Hendaye. It was hardly believable to the trio that a town could display itself to the sky, that people could be walking about the streets, confident that no bombs would fall. They remembered then that the Spanish had had their ghastly war and it was over, with Franco now in charge. By four a.m. they had crossed the ridge of hills and were looking down a wide valley that ran all the way to the sea with the coastal town of San Sebastian at its foot. Jean led them downwards now and made for a little village. Once in the village, they were guided to a small house where they waited in the darkness, crouching in the garden while Jean roused the inmates and let them know they had arrived.

While breakfast was cooking, Andrée took the fugitives upstairs to wash and change. They had been wearing blue trousers and shirts, which were now positively disreputable. After cleaning themselves, the British officers changed into the smart Brussels suitings and shirts they had previously worn. Once downstairs again, as dawn broke, a small Morris four-seater car arrived. The four men were bundled into the car and the driver, a jovial spiv-like man by name Federico, drove them into San Sebastian. That day and night was spent at his house. Andrée and François were staying elsewhere but visited them for meals. On the following day they were also visited by the British Consul from Bilbao, a reassuring and sober Scotsman. He told them that in a day or two a car would arrive to take them back to Madrid.

It is understandable that the trio were by now practically jumping up and down with impatience at any delay or inactivity. But they had spent two months on their journey to freedom and now that they were safe in a neutral country, the thought of even a day without onward travel, in spite of their hosts' splendid hospitality, ground down upon them. Eventually, taking precautions not to be seen leaving Federico's house, they were led to a place where he was waiting with his car. He drove them out into the open countryside, past a car apparently suffering from engine trouble. Federico explained to them that the vehicle belonged to a German firm and that the driver was strangely interested in small parties of tourists seen leaving the town. They had scarcely turned the next corner and were out of sight of the German car when they came across a second stationary car, whose driver also seemed to be in trouble. It was the Embassy car. Quickly they transferred themselves to it. As they settled back, they had the most glorious feeling of joy to be safely in a car flying the Union flag. For they were now technically in British territory. From being for so long fugitives, outcasts and imposters, they – apart from Stalin of course! – were now out-and-out Britishers.

The car was a powerful Sunbeam Talbot and for part of the way they travelled at a speed between seventy and eighty miles per hour. Mr Marshal produced a wide variety of food and a skinful of wine which they did justice to.

They arrived in Madrid about five o'clock at Marshal's house. One reason why he took them there was because his wife was Russian and he wanted her to have a talk with Stalin. After a meal she and Stalin talked at length. She was of the old pre-revolution aristocracy; Stalin was of the nation reborn. Although of such different origins, they got on excellently together. Stalin was warmly grateful, after all his vicissitudes, for the opportunity of speaking his own language with someone of his own country. Marshal asked Arkwright to stay the night but took the other three down to the Embassy. Arkwright therefore had the almost bemusing experience of a truly leisurely English dinner, with sherry to begin with, port and coffee to end it and interesting and informative conversation throughout.

The following morning he was reunited with his comrades at the Embassy, finding that there were about twenty others sheltering there, of various nationalities – Frenchmen, Canadians, Poles – all with the ambition to get to Great Britain. It was an ongoing operation and the Embassy staff had reduced it to a fine art. They had diversions such as reading, catching up with the news and playing cards. Henry became involved in a poker school with some of their companions, which occupied him for several hours every day. But at length the day of departure arrived and the trio, with six of their companions, a member of the Embassy staff and a member of the Spanish police, left Madrid by train that evening. The journey took them all that night and it was not until ten the following morning that they reached La Linea, the last stop before Gibraltar. They found that they were still so conditioned by their previous hazardous long travel through Germany and occupied Europe that during the journey, even although rationally they knew they were definitely in a neutral country, there still occasionally surfaced in their minds feelings of foreboding, feelings that did not die until, after a short rickety bus ride and formalities at two police stations – one Spanish, one British – they were inside the final barrier and within the towering fortress that was Gibraltar.

The officers stayed in Gibraltar for only three or four days. Assigned batmen, given enough money by the Army Pay Department to kit themselves out as British officers, they bought battledress, shirts, shoes and the like. They then realised as they walked about the streets of Gibraltar town that, at that time in the war, Gibraltar shops were still exceedingly well stocked. What a joke it would be to arrive back home from a German POW camp laden with all kinds of luxury articles absolutely unobtainable since the start of the war. Common sense prevailed and they finally contented themselves with luxuries that were sure to be appreciated at home and were small in weight and bulk.

Their plane made one overnight stop in Lisbon before journeying on to England. As the hours passed, the drone of the plane's engines and the comfort of their seats must have brought to all of them a state almost of unreality in which episodes of their nine weeks' experiences surfaced, not in any particular order – the weeks of planning and preparation for the escape from the Oflag, the hopes and fears and recovery, the night of the escape, their dogged, grim trudge by night through Germany to the Dutch frontier, the fantastic organisation of the underground, the onward progress by foot, by bicycle, by train and by car, the unforgettable faces of their helpers. Now the plane was descending. A member of the crew came into the cabin and began putting little blackout shutters over the windows. 'For reasons of security,' he said with a smile. They settled back in their seats and before long, they felt a bump as the plane touched down. Their journey was over.

Even muffled up it was bitterly cold in the aircraft. Outside, the night reigned, an impenetrable black void. The steady drone of the engines was of little reassurance.

Hope my shivering is not put down to fear. But I'm not the only one. Anyway, we're all afraid. You'd be an idiot not to be. I'm sure even the pilot is tense, even if he's done this trip many times. Probably has engraved on his mind the pitcher going to the well once too often. The hymn-writer didn't know how truly he wrote: 'When danger calls or battle, be never *wanting* there!' One time when the modern meaning is more appropriate than the older! So many uncertainties. Not to know if we'll be shot down, or if the parachute will open or if I'll hit the right place or drop 'in another part of the forest' – after all it is the Ardennes! – or if the Maquis will meet me or if a reception committee from the Germans will be there with their nasty little ways. Glad I never had much aptitude for statistics and could calculate the probability of it all going wrong. Somehow not even a double first at Cambridge in Moral Sciences nor a training in philosophy seems the best preparation for this caper.

What a change from the debacle in France in 1940! When we were in Gib we didn't know then that within a few days two major turning points in the war were going to occur – the Battle of El-Alamein and the Allied invasion of North Africa. Churchill put it well – El-Alamein was the end of the beginning, he said, and he allowed the church bells to be rung for the first time since 1940 to celebrate. That in itself was a major indication of the distance Britain has come from the 1940 debacle when the sound of church bells would have been a signal that the invasion of Britain had begun. Now with the Second Front in full swing and Uncle Joe pushing ever closer to the Reich, we do know that we will win eventually. But what will we win? What does winning mean in a modern war? Europe will end up a total disaster area. If the first casualty of war is truth, the second is morality and the third is civilisation. He thought again of the deliberate descent of Germany under the Nazis into organised barbarism. Sometimes, he thought, you learn things in Intelligence you'd perhaps be better off not knowing.

It was obvious to him that he was recalling these memories to take his mind off what lay ahead. At least, he thought, his formidable mother had no idea where he was at that moment. As far as she knew, he was safe in England, on essential and important war work. Mrs Winifred Coombe-Tennant of Cadoxton Lodge, Wales, was no doubt still giving her ungrateful servants hell and complaining about the dreadful vicissitudes in her life caused by wartime conditions.

He smiled. I wonder if I shall ever see her again, or Alexander, or the Balfours? In surprisingly sharp, clear images, he recalled his visit with his mother in September 1930 to Whittingehame. How welcome they made me – Gerald, Ral, Jean. Yet it was strange. But for some reason, Mother was not satisfied. At that time he had not got to the age when he could question her. Though even now she could clam up and simply refuse to discuss a topic if she had no intention of being drawn on it. And make you feel guilty that you had even thought of questioning her. She would have done well in Intelligence, he thought. She really operated on a 'need to know' basis. What was it that she was hiding? He remembered that he had once been visited at Eton by a friend of his mother, Dame Edith Lyttelton. She had hinted that there was something to do with his mother – and himself – that very few people knew about. But he had made nothing of it at the time and now, well, he had other things to think about. He must ask Alexander about it when – if – he got back.

Almost as if the pilot had been waiting for him to get to this point in his thoughts he heard him announce: 'Five minutes to the drop zone.' Somehow the drone of the engines seemed louder. From then on the final check and a final rehearsal of mission data dominated his thoughts.

Even if the drop went well, even if most of his fears were unfounded, even if the parachutist was met by a resistance group, there was no guarantee that his troubles would be over. Henry's mission was to help the Maquis in every way he could, attempting to coordinate their sabotage and military efforts with those of the Allied forces pushing through France after the D-Day initial invasion, organising drops of material to them. There were, of course, Maquis groups and Maquis groups. Some, whose true allegiance was communist, their eyes turned northwards to Russia, had no intention of fighting and dying to kick the Nazi forces out of France if the result was merely to reintroduce a government composed of politicians of a calibre similar to the pre-war, self-serving, corrupt, cowardly incompetents who had contributed to the fall of France. They wanted a communist government in place of the Vichy 'government' led by Pétain and Laval which had cooperated so faithfully with the occupying power. Such Maquis groups were not by any means singing from the same hymn sheet as the Allies. They would cooperate – certainly they wanted the hated Germans out of France – but would keep an eye on the future that would result from their actions. If, during the course of their operations, they could help on that future by knobbling some of their fellow Frenchmen who might be awkward opponents after the victory, they would do so.

The history of the Resistance and its British Special Operations Executive helpers in Western Europe during 1943 and the first half of 1944 was an astounding mixture of heroism, betrayal, and unbelievable negligence at home of fail-safe provisions, such as agreed tell-tales to provide proof of capture, to be used in wireless signals sent under extreme duress, which had resulted in a high proportion of agents being killed, or taken and interrogated by the Gestapo and its collaborators before they were transported to a

387

concentration camp to die. Even today, it is not generally understood how some fifty agents, dropped in succession into Holland, were met and captured by the German anti-espionage service on arrival, in what the Germans called the *England-Spiel* (the 'England-Game').

The majority of the resistance groups, however, were not looking to the postwar future. Their sole, pure, burning aim was to defeat the Nazi occupation and achieve the freedom of France. The German decision to conscript French workers and ship them to the Reich led to many of them taking to the hills where they joined guerrilla groups. The Maquis (underbrush) took their name from the scrubland (*maquis*) they hid in. By June 6th, 1944, quite large areas of the countryside were held by Maquis forces up to 2,000-strong. Pitched battles against SS forces, though avoided, inevitably happened. On other occasions in the two months following D-Day, the Maquis and their advisers might also utilise persuasion. After July 30th, they were able to point out to the French officials they negotiated with that with the Nazi occupation fast disintegrating, only their cooperation would save their necks or diminish their sentences.

The Normandy landings on June 6th had envisaged a swift occupation of the Cherbourg peninsula on the west and Caen and the Orne estuary on the east. Thereafter, the main enemy reserves were to be drawn to the east to face a threat by the Allies to break out there. In fact, this would enable the western forces to break out, first driving southwards to the Loire, then swinging east and sweeping up to the Seine near Paris.

The Americans took Cherbourg on June 27th. The British and Canadians had captured all of Caen by July 8th. On July 25th, the Americans broke out west of St-Lô and began the southward part of their sweep. On July 30th British armour and infantry launched a major attack to the left of the Americans. It was not until August 8th, however, that this period of fierce advance, counterattack and further advance was completed and the great surge forward of the Allied forces could begin. On August 30th, after a seventy-mile drive that day, the Guards Armoured Division reached the Seine, which they crossed near Vernon that evening. British and Canadian forces had won crossings on August 24th and 25th; the Americans reached the Seine south of Paris on August 19th; the capital itself had been liberated by August 26th, mainly by Maquis and a French Armoured Division.

It was time for the next phase: the clearing of northern France with its V-bomb sites from which, all during the Normandy battle, the Germans had launched a constant stream of these indiscriminate killers. During that time 5,500 people in southern England had been killed and over 16,000 seriously injured.

The Second British Army crossed the Seine on August 30th. On August 31st the Guards Armoured Division advanced over eighty miles, the following day reaching Arras. By September 2nd they were in Douai. On the fourth day of their record-breaking pace, overcoming all opposition, they liberated Brussels as night was falling. An entry in Lieutenant Colonel J.C. Windsor Lewis's personal diary for this date reads: 'The last time I had been in Brussels was in July, 1940, as a fugitive escaping from the Germans. On that occasion I had entered the city from the east in a tram. Today I entered it from the west in a tank.'

Other Allied forces had also been making remarkable advances. To the right of the Welsh Guards on the Seine, two American armies were forging ahead while a third, landed on the Mediterranean coast near Marseille, had already driven 200 miles northwards up the Rhone valley.

The armies of the USSR had also made spectacular advances throughout this period, pushing the fiercely resisting enemy back to the west. But when they arrived on the east bank of the Vistula they halted under orders from Stalin. Stalin now typically produced an atrocity of monstrous proportions. Rising against their ruthless oppressors in Warsaw, the Polish Home Army, outnumbered, short on food, arms and munitions, fought heroically for over two months, finally succumbing to the overwhelming German forces on October 2nd. They had lost 200,000 men in the struggle, most of Warsaw was destroyed and the remaining 500,000 people deported. While the rising was taking place, the Russians were so near that they could watch events through their binoculars. During the conflict, Flight Lieutenant John Ward, a wireless operator in the RAF, who had escaped from a POW camp in Poland and had managed to reach Warsaw, sent more than one hundred messages to London. In them he gave details of what was taking place, the overwhelming need for food and munitions, the need for Churchill and Roosevelt to get Stalin to intervene in the conflict. Stalin refused. He had plans to make Poland part of the Soviet's sphere of influence. He refused to order airdrops of munitions to be made from an airbase no more than five minutes' flying time from Warsaw.

Ward's messages to the West became increasingly desperate. 'About 40 per cent of the city centre is already completely destroyed. The German forces make no difference between civilians and troops of the Home Army.' In another report he told how 500 Polish women and children were used as human shields in front of a German panzer column. Abandoning hope of Soviet airdrops he urged that food and arms be dropped from newly captured areas in Italy. Very few flights of this nature were attempted and RAF pilots on one run from the Italian port of Brindisi to Warsaw were fired upon by the Soviets. High-level telegram exchanges from this time reveal that Stalin refused to let the Allies use his airfields. Starving, wounded and out of ammunition, Ward used one of his last dispatches to warn that the Nazis were planning to destroy the Auschwitz extermination camp to wipe out evidence of the mass murders carried out there.

Against all the odds, John Ward survived the defeat of the Home Army and died as recently as 1995.

With the final clearing of German forces from France, Henry's activities with his Maquis were at an end. He therefore found out where the 1st Battalion of the Welsh Guards was stationed and got permission to report to it for duty. At that time the battalion was stationed in 'The Island', the name they gave to the land between the Waal and the Lower Rhine. It was typical Low Country land, absolutely flat and criss-crossed by innumerable ditches making it unusable for tanks. When Henry reached the battalion he was given command of Prince of Wales Company.

They were in the 'Island' until October 6th. A month later the 1st Battalion was stationed at Veulen, about forty miles south of Arnhem. On the surface their role was largely static but it involved endless patrols by day and night in the no man's land between them and the enemy. It was a time of strain and discomfort and the weather was noticeably deteriorating. It was also a time of booby traps, mining and sniping. On November 7th, Henry was slightly wounded but, after spending a night in hospital, he returned to duty.

Six months remained of the war in Europe. On May 7th, at 2.40 a.m., the representatives of Admiral Dönitz finally agreed to unconditional surrender to the Allies on all fronts. The final act of surrender of the remaining forces of the hell of death, retribution, starvation and destruction Germany had now become was signed in Berlin on the night of May 9th.

By then Henry and his company, after sustained and savage fighting in their advance through Germany against a ferocious last-ditch defence, were in its north-west region near the ruins of Hamburg.

Japan's surrender later that same year after the destruction of Hiroshima and Nagasaki cut short his preliminary training for a part in the invasion of that country. Quite soon after that, Major A.H.S. Coombe-Tennant, MC (mentioned in despatches), Croix de Guerre (France) was assigned with his company to new duties that included postings to the Middle East. Though officially in the Welsh Guards, he was still in Intelligence. Nevertheless he had time then to try to reassess his attitudes to life and to try to understand better his relationship with his mother and the Balfours. He would be faced with fresh and astonishing information just a few years down the line of his life.

18

Saving the Scripts – Seeking the Successors

Watch thee, stand fast in the faith, quit you like men, be strong.

1 Corinthians 16.13

Carved over the entrance to Selwyn College, Cambridge is the Greek original of the middle part of the above text: 'stand fast in the faith, quit you like men'. It was seen by Frederic Myers whenever he passed by the entrance on the occasions when he left his own house to visit the Verralls or the Sidgwicks. There is a small mistake in the Greek text, as carved, which offended Myers' scholarly sense.

The verse is singularly appropriate to the ethos of the Sidgwick Group in the years following Mrs Verrall's death in 1916. They faced a problem that nagged at them with increasing persistence, one that has faced many small groups who believe that they hold a secret of great value, one they are pledged to protect. All the members of the Sidgwick Group were middle-aged or elderly. In a real sense, they were Victorians. They had been born in Victoria's reign and they remained Victorians. Eleanor Sidgwick had been born in 1845, her brothers Arthur and Gerald in 1848 and 1853. Sir Oliver Lodge was born in 1851, J.G. Piddington in 1869, and Mrs Coombe-Tennant in 1874. As the years went on, successive deaths among them diminished their number, raising ever more urgently a problem that had to be solved. How could they enlist reliable successors who would have the necessary learning to continue their work of interpretation and be able to protect the vast, ever larger number of scripts and privately printed volumes that had accrued from their years of work at the never-ending task

392

of teasing out the enigmatic meanings woven into the band of automatists' continuing production of scripts?

But there were other facets to the problem. Where should the written material eventually be stored? This was not an immediate problem throughout the First World War or during the following fifteen years where everything could be stored at Fishers Hill, but the rise of the dictators and the threat of a second war with the possibility of air raids of devastating power began to exercise their minds – the destruction of Guernica in the Spanish Civil War seemed to many people the shape of things to come. There was also the conflict between their perceived need for secrecy – this was an ever-present driving force in Winifred Coombe-Tennant's mind – and the need to search for younger, suitable people to enlist. Several possibilities were identified but turned down for various reasons. Were they not *too* young? Could they keep their mouths shut? There surfaces in one's mind the thought of Mrs Thatcher, when a certain person was proposed for Cabinet membership, leaning forward and asking searchingly, 'But is he one of *us*?'

After her marriage in 1925, Jean Balfour, Gerald Balfour's daughter-in-law, *was* accepted as a trustworthy person ultimately becoming the archivist of the Sidgwick Group. Every member of the group came to depend upon her absolutely.

On August 4th, 1935, Piddington prepared a report concerning the material brought to Fishers Hill on November 29th, 1933, by Oliver Lodge at Piddington's request and subsequently examined in detail by Mrs Winifred Coombe-Tennant and Mr Piddington between July 24th and July 29th, 1935. The material, contained in fifteen cases and two packets, comprised correspondence between Lodge and Mrs Coombe-Tennant; several originals of Willett scripts (some unprinted); originals of Lodge's records of Willett 'Daylight Impressions' (D.I.s); original records and/or copies of records of some sittings with Mrs Piper, Mrs Leonard and Miss Bacon; letters to Lodge from Mrs Verrall, Miss Alice Johnson, Gerald W. Balfour and others, and copies of his replies; many typed Willett scripts that had been printed or D.I.s that had been printed; and numerous notes on Willett scripts chiefly by Lodge, Mrs Verrall, G.W. Balfour and Miss Johnson.

During the examination of the Lodge material, Mrs Coombe-Tennant either showed Piddington or read to him all her letters to Lodge and all of his to her. A great many of the letters were of no importance and it was agreed to destroy them. Sometimes they could not come to an agreement over a letter's importance, and letters like these were kept. Mrs Coombe-Tennant also kept a few papers, letters, or newspaper cuttings, which were merely of personal interest to her, after showing them to Piddington.

Piddington claimed that she did not examine anything that was not in her own handwriting or that was not addressed to her, except such things as records of her sittings with Mrs Piper, Mrs Leonard, Miss Bacon, and the typed records of her scripts and D.I.s in 1918, the greater part of which had not been printed at that date. Piddington later remarked that she had already been supplied with typed copies of these 1918 scripts and D.I.s, except that a page or so of the copies had been withheld from her. But, he said, she glanced at them so quickly that he was sure that she did not notice that they contained pages hitherto withheld from her, and in any case he did not think that it mattered. In his report, Piddington gives a detailed list showing at what dates the contents of all the cases, boxes and packets were examined by Winifred and him. He also describes the nature of the letters – mostly letters fixing dates for Winifred's sittings with Mrs Leonard – and documents – mainly extra copies – that he subsequently destroyed.

In the complete list of volumes of scripts by the automatists (see Appendix 1) it appears that volume 6 of the Willett scripts containing scripts 419–30 were written between October 1929 and March 1936. Willett 420 was the famous Palm Sunday script of October 18th, 1929. It is evident that Winifred's mediumship was effectively finished when she saw the Oliver Lodge material in 1935 considering that in the six and a half years after October 18, 1929, she wrote a mere ten scripts, a meagre output highlighted by the two hundred scripts she produced in the six year period from May 1910 to July 1917. One might say that for whatever reason, Mrs Willett no longer surfaced or did so on rare occasions with extreme difficulty. Mrs Winifred Coombe-Tennant, the lady involved in public affairs, was firmly in charge. It was the administrator who helped Piddington look through the contents of the cases and packets, the person always anxious that nothing of a private nature referring to herself should fall into the wrong hands.

On March 23rd, 1936, Winifred wrote a memorandum of a discussion she had had with Edith Lyttelton regarding what should be done with the Willett material. She gave a copy to Gerald Balfour:

Dined last night with D.D. Lyttelton tete a tete. After dinner long conversation re Willett stuff recently seen by her at Fishers Hill.

She advocated complete collection of printed and mss documents (including original scripts) to be deposited in British Museum with provision that nothing be opened for 80 years, such papers to include her own scripts, H.V. and M.V. and others where procurable – and a statement to be drawn up by GWB or JGP to be placed among them giving my name and other information. From this, talk arose on the present holders of material outside Fishers Hill – Jean and the Salters. It became clear all should be withdrawn from both, neither being likely to make such an outstanding contribution to their study as would outweigh the disadvantages of copies being out and about. DD and I agreed complete secrecy was part of the plan, extending over certain lives – all of which would have terminated in 80 years.

When deposited with British Museum a sum of £1000, to be contributed by me anonymously, would be made over to the British Museum to accumulate on compound interest during the 80 years, the capital then becoming available to be spent on securing a person or persons expert in either psychical research or psychology to go over and deal with the whole of the papers, with power to publish at their or his discretion.

Set down in this bare way is the plan – but it came in a curious ... manner, DD contributing something and then I myself 'catching' as it were something from outside.

It is the first and only time I have felt a clear and compelling lead about the disposition of the accumulated papers and printed material and after sleeping on it I feel it even more strongly today.

GWB came to tea today and I told him briefly what the plan had formed itself into and how it had come about.

Delta's M. [Delta = Daphne, M = Mother; H.V. = Helen Verrall; M.V. = Margaret Verrall; GWB = Gerald Balfour; J.G.P. = Piddington]

                                              Fishers Hill,
                                                   Woking.
                                            March 25 / 36
My dear Pid,
The enclosed will interest you. As you will see it is in the
nature of a 'record', and must be carefully kept.
    I have provisionally suggested to D.M. that she should come
here for Tuesday and Wednesday, April 7 and 8, and we will
try to get D.D. here at the same time, for a confabulation.
    Glad you are coming back on Saturday.
                              Ever yours,
                         B. [Gerald Balfour]

                                               March 1936
In D.D.'s writing: Mrs Alfred Lyttelton = 'Mrs King'
Question whether a statement should be drawn up for the SPR
to make public in the event of pressing inquiries presenting
the fact that the papers are deposited with a competent authority
for a certain number of years. / Custody of the papers for a
certain number of years / Note by J.G.P. Mrs A.L. suggests
(a) biographical details of H.T.'s [Henry Tennant] youth to be
written by his mother (b) collection of photos of chief people
concerned (c) box of hair.
    J.G.P.

Destruction of unnecessary copies? including copies at
MacLehose's [Robert MacLehose and Company, the University
Press Glasgow, printers of the *Journal and Proceedings of the
Society for Psychical Research*]
    Should duplicate copies of the printed stuff be deposited in
another museum?
                         List of paper
    HMV original RM? originals
    MV originals
    Holland „
    Wilson „
    Macs „
    King „
    Willett „ stuff
    Fred's memoir True (ref. to published version)

                              396

Christopher T. (portrait of)
Cadoxton (photograph of)

There is obviously an increasing urgency in the air. Apart from the fact that the world was becoming an even more dangerous place, there had been a number of deaths in the years since the end of the First World War that had brought home to the Sidgwick Group that many of those who belonged to the old guard and were at least sympathetic to their way of mind and beliefs had gone. Sir William Crookes had died in 1919. Within two months, Lord Rayleigh followed him. In 1925 Sir William Barrett, one of the principal founding fathers of the SPR, died. In 1930 Arthur James Balfour passed away. But it might be argued that when his sister, Mrs Sidgwick, died on February 10th, 1936, the shock was strongest not only to the Balfours and Piddington but also to many in the SPR. It was somewhat akin to the death of Queen Victoria. It was undoubtedly the end of an era that had lasted from the beginnings of the SPR in 1882 to 1936, a period of over fifty years.

Although Mrs Sidgwick had never had any urge to push herself to the forefront of the psychical research scene, her contributions, the fruit of an exceptional intelligence and wide experience in every part of psychical research, had made her known and respected by its practitioners throughout the Western world. In addition, her influence on the education of women and her principalship of Newnham College, Cambridge had added to her formidable reputation.

Tributes to her and her work occupy no less than forty-four pages of the SPR *Proceedings*. Many of these were written by Alice Johnson who had known her well when she herself worked for the SPR. Shorter contributions were given by W.H. Salter and Theodore Besterman. It is worth giving Besterman's contribution:

I first met Mrs Sidgwick in the autumn or winter of the year 1926. She had already entered her ninth decade, and I looked at this great lady of whom I had read and heard so much across the chasm of nearly sixty years. It was a Committee Meeting at which somewhat uninteresting technical details were being discussed. Mrs Sidgwick said little, but she was very attentive and her gently, but accurately observant eyes studied the speaker. It was clear that she was considering not only

397

the merits of the case, but also the motives and intentions of the proposer. At the end of the meeting Mrs Sidgwick, having said less but thought more than anyone else, quietly put forward a motion which met the situation to everyone's satisfaction.

In the following years this experience was often repeated and this first impression was as often confirmed. Mrs Sidgwick put her faith more in reflection than in superfluous discussion, and character was at least as important to her as ability. This feeling was in a sense a projection of her own personality, for Mrs Sidgwick's greatness was in fact due to the union in her of brilliant ability and outstanding character. These things were so perfectly blended in her that one was often at a loss whether to admire more the accuracy or the justice of her judgment.

The accident of birth and the process of time added to Mrs Sidgwick's mental and moral qualities what was almost as valuable, an exceptional range and depth of experience. Thus it is not surprising that those who had the privilege of knowing her quality took Mrs Sidgwick as their touchstone. Certainly during the years in which I was an official of the society, I avoided many a hasty decision, many an unwise step, by testing it against what I knew of Mrs Sidgwick's opinions. And when I did act in a manner of which I knew she would not approve, that knowledge was the obstacle most difficult to overcome. This was true, I think, of every one who was capable of appreciating her singular <u>fineness</u>, a quality, in my experience, peculiar to her, and one which seemed unaffected by the passage of time.

History will no doubt record some, at least, of the perceptible influence exercised by Mrs Sidgwick on psychical research. Greater even than this was her personal influence on those practitioners of psychical research who have most usefully contributed to this nascent science. If part of the subject matter of psychical research ever attains to the dignity of general recognition, this result will be due to no one individual anywhere so much as to the calm enthusiasm, the steady persistence, the bold but sober judgement, and the intellectual quality and charm of Eleanor Mildred Sidgwick.

In her tribute to Mrs Sidgwick, Alice Johnson remarks that Mrs

Sidgwick's first scientific work with her brother-in-law Lord Rayleigh, in the years from 1879 to 1884, when he was Professor of Experimental Physics at Cambridge, helped him to establish definitely the units of electrical resistance, current and electromotive force. They published jointly three papers in the *Philosophical Transactions of the Royal Society*. The last important paper by her, contributed to the SPR *Proceedings* and written at the age of eighty-seven, was the 'History of the S.P.R.', compiled for the society's Jubilee in 1932. But as Alice Johnson puts it, '[that history] must have seemed to older members not unlike the tragedy of Hamlet with the Prince of Denmark left out, for there is hardly anything in it about her own share in the history, beyond the general statement that she was cognisant from the beginning of what was in the minds of the founders of the society and was herself in the inner circle of workers.'

Thereupon Miss Johnson, in her tribute, demonstrates the truth of the matter, namely that Mrs Sidgwick participated in every aspect of psychical research, making significant contributions to them all, publishing innumerable papers (she thought nothing of writing papers of length many hundreds of pages), serving on many committees, defending the subject, carrying out for many years the office work, refereeing and editing the papers of others, writing countless letters. She also wrote a comprehensive history of spiritualism for the ninth edition of the *Encyclopaedia Britannica*. Among the experimental subjects she participated in were the physical phenomena of spiritualism, the question of fraudulent mediums, telepathy, phantasms of the living, phantasms of the dead, an investigation of theosophy, premonitions, the Brighton experiments in thought-transference using people in the hypnotic state, clairvoyance, spirit photography, the Census of Hallucinations, the study of Eusapia Palladino, sittings with Mrs Piper – her paper 'Contribution to the Study of the Psychology of Mrs Piper's Trance Phenomena' runs to 676 pages! – the study of automatic scripts and the Cross-Correspondences, book tests, analysis of Professor Murray's experiments, and so on.

In 1932, when Sir Oliver Lodge was President, Mrs Sidgwick was elected by Council as President of Honour. It was then that she wrote the 'History of the S.P.R.'. Its concluding sentence states that, upon the evidence before her, she was 'a firm believer both in survival and in the reality of communication between the living and the dead'. To the end of her long life her continued openness to new conceptions was remarkable. 'If this is so, we may have to revise our ideas,' she used to say, and clearly, Alice Johnson believed, there was no opinion that she would not have revised, if the freshly alleged facts had satisfied her critical mind.

'Yet,' Miss Johnson wrote,

> it must not be supposed that the essence of her nature was pure intellect. She valued human beings far more than ideas, or even than the causes for which she would spend herself. Her own standard seemed beyond the reach of ordinary mortals, but she had an infinite tolerance and charity for other people's weaknesses, and a most generous appreciation of their capacities and achievements. Her life might perhaps be summed up in the words:
>
> > 'Mercy and truth are met together;
> > righteousness and peace have kissed each other.'

The world was certainly a different place in the years after Mrs Sidgwick's death. It was an increasingly menacing, brutal and treacherous place, with no room on the international stage for Miss Johnson's couplet. The dictators continued their aggressions – the re-occupation of the Saar, the Anschluss with Austria, the invasion and conquest of Ethiopia, the Spanish Civil War – while the League of Nations talked and talked – the old talking shop Mrs Coombe-Tennant had become disillusioned with so many years before – and the British and French politicians postured and promised, waving the toothless weapon of sanctions. They still avoided the truth that Germany, no longer with any vestige of democratic process, was now a powerful totalitarian weapon, wielded by a group of psychopaths with not a trace of civilised moral standards, driven by hatred, racism and a mish-mash of Nordic myths. The British and French governments still clung to the shreds of their belief that appeasement might yet satisfy the aggressors, that they could preserve the illusion spun to the electorate that they were dealing with rational statesmen, and might even persuade the Nazis to behave like statesmen. In the bleak desert that is the politician's out-of-office fate, Churchill unceasingly watched, waited and warned, seeing clearly and despairingly the inevitable consequences if the sell-out continued.

400

*   *   *

When war was declared on September 3rd, 1939, J.G. Piddington was seventy years of age. He had lived at Fishers Hill since 1919, collaborating with Gerald Balfour in the never-ending task of interpreting the Scripts and attempting to obtain a clear understanding of the precise meaning of 'the Plan'. Balfour himself was eighty-six years old: his health was deteriorating quite rapidly and his last major paper, 'A Study of the Psychological Aspects of Mrs Willett's Mediumship', had been published in 1935. His eyesight was giving him trouble and although he still took a keen interest in the Scripts, and still believed firmly that Henry was destined to be a great world leader of Messianic proportions, he was content now to leave much of the work of interpretation of the Scripts to Piddington, discussing with him his old friend's findings when asked to do so. Piddington, in his turn, though still dedicated to his task, felt rather overwhelmed by the continuing output of scripts from the automatists and in the early thirties asked them to cease their efforts. Thereafter, the flow largely dried up and Piddington was able to give more of his time to the preparation and annotation of the Scripts and commentaries for private printing.

The 'phoney war' was worrying enough to the people at Fishers Hill. After the shattering German offensive of May 1940 and the capitulation of France, raising the prospects of invasion or defeat, followed by the Battle of Britain and the aerial blitz by Goering's Luftwaffe on London that autumn, major changes took place at Fishers Hill. Piddington left for the last time, to spend his last years with his daughter Leo in Somerset. Gerald Balfour for a time lived at Fishers Hill Cottage, the large house now being full of soldiers for the duration. Later in the war, he left the cottage and travelled to Scotland to be with his son Ral and daughter-in-law Jean at Whittingehame.

The correspondence between Piddington and Gerald Balfour in those years shows quite clearly the devoted friendship between them, also their anxiety regarding the fate of the Scripts to which they had given their labours for so many years. There is also reference to the unprinted Willett trance-script of March 5th, 1912, which alludes to 'children of the spirit'. This may have been eventually decided by Mrs Coombe-Tennant to be left in the care of her lawyers, along with one year of her journal, and other

401

documents to be kept for a considerable number of years after her death. Many of the letters to Balfour and also to Jean Balfour over these years reveal Piddington's delightful self-deprecating sense of humour. All the letters are to be found in the Kremer Archive. In the present work several are given in their entirety, not only to provide data but also to illustrate the flavour of wartime letters written by an old, well-educated English gentleman. Excerpts are given of others where important decisions or data are given but without the chatty comments on the weather, the progress of the war or his ironic overtones as he comes to acknowledge his increasing age, growing infirmity and stoic acceptance that he could not hope to finish the work he began so many years before.

> Pardlestone, Holford, near Bridgewater, Somerset.
> 2 Jan., 1941

Dear G.W.B.

Your letter for the new year deeply touched me, – how deeply I think you could hardly realize. The more than twenty years that I lived at Fishers Hill were by far the happiest of my life. If I were a curate (which, thank heaven, I'm not), I should say that it was a 'great privilege' to have passed those years with you. I often and often wish I were back there again; but I'm glad after all that I didn't accept your offer of the cottage next door, for, if I had, Nellie would have gone to London, and you wouldn't have had her near you...

Like you I shall not regret the time we have spent over scripts because I remain intellectually convinced that they are in the main inspired by the group of people who claim to have inspired them, and who had a plan to bring about peace and goodwill among men. This plan may fail; but that won't shake my conviction that they had a plan.

Your words 'Our joint labour may prove vanity' indicate, I imagine, that you are feeling very much what I am feeling: namely, the seeming hopelessness of Henry, or any one else for that matter, bringing about the return of a Golden Age within, say, 30 years' time. Nevertheless I don't despair...

One point that struck me months ago and which I thought several times of mentioning to you, is that in neither Mrs Verrall's nor Mrs W.'s scripts – and both were strangely pro-

French – is there, I believe, a word about the part played by the French in the last war, whereas there is plenty, especially in M.V. scripts, about the part played by this country.

I do think Winston Churchill's broad-cast to the Italian people, followed as it has been by Roosevelt's New Year message to the King of Italy, very curious. Both seem to me useless, <u>unless</u> they know that there is a greater degree of dissatisfaction with the Fascist regime in Italy than is generally known...

I return Mrs T.'s letter of Dec. 24, 1940. I can't form any opinion about the Red Cross, because I don't know what difficulties they may have to encounter. They did very well in the last war, and I don't see why their organization should have deteriorated now. I suspect that the Germans put far more difficulties in their way now than they did in 1914–1918.

Leo thanks you for your message, and sends her love to you. I hope that the Clothworkers' Hall escaped, although it is obviously a military objective.

Yours ever
J.G.P.

Note by Jean Balfour:

Letter from J.G.P. to G.W.B. dated April 1942, about the destruction of Willett originals, upon G.W.B. leaving Fishers Hill to live in Scotland: and on an unprinted Willett trance-script (date March 5, 1912) which contains reference to Phyllis, Myers, and 'unborn children', & the question of its being kept or destroyed. This evidently being considered to be very important by G.W.B. & J.G.P., the matter was almost certainly referred to Mrs Willett herself to decide.

Pardlestone, Holford, near Bridgewater,
Somerset.
25 April, 1942.

Dear G.W.B.,
I am glad that Mrs T. didn't object to the destruction of the original scripts.

I didn't know – or at any rate I don't now remember, that you had any papers in your possession relating to Mrs T's sittings with Mrs Piper. My feeling is that these should be preserved.

I don't quite understand what you mean by 'we have to consider only the disposal of the printed volumes'. Do you mean your own set of the printed volumes, or other spare sets that are in your possession?

I've got several sets of the printed volumes, besides my own, here; and all these will eventually on my death go to my Executors, the Royal Exchange Assurance, to whom I have given instructions as to their disposal. I have instructed my executors to hand them over, as well as all other papers that I have relating to the Great Subject, to Salter, or Mrs Salter, or Jean. (I can't remember in what order I gave these three names.) I think that as many sets of the printed Volumes of Scripts and the Notes & Excursuses as are in existence should be preserved, because, if even the predictions in the scripts come off, it will be desirable that there should be as many of the printed volumes available for study by various people as possible.

There is one other document that I should like to see preserved, although I realize the difficulty of finding the proper depository. It is the Willett trance-script of March 5, 1912 (not printed) which contains the following passage:

> 'Do you understand that she [Mrs W.] has caught without realising some vital truth in regard to the connection of A— (Phyllis) ... but she does not perceive the connection between the PLAN & the unborn children of A which F and she bore spiritually.'

The importance of this extract from the Trance-Script seems to me to lie in the fact that this is the only passage in all the scripts that really throws any light on the constant references in scripts to Phyllis and Myers. With your leave I quoted the extract as given above (i.e. with the dots representing an omission) in one of the chapters forming part of the additional volumes of N.&E. that I still hope I may be able to get printed, and those I shall anyhow leave in MS to my executors.

The difficulty arises over the omitted words represented by dots. I don't see how you could entrust the <u>whole</u> passsage to Jean, or to any one else than Mrs T., leaving her to decide whether it should be preserved or not.

Sorry to write at such length.

The weather here for the past two days, and also to-day, is just like winter. Lots of sunshine, but a <u>most</u> bitter N.E. wind. I hope to goodness that you won't have such weather for your journey to Scotland, and, whatever weather you may have, I do hope that you won't be too frightfully tired by the journey.

I feel like a worm for having decided not to come to see you; but all the same I also feel that my decision was a right one.

If this requires an answer, don't think of answering it till you have got to Whittingehame, and have had a thorough rest. I should, however, be most grateful to Nellie if she would send me a line to let me know how you have stood the journey...

I shall go to the village to post this this afternoon, so you ought to get it on Monday.

Yours ever
J.G.P.

Pardlestone, Holford, near Bridgewater, Somerset.
Feb. 27, 1943, (but not posted till March 1.)

Dear G.W.B.,

For a week past, at least, I've been saying to myself every morning 'I must write to G.W.B.', and for lack of anything to say, my good resolutions have come to nothing. Or rather I did have one thing to say, and that was how much I miss you: for, though I should not have expected it to be so, I miss you more, and not less, as time goes on.

Although I still feel that I was a beast to urge you to write to Mrs L., I'm glad that you did write, for the effect of your letter is satisfactory. I'm specially glad to learn from Mrs L.'s letter that she has never spoken to Zoe Richmond about 'Excalibur', etc...

In her letter to you Mrs L. writes: 'I am almost sure I never told anything to Florence Upton about it [i.e. about the Antony

405

Carew references] – for one thing she died in 22 – & I had not then been shown any of the Scripts concerning the big story'. It is quite true that before Florence Upton's death she had not been shown any of the Scripts 'concerning the big story'; but <u>before</u> F.U.'s death she had been told by me about the Antony Carew references, and <u>shortly after</u> her death Mrs L. told me that she believed that she told F.U. as much as she could remember of what I had told her.

I am making a copy of the part of Mrs L.'s letter marked 'Private'; but if you tell me to destroy it I shall do so at once...

These scripts of the Richmonds rather weigh on my mind. I've typed <u>nearly</u> all of them (they number about 160), but have annotated only 80, and these annotations need no end of revision. I know that I shall never revise these annotations, or annotate the remaining 80 scripts. I haven't the necessary books here to do work of this kind, and anyhow I haven't the energy. What energy I have I must devote to getting the three new volumes of <u>N.&.E.</u> through the press. About 2/3 rds is now in slip proof, and the remaining 1/3 rd will, I suppose, be finished some time this summer. I don't mind the proof-correcting, but I look forward with horror to the task of inserting all the hundreds, and it may be thousands, of page-references; and this can't be done till the whole thing is paged proof.

Yours ever,
J.G.P.

[Long postscript omitted.]

Pardlestone, Holford, near Bridgewater, Somerset.
9 April, 1943

Dear Jean,

I was delighted to get a letter – and such a long one – from you, and to hear news of you and the family.

Not only had I heard of the 'most excellent elderly maid' at the Cottage, but I know her almost – not quite – filmstar-like name: Roberta Robertson.

Your account of G.W.B., <u>alias</u> Nunkie G., <u>alias</u> Father, is on the whole good; though it's sad about the eyes. Still at his age what else can one expect?

I am very glad that all the privately printed volumes etc., and the Casket [Marginal note: 'Containing M.L.'s hair'], are to be put into your keeping. You say 'I think there will be no difficulty at all about this'. I hope and think that there won't be; but executors are sometimes troublesome, and I wonder whether it might not be a good thing for G.W.B. to write a few lines to say that you are to have these volumes, etc. Don't suggest this to him if you think that it would bother him. (I don't mean add anything to his Will, but just a private note.)

I understand your being rather worried over the problem of deciding on someone of the next generation to whom to entrust the volumes, etc., and to tell the story. David would be an excellent choice because I'm sure that he can keep his mouth shut. (I have learnt from experience that people who can keep their mouths shut are rarities.) I can't judge about Gerald, but, as you say, he is as yet far too young. (If he is like he used to be, he would have one admirable qualification: that of rarely opening his mouth, except to say 'may be'.) You must arrange to live a long time, and then it will be easier for you to come to a decision.

I don't know whether the Salters have anyone in mind. I think it would be an admirable thing if you were to meet Helen Salter and talk things over with her; and you could then find out whether she and her husband have fixed on anyone to whom to leave the volumes, and various papers, etc. in their possession.

When the time for your holiday comes near, you might write to her, and suggest a meeting. Her address is

Mrs W.H. Salter,
The Crown House,
Newport, Essex.

I don't imagine that you would have any hesitation in writing to her, but if you have and if you would like me to do so, I could write to her and tell her that you want to meet her.

You ask whether I have finished editing Richmond Scripts. Alas! No. They number about 160, and I have typed notes to the first 80; but these notes will need a tremendous lot of revision, and I know that I haven't the energy left to do the revision, let alone annotating the remaining 80... I shall just have to leave the Richmond scripts in their present state and hope that someone in the future may deal with them.

Pardlestone, Holford, near Bridgewater, Somerset.

16 August, 1943

Dear G.W.B.,

I haven't used my typewriter for a year or more, and I'm using it now to see whether it is in decent enough order to work.

On Thursday July 22, I sent off to MacLehose the finally corrected page proofs of Vols. VII. and VIII. of <u>Notes &</u> <u>Excursuses</u>. I knew that they wouldn't receive the proofs before Monday July 26, because the firm was closed until that date for their annual summer holiday. I asked MacLehose to send me a line on a postcard, acknowledging receipt of the parcel, & so I didn't expect to hear from them till Wednesday July 28, or Thursday July 29. As a matter of fact I received their <u>written</u> acknowledgement on July 29. Meanwhile just before 6 p.m. on Monday July 26, I received a telegram from them saying that the proofs had arrived safely. You'll be wondering why I tell you these dull facts, but you'll soon see why I do. When I got the telegram on the evening of July 26, I said to myself 'I must write to Salter tomorrow to tell him that the last corrected page proofs of the new Vols. of <u>N</u>. &. <u>E</u>. are in the printer's hands'. My reason for informing Salter was that in early May <u>last</u> year I had asked him or Helen Salter whether in the event of my not being up to seeing the new Vols. through the press – and at that time I hadn't sent my MS. to the printers – one or other of them would complete the work which I might have to leave undone. They replied that, though they would give no definite promise, they would seriously think of doing what I asked. From early May 1942, until the present time I haven't written a single word to either of the Salters to tell them how the work was getting on. Now here comes the point. I received MacLehose's telegram in the evening of Monday 26. By the morning post of Tuesday July 27, I received a letter from Salter written on July 25; and in this letter to my great surprise he wrote 'I should rather like to have a talk with you about scripts, if I could get quarters for a day or two near your present abode'. He also said that he had been thinking lately that at some future date he might be called upon to make closer acquaintance with the whole body of scripts, and that he would like as soon as practicable to be told in what form, and in whose custody, the various volumes of Scripts and of <u>Notes</u> <u>and</u> <u>Excursuses</u>, and the various confidential papers, memoranda, etc. were preserved.

That Salter should have written to me just three days after I had sent the finally corrected page proofs to the printers strikes me as being what Mrs. Richmond calls 'plannish' ...

In my Will as long ago as 1933 – as I almost certainly must have told you at the time – I left all the printed Vols. of Scripts and all the copies of <u>N.</u> & <u>E.</u> in my possession, as well as all private letters, memoranda, notes, etc., to my executors, the Royal Exchange Assurance. I also gave my Executors instructions to hand over, if requested, all these books, papers, etc. in the first place to you, in the second to Jean, and in the third to Helen Salter. In July 1940, I altered these instructions, and told my Executors that the books, etc., were, at my death, to be handed over to Jean in the first place, to Helen Salter in the second, and in the third place to H.W. Salter. I shall almost certainly give fresh instructions, putting W.H. Salter first on the list; Helen Salter second; and Jean third. My reason for making this change is that it will probably be so much easier for Salter or Helen Salter to come down here to deal with the books, documents, etc., or to deal with the R.E.A. in London, than it would be for Jean.

I have been a good deal worried lately by the problem of how and where all this stuff is to be stored. It is practically certain that the Salters couldn't find room for it; and Jean, I should imagine, wouldn't want to store it either. It is not likely that anything concerning the Great Subject can be made public at the very earliest for thirty years; and by that time Salter, if alive, will be 90 years old, and Helen getting on for 90, and Jean will not be anxious to undertake a lot of hard work. I think we have got to allow for nothing being made public until fifty years hence. If by that time there is no sign of the predictions in the scripts being fulfilled, it will be best to destroy all the printed volumes, private memoranda, etc, etc.

I am thinking of adding a Codicil to my Will empowering

the Royal Exchange Assurance to pay for the cost of storing all this material out of my Estate. As my Will stands, the R.E.A. would not, I believe, be entitled to do so. Salter is going to see whether he can induce Trinity College, Cambridge, or some other College, or possibly, say, the British Museum, to accept the guardianship of the books, etc. But even if he were successful, it might well be that an annual charge would be made for the storage. Accordingly I shall probably add a clause to the new Codicil to my Will empowering such charge to be paid out of my Estate.

Like Jean, the Salters are much bothered over the question of appointing a successor to whom, on their death the Royal Exchange Assurance can on demand make over the books, papers, etc. When they do settle on a successor, or successors, they will have to inform the R.E.A. ... Obviously both the Salters and Jean had better choose a <u>young</u> person, or young persons. Salter thinks that his son may be a suitable choice.

Some months ago Jean told me that when she takes her holiday in October she would like to meet the Salters in order to discuss this difficult problem with them. I told this to Salter, who said that he had long been wanting to discuss the matter with her.

I have for some time past wanted Salter to write a sort of Introduction to the study of Scripts and <u>Notes</u> & <u>Excursuses</u>: my idea being that without some such guidance future students (if there ever are any) would find the job an infernally tiresome and difficult one. I told Salter of my idea when he was here, little thinking that there would be any chance of his regarding it favourably. Not only did he regard the idea favourably, but – curiously enough – he had quite independently been contemplating doing something of the sort. He has not promised to do the work, and anyhow he couldn't, as he said, begin until he had read the three new vols. of <u>N.</u> & <u>E.</u> My impression is that he will undertake the task; and if he does, he will, I believe, do it well.

I think that you know, but in case you don't, I had better tell you, that ten copies of all – or practically all – volumes of Scripts and of volumes of <u>N.</u> & <u>E.</u> are stored at MacLehose's. They are divided into two groups; 5 copies of each volume in one warehouse, and five in another, and they have been most carefully packed so as to prevent their being damaged by damp, or rats, and so on. I must let Jean know about this. So far MacLehoses have never charged a penny for the storage, and my impression is that they never will. I think that MacLehoses can be trusted absolutely.

I had originally intended to include an Index of the three new vols. of <u>N. & E.</u> at the end of Vol. VIII.; but after filling in between 3000 or 4000 page references in the final revision of the page proofs, I just felt that I could do no more... Possibly I may pluck up courage to do this work later; and if I do, and if I've enough money left to pay for it, I should have the Index printed as a small additional volume. But if I ever do this, it will, I think, be the last work that I shall undertake.

Yours ever,
J.G.P.

Copy of a letter dated September 2nd, 1943, from W.H. Salter:

Lady Traprain [Jean Balfour] will probably come here to stay a night some time in the latter part of October.

It seemed to me that it would be a good thing, before her visit, to explore (pedetemptim) the possibility of Trinity housing the documents, & accordingly I asked Broad to let me have a talk with him. Over the tea-table yesterday I gave him a general description of the quantity and nature of the documents, printed & MS., & stated the reason for keeping them 30 or 50 years. I reminded him that, as has already been stated in <u>Proceedings</u>, there were both private, personal matters, and 'prophetic' matters in the scripts, adding that these were mixed together, & concerned persons now alive.

He already knew a good deal about the documents: (a) I think he has for some time known who Mrs Willett is, though her identity was not discussed between us yesterday: (b) on my referring to the number of Trinity 'communicators', some of whom I named, he said 'Yes, & then there's the "dark young man"', clearly knowing who he was: (c) he said 'I don't want to press you for information, but isn't there some private matter connected with the Balfour family?': I admitted

411

this, & he said he had been told so by Oldfield. Just how much Oldfield has told him I don't know, but I suspect that he (Broad) knows the scripts refer to a romance of the Knight, & who the lady was: to the story in fact which Mrs Dugdale published.

I didn't detect any knowledge on his part that Mrs W. comes into the story otherwise than as an automatist, & that is, I suppose, the only thing as to which continued secrecy is essential. At the same time, if there is too much talk of Mrs W., & the Knight's romance, the chances of the rest leaking out are much increased.

Broad himself, is, of course, extremely discreet. I asked him to keep our conversation to himself.

He said he could not, naturally, say whether the College would accept custody of the documents, though he thought they would approach the question with an open mind, & without any anti-S.P.R. bias. A personal letter from G.W.B. would probably carry great weight. He felt sure that they would stipulate that their responsibility should be confined to custody, & that they should be satisfied that arrangements had been made by you & G.W.B. defining, beyond any possibility of doubt, what person or persons at any given time had access to the documents, & the right to decide for or against making a public statement regarding their contents, & also that such person or persons should be awake to their responsibilities & not just let things drift. I assured him that you and G.W.B. were equally anxious as to this.

Pardlestone, Holford, near Bridgewater, Somerset.
8 Sept., 1943.

Dear G.W.B.,

I'm sorry to inflict another bothersome letter upon you.

I enclose a typed copy of a letter which Salter wrote me on Sept 2. Perhaps you had better read it at this point, as that will make it easier to follow what I say.

I wrote to Salter and asked him whether he had any objection to my sending you a copy of his letter. He has replied that he has no objection.

I also asked Salter whether in his conversation with Broad

412

he had referred to the books, documents, etc., which are at present here in my possession, <u>only</u> which were in question.

I also asked Salter who had suggested that a personal letter from you would carry great weight: himself or Broad. He replied that it was Broad who made the suggestion.

I further asked Salter to whom in his opinion the letter should be addressed: to Broad, to the Librarian, or to the Master. He replied that both Helen Salter and himself think that the letter should be addressed to the Master, and a copy of it sent to Broad.

I suggested to Salter that, when he next saw Broad, he should sound him as to the likelihood of the College charging for the storage of the books, etc., in the event of their agreeing to store them. Salter tells me that he did raise this point during his talk with Broad, and that Broad waived it aside.

I don't know, of course, whether you would care to write such a letter as Broad suggests; but I agree that it would carry much weight. I shall be glad, in one way, and sorry in another, for I hate giving you trouble.

The difficulty about the books, etc., etc., that I have here is that I have no one in my family to entrust them to. Leo knows nothing about them, except that they are private and have to do with 'spooks', in which she has no interest. And even if I did leave them in her charge, that wouldn't meet the difficulty for two reasons:

(1) I think it is likely that after my death she will go and live in the United States; (2) if the books, etc., have to be kept for many years – as seems likely – she herself might well be dead, and she has no relations to whom she could possibly hand over the care of them.

[...]

You will probably want to reply to this letter. Couldn't you save yourself the trouble of writing by dictating to Jean?

I think that you know that Broad knows who Mrs Willett is. I knew, and I must have been told either by you or Salter; and, if it was Salter who told me, then I should certainly have told you.

No need to return the copy of Salter's letter...

Yours ever,
J.G.P.

Pardlestone, Holford, near Bridgewater, Somerset
23 Sept., 1943

Dear G.W.B.

I wish to goodness that we could have a talk together over what's to be done with the private books and papers at present here. It's so difficult to discuss these matters in writing. Still, as a meeting is out of the question, I must do my best to answer your letter of Sept. 19, which I did not receive till this morning.

Personally, of course, I shouldn't have the slightest objection to leaving the books and papers to Jean: in fact, I should be only too glad to do so, if I felt assured of their custody in the future. I'm not particularly keen about the Trinity College proposal, which was Salter's, not mine. But if I leave the books & papers to Jean, two questions arise. First, what will happen if Jean dies? If she died within the next 5 or 10 years, to whom would the books and papers pass? It seems to me essential that if I leave them to her in my Will, she ought to add a Codicil to her Will without delay in which she would name the person or persons to whom the books, etc., are to pass on her death. But can she now name any such person or persons?

Secondly, I am not sure that you realize the number of copies of printed Scripts & of N. & E., of the Delta Case & of Mrs Willett's Phenomena that I have here: all of which, I think, ought to be kept. I will try to count the numbers of books, and to give you an idea of the space occupied by the papers, etc. But I can't do that today, as I want this letter to go by the afternoon post. I will try to draw up a list tomorrow, & send it to you.

The advantage of leaving the books, papers, etc., to some institution like Trinity College, is that they would then be in the custody of an institution which, so far as one can foresee, is not likely to disappear in the next 40 or 50 years.

I don't yet know whether my solicitor comes here on Tuesday, Sept. 28, or on Tuesday, Oct. 5... If my solicitor doesn't come here till Oct. 5, then there would perhaps be time for you to write to tell me what opinion you have reached in talking the matter over with Jean. If I hear that my solicitor is coming here on Oct. 5, I shall let you know by telegram.

414

If, however, you don't receive a telegram, you will know that he had come on Sept. 28.

In your letter you mention the possibility of Jean destroying the privately [printed] volumes now in her possession in order to make more room for your and my volumes & papers. It is this sentence in your letter that makes me doubt whether you realize the number of volumes that I have here. I should imagine that Jean hasn't got more than about 24 volumes, and that is a small number compared to the number that you and I, especially, have.

When I wrote above about the advantage of leaving the books, papers, etc. to some permanent institution like Trinity College, I wasn't meaning to press the Trinity College proposal. I would rather leave them to Jean, provided that their future custody can be assured.

Yours ever   P.T.O. [missing]

J.G.P.

Pardlestone, Holford, near Bridgewater, Somerset.
6 Oct., 1943

Dear G.W.B.,

Many thanks for your answers to my questions.

I assume that Jean will eventually – that is when she can fix upon some one a good deal younger than herself and Ral – name this some one as well as Ral, as custodian of the books and papers.

I did wonder how room could be found for all the books & papers at Redcliff. I suppose that the room in the Old Tower is fairly dry and warm, for if it isn't the books and papers might easily become mouldy. This would never have occurred to me if I hadn't known of the precautions that MacLehose & Co. have taken to protect the volumes stored in their warehouses against damp. They did this several years ago before they knew that the volumes will probably have to be stored for many years.

As regards the problems raised in the last paragraph of Salter's letter of Sept. 2, 1943 (of which you have a copy) so far as I can see neither you nor I can deal with them, and they will have to be solved by Jean and/or Ral after consultation

415

with the Salters or their successors. By the Salters' successors I mean whomever they leave in charge of the books and papers which are in their possession at the present time. I hope that Jean will be able to meet the Salters this autumn, for then they would have an opportunity to discuss these problems.

[...]

Yours ever
J.G.P.

Note by Jean Balfour.
Record March 1944.
I visited the Salters at the Crown House, Newport, in March 1944, made better acquaintance with them, had very interesting talks, on points as follows:–

1) They are in favour of all Mr Pidd's material and also G.W.B.'s coming straight to me, as they feel first they have no room for it, second they are preoccupied enough with the question of what to do with all theirs, and third, they feel I am more remote from the S.P.R. members, many of whom are eager to investigate it themselves in the possible future! I agreed I could store it all safely, either in the Old Tower, or at Redcliff, Whittingehame: we also agreed that in the future, anything we should have to have access to, with the consent and knowledge of the other two. Should this be put in writing? Decided not but agreed that nothing should be done with any of it (such as publication) without the consent of the others.

2) Question of what person or persons of the next generation should be included in our association, that is to say, let into the secret and be permitted to read the material, in order to continue, after our respective deaths, to safeguard it all, and give or withhold permission for anything to be published?

We came to the conclusion that at the present moment it was hopeless to appoint anyone.

3) Question whether some of the subjects embedded in the Scripts could be picked out from the bulk of the material and published in the S.P.R. Proceedings once the War is over? – Cases such as the 'Palm Sunday' Story – the Myers – Phyllis story, which are complete in themselves, all persons in them now being dead. We were all strongly in favour of this, but

agreed that it must be deferred to the end of the War. The consent of Myers' family to the publication of parts of the privately printed 'Autobiography', (which Mrs Eveleen Myers attempted to suppress) would have to be obtained.

Mr Salter at present engaged in writing an 'Introduction to the study of the Scripts' which will be of great value to any future student.

J.B.

Pardlestone, Holford, near Bridgewater, Somerset.
18 April, 1944.

Dear Jean,

Business first. I am sending you herewith two typed Notes on two Holland Scr. Don't bother to read them, for they are duller than ditchwater, and until you receive Vol. VI of N.&.E., you wouldn't understand why I have taken the trouble of writing them. My only reason for writing these Notes is that for the first time on April 12, 1944, I came across two bits of information which, had I learnt them earlier, I should certainly have mentioned in Vol. VI. Keep them until you receive Vol. VI., and then you can shove them in this volume. I've sent a copy of the Notes to the Salters, but am keeping no copy myself.

[...]

I agree with your impressions about the Salters. I am now sure that _he_ is deeply interested, though I never realized that he was until lately. Helen's attitude towards Scripts has always been curiously detached, and I suspect that it is this odd aloofness that has helped to make her own scripts so good. I think that she has always been more interested in practical things than in spooks. I'm not a bit surprised if it is really the case that she doubts whether scripts, as you put it, 'really do mean as much as we all believe they do'; and the reason why I'm not surprised is that I often feel extremely sceptical too. I don't doubt that the scripts foretold the crisis through which the world is passing, nor do I doubt that they predict that a Messianic type of man would arise to bring peace to a distracted world, nor do I doubt who this man is. Where I feel sceptical is whether this – or any other – man will succeed in his task. Henry is a <u>very</u> difficult person to know: partly, perhaps, because he doesn't know himself. His apparent – perhaps real – want of enthusiasm is, I think, in part due to his innate scepticism.

[...]

Yes, I am most anxious that Salter should write an introduction to the study of Scripts. One is <u>very</u> badly needed, and Salter would do it well.

By the same post as your letter arrived came a letter from Mary, and enclosed in it was a short one from her father, which he had dictated to her; and with his letter was a typed memorandum which he had dictated to Mary on April 3, 1944, of a conversation with Henry on the subject of survival. Mary in her letter says that her father's sight is 'failing badly now, and he really can't read to himself any more'. Now here I want your advice, for I don't know what the position is. If I write to her father about <u>private</u> matters in scripts, it seems likely that Mary will read the letter to him, and I don't know how much Mary knows. She must know something, but <u>how much</u> I don't know; just as I never knew how much Nelly knew. Sorry to trouble you, as the telephone operator says, but I wish you'd let me know; and if you don't know, will you consult G.W.B.

As to the re-publication of G.W.B.'s SPR papers, that was proposed to the Council of the SPR not long ago, and turned down on account of the paper shortage. If later on they are re-published in a handy form, I think that it would be better to make a <u>selection</u>, and not publish all of them.

I was delighted and immensely surprised by your saying that you were wondering whether you might come and see me 'one day this summer'. Of course you might, and not only I but Leo too would be delighted to see you, though not for 'one day'. That 'one day' made me laugh, because it shows that you don't realize what an un-get-at-able place this is. (Leo has warned me in her most emphatic manner that I'm not to put you off by exaggerating the difficulties; but I'm not going to let you come down here under the impression that you just take a convenient express train to Pardlestone or Holford, and then just take a nice little taxi and drive to this house.) If you come – and I've been longing to talk to you about lots of things – you must come for at least 2 or 3 days. The nearest station is Bridgewater, and this over 13 miles away. Leo has only enough petrol to go to Bridgewater once a week, and nearly always she goes there on Tuesdays to shop. So if you could come on a Tuesday, she could meet you. But if you came on another day of the week, you might not be able to get a taxi, and would have to take a 'bus, and the 'bus would land you at the Hood Arms, <u>Kilve</u>, and from there it's a mile's walk up-hill to this bungalow. If Leo hadn't enough petrol to fetch you from Kilve, you'd have to walk. Your luggage, of course, could be fetched. (Don't bring more than 3 evening dresses.) If you had to take the 'bus, <u>don't</u> get out at Holford, for that is 2 1/2 miles away, or more. But come on a Tuesday, if you can [...] for it's not good for people with backbones to ride in 'buses, or to walk a mile up a very steep hill. I think that we could almost certainly get you a taxi for the return journey. Meanwhile I'll say no more about the journey until you've fixed that 'one day this summer'.

While I remember it. If you do come here, you must bear in mind that – <u>so</u> <u>far</u> <u>as</u> <u>I</u> <u>am</u> <u>aware</u> – Leo knows nothing about scripts. She may have picked up things at Fishers Hill, but I've never said a word to her about <u>private</u> matters in scripts and I've never asked her whether she knows anything. She knows, of course, that this place is crammed with printed volumes of Scripts, etc., and papers, and that these are all private; but otherwise, so far as I know, she knows nothing else.* She is obviously curious about Henry, but she could hardly be otherwise in view of the interest displayed in him at Fishers Hill.

Well, I had better stop. I hope that I've answered all the points in your letter.

Yours ever – or at least till 'one day this summer' –

J.G.P.

*Curiously enough, a few days ago, I purposely said to her <u>in</u> <u>a</u> <u>casual</u> <u>way</u> that I wished that, as soon as this war was finished, I could send all the Vols. of Scripts, etc., that are here to you to keep at Whittingehame; and I explained that they would anyhow go to you after my death. So she knows that much.

This letter is followed by a four-page typed note by J.G.P. on Hld. [Holland] script 155 regarding obscure references to Lady Mounttemple, Broadlands, in the Myers and Phyllis story.

Pardlestone, Holford, near Bridgewater, Somerset.
14 June (or January), 1944.

Dear Jean,

I look forward with great interest to reading the note about Guinevere and the 'recantation' references, for I have long felt we have never really got to the bottom of those 'recantation' references. Of course I understand that G.W.B. may not be up to dictating it, and that anyhow it may be some time before it's finished. I believe that the explanation of 'I, I too have written swift iambics' in Note A to W. 417 is right as far as it goes, but that it doesn't clear up the whole problem. It seems so odd to represent the Palm Maiden as '<u>recanting</u>' views about a future life which there seems no reason for supposing that she ever held. If I have energy enough I may add a note about the connexion in W. 415 of 'I, I too, have written swift iambics' with A.W. Verrall.

It's extraordinarily kind of you, overburdened, as you are, with family and other cares, to ask me to stay at Redcliff for a month in October; and most kind of Ral to think of trying to get me a first class sleeper from London to Scotland. But to my very real and deep regret I know that it's no use attempting the journey. I'm just not up to it. I should long ago have gone up to London to see my solicitor (who still has not been able to come down here) if I had felt that I could stand the journey, but I know that I couldn't, and still less a journey to Scotland. I'd give much to see you all at Whittingehame again, and especially G.W.B. (as you won't, I know, mind my adding). Since I came here in June 1940, I have left this place only 6 times...

By the way, a few days ago, I received from MacLehose the reader's queries relating to the final proofs of Vol. VIII. (the last volume) of <u>Notes</u> & <u>Excursuses</u>. So I hope that within the next 3 months you'll receive vols. VI, VII, & VIII. But MacLehose & Co. are, as their letters to me show, evidently in great difficulties owing to shortage of staff and materials.

I am still most awfully puzzled over the Holy Grail references in scripts. I am clear that the Grail in many instances must be a symbol of the Palm Maiden, in spite of the fact that in W. 323 (25) there is the clearest reference to Percival's sister's own vision of the Grail. Yet there are other passages that strongly suggest that the Grail is a Messianic symbol. It seems just possible that the Grail is a sort of composite symbol applied to the Palm Maiden and the Child. The Grail in scripts is clearly connected with a lot of other topics: e.g. the Golden Fleece, the order of the Golden Fleece, the Argonauts and the Argo, and with argosies (which have nothing to do with the Argo), & also with the Golden Bough, the Transfiguration, the White Lady of Avenel, & so on. Some years ago I wrote a long Note on these connected topics which I meant to include in the new vols. of N. & E., but I gave it up as a bad job. Most of the interconnexions are clear enough, but I just can't make sense of them.

[...]

Yours ever

J.G.P.

At the end of this letter J.G.P. adds the note about Verrall & the iambics, heavily Classical in its references.

Jean Balfour's letter to J.G.P. about G.W.B.'s beliefs on the meaning of the 'Guinevere' references in the Scripts, returned to him to Whittingehame for safe keeping.
Page 1 is missing.

Whittingehame
Haddington
Scotland
July 4, 1944

[...] perhaps you had better not comment on it – just keep it: because he does intend eventually to express his opinion to you on the Subject of Guinevere & its connexion with the Recantation topic. So if I write it now, while it is fresh in my mind, at least we shall have a record of what he remembers and believes, and I think that is so important that I hope I am justified in doing so.

He has very interesting views on the personality of M.L. and he thinks that the Guinevere references in the scripts are quite deliberate: and that, taken together with the Recantation references, they attempt to draw attention to a very profound change of opinion which he believes M.L. realised at the time of the experience of her death. He remembers her, of course, and in his description of her to me, said that he wished to point out that she was very attractive, very full of life, and that she was of an amorous disposition: she had had, he said, at least 2 love affairs before she died (as you know). He thought A.J.B. had managed his courting very badly, for he never made any strong attempt to win her, and after several years, there was still no declaration between them. I said, 'He was always so very modest, perhaps that diffidence prevented him.' But G.W.B. felt that A.J.B. had never realised what a passionate nature hers was, and he could not have won her by just looking at her with his love and admiration in his eyes. He referred to the letter written by A.J.B. to the Warden only a week after her death; (which you have seen, it came into our possession about 2 years ago through one of the Talbot daughters having given it along with other letters to Baffy Dugdale;) A.J.B. seems in his letter hardly to have believed that he could ever have been loved by her, and to think that it might not have been within his power ever to have made her happy. G.W.B. thinks that her temperament had a strong need of physical demonstration, and that is where the simile of Guinevere is not out of place. He thinks that the man to whom she had been engaged understood and appealed to her nature better than A.J.B. ever did – 'a lesser man,' (a sort of Launcelot). He died (as you know) and still A.J.B. did not press his suit, for he feared to intrude on her private feelings, he did not know how much she had really cared for him. I remember that a long time ago Aunt Nora told me that Mrs Talbot had told her that M.L. had once said, about Arthur 'I wish he had a little more backbone.' It is almost as if A.J.B. had been under a spell, always thinking there was plenty of time. G.W.B. believes she must have thought him 'high, self-contained and passionless.'

But, just before she became ill, it seems that she was beginning to think of A.J.B. in a different way, & to perceive

422

the deep strength of his feelings and the essential fineness of his nature. I said 'As if at last she was ripening into a sort of spiritual maturity?' and he agreed, and added that he thought she had begun to <u>compare</u> her lovers, & the different kinds of love. 'We needs must love the highest when we see it,' fits in here. The previous lovers ('not Launcelot nor another') had never touched the spiritual fires which in one of her ardent temperament would be just as strong as physical passion, and G.W.B. believes that it needed the <u>crisis of death</u> to fully awaken this new love: he thinks that the change of opinion about love and the experience of a different kind of love (a very <u>great</u> love, essentially spiritual) was just dawning in her but it had not time even to crystallize into conscious realisation before death put an end to all hope of its fulfilment on earth. He quoted 'she never fully realised until she got here (across the sands of Dee)' which he feels is a very important point.

It needed the same sort of crisis, the experience of an utter loss by her death, to awaken A.J.B. to a realisation of the greatness of his love for her: 'on both sides' the shock of death seems to have provided the motive spring for the continuous growth of a spiritual love which according to the scripts seems to have strengthened as years went on. Cf: Guinevere's hope that she would 'be his mate hereafter in the heavens.'

I expect most of this is not new to you: probably G.W.B. has told you these facts. I suppose his intimate knowledge of M.L.'s state of mind is based on conversations with the Talbots long ago, for he seems to have met them & discussed very fully all the circumstances relating to the time of her death. I do think the analogies of the 'quotations' from Tennyson's Guinevere are very remarkable, and I felt what a good thing it is that G.W.B. is still alive, still able to remember, and that I am here to talk over these things with him and to set down what he thinks in writing: also that the letter from A.J.B. of March 31st 1871(?) 1875 has come into our keeping. G.W.B. thinks that the Recantation references can be interpreted as attempts to describe the <u>change</u> of the opinion held by M.L. before, and after, the crisis of death – her opinion, I suppose, of love, though he has not so far spoken very fully upon his views on this subject. As allusions to the 'Recantation topic' are scattered all over the scripts, it would take a long time to look them up, and he wants to go through Willett first, following the revelation of the personality of M.L. In your latest paper, 'Horace's' Swift Iambics '& A.W. Verrall', you draw attention to Socrates' recantation, after having spoken ill of love in Plato's 'Phaedrus' in which the celebrated lines of Stesichorus were quoted: and (though alas, I know nothing of Greek & Latin, so that I realise I miss the real point every time.) I think this must be extremely significant, because the Palm Maiden, G.W.B. believes, made a sort of recantation when she came to compare her former experience of love with the new love just dawning when she died: but she could not make that recantation clear till after death.

I do hope all this makes sense to you, and I do hope, too, that eventually G.W.B. will be up to dictating.
[Rest of letter missing.]

Note added by Jean Balfour: '[G.W.B] died at end of Jan: 1945'

Pardlestone, Holford, near Bridgewater, Somerset.
11 July 1944.

Dear Jean,
This is a <u>private</u> letter, and I think you had better destroy it after it is read.

I am returning you pages 2, 3 and 4 of your letter dated 4 July; my reason for doing so being that I don't want a letter dealing with such private matters to be kept here. After my death my executors will have to collect and pack the books, papers, etc., which are to go to you. From most of them they could gain little or no information, but from your letter of July 4 they could learn things which must be kept private. I advise you to keep these sheets, as it will save you making another record of what G.W.B. has told you about the Palm Maiden.

I knew of the two love affairs, and I think that I knew that A.J.B. was too backward a lover; but what you tell me about the Palm Maiden's nature is new to me.

I wish that neither G.W.B. nor you had felt that you were

keeping me waiting a long time for comments on my 'Duck Associations' note. I had absolutely no feeling of being kept waiting, and indeed I hardly expected any comments. And I wish that G.W.B. wouldn't undergo the strain of writing about the Recantation & Guinevere topic. I'm never going to have anything more <u>printed</u> about scripts, and I imagine that G.W.B. isn't either; and it's no use adding to the mass of MS. notes or comments. I'm afraid that this may sound very ungracious; but it certainly isn't meant to be so. I'm <u>interested</u>, of course, by G.W.B.'s comments; but I feel that the effort which it costs him to make them is not worth while.

I shall write you a <u>non</u>-private reply to your letter of July 4, which <u>possibly</u> I may enclose with this letter; but more probably I shall send this <u>private</u> letter off to-day, and post the non-private one later.

[...]

Yours ever
J.G.P.

Pardlestone, Holford, near Bridgewater,
Somerset.
17 Sept., 1944

Dear Jean,

I have at last got that new Will of mine finished, and it is now in the keeping of the Royal Exchange Assurance.

In my previous Will I had left all the privately printed vols. of scripts and of <u>Notes & Excursuses</u>, and all notes, papers, letters, etc., etc., to the Royal Exchange Assurance as my Executors with instructions to hand them to you, or, in the event of your death, to Mrs Salter, and in the event of her death, to Salter. You will realise that by my new Will all these books, papers, etc. become your property; and so you'll have to consider to whom they are to pass in the event of your death.

According to my new Will all the books and papers are bequeathed to you, if they have not already been sent to you during my lifetime. That's one of the points we shall have to discuss when you come here...

In my old Will the nature of the books, papers, etc., etc.,

was described. In my new Will their nature is <u>not</u> described, and the Will merely says that a list of the books, etc., etc., is given in a letter addressed to my Executors. The advantage of this change is that no one reading the Will (and any one can read it by applying to Somerset House) can tell what the books, etc., are. The letter to my Executors will not have to be deposited at Somerset House.

I do not mention the Salters in my new Will, and the Will does not give them the right of access to the books, papers, etc. Neither of them would want to have access to the printed volumes, for they have copies of all of them. But they do want to have the right to see any of the papers, etc., etc., and when Salter was here a year ago I promised that they should have. I'm sure that you will let them see any of the papers. etc., that they may wish to see. Salter has seen most of them, and he has copies at any rate of some of the more important ones. So if the Salters want to see any of the rest (and many I'm sure they wont want to see), it wouldn't be much bother for you to send any papers that they might want to see by post to them.

During the autumn and winter I'll try to make out a complete list of all the papers, documents, notes, letters, memoranda, etc., etc. (a loathsome job.)

One of the matters that I want to discuss with you is what is ultimately to be done about the copies of Scripts and <u>N. & E.</u> stored at MacLehose's in Glasgow. So far no charge is made for the storage of these books (which by now amount to about 300 copies), and none is likely to be made so long as Mr Hamish MacLehose is alive. But he can't answer for what his firm may do after he is dead, and as the books may have to be stored for 25, 30, 40 or even 50 years, there may well be an annual charge to storage made. I don't want you or your successor to bear this expense, and yet I couldn't see how to arrange for my Executors to pay the charge if made. It has occurred to me that I might pay you a sum of money to meet possible storage expenses; but even if I did, what would become of this sum if you died before the books were removed from MacLehose & Co's warehouses? It's a knotty problem; and you might send yourself to sleep o' nights by trying to solve it.

No time or energy for more. Please, if you've time, read this letter to G.W.B., and give him my love.

Yours ever,
J.G.P

Note by Jean Balfour regarding the correspondence in 1943 on the question of the future storage and care of the Scripts and also recording the meeting between her and the Salters in March 1944:

Re Storage in Glasgow of Surplus Vols. of Scripts

A letter from J.G.P. to Mr Salter dated <u>September 1945</u> says that he had lately paid a sum of money to MacLehose's to cover storage for 50 years. The sum paid was to cover the cost not only of storing but of opening, examining, repacking and, if necessary, cleaning the volumes from time to time. They are <u>*not insured*</u> against risk of fire or other damage (of what value would insurance be?)

Sir Hamish MacLehose gave it as his opinion that the continuance of his firm seemed to be well assured for a very considerable period.

Mr Salter has this letter: this is a rough copy I took when I read it.

J.B. 1945

Note by Jean Balfour, February 1945, on notepaper headed Whittingehame, Haddington, Scotland:

G.W.B. died in January 1945. For the last 3 years of his life he lived in the cottage next door to us, and there I used to read Scripts to him almost daily & we went all through the Willett volumes, and all his works; and had many intimate discussions on subjects that deeply interested him, both long ago & at the present time.

At his death, in accordance with his wish, I received all books, papers, letters, etc., to do with Scripts. I looked carefully through them and set them in order & shall faithfully guard them henceforth.

I wish to put on record certain things. In my talks with G.W.B., he referred quite openly to his past relations with Mrs Willett, (for he knew that I knew) and also revealed to me his intense affection for Henry & pride in him, a great deal of which I could share. Over his tremendous convictions on the meaning of the Scripts, and what they foretold for Henry, he knew that I was not as certain as he; but of one thing I am quite convinced, viz. that ever since M.L. died, the activities of the group on the 'Other Side', responsible for all these Scripts, has been concerned with the production of a special type of child: and that several children have undoubtedly, been deliberately produced, but were, for some reason or other, failures; these are clearly regarded as 'sacrifices to fate', and that finally their efforts culminated in the production of Henry, whose origin and conditions of birth were evidently regarded as perfect and hopeful.

Perhaps I should not have said 'culminated' because to me, the tone of the Scripts suggests that the 'incarnation of the divine', and the motif of the 'Christchild's birth' was still going on, even after Augustus had appeared. G.W.B. believed that the 'Holy Grail references' referred to an event – not to any personage – and that this event was Birth – the 'descent into generation', which is always going on, though at certain periods in the world's history, it rises to a peak in the number of geniuses, or men of special calibre, produced – such as took place in the Greco-Roman epoch. 'The Blossoming Rod' topic, he thought, had a place here, and was to be understood as referring to these periods, both past and to come, when many great men appeared on the earth, and when the invasion of spiritual influence into our world became especially compelling.

I have therefore included his note on the Incarnation topic at which he was working up to the time of his death, with these records of Willett private papers, for they evidently belong here.

In the course of my acquaintance with Mrs Tennant, I became fond of her; but during my readings with G.W.B. of the whole series of Willett Phenomena, I realised that I never knew Mrs Willett. Only G.W.B., Mrs Verrall, Miss Johnson, Sir O.J.L. [Oliver Lodge] had known her. It was however, only when I

428

had possession of these papers, and <u>saw the photographs</u>, that I knew this: when I looked at the picture of Mrs Tennant standing sideways, I had a very strange feeling that I was looking at someone else, not Mrs Tennant, but the other being, in <u>her</u> body. I felt I could love and almost worship this one; I had never felt that (except when I read the Willett scripts of 1912 till 1918) over the one I knew. It explained a great deal: I think, of course, that Mrs Willett and Mrs Tennant were 2 distinct facets of personality, alternately having possession of the same body, during that mediumistic period of Mrs Tennant's life: and though Mrs Willett only gained full ascendency during trance, still she very profoundly influenced Mrs Tennant's waking life, and may be said to have been the mother of Henry in a special sense.

G.W.B. told me of the subjects of these private papers before he died, and in the light of all that I know, & have myself experienced, it seems clear to me that to the Group on the Other Side – whoever & whatever they are – the only way for them to obtain this pre-ordained child – who had a better chance than all the others by reason of the working experience thereby gained – was by raising up a new husband for Mrs Tennant to be the father of Mrs Willett's child.

The Piper–Willett Sittings introduce the idea of having another child to her, at first a repugnant idea: her dream of February 1912 reveals that she has suffered a change of view and coincides with the love affair of that time just opening in her life: and in that sense the dream is certainly a premonitory one: Henry was not actually conceived till July 1912.

These considerations colour the thoughts in connexion with Henry which I have lately had, especially since reading certain letters of 1931 written by his mother: these I shall try later on to embody in a paper which I shall call 'Further Questions in a New Light.' The subject of my contention is that Henry was certainly the child of Mrs Willett but that it was Mrs Tennant who has brought him up.

J.B.

Advice from J.G.P. on reading volumes 6, 7 & 8 of *Notes and Excursuses*.

I expect that so long as the war lasts you won't have time to read the 3 new vols. of <u>N. & E.</u>; but a time may come when after the war is over you will summon up the courage to read them. So I give you the following advice:–

Read the Preface to the 3 vols. and the <u>Introduction</u> to ch. I. But you had better skip ch.1 itself because there is too much Greek in it. Don't try to read ch. II., with its awful 13 Sections. Skip it and go straight on to chs. III and IV (omitting the Appendix to ch. III), and then read ch. V. up to the point where I begin to discuss Mrs Salter's 'Martinmas' script, H.V. 538. Ch. VI., which is poor stuff, you had better skip; but ch. VII & the comparatively short Notes which follow it might interest you. By far the least unsatisfactory thing in the three vols. is the first half of ch. V.: by which I mean up to the 'Martinmas' script. I think it will interest you, and I hope that you will find it convincing.

If ever in an heroic mood you should try to wade through ch. II., I advise you to read the <u>last</u> Section of it, called 'A Bye-Election at Brighton', <u>first</u>, for if you do it will help you to understand why in the preceeding Sections I discuss the references in scripts to Henry Fawcett, Leslie Stephen, Merrifield, F. W. Maitland, and 'Various People Named Tennant'.

I shall answer Nellie's letter when I have recovered from writing this long one to you.

Yours ever
J.G.P.

Re disposition of Private Documents

<u>Note by Jean Balfour.</u> The first idea was to store them and all volumes of scripts in the British Museum, then the War having broken out in 1939 and London being bombed, a new idea of storing them in Trinity College was entertained. But Professor Broad seeming to G.W.B. & J.G.P's ideas somewhat too interested in the little that was known of them by the public (i.e. the SPR members) caused this idea to be abandoned, and it was finally decided to leave them all to me (Jean Balfour) and that I should store them in the Tower Room at Whittingehame, in far Scotland, where they would be safe and

kept out of the reach of the SPR until such time as it would be proved whether what the interpreters (G.W.B. and J.G.P.) believed them to foretell, was true.

Piddington died in April 1952. With his death, one of the last links with the founders of the SPR had been broken. (For the enormous strength, care and dedication he had brought to the service of the SPR, reference may be made to Chapter 7.) Valuable as were his administrative services to the society, it is his part in interpreting the Scripts that calls for special notice. This was the task of the team that included Mrs Sidgwick, Oliver Lodge, Alice Johnson and G.W. Balfour, but as time passed, the main work fell on Piddington, and increasingly so as ill-health or advancing years compelled the withdrawal of the others. This is not the place in this narrative to attempt a final appraisement of the significance of the Scripts, but readers may refresh their memories by turning back to Chapter 9 where W.H. Salter's assessment in 1952 of the work done by Piddington and his colleagues is given.

Salter points out that Piddington had in full measure two indispensibles for psychical research, human sympathy and a sense of humour. Because of his sympathy and his obvious trustworthiness and discretion, whenever, as often happened, it was necessary to verify some personal allusion in the scripts, he had no difficulty in getting people to answer questions as to their private affairs or to allow him to inspect their confidential diaries. His keen sense of humour made him a delightful companion and correspondent as soon as one penetrated his natural shyness and the reserve that went with it.

The poor health from which he suffered for many years did not prevent his deriving much quiet enjoyment from country life, golf and music, all of which he found at Fisher's Hill. From the windows of his book-lined study there he could enjoy delightful views of garden, woodland and down, and there, whenever scripts became a weariness to the flesh, he could console himself at the piano. But above all Fisher's Hill gave him the company of like-minded friends. The last few years of his long life were spent in his daughter's charming house overlooking the Bristol Channel.

The scripts had come to an end many years before his death. All his close friends and comrades in the 'Great Work', apart from

Jean Balfour and Mrs Coombe-Tennant, who really was never all that close to him, had departed. Nevertheless, he had remained faithful to the end to that text carved over the entrance to Selwyn College. As long as he was able to do so, he had doggedly worked on throughout the disturbing, distressing years of the war – perhaps the 'Second Great War' predicted by the Scripts – but even he was beginning to have doubts. Jean noted that on occasion he used to say: 'Time will show if we are right. It all depends on Henry. But if nothing happens, all our work will have been a great waste of time . . .'

19

Salter

The question one often hears put, 'Is death the end?' is too
stupid to deserve an answer. After the death of anyone things
are different from what they would have been if he had never
lived, and that is true whether the death be of Socrates, Caesar,
or Shakespeare, or the veriest Simple Simon. Something
continues, and the question that needs an answer is, what is
that something?'

Zoar, W.H. Salter

At the little bistro in Montmartre the small group had dined well.
The evening had been convivial: one member of the party of
psychical researchers had cast aside his customary seriousness and
had kept the members of his party in fits of laughter with his
stories. The hilarity of the party caught the attention of a group
of young French men and women nearby who came up to the
group of happy diners and, to the speaker's embarrassment and the
delight of his friends, decked him out with a crown of flowers
taken from vases on the tables around. Kathleen Goldney always
remembered that happy evening in Paris in 1953. She also recalled
another occasion, at another of the medium and psychical researcher
Mrs Eileen Garrett's Conferences, in 1955, when the SPR acted
as host in Cambridge, and they lodged in Newnham College. She
remembered her delight in meeting members of the American SPR,
the yarns they had had, often long into the night, the sightseeing
in Cambridge, Professor Broad entertaining them to tea in his rooms
at Trinity, strawberries and cream on the lawn at the Garden House
Hotel on a perfect summer's afternoon. She also remembered the

man who had been the storyteller in the bistro in Montmartre perspiringly rowing some of them on the river one afternoon.

Kathleen Goldney joined the SPR while she was living in India. When she returned to England and worked part-time for eight years as Organising Secretary at the SPR – most of them in Tavistock Square – she would meet him once or twice a week when he came up regularly from his home in Newport, Essex, to deal with correspondence and SPR matters generally and to discuss with Miss Horsell, the Secretary, any matters requiring his guidance and advice. On these occasions she and he would lunch at a nearby restaurant and frequently she would say to him: 'Willy, what are we going to talk about today? Tell me about all the people I never knew; about the Verralls ... and Mr Piddington ... and Mr Podmore ... and what do you think about the cross-correspondences? ... and about such and such a medium?' She recalled:

> he'd hold forth (he was a *great* talker) and I would listen all ears to all he had to tell me and, on getting back to the office, would go straight to my typewriter to write down all he had said before getting back to work and while it was only half-an-hour old in my memory. I have a big file of these notes marked 'W.H.S.'s Information' and many letters from him.
>
> On one such occasion my question was 'Tell me who 'Mrs Willett' really is.' But that one got no answer. 'No,' he said, 'I'm not going to tell you that, and you're not to ask me again and you're to stop anyone else being curious about it.' And he explained that keeping her name secret at that time was not only for personal reasons but for research reasons too. This led to an amusing coincidence when for fun I made a note 'guessing' Mrs Willett's real name (correctly) but for quite false reasons and from completely inaccurate premises, assigning her to the wrong Tennant family.

William Henry Salter was born in London on March 19th, 1880. His father was William Henry Gurney Salter, a barrister and shorthand writer to the Houses of Parliament. Professor C.D. Broad was told by Salter that he was related to Edmund Gurney. Broad could well accept this, not only by Salter's father's middle name but also by Edmund Gurney's family history. For Gurney's ancestors

434

William H. Salter   Helen Salter (Mrs Salter)

first came to prominence and prosperity through inventing a system of shorthand, and several of them in succession had been shorthand writers to the House of Commons.

Salter was destined to be one of the last survivors of the several generations of Trinity College graduates who have played a major part in the SPR. Educated first at St Paul's School and then at Trinity College, Cambridge, he became a Classical Scholar of the college in 1899, and in 1901 was placed in the first class of the Classical tripos. Thereafter, having acquired a major Classical education that was to serve him well in later years in his researches, he turned his attention to the law. Obtaining his law degree in 1902, he was called to the Bar at Lincoln's Inn on July 5th, 1905. His younger brother, F.R. Salter, was also educated at St Paul's and Trinity. As Broad put it in an obituary, 'The Salters were typical intelligent, cultured, Liberal Nonconformists; and both brothers exhibited throughout their lives the many virtues and the occasional angularities of that once powerful and now almost extinct Victorian species.'

On September 28th, 1915, Salter married Helen de G. Verrall, the only surviving child of Professor and Mrs Verrall. Arthur Woollgar Verrall had been a Classical scholar at Trinity; he had read for the Bar but returned to Cambridge in 1877. He was one of the most accomplished and original Classical scholars of his day, a man of marked wit and humour. A tutor and classical lecturer at Trinity College, he lived there until his death on June 18th, 1912, only a year after having been appointed first King Edward VII Professor of English Literature. Helen Verrall's mother was, of course, Margaret de Gaudrion Verrall, herself a Classical scholar and a lecturer in Classics at her own college, Newnham, Cambridge. It was she, it will be recalled, who began the long series of automatic writings in order to give her friend Frederic Myers, after

435

his death on January 17th, 1901, a chance to communicate evidence of his survival of death.

Their daughter Helen, also a Classical scholar, likewise possessed the ability to write automatically and it seems probable that Salter's first introduction to psychical research in general and the SPR in particular was from the Verralls and his wife. A year after his marriage he joined the SPR. His wife had already been an Associate Member since October 1905, when she was twenty-two, and became a Life Member in 1917. In 1916 she was appointed Honorary Research Officer on the retirement of Miss Alice Johnson.

During the First World War, Salter held various posts in the Ministry of Munitions, being in turn in the Labour Section, the Legal Department and the Secretariat. In 1918 he was awarded the MBE.

Mrs Verrall died in 1916. Early in 1925, the Salters moved to Newport, near Saffron Walden, in Essex, and the rest of the lives of both of them were spent in the beautiful old Crown House there. They had two children, a daughter and a son. The daughter, Imogen, was born in 1926 and was the third in succession in her mother's family to be a student at Newnham. The son, Martin, was born in 1929. Both Salter and his wife played important parts in the local affairs of Essex. Among other things, Salter was for many years a governor of the Newport Grammar School, and for a time chairman of the Board of Governors. He was chairman of the Newport Parish Council for several years, and for more than twenty years chairman of the managers of the Newport Primary School.

Mrs Salter died, unexpectedly and in her sleep, on April 22nd, 1959. For a period after her death Salter was strongly inclined to give up their house, but eventually he decided to stay on there, and there he spent the rest of his life.

From the end of the First World War until very near the end of his life, Salter devoted the greater part of his time and energy to the honorary service of the SPR. He first became a member of Council, by cooptation, in December 1919. He became Honorary Treasurer on December 9th, 1920, in succession to Piddington, and he held that office until September 30th, 1931, when he resigned. In March 1924 he was appointed Honorary Secretary and he occupied that post continuously until 1958. He was President of the society for the years 1947–8, and in his later years a Vice-President.

By education, training, family and active participation in the SPR, Salter was for many years on intimate terms with some of the main producers of the scripts which became the basis of the Cross-Correspondences, including Mrs Verrall, his wife, Helen, and 'Mrs Willett'. He also was in constant touch with the investigators and interpreters of the scripts such as Gerald Balfour, Piddington and Mrs Sidgwick. And he had, of course, the necessary Classical knowledge to appreciate the more recondite references in the scripts and to assess the meanings that the investigators believed they had found in the scripts. Over the years, therefore, while he did not invest in them the measure of total involvement the investigators had devoted to them, and retained throughout these years a marked, almost legal degree of detachment, after the death of the 'old guard' he ended by becoming the repository of their knowledge and theories, and a person whose knowledge of the Cross-Correspondences and their ramifications went far beyond what anyone else – even Jean Balfour – possessed.

Just before the beginning of the Second World War, the publishers G. Bell & Son brought out a series of small books on various aspects of psychic phenomena. Based on material in the possession of the SPR, they were published with the consent of Council, but with their traditional caution the SPR insisted that it was explicitly stated in them that the society was in no way responsible for any of the deductions made or the theories advanced by the authors. They need not have worried. The authors were careful to write measured and instructive books. One of them, *Some Cases of Prediction* (1937), was written by Dame Edith Lyttelton; another, *Ghosts and Apparitions* (1938), was written by W.H. Salter.

In 1961 Salter wrote a book published by Sidgwick & Jackson, with the cryptic title *Zoar*. For that dwindling fraction of the present generation who still know their Bible (see Genesis 19.20–22 and Deuteronomy 34.3) it is not an inappropriate title, especially when one reads the sub-title 'The Evidence of Psychical Research Concerning Survival'. It is dedicated 'to Helen and all who are working to complete Man's knowledge of his Nature.' In his introduction, Salter points out that the material in the book is based on forty years' experience of the work of the SPR, half of the book being written before the crushing blow of his wife Helen's sudden and totally unexpected death in 1959. He states honestly: 'I can no longer therefore claim to write with emotional detachment but will most positively assert that the opinions I now put forward are substantially the same as those that my wife and I often discussed together, and that I formed when the end of earthly life seemed far off for either of us.'

Zoar is an important book which no one who is interested in obtaining an intelligent, cautious examination of the scope and findings of psychical research can afford to ignore. It has much in it that is reminiscent of Myers' major work, *Human Personality and Its Survival of Bodily Death*, but contains a great deal more, gleaned and assessed from a further sixty years of psychical research, including, of course, the Cross-Correspondences and the efforts of the interpreters to decode them.

Salter does not devote much space to physical phenomena beyond giving a short historical summary of the more important phases such as the Fox sisters' lives and Daniel Dunglas Home's career. After acknowledging the work done by Crookes and his colleagues and other investigators in studying Home, Salter, with characteristic robust sense and a touch of his dry humour, writes:

Many of Home's 'physical' phenomena are extremely difficult to explain away by normal means, unless one attributes to the many eminent witnesses of them astounding incompetence as observers and as recorders of what they observed. But while these witnesses have recorded the deep impression made on them by such feats as Home's taking in his hands a red-hot coal from the fire and placing it on the head of an old gentleman without doing an injury to his own hand or the other's head, it is not, I think, reported that while doing this, any of those who saw it exclaimed, 'How characteristic of poor dear So-and-so! Just how he used to behave!' Physical phenomena may, possibly, provide evidence of the existence of some physical force not at present recognised by science; they are no evidence at all of the survival of any person who has departed this life, unless *either* there is present at the sitting a form perceptible to the sitters' senses and such as the surviving spirit may reasonably be supposed to inhabit, *or* else there occurs behaviour distinctive of the bodily activity of that person... As to physical phenomena purporting to be produced by a surviving spirit, the more paranormal they are the less likely they are to be distinctive or even appropriate, and *vice versa*, since the conditions of ordinary life are very different from those of a properly controlled seance. It is, for example, a common occurrence in seances held in the dark for a tambourine to be shaken, ostensibly by the communicating spirit. The number of persons addicted to this practice in life cannot be considerable. It is a habit which, if the phenomena are genuine, we must suppose we adopt when we join the Choir Invisible.

A third book, also very important but not ever printed by a publishing house – it is difficult to see how it could have been of any commercial value whatsoever! – was completed in May 1948 and privately printed. This is W.H. Salter's *An Introduction to the Study of Scripts*. It is invaluable to anyone contemplating any serious study of the Cross-Correspondences. Just over a hundred pages in length, it is in six parts, together with a preface explaining what the six parts contain. Part 1 gives a short narrative concerning events leading up to the production of the first script in 1901. Further developments are then given up to the scripts of 1912 and 1913 which referred to past events and which required the previous scripts to be reexamined. Part 2 gives a summary of the Story and the Plan. Part 3 deals with the interpretation of scripts, drawing attention to the cryptic nature of trance scripts, their difficulties and the interpreters' methods of overcoming these. Part 4 describes how the interpretations were tested by referring to the earlier scripts – the acid test. In Part 5 the narrative is carried to later developments, the scripts of Mrs Wilson, who knew nothing of the Story or the Plan being discussed. Part 6, written in 1948 or earlier, is inevitably out of date, dealing as it does with the locations of the Scripts, published papers, printed volumes, diaries, copybooks, and so on but is still at the very least indicative of the extreme care Salter took in preparing his introductory book. The final section of Part 6 – the last twenty pages of the book – is a very useful set of short biographical notes of over fifty of the principal 'players'. It gives a wealth of relevant information regarding events in their lives, their 'scriptic role' and a note as to which scriptic incidents that player was particularly concerned in. There are also valuable cross-linking data.

Between 1924 and 1963, Salter also published a number of significant papers on the Cross-Correspondences and related topics in the *Journal* and the *Proceedings* of the SPR. They include 'Elucidation of Two Points in the "One Horse Dawn Scripts"';

'F.W.H. Myers' Posthumous Message'; 'The Palm Sunday Case – A Note on the Interpretation of Automatic Writings', and 'The Rose of Sharon'. He also wrote the obituary, 'J.G. Piddington and His Work on the "Cross-Correspondence" Scripts'.

As a result of his discussions with J.G. Piddington and Jean Balfour about the disposition and safeguarding of sensitive material concerned with the scripts and their interpretations, Salter ultimately made two deposits with the Library of Trinity College, Cambridge, to be retained unopened for a certain period of time and then to become available under certain conditions. These restrictions were imposed in order to avoid possible embarrassment to people still living or to their relatives in the next generation. The first package of material was labelled 'Reminiscences of The Society for Psychical Research'. It was accepted for custody by the College after considerable correspondence, being received on December 1956. It was labelled 'Not to be opened until 1996'.

The second package of material contained important papers in connexion with the 'Cross-Correspondences'. In discussions with Professor Broad, Salter agreed to submit it to the then Master, Lord Adrian, on May 30th, 1963. After a considerable amount of negotiation and correspondence, the conditions of acceptance were finally agreed between him and the college in a letter from him to the Master of July 21st, 1963. The conditions of acceptance finally agreed between Salter and Trinity College were as follows:

The College will accept the gift of Mr W.H. Salter's 'cross-correspondence' material for the Library, on the condition that they are sent in a sealed case or cases; and with the assurance that they should not be examined until 1995, and that in the 6 months following the beginning of that year they may be examined by the donor's son, Mr Martin Salter, or by the representative whom he may have appointed for that purpose. If, within that period of six months, no decision to publish shall have been communicated to the College by Mr Martin Salter or his representative, the material shall become available for study or loan to any serious student whom the Librarian may approve.

The 1963 material consisted of:
Unprinted:

440

Mrs Verrall's original scripts from 1901 to 1906

Mrs Verrall's M.S. transcripts of her original scripts from 1901 to 1916

A sort of diary kept by Mrs Verrall, in which she recorded things that seemed to have a bearing on her scripts (9 vols).

Four books of transcripts (1906 to 1932) of the original scripts (including trance-utterances) of Helen Verrall

Helen Verrall's 'script-diary' (1 vol.)

A small quantity of letters and other documents relating to the scripts

An Index, by Helen Verrall, of Mrs Wilson's scripts (1 notebook)

Printed:

Printed volumes of scripts, with footnotes:
  (a) Mrs Verrall   4 vols
  (b) Helen Verrall   2 vols
  (c) Mrs 'Holland'   2 vols
  (d) 'Mrs Willett'   6 vols
  (e) Mrs Wilson   2 vols
  (f) 'The Macs'   1 vol.

'Notes and Excursuses', 8 vols with index

Introduction to the Study of the Scripts by W.H. Salter, 1 vol.

The Delta Case and two other volumes by Mrs Verrall relating to 'Mrs Willett'.

It has already been seen that the problem of safeguarding the security of the Scripts and other documents for the future had been looming with ever increasing urgency over Piddington's and Gerald Balfour's lives as they grew older and observed the destructive and disruptive effect of the war on every facet of society. Salter's proferred help had been more than welcome to them; he had injected a businesslike, calm and detached attitude to every question they had been faced with. When Winifred Coombe-Tennant died in 1956 and the question arose, some time after the obituary in *The Times*, of disclosing in a second obituary in the SPR *Journal* that she had been 'Mrs Willett', he obtained the necessary permission from her sons to do so. When Henry suggested that it seemed reasonable to give her the opportunity, if she had survived her death, to communicate the fact through a medium, it was Salter who arranged the proxy sittings with Geraldine Cummins. On May 26th, 1957, he sent Jean Balfour a copy of a note he prepared for Alexander and Henry Tennant concerning the SPR group of automatists, the Story and the Plan. He also included a summary of the long talk he and his wife Helen had had with Alexander when the latter had come to lunch with them at Newport.

A.T. came to lunch today and had a long talk with H. (Mrs Salter) and me. He brought with him two volumes (ledger size) of his mother's Journal, one bound in white, running from 6th March 1897–20th Sep. 1908: the other, in dark blue, from 3rd Jan. 1909–27th Sep. 1910. These he left with us: he took away with him from us, the following printed volumes of scripts:

M.V	4
H. V	4
Hld	2
W.	6
Macs	1
Wil.	2

Also, the typewritten notes O.J.L. [Oliver Lodge] had given us containing the parts of Myers' autobiography left out of the Fragments published after his death by his wife, and a copy of Note for Alexander and Henry Tennant [which Salter himself had drafted and of which this is a copy – J.B.] which he will send on to Henry.

The talk covered a wide field. The following points emerged:

(1) That Alexander, though very fond of his mother and looking on her as a 'genius', said that there had been tension between her and him. [For instance, Mrs Salter, later staying at Redcliff, Whittingehame, told Jean that with regard to his marriage a few years ago, Alexander had said: 'Before I could marry, which I would have liked to do before, I had to push my mother away from me.']

(2) That he and Henry were very different people both in intellectual capacity and temperament, but that they had drawn closer together in recent years.

(3) That there was a likeness between Henry and G.W.B. – [the Salters are not sure how far he (Alexander) intended this to include physical likeness.]

(4) That Henry would be more interested in the study of scripts and better qualified to understand them than he himself.

He knew that A.J.B. came into the scripts, and also about F.W.H.M.'s will and the mutilation of his autobiography. Being pressed by him, I told him that he had the Sidgwick copy of this, and that Lady Balfour had Lodge's copy.

As Lady Balfour had requested, we told him that she had received from his mother under protest her copy of the Willett script-volumes, and that she was willing to send them to A.T. [Alexander Tennant] if he wished, also that she had urged Mrs Willett to disclose her identity to her sons. Alexander said that he would leave it to Henry to accept the script volumes from Lady B. if he wanted them.

He said <u>he</u> would have no objection to the SPR disclosing his mother's identity. I mentioned that Lady B. had been working on a case relating to AJB in the scripts of several automatists: that these references, cryptic at first, became plain through his mother's scripts, and that if this was ever published, it would be essential that her name should be given.

[Signed W.H.S.]

May 1957. Draft copy of Mr W. H. Salter's <u>Note for Alexander and Henry Coombe-Tennant</u> upon the Scripts relating to 'The Story' and to 'The Plan'.

[Obviously this is based upon Salter's 1948 book on the interpretation of Scripts.]

May 1957
Note for Alexander & Henry Tennant (copy) by W.H.S.

This is an extremely complicated affair which this note is intended to simplify, so that you can more easily read up the voluminous literature.

I Composition of the S.P.R. group of automatists.
It began with Mrs Verrall (M.V.) starting to write automatically

in the spring of 1901, so as to give F.W.H. Myers an opportunity to communicate, if he could. He died 17th Jan. 1901: her first script was written on 5th March 1901 and her scripts continued till shortly before her death in July 1916.

In 1903 Mrs Holland (HLD) began writing. She was the wife of an officer serving in India, named Fleming and the sister of Rudyard Kipling. Her scripts continued till 1910, when her health broke down.

Also in 1903 Helen Verrall, now Mrs Salter (H.V.) began writing. Her scripts continued till about 1930, when Mr Piddington invited her and also Mrs Stuart Wilson (see post.) to discontinue as he had more to annotate than he could manage.

In 1908 Mrs Willett (I will continue to use this name) got in touch with M.V. in circumstances you have already learnt from 'The Delta Case'.

In 1915 Mrs Stuart Wilson (WIL) the American wife of Brig. Gen. Wilson (British Army) began telepathy experiments with H.V. Her scripts, which were contemporary records of impressions received before going to sleep, showed signs of connection with the scripts of earlier members of the group, of whom only H.V. was known to her. Her scripts continued until about 1930.

There was also a family group in Scotland, known as 'the Macs' (their real name was Mackinnon) who wrote a few scripts, that also fitted in, between 1908 and 1911.

All the scripts of the above automatists were privately printed in volumes edited by Alice Johnson, J.G. Piddington, Mrs Verrall and G.W. Balfour (who edited the Willett vols). After printing the originals were mostly destroyed; a few private scripts of Mrs Willett's were omitted from printing at her request (in the keeping of Lady Balfour), and a few scripts of H.V. written later than the last scripts in the printed volumes, (these are with Mrs Salter). We have duplicate sets of all the script volumes which we would willingly hand over to you. Lady Balfour has Mrs Willett's own copy of the vols. of Willett Scripts which Mrs W. insisted in giving to her which she accepted unwillingly as she felt they ought to belong to your family: these she will gladly send if you wish.

Besides the automatists already named, various other persons took part in the affair, but as their part was a minor one, their scripts have not been printed in extenso. They included (1) Dame Edith Lyttelton (Mrs King). Her scripts began in 1913 and are numerous: she gave the complete set of them to Mrs Zoe Richmond, who still has them and would let you see them if you wish. They are very hard to read.

(2) Mr & Mrs Richmond, who were great friends of Dame Edith's. Kenneth Richmond died in 1945: J.G.P. was engaged in indexing his scripts up to the time when he became too old to continue, and they are not fully annotated. Zoe Richmond's scripts may be said to be telepathically in close touch with his (her husband).

(3) Mrs Piper, the only professional medium concerned.

(4) Mrs 'Forbes'. She was really Mrs Raikes, wife of Judge Raikes: there was also Mrs Howe[?] and a few others. Some of their work was published in SPR Proceedings.

II The contents of the Scripts involves a Story and a Plan.
(1) The group of 'communicators' who revealed the Story.

M.V., as already said, wished to give <u>Myers</u> an opportunity to communicate and her early scripts until the end of 1904 are mainly concerned with communications from him: she had of course known him very well. Her scripts are polyglot, consisting largely of tags of Latin, Greek and English quotations, giving an appearance at least of intelligibility. By putting together bits which fitted, a fairly clear meaning can be found. References are made to unpublished writings of F.W.H.M.'s, which she had never seen, in particular:

(A) passages in his privately printed autobiographical fragment in which he describes his love for 'Phyllis', and the effect on his character and outlook on life of this love, and her death in 1876, i.e. several years before he met his wife. [These passages were unfortunately suppressed by Mrs Myers when she published 'Fragments of Prose and Poetry' in 1904.]

(B) The summary of Plato's Symposium printed on pp. 113–115, written by Myers, in 'Human Personality', which was published in 1903. It would interest you to read the suppressed portions of Myers' autobiography: we could lend you our typed copy of this, made by Sir Oliver Lodge & given to us by him. Also a note I made several years ago, on the references to 'Phyllis' in H.V. scripts. Myers' posthumous envelope opened in December 1904, contained a statement that if he could return to earth he would revisit the garden of the country house where he met 'Phyllis'. M.V. scripts of July 1904 had predicted that the contents of this envelope would refer to a passage from the Symposium. There was no patent connection between the scripts and the posthumous message, but a definite although indirect connection between them can be traced.

Besides Myers & 'Phyllis', the communicating group consisted of Henry Sidgwick and Edmund Gurney, who with Myers, were the principal founders of the S.P.R.; Francis Maitland Balfour, elder brother of G.W.B., who was killed in an Alpine accident in 1882; Mary Catherine Lyttelton, who died on Palm Sunday 1875; and Laura Tennent, of the Glenconner family, who was the first wife of Alfred Lyttelton, and died in 1886.

The references to the two last-named are cryptic in M.V. scripts and she did not recognise them. There were also cryptic references to Arthur Balfour, who as a young man had been deeply in love with Mary Lyttelton (M.L.). These references to M.L., A.J.B. and to some curious particulars connected with her final illness, death, and burial, only became intelligible many years later through the more explicit references in Mrs Willett's scripts beginning Palm Sunday 1912. This is one of the most important developments in the whole affair. Thus the identification of this group of seven, i.e. Myers, Sidgwick, Gurney, F.M. Balfour, 'Phyllis', M.L. and Laura, constitutes what is called 'The Story'.

(2) The Plan.

This group of seven, all dead when the scripts began, is represented as being engaged in one Plan of worldwide importance. They are not represented as being the only persons so engaged, but as a group standing in a special relation to the group of automatists, and to the group of interpreters, i.e. G.W. Balfour, J.G. Piddington, Alice Johnson, etc. Many other persons, not named, are said to be acting with them, and friends dying since the scripts began, such as A.W. Verrall & S.H. Butcher, are regarded as additions to the group.

The ultimate purpose of the Plan is to bring about a state of peace between nations and of social justice. This was of course a matter of great interest to Mrs Willett [(x)] but there are clear references to it in the quite early M.V. scripts. The allusions are made in various ways, especially through references to the predictions of the 'Pax Augusta' to be found in Vergil's Eclogue (4th) and several passages of the Aeneid e.g. I 257–, VI and VIII.

Before, however, this can come about, two things must happen: first, there are to be wars – note the plural. This is all discussed in Piddington's paper, in Proceedings XXXIII, which you should read. Second, a breed of human beings fit to live in a world of peace has to be born. This is a matter of 'psychological eugenics' as the scripts call it, in which the pioneer psychological work of Gurney, and the researches in genetics of F.M. Balfour, will be of importance. This is concisely treated by H.V. in a talk she gave [to] the American S.P.R. in 1950; a summary is printed in A.S.P.R. Journal for April 1951. We can lend you this: it might interest you.

A very difficult problem of interpretation is connected with 'psychological eugenics'. Is the Plan intended to produce a race or breed of 'children of the spirit', fitted to introduce the Age of Peace, not of course a race in the national sense, but a number of persons with the requisite gifts of mind and character?

Or has it a more restricted personal aim?

Different passages in the whole body of scripts could be quoted to support either interpretation. The wider aim seems to me to be supported by Vergil's lines 'Romanos, rerum dominos, gentunque togatam' ['Romans, lords of the world, the race that wears the toga'], in early M.V. scripts. Mrs Willett's scripts, however, favour the more personal view, and point with increasing emphasis, first to Alexander and then to Henry as being of very special, one might say, unique importance in the Plan. In this view G.W. Balfour, interpreter of her scripts, concurred; but some others, who have read the scripts, H.V. and I, for instance, and I believe Lady Balfour, are not entirely convinced.

I have said nothing about cross-correspondences. There is no doubt that in the main the exposition of them in Proceedings XXI, XXII, etc. is correct as far as it goes. In the light of later developments in the scripts, however, they cannot now

447

be regarded as isolated incidents, or as the most important elements in the scripts: but they must be taken <u>with the whole scriptic context</u> as being inseparable from the Story and the Plan.

[signed] W.H.S.

(x) Note by J.B.: 'Why to her specially? I think that insofar as the Plan pointed to the world's betterment in terms of a great leader – an inaugurator of the Golden Age, it had her interest but apart from the personal aspect, it meant very little to her.'

In September, 1957, Salter wrote to Jean Balfour, expressing interest in her forthcoming book – obviously on the Palm Sunday Story – and reporting to her with characteristic caution developments regarding the 'second' Mrs Coombe-Tennant obituary and the early scripts obtained from Geraldine Cummins:

17/9/57

Dear Lady Balfour,
We hope all goes well with you and with your book

You may be interested to hear of recent developments as the disclosure of 'Mrs Willett's' identity. Alexander and Henry have now both given their consent to this, and it is proposed to put a short Obituary in the winter issue of the <u>Journal</u>. When the form of this has been settled, I will send you a copy.

We think it would be a good thing to tell Shackleton Bailey too, before he reads it in the <u>Journal</u>. We shall try to arrange a meeting with him early in the Cambridge term, & will show him the Obituary.

Henry, who is very sceptical about survival, wished before anything about his mother was published, to give her a chance to send him a message. It was possible to arrange for him to have an 'absent sitting' with Geraldine Cummins, who is now in Ireland. She was told nothing more than his name & rank, & that he wished to try for a message from his mother who had died 'some months ago'.

She has now sent me 3 scripts which strike both Helen & me as remarkable, & have impressed Henry still more. She has got on (1) to the name Winifred, (2) to the fact that she

448

wrote automatically, (3) that she was friendly with G.W.B., (4) that she met & recognised F.M.B. after death (this passage impressed H. and me a lot), (5) that a son aged 19 was killed in World War I & that her youngest (Henry) fought in World War II, (6) that she had been a J.P.

She has not so far made any allusion to her Welsh interests, her public work (other than as J.P.), her connection with Mrs Verrall, or (most surprising) Daphne.

With Miss Cummins I am always on the look out for cryptomnesia [the recollection of forgotten or supressed memories], which seemed to me to account for a lot of what she told me about my family some years ago. But the omissions seem to us to suggest that latent memory of Lodge's book Christopher does not come in to the story. On the other hand, she knew D.D. personally & D.D. was not always as discreet as she should have been.

It is the aptness of her appreciation of the psychological position that most impresses H. and me.

She joins with me in sending our best wishes, Yours sincerely

W. H. Salter.

Just over a month later Salter sent Jean Balfour a second progress report:

23/10/57

Dear Lady Balfour,

Mr Shackleton Bailey was here to lunch on Sunday, and we had a long chat. He does not think there is much to be done, by him, at the moment. I think myself there is a good deal he could do, if he had more time, by applying a fresh mind to some of the interpretations G.W.B. and J.G.P. placed on the scripts. He seemed to think that what was needed was to concentrate on a few outstanding points, like the Palm Maiden case in particular, and to a less extent, the Phyllis Story.

He took away with him a copy of my Introduction with a number of Misprints & slips corrected, & a few dates of recent events filled in: he had better keep this. He also borrowed my partly typed partly manuscript note on Phyllis.

When your book has been vetted by your family, it might

be a good thing if Shackleton Bailey, Helen and I all saw it, and then met again and talked it over. [This was done]* Geraldine Cummins has now produced seven scripts for Henry. They contain some very interesting material, partly romancing on her part, partly cryptomnesia, but some accurate statements on things which we don't see how she could have acquired normal knowledge of. As both in her scripts and in conversation it was quite clear that she knew that Mrs Coombe-Tennant was 'Mrs Willett', I thought it sensible to tell her that straight, and also to tell her, what I should think she had certainly known at some time, that she was sister-in-law to Mrs F.W.H. Myers, whose first name [Eveleen] had come more than once in the scripts. Odd there has been no mention, or even hint, of Daphne, & Christopher is always called by his first name, George, which hardly anyone used.

Henry & Alexander are critical but up to a point, impressed. They have agreed the wording of a short notice of Winifred to appear in the next but one issue of the <u>Journal</u>. We will send you a copy in proof.

Helen joins in good wishes.
Yours sincerely,
W.H. Salter

* Inserted by Lady Balfour.

A third report was sent to Jean a fortnight later:

6/11/57

Dear Lady Balfour,

I don't think there is any urgency in returning the two vols of ASPR <u>Proceedings</u> as they are not at the moment in great demand. If they should become so, you will get a reminder from the Secretary, who will also charge you the postage in due course. [He never did!]*

On looking through one of Geraldine Cummins's books (<u>Unseen Adventures</u>) I find that she evidently saw a good deal of D.D. in 1938 & 1939 & that in the latter year D.D. took her to Fishers Hill for a sitting with G.W.B. & B.B., both of whom were of course discreet.

450

[Doubtful about this]*

I doubt however whether D.D. or any one else, until quite recently, ever definitely identified Mrs Willett with Winifred C.T., but I think her mind, both conscious & subconscious, is very quick at putting together scraps of information. The realisation of the identity came to her, I suspect, gradually & as a result of some kind of telepathy, possibly from me, combining with subconscious memories of what she had picked up from D.D., and also from Mrs F.W.H. Myers whom she knew, but not intimately.

Helen is giving a talk on apparitions to-night to the Cambridge S.P.R.

Yours very sincerely
W.H. Salter

*Inserted by Jean Balfour. There is also a note by her in the Salter letter saying: 'In answer to my question – how did Miss Geraldine Cummins know that Mrs W. = Mrs Tennant? Had she known D.D. and could D.D. have told her?'

It has been revealed that Jean Balfour, at intervals throughout her life, set down her thoughts on paper regarding Henry and Alexander Coombe-Tennant, their mother Winifred (in particular the psychological differences between Mrs Willett and Mrs Coombe-Tennant), her own changing perspectives on the interpretations of the scripts by G.W.B. and J.G. Piddington and the probability of the Plan ever achieving reality. (It is of course well known that writing a memorandum is one of the best ways of assessing one's understanding of a complex situation. An even better one is by writing a textbook!) In her notes, Jean included various other topics. Now, having long had full confidence on the good faith and sound advice of Salter, she sent him two of her latest attempts at this exercise. His replies are of great interest, giving as they do his opinion of her work and also his own measured viewpoint on a number of the topics.

The Crown House,
Newport, Essex

Dear Lady Balfour,

I have found your paper 'Thoughts on Mrs Willett' exceedingly interesting, & so I have no doubt it will prove to future students of the scripts, if there ever are any! My personal knowledge of her was negligible, a short day at Cadoxton in 1919 when Helen & I were taking a holiday at Gowar [*sic*], but putting together what it said about her in G.W.B.'s comments on her scripts, and what Helen said of her, I formed an impression closely corresponding to the picture you give. I think if I had known her better I should have disliked her intensely.

As you know I have parted with all the privately printed volumes, but from extracts I made from the Volume of N. & E. which gives at the beginning a list of important dates, I think there are some errors on pages 13, 14 & 15 of your Notes: Perhaps you would check these pages against the N. & E. volume.

p.13   Christopher born 1897, killed 1917, so 20 years old approx.
        Daphne born Jan. 1907, died July 1908, <u>18</u> months old
   14   Mrs W. became Associate of SPR in <u>1901</u>, resigning 1905
        I think as to 1905 you confuse her & Mrs Myers, who was certainly an SPR member long after that, until her death, which occurred in 1937, if I remember right
   15   Henry is described as the 4th son: he was 4th child but 3rd son.

I think on p. 16 where you refer to the book 'Christopher', you might mention Oliver Lodge's authorship. p.17. I do not know when Alex learnt of Henry's paternity. You will remember telling Helen & me about it on our visit to Whittingehame in the autumn of 1945. We had not seen Henry since his undergraduate days, or we might have guessed it sooner.

I think I must summon up energy to write a personal impression of Mrs Verrall. Fishers Hill was too inclined to underestimate her. Her only defect as an automatist was, I think, her good nature, which led her to wasting time and energy in all sorts of experiments with other automatists, often with no results.

It was natural for her to discuss Helen's scripts with her, when Helen, then aged 20, began her automatism & might have felt nervous about taking up a practise still often supposed to be uncanny. They should after a year or two have dropped it. I do not think its continuance in fact appreciably distorted the product of either of them, but for evidential purposes they cannot be regarded as independent; i.e. no cross-correspondence between those two would have any significance. This would not however affect any situation in which a third person, Mrs Holland, say, or Mrs Willett were involved.

I have always thought the communication of their, & also Mrs Holland's, scripts to Mrs Willett a great mistake.

As to the 'sacrifice' topic in the scripts, I did not of course deal with this in the <u>Rose of Sharon</u>, but I believe that 'Those Above' (to use J.G.P's convenient phrase) do preach it, however one shrinks from accepting it except in a very allegorical way. I told J.G.P. I disliked (as H. and her mother did) the idea that Daphne had been born just to die 18 months later, & J.G.P. said, 'Would you say that, if it was the only way to bring peace to the world?' Helen, probably voicing her mother's views, also took the script doctrine to be that there were three attempts to produce a human being well balanced in mind, soul and body, (1) Daphne, in whom soul outweighed body, (2) Alex, body outweighing soul & (3) Henry well-balanced body and soul, with mind too. As a doctrine H. was prepared to accept it, provisionally; i.e. if Henry brought it off.

In the <u>Rose of Sharon</u>, I referred to but did not press the Lycidas quotations, which are however remarkable. H.V. 52 of 22/11/07 Once more ye laurels (the first line of <u>Lycidas</u>), Mac 1 (19/7/08 the day before Daphne's death) Age me I fondly dream. Mac 8 (26/7/08) Lesbian shore. These last two phrases are the first and last words of the section of <u>Lycidas</u> referring to the death of Orpheus, the son of a muse, i.e. a goddess, who could not save him from death. The parallel is in my opinion with Daphne whom Those Above brought to birth but could not keep alive.

Oddly enough Mrs Verrall, annotating this Mac script, did not give the <u>Lycidas</u> reference, but attributed 'Lesbian shore' to a passage from the Myers autobiography in which he recalls a visit to that island. This I am sure is wrong.

In short, with a few reservations I am prepared to accept the interpretation of the scripts put forward by G.W.B. & J.G.P. <u>as a true interpretation</u> without any great assurance that it is objectively true. It can, by and large, be supported, as interpretation, from the scripts of the other automatists, leaving Mrs W out of account. My principal reservation would be, not as to children of the Spirit, but as to particular persons, Henry or another, being the spiritual children of particular persons, A.J.B, the Palm Maiden, or any other pair. It seems to me that, apart from Mrs W., the scripts point, as you say, to something more universal. That A.J.B. and Mary L. come into both Story and Plan is certainly stated in the scripts of Mrs V & others, but not as having, I think, that particular function. That notion is probably due to Mrs W.'s maternal megalomania, reinforced by her snobbery to which you rightly draw attention.

I doubt whether anyone trained in modern psychology would make a better job of it than G.W.B. & J.G.P. did. Psychologists, academics or medical, can be extremely narrow-minded, & do not mostly have as much literary flair as those two had. But those two had their failings: Helen used often to say to J.G.P. (she was too much in awe of G.W.B. ever to criticise <u>him</u>) 'You wouldn't say that if you were an automatist yourself'. Also she thought they underestimated people's ability, especially women's ability, to put two and two together.

I have often wondered what Mrs Sidgwick, and what J.G.P. personally thought of Mrs W. I never discussed her with Mrs S., but got the idea that J.G.P., though he said nothing definite, did not much care for her: he did however impress on me that her automatism was genuine.

Well, all we have to do is to wait another 30 years until all the documents are made available for general examination: will it be in the light of a New World Order?

With renewed thanks for showing me the Notes.

Yours sincerely,

W. H. Salter

Mr Salter's comments on the paper about Augustus Henry arrived in January 1967:

The Crown House, Newport, Essex.
14 Jan. 67

Dear Jean,

I am most sorry to hear of your flu & hope it is now passing off. So far this winter I have escaped flu and other ailments, except, earlier in the winter, some recurrent digestive upsets.

The papers you have sent me are of absorbing interest, both the letters and your summing up the position as to Henry. It is rather like some of the old fairy tales in which the hero receives at birth every sort of endowment, except one. In his case health, good looks, physical courage, first-rate brains, but not somehow what our ancestors called, if I may be excused the vulgarism, 'a fire in his belly'. He may have been born with that, and had it damped down by 'smother love'. I still think he may do something really important. It would be something if he could tidy up religion so as to make it really alive to most thinking people all over the world (N.B. I am not an enthusiast for what is called 'South Bank Theology'.) There is perhaps more possibility of advance towards reconciliation between nations on that line, than on more definitely political lines. I ought perhaps to say that I am not particularly devout & have a traceable anti-clerical bias.

Winifred's wish, as expressed in her letters, that her sons should marry, surprises me, as I understood from Alexander that he felt a good deal of opposition in that quarter. [True. J.B.] I doubt whether she would have been, over a long period, a comfortable mother-in-law, though she evidently had a proper appreciation of Jenifer.

I am sending you under separate cover my copy of Ian Stevenson's book on reincarnation. There need be no hurry in returning it.

Yours sincerely,
W.H. Salter

W.H. Salter died on July 21st, 1969. He was in his ninetieth year. In his passing the SPR lost a devoted friend and colleague whose knowledge of the history and day-to-day administration of the society was equalled by no other living member. Probably, more than anyone in his generation, he worked to maintain the society on the course on which it was originally set by its illustrious founders. It was not in pursuance of any preconceived theory of his own that he became deeply involved in psychical research, mastered the subject and in addition to his own work spent much time and energy helping others to further their own enquiries. Apart from his papers and books, still of great value in helping to form some appreciation of the importance of the Cross-Correspondences in psychical research and the understanding of human personality in all its multifarious ramifications, his meticulous attitude to the subject, never going beyond what, in his considered opinion, the evidence justified, embodied the best traditions of the law and science.

Though much of this Chapter material is taken from the Kremer Archive, Salter's own published work gives ample evidence of the intelligence, knowledge and character of this remarkable man. His obituary by Professor C.D. Broad, and the additional tributes to him in the pages following Broad's, demonstrate his capabilities and the value of the work he performed for the Society for Psychical Research and for psychical research itself. Although he could never have been classed as a member of the Sidgwick Group, his views are all the more important for that, for it enabled him to form a firm opinion, calmly and without their emotional investment, about the plausibility of their deductions. He also knew Henry Coombe-Tennant and his brother Alexander and had a number of meetings with them as a consequence of the *Swan on a Black Sea* Case.

20

Swan on a Black Sea

Is there an entity called a soul that rises like a swan above the Black Sea of Death?

Swan on a Black Sea, Geraldine Cummins

In the ecclesiastical study there were seven clergymen waiting for her including the Bishop of Kensington, Dr Maude and Prebendary W.O.E. Oesterley of King's College, London, the most eminent theological scholar of that time in England. A thunderstorm began to crash outside and the fear that she would not be able to achieve anything in the presence of such cautious and critical witnesses and in such disturbing conditions threatened to destroy the automatist's calmness. The clergymen were not by nature condemnatory or hostilely sceptical but in the circumstances who could have blamed them, for the woman claimed to produce scripts purporting to be from people who had departed this life almost eighteen hundred years before.

But on that day in the year 1925 the fears she had fought night after night to dispel before the test were displaced by a merciful tranquillity once she was seated at the table. Before her was the supply of blank paper; she shaded her eyes with one hand and waited, pen ready. The other silent occupants of the room were forgotten, the storm raged unheard as she became attuned to the Messenger and for an hour and a half the writing continued, the pen moving swiftly over the paper until some 2500 words had been written. As each sheet was filled with the script, it was passed by the attendant sitter to the witnesses for a first assessment. That section of automatic writing ultimately became part of *The Scripts*

457

of Cleophas, one of a number of books such as *Paul in Athens* and *The Great Days of Ephesus* written under similar circumstances.

Geraldine Cummins was proud of her Celtic ancestry. Born at 17 St Patrick's Place, in Cork, Ireland, she was satisfied that not one Cromwellian settler figured in her racial past. Her parents, Professor and Mrs Ashley Cummins, came respectively from an old Irish clan and a family, the Aylmers, who arrived in Ireland from Cornwall in the eleventh century. Her father was Professor of Medicine at the University of Cork. One uncle became Professor of Botany at the same university while another was Professor of Pathology at Millbank. Two brothers and two sisters likewise became members of the medical profession. She believed that it was probably her medical environment that gave her the insatiable curiosity as to the nature of man which haunted her all her life.

Geraldine was a member of a large and intelligent family. She had four sisters and six brothers. All six brothers served in the First World War, two of them being killed in action. She was privately educated, in succession among her teachers being two resident English governesses and a French mademoiselle. Her insatiable curiosity supplemented their mixed educational legacies by forays into the Cork Public Library where she devoured works of fiction, Irish tales and plays. Her interest in psychic phenomena was first aroused at the age of five when her father's coachman, John Dempsey, told her in sober terms stories of fairies and ghosts he claimed to have seen.

Small and wiry in build, she excelled at sport playing football, tennis and cricket, and by the age of eighteen had won her place on the Irish Women's international hockey team. Unlike many psychics, she does not seem to have experienced psychic events from an early age. She claimed that she only saw one ghost but even so, she knew from youth onwards that human beings were not simply flesh and blood and that the mind was more than a mere function of the brain.

Geraldine's early ambition to follow a career in medicine changed to a desire for a career in literature. She wrote plays in collaboration with Miss S.R. Day and at the age of twenty-two experienced the joy of seeing one of them, *Broken Faith*, being rehearsed by the poet W.B.Yeats and the playwright Lennox Robinson at the Abbey Theatre, Dublin. She also wrote an Irish peasant novel, *The Land They Loved*, and also produced short stories, articles and book

458

reviews. But it was the product of her other life as a psychic and automatist for which she is renowned.

Towards the end of the First World War she was working in the National Library in Dublin and staying with Mrs Hester Dowden, a highly educated woman, who was also a musician and a medium. Evening experiments with a ouija board led to Geraldine getting messages, messages she evaluated with a healthy scepticism. An alleged control, by name Astor, became a regular communicator and took on the role of Miss Cummins' personal control. She herself, with a true Irish spirit of independence, expressed her dislike for the word 'control', maintaining that Astor never controlled her but likened the guide to Socrates' 'daimon' who advised him.

The experiments also included attempts at psychometry and her psychic talent was undoubtedly helped in its development by such sessions. Her really active psychic work, however, began when she met Miss E.B. Gibbes in Chelsea. A large, frank, strong-minded English woman and a member of the SPR, she had a thorough knowledge of the methods of psychical research and had sat with Mrs Leonard, Mrs Blanche Cooper and most of the leading mediums in London. She recognised the power of Miss Cummins's psychic gift and took remarkable steps to encourage it, to study it scientifically and to protect its possessor. In truth, for the next quarter of a century she largely devoted her life to Geraldine. She took her to live in her London house for about eight months in each year; she watched over her, helped her talent to burgeon, kept exhaustive records of all sittings and spent an enormous amount of time and labour in checking on the evidence obtained by her protégé. An important part of her role was to filter the stream of would-be sitters, allowing through for the most part only those she felt to be in real need. She also ensured that after her death Geraldine should have the use of her house for the rest of her life. A month before she died on December 18th, 1951, Miss Gibbes implored her friend to give up any further attempts at literary work and devote her time to her psychic work.

Geraldine Cummins herself has described the complete contrast between the ways in which her literary work and her psychic writings were obtained. Her literary work was always a long and painful struggle, composition being difficult with much revision being required. By no means was it spontaneous. Often the output of seven or eight hours' work amounted to no more than 800 words. These labourings of the conscious mind were in marked contrast to the process by which she received script when in an hour and a half she might write 2000 words. She would sit at a table, cover her eyes with her left hand, concentrate on stillness and then, in her own words:

> soon I am in a condition of half-sleep, a kind of dream-state that yet, in its peculiar way, has more illumination than one's waking state. I have at times distinctly the sensation of a dreamer who has no conscious creative control over the ideas that are being formulated in words. I am a mere listener, and through my stillness and passivity, I lend my aid to the stranger who is speaking. It is hard to put such a psychological condition into words. I have the consciousness that my brain is being used by a stranger all the time. It is just as if an endless telegram is being tapped out on it. The great speed of the writing suggests actual dictation, as though some ready prepared essay were being read out to my brain. But something more than the faculty of amanuensis seems to be required. Whatever intelligence is operating, it may use my subconscious mind as an interpreter, may communicate in the language of thoughts or images and not of words.

With her right hand resting on the block of foolscap paper, her state of mind being a slight trance or dream-state, her hand then began to write. Her control Astor would make a few introductory remarks then announce that another entity was present and waiting to speak. It was the task of the person sitting beside Miss Cummins to remove each sheet of paper when it was filled up. Miss Gibbes, whose job this very often was, would do so, quickly lifting up Geraldine's right hand to the top of the new blank sheet so that the writing could continue with no perceptible break. Invariably the automatic writing was larger than Miss Cummins' normal script, no gap being left between words. The paragraphing and punctuation had to be inserted later.

Her total output of script was enormous over the years, covering a wide variety of subjects, people, places and eras. In her psychic work the scores of people who appeared and purported to have survived death were markedly convincing. As Rosalind Heywood, herself a talented sensitive, put it:

Outside the Irish scene [her work] showed little talent for characterisation. As against this her automatic writing produced authentic-seeming early Christians, a Frederic Myers convincing to his friends Sir Oliver Lodge and Sir Lawrence Jones... an Australian Ambrose Pratt and above all, a Mrs Coombe-Tennant (Mrs Willett) of whom Professor C.D. Broad has written that 'the very marked personality which emerged in the scripts' seems to him, 'as a largely external but not wholly ignorant observer, to fit like a glove' the Mrs Coombe-Tennant he had known.

By 1932 when her book *The Road to Immortality*, was published, Geraldine had become well known as a respected psychic. The book, purporting to be a description of the afterlife by Frederic W.H. Myers, communicated through Miss Cummins' hand, remains after seventy years one any searcher after truth should study. Sir Oliver Lodge, in his preface to the book, points out that neither Miss Cummins nor Miss Gibbes new Myers personally. Yet Lodge's examination of the scripts convinced him that they were in many respects characteristic of Myers, his ideas, mode of expression and worthy of his intelligence. Lodge also had sittings with Mrs Osborne Leonard at the time and found that the Myers communicator through Mrs Leonard not only claimed to be speaking through Miss Cummins but communicated many of the same views. In particular the Myers communicator on one occasion tried to describe the ways in which those on the other side attempted to impress their thoughts on the automatist's or medium's inner mind (it is of interest that the Myers and Gurney communicators through Mrs Willett gave not dissimilar descriptions of the *modus operandi*):

The inner mind is very difficult to deal with from this side. We impress it with our message. We never impress the brain of the medium directly. That is out of the question. But the inner mind receives our message and sends it on to the brain. The brain is a mere mechanism. The inner mind is like soft wax, it receives our thoughts, their whole content, but it must produce the words that clothe it. That is what makes cross-correspondence so very difficult. We may succeed in sending the thought through, but the actual words depend largely on the inner mind's content, on what words will frame the thought.

461

If I am to send half a sentence through one medium and half through another, I can only send the same thought with the suggestion that a part of it will come through one medium and a part through another... We communicate an impression through the inner mind of the medium. It receives the impression in a curious way. It has to contribute to the body of the message, we furnish the spirit of it. In other words. we send the thoughts and the words usually in which they must be framed, but the actual letters or spelling of the words are drawn from the medium's memory. Sometimes we only send the thoughts and the medium's unconscious mind clothes them in words.

A second book, *Beyond Human personality*, published the following year, continued the Myers communicator's attempt to describe the afterlife. There are those who say that mediumistic material is all waffle and banal, pious blather. Such critics of mediumistic material, facilely dismissing all of it as worthless, have obviously never read these two books or indeed much of the highly intelligent metaphysical conversations held by Lodge, Balfour, Hodgson and other investigators with communicators claiming to be Gurney, Myers and Sidgwick.

During these years the material for eight books was received which became collectively known as 'The Scripts of Cleophas'. Given by communicators who called themselves the Messengers, it described historical events in the rise of Christianity during the first century AD. These scripts were subsequently published as *The Scripts of Cleophas*, *Paul in Athens*, *The Great Days of Ephesus*, with other volumes in the series. Those who say that Miss Cummins' undoubtedly literary talent simply gathered everything she had ever read about the early Christian church and unconsciously dramatised it do not even begin to understand the nature of the problem. A wealth of historical, geographical, ecclesiastical facts, many of them decidedly obscure, appears in the material. Expert English and Scottish theological scholars who studied the scripts testified to their accuracy and deep knowledge of the times. For example, Dr W.O.E. Oesterley, Professor of Hebrew at King's College, London, pointed out places in them where casual references were made to the local government of Jerusalem. In one case, the word 'Archon' is used, correct as the title of the head of the Jewish city communities, but it had only superseded the former title 'Ethnarch' in 11 AD.

462

Again, all relevant early literature, including the New Testament, gives the name of the High Priest of the time as 'Annas' (the Greek form) whereas the Jews of the day would have known him as 'Hanan', the form used in the scripts. Miss Cummins' patchy education had been such that she lacked the required knowledge of Greek, Latin or Hebrew history to fabricate these scripts, consciously or subconsciously, unless one falls back on the old super-ESP hypothesis and says that by some such means, her dramatic will fished for the necessary facts in the minds of great theological and ecclesiastical scholars. In fact, the problems raised by this automatic script are similar to the problems set up by the novels Mrs Curran produced by automatic writing. Ostensibly composed by the entity Patience Worth, they, likewise, especially the first one, 'A Sorry Tale', set in the time of Christ, were packed with veridical details and facts of that era Mrs Curran simply could not have learned in any normal way.

But who or what were Cleophas and his fellow scribes who communicated their accounts of life in the early Christian church? If they were not dramatisations by Miss Cummins' subconscious did they once live and were they recalling correctly events in their own lives? The Myers entity, who dictated the scripts that formed *The Road to Immortality* and *Beyond Human Personality*, had himself firm views on their nature. They were a response, he said, to the hunger for spiritual truth in the hearts of human beings traumatised by the tragedy of the recent world war. A group-soul in the afterlife responded, one composed of the scribes of Cleophas. 'Myers' went on to say that no age vanishes or passes away completely. The experiences and beliefs of the men of that age are imprinted on the Great Memory. The group-soul of the Cleophas scribes put the medium in touch with the relevant parts of the Great Memory in the belief that it was giving to the world the help it required. Nevertheless, 'Myers' was careful to add that the group-soul was not necessarily infallible, nor was the Great Memory a totally true account of what actually happened in those early days of the Christian church. It was 'not as it was, but as man imaged it, in the heart of the universe'. Again, he says 'Cleophas might be described as a unit, and yet as many ... he is the expression of a certain stage in the long journey of evolution, of a number of fervent Christians who lived in that early period. He is not an individual, as are the souls of those who have of recent times passed over. He is a collective soul ... and he is able to draw from the Great Ether Memory the pageantry of that early Christian period; not as set down by a cold detached historian, but as the passionate outpouring of fanatical and holy Christians, who strove to state in writing their own emotional view of the period in which they lived.'

Other kinds of psychic work were being carried out by Miss Cummins in those years: experiments in precognition, psychometry and sittings with Miss Gibbes or those whom Miss Gibbes felt were in real need of help. Geraldine continued the last category after Miss Gibbes's death. In that last category of psychic work she on occasion had 'drop-in' communicators who gate-crashed the sittings, those communicators being unknown to herself or any of the sitters. One such case is instructive and, to put it mildly, extremely difficult to fit into the super-ESP theory.

Scripts were received for a 'Mrs Grant' (a pseudonym) and were posted to her. In them a Dr Tomlin gave names and facts about himself, his wife and daughter. A number of the facts were unknown to Mrs Grant, who had them verified by Dr Tomlin's daughter. The daughter confirmed that her life as given in the scripts was accurately described and also that not only had she never met or heard of Miss Cummins but also knew no one acquainted with Miss Cummins but Mrs Grant. Miss Cummins wrote of this case:

According to one anti-survival theory, Dr Tomlin was extinct as an individual, and I was merely stealing his neatly tabulated memories from an alleged Common Unconscious. But how then in these scripts did this static Great Memory demonstrate a very active survival in Tomlin's case, showing his characteristic jealousy of his daughter's husband and exhibiting in unscrupulous action an agitated mind tormented by hatred and frustration?

This case and others show that when an intruding stranger is driven by a powerful emotion of love, jealousy or hatred he appears to be able, through its power, to overcome all difficulties of transmission and to be able to convey verifiable facts, as did Tomlin. His active, hate-driven mind endeavoured with threats to break up the happy marriage of a living couple. We do not seem to have static existence in the Hereafter, but continue our progress either for evil or for good. I felt extremely

464

repelled by the unpleasant personality of Dr Tomlin and I stopped his later attempts to write through me.

For many years Miss Cummins collaborated with Dr Connell, a Fellow of the Royal College of Physicians, Ireland, on the diagnosis of the hidden background to patients' mental illnesses. She practised psychometry on a sheet of the patient's handwriting and an object belonging to the patient sent to her by Dr Connell. The patients suffered from a wide variety of ailments, including claustrophobia, anorexia nervosa, alcoholism, or a number of obsessional neuroses. Miss Cummins never saw the patient. Her diagnoses were sent to the physician who was thus guided in his treatment of the underlying causes of the patient's distressing state. In his book *Healing the Mind*, Dr Connell described a number of these experiments and their outcome.

It goes without saying that all of this work by Geraldine Cummins and her collaborators is still worthy of careful study by psychical researchers. And it is only by comparing the forms her psychic gift took with those presented by other sensitives such as Mrs Piper, Mrs Leonard, Mrs Curran, Mrs Garrett and Mrs Willett that we can begin to see 'family resemblances' and detect features that hopefully will lead us to a more complete exploration and understanding of the dark continent of the human psyche.

In Geraldine Cummins' case, however, one section of her work stands out, a section that has intrigued and fascinated all who have encountered it. It is the Cummins–Willett scripts, published in Cummins' book *Swan on a Black Sea*. Edited by the biographer Signe Toksvig and with a foreword by Professor C.D. Broad, it is a series of forty-four scripts received through Miss Cummins' hand over the period August 1957 to March 1960 and purporting to come from the surviving spirit of Mrs Winifred Coombe-Tennant.

Before considering the circumstances in which the scripts were written, the opinions of two people who studied them are worth quoting. Dr R.H. Thouless, former Reader in Educational Psychology, a fellow of Corpus Christi College, Cambridge and a former President of the SPR, wrote in the foreword: 'I find this series of scripts of absorbing interest. It seems to me to be the strongest evidence for a real communicator that I have ever seen. It shows ... the great gifts of Geraldine Cummins as a medium (or interpreter), although its success may also be attributed to the unique gifts of

Mrs Tennant as a communicator.' Broad, fellow of Trinity College, Cambridge, a philosopher with an international reputation, an expert in all aspects of psychical research and soon for the second time to be President of the SPR, also wrote in the foreword: 'I believe that these automatic scripts are a very important addition to the vast mass of such material which prima facie suggests rather strongly that certain human beings have survived the death of their physical bodies and have been able to communicate with certain others who are still in the flesh.' These are strong statements from two people of high intelligence and qualifications, wellknown for their professional and innate caution in pronouncing firmly on *any* matter.

We have seen that Mrs Coombe-Tennant ('Mrs Willett') in particular was closely involved in the Palm Sunday Case which to many has given strong support to the belief that the communicator Mary Lyttelton was trying to transmit to Arthur Balfour her undying love for him, and her longing for his reunion with her on the other side of death. Winifred Coombe-Tennant died on August 31st, 1956 at her home in London and the following day her obituary appeared in *The Times*, giving a full account of her long and active life of public service. But it was not until December of the following year that a closely guarded secret of almost half a century's duration came to light in a further obituary. It was published in the *Journal* of the SPR and revealed for the first time that she had been 'Mrs Willett'.

The Cummins-Willett scripts were initiated by Mr W.H. Salter, the Honorary Secretary of the SPR. He had gained the approval of Henry Coombe-Tennant to reveal Mrs Willett's identity in the second obituary published in the *Journal*. As we have seen, Henry himself, though at this time a disbeliever in survival, felt that if it was possible, he should give his mother a chance to communicate from the other side if she had indeed survived. He therefore asked Salter if he could arrange proxy sittings with a medium of good reputation. In other words, he did not intend to be present during the sittings. At this time his older brother Alexander knew nothing of this approach and had no idea of Mrs Willett's true identity until subsequently informed by Salter.

Salter wrote to Geraldine Cummins on August 7th, 1957, almost a year after Mrs Coombe-Tennant's death, asking her, as an experiment, to try to get a message from a deceased mother for her son:

The Crown House, Newport, Essex.
7 August, 1957

Dear Miss Cummins,

A member of the S.P.R., who lost his mother some months ago, would like to give her an opportunity of sending him a message. I believe that this is a case that would interest you evidentially; I mean because the circumstances are peculiar. I am wondering whether you would be willing to consult Astor on his behalf.

I certainly should not wish to press on you any work that you might find a strain, but the facts so far known to me are definitely curious and of a kind to rouse your keenness in the search for convincing evidence. Would you let me know how you feel about it?

Perhaps you might feel moved to have a try while in Ireland. By the end of the year the evidential significance of the case will probably have declined through the publication of some facts at present known to very few persons, so that if you were so good as to try for a message you might feel disposed to do so fairly soon.

I should propose to restrict the information given you to the name of 'the absent sitter', so as to make a success all the more striking.

My wife joins in good wishes and hopes that your health will benefit from your stay in Ireland.

Yours sincerely,
W.H. Salter.

Miss Cummins agreed to Salter's request and in a second letter dated August 22nd, she was given a little more information.

Crown House, 22 Aug. '57

Dear Miss Cummins,

The member about whom I wrote to you, Major Henry Tennant, expresses himself as most gratified that you consent to try for a message from his mother. He has sent me four papers in her handwriting. Would you prefer to have these sent to you open for inspection, or would you for evidential reasons wish to have them forwarded in a sealed envelope?

Yours very sincerely,
W.H. Salter.

467

Miss Cummins had met Mr Salter twice and had corresponded with him. The request from such a distinguished researcher persuaded her to try to get one or two scripts, though in the event she preferred to try without the specimens of the mother's handwriting. Nevertheless, as Montague Keen puts it, she was 'far from enthusiastic. She was over 70 at the time the scripts began, "tired, busy, preyed upon by an ailing family and somewhat scared of the cold-blooded approach of the SPR", according to Rosalind Heywood, who knew her well (Heywood, 1965)'. In the event, she quickly produced from her home in Ireland three scripts. In a letter to Jean Balfour, Salter records that, while he and his wife Helen considered them remarkable, they had impressed Henry still more. Indeed the personality of the script communicator so intrigued Geraldine Cummins herself that she went on to obtain a total of forty-four.

It was not until she had completed six that her attention was drawn to the obituary that appeared in the SPR *Journal* in December 1957 and revealed her identity as Mrs Willett. But by September of that year, Geraldine had already become practically certain that the formidable, intelligent communicator who had already given so much data concerning her life was the medium known as Mrs Willett. At the end of October, Mr W.H. Salter called on Geraldine and acknowledged that Mrs Willett had in truth been Mrs Winifred Coombe-Tennant.

A study of the first six scripts reveals a very large number of details correct for the life and characteristics of Winifred Coombe-Tennant, her family and friends. The first three scripts are by Astor, Geraldine Cummins' guide, who describes Mrs Willett at first as an old woman who even in her new state surprises the guide by her speed in organising herself, going over the memories of her life, conveying recollections about her sons and facing up to the possibility that she may have been too possessive in her love for her youngest son. Names are given, 'Wyn' or 'Win', 'Gerald' partly Scottish, English mother; a person, 'Francis' who died young in a fall in a foreign country. She transmits her name 'Winifred', the name of her son 'Henry', that he fought in World War Two, that she had been a magistrate.

From script four onwards, this forceful communicator, unflinching in her self-criticism, takes charge of the automatist's hand and mind and reflects upon her life, so that even before script seven, by which time Geraldine Cummins had been told that Mrs Willett had been Mrs Winifred Coombe-Tennant, names and episodes in the family life and in the psychic career of Mrs Willett had come pouring out through Miss Cummins' hand. In particular may be mentioned Cadox Lodge, Morganwg, Dorothy, Eveleen, Fred, Charles, the Cambridge group, all highly relevant to Mrs Coombe-Tennant's life in both its aspects. Script six, September 26th, 1957, in particular, demonstrates clearly and movingly Winifred's yearning to explain herself to her youngest son, offering no excuses but anxious to convince him of her continued existence and undying love for him:

Astor is here. Winifred has asked to be allowed to write to her son one more letter. She tells me that she endeavoured to communicate through other mediums since her passing, that she knocked at Mrs L.'s door and sought also Mrs W.H. She says that she finds it very difficult through not always knowing what has been picked up and what has been missed. How far the medium has picked up what might be likened to radar signals.

(Writing changes.)

Winifred T.
My dearest H.
I want this to be a personal note and to make in it my little confession to you. I long more than anything to convince you that I am alive and no longer the tiresome old lady, but Winifred in her prime. To do this my friend Gerald B. advised me to give general facts about the family and myself in this way. But today I shall write more intimately.

Three sons were mine and I ask myself did I fail them when they were growing up. I am rather worried about that. There was my eldest, George. My pride was mingled with love for him. Pride was, I think, a fault in my character.

Perhaps that was why his loss in the war was such a blow. My pride as well as my love was abominably hurt by it. Then, being older than you, Alex was more self-sufficient. But you were so small, so completely mine, my creation. The sight of you playing somehow helped me back to life. But I must not dwell on that time as I want to make my confession.

I feel that during the times you three were growing up in

469

those important early years of your early life I was not enough with you, and when I was with my children I expressed too little of that deep love I felt for them. If I failed, for this failure forgive me. I see now my weakness. I was the victim of several fears. I will write of one fear in particular. When you were children I had a fear of being too possessive in my love for you. A mother's possessive love can do more injury to a son's character than anything else she can do to him. I had the example before me of certain members of your father's family. One was your aunt Eveleen. She had inherited from an ancestor, the financier, a terribly possessive instinct. He satisfied it by acquiring possessions, making a great deal of money. But Eveleen satisfied the same instinct by loving possessively. She used to be so jealous if her husband paid any attention to any particular woman. He was a saint, and she failed to injure him through her possessive love. But it was different in the case of her son L., when he was a boy.

She has now in this life slowly and painfully realised how much she injured L. in his early years through her possessive love for him. It has indeed been her purgatory to see how much she contributed to the ruin of his life on earth, and how unhappy were the consequences for him after his death. His suicide led to him being plunged into darkness and isolation here for a very long time. L. had as well inherited the instability of abnormal possessiveness from his mother. It was not expressed in the desire for property, money, but in other ways and in a self-centredness. But I cannot go into these details now. It is sufficient to say that your aunt Eveleen's possessive love even led her subtly to antagonise the boy L. against his father. His father was idealistic, devoted to spiritual things, so L., disliking his father largely through his mother's jealous influence, became a materialist when he was a man. Later in life he developed a passion for a very beautiful married woman, who also was spiritually minded, and of course rejected his passionate possessive love. All this – her spirituality, his father's spirituality, failure to possess this woman, drove him to unbelief and gave him a tortured mind. Eventually he took to drugs and, as you know, killed himself. That is a mortal sin. He took into this life his crude ego that hated and hated, and denied love. So he suffered much. Poor Eveleen some time after coming here

470

had to perceive, as we all have to, the consequences resulting from her life on earth. She saw how much she was responsible for her son's ruined life on earth. She has been very brave about it and, though her reception by L. was grim, she sought him out and tried to help him out of his hell of her and his creation. She has done much to improve things for him.

But now you may ask, why do I tell you all this about Eveleen and L. her son? It is to explain things in connection with myself. Long ago, quite soon I perceived intuitively more than by reason the harm Eveleen was doing through her possessive love. So when you were all children I tried to avoid possessing you, tried to make you three independent little mortals. But I may have gone to the other extreme and not showed you enough of the deep love I felt for you. So forgive me please if I failed you in loving when you were a small boy.

I am thankful that your father did not inherit from that ancestor as unfortunate Eveleen did. But bear in mind always that the danger in the T. family is this possessive instinct. If it is there, it is a force that can be used for good as well as for evil.

St Paul was so right when he said 'We are members one of another.' We cannot live a day on earth without affecting in some way some person in our circle. The little builds into the great as time goes by, and our influence may precipitate some other soul's downfall, through the accumulation of the little, through the building up of the bricks of time.

And indeed there can be much jerry-building, bad workmanship, thin walls that crash into ruins.

Now I have preached enough, my dearest, to you. But I may not have another opportunity to write of these things and they are important.

Gerald B. has been so good to me, helping me to make all this out so that you may understand .

'I need not send my love as it is with you always.

G.C. Pray give this to W.H. for my son.'

(Note: Script is endorsed as follows: 'This script was written at Woodville, Glanmire, Co. Cork, on 26.9.57. Iris A. Cummins.')

All the names in the script are readily identifiable. 'H.' of course is Henry, Winifred's youngest son. Gerald B. is Gerald. George was her eldest son, killed in World War One. The material about Eveleen, Mrs Coombe-Tennant's sister-in-law, is exactly right in its description of her possessive, jealous attitude to her husband Frederic Myers, and her son Leo ('L'), who committed suicide in 1944. 'Mrs L.' refers to Mrs Gladys Leonard and Mrs W.H. to Mrs W.H. Salter, the former Helen Verrall, the daughter of Mrs Margaret Verrall, both of whom Winifred had known. 'W.H.' is of course W.H. Salter.

As the weeks and months passed, the scripts continued to come from the Winifred communicator, sometimes one a day, sometimes after a gap of a fortnight. They ranged fully and accurately over Winifred's life on earth and it seemed that the communicator in some way was being presented on request with scenes from her life as if staged before her. The development of her personality in her family and public life and her work with Lodge, Gerald and Arthur Balfour and the other psychical researchers is not only described vividly in the scripts by her but in an unflinchingly honest manner. Her continued effort to meet the challenge of convincing Henry of her existence on the other side is couched in a humorous and wry acceptance that she, in a sense, as she puts it, is on trial – the former magistrate is in the dock!

Many of the experiences she claims to have had since she passed over are of extreme interest. Mrs Coombe-Tennant was a very old woman when she died. Almost all the people she had known and had worked with as Mrs Coombe-Tennant or as 'Mrs Willett' had died long before her. Now she claimed to have met many of her old friends and renewed those friendships, for all the world like someone who had arrived in a country his or her friends emigrated to long ago and is catching up on their experiences there. One meeting, however, was not successful. The death in 1908 of Winifred's young daughter Daphne had been a shattering blow to her. If we are dealing in truth with the survival of death, then Daphne had been in the afterlife for some forty-eight years when Winifred herself passed over. In script 19, Winifred described her devastating disappointment when she had a meeting with Daphne, grown-up, a stranger, indifferent to her mother with no apparent daughterly affection for her. 'Perhaps after all', muses Winifred, 'any connection with her was only through the physical maternal link, but how powerful that can be. I deeply mourned her death.'

Other meetings were more rewarding. In script 7 she recalls how:

Many years ago I spent a strange hour in a room being one of a trio. We were listening to great music. All was peaceful. But music did not carry me away. It peopled the room with the invisible dead. But at first I felt rather than perceived their presences. As I know now, I became linked with the third in the trio, the deeper mind of a living man, who was resting and relaxing and appeared to be half asleep. And suddenly the presences of the dead I sensed became one visible presence from another life. I saw nothing ghostly. It was as real to me as my hand – simply a woman wearing an old-fashioned costume. She was of another period. But I want you to realise that it was the third of the trio – this old man of eighty years or so – who gave me the power in some curious way to see this young woman, so attractive, the embodiment of youth, who literally shone down upon him as she stood beside him – rays of a hidden sun, as it were, emanating from her body, as she stood looking down at him.

To me the effect was utterly strange, non-human, yet in appearance she was wholly human, with hair thick and beautiful. In that period women cherished their long hair, of course, she was so dated by that dress she wore. But the old man was old enough to be her grandfather, yet he was her contemporary and I felt from this illumination she cast upon him that she loved him not as one loves a grandfather, but as a woman loves a man greatly of her own generation. He so ancient and she so young, yet they had been young once together. There's a riddle for you! But I later learnt that I had seen and described to my companion, the second in the trio, one dead many years. That this vision of mine meant much to this old man who was lying down resting oblivious of this visitor. She was of his early manhood, and there had been no other in his long life! Incredible, you will say. But when I met him, he was cold and austere, and I was in awe of his admirable intellect. He had schooled himself, punished himself, like a flagellating saint, and so had kept himself immaculate for her.

473

That scene I have described took its toll of me. As she you will call the ghost appeared beside the aged man, I felt myself slipping, fading, passing into the sleep of trance. Oh! I was always afraid of losing control, of being banished. It meant I might unfit myself for my work in life, which was dear to me. So I struggled frantically to keep my hold on my self. I got back, but that meant the ghost disappeared.

My companion learnt from me what had happened, and imparted my experience to the old man. For me, then, it removed their masks. I looked into their souls and perceived behind the aloof manner there was within warmth and a fine humanity; they were not by any means merely intellect and courteous manners.

So that memory I drew out from the cupboard was still informed with life, because of the emotions roused by the coming of the lady into my perceptive life. Oh! How strong their emotions were! The younger man was devoted to the elder man and was moved because he was moved by my presentation of the presence.

Brothers are seldom so linked. But they were.

It is important to note that this script, written on February 14th, 1958, gives correctly a wealth of information concerning the experience Mrs Coombe-Tennant had during the visit to Gerald Balfour's home on October 16, 1929. This experience was mentioned briefly but not explained in detail in Gerald Balfour's *Study of the Psychological Aspects of Mrs Willett's Mediumship*, published in 1935. A full description did not appear until the publication of Jean Balfour's *The 'Palm Sunday' Case* in February 1960.

In script 8, written on February 15th, 1958, Winifred speaks with great happiness of the reunion of Mary Lyttelton and Arthur Balfour on the other side.

A quite early experience of mine, after I had left behind me my ancient bones and become a risen mind, was to meet and be greeted by the gracious youth of the lady with the old-fashioned dress. She deliberately adopted the cast-off shell, put on the ancient costume and appearance in order to re-introduce herself, and thank me for imparting faith in her resurrected self to that wearied, bored and apprehensive man

I described in the early scene of the trio listening to the music thirty or more years ago.

Words commonly used have such different meanings for people. There is the ancient definition of man – spirit, soul and body. I prefer to call what spiritually influences composite man for evil or for good the anti-self, for it is not egocentric, it is not literally incarnate. It is outside the human being and reveals itself to him only in flashes. It can be inspiration, intuition, prophecy, even wisdom, and these flashes are used for evil or good by the receiving human being.

There is, you may not know, gossip in this life. I shall gossip now.

I have encountered A.J.B.'s friend. I am free to tell you of their intrinsic inviolable unity. They shared the one anti-self, while consciously separated by her early death.

So many years parted after her passing. An emptiness, a dissatisfaction continually then for him. No joy. He merely put in time with hard and varied mental work. Such faithfulness, such patient waiting. Then at last, after sixty years or fifty by the clock, the meeting at the other side of death when his old age dropped from him like a ragged garment. But oh! It was well worth while to wait so long for that event. If they had not been parted by her death, he would never have worked with that industry, that brilliance that made a name for him. Work was his escape for intolerable memory. Oh! He was so idle before she passed.

If she had lived, she would have been his all-absorbing play-mate, life brilliant in the sunshine of just being, instead of doing, instead of a rough path each followed solitarily of struggle, and in his case of fine achievement.

But hers was also fine; they tell me that she remained waiting, waiting at the border for him, returned from the higher level, at what sacrifice! A world so tempting, beckoning, but she ignored it. She put all that away from her so as to meet an old man's soul. Therefore it need hardly be said that she was the first to greet A.J.B. when he came home to her. A lonely man throughout his life until then. They have gone to that other level together. Happiness incomparable for them...

Now I can't hold on.

Winifred T.

What can we make of all this? The total sceptic clutches to himself or herself the multi-coloured comfort blanket of hoax or monumental gullibility and wish-fulfilment acceptance by ostensible psychic and investigator, or limitless super-ESP coupled to a super-talent of unconscious dramatisation. But surely, not even the most shameless sceptic will tout the explanation of coincidence to 'explain' the work of the great mediums? In the case of the Willett-Cummins scripts, Montague Keen has with characteristic care and industry listed in a table some of the data given in the scripts of particular dates and assessed their accuracy. The table he sent me speaks for itself as a total negation of the hypothesis of coincidence:

Script 9, February 16th, 1958
'Mary' and 'Dear George': a reference to her parents. *Correct.*

Derwen House, W's grandfather's house which she visited as a small child. *Correct.*

The youngest child. W. was *the youngest child.* [She had older half-sisters.]

Had elder sister to play with. *Correct.*

Desired to paint. *Correct.*

Script 10, February 17th, 1958
'Margaret', the name given to her by the medium's control, Astor, who summoned and guided the recently reborn spirit. *This was in fact W's second name.* 'Eveleen' and 'Dorothy'. These were the correct names of two of her three sisters-in-law. Both sisters-in-law were disdainful of the 22 year gap between their brother and W. *Correct.*

Dorothy's husband was famous for his African exploits. *Correct. H.M. Stanley's meeting with David Livingstone had made him a household name.*

Gertrude, her mother-in-law's name. *Correct.*

1908, the year of her first great loss. *Correct. This was the year of Daphne's death.*

1918. A year of great change. *This followed the death on the Western Front of her son Christopher and her decision to throw herself vigorously into public life.*

Relative neglect of children 1918–19??. *This was a period of intense public activity for W. both in Wales and internationally.*

Talking in the talking-shop of Geneva. *She was the first woman*

476

delegate from the U.K. to the League of Nations, whose activities and endless conferences eventually appeared to bore and disillusion her.

Script 11, February 18th, 1958
Widowed in 1928. *Correct.*

Concern over Henry's residence at Eton. *Correct.*

No ancestor in the male succession had ever been a soldier until Henry. *Confirmed by Henry.*

They came from the heart of Yorkshire. *The Coombe-Tennants did come from Yorkshire.*

Henry's service as an officer in the Guards. *Correct.*

Comment on Alma Mater. *Correct as a frequent reference by W. to Cambridge University.*

Script 12, March 1st, 1958
[This has a good deal of unpublished evidence in which W. discusses correctly certain changes in the family surnames and some events in her son's life, knowledge of a property owned in Africa by a member of the family, and names relevant to the problem of a career. Details, however, are currently unavailable.]

Script 13, March 2nd, 1958
Detailed description of W.'s quarrrels with Mrs Ford. *Correct. Likewise Christian names and initials of surname and place names.*

Identification of Henry as a bachelor. *Correct.*

W.'s role in the Cross-Correspondences for thirty years. *Correct.*

W.'s account of the Palm Sunday event at Arthur Balfour's bedside. *This was so vivid and detailed that Geraldine Cummins initially took it to be subliminal fiction from her own psyche.*

Script 16, April 16th, 1958
Correct reference to the Salters' Elizabethan home, which was unknown to G.C.

Script 17, April 19th, 1958
References to Lob (derived from a cricketing term to represent

the Lyttelton family, whose members were prominently associated with that game). *Lob was the name W. applied specifically to the headmaster of Eton, a member of the Lyttelton family, whom she disliked.*

Another member of the Lyttelton family is correctly identified as having married Edith. *This was a correct reference to Dame Edith Lyttelton who had succeeded Laura as Alfred Lyttelton's wife.*

A second Edith was married to another Lyttelton, Bob, and was known as D. *This is correct. Dame Edith was known as D.D.*

Script 18, April 20th, 1958

A reference to 'the Presbyterian Churches preserved the Welsh Language under Cymanfa Gyfredinol'. *Remarkably no attempt ever appears to have been made to check the accuracy of this highly specific name. According to the General Secretary of the Presbyterian Church of Wales, 'The term Y Gymanfa Gyffredinol refers to the General Assembly highest court of the Presbyterian Church of Wales'.*

References to W.'s work at music festivals and picture exhibitions in Wales. *Correct.*

Script 19, May 3rd, 1958

Sudden death prompted the resumption of W.'s automatic writing. *Correct. This was Daphne's death in 1908.*

Staying with 'Pry – Pryse ... in their lovely country house.' *Pryce was the maiden name of Mrs Douglas Fawcett at whose country home Winifred used to stay soon after she married in 1895.*

Closeness of W.'s attachment to Helen Salter's mother, Mrs Margaret Verrall. *Correct.*

Correct date given of birth of Alexander Coombe-Tennant.

Script 20, May 4th, 1958

W. correctly notes and sardonically comments on the inverted commas placed round her name in a second letter to her via G.C.

W. refers to her querying as a child the appropriateness of the prayer to be delivered from sudden death: one in which she never joined. *A.C.T. confirms that his mother used to omit this prayer. Miss Barrington's [S.P.R] Journal critique cites this as an example of the strain such information places on the subliminal recollection theory.*

W. refers to being bullied and coerced by 'Myers' and 'Gurney' in January 1909 to write scripts. She did so, from 'Myers', but the results were so private she did not even tell Mrs Verrall, her chief confidant. *This is true, but has been unknown until now.*

W.'s account of Myers' pre-marital love for Annie Marshall is given correctly.

Eveleen Myers' role as secondary to the long deceased Annie in Myers' love is discussed. *The effect this had on her and her conduct is correctly described.*

A number of small but highly significant passages in the scripts have been overlooked by commentators, chiefly because their importance could be recognised only through knowledge of events unknown at that time. In Script 24 (June 8th, 1958), for example, which was an entirely unprepared response for information about W.'s sittings with scientists, she writes: 'Fred, my brother-in-law, wrote in that fateful year of 1909 that he was going to make me hear without my writing.' This is now apparent from the accounts which at that time were still unavailable.

End of extract from M. Keen Table

Nevertheless, neither Montague Keen's table nor the account of the Willett-Cummins scripts given in the present chapter can do justice to the importance of these scripts and their analysis and assessment given in the book *Swan on a Black Sea*. To the open-minded person who reads it, a person perhaps unfamiliar with the field of psychical research, it becomes akin to one of those archaeological treasures stumbled across that leads to the uncovering of a vastly greater horde – the careful and patient study by psychical researchers of the mediumship of the great sensitives.

And as one proceeds in the study of the field, one finds that to invoke the notion of a hoax involving so many, in so many countries, and by so many cautious and intelligent people of good reputation is simply untenable – as untenable, indeed, as the idea that all these mediums were brilliant frauds investigated by gullible, happy-clappy researchers. In the end we seem to be forced back again upon some version of the classic three theories – survival, the super-ESP theory and the William James cosmic reservoir theory, with the super-ESP theory puffing along breathlessly, singularly failing to keep up with its two strolling companions.

There is one more point that demands attention when we confront the Cummins–Willett scripts, one best expressed in Professor C.D. Broad's typically dry tones:

> If there be an after-world, the scripts must present an extremely narrow and peculiar corner of it. All the persons whom we meet in them are particularly cultured and intelligent members of the English upper or upper-middle classes, whose earthly lives were lived in a certain brief period of English history. It is platitudinous, but not superfluous, to point out that most human beings are not Victorian ladies and gentlemen, and that a good many of them are savages. Even if we quite arbitrarily confine our attention to our contemporary fellow-countrymen we must remember that a certain proportion of them are actual or potential criminals; that a much larger proportion are feeble-minded or neurotic or downright crazy; and that the vast majority of the rest are more or less amiable nit-wits, with no intellectual or cultural interests whatever. If all or most human beings survive the death of their bodies, there must presumably be, among the many mansions of their Father's house, places prepared for such as these. And they must be very unlike those gentlemanly and academic apartments to which alone the scripts introduce us.

Swan on a Black Sea spurred three important contributions to the SPR *Journal* between June 1966 and December 1967. The first contribution, by Mary Rose Barrington, discusses the question 'How much could Miss Cummins have known?' and lists four questions she believed merited particular consideration:

1. *Could Miss Cummins have known that Mrs Willett was Mrs Coombe-Tennant?*
2. *Could she have been aware of expressions used in the Balfour paper: 'Study of the Psychological Aspects of Mrs Willett's Mediumship' (Proceedings May 1935)?*

3. *Could she have known details of the A.J. Balfour – May Lyttelton love story (Palm Sunday case, Proceedings February 1960)?*
4. *How much could Miss Cummins have known about Mrs Coombe-Tennant's personality and private life?*

In her adopted role of devil's advocate, Mary Barrington answered these questions as best she could, attempting to show that Cummins could have amassed over many years, a host of memories from many scattered human and documentary sources, the stored memories being fragmentary and beyond the ability of conscious effort to recall. In our absence even today of the necessary knowledge of the powers of the mind and brain, we cannot state that they could not have been associated subconsciously like the pieces of a jigsaw, becoming capable, when Miss Cummins was in trance, of being used to dramatise and produce a very reasonable representation of Winifred Coombe-Tennant. Barrington also gave a number of specific details that, if answered by people involved in the case, would provide a better understanding of the paranormality or otherwise of the case. Nevertheless, she adds: '... it is meaningful to say that if Winifred is Miss Cummins' fiction, then some of the Winifred material must have reached the medium's mind by some very improbable ways and means; to say that however improbable the ways and means, survival must be considered even more improbable is not meaningful.'

Alexander Coombe-Tennant responded to her paper in a long letter, published in the *Journal* of the SPR in 1966, that went a long way to answering a number of the points Miss Barrington had raised. It is a valuable response and is given here in full:

Sir, – Certain questions of fact have been submitted to me, as possessor of the diaries of the late Mrs Winifred Coombe-Tennant, by readers of Geraldine Cummins' *Swan on a Black Sea* (Routledge, London, 1965). The questions are principally concerned with the reproduction in two places in Miss Cummins' scripts of wording to be found in Mrs Coombe-Tennant's private diaries. The relevant passages are these:

(a) *Script 23, June 7th, 1958, p.86.* 'Now I am travelling a road beyond Dollygelly, up through wooded glens. One emerges from them into the warm sunlight. And here come the wide

481

spaces; far below the climbing road lies a great sweep of lowland country, placid and silent. In the distance the mountains stand massive and aloof, a blue wall stretching along the west.'

Annotation to Script 23, p.88. ' "Dollygelly" is mentioned in a diary. A[lexander] T[ennant] says the view is marvellous beyond it.'

(b) *Script 26, June 13th, 1958, p.96.* 'I think that my son's question refers to a number of sittings I gave to Sir Oliver Lodge in 1910. I wrote scripts dictated to me at them, but I also repeated messages aloud.

'I must mention that I took part in my D.D.I. ("Daylight Impression") talks with my communicators. I continued to make remarks to my communicators at my first sittings with Sir Oliver, which took place when the Mayflower was out.'

Annotation to Script 26, p.100. 'In her diary for May, 1910, she mentions that the Mayflower is out. Page 55 in the Balfour Study mentions that she gave three sittings to Lodge in May, 1910.'

I will now take in turn each of the questions which have been raised, and answer them to the best of my ability.

1. *When were Mrs Coombe-Tennant's diaries first seen by anyone?*

My wife and I, who lived at 18 Cottesmore Gardens, London, W.8., from October 1956 to August 1962, opened the many tin boxes and safes after my mother's death at about the time of Suez in 1956. We merely saw that a small safe was filled with diaries, but we did not open any or read them at that time

I first read some of the diaries in the early months of 1958. My brother sent comments on a number of scripts to Mr Salter on 5th April 1958, and these incorporated some of my observations. I checked that there were many references in the diaries to a row with Mrs R. with whom my mother stayed during the war at Y. (*Swan*, p.52).

2. *Has Miss Cummins ever seen the diaries?*

I first met Miss Cummins in February 1960. On 23rd January 1960 she wrote to 'Alexander Tennant' at an address in Albert Court S.W.7., and the letter was sent on to me by a Mrs Tennant of that address.

When Miss Cummins came to see me at Cottesmore Gardens

482

I showed her some of the diaries and the book Christopher, which she told me she had never read.

3. *At what date did Signe Toksvig first see the diaries?*

Miss Toksvig first saw the diaries in the autumn of 1962. She came to London in September, and at my invitation subsequently stayed with my wife and myself. It was then that she had free access to the diaries, and discovered the correspondences between the diaries and the scripts.

4. *Can we be quite certain that at the times when (a) Miss Cummins first saw the diaries, and (b) Miss Toksvig discovered the correspondences between the scripts and the diaries, the scripts had been written and were out of Miss Cummins' possession?*

The early scripts (Nos. 1–9, August 28th, 1957 to February 16th, 1958) were sent by Miss Cummins to Mr W.H. Salter, but after my brother (Major Henry Coombe-Tennant) had written to Miss Cummins on 20th January, 1958 saying that the scripts were of interest and suggesting that she should try and continue the experiment, she began to send the originals of further scripts to H.C.T. direct. This is confirmed by a letter from Mr Salter to Mrs Gay written on 4th March, 1958.

Miss Cummins sent script 23 (June 7th, 1958), together with scripts 22 and 24, to my brother at the Hague, and he forwarded them to me on June 15th. Miss Cummins enclosed script 26 (June 13th, 1958) with a letter which she sent to my brother on June 15th; and my brother sent this script, together with scripts 25 and 27, which he had also received, to Mr Salter on July 14th, 1958.

[Here the *Journal* editor has appended the following footnote: 'Mr A. Coombe-Tennant has kindly shown me the correspondence concerned. Relevant extracts are these. H.C.T. to A.C.T. 15th June, 1958: "I enclose three scripts from Miss Cummins... The second script [script 23] contains some descriptive writing about Wales... There is another bit of childhood reminiscence about George Washington, which I cannot confirm." H.C.T. to W.H.S. 14th July, 1958: "I have received 6 scripts from Miss Cummins since I met you in London. The first two [22 and 23] are mainly about childhood memories, and the other four [24 to 27] are in response to a request that 'Winifred' should say something about her sittings with Lodge... So much for the first of the Lodge scripts [24]. The next three are enclosed... One point of interest is that Winifred corrects a misstatement in an earlier script about Christopher's education. In the script of April 20th, Winifred states, writing about the 'Lob' who was a headmaster of Eton, 'I was in awe of him but did not like him on the occasion my husband and I deposited our son in the educational establishment over which he reigned'. She now says that because she did not like him, she and my father decided to send Christopher to Winchester." This clearly refers to the contents of script 26. – Ed.']

The originals of all the scripts have been in the possession of my brother or myself ever since they left Miss Cummins' hands, apart from times when they were being examined by Mr Salter, or being copied under his direction.

Miss Cummins did not in fact see the diaries until February 1960, and the series of 39 scripts was completed on November 23rd 1959 (as is stated on p.140 of *Swan*). I think that she will have received from Mr Salter typed copies of the originals of the scripts from February 1959 onwards.

Miss Toksvig did not see the diaries until the autumn of 1962 (see above).

Some further questions are raised in Miss M.R. Barrington's article *Swan on a Black Sea: How Much Could Miss Cummins Have Known?* (*Journal* SPR, June 1966, 289–300).

1. *Is 'Dolgelly', which is spelled 'Dollygelly' in script 23 (see (a) above), spelled in the same unusual way in the diaries?*

'Dolgelly' is indeed misspelt in this way in the original of script 23; but I can find no evidence in the diaries or elsewhere that my mother ever misspelt it so. The annotation on p.88 of *Swan* is therefore inaccurate.

2. *Is 'Mayflower', which is spelled out with a capital 'M' in script 26, spelled with one in the diaries? (cp (b) above).*

The relevant extracts from the diary are as follows:

Wed. 25th May, 1910. 'Long to have time to rest and feel. Laburnum and pink May out in blossom, divine birds, scents, clouds!'

Thur. 26th May, 1910. 'Glorious weather, enchantment of the song of birds, the budding of the May, the scents and sounds of summer – contrasts – wrote to schoolmistress whose daughter at 7 died last week, God help her.'

484

These entries were written at Cadoxton Lodge, Neath, to which Mrs Coombe-Tennant had travelled on 24th from London. Oliver Lodge came to see her on May 6th, and the diary notes 'Second D. I.' On 21st diary notes 'Oliver Lodge 3rd D.I.'

There is no reference to 'the Mayflower' in the diaries, but only to 'the May' and 'pink May'. The annotation on p.100 of *Swan* is therefore not strictly accurate. It is impossible to say definitely if 'May' is written with a capital letter in the diaries, but my wife and I think that it is.

3. *Was Mrs Coombe-Tennant known to refer to the W.8. district as 'West Kensington' (as in Script 33)?*

Not as far as I know. I think that the reference to 'West Kensington' was an error.

4. *From correspondence in the SPR archives it appears that Mrs Coombe-Tennant was liable to spell 'across' as 'accross'. Are there any signs of the same mistake occurring in the scripts?*

My wife and I can confirm that in some of the diaries before 1913 the word 'across' is spelt 'accross'; but we have not found instances of this mistake in the scripts.

Alexander Coombe-Tennant

In the March 1967 issue of the *Journal* the correspondence continued with a useful input, by Geraldine Cummins herself.

Sir, – In Miss Barrington's study of *The Swan on the Black Sea* scripts in the Journal for June, 1966, she considers various theoretically possible sensory means by which I might have obtained information about Mrs Coombe-Tennant. There seems no point in asking for space to repeat my own unsupported recollections about myself: here, like the experimental researchers, I shall be believed or not according to the outlook of the enquirer. But I should like to give my recollections of the 'social contacts' which Miss Barrington fears might have enabled me to obtain such information, through lack of discretion in persons who knew us both. I would not wish what I believe to be unjustified doubts as to their discretion to arise as a result of scripts written by me.

Sir Oliver Lodge
I saw him twice. In 1932 he visited me for about half an hour

to offer to write a foreword for a forth-coming book of mine. We talked about the book. In 1933 he asked me for a sitting. He arrived looking very ill indeed and was with great difficulty helped up my stairs. His object was to ask 'Myers' views about a matter connected with Harry Price and the SPR. Having answered, 'Myers' began to describe his present situation, but Miss Gibbes noticed that Sir Oliver was looking so much worse that she cut short the sitting. He was helped down-stairs and into his car and, I believe, driven straight to his doctor. I never saw him again.

Dame Edith Lyttelton

She first came to see me in 1938, because she was interested in a book I had written called *The Childhood of Jesus*, which she reviewed very kindly in the *Spectator*. We talked about the book. On a second occasion she came to ask me to give a lecture about 'Influenced Books'. She also had two sittings in connection with her late husband, Alfred Lyttelton. At one of these a niece of Lord Balfour's, who had recently died, appeared to communicate. This led to the one and only sitting I gave Lord and Lady Balfour at Fisher's Hill in June 1939. Their alleged communicators were his niece and a sister of Lady Balfour, Lady Constance Lytton.

The Balfour Sitting

Miss Gibbes and I were met in the hall by Mrs Lyttelton and at once taken into the room where the sitting was to be held. Lord and Lady Balfour came in straight away, looking very old, and sat down without speaking. They did not speak a single word during the sitting and silently left the room when my automatic writing ceased. It was concerned with the manner of death of the young relative. At once afterwards we had a hasty luncheon, as I had urgently to return to London. We spoke a little about Ireland, which I was glad to do as I felt a great veneration for both Lord Balfour and his elder brother, Arthur, for the wonderful work they had done to prevent a second Irish Famine. There was neither time nor inclination to discuss personalities about whom I knew nothing. I left for my home in Ireland two days later. The War broke out in September. The Balfours died during the War, and I never saw them again.

486

Miss Gibbes

It is suggested that I might have looked through Lord Balfour's report on Mrs Willett's mediumship. Obviously I cannot prove that I did not. But it should perhaps be remembered that in those days it was a well known ruling by the S.P.R. that no medium could be a member, for fear that information gleaned, even in all honesty, from its literature might invalidate subsequent 'communications' through him or her. Miss Gibbes was an upright woman, a careful investigator and a member of the S.P.R., and certainly would have known this. Moreover, she always took particular care to keep from me *any* information she thought might reduce the value of my scripts.

Perhaps I should add that I do not take *The Times*. Indeed, I seldom read more than an occasional evening paper in London, or *The Cork Examiner* in Eire. But in many of these matters one can only get probabilities, not certainties, but, of course, I can not rule out that I did not subconsciously study the details of Mrs Coombe-Tennant's obituary in somebody else's paper opposite me in a bus. I was at home in Co. Cork in Ireland during August, September and part of October when *The Times* obituary appeared, so I could only have read it clairvoyantly. There are two more suggested possibilities which I cannot rule out for other people, though I can for myself. One is that my path, or indeed orbit, ever crossed with those of Mrs Myers, and that she discovered and spread abroad that Mrs Willett and Mrs Coombe-Tennant were one. But if she did, it seems very curious that it never reached the ears of Mr and Mrs Salter who were in contact with her relatives. The second possibility is that I might actually have met Mrs Coombe-Tennant. I can only say that I am quite sure that I did not, and enquiry will confirm that we lived in entirely different worlds.

My home was in Ireland and I was by profession an Irish Author and had published novels, short stories and articles about Irish country folk mostly talking in their picturesque dialect. Also at intervals I had Irish Plays of mine performed, three of them first produced in Dublin or Cork and a fourth at the Court Theatre, London.

Because of my Irish literary work, experiments in psychical research took a very secondary place in my life.

Geraldine Cummins.

The above contributions by Mary Rose Barrington, Alexander Coombe-Tennant and Geraldine Cummins were valuable. The correspondence thereafter tailed off into a point-scoring exercise by Dr Dingwall and the editor of the *Journal* was forced to apply the time-worn instruction: 'This correspondence is now closed.'

Geraldine Cummins died in 1968. She left an enormous legacy of material relevant to the age-old problem of the survival of bodily death. I am sure that much of that material was paranormally acquired. Those who have read and studied her output must form their own opinion as to its meaning; those who haven't must face the fact that they have no opinion of value whatsoever to offer about her work.

21

Letters from Henry

Shaken, but not stirred.

The Bond Martini

Heads in the clouds and feet firmly planted on the ground.

Henry Coombe-Tennant

In December 1966, Jean Balfour was living in Edinburgh. Twenty years had passed since the end of the war in Europe and the Far East but the world was certainly not at peace. In its icy grip, the Cold War had the human race by the scruff of its neck, forcing the principal players, the Soviet Union and the United States, into an ever closer eyeball-to-eyeball confrontation. Churchill's Iron Curtain split Europe, with NATO and Warsaw Pact powers on permanent alert on either side of it. Rank upon rank of ICBMs in their buried silos stood in a state of readiness, promising the death of tens of millions of human beings in the first few hours of transition from Cold War to Hot War. In the American air, bombers of the Strategic Air Command endlessly patrolled, waiting for the signal to take part in the mass retaliation, while under the waves of the oceans, submarines played cat and mouse with each other, many of them carrying an armament outpowering the destructive effect of the Royal Air Force's Bomber Command in the latter days of the Second World War. Across the world, each side bolstered up vile, repressive regimes, stifling the human rights of their oppressed and wretched populations, under the pragmatic, hopeful and ruthless philosophy that these regimes' leaders were our bastards, not theirs.

Even outer space and the Moon were not immune to this knife-edge threat of mutually assured destruction (known wryly by its acronym of MAD). Relatively few of the increasing number of artificial satellites now successfully launched by the Americans and the Russians were totally dedicated to scientific research. When the Americans in 1956 proudly announced that they would put into low Earth orbit a number of satellites dedicated to playing a distinguished part in the forthcoming International Geophysical Year, they were shocked when the Russians put Sputnik 1 in orbit on October 4th, 1957. Less than a month later, the Russians put up a half-ton satellite with the dog Laika in it.

It would be almost a year before the Americans got their space act in order, with the aid of Wernher von Braun, whose wartime V2 rockets, the first successful ICBMs, had bombarded London, causing almost as many deaths as those inflicted in the collapse of the twin towers of the New York Trade Center on September 11th, 2001. By now, astronauts and cosmonauts had orbited the Earth and John F. Kennedy had announced that before the end of the decade, the Americans would put a man on the Moon and bring him back safely. In the United Kingdom, the betting firm William Hill was offering 100 to 1 against a Russian being landed on the Moon by the end of 1971, 150 to 1 against an American and 2000 to 1 against anyone else. One can see from the odds who was the favourite at that time.

It was a world of stupendous scientific and technological achievements, far beyond anything the nineteenth century's Victorian scientists of the X Club could ever have imagined. It was a world of colossal dangers where the same types of political dinosaurs, flawed and fallible, struggled to control or extinguish incipient or actual conflagrations by pouring upon them the teacupfuls of their talents.

It was also a world that seemed utterly remote, Jean thought, from the Sidgwick Group and their hopes for Henry. Their world, the Victorian world, had still had momentum and relevance to last some way into the twentieth century, perhaps even until the end of the Second World War. But did their ethos and hopes have any relevance to the terrifying world that now existed, a world that made a despairing H.G. Wells at the end of his life write his last, deeply pessimistic work, *Mind at the End of Its Tether*? Was it even a remote possibility that in such a world, any one man could make any difference, could go any way towards solving the world's problems, could in some totally unexpected way implement the Scripts' promise of a glorious new era?

It was forty years since she had first met Henry Coombe-Tennant. In that time so many things had happened, including the deaths of Arthur James Balfour, Gerald W. Balfour, Eleanor M. Sidgwick, J.G. Piddington and Mrs W. Coombe-Tennant. The Palm Sunday Case had been issued in the SPR *Proceedings* in 1960 and Geraldine Cummins' book *Swan on a Black Sea* had been published in 1965. And Henry's career had taken a totally unexpected twist.

On two previous occasions since that first meeting with Henry, she had set down her thoughts in memoranda concerning him and those surrounding him and trying to influence him. The first time had been in 1931 when she had written the 'letter' to Henry, inspired by her realisation that he was Ral's half-brother, a letter that in the event had never been given to him. The second time had been towards the end of the war, when she felt such admiration for him for his military record and pity for his unhappiness. The time had come, she thought, to write a third memorandum. It might help to clarify her thoughts about him, his life and people's reactions to him. Many of the memories were very old but as archivist to the Sidgwick Group the letters in her possession would help.

Thoughts on Augustus Henry by Jean Balfour,
December, 1966, Edinburgh.

I met him first, soon after I married, in 1925, on one of his occasional visits to Fishers Hill, when he was still at Eton. Afterwards he was at Trinity, Cambridge, and then he went into the Welsh Guards: we saw him from time to time during all those years.

Many people thought he was the most beautiful human being they had ever seen, and it was probably true. He was extremely good-looking, tall, slender and well-built, with dark-brown hair, very fine deep-blue eyes, and a real 'presence'. Added to that, he had absolutely first-class brains, and was one of the most brilliant young men of his time at Trinity. Professor Broad thought most highly of him, and was very interested in his future: he had however a strong antipathy to his mother! I expect this was largely because Mrs Tennant was such a dragon where Henry was concerned, and was inclined to bother his tutors un-necessarily.

Henry's manners were gentle and he had a pleasant voice: but he was not a helpful guest, I used to think. He never made any effort to make a party 'go', and he had no 'small-talk', though he never omitted to open the door to a lady, for he was trained in social grace. He would listen attentively, but I never heard him contribute anything really interesting, or startling, to the conversation. I never saw him get really animated or 'worked up' about anything. We young ones of the Fishers Hill crowd felt that he was somehow above that, because he was so awfully clever! He was however fond of discussing philosophy and allied subjects and used to have lengthy talks with his god-father G.W.B.: these were subjects that didn't interest us. But I recollect having a discussion with him once on Dunne's book on Time, [*An Experiment with Time*, 1934], which interested him very much at the time when it came out: the date, however, was a good deal later than the period I am trying to remember just now.

I was told by Ral, my husband, that when they were all much younger, Eve would be admonished to look after Henry, and if he got very dirty, they all got into trouble with Mrs Tennant. In consequence they took delight in taking Henry on the grubbiest escapades, in which he got filthy, or soaked. What he really thought of the young Balfours, whether, when he was grown-up and I knew him, he really liked us, I don't know: I think he accepted us, as part of Fishers Hill, which was such a familiar place to him, and as he seemed to accept everybody, calmly. Years afterwards Mrs Tennant told me that Henry had always liked Ral best (and it is to be noted that Ral was so frail with asthma that he often had to stay behind from the more arduous adventures Eve organised) but I don't believe that Henry ever complained, or attempted to avoid Eve's society – which all goes to show what a <u>very nice</u> nature he was: and I never heard of him being unkind, sharp, or out of temper.

The young ones in the Balfour family cordially disliked Mrs Tennant, partly, I suppose, because she was so critical of them; partly, no doubt, because of the extraordinary way she brought up Henry, guarding him from wet & cold, which they found ridiculous; and also because, whenever she came, a great fuss was made over her, and she would be closetted with G.W.B. for private sittings. The generation to which I belonged, Mary, Eve and Ral, were all aware of the 'prophecies' concerning Augustus Henry, which G.W.B. and J.G.P. believed were to be found in the Scripts of the SPR group of automatists, of whom Mrs Tennant, as 'Mrs Willett', was one. Their mother B.B. [Betty Balfour] had told them. It was of course a great secret. Of course at that date I accepted everything as I found it: but years later, I wondered why their mother had told them something that was so secret and important?

I think the reason lay in the circumstances of that household in the Edwardian age. B.B. minded deeply her husband's infidelity; although she learnt to accept Mrs Tennant as part of life, she wished above all to hide it up. The child and his mother were a living sign, and the presence of Augustus Henry, so frequently at Fishers Hill, coupled with the fact that to his 'god-father' (G.W.B.) he was all-in-all, to the exclusion of his other son by B.B. (Ral), was suspicious to anyone familiar, but observant, in those days. I think that she was so afraid that the children might put two and two together and find out, that to divulge to them the secret of the prophecies concerning Henry was a safeguard, because it explained the interest focussing on the boy, and the reverence in which 'Mrs Willett' was held by the Fishers Hill trio (G.W.B., J.G.P. and to a very much less extent E.M.S.).

When in 1930, five years after my marriage, I told B.B. that we had guessed that Henry was Ral's half-brother, she said, 'I've never told anyone, I never breathed a word, all these years!'

The idea that Augustus Henry might be a superior being and that 'the people on the Other Side' had had a hand in his birth and spiritual constitution was not so strange in those days (from the end of the First World War, 1918, over about 14 years to Hitler's time) as it seems to us now. Granted we were all young and romantic, we were amused rather than critical and not in the least antagonistic. Sometimes, while brushing our hair at bedtime, we used to discuss with B.B. these ideas, that Henry had been born at the will of the Gods, and that he was destined to become a great world-leader, and inaugurate the coming 'Golden Age'. Nevertheless, as I recollect, there used to be an almost invisible twinkle in B.B.'s eye!

Her sister, Emily Lutyens ('Aunt Emmie') was an ardent theosophist and the expectation of a new Messiah was perfectly familiar to the Balfour circle. I think it is true to say that all over the world at that period, a movement existed creating a mental atmosphere, in which some sort of spiritual intervention in the affairs of the world was tacitly assumed: and lots of people held the belief that a universal Saviour was about to arise.

Not long after I married (about 1927 I think), 'Aunt Emmie' brought the young Indian Krishnamurti – the hope of the Theosophist movement – to Fishers Hill when I was staying there with my baby son Gerald. Krishnamurti was about 17 years old at the time, and one could not have met a more charming, gentle creature, full of wisdom and spiritual depth; but B.B. told me afterwards that G.W.B. was quite sure that Augustus Henry's prospects were quite superior! (Of course before long the Indian went off on his own to the U.S.A.)

So it must be borne in mind that the possibility of a remarkable human being sent by God was 'in the air', and we young ones were expectant, not to say convinced.

The first time I met Henry, when he was about 14 and at Eton, we had a conversation in the garden at Fishers Hill, about God and mysticism; and I remember that he said to me quite seriously, 'I have always felt my hand was held in God's.' I myself felt that I could tell him anything, and I liked him very much. Afterwards B.B. told me that Mrs Tennant very much approved of Henry's friendship with me(!) At a later date, when he was about 18, during his last year at Eton (for he remained there till he was 19, which _we_ always thought was too long for a public school) he came to stay with us for a Shoot at Whittingehame, and we tried some tabletilting, very unsuccessfully. Now it was with Ral that he was more intimate. In one of their conversations, recounted to me by Ral, he remarked that he could well understand the attraction of homosexuality, though it was not a temptation he found difficult to resist himself; for when it came to the question of beauty and aesthetic satisfaction he didn't think the female body was a patch on that of the male, and that he didn't feel himself to be stirred at all by the bodies of girls. Ral of course took a very different view of women.

Henry was a remarkably good piano player: he made a thorough study of Jazz, which about 1930 was coming from the U.S.A. with increasing popularity. He would play it by the hour! and later, in the Prison Camp in Germany, it was a solace to other men besides himself.

Again we heard a report that Mrs Tennant regarded us as being suitable friends for Henry, or words to that effect: but I remember reflecting that if I had not been safely married, she would certainly have been suspicious of me! Her influence over him was so profound and extended into every field – and yet I don't believe he ever noticed it; he did not seem to realise it until after the War, when he had led an independent life, so that when he returned to her side, he seemed to have quite quietly grown out of it. But my own opinion is that during those formative years, her influence was so strong that, unconsciously, it simply extinguished those sexual drives that bring about the individualisation of a young man.

The next time he came, again to shoot, during one of his leaves in the early days of the Second World War, Olga Petro was staying with us, and we were living in Redcliff. She could stir any man's blood, and she turned on all her charm; but afterwards, talking about him to Ral she remarked, 'I never met anyone like him: he's like an Angel, so very handsome and completely impervious!'

And I remember that at that time I began to wonder if that had been one of the aims of the 'Group over there' and of their 'psychological eugenics' – to create a human being who would be sexless?

Henry's worldly successes were great; he was picked for Army duties needing dignity and responsibility; he was acclaimed for the brilliance of his intellectual ability; he was respected, admired, and loved by many: but I never felt that he possessed that inward fire, and drive, that makes a great leader of men, nor did this ever show any sign of developing in him; and my doubt began to grow that perhaps the prophecies would never come off, or that the interpretation of them had gone amiss. Not that I consider sexuality necessary for inner growth, but there seemed to me to be some sort of psychological hold-

495

up – it seemed evident all through his character. His intellect was always ready to play on any question; but he was never emotionally involved, and I looked in vain for signs of the rebelliousness and mental adventurousness that one expects in the young and ardent.

Ral never had any illusions: as he grew older he became increasingly sceptical about the Scripts.

The Second World War started in 1939. What it meant to Mrs Tennant – that Henry should go to the Front, and be in danger, could only be imagined. It must have been Hell for her.

He was taken prisoner almost at once, and did not have too bad a time in the P.O.W. camp in Germany. I remember he told me afterwards that in Belgium, the Germans had such <u>lots</u> of prisoners, that an attempt [presumably 'opportunity'] to escape presented itself again and again, but that something seemed to inhibit him from seizing any of these opportunities – he did not really want to escape when it came to the point. He also told us that he was quite happy in the P.O.W. camp: his health for one thing was better than it had ever been before, and he put this down to the fact that all his life he had been given too rich food, and the sparse prison diet suited him! Also there was a piano there, on which he loved to play, and he was able to get books for study. In fact, when the question of his escape came up, he had not been interested in the idea and was only persuaded to join the trio, because one of them had taken ill at the time of departure, and they needed him to go together for the best advantage. It was a lengthy ordeal, needing considerable 'guts' but all went according to plan. I think it is true to say that his physical courage was never in question; and in this escape, which involved walking through Germany, across France, over the Pyrenees and into Portugal [in fact, Spain], the fact that he had had no preliminary training, like the other two, was never allowed to be a drag on his companions.

B.B. died during the War and G.W.B., with his daughter Nellie Cole, came to live in the cottage at Whittingehame. I think it was in 1944 in the summer before he died, that Henry came to see his godfather, and stayed 2 nights with us next door in Redcliff. G.W.B.'s joy was great: the flush on his cheeks made him look most lovely. They sat together peacefully, often without speaking for long periods, completely contented with each other's society. I believe that this visit cemented all G.W.B's passionate belief that Henry's future would be instrumental in bringing about the glorious era that would follow the end of the War. At his request I read aloud to him during the last six months of his life the 'Willett' scripts from beginning to end, and I felt that he was re-living all his life's dreams.

On this occasion Henry seemed to us very much a man, and with a man's reserves. Neither of us had any talk of an intimate sort with him. He was as always, tremendously interested in psychical research, and we had several conversations on that subject. Thinking about it all afterwards, I remember that I did feel, this time, that perhaps Henry would become a great <u>spiritual</u> leader: there was a depth in him now, after all these experiences. At the same time I could not help discerning that the world situation, when the War ended, would be too vast and too confused, for any <u>one</u> human being, however gifted, to handle. So I relinquished now the material prophecies, and decided that the interpretation must have been at fault; and set my hopes on the possibility of a great spiritual revival when peace came which perhaps Henry would somehow inspire. But (as I see now) the world was too tired, people were bitter and unhopeful; and when Henry's release came, with the death of his mother after a long illness, in 1956, what I have felt might be a pregnant moment in him, had passed: the consolidation of middle age had set in, I suppose. He was then forty-three.

I visited Mrs Tennant in London, at 18 Cottesmore Gardens, W.8. some time after G.W.B.'s death, I think about 1949. On this occasion she spoke very bitterly about Henry, said he had 'been ruined by his Army friends', and that he had never been the same since the War. (Of course the truth was that he was now grown-up.) She seemed to be deeply perturbed, and much troubled by the changes and problems of the aftermath of the War. I could not help wondering whether she, like the rest of us, had doubts now about the meaning of the Scripts, but of course I said nothing. But I did tell her that I knew that Henry was tremendously interested in psychical research; and that I hoped, now that he was living again at home, that she would let him know about her own psychic experiences; I felt that he ought to know what a wonderful medium his mother had been. But this seemed to agitate her and she declared vehemently that Henry must never know <u>anything</u> about that side of her life. I thought it strange, and also a great pity, that she should refuse to share with her son, who was so really interested, the story of A.J.B.'s inner life, in which her psychic powers had played so large a part: but I didn't want to upset her. I had not reckoned on how strongly she would react on my suggestion, but thinking it over later, I realised that to <u>her</u>, it would be unthinkable to run any risk that Henry should guess at the relationship which she and G.W.B. supposed to exist between himself and A.J.B. – that is to say, that he was the 'spiritual son' of A.J.B. and M.L. I had forgotten about this idea, which to me and Ral was <u>so</u> fantastic (as indeed it was to A.J.B. himself when informed of it on his death-bed – see my notes on the record made by B.B. at the time) that we had never attached any weight to it whatever.

I then asked her if she would agree that I should prepare parts of the 'Palm Sunday Case' for publication in the SPR Proceedings: this would involve picking out what was apposite from the main body of the Scripts, and excluding the prophecies concerning Henry. But to this she gave an emphatic refusal, and declared that the one <u>could not</u> be separated from the other, and that the whole aim and end of the Palm Maiden's story led on to the birth of Augustus Henry.

Finally we agreed that the Scripts must be safeguarded, and that Ral and I and the Salters must go on looking for wise young men, who would take care of them in the future. However, back in Scotland I continued to work upon the 'Palm Sunday' material: for I felt that <u>that</u>, apart from anything else in the Scripts, might be presented to the world in this generation: and it seemed to me, that the supposition that Henry was the spiritual offspring of that mystical union could wait upon the fulfilment of the prophetic interpretation.

His mother had accused him in one of her letters to Jean Balfour (June 4th, 1945) of not being a letter writer. In fact this was unfair. When in a busy life he did write his mother, his letters were full of interest, not only because of his descriptive talent but also by his capabilities as an observer. For of course he was hyper-observant, as a man whose life in Intelligence work in the field had had to be to survive from day to day and he was highly literate. His letters also revealed facets of his complex reserved personality, possibly also a sense of detachment coupled paradoxically with a yearning to belong in some way. Perhaps he did not write as often as she would have wished him to: undoubtedly she wanted him to be a compass needle always pointing in the direction of her magnetic polarity, continually communicating to her every detail of his career. There was no doubt that she was ever anxious to detect the slightest indication of the beginning of the messianic role she had believed from before his birth he was destined to play in world affairs. And no doubt his exploits kept the flame of her belief alive, firstly his escape in 1942 from the prisoner of war camp with his two comrades, and their success in making their way through occupied Europe to Britain, then his involvement in Intelligence work and being dropped behind the enemy lines in France in 1944 to aid the Maquis, together with his subsequent post-war military and Intelligence career. His letters did let her know in a colourful way the activities that he could safely reveal to her in the countries in which he did tours of duty.

From 1944 to 1945 he was Company Commander, the Welsh Guards, in Belgium, Holland and Germany. In 1945 to 1946 and in 1948 he was Company Commander, the Welsh Guards in Palestine while in 1947 he was the Administrative Officer of the British Military Mission to Saudi Arabia. From 1948 to 1952 and from 1955 to 1956 he served in Military Intelligence at the War Office. In 1952–3 he was attached to the Control Commission in Germany while from 1953 to 1954 he was posted to the headquarters of the British troops in Austria. In 1956 he retired from the Army with the rank of Major. From 1956 to 1960 he served in HM Foreign Service being Second Secretary at The Hague from 1956 to 1958 and First Secretary in Baghdad, from 1958 to 1960. It was after that time that he retired and took up the new profession that so surprised Jean and Ral.

Prince of Wales Company
1st Batallion Welsh Guards
M.E.F.

12 November 1945

Dear Mother,

We are up on the Syrian Frontier at Metullah, in a Camp –
half tents & half huts and nearby is a Camp of the Transjordan
Frontier Force, where I get a horse to ride every morning. It
is very like Kalgan here [on the Great Wall in China where
he was in 1935] with the same dim-coloured mountains, clear
pure air & vast sweeping views. To the North lies a huge sort
of amphitheatre 5 miles across, with the first hills of Lebanon
beyond; to the South the valley of the Jordan with the lake
Hula 15 miles away, looking like the Round Pond in Kensington
Gardens. There is excellent shooting of snipe in the valley.
We do a certain amount of patrolling by day & night. There
are a number of Jewish Communist Settlements in the valley
and on the mountain tops: they vary in size from big ones
with 500 people of both sexes & all ages, to the tiny offshoots
that have only just started, with 30 or 40 young men. The
principle of communal ownership extends to having all the
infants and children in communal kindergartens. It is a very
interesting experiment, and I have always been warmly welcomed
when I have visited them.

I have also had dinner with 2 prominent Arabs, one an Emir
who represented the Arab world at the San Francisco Conference.
My sympathies lie with both sides, but rather more with the
Jews, who seem to me to be industrious, able and charming.
The younger settlements remind me very much of the Maquis
groups of France. I have no doubt that they will wage guerilla
warfare against us, if ordered, with equal intensity and patriotism,
but that does not make me like them any the less, on the one
hand, or feel reluctant to fight them, if necessary, on the other.
At present everything here is quiet.

I am completely captivated by this lovely country. I feel
increasingly that modern England has nothing to offer me. I
have given up all idea of leaving the Army provided I can
avoid regimental soldiering in a home station. But no other
form of soldiering is so satisfactory as regimental soldiering

500

in the Brigade. I am an oddly shaped key but I fit that particular lock now as though it were made for me and I for it.

[rest of letter missing]

Trans-Jordan, 20th October, 1946

Dear Mother,

We are nearing the end of our training in Trans-Jordan, with a big exercise starting tomorrow and finishing on Wednesday. I shall be sorry to go back to Palestine, as I have enjoyed being here very much. The other day I went shooting at Azrak, which is a famous oasis about 60 miles S.E. of here. There are several desert tracks leading to it – the main one crosses some huge mud flats over which one can drive a car at any speed, and for the last twenty miles passes through a flat desolate wilderness carpeted with black flints – passable anywhere to vehicles – which has an austere and incommunicable beauty of its own.

We reached Azrak about 7.30 a.m. – still bitterly cold in spite of the clear sky and the rising sun. Leaving the two villages on our left – the small one below the modern Arab Legion Fort and the large straggling one built around the old Roman Fort with its palm trees which was Lawrence's H.Q. in 1917/18 winter – we past [sic] on to a vast plain of hard mud north of which lie the two main marshes where the duck flight. Near the southern marsh we came upon a concourse of camels – hundreds of them – and black camel hair tents of a tribe; the Beni-Sakr, so one of them said. The camels were on the move a few minutes late – endless strings of them in single file padding out into the desert towards Arabia, each string controlled apparently by a youth sitting on the tail camel. We spent an hour or so shooting sand grouse. They were sitting in coveys all over the plain sunning themselves, and so tame that the technique is to drive a jeep up, stop near the covey, wait till they rise and fly away, and shoot out of the car. Rather an easy business and not very sporting. Then we went into the marsh and waited for them to flight over – going fast and high they are hard to shoot. I had a few shots but only got one – a high bird that fell with a whistling noise like a bomb to fall almost at my feet. At about 10 a.m. we were more than ready for breakfast – cold turkey, eggs, bread and butter and marmalade and tea and beer. Later we moved to the northern marsh to try for the duck, and I walked over to look at Lawrence's fort. I should think it must have been bitterly cold that winter.

All this after a night exercise that finished at 2 a.m. – so you can imagine how well I slept that night.

Last Sunday I went out into the desert about 30 miles from the Wadi el Harith. Approaching a strange little grove of old bay trees – the only ones in sight for miles – an enormous covey of chicken flew out of the biggest tree: of course the gun was not loaded, and they never came back, though we sat in the shade waiting for them eating sandwiches and beer and staring out into the desolate distance. Today also I have been out, to try and find a 'Bir' or water cistern marked on the map some miles off any recorded track. We found a spot that was identifiable on the map, took a compass bearing off the map and measured the distance in miles, noted the speedometer reading and then started straight across country on the required bearing. We eventually bumped along up a Wadi and over a saddle into the heart of a range of low hills. Nothing that looked like a cistern could be seen, but we went on following our compass bearing till the speedometer registered the required fraction of a mile. We stopped and could see nothing except a little group of boulders that might mark the lip of a narrow well, and what looked like a shallow dewpit minus water about 100 yards to our right. We tried the stones first and drew blank: then we motored over to the dewpond. It was the edge of a great crater, at the bottom of which was the narrow entrance and an underground chamber about 20 foot deep. This must be the cistern, and as we drew up on the edge, congratulating ourselves on our accurate navigation, about 500 rock pigeons rose from the bowels of the earth and flew away with a great flutter of wings. Again we had been caught napping with an unloaded gun, but this time I just managed to load and bring one down. We got another presently but had not time to wait for them to come back. Today has been cold and fresh after light rain in the night. A faint – the faintest possible – bloom of green on the khaki on the desert

502

is the result: it can only be seen from a great distance from a flat angle, for looking straight down on the ground nothing but the scattered harsh scrub can be seen growing. In the spring, I believe, it goes green all over. I find this country enchanting. Its great empty spaces are more to my taste than the most lovesome garden in creation.

[rest of the letter missing]

> The British Military Mission to
> Saudi Arabia,Taif,
> Saudi Arabia
> 25th April 1947

Dear Mother,

I have just returned from a trip to Jedda to fetch some of our stores. A Moslem pilot, flying over Mecca, would do the trip in under half an hour, but for a Christian in a jeep, obliged to take the long detour round Mecca, it takes a good eight hours over rough desert tracks. The long slow descent through the broad valley that winds its way through the mountains to within 30 miles of Mecca is a drive of great beauty and ever increasing heat. From this point the 'Christian's Way' turns north from the Mecca road, a bad track, barely discernible at times, through the sandy Wadi Fatima. Ten miles of bad going brings you to 'Sheikh Abdulla's' – a clay building near a well said to contain the purest water in Arabia, and sold to the neighbouring Beduins by the Sheikh. Here the 'Engleesy' can always rest in the shade and be served with coffee and tea free of charge. The temperature in the shade here was 102. It is a pleasant spot surrounded by mountains and filled with the cries of the wild-looking Arabs as they haul their goatskin buckets up from the depths of the well. Further on the Wadi gradually broadens out to the vast white sandy plain enclosed by the faint delicate outlines of distant hills. The heat here was terrific, with a scorching wind like the breath of a furnace. Some miles further on the track rejoins the Mecca-Jedda road which is tarmac all the way from here on. As we approached Jedda a cool damp wind from the sea began to refresh us, and Jedda itself, although so humid that paper flops with

503

moisture, was for the two days we were there no hotter than Haifa or Nathanya. It is a tightly packed town, with narrow sandy streets and tall houses with highly decorative wooden balconies. The hotels were full – I managed to get accommodation for the drivers, and I stayed with one of the people from the Legation. 'Dorothy is throwing a party – you must come!' so I went to Dorothy's party, where two elderly ladies and about a dozen men in white duck trousers kept up by broad black cummerbunds, with white shirts open at the neck (the correct evening wear in Jedda) sat around on sofas or on the floor drinking, talking or occasionally dancing. One man was detailed to see that the gramophone was never silent, and in this friendly babel I sat drinking endless whiskies and sodas and trying to carry on a conversation against the gramophone with various quite interesting people. There were a few rather pansy young men from the Legation, some Americans, the Manager of the shipping agents, Gollatly & Hankey, and the new eye-specialist who is opening a clinic in Jedda and has already been presented with a gold watch by the Saud for treating him at Riyadh. Somebody gives a party practically every night in Jedda. You meet the same people, eat the same snacks, drink the same drinks – the only difference, as someone has said, being the colour of the wall-paper. Not my world!!

I got to bed about 2 a.m. and was up early next morning to see about getting our stores out of the customs. I had to get a delivery note from the shipping agents, and customs clearance from the Legation, then fetch the 10 ton lorries lent us by the Saudis from the barracks and take them down to the Customs Sheds. With the help of the Cavasse from the Legation I engaged the necessary 'coolies' and started loading our stores onto the trucks. There were bits and pieces lying about everywhere, and three huge cases weighing half a ton each which had to be man-handled – can you imagine having no lifting-gear of any sort at the principal port of the country?! After a long day's work it was all loaded. In the evening I called on the Minister, Geoffrey-Smith, and had a chat with him – later we went to a cinema show given on the roof of the American Legation.

Next morning we filled six 40 gallon drums with our petrol, which is held in store for us at a dump outside the town, and at

10 a.m. we got away. Fifteen miles inland the heat hit us like a sledge-hammer, and we had to close up the windscreens as a protection from the searing wind. We boiled over twice before reaching Abdulla's, and had to use some of our precious drinking water. However we filled up at Abdulla's and had no more trouble afterwards. We drove up the Wadi onto the Taif plateau in the cool of the evening, reaching Taif about 9 p.m.

It had been an enjoyable trip, although strenuous, and I was left with a legacy of innumerable bites, some from mosquitos, some from harvesters, and not a few, I fear, from bugs, some of which probably came from the carpets spread out for us at Sheikh Abdulla's.

The Brigadier and the Colonel flew to Riyadh recently for an audience with the King. I hope I shall have a chance to go there some time. Instruction is closing down during Ramadan in July, and I am planning a Jeep trip with Norman Smith up to Hayil in Northern Arabia. This morning (our Sunday) I went for a ride, and after tea we are going out to the aerodrome to try and shoot a few hares. On all journeys outside the immediate vicinity of Taif one has to take a guide – his main preoccupation on the journey to Jedda being to see that the infidels do not enter the precincts of Mecca. It is hot here today, and the nights, despite the heights, are beginning to be sultry. Will continue this tonight...

Sorry, no time but to catch the post, will reply to your letter re Cots etc next mail.

H. C-T.

After Winifred's death in 1956, Henry continued to write to Jean and Ral Balfour. Apart from his brother, Alexander, who remained close to him, it is possible that he felt most at home with Jean and Ral. Their warmth and deep friendship for him seems to have been a source of great comfort to him, enabling him to relax as far as he was ever capable of doing. The Intelligence officer may have inherited his mother's innate 'only on a need to know' reserve at giving away information, especially of one's private life and if so, his work continually reinforced that reserve, making it impossible for him to 'open up' to anyone. It is even possible that he was most relaxed with his dogs and horses.

505

A letter to Jean not long after the end of the Second World War suggests a lingering caution at the unexpected outcome of the general election, almost an unease at the sweeping changes in the political field.

Kingston Camp,
Hereford.
4 Sep. '45

Dear Jean,

After all I was only in Scotland for a very short time: I had intended to propose myself for a weekend at the end of July, but was whisked away too soon. Instead of returning to Scotland at the end of August, the Bn [battalion] has now come here, & is preparing to go overseas. So I don't know when I shall be able to see you.

It was good to hear from you & to learn the family news. I hope Mary will be happy in her new job. I wondered when I read an article on Conservative policy by Lord Balfour of Inchrye, what relation he might be to Ral. What did you think of the election? The men here took no interest in it, only 17 men in my company of 250 voted. The officers were rather pained, not to say shocked, but personally I think it is not a bad thing. The Conservative party has had a good innings, or at any rate a long one, & the ineptitude of its election policy suggested that perhaps it was time it gave place to a party more in touch with the common people of England.

I am true-blue by nature, but even I have been turned slightly pink by Beaverbrook's blatherings. Though to be sure Laski is even more dangerous & mischievous.

I think this is a very good time for ignorant & opinionated soldiers to take two years abroad improving their polo, & leave their elders and betters to clear up the mess!!

Yours ever
    Henry.

To Jean Balfour:

My dear Jean,
Thank you very much for your letter and for the assortment
of books. I am so glad to have the little memoir of Andrew
– I don't think I ever knew him, but I also learnt from old
Tom the rudiments of fishing, and caught my first trout in the
Burn, before the War.

Mick Brander's book looks fascinating and I have read quite
a bit of it already. I have looked through Mr Pid's Paper,
which is most interesting. It is difficult to know what to make
of these cross correspondences but most difficult of all is to
see what the purpose of these communications (if such they
were) really was. If it is true that the communicators, as Pid
suggests, did not want their meaning to be understood at the
time either by the mediums or the interpreters, are we to
suppose that the whole thing was an elaborately devised scheme
to prove to the ultimate readers of the riddle that it really was
a case of communication from the dead, and that the content
of the messages was of secondary importance? It must be
admitted that this kind of elaborate literary cryptogram-game
was a good choice for evidential purposes, but if the
communicators were really trying to convey that the War would
be followed by Utopia, it shows that they were not much
better at reading the future than living persons. I must try to
study the whole work of the SPR group sometime.

I was most interested to read the review of Lady Emily's
book. There is no doubt that the whole field of Psychical
Research is a happy hunting ground not only for crooks and
deliberately fraudulent persons, but also for those who wish
to believe various things and can persuade themselves that
they have good reason to do so. In the scientific study of what
is measurable – e.g. card guessing and probability – one escapes
all this, but that is not the most interesting side of the subject.

After your visit, which I much enjoyed, I thought very
carefully about the question of publishing Mrs Willett's identity,
and finally wrote to Salter agreeing to it. I added that I felt
it might be worth while, now that almost all the original
mediums and investigators were on the same side of the fence

as the communicators, to give the whole group a chance to communicate, and that possibly the best way would be for me to take a proxy sitting as an invitation to my mother to do so. Salter agreed with this idea and felt that the attempt should be made before the publication of Mrs W's identity – if necessary postponing the latter until the winter. He is trying to arrange something as soon as possible.

All well here – the explosions only lasted for a week, but recently we have had a lot of thunder, which has upset poor Toby quite a lot. However he soon recovers! I think of you tucked away quietly in the calm before the storm of family and guests. I hope you will get some useful work done.

With love from Henry

To Jean Balfour:

British Embassy, The Hague, 10 Nov. 57

My dear Jean,

I am sorry to have been so long in answering your letter, but my leave plans have only just been settled, & I much want to see [you] when I come over.

I should like to shoot, but I am such a bad shot that I am always rather reluctant to take anyone else's place. However, if Ral can fit me in I will spend an hour at a shooting school & see if I can discover what I am doing wrong. I would suggest either the week end of the 7th or the 14th December. I would try to come up on the Thursday night or possibly a morning plane on the Friday, as I would like to show you and discuss the results of the Geraldine Cummins experiment to date. I am so glad that Salter has spoken to you about it: I did not like to say anything to anyone else while the experiment was in progress without his agreement, but I intended to suggest that at a certain point you should be shown the results. There have been no 'sittings' in the ordinary sense of the word, & I have not communicated with Miss Cummins myself. Salter sent her my name and asked her to try for a message. After the first script he sent some not very revealing examples of my mother's handwriting. Miss Cummins has produced 7 scripts in all so far, of varying quality, but which

508

show an awareness of family matters that – unless she is dishonest – could scarcely have been acquired by normal means. She very soon got out the fact that my mother was Mrs Willett. G.W.B. appears constantly in the scripts – not always very characteristically – and there are appropriate references to others in the Group. There are references to Christopher (as 'George' – his first name, which was never used) and to Alexander, but surprisingly none whatever to Daphne. Salter does not think Miss C. has drawn upon conscious or unconscious memories of reading 'Christopher' – in fact we all doubt whether she has ever read it. There seems hardly any doubt that some paranormal faculty is at work, and I would say there is some evidence that she has had direct access to my mother's memories; I am not convinced that she has had direct or indirect access to my mother herself i.e. to a personality that has persisted through death. The survival of memory is no doubt a necessary condition of the survival of personality, but I doubt whether it is a sufficient condition. It seems possible that individual personality may come to an end though memories persist in a form accessible to mediums. All this, and indeed the meaning of 'survival', is bound up with our notions of time, & it may well be that these do not really apply.

Gardner Murphy seems to me to have summed up these reflections very well on page 132 of the Journal you sent me: 'Maybe some of the aspects of personality are not in the time dimension, and that the question of continuity beyond death is wrongly stated.'

I would like just to ask you one question. Miss C. refers to an occasion when my father asked to be present while my mother was getting automatic writing, & on this occasion she passed out completely into a trance, which rather upset her. I seem to remember reading about such an incident, but cannot find it in the Delta case. Could it have been in the Palm Sunday case?

Would you like me to send you the scripts and correspondence about them, or shall I bring them with me? I am so looking forward to seeing you both again.

Yours ever,
    Henry.

To Jean Balfour:

British Embassy, The Hague, 18th December 57
My dear Jean,
I did enjoy my short stay at Whittingehame & the opportunity
of seeing you and Ral again & discuss the strange affair of
the scripts.

If you have a spare set of the curiously titled 'Notes and
Excursuses' I should like some time to add them to my
collection of the volumes of scripts which Mr Sadler gave
to my brother. Whether I shall ever have time to study the
whole of the material, I do not know. I am rather daunted
by the vast literary knowledge which the interpreters drew
upon in their attempts to connect the scripts with each other
and with the Story and the Plan. I wonder if anything could
be achieved by approaching the scripts from a different angle.
I was interested, for example, to notice in 2 of the scripts
quoted in 'Notes and Excursuses' what seemed to me to
be possible references to events in my own life. Neither
of those were Willett scripts, & both of them were written
I think between 1910 and 1920. One mentioned a happy
band of 3 brothers (or words to that effect) in connexion with
escape from captivity. The other – quite a short script –
mentioned ravens (referring to them as a portent of doom),
then something about a small procession led by someone with
a lantern then referred to the 'Forest of Arden'. These references
immediately reminded me (a) of the Tower of London (whose
ravens are like the Gibraltar apes) where I started my time in
the Army & where, a few years later, I heard the declaration
of war & the first air-raid syren; (b) of the officers' 'rounds'
on King's Guard, a small party, led by a drummer-boy with
a lantern, which visits the sentries at intervals during the night;
(c) the forests of the French Ardennes, where I was dropped
by parachute in 1944. All this may be pure coincidence of
course.

I had a good flight of just over an hour to London. The
weather was clear most of the way, and flying at 20 000 feet
over Solway Firth one could see the Isle of Man clearly.

Alas, after all the frost robbed me of my last day's hunting,
which was most disappointing.

510

22 Dec.

Since returning here I have been on the go without stopping. Masses of work that I feel I shall never catch up with. That is the trouble about going away for more than a week at a time!

I do hope I shall see you here sometime next year. Perhaps you will all sail over to the Zuider Zee, or what is left of it.

Love and best wishes from

Henry

To Ral:

British Embassy, The Hague, 22 Dec 57

My dear Ral,

I did enjoy my visit to Whit, and it was very kind to include me in the shoot. This I particularly enjoyed, and though I couldn't hit the high pheasants I wasn't quite as hopeless as usual at the others. There's hope yet, if only I can get some practice!

I was most interested in your views on the Middle East, and would like to have had more time to discuss this with you. Would you please let me know what happens to your idea of forming a sort of pressure group to gain currency for your views. I had only one additional idea after I left – that it might be well to make any guarantee of the Western Powers to Israel conditional on her respecting the present Arab frontiers. Guarantees to both sides by the Western Powers alone would I think be unrealistic. We should have to bring Russia in for that. But if Russia won't play, a guarantee of the Western Powers to Israel alone without any conditions might alienate Arab feeling and drive the Arabs into the Russian camp. I don't think we want a situation where Russia and the Arab States on one side, and the Western Powers and Israel on the other, make faces at each other. This would be very insecure. If our aim is to ensure 10 years cease-fire in the M.E. during which passions can cool, the best way is to include Russia in a pact to put out any flames that start in the area irrespective of race. The next best thing is to make Russia and the Arabs understand that an attack on Israel would be resisted with the

511

full force of the Western Powers, while making it quite clear to the Arab States and to Israel that Israel would forfeit Western support immediately if she indulged in any military adventures a la Suez.

Best wishes for Christmas and the New Year to you all, & hoping to see you here next year.

Yours ever
    Henry

To Jean Balfour:

19 Feb 58

My dear Jean,
I wrote to Miss Cummins last month suggesting she should continue trying for script from my mother, and explaining why I thought it inadvisable to give her my comments on previous scripts. She agreed & has since produced two scripts, copies of which I enclose. I have also sent copies to Alexander & to Mr Salter. If Miss Cummins has had no normal access to the facts of the Palm Sunday case (& you will see from her covering letter that it all means nothing to her conscious mind) I suppose it is possible that she derived the material in the scripts from Mr Salter by telepathy. But there is a good deal here that is quite characteristic of WCT & that gives the impression of having been written from the inside of the person taking part in the scene described. I will send you further scripts when received. Hope you are all well & that the snowstorms have not affected you up in Scotland. My love to Ral. My boxer has had an operation for removal of a tumour, but is recovering well.

Love
    Henry

Comments by Jean written on the letter:

This refers to the Cummins Willett Script describing the vision in the room of the old man (?AJB).
It is true that Helen Salter had been reading the finished draft of my Palm Sunday Case at just about the same date.

512

To Jean Balfour:

23 March 58

My dear Jean,

Many thanks for your letter. I was most interested in your comments on the scripts. I do not recall very clearly the order of the events in the Palm Sunday Case, but I gather from what you say that the only part reproduced in Miss Cummins' scripts is that which was consciously experienced by Mrs Willett, & that the impressions received & communicated in trance (of which my mother would have had no conscious memory) do not appear in the Cummins' scripts. If we assume that the trance experience is still unavailable to my mother if she has survived, its absence from the scripts rather supports the possibility of communication as opposed to telepathy – or, as you say, the alternative possibility of 'memory reading'. For if it was telepathy from Helen, one would not have expected the trance part to be excluded altogether.

I have looked again at the script, & there is no doubt that 'bored' is the word. No doubt you are right in saying that A.J.B. never was bored, but may he not have seemed bored on that occasion? I do not recall the circumstances exactly, but was the sitting not given at GWB's persuasion to a somewhat unwilling A.J.B.?

Further material of great interest has been provided in 3 more scripts on which I am awaiting Alexander's comments. Part of this seems to me almost impossible to have been produced (apart from communication or memory reading) except by cryptomnesia which would imply remarkable forgetfulness in the part of Miss Cummins, or by deliberate fraud involving personal enquiries of a most searching nature.

Yes, keep the scripts as long as you like. I shall be interested to hear Ral's comments.

I hope to be in London for Broad's SPR lecture on 15 May. Any chance of meeting then?

Love from Henry

To Jean Balfour:

British Embassy, The Hague, 26 May 58

My dear Jean,

I did not have time to give the Palm Sunday Case the study it deserved, but we (Mr Salter and I) gave the manuscript to Professor Broad at the lecture on 15th with your letter. I very much hope it will be published & look forward to reading it more carefully.

Miss Cummins has produced some remarkable scripts in response to a request from me, at Mr Salter's suggestion, that 'Winifred' should be asked to say more about the beginning of her work as Mrs Willett. In these scripts Daphne is mentioned for the first time – not by name, but as 'my daughter' and (more characteristically) 'my darling'. It had always struck us as very odd that no reference had been made to her in the Cummins' scripts, & I had wondered if (assuming the scripts to be from my mother) there had been a reluctance on the part of the communicator to dwell on these very painful memories. This, according to the latest scripts, was indeed the case, but there seems to have been a further reason why the whole subject of Daphne was being avoided. It seems that when 'Winifred' met Daphne after her death, she got a great shock, as she found her quite changed and entirely attached to her father. No doubt the image of Daphne as a baby had dominated all my mother's memories of her, and it seems quite possible that the discovery that this image no longer corresponded to reality would have been a severe shock.

There is one very striking reference in the Scripts to an incident in Christopher's Christmas holidays 1908/9 when 'Winifred' claims to have received a mental message from Myers telling her not to worry about 'George's' illness as he would be fit enough to go back to school. This incident is described in the privately printed Willett volumes, & was entirely unknown to Alexander or myself. Mr Salter does not think Miss C. can have had access to these Willett volumes, and considers this a very remarkable success. With the Willett volumes and my mother's daily diaries from 1908 onwards (1912–15, I think, are missing & have either been destroyed or hidden away) we have ample material to check the accuracy

514

of 'Winifred's' statements about her work as Mrs Willett, & I have urged Miss Cummins to continue the experiment.

A great deal of study and research would be involved in trying to prepare any paper for the Journal on the results achieved, & unfortunately I haven't at present the time to do it properly.

I found Broad's lecture very interesting, & I dined afterwards with those members of the Council who were present.

Poor Mandy the Boxer died of cancer in March, which was very sad for me and Mr Toby, who was so attached to her. My horse is out at grass, but unfortunately has cut his knee very badly on barbed wire. Otherwise all well.

My love to you and Ral. Any chance of seeing you here this summer?

Yours ever
        Henry

Comment by Jean written on the letter: 'These [the diaries] are in the keeping of the C.T. family lawyer in accordance with her will for 50 years.'

Continuation of Jean Balfour's memorandum:

Not long after Mrs Tennant died, Ral had business in Holland – in 1957, I think – where Henry was then living, being at that time engaged in secret service work for the Foreign Office; and we stayed 2 nights at the Hague. At this time Henry had a most charming house at Wassensee, and a Dutch couple looked after him. He was particularly proud of his garden, which he showed me minutely: he had a beautiful grand piano and very nice furniture, and the company of his beloved dogs. I think he really loved it there. Later on he took a pleasant house in Leicestershire with a stable for his horse, where he had local friends who followed the hunt, but I don't think he lived there for longer than about 2 years before he decided to take monastic vows.

I spent the days with Henry [in Holland], and took with me a rough draft of the essentials of the 'Palm Sunday' case, which included copies of the more important 'Willett' scripts.

In all this Henry was tremendously interested. I think that it was rather a revelation to him, for it shed light on his mother's private activities, which in the past it appeared he had dimly suspected. Since her death, he told me, he and Alexander, his elder brother, had come across the 'Journal' which she had kept for many years, and other significant material that hinted at an extensive secret life. But what had really opened a door to him was something he remembered had been said to him by D.D. Lyttelton while he was still at Eton!

Note on Dame Edith Lyttelton. She was the 'Mrs King' of J.G.P.'s paper on 'Forecasts in Scripts concerning the First World War', and had considerable mediumistic ability. At the same time she was a very active woman of affairs, an excellent talker, and at one time Henry saw quite a lot of her. She was the second wife of Alfred Lyttelton (brother of M.L.) and knew both the Lyttelton and Balfour families when they were young. She alone of the Balfour entourage could perceive the astonishing likeness between Henry and his 'godfather' (G.W.B.) for she had known the latter in his youth when his hair was black – not silver. She once remarked on this to poor B.B. who immediately passed it off by pretending not to understand what she meant. B.B. told me long ago that she was sure D.D. knew. At one period she was rather a close friend of Mrs Tennant's, I think at the time of the 'Delta' Case and when Alexander was a baby, but later a chasm opened between them, I don't know from what cause. Possibly D.D. was tactless; she was (I would say from my own observance of her on the few occasions I met her) a bit of a gossip; and I knew that G.W.B. considered her indiscreet. She was very much hurt (she confided to B.B.) that the Fishers Hill interpreters never included her as one of the SPR mediumistic group: but of course her association with the Lyttelton family rendered her scripts of less value as evidence for the 'Palm Sunday' material at least.

Henry told me that on one occasion when D.D. took him out from Eton for the day, they had 'talked S.P.R.' – and she had told him that 'Mrs Willett' was his mother, but that he must never tell it to anyone. At the time, he said, he had not really understood what this meant, for he knew very little about mediumship, his interest in psychic matters being then

516

mostly in ghosts and table-tilting. He had been flattered by the grown-up way she talked to him, and by her interest in him. But afterwards he remembered, and when the War was over, he read everything he could find about 'Mrs Willett', including G.W.B.'s paper in the S.P.R. *Proceedings* on the psychological aspects of her phenomena.

Again and again, he told me bitterly, he had tried to draw out his mother on these subjects (without however letting her know that he had some actual knowledge) but he met with no success. She resolutely refused to discuss anything of the sort with him, and when he wished to argue, or to question some point, especially upon the evidence for survival, (which in common with so many young men who had been through the War, both attracted and repelled him), she declared that her personal conviction was so profound, that she had no need of evidence; yet she would not give him the benefit of what had convinced her. The consequence was that he was so deeply irritated that the subject was voluntarily closed between them: and knowing what it always meant to Henry to have free intellectual discussion, I could see that his resentment must have been great: from the way he spoke, I realised that her passing, although no doubt it brought him regret, had not really shaken him; she had lost his spontaneous affection long ago.

Henry himself saw no objection to the 'Palm Sunday' Case coming out in the S.P.R. *Proceedings*. I told him, of course, that his mother had definitely refused her consent. I then took it to London to get permission from Alexander. This was the first time I had met the brother. Alexander was at first immensely surprised, and later extremely interested, in the history of his mother's mediumship.

Later on, at Henry's request (I wondered whether it was partly to obtain some guidance as to what, if any, view was held by the 'Other Side', on the question of publication of the Palm Sunday scripts) Mr Salter arranged for some proxy sittings on Henry's behalf with the Irish medium Miss Geraldine Cummins. From the summer of 1957 for about 3 years, the series of 'Cummins–Willett' scripts developed, which were published in 1966 under the title of 'Swan on a Black Sea'.

A good deal of these scripts must have been somewhat

painful, I should imagine, for the brothers to annotate, but although as a build-up of Mrs Tennant's personality, it is remarkable, Henry himself seems to have remained sceptical as to her genuine survival. [From my own knowledge of Mrs Tennant, I personally cannot believe that she would ever have given permission to let the 'Palm Sunday' Case see the light of day. Yet her consent is clearly granted in these scripts! It would, however, be almost impossible, I think, for a medium (especially for one as fond of the lime-light as G.C.) to withhold from the public such a good case for survival, and I believe that this mediumistic propensity almost certainly played into my hands.]

Sometime in 1958, Henry came for a night to Redcliff and brought me two of the 'Cummins–Willett' scripts – he was on his way to shoot with some friends in Scotland. Ral was away that evening on Masonic business, if I remember right.

Henry and I talked about G.W.B. and of his long-lasting deep interest in 'the Scripts'. Although Henry himself was sceptical as to whether they emanated from the 'Other World', he was very interested in them too, as his letter of this date shows. He spoke again at some length of his mother, and her absorption in the psychic sphere, and evidently he still resented the fact that he had been deliberately kept in the dark: I felt awfully sorry for him. I mentioned to him what he was already aware of, that both G.W.B. and his mother had anticipated a very great and brilliant future for him. From what he said now, it seemed that he had been aware for a long time that certain things, mysterious to him, for he could not have named them, had always been expected of him: he had felt it, not known it consciously, and it had puzzled and disquieted him. This was especially during the last period of his time at Eton, and at Cambridge.

When G.W.B. died, his volumes of Willett script, and a leather box, with his copy of N. and E. Vol II (in which he compiled the introduction, where 'the Plan' is set forth in plain language) came into my keeping, at his wish. In the box there were some little snapshots of Henry as a baby and a young child: and a few letters from his mother. Ral and I did not read the letters, but one could see, by a cursory glance, that they were about Henry, and one, very long one, concerned him at Eton. We both felt strongly that, should the opportunity ever arise, we ought to free Henry from the domination of the past. We were of the same generation as he was – we could not stand by and keep from him letters to which only he had right, or knowledge that would bring him peace from questioning, for if he really understood how much his mother had loved him or expected of him, he would be able to forgive her, and have peace of mind.

So I told him now, that there were letters that we had not ourselves read, but that we felt ought to be given to him. He carried them off, and I have no doubt shared them with Alexander. Together no doubt they must have guessed the truth, if they had not already known. Alexander certainly knew: at a slightly later date, Mr Salter had it from his own mouth. Poor Henry! Though he had all the world's goods and successes, I don't believe he was a very happy person: and that possibly the only person who ever treated him entirely <u>naturally</u>, without any preconceptions, was his brother.

Not long after these events, and as a result, I am sure, of the welter of emotions arising from his mother's death, the Roman Catholic religion began to exercise a powerful attraction on him. In his letter to me, dated June 1960, he describes an arduous time of mental questioning; he was too honest and sincere a person to take such a step as conversion lightly. Besides, he had always evinced himself as lacking in psychic perception (and in this, perhaps, he took after the Balfours who were apparently impervious, consciously, at any rate), so that he cannot have had mystical experiences to help him. When one reflects on the torment he had been in, because of his mother, both before and after her death, it did not surprise me in the least to hear, only a little over a year later, that he had entered Downside Abbey as a monk.

To Jean Balfour:

> 12 Olegsmanlaan[?], Wassenaar, Holland
> 16 June 1960

My dear Jean,
I have left Baghdad for good, and am on leave here. Shall

probably be in London for the winter, & further plans rather uncertain for the moment.

I hope we may meet. Perhaps Ral will be visiting his agent or you may both be in the neighbourhood during a sailing holiday. I expect to be here, apart from the first half of June & the last week of August, until September.

I have been reading the Palm Sunday Case in the Proceedings. It is much expanded, I think, from the original version, & represents a tremendous amount of research and selection. The difficulty must have been to avoid over simplification on the one hand, & on the other too full a treatment which would have obscured the narrative aspect of the case. It seems to me that the Paper succeeds in striking the right sort of mean. It is a fascinating case, & I hope that someone like Broad will attempt a critical study of it. It is impossible not to feel that the scripts of the various automatists had a common cause; whether this common cause can be equated with a fusion of the surviving souls of the communicators into a single 'script intelligence', as Mr Salter suggests, seems to me more doubtful. I am not sure that I understand this idea, or that it is any more plausible than to suppose that the common cause was A.J.B. himself in unconscious telepathic communication with the automatists.

You and Ral will probably be surprised to hear that I have become a Roman Catholic. Needless to say this step was not taken lightly. It was preceded by about eight months of reflection, study and instruction, starting from scratch – i.e. a position of agnosticism and ignorance. This study was not begun or pursued as a purely intellectual exercise, & the whole process has involved a considerable inner upheaval. I have not consciously been influenced by the existence of the SPR Scripts or by anything I can remember of their contents, nor by the Cummins' Scripts. Nor do I imagine that such a development fits what is called 'The Plan'. As you probably know, the Roman Catholic Church forbids recourse to mediums, and I should not feel able to invite Miss Cummins to produce any more scripts. This prohibition is of course directed against 'Spiritualism' rather than Psychical Research. I do not think it implies that persons who (say) do automatic writing in good faith, are acting wrongly, but that there is a danger in such activities, & that it is best for ordinary folk to avoid them.

Hoping to see you soon & with love to you both
Yours ever,
Henry.

P.S. Toby is well & the explosions, happily, are a thing of the past.

Although Henry maintained, and possibly sincerely believed it to be the case, that the Scripts and the interpreters' conclusions about the meanings hidden within them did not consciously influence his decision to embrace the Roman Catholic faith, it seems probable that Henry was intensely affected by his experience. He had certainly been deeply interested in psychical research, and deeply frustrated that his domineering mother had resolutely concealed her past as a psychic from him. There is no doubt that he had been shaken and moved by the Willett–Cummins scripts in particular, where he had had to consider the possibility that she had survived death and was trying to prove it to the son who had given her the chance to do so. It also seems fair to say that with his particular psychological make-up, it must have been a peak experience for him in the transpersonal psychology sense. He could not be the same man that he was before, as his subsequent decisions demonstrated.

Continuation of Jean Balfour's memorandum:

I met him once again, in the late summer of 1960, at Alexander's house in London: he looked a great deal older, and it struck me at once that he was more at peace within. Ral had gone off with Elizabeth Harker, and the 'Palm Sunday' Case had been issued in the SPR Proceedings the previous spring. On motoring me back to where I was staying in London, he spoke comforting words to me about Ral that he was sure that his present behaviour was not that of the real true person, and that all would come right in the end. It was like him to be so kind. The next time I heard from him was to tell me that he had 'cut his ties' and entered the monastery.

521

The letter, describing his duties and sense of peace reveals his usual disposition of mind, how much he valued the safety of discipline; he had found his vocation, and for him, henceforth, one felt, the R.C. religion would hold all the answers: the disturbing questions of psychical research were also forbidden things.

To Jean Balfour:

> Downside Abbey, Stratton on the Fosse, Bath
> 28 Dec 61

My dear Jean,

Thank you so much for your card. I have not been able to send my usual quota this year, & I was in any case not sure of your address.

What changes in our lives since we three lay in the sunshine in the dunes in Holland during your visit. I am of course desperately sorry about the whole business for you and Ral. I cannot say more. As for me, I have left my home and cut my ties with the world, to become a Benedictine monk. I am in my first year as a Novice, & then have 3 more years before taking final vows, so that I can always come back to the world during those 4 years. But I do not think I shall do so. I have at last found happiness and a vocation.

The motto of the Benedictines is PAX – actually the full motto I believe is Pax inter spinis – ('peace among thorns') – but there is not much peace, as the world understands the term, in a novice's life. It is more like being a recruit at the Guards Depot than anything else – on the go the whole time, usually working against the clock to get everything done in time. About 4 hours a day are spent chanting the Office in Choir, or assisting at Mass. Then there is study, manual labour, prayer, & for the novitiate the complicated procedure of sacristy work – vestments to be laid out, candles scraped, wicks trimmed, lamps oiled, missals marked, silver polished, things of every description to be placed in the right place at the right time & taken back again afterwards – etc, etc. A very practical down to earth existence in one way – but everything referred to the glory of God. Heads in the clouds and feet firmly planted on the ground – that is perhaps not a bad description of what has to be attempted in the monastic life.

Looking back over my life I feel that most of my past varied activities have a more or less direct bearing on my present ones – military life is a good natural preparation for monastic discipline and community life, & of course my philosophy training will come in useful when I begin my studies of philosophy and theology. And the 2 and a 1/2 years as a prisoner of war were most useful too.

So, though I am clear enough on the question of vocation to feel that in one way I ought to have become a monk as soon as I left Cambridge, yet I do not regret the 25 years spent as a rather rolling stone since then.

Do keep in touch & let me have your address. I am restricted as to letter writing in this first year, which is one of 'retreat'; but I do not want to lose contact with my friends.

May the New Year bring you God's blessing and Peace.

Yours ever
    Henry

To Jean Balfour:

> Downside Abbey, Stratton on the Fosse, Bath
> 20 Jan 63

My dear Jean,

Thank you very much for your card. I am so glad to have your address & news of you and Ral. You are both much in my thoughts & prayers & I hope that all will turn out well in the end.

I was professed in simple vows last September for a period of 3 years. The next step is in 1965 when I become due for solemn profession in perpetual vows. I have some hope that I may be released from the novitiate by the end of this year, & this will be most welcome. No one could really call the novitiate a 'hard' life, but it is not meant to be easy, & has elements both of the nursery & of the prison which make it trying at times for the rare middle aged entrant. But I do not have any doubt that I have at last found my vocation, and although it is one that inevitably separates one physically from family and friends, it is good to keep up old friendships by correspondence at least. I had a visit from Alex and Jenifer last October & also one from my Dutch couple whom I have pensioned off & who are living in my cottage at Foxton. The house itself is let to my neighbour's mother, a most satisfactory arrangement for all concerned.

I am glad that you manage to get out to Whittingehame for weekends & that you have visits from the family. I had a letter from Nelly – apart from that I have heard no Balfour news.

I hope that we may meet again one day. I do not get any leave of absence until just before solemn profession, when I have 10 days to settle my affairs; but later on, when I am a priest, I get a month every year, so that it should be possible to see some of my friends occasionally.

All my good wishes for 1963, & do write when the spirit moves you, especially as I know that you will understand if I am very slow in replying. Incidentally I much appreciated your letter last April on my and GWB's birthday.

    With love
        Henry

To Jean Balfour:

                Downside Abbey, Stratton on the Fosse, Bath
                                    29 Dec 63
My dear Jean,
Many thanks for your card. I am sending this to the old address in the hope that it finds you. I am so glad that you may see something of Alex and Jenifer, although I think that they now seldom spend a night in London as they live in Sussex and just keep a pied-a-terre at Cottesmore Gardens. All goes well here. I was released from the Novitiate in September & am now embarked in my second year of theology. As far as I can see I am likely to take the monastic vows in perpetuity in September 1965 & to be ordained Priest a year later.

I am keeping up my Philosophy, & this will be a permanent interest, though I have a good deal of ground to make up in the very important field of modern analytical philosophy in

524

the last 30 years. Thomist philosophy was not taught at all at Cambridge but remains, I think, of permanent value to human thought provided it is not fossilised and divorced from later currents of thought.

I have some contact with the School, including running a Shooting Society. We have about 80 acres to shoot over but there is practically nothing to shoot – pigeons are so scarce this year.

I think of you often & hope that all goes as well as it could. Do let me have your news as & when you feel inclined. All good wishes for the New Year.

Yours ever,
  Henry.

Conclusion of Jean's memorandum:

[Why did he become a monk?] Was it an escape from a world that I do not think had ever meant a very great deal to him? Or was it an expiation for 'the sins of the fathers'? A little of both, I suppose: but when I remember how he said as a boy, 'I always felt my hand was held in God's,' I can think that perhaps he has still kept that childlike faith. I do believe that he is happy: and he <u>deserves</u> happiness, more than most people do.

For a while, I harboured the hope that even if the old interpretation of the Scripts was wrong, over the <u>method</u> by which a great world-leader might come, there was still the possibility that in the religious sphere, Henry might have a special mission – if he eventually became Pope, mightn't he wield tremendous power?

But that is clearly not what the Scripts meant, if they really meant anything at all, in relation to an individual.

Jean Balfour   Dec: 1966. Edinburgh

The members of the Sidgwick Group by now had all departed this life. Jean, Henry and Alexander, though still alive and obviously involved implicitly or explicitly in the Plan, strictly speaking could not be considered to have been original members of the Group.

Professor C.D. Broad

Professor C.D. Broad died in 1971. He had never been a member of the Group but had strongly influenced Henry in a number of ways. Though he had been enormously helpful when approached by people such as Salter, he had been considered unjustifiably as too inquisitive by Mrs Coombe-Tennant, driven by her obsessive, secretive 'need to know' caution, and had never been invited to become one of the Cross-Correspondences researchers and interpreters. Which was a pity. For C.D. Broad had one of the most brilliant minds of his generation. He had an unparalleled knowledge not only of psychical research and philosophy, but by his nature and gentleness, though he possessed a delicate dry wit, 'which was somewhat barbed for those wise in their own conceit', he would respond to requests for help and advice with an almost inexhaustible store of patience, a patience extended even to the most woolly-headed. And to the intellectual undergraduate, he was quite simply an inspiration. Ten pages in the June 1971 SPR *Journal* are devoted to his life and accomplishments, written by luminaries such as Alan Gauld, E. Garth Moore, H.H. Price, Rosalind Heywood, C.T.K. Chari and Henry Coombe-Tennant himself.

Essentially Broad was a shy man. After an initial desire to become an engineer he decided that, though he took at Trinity College, Cambridge, a first class in Part 1 of the Natural Sciences tripos, he lacked the mathematical talent to become an outstanding physicist and turned instead to philosophy. In 1910 he obtained a first class with special distinction in Part II of the Moral Sciences tripos and in 1911 he was elected to a prize fellowship at Trinity for an essay which was subsequently enlarged into his first book, *Perception, Physics and Reality* (1914). After spells at the University of St Andrews and Dundee University College, and First World War work for the Ministry of Munitions, he became Professor of Philosophy at Bristol University. In 1923, however, he returned to

526

Trinity as fellow and college lecturer in Moral Sciences. In 1933 he was elected to the Knightsbridge Professorship in Moral Philosophy.

It is probable, Gauld writes, that Broad 'recognised his own intellectual capacities as being on a par with those of the many gifted men who had been and were Fellows of Trinity, and felt that he BELONGED in their fellowship as nowhere else.' He lived there for some fifty years, his rooms having once been occupied by Sir Isaac Newton. During that half century he, to many, did not appear to change in appearance, having seemed at the start of his occupancy to be much older than he really was and, as Garth Moore put it, 'he looked exactly the same when, in the same set of rooms, he died peacefully and suddenly, aged over eighty. To the last his mind was as alert as ever.'

He himself claimed in his autobiography that his interest in psychical research was 'almost life-long' and added, 'I do not know when it began, but I can hardly remember a time when it did not exist.' In another place in his autobiography he took pains to emphasise his faults of character, among them moral and physical cowardice. He felt himself ill-fitted for any life more exacting than that of a don, or perhaps a civil servant. Having, as he once said, been fortunate enough this time to put his hand into a sackfull of adders, plus one eel, he had been able to pull the eel from the bag. He did not desire to put his hand in the bag for a second trial. He was entirely too hard on himself and one can say that if there were more people around with Broad's character, the world would be a better place. Gauld puts the matter more clearly:

Broad judged himself morally, as in all other ways, only by the highest standards, and before one takes his self-strictures too seriously one should perhaps reflect that there may be more than one kind of courage and more than one kind of cowardice. Intellectually he shirked nothing. He possessed in the highest degree the capacity to weigh arguments, and to accept conclusions, without being in the least influenced by his own feelings and preferences. The conclusions which he reached must have been in some instances, and not least upon questions related to psychical research, altogether distasteful to him; and to reach and face such conclusions surely requires courage of no common kind. The capacity to argue dispassionately is one which both psychical research and philosophy could

527

and should foster; in practice they rarely do so, and one looks to Broad's example, as to that of Henry Sidgwick the predecessor whom he so much admired, more in the hope than in the expectation that it will be followed.

He did little practical work in psychical research beyond participating in a few investigations of allegedly haunted houses. He also had sittings with mediums. But his lasting contribution was his calm, considered assessment of the evidence for paranormal phenomena collected by psychical researchers of the highest standard over the best part of a century, and its relevance towards an understanding of human personality. His studies culminated in his *Lectures on Psychical Research* (1962), based on the Perrott Lectures given at Cambridge in the years 1959 and 1960. Alan Gauld vividly remembers the rustle of astonishment which went round the room during one of his Perrott Lectures when, after describing Mrs Leonard's 'independent voice', Broad looked up from his notes to remark that he had heard it himself.

Garth Moore noted that an important part of Broad's contribution to psychical research lies in the serious interest he took in it. It is a subject that even today is misunderstood, barely known in its findings and not considered to be respectable:

> But this is an attitude which can scarcely be maintained, when men of Broad's intellectual calibre are seen to take the subject so seriously and are prepared to spend so much time on it. It will always be to the credit of Cambridge (and of Trinity in particular) that it has been the pioneer in serious psychical research, and Broad takes his place in the distinguished company of Cambridge researchers, among whom are to be numbered F.W.H. Myers, the Sidgwicks, Arthur Balfour, Stratton and many others.

H.H. Price, in his in memoriam contribution, states:

> [Broad's] views about life after death are probably shared by a good many other people. But there are few who would state them so candidly as he did... He said 'so far as I can tell, I have no desire to survive the death of my present body, and I should be considerably relieved if I could feel much surer than I do that no kind of survival is possible.'

It was this quiet, unassuming, unflinching, massively erudite man who, in spite of his decades of training in philosophy and psychical research, had been shut out, so to speak, from taking an active, collaborative part in the Sidgwick Group's activities. It is obvious, however, whenever he had come into contact with people such as Salter seeking help in safeguarding the Scripts, and prepared to discuss with him matters relating to the whole question of the significance of the Cross-Correspondences, that he already had spent a great deal of careful thought upon them and had elucidated the basic background of the Story and the Plan. But in his innate disposition and because of Mrs Coombe-Tennant's almost paranoic suspicions, he had remained, to a large extent, remote and detached from their interests, until her youngest son Henry entered Trinity College as an undergraduate in 1932.

Almost forty years later, Henry Coombe-Tennant's contribution to the 'in memoriam' to Broad is illuminating, not only about Broad, but also to the influence Broad had on his student and friend.

I was Broad's pupil at Cambridge in the early thirties, and learnt much from his companionship. He gave me an interest in philosophical questions which has not diminished with the years, but which was to be no more than a hobby, so that I am not qualified to appraise his contribution to philosophy. As a teacher he was not, perhaps, so stimulating as Moore or Wisdom, nor so original as Wittgenstein, but from him more than from anyone else I learnt to discipline my thinking and free it from the pressures of emotion and prejudice, and not to be taken in by superficial arguments, half truths and bogus attitudes. We shared an interest in psychical research, especially in the conceptual problems raised by the notion of personal survival after death, and during my time at Cambridge we had many interesting conversations on religion.

I formed my first impression of Broad from his rooms in Trinity where I waited for my first interview with him in 1932. I expected someone tall, saturnine and remote, and it was a surprise when I found him in his study, mild and cherubic, playing with a yo-yo. This was the beginning of a three year friendship which was one of the formative influences in my life. Broad was a man of wide culture and acute judgment, and though his humour was often barbed he was fundamentally gentle and kind.

529

Yet he could be severe. His own standard of conduct and consideration for others was high, and he expected it to be reciprocated. Lapses were apt to be met with freezing displeasure. I once earned this by a brash criticism of the College kitchen arrangements over which he presided. And when in our first summer he took me to a garden where he had constructed a model railway complete with a miniature steam engine, which I managed to run at full speed into the buffers, he said nothing, but I was not asked again. Some of my clearest Cambridge memories are of the afternoon walks we often took together, discoursing on all manner of subjects, followed by tea and crumpets in his rooms, and often, in summer, a game at bowls at which I was no match for his patience and accuracy.

After going down in 1935 I saw him only at intervals. I think he was disappointed when I took a commission in the Regular Army instead of trying for a fellowship; and he must have been puzzled when twenty five years later I became a Roman Catholic and a Benedictine monk, though he kindly came to see me as soon as my novitiate was over, and later took a lot of trouble over two matters in which I was concerned. The first was the publication in 1965 of *Swan on a Black Sea*, the collection of scripts ostensibly communicated by my mother through Geraldine Cummins, to which Broad wrote a long and interesting Foreword. The second arose out of my revived interest in philosophy: from time to time I would write to him about my theories or those of philosophers in whom I was interested; he always replied quickly and often at great length, having given many hours of thought to what a lesser man might have treated with perfunctory interest.

As far as I know, Broad had no religious belief of any kind, though he would have called himself an agnostic rather than an atheist. His attitude to the possibility of human survival after death was complex. He obviously found it difficult to make sense of the idea and had no desire to survive himself; yet he seemed to be fascinated by the subject. For traditional Christianity, as opposed to its contemporary attenuations, he had a certain reluctant respect. He would have thought himself unworthy of a place in the Christian heaven; but in this, unless my reading of the Gospels is very much at fault, I believe he was mistaken.

530

22

The Soldier Monk

Pax inter spinis – peace among thorns.

The motto of the Benedictines

Fear no more the heat o' the sun
Nor the furious winter's rages;
Thou thy worldly task hast done,
Home art gone and ta'en thy wages:
Golden lads and girls all must,
As chimney-sweepers, come to dust.

Fear no more the frown o' the great,
Thou art past the tyrant's stroke;
Care no more to clothe and eat;
To thee the reed is as the oak:
The sceptre, learning, physic, must
All follow this, and come to dust.

Fear no more the lightning flash
Nor the all-dreaded thunder-stone;
Fear not slander, censure rash;
Thou hast finish'd joy and moan;
All lovers young, all lovers must
Consign to thee, and come to dust

. . . Quiet consummation have,
And renowned be thy grave.

Fidele from *Cymbeline* by William Shakespeare

In preparing this book I met, during the years of research, many memorable and helpful persons. Perhaps the most memorable, however, were two I never met in life, namely Jean Balfour and Henry Coombe-Tennant. Nevertheless, by the time I had completed the text I believed I knew them more clearly and intimately than many friends and colleagues whom I have encountered and cherished in my life, not only by Jean, and Henry's own written words but also what those who knew them told me about them.

I visited Downside Abbey, Stratton-on-the-Fosse, Somerset, on June 9th, 2004, with Lady Kremer, Jean's daughter, and my colleague Tricia Robertson. By that date the three remaining people who in their own very different ways had long been directly involved in Henry Coombe-Tennant's life and provided for him friendship, love and help had died. Jean Balfour departed this life on October 17th, 1981. Ral died on November 27th, 1968. And Henry's brother Alexander's death had occurred in November 2003.

It was the morning of a warm sunny day when we met Dom Philip Jebb at the beautiful abbey church. He is the archivist at Downside and also knew Henry during the quarter of a century he spent as the monk Dom Joseph Coombe-Tennant. Unstintingly Dom Philip gave us his time and help, discussing with us the life of Dom Joseph who had been for so long Henry the solitary traveller. Apart from giving us a valuable and detailed inventory of Henry's life, confirming his education, posts he had held in his Army career and Intelligence service, he told us much about Henry's character and warmly and affectionately related incidents in Henry's life as a monk and parish priest.

On 25th May, 1960, Henry was received into the Catholic Church. Successive dates in his progress to becoming a monk were as follows:

1961 September 24th. Clothed by Abbot Butler.
1962 September 25th. Simple Profession by Abbot Butler.
1963 Teaching in School.
1965 September 25th. Solemn Profession by Wilfrid Passmore, Claustral Prior.
1966 July 16th. Ordained by the Bishop of Clifton.
1969 September. Priest in charge at Radstock.
1973 December. Went to Little Malvern as Parish priest on the death of Dom Everard Faulkner.

1976 August. Returned to Downside to be Junior Master (looking after junior monks), in succession to Dom Edmund Lee, and Guest Master, in succession to Dom Richard Yeo. Assistant to Dom Dominic Mansi on the Radstock Mission.

1979 September. Ceased to be Guest Master and Junior Master.

It would appear then that as in all other organisations Henry had been part of in his life, he gave more than he was asked to do, going that extra mile that singles out the dedicated, dependable and justly valued comrade.

Dom Philip related how it was some time in 1961 that Henry rang a friend of his and in his characteristic understated way said 'Tell me about this Catholic thing!' followed some time later by a similar phone call: 'Tell me about this monk thing.' As a consequence of these enquiries he was accepted as a novitiate of Downside. It was as a novitiate he was given his new name Joseph. The novitiate stage lasted a year, and being found suitable and wishing to continue with this life, he took his solemn vows committing him to three years of obedience, stability and conversion. Again, being found suitable and wishing to continue, he took his final vows for life in 1965. It was also part of the process of becoming a full monk at Downside to train and become ordained as a priest. It was also a duty to teach in Downside Abbey School. Joseph did not enjoy teaching. He did it as a duty. Later, to the amusement of his colleagues, he said the best class he ever took was with a particularly tiresome lot of sixteen-year-olds he was supposed to teach the foundations of the faith. Having struggled with them, he came in one day and said, 'I have nothing to say to you. But if you have something to say to me, please do so.' Complete silence for the full forty minutes.

Joseph was a very private man, as he had been in the earlier parts of his life, yet he was much loved and respected by his new community. They particularly enjoyed him for his humour and his delightful vagueness: the proverbial professorial impractical person. Perhaps part of the reason for this vagueness was again a wish to protect his privacy. A charming story is told of him. He had just come in from driving his car (he was a very haphazard driver) and couldn't find his car keys. The others remonstrated with him: they can't be far: visualise exactly what you did when you left

533

the car; they must be just to hand, not to worry. Later he came and thanked them for their help, but added, 'I must take credit for finding the keys in the waste-paper basket!'

He once said of himself, again with characteristic understatement: 'I am a very boring person to whom very interesting things have happened.'

Downside has several parishes attached to it and in September 1969 Joseph became the parish priest to Radstock. He clearly must have enjoyed this new work, and although he was a man of remarkable intellect, he obviously had no trouble at all in connecting with the relatively uneducated, quite rough mining community, drinking endless cups of tea in their living rooms, bringing real comfort and understanding to their problems. Later he became the priest of Malvern, a rural community. Both communities got to love him very much. Even twenty years later, people living in Radstock and Malvern remember him with love and affection.

It was while Henry was in Baghdad that he fell into what might loosely yet accurately be called the 'dark night of the soul'. Much later, he gave a talk at Downside to the Association for the Propagation of the Faith (APF) in which he tried to explain the circumstances that brought him to drop agnosticism and embrace Christianity.

During the time we were with Dom Philip, he brought from the archives four large boxes that contained all the papers that had belonged to Henry and had been collected after his death in 1989. They had then been filed away in the archives of the Abbey. Dom Philip told us that as far as he knew, the boxes' contents had never been looked at since Henry's death.

With Dom Philip's permission, we opened the boxes. They contained letters, many addressed to Major Henry Coombe-Tennant, lecture notes, music manuscripts and unframed paintings he himself had created. On the top of the items in the box I opened was a manuscript. It was Henry's lecture notes for the talk he gave at Downside to the APF in January 1965. Reading the notes aroused strong feelings within me. For me it was a deeply poignant moment: it almost seemed that the man whom I had studied for so long was talking to me. My years of research and study of the letters, documents and papers in the Kremer Archive and elsewhere had already produced a close, sympathetic involvement, certainly an empathy, with Henry, who had always, in often difficult and dangerous circumstances, striven to do the best he could. Now the notes, in his handwriting, filled in a few more facets of the life, and inner life, of the man who had been Augustus Henry Coombe-Tennant. He had told the APF audience:

I have been asked to talk to you tonight on why I was an agnostic – which I was for nearly 30 years.

If I was in a flippant mood, I might say a possible short answer off-the-cuff would be mainly because I was made to go to Chapel every day at Eton and, secondarily, because I came to feel that the existence of God, as a hypothesis, was superfluous: that one could get along all right without it.

But if you then asked why I found my faith again at the end, in all fairness I would have to reply mainly because I found God was not superfluous but secondarily because I had been made to go to Chapel every day at Eton. So you see that the difficult question of compulsory religious services at school is as broad as it's long!

I was born and brought up in a Welsh village, and baptised in the Anglican village church. My father was a strict Sunday church-goer. How deep his religion went I never discovered. He was sixty when I was born, and nearly stone deaf when I grew old enough to talk. I enjoyed his company, but the deafness and the difference in our ages made serious conversation difficult.

My mother was a deeply religious woman but she did not go to Church. My father and I and my brother would go every Sunday at least once. Mr James, the elderly vicar, was a scholar and an expert on Welsh mediaeval poetry. His sermons were hard to understand, and an impediment in his speech made them difficult to hear. I did not like the archaic language of the prayer book, the Victorian hymns and anthems, and the sentimental harmonies of the village organist. I was bored, and in the winter cold. I acquired a dislike of church services which, to be candid, I have never really lost.

When at the age of 11 I entered a 'religious' phase, it took the form of sitting for half an hour in the evening in my room in front of a statue of Buddha, with candles lit and an incense-stick burning. I was not, of course, a Buddhist. I was groping for God. Had I been a Catholic I would have been sitting in

535

front of the Tabernacle – but in those days I knew nothing of Tabernacles or their contents. My parents wisely let this phase run its course, and it culminated a year later in my desire to be confirmed. As you know, it is not customary for Anglican boys to be confirmed before the age of 15, a practice which I still think has much to recommend it. I have a theory that one cannot begin to understand religion before the age of puberty. Certainly I do not think I understood much of the instruction I was given at the age of 12, and the fact that I remember nothing of it now shows that it made little intellectual impression on me. I made my first Communion with much devotion, but doctrinally I was weak.

I went to Eton when I was 13. I do not remember receiving any RI [Religious Instruction] at Eton. My impression was that it was given to boys when they were being prepared for confirmation so of course I missed it. Sc. [Scripture] was studied as a subject under the title of 'Divinity'. I found this subject very boring. I did not like Chapel services at Eton any better than those at my village church, and I resented having to go – once a day and twice on Sundays. However I did from time to time get up early on Sundays to go to Holy Communion, which was voluntary. I think I ceased to do so about the age of 17, and after I left Eton I seldom set foot in a church until nearly thirty years later. Oddly enough, however, towards the end of my time at Eton, I became a member of the Toc H – an interdenominational Christian society organised in regional branches and groups, and devoted to fellowship and good works – and continued actively a member during my time at Cambridge.

I used to go and visit the old and the sick, and when I was 21 I helped to organise a holiday camp for unemployed men near Durham. This experience made a profound impression on me, and led me to give up my idea of taking a fellowship in Philosophy at Trinity College, and to join the Army instead as a regular officer.

I had a remarkably interesting, exciting and often dangerous time during the war, but it never occurred to me to thank God for what I attributed to my own powers, to the help of others, or just to luck. For by this time I was a complete agnostic. I was not, and never have been an atheist. I kept an open mind

536

on the subject, and never considered religious belief and practice as simply the survival of a primitive superstition. On the contrary, I held that religion was an excellent thing – for those who needed it or were drawn to it – whether there was a God or not. Nor did my agnosticism affect my conceptions of duty, right and wrong. It seemed to me, then, as it seems to me now, that theism and morality are logically independent. Some people think that to say that an action is right or wrong simply means that God commands it or forbids it. I have never understood this. It is certainly not what these words mean in ordinary English usage. Nor does it seem natural to say that actions are only right or wrong insofar as they are commanded or forbidden by God. It would be better to say that God commands them because they are right, or forbids them because they are wrong. But it has always seemed to me that what is good and right would be so whether there was a God or not.

As an agnostic I found it just as difficult as anybody else – but no more difficult – to keep to what is so inappropriately called the 'straight and narrow path' of virtue. But I never questioned my duty to do so, and I think it was this sense of duty – derived no doubt from my upbringing at home and school – that saved me from going to the bad, which I might otherwise have done.

As an agnostic I had no belief or hope in life after death. But this did not lead me, as it leads some, to question the value of human relationships and right conduct. Even now, as a monk, fear of Hell is not a serious factor in my life (though perhaps it ought to be), nor is the prospect of eternal bliss one that I find particularly stirring. As far as I can make out from my younger colleagues, if I attain to the Beautific Vision I shall find myself one of countless millions of souls, all absorbed in the contemplation of God and at the same time all madly in love with each other. I cannot form a clear enough concept of this state of affairs to be strongly attracted by the prospect of its realisation.

I do not remember, as an agnostic, ever having made a serious study of the so-called 'proofs' of the existence of God. Had I done so, I would no doubt have found them even less impressive than I do now.

The root cause of my agnosticism was, I think, the notion

that religious behaviour is something one does in Church on Sundays, as an optional extra to one's ordinary duties to one's fellow men during the week, and that religious belief, where it exists, is largely a conventional attitude to a matter of purely speculative interest. In this, so, I am afraid, it seems to me, I was in the same position as the majority of my non-Catholic countrymen. Some would put the proportion as high as 90%. It is probably higher than it was 30 years ago.

How did I get out of this position? Six years ago, when I was serving in Baghdad, I became involved in a sequence of events and experiences whose significance seemed to me to transcend their actual content. I don't want to be questioned about these events or experiences. It will be sufficient to say that there was a period of profound mental and physical suffering, during which (if I may put it this way) my own ego, which had for so long been the self-sufficient centre of my inner life, disintegrated. I have grown a new ego since, of course, though not a self-sufficient one, but at that time there was nothing to hold me together. I was in pieces, and if the pieces were to be reassembled, a new principle of unity would have to be found.

I began the task that autumn by praying to a God in whose existence I did not believe. This remarkable performance seemed to work. I continued to pray, and also to think. I read some books about Christianity. I chose Catholic books, because I had often thought that if I ever turned to religion, it would be to the Catholic Church, who seemed to know her own mind. (I wonder if one can say that today.) At the end of the year I asked for instruction, and in May 1960 I was received into the Church by the Principal of the American Jesuit College in Baghdad.

When you find God at my age, and after my kind of life, you may feel a somewhat dramatic desire to give him all you have and keep nothing back. At first it seems that you can accomplish this at a single stroke by entering a monastery. It takes time to realise that it is the work of a lifetime. [I entered this monastery as a postulant in May 1960, and in September of that year I was clothed as a Novice, and so started on the long grind that is called the Religious life.] [Stroked out by Henry.]

I would ask for your prayers that I may stay the course.

538

At my request, Dom Philip kindly photocopied the manuscript and other documents for us. One of these was the long obituary written shortly after Henry's death. It follows in full and gives a vivid synoptic view of the life of Henry, the solitary traveller:

Obituary of Dom Joseph Coombe-Tennant, 1913–1989

Dom Joseph – Henry to those who knew him before he came to Downside – Coombe-Tennant was born in Neath, Glamorgan, on 9th April, 1913. His father, Charles Coombe-Tennant, of Cadoxton Lodge, belonged to a family long established in Wales and possessed of a wealth that seemed inexhaustible; and his mother, Winifred Pearce-Serocold, was a descendent of Oliver Cromwell. 'You know, I always feel people did what they thought best at the time', was how Henry once referred in an aside to his famous ancestor.

From Sir Oliver Lodge's memoir of Henry's elder brother, 'Christopher', who was killed with the Welsh Guards in Flanders in 1917, we learn that Henry was already demonstrating an exceptional intellect at the age of five, and even then was spoken of within his family as 'the wise one'. While Charles Coombe-Tennant died in 1929 when Henry was only sixteen, it is unusual to be able to record that his grandfather, another Charles, was born as long ago as 1796.

After West Downs he was sent to Eton where he shone as an academic and a chessplayer, twice winning the school cup. As a scholar, in 1932, he went up to Trinity College, Cambridge, and it was here, reading Philosophy that he first came into contact with Ludwig Wittgenstein, who was then lecturing at Cambridge, Guy Burgess, with whom he had also been at Eton, Donald Maclean, Anthony Blunt and Kim Philby. Although approached by The Apostles, 'after attending one of their sessions, I felt they weren't for me'. In later life, at the Foreign Office, he was to work alongside Burgess, Maclean and Blunt, and came to know Philby very well.

It was, however, the philosopher Ludwig Wittgenstein, and to a lesser extent his tutor Charlie Broad, who were to leave the strongest impression. Of Broad Henry was later to opine that his was the most powerful mind with which he had ever been brought into contact; while Wittgenstein remained for

Henry 'the only genius the twentieth century has produced'. His own philosophical abilities were made manifest when in 1935 he took a double first. 'I was fed up with much that had gone before', he remarked with the pronounced understatement that was all his own, 'and I said so'. And it was while he was at Trinity that he contributed to the philosophical journal *Mind* a paper dealing with specific aspects of linguistic analysis, which remains of significance to this day.

During his time at University, he took a term off to act as personal assistant to Archie Rose – a former diplomat who had spent much of his career in the Far East and had witnessed the Siege of Peking in 1900 and who at this time was working for the British Council in a world-wide attempt to improve international relations between students. After a short spell in Montreal, they crossed the Pacific to Northern China, and from there travelled for some six weeks by road and rail throughout the North-South axis of Eastern China, until reaching their final destination in Hong Kong.

A few months after coming down from Cambridge he joined the Welsh Guards, in which his eldest brother, Christopher, had served so briefly, before being killed in action eighteen years earlier. If Henry's pre-war service was straightforward and unspectacular, what followed after 1940 was anything but. In May of that year he played a personal part in ensuring the safe transit from Holland to Great Britain of the Dutch Queen Wilhelmina, which gained him his first wartime decoration.

Later in 1940, with a section of his regiment near Boulogne, he faced a German tank at point-blank range. 'The Germans gave us a time limit to surrender, failing which they threatened to destroy us. We were in no position to call their bluff; it would have been pointless to resist.'

He spent the next two-and-a-half years in various German prison camps, which he found dreary though not uninteresting. 'Prison camp life allowed many to take on roles they could only ever have dreamed about in normal life. Some men had always wanted to be musicians, but had never been able to earn a living by doing so. Now, in prison camp, some found themselves not just musicians but in charge of their own orchestra. There were many instances like this.' He himself, a fine pianist, was responsible time and again for enlivening the existence of those around him as he played piece after piece for hours on end.

Above all, though, it was his escape from Oflag VI B, in Warburg, near Kassel, and his successful return to England in the autumn of 1942 that marked for him personally the war's real turning point. The account of his *Return Journey* with two other officers was set down in a book of the same name by Major A.S.B. Arkwright, one of the three escapees. For Henry it was a lucky break, as his selection was only the result of another's last minute inability to make up the original trio. It was a journey of much suspense and tense moments, but crowned with success; and thereafter the Military Cross was held by all three men.

On his return to England he was keen to continue normal service with his regiment. But his fluency in French and overall ability saw him quickly chosen for underground work with the French and Belgian resistance movements, in advance of the D-Day landings of June 1944.

During the months of preparation a mechanical failure involved him in a chance meeting which was to remain unforgettable. Visiting his mother in Norfolk one weekend with a brother officer, their car broke down in a lonely lane in an area quite unknown to either of them. They started walking in search of help or a telephone. They had not walked far before a car drew up beside them; they were asked to get inside and driven on to a splendid house where they were served a memorable tea with, as Henry recalled vividly, 'the most charming hosts imaginable – the girl who had rescued us and her parents'. The house was Sandringham; the girl, H.R.H. Princess Elizabeth; and her parents, the King and Queen of England.

He dropped by parachute a few weeks prior to the invasion of Normandy; and during his period of training he had devised a special parachute for his terrier which he seriously intended taking with him. 'At the last moment I realized it would be impractical', he remarked laconically many years afterwards, 'and so I abandoned the idea.' Eccentricities like this peppered his whole life. Another one was that, when driving a car at night and coming to a road junction, he would switch off all his lights, ' because then I can see if anyone else is coming.' To add to his M.C., he was awarded the Croix de Guerre for his service with the 'Maquis'.

He ended the war as a Major, and from 1945 to 1948 served with the Welsh Guards in Palestine. Then after thirteen years' service, he left the Army and entered the Foreign Office, spending the next twelve years in the Special Intelligence Service, better known as MI6. As distinct from MI5 whose task is to catch enemy agents, that of the S.I.S. is to gather information about the enemy.

It is, understandingly, impossible to disclose anything in detail, certainly at this stage, about his work in that field, except to emphasise how highly esteemed it was on both sides of the Atlantic. No secrecy is violated, however, in recording that now came the time when he was to work closely with Burgess, Maclean, Blunt and, most of all, Kim Philby, 'Burgess was never my favourite person'. For Philby, however, he had agreeable personal memories, 'and if I ever saw him in the street today', he recalled in 1970, 'I'd have little hesitation in approaching him genially and asking "Hello, Kim. How are you?" '

When in the 1980s the Hollis and Blunt affairs hit the headlines of the national press – and in recent times there were mutterings about a 'fifth man' – certainly more than one voice was heard to muse smilingly: Could that man be at Downside Abbey? [According to Alan Gauld, even Professor C.D. Broad was accused as being the Fifth Man according to a newspaper cutting he has in his possession. He adds that he can't imagine anyone less likely than Broad to have fallen for Marxist propaganda.] As for Roger Hollis, Henry had little doubt of his innocence; while time will tell whether his high opinion of President Gorbachev was apposite.

He was serving as Second Secretary in the British Embassy in Baghdad at the time of the revolution of 1958; and he ended his service in the Foreign Office at the Hague, in 1960, where he had engaged a couple, Mickey and Gladys de Lange, to look after him, to whom he was to remain dedicated until the end of their lives. In this same year of 1960 he had bought a house in the village of Foxton, near Market Harborough in Leicestershire; he had installed the de Langes to manage the house and garden and there kept a couple of hunters with which to continue one of his favourite occupations with the Fernie. In sum, he had planned to settle down to conventional affairs – small, local and kindly – at which he would have been undoubtedly adept.

Two years previously, while in Iraq, and after a lifelong adhesion to agnosticism, he had become a Roman Catholic. 'I then felt that, as I had just about reached the end of my career in the Foreign office and as I had become a Catholic and was unmarried and had presumably a good number of years ahead of me, I might as well go the whole hog. So I decided to become a monk. My problem was where to go.' The choice of Downside was very much the result of discussions he had with today's Archbishop of Liverpool, The Most Revd Derek Worlock, 'who insisted Downside was the place for me. And how right he was! I would certainly not have been happy anywhere else.'

Apart, however, from Derek Worlock's insistence, an experience as a postulant also struck Henry as providential. Late one evening a solitary light was shining in the choir stalls of an otherwise pitch-black Abbey Church. Doing his tour of duties, Henry could not fail to notice the light, and promptly switched it off. In an instant a furious growl bellowed from the darkness: 'Turn on the light, you bloody fool'. 'When I heard that', smiled Henry, 'I knew at once Downside was the place for me.'

He was very fortunate in having Dom Ralph Russell as his novice master, a monk for whom Henry had great affection and regard. At the same time, recollection of his first year in the monastery was succinctly put when he once cited the three greatest days of his life: 'The day I left Eton; the day I escaped from prison camp; and the day I came out of the novitiate at Downside.'

In almost thirty years at Downside, he touched its activities at many points: as secretary to Abbot Passmore; as guestmaster; as parish priest of Little Malvern and Radstock; and as a man who from the beginning won the friendship and trust of all. Teaching he did not like, and he made no bones about it. He more than once remarked how he was 'not a schoolmaster', and it may be fairly stated that his few attempts to teach boys

Religious Instruction and General Paper were among the least successful features of his life. Where, however, school activities of a non-teaching type were involved, he could immerse himself with real and not synthetic enthusiasm. No one could have taken greater pleasure in running the Shooting Society, or delighted more in his evenings spent with The Vintners.

His house in Leicestershire, staffed and equipped in 1960 to see him through the evening of life, lasted merely 6 months, and thus never led to the traditional tedium he had vaguely intended. But before moving to Downside and renouncing his material possessions – and Henry was an unusually rich man – he was intent on providing for the de Langes for life. Realising that Mickey de Lange had a mercurial temperament, largely caused by a wartime wound while serving in the Dutch Navy, that would make further employment for him and his wife very uncertain, he characteristically set about ensuring their future. He bought them a house in Bristol, which was Gladys's birthplace; took pains to establish a trust in their favour; and from Downside kept a more than watchful eye on them for the next twenty-five years. When Mickey went blind temporarily in the 1970s, Henry was endlessly at his bedside, and undertook all the awkward negotiations with his surgeon; while simultaneously he comforted Gladys by visiting her repeatedly while Mickey was in hospital. After Mickey's death and when her arthritis had made her almost bed-ridden, Henry would drive over to Bristol once a fortnight with unfailing regularity to do her gardening. And towards her own end he arranged for a special staircase lift to be installed in her little house.

A scholar, an intellectual in the fullest sense of the word, soldier, intelligence agent, monk and parish priest, he had tested life at many levels. But those who knew him best will remember him not so much for what he did but for what he was. What he was was best set forth in his unforgettable personality and force of character. Tall, slim, of distinguished appearance and rivalling Teilhard de Chardin with his engaging and disarming smile, he was a gentle man of few words, softly spoken and aptly chosen, of patent integrity, modesty and natural charm – with the sugar taken out. Such integrity made him a man of secrets, and his lifetime facility for maintaining sealed lips turned him into a pillar of trust.

A gifted mathematician, he was equally accomplished as a philosopher, pianist, chess problemist and bridge player, with a love and profound knowledge of wine and food, of hunting, shooting and skiing, and, in his last years, of croquet. In his pre-Downside days a member of White's, Pratt's, the Athenaeum and Guards clubs: few men who are so often labelled – erroneously – as escaping the world had been more a part of it. As he once so tersely related monasticism to the big wide world: 'If you can't face up to problems out there, you'll never face up to them in here.'

In 1986 and 1987 he underwent hip replacement surgery – with disastrous results. The two operations were in themselves completely successful; but the side-effects of the immediate and marked reduction in his mobility, which made him largely dependent on others, brought about a new illness – a black and most terrible depression. Always a quiet man, he now became close to a mute and withdrew into himself. Henceforth his mind was being driven by a flagging willpower and he appeared to have lost his zest for living. While Lord Peyton is surely right in asserting that 'the pain which he endured towards the end never diminished the grace and serenity which he carried everywhere with him', it still became pitiful to watch so brilliant a light being slowly snuffed out.

He died at St Dunstan's, Stratton-on-the-Fosse, in the small hours of 6th November, 1989, while reciting prayers with the sister-in-charge. His funeral took place a week later in the Abbey Church, with the Abbot, the Rt Revd John Roberts – who by strange coincidence had been in the same wartime prison camp as Henry – concelebrating with other members of the Community. Many of the mourners had travelled a great distance and had risked foggy and unpredictable November weather, determined to pay a final tribute and be present at the graveside of their dear old friend. The closing words of the Abbot's address were poignantly put: 'He was a good man; a dear man. And we shall remember him until one day when we shall meet him again.'

If the definition of greatness is to grow old beloved, then Henry Joseph Coombe-Tennant serves as the textbook example. He was something special, met with perhaps only once in a lifetime; and those who had that privilege will treasure his memory till their own time is come.

This account of Henry's last days and end inevitably brings back to mind the death of Frederic Myers in 1901 when he died in the clinic in Rome in the presence of his family. In his tribute to Myers, published in the SPR *Proceedings*, Oliver Lodge wrote:

The termination of his life ... was physically painful ... but his bearing under it all was so patient and elevated as to extort admiration from the excellent Italian doctor who attended him... In the intervals of painful breathing he quoted from one of his own poems (The Renewal of Youth)...

'Ah, welcome then that hour which bids thee lie
In anguish of thy last infirmity!
Welcome the toss for ease, the gasp for air,
The visage drawn, the Hippocratic stare;
Welcome the darkening dream, the lost control,
The sleep, the swoon, the arousal of the soul!'

Thirty-two years before Henry's passing, on August 14th, 1957, the First World War poet Siegfried Sassoon was received into the Roman Catholic Church at Downside, in Somerset, from his house at Heytesbury on the edge of Salisbury Plain. On August 26th, Sassoon was hopelessly ill with stomach cancer. He died on September 1st, a week before his eighty-first birthday. One would like to believe that Dom Joseph, formerly Henry, the solitary traveller, on his deathbed had the experience described by Sassoon in his wonderful poem of the release of the spirit from the body: 'Everyone Sang'.

Everyone suddenly burst out singing;
And I was fill'd with such delight
As prison'd birds must find in freedom
Winging wildly across the white
Orchards and dark green fields; on – on – and out of sight.

Everyone's voice was suddenly lifted;
And beauty came like the setting sun:
My heart was shaken with tears; And horror
Drifted away... O but everyone
Was a bird; and the song was wordless; the singing will never
    be done.

PART 4

THROUGH A GLASS DARKLY

23

That Bourn from Which No Traveller Returns?

To sleep, perchance to dream, aye, there's the rub.
For in that sleep of death what dreams may come.

Hamlet, 3.1, William Shakespeare

The Eager Dead – A Study in Haunting. How appropriate is the title?

On the face of it, this book has been about people who became convinced that we survive death; it is also about people who, without holding that conviction, were influenced throughout a large part of their lives not only by those who held that belief but also because they themselves were totally convinced that a wide variety of paranormal phenomena had been observed and recorded in a scientific manner.

The former group, moreover, was also convinced that those on the other side had not lost their interest or concern for the people in the world they had left but strove to implement new agendas formed by experience gained by a wider perspective and bring to fruition on this side unfinished business interrupted by their deaths. The former group also believed that the other world people could do this by contacting the living, convincing them that their friends now beyond the veil still existed, and by persuading them to carry out certain actions. These actions, they maintained, were of crucial importance to the well-being and happiness of a large number of human beings. Indeed, if the Plan were realised in this world, it would benefit enormously the universal human situation.

The latter group of people contained those who had also studied in depth the evidence for the occurrence of events of massive

549

paranormality but, while accepting that these events had taken place and were still occurring, never could bring themselves to take the final step and accept a total belief that survival of death was a certainty. Some accepted it as a probability but could not decisively dismiss the alternative theory that perhaps a form of super-ESP might, just might, also cover the phenomena.

Nevertheless, at this level, the title of the book is appropriate for it is certainly true that most of the members of both groups could be said to have been *haunted* for much of their lives, even if some of them could not quite bring themselves to accept the reality of the eager dead.

It is not possible to put the main players in this story categorically into one appropriate group, for some of them at times slipped from one group to the other. There are very few intelligent people who have never ever questioned their strongest convictions or found that they have changed their opinion about some matter only to find that, in time, they have slipped back into the former opinion. The ultimate doubt is, of course, solipsism: where one is certain of only one thing, namely that one exists. As Descartes put it: 'I think, therefore I am.' As far as one knows, everything else may be a creation of one's imagination.

Nevertheless in the light of the above caveat let us look at the composition and calibre of the two groups.

In the first group can be found Frederic Myers, Arthur James Balfour, Gerald William Balfour, Mrs Sidgwick, Lady Jean Balfour, Sir Oliver Lodge, Mrs Verrall, Helen Verrall, J.G. Piddington, Richard Hodgson, Mrs Winifred Coombe-Tennant and Alice Johnson. It should be remembered that many of them came to their belief in survival of bodily death only after many years of careful, cautious study of well-authenticated paranormal phenomena. Indeed in Richard Hodgson's case the slow cautious transition was from a status of total scepticism and hyper-alertness to fraud to a final conviction that survival of death took place.

In the second group can be found Edmund Gurney, Professor Henry Sidgwick, Professor William James, W.H. Salter, Professor C.D. Broad, Professor Charles Richet, Henry Coombe-Tennant and possibly his brother, Alexander.

Apart from the deep personal involvement of a number of people in these groups with the Palm Sunday Case and the Plan, the members of both groups were associated for much of their lives

550

with the Society for Psychical Research. It is worth remembering and repeating the fact concerning that society that throughout its existence from its origin in 1882 to the present date, the SPR has enjoyed the allegiance and expertise of some of the most gifted scientists, psychologists, physicians, philosophers and statesmen who have existed during that period of time. Brian Inglis's assessment of the calibre of the membership of the society, given in Chapter 4 of this book, is worth reading again to remind oneself that, in the first century of the SPR's existence, among the 51 Presidents of the society there were 19 Professors, 10 Fellows of the Royal Society, 5 Fellows of the British Academy, 4 holders of the Order of Merit and one Nobel prizewinner.

It has also been seen that the careful and prolonged studies by psychical researchers, sometimes over decades, of mediums such as Mrs Piper, Mrs Leonard, Mrs Willett, Mrs Garrett, and Miss Cummins have demonstrated beyond any reasonable shadow of doubt to anyone of open mind that these psychics again and again could acquire knowledge in a paranormal manner. The majority of the psychical researchers who participated in such studies or, coming later into psychical research and studying carefully the detailed, thoughtful, numerous and varied case reports in the literature, came to the conclusion that unless one accepted a variation of super-telepathy, clairvoyance and precognition, the so-called super-ESP theory, the possibility that some people survive death, retaining their essential personalities, memory, characteristics, skills and concern for those they have left behind, had to be taken very seriously indeed.

If we accept however that the varied, uncommon, bewildering phenomena of the paranormal are as real as those of any other scientific field of study, we are of course faced with the enormous problem of making sense of it all. The distinguished first President of the SPR, Professor Henry Sidgwick, once remarked that, 'Facts without a theory simply form a mob.' In a parallel great enterprise in science taking shape at the beginnings of the twentieth century – quantum mechanics – one of its pioneers, Erwin Schrodinger, stated: 'I can see no other escape from this dilemma ... that some of us should venture to embark on a synthesis of facts and theories, albeit with second-hand and incomplete knowledge of some of them and at the risk of making fools of ourselves.' Carl Gustav Jung himself, in his scathing statement 'I shall not commit the fashionable stupidity of regarding everything I cannot explain as fraud' also dismissed the facile argument of the negative sceptics that what they could not swallow must be attributed to fraud.

In other words, in any nascent science, the pioneer theorist at the cutting edge is trying to make sense of a bewilderingly diverse range of phenomena, conscious that at least the majority of the observations are honestly reported, but possibly a fraction of them inadequately or even misleadingly from a lack of the proper equipment and understanding, with a further fraction mendaciously fabricated by knaves for career.

For the above reasons, and the data given in this book, we see then that the respective opinions of the two groups of people listed at the beginning of this chapter were based on critical, intelligent examinations of the phenomena, not merely passively studied but often conducted interactively with the communicators professing to be their deceased friends. But the outstanding question that faces us would then appear to be:

If we accept that the Sidgwick Group was correct and there was an active, planning body of intelligent beings on the other side of death, why did these beings fail to achieve their purpose, stated with so much confidence? Why did the Plan fail?

24

The Best-laid Schemes

The best-laid schemes o' mice and men gang aft agley,
And leave us naught but grief and pain for promised joy.

Robert Burns, 'To a Mouse'

There seems little doubt to anyone familiar with the Cross-Correspondences that if the Sidgwick Group and W.H. Salter were correct in accepting that the Cross-Correspondences contained an ambitious plan, claimed to have been conceived on the other side of death, a Plan predicting the birth of a Messianic human being – a designer baby, to use a modern term – who would save the world and usher in a new Augustan Age, then something went drastically wrong. If Henry was indeed the 'designed' and chosen one, he did not succeed in transforming the world into a markedly better place for the human race. Certainly his life was exemplary. He was highly intelligent, totally conscientious, a courageous soldier with an exceptional war record, who also for many years served his country post-war as a military man involved in Intelligence work. In his subsequent life as a Benedictine monk at Downside Abbey he was much loved, and as a Roman Catholic priest, he was devoted to his parishioners at West Malvern and Radstock. A man richly endowed with great talents, he placed these qualities unreservedly and unselfishly at the disposal of his parishioners in a life of natural grace and serenity. He must have helped and comforted many in distress. If any of us could have all of that, or an equivalent selfless exemplary lifetime of actions, said about us in our obituary, I feel that most of us would be satisfied – and rather surprised.

But Henry Coombe-Tennant did not save the world.

Did the communicators who promised such great things totally misunderstand their limitations? If they did exist in a post-mortem dimension, was their state as deluding as a living person's dream, which, when the person is asleep, is acceptable in its entirety as real, even a state in which seemingly intelligent, logical and practical plans can be made by himself or with other people he encounters in the dream. When that person wakens, however, the dream state is perceived to be fanciful, irrational and untrustworthy, the plans full of flaws or contradictions.

It also has to be said that the communicators themselves, as if at some times they experienced a clearer understanding of their state, gave warnings of their limited powers. On one occasion Gurney said through Mrs Willett: 'You never seem to realise how little we know. I'm not – sometimes I know and can't get it through, but very often I don't know.' Nevertheless, they stated their sense of taking part in a series of experiments, some of which had failed; it was their *hope*, not certainty, that they, in particular Francis Maitland Balfour and Edmund Gurney, by their expanded expertise, could bring about the birth of the genetically endowed child and influence him psychically during his lifetime. As a result of their studies, both Jean Balfour and Gerald Balfour came to believe in the Plan. In the memorandum Jean wrote at Whittingehame in February 1945, she stated:

ever since M.L. died, the activities of the group on the 'Other Side', responsible for all these Scripts, have been concerned with the production of a special type of child: and that several children have undoubtedly been deliberately produced, but were, for some reason or other, failures ... finally their efforts culminated in the production of Henry 'Augustus', whose origin and conditions of birth were evidently regarded as perfect and hopeful.

It was during the sittings with Mrs Piper in Birmingham in October 1910 that the Gurney communicator through Mrs Piper urged Winifred Coombe-Tennant to have another child, while in a Willett script Gurney maintained that the child the group entreated Winifred to have had long been planned, planned in the highest quarters, to an extent which it was difficult to exaggerate, and that the child would possess a remarkable personality – a genius, in fact, of high order – and would prove to be the greatest of his psychic works, to which all else had been leading up. This was not at all an unbelievable idea in that part of the twentieth century between the two world wars. Jean Balfour wrote:

> The idea that Augustus Henry might be a superior being and that 'the people on the Other Side' had had a hand in his birth and spiritual constitution was not so strange in those days (from the end of the First World War, 1918, over about 14 years to Hitler's time) as it seems to us now. Granted we were all young and romantic, we were amused rather than critical and not in the least antagonistic. Sometimes, while brushing our hair at bedtime, we used to discuss with B.B. [Betty Balfour] these ideas, that Henry had been born at the will of the Gods, and that he was destined to become a great world-leader, and inaugurate the coming 'Golden Age'. Nevertheless, as I recollect, there used to be an almost invisible twinkle in B.B.'s eye!
>
> Her sister, Emily Lutyens ('Aunt Emmie') was an ardent theosophist and the expectation of a new Messiah was perfectly familiar to the Balfour circle. I think it is true to say that all over the world at that period, a movement existed creating a mental atmosphere, in which some sort of spiritual intervention in the affairs of the world was tacitly assumed: and lots of people held the belief that a universal Saviour was about to arise.
>
> Not long after I married, (about 1927 I think) 'Aunt Emmie' brought the young Indian Krishnamurti – the hope of the Theosophist movement – to Fishers Hill when I was staying there with my baby son Gerald. Krishnamurti was about 17 years old at the time, and one could not have met a more charming, gentle creature, full of wisdom and spiritual depth; but B.B. told me afterwards that G.W.B. was quite sure that Augustus Henry's prospects were quite superior...
>
> So it must be borne in mind that the possibility of a remarkable human being sent by God was 'in the air', and we young ones were expectant, not to say convinced.

As the twentieth century progressed, and the social climate

changed, various factors in the Plan formerly accepted without qualms by many on this side of the grave began to lose their attraction and even respectability. In the thirties and forties of the century there were elements in it that became repellant and even unpleasantly and unacceptably immoral, sickened as people were by the atrocities committed by the Nazis in their unhinged fantasy of producing a pure Aryan race, murdering in the vilest conditions millions of people they considered to be members of a sub-species. But in the early years of the century, still thrilled by the achievements of science and technology, and enthusiasm for the Darwinist doctrine of the survival of the fittest, the idea of using genetic influence intelligently as guidance for the improvement of humanity, by the discouragement of the genetically disabled and mentally handicapped from reproducing, was accepted by many as desirable. Arthur Balfour himself had chaired a Conference on Genetics and Eugenics in the first decade of the twentieth century. Naturally the Rayleigh-Strutt herd of cattle used genetic breeding to improve the stock. Indeed Alexander Coombe-Tennant's own herd contained some cattle from the Rayleigh-Strutt herd. But was it right, if the Plan had been correctly interpreted, to design and influence in life for a specific purpose a human being? Nevertheless, Winifred's account of her strange dream of the night of February 1st–2nd, 1912, is another factor to be taken into consideration. She recalled that the Majestic Figure:

> came towards me and took my face between its hands and gazed into my very soul and I into its soul. (I don't know whether it was a man or woman). I can't describe what follows because it was all 'feelings' and escapes definition. But I felt just worship, then amazement, then joy – and the figure seemed to feel no amazement but great tenderness, and it said these words: 'You have not chosen me but I have chosen you' and then the word 'Mother' is the next I remember. I knew it was speaking to me and I only remember that the last words meant (I don't remember the actual ones) that when I next saw it, it would be in the likeness of a human Babe and that what was written on the thing picked up was a destiny that it should come into the world through me.

One version of religious teaching, of course, is that if we do have more than one life on this planet, we may choose for a specific purpose the circumstances into which we will be born, though in entering the next life that purpose may be forgotten. It is not an idea that concerned many people in the West but, ironically, at the beginning of the twenty-first century, with the decoding of the genome and the increasing mastery in cloning species, including human beings, moral questions have arisen that ever more urgently need acceptable answers. Designer babies once again confront us, not so much trailing clouds of glory but fogs of foreboding.

On the other hand, perhaps the failure of the Plan was due to a lack of some vital spark in Henry himself? As time went on, several of the 'watchers' began to suspect that this was the main defect. W.H. Salter's letter to Jean Balfour of January 14th, 1967, puts it neatly:

> The papers you have sent me are of absorbing interest, both the letters and your summing up the position as to Henry. It is rather like some of the old fairy tales in which the hero receives at birth every sort of endowment, except one. In his case health, good looks, physical courage, first-rate brains, but not somehow what our ancestors called, ... 'a fire in his belly'. He may have been born with that, and had it damped down by 'smother love'. I still think he may do something really important.

Jean herself had worried about Henry's potential ability to emerge as a messiah.

> I once asked G.W.B. if he thought Henry had any inkling of what the Scripts led us to expect would develop in him? He replied 'Yes, he had little doubt that Henry had a fairly good idea of it: neither D.D. [Dame Edith Lyttelton] nor his mother (the two people closely in touch with him always) were in the least what one would describe as discreet, and he felt certain they had long ago dropped broad hints.' I very much regret that he should have any knowledge whatever of the possibility that he is fated to play a great part in human affairs, for such a knowledge, if taken seriously, would be bound to set any young man apart from his fellows. In one destined to be a Messiah, of the traditional sort, the passionate conviction of being 'chosen and sent', arises *from within*.

557

She too, had also puzzled over the many sterling qualities in Henry, coupled with a seeming lack of passion. She wrote:

> And yet, in spite of good looks, perfect manners, fine achievement, brilliant brains and lots of experience, he strikes one as a singularly passion-less creature, without any great enthusiasms. Yet he is rare, and good: and there is lots of time still for him to develop in startling ways. Only nothing about him just *now* gives me the feeling that a mere spark is needed to light up a great blaze in him. But suppose, if he should fall in love? – *That* might provide the spark. But will he, ever? I think myself it would take some courage to bring home a wife to that wonderful almighty mother of his! A perusal of these letters alone gives one a picture of the especial problems she herself creates in the life of those around her. These letters made me wonder with infinite pity for her son. Whether the possibility of failure of the Great Plan, (a possibility which was always present) has augmented with the years: and whether the Group, having succeeded in producing their new being in the first place, could not extend their influence sufficiently far into this world of flesh, to dominate his growth all the way. If his mother could always have remained 'Mrs Willett', they might have been able to do so much more than could ever have been the case when Mrs Tennant took possession of the field.

Whatever his gifts, the spark that lit the blue touch-paper in the cases of Swedenborg and Andrew Jackson Davis always seemed to have missed him.

Nevertheless, he did join the Roman Catholic Church and enter the Benedictine Order. Why did he do so after so many years during which he was so obviously uncommitted to any firm religious belief? Although he had admitted to a long-term deep interest in psychical research and its implications concerning human personality, and although the Cummins scripts had obviously deeply impressed him, he had also written to Jean:

> I am not convinced that she [Geraldine Cummins] has had direct or indirect access to my mother herself i.e. to a personality that has persisted through death. The survival of memory is

no doubt a necessary condition of the survival of personality, but I doubt whether it is a sufficient condition. It seems possible that individual personality may come to an end though memories persist in a form accessible to mediums.

In his June 16th, 1960 letter to Jean Balfour, he wrote:

> You and Ral will probably be surprised to hear that I have become a Roman Catholic. Needless to say this step was not taken lightly. It was preceded by about eight months of reflection, study and instruction, starting from scratch – i.e. a position of agnosticism and ignorance. This study was not begun or pursued as a purely intellectual exercise, & the whole process has involved a considerable inner upheaval. I have not consciously been influenced by the existence of the SPR Scripts or by anything I can remember of their contents, nor by the Cummins' Scripts. Nor do I imagine that such a development fits what is called 'The Plan'. As you probably know, the Roman Catholic Church forbids recourse to mediums, and I should not feel able to invite Miss Cummins to produce any more scripts. This prohibition is of course directed against 'Spiritualism' rather than Psychical Research.

Even in this letter to Jean there is a suggestion that he was employing his usual understatement regarding the exact motivation of his conversion to Roman Catholicism. Certainly in his Downside talk to the Association for the Propagation of the Faith he mentions the trauma he endured in Baghdad during a period of profound mental and physical suffering but resolutely refuses to be questioned about its cause.

It is possible of course that it was his increasing distaste for his endless tours of duty in Intelligence work and his inside knowledge of the murky spins and actions in the Middle East following from such work that persuaded him to seek a more satisfactory service to enrol in. He had always seemed to have a need to serve in an organisation with rules and regulations and the Catholic Church certainly had these. It is also possible that the upheaval he refers to in his letter to Jean could have originated at least to some extent in his exposure to the Cummins' scripts, enhanced by the ever-present influence of his mother, even after her death, or even to his realisation of who his father really was. Or perhaps those traumatic experiences in Baghdad he refused to speak about that resulted in a complete nervous breakdown were real and were the key events, far more important than any other life-events for his complete change of career.

Or could it be that the discarnate group, still trying to influence Henry, managed to steer him in his decision in the hope that in the Roman Catholic Church the best opportunity would present itself for the Plan to succeed? *If he could have become Pope?* The thought had occurred to Jean but had subsequently been dismissed by her as unconvincing.

Even if a modern person is knowledgeable concerning psychical research and its importance with respect to our understanding of human personality, it is probable that that person, if they have heard of the Cross-Correspondences, will have little or no appreciation in depth of the literature and the Classics quoted so frequently in them, those truffle quotations carefully and cautiously identified and correlated among the scripts by the interpreters over so many years. From our perspective of the best part of a century later and a knowledge of progress made in that time in psychical research and parapsychology we are aware of at least some factors that the Sidgwick Group were probably unaware of. As Alan Gauld has put it (in a private communication to the author):

Once the Plan in respect of Henry had been spelled out in the 'Willett' scripts of 1912–13 (which it was pretty un-equivocally) and had become known to the leading interpreters, how far could hope and expectation have led to interpretation of both past and subsequent scripts in the light of it? Remember how closely bound by ties of blood or friendship and indeed paternity/maternity were the leading interpreters to persons mentioned in or supposedly behind the scripts as well to each other. G.W. Balfour, the father of the destined one, states on p. xxii of his very useful introduction to Volume II of 'Notes and Excursuses' that he has assumed as 'a working hypothesis' that the communicators 'really are what they claim to be.' And there is the question of how much the various automatists could have learned or picked up about the drift of the interpretations. An essential paper here is the long one contributed by Mrs Sidgwick to volume 1 of 'Notes and Excursuses' on the dates on which the various automatists were first shown scripts produced by the others (if of course they were ever shown them at all). Mrs Verrall didn't learn about the Plan etc. until her career as an automatist was nearly over, Mrs Salter not until much later... All the interpreters of course did their best not to be influenced by their own beliefs and hopes. But the subtleties of many 'experimenter effects' and the devious and hidden pathways by which they may operate have only become fully realised in the last few decades, and we now know that hints and promptings can be given and taken up unawares by experimenters and subjects alike, even in apparently strict experimental situations.

Gauld also states that he would have been far more impressed with the Cross-Correspondences if they had come to an end about 1912. He regards some of the scripts prior to that date as extraordinary and notes (see above) that by 1912–13 the Plan in respect to Henry had been spelled out in the 'Willett' scripts of those years. On the other hand it must be pointed out that those scripts by Mrs Willett from 1912 to 1929 pertaining to the Palm Sunday Story are remarkably relevant to the events of Mary Lyttelton's death and the events immediately following from that death.

But it also has to be said, as those of us who have sat in mediumistic circles have had to note, there are sometimes features that can shake our confidence. One is the fraction of such circles where the sitters are solemnly assured from time to time by the communicators that there is something very special about this circle, that if the sitters only have patience matters of great importance will result. It is also of concern that when some circles of this nature end, the reasons given for this unexpected cessation sometimes verge on the utterly ludicrous. The important Scole circle ended because the sitters were solemnly told that it had to be shut down because it was causing time travel difficulties for intelligent aliens in another galaxy!

Perhaps a further cause for concern is that some of the communicators, going under such high-sounding names as Imperator, or Moses of Old, or John Sebastian Bach, or Longfellow, can at times spout the most appalling nonsense. Imperator, despite his arrogant name, was often guilty of producing great quantities of pseudoscientific and inflated religious nonsense. Nevertheless the Sidgwick Group of investigators, who had known and worked for years with Myers, Gurney and Sidgwick in life, were reluctantly forced to the conclusion that these communicators displayed the intelligence, personality characteristics, skills and knowledge they had possessed in life, being able to discuss with G.W. Balfour, Sir Oliver Lodge and others in the Group recondite topics relevant to the problems of communication and the implementation of their agendas. My own study over the years of quite a number of the scripts, among them many where such conversations and discussions between incarnate and discarnate are taking place produces firm conviction that the members of the Sidgwick Group taking part in them were indeed, in spite of their innate caution, slowly and reasonably persuaded that they were talking with their old friends, even in spite of the 'noisy' communication channels the friends were using.

Through some mediums, communicators manifest who claim to be advanced teachers. They talk of spiritual levels of development, of levels as far above them as they are above us. Perhaps the communicators claiming to be the surviving spirits of Sidgwick, Gurney and Myers did struggle to understand the teachings of others, perhaps their hope was moulded to some extent by their religious and Classical upbringings that a messianic child could be born and would by his life initiate a major leap in the spiritual level of the human race.

The richness of human personality, both supraliminal and subliminal, is still largely unexplored. The question of whether a human being survives the death of his or her body is one, thanks to the well-authenticated evidence gathered by that century of psychical researchers led by the great pioneers Sidgwick, Gurney and Myers, that any intelligent and well-read person must take seriously. Moreover, that person must take as highly probable the proposition that survival of some sort *does* take place. The accumulation of databases from more recent studies of paranormal phenomena in the field of human personality beyond the laboratory made by Stevenson, Haraldsson, Gauld and others, has forced many psychical researchers to take seriously the concepts of obsession, possession, 'drop-in' communications and children who very convincingly display detailed memories of a past life. Far from such studies negating the importance of the Cross-Correspondences, they support the C.C.'s challenge and importance for study, even though many questions raised still remain unanswered, any proposed answers still debatable.

Were the communicators who they claimed to be? The investigators' many years of cautious study finally convinced them that they were.

Had they, even if they did survive, a clear perception of their state or is it that although there is survival, with 'special interest' groups, who converse and remember unfinished business and plan strategies to complete it, they exist in a confusing, dreamlike state, a state so strange as to be impossible for them to give us any real understanding of its nature? The statements on occasion by Gurney and Myers seemed to convey a sense of a somewhat restricted perception and limited knowledge.

Even if their ingenious and intricate puzzle was genuine, was the communicators' Plan feasible? Even if it was, it failed.

Was her mother instinct so powerful, and was she so convinced of the almost god-like talents of each of her children, that, even if they did exist, the communicators' flow of information through her *and any other medium* was constantly being perturbed strongly by the most primitive desires of the mother? And did what some of the investigators called her 'smother-love' also contribute significantly to that failure?

Broad talked somewhere of Winifred Coombe-Tennant's 'maternal megalomania' and this was obviously very marked. Although her close relationship with Gerald Balfour had lasted a considerable number of years, it was largely shattered when Balfour wrote what to Winifred was a totally insufficiently eulogistic preface to her memorial book concerning her first son, Christopher. It is probably not irrelevant that, following the death of her young daughter Daphne, she suffered an acute and quite long-lasting depression. It was after this that she took up automatic writing, and doubtless harboured the idea that Daphne's short life had some kind of point and purpose. Filtering into her script came the concept that Daphne's birth and life was an attempt guided from the beyond to create a very special human being. She told Mrs Verrall about this long before Henry was conceived or even thought of and Mrs Verrall agonized in her diary over the possibility, which she found morally repellent, that Daphne had been created as a sort of experiment in psychological eugenics by beings who were prepared to discard her as a failure. Later Mrs Verrall concluded that she had misunderstood matters. One can understand why Winifred might have been open, consciously, subconsciously, half-consciously to this idea, and how it might have stuck and been developed.

There is also the debateable point that if there were a Plan and an experiment in psychological eugenics of which Henry was the result (and one must remember here that such a plan, which even modern genetics is not yet capable of implementing *in utero*, becomes yet more implausible when supposedly conducted by a C19 embryologist who predated the very concept of modern 'genetics', and a psychologist whose only claim to expertise in developmental psychology was having one baby daughter) that experiment failed completely, or at any rate yielded no obvious evidence of success. Of course Henry was a remarkably gifted and impressive man, but his ordinary heredity and his excellent education are surely quite sufficient to account for that.

So many questions still arise from this particular study, to add to all those other unanswered questions debated for thousands of years concerning the nature of human personality and summarised in the philosophical yet sombre words of Pindar:

> 'What is a man? What is he not?
> He is but a shadow in a dream.
> But when the gods smile upon him,
> There is a light upon Earth,
> And life is sweet as honey'.

If the gods (mortal or immortal) did smile upon Henry, it brought him little light and a life often fraught with worry and pain

Fraser Nicol suggested that Frederic Myers was the Coleridge of psychical research. He was able, in his prodigious output of daring, highly skilled deductions of the nature of human personality from the evidence of psychical research, even in those early years of its existence, to enlist, together with his largely self-taught expertise in philosophy, psychology, logic, and those other disciplines he mastered, his poetic intuition, his own experience of what he called 'subliminal upsurges', to create the lasting, still invaluable legacy he left us. He himself was well aware of the words of the person I would term the psychical researcher of poets, namely Wordsworth:

'Those obstinate questionings
Of sense and outward things,
Fallings from us, vanishings;
Blank misgivings of a creature
Moving about in worlds not realised,
High instincts, before which our mortal nature
Did tremble like a guilty thing surprised:
'Those shadowy recollections,
Which, be they what they may,
Are yet the fountain-light of all our day,
Are yet a master-light of all our seeing;
Uphold us, cherish, and have power to make
Our noisy years seem moments in the being
Of the eternal Silence: truths that wake
To perish never;
Which neither listlessness, nor mad endeavour,
Nor man nor boy,
Nor all that is at enmity with joy,
Can utterly abolish or destroy!'

To perceive these intangible yet powerful indications of other dimensions and feel impelled to try to map them and understand their nature is and remains the impetus driving the true psychical researcher. I hope that I may be forgiven for adding that although much has been achieved by successive psychical researchers since the days of Frederic Myers, none has surpassed his priceless legacy to us. He was indeed, as that young parapsychologist at the SPR Conference at Northhampton University unconsciously but truly termed him, 'some guy'!

But still there remains, even yet incompletely answered, that question from *Lord Halifax's Ghost Book*, the question with which this book began, the question every human being has to face and consider at some time in his or her life:

'Where are the dead – those who have loved us and whom we have loved; and those to whom we have done some irreparable injury? Are they gone from us for ever, or do they return?'

Time Chart

Date:	Initials frequently used in book	Event
1809, February 12		Birth of Charles Darwin
1819, May 24		Birth of Queen Victoria
1819, August 26		Birth of Albert, Prince Consort
1822, February 16		Birth of Sir Francis Galton
1823, January 8		Birth of Alfred Russel Wallace
1825, May 4		Birth of Thomas Henry Huxley
1832, June 17	W.C.	Birth of Sir William Crookes
1833, March 20	D.D.H.	Birth of Daniel Dunglas Home
1838, May 31	H.S.	Birth of Henry Sidgwick
1842, November 12		Birth of Lord Rayleigh (John William Strutt, Baron Rayleigh)
1843, February 6	F.W.H.M.	Birth of Frederic Myers
1844, February 10		Birth of Sir William Fletcher Barrett
1845, March 11	E.M.B. = Mrs H.S.	Birth of Eleanor Mildred Balfour
1845, March 22		Birth of Anne Eliza Hill (Annie Marshall)
1847, March 23	E.G.	Birth of Edmund Gurney
1848, July 25	A.J.B.	Birth of Arthur James Balfour
1850	S.H.B.	Birth of Samuel Henry Butcher
1850, May 26	M.C.L.	Birth of Mary Catherine Lyttelton
1851, February 5	A.W.V.	Birth of Arthur Woollgar Verrall
1851, November 10	F.M.B.	Birth of Francis Maitland Balfour
1851, June 12	O.J.L.	Birth of Sir Oliver Lodge
1852, July 31	C.C.-T.	Birth of Charles Coombe-Tennant
1853, April 9	G.W.B.	Birth of Gerald William Balfour
1854, January 21		Birth of Eusapia Palladino
1855, September 24	R.H.	Birth of Richard Hodgson
1856, February 5	F.P.	Birth of Frank Podmore
1859, June 27		Birth of Leonora Simonds (Mrs Piper)

1859	M.V.	Birth of Mrs Margaret de Gaudrion Verrall
1861, December 14		Death of Albert, Prince Consort
1869, January 24	J.G.P.	Birth of John George Piddington
1874, November 1	W.C.-T.	Birth of Mrs Winifred Coombe-Tennant
1875, March 21 (Palm Sunday)		Death of Mary Catherine Lyttelton
1876, August 29		Death of Annie Marshall
1880, March 19	W.H.S.	Birth of William Henry Salter
1882, April 19		Death of Charles Darwin
1882, May 28		Birth of Mrs Gladys Osborne Leonard
1882, July 19		Death of Francis Maitland Balfour
1883, July 4	H.V. = Mrs H. Salter	Birth of Helen Woollgar de Gaudrion Verrall (Mrs Salter)
1886, June 21	D.D.H.	Death of Daniel Dunglas Home
1887, December 30	C.B.	Birth of Charlie Dunbar Broad
1888, June 23		Death of Edmund Gurney
1891, November 1		Death of Leah Fox
1892, July 2		Death of Katie Fox
1893, March 8		Death of Margaret Fox
1895, June 29		Death of Thomas Henry Huxley
1897, October 10	C.C.-T.	Birth of Christopher Coombe-Tennant
1900, February 2	J.B.	Birth of Jean Balfour (Countess of Balfour)
1900, August 28		Death of Henry Sidgwick
1901, January 17		Death of Frederic Myers
1901, January 22		Death of Queen Victoria
1902, December 31	Ral	Birth of Robert Arthur Lytton ('Ral') Balfour
1905, December 20	R.H.	Death of Richard Hodgson
1907, January 6	Delta	Birth of Daphne Coombe-Tennant
1908, July 21		Death of Daphne Coombe-Tennant
1909, November 20	A.C.-T.	Birth of Alexander Coombe-Tennant
1910, August 14		Death of Frank Podmore
1910, August 26		Death of William James
1910, December 29		Death of Samuel Henry Butcher
1911, January 17		Death of Sir Francis Galton
1912, June 18		Death of Arthur Woollgar Verrall
1913, April 9	H.C.-T.	Birth of Augustus Henry Coombe-Tennant
1913, November 7		Death of Alfred Russel Wallace
1916, July 2		Death of Mrs Margaret Verrall

567

1917, September 3		Death of Christopher Coombe-Tennant
1918, May 16		Death of Eusapia Palladino
1919, April 4		Death of Sir William Crookes
1919, June 30		Death of Lord Rayleigh
1925, May 26		Death of Sir William Fletcher Barrett
1928, November 5		Death of Charles Coombe-Tennant
1930, March 19		Death of Arthur James Balfour
1936, February 10		Death of Mrs Henry Sidgwick
1937, March 12		Death of Eveleen Tennant (Mrs F.W.H. Myers)
1940, January 13	A.J.	Death of Alice Johnson
1940, August 22		Death of Sir Oliver Lodge
1945, January		Death of Gerald William Balfour
1950, July 3		Death of Mrs Leonora Piper
1952, April		Death of John George Piddington
1956, August 31		Death of Mrs Winifred Coombe-Tennant
1968, March 10		Death of Mrs Gladys Osborne Leonard
1968	G.C.	Death of Geraldine Cummins
1968, November 27		Death of Robert Arthur Lytton (Ral) Balfour
1969, July 21		Death of William Henry Salter
1971, March 11		Death of Charlie Dunbar Broad
1981, October 17		Death of Jean Balfour (Countess of Balfour)
1989, November 6		Death of Augustus Henry Coombe-Tennant
2003, November		Death of Alexander Coombe-Tennant

Archive Material

The following bodies and individuals hold important collections of materials relating to the Scripts:

Trinity College Library, Cambridge – W.H. Salter's complete set,* together with Mrs Verrall's notebooks
Cambridge University Library – the SPR's complete set
Edinburgh University Library
The Harry Price Library, University of London Library
The National Library of Wales – papers of 'Mrs Willett' (Mrs Coombe-Tennant)
Nottingham University Library
University of Virginia, Charlottesville, USA
Martin Salter, Oracle, Arizona, USA
Lady Alison Kremer (The Kremer Archive), Widworthy Barton, Devon – complete set, together with extensive archive of handwritten letters, notes and commentaries from *c.*1908–80; given to Lady Kremer by Jean, Countess of Balfour
Dr Alan Gauld, Dept. of Psychology, University of Nottingham
The Earl of Balfour, Whittingehame – complete set, together with other Script materials including indexes and references
The Society for Psychical Research, Kensington, London – complete set
College of Psychic Studies, Kensington, London – complete set
Parapsychology Foundation of New York, USA – complete set

*Note: A complete set of privately printed SPR volumes comprises:

569

- 19 volumes of scripts (Mrs Willett scripts, 6 vols, 1908–36; Miss Verrall scripts, 4 vols, 1903 – script 625; Mrs Verrall, 4 vols, 1905–16; Mrs Holland scripts, 2 vols, 1903–10; Mrs Wilson scripts, 2 vols, 1915–31; Mac Scripts, 1 vol., 1908–11)
- *Notes and Excursuses* (9 vols; vol. 9 = Index)
- 2 volumes of Mrs Willett's automatic phenomena

Bibliography

The following abbreviations are used:

JSPR   *Journal of the Society for Psychical Research*
PSPR   *Proceedings of the Society for Psychical Research*
JASPR   *Journal of the American Society for Psychical Research*
PASPR *Proceedings of the American Society for Psychical Research*

Published works:

Akolkar, V.V., 'Search for Sharada: Report of a Case and its Investigation', *JASPR*, **86**, 1992, 209–47.

Arkwright, A.S.B., *Return Journey*, Seeley, Service & Co., n.d.

Balfour, G.W., *The Ear of Dionysius*, Henry Holt, New York, 1920.

Balfour, G.W., 'A Study of the Psychological Aspects of Mrs Willett's Mediumship and the Statements of the Communicators Concerning Process', *PSPR*, **43**, 1935, 41–318.

Balfour, Jean, 'The 'Palm Sunday' Case: New Light on an Old Love Story', *PSPR*, **52**, 1960, 79–267.

Barrett, W.F., 'The Origin of the Society for Psychical Research', *Light*, **13**, 1893.

Barrett, W.F., *On the Threshold of the Unseen*, London, 1920.

Barrington, M.R., '*Swan on a Black Sea*: How Much Could Miss Cummins Have Known?', *JSPR*, **43**: 728, 1966, 289–300.

Beard, Paul, *Survival of Death*, Hodder & Stoughton, London, 1966.

Beard, Paul, *Living On*, Allen & Unwin, London, 1980.

Beard, Paul, *Hidden Man*, Pilgrim Books, Norwich, 1986.

Beer, John, *Providence and Love: Studies in Wordsworth, Channing, Myers, George Eliot, and Ruskin*, Clarendon Press, Oxford, 2000.

Bernstein, M., *The Search for Bridey Murphy*, Doubleday, Garden City, NY: Doubleday, 1956.

Broad, C.D., *Lectures on Psychical Research*, Routledge and Kegan Paul, London, 1962.

Broad, C.D., 'Obituary: Mr W.H. Salter', *JSPR*, **45**: 743, 1970, 203–7.

Burton, J., *Heyday of a Wizard*, Harrap & Co., London, 1948.

Carrington, Hereward, *Eusapia Palladino and Her Phenomena*, B.W. Dodge, New York, 1909.

Connell, R., and Cummins, Geraldine, *Healing the Mind*, The Aquarian Press, London, 1957.

Coombe-Tennant, A., '*Swan on a Black Sea* – Some Questions Answered', *JSPR*, **43**: 729, 1966, 378–81.

Courtier, J., *Rapport sur les Séances d'Eusapia Palladino à l'Institut General Psychologique en 1905, 1906, 1907 et 1908*, Institut General Psychologique, Section des Recherches Psychique et Physiologiques, November 1908.

Crookes, Sir William, 'Notes of Seances with D.D. Home', *PSPR*, Part XV (December 1889), 98–127.

Cummins, G., *The Road to Immortality*, Ivor Nicholson and Watson, London, 1933.

Cummins, G., *Swan on a Black Sea*, Routledge & Kegan Paul, London, 1965.

Darwin, Charles, *On the Origin of Species by Means of Natural Selection*, 1859.

Dodds, E.R., *Supernormal Phenomena in Classical Antiquity*, JSPR, XVII, 216.

Ducasse, C.J., 'How the Case of *The Search for Bridey Murphy* Stands Today', *JASPR*, **54**, 1960, 3–22.

Ducasse, C.J., *A Critical Examination of a Belief in a Life after Death*, C.C. Thomas, Springfield, IL, 1961.

Ducasse, C.J., 'What Would Constitute Conclusive Evidence of Survival?', *JSPR*, **41**, 1962, 714, 401–06.

Dunne, J.W., *An Experiment with Time*, A. & C. Black, London, 1927.

Dunraven, the Earl of, 'Experiences in Spiritualism with D.D. Home', *PSPR*, **XXXV**: Part XCIII, 1924, 1–285.

Dusen, Wilson van, *The Presence of Other Worlds*, Wildwood House, London, 1975.

Ellis, L.F., *The Welsh Guards at War*, Aldershot, 1946.

Feilding, Everard, *Sittings with Eusapia Palladino and Other Studies*, University Books, Hyde Park, NY, 1963.

Feilding, E., Baggally, W.W., and Carrington, H., 'Report on a series of sittings with Eusapia Palladino', *PSPR*, **23**, 1909, 309–569.

Findlay, Arthur, *Looking Back*, Psychic Press, London, 1988.

Fuller, J.G., *The Airmen Who Would Not Die*, G.P. Putnam's Sons, New York, 1979.

Gauld, A., *The Founders of Psychical Research*, London, Routledge and Kegan Paul, 1968.

Gauld, A., 'A Series of "Drop-In" Communicators', *PSPR*, **55**, 1971, 273–340.

Gauld, A., *Mediumship and Survival*, William Heinemann, London, 1982.

Gauld, A., 'The Function of a Society for Psychical Research at the Present Time', *PSPR*, **57**, 1993, 253–73.

Gay, K., 'The Case of Edgar Vandy', *JSPR*, **39**, 1957, 1–64.

Glenconner, Pamela, *The Earthen Vessel*, John Lane Co., New York, 1921.

Gurney, E., Myers, F.W.H., and Podmore, F., *Phantasms of the Living*, London, 1886.

Halifax, Lord, *Ghost Book* (2 vols), London, 1936 & 1937.

Haraldsson, E., 'Apparitions of the Dead: A Representative Survey in Iceland' in Roll, W.G., Beloff, J., and McAllister, J., eds, *Research in Parapsychology 1980*, The Scarecrow Press, Metuchen, N.J, 1981.

Haraldsson, E., 'Birthmarks and Claims of Previous-Life Memories 1. The Case of Purnima Ekanayake', *JSPR*, **64**: 1, 2000, 16–25.

Haraldsson, E., and Stevenson, I., 'A Communicator of the "Drop-in" Type in Iceland: The Case of Runolfur Runolfsson', *JASPR*, **69**, 1975, 33–59.

Haraldsson, E., and Stevenson, I., 'A Communicator of the "Drop-in" Type in Iceland: The Case of Gudni Magnusson', *JASPR*, **69**, 1975, 245–61.

Hart, Hornell, *The Enigma of Survival,*: C.C. Thomas, Springfield, IL, 1959.

Haynes, Renee, *The Society for Psychical Research, 1882–1982: A History*, Heinemann, London, 1982.

Heywood, Rosalind, 'The Palm Sunday Case: A Tangle for Unravelling', *JSPR*, **40**: 704, 1960, 285–91.

Hodgson, R., 'A Record of Observation of Certain Phenomena of Trance', *PSPR* **8**, 1892, 1–167.

Hodgson, R., 'A Further Record of Observation of Certain Phenomena of Trance', *PSPR*, **13**, 1897–8, 284–582.

Hodgson, R., 'Report on Mrs Piper's mediumship', *PSPR*, **6**, 1889, 436–59.

Hodgson, R., 'Mr Davey's Imitations by Conjuring of Phenomena Sometimes Attributed to Spirit Agency', *PSPR*, **8**, 1892–7, 253–310.

Hodgson, R., and Davey, S.J., 'The Possibilities of Malobservation and Lapse of Memory from a Practical Point of View', *PSPR*, **4**, 1887, 381–495.

Hyslop, J.H., 'A Further Record of Observations of Certain Trance Phenomena', *PSPR*, **16**, 1901, 1–649.

Hyslop, J.H., 'A Case of Veridical Hallucinations', *PASPR*, **3**, 1909, 1–469.

Hyslop, J.H., 'The Doris Case of Multiple Personality', *PASPR*, **11**, 1917, 5–866.

Inglis, Brian, *Natural and Supernatural*, Hodder & Stoughton, London, 1977.

Inglis, Brian, *Science and Parascience*, Hodder & Stoughton, London, 1984.

James, William, 'Frederic Myers' Service to Psychology', *PSPR*, **XLII**, 1901.

James, William, 'Report on Mrs Piper's Hodgson Control', *PSPR*, **23**, 1909, 2–121.

James, W., Piddington, J.G., and Lodge, Sir O., 'Report on Mrs Piper's Hodgson Control', *PSPR*, **23**, 1909, 1–285.

Keen, M., 'The Case of Edgar Vandy: Defending the Evidence', *JSPR*, **64**: 3, 2002, 247–59.

Keynes, Randal, *Annie's Box: Charles Darwin, His Daughter, and Human Evolution*, Fourth Estate, London, 2001.

Klimo, Jon, *Psychics, Prophets and Mystics: Receiving Information from Paranormal Sources*, The Aquarian Press, Grafton Books, 1991.

Koestler, Arthur, *The Challenge of Chance*, Hutchinson and Co., London, 1973.

Larusdottir, E., *Midillinn Hafsteinn Bjornsson*, Nordri, Iceland, 1946.

Leonard, Gladys Osborne, *My Life in Two Worlds*, Cassell & Co., London, 1931.

Litvig, I., *Singer in the Shadows*, Macmillan, New York, 1972.

Lodge, Oliver, 'In Memory of F.W.H. Myers', *PSPR*, **XLII**, 1901.

Lodge, Oliver, *Survival of Man*, Methuen, London, 1909.

Lodge, Oliver, 'Report on Some Trance Communications Received Chiefly through Mrs Piper', *PSPR*, **23**, 1909, 127–280.

Lodge, Oliver, 'Evidence of Classical Scholarship and of Cross- Correspondence in some New Automatic Writing', *PSPR*, **25**, 1911, 113–75.

Lodge, Oliver, *Raymond or Life and Death*, Methuen & Co., London, 1916.

Lodge, Oliver, *Christopher*, Cassell, London, 1918.

Lyttelton, Edith, *Some Cases of Prediction*, G. Bell & Son, 1937.

Mackenzie, A., 'An Edgar Vandy Proxy Sitting', *JSPR*, **46**, 1971, 166–73.

Manning, Matthew, *The Strangers*, W.H. Allen, London, 1978.

Murphy, Gardner, *The Challenge of Psychical Research*, Harper and Bros., New York, 1961.

Myers, F.W.H., Lodge, Sir O., Leaf, W. and James, W., 'A Record of Observations of Certain Phenomena of Trance', *PSPR*, **6**, 1890, 436–659.

Myers, F.W.H., *Fragments of Inner Life,* privately printed, 1890.

Myers, F.W.H., 'In Memory of Henry Sidgwick', *PSPR*, **XXXIX**, 1900.

Myers, F.W.H., *Human Personality and Its Survival of Bodily Death* (2 vols), Longmans, Green, London, 1903.

Myers, F.W.H., *Essays (Classical and Modern)*, Macmillan, London, 1883.

Myers, F.W.H., *Fragments of Prose and Poetry*, ed. Eveleen Myers, Macmillan, London, 1904.

Nichol, J., and Rennell, T., *The Last Escape*, Penguin/Viking, London, 2002.

Nicol, Fraser, 'The Founders of the SPR', *PSPR*, **55**, 1972, 341–7.

Piddington, J.G., with Mrs H. Sidgwick, 'Note on Mrs Piper's Hodgson-Control in England in 1906–7', *PSPR*, **23**, 1909, 122–6.

Piddington, J.G., 'Three Incidents from the Sittings', *PSPR*, **24**, 1910, 86–143.

Piper, A.L., *The Life and Work of Mrs Piper*, Kegan Paul, London, 1929.

Prince, M., *The Dissociation of a Personality*, Oxford University Press, 1978.

Prince, W.F., 'The Doris Case of Multiple Personality', *PASPR*, **9**, 1915, 1–700.

Prince, W.F., 'The Doris Case of Multiple Personality', *PASPR*, **10**, 1916, 701–1419.

574

Prince, W.F., 'The Doris Case of Quintuple Personality', *Journal of Abnormal Psychology*, **11**, 1916, 73–122.

Prince, W.F., *The Case of Patience Worth*, Boston Society for Psychical Research, 1927.

Radclyffe-Hall, M., and Troubridge, Una, Lady, 'On a Series of Sittings with Mrs Osbourne Leonard', *PSPR*, **30**, 1919, 339–554.

Richet, C., *Thirty Years of Psychical Research: Being a Treatise on Metapsychics*, tr. de Brath, S., Macmillan, New York, 1923.

Rogo, D. Scott, *The Infinite Boundary*, The Aquarian Press, Wellingborough, 1988.

Roy, A.E., *The Archives of the Mind*, Psychic Press, Stansted Mountfitchet, 1996 (reprinted 2005).

Salter, W.H., 'Elucidation of two points in the "One Horse Dawn Scripts"', *PSPR*, **XXXIV**, 1924.

Salter, W.H., *Ghosts and Apparitions*, G. Bell & Son, 1938.

Salter, W.H., *An Introduction to the Study of Scripts*. privately printed, 1948.

Salter, W.H., *Trance Mediumship*, The Society for Psychical Research, London, 1950.

Salter, W.H., '*J.G. Piddington and his Work on the "Cross-Correspondence" Scripts*', *JSPR*, **XXVI**, 1951–2.

Salter, W.H., 'F.W. Myers' Posthumous Message', *PSPR*, **52**, 1958, 1–32.

Salter, W.H., 'The Palm Sunday Case – A Note on the Interpretation of Automatic Writings', *JSPR*, **XXX**, 1959–1960.

Salter, W.H., *Zoar*, Sidgwick & Jackson, London, 1961.

Salter, W.H., 'The Rose of Sharon', *PSPR*, **54**, 1963, 1–22.

Saltmarsh, H.F., *Evidence of Personal Survival from Cross-Correspondences*, G. Bell & Sons, London, 1938.

Sidgwick, E.M., 'Discussion of the Trance Phenomena of Mrs Piper', *PSPR*, **15**, 1900–1, 16–38.

Sidgwick, E.M., 'A Contribution to the Study of the Psychology of Mrs Piper's Trance Phenomena', *PSPR*, **28**, 1915, 1–657.

Sidgwick, E.M., 'An Examination of Book-tests Obtained in Sittings with Mrs Leonard', *PSPR*, **31**, 1921, 241–400.

Sidgwick, E.M., 'A History of the S.P.R.', *PSPR*, 1932.

Sidgwick, H., *The Methods of Ethics*, 1874.

Sidgwick, H., Sidgwick, E.M., and Johnson, A., 'Report on the Census of Hallucinations', *PSPR*, **10**, 1894, 25–422.

Sidgwick, Mrs H., Verrall, A.W., and Piddington, J.G., 'Further Experiments with Mrs Piper in 1908', *PSPR*, **24**, 1910, 31–200.

Stevens, E.W., *The Watseka Wonder*, The Religio-Philosophical Publishing House, Chicago, 1887.

Stevenson, I., 'A Review and Analysis of Paranormal Experiences Connected with the Sinking of the *Titanic*', *JASPR*, **54**, 1960.

Stevenson, I., 'Seven More Paranormal Experiences Associated with the Sinking of the *Titanic*, *JASPR*, **59**, 1965.

Stevenson, I., 'A Communicator Unknown to Medium and Sitters', *JASPR*, **64**, 1970, 53–65.

Stevenson, I., *Twenty Cases Suggestive of Reincarnation*, 2nd edn, University Press of Virginia, Charlottesville, 1974.

Stevenson, I., *Cases of the Reincarnation Type. Vol. 1. Ten Cases in India*, University Press of Virginia, Charlottesville, 1975.

Stevenson, I., *Cases of the Reincarnation Type. Vol. 2. Ten Cases in Sri Lanka*, University Press of Virginia, Charlottesville, 1977.

Stevenson, I., *Cases of the Reincarnation Type. Vol. 3. Twelve Cases in Lebanon and Turkey*, University Press of Virginia, Charlottesville, 1980.

Stevenson, I., *Unlearned Language: New Studies in Xenoglossy*, University Press of Virginia, Charlottesville, 1984.

Stevenson, I., *Children Who Remember Previous Lives*, University Press of Virginia, Charlottesville, 1987.

Stevenson I., *Reincarnation and Biology: A Contribution to the Etiology of Birthmarks and Birth Defects*, 2 vols, Praeger, Westport, CT, 1997.

Stevenson I., *Where Reincarnation and Biology Intersect*, Praeger, Westport, CT, 1997.

Stevenson, I., and Pasricha, S., 'A Case of Secondary Personality with Xenoglossy', *American Journal of Psychiatry*, **136**, 1979, 1591–2.

Stevenson, I., and Pasricha, S., 'A Preliminary Report on an Unusual Case of the Reincarnation Type with Xenoglossy', *JASPR* **74**, 1980, 331–48.

Stevenson, I., Pasricha, S., and McClean-Rice, N., 'A Case of the Possession Type in India with Evidence of Paranormal Knowledge', *Journal of Scientific Exploration*, **3**, 1989, 81–101.

Swedenborg, Emanuel, *Divine Love and Wisdom*, American Swedenborg Printing and Publishing Society, New York, 1904, [1763].

Swedenborg, Emanuel, *The Four Doctrines*, The Swedenborg Foundation, New York, 1976, [1763].

Swedenborg, Emanuel, *Divine Providence*, The Swedenborg Foundation, New York, 1972 [1764].

Tarazi, Linda, 'An Unusual Case of Hypnotic Regression with Some Unexplained Contents', *JASPR*, **84**, 1990, 309–44.

Thomas, C.D., *Life Beyond Death with Evidence*, W. Collins & Sons, London, 1928.

Thomas, C.D., 'The *Modus Operandi* of Trance-Communication According to Descriptions Received through Mrs Osborne Leonard', *PSPR*, **38**, 1928–9, 49–100.

Thomas, C.D., 'A Consideration of a Series of Proxy Sittings', *PSPR*, **41**, 1932–3, 139–185.

Thomas, C.D., 'A Proxy Case Extending over Eleven Sittings with Mrs Osborne Leonard', *PSPR*, **43**, 1935, 257–306.

Thomas, C.D., 'A New Hypothesis Concerning Trance Communication', *PSPR*, **48**, 1946–7, 121–163.

576

Troubridge, U., 'The *Modus Operandi* in So-called Mediumistic Trance', *PSPR*, **32**, 1922, 344–78.

Troubridge, U., 'Some Further Considerations of the *Modus Operandi* in Trance Mediumship', *PSPR*, **34**, 1924, 298–309.

Tyrrell, G.N.M., *The Personality of Man*, Pelican Books, London, 1947.

Tyrrell, G.N.M., *Apparitions*, Gerald Duckworth, London, 1953.

Underwood, P., *Queen Victoria's Other World*.

Verrall, Margaret de G., *Mrs Willett's Automatic Phenomena,* 2 vols, printed privately, 1912.

Verrall, H. de G., 'Report on the Junot Sittings with Mrs Piper', *PSPR*, **24**, 1910, 351–664.

Walker, Nea, *The Bridge*, Cassell & Co, London, 1927.

Walker, Nea, *Through A Stranger's Hands*, Hutchinson, London, 1935.

Wilson, Ian, *The Bleeding Mind*, Weidenfeld & Nicolson, London, 1988.

Worth, Patience, *The Sorry Tale*, Henry Holt & Co., New York, 1917.

Index

Note: The filing of a communicator claiming to be a particular person is listed under that person's name. This does not mean that the communicator is necessarily taken by the author to be that person.

579

Browning, Elizabeth Barrett, 196, 212, 224
Brunel, Isambard Kingdom, 29
Brunel, Sir Marc Isambard, 29
Bryant, William Cullen, 65
Buckingham Palace, 1
Buddha, the, 535
Burgess, Guy, 539, 542
Burgoyne, 5
Burlington House, 4, 199
Burns, Robert, 103, 553
Burr, Frank L. 65
Bush, DrGeorge, 63
Busk, George, 37
Butcher, Prof. Samuel Henry Butler, 96, 140, 152, 169, 170, 172, 282, 446
Butler, Abbot, 532
Butler, George, 104
Butler, Mrs Josephine Butler, 104, 106

Cadoc, 226
Cadoxton Lodge, 22, 226, 235, 285, 303, 331, 332, 341, 345, 386, 452, 484, 485
Caesar, Julius, 21
Cahan, 20
Calder, Alexander, 79
Cambridge, Duke of, 46
Cambridge, Massachusetts, 39
Cambridge University, 6, 91, 198, 385, 518, 523, 525, 530
Cambridge Ghost Club, 91
Carew, Antony, 405–6
Carnot, Sadi, 28
Carpenter, Dr, 74, 75
Carrington, Hereward, 87
casket, 206, 207–8, 212, 223, 407
Catherine the Great, 61
Catullus, 211
Census of Hallucinations, 399
Chambers, Robert, 66
chaos theory, 338–9
Chari, C. T. K., 526
Charles XII, King, 58
Chateaubriand, 240
Cheltenham College, 103
Cheves, Mrs, 313
'Chlorine', 124
Churchill, Mrs, 368

Churchill, Lord Randolph 338
Churchill, Winston, 317, 338, 358, 386, 389, 400, 403, 489
Civil List, 35
clairvoyance, 173, 196, 223, 551
Clarendon, Lord, 2
Cleophas, The Scripts of Cleophas, 457–8, 462–4
Clifford, W.K., 96
Clifton, Bishop of, 532
Clifton, Nellie, 44
Clotho, 1
Club, The Metaphysical, 39
Cocke, J.R., 124
Coffin, Walter H., 79
Coleridge, 564
Collier, Gertrude Barbara Rich, 227
communicators, 507, 562, 563
Connell, Dr, 465
Conroy, Sir John, 42, 45
controls, of mediums, 125, 314–6
Cook, Florence, 50, 74
Cooke-Yarborough, Jean Lily, (Countess of Balfour), 321
Coombe-Tennant, Alexander, 20–2, 228, 230, 236, 237, 238, 239, 244, 246, 263, 267, 271, 273, 276, 284, 287, 318, 340, 362–4, 386, 442, 443, 448, 450, 451, 452, 453, 455, 465, 466, 481–5, 488, 505, 509, 514, 516, 519, 521, 524, 525, 532, 550, 556
Coombe-Tennant, Augustus Henry, (Dom Joseph),13–14, 15–22, 226, 230, 231, 234–46, 249, 294–302, 318, 321–37, 339–57, 358–91, 396, 401, 402, 418–9, 429, 432, 442, 443, 448, 450, 451, 452, 453, 455, 456, 466, 467, 468, 483, 489–530, 531–46, 550, 553–65
Coombe-Tennant, Charles, 226, 227, 229, 230, 356, 539
Coombe-Tennant, Christopher, 227, 228–30, 233, 316–7, 334, 358, 367, 449, 450, 452, 472, 509, 514, 539, 540, 563
Coombe-Tennant, Daphne, 7–8, 228–9, 276, 284, 288, 301, 302–4, 316, 450, 452, 453, 472, 509, 514, 563
Coombe-Tennant, Dorothy, 227

Greeley, Horace, 55
Grey, Sir Edward, 305
Grigg, Sir James, 372
Guinevere, 420, 421, 422, 423, 425
Gurney, Alfred 88, 100
Gurney, Edmund, 8, 10, 78, 79, 80, 82,
    84, 90, 91, 92, 93, 96, 97–101, 114,
    118, 140, 141, 142, 168, 173, 177,
    178, 188, 193, 197, 200–2, 222, 250,
    253, 256, 258–61, 264, 266, 267,
    268, 270–2, 273–90, 292, 317, 318,
    434, 446, 447, 461, 550, 554, 562,
    563
Gurney, Helen May, 99
Gurney, Kate, 98
Gurney, Rev John Hampden, 97

Hague, The, 499, 508–12, 542
hair, lock of, 207–8
Hall, Dr Hall, 107
Hall, Mr and Mrs, 67, 68
Hall, Trevor, 101
Hamilton, William, 310
Hamlet, 399
Hammill, Faye, 110
Handel, G. F., 294
Haraldsson, Erlendur, 562
Hardy, Sir Alister, 81
Hardy, Thomas, 227
Harker, Elizabeth, 521
Harris, Thomas Lake, 63
Harrison, Thomas, 57
Harrison, Vernon, 85
Hartford Times, 65
Hart, John, 130, 131
Haunted houses, 80, 82
Herschel, Sir William, 31
Heywood, Rosalind, 460, 468, 526
Hill, Annie Eliza (*see* Annie Eliza
    Marshall), 105–7
Hill, J. Arthur, 144
Hill, William, 490
Hirst, T.A., 37
Hitler, Adolf, 25, 351, 493, 555
Hodge, General, 234
Hodgson-Davey study, 88
Hodgson, Richard, 80, 82, 84, 85, 86,
    87, 88, 91, 115, 121–39, 140, 150,
    179, 188, 271, 462, 550

Hollis, Roger, 542
Holmes, Oliver Wendell, 39
'Holland', Mrs (Alice Fleming), 89,
    147, 165, 166, 167, 169, 187, 192,
    198, 206, 300, 304, 444, 453
Home, Alexandrina, 66
Home, Daniel Dunglas, 2, 49, 50,
    64–74, 77, 86, 258, 438
Homer, 103, 112, 172, 257
Hood, Thomas, 202
Hooker, Sir Joseph Dalton, 37
Horace, 103
Horsell, Miss, 434
Howard, James and Mary, 131–3
Howard, Katherine, 131
Howitt, William, 69
Huggins, William, 74
Human personality, 562
*Human Personality and its Survival of
    Bodily Death*, 115–7, 165, 166, 197,
    282, 321, 438
Hume, David 154, 185
Humphries, H.T., 67, 68
Huxley, George, 75
Huxley, Thomas Henry, 5, 25, 33, 34,
    35, 37, 53, 76–7
Hydesville, 54, 85
hypnotism, 82, 99, 100, 101, 114–15,
    168

Iamblichus, 56
Imperator, 136, 139, 277, 561
Inglis, Brian, 56, 81, 551
Ingraham, Dr Lena V., 128
Interactionalism, 174–7
International Congress of Psychology,
    83
Irish Guards, 359, 363, 364–6
Irish Potato Famine, 38, 486

Jackson, Henry, 96
James, Henry, 41
James, Mr, 535
James, Prof. William, 39, 79, 81, 112,
    113, 121, 122, 123, 137, 138, 139,
    140, 258, 308, 480, 550
Janet, P., 115
Jean, 380
Jebb, Dom Philip, 532–4, 539

584

Jebb, R.C., 96
Jencken, H.D., 67
Jenner, Edward, 52
Jinadasa 500
Johnson, Alice, 83, 115, 140, 146–8,
    149, 162, 165, 166, 168, 170, 187,
    188, 198, 223, 250, 259–61, 267,
    285, 287–90, 295–302, 317, 393,
    397–400, 428, 431, 436, 444, 446,
    550
Johnston, Samuel, 15
Jones, Sir Lawrence, 461
Jongh, Andree de, 380–3
Jonson, Ben, 206
Joule, James, 28
Jung, Carl Gustav, 78, 81, 551–2

Kant, Immanuel, 60
Keats, John, 180, 181
Keen, Montague, 170, 187, 303–4, 468,
    476–9
Keen, Montague, accuracy of data in
    Cummins' Willett scripts, 476–9
Kelman, J. Harvey, 316
Kempis, Thomas a, 4, 107
Kennedy, John F., 490
Kent, Duchess of, 41
Kent, Duke of, 41, 42
Keynes, Randal, 36
King of Italy, 403
Kingsley, Charles, 206
Kipling, Rudyard, 165, 364–5, 444
Koot Hoomi letters, 85
Koucheleff, Count Gregoire de, 66
Koestler, Arthur, 56, 81, 351
Kremer Archive, 402, 456
Kremer, Lady Alison, 532
Krishnamurti, 494, 555
Kroll, Alexandrina de, 66

Lachesis, 1
Landseer, Sir Edwin, 66
Lang, Andrew, 81
Laski, Harold, 505
Laura (Petrarch's Laura), 209
Laval, Pierre, 387
Lawrence, T.E., 241, 501
Leaf, Walter, 96
League of Nations, 317, 400

Lee, Dom Edmund, 533
Lees, Eva, 48
Lees, Robert James, 48–9, 50, 51
Leeuwenhoek, Antonie van, 248
Lehzen, Louise, 42
Leonard, Frederick, 310, 311
Leonard, Mrs Gladys Osborne, 89, 144,
    250, 308–16, 393, 394, 459, 461,
    465, 528, 551
Leopold, Prince, (Duke of Albany), 46
Leopold, Prince, (King of Belgium, 42,
    44
Lethe Case, 178–82, 188, 269, 304
Leverrier, Urbain J.J., 31
'Leviathan', 32
Levin, Bernard, 56
Levingston, William, 62
Lewes, George, 75
Lewis, Major J.C. Windsor, 389
Light Brigade, Charge of, 38
Lindsay, Master of, 66, 67
Linnean Society, 34, 35
Little Malvern, 532, 534, 543, 553
Livingstone, David, 30–1, 33
Llangattock, 226, 227, 303
Lob, 484
Lodge, Brodie, 141
Lodge, Lady, 142, 311
Lodge, Prof. Sir Oliver, 80, 81, 82, 86,
    91, 101, 111, 117, 118, 123, 127,
    138, 140–5, 152, 166, 168, 174, 181,
    187, 188, 196, 198, 228, 229, 250,
    252, 254–64, 267, 269–78, 302,
    311–4, 317, 392, 393, 399, 428, 431,
    445, 449, 452, 461, 462, 482, 483,
    485–6, 539, 546, 550, 562
Lodge, Raymond, 141, 144, 311–14
Logue, Lionel, 51
Lombroso, Cesare, 86
London Palladium, 310
London Zoo, 36
Longfellow, Henry Wadsworth, 66, 124,
    561
Lord Halifax's Ghost Book, 565
Lord Lytton, 66
Lubbock, John, 37
Lucretius, 103,
Lutyens, Lady Emily, 494, 507, 555
Lyon, S. Silas, 62–3

Lyttelton, Alfred, 198, 216, 486, 516
Lyttelton, Hon Mrs Alfred, 81
Lyttelton, Dame Edith, 22, 198, 223,
    232, 240, 334, 340, 349, 386, 394–5,
    437, 445, 450, 451, 486, 516, 557
Lyttelton, Laura, 197, 198, 206, 222,
    446
Lyttelton, Lavinia, 3–4, 199, 205, 207
Lyttelton, Mary Catherine, 3–4, 197–24,
    317, 323, 352–4, 421–24, 446, 466,
    474, 498, 516, 561
Lytton, Lady Constance, 486

MacLehose and Company, 154, 396,
    408, 410–11, 415, 420, 426
MacLehose, Sir Hamish, 426, 427
Mackinnon family, 167, 444
Maclean, Donald, 539, 542
Maitland, F.W., 96, 98
Maitland, Mrs, 299
Mansi, Dom Dominic, 533
Maquis, 234, 385, 388, 387, 390, 499,
    500, 542
Marshall, Annie Eliza, 4–5, 117, 118,
    197, 198, 206, 222, 446, 449
Marshall, John, 102
Marshal, Mr, 383–4
Marshall, Walter James, 4, 105, 106,
    107
Marte (John Fiske), 134
Maskelyne, J.N., 88
Massey, C.C., 79
Maude, Dr, 457
Maxwell, James Clerk, 28
McDougall, William, 81
medium, 56, 85–9
mediumistic phenomena, 85–9
mediumship, mental, 82, 89, 122–39,
    151, 248–68, 269–93, 308–16
mediumship, physical, 80, 82, 85–9
Melbourne, Lord, 2, 49–50
Merrifield, 430
mesmerism, 62–3, 80
Metternich, Princess, 66
MI6, 542
Millennium Dome, 26
Milner-Gibson, Mrs, 66
Moore, E. Garth, 526, 527, 528, 529
Moreman, Christopher, 184

Moses, Rev. W. Stainton, 50, 79, 80
Moses of Old, 561
Mounttemple, Lady, 420
Mozart, W.A., 115
Murat, Prince, 66
Murphy, Gardner, 81, 509
Murray, Prof. Gilbert, 81, 399
Mussolini, Benito, 351
Myers, Dr A.T, 83, 100, 107
Myers, Eveleen, 111, 117, 118, 148,
    445, 450, 470–2, 487
Myers, Rev Frederic, 102
Myers, Frederic W.H., 8, 53, 78, 79,
    80, 82, 83, 86, 87, 91, 92, 93, 95–7,
    98, 101–18, 123, 127, 137, 140, 141,
    142, 145, 146, 148, 150, 161, 162,
    166, 167, 168, 169, 170, 173, 177,
    178–82, 188, 193, 197, 198, 222,
    227, 229, 249, 250, 253–8, 262–3,
    265–6, 267, 269, 270–2, 273–4, 281,
    288–9, 302, 317, 318, 321, 392,
    435–6, 444, 445–6, 461, 463, 486,
    514, 546, 550, 562, 563, 564, 565
Myers, Leo, 470–2
Myers, Susan, 102, 105, 107

Napoleon III, Emperor, 1, 49, 66
NATO, 489
Neo-Platonists, 56
Neptune, 31–2
New York Times, 39
New York Tribune, 55
Newcomb, Simon, 79
Newnham College, Cambridge, 95, 146,
    148, 150, 152, 181, 265, 397, 433,
    435
Newton, Sir Isaac, 28, 32, 77, 527
Newton, Isobel, 147
Nichol, Prof. John, 32
Nicholas, Czar, 66,
Nicol, Fraser, 79, 80, 92, 100, 116,
    564
Nightingale, Florence, 38
Northampton University, 565
Notes and Excursuses, 156, 157, 159,
    162, 183–4, 404, 408–11, 420, 425,
    426, 429–30, 452, 510, 518, 560

Obsession, 562

586

589

THE RAPE OF SOCIALISM

'It is your duty to know and to be haunted by your knowledge.'

Arthur Koestler

'The only thing necessary for the triumph of evil is for good men to do nothing.'

Edmund Burke

'None are more hopelessly enslaved than those who falsely believe they are free.'

Goethe

'It is not the King and the generals who make history, but the masses of the people.'

Nelson Mandela

THE RAPE OF SOCIALISM

How Labour Lost the Millennium

by

DONOVAN PEDELTY

Prometheus Press
Powys, Wales

Prometheus Press
Tir Celyn
Aberedw
Builth Wells Powys LD2 3SQ

Published by Prometheus Press 1997

A catalogue record for this book is available from the British Library

ISBN 0 9529993 1 5

Printed and bound in Great Britain by T. J. International Ltd, Padstow, Cornwall

CONTENTS

CONTENTS

LOOKING BACKWARD

In September 1987 a young man who had lived since his birth, in 1857, in Boston, Massachusetts, awoke from a state of suspended animation to find his native city changed beyond all recognition, had it not been that, raising his eyes towards the horizon, he could discern, to the west, the familiar blue ribbon of the sinuous River Charles winding away to the sunset and, to the east, Boston harbour, stretching before him within its headlands, not one of its green islets missing. In the course of the next seven days, however, young Julian West was to discover that, if the fabric of the city was so greatly changed, the society it sustained was utterly transformed. And it is on this transformation of the social ethos that his own account concentrates.

He comes to see that the common assumptions of his social class that had kept the toiling masses in or on the verge of destitution throughout the nineteenth century were not only false but were themselves the primary causes of the most pernicious ills of society. The two principal beliefs underpinning the dominant ideology at the time of his birth and upbringing had concerned human nature and the 'laws' of economics. What the latter were conceived to be is explained in the opening pages of the account, in which the author outlines his own privileged position in society, conferred on him by an inheritance that had come down to him from his great-grandfather and that, despite having already supported three generations in idleness, had, strangely, not diminished, but actually grown in size - a mystery revealed as being due to an 'unnatural and preposterous arrangement' of giving what was called 'interest on investments' and which amounted to 'a species of tax in perpetuity upon the product of those engaged in industry which a person possessing or inheriting money was able to levy.'

He then turns to the condition of the common people and refers to the great 'labor troubles' of those days, which had particularly exercised him because a strike of building workers, some of whom were engaged in putting up a new house for him, had caused a delay in his intended marriage. 'The working classes had quite suddenly and very generally become infected with a profound discontent with their condition, and an idea that it could be greatly bettered if they only

1

knew how to go about it.' The trouble was that, however understandable they might be, their aspirations were in fact 'chimerical' since 'it was in the very nature of things impossible that the new hopes of the workingmen could be satisfied, simply because the world had not the wherewithal to satisfy them. It was only because the masses worked very hard and lived on short commons that the race did not starve outright, and no considerable improvement in their condition was possible while the world, as a whole, remained so poor. *It was not the capitalists whom the laboringmen were contending with...but the iron-bound environment of humanity, and it was merely a question of the thickness of their skulls when they would discover the fact and make up their minds to endure what they could not cure.'* [my emphasis]

In addition to this apparently perpetual social condition of mass deprivation, the young Julian West and his contemporaries had accepted, as though they were natural disasters, the five- to ten-year devastations of severe trade depression. Unable to prevent or control these calamities, 'it only remained to endure them as necessary evils, and when they had passed over, to build up again the shattered structure of industry, as dwellers in an earthquake country keep on rebuilding their cities on the same site.'

Most of West's account of those troubled times, and of the almost unbelievable contrast they present when compared with the modern age he has so miraculously survived to enjoy, take the form of conversations with his new-found friend Dr Leete, in whose home he is now living. 'In our day,' he tells his host, 'the market rate determined the price of labor of all sorts, as well as of goods. The employer paid as little as he could, and the worker got as much. It was not a pretty system ethically, I admit; but...there seemed to be no other practicable way of doing it.'

'It would have been a pity if humanity could never have devised a better plan,' replies Dr Leete, 'for yours was simply the application to the mutual relations of men of the devil's maxim, "Your necessity is my opportunity." The reward of any service depended not upon its difficulty, danger, or hardship, for throughout the world it seems that the most perilous, severe, and repulsive labor was done by the worst paid classes...' And he goes on to astonish his young friend by telling him that nowadays all people get the same share of the social product for their services to the community.

To West's objections that 'some men do twice the work of others' and that while some are clever, others are indifferent workers, Dr Leete replies: 'We require of each that he shall make the same effort; that is, we demand of him the best service it is in his power to give.' He points out that 'desert is a moral question' and that the amount of the effort alone is pertinent to the question of desert. All men who do their best, do the same. A man's endowments, however godlike, merely fix the measure of his duty. The man of great endowments who does not do all he might, though he may do more than a man of small endowments who does his best, is deemed a less deserving worker than the latter, and dies a debtor to his fellows.'

And he draws West's attention to a number of other advantages of the modern way of dealing with rewards for services rendered. No longer need a worker demean himself by haggling for his price in the marketplace, as he was formerly obliged to do, whatever his calling. No longer is every member of society 'in a position of galling personal dependence upon others as to the very means of life, the poor upon the rich, or employed upon employer, women upon men, children upon parents...' No longer are natural aptitudes wasted by force of circumstance and talents perverted by mercenary considerations. No longer do bribery and corruption flourish, while venal crimes in general, 'which the machinery of law, courts, and police could barely prevent from choking your civilization outright,' have effectively been abolished. This means the virtual eradication of crime as a whole, since 'in your day fully nineteen twentieths of the crime...resulted from the inequality in the possessions of individuals: want tempted the poor, lust of greater gains, or the desire to preserve former gains, tempted the well-to-do.'

He said that such great social changes had combined to produce a transformation in people's attitudes to one another; they were no longer supercilious or patronising, servile or malevolent, but reflected mutual esteem. For, Dr Leete declares, 'It is the worst thing about any system which divides men, or allows them to be divided, into classes and castes, that it weakens the sense of a common humanity. Unequal distribution of wealth, and, still more effectually, unequal opportunities of education and culture, divided society in your day into classes which, in many respects, regarded each other as distinct races.'

On another occasion he remarks to West: 'If I were to give you, in one sentence, a key to what may seem the mysteries of our civilization as compared with that of your age, I should say that it is the fact that the solidarity of the race and the brotherhood of man, which to you were but fine phrases, are, to our thinking and feeling, ties as real and vital as physical fraternity.' Such perceptions, he has already made clear, have made war a thing of the past, for 'in heaven's name, who are the public enemies? Are they France, England, Germany, or hunger, cold and nakedness?'

And they are perceptions rooted in a clear understanding of the realities of social life. 'Who is capable of self-support?' he demands, when West starts to talk of charity. 'There is no such thing in a civilized society as self-support... As men grow more civilized, and the subdivision of occupations and services is carried out, a complex mutual dependence becomes the universal rule. Every man, however solitary may seem his occupation, is a member of a vast industrial partnership, as large as the nation, as large as humanity. The necessity of mutual dependence should imply the duty and guarantee of mutual support; and that it did not in your day, constituted the essential cruelty and unreason of your system.'

Accompanying this growth in understanding of social realities and their implications was a new perception of human nature. This is most fully and explicitly expressed in the author's report of a sermon he has heard. The preacher, a Mr Barton, stresses the cruel necessity that people of former times were driven by to fight for survival. 'For the sake of those dependent on him, a man might not choose, but must plunge into the foul fight - cheat, overreach, supplant, defraud, buy below worth and sell above...grind his laborers, sweat his debtors, cozen his creditors. Though a man sought it carefully with tears, it was hard to find a way in which he could earn a living and provide for his family except by pressing in before some weaker rival and taking the food from his mouth.'

Mr Barton attributes this savage situation to a most extraordinary assumption made by most people in those unhappy times. 'It was the sincere belief of even the best of men at that epoch that the only stable elements in human nature, on which a social system could be safely founded, were its worst propensities. They had been taught and believed that greed and self-seeking were all that held mankind together, and that all human associations would fall to pieces if anything were done to blunt the edge of these motives or curb their operation. In a word, they believed - even those who longed to believe otherwise - the exact reverse of what seems to us to be self-evident; they believed, that is, that the anti-social qualities of men, and not their social qualities, were what furnished the cohesive force of society. It seemed reasonable

4

to them that men lived together solely for the purpose of overreaching and oppressing one another, and of being overreached and oppressed, and that while a society that gave full scope to these propensities could stand, there would be little chance for one based on the idea of co-operation for the benefit of all.'

Looking on the 'inhuman spectacle' of that society, ministers of religion 'bitterly bemoaned *the depravity of human nature*; as if angelic nature would not have been debauched in such a devil's school!' [my emphasis] So we should not think of 'the stupendous change' that has taken place since those tragic times as some kind of miracle. 'It is not necessary to suppose a moral new birth of humanity, or a wholesale destruction of the wicked, and survival of the good, to account for the fact before us. It finds its simple and obvious explanation in the reaction of a changed environment upon human nature...Ceasing to be predatory in their habits,' the people of our age have become 'co-workers, and found in fraternity, at once, the science of wealth and of happiness.'

Mr Barton is right, of course, to curb whatever childish tendencies we may still have to jump to supernatural conclusions when amazed; and Julian West's account of the stark contrast between his times and ours provides ample explanation for the transformation of human conduct. Nevertheless, the differences are of such magnitude that it requires a prodigious feat of the imagination to think ourselves back into those distressful days. Mr West's vivid account of his strange experience and its profound effects on him helps us to take that great leap in time and to realise how nearly we have come to the millennium of which men have dreamt throughout the ages.

Wye Valley
Mid-Wales
Autumn 1987

5

PROLOGUE II

UTOPIA AND REALITY

Mr Barton shared with his audience his reflections on the extraordinary fact that they had amongst them 'a living representative of the epoch of our great- grandparents' - a fact which, he suggested, could only 'leave us more than ever amazed at the stupendous change which one brief century has made in the material and moral conditions of humanity.' But whatever may be thought about the material changes that have occurred during the past hundred years - and in certain respects they have unquestionably been very great - such a remark could only have been made in 1987 (and could only be made now) with satirical intent. In fact, like Dr Leete and his family, and like Julian West himself, Mr Barton is of course a fictitious character, and the book he comes from was first published in 1888. Its author's intentions were not satirical at all; they were to portray 'a social order at once so simple and logical that it seems but the triumph of common sense.' It was, in short, a utopia, a dream of better times, written not as mere fantasy or escapism, but in the firm conviction that such times could be brought about.

Utopias are of course quite out of fashion. But Edward Bellamy's *Looking Backward: 2000-1887* was not only a great success in its own time and place (it sold more than 300,000 copies in America within two years of its first appearance and spawned a movement known - confusingly to our ears, living as we do in an age which has witnessed the rebirth of fierce, not to say ferocious, nationalistic feuds in several part of the world, including that old powder-keg the Balkans, at the same time as frontiers are fast becoming essentially irrelevant - as Nationalism, to promote its ideas on the 'nationalisation' of the production and distribution of wealth), but it was translated into many foreign languages and was given a new lease of life at the end of the Second World War, when, as Bellamy's son Paul wrote in 1945 in the introduction to a new edition, 'The yeast of social change is working in every country of the globe' and 'every statesman is drawing up blueprints, if not of Utopia, at

6

least of something different and better than the economic order we have.'

If this quite restrained statement be accepted - and it would be difficult to deny that the upheaval of war waged on every inhabited continent, following as it did the great trade depression of the thirties and the unrelenting repression and exploitation of colonial peoples by European powers, as well of course as the ravages of the dictatorships, produced an all but universal clamour for a better life - we owe it to ourselves to stop our ears to the jeers and sneers of those who haven't the imagination to envisage a better world, and to ask in all seriousness why so little has changed in the common lot of mankind in the hundred years since Bellamy dreamt and wrote. For even if we turn our backs on the three-quarters of the human race who live in the 'underdeveloped world' (to use one euphemism) and further restrict our consideration to the 'free world' (to use a bigger one), we cannot justly claim that the condition of mankind has in most respects fundamentally improved. If we took as our yardstick Franklin D. Roosevelt's 'Four Freedoms' - freedom of speech and expression, freedom of worship, freedom from fear, and freedom from want - we might maintain with some plausibility that in the more genuine 'parliamentary democracies' the first two were substantially guaranteed (although even in the freest bits of the 'free world', anybody who has made a habit of exercising the first of these hard-won constitutional rights will know that to do so can cost one dearly in one's working life, leave one open to financial ruin from libel action, and in some circumstances bring one directly into conflict with the forces of the State); but we would have to admit that the other two were far from assured.

In the closing pages of Bellamy's utopia, his hero dreams that he has been dreaming and has woken up in nineteenth-century Boston. Before going in his dream out into the streets of the city and looking again (but with his perceptions awakened by having seen a nobler future) at the nightmare spectacle of 'the festering mass of human wretchedness' about him, and then suffering the scorn of his own social circle when he pleads the cause of the dispossessed, he glances at a summary of world events in his morning newspaper which reads as follows:

7

'FOREIGN AFFAIRS. - The impending war between France and Germany. The French Chambers asked for new military credits to meet Germany's increase of her army. - Great suffering among the unemployed in London. They demand work. Monster demonstration to be made. The authorities uneasy. - Great strikes in Belgium. The government preparing to repress outbreaks. Shocking facts in regard to the employment of girls in Belgian coal mines. - Wholesale evictions in Ireland.

'HOME AFFAIRS.- The epidemic of fraud unchecked. Embezzlement of half a million in New York. - Misappropriation of a trust fund by executors. Orphans left penniless. - Clever system of thefts by a bank teller; $50,000 gone. - The coal barons decide to advance the price of coal and reduce production. - Speculators engineering a great wheat corner at Chicago. - A clique forcing up the price of coffee. - Enormous land grabs of Western syndicates. - Revelations of shocking corruption among Chicago officials. Systematic bribery. - The trial of the Boodle aldermen to go on at New York. - Large failures of business houses. Fears of a business crisis. - A large grist of burglaries and larcenies. - A woman murdered in cold blood for her money at New Haven. A householder shot by a burglar in this city last night. - A man shoots himself in Worcester because he could not get work. A large family left destitute. - An aged couple in New Jersey commit suicide rather than go to the workhouse. - Pitiable destitution among the women wage-workers in the great cities. - Startling growth of illiteracy in Massachusetts. - More insane asylums wanted. - Decoration Day addresses. Professor Brown's oration on the moral grandeur of nineteenth century civilisation.'

The remarkable fact is that the picture of the world reflected in this 1887 news summary, far from seeming a historical curiosity, remains chillingly close to experienced reality a century later. Making due allowance for the big geopolitical changes that have made military conflict between the Western-style powers improbable, for major reforms concerning the rights of women and children in the advanced 'democracies' and for the general provision in such countries of safety- nets that has made utter destitution largely a thing of the past, most of the items in Julian West's paper have their shocking parallels today.

On the eve of what was to prove a third successive general election victory for the Tory Party led by Margaret Thatcher, Britain's second biggest circulation daily paper, *The Daily Mirror*, published a special edition dedicated to the millions living in or on the margins of poverty. Its photographs of inner city poverty and squalor recalled irresistibly those social campaigning issues of *Picture Post* that had once so shocked the conscience of the nation. 'Britain is divided, the *Mirror* editorial roundly declared, between those who have and those who will never have. Between those who hope and those who have no hope.' It is 'the Britain of her creation,' the indictment of the Tory leader read, and 'She doesn't care. Do you?' Too many of those who used their vote either did not know what they were doing or didn't care, so that with only 43 per cent of the total poll in their pockets, Maggie Thatcher's New Model Tories were given a third term in office. Five years later, in defiance of the opinion polls, they won yet again - even if, as some argued, their victory was largely due to the assumption of gullible voters that having a new leader, decent little John Major, made them to all intents and purposes a new party.

The years in between those two British general elections brought two sequences of events of epic, mould-breaking dimensions: in southern Africa the dismantling of the laager of apartheid, in eastern Europe and the Russian empire the collapse of 'Soviet Communism'. The capitalist 'democracies' of the Western alliance had won the Cold War which had cost their citizens and many others so dearly. Surely that famous victory meant, for 'the free world' at any rate, that 'the market' would at last be able to deliver that milk and honey? Of the 'moral grandeur' of civilisation in America, Britain, and the world at large as the twentieth century draws to a close, we may judge from the following facts and comments (all of which appeared in the columns of one of the world's great liberal newspapers, *The Guardian*, which Julian West might have known as *The Manchester Guardian*), mainly from 1996, which the United Nations had designated the International Year for the Eradication of Poverty:

> THE TRIUMPH OF GLOBAL CAPITALISM - 'If you choose a day and make a total of the movement of money that has taken place that day, and you then calculate the sum of all the transfer of merchandise that has taken place, you will find it represents only one thousandth part of monetary movement. This is terrifying.' (French political economist Alain Minc, talking to Peter Lennon, *Guardian* 31st January 1994) - Transnational corporations account for one third of global output. TNC sales, at $4,000 billion worth, exceed the market value of total international trade. (UN Conference on Trade and Development, World Investment Report, 1994) - The top ten British supermarkets have an annual turnover equal to the income of the world's poorest 35 countries. (Alex Bellos, *Guardian* 28th October 1996) - The wealth of the world's 358 billionaires is greater than the combined annual incomes of countries with nearly half the world's people. In 1961 the richest 20 per cent of the world's population were 30 times better off than the poorest 20 per cent; in 1996 they were 61 times better off. The share of global income received by the poorest 20 per cent fell from 2.3 per cent to 1.4 per cent. (UN Human Development Report 1996) - In the financial year 1995/96 the World Bank lent a record $19 billion to help countries develop their economies. Through the payment of interest and other debts, it recouped $1.7 billion more from Third World countries than it lent. (Annual Report of the World Bank, 1996) - 'Although I have made a fortune in the financial markets, I now fear that the untrammelled intensification of laissez-faire capitalism and the spread of market values into all areas of life is endangering our open and democratic

10

society. The main enemy of the open society, I believe, is no longer the communist but the capitalist threat.' (George Soros, *Guardian* 18th January 1997).

CAPITALIST DEMOCRACY LIBERATES LATIN AMERICA - 'The US and capitalism have won, and in few areas of the world is that victory so clear- cut, sweet, and spectacular as in Latin America. Democracy, free market economies, and pro-American outpourings of sentiment and policy dot the landscape...' Such euphoria seems distant now...By 1990, 240 million people in Latin America were believed to be living below the poverty line. (Martin Woollacott comments on Jorge Castañeda's reflections on the dividend from the end of the Cold War, *Guardian* 1st February 1995) - Some 86 million Latin Americans survive on less than a dollar a day, and if income distribution is left to market forces, everything indicates that their number can only increase. There are 35 dollar billionaires in Latin America according to Forbes [magazine], of whom 15 are Mexicans. A country in which, according to United Nations figures, half the population cannot afford an adequate calorie intake ranks fifth in the world by number of billionaires, behind the United States, Germany, Japan and Hong Kong...Between 1960 and 1990 the share of Brazil's national income received by the poorest 50 per cent fell from 17.7 per cent to 10.4 per cent of the total. (Phil Gunson, *Guardian* 15th July 1996).

PROPAGANDA BY DEED - Peru is a country where half the 24 million population live in poverty and four million of these cannot satisfy basic food and health requirements. Next week's news magazines will prove the point: a dramatic piece of guerrilla action does wonders for the world media's social consciousness. (*Guardian* leader of 21st December 1996 on the seizing of the Japanese embassy in Lima by Tupac Amaru revolutionaries) - 1; This is that brief moment when the hundreds of millions of poor and illiterate people, through sheer force of numbers, have an equal voice to the privileged few who generally dominate public life. 2: On a lane leading to an Allahabad slum, local people have put up barricades of wood and rubbish and a sign, 'Political leaders prohibited. Give us water, and then come and ask us for our vote.' (Suzanne Goldenberg reporting on the 1996 general election campaign in the world's largest parliamentary democracy, *Guardian* 30th March 1996 and 27th April 1996).

THE PEACE DIVIDEND - Annual military spending around the world amounted to $778 billion. (*UN Human Development Report 1996*) - With a slump in the arms trade from the 1988 peak of $61 billion during the Gulf War down to $15.4 billion in 1995, Russian arms sales to the developing world for the first time overtook US sales. At $6 billion Russian sales equalled 40 per cent of the total, followed by the US at $3.8 billion, France at $2.4 billion, Italy at $800 million, and Britain at $500 million. (Congressional Research Service, Washington DC, 20th August 1996) - Contrary to an assurance by Prime Minister John Major, British-made armoured vehicles supplied in the 1960s were used to repress the democratic movement in Indonesia, the Ministry of Defence has admitted. (*Guardian* 19th October 1996).

BUYING HEALTH - One sixth of the world's population, 800 million or so people, have no access to health care. It costs at least £8 a person a year to provide basic health care. Sixteen countries spend less than this, as do Bangladesh, Nepal, India, Vietnam, and Pakistan. Britain spends £723 a head a year. The worst decline in health services in fifty years means that simple, preventable diseases will be killing more children by the end of the century.

Immunisation costs 40p per head of population, more than half the entire national health budget for countries like Mozambique and Uganda. Most African countries spend considerably or hugely more on 'defence' than on health. Zaire spends per capita 26.5p on health and £6.50 on defence, Liberia 46.5p to £11.10, Tanzania 46.5p to £70...Aid as a proportion of the income of donor countries is at its lowest level for twenty years, with Britain's contribution standing at about 0.26 per cent of GNP, scarcely more than a third of the way to the target of 0.7 per cent. (Save the Children report, April 1996).

OUR SHELTER FROM THE STORMY BLAST - 'Send these, the homeless, tempest-tossed, to me.' (One of the lines of verse by Emma Lazarus inscribed on the Statue of Liberty) - On any given night there are about 700,000 homeless people sleeping out in America. Here in New Orleans and in more than forty cities across the United States the homeless are facing a determined push of new laws aimed at banishing them from the streets. 'The general public is fed up. We have certain standards we must uphold. People should be able to use public spaces. When other people come in and build cardboard tents and so on, the area becomes inaccessible for everyone else,' said New Orleans city council president Peggy Wilson, author of the [eviction] proposal. (Sue Anne Pressley, *The Washington Post* 2nd January 1996) - President Clinton deprived America's poor of a 61-year-old safety net yesterday when he signed into law a radical overhaul of the United States welfare system. The law removes the guarantee of federal cash for the poor for the first time since the New Deal. It was condemned by trade unions, women's groups, ethnic minorities and immigrant organisations as a betrayal of the Democratic Party's heritage and a shameless attempt to outflank his Republican rival, Bob Dole. Mr Clinton said he hoped his action would help reduce 'the terrible, almost physical isolation' of the poor from the rest of American society. (Joseph Freedland, reporting from Washington DC, *Guardian* 3rd August 1996).

SUFFER LITTLE CHILDREN - Intolerable forms of child labour are so grave an abuse of human rights that the world must come to regard them in the way it does slavery, as unjustifiable under any circumstance. (From a UNICEF report published on its fiftieth birthday, 12th December 1996) - In very poor countries every family member has to work if they are to survive. (Oxfam comment) - Britain prevented the final communiqué at the Lille G7 jobs summit from including a call for the World Trade Organisation to investigate whether some developing countries win markets by using slave or child labour. (Larry Elliott, *Guardian* 3rd April 1996) - Reebok yesterday called on its arch rival Nike, the market leader in trainers, to join it in a bid to end child labour and improve working conditions at their Asian factories. Christian Aid says only £1.20 from the price of a £50 pair typically goes to workers who made the shoes and Chinese workers would have to work nine hours a day, six days a week for fifteen centuries to earn the £929,113 paid to Nike boss Phil Knight last year. (Roger Cowe, *Guardian* 28th September 1996) - One in three children in Britain is growing up in a family without anybody in a full-time job. (*Households Below Average Income*, Stationery Office, 14th November 1996) - According to Barnardo's one in four children in Britain, around three million, is growing up in poverty. 'The shocking reality is that many of the problems Thomas Barnardo faced in the East End of the 1860s are still facts of life in London today. Homeless children carving out a meagre existence on London's streets, begging for their supper in the West End, sleeping rough in parks and subways, they're easy victims for the pimps who prey on their vulnerability.' (Roger Singleton, director of Barnardo's, in conversation with Margaret Hughes, *Guardian* 30th September 1995).

GIVE US THIS DAY... - At an aggregate level, the world still has enough to eat. But individual people do not eat around an aggregate table. Many dine in comfort. Others continue to get by. And a large minority, 800 million, struggle for food in overcrowded slums, on impoverished soils, often amidst an abundance which they cannot afford...The World Development Movement points out that even in the US an estimated 30 million people suffer from malnutrition. (*Guardian* leader of 12th November 1996 on the forthcoming World Food Summit in Rome) - The World Food Summit opens here today to a chorus of protest from charities who argue it will merely serve to endorse a set of free-market principles favouring the richer countries...Save the Children denounced the summit as a 'forum for legitimising a new international code of practice which basically subordinates basic rights to the market philosophy.' (John Hooper, *Guardian* 13th November 1996).

THE POOR ARE ALWAYS WITH US - Nearly one household in six in Britain is living below the poverty line [half average income], putting the country on a par with the poorest states in the European Union. (European Commission report, 6th November 1996) - Between 1979 and 1993 the number of people living below the poverty line in Britain rose from 5 million to 14.1 million. The fall of 400,000 during the next two years marks the first time the gap between rich and poor stopped widening since *1976*. [my emphasis] Average real income after allowing for housing costs rose by 40 per cent from its 1979 level, but while the richest tenth of the population enjoyed a 65 per cent rise, the poorest tenth suffered a 13 per cent fall. (*Households Below Average Income*, 1996) The US system of state provision is driven and defined by politics rather than principles...the American poor are the least likely [to vote], and children cannot vote at all. Accordingly, 21 per cent

15

of US children live in poverty, double the rate of any other industrialised country, Unicef reported last year. (Martin Walker, *Guardian* 27th January 1996).

THE RESERVE WORKFORCE - Worldwide unemployment has reached one billion, representing crisis levels not experienced since the depths of the 1930s depression...almost one in three of the global labour force is now out of work or underemployed...At least 34 million people in the world's richest nations which belong to the Organisation for Economic Co-operation and Development are jobless. Unemployment rose to an average 11.3 per cent in European countries last year, compared with 2 per cent in the 1960s. (International Labour Organisation report, 26th November 1996) - The number of people out of work in Britain is twice the level suggested by official unemployment figures: 4.2 million men and women who want paid work are currently out of a job, compared to the Government's figure of 2.16 million. (The Employment Policy Institute, 16th July 1996) - 'For nearly 200 years, the heart of the social contract and the measure of individual human worth have centred on the value of each person's labour. Every nation will have to grapple with the question of what to do with the millions of people whose labour is needed less, or not at all.' (Jeremy Rifkin, *Los Angeles Times* 17th October 1995).

THE PARTNERSHIP OF CAPITAL AND LABOUR - In 1995/96 the ten most highly remunerated of Britain's bosses all earned more than £1 million, the equivalent of £19,230 every week, almost exactly what the average full-time male worker earns in a year. Top executives gave themselves pay rises last year of nearly 19 per cent, roughly five times both inflation and the average increase in earnings. (Lisa Buckingham and Sarah Whitebloom, *Guardian* 1st June 1996) - Directors of the UK's 250 largest quoted companies received a median increase of 8.6 per cent in total earnings...in the most recent financial year...well over twice the 3.75 increase in average earnings over the same period...Top earners received an *increase* last year worth twice as much as the entire pay of an average worker. (*Guardian* leader 28th December 1996) - A group of power industry executives scooped £26.9 million in pay-offs and compensation payments as a result of last year's takeovers and mergers in the electricity industry. One executive, former Norweb chairman Ken Harvey, received a total package of nearly £3 million including a last-minute pay rise of £377,000, enough to pay the power bill of an average family for 1,350 years...The huge payouts will infuriate unions in an industry which has seen 50,000 jobs axed in the six years since privatisation. They are braced for further job cuts following the takeovers. (Chris Cowe, *Guardian* 15th November 1996) - Estimates of people who cannot afford to heat their homes, people in 'fuel poverty', run to about 6.6 to 8 million. Winter deaths, associated with cold temperatures and poorly-insulated homes, exceed summer deaths by around 30,000 annually. This is a particularly British problem not seen in a range of other countries with much more severe winter weather. (Dr Hugh Crombie, Research Manager, Royal Society of Health, in a letter to *The Guardian*, 19th April 1996) - Chief executives in top American corporations earn 120 times more than the average worker, compared with 35 times more in the 1970s. Among men about 70 per cent of all earnings growth has been captured by the top one per cent of earners. (Robert Frank of Cornell University to the American Association for the Advancement of Science, reported by Tim Radford, *Guardian* 10th February 1996).

OUR SENIOR CITIZENS - Britain's top directors are being given company pension contributions worth on average half their salaries, more than five times the

value of pension payments for most employees...
More than forty companies gave their executives
contributions running into six figures in their latest
financial year, nearly 60 per cent up on the previous
12-month period. (Labour Research report, 2nd
January 1997) - Some 5 million people out of the 8
million people, half the working population,
employed by smaller British companies are facing an
impoverished old age because of a huge shortfall in
the pension provision. (Association of Consulting
Actuaries report, 17th September 1996) - Of Britain's
10 million or so pensioners, 3.8 million 'only survive
through means-tested benefits and another 600,000
who should be claiming, either through pride or
ignorance, do not. Where the basic pension
represented 21 per cent of average earnings in 1979,
it has now shrunk to 14 per cent today because of the
1980 decision by ministers to break its link to the
earnings index. On current trends it will shrink to 9
per cent by 2020. (*Guardian* leader, 13th September
1996).

In its 1987 election campaign special edition *The Daily
Mirror* numbered the have-nots for whom it was pleading at 18
million - near to a third of the nation. In the lifetime of Edward
Bellamy and his English contemporary George Gissing, whose
fiction is a sustained threnody on the plight of the disinherited,
these 'submerged classes' constituted a clear majority in all the
wealthiest nations. To that extent George Orwell was right in
saying in his 1948 essay on Gissing that his novels were one
reason 'for thinking that the present age is a good deal better
than the last one' and that 'we have improved perceptibly on
that black- coated, money-ruled world of only sixty years ago.'
But despite 'the shadow of the atomic bomb', he was writing at
a time of hope replenished, a new dawn after a long dark night.
Had he foreseen how degraded and fettered life would still be
for millions of his fellow countrymen forty years on, we may be
sure that his comments on Britain's social progress would have
been a deal more abrasive. In the concluding passage of the
grimmest of Gissing's novels, published in 1889, he reflects on

the blighted hopes of his two principal characters that 'at least their lives would remain a protest against those brute forces of society which fill with wreck the abysses of the nether world.' A century later such language may sound melodramatic; but to our shame we still have that 'nether world' and those insensately consigned to it. How is this possible, when at any rate since Orwell was writing those encouraging words, Britain has had the benefit of having one of the strongest 'democratic socialist' movements in the world? The purpose of this book is to answer that question.

PART ONE

MAKING AND MARRING A NATURAL PARTY OF GOVERNMENT

'I remember very well, in a discourse one day with the King, when I happened to say there were several thousand books among us written upon the *Art of Government*, it gave him (directly contrary to my intention) a very mean opinion of our understandings. He professed to despise all *mystery*, *refinement*, and *intrigue*, either in a prince or in a minister. He could not tell what I meant by *Secrets of State*, where an enemy or some rival nation were not in the case. He confined the knowledge of governing within very *narrow bounds*; to common sense and reason, to justice and lenity, to the speedy determination of civil and criminal cases; with some other obvious topics which are not worth considering. And, he gave it for his opinion, that whoever could make two ears of corn, or two blades of grass to grow upon a spot of ground where only one grew before, would deserve better of mankind, and do more essential service to his country, than the whole race of politicians put together.'

**Jonathan Swift, *Gulliver's Travels*
(A Voyage to Brobdingnag)**

CHAPTER 1

The hijacking of the Tory Party

'The Tories have ceased to be gentlemen without
becoming democrats.'

William Rees-Mogg (1963)

'Melmotte was the Conservative candidate for
Westminster. It is needless to say that his committee
was made up of peers, bankers, and publicans, with all
that absence of class prejudice for which the party
has become famous since the ballot was introduced
among us.'

Anthony Trollope, *The Way We Live Now* (1875)

If the Labour Party is, as is often said, a 'broad church', embracing
very diverse points of view on the kind of polity at which it should
aim ('a house divided', as its enemies gleefully proclaim), then the
Conservative Party is close to being an inexplicable enigma, since
it succeeds in uniting for political action social groups, economic
interests, and ideological persuasions that are almost totally
disparate. Tory zealots hail this as their party's greatest glory. Its
more thoughtful supporters might secretly subscribe to the view of
opponents that in its ability to mean 'all things to all men' (of any
sex, of course) the party is a masterpiece of Machiavellian
statesmanship. At all events, the Thatcherite Revolution has
dangerously exposed the deep fissures in the Conservative Party.

It is a little too early to predict the demise of the Conservative
Party, but should its latter-day history come to be seen in this way,
the supreme irony which will have to be recorded is that its *first
cause* is to be found in the machinations of its demi-gods, the inner
circle of grandees who had controlled the party throughout most of
its life. When Harold Macmillan announced his resignation of the
leadership to the party conference at Blackpool in the autumn of
1963 (a resignation determined not by illness, as was given out,
but by a loss of will, of that spirit which had made him revel in the
mocking nickname 'Supermac') a train of events was set in motion
that was to lead to a wholly unforeseen revolution in the

Conservatives' collective concept of the *final cause*, the kind of polity for which they should strive. At that time the Party picked its leader by what Bernard Levin, in *The Pendulum Years*, has described as 'a mysterious and undefinable process' and Iain Macleod characterised as a 'magic circle of Old Etonians'. There was at the time a handful of credible claimants to the succession. The one who emerged from the dubious straw-poll procedures of Cabinet, MPs, peers, and executive committee members of the National Union of Conservative and Constitutional Associations (the Party's approximation to a national organisation of members) as the most credible consensus candidate was, for a party striving for a modern image, quite *in*credible, as he himself was later to admit.

Amongst the credible claimants, foremost by right of experience and distinction in office, of standing with the nation, and ironically, of the kindredness of his concept of modern Conservatism to Macmillan's own 'middle way' stance, was Rab Butler. His selection as leader to succeed the man chosen in preference to him on Anthony Eden's resignation following the Suez debacle, might have ensured both the continuance of progressive paternalism in a democratic packaging *and* (for a while at least) of a preponderant influence in the party for its grandees. In his memoirs, Macmillan records his surprise that Lord Home had come out of the consultation proceedings as the favourite, but the suspicion remains that the mantle fell on him because Supermac was, as Macleod believed, 'determined that Butler, although incomparably the best qualified of the contenders, should not succeed him,' and so cast his 'blockvote' against him.

Inevitably, Home's consequential elevation to the pinnacle of power prompted a repeat performance of the protest and derision that had erupted in 1960. Then Macmillan had promoted him to one of the highest and most politically important offices in the realm, the post of Foreign Secretary, contrary, as it was claimed, to what had become the accepted constitutional practice of only filling such posts from the elected chamber. Now the newly-elected Labour leader, Harold Wilson, made much of the fact that his opponent was a hereditary peer, 'the fourteenth earl' and mocked him as an 'elegant anachronism'. Home retorted with spirit that he supposed that when you came to think of it Mr Wilson was 'the fourteenth Mr Wilson' and asked, ironically, 'Are we to say that all men are equal except peers?' Nevertheless, to reach the summit he was obliged to cast aside the ermine and reappear centre stage in commoner's guise as Sir Alec Douglas-Home.

In an unseemly scramble for top-billing, one of his rivals, Lord Hailsham, had actually announced at the Blackpool Conference that he was on the point of divesting himself of his peer's robes so that he might run - or 'streak' perhaps - in the race for the premiership. Like Home, he proved adept at the quick-change act, gliding from 'Lord Hailsham' to 'Quintin Hogg' (an unavailing enticement as it turned out) and back again, with consummate artistry, thus allowing him eventually to sit, like his father before him, on the Woolsack. History's bigger joke, however, was that these noble scions were enabled to compete for the top job through the determination of another politician (who, notwithstanding his personal ambitions, undoubtedly had better credentials for taking on the role of true commoner) to renounce his succession to the peerage, in order to retain his seat in the Commons. Disqualified from sitting when his father, the first Viscount Stansgate, died, Anthony Wedgwood Benn appealed to his Bristol constituents in the ensuing by-election and was voted in again, but his election was declared invalid and his Tory opponent returned for Bristol South-West. The disquiet caused, however, by this frustration of the will of the electorate, led to the Peerage Act, passed with perfect timing for the climax of the Tory leadership pantomime (while Benn regained his seat unopposed when his former adversary honoured his pledge to resign if the law were changed).

Whether or not the antics attendant on choosing a new leader played any part in the Tories being pipped at the post in the general election of October 1964, it cannot have done them any good that their old leader was so clearly disinclined to allow 'the winds of change' to blow away the cobwebs of his own party's rituals. 'The way in which Home had been chosen did the Conservatives no good,' one historian (T.O. Lloyd) comments. 'Wilson had been elected leader of the Labour Party in a straightforward way that everybody could understand; Home had been presented as Prime Minister after consultations that were never intended to be understood by the public. Being elected gives a leader legitimacy in the modern world; emerging as the result of consultations is not a process that commands general respect.' Another historian (C.J. Bartlett) tartly observes: 'Significantly the Conservatives never used this system to choose a leader again.'

23

Their removal from office (even though it was by such a small margin that the new government had the smallest ever overall majority won in a British general election - four seats precisely) made it clear to all but the most incorrigible traditionalists amongst them that they must do something to tart up their image; above all, that they must show that no future Tory government would be open to the gibe that the fate of nation and empire (or what was left of it) was settled on the grouse-moors of England or Scotland. Especially so as they were now confronted by a party led by a dynamic economist who spoke with evident conviction of reshaping the country in the 'white heat of the technological revolution.' Home was to say later, in explaining his relinquishment of the leadership: 'One of the reasons why I resigned was just that I'd been on the scene a long time, and I thought that the Tory Party needed somebody else who would have a slightly more modern outlook, perhaps, or be *thought* to have a more modern outlook.'

After an inquiry had been set up by Home, it had been agreed that in future the Tories would follow the practice of the other principal political parties in leaving it to their parliamentary party to choose the leader. And so it was that Edward Heath, victor of a three-way contest with Reginald Maudling and Enoch Powell, became the first leader of the Conservative Party to be elected instead of 'emerging' from the steaming cauldron of the 'magic circle'.

The change in the procedure of appointing the leader naturally helped to give Heath the appearance of having 'a more modern outlook'; but his elevation did in fact mark a major - and almost certainly irreversible - change in the nature of the Tory Party leadership. The landed gentry had given way to the class that had long formed the party's backbone of loyal ensigns; public school *noblesse oblige* had retired in favour of grammar school commonsensical assumptions of the civic rights and responsibilities of 'the responsible classes'. And in keeping with this, Ted Heath authentically represented a newer managerial breed of Tory to match the 'new model socialist' elite, fired not by millennial dreams of social justice and a true commonwealth, but by Vorticist visions of social order and scientific revolution. 'Butskellism' had paved the way; but now was the real apotheosis of post-war consensual politics, for each of the leading protagonists, despite their strenuous efforts at differentiation, equally embodied the spirit of the age.

What inevitably ensued - teasing steps to left or right notwithstanding - was a decade of manoeuvring to occupy the middle ground, not simply because it was generally accepted that the party which succeeded in doing so would govern (though a strongly pragmatic approach to politics was one of the things the top contenders had in common), but because of the genuine similarity of outlook between these modern men of affairs. Each was so essentially 'moderate' that to talk of one as of the Left and the other as of the Right obscures rather than illuminates the reality. If one were to remove the shadow cast by opposing rhetoric and consider the substance only, one might well muddle up in one's mind the measures taken by Heath's administration and those taken by the Wilson and Callaghan governments. And the truth was that their underlying political philosophies of a 'mixed economy' supervised by government as and when it considered it necessary in the interests of national prosperity, abetted by such adjustments from time to time in the provision of incentives and disincentives as were felt to promote this, accompanied by paternalistic concern for the provision of 'decent' standards of welfare (or as some would say, of indigence) for the less successful members of society - these politician philosophies, or concepts of wise 'governance' (to use one of Wilson's favourite words) were difficult to distinguish except in detail and emphasis.

To prepare to demolish, brick by brick, the consensus they so hated but which seemed at the time so solidly built, the Thatcherite faction (as we may now call them) in the Tory Party had first to oust their own leader. And it suited their purpose to charge Heath with reneging on his election promises, with caving in to opposition forces and making a series of U-turns. 'The free-market philosophy on which he was elected in 1970,' says Patrick Cosgrave in *Thatcher: The First Term*, 'was not all that dissimilar to the one on which she was elected in 1979. But Heath changed - indeed reversed - his policies in 1972, because he had become convinced that they did not work.' It is, of course, a matter of historical record that he came into office with a strategy of removing shackles on business enterprise, but as for his 'free-market philosophy', it is of a markedly different species from that of Thatcherism. As he himself put it in 1966: 'It is the job of Government to help industry overcome problems and to help modern capitalism to work...our task is to remove the obstructions...to enterprise and competition in our business world.' However disinclined they might be to put it quite like that, that is the position of every modern social democrat and of the great majority of leading Labour politicians. And there is no more reason to think that, speaking honestly, they would need to qualify Heath's words to make their own political creed clear than would Heath himself. In short, such a statement is itself an expression of the consensus which the Thatcherites were bent on destroying, since for them it was 'the hidden hand' of 'spontaneous market forces', not the helping hand of government, that makes the magic of capitalism.

Put simply, while impatient of custom and practice that impeded efficiency, it is clear that Heath always was a paternalist Conservative, not a 'free-for-aller'. He is also a reasonable man who, despite strong and durable convictions which some feel distinguish him from that master pragmatist Harold Wilson, has shown himself capable of learning from his mistakes and changing his mind, a virtue to which Cosgrave's caustic comments on Heath's changes of policy pay unintended tribute. Considering his obviously fundamental belief in the democratic virtue of compromise, it is highly ironic (and not a little tragic - and not only in a personal sense either) that a leader in effect accused of funk by enemies within his own party, should at the same time have gone down in history for practising what Alan Sked and Chris Cook call in the chapter on his government in their *Post-War Britain*, 'The Politics of Confrontation'.

However much the 'hidden hand' Tories might grind their teeth at Heath's unnatural practices in propping up 'lame ducks' and so forth, they could hardly deny that in such matters he was in large measure a victim of circumstances beyond his control. In interfering with the natural *dis*order of the market in respect of prices and incomes, on the other hand, Heath chose to confront the unions, appealed to the country in the 'Who Governs Britain?' election of February 1974 when they would not knuckle under, and lost power for his party by a whisker. (The Tories actually secured the highest number of votes, nearly a quarter of a million more than Labour, but five fewer seats, with the Liberal and nationalist parties holding the balance but declining to use it to sustain the Tories in power.) Needless to say, it was not the confrontation with the unions as such to which the Tory troops objected, only to the fact that, in a situation far less favourable to State power than that enjoyed by Margaret Thatcher in her relentless campaigns to bring the unions to heel, Heath lost.

Clearly ripe for a bit of the Brutus treatment, Heath engineered his own downfall in more specific way. Beaten on points in a return bout in October with Wilson (who gambled on securing an overall majority and got it, by just three seats), Heath clung to his dignity. He agreed under heavy pressure to the setting up of a committee under Lord Home to consider changes to the Party's leadership election procedures (at that time they contained no formal provision for removing a leader who was not prepared to fall on his own sword after defeat in battle) and accepted the committee's recommendations, with the greatest reluctance, after sitting on them for over a month.

The reluctance was understandable. Under the procedures then implemented, a formal challenge for the party leadership could be made once a year. No party with democratic pretensions could take exception to this; but one particular provision for entering the contest was another matter and led to its being called a 'coward's charter'. This allowed for the entry of previously undeclared candidates in the event of no one gaining a lead of at least 15 per cent over the nearest challenger in the previous ballot. Which is precisely what happened in the scramble for the succession to Heath. Though not obliged to withdraw on being beaten in the first ballot (by 130 votes to 119, with Hugh Fraser picking up 11 as a stalking-horse and 12 MPs abstaining) by the woman he had appointed his Secretary of State for Education, Heath rightly took it as a vote of no confidence. At this stage, with Fraser and Heath himself dropping out, four more former cabinet ministers, William Whitelaw, Sir Geoffrey Howe, James Prior, and John Peyton, each of them with greater experience and - or so it was thought - carrying more weight in the party than Margaret Thatcher, entered the contest. In the second ballot they were routed. Thatcher won an overall majority with 146 votes out of the 271 cast, Willie Whitelaw (whose awesome fate was to be nominated by Mrs Thatcher as 'my Willie') collected 76, Howe and Prior 19 each, and Peyton trailed with 11. The first woman to become leader of a major British political party had won the position because, as Geoffrey Rippon put it: 'She had the courage to declare herself in time. I think people respected that.'

That at least is undeniably half the story. The other half, however, is of greater importance in considering the fate of the Conservative Party and the consequences for the country. Those in the know are agreed that Thatcher's commanding lead (only nine votes short of an absolute majority) in the first ballot did not reflect a general infatuation with Maggie but rather a general jilting of Ted. It appears that a decisive proportion of the parliamentary party voted tactically to try to ensure a second ballot. Cosgrave claims to have identified at least sixteen backbenchers who were determined to get rid of Heath, but 'did not want a Thatcher victory either: they wanted her to damage Edward Heath sufficiently to allow the entry of further candidates the second time around.' But in employing what Phillip Whitehead, in *The Writing on the Wall*, calls this 'ingenious way of smoking out an unpopular leader' which was provided by the new election procedures, they failed to reckon with the disinformation stratagems of Thatcher's master-agent, Airey Neave (who had been, as Whitehead puts it, 'left to rust by Heath'), or to calculate the possible consequences of the kind of runaway lead the lady took in the first ballot. The amateur plotters, along with whichever of the heavyweights who hung around outside the ropes had calculated all along to be in the ring for the final round, had hoist themselves with their own petard.

Beyond the frisson it gave them at having, to the amazement of everyone, outpaced the parvenu parties by becoming the first party to pick a woman to lead them into battle, it is doubtful if more than a handful or two of the more thoughtful Tory legionaries had much conception of what they had done. In tribute to her intuitive mastery of political timing we now need to remind ourselves that, while forceful and effective enough on the floor of the House, Margaret Thatcher had been admirably discreet in the airing of her fundamental views of society. Only her intimates had much idea what she really stood for. As I have already made clear, while Heath's election as leader marked a significant sociological shift in the nature of the Tory Party, it did *not* mean a major change in the ideology that sustained it. Now the brigadiers of the Old Guard had lost more than a skirmish for the leadership: without yet realising it, they had lost the commanding heights where the strategic decisions were taken and the war aims declared. As a discreetly anonymous dissident was to put it, the party had been 'hijacked'.

The Tory Party had been such an effective instrument for the subliminal control by the Elders of affairs of state in a representative democracy precisely because it was *not* a democratic machine. Until the wisest and most astute of the party's twentieth-century statesmen drew attention to the artifice, by allowing his personal prejudice to cloud his judgement, it worked like a dream. The very obscurity of the grandees' deliberations - including their arrogation of the right to choose the party's leader - somehow seemed (as with the election of Popes) to legitimise them. In the not-so-long run, however, the constitutional metamorphosis from 'magic circle' ministrations to the elevation of leaders with a clear mandate from the parliamentary party, was to let the populist genie out of the Tory bottle. After which, we did not have to wait long to witness the forging of an unholy alliance between popular prejudice and militant capitalist individualism.

CHAPTER 2

New model Tories

> 'Mrs Thatcher undoubtedly inserted into Conservative
> policy an ideological, if not religious, fervour and
> a dogmatic tone that had previously been lacking...
> Thatcherism largely consisted of nineteenth-century
> individualism dressed up in twentieth-century
> clothes. As with the Manchester Liberalism of the
> last century, economic dogma was at its core.'
>
> **Ian Gilmour, *Dancing with Dogma***

When our discreet dissident spoke of the hijacking of the Tory Party, he was saying a lot more than 'this woman outsmarted us in seizing the reins'. Maggie's coup it was. But she and her henchmen had not broken the rules of the game. The real point was much more fundamental. It denoted a radical change in destination for the Conservative omnibus, since what the more immediate changes in style and stress were ultimately to add up to was a change in ideology.

While the changes in style and stress that occurred between Mrs Thatcher's startling triumph in the party leadership contest and her first victory at the polls were obvious enough, they did not in themselves constitute a break with the past. Tory rhetoric, especially since the great social upheaval of the French Revolution, has always played heavily on the themes of freedom and individual rights being under threat from absolutist or collectivist power embodied in the State or in political creeds dependent on capturing the State as a weapon or instrument to further their aims. The preservation of the citizen's rights and liberties by maintaining the 'proper constitutional balance' between the three estates of the realm - sovereign, peers, and the people's representatives in the Commons - has always been represented as the party's paramount concern. Until the Russian Revolution its bogeymen were generally dubbed Jacobins; since then they have more commonly been called Reds.

As a rule Tory ideologues do not speak plainly (and advisedly so); but they *see* very clearly: that the capture of the citadel of State power by those intent (or purportedly intent) on the redistribution of wealth threatens the very core of the Tories' *real* concern, which is with 'property rights'. Against egalitarian charges of defending privilege and perpetuating social injustice, they have only the 'freedom' card to play; but for two centuries, from the days of Burke and the Younger Pitt till our own times, they have used it again and again triumphantly to trump the 'equality' card of their collectivist opponents. (Even though, in the representative democracies, the collectivists have won a trick or two, as, notably, Labour did in 1945 when Churchill, unscrupulously conflating black-shirted National Socialism with State Socialism of whatever hue, flung down his impending- 'Gestapo-State' challenge but failed to frighten the voters into the arms of the Conservatives.) So in using, with great seductive force, the 'our ancient liberties' rhetoric in the 1979 campaign, Margaret Thatcher was in the mainstream of Conservative tradition.

At the time it was not so easy to see that a radical break with the past had already been made, especially since, although the leading lady was for most of the action centre stage, the old praetorian guard of Willie Whitelaw, Jim Prior, Peter Walker, Francis Pym, Ian Gilmour, and the like, still surrounded her, providing a reassuring connection with family traditions, while, from the wings, the speeches of the ousted autocrat seemed not so very different in substance, however dissimilar they might be in tone. And after the victory, Mrs Thatcher's first appointments to office appeared to promise a considerable measure of continuity, not to presage violent change. We might go even further than this and aver that if fate or the electorate had deprived her of a second term, we would hardly now talk of 'the Thatcherite Revolution'.

Furthermore, in her campaign speeches Mrs Thatcher brought out equally strongly the Tories' traditional claim to being England's truly national party, the party best able to hold the country together and to lead it in pursuing generally recognised common purposes. They concede the special concern of the Liberals for individual liberties and of Labour for social welfare; but their party alone, they aver, by appropriately qualifying enthusiasm for these ideals with equal concern for national prosperity and stability and sufficient skill in maintaining them, assures concord at home and concerted action abroad. Civil strife and national disunity, according to this view, are primarily the consequence of sectional interests pressing their claims too imperiously or too impatiently: where change in the balance of advantage between social groups or classes is desirable, it should be brought about gradually and with the general consent of those affected. Thus, in her adoption speech on the opening day of the official general election campaign in 1979, Mrs Thatcher declared: 'I seek confrontation with no one...Our Conservative message is not one of strife but of reconciliation. The things we have in common as a nation far outnumber those that divide us. We want not to uproot or destroy, but to rebuild.' More memorably (but some might think more hubristically), on taking possession of the keys of No.10 she quoted the celebrated prayer of St. Francis of Assisi: 'Where there is discord, may we bring harmony. Where there is error, may we bring truth. Where there is doubt, may we bring faith. Where there is despair, may we bring hope.'

The Tories' 1979 manifesto, and their whole campaign, did of course lay great stress on what they saw as the need to restore incentives (especially in the form of tax cuts) for the creation of wealth; but, needless to say, the emphasis was not put primarily on the vulgar right to make money (which could be the one kind of equality in which modern Conservatives of every degree of humidity really believe) but on what this would do for national prosperity. 'The State takes too much of the nation's income. Its share must be steadily reduced. When it spends and borrows too much, taxes, interest rates, prices and unemployment rise, so that in the long run there is less wealth with which to improve *our standard of living* and our social services,' the manifesto argued. (My emphasis: as with the word *national*, *our* does not reveal reality but obscures it. There is, of course, no common standard of living but a multitude of almost infinitely diverse standards of living.) The tasks were: 'to restore the health of our economic and social life...'; to ensure that 'genuine new jobs are created in an expanding economy'; and, most cosily of all, 'to support family life' and raise standards of education, while 'concentrating welfare services on the effective support of the old, the sick, the disabled and those who are in real need.' Far from heralding the end of caring, the objective presented was to construct a better, more effective as well as less bossy, Welfare State. No one could say this was not wholly in accord with Disraeli's declaration that 'another great object of the Tory Party, and one not inferior to the maintenance of the Empire, or the upholding of our institutions, is the elevation of the condition of the people.'

Yet the portents *were* there, in the spring of '79 (not to mention earlier indicators in speeches by Margaret Thatcher and her henchmen). They pointed to a change in the nature of the Tory beast as big as those signposted by Peel's Tamworth Manifesto and the 'two nations' admonishments of Disraeli - and notwithstanding the populist character of Thatcherism, in one fundamental sense, to a change in the opposite direction!

'A change in style, stress, and ideology,' I called it. But there is a sense peculiar to conservative political philosophies in which it is not really possible to distinguish between these three terms. Their adherents commonly disclaim having any ideology at all, and normally employ words like 'doctrine' and 'dogma' only as sticks with which to goad and beat their opponents. Conservatives have a weakness for emotive abstractions like 'loyalty' and 'patriotism' and for what one might call institutional abstractions like 'Crown' and 'constitution' but distrust purer ideological abstractions. For example, although they have been obliged by historical 'progress' to let 'democracy', 'freedom' and even 'equality' out on probation, they display an almost invincible disinclination to defining them.

'It is easier to identify a Conservative than it is to define Conservatism,' writes Philip Buck in the introduction to his anthology *How Conservatives Think*. 'Indeed, this might be pressed further: it is easier for a Conservative to identify a fellow-Conservative than it is for either of them to define what each, or both, believe to be Conservatism, as a political theory or a system of ideas. The problem of definition is as great, or greater, if an attempt is made to trace the history of Conservative thought.' Similarly, R.J. White describes Conservatism as 'less a political doctrine than a habit of mind, a mode of feeling, a way of living'; while Lord Coleraine says it is 'an attitude of mind, not a corpus of doctrine or a carefully worked out system of political theory.'

All of which helps to explain the difficulties the Conservatives tend to have with the intelligentsia. Conservative thinking is religious rather than philosophical in the Western sense, if only because their basic premises (or perhaps one should say, even if it arguably puts the cart before the horse, basic purposes) force them into the philosophically absurd position of having to make virtues of inconsistency and illogicality. Well the truth is that, in the *expression* (if not in the thinking) of Conservative political philosophy, they *are* virtues (political virtues, that is), precisely because they do not illuminate but obscure the realities they purport to represent.

Nevertheless, Tory ideology is real enough, and like any other ideology with some claim to sense, it prides itself on addressing itself to the harsh realities of life. In essence, these concern Tory perceptions of 'human nature' and 'economic laws' and the interaction of these two intractables. The former, as they see it, is more or less immutable and determines the economic relationships between one human being and another unless those 'natural' relationships are distorted by the intervention of 'artificial' (i.e. devised or imposed) practices or institutions. Inasmuch as they are so distorted by meddlers, the inescapable consequence is waste and inefficiency, i.e. bad economics, since (according to this view) economics is just as much subject to 'laws' as is physics.

In one *extreme* view, this means that society is of its nature essentially atomistic; which is to say that it does not really exist. In Margaret Thatcher's words: 'There is no such thing as society; only individuals and families.' The paradox is, of course, that every political party or grouping, of whatever persuasion, must in some measure strive to refute the assumption of atomism; and in fact the bonds of nationhood which are so strongly felt (or so they tell us) and so insistently invoked by Conservatives are utterly incompatible with such a divisive view of human relationships.

The Tory manifesto which heralded the country's resounding rebuff to a divided, dispirited, and above all directionless Labour Movement declared: 'We want to work with the grain of human nature, helping people to restore that self-reliance and self-confidence which are the basis of personal responsibility and national success,' going on to argue, in a passage quoted above, that in taking too much of the nation's income, the State reduces the nation's wealth, and therefore its standard of living. As I have already observed, such arguments marked no break with Tory tradition. However, in retrospect at least (and precisely because of the pains taken to emphasise the continuity of the new Tory administration with its predecessors) it is easy to see a momentous shift in stress, barely a year after

34

the election, in the words of the man who was to become the key figure - second only to Herself - in implementing the Thatcherite Revolution.

In a lecture given to the Bow Group in August 1980, Nigel Lawson (at that time a junior minister in the Treasury) concluded:

> 'All that is new is that the new Conservatism has embarked on the task - it is not an easy one: nothing worthwhile in politics is; but at least it runs with rather than against the grain of human nature - of re-educating the people in some old truths. They are no less true for being old.'

The lecture was published by the Centre for Policy Studies under the title *The New Conservatism*, and the very fact that it was given to a Tory ginger group especially characterised by its concern for 'the condition of the people' made it a clear declaration of intent to capture the party for the new thinking - thinking which is rooted not in Tory tradition but in classical economics and the Manchester school of liberalism.

Patrick Cosgrave says of Thatcherism that its combination of market-place liberalism in domestic policy and nationalism in foreign (including foreign economic) policy 'has been unknown in British politics since the middle of the nineteenth century.' But while conceding that Mrs Thatcher's Tory critics are right in saying that 'she has by her words and actions sought to establish a strand of Conservatism as the whole tradition,' he stresses that 'at least it *is* a strand, and an important one.'

So lenient a judgement comes close to a Humpty Dumpty effrontery with regard to terminology. None of the British political parties represented in Parliament subscribes, as a party, to anything approaching a clearly defined ideology. Some of them, indeed, glory in this haziness, while the leader of one party is embarrassed that he cannot pronounce his party totally free of such foreign infections. For practical, psychological, and historical reasons the Conservative Party is in most respects even more of a pantechnicon than its rivals. This does not mean, however, that anything goes, that it is a mere transitory alliance of shifting sectional interests. Such expediency could never have brought it such enduring success. Equally, however, it can never be itself by leaning too far in one particular direction. If ever it does so, its innate centrifugal forces threaten to fragment it.

Nigel Lawson was perfectly right to reject, in his Bow Group lecture, the notion 'that Conservatism is nothing more than a technique of government.' (Though it is that and, in a sense, centrally so.) But to do so in the context of repudiating consensus politics in the name of conviction politics was to pose a false antithesis. Strong (and even contradictory) convictions can accommodate themselves to the politics of conservatism; blind obsessions cannot.

The whole point about British Conservatism is its fine sense of balance - between the estates of the realm, between social classes, between self-interest and communal concerns, between privilege and duty, and so on and so forth. It is precisely its generally skilful balancing of interests and concerns that has enabled the Conservative Party to pose so successfully for a hundred and fifty years as a (even as *the*) truly national party. There is even a sense in which it can rightfully claim to have been, during the historical period of 'representative democracy', the natural party of government.

If we dig beneath those great accretions of sentiment regarding King, Country, Church, and suchlike (which are admittedly of real concern to true Conservatives) for the keystones of the old Conservatism, we will find that they are PROPERTY & PATERNALISM. Enough of the latter, at least, to preserve the former! In their boundless enthusiasm for the shining splendours of capitalism, the cohorts of Thatcherism have upset the 'natural' balance of traditional Conservatism by knocking out the keystone of 'paternalism' and replacing it with 'economic liberty', the better to accumulate 'property' - which, needless to say, *does* remain safe in their hands! In practical terms this boils down to one all-embracing slogan, namely, PROPERTY: The Right to Procure, Deploy, and Dispose of it as one pleases; or, in the universal question-begging phrase: the right to do what one likes with one's own.

Just so long as 'the New Conservatism' appears to be delivering general prosperity, it may continue to be widely popular; and since it has been instrumental in dispersing the mists concealing the realities of the old Conservatism (while at the same time laying down some of its own), it is doubtful if the old kind of Conservative equilibrium can ever be restored. That is no reason for not recognising that, despite having some important constituents in common, the old and the new Conservatisms are quite distinct creeds. And, since, despite the triumphant ascendancy of the Thatcherites, the battle for the soul of the Tory Party is not by any means over and may still result in a major realignment of political forces, it is of some practical importance to understand the issues dividing the new from the old and the drys from the wets.

CHAPTER 3

The Tory heritage

'Every history of the creation, and every traditionary
account, whether from the lettered or unlettered
world, however they may vary in their opinion or
belief of certain particulars, all agree in establishing
onepoint, *the unity of man*; by which I mean, that all
men are of *one degree*, and consequently that all men
are born equal, and with equal natural right, in the
same manner as if posterity had been continued by
creation instead of *generation...*'

Tom Paine, *The Rights of Man* (1791-92)

That Thatcherism is just a strand or two ripped out of the whole
complex tapestry of Conservatism can be easily seen by a brief
survey of the salient ideas of the twenty-five Conservative
thinkers, spanning nearly three hundred years of British politics,
represented in Philip Buck's anthology.

Buck starts in Restoration times with George Savile, the
first Marquis of Halifax (1633-1695), of whose influence on
bringing about what came to be called by its beneficiaries 'the
Glorious Revolution' Macaulay was to write: 'The revolution,
as far as it can be said to bear the character of any single mind,
assuredly bears the character of the large yet cautious mind of
Halifax.' Macaulay also said of him that: 'Through frequent and
violent revolutions of public feeling, he almost invariably took
that view of the great questions of his time which history has
finally adopted.'

In the most important of his political works, *The Character
of a Trimmer* (which was really a kind of open letter to Charles
II), Halifax not only slyly turns his enemies' taunts back on
themselves by affecting to understand 'trimmer' as a tribute to
his prudent handling of the ship of state, but adopts the term to
characterise his principles of good government and political
stability. In doing so, he expresses some of the most central and
most enduring precepts of Conservatism: respect for the rule of
law ('the laws are jewels' and 'chains of gold' that 'tie up our

unruly passions'), the maintaining of a balance of power between Crown and Parliament to ensure both order and liberty ('our Government is in a just proportion, no tympany, no unnatural swelling either of power or liberty') and government by consent of the governed ('the virtual consent of the whole being included in their representatives' who express 'the united sense of the people' so that 'every act done by such an authority seemeth to be an effect of their choice as well as part of their duty' and spurs them on to 'execute whatsoever is so enjoined *as their own will, better explained by Parliament*, rather than from the terror of incurring the penalty of the law for omitting it'). [my emphasis]

Such is the art of representative government as proffered by the Marquis of Halifax. Leaving out of account the awkward fact that in his times representation through parliamentary elections was a sorry jest in which few could join and averting our eyes from such mercenary considerations as the spoils of office, one passage in his essay (where he contrasts the virtues and vices of 'Monarchy', i.e. absolute monarchy, and 'Commonwealth', i.e. a so-called democratic republic, and rejects both in favour of 'our blessed constitution, in which dominion and liberty are so well reconciled') underlines the essentially oligarchical nature of representative government so conceived:

> 'The Rules of a Commonwealth are too hard for the bulk of mankind to come up to; that form of government requireth such a spirit to carry it on as doth not dwell in great numbers, but is restrained to so very few, especially in this age, that let the methods appear never so reasonable in paper, they must fail in practice, which will ever be more suited to men's nature as it is, than as it should be...'

For all the wit and elegance of his prose, Halifax *examines* nothing. His arguments are but eulogies of the 'this blessed plot of land' variety. ('The Crown has power sufficient to protect our liberties; the People have so much liberty as is necessary to make them useful to the Crown,' runs a typical Halifax clincher). What he does do, however, as I have already observed, is clearly to enunciate the basic constitutional precepts and fine loyal and patriotic sentiments which every Tory holds dear to this day - though just how a latter-day Tory would reconcile his conflicting allegiances should the Crown ever decline to assent to a bill passed by Parliament is the conundrum of conundrums.

Buck's second representative Conservative thinker is Henry St. John, the first Viscount Bolingbroke (1678-1751), a politician much admired by Disraeli. Chief architect of the Treaty of Utrecht which ended Britain's involvement in the War of the Spanish Succession, Bolingbroke shared with Robert Harley, Earl of Oxford, the leadership of the Tory ministry of 1710-1714. Impeached by his enemies after the death of Queen Anne, Bolingbroke lived in exile in France until 1723.

The range of his writings is wider and more philosophical than Halifax's but their political concerns and conclusions are broadly similar, as the three following excerpts (the first from *A Dissertation on Parties*, the second and third from *The Idea of a Patriot King*) show:

'Absolute monarchy is tyranny; but absolute democracy is tyranny and anarchy both. If aristocracy be placed between these two extremes, it is placed on a slippery ridge and must fall into one or the other, according to the natural course of human affairs; if the few who govern are united, into tyranny, perhaps more severe than any other; if they are disunited, into factions and disorders as great as those of the most tumultuous democracy.'

'It is by this mixture of monarchical, aristocratical and democratical power, blended together in one system, and by these three estates balancing one another, that our free constitution of government hath been preserved so long inviolate, or hath been brought back, having suffered violations, to its original principles, and been renewed, and improved too, by frequent and salutary revolutions.'

'To espouse no party, but to govern like the common father of his people, is so essential to the character of a

> PATRIOT KING, that he who does otherwise forfeits
> the title...The true image of a free people, governed by a
> PATRIOT KING, is that of a patriarchal family, where
> the head and all the members are united by one common
> interest...'

Bolingbroke rejected Hobbes' preposterous notion of an antediluvian state of 'absolute individuality', considering society to be natural, and, in accordance with this, presupposing a kind of original commonwealth. From which it follows that his Patriot King 'can have a right to no more than is trusted to him by the constitution: and that his people, *who had an original right to the whole by the law of nature*, can have the sole indefeasible right to that part which they have reserved to themselves.' [my emphasis]

Such speculations (in which, incidentally, as with most thinkers of the Age of Enlightenment, a consideration of historical processes did not seriously figure) might have led to revolutionary conclusions. But in his thinking they coalesce into the 'one close system of Benevolence', into a 'gen'ral good...all serv'd, all serving', each in his allotted place in an 'order' in which 'some are, and must be greater than the rest' - the 'Heav'n's first law' of Pope's *Essay on Man*, for which, indeed, Bolingbroke had provided the philosophy. For democrats, perhaps his most thought-provoking words are: 'Parliaments have had a good effect on the people, by keeping them quiet...'

Just as, in the late seventeenth century, under the pressures of continuing religious conflict and a renewed struggle for supremacy between King and Parliament, the Marquis of Halifax moved from moderate Toryism to at least temporary accommodation with the Whigs so, at the end of the eighteenth century, under the pressures of the continent-wide upheaval ignited by the French Revolution, Edmund Burke (1729-1797) began his political career as a reforming Whig and ended it, to all intents and purposes, as a Tory. Ironically enough, Burke has indeed been placed by many Tories at the very pinnacle of the party's pantheon. (Even more ironically, his spirit is still invoked by parliamentarians of divers parties as one of the greatest of their brotherhood).

Buck goes so far as to say of him: 'The great contribution to Conservative political thought in the eighteenth century, and for succeeding centuries as well, was made by Edmund Burke'; and:

'The most telling statement of the Conservative position is embodied in Burke's *Reflections* and not much is added to these fundamental ideas during the nineteenth and twentieth centuries.' In discussing the contributions of the four politicians he uses to represent Conservative political ideas in the nineteenth century - Peel, Disraeli, Randolph Churchill, and Salisbury - Buck points out that 'they maintained the general framework of political thought which had been stated by Burke.' He usefully summarises this as: 'the respect for the mixed or balanced constitution; the three estates of the realm; the importance of religion; the belief in an aristocracy; the belief in personal rights and property rights; and the recognition of the need for gradual change in institutions as conditions change.' Burke's principles and precepts with regard to the first two of these were, in their essence at least, largely anticipated by Halifax. I shall therefore concentrate on illustrating the last three points as well as Burke's notions of how society began and its organic nature, which have a particularly strong bearing on his views on political stability.

The odd thing is that, notwithstanding the vehemence with which he warns us of the dangers of social engineering because society is to him like a living body, he insists (without offering any evidence and contrary to reasonable assumptions) that society was *not*, and then suddenly, through men's volition, *was*. Thus he accepts the common (and convenient!) idea of his age of the social contract, but utterly rejects Bolingbroke's argument, in his *Origin of Civil Society*, that, since man is by nature a social animal, 'In general we may say, that the foundations of civil or political societies were laid by nature, though they are the creatures of art. Societies were begun by instinct, and improved by experience.' Which is in effect to say that human society has existed for as long as human beings, however long it may have taken to evolve its present forms.

For Burke, the contrary applies - and it is clearly a matter of the greatest concern to him. 'In a state of *rude* Nature there is no such thing as a people,' and he goes on to call this a 'wholly artificial' idea. He maintains (or perhaps one had better say 'supposes') that 'a people' is constituted when 'loose individuals...form themselves into a mass' or 'corporation' by '*common* agreement' [my emphasis], 'covenant' or 'original compact'. Only then do they have 'a true politic personality' which entitles them to be called 'a people'. They may then be said to have a 'general will'. By breaking the covenant between them, they destroy their nationhood - which is what the French had done in overthrowing their monarchy. Such are his arguments in *An Appeal from the New to the Old Whigs* (1791).

Furthermore, the social contract should be looked on with reverence because

> 'It is a partnership in all science, a partnership in all
> art, a partnership in every virtue and in all perfection.
> As the ends of such a partnership cannot be obtained
> in many generations, it becomes a partnership not
> only between those who are living, but between those
> who are living, those who are dead, and those who
> are to be born. Each contract of each particular state
> is but a clause in the great primaeval contract of
> eternal society, linking the lower with the higher
> natures, connecting the visible and invisible world,
> according to a fixed compact sanctioned by the
> inviolable oath which holds all physical and all moral
> natures each in their appointed place.'

Thus, at any rate by the time he came to write his most celebrated work, *Reflections on the Revolution in France* (1790), from which the above passage is taken, Burke's feelings about society partake of the sacerdotal. He is evidently oblivious to how ill such thoughts consort with ideas that, however debatable they may be, are certainly more rational, such as his preceding statement that: 'Government is a contrivance of human wisdom to provide for human *wants*. Men have a right that these wants should be provided for by this wisdom.'

Despite his ardour for reform during his first twenty-three years in Parliament as (to use his own label) a 'Rockingham Whig' and, despite his own protestation, in a speech made early in the year in which he wrote his *Reflections*, that he was 'no enemy to reformation', it is difficult to avoid the conclusion that, consequent to the French Revolution, Burke recognised, not so much the need for change as a regrettable unavoidability which made it imperative that every constitution incorporated the machinery for peaceful change:

'A state without the means of some change is without the means of its conservation...By a constitutional policy working after the pattern of Nature, we receive, we hold, we transmit our government and our privileges, in the same manner in which we enjoy and transmit our property and our lives...Thus, by reserving the method of Nature in the conduct of the state, in what we improve we are never wholly new, in what we retain we are never wholly obsolete.'

Strictly speaking, 'conservation' and hence 'conservatism' are in themselves politically neutral ideas, in the sense that they simply endorse the value of some thing or situation that at present exists or obtains. In a class society, however, they express approval of inequality. Enormous changes in social relationships have occurred, of course, since Burke's day, when even a blind man could see that society was highly hierarchical. Nevertheless - and notwithstanding what may at first sight appear to be an antiquated and wholly superseded attitude to the *demos* - Burke's views on class mirror with astonishing accuracy Conservative views two hundred years later. 'Belief in an aristocracy' was listed above as one of the elements in 'the general framework of political thought' which he handed down to his successors, and like them, he endorses the idea of aristocracy both in the literal or hereditary and in the figurative or natural sense of the term. Of the former he writes in his *Reflections*: 'Some decent regulated pre-eminence, some preference...given to birth, is neither unnatural, nor unjust, nor impolitic...'; while later in the same work, having contemptuously dismissed the case made by Rousseau, Voltaire, and Helvetius (characteristically, without giving them a hearing, but on the conclusive grounds, one gathers, that they are foreigners), he nails his colours firmly to the mast of the *status quo* by roundly declaring: 'We are resolved to keep an established church, an established monarchy, an established aristocracy, and an established democracy, each in the degree it exists, *and in no greater.*' [my emphasis]

With regard to what Burke himself calls 'natural aristocracy', considering his own relatively humble origins, he could hardly but subscribe to what Napoleon, reflecting on his own meteoric career from a distant exile, was to epitomise as *'la carriére ouverte aux talents.'* In his *Reflections*, Burke nominates 'virtue and wisdom...wherever they are actually found' - not 'blood', 'names', and 'titles' - as the sole qualifications for government. However, it should be added that he assumes them to be quite liberally distributed amongst the gentry (since, as he explains in *An Appeal from the New to the Old Whigs*, they have among other advantages 'leisure to read' and are able 'to take a large view...of society') and nowhere declares that the not infrequent absence of such moral qualifications should disqualify the well-bred from office or influence. In his *Appeal*, he defines, or rather describes, 'natural aristocracy' as excellence in a variety of positions of leadership - military, judicial, academic, commercial, simply social, and so forth - and goes on:

> 'Men, qualified in the manner I have just described, form in Nature, as she operates in the common modification of society, the leading, guiding, and governing part. It is the soul to the body, without which the man does not exist. To give, therefore, no more importance, in the social order, to such descriptions of men than that of so many units is a horrible usurpation.'

One could not get much further away than that from the modern idea of democracy as meaning 'one man (or woman), one vote'!

A few lines later, after summoning up a vision of 'great multitudes' acting together 'under the discipline of Nature' and of 'the voice of this grand chorus of national harmony', Burke's rhetoric impersonating reason reaches a crescendo of hatred and hysteria towards the new democratic doctrines:

> 'But when you disturb this harmony, - when you break up this beautiful order, this array of truth and Nature, as well as of habit and *prejudice*, when you separate the common sort of men from the *proper chieftains*, so as to form them into an adverse army, - I no longer know that venerable object called the

people in such a disbanded race of deserters and
vagabonds...Those who attempt by outrage and
violence to deprive men of any advantage which they
hold under the laws, and to destroy the natural order
of life, proclaim war against them.' [my emphases]

Burke's remarkable insight into how the apparently divisive
forces in a capitalist society can, by the harnessing of political
inequality to economic inequality, actually make for political
stability is shown in a passage from his *Reflections* in which
four fundamental tenets of Conservatism - hereditary aristocracy,
meritocracy or natural aristocracy (in a secondary, supportive
role, be it noted, to the fourteen-carat variety), economic
inequality, and political inequality - are seen as acting together
in support of what was summarised above as 'the belief in
personal rights and property rights':

'Nothing is due and adequate representation of a
state, that does not represent its ability, as well as its
property. But as ability is a vigorous and active
principle, and as property is sluggish, inert, and
timid, it never can be safe from the invasions of
ability, unless it be, out of all proportion,
predominant in the representation. It must be
represented too in great masses of accumulation, or it
is not rightly protected. The characteristic essence of
property, formed out of the combined principles of its
acquisition and conservation, is to be *unequal*. The
great masses therefore which excite envy, and tempt
rapacity, must be put out of the possibility of danger.
They then form a natural rampart about the lesser
properties in all their gradations.'

In the context in which we are considering Burke's views
- that of his lasting contribution to Conservative political thought
- it should be remarked that in much of what he has to say he is
speaking for 'men of property' (that is to say, for those who are
markedly better endowed with possessions than the average
person) of *whatever party or none*, and in his or any other time.
In particular, he is a spokesman for the virtues of capitalism.

What he feared above all from the wildfire spread of Jacobinical ideas was that they might eventually lead, via revolution, to State expropriation of property in England. Of the French Assembly he writes:

> 'We entertain an high opinion of the legislative authority; but we have never dreamt that parliaments had any right whatever to violate property...this legislative assembly of a free nation sits, not for security, but for the destruction of property, and not of property only, but of every rule and maxim which can give it stability.'

And a little later he makes his fears absolutely specific:

> 'The great source of my solicitude is, lest it should ever be considered in England as the policy of the state, to seek a resource in confiscations of any kind; or that any one description of citizens should be brought to regard any of the others, as their proper *prey*...Revolutions are favourable to confiscation; and it is impossible to know under what obnoxious names the next confiscations will be authorised. I am sure that the principles predominant in France extend to very many persons and descriptions of persons in all countries who think their *innoxious indolence* their security. This kind of innocence in proprietors may be argued into inutility; and inutility into an unfitness for their estates.' [my emphases]

It is entertaining to recall that within eighteen months of Burke's death Pitt persuaded the Commons, against fierce opposition, to accept a modest proposal for confiscation, namely a tax on incomes of sixty pounds a year and above, 'as an aid for the prosecution of the war' with France, though without any of the dire consequences on the redistribution of property that Burke feared. Income tax was, in any case, repealed at the end of the Napoleonic Wars (on a motion put by one of the leading Whig reformers in the House, Henry Brougham) and it was not reintroduced until the first true Conservative (as distinct from

Tory) administration took office under Sir Robert Peel. Since then - for the first half century mostly at the crippling rate of between 5d and 7d in the pound - it has been a permanent part of 'the social contract'.

In the long view, most of the great parliamentary battles of the century and a half between the Restoration of the Stuart dynasty and that of the Bourbons may be pronounced as 'sound and fury, signifying nothing.' One might consider it fair cause for wry raillery that (despite Philip Buck's confident assertion that from around 1678, when the mutual mudslinging names 'Whig' and 'Tory' came into general use to refer to the two contending bourgeois factions in the English parliament, 'the Tory party shows a fairly continuous development to the present day') before the nineteenth century it is in fact often difficult to distinguish one from the other, except in matters of little moment to most of us today, chiefly concerning loyalty to the Stuart line and, sometimes, though by no means consistently so, adherence to the old faith.

And even then, they might pass back and forth, like actors in a small company playing many parts, or hover in the wings, like the Vicar of Bray, in order to see from which side they might get preferment, since everything ultimately depended on the royal favour. 'The question is,' says Humpty Dumpty in Lewis Carroll's great political satire *Through the Looking-Glass*, 'which is to be the master - that's all.' From our distance in time and outlook, quite contrary to the parliamentary brouhaha and flummery on the occasion of the tercentenary of 'the Glorious Revolution', there seems little sense in awarding marks to one side or the other. As Dryden puts it in his address to the reader prefacing *Absolam and Achitophel* (1681): 'For, Wit and Fool, are consequents of Whig and Tory: And every man is a Knave or an Ass to the contrary side.'

There is a serious point to be made here, though: that the central constitutional precepts and principles characterised above as 'Tory' or 'Conservative' were - and *are still* - more or less common currency among British parliamentarians, so they cannot be used to distinguish between the fundamental aims and values of different parties. In the hunt for these, we might look first at the metamorphoses of Whig and Tory caterpillars into Liberal and Conservative butterflies and see how they hatched in the heat of unrelenting pressure for the extension of the suffrage during the nineteenth and well into the twentieth centuries.

In considering the effects on the nature of the old political parties of their striving, willy-nilly and piecemeal, to accommodate the amorphous masses to the British heritage of constitutional government *without* altering the essential structure of society, it might help to glance first at one other aspect of Burke's attitude to the great 'silent majority' whose interests he (and those of his fellow parliamentarians who ever gave the question any thought) maintained were already properly represented by the three estates whose deliberations determined the 'national interest' and destiny.

Burke acknowledged the truth, laid down by Adam Smith and other economists and by that time generally recognised by thinking people, that labour was the source of all wealth and that, as Burke puts it in *Thoughts and Details on Scarcity*, an essay written in the famine year of 1795 to attract the attention of William Pitt: 'Those who labour...in reality feed both the pensioners called the rich and themselves.' If we knew nothing else about his ideas, such observations, particularly when set alongside such an unequivocal declaration as that in the *Reflections* that 'men have a right to the fruits of their industry,' might lead us to suppose that he was some kind of prototype Socialist.

But as we have already seen, Burke accepted without qualm or question the class and property structure of his society. And as we would expect from such a complete and consummate apologist for capitalism, he was also quite satisfied that what he quaintly called 'commutative justice' generally obtained in eighteenth-century England. In the essay on *Scarcity* he also declaims, with that characteristic way he has of elevating the most mundane and material things into the empyrean: 'The laws of commerce are the laws of nature and therefore the laws of God.' Which flight of fancy was to earn him, from the blistering tongue of Karl Marx, the remark that, 'To the very marrow, he was a commonplace bourgeois.'

Whether or not this son of Ireland felt any compassion for the great ragged army commonly called in his time 'the labouring poor' and whether or not E.P. Thompson is too gentle with him

49

in describing as an 'epochal indiscretion' his most infamous allusion to the masses (in the *Reflections*) as 'the swinish multitude', he certainly seems to have successfully sublimated whatever real concern he might have felt for 'the PEOPLE' in the kind of sublime and vacuous formulae I have cited above. At any rate, the counsel he considered should be given to the labouring poor, in that year of even greater suffering than was their normal lot, was: 'Patience, labour, sobriety, frugality and religion.' In his opinion, 'All the rest is downright fraud.'

CHAPTER 4

The forging of the Conservative Party

> 'Where honest and laborious men can be *compelled to starve quietly*, whether all at once or by inches, with old wheat ricks and fat cattle under their eye, it is mockery to talk of their "*liberty*", of any sort; for the sum total of their state is this, they have "*liberty*" to choose between death by starvation (quick or slow) and death by the halter!'
>
> **William Cobbett, *Rural Rides* (1830)**

Burke's modest origins absolve him of the charge of not living up to the ideal of *noblesse oblige.* Whether or not this has anything to do with his attitude to the masses, these aspects of his mind draw our attention to a missing element in his thinking which was to be of major importance in the development of the Conservative Party - the element of paternalism, or what Disraeli generally referred to as concern for 'the condition of the people'.

Such a charge (of practical, if not of theoretical, neglect of the common people) could not be made against Sir Robert Peel (1788-1850), the politician who, *pace* Buck, has the most genuine claim to be considered the father of the Conservative Party. Not least because, by changing his mind and his policies on major issues on at least three momentous occasions, he split his party - on the first two (concerning Catholic emancipation and parliamentary reform) seriously though temporarily, on the last (the repeal of the corn laws) so fundamentally that it caused a radical realignment of political forces and disabled the Conservatives from serious contention for power for the next twenty years.

Paradoxically, however, in so doing, Peel acted in what has come to be widely seen as the best traditions of his party:

(1) A resolve to put the perceived long-term interests of the country above the interests of the party:

> 'As a minister of the crown I reserve to myself, distinctly and unequivocally, the right of adapting my conduct to the exigency of the moment, and to the wants of the country.' - Peel in 1829.

'When I fall, I shall have the satisfaction of reflecting that I do not fall because I have shown subservience to a party. I shall not fall because I preferred the interests of party to the general interests of the community.' - Peel in 1846, during the debate on the repeal of the corn laws.

(2) The maintenance of political stability through a balanced constitution:

'My object for some years past has been to lay the foundations of a great party, which, existing in the House of Commons, and deriving its strength from the popular will, should diminish the risk and deaden the shock of collisions between the two deliberative branches of the legislature.' - Peel in 1838.

During the debate on the repeal of the corn laws, Peel told the House that, as a Conservative minister, he had done his best 'to ensure the united action of an ancient monarchy, a proud aristocracy, and a reformed constituency.'

(3) The pragmatic adjustment to inevitable change in order to conserve as much as possible of what is cherished. The three most striking illustrations in Peel's career are:

(i) His letter of 11 August 1828 to Wellington arguing that although Catholic emancipation was a great danger, civil strife was a greater one.
(ii) His action to forestall the creation of Whig peers to force through the Reform Bill - a scenario replayed nearly eighty years later in the struggle between the Commons and the Lords over the Lloyd George 'people's budget' of 1909.
(iii) His abandonment of support for the corn laws, defusing a potentially revolutionary situation resulting from the aggregated pressures of labour militancy, the Chartist movement, and agitation against the corn laws.

(4) A real and active concern for 'the condition of the people':

As well as by his conversion to the repeal of the corn laws

and to free trade in general, this was shown in his fiscal reforms (particularly in the introduction of income tax), largely motivated by a desire to cut the cost of living of the working classes by reducing indirect taxation.

All four principles and concerns find expression in his speech of resignation after the irredeemably protectionist Tories, outraged by the repeal of the corn laws, had combined with the Whigs to throw out a government bill on Ireland:

> 'I shall leave a name severely censured, I fear, by many who, on public grounds, deeply regret the severance of party ties - deeply regret that severance not from interested or personal motives, but from the firm conviction that fidelity to party engagements - the existence and maintenance of a great party - constitutes a powerful instrument of government. I shall surrender power severely censured by others who, from no interested motive, adhere to the principle of protection, considering the maintenance of it to be essential to the welfare and interests of the country; I shall leave a name execrated by every monopolist who, from less honourable motives, clamours for protection because it conduces to his own individual benefit; but it may be that I shall leave a name sometimes remembered with expressions of goodwill in the abodes of those whose lot it is to labour and to earn their daily bread with the sweat of their brow, when they shall recruit their exhausted strength with abundant and untaxed food, the sweeter because it is no longer leavened with a sense of injustice.'

As the son and grandson of manufacturers (his father, the first baronet, has his place in history as a forerunner of all the legislation designed to protect factory workers), in his antecedents and in his own career, Peel graphically illustrates the great economic and social changes of his time - the Industrial Revolution, the rise of the middle classes, and (with special relevance to our context) the effect of these changes on the character of the political parties. Considering his origins, it is ironic that his destiny was to lead the party most closely associated with the country gentry and ultimately to be accused by fellow Tories of having 'thrown over the landed interest'.

Of deeper interest is the point that, because of the very fact that his life represents the Tory gentleman at his best, it also demonstrates conclusively the ultimate inadequacy of benevolent paternalism in general and exposes, in particular, the crippling circumscriptions of the Conservative approach to politics. He had the courage to change his mind and his course in the teeth of his most cherished convictions, and that is, especially in a politician, a most admirable quality. Yet not only his career but his most famous testament, the *Tamworth Manifesto* (both in what it does say and in what it fails to say), show that there is no substitute for unfettered thought.

Honourable, scrupulous, conscientious and concerned though he was, lack of foresight led to his inchworm measures for the reform of crying evils, as instanced by years of tinkering with the mechanism of protective restrictions on importing corn until the Irish potato famine forced his hand; lack of imagination dammed up his understanding of the aspirations of the common people; and lack of vision or hard thinking disabled his capacity to search for lasting solutions to the great social problems of his time, as is surely always the case where speculation, theory, and the painstaking construction of ideology are scorned or neglected. Only such deficiencies made it possible for Peel (whom no one could accuse of being a die-hard) to make the extraordinary statement, in the *Manifesto*: 'I consider the Reform Bill a *final* and irrevocable settlement of a great constitutional question - a settlement which no friend to the peace and welfare of this country would attempt to disturb, either by direct or by insidious means.'[my emphasis] Unless it were an appreciation, conscious or unconscious, of self- and class-interest, only a wanton circumscription of his natural powers of intellect could have led him to insist (again in the *Manifesto*) that reason and the righting of wrongs must give way to such Burkean precepts as 'the respect for ancient rights, and the deference to prescriptive authority'. And granting the genuineness of his concern, only one blinkered by the conditioned assumptions and the prejudicial economic doctrines of his time and class (assumptions and doctrines which, it has to be said, served admirably the interests of those who held them) could have got no further in thought and deed than how to ameliorate the harsh conditions of life of 'those whose lot it is to labour'.

If the story of the forging of the Conservative Party out of the old Tories abounds with irony, which it does, it is in large measure a consequence of the internal inconsistencies of Conservative thought. No one illustrates this better than the second of the modern party's founding fathers, Benjamin Disraeli (1804-1881), who played such a prominent part in the sundering of Peel's post-Industrial-Revolution party and subsequently succeeded in re-creating it more nearly in his own image. Political expediency, self-advancement and resentment at Peel's snubbing of his bid for promotion doubtless partly account for the virulence of Disraeli's attack on his leader. However, they do not detract from the sincerity of Disraeli's stance and arguments in declaiming:

> 'Let men stand by the principle by which they rise - right or wrong...It is not a legitimate trial of the principles of free trade against the principle of protection, if a Parliament, the majority of which are elected to support protection, be gained over to free trade by the arts of the very individual whom they were elected to support in an opposite career. It is not fair to the people of England.'

Ironies abound. Disraeli no less than Peel subscribed to a restricted suffrage but was not one of those given, thoughtlessly or disingenuously, to confuse 'the electorate' with 'the people'. Neither had a vested interest in protection for agriculture. Disraeli's concern had more to do with his romantic conception of an English constitution that had always rested on the leading part played by the landed gentry in affairs of state - a political reality until relatively recently not seriously challenged by other social groups (except perhaps in the Civil War) and one which Disraeli sincerely believed to be in the best interests of the whole nation so long as that section of society remained true to its stewardship. Peel, on the other hand, though the son of a manufacturer, was not moved to the major policy change which split his own party through that desire for cheap bread in order to lower the cost of subsistence wages that polluted the motives of so many of the corn law abolitionists. Above all, both of the protagonists had the welfare of the common people at heart.

Despite his severe shortcomings as a thinker - due mainly no doubt to the unremitting pressures of high office in an era of enormous and near-cataclysmic social change - Peel was the greater realist, the one more sensible to the irreversible shift in the balance of social forces that was inexorably making the middle classes, not the landed gentry, the fulcrum of the future. Disraeli combined dazzling parliamentary and political gifts with a profound critique of the present and a powerful vision of the future; he scorned the expedient manoeuvrings of most of his fellow party members, who were concerned at all costs to remain in office or return to power as quickly as possible if ousted. But his vision, fired by a largely mythical past, was of an impossible future, so that despite his great and lasting influence on his party, events carried both it and the country in a quite different direction. Nevertheless, he maintained the four traditions enunciated above with regard to Peel, and (which is our present principal concern) consolidated PROPERTY & PATERNALISM as keystones of Conservatism.

Disraeli's subscription to these central tenets in the Conservative heritage is expressed most cogently (and that this should be so is itself revealing of the cast of his mind) in his novel *Sybil*. But before looking at this it would be as well to glance at two more direct expressions of his political philosophy included in Buck's symposium, since they so well exemplify both the substance and the style of Conservative thinking up to the apotheosis of the Blessed Margaret - its romantic rhetoric, its disinclination to definition, the misty elusiveness (*not* the absence) of its dogma. That a lifetime in politics did not serve to eradicate the protective vagueness of Disraeli's declared views on English 'democracy' is shown by the fact that the first of these two declarations, his *Vindication of the English Constitution in a letter to a noble and learned Lord*, dates from 1835, the year of his fourth unsuccessful attempt to get into Parliament; while the second, a *Speech at the Banquet of the National Union of Conservative and Constitutional Associations* at Crystal Palace, dates from 1872, two years before the start of his second and last ministry.

Nor - despite his attempt to convince the public of his commitment to democracy in his pamphlet *What is He?* (written to explain why, after standing in an 1832 by-election as a Radical, he had thrown in his lot with the Tories); despite his idiosyncratic definition of a democracy (in the *Vindication*) as a 'country where the legislative and even the executive office may be constitutionally obtained by every subject of the land'; and despite the fact that it was under his leadership in the Commons that, in 1867, the second major extension of the suffrage was carried - did he ever become what would be recognised nowadays as a democrat, even of the parliamentary breed.

But this rejection of what he dismissed as the 'democracy of numbers' was, of course, entirely consistent with his paternalism, and indeed its logical concomitant. In his *Vindication* he pointedly distinguishes the 'Commons' - 'an estate of the realm privileged as the other estates...and constituting, even with its late considerable accession of members, only a small section of the nation' - from 'the people'. His point is that the elected members of Parliament, constituting the House of Commons, were not and never had been the representatives of the people (which was an undeniable constitutional fact) although, according to him, Members of Parliament were, together with the Peers, 'the trustees of the nation, not its masters'. And while he abhorred the failure of Parliament properly to protect the interests of the common people (a dereliction of duty dating, he considered, primarily from Parliament's usurpation of the powers of the Crown to act as the nation's umpire - he greatly admired Bolingbroke and particularly his concept of the 'patriot king' - and secondarily from the relinquishment by the Peers of a leading, or at least equal, role in Parliament) he did not, either then or later, disapprove of limitations on the franchise which deprived most of the common people of formal representation in their own governance. In his 1872 *Banquet* speech, alluding to the second Reform Bill which Lord Derby and he had hijacked from Gladstone and his supporters and manoeuvred through Parliament, he declared that 'the great body of the working classes of this country', having 'recently' and 'wisely' obtained 'a great extension of political rights', were now 'in possession of personal privileges - of personal rights and liberties - which are not enjoyed by the aristocracies of other countries'. He described this as 'an adequate concession of political rights' and claimed, revealingly, that such was 'the conviction of the whole country'.

Assumptions of omniscience with regard to the state of public opinion, together with arrogation of the right to speak for others, are, of course, classic symptoms of the sickness of megalomania that so frequently strikes politicians and pressmen. But perhaps the blithe confidence of Disraeli's asseveration is rather to be attributed to the even more dangerous delusion that there is something called 'the country' on the pulse of which it is possible to have one's finger; that such abstractions as 'the mother/fatherland', 'the French nation', 'the German race', 'the English people', and so on, have a reality beyond and above their utility (when used scrupulously and intelligently) as generalisations - and one to which, it goes without saying, these deluded pundits believe themselves to be uniquely attuned. Thus the *Vindication*, without the slightest warrant in the historical record, speaks of 'the English nation' having 'established a popular throne' and having 'invested certain orders of their fellow-subjects with legislative functions', and then proceeds to praise the supposed consequences of a supposed happening that has blessed us with a constitution - 'the matchless creation of our ancestors' - which has 'united equality with freedom' and conferred on us an 'administration of justice...so pure that its exercise has realised the dreams of some Utopian romance...' Who, one might well ask, are the real Utopians - Socialist 'dreamers' or the spinners of conservative myths?

The flowery and fanciful language of the *Vindication* was penned during Disraeli's political immaturity; though, as we have seen, this kind of childishness is not uncommon amongst subscribers to theories of an actual or implicit 'social contract' rooted in the very history of 'the nation'. But if it vitiates his contribution to political thought, his concern for 'the condition of the people' and his championship of 'the rights of labour', however paternalistic their nature, are much to his credit. In his Crystal Palace speech, having enunciated two great objects of his party as 'to maintain the institutions of the country' and 'to uphold the Empire', Disraeli goes on to tell his audience that 'another great object of the Tory party, and one not inferior` to those of which he has been speaking, 'is the elevation of the condition of the people', a prerequisite of which was to 'effect some reduction of their hours of labour and humanise their toil'.

Apart, of course, from the record of relevant reforms during his two administrations (which we shall consider in a moment), there is no surer testimony to the sincerity of his commitment to this cause than the passionate pages of his crusading novel, *Sybil, or The Two Nations*, which projects a remarkably comprehensive picture of the state of England in the early years of Queen Victoria's reign. Disraeli, who had already won a name for himself as a fashionable novelist, was persuaded to write *Sybil* (and the two political novels which flanked it, *Conrad, or The New Generation* and *Tancred, or The New Crusade*) to promote the views of the 'Young England' group of Tory Radicals, who believed that the country's ills were mainly due to the growing predominance of the commercial middle classes (especially since the Reform Act of 1832) and that they could be cured by rallying the working classes under the banner of a benevolent paternalism administered by a rehabilitated monarchy, a regenerated church and a reconstituted aristocracy composed of the more enlightened elements of both the hereditary peers and the captains of industry - an alliance which would have amounted to a kind of semi-feudalistic Welfare State managed through a system of 'guided democracy'.

Sybil (published in 1845) was in part the fruit of a tour through the North of England during which Disraeli and his companions, Lord John Manners and the Hon. George Smythe, saw the factory system at first hand. It tells the story of the awakening of a young nobleman, Charles Egremont, to the condition of the people, largely through his friendship with two Chartist leaders, Stephen Morley and Walter Gerard, and his love for Gerard's daughter Sybil. Thrown into a reflective mood by an outbreak of rick-burning and a disturbing conversation with a tenant farmer on his elder brother's estate, Egremont asks himself:

> 'And the People - the millions of Toil, on whose unconscious energies during these changeful centuries all rested - what changes had these centuries brought to them? Had their advance in the national scale borne a due relation to that progress of their rulers, which had accumulated in the treasuries of a limited class the riches of the world, and made their possessors boast that they were the first of nations: the most powerful and the most free, the most enlightened, the most moral, and the most religious?'

At his first meeting with the two Chartists, Egremont says to Morley: 'Say what you like, our Queen reigns over the greatest nation that ever existed.' But Morley replies (in a passage which focuses on the very heart of the novel and which gives it its second title) that she reigns over not one nation but two, 'THE RICH AND THE POOR', and he stresses how utterly alien each is to the other:

> 'Two nations; between whom there is no intercourse and no sympathy; who are as ignorant of each other's habits, thoughts, and feelings, as if they were dwellers in different zones, or inhabitants of different planets; who are formed by a different breeding, are fed by a different food, are ordered by different manners, and are not governed by the same laws.'

Egremont comes to see that it is so and that the abundant pleasures of life, which he has unthinkingly accepted as his birthright, are rooted in the exploitation of the common people. Philip Warner, a weaver who, despite toiling at his handloom for twelve hours a day for a penny an hour, despairs of being able to keep a roof over the heads of himself and his family much longer, is the very archetype of the dispossessed. 'How did honesty and industry bring us to this?' he muses, and answers himself:

> 'It is that the capitalist has found a slave that has
> supplanted the labour and ingenuity of man. Once he
> was an artisan: at the best, he now only watches
> machines; and even that occupation slips from his grasp,
> to the woman and the child. The capitalist flourishes, he
> amasses immense wealth; we sink, lower and lower;
> lower than the beasts of burthen; for they are fed better
> than we are, cared for more. And it is just, for according
> to the present system they are more precious.'

He bitterly repudiates the fraudulent claim that 'the interests of capital and labour are identical', and declares that:

> 'If a society that has been created by labour suddenly
> becomes independent of it, that society is bound to maintain
> the race whose only property is labour, out of the proceeds of
> that other property, which has not ceased to be productive.'

In scene after vivid scene of high and low life, *Sybil* delivers a withering indictment of a society (whose outlines we can hardly fail to recognise when we look around us today, however changed the detail) in which property comes before people. Then, through the agency of the young parliamentarian Egremont - in the report of a speech that echoes the young Disraeli's speech to the House calling on it to receive the Chartists' National Petition - the author makes a forthright declaration of where he himself stands:

> 'Yes! there was one voice that had sounded in that
> proud Parliament, that, free from the slang of faction,
> had dared to express immortal truths: the voice of a
> noble who, without being a demagogue, had upheld

60

the popular cause; had pronounced his conviction that the rights of labour were as sacred as those of property; that if a difference were to be established, the interests of the living wealth ought to be preferred; who had declared that the social happiness of the millions should be the first object of a statesman, and that, if this were not achieved, thrones and dominions, the pomp and power of courts and empires, were alike worthless.'

Disraeli/Egremont felt his own party was moribund and aspired to lead its regeneration, to restore it to that noble sense of stewardship which he believed had once characterised it:

'Even now it is not dead, but sleepeth; and, in an age of political materialism, of confused purposes and perplexed intelligence, that aspires only to wealth because it has faith in no other accomplishment... Toryism will yet arise from the tomb...to bring back strength to the Crown, liberty to the subject, and to announce that power has only one duty - to secure the social welfare of the PEOPLE.'

The degradation Disraeli describes in *Sybil* mirrors the same inglorious England that Engels portrayed in *The Condition of the Working Class in England*, which was also first published in 1845 - but in Germany, the Victorian reading public being spared this salutary scourge until a translation was issued forty years later. The varied and conflicting attitudes and arguments (not least, for example, over the question of whether poverty is poverty until it is absolute) *Sybil* presents, as well as the range of material conditions - from splendour to squalor - that it portrays, are not so greatly different from those encountered in our own splintered society. That is why Disraeli's expression 'The Two Nations' still strikes home today. And never more so than in differentiating paternalist Tories (or 'One-Nation Tories' as they prefer to call themselves) from 'the New Conservatives'.

Of course, the crusading zeal of the aspiring young politician might have evaporated with the growing triumph of his own career from derided parvenu to honoured elder statesman. How seldom do such youthful ideals survive the surmounting of the slippery slope to success! In Disraeli's case they did, so that his second (and only substantial) ministry, from February 1874 to March 1880, saw the passing of a whole series of laws to improve the lives and labour of the working classes: Factory Acts, an Artisans' Dwelling Act, a Public Health Act, and a Trade Union Act which gave to union funds some protection against claims for damages and granted the right of peaceful picketing.

From this side of the historic watershed of the great Liberal reforming governments of 1906-1914, which laid the foundations of a Welfare State in alliance with a lusty young Labour Party, it is difficult not to think of the Liberals as markedly more sympathetic to the working classes than the Tories. But taken as a whole, the record tells us otherwise. That is no more than we should expect when we consider how the manufacturing and commercial interests were more powerfully represented in the Liberal Party. The miners' leader Alexander Macdonald, who was elected MP for Stafford in the 1874 general election (becoming, in effect, along with another miner who won Morpeth, one of the first two Labour MPs, although officially they sat in the House as Liberals), said of Disraeli's great reforming ministry: 'The Conservative Party have done more for the working classes in five years than the Liberals have in fifty.' Writing about representation of the trade union movement in Parliament after the extension of the franchise to the ever-last-in-the-queue group of workers, the farm labourers, in 1884, Henry Pelling remarks: 'It was not at all clear that the Liberal Party as a whole was more likely to espouse the labour cause than the Conservatives.' He illustrates his point by referring to the 'fair wages' resolution passed by a House of Commons under Tory control in 1891, 'whereby it was agreed that in the awarding of government contracts every effort should be made "to secure the payment of such wages as are generally accepted as current in each trade for competent workmen"'. He describes this as a 'major service for labour.'

In fact - although the 1884 Reform Act was the work of Gladstone's administration, although the 1867 Reform Act of the Derby/Disraeli ministry was the indirect result of the defeat of the Russell/Gladstone Reform Bill of 1866 and although Grey's 1832 Reform Act was only passed when Wellington's forces retreated in face of the King's threat to wipe out the Tory majority in the Lords by creating more Whig peers - the truth is that even when it came to the extension of the franchise, the nineteenth-century Liberals were scarcely less equivocal than the Tories. While Gladstone expressed his belief, as early as 1864, in the right of every man to have the vote, thereby provoking Disraeli's taunt that he had 'revived the doctrine of Tom Paine'; and while unremitting pressure from the radical section of the Liberal Party forced the pace of electoral reform, there was scarcely less opposition to the enfranchisement of the masses among the Liberals than there was in the ranks of the Tories. Robert Lowe (a distinguished frontbencher, subsequently Chancellor of the Exchequer and then Home Secretary), who led the Liberal faction which frustrated the attempt by Lord Russell and Gladstone to widen the franchise in 1866, expressed his aversion, in terms reminiscent of Burke's 'epochal indiscretion', to having his seat dependent on the votes of a class of men he regarded as 'impulsive, unreflecting, and violent' and a prey to 'venality, ignorance, and drunkenness'. Suffice it to say that Hazlitt's sardonic simile likening the Whigs and Tories to rival stagecoaches splashing each other with mud but travelling by the same road to the same destination was almost as pertinent in mid-Victorian Britain as it had been when he made it before the so-called Great Reform Act of 1832.

CHAPTER 5

Radical Liberals and Tory democrats

> 'The 'Fissical Policy' emanated from the Tory party.
> That was the reason some of them were strongly in
> favour of it, and for the same reason others were
> opposed to it. Some of them were under the delusion
> that they were Conservatives: similarly, others imagined
> themselves to be Liberals. As a matter of a fact, most of
> them were nothing. They knew as much about the
> public affairs of their own country as they did of the
> condition of affairs in the planet Jupiter.'
>
> **Robert Tressell,**
> ***The Ragged Trousered Philanthropists* (1914)**

In short, it is a peculiarly purblind and simplistic kind of historical hindsight that promotes the Liberals as the party of reform in Victorian England, mainly to be accounted for, perhaps, by the hold taken on the popular imagination by Gladstone's crusading zeal. One needs to remember, however, that - with the important exception of the extension of the franchise - this zeal was principally focused on foreign parts, across the Irish Channel or further overseas (reminding one a little of Wilberforce's discrimination in favour of slaves in the West Indies, while the toiling masses at home awakened in his breast no comparable compassion). In *The Common People*, their masterly narrative of two centuries (1746-1946) in the life and struggles of Britain's working classes, G.D.H. Cole and Raymond Postgate declare bluntly that 'Gladstone had never understood or sympathised with the economic claims of the workers.'

Even on the issue of male suffrage, radicals were to be found on both sides of the House; while when it came to questions of social reform to ameliorate 'the condition of the people', neither side could be said to stand unequivocally for progress. What else should one expect from an assembly that, until the election of *two* working-class members in 1874, was wholly composed of representatives of property interests? In other words, in considering the development of democracy and the piecemeal construction of a welfare state, what counts is not the perpetual ritualistic combat between Liberals and Conservatives, but the struggle between social radicals and small-c conservatives of whatever party.

Just as parallel lines (or so we are told by those who understand such abstruse matters) meet in infinity, so do the careers of two political comets - Lord Randolph Churchill and Joseph Chamberlain - apparently travelling in quite separate orbits, converge to illustrate the conflict that was of real historical moment. Son of a leading boot and shoe manufacturer and of the daughter of a London provision merchant, Joseph Chamberlain (1836-1914) sat as a Liberal MP for only ten years and held only two ministerial posts (President of the Board of Trade, 1880-85, and President of the Local Government Board, 1886) in Liberal administrations. Then he broke with Gladstone over the Irish Home Rule issue and crossed the floor of the House, subsequently to serve as Colonial Secretary for Conservative ministries from 1895-1903. Yet his programme of radical reform had a profound influence on both parties and on the social development of the whole country in the second half of the Victorian Age. His most indisputable achievement was, as Mayor of Birmingham from 1873-76, to guide the city into making itself a model for municipal reform, 'parked, paved, assized, marketed, Gas-and-watered, and *improved* - all as the result of three years' active work', as he put it himself. Too modestly, as it happens, since he left out of the account major advances in the provision of educational and cultural facilities and an ongoing commitment to 'the increase of the comfort and happiness of the community'.

In his *Victorian Cities* Asa Briggs draws attention to Chamberlain's doubts that he could do as much, let alone more, for his fellow men as an actor on the national stage as he had done for the citizens of his adopted city. On his election to Parliament in 1876 he remarked to his friend Jesse Collings (a doughty champion of the poor in general and of the agricultural labourer and the smallholder in particular): 'What a fool I am to be willing to go to Parliament and give up the opportunity of influencing the only constructive legislation in the country for the sake of tacking M.P. to my name'; and, while serving as President of the Board of Trade, he commented on the progress of his career to the eminent biographer and statesman John Morley: 'Unless I can secure for the nation results similar to those which have followed the adoption of my policy in

Birmingham, it will have been a very sorry exchange to give up the Town Council for the Cabinet.'

At all events, his commitment to social reform endured (surviving, indeed, his subsequent defection to the Conservatives, with whose views he was more in sympathy when it came to foreign and colonial affairs and also to the question of free trade versus protection) and was forcefully expressed in the general election campaign of autumn 1885, in which Chamberlain's dazzlingly bold 'unauthorised programme', appealing to the have-nots and the have-littles, and especially to the newly enfranchised rural labourers, is generally credited with returning the Liberals to power. Chamberlain argued that, as a consequence of the development of industry, private property had usurped the place of communal ownership; and he counselled the haves to pay 'ransom', that they might continue to enjoy security of property. This they could only do by raising the condition of 'the lower orders' - through the provision of good housing at fair rents; free education; compulsory land purchase to set up a scheme for smallholdings (which was popularised under Jesse Collings' slogan 'three acres and a cow'); security of tenure for farmers; radical revision of the system of taxation; and other measures, including the old Chartist demand for the payment of MPs. 'It went to the extreme limits to which Radicalism could go without becoming Socialism,' say Cole and Postgate in *The Common People*. To which one might add that in one respect of fundamental importance - its challenge to the market basis of landholding and its aspiration to the creation of a protected class of smallholders - it went further than any British government laying claim to Socialist credentials has ever dared to go.

It was such Jacobinical talk that led the moderate Liberal George Joachim Goschen (an ex-merchant banker and director of the Bank of England who, ironically, like Chamberlain broke with Gladstone over Irish Home Rule, became, as a Liberal Unionist, Chancellor of the Exchequer under Salisbury, and, again like Chamberlain, moved all the way into the Conservative Party) to charge his Radical colleague with (says his biographer A. D. Elliot) 'setting class against class; all against property; which he implies but does not actually say is *landed* property.' (Goschen, incidentally, had voted against giving farm labourers the vote). And there is no doubt that the Radicals' efforts to take over the Liberal Party platform, which came so near to success, were mainly responsible for the growing number of defections of businessmen to the

Conservatives. This changing party allegiance of the capitalist classes is clearly capitulated by Harold Perkin in *The Origins of Modern English Society*:

> 'The threat to passive property mounted by the left wing of the Liberal Party, however innocuous it looks at this distance, was enough to frighten some of them into the arms of the Conservatives. Long before the geological shift in the structure of British politics centred around the Liberal split of 1886 [over Irish Home Rule], which took so many business men as well as landowners into the Tory Party, it is possible, beneath the overwhelming Liberalism of the mid-Victorian business class, to detect anticipatory traces of the drift... The Liberals of course retained a majority of all categories of business MPs except the brewers down to 1885, but the Tory share steadily rose, and when the main break came in 1886 it was the typically corporate interests, finance, railways, shipping and transport, which first gave a majority to the Tories, and the more typically entrepreneurial categories. cotton, coal, metals, engineering, and the merchants, which still remained marginally more loyal to the Liberals. The remoter origins of the modern social structure of politics and particularly the equation of big business and Conservatism, can be traced to the mid-Victorian age.'

On the other hand, it would seem probable that for every disaffected bourgeois it drove away, the populist programme of the Radicals attracted a handful of supporters from the newly enfranchised classes. Thus, had the Liberal Party wholeheartedly embraced a radical agenda in the 1880s, it might have secured the allegiance of 'the lower orders', pre-empted the birth of a workers' party with potential mass support and made itself the natural party of government in a 'fully representative democracy'.

As for Chamberlain's efforts to rally support for the Liberals, far from resting on the appeal of radical manifestos alone, they took the most practical of forms: fostering the recruiting of supporters into local associations and, from 1877, the co-ordination of their activities by the National Liberal Federation, with Francis Schnadhorst, Birmingham-born-and-bred despite his name, as its organising secretary.

Having given working men the vote, not through a process of wise and generous-hearted deliberation but in a succession of political auctions in which the convention-shackled core of each party feared it would be outbid by the other in the contest for popularity, the two illustrious rival parties which together had composed England's competitive oligarchy for so long, were now obliged to set out their stalls to catch - and if they could to hold - the masses on whom their chances of another turn in the seats of political power now principally depended.

Each party emulated the other. In building up a nation-wide grassroots organisation the Liberals were following in the footsteps of the Conservatives, who, with the active encouragement of Disraeli himself, had - to cite only the most salient organisational measure - established the National Union of Conservative and Constitutional Associations ten years earlier, with John Gorst, who had already played a leading part in redesigning the Conservative Party machine, as its honorary secretary. (Gorst was eventually to turn free-trader, break with the Conservatives and, in 1910, to stand unsuccessfully as a Liberal candidate; but during the handful of years during which Lord Randolph Churchill strove to put the imprint of 'Tory Democracy' on the party, Gorst was one of his 'Fourth Party' paladins).

The Tories in turn learned from the tighter organisation of supporters introduced by Chamberlain and his confederates. Lord Randolph Churchill (1849-1895) was among those who had attacked Chamberlain's methods of mustering his forces as 'caucusing'; but he soon came to the conclusion that - as he wrote in a letter to Salisbury - it was 'undeniably the only form of political organisation which can collect, guide, and control for common objects large masses of electors.' Moreover, like Chamberlain, Churchill played the recruiting sergeant, not only by fostering the enlistment of supporters into the party ranks (notably through the setting up of working men's clubs) but through propaganda. And in promoting his own 'unauthorised programme' (the 'Dartford programme', as it came to be called from the place where it was first promulgated) of populist proposals, he followed the example of his illustrious mentor Disraeli by stealing the thunder of reforming Liberals. As we reach this episode in the tedious tale of the jockeying for power between England's two great oligarchical factions, the young Disraeli's derisive charge that Peel had 'caught the Whigs bathing, and walked away with their clothes' echoes mockingly in our ears.

'The dreary negatives of contemporary Toryism,' to quote Philip Guedalla's comment in *Mr Churchill: A Portrait*, were not for the dashing Lord Randolph, and his impatience with them fuelled 'his effort to modernise Lord Salisbury by inoculation with the elastic ideals of Tory Democracy'. Just two months before his political self-immolation, when, as Chancellor of the Exchequer, he had reached the pinnacle of his career, Randolph Churchill, expressing his thoughts in words which, ironically, are reminiscent of Marx's famous comment on philosophy that the point is not to understand the world but to change it, roundly proclaimed: 'Politics is not a science of the past. You must use the past as a lever with which to manufacture the future.' Which is exactly what he tried to do (with the object of furthering his own career as well as his aspirations for his country) in setting out his 'Dartford programme'. Amongst other things, it proposed local government reforms, legislation on land transfer and on tithes, the sale of glebe land and measures to provide agricultural labourers with allotments and smallholdings.

The resemblance of all this to the 'unauthorised programme' which Joseph Chamberlain promoted when he was still a Liberal is striking. And it should be noted that the populist proposals of the 'Dartford programme', emanating from what might be thought of as a distinctly pinkish extreme of the Tory Party, were subsequently adopted as official party policy; just as we need to keep pinching ourselves over the rather astonishing fact that in those palmy days of 'Victorian values' a hundred years ago, the foremost champion of this decidedly radical Conservatism reached the highest elected office within the party, chairman of the council of the National Union of Conservative and Constitutional Associations.

When we turn from particular proposals to seek out the principles underlying Randolph Churchill's 'Tory Democracy', however, we find that, from the point of view of conceptual thinking, they are as insubstantial and as wayward as the 'clouds without water, blown by the wind' to which he scornfully compared his Liberal opponents in a characteristic blast of bombast discharged in a campaign speech at Carlisle in October 1884. At a time of schism in the Liberal ranks over the Irish question and apprehensions concerning democracy and radicalism, he assured his audience and himself that the 'helplessness' of the Liberals 'would compel the English people to turn to the united and historic party, which can alone re-establish your social and imperial interests, and can alone proceed safely, steadily, and surely along the broad path of social progress and reform.'

An address delivered in April of the same year to the Birmingham Conservative Association reveals the thoroughly Disraelian cast of his thinking on the Constitution. Charging 'the Radicals' (and, of course, through insinuated guilt by association, the whole Liberal Party) with 'aversion' to 'the institutions of our country' and with giving 'reasons for their destruction' which - without specifying them, let alone answering them - he characterises as 'multitudinous and specious', he claims that Conservatives defend the Constitution 'on the ground of its *utility to the people*' and on that alone. 'An hereditary throne,' he declares, 'is the surest device which has ever been imagined or invented for the perpetuation of civil order and for that first necessity of civilised society - continuity of government,' while the House of Lords constitutes 'an aggregation of political wisdom and experience such as no other country can produce' and provides '*a powerful check on popular impulses arising from imperfect information.*' Such unexamined arguments are, of course, the staple fare of Tory speechifying. Nor can it be said, however fanciful the dish, that he departs radically from the standard menu in affirming of the Peers that they '*are essentially of the people*,' so that 'every privilege, every franchise, every liberty which is gained by the people, is treasured up and guarded by those who, animated by tradition and custom, by long descent and lofty name, fear neither monarchs, nor ministers, nor men, but only the people, *whose trustees they are...*' [my emphases in the above and following extracts from this speech]

Conservative apologists never have been unduly concerned by problems of consistency in projecting their vision of the good society, so there is no reason to fear that either Lord Randolph or his audience were troubled when he glided on from celebrating 'the glories of our blood and state' as represented by the Crown and the Peers of the Realm to commending the Established Church as 'a centre, a source, a guide of *charitable effort, mitigating* by its mendicant importunity *the violence of human misery*, whether mental or physical, and contributing to the work of alleviation from its own not superfluous resources.' If we feel that talk of charity and the mitigation of human misery (or that part of it at least that is the child of poverty) hardly gets to the root of the problem, at least the injunction that follows - 'And I urge upon you not to throw that source of charity upon *the haphazard almsgiving of a busy and selfish world*' - makes for salutary reading in an age when trickle-down theories of the distribution of wealth are once again in fashion and when private generosity and public parsimony are recommended as the proper palliatives for socially-generated misery. And at least Lord Randolph floated one real remedy on the torrent of his rhetoric: a proposal for 'a large redistribution of the incidence of taxation.'

Despite the disparity in achievement, Lord Randolph Churchill irresistibly recalls Disraeli. Like him, he forced the Elders of the Party to pay attention to him by the sheer brilliance of his attacks on the Opposition - and even more, perhaps, by the derisive darts directed at his own party establishment. Just as the young Disraeli had captained the 'Young England' partisans, so Lord Randolph dashingly deployed his dissident ginger group, which was derisively dubbed the 'Fourth Party' (Parnell's Irish group being the third) but which repaid the mockers in their own coin - and with interest. Both of these Tory young turks were witty and irreverent; neither was over-scrupulous in striking their targets in the House.

As I have demonstrated, they were alike too in their agitprop excursions in the grandiloquent mode, in which sound largely substituted for sense. In fact Lord Randolph Churchill has nothing to contribute to the history of political philosophy but a great deal to contribute to the history of practical politics. At a crucial period in the development of 'representative democracy' he recognised the necessity of roping in the masses and set about it with energy and flair. Since he does not appear to have done this in a spirit of cynical calculation, we may conclude that - as is not infrequently the case in politics - it was his very lack of penetration as a thinker that afforded him the transparency of purpose which made him successful as a tribune of the people. *'No class interests should be allowed to stand in the way of this mighty movement*, [of the people]', he told his Birmingham audience of 'men well acquainted with business, commerce, and trade', who hardly needed his reminder that 'the Tory party of today is no longer identified with that small and narrow class which is connected with the ownership of land', but were doubtless flattered by the recitation. *'Trust the people*,' he enjoined the assembled entrepreneurs, *'and they will trust you* - and they will follow you and join in the defence of that Constitution against any and every foe. *I have no fear of democracy*...To rally the people round the Throne and a patriotic people, that is our policy and that is our faith.'

The idioms have changed a little, but such slogans, such rhetoric, have survived as central elements in Tory Party propaganda, and evidently they have lost little of their persuasive power. As for the elusive nature of the philosophy behind the Birmingham speech, I have already remarked that such vagueness, whether studied or involuntary, is, and will remain, a political asset for as long as the great mass of the electorate remains incapable of rational analysis of the society they live in. Which regrettably is still the case, no matter how many contending politicians may unctuously compliment the public on its good sense.

Nevertheless, for all his faults and all his demagoguery, it seems to me, even if I risk the charge of naiveté in saying so, that Randolph Churchill shared with Disraeli a genuine commitment to 'improving the condition of the people'. And what is more important, under his influence the Tory approach to the problem of the common people shifted perceptibly from pure paternalism to a kind of hybrid solution we might describe as 'paternalistic democracy'. Or to put it another way, he contributed greatly to ensuring that Tory paternalism successfully accommodated itself to the demands of a parliamentary democracy accelerating towards universal suffrage. And that was a major political achievement.

CHAPTER 6

Fear the people

'There is no period in history - with the exception, perhaps, of the period of insurrections in the twelfth and thirteenth centuries, which led to the birth of the mediaeval Communes - during which a similarly deep change has taken place in the current conceptions of society...a chance combination of accidental circumstances may bring about in Europe a revolution as widespread as that of 1848, and far more important; not in the sense of mere fighting...but in the sense of a profound and rapid social reconstruction...'

Peter Kropotkin, *Memoirs of a Revolutionist* **(1899)**

There is a long-standing and comforting myth that the 'character' of the English people - in blessed contrast to that of more volatile Continental races - has preserved the country from revolution. And considering the monstrous provocations they have repeatedly endured without ever rising 'in unvanquishable NUMBER', there seem to be solid grounds for thinking this. But such serene assurance has by no means always held sway in the minds of the bourgeoisie and may even have been the exception rather than the rule throughout the Victorian Age (not to speak of earlier times) and right up to our 'thirties. On quite a few occasions bourgeois self-confidence must have turned distinctly pale.

'The first and highest duty of a government is to prevent revolution rather than to repress it, to sustain law rather than to revive it, to preserve order rather than to restore it,' Lord Randolph Churchill told a Manchester audience estimated at no less than 12,000 people, in December 1881. The context of his speech was the Irish problem; but nevertheless, when, in his address to the Birmingham Conservative Association referred to above, he commended the exhortation to the House of Commons of their arch opponent, Gladstone, to 'trust the people', surely Lord Randolph's counsel conveyed to the party faithful a subliminal message too - 'or fear them'!

Certainly fear of the people served to remind the combatants in the forever recurring parliamentary mêlée over the question of the suffrage that they had a great deal more in common with their Westminster opponents than they had with the unfathomable working classes whom Disraeli had called through his fictional hero 'inhabitants of a different planet'. And nearly a century after Disraeli raised the spectre of 'the two nations', George Orwell was to comment on 'the idea that there is some mysterious, fundamental difference between rich and poor, as though they were two different races', to which fallacy he ascribed the 'fear of a supposedly dangerous mob that makes nearly all intelligent [i.e. cultivated] people conservative in their opinions.'

To the very considerable extent to which this fear was rooted in sheer ignorance of how the other half lived, felt, and thought, he was right to describe it as 'superstitious'. But that is far from saying it had no rational basis. And if there was still good cause for fear in 1933, when Orwell's *Down and Out in Paris and London* was published, how much more was that true in Victorian England. In fact, despite the clouds of steam produced in all too many instances by panic and prejudice, two eminently reasonable objections (or at least wholly understandable reservations) to proposals to extend the franchise to the working classes stand out starkly enough. Was it wise to admit either the ignorant or the property-less to the body of electors? Since the first of these two deficiencies is the least easily remedied (as we can bear witness to a century later), it is not to be lightly dismissed. For the time being, however, let us simply listen to a few voices objecting to the ill-informed being allowed a say in the government of the country, before tackling the more contentious opinion that the have-nots should not have a vote either.

As we have seen, Gladstone had made it absolutely clear where he stood in principal when, in 1864, he put the burden of proof firmly on the opponents of manhood suffrage. He was far from being either blind or dismissive, however, to the problems that would stem from its introduction. While fully appreciating that the special social disabilities of labouring men were in large measure the cause of their unfitness for much more than a passive role in politics, in an article published in the monthly review *The Nineteenth Century* in July 1878, he expressed concern that in many instances their value as electors would suffer, not only from lack of information and thought, but from 'a degree of subserviency' inseparable from their exceptional dependency on the goodwill of others, in particular employers and landlords. This and other issues he raises in this article remain of central relevance to the question of what 'representative democracy' really amounts to.

Gladstone's mind was made up, then, but it was still full of misgivings. Like him, John Stuart Mill, the foremost liberal philosopher of the mid-Victorian age, certainly wanted to see the extension of the franchise. Indeed, in his *Considerations on Representative Government*, published in 1861, he maintained the equal right of women to have the vote and, in principle, endorsed a fully representative democracy. But he contended that although 'the opinions and wishes of the poorest and rudest class of labourers may be very useful as one influence among others on the minds of the voters, as well as on those of the Legislature...it might be highly mischievous to give them the preponderant influence, by admitting them, in their present state of morals and intelligence, to the full exercise of the suffrage.' This was exactly the point that Lord Randolph Churchill was to make when, in the opening debate on Gladstone's 1884 bill to enfranchise the rural labourers, he inveighed against the swamping of the electorate by the addition of some two millions of poor and grossly ignorant voters; though - doubtless primarily for tactical reasons - he had changed his mind by the time the House voted.

Naturally a host of less sympathetic and not a few wholly hostile politicians and political thinkers employed arguments against the extension of the franchise that were based on the disadvantages which were inseparable from having a great number of voters 'whose minds are unused to thought and undisciplined to study' (to quote Robert Cecil, the future third Marquis of Salisbury). Such arguments, notwithstanding the mixed and not infrequently ulterior motives of their proponents, included many pertinent points concerning the dangers of demagoguery, and collectively they composed a powerful critique of the whole concept of democratic government. For the moment one quite unpartisan comment may suffice to represent these particular fears. In the introduction to the second edition (1872) of *The English Constitution,* Walter Bagehot wrote: 'What I fear is that both our political parties will bid for the support of the working man; that both of them will promise to do as he likes, if he will only tell them what that is; that, as he now holds the casting vote in our affairs, both parties will beg and pray him to give that vote to them.'

After the passing of the Second Reform Act, in the year in which Bagehot's classic study first appeared, the increasingly desperate attempt to stem the tide, flowing, apparently inexorably, towards manhood suffrage, mostly took the form of advocating what Cecil had called, in 1864, a 'graduated suffrage' - a form of progress which, in less specific but also less grudging terms, his party leaders, Lord Derby and Disraeli, had in fact already conceded. Amongst the qualifications nominated as requisite for the privilege of voting were education, intelligence, wisdom, integrity, and virtue (the last unspecified, but doubtless intended to denote subscription, in word if not in deed, to conventional standards of decency in sexual and marital conduct). Let a wry smile suffice, for the time being, as comment, while we turn to look at what surely must have loomed in the minds of the anti-democrats as quite the gravest objection to manhood suffrage: the horrendous prospect it appeared to open up of the radical redistribution of wealth and income.

Again and again we detect - at the very heart of the host of arguments deployed against a wider suffrage - that vindication of inequality in the interests of political stability (that is to say, of the *status quo!*) which Burke made with unexampled effrontery in implicitly equating rapacity with the dispossessed. As with Burke himself, it is by no means always easy to disentangle the gut concern for self from the lofty thoughts of liberty and the like or the pseudo-scientific claptrap concerning 'hidden hands' or 'the characteristic essence of property' into which it is woven. Thus it is quite a relief to read such blunt objections as Robert Lowe's fearful remark that, 'Once give the working man the vote, and the machinery is ready to launch those votes in one compact mass upon the institutions of property in this country.'

A proud distaste for pompous or mealy-mouthed declamation is also one of the attractions of the man who led the Conservatives into the twentieth century, the Marquis of Salisbury (1830-1903). Not that his political testimony is wholly free of humbug. In one of his *Quarterly Review* pieces in particular (published in July 1864), he, whose whole case was based on the defence of property, had the gall to charge his opponents with taking a 'Joint-stock Company' approach to politics. He accused them of leading 'agitation for the extension of the franchise' that is 'purely a struggle for material advantages', while men such as himself (it was implied) were moved by 'emotions far higher than self-interest', by 'self-sacrifice and heroism'. In a passage that might almost have been designed to conjure up the applauding ghost of Coriolanus and reminds one of Lord Valentine's assertion (in *Sybil*) that it was men like his ancestors who had made England what it was - a presumptuous claim which provokes from Stephen Morley such a stinging rebuttal - Salisbury declares:

> 'The sacrifices required of an English politician are heavy enough as matters stand. It is surely enough that he should give his time, his money, and his health to his country, and devote himself to an exhausting labour without reward. To require of him, in addition to all this, that he shall seek the privilege of being permitted to do it by solicitations and compliances which he feels to be degrading, is a heavier trial than the patriotism of the better spirits among the educated classes will bear for any length of time.'

For all that, Salisbury's animadversions against democracy have the great merit of taking us straight to the heart of the matter. 'Revolutions are favourable to confiscation,' Burke had somewhat superfluously proclaimed. His 'solicitude...lest it should ever be considered in England as the policy of the state, to seek a resource in confiscations of any kind...' was now echoed, in the rather less cataclysmic context of parliamentary reform, by Salisbury's warning:

> 'We have now entered upon the descent of the smooth, easy, sloping path of popular finance, on which there is no halting-place to check our career short of *confiscation*. This question of the incidence of taxation is in truth the vital question of modern politics. It is the field on which the contending classes of this generation will do battle...The *proletariat* will not now fight for a *barren share in the business of legislation*, unless it is to bear to each of them a substantial and palpable fruit. The issue between the conflicting forces of society is becoming narrower and more distinct. *The mists of mere political theory* are clearing away, and the true character of the battleground, and the real nature of the prize that is at stake, are standing out more and more distinctly every year...The struggle between the English constitution on the one hand, and *the democratic forces*

that are now labouring to subvert it on the other, is now, in reality, when reduced to its simplest elements and stated in its most prosaic form, *a struggle between those who have, to keep what they have got, and those who have not, to get it.*' [my emphases in the above and subsequent quotations from Salisbury's writings]

And just as Burke had drolly dreamed of the rich and powerful becoming '*prey*' to the destitute, so did Salisbury foresee a 'rising storm of Democratic *spoliation*' in which taxation would be wielded 'as an instrument of *plunder.*' All this was, of course, nothing more than an appeal to the healthily possessive instincts of the possessors. Nor can he be said to have plumbed the philosophical depths when he did cast around for decent arguments to clothe the naked interests of his class. For this very reason, the case he makes (in the July 1864 *Quarterly Review* article mentioned above) against 'a wide extension of the franchise', in fact constitutes as telling an advocacy of universal suffrage as his most ardent democratic opponents could have desired:

'To give 'the suffrage' to a poor man is to give him as large a part in determining *that legislation which is mainly concerned with property* as the banker whose name is known on every Exchange in Europe, as the merchant whose ships are in every sea, as the landowner *who owns the soil of a whole manufacturing town.* An extension of the suffrage to the working classes means that upon a question of taxation, or expenditure, or upon a measure vitally affecting commerce, *two day-labourers shall outvote Rothschild.*'

The gravamen of Salisbury's argument - and one cannot doubt that if it were a necessary buttress for the continued hegemony of capitalism its apostles would maintain so still - was that political power should be proportionate to a man's 'stake in the country', with 'stake' carrying, of course, the venal and vulgar connotations not of his life's blood but of his property and his pecuniary holdings and investments. Such utterly materialistic measurements of a man's worth - *not* fine considerations of his intellectual, moral, or spiritual calibre - were foremost in Salisbury's mind in proposing a 'graduated suffrage' and in claiming, with breath-taking confidence, to know and to share the general opinion of mankind on how its affairs should be ordered. '*The common consent of mankind*,' he intoned, 'expressed in the management of their own concerns, has agreed that in the government and administration of *common property*, men should vote in proportion to their shares.'

His most uncompromising dictum on the proper relationship between property ownership and political participation (as manifested, that is, in the periodic privilege of choosing the lawmakers) proclaims: 'Natural right, then, cannot be made to justify an equal suffrage, *so long as there is not equal property to protect.*' But if, without challenging his insolently arbitrary premises, we simply follow where his own logic leads, we see at once that he utterly undermines his own argument (which is of course circular, not to say either simple-minded or disingenuous) by drawing our attention to the possibility, and our thoughts to the desirability, of a drastic redistribution of the nation's 'common wealth'.

The real value of Salisbury's contribution to political thought is that, in his anxiety to defend the *status quo*, he inadvertently illuminates the inescapably fraudulent nature of what purports to be democratic political representation in societies constructed on a system of gross economic inequalities. In short, in complete contradiction to his intentions, he presents us with a formidable critique of 'capitalist democracy'.

How little Salisbury and his class had to fear the supposed rapacity of a predominantly working-class electorate we can testify a century later. As Harold Perkin points out in *The Origins of Modern English Society*, not only Gladstone but also Disraeli took a much more relaxed attitude to the prospect of proletarian voters. As early as 1859, paying tribute to the 'virtue, prudence, intelligence, and frugality' of the artisans who had played such a great part in making Britain pre-eminent among the industrialised nations, Disraeli had recommended that they be permitted 'to enter the privileged pale of the constituent body of the country'. Gladstone went further in speaking of the working classes as 'our fellow-subjects, our fellow-Christians, *our own flesh and blood*, who have been lauded to the skies for their good conduct.' On which words Perkin comments, 'that is, were believed to have accepted so much of the entrepreneurial ideal of a class society based on capital and competition as to be trusted not to use their voting power to undermine it.'

When, with remarkable political agility, Disraeli and Derby 'dished the Whigs' by capturing the credit for the second Reform Bill, the future Lord Salisbury called their coup 'a political betrayal which has no parallel in our annals.' So out of tune with the times did he feel, that he even contemplated abandoning politics. He was to live long enough (besides rising to the highest possible political vantage point) to come to realise that his fears had been childish, to see clearly that the fabric of society remained essentially unaltered by the advance of 'representative democracy'. Indeed, by the time it came to the third major extension of the franchise, the third Reform Bill of 1884, Salisbury, who was blessed with the capacity for philosophical acceptance of the inevitable, had so well readjusted his sense of political balance as to do a deal with Gladstone behind the scenes to ease the passage of the bill through Parliament. His political career, in fact, is quite in consonance with the four political virtues of his party which I enumerated in discussing Peel. It only needs to be added that, as with Disraeli, his opposition to the extension of the franchise, although more unyielding, underlines rather than detracts from his active subscription to the Tory tradition of paternalism.

The centrality of this tradition to whatever can properly be called Conservative philosophy has now been traced from pre-Victorian times into the early years of our century. Since, apart from the partisan opposition to social reform during the Liberal hegemony of 1906-1914, there are no major departures from this paternalist tradition until the Thatcherite hijack of the party, I propose to pick up the thread in the age of consensus that preceded that event and may be said to date from the Second World War, or arguably from the National Government formed in 1931. Before doing so, however, it might be illuminating to glance at one of the most uncompromising of the anti-democrats, one who actually believed that the world had never 'seen a better Constitution than England enjoyed between the Reform Bill of 1832 and the Reform Bill of 1867'. His contribution to the debate, for all its unperceived tendentiousness and its blinkered class bias, stands out, nearly a hundred years after he was writing, as in some ways remarkably prophetic. Let Lecky stand, if you like, for that single strand of

Conservatism of which Cosgrave speaks, for he is, to be sure, the very prototype of a Thatcherite.

William Edward Hartpole Lecky (1838-1903) was, like John Stuart Mill, an intellectual of private means, not a man of affairs. However, in his final years, from 1895 until his resignation through ill-health in 1902, he did sit in the Commons as a Liberal Unionist member of Parliament for his alma mater, Trinity College, Dublin. His most notable works are histories of rationalism and of morals in Europe, a history of England and Ireland in the eighteenth century, and the study with which we are concerned, *Democracy and Liberty* (1896). I shall leave aside his often searching criticisms of the basic concept of democracy in order to concentrate on a few passages which - because they focus more sharply on the trends of the time (in particular on the growing challenge of the trade unions and the evolution of an interventionist and paternalist State) than the writings of most of his conservative contemporaries - are also exceptionally prescient; even though, like Salisbury's animadversions on representative democracy, they grossly exaggerate the threat to the privileges of the bourgeoisie.

> 'In our own day, no fact is more incontestable and
> conspicuous than the love of democracy for
> authoritative regulation. The two things that men in
> middle age have seen most discredited among their
> contemporaries are probably free contract and free trade.
> The great majority of the democracies of the world are
> now frankly protectionist, and even in free trade
> countries the multiplication of laws regulating,
> restricting, and interfering with industry in all its
> departments is one of the most marked characteristics of
> our time.'

The widespread revulsion against the crying injustices associated with the Industrial Revolution is then alluded to in the most offhand manner imaginable, with the casual remark: 'Nor are these regulations solely due to sanitary or humanitarian motives.' This airy dismissal of a revulsion that in truth provided the driving force which many felt obliged the State to become a guardian of the working classes whose welfare the employing classes had so shamefully neglected, serves for Lecky merely as a preface to a slanderous swipe at the trade union movement - one that is remarkably reminiscent of that guru of the Thatcherites, Friedrich Hayek, not to mention legions of leader writers in the capitalist press.

> 'Among large classes of those who advocate them [regulations] another motive is very perceptible. A school has arisen among popular working-class leaders which no longer desires that superior skill, or industry, or providence should reap extraordinary rewards. Their ideal is to restrict by the strongest trade-union regulations the amount of work and the amount of the produce of work, to introduce the principle of legal compulsion into every branch of industry, to give the trade union an absolute coercive power over its members, to attain a high average, but to permit no superiorities.'

In one of those self-revealing (and *class*-revealing) remarks that presumably explains Lecky's reputation among some commentators for impartiality, he charges the chosen champions of the working classes to whom he has been alluding with having too much power and too little concern for liberty. 'It may be permitted to doubt whether liberty in other forms is likely to be very secure if power is mainly placed in the hands of men who, in their own sphere, value it so little.'

Having summarily disposed of the little matter of the common people and their leaders, Lecky turns again to the issue of the State as an enemy of freedom. The following passage echoes Burke and Salisbury in its fear of democratic depredations on the current distribution of wealth through the deployment of the power of levying taxes, as is stressed by my emphases:

> 'The expansion of the authority and the multiplication of the functions of the State in other fields, and especially in the field of social regulation, is an equally apparent accompaniment of modern democracy. This increase of State power means a multiplication of restrictions imposed upon the various forms of human action. It means an increase of bureaucracy, or, in other

words, of the number and power of State officials. It means also a constant increase of taxation, which is in reality a constant restriction of liberty...*The question of taxation is in the highest degree a question of liberty, and taxation under a democracy is likely to take forms that are peculiarly hostile to liberty...We are steadily advancing to a state in which one class will impose the taxes, while another class will be mainly compelled to pay them.* It is obvious that taxation is more and more employed for objects that are *not common interests of the whole community*, and that there is a growing tendency to look upon it as a possible means of *confiscation*; to make use of it to break down the power, influence, and wealth of particular classes...'

So much for Lecky's foreshadowing of Thatcherism's clarion call to return to *selected* 'Victorian values'. Now for his forewarnings of fascism - ever-impending wherever a would be democratic polity tries to share an estate with the cupidities of capitalism:

'There are other ways in which de*mocracy does not harmonise well with liberty.* To place *the chief power in the most ignorant classes* is to place it in the hands of those who naturally care least for political liberty, and *who are most likely to follow with an absolute devotion some strong leader.* The sentiment of nationality penetrates very deeply into all classes; but in all countries and ages *it is the upper and middle classes who have chiefly valued constitutional liberty*, and those classes it is the work of democracy to dethrone. *At the same time democracy does much to weaken among these also the love of liberty.* The instability and insecurity of democratic politics; the spectacle of *dishonest and predatory adventurers climbing by popular suffrage into positions of great power* in the State; the alarm which attacks on property seldom fail to produce among *those who have something to lose,* may easily scare to the side of despotism large classes who, under other circumstances, would have been steady

83

supporters of liberty. A despotism which secures order, property, and industry, which leaves the liberty of religion and of private life unimpaired, and which enables quiet and industrious men to pass through life untroubled and unmolested will always appear to many very preferable to a democratic republic which is constantly menacing, disturbing, or *plundering* them.'
[my emphases]

It is true that Lecky's apprehensions of democracy leading to despotism are based on his assessment of the causes that led to the Second Empire. 'It would be a great mistake,' he writes, 'to suppose that the French despotic Empire after 1852 rested on bayonets alone. It rested partly on the genuine consent of those large agricultural classes who cared greatly for material prosperity and very little for constitutional liberty, and partly on the panic produced among the middle classes by the socialist preaching of 1848.' But for all that, it is remarkable how he foreshadows the rise of fascist states in the 1920s and 30s. One notes, too, his blithe indifference to the inconsistency of his contentions. On the one hand, it is the lower orders (for it is, of course, to these he refers when he speaks of 'the most ignorant classes') who are most disposed to look to dictatorship for their salvation, while the love of liberty is an upper- and middle-class virtue; but that, on the other hand, 'those who have something to lose' will if they can most likely make sure it is their virtue rather than their property! To generations affronted by apologia for well-heeled fellow-travellers of the far right, especially in the years between the two world wars, it all sounds frighteningly familiar.

We could contrast with Lecky's utterly property-centred and negative interpretation of freedom, the reflections of a contemporary of his own class who was also an essentially conservative thinker, but who did at least make some effort to understand the situation and attitude of those who had little or nothing to lose. While personally sharing the concept of freedom that was natural to Lecky's and his own class, Matthew Arnold recognised that democracy was opening up for the lower orders the prospect of another kind of freedom - 'social freedom' or 'equality' - with its own validity. And he refused to accept that this kind of freedom necessarily implied what its detractors slanderously call 'the politics of envy'.

Most damaging of all, in fact, to Lecky's whole thesis is the eloquent commentary such passages as I have cited provide on the true significance of what he - *like all persons of his class and time who were either Conservative or Liberal by persuasion or oversight* - called *'constitutional* liberty', which is to say, a kind of liberty that can live very comfortably alongside the harshest deprivation *for others*. Shamefully, nearly a century on, we still cannot claim to have even begun to construct a community in which there is no distinction and no enforced choice - as there should never be - between bread and freedom, liberty and equality.

CHAPTER 7

The age of convergence

'However much it was despised by some in the seventies and eighties, consensus has usually been considered one of the marks that distinguish liberal democracies from less civilized states...Perhaps the chief difference...Between consensus and conviction politicians is that the former weigh the consequences of carrying their convictions into practice or law, while the latter are determined to implement their convictions whatever their cost to other people.'

Ian Gilmour, *Dancing with Dogma*

'If you do not give the people social reform, they are going to give you social revolution,' Quintin Hogg warned his own party during the debate on the Beveridge Report in the House of Commons in February 1943. This debate, its circumstances and its outcome, provides a model lesson in the limitations of parliamentary democracy. What we are concerned with at present, however, is what it tells us about the Conservative Party and its capacity to adapt and survive. As a prominent member of the forty-odd-strong Tory Reform Group, Hogg was not, of course, a typical Tory member of the House. But no more, as a general rule, are the official leaders of any party. For the most part the rank and file take their cue, willingly or unwillingly, from those who by appointment or by sheer force of character have won prestige and thus become opinion-leaders. Perhaps we need to remind ourselves now and again that in talking about the doctrines and philosophy of a political party we are, strictly speaking, talking about the views of a minority of that party. As in society at large, the mass is normally more or less conformist and politically speaking more or less inert; but that very fact means that when there is change, it is almost always an active minority which determines the direction in which the party moves.

In any case, without falling into the trap of historicism and treating History as a protagonist in its own chronicles, we may fairly say that, as Lecky had clearly foreseen, the concatenation of evolving social and economic forces was pushing all political parties, however disparate their premises, in the same general direction - towards ever-increasing State intervention. It may have taken the common run of men in the property-owning classes a long time to see what was obvious to Socialists from the start: that 'invisible hand' thinking was all very well for eighteenth-century economists but would hardly serve today to save society from disaster in any highly-developed industrialised and capitalist economy; but come to it they had to at the last, though some of them may be kicking and screaming still. Nor should we allow ourselves to be deceived by 'rolling back the State' rhetoric into thinking that the essential reality has been changed by the Thatcherite counter-revolution. However limited its influence on velocity and destination, for the State simply to take its hands off the controls in any modern economy would be to career towards catastrophe.

Values and viewpoints are not confined by party boundaries; but it is still pertinent to recall that 'economic liberty' in anything approaching an absolute sense is historically a Liberal doctrine, while notwithstanding Lecky and his like, their paternalistic traditions made it easier for true Tories to accept the encroachment of the State on economic affairs. In his classic study *Modern British Politics*, Samuel Beer draws attention to this in recounting one of those rare occasions on which fundamental political ideas have been explicitly and directly discussed in Parliament, the 1923 House of Commons debate on Philip Snowden's motion on 'the failure of the capitalist system'. It was the Liberals who led the counterattack, with Sir Alfred Mond, in tabling the only amendment to the motion, admonishing the House that they were faced with 'a clear issue between Individualism and Socialism' and deploying (in Beer's words) 'the old and familiar arguments for free enterprise and free trade that constituted the Liberal orthodoxy.' And Beer points out that while the Conservatives 'attacked Socialism and defended private ownership', that did not mean that they unanimously accepted the Liberal orthodoxy. One distinguished member of the Tory Party, Leopold Amery, not only held forth on the merits of protection (in particular for British farmers) and of Empire development, which were of course old

Tory concerns, but openly advocated State guidance of the economy.

In like manner, Neville Chamberlain, introducing his Import Duties bill of 1932, as Chancellor of the Exchequer in Ramsay MacDonald's second National Cabinet, had no qualms about talking in terms of 'inducing or, if you like, forcing industry to set its house in order'. He was making particular reference to the deplorable state of cotton manufacture and the iron and steel industry, which he considered required 'a thorough reorganisation...if they are even to keep their heads above water in the future.' In fact, as Professor Beer points out in writing about the Conservative Party's 'adaptation' in not only accepting 'the financial burdens of the post-war Welfare State' but in adopting 'the methods and responsibilities of the Managed Economy', its supporters had had time to prepare their minds for further adjustment, since 'interwar Conservatism had taken major steps toward control of the economy.'

Just how far - under the pressure of mass unemployment, declining industries, and increasing balance of trade problems; of the unifying experience of national co-operation in the struggle against Nazi Germany and Japan; and, perhaps above all, of the shock of rejection at the polls in July 1945 - the Conservative Party eventually moved towards Labour's conception of a managed economy, was shown by the *Industrial Charter* drawn up by an Industrial Policy Committee appointed by Churchill. It was composed of five members of the Shadow Cabinet (Butler as chairman, plus Macmillan, Lyttleton, Oliver Stanley, and Maxwell Fyfe) and four back-benchers (David Eccles, Heathcoat Amory, Sir Peter Bennett, and J.R.H. Hutchison). Remarkably, amidst a fusillade of denunciation from the Beaverbrook press and other right-wing quarters for its 'pink socialism' and 'totalitarianism', when this Charter (endorsing the nationalisation of the mines, the railways, and the Bank of England, and proposing new machinery for economic planning and wage-fixing) was put to the 1947 Conservative Party Conference, only three hands were raised against it in an assembly of around 5000 delegates. In the following year, conference accepted an Agricultural Charter which endorsed the principle of guaranteed price supports for farm produce introduced under the Labour Government's 1947 Agriculture Act.

Butler was subsequently to describe the *Industrial Charter* as 'an assurance that, in the interests of full employment and social security, modern Conservatism would maintain strong central

guidance over the operation of the economy.' The proponents of
the Charter were admittedly on the left of the party; but it would be
a mistake to deduce from this either that they in some way misled
rather than represented party opinion at the time, or that the Charter
was primarily a reactive exercise in self-preservation, designed to
strike a note in tune with the spirit of the age - though it was that as
well. While it certainly went considerably further than ever before
in frankly embracing the policy of State control over the economic
health of the nation - and while Churchill certainly spoke for all
Conservatives in telling the 1946 party conference that among the
party's objectives was: 'To support *as a general rule* free enterprise
and initiative against State trading and nationalisation of industries'
[my emphasis] - the Charter was equally certainly not at variance
with Tory tradition. That was faithfully reflected in Butler's
declaration to the House during a debate in March 1947 that 'a
good Tory has never been in history afraid of the use of the State.'

And the historical reasons for this readiness to use the State
to intervene in the economic life of the nation had more to do with
concern, from whatever motives, for improving 'the health and
social conditions of the people' (to cite the objective that preceded
support for free enterprise in Churchill's statement of aims referred
to above) than with questions of economic efficiency or
entrepreneurial rights. To put it rather more bluntly than Edward
Heath did in his celebrated apology for 'the unacceptable face of
capitalism', State intervention had always been necessary to protect
the working classes - men, women, and children - from the ruthless
exploitation endemic to unregulated free enterprise economic
systems. Anthony Eden implicitly admitted as much in commending
the *Industrial Charter* to conference:

'We are not a party of unbridled, brutal capitalism, and
never have been. Although we believe in personal
responsibility and personal initiative in business, we are
not the political children of the *laissez-faire* school. We
opposed them decade after decade. Where did the Tories
stand when the greed and squalor of the Industrial
Revolution were darkening the land? I am content with
Keir Hardie's testimony: "As a matter of hard dry fact,
from which there can be no getting away, there is more
labour legislation standing to the credit account of the

Conservative Party on the Statute Book than there is to that of their opponents.'"

Such views were by no means confined to Conservatives on the left of the party spectrum, as Leopold Amery, the independent-minded but in general decidedly right-wing thinker cited above, bears witness in a policy pamphlet entitled *The Conservative Future* and published by the Conservative Political Centre in 1945:

> 'The aim of freedom is the development of human personality. The old *laissez-faire* individualism exalted freedom and personality in principle. But experience has proved that individualism, unchecked and unbalanced, can destroy both freedom and individuality for the majority. In the economic field, indeed, *the old capitalist orthodoxy habitually tended to relegate the majority, under the designation of Labour, to the position of a mere commodity governed by the laws of supply and demand.*' [my emphasis]

As for the question of national economic planning, far from having changed his mind after a lifetime in politics, Amery declares in this policy outline that 'in industry it is for the State to set the course.' And, while clearly sharing the preference for free enterprise expressed in Churchill's conference speech mentioned above, he by no means ruled out public ownership or control, specifically distinguishing the Conservative approach to economic problems from Liberal attitudes on this very point:

> 'Conservatism has none of the old Liberal objection to the direction and control of industry in the national interest, or even a theoretical objection to nationalisation as such, if the national interest cannot be equally well served without it. But it recognises the greatness of the achievement of individual enterprise in the past and the ordinary Englishman's instinct for doing things his own way, and wishes to give the fullest play to that instinct that the national well-being will allow.'

90

Amery's pamphlet expresses some weighty reservations concerning nationalisation as a general policy and makes some severe strictures on State Socialism, but at the same time pays tribute to Socialism for having seized the initiative in the field of economics:

> 'It is on economic policy that Socialism has won its victories, and will continue to win them so long as we confine ourselves to mere negative criticism of nationalisation. We can only win ourselves if we have a better alternative policy for securing both prosperity and stability of employment and are prepared to preach that policy as wholeheartedly and consistently as the Socialists have preached theirs.'

Probably the most startling statement ever made by a Conservative on the relationship between his credo and Socialism is Harold Macmillan's remark, in the course of an interview by *The Star* in June 1936, that 'Toryism has always been a form of paternal Socialism.' This may not quite stand up to serious examination; but if instead of simply dismissing it as mischievous one tries transposing the isms, one sees at once that it is rather more than just provocative. For all his predilection for elfishness, Macmillan had, as usual, a serious intent, which he was to spell out two years later in *The Middle Way*, harbinger of the 'mixed economy' approach to the nation's problems that - amidst all the flowing and ebbing of the tides of nationalisation, denationalisation, renationalisation, and so on and so forth, which caused such turbulence on the surface - underpinned the Age of Consensus which characterised the political scene until the Thatcherite *coup de partie*. With more fidelity to the truth of the matter than his Labour Party opponents, Macmillan called this approach 'planned Capitalism', while freely acknowledging the contribution of Socialist ideas to his own thinking:

> 'I am led to the conclusion that, for as far ahead as we can see, it is both possible and desirable to find a solution of our economic difficulties in a mixed system which combines State ownership, regulation or control of certain aspects of economic activity with the drive

and initiative of private enterprise in those realms of origination and expansion for which it is, by general admission, so admirably suited...The Socialist remedy should on the other hand be accepted in regard to the industries and services...where it is obvious that private enterprise has exhausted its social usefulness, or where the general welfare of the economy requires that *certain basic industries and services need now to be conducted in the light of broader social considerations than the profit motive will supply.*' [my emphasis]

Macmillan's attitude to the questions of State intervention, to planning and social engineering, always had been undoctrinaire. In 1927, in collaboration with Robert Boothby, Oliver Stanley, and John Loder, he had produced a book entitled *Industry and State* which he describes in the first volume of his autobiography, *Winds of Change*, as 'a first essay in devising some coherent system lying in between unadulterated private enterprise and collectivism.' This was at a time when, according to his own testimony, 'the Conservative Party as a whole seemed to have absorbed the old Liberal *laissez-faire* concepts,' and the book was severely handled by the right-wing press, the *Sunday Pictorial* going so far as to call it 'nothing more or less than thinly-veiled Socialism.' Such gibes left him unmoved. Speaking in the 1938 Budget debate, Macmillan told the House:

'Right through the whole national system of industry the State, *whether we call it individualism or Socialism I do not care*, is a partner with the people, and the State today from its own interest has a duty as well as a right to demand effective organisation of commerce and industry in order to produce the results from which the Government may secure its revenue...All modern governments today, *whether of the Right or Left*, must be partners in production and distribution. If we do that, we are going to do far more than by making speeches about democracy which we are so fond of making; about the great advantages it has over dictatorships. We shall be proving that in a Parliamentary and democratic system we are able to organise the system of production more effectively than any other system, that we are able to use the powers of science and technique to develop wealth unknown before. In this new world, there is no conflict between government and industry: it is a partnership between all classes in the nation to achieve the only means by which we can carry these staggering burdens and that is to make them relatively smaller by a continual expansion of the national economy.' [my emphases]

In the passages cited, the emphasis is on Macmillan's recognition that free enterprise capitalism unguided by the State had failed to deliver national prosperity. Bizarre though it may be, concern for 'the national interest' - and the part played in this by efficiency in industrial and commercial affairs - by no means guarantees concern for the welfare of all the nation's citizens, as Oliver Goldsmith caustically observed a couple of hundred years ago. But not for nothing was Macmillan the Member of Parliament for Stockton-on-Tees throughout the years of the Great Depression. When he writes in *Winds of Change* of 'a world which seemed now, economically speaking, to have fallen apart', it is clear that what affected him most deeply was what he calls (in describing the main theme of *The Middle Way*) 'the twin evils of poverty and insecurity'. Of the discarded workers of his own constituency he says, 'I shall never forget those despairing faces, as the men tramped up and down the High Street in Stockton or gathered round the Five Lamps in Thornaby'; and of the 'unequalled' relief campaign he writes, 'But charity, whether of the nation as a whole or from their neighbours, was not what the men wanted. They wanted work.'

If there was one question above all others on which, by the end of the Second World War, all but the most benighted of politicians had come to agree, it was the utter unacceptability of mass unemployment, an accord which - along with a general acceptance of the need for some degree of national planning to secure economic efficiency - formed the keystone of the Age of Consensus for the next generation. Professor Beer cites a memorandum from Sir Anthony Eden to his Chancellor of the Exchequer, Harold Macmillan (who within nine months was to replace him as Prime Minister), concerning the inflationary pressures of excessive demand and of wage claims, but which nonetheless ruled out measures that would lead to dishonouring the Conservatives' commitment to 'full employment'. Eden called such a solution to the country's problems 'politically intolerable'.

One whose ministerial career spanned the great divide between the Age of Consensus and the Thatcherite hegemony (and who may therefore be presumed to have changed his mind and found such a social situation tolerable after all!) is Lord Hailsham, who, as Quintin Hogg, produced one of the most notable statements of consensus-style Conservatism. At any rate, in *The Case for Conservatism*, published in 1947, he quotes without dissent Beveridge's judgement, in *Full Employment in a Free Society* (1944), that few would deny that unemployment, which 'before the first World War appeared as an evil calling for remedy', had come to be considered between the wars 'as the most serious economic problem of its time.' And Hogg concludes his chapters that focus on the problem of ensuring full employment with the hope and conviction that, 'given low rates of interest, high wages, adequate social security (for that is what redistribution means) this terrible scourge can be relegated to the category of minor nuisances.'

As a closely-argued polemic in which conflicting political ideas are presented quite fully, if not quite fairly, *The Case for Conservatism* warrants some scrutiny. In the context of the present polemic, however, I wish simply to record its substantial agreement with the views of other thinking Tories noted above - views which concede a considerable area of common ground between what had become by the 1940s the two principal contenders for power, and at the same time making clear their mutual repudiation of nineteenth-century Liberalism. 'The great heresy of the nineteenth century was self-interest,' writes Hogg, alluding to the long hegemony of Mancunian Liberalism; and in another place, putting the matter in the context of the first two Commandments, he says that Liberalism stands condemned 'because it ignored God and believed that self love was an adequate substitute for our duty towards our neighbour.'

The defection of businessmen from the Liberals which was in the course of time to make the Conservative Party the businessmen's party *par excellence* has already been noted, and in their book on *The English Middle Classes* (1947), Roy Lewis and Angus Maude complain that this had had 'a profound effect on the [Conservative] party, purging it of most of its Tory philosophy and indoctrinating it with that peculiar blend of Whiggery and *laissez-faire* Liberalism which still colours the speeches of some of its leaders.' But Hogg, writing at the same time, had no hesitation in pronouncing *laissez-faire* attitudes as contrary to Conservatism. In a passage referring to Macmillan's book *The Middle Way* and surveying the 'variety of forms of Conservative public ownership as at 1939', he declares: 'It was the Liberals who believed in the essentially unbalanced theory of *laissez faire*,' a principle which (he remarks elsewhere), if 'consistently applied', is 'the mother of economic chaos'. On the other hand, he declares: 'It is completely false to say that Socialism has the monopoly of "planning" in politics.' He points out that neither Churchill nor Eden had a doctrinaire attitude to nationalisation and cites Churchill's wartime statement which emphasises that it would be 'vital to revive at the earliest moment a widespread healthy and vigorous private enterprise' but recognises the increasing role of the State in promoting 'the economic well-being of the nation' and even that 'there is a broadening field for State ownership and enterprise, especially in relation to monopolies of all kinds.'

Just how close the convergence of the contending political philosophies had become Hogg himself makes clear in a chapter on the general election of 1945:

> 'I cannot accept the facile view that the election of 1945 was a choice for or against planning. If it had been, I too, would have found myself among the planners. *Laissez faire* has never been good Conservative doctrine, and though there is much to be said for it in an era of prosperity - in the fierce atmosphere of post-war reconstruction it would have been a fantastic folly to which none but extremists would have subscribed...The key to the nature of the decision in 1945 can be found in a comparison of the two election programmes, contained in the Conservative Manifesto and *Let Us Face the Future*. The most significant fact which emerges from a comparison of these documents is not so much the points of difference, as *the extensive area of agreement*.' [my emphases]

Hogg gives chapter and verse - with regard to foreign affairs and 'Imperial policies', and to the 'reconstruction programme...worked out during the Coalition' for 'full employment' and social security, 'a comprehensive National Health Service', and the provision of decent housing for all - to demonstrate the extent of the consensus. He goes so far as to claim that in 'over 80 per cent of the field of politics the great mass of decent opinion of all parties was agreed as to the best practicable course to take.' And that, if we are to trust his judgement, was a pretty remarkable and utterly unprecedented state of affairs, even allowing for a sizeable deduction from the presumed level of consensus for that prejudicial rider 'decent opinion'. In answer to the questions he began with - 'what was the real choice?' before the electors, and 'what did it amount to?' - he concludes that it was a choice between differences in emphasis rather than in substance:

> 'There was one further point of identity which tended to be obscured in the flood of ideological controversy. Neither side was committed to the abolition of all controls. Both sides who had manned the Coalition Government were committed to the retention of a fairly full set of wartime controls for a period of years at least from the end of the existing hostilities with Japan. Even after that there was no reasonable authority for claiming that Conservatives were in the least likely to return to a full *laissez faire* economy. The whole trend of our policy for twenty years had been against it. The legislative programme for pensions, housing, the National Health Service, and full employment to which we were fully committed absolutely precluded any such possibility. Wherein, therefore, lay the choice, the vital difference, between the programme of the two parties? It lay in the promise, or threat, of the Labour Party to nationalise the vital industries of the country, and the refusal of the Conservative Party to agree to this course.'

As he remarks in his chapter on Planning, '*Laissez faire* economics were never orthodox Conservative teaching, and Conservatives have only begun to defend them when there appears to be a danger of society swinging too far to the other extreme.' And while the Conservative Party officially accepted the concepts of State guidance over the economy, and even, in certain circumstances, of public ownership, it saw a threat to private enterprise and to individual liberty in the extensive nationalisation programme it feared would ensue from prolonged Labour hegemony.

The *Case for Conservatism* contains some trenchant criticism of the only kind of Socialism that Hogg understands (the State 'Socialism' which is, indeed, the only kind that he shows any signs of knowing anything about). At the same time, it does pay tribute to the humanitarian motivation of much Socialist thinking (though Liberals might protest with some justice that it pays scant regard, if any, to the transformation in this respect of the central values of their creed). It is only right, therefore, to accept at face value the oft-expressed concern for the disadvantaged, with the author recurring again and again to Disraeli's denunciation in *Sybil* of his times' 'triple worship' of acquisition, accumulation, and plunder before 'the altar of Mammon' and his anguish at 'the wail of intolerable serfage' which accompanied it. While one may question how seriously Hogg's book faces up to the problems of achieving social justice (as opposed to what is always the absolute priority for Conservatives: preserving 'the essential fabric of society' - society as it is, of course, based on Property and the grossly unequal shares of Power and Wealth which the capitalist notion of property entails), it is unquestionably a testament in the tradition of Disraelian Conservatism. Such a tradition continued to reign supreme until the bourgeois reaction of our time which thrust into our political vocabulary the appropriately unmelodious term 'Thatcherism', though we might just as aptly describe that harsh philistine creed as 'the neo-Liberal heresy'. To sum up: it is not old-style Tory paternalism but Thatcherite 'libertarianism' that is the foreign body in today's Conservatism.

PART TWO

THE WANING OF THE LABOUR MOVEMENT

'I was at much pains to describe to him the use of *money*, the materials it was made of, and the value of the metals; that when a Yahoo had got a great store of this precious substance, he was able to purchase whatever he had mind to, the finest clothing, the noblest houses, great tracts of land, the most costly meats and drinks, and have his choice of the most beautiful females. Therefore since *money* alone was able to perform all these feats, our Yahoos thought they could never have enough of it to spend or to save, as they found themselves inclined from their natural bent either to profusion or avarice. That the rich man enjoyed the fruit of the poor man's labour, and the latter were a thousand to one in proportion to the former. That the bulk of our people was forced to live miserably, by labouring every day for small wages to make a few live plentifully. I enlarged myself much on these and many other particulars to the same purpose: but his Honour was still to seek: for he went upon a supposition that all animals had a share in the productions of the earth...'

Jonathan Swift, *Gulliver's Travels*
(A Voyage to the Houyhnhnms)

CHAPTER 8

A party in search of an identity

'The fact of the matter is: modern capitalism has not succeeded; it has failed. We are asked in 1959 to believe that if we are only patient, if we only work hard, we will double the standard of living in twenty- five years. That is the same rate of progress as before the war. With all the techniques of modern production...the capitalists of Great Britain can promise us exactly the same rate of progress as before the war.'

Aneurin Bevan at the 1959 Labour Party Conference

'We cannot remove the evils of capitalism without taking its source of power - ownership.'

Neil Kinnock, 1975

In the absolute dog-end days of the Labour Party's supposed endeavour to build a Socialist society through parliamentary power and barely a month before the resurgent forces of Conservatism, largely refashioned in the image of its militant new leader, swept Labour from power, Prime Minister James Callaghan startled the Commons with a challenge that raised the most fundamental issue in political philosophy. 'The question we have to ask ourselves,' he shouted above the uproar of his baying opponents, 'is what kind of society we want in this country. What we have got,' he told them, 'is a totally acquisitive society, and some people are now practising what the Opposition preaches.'

A decade and some down the road to total acquisitiveness, one might ask at whom Callaghan was pointing the finger, and how justly; but the essential truth and the unevadable challenge stand. In that fateful spring of 1979, the people rejected Uncle Jim and bought the glamorous New Conservatism of Maggie Thatcher. It is of continuing importance to consider not only what they got but why they made the choice they did and what they thought they were buying. Accurate answers to these last two questions will uncover the basic values of the nation, while as for what they got, the degree of correspondence between the product progressively unwrapped and the message that sold it is a measure of the maturity of judgement of the British electorate.

Callaghan's impassioned interjection in the debate on an Opposition motion taking the Government to task for its failure to cope with the widespread industrial unrest and the rapidly deteriorating economic situation of that 'winter of discontent' was described by Ian Aitken of *The Guardian* as 'a sudden and highly unexpected flash of old-fashioned Socialist principle.' But the biggest irony is the failure of the Labour Party and of successive Labour governments (since the triumphant post-war days at least) clearly and cogently to project a distinctive vision of the good society. Like the leaders he succeeded, Callaghan had neglected publicly to answer his own question in such a way that any conscientious and reasonably intelligent voter would know what his party stood for. On the contrary, for a not that politically well-educated electorate considering how to cast their votes at the end of a decade or more of manifest national decline, it was not altogether unreasonable to conclude that the Labour Party had little idea where it was going and even less idea of how to get there. It followed that it should therefore give way to a revitalised Conservative Party which at least had the virtue of propagating its notions of how to achieve national prosperity with confidence and enthusiasm - which had, in short, the courage of its convictions. After all, a dynamic approach to problems is attractive and infectious, even if it does tend to distract attention from the need to examine its premises closely.

In rueful contrast, it is a relatively slight and wholly pardonable exaggeration to say that, long before the debacle of May 1979, the Labour Party looked as if it had little left other than a sense of moral superiority to comfort it for its gigantic loss of the faith and fervour of its forebears and its manifest failure to found a Socialist Jerusalem. To persuade a weary electorate to entrust power to it once again, the Party needed to examine itself much more rigorously on what, *in practice*, it had to offer the country which would distinguish its rule from that of its rivals. Whether the voters would then have bought it or not, surely only something that was recognisably *some* brand of Socialism could possibly have fulfilled that requirement.

The story of the uneasy marital relations between the Labour Party and Socialism will be traced in more detail later; but to explain the Party's fateful loss of power in the spring of '79 in terms other than that of the fickleness or the callowness of the electorate, it is necessary to establish Labour's failure to measure up to certain fundamental criteria concerning wealth, work, wages and welfare. A true picture of the state of a nation in these respects, taken together with an accurate analysis of its situation with regard to power and to participation in the polity, will go far to answer the question: what kind of society do its citizens enjoy?

Remarkably, two centuries after the banner of the French Revolution was first raised aloft, the ideals it proclaimed still represent the most quintessential challenge to all societies, whether earlier or later in time. How they rate on the scales of liberty, equality, and fraternity is a question for every ideology and for every polity as it is practised. Spelt out in greater particularity, we are confronted with questions about the relations of State and Government with the people - as citizens, as producers, as consumers, as involuntary supplicants through sickness or other forms of distress, as fledglings and pupils, and as actual or potential dissidents: e.g. as individuals when dissent makes them most individualistic or, most challengingly of all, when they join, form themselves into, or simply constitute through acting as such (as is commonly the case with families) alternative centres of power. (A moment's consideration of this last, family solidarity, aspect of all societies, incidentally, exposes the hollowness of the standard antithesis, which bourgeois liberals are particularly fond of making - as an indictment of Socialism as allegedly inimical to liberty - between individualism and collectivism.) Beyond all this lies the question of the relations of one State with other States and their citizens, and whether these are conducted according to the principles of particularism or universalism.

Another way of approaching the question is through consideration of the distribution of both political and economic power. To take the second kind of power first, all nation-states may be said to imply a commonwealth of sorts, but the vital question is in what sense and in what manner the nation's wealth is held in common. Obviously all nation-states wish to sustain and generally to increase their wealth through commerce and productive labour - but for what and for whom? As for political power, the theoretical scale of its distribution runs all the way from total concentration in the hands of one person, or absolute autocracy, to equal distribution amongst all, or perfect democracy.

From the answers to such general questions we may characterise all political parties, distinguishing in doing so, of course, between precept and practice. In the case of the Labour Party we are obliged to judge its achievements by criteria derived from its origins and history, as well as by its proclaimed principles. At the heart of these, however it is defined and however the definition may shift, lies the idea of equality that is central to all Socialist ideologies. However attenuated this may become in, say, the minds of those who describe themselves as Social Democrats rather than Socialists, it cannot be discarded without changing the character of the party beyond recognition. Nor can it exclude from consideration the more specific idea of economic equality, since it is precisely the importance which the Labour Party attaches to this aspect of equality that most clearly distinguishes it from its principal opponents. Nominal concepts of political equality, equality before the law, social equality and equality of opportunity may suffice for other 'democratic' parties but not for Labour. That party's *raison d'être* may be said to be the conviction that economic equality is the indispensable bedrock of all other aspects of equality.

So we may refine our yardstick to measure Labour's record on more specific issues, especially those concerning social justice, such as the redistribution of wealth and helping the disadvantaged. We may ask such questions as: How does Labour in office treat its own employees - in administration, in the social services, and in the public sector in general? And, in particular, how does it get on with the trade unions? This has to be a touchstone for Labour's success in seeking and holding office, since however many problems the trade unions may cause the Party, they are and always have been a major and integral part of the Labour Movement.

At the same time, just so long as it remains as a whole healthy and vigorous, the trade union movement constitutes a major alternative centre of power to Labour governments, just as it does to governments of any other political hue. So we are brought back from questions of economic power to consideration of the distribution of political power, and we must ask whether, in general, Labour governments try to subordinate other forces that are part of the Labour Movement or seek to co-operate with them as equal partners.

The same question may be asked with regard to other extra-parliamentary forces. Does the Labour record show a commitment to participatory democracy, in respect of both individuals and collectives? All parties in multi-party representative democracies have to pay lip-service at least to civil liberties. The other side of that coin, the more positive concept of people power, is for parties with a stronger emphasis on endorsement of equality. And what of industrial democracy? This is, after all, essentially participatory democracy in the workplace, and so, one might argue, a prerequisite for an equitable distribution of economic power in the widest sense of the term and, more particularly, of wealth, wages, and welfare provision. What part has the Labour Party played in the struggle for industrial democracy?

The following section will give some account of post-World War Labour governments, focusing especially on the Callaghan Government and its demise, with the above questions particularly in mind. At the same time - and unavoidably so - it will highlight the melancholy truth that Labour's story is the story of a party in search of an identity. After the debacle of '79, this became a fact impossible to hide; but the record shows that this uncertainty of purpose, punctuated by explosive discord, stretches right back to the loss of will clearly displayed even before the first majority Labour government had completed a full term in office. And the roots of this identity crisis go back much deeper into the party's past.

CHAPTER 9

How capitalism passed peacefully away

'The truth is that we have had a barrier put to our aspirations, for now the individual is no longer important, whether here or in the East. In Germany, in America, to a lesser extent in Britain, the individual has long been little more than a marketing unit, a gullet that needs feeding, a body that needs clothing, housing, transporting and providing with as much medicinal pap and prepacked pleasure as it can be induced to swallow - all in the interests of higher company profits. In the so-called Socialist states he is an integer of another sort, an underpaid, undertrained, undervalued and completely unindividual unit in the service of a state that as far as one can tell has no function except to exist.'

William Woods, ***Poland: Eagle in the East*** **(1969)**

Flashes of 'old Socialist principle' notwithstanding, it was evident enough by the seventies that the Labour leadership had come to terms with the fundamental realities of society as they found it. Reform might still be on the agenda; but anything approaching radical restructuring had long since been ruled out as utopian. It was not simply that a consensus with the other parties on the desirability of a mixed economy was apparently permanently established (for although the balance of the mix remained a matter of significant debate, only the political equivalent of a mad inventor could ever have aimed altogether - or even largely - to eliminate private enterprise), but that the basic features of capitalism had come to be accepted as not so bad as long as society provided a safety-net for the casualties, and, in any case, as probably incapable of transformation except under a dictatorship, as the terrible example of Russia's fate reminded us all.

There was even a tendency to try to talk the facts of life under capitalism out of existence. As early as 1950 Anthony Crosland, who within a few years was to become a leader of opinion in the Party and was to end up as Callaghan's first Foreign Secretary, was proclaiming: 'Britain has *in all essentials* ceased to be a capitalist country.' [my emphasis] And by the time he came to write what has been called 'the revisionists' bible', *The Future of Socialism* (1956), he was even more emphatic, asserting: 'It is manifestly inaccurate to call contemporary Britain a capitalist society.' His more unperceptive comrades had not noticed but capitalism had passed peacefully away.

The nub of his argument was that the intervention of the State in the economic affairs of the nation, employing the tool of Keynesian demand management, had so changed the parameters that it was misleading to use the same term for contemporary Britain as was used to describe the economic organisation of society between the 1830s and the 1930s. And it is undeniable that very substantial changes had taken place in the nature of capitalism, especially (though by no means exclusively) in the crucible of the Second World War and under the planned reconstruction of the Attlee administration that followed. However, a critical intelligence is bound to suspect Crosland's motives in so seismologically shifting the ground of the most elemental ideological contest of the eighteenth and nineteenth centuries as to disarm Socialist thought by the simple expedient of transmuting its infernal old enemy into a quite innocuous old gentleman.

The point I want to stress at the moment though is simply that Crosland's large claim, magnified if anything by his rider 'in all essentials', received a remarkable measure of credence in the higher echelons of the Party (Hugh Gaitskell himself, the Party's leader since Attlee's retirement in December 1955, told a two-day post-mortem conference following Labour's defeat in the 1959 general election: 'In my opinion, capitalism has significantly changed, largely as a result of our own effort') and that this had an enervating influence on its strategy. The implications of this dangerous underestimation of the enemy are most clearly seen by considering the then still surviving Labour objectives of equality in general and of the elimination of poverty in particular.

Contrary to the traditions of the Party, Crosland undervalued (not to mention underestimated the significance of) the very touchstone of Socialism, economic equality, in favour of an ill-defined and sentimental concept of social equality together with a commitment to equality of opportunity viewed most centrally in terms of education. As for Labour as the champion of society's most luckless, in *The Future of Socialism*, Crosland almost seemed to look on poverty as a problem that, through economic growth, would virtually evaporate within a decade or so (note the similarity to the 'trickle-down' talk of apologists for capitalism who are concerned to leave the impression that they *do* give a monkey's about the least advantaged) leaving only so-called secondary poverty, arising from personal disability or misfortune, to be tackled.

Moreover, he gave the impression of looking on class divisions as primarily a subjective phenomenon ('nothing is but thinking makes it so'), writing with some contempt of the curious obsessiveness of 'militant, class-conscious Leftism'. It is true that the best part of two decades later he was admitting, in *Socialism Now* (1974), that extreme class inequalities remained and that poverty was far from eliminated. However, he appeared to attribute the thwarting of his earlier and astonishingly sanguine hopes to rampant inflation and the 'semi-permanent crisis' of the national economy as a whole, rather than to the failure of Labour policies to reflect and of Labour governments effectively to demonstrate that 'exceptional priority' to the elimination of poverty, which he himself had nominated as the defining characteristic of Socialism.

One might remark, in passing, that papal pronouncements have likewise repeatedly avowed a bias towards the poor on the part of the universal church, with similarly disappointing results. But it is more pertinent to highlight a logical flaw of such monstrous proportions in Crosland's thinking that it destroyed his whole case for a laid-back approach to constructing a Socialist society. If no government, Conservative or Labour, appeared to be capable of solving these problems, regardless of whether or not they were to be ascribed to capitalist economics, how was anything that even he might describe as Socialism ever to come about? It was all very well to mock Marxist or other historicist concepts implying some inevitable historical progression towards Socialism, but at least they did offer 'progress'; whereas here, surely, one was left with little more than the politics of historical fatalism?

What all this adds up to, indisputably, is a lowering of the sights of Socialism and, even then, a failure to hit the target. Looking around him in the fifties, Crosland had asked himself: 'Is this still capitalism?' and confidently answered: 'No.' We might more pertinently scrutinise his diagnosis of social ills along with his prescribed remedies and ask ourselves: 'Is this really Socialism?' As a portent of what the Labour Party was to become in the sixties and seventies (not to mention the eighties and nineties) however, *The Future of Socialism* was all too prophetic. From a party promoting Socialist ideas of some sort at least, Labour was reduced to just another Party of social reform, with a mite more, perhaps, of special concern for the poor and, though decreasingly so, for the working class. Nothing more - outside the ranks of its curiously class-conscious Leftists, that is!

CHAPTER 10

Pathfinders for Thatcherism

'For a British government (and nearly every other government)...[before Mrs Thatcher's] dogmatism was unusual. In formulating their policies, previous British governments had traditionally avoided the extremes of a command economy on the left and of uncontrolled market forces on the right. Whatever their ideological banner, Labour governments have never attempted a fully socialist economy, and indeed have often shown at least as much respect for market forces as their opponents.'

Ian Gilmour, *Dancing with Dogma*

Looking back after a decade of Thatcherism at the Labour governments that preceded it, it is the continuity, not the differences in financial policy that strikes one most forcibly. An obsessive and overriding fear of the debilitating effects of inflation dominated the decisions of the Wilson and Callaghan regimes, sapping their Socialist will, such as it was. They suffered, in fact, from the common mental confusion of modern British politicians that conflates finance with economics and allows the world of finance to dominate, instead of obliging it to serve, economic purpose. How ironic that this financial consensus should survive the storm of Thatcherism; while those elements of social and political consensus (over such matters as full employment, health and welfare provision, and even over the rights and due status of trade unions) that - whatever part concern for maintaining a degree of consensus may have played in emasculating the Socialist drive - had at least tempered the ravages of capitalist economics for two generations, were insidiously eroded or frontally assaulted! Worse still, under the spell of those peddling the newly fashionable remedy for inflation, Callaghan and his Chancellor of the Exchequer, Denis Healey, actually acted as pathfinders for those who were to supplant them.

With the loss of faith in Keynesian demand management brought about by the stubborn world-wide recession sparked off in

October 1973 by the Arab nations' use of oil supply and prices as a weapon in the war with Israel and its allies, monetarism, with its seductively simple prescription of curbing inflation through tight controls on money supply, became for many the cure-all. In the words of its arch-priest, Professor Milton Friedman of Chicago University: 'Just as an excessive increase in the quantity of money is the one and only important cause of inflation, so a reduction in the rate of monetary growth is the one and only cure for inflation.' This old doctrine in new guise was enthusiastically embraced by Mrs Thatcher's economic tutors, among them Sir Keith Joseph and Sir Geoffrey Howe, her Shadow Chancellor. The secret subscription to the same doctrine by Callaghan and Healey provoked Labour left-winger Stuart Holland to dub the unholy alliance of supposed political opposites Howleyism, with ironic allusion to the ousted consensus, which had been nicknamed Butskellism after its two leading protagonists, R.A. Butler and Hugh Gaitskell.

'If there has been a Thatcher experiment, it was launched by Denis Healey,' the political editor of *The Financial Times* was to write later. Perhaps the moment when the conversion of Labour's leaders to the new orthodoxy was first clearly exposed was in May 1978. It followed the Chancellor's explanation to the House of his new letter of intent to the International Monetary Fund, concerning the $4.1 billion standby credit it had granted Britain in 1976, in which he reiterated his commitment to maintain monetary control. Under fire from Howe and Kenneth Baker over a six-month growth in the money supply that would mean an annual rate of over 20 per cent, Callaghan declared: 'I am not going to have the great success we have had on inflation dissipated by an increase in the money supply that cannot be contained.' And to Baker's insinuation that the Prime Minister's only way out was to call a general election 'before your chickens come home to roost', Callaghan retorted: 'Your eyes may be fixed on some distant general election, but that is not going to deflect this government from taking any action necessary to keep inflation under control. You can be sure of that.' Five months later, in a Mansion House speech, Healey publicly endorsed monetary policy as the main defence against inflation. (*See Chapter 22*)

It is true that one important difference remained between those determining the Government's financial policies and their shadow opponents. This was over the issue of whether or not fiscal and monetary manipulation were, as ordained by Monetarism's high-priest, the *sole* weapons available to government to curb inflation. By chance, at about the same moment that Denis Healey was spicing his *cordon bleu* Mansion House dinner with a liberal sprinkling of self-gratulation, Ted Heath, the loss-leader of the Tory Party (having travelled his own 'road to Damascus' and renounced his Selsdon Park zealotry) was curdling the blood of a gathering of the faithful in Chelsea with a recitation of the fearful scenario that would face them all should inflation let rip. A new wages' explosion of as little as 10 per cent, he warned them, would double prices in less than eight years, while a return to 20 per cent rises would slash the value of the pound to 50 pence in four years, 25 pence in eight years, and less than 10 pence in thirteen years.

This latest barrage in Ted Heath's dogged campaign to reconvert his party to its old belief in the need for an incomes policy was directed not at the Labour Government, which was still striving to reach an agreement on pay with the trade union movement that would stick, but at the leadership of his own party, at those who had ousted him. In a ringing reaffirmation of the old Tory virtue of pragmatism, he told them: 'We are not having to choose between competing dogmas. We are concerned with the practical questions of running the economy.'

He made his own position absolutely clear in two passages. 'One does not have to agree with all the details of the present policy,' he contended, 'to believe that if that policy fails and wages soar out of control once again we will be taking one giant step back towards the disaster from which we thought we had escaped.' And as for the simplistic fundamentalism of pure monetarism, he demolished it with one hefty swipe of brutal realism: 'I know it is argued that with sound monetary and fiscal policies prevailing, negotiators will come to see the dire consequences of their own actions and learn to behave responsibly. The truth is that, time and again, negotiators, faced with the consequences of inflation and unemployment in the absence of an incomes policy, have made inflationary settlements.'

Ted's target may have been those who had siphoned the Old Liberalism tonic into new bottles labelled New Conservatism, but there were many, both within Labour's ranks and outside them, who were now convinced that the rubicund Denis and even the teetotal, tobacco-shunning, cheery chapel-goer Jim had become hooked on the stuff. It affords wry amusement a Thatcher-Howe-

Lawson-Major-minted 15-per-cent world away to read of the reproachful response of the then director-general of the Confederation of British Industries, Sir John Methven, to the raising of the Minimum Lending Rate to 12½ per cent in November 1978. Speaking for an organisation that was to become quite cravenly reluctant to defend the interests of its own members against the ravages of Thatcherism, Sir John expressed the fear that the Government was relying solely on monetary restraint in its fight against inflation, and that, if this was so, it would gravely damage business investment and the drive to create new jobs in order to cut unemployment and boost economic growth.

The Guardian called the jacking up of the Bank Rate 'a further ominous stride down the monetarist path.' It hoped that the measures were temporary and would jolt the unions into recognising 'the painful alternative of an incomes policy' but could not hide its own fear 'that the squeeze contains an element of overkill which could do long term damage to the British economy.' Three months later, on 8th February 1979, the MLR was raised again to 14 per cent, bestowing on Britain the gift of what were then the highest real interest rates on record.

In a leader entitled 'Between the City and Charybdis', *The Guardian* (10th February 1979) spoke of 'the most savage monetary squeeze in recent memory,' and declared: 'The Government finds itself uncomfortably squeezed between the City, which increasingly controls financial policy (by refusing to buy gilt edge stock to fund the Government's deficit) and the unions, which increasingly control the supply side of the economy.' The paper's principal political commentator, Peter Jenkins, had addressed the threat to national prosperity posed by these two alternative power centres on the previous day, in the course of a trenchant attack on Healey's handling of the economy. Pivoting his commentary on Sir Keith Joseph's sudden and transient conversion to the view that 'monetarism is not enough', Jenkins witheringly declared that, in the depredations of bankruptcy and unemployment it would inflict on the economy, 'Mr Healey's monetarism is the economic equivalent of decimation as a technique of military discipline.' In the event, of course, since Labour was itself wobbling on the brink of decimation at the polls, it was left to Mrs Thatcher's evangelists, from whom Jenkins evidently hoped for national salvation, to decimate British industry as a by-product of its 'economic miracle'.

The Labour left did not take this unholy alliance of its leaders with the City lying down. One of the Government's most persistent critics was Bryan Gould, who at the time of the skirmish in the House of Commons over the money supply referred to above, wrote:

'It is often said that Denis Healey is not really a monetarist but goes through the motions in order to placate the City. The trouble with this, if true, is that he makes such a convincing job of the deception that he simply reinforces monetarist superstitions. Whatever the explanation, the regime over which he has presided in the past year has been even harsher and more damaging than that which would have applied under the Gold Standard itself.'

At the end of the year, as a tidal wave of strikes threatened to engulf Callaghan's struggling administration, Gould castigated the Chancellor for foolishly encouraging 'the myth that the touchstone of success or failure is the monthly figure for growth in M3. Since this figure is entirely at the mercy of the money markets (who can raise it or lower it according to their willingness or otherwise to buy gilts) it is effectively the money markets which now determine the level of deflation required.' In any case, he argued in March 1979, in the Left's last-ditch-before-the-debacle campaign for an expansionary budget which 'would not only improve Labour's election chances and be consistent with Labour's objectives...but would...lay the foundation for desperately needed industrial regeneration,' that deflation was the last thing needed on the brink of a recession:

'The truth is that monetarism is no more than old-fashioned deflation dressed up in a newly fashionable guise. We have a uniquely long and depressing experience of trying to deflate our way out of our problems. It never has worked and it is not working now; manufacturing output is lower now than during the three-day week and is probably falling rather than rising at this very moment.'

With unflagging zeal Gould chastised the Chancellor for so tamely submitting to the City. 'At least in the 1960s and earlier,' he observed, 'deflationary policies were imposed by governments; now it is the money markets which decide policy and the Government has become a helpless bystander.' The present Chancellor 'has handed over control of the economy to the money markets. In two major areas of policy, the exchange rate and domestic money supply, it is the markets rather than the Chancellor who are in control,' he charged. Then he went on to complain that Healey's insistence on 'a stable (and overvalued) exchange rate' for sterling 'means that the foreign exchange markets have a power of veto over anything which might induce them to take a less optimistic view of the pound.'

The strength of Gould's conviction that by bowing down before financial orthodoxy the Government was betraying the whole Labour Movement comes out in rueful reflections on earlier Labour administrations:

> 'The danger for this Government is that the Public
> Sector Borrowing Requirement will become as much an
> albatross around its neck as the balance of payments
> was for the 1964-70 Government and adherence to the
> Gold Standard was for Philip Snowden in 1929-31. In
> conditions of substantial under-utilisation of resources
> of men and money, it is the merest common sense to try
> to put those resources to work.'

And again:

> 'It is...bitterly disappointing to see a Labour
> Government...once again succumbing to the doctrines of
> financial orthodoxy, which are so congenial to Labour's
> opponents both in Parliament and in the City but which
> are so damaging to Labour's aspirations.'

Anyone disposed to dismiss Bryan Gould's scourging of the Callaghan Government for its financial (and hence, in the final analysis, its economic) policies as just the kind of intemperate attacks that were to be expected from an ambitious Labour left-winger could do worse than consider the remarkably similar strictures of that solid, sensible, centrist journalist Peter Jenkins in the article referred to above:

'One aspect of the situation worthy of note is the extent
to which what used to be called the 'management of the
economy' has passed to the City of London. It is
markets which now make policies, not elected
governments. For this Mr Healey has himself partly to
blame for he has in the past encouraged the financiers in
their belief that the Government can be made to dance
to the tunes of M3 and the PSBR...Once more a Labour
government will have impaled itself upon the financial
orthodoxy of the day.'

Despite this intellectual grasp of the half-nelson exercised on 'the
financial mind' by a 'money religion' that engendered 'the
supposedly sacred nature of certain connections - between the
money supply and the level of government borrowing and the
external value of the pound,' however, Jenkins had no solutions to
offer for overcoming the perils presented by the Scylla of the City.
He was far more intent on belabouring Charybdis, i.e. bashing the
unions, which, like all respectable citizens, he held to have become
a veritable Leviathan.

Where Peter Jenkins and his *Guardian* stable-mate Hamish
McRae abruptly parted company with Bryan Gould was in their
assumption that, for the present at least, there was nothing for it
but to submit to the thumbscrews of the monetarists. McRae was
particularly emphatic about this. In a kind of pre-echoing of words
that were to become wearisomely familiar, he gave it as his opinion
that 'if the general economic policies of a Callaghan/Healey
government are broadly similar to those of, say, a Thatcher/
Joseph/Howe one it is because there is no realistic alternative.
And the same discipline would act on a Shore/Benn government
too.'

Further on in his article on 'Elections and the City' (*Guardian*,
2nd January 1979) he threw in the rhetorical question: 'And is there
any evidence that the City could not prove as effective at blocking
a *rabid* left-wing Labour government's efforts to control it as the
trade unions were in blocking the efforts of both the 1966 Wilson
government and its Conservative successor to change the framework
of industrial relations?' [my emphasis] No Labour government has
ever had the bottle to seriously take on the City in the name of
Socialism - nor has the Labour Movement as a whole - and until

that millennium arrives we cannot know whether McRae is right or not.

Meanwhile, in the later light of the prodigious feats of prestidigitation performed by Nigel Lawson before he discreetly took himself off in a huff as the storm clouds gathered, there is a melancholy pleasure to be had from reading McRae's equally assured judgement that: 'The punishment that the markets can inflict on a spendthrift Government - by driving down the exchange rate and pushing up interest rates - is so great and takes place so rapidly that it has become virtually impossible to imagine a Government being able to set up a short-lived boom by lax fiscal and monetary policies.'

CHAPTER 11

The State as the instrument of Property

'From the moment in which Mr Melmotte had declared his purpose of standing for Westminster in the Conservative interest, an attempt was made to drive him down the throats of the electors by clamorous assertions of his unprecedented commercial greatness. It seemed that there was but one virtue in the world, commercial enterprise - and that Melmotte was its prophet. It seemed, too...that Melmotte treated his great affairs in a spirit very different from that which animates the bosoms of merchants in general. He had risen above any feeling of personal profit...But by carrying on the enormous affairs which he held in his hands, he would be able to open up new worlds, to afford relief to the oppressed nationalities of the over-populated old countries.'

Anthony Trollope, *The Way We Live Now*

It may no longer be *literally* true that in the developed countries of the world the masses have nothing to sell but their labour. But it *is* true that (whatever aberrations may occur, as a consequence, for example, of arbitrary or lawful confiscation) it is and always has been part of the nature of the State - arguably, indeed, its primary role - to protect property. If 'the State' simply stood for the political institutions of a genuinely classless society, one might reply, 'Fair enough!' But, with the arguable exception of a few so-called primitive societies, we have no record of such a society, either past or present. The problem with the concept of a 'property-owning democracy' is that it is a contradiction in terms where property is held unequally, unless, of course, one adopts the absurd or fraudulent position that *real* political equality has nothing to do with democracy.

Inasmuch as property-owners - and in particular larger property-owners - have a preponderant influence on the actions of the State (as two hundred years ago Edmund Burke insisted was right and proper - see Chapter 3 - though he really need not have been so worried about the dangers of this state of affairs being overthrown), regardless of the purposes of any particular government, it is as true now as when the charge was first made that the State is for the most part the instrument of the property-owning classes. Short of revolution, only the most resolute, persistent and sagacious measures of government could significantly shift the balance of control over the machinery of the State away from the large property-owners towards the little people whose principal bargaining power is still their labour. Which is why, of course, any attack on organised labour should arouse the suspicion that it is an attack on the fundamental liberties of the people. The outstanding achievement of the Callaghan regime was that, through its resolution, its tenacity, and its incurable myopia, it gave the Labour Movement as a whole an opportunity to demonstrate its huge potential as a countervailing force.

Despite their submission to the new financial orthodoxy and their consequent catching of a dose of monetarist mania, at least the Labour leaders of those far-off days still believed in the Butskellite concept of 'the management of the economy', a now heretical concept. The New Conservatives, those economic Doctor Panglosses, were already busily deriding this as contradicting Adam Smith's self-evident truth that there is nothing for it but to put one's trust in the 'invisible hand', i.e. in market forces. However, their weakness of will in the presence of the captains of industry rendered the Labour leaders' obdurate adherence to the 'management' tenet of the old faith somewhat nugatory.

Labour's 1974 Manifesto commitment to compulsory planning, which had pledged to strike more than a hundred bargains with key companies, had, by unilateral decision of Harold Wilson and his henchmen, been watered down in the 1975 Industry Act to seeking agreements on medium-term targets and the means of achieving them through a voluntary approach. Tony Benn's fight to uphold the decision of Conference and the Manifesto pledge consequently foisted on the leadership was one of the principal reasons for his transference from the post of Secretary of State for Industry to the less sensitive Department of Energy, an effective demotion that prompted Barbara Castle to commit to her diary the vitriolic but revealing comment: 'We have all suffered from his habit of writing Labour policy by ministerial edict. The Department of Industry enabled him to be all things to the Labour movement with none of the restraints the rest of us face.' With their predominant hold on the Party's National Executive Committee, the Left took up the cudgels again under Callaghan's

117

premiership. But all it could wrest from the leadership was acceptance of the compromise proposed by a joint NEC-Cabinet working party for the passing of back-up legislation empowering the Government to enforce planning agreements where the voluntary approach had failed, should it be thought necessary.

Just how meaningless this watered-down approach had proved to be is made clear by the *Guardian* leader of 22nd August 1978, which asked: 'But why are there so few volunteers?' The writer went on to say: 'The Government lost interest in central planning and the Confederation of British Industry made it clear that compulsory agreements would mean the end of voluntary co-operation elsewhere in the industrial jungle...Agreements became voluntary and there have been few volunteers. Only, to be precise, State-aided Chrysler and State-owned coal.'

Worse still, the Government's one apparent success (outside the public sector) at getting industry to co-operate in planning through friendly persuasion had now turned out to be its deepest humiliation. The disdain of the potentates of capitalism for the views of elected government was impudently demonstrated by the Chrysler management who, having pocketed well over £150 millions in subsidy from the British State since the 1975 rescue operation, proceeded to do a £250-million sell-off deal with the French firm Peugeot-Citroen. It was done behind the backs of the Callaghan Government, who were notified just four days before it was to take effect.

A sharply-etched vignette of the Detroit bosses running rings around the Westminster statesmen is provided by an interchange in the Commons between Labour back-bencher Tom Litterick and the Minister of State for Industry, Alan Williams. 'Why are you in the dark, then?' retorted the back-bencher in response to the Minister's denial that the directors appointed by the Government to the UK subsidiary to keep an eye on British interests as part of the funding agreement had not been consulted. The Minister's somewhat disingenuous explanation was that Chrysler had conducted negotiations with the French motor manufacturers at an international rather than a national level, 'and in this sense...they were less than straightforward.' The comic-cartoon character of the affair is completed by the fact that the Government had neglected to buy an equity stake in Chrysler with its subsidies and was now faced with the probability of having to write off over £50 millions and perhaps more than twice that. For the 23,000 British workers whose jobs were being diced with, however, there was little to smile about. Even when Peugeot-Citroen agreed to take over the UK Chrysler debt, no one assured *them* of a future livelihood.

Another example of this kid-glove approach to employers concerns the notoriously anarchic building industry, which has always operated largely on the basis of casual and temporary labour piped in from pools of unemployed workers. In the interests both of the workers (especially with regard to health and safety and to insurance issues) and, perhaps more significantly, of its own revenue, the Government opened a register of firms in the industry. Unfortunately, however, it decided that registration should be voluntary, with the entirely predictable result (especially as the building bosses became increasingly confident that the Tories would win the next general election and scrap the scheme) that it became yet again a question of 'But where are the volunteers?'

The CBI president, John Greenborough, was technically right, of course, to stress that his organisation was not a party political one, as he did in launching the pamphlet *Britain Means Business*, with its advice to the Government on how to maintain economic growth through tax cuts and the like. But it is a deal more to the point to note the exhortation of Sir John Methven, CBI's director-general, to the bosses attending the 1978 Conference, to stop being apologetic about the way they made their money. For thirty years, he told them (in a side-swipe at those stuck in the mud of consensus politics), employers had not defended the capitalist system properly and it was high time they did.

For Labour's crazy mixed-up-economy kids the times were becoming increasingly difficult. But they knew well enough on which side *their* bread was buttered. As Victor Keegan put it in his *Guardian Notebook* (6th September 1978): 'The CBI's influence tends to be in inverse proportion to the friendliness of the Government in power. It can more easily exploit Labour's desperate need to court industry than it can the natural friendliness of the Tories.' He was even prepared to quantify the arm-twisting powers of this particular capitalists' club as set against the influence of the Left:

> 'Indeed, it could be argued that the Confederation of British Industry has at least 10 times more influence on the Government than Labour's Left. Most of the Left's designs - more nationalisation, more public expenditure and a return to free collective bargaining - have been ignored almost contemptuously by the present Government. Indeed

it is difficult to think of any important concession to the Left that might not have happened anyway as a result of the implementation of centrist Labour policies.'

A similar conclusion was reached in Ian Aitken's commentary (*Guardian*, 7th September 1978) on a book by Michael Hatfield entitled *The House the Left Built* (1978). It chronicled the failure of the Left to make its strength in the Party really tell, despite its success in securing 'the endorsement of a whole catalogue of left-wing policy documents' as Party policy:

'The fact is that very few of the radical proposals incorporated in Labour's programme before 1974 have been even remotely reflected in the subsequent actions of the Labour Government...The conclusion to be drawn from all this is that The House the Left Built now looks more like one of those cardboard cutouts than anything really substantial in brickwork and mortar.'

Of course, besides the bitter foes outside the Party who were intent on demonstrating that the milk-and-water Labourism of Uncle Jim & Co. was actually composed of red blood leeched from enterprising citizens, there were those in the Party ranks who defended the Government's record for perfectly honourable reasons, even if awkward facts obliged them to be a little 'economical with the truth' (to use a then uncoined but now immortal phrase). Around the middle of November 1978 *Labour Weekly* published a checklist claiming that no fewer than 53 out of 68 commitments made in Labour's 1974 Manifesto had been more or less 'carried out'. Then one of the Party's prospective parliamentary candidates, Timothy Sherwen, delivered a stinging (and deserved) rebuke to *The Guardian* for its 'cynical attack', in its first leader of 11th December, on Labour's NEC, together with a spirited but somewhat less deserved rebuke for the paper's claim that Labour's promises had received 'pretty short shrift'. Achievements there undeniably were to the Labour Government's credit; but there can be no doubt that the verdict of the *Guardian* writers was broadly speaking correct.

Among those who supported what had come to be called the Alternative Economic Strategy (which the radical decisions of the 1973 Labour Party Conference substantially embodied) was Stan Orme, by now Minister for Social Security. In the week before the crucial Party Conference of 1978, he argued strongly for a commitment to use the fast-growing Government revenue from North Sea oil to invest more both in industry and in social welfare provision. 'On the industrial front,' he wrote (*Guardian*, 29th September 1978), 'our support for industry must become conditional on industry accepting a more interventionist policy,' and that the National Enterprise Board should be provided with more funds to back 'winners'. He went on to declare: 'Planning agreements should become a reality in our major firms and a solid start on the road to industrial democracy is needed.' This may sound like pretty radical stuff. But when we set it against the original demands of the supporters of the AES (which, as noted, had received substantial endorsement from Conference); when we consider how negligible - and indeed disdainful - had been the leaders' efforts to carry out the declared wishes of the Party; and when we note Orme's forbearing to point out that Party policy had called for planning agreements that would be enforceable by law; then it becomes difficult to describe it as anything but timid and defeatist. As for the reference to 'a solid start on the road to industrial democracy,' anyone acquainted with the Government's record on this score would be inclined to dismiss it as yet another mocking obeisance to one of the Labour Party's oldest, most hallowed, and most neglected ideals.

Even more eloquent of the dispirited state of the Left, however, was the character of the Minister's plea for more resources for his own allotted province; the more so since he was one of those still ready to speak unabashedly in the romantic terms of 'our egalitarian battle-cry'. Calling on his comrades to defy the Tory clamour for tax cuts based on further reduction in government spending (a monetarist policy which, he argued, would not only cut still deeper into investment in the social and industrial infrastructure, but would by the same token accelerate the recession), Orme declared:

> 'Public spending laid the foundation of the Welfare State. It formed the basis of our caring society *by moderating the insecurity* associated with illness, unemployment, disability, and old age. In doing so it provided, and continues to provide, *an important redistribution of income*. Public spending helps ensure that *nearly everyone has the basic minimum*. This role for public spending must be strengthened. We must recognise that the basic

minimum which was tolerable a decade ago is no longer adequate. The aspirations of our society - *of all families in our society, not just the rich* - move upwards all the time.' [my emphases]

Throughout thirty years of consensus politics such a statement would hardly have been thought controversial coming from the lips of any politician - left, right, or centre - of any party. Indeed, it was a Tory government, Macmillan's, which (in connection with the National Insurance Act of 1959, which in some measure anticipated Wilson's SERPS reform - see Chapter 19 - by introducing into the State's old age pension scheme, with effect from 1961, a system of graduating contributions according to earnings, with subsequent graduated retirement pensions) first proclaimed as a principle that the living standards of the poorest sections of the community should rise at the same rate at which average living standards rose. That Orme's remarks in defending the Welfare State in the speech cited above should have been considered in the least controversial (and, indeed, that he felt they needed to be made at all), is a measure of the vicious swing to both the right and the past which was taking place now that Margaret Thatcher had hijacked the Tory Party. What shocks one, however, is the extreme moderation of those demands for social justice, coming as they do from a Labour left-winger. Was it by such standards that, after three quarters of a century of struggle, the achievements of the Labour Party were to be measured?. Where - or what - was the Socialism? Crosland himself could hardly have demurred at this moderate plea for moderating the ills of capitalism.

After Jim Callaghan had taken the helm, even the most timid hopes of a partial reconversion to Keynesian 'socialism' became childish dreams, as his blunt statement to his first Conference (that of 1976) as leader of the Party and the nation should have made abundantly clear. (See Chapter 21). By the spring of 1979, as Britain began to breathe again after the storm of strikes that has gone down in the history books as the Winter of Discontent, and as the Tories rode ever higher in the opinion polls, it was simply unimaginable that party leaders of the calibre of Callaghan and Healey would go to the country on a Socialist platform.

To their credit, the Left kept up the fight to the bitter end. Early in March, three weeks before the Government was forced by a no-confidence vote in the Commons to declare a general election, the

Labour Co-ordinating Committee, set up at the end of the previous September to mobilise constituency and union support for Benn and other left-wingers on the NEC, launched its own manifesto. It called for an election campaign based on authentically Socialist measures which contrasted with the essentially palliative proposals of the Party leaders. And it spoke up unashamedly for 'labour' as opposed to 'management':

> 'Behind the daily attacks on working people mounted by the newspapers lies a Tory establishment which has no idea what to do next. Industrial management is preoccupied with closure and redundancy, and Britain's plentiful banking and pension funds are flowing abroad or else being invested in pictures, property and other non-productive items at home. Labour has the only answer.'

The unauthorised version of Labour's appeal to the people demanded that the defeat of unemployment be given priority over bringing down inflation, arguing that growing unemployment and under-utilisation of productive capacity were making inflation worse. It called for higher public expenditure, more extensive economic planning and import controls; in short, that the Party should directly challenge the current received wisdom for ensuring national survival in a period of world recession.

The radically democratic thrust of the rebel manifesto is shown by its call for the abolition of the House of Lords, annual election of Labour Cabinets by the Parliamentary Labour Party, meaningful progress towards workers' control, the breaking up of the press monopolies into smaller units to be run by trusts and co-operatives, the abolition of private education, and a Socialist foreign policy that would involve, amongst other objectives, the phasing out of arms exports. Needless to say, none of these near-revolutionary propositions was given the imprimatur of respectability by being officially adopted as part of the Labour Party's appeal to the voters to return it to office.

The Labour Left's failure to make its strength really count is most simply explained by its fear that rocking the boat too violently when the Party was clinging on to power by the skin of its teeth and the courtesy of Liberals, Scottish and Welsh nationalists, and even at times Ulster Unionists, would tip them all into the water. Less superficially, however, it stemmed inexorably from the hierarchical and, in the final analysis, anti-democratic nature of the Labour Party. At the deepest level of all, the failure simply reflected the fundamental flaw in parliamentary democracy and parliamentary Socialism in general and in the Labour Movement in particular, all of which give the last word - and most of the others too! - to Westminster and Whitehall, not to the workers in the street or riding on the proverbial Clapham omnibus.

That I consider the strategy of the Labour Left (even from its own parliamentary-road-to-Socialism point of view) in certain respects misconceived, even to the extent of allowing the Right to pose, with some plausibility, as the true champions of social justice, will become apparent in the course of this essay. But it does not alter the more fundamental fact that the Left was still motivated by a vision of Socialism of sorts, while Centre and Right had effectively abandoned all pretensions to Socialist objectives in favour of 'realism' - i.e. a lowering of sights to seeking the amelioration of the immanent injustices of capitalist society by gaining power through the ballot box. And that is a generous judgement upon the motives of these moderate Labour politicians, taking their expressed concern for the common people at face value.

CHAPTER 12

Juggling with a mixed economy

'...that foul itch of covetousness which is the
explanation of the greater part of the world's activity.'
George Gissing, *The Nether World,* 1889

'If Labour attains an electoral majority and thus dominates the House of Commons, will capitalism meekly abdicate before the onset?' asked the turbulent left-wing professor Harold Laski in the year that Adolph Hitler came to power, *constitutionally*, in Germany. But when, at long last, the Labour Party did, for the first time, capture an absolute majority of seats in the Commons, capitalism was never faced with the awful choice of abdication or the overthrowing of parliamentary democracy by right-wing irreconcilables, since 'the onset' never came. It quickly became clear, even to the most apprehensive of businessmen, that economic enterprise was to remain overwhelmingly in their hands. Indeed, as Ralph Miliband wryly remarks in his study of *Parliamentary Socialism*: 'Private industry enjoyed the co-operation of the Government.'

Since the central tenet of the Labour Party (the notorious Clause IV (4), calling for the workers to receive 'the full fruits of their industry' through 'the common ownership of the means of production, distribution, and exchange') had come to be almost universally interpreted primarily in terms of nationalisation, the extent and degree of success of its nationalisation measures must be a principal touchstone in assessing the seriousness of the efforts of the Attlee administrations to lay the foundations of a Socialist society. At the time he wrote his brilliantly simple exposition of Labour's case, *The Labour Party in Perspective* (1937), Attlee envisaged by far the greater part of industry being taken into public ownership. 'All the major industries will be owned and controlled by the community,' he declared unequivocally, although he did go on to say, 'but there may well exist for a long time many smaller enterprises which are left to be carried on individually.' From other statements in the book, it is clear that it was his absolute conviction that public ownership of the greater part of industry and commerce was indispensable to the building of a Socialist society. 'The root cause' of 'the evils of Capitalism...is the private ownership of the means of life; the remedy is public ownership.' Furthermore, the *primary* purpose of public ownership, as of Socialist planning and economic controls in general, was not to gain efficiency, but to drive towards the goal of equality, with 'the service of the community' displacing 'private profit' as the 'actuating motive' of economic enterprise:

> 'It is the business of the Government to see that the resources of the country, material and human, are utilised so as to produce the greatest amount of well-being for all...I say "for all" because here is the essential difference between Socialist planning and Capitalist planning. There are many advocates of a planned economy who join with Socialists in denouncing the waste and chaos of wealth production. They would seek to substitute for the anarchy of competitive industrialism a planned and organised system, but they still retain their belief in a class society. Socialists believe in a classless society, and the plan which they put forward will envisage a steady progress towards greater equalisation of wealth. In considering what it is desirable to produce in this country they will consider who are to be the consumers. It is no use planning production for a society with its present gross inequalities if your intention is to develop society more and more on lines of equality.'

In other words, State intervention in general and nationalisation in particular were to be recommended not simply to bring greater order and rationality into the nation's economic affairs but to promote social justice.

By the time Labour had the opportunity to put its ideas into practice, the exigencies of war and its aftermath had ensured that the need for a considerable measure of economic planning by the State had become common ground for politicians of all parties, and in some areas even the case for outright nationalisation had been widely conceded. This widespread acceptance of the concept of public ownership, together with subsequent widespread disillusionment, make it all the more important to distinguish between what we might describe as purely economic reasons for support or opposition to such policies and what are at bottom social reasons that might answer in one way or another Callaghan's challenging question, more than thirty years later, 'What kind of society do we want?'

But in those jubilant days of power at last, the Labour Movement was at least united in the belief that a substantial measure of public ownership was desirable. As Kenneth O. Morgan puts it in his study *Labour in Power: 1945-1951*: 'The Labour government in 1945 was bent on implementing socialism as it conceived it, in place of the stagnation and unemployment of the past. Nationalisation was generally agreed to be the vital mechanism in the achievement of this historic objective.' However, the unity was more apparent than real, or perhaps it would be truer to say, more superficial than fundamental, for as Morgan also points out: 'The single most striking difference between the Labour Party's programme in 1945 and that in all subsequent elections down to 1979 [i.e. the latest election at the time he wrote this, for clearly the statement could still stand] is the centrality of nationalization in its overall grand design.' Moreover, as early as the first post-victory Party Conference, that of June 1946 at Bournemouth, with only around one-fifth of industry earmarked for nationalisation, Attlee was telling the comrades: 'The Government has gone as far left as is consistent with sound reason and the national interest.'

Ironically, it would seem that their experience in office in Churchill's wartime coalition government had cooled the ardour of Labour's leaders for outright nationalisation. At any rate, in *The Road to 1945*, Paul Addison cites a letter, dated 12th October 1944, to Richard Acland from Stafford Cripps in which he declares: 'Oh, no, my dear Richard. We have learnt in the war that we *can* control industry.' The same foolish boast was being made, with less excuse, almost thirty-five years later, as Labour slithered towards its most cataclysmic defeat. But in any case, leaving aside the major point that controlling industry in peacetime was a very different matter from controlling it at a time of universally recognised national emergency (and it would be perfectly reasonable to maintain that this extended into the period of post-war reconstruction), just what was the purpose of control? Was it economic efficiency alone, or social transformation too? In Cripps's case a somewhat sombre light will be thrown on this question when we come to consider the thinking of Labour leaders on the status of labour in industry.

In a chapter entitled 'Economic Socialisation' (the term he preferred to 'nationalisation') which he contributed to a three-volume study of *The British Labour Party* published in 1948, Herbert Morrison wrote:

> 'Socialisation should not be regarded as an end in itself. The mere transfer of ownership from private persons or companies to a public authority and management by that public authority is a means to an end - not *the* end. The essential aims are better public service, greater efficiency and economy, and the well-being and dignity of the workers employed in the industry or service. That we should socialise for the sake of socialisation or for the purpose of satisfying a political dogma or slogan would be silly; socialisation for the advantage of the nation is sense.'

As far as it goes, there is not much to quarrel with there. Certainly it is no part of my thesis to insist that nationalisation necessarily equates with Socialism. Perhaps it may in certain circumstances, though there neither is nor has been a single instance of its doing so, which, to say the least, leaves it open to doubt. (And, equally, there are many examples of nationalisation as a key element in the structure of authoritarian States - by which I mean all those that make no bones about banning dissent - and not a few of so-called liberal or social democracies in which it serves as a foundation for private capitalist enterprise and profit.) The issue has been posed in these terms simply because the Labour Party has so posed it by its eternal internecine feud between proponents brandishing it as testimony to their Socialist virility and opponents who may be rationalising their loss of faith in Socialism under the cover of 'realism'. The questions to be put to proponents and opponents alike are:

1) Has nationalisation advanced the cause of Socialism and would more nationalisation advance it further?

2) If it has not, or has only marginally done so, might it produce progress in the desired direction if suitably modified?

3) If it is, by its nature or as a consequence of its misuse, not a vital but a moribund mechanism for implementing Socialism, what other means are there to this end?

4) If some measure of community control over production, distribution and exchange is a prerequisite for Socialist progress, can any of the orthodox mechanisms for such control, or any conceivable modifications of them, serve the advancement of Socialism, without a radical re-ordering of the present system of social relationships and economic ownership?

Uninhibited cynicism might prompt one to ask if this whole argument is anything more than a debate between self-deluding impossibilists on the one hand and open-eyed but button-lipped apostates on the other. However, to jump to that conclusion would not simply painlessly dispose of the questions I have posed, but would beg not a few others in the process. So let us continue to treat them as serious questions and to bear them in mind in further examining Labour's last administration.

The challenge that rings again and again in Labour's interminable debates over nationalisation is Aneurin Bevan's call to hold 'the commanding heights of the economy'. Let us concede at once that such a gain could have been decisive, and that Attlee's pre-war vision of something much nearer to total nationalisation would be superfluous if those 'heights' could be captured without a wholesale State take-over of industry. The verdict of Alan Sked and Chris Cook on how near the first majority Labour ministries came to fulfilling Bevan's more modest ambitions is that: 'The Government, in fact, despite their efforts, had succeeded neither in 'controlling' nor even in capturing the commanding heights...in spite of all the fuss the commanding heights had never really been attacked. The twenty per cent of the economy taken over by the government was to a large extent the unprofitable part, while the profitable sector remained firmly in the hands of private enterprise. Socialist planning of this type was acceptable even to Conservatives.'

Putting aside for the moment the even harsher judgements Sked and Cook make in the same passage of *Post-War Britain: A Political History*, the implications of their verdict clearly go well beyond questions of quantification in nationalising industry and commerce. But, bearing in mind Herbert Morrison's injunctions against a doctrinaire approach to the issue, and focusing on the objectives of nationalisation (to employ Morrison's formula, 'better public service, greater efficiency and economy, and the well-being and dignity of the workers employed in the industry or service'), now that we have been led up the mountain by Bevan's eloquent sermonising, let us descend with him to the plains of practical living. In an NEC debate of 25th November 1947 on a policy document entitled 'Socialism and Private Enterprise', Bevan counselled the comrades: 'What we have to do is to create a framework within which private enterprise can operate efficiently.' As it happens, that is a pretty accurate description of the approach to nationalisation taken by every post-war Labour government, and provided we do not look too closely into the meaning of 'efficient private enterprise', it may even be fairly claimed that to a very large extent nationalisation has achieved that objective. However, whether that means that it has fulfilled the aims set out by Morrison, let alone whether it has assisted in the advance to Socialism, are very different questions.

Of course, once it has been conceded that total or even massively predominant nationalisation of industry and commerce is, under representative government, neither practicable nor desirable, there is nothing to object to, *per se*, in Bevan's formula. But the extraordinary thing is - given the voluminous literature and the interminable talk that had been expended on the subject during the years of preparing for power - that Labour crossed the portals of State power with such a lack of clarity regarding the objectives of nationalisation and the structures best suited to achieving them. (Indeed, until almost the last minute, when, through left-wing pressure in the National Executive Committee, the iron and steel industry was added to the list of coal, gas, electricity, railways, road haulage, Cable and Wireless and the Bank of England, not even the initial targets for take-over had been agreed.)

The consequences of what Kenneth O. Morgan calls the Party's 'extreme and studious vagueness' were seriously disabling, not simply during those pioneering days, but in later Labour administrations and, above all, for the long-term interests of the Labour Party and Movement. In the first place, imprecision, irresolution and poverty of imagination in official thinking led to a complacent falling back on the model of the autonomous public corporation, as advocated by Herbert Morrison. He, as principal architect of the London Passenger Transport Board which had taken over the capital's public transport system in 1933, had the inestimable forensic advantage of having an actual 'socialisation' scalp to his credit. But the trouble with taking the LPTB as a model (or, for that matter, any other existing public corporation - for by 1939 there was a whole string of such bodies, including the Port of London Authority, the Forestry Commission, the British Broadcasting Corporation, the Central Generating Electricity Board, the British Overseas Airways Corporation, the Agricultural Marketing Boards, and a General Post Office which was already evolving in that direction) was that what was needed for each candidate for State take-over was bespoke tailoring to fit its particular needs. And first there had to be agreement as to what those needs were, while those needs in turn could only be rationally articulated in terms of agreed aims.

State regulation was considered desirable to generate 'greater efficiency and economy' (which may be taken as self-evident virtues, even if they do need balancing against other desirables), in the interests of 'better public service', and to provide - in Bevan's formula - 'a framework within which private enterprise can operate efficiently.' Such aims would surely win general assent, as would a proper concern (however that might be defined) for the welfare of those who worked in the public sector enterprises. But even supposing the needs of each particular public enterprise to have been met and its aims fulfilled, unless those separate enterprises worked together to fulfil a general plan, they would be doing little more than aping the beggar-my-neighbour competition of the private sector. For example, in *The Labour Party in Perspective*, Attlee had stressed the need for the co-ordination of transport services:

> 'Road, rail, and sea transport should not be regarded as separate undertakings. They form part of a single whole. At the present time there is nothing to prevent one port being neglected and another developed according to the immediate interests of profit-makers. There is a scramble for business between the various agencies so that goods which ought to go by rail go by road, and vice versa. In a short time the development of air services will bring yet another competitor into the field. The Labour Government will end this chaos.'

Similarly, in discussing Labour's policy for fuel, Attlee treated fuel production as one industry as a matter of course. Yet the need for co-ordination in these two crucially important sections of the nation's economic infrastructure was grossly neglected in those formative post-war years of Labour power. Not until 1965 did any government draw up a long-term development plan for fuel; while no British government has ever got to grips with national transport planning. The chaos of the market still rules! As John Westergaard and Henrietta Resler point out in *Class in a Capitalist Society*, the fact that nationalisation has provided 'a central framework for the long-term development of services and supplies on which the business economy at large depends' itself validates 'the rationale of co-ordination and growth' on businessmen's own terms. This they would all see if they were not blinded by a quite unfounded fear that there is a 'thick socialist end to the thin wedge of *pro-capitalist* public ownership.' [my emphasis] In practice, however, such co-ordination has been rudimentary. What has prevailed instead has been 'the insistence that the nationalized industries should, in normal practice, follow the principles of private commercial enterprise, each pursuing profit maximization for itself', with State-owned industries competing vigorously with one another for business. Only those suffering from the quasi-religious delusions of market mania can seriously believe that such a situation could possibly be in the best interests of a national (let alone an international) community.

The ultimate irony, however, is that notwithstanding this submission of 'Socialist statesmen' to the juju jurisdiction of orthodox economics, market forces have *not* been allowed the same sway in transactions between public and private industry. On the contrary, the prices of products supplied by the nationalised enterprises have not uncommonly been kept so much below what the market would bear that public sector losses have subsidised private sector profit. However deficient Bevan's formula of a publicly-maintained framework for private enterprise to profit from might be felt to be, surely this could not be what he intended? Naturally, this situation of generally low profits - not to mention deficits made good, as well as investment for development provided, through subsidies drawn from the general revenue - has fostered the myth of public sector failure; and that in turn has eroded support for Labour Party policy as a whole. And of course it has been exploited without scruple and frequently without sense by the anti-Socialist parties. Churchill was already wielding this weapon in the general election campaign of 1950:

'Socialism, with its vast network of regulations and restrictions and its incompetent planning and purchasing by Whitehall officials, [is] proving itself every day to be a dangerous and costly fallacy. Every major industry which the Socialists have nationalized, without exception, has passed from the profitable or self-supporting side of the balance sheet to the loss-making, debit side.'

But as Morgan points out:

'Despite all the hostile propaganda from 'Aims of Industry', the FBI, and Fleet Street, it was significant that there was no general move by the Conservatives after 1951 to reverse the nationalization already achieved, apart from the controversial case of steel, and the separate, limited issue of road haulage. In effect, Churchill and his ministers implicitly admitted the unfairness of many past attacks on industries taken into public ownership in highly adverse financial circumstances, and with, in the case of the railways and the mines, a background of under-capitalization, under-investment, and long-term failure.'

Three decades later, the same kind of propaganda against nationalisation was still being spewed out, not just by party hacks, Grub Street journalists, and businessmen, but by economists of repute. In his *Guardian* 'Notebook' for 4th January 1979, Hamish McRae reflected on an article in *Lloyds Bank Review* by Walter Eltis, a Fellow of Exeter College, Oxford, which appeared to prove conclusively that nationalised industries cost the country more than they produced. McRae's conclusions were somewhat different:

'The trouble is (as Mr Eltis partially concedes) the figures do not necessarily prove what they are supposed to. Many nationalised corporations (like coal and the railways) were not profitable producers of wealth even when they were in the private sector - and it was partly for that reason that they fell into public hands. Some, like steel, were inevitably heading for a deficit as a result of world pressures. Others, like atomic energy, have such a long gestation period that it is unfair to compare their sales so far with their cost to the public purse.'

He went on to draw attention to the standard State industry situation of uncommercial pricing policies:

'More to the point all of the sales figures for nationalised corporations ought to be adjusted sharply upwards to make up for what sales would have been worth if successive governments had not imposed policies of price restraint - policies that were ultimately self-defeating.'

Such policies may have been (from any sane and Socialist viewpoint) profoundly misconceived; but they are certainly not illustrations of the failure of the public sector to operate efficiently. They have been deliberately imposed for two purposes. One of these, the holding down of State industry prices as a counter-inflationary measure, at least has the merit of not being in itself an *anti*-Socialist objective, though as we shall see it commonly has dire (and most anti-Socialist) consequences for the workforce in the public sector. The second purpose is to provide a good springboard for private enterprise; and an added irony here is that it is the once-upon-a-time anti-capitalist party that has been the most assiduous advocate of such a policy. As Westergaard and Resler so trenchantly put the matter:

'The more complex [the] economy and the more interdependent its different parts, the greater the need for some sort of common framework...in the interests of private industry itself...The case for using public enterprise - nationalized industry as well as other state agencies and devices - to provide the preconditions of 'modernization', economic growth and business prosperity came to be stressed increasingly during the 1960s, with Labour as the main spokesman for state stimulation of private capitalism.'

The thrust of Labour government - if not of Labour Party - policy is most clearly seen in the years in which Harold Wilson convinced himself, and quite a few others, that Labour, not the Tory party, was after all the natural party of government. Wilson, the supreme political pragmatist, rose to power on the hot air of techno-babble, by capitalising on the obvious connection between modernisation and technological progress and playing up the more ludicrous anachronistic aspects of the gentlemen's party. In the age of the sputnik, the shooting-stick had become an inappropriate symbol for the qualities that made men fit to govern others. In the very autumn when Harold Macmillan relinquished the reins of party and national leadership to the Earl of Home (see Chapter 1), the other Harold summoned up the blood of his troops, in a Party Conference debate on an NEC document entitled *Labour and the Scientific Revolution*, with the exhortation: 'We must harness Socialism to science and science to Socialism', to forge a new Britain 'in the white heat of technological revolution.'

At one stroke the Party had wrought the perfect emblem for electoral success. If the nation was to prosper in the modern world, it needed to exploit fully advanced technology in the common cause. Who could argue with that? And here, miraculously, was a party united in the will to see Science harnessed to Socialism, as the 'workers' State' of Soviet Russia was said to have done. As Bartlett puts it (op. cit.), the document 'could be read by the left as denoting new interest in public ownership and initiative, and by the centre and right as a pragmatic bid for modernisation. Crossman applauded this bridging of party differences with science-based socialism to make men masters of technological change. Editorials in *The New Statesman* took the same line, enthusiastically acclaiming scepticism, science and reason as the high road to socialism.'

Unfortunately, however, scepticism was in short supply on all sides. Its absence was exactly what made the document the perfect device for dealing with irreconcilable differences in the Party by promoting an attractively packaged and genuinely unconscious fudge. 'Socialists' of widely varying hues, from pallid parliamentary reformists to revolutionary Marxists, share a susceptibility to the allures of Science. Labour's illusion that it again had a banner to rally round (and as is often the case with illusions, this one did have a striking if transient success) and, moreover, that waving it vigorously might induce swathes of businessmen to sign up as camp-followers, is well illustrated by the reflections which Tony Benn (recently appointed supremo in Wilson's newly-minted Ministry of Technology to replace the left-wing trade union leader Frank Cousins, who, ominously, had resigned in protest at the Government's incomes legislation) imparted to, of all bodies, the American Chamber of Commerce:

> 'Technology challenges governments, whether capitalist, communist, or socialist, and industry whether publicly or privately owned, in such a direct fashion that the common interest uniting them is stronger and more important than the disagreements which divide them. Every society will seek to express this common interest in its own way and in the light of its own history. Here in Britain we start with a mixed economy, and we shall have one as far ahead as I can see. We must therefore make a mixed economy work. Make it successful; make it competitive; look to it to create the wealth we need to do the things we want to do.'

Benn was later to redeem himself from the alternative or combined charges of intent merely to manage capitalism better than the capitalists or of criminal naiveté that such words invited. But for the time being, both for him and for others seeking Socialism along the highway of modernism, such thinking was crippling. It compounded subjection to the partnership myth camouflaging the reality that the State provides the infrastructure (including, let it be noted, that of the Welfare State in general and the social security system in particular) while capitalist tycoons call the shots, with subjection to what Stuart Holland has dubbed the 'mixed economy myth' because of the gross imbalance between public and private sectors, itself reflecting the failure of political will that has allowed multinational firms to capture 'the commanding heights' of Britain's economy.

For however millennial its prospect had already become, those 'heights' remained (doctrinally speaking) the Labour Party's strategic objective right up to the reign of Neil Kinnock. When, following Labour's third successive post-war general election defeat (with the scoreboard showing a loss to Labour since it was last in office of over a million votes), Hugh Gaitskell tried to persuade the Party to ditch Clause IV as user-unfriendly at the hustings, he was heavily rebuffed, but he persisted in his efforts to have it amended so that it should, in his eyes, more accurately reflect the modern Party's aims. He did not succeed in this endeavour; but the 1960 Scarborough Conference (more renowned for the battle over the issue of unilateral nuclear disarmament and for Gaitskell's vow to 'fight and fight and fight again to save the Party we love' from pacifists, fellow-travellers, and - by implication - lunatics) did adopt a statement endorsing both a mixed economy and the 'commanding heights' strategy. The key passage on these issues declares that the Party's:

> '...social and economic objectives can be achieved only through an expansion of common ownership substantial enough to give the community power over the commanding heights of the economy. Common ownership takes varying forms, including state-owned industries and firms, producer and consumer co-operation, municipal ownership and public participation in private concerns. Recognizing that both public and private enterprise have a place in the economy it believes that further extension of common ownership should be decided from time to time in the light of these objectives and according to circumstances, with due regard for the views of the workers and consumers concerned.'

The statement makes clear enough that Labour was not pursuing a policy of wholesale nationalisation and, moreover, that its views on public ownership and control were flexible, not doctrinaire. Before considering whether such an approach could have become a viable route by which to storm the 'commanding heights', let us look more closely at Labour's record in juggling with the mixed economy.

Some of the handicaps that Labour governments have imposed upon themselves in their drive towards the 'commanding heights' (always supposing that this still remained a serious objective after the first flush of enthusiasm for nationalisation had begun to evaporate, as early, according to Morgan, as 1948) have already been noticed. They include the incongruous sack-race stance of price restraint for State-owned industries when dealing with the private sector, on the one hand, and knockabout competition between themselves (as in the case of the power industries) on the other. They also include the related negligent or perverse failure to closely co-ordinate their policy and practice to accord with an overall plan. (That such a plan never really got on to the drawing-board, let alone reaching the assembly lines, seems to argue a lack of conviction in Labour's declared commitment to planning.) Arguably more crippling than these defects was the failure to grasp the nettle of accountability. But before examining that fundamental issue, let us look at the bounds the Labour leadership tacitly set in selecting targets for nationalisation and the circumstances in which they at times transgressed them.

Firstly, just because the issue now seems to have disappeared into a black hole, it should not be overlooked that the national resource which had (along with the railways and minerals) been longest targeted by the Labour Movement was land. The intention of taking land into public ownership - unquestionably the nationalisation proposal with the greatest revolutionary potential of them all - was reaffirmed as Party policy in the 1945 Manifesto, but effectively shunted on to a track terminating (as they tell us parallel lines do) in infinity. At the last Party Conference before the debacle of '79, when a motion calling for farmland to be taken into public ownership, put by the National Union of Agricultural Workers with NEC backing, was once again received with acclamation, Joan Maynard reminded delegates that the Attlee Government had promised in 1946 that the policy would be implemented in the next session. Instead, it had become yet another instance of ritualistic reciting of the creed in place of serious efforts to turn it into reality. It is true that measures had been taken to strengthen the control of representative bodies over land development and that local authorities had been given greater powers to acquire land for public purposes, but the goal of giving the land back to the People was almost as far away as ever.

Secondly, the tacit acceptance that public ownership should be restricted to the infrastructure industries - a growing conviction in the thinking of the core of the Labour leadership that dates back at least to the dispute over steel nationalisation (Hugh Dalton records that despite a clear call from Conference, Herbert Morrison and Arthur Greenwood resisted its inclusion in the '45 Manifesto on the grounds that the City was opposed to the extension of public ownership to manufacturing industry, although the efficient production and supply of steel at reasonable prices was, of course, a basic requirement of almost every other manufacturing enterprise) - deprived Labour (at any rate when conjoined with the policy of public sector price restraint and a predominant motivation of providing a sound framework for private enterprise) of the opportunity of generating profit for the public purse.

Generally speaking, the bounds set by Labour - with a few exceptions justified on such grounds as market domination, as in the abortive and counterproductive attempt to take sugar into public ownership - have been overstepped only to rescue the failures of private capitalism, or perhaps it would be fairer to say, of the capitalist system. (The most famous of these 'failures', Rolls Royce, was saved from bankruptcy by the leaders of the party that had poured so much scorn on the idea of coming to the assistance of 'lame ducks'. This demonstrated that the Tories too were not prepared to see Britain's industrial flagships go down, though some of them would never forgive Ted Heath for the chagrin this caused them.) As Westergaard and Resler point out, the unhappy permutation of piecemeal nationalisation, the taking over of declining industries and 'lame ducks', and uncompetitive pricing policies, has served to discredit 'the goal of full public ownership', since they 'cannot produce commensurate redistribution' of wealth and power. 'In fact, if not by explicit design, it...neatly helps to undermine popular support for the public appropriation of capitalist enterprise at large.'

It is true that, with the confirmation of Wilson & Co. in office in the second (October) general election of 1974, and the subsequent enactment just over a year later of the Industry Bill, Labour appeared to be poised to implement what Phillip Whitehead describes as 'its most radical programme since the war, centred on a National Enterprise Board and a system of compulsory agreements with private industry.' However, the CBI's fear of 'a policy which might shift power fundamentally towards trade unions and away from management' proved to be a 'painted devil'. By subterfuge, stonewalling, and undisguised diktat, Wilson so emasculated the NEB that it could not possibly act as 'the investment primer for the whole economy (let alone take over twenty-five leading companies across the whole spectrum of industry) which Benn and his aides had envisaged.' Instead, it 'was left dealing with the walking wounded of the industrial collapse.' The titanic dimensions of Wilson's autocratic behaviour are graphically illustrated by the fact that the junior minister handling the Bill in committee, Michael Meacher, only discovered that a mere £50 million had been allocated for the Board's use in its first year when a Tory member of the committee challenged him to explain how that figure had been arrived at. Meacher himself considered that 'if it was going to be effective, it probably needed about £1 billion in the first year, and a further billion in each of the next five.'

In the band-aid role it had been reduced to, the NEB did in fact perform a valuable service to the nation - of a kind that any less unintelligently doctrinaire capitalist political party than the Tories had become under the Grantham grocer's daughter would have properly appreciated. Amongst the industries and enterprises Labour's policy of planned investment kept alive, resuscitated, or gave a boost to were coal, oil, steel, shipbuilding, aircraft manufacture, and the motor industry (including BL, of course, as well as the unhappy cases of Chrysler and De Lorean, in which government and nation were ripped off by the beneficiaries). It also gave vital support to sunrise industries (most notably in the micro-chip field) of the kind provided by the State as a matter of course in other capitalist economies, although this public investment was wantonly wasted by the Thatcherites' anorexic approach to the problems of British industry.

The Government's two main objectives were to ensure that the conditions necessary to long-term growth and prosperity were created or consolidated (in which matter they were incomparably more far-sighted than the free-market buccaneers who followed them in office) and to maintain as high a level of employment as possible. Callaghan inherited from Wilson an unemployment burden of well over a million (already the highest figure since the war) which had peaked in September 1977 at over 1.6 million. So it was entirely understandable that bringing it down was a Government priority, since the nation had not yet learned to welcome mass unemployment as a salutary remedy for overindulgence in job-security that would assuredly restore well-being to the body politic. These two objectives (which Labour thought of as mutually reinforcing and the New Conservatives as wholly inconsistent) were very clearly spelt out in a speech made by the Prime Minister in opening a new factory in Birmingham. Defending job-preservation and job-creation measures which were, he said, keeping 300,000 people off the dole, he told his audience:

'We are told that these [job-creation] measures should be
swept away. But I say to you that the simple- minded
recipe of leaving firms to sink or swim unaided in the free
market in a world trading recession, where every country is
scrambling for orders, would mean bankruptcy for many

firms in the Midlands and unemployment for thousands. So we take action to help the firms through this period so that they can emerge healthy and viable at the end of it.'

Under the hammer blows of the worsening world-wide recession, Labour had at least reforged the National Enterprise Board into a more credible shield, even if it was still in essence what Bernard Donoghue, head of the No 10 Policy Unit, described as 'a convenient casualty ward for firms the Government wished to rescue from bankruptcy.' The pitiful £50 million launch budget had been multiplied until its total expenditure and commitments topped £2.5 billion, and on the eve of the Government's demise another Industry Bill was introduced to raise its financial limit to £3 billion, with provision for a further increase to £4.5 billion. An increase in the financial limits of the Welsh and Scottish Development Agencies was also sought. In the Lords debate on the Bill, one crusty Tory peer, Lord Campbell of Croy, with closer approximation to honestly admitting his own hang-ups than to giving an accurate account of the real world, inveighed against the NEB as a bureaucratic institution licensed to 'set forth on pillaging forays in profitable private enterprises', provoking Labour peer Lord Jacques to the even more bizarre observation that if the Opposition resisted all public control they would 'drive people towards communism'!

Official on-the-record Tory policy was more ambivalent but decidedly sour. Speaking as one who would rather die than confess that he was glad that State intervention had saved such prestigious firms as Rolls Royce and Ferranti from the auction rooms if not the scrap-heap, 'Stormin' Norman Lamont, in telling the House that the Opposition would limit the NEB's borrowing power to £3 billion, both complained that the level of return on the Board's investment was well below the average for British industry *and* demanded that it release its holdings in turned-around Ferranti and in the successfully-launched pioneering firm International Computers Ltd. The astounding acumen of the businessmen's party was dazzlingly displayed in both of these instances after it was back in power. Ferranti, flying free of State supervision, was taken to the cleaners by a parasitic entrepreneur, while ICL, Britain's only major computer company, was taken over by a company at the time largely owned by the US multinational ITT, STC, who, in 1990, flogged it off to the giant Japanese electronics firm Fujitsu.

141

As for the use of public subsidy to sustain livelihoods, to make the right to work a reality, the Tories now making the running were scornful. Thatcherite guru, Sir Keith Joseph, opening a debate on an Opposition censure motion, on the one hand accused the Government of preserving low-paid and unstable jobs at the expense of creating 'new worthwhile jobs', thereby leaving the nation poor and divided, stifling enterprise, and through its 'Socialist' policies paralysing 'adaptation which is the heart of industrial success'; while, on the other hand, he advised the Government not to try to compete with the Japanese and the Americans in the mass-production of what has been called as revolutionary an invention for our age as the wheel once was - the silicon chip. Thus did Sir Keith adapt for a sceptical age the old counsel, 'Let not your right hand know what your left hand doeth.'

To sum up, in judging between the policies of Labour and the Thatcherite Tories, with the long-term prosperity of the nation *and* of industry as the criteria, any mentally sound and moderately detached adjudicator would be bound to award the palm to Labour. The Tories, in fact, have been collectively in the grip of a competition-at-all-costs fever from which few have escaped contamination. From any tolerably sane view of national interests, Labour deserved credit for making some things better than they would otherwise have been and preventing other things from becoming even worse than they did. From the point of view of securing more direct and more enduring benefits to the community from State support for private enterprises, however, the Wilson and Callaghan administrations behaved with selfless generosity in giving away the public's money with scarcely a thought of return. As, for example, in the Chrysler affair referred to in the previous section and in the case of the electronics company Ferranti, a family firm which made huge profits from Britain's *folie de grandeur* 'defence' expenditure. And as for the potential of the NEB and the other State intervention agencies to contribute to progress towards Socialism, the way they were deployed ensured that they supplied still more examples of Labour's almost perverse determination to see (to borrow the title of John Mortimer's novel) 'paradise postponed'.

So does it follow (as the strictures of Westergaard and Resler seem to insist) that having settled for a mixed economy with the cautious option of a 'considering each case on its merits' approach to nationalisation, that the Labour left had unwittingly relinquished all realistic hope of securing sufficient control over the economy to ensure that effective planning would be much more than a paper game? Or had there been all along (as those who framed the Scarborough Conference resolution referred to above apparently believed) an alternative route to the summit that might well have called for more but certainly did not demand wholesale nationalisation? These questions became particularly pertinent in the light of declining public support for nationalisation, which was already down to only around a fifth of the electorate by the mid seventies.

Not only are there good reasons for thinking that the Scarborough resolutionaries were right, but a credible case can be made for maintaining that, even without any further nationalisation, Labour governments could have succeeded in making community interests paramount if they had had the will to do so. The reasons for believing this are in essence very simple and can be summed up by pointing to the enormous clout that, for good or ill, the modern State wields with respect to the economic activities within its ambit. Notwithstanding the powerful and important case made by Stuart Holland in his book *The Socialist Challenge* (1975) to the effect that the multinationals dominating what he calls the mesoeconomic sector were escaping from the control of the nation-state - a case which is even stronger now, as the century draws to a close - this point remains true whenever and wherever a representative government makes up its mind that the State it controls will not be held to ransom by private sector interests.

Consider first the historical growth in central and local government employment. Excluding the armed services, this only absorbed some 2 per cent of the workforce in 1891, about 5 per cent in the years leading up to the First World War, about 8 per cent between the wars, over 11 per cent in 1950, and 17 per cent by 1971. With the 7 to 8 per cent of workers in the nationalised industries added, public sector employment had reached about 25 per cent by the early seventies and around 30 per cent by the end of the decade. As for the State's financial muscle (without taking into account its fiscal powers), writing in the mid seventies, Westergaard and Resler calculated that 'the state in one way or another has passing through its hands nearly one-half of the funds generated by economic activity in the country,' and that 'the public sector's contribution to capital investment for the future is on much the same scale.' And this is to leave out of the equation the overwhelming investment of the State in the present and future prosperity of its citizens represented by benefits in kind received through the whole welfare infrastructure - education, health care, and so on.

Of course, for a representative government to wield such clout wantonly would be to invite confrontation and court disaster. But that does not alter the fact that the State carries a most terrific clout which might have been used in alliance with a united Labour Movement to shove society in a Socialist direction. For Labour to have renounced all thought of a 'command economy' was one thing, and wise. For it to have failed to stand up to capitalism on behalf of the community was to reduce the State in which it had put its faith from a paramount power to a supplicant to private privilege. That is what, with a progressive bending of the knee, the Labour governments of the sixties and seventies became.

CHAPTER 13

Labour plays the Great Power game

'Be it thy course to busy giddy minds
With foreign quarrels...'
**The King's advice to Prince Harry,
Part Two of** *Henry IV*

'The cold war was a marvellous device by means of
which the domestic population could be mobilised in
support of aggressive and interventionist policies under
the threat of the superpower enemy...a highly functional
system by which the superpowers control their own
domains...The question now is whether people can
overcome the attempt to beat the workforce and the poor
into a chauvinist mood so as to tolerate the attack being
launched against them.'

Noam Chomsky (1981)

All political parties, in all countries and at all times, lay claim to
patriotism, to having the best interests of the nation at heart. How
could it be otherwise? (And in a sense the claim is always genuine,
since they sincerely believe it to be so, as, for example, the Petainists
did in Nazi-occupied France). True Socialist parties, however, differ
from other political parties in being at the same time of their very
essence internationalist. (Which is one reason, besides its monstrous
travesty of Socialist ideas and values, why 'National Socialism'
always was a preposterous contradiction in terms, and why
'Socialism in one country' never could be more than a dubious
slogan). This internationalism necessarily arises from the Socialist
analysis of society, which perceives the hierarchical and class-based
character of all capitalist social structures and identifies with the
majority class. However fragmented by the more or less favoured
place of individual members in the hierarchy, that is still in the
final analysis a working class, not an employing class. This in turn
implicates the recognition of common class interests that transcend
national frontiers. (This is just as true of bourgeois parties, of course,
but certain complicating factors inhibit open recognition and

sometimes even awareness on their part.) Socialism, in short, considered as a historical movement reacting to capitalism, always has been a movement placing great value on international contacts and solidarity.

'The Labour Party is the expression in Great Britain of a world-wide movement,' says Attlee in *The Labour Party in Perspective*, and he cites with approbation Bertrand Russell's summary of the essentials of Socialism, with its concluding point that: 'To be fully realised it must be international.' Of course, one is entitled to challenge every value-centred or ideology-centred group or organisation (political, religious, or whatever) on the grounds of whether or not it applies the principles it professes consistently and universally; but this is peculiarly true of Socialist parties when it comes to their handling of foreign affairs, especially when they are in power, for it could be said that their commitment to international working-class solidarity should effectively remove the term 'foreign' from their vocabulary.

It might as well be said at once, that in this respect Labour's record is lamentable. And making every reasonable allowance for the daunting problems of playing a part in restructuring a fractured world order that it faced on coming to power, besides giving it due credit for some positive achievements (making a start, for instance, on the dismantling of empire), the Attlee regime is not simply implicated in this judgement, but it was responsible for laying down the lines (or rather, it would be more correct to say, for faithfully following established custom and practice) by which later Labour governments were generally content to be guided.

The stark contrast between Labour's youthful idealism and its cynical maturity could hardly be highlighted better than by following Tony Cliff and Donny Gluckstein, in *The Labour Party - a Marxist History*, in citing a fire-in-the-belly speech by a constituency delegate at the Labour Party Conference of May 1945:

> 'The Labour Party should have a clear foreign policy of
> its own, which is completely distinct from that of the
> Tory Party. The Socialist revolution had already begun
> in Europe and was firmly established in many countries
> in Eastern and Southern Europe. The crucial principle of
> our foreign policy should be to protect, assist, encourage
> and aid in every way the Socialist revolution wherever it

appears...The upper class in every country are selfish, depraved, dissolute and decadent. These upper classes look to the British Army and the British people to protect them against the just wrath of the people who have been fighting underground against them for...four years. We must see that that does not happen. The penalty for entertaining any hesitation about the support for the revolution would be that Labour would wake one day to find itself "running with the Red Flag in front of the armoured car of Tory imperialism and counter-revolution."'

History was to transform that 'bliss was it in that dawn to be alive' speaker into one of the Party's elder statesmen, deeply implicated (in particular as Defence Secretary and as Chancellor of the Exchequer) in its crimes and blunders, for it was none other than the young Denis Healey, back from playing an honourable part in the war against fascism.

If expecting the Party to promote revolution was a bit starry-eyed, its young turks had every right to expect their leaders to strive to live up to its principles. They had every right to demand that the Party's triumph at the polls should make a qualitative difference to history, not just with respect to domestic issues but in the conduct of foreign and Commonwealth affairs. There is little if any evidence that it did so. From the start the Attlee Government was ready to spend - and to do - whatever it took to keep Great Britain in the Great Powers' League. It was all very well for the golden-tongued hero of the Labour left, Aneurin Bevan, to proclaim (in July 1948): 'We now have the moral leadership of the world, and before many years we shall have people coming here as to a modern Mecca...' The reality was that, whatever good examples it might have been setting at home, the regime which purported to be the first Socialist government with a clear mandate from the British electorate was no moral force abroad; just another tawdry example of the nation-state rampant. A laundry list of sordid episodes must suffice as evidence.

With the defeat of Japan in August 1945, the British Empire and Commonwealth once again embraced a quarter of the world's population and territory; but over vast tracts of it British rule was already untenable. In 1947-48 Britain pulled out of India,

Ceylon, and Burma, and abandoned its mandate in Palestine. Forces beyond its control largely absolve the Attlee Government of guilt over the bloody partitioning of India and, perhaps, over the tragic fate of the Palestinian Arabs. However, the catalogue of continuing repression in Britain's other colonies makes sorry reading, with, *inter alia*, the imposition of states of emergency, curfews and the banning of demonstrations; the proscribing of political parties; the banning of newspapers and prosecutions for publishing seditious literature; the shackling of trade unions; the jailing, 'preventive detention', or banishment - not to mention the committing of GBH and lawful murder - of nationalists; and so on (in short, a chronicle of the kind of crimes committed by the British State against its own people a century or so earlier when most of *them* were voteless), in East and West Africa and in colonial territories in the New World.

A charge-sheet of State crimes could include the shooting dead of six African mutineers striking in protest at delays in demobilisation (Kenya, January 1947); an armed police assault on miners taking part in a sit-down strike, in which 21 workers were killed and 51 wounded (Nigeria, November 1949); killings, mass arrests, and savage prison sentences in response to widespread unrest in Buganda (Uganda, 1949-50); a whole series of repressive measures to keep the lid on liberation movements in Nigeria and the Gold Coast; the collective punishment of whole villages during the Malayan emergency (1948-60); and the imprisonment of twelve trade unionists for belonging to an unlawful association (Cyprus, January 1946).

Years later, in 1959, during the Commons debate on the agreement under which Cyprus became independent, with Archbishop Makarios, who had been exiled for a year (1956-57), as its first president, Nye Bevan, now shadow foreign secretary, was to receive a most unwelcome reminder that he had himself been an accomplice in the Attlee regime's repression of freedom fighters. In the midst of a withering attack on the Tories for their folly in suppressing nationalist leaders in the colonies with whom they later had to come to terms, he was 'hoist with his own petard' when he cited the case of Kwame Nkrumah, the first prime minister of the Gold Coast and of Ghana (as the Gold Coast had become on gaining independence in 1957). As the Government benches rocked with mocking laughter, Bevan's mortified colleagues were obliged to break into his cocoon of selective amnesia, though nothing, it seemed, could puncture his impudence. 'All right!' he exclaimed. 'We shoved him in jail. Yes, certainly! If honourable members will restrain their hilarity for a moment, I said this is part of the classic story of these struggles.'

Perhaps only Patrick Gordon-Walker, Secretary of State for Commonwealth Relations in Attlee's second administration, could match such effrontery. Although he was up to his ears in the plot that had enticed Seretse Khama, elected chief of the Bamangwato tribe of Bechuanaland (now Botswana), to England so that he could be banned from the protectorate to placate the South African authorities because he had had the temerity to fall in love with a white woman and marry her, Gordon-Walker denied deceit. He told the House: 'I have done my utmost throughout to preserve honour between man and man in this matter.' Seretse Khama - like Nkrumah and Makarios, and like Jomo Kenyatta in Kenya, among other 'classic' cases - rose in time to the pinnacle of power in his own country through a measure of martyrdom conferred on him by his colonial masters; so perhaps they all had reason to be grateful. Is it not meet then that we outdo Mark Anthony by calling our Statesmen 'Right Honourable'? (Gordon-Walker's frugal habits with respect to open government may be admired again in the context of the sanctions-busting which kept the Rhodesian rebels on the road, recounted in Chapter 30; and further testimony to his dedication to democratic principles surfaced in January 1997 with the 30-years-later rule revelations for 1966, in his words of advice to Harold Wilson on how to handle the embarrassing matter of the war in Vietnam: 'We should search for a policy which, while backing America loyally, allows us a certain more apparent independence of view.')

What we are searching for however, like Diogenes with his lamp in the daylight despondently looking for an honest man, is that 'qualitative difference' alluded to above, and with this in mind it would seem more pertinent to quote the verdict of the authors of *How Labour Governed, 1945-1951*, a seditious if not scurrilous pamphlet that recounts these and other unsavoury stories in some detail:

'To what extent the British Government, as opposed to the colonial governments, was directly responsible for all these colonial crimes is not the main point at issue, although its ultimate responsibility is inescapable. The

149

significant fact is that they could, and did, happen again and again while a Labour Government was in power, no less than they have done under the Tories.'

Perhaps even more shameful was the assistance given to other European powers to regain their right to exploit colonial peoples. British, Indian, and what were described as 'controlled' Japanese troops were used to put down insurrection in the Dutch East Indies and to restore the *status quo ante* until Holland could send troops. As late as 1947 Britain was training and equipping units for a Dutch expeditionary force that grew to over 100,000 strong but none the less failed to prevail over the Indonesian nationalists. Similarly in Indo-China, British along with surrendered Japanese forces operating under their command helped the French to suppress an Annamite rebellion and 'to restore order'.

The current Labour Party Chairman, Harold Laski, spoke for the true Socialists in the Party when he commented on Britain's intervention in Indonesia that it 'makes the British claim to have been engaged in a war for democracy and freedom a hollow mockery all over Southeast Asia'; but there was nothing they could do to control the new masters of State power. This was particularly true in the Middle East. Where Britain's strategic or economic interests were felt to be at stake, the Labour Government made the same assumptions that they must prevail over the rights and interests of other nations as a Tory government would have done. When, on 2nd May 1951, Dr Mossadeq's government asserted Iran's right to her own natural resources by nationalising the Anglo-Iranian Oil Company which controlled the country's oil fields (a measure described by Sked and Cook as 'an act of socialism much bolder than anything ever contemplated by Britain's Labour leaders'), the British Government responded by despatching warships to the Persian Gulf and imposing economic sanctions. Herbert Morrison, who had succeeded Ernest Bevin as Foreign Secretary, was evidently more in sympathy with the kind of British upper-class arrogance displayed by Lord Fraser, the First Sea Lord, when he told a meeting of ministers and the Chiefs of Staff that 'the British public... were tired of being pushed around by Persian pipsqueaks,' than with Labour back-benchers whose consciences were troubling them. At any rate, when Emrys Hughes suggested that Britain's actions smacked of 'nineteenth century imperialism', Morrison coolly replied: 'I think in this case the imperialism is in some respects the other way round.' American diplomacy, combined with cooler consideration of the extent of Britain's military commitments elsewhere, particularly in Korea and Malaya, defused the crisis, and eventually (it was not finalised until 1954) a new deal was worked out. It guaranteed the bulk of Britain's oil supplies, more or less satisfied Iran's honour, and allowed the Americans to get a large finger in the pie. But with such a 'cocky and reactionary pseudo-Pam' (as Hugh Dalton called Morrison, in a mocking comparison with the famous Lord Palmerston of the nation's great-power past) at the Foreign Office helm, Britain had come close to drifting into an imperialistic war.

Quite as bellicose as Morrison was the Minister of Defence, Emmanuel Shinwell (yes, Manny Shinwell, that spunky little Glaswegian Jew who had been one of the leaders of the Red Clydesiders striking for a forty-hour week in 1919), who argued that not standing up to the Persians might embolden nationalists elsewhere and culminate in the nationalisation of the Suez Canal and the collapse of British power throughout the Middle East. Suez was indeed the part of the world where lightning next struck Labour's twilight imperialists. In the middle of the British general election campaign of October 1951, the Egyptian parliament abrogated both the Anglo-Egyptian Treaty of 1936, under which British troops were stationed in the Suez Canal Zone, and the agreement under which the Sudan had been an Anglo-Egyptian condominium since 1899. Again troops, tanks, and warships were promptly deployed against the patriots of another country. 'Morrison's instinctive response,' says Kenneth O. Morgan, 'was again belligerent; echoes of Wolseley and General Gordon were heard in the land,' and the 'bloody little fool' (as Dalton called him on this occasion) had to be overruled by the Prime Minister when he pressed for the escalation of military action. Attlee was at least fortunate in having this crisis taken out of his hands by Labour's defeat at the polls. Five years later, under Sir Anthony Eden, Britain, in collusion with France and Israel, would go to war with Egypt in answer to Nasser's nationalisation of the Suez Canal, much to the official indignation of the Labour opposition; but the truth is that these two incidents in the Middle East in 1951 showed clearly that having a Labour government in power in Britain was no guarantee against gunboat diplomacy.

If Labour's leaders failed to grasp the fact that the Second World War - much more definitively than the First - marked not simply a break in a historical progression, but a total transformation of the international scene; that victory over Germany and Japan did not even offer the option of restoring the *status quo ante*, never mind whether this was to be considered desirable or not; then they are less to be blamed for that (although a greater degree of perspicacity might reasonably have been expected of statesmen who supposedly had a Socialist perspective on the world) than for sharing both the emotional commitment of their political opponents to Britain's 'glorious past' as a great power and their illusion that this role could be sustained in the mid-century world. Socialism in one country may be an unobtainable goal; but had they been wise enough to recognise that Britain was now only cut out to be a bit-part player, had they not been so avid in their desire to strut their hour upon the stage of history, then they might have done far more than they did, both at home and abroad, to further the cause they professed. At least they would not have so tarnished its name by making their country an accomplice in acts wholly inimical to Socialist principles and purposes and, in doing so, come close to reducing Great Britain to the status of a satellite of the United States.

The Labour left saw this danger clearly enough. In November 1946, 58 Labour MPs put their names to an amendment calling on the Government to 'review and recast its conduct of international affairs' in such a way as to 'provide a democratic and constructive alternative to an otherwise inevitable conflict between American capitalism and Soviet Communism, in which all hope of World Government would be destroyed.' In moving the amendment, Richard Crossman accused the Government of drifting away from Labour's election pledges towards an 'exclusive Anglo-American tie-up and of a tie-up between the two front benches.' The bipartisan character of the Government's foreign policy was promptly confirmed by a Tory MP, Captain Crookshank, who declared: 'The Government's foreign policy is, broadly speaking, supported by the Opposition,' and expressed his sympathy for the Foreign Secretary, Ernest Bevin, over the 'stabs in the back' he was suffering 'from his so-called friends.' The conspirators, however, were using rubber daggers: not one of them went into the division lobbies to vote against the Government.

As for the autocrat they had targeted, he was impervious to

their blows and contemptuous of their opinions. On the very day the 1945 general election results were declared, the foreign-secretary-in-waiting had announced: 'British foreign policy will not be altered in any way under the Labour Government.' It is true that the particular policy to which he was referring was that agreed by the wartime Coalition Government of which he had been a member, as he made clear to the House in a mutual backslapping display with the former foreign secretary, Sir Anthony Eden. But despite the important changes in attitude instilled by the chastening experiences of war and the general recognition that Britain's imperial sway could no longer be exercised in the same untrammelled way, that still meant that, in essence, Britain's foreign policy would be Tory foreign policy. Having been let into the club, the Labour statesmen would show they were gentlemen by playing by the rules.

The virtues of a bipartisan foreign policy are commonly taken as self-evident in all countries; but that only highlights the fact that the nation-state is an instrument of tribalism. Parties that profess internationalism yet fail radically to alter their country's foreign policy when they get into power simply illustrate the cynical truth that in politics practice seldom follows precept. But politicians live by the word and, if they dishonour it, deserve to die by it. So whatever allowances may reasonably be made for the practical difficulties of following their principles when in office, it is fitting that the powerless - the ordinary citizens - should constantly rub the politicians' noses in what they have said.

The 'Foreign Policy' chapter in *The Labour Party in Perspective*, for example, opens with the ringing declaration: 'Socialists in all countries are united by a common rejection of the doctrines and ideals of militarism and imperialism,' and goes on to affirm: 'Social justice must be the basis of a peaceful world.' Following a brief but thoughtful survey of the reactions of Labour's supporters to British foreign policy from Victorian times up to the rise of fascism and the civil war in Spain that was still raging when the book was written, Attlee outlines the principal points of the Party's 1934 Conference statement on 'War and Peace', which, he says, 'stands today [1937] as the official policy of the Party...' and 'which it would pursue when given power':

'It based Labour's foreign policy on the collective peace

153

system through the League of Nations...It regarded the League as a first step towards a co-operative world commonwealth. It rejected the theory of the balance of power and demanded the subordination of national sovereignty to world obligations. It stressed the need for basing the new world order on social justice and demanded far-reaching measures of economic co-operation and world control in economic and financial matters...It declared for an international police force. It stressed the need for world loyalty as against national loyalty. It regarded war resistance as the duty of every citizen, and not merely of organised Labour.'

Attlee makes a special point of declaring that, besides its rejection of Britain's traditional balance of power policy, the Party would not countenance the concept of bipartisan foreign policy:

'It does not agree that there is some policy to be pursued by this country irrespective of what party is in power, a policy which is national and so transcends party differences. There is a deep difference of opinion between the Labour Party and the Capitalist parties on foreign as well as on home policy. *The foreign policy of a Government is the reflection of its internal policy.* Imperialism is the form which Capitalism takes in relation to other nations. A Capitalist Government in Britain...does not consider it [the League of Nations] as a world commonwealth in embryo, because its outlook is nationalist, not internationalist.' [my emphasis]

With respect to these antithetical concepts, in his next chapter, 'The Commonwealth and the Empire', Attlee puts it beyond all possible doubt that his party's principles are to be applied universally, without regard to nation or race. The chapter opens with a frank acknowledgement of Labour's involuntary association with the guilt of imperialism: 'While, on the one hand, it is the protagonist at home of the struggle of the workers against the Capitalists, it is, in relation to the less developed peoples of the world, part of the dominant race which collectively exploits them.' It concludes with a declaration of solidarity with the whole human race:

'One of the vital questions for the future of world peace is the reconciliation of the interests of the white, the black, the brown, and the yellow races. The Labour Party fearlessly applies to this problem the principle of the brotherhood of man. It does not admit that the white race has any right of primogeniture in the world. It holds that the resources of the world must be developed in the interests of all people, and that the standard of life of the inhabitants of Asia and Africa must be raised, and not kept always below those of Europe, America, and Australia.'

Of course, one possible reaction to such elevated declarations is cynicism and sheer disbelief - all too well founded on the observation that politics is a dirty game, and on the suspicion that the only concern of politicians is to persuade others to support them, and that they will say and do anything to secure power. But to take this line, in a society in which we have at least the right openly to debate issues, is to surrender to despair and to become probably more cynical than the worst of those we suspect. Better to take them at their word until we have grounds for disbelieving, and then, piecemeal, to withdraw the credit we have extended them. By treating them as sincere in the first place, we can at least tax them with falling from grace. Besides, like the rest of us, they are more likely to be partly honourable and partly dishonourable than wholly one or the other, and capable of insight as well as subject to self-deception. There is an interesting passage in *The Labour Party in Perspective* in which Attlee takes to task those Labour supporters who, transfixed by the menace of Fascism, were adopting a lesser-of-two-evils attitude to their own government; by so doing they were underestimating the struggle between Socialism and Capitalism, magnifying the differences between Capitalist States and Fascist States, and in their prepossession with national unity encouraging, however unintentionally, 'the subtle introduction of Fascism' at home. The irony and the tragedy is that, ten years later and no longer in opposition but in power, he evidently saw no parallel, but responded to a new menace, that of Soviet Communism, by himself choosing the lesser of two evils, while minimising the distance between his own values and those of American capitalism.

There were, of course, strongly extenuating circumstances to plead in reply to Crossman's charge of an 'exclusive Anglo-American tie-up.' The hot war with the Axis powers had been succeeded, virtually without an interlude of peace, by the Cold War with Soviet power and, to put it mildly, there were already reasons enough for a democratic Socialist State to distrust the intentions of Stalin. Poland, Bulgaria, and Romania were already effectively in the Soviet camp, and within fifteen months the salami tactics of the Communists in Hungary and Czechoslovakia would enmesh those countries too. That is not to say, however, that fear of a Russian attack on the West (inasmuch as it was ever genuinely felt by the Western leaders) was warranted. Sked and Cook bluntly call it 'nonsense' in writing of the panic in Western Europe caused by the invasion of South Korea. Common sense and the evidence concur in concluding that the Russians were as little inclined (if not less!) as their erstwhile allies to plunge themselves into a third world war. The probing and manoeuvring on both sides were part of the age-old balance-of-power game, with neither side now willing to test the other's weakness to destruction, as level-headed peace campaigners well understood long before the amazing Mikhail Gorbachev transformed it into the new received wisdom.

Nor did the rapidly vanishing hopes of reaching an acceptable accommodation with Stalin justify the Attlee Government in coupling Britain to the American chariot. It might even be remarked in passing that the only major demonstration of independence in British foreign policy, the Suez invasion of 1956, which the United States opposed not on ideological or ethical but on pragmatic grounds concerning its own interests in the Middle East, was the act of a Tory government. Although it is only fair to add that their doughty opponents made valiant efforts to rise to the occasion, with Gaitskell comparing Nasser to Mussolini and Hitler because of his take-over of the Canal, and the effervescent Nye regaling the House with such excellent buffoonery as the crack that: 'If the sending of one's police and soldiers into the darkness of the night to seize somebody else's property is nationalisation, then Ali Baba used the wrong terminology.'

The hopes of a better world to come which had helped so many to get through the nightmare years of the war were certainly blighted by the ruthless internal repression and external aggression of the Soviet Union. But they were also blighted by the malign consequences of America's determination to remake the world in its own image. Two days after the opening, on 10th March 1947, of the Moscow Conference of foreign ministers of the wartime allies, at which the future of Germany - still officially envisaged as one country - was the main issue, President Truman, in a speech to a joint session of Congress that was broadcast live nation-wide, assumed on behalf of America the role of global sheriff. The Truman Doctrine, as it came to be called, was full of fine phrases about the choice facing nearly every nation between two ways of life, one 'based upon the will of the majority' and bringing freedom, the other 'based upon the will of a minority' employing 'terror and oppression' to rule the majority. 'I believe that it must be the policy of the United States to support free peoples who are resisting attempted subjugation by armed minorities or by outside pressures,' Truman declared.

The trouble was (leaving aside the megalomaniacal putting-the-world-to-rights presumption involved) that, as Stephen Ambrose says in *Rise to Globalism*: 'The Truman Doctrine came close to shutting the door against any revolution, since the terms 'free peoples' and 'anti-Communist' were thought to be synonymous. All the Greek government, or any dictatorship, had to do to get American aid was to claim that its opponents were Communist.' And so it was to prove, across the continents and for the best part of the next half-century, that the Truman Doctrine became not a torch of freedom to the subject peoples of the world but a terrible threat, reinforcing repression and contributing directly or indirectly to millions of deaths - in Korea, in Indo-China, in Afghanistan, in Angola, and in parts of Latin America, to name just a few of the bloodiest cockpits.

Truth as well as justice was a victim. Ambrose draws attention to the crusading character of the Americans when operating in their idealistic mode, to that Manichaean simple-mindedness that makes them tend to see things in terms of 'a struggle between light and darkness' and equally prone to double-think:

> 'It was difficult for other outsiders, not just Stalin, to understand the American position. Throughout the war Americans had denounced sphere-of-influence and balance-of-power concepts, calling instead for a new era of peace backed by the collective security of the United

Nations, an organization open to all democratic nations. Yet in practice the United States maintained a near hegemony over Central and South America (through the instrument of military dictatorships in most cases). It was true that free elections in East Europe would result in anti-Soviet governments, but it was equally true that free elections in Latin America probably would bring power to anti-American governments.'

To a greater or lesser extent, Britain has been implicated in all of America's post-World-War-II crimes against humanity, since even when its government has not actively collaborated with the United States, it has taken the view that, as a loyal ally, Britain should not oppose them. This is no less true of Labour when in power than of the Tories, who have at least had the excuse that they were not radically departing from their own principles. Indeed, in one crucial case (in addition, that is, to the colonial spats already noted) a Labour government led the way and set the pace for the United States. When the Germans withdrew from Greece in October 1944, Churchill had sent 60,000 British troops to keep the Communist-led resistance movement out of power. As A.J.P. Taylor puts it in *English History, 1914-1945*: 'The British government backed the king of Greece in the name of democracy; though the king's past was far from democratic.' A Commons censure motion protesting at Britain's intervention was backed by 24 Labour MPs, with 23 Labour MPs supporting the Coalition Government and the rest abstaining.

But if that denoted dissent, however feeble, on the Labour benches, the Party's accession to power in July 1945 made not a scrap of difference to the official British position on the issue. In another Commons debate, on 23rd November 1945, Bevin said that the holding of a plebiscite on the controversial issue of the future of the Greek monarchy must await pacification, and with characteristic arrogance told the House that the question was: 'In what reasonable period can I get this country into a tranquil state?' In fact British troops remained in Greece, collaborating with the royalists throughout a bitter civil war that waged from May 1946 to October 1949, the last contingents not being withdrawn until 1950. This shameful episode was instrumental in the proclamation that stood the Monroe Doctrine on its head, since Britain's warning, in February 1947, that it could no longer sustain the burden of military and economic aid to Greece and Turkey led to the United States donning Britain's traditional mantle of paymaster to foreign armies in the balance-of-power game and to the proclamation of the Truman Doctrine as its justification.

In considering the outbreak of the Cold War, the historical record demands recognition of the fact that the Truman Doctrine - like Churchill's earlier 'iron curtain' speech, made in Truman's presence to a university audience at Fulton, Missouri - preceded any clear act of Russian expansionism or aggression, with the arguable exceptions of the Soviet Union's attempts (1) to obtain oil concessions from Iran by postponing the withdrawal of its troops deployed there during the war, and (2) to secure joint control with Turkey over the Dardanelles. The first of these *démarches* was nothing but a mirror image of rights over Middle East oil obtained by Western pressure, while the second reflected the old Tsarist claims to guaranteed passage for Russian ships between the Black Sea and the Mediterranean. In both cases the Russians backed down when their former allies protested. Ambrose comments: 'Stalin was no more ready for war than Truman'; then goes on to record the despatch of America's newest aircraft carrier through the Straits and Truman's remark: 'We might as well find out whether the Russians were bent on world conquest now as in five years or ten years.' In the case of the Iranian oil imbroglio, all the Americans needed to despatch was a stiff note from Secretary of State James Byrnes.

The Truman Doctrine raised the stakes in the poker game with the Russians from an undeclared policy of containment through diplomatic pressures to an open declaration of confrontation. It was America's declaration of Cold War on the Soviet Union. The principal cockpit of this confrontation was Germany, and even if we leave out of account the failure of the United States to take up Stalin's offer of an agreement for a united but neutral Germany (a failure to call his bluff, if bluff is what it was) there are grounds for asserting that America and her principal allies were as responsible as Russia for Germany's forty-five-year division. Perhaps the most telling evidence which supports this view relates to the machinations of General Lucius Clay, the administrator of the American occupation zone. Ambrose - citing Clay's failure to enforce denazification, his inaction with regard to breaking up the industrial cartel system, his ignoring of the Potsdam agreement to limit German industrial production, and his explicit comment that, 'In the event of another war, the Germans probably would be the only Continental peoples upon whom we could rely' - remarks that Clay 'had made the Germans into allies, at a time when most Americans still regarded them as enemies who needed to be punished and re-educated.'

Whatever qualms they still felt about the resurrection of German power and about a permanent rupturing of the wartime alliance with Russia, Bevin and Attlee were in general accord with this pugnacious American stance. 'Both responded to Truman's message [the Truman Doctrine] with enthusiasm,' Morgan says, while Attlee had 'refused to condemn Churchill's ['iron curtain'] speech' when invited to do so in the Commons and Bevin viewed it 'with grim satisfaction.' The House of Commons voted on ratification of the North Atlantic Treaty Organisation on 12th May 1949 (which was, with ironic coincidence, the same day that the Russians lifted their 324-day land blockade of West Berlin). Churchill took the opportunity to taunt the 105 left-wingers who had supported a motion of censure against him for the Fulton speech, in which he had apocalyptically assigned the atomic bomb as God's gift to America so that, in alliance with the other English-speaking nations, it could liberate Eastern Europe and stem the Russian hordes. 'Where are they all now?' he asked. About a hundred simply sat on their hands, with only four voting against ratification.

The influence of Ernest Bevin on the events leading up to the establishment of NATO - and with it the decisive defeat of the American isolationists - was enormous. His advocacy of Western Union in a speech in the Commons in January 1948 led directly to the Brussels Treaty of March 1948 between Britain, France and the three Benelux countries, which alliance became in turn the core of NATO. His prompt response to the proposal of General George Marshall (successor to James Byrnes as US Secretary of State) - in a visionary speech, 'directed not against any country or doctrine but against hunger, poverty, desperation, and chaos,' made at Harvard on 5th June 1947 - 'that the United States should do whatever it is able to do to assist in the return of normal economic health in the world, without which there can be no political stability and no assured peace,' ensured a speedy launch for the Marshall Plan. This was to prove of great importance not only for the rapid recovery of the countries of Western Europe, but also for their continuing co-operation and hence, ultimately, for the European Economic Community and the Organisation for Economic Co-operation and Development.

Historians differ over whether or not Bevin genuinely hoped (as Marshall himself did) that Russia would accept Marshall Aid and encourage the countries of Eastern Europe to do so too, though there is evidence in his favour. Be that as it may, given the intransigence and miscalculation of the Soviet leadership, the consequences of the Marshall Plan were not wholly benign, but divisive too; while with the establishment of NATO, to quote Morgan: 'The polarization of the world between East and West was finally confirmed.'

The consequences of the Cold War for the world as a whole, but especially for the dispossessed masses of the Third World, are incalculable but horrendous. The consequences for Britain are in some respects all too calculable. In collusion with the Great Power delusions of British statesmen, they meant - besides the follies and crimes already chronicled - direct involvement in the devastating war in Korea; complicity in the even more terrible war in Vietnam that spilt over into Laos and tragic Cambodia; complicity in many other acts of slaughter and repression carried out or fostered by the world's preceptor and policeman; the continuation of military conscription for seventeen years after the end of the Second World War; and the imposition of a burden of so-called defence expenditure which was at times greater per head of population than that borne by the United States and which always substantially exceeded that of our other NATO allies. This distorted the economy, constantly diverting precious human, material, and financial resources from being deployed to better the life of the people. It made it more difficult for us to pay our way in the world by trading successfully, let alone to afford much help to less fortunate nations. More directly, our swollen defence budget led to a sickening series of shameful arms deals, in which 'helping our balance of payments' jockeyed with 'sustaining our defence industries and defence jobs' and the age-old shibboleth of 'strategic interests' as justification. (A noisome specimen or two of gun-running deals made by the Callaghan Government on such morally shaky grounds will be examined later.)

The culminating folly of the struggle to retain Great Power status was the development of Britain's own nuclear deterrent, an act mocked, as proliferation gathered pace, in Tom Lehrer's song 'I wanna have a little bomb like you.' With America refusing to share its nuclear power know-how with Britain, despite the substantial contribution British scientists had made to it, Attlee and Bevin (who apparently deployed the cogent argument that it was important for the Union Jack to fly over a British atom bomb), launched this project in secret, without even Cabinet discussion at any stage. It only became public - and indeed parliamentary - knowledge after the Tories had returned to power. After the successful explosion of Britain's prototype atom bomb on the Montebello Islands, off the north-west coast of Australia, in October 1952, Churchill (once again Prime Minister) in a Commons statement, warmly congratulated all those concerned in arming Great Britain with this fiendish weapon, adding: 'I should no doubt pay my compliments to the Leader of the Opposition and the party opposite for initiating it.'

To at least some of those on the Opposition benches this must have been mortifying; but the Labour leaders' love-in with the bomb went on and on. It endured through Nye Bevan's volte-face at Brighton in 1957, when, anticipating his transmutation from shadow to substance following the next general election, he told Conference that to pass the unilateral nuclear disarmament motion they were debating would be to propose sending the next foreign secretary 'naked into the conference chamber...to preach sermons'; through Hugh Gaitskell's contemptuous defiance of Conference when it did vote for unilateralism at Scarborough in 1960; through Wilson's and Callaghan's under-the-counter Polaris submarine nuclear missile development programme code-named Chevaline, pursued with scornful disregard of Labour's 1974 Manifesto pledge not to develop a new generation of nuclear weapons; through Neil Kinnock's neurotic nuclear juggling act ('now you see the bomb, now you don't...') - impelled, like his hesitancy in making anything of the 'peace dividend' which the end of the Cold War offered, by his fear that his political opponents would call him unpatriotic - as he approached, apparently, the threshold of power at the very moment when it was plain for all to see that so far as those in this little island are concerned the unilateralist case had been vindicated by history.

The heart sickens. But what was to be expected from a party whose leaders could have found no answer to the insane logic of Winston Churchill's son Randolph, who, when Britain's strike-force of Vulcan bombers armed with hydrogen bombs became fully operational in 1958, rejoiced because: 'Britain can knock down twelve cities in the region of Stalingrad and Moscow from bases in Britain and another dozen in the Crimea from bases in Cyprus. We did not have that power at the time of Suez. We are a major power again.'? Commenting on Truman's spine-chilling reassurance to General de Gaulle when he expressed his apprehensions of Russian military aggression in Central Europe, that there was nothing to fear, since America would use the atom bomb against any nation that became aggressive, Ambrose writes:

> 'The strategy would later be called massive retaliation. The trouble with it was that even as early as 1945 it bore little relation to reality... Should the Russians realise the West's worst fears and march across the Elbe, the most that bombs could achieve would be retaliation on principal Russian population centers, which would kill tens of thousands but which would not hamstring the Russian war machine. Stalin would match American destruction of Moscow with Soviet occupation of Western Europe. The Red Army was just as effective a deterrent as the atomic bomb.'

All that the nuclear arms race ever did achieve was the ultimate abomination of the doctrine of 'mutual assured destruction', a kind of mutual suicide pact that in the event would willy-nilly take the rest of the world along with the subscribers. Madness there has been aplenty, but as yet no superpower leader mad enough to activate that pact.

Of her own volition - or rather that of her rulers - Britain made as big a contribution to this folly as she was able - punching, indeed, not only above her weight but well above her wit! And by the roll of the historical dice it fell to the first Labour leaders with plenary powers to make the choices that determined Britain's role in the world for the next half-century. Had they chosen differently, and more in accordance with their proclaimed principles, it may well have been too late by the time the Tories returned to office for them to try to reclaim Britain's great power status with any credibility at all. Kenneth O. Morgan rightly says: 'It is easy to go too far in criticizing or debunking the Attlee government.'

Nevertheless, he himself is severe enough in assessing its record on foreign affairs and defence. 'Caught up in cold-war postures' and the defence of 'old imperialist commitments', and responding to a perceived threat from Russia which time 'seemed to show to be increasingly illusory,' he says:

> '...the Attlee government committed Britain to a rearmament programme which was economically damaging and politically naive. The secret decision to commit the country to an independent nuclear weapons programme, which no government minister had the scientific expertise to understand, consorted ill with the proclaimed desire to promote world peace and disarmament.'

He expresses the widespread revulsion against these policies that gathered force in the 'fifties, especially after the launching of the Campaign for Nuclear Disarmament: 'That a British Labour government could involve itself covertly in producing so horrendous an arsenal of destructive weapons seemed at variance with the moral and humanitarian instincts of a party calling itself, in any meaningful sense, socialist.' And he concludes that this 'passionate debate over major aspects of foreign and defence policy...did the party prolonged, perhaps irretrievable, damage.'

As for the long-term consequences for the cause of Socialism in Britain, since the Labour Party, however imperfect, was its main channel, they were baleful indeed. The sad truth is that, far from enabling Britain to claim 'the moral leadership of the world', Labour's adjustment 'to the realities and torments of power' (to quote Morgan again) has meant the sacrifice of more and more of its 'moral capital'. Instead of instilling the courage born of hope and feelings of fraternity, one Labour government after another has collaborated in the conditioning of its subjects - and all citizens of the self-styled 'free world' - to fear and hatred.

CHAPTER 14

Trade wars and tribalism

'Within the tribe the rule of "each for all" is supreme so long as the separate family has not yet broken up the tribal unity. But that rule is not extended to the neighbouring clans, or tribes...Each tribe, or clan, is a separate unity...Therefore, when it comes to a war the most revolting cruelties may be considered as so many claims upon the admiration of the tribe. This double conception of morality passes through the whole evolution of mankind, and maintains itself until now.'

Peter Kropotkin, *Mutual Aid* **(1902)**

If the world at large were like the Bourbons, damned by the verdict that they forgot nothing and learned nothing, we should have cause to despair. But whether or not history signifies anything, the record is not quite as black as that. It suggests, rather, that man learns from the past, but too slowly to keep pace with events, so that the lesson he is learning is perpetually out of date, appropriate for yesterday but not quite applicable today. Like warriors from dragons' teeth, aggressors may spring up anywhere at any time. Conversely, as one of the speakers (though I forget which one - Fenner Brockway, I think, though it might have been Bronowski) so memorably declared at a meeting I went to in my youth to protest at the impending execution of a group of Spanish Anarchists, 'Freedom is indivisible.' It has no frontiers and is nothing essentially to do with national sovereignty. The nation-state is simply the tribe writ large: it partitions mankind on the adventitious grounds of nationality. The struggle for national independence was one of the great epics of the nineteenth century, from the Congress of Vienna to the Treaty of Versailles and, especially for 'colonial peoples', till much more recent times. A historically imperative aspect of the fight for freedom, it was and is none the less far from being coterminous with that struggle, as the early Socialists intuitively understood. It is therefore a matter of particular poignancy to be obliged to look on as statesmen who claim to be Socialists act like any other tribal elders.

Where the 'national interest' more or less coincides with

equity, such primitive viewpoints, though still regrettable, are tolerable. One instance of this state of affairs obtaining during Callaghan's chieftainship was the demand that Britain's burden of contributions to the European Economic Community be lightened on the grounds that it was disproportionate both to the benefits received by Britain and to the country's ability to pay without seriously undermining efforts to improve national prosperity. (One cross-party faction amongst the Brits even appeared to regard the EEC levy as a modern equivalent of Danegeld!) At the time Britain stood third from the bottom of the Community's nine members in terms of gross national product, yet she was easily the main contributor to the EEC budget, with an annual deficit of £1.1 billion (around £20 for every man, woman, and child) between payments levied and payments received, effectively wiping out the whole of the balance of trade in her favour gained from her North Sea oil assets. At the same time her deficit on trade with the other EEC countries was twice the size of her EEC budget payment's deficit, £2.2 billion. Without adding in the folly of the mountainous stocks of surplus food (rising to as much as 5,000,000 tonnes of wheat, 1,500,000 of beet-sugar, 800,000 of milk powder, and 500,000 of butter, some of which was, in November 1978, flogged off to Soviet Russia and Poland at only two-thirds of the price British consumers had to pay for butter in the shops, and at a cost of £25 million to the EEC) and the fact that three-quarters of the EEC's budget was devoted to bolstering farm prices - and hence in EEC domestic terms to overproduction and in global terms to subsidised dumping on the world market - there was reason enough in Britain's extremely unfavourable situation *vis à vis* the Common Market for the tough stance taken by Jim Callaghan and his Minister of Agriculture, John Silkin, against a 2 to 2½ per cent rise in farm support prices demanded by West Germany and France and some cause for congratulations that, with the support of the EEC Commission and Italy, Britain's negotiators secured the promise of a freeze on prices until at least the second half of 1979.

Looking back at what was at the time billed as the mother and father of a row, it is both instructive and wryly amusing to recall the party manoeuvring, factional fisticuffs, and unabashed rationalisations it occasioned. Britain's Minister of Agriculture was charged by his Dutch counterpart with 'pursuing the policies of nineteenth-century capitalism in attacking the small farmers of Europe' for electoral advantage. And while Labour's NEC adopted by the sweeping majority of 19 to 4 a document describing the Common Market as 'an instrument of private profit seeking', the Tories' trade spokesman, John Nott, denounced 'the inherently Socialist manner' in which EEC monies were disbursed and vowed that when they were back in power his party would be 'fighting for the liberal policies of the Rome treaty' against 'the creeping dirigism, the electoral cynicism and the wholly unwarranted destruction of British national interests.' Almost simultaneously, his leaderene, that renowned exemplar of the counsel that the 'soft answer turneth away wrath', rebuffing Callaghan's charge that the Tories' attitude to the Market had been 'acquiescent', sanctimoniously advised the Prime Minister and his colleagues to drop 'their abrasive and critical attitude towards our partners' and to behave 'genuinely as partners'.

In this maelstrom of political manoeuvring, very few could be credited with that 'virtue of small minds', consistency; even fewer with clear-sightedness. Greater truths, such as the long-term development interests of Third World countries and the welfare of peasant farmers - not to mention the landless poor - in far-away places convenient for dumping excess EEC products, got quite drowned out in the din of reciprocal denunciation between members of the exclusive club of EEC politicians.

The ambivalent state of mind of Euro-politicians when called upon to consider the interests of underdeveloped (or as the politicially correct terminology has it, 'developing') countries was thrown into sharp relief in November 1978, during negotiations for a new trade and aid agreement between the EEC and some fifty African, Caribbean, and Pacific nations, to update the Lomé Convention. A proposal to make the new agreement subject to suspension in the event of persistent violation of human rights was strongly opposed not only by the former colonies (whose governments were understandably sensitive to any conditions that appeared to infringe their sovereignty), but by some EEC members too, especially France, while Britain's Foreign Secretary, Dr David Owen, strongly endorsed the proposal. On the other hand, the Callaghan Government was not prepared to accept the argument of the Commons Select Committee on Overseas Development that Britain should actively pursue a policy of industrial adjustment that would foster the importation of manufactured goods from the Third World; while for its part the Select Committee was sceptical of the value of the proposed human rights clause.

The human rights issue had already figured in an attempt by the Labour Government to set a good example to the major non-Communist industrialised nations in their handling of aid to the Third World. In July 1978, following the Group of Seven meeting in Bonn, Judith Hart, Minister for Overseas Development, announced that debts totalling £928 million owed to Britain by seventeen of the world's poorest nations (as defined by the United Nations' poverty yardstick of having an annual per capita income of less than 280 dollars) were to be written off. Five other 'poorest nations' were excluded from this bountifulness because of their serious violations of human rights. The unforgiven were Uganda, Ethiopia, South Yemen, Kampuchea and Vietnam. But amongst those which apparently passed the 'decent society' test were Dr Hastings Banda's squalid little autocracy, Malawi; the military dictatorship of Zia ul-Haq, Pakistan, whose deposed prime minister, Zulfikar Ali Bhutto, was languishing in prison under sentence of death; and a very poor nation-state, Indonesia, whose appalling human rights record may serve to illustrate how tortuous the reasoning, how devious the adjudication must have been in deciding whether to forgive or not to forgive the debtor nations for being too poor to repay the capitalist moneylenders.

In a report published by Amnesty in January 1979 (to mark the thirtieth anniversary of the Universal Declaration of Human Rights) in which at least 110 countries were indicted for abuses, Argentina and Indonesia were singled out for special mention, the former for the disappearance of 15,000 people in the previous two years, the latter for having had no less than 55,000 political prisoners in October 1977. The majority of them had been incarcerated since the abortive Communist uprising of 1965; others were members of different resistance movements, including guerrillas who had fought against Indonesia's illegal annexation of East Timor. At the end of 1978 the Suharto regime announced that it had freed more than 10,000 detainees during that year and that it was now holding 9,700, who it said would be released by the end of 1979.

As a meaningful act of solidarity with the Third World as a whole the Labour Government's debt-forgiveness decision (reached after much debate between ministers over the anticipated loss of 2,400 British jobs over a three-year period) was in any case little more than an encouraging gesture. Responding to a challenge from Robert Rhodes James on the Opposition benches that the House should not have been simply informed of the decision by the

Minister but that parliamentary approval should have been sought for a measure costing the country around £60 million a year, Mrs Hart assured him that the cost would be met from the aid programme already announced and would not entail new expenditure.

Such a rob-Peter-to-pay-Paul approach to figures, such a juggling of monies to counterfeit generosity, always makes it difficult to know just what a government is so virtuously spending, or alternatively and equally virtuously, saving. But judging Labour on its own best self-presentation, as in the challenge of supreme stinginess hurled at the Tories by Labour's spokesperson for Overseas Development and Co-operation, Ann Clwyd, in December 1990, it would appear that Britain came the closest it ever did to hitting the target of 0.7 per cent of GNP set as the UN Second Development Decade (i.e. the 1970s) target for aid from the richer nations to the poorer, in the Wilson/Callaghan years, with 'an all-time high' of 0.51 per cent of GNP. That fell to 0.31 under the tender care of Thatcher & Co. It should be said at once, however, that the top figure claimed for Labour by Ann Clwyd (which is in any case nothing to boast about) is at least a third higher than the generally accepted figures for official British aid during the 1970s, and that Britain's recognised peak performances of over 0.5 per cent occurred in the early sixties under the other Harold, Macmillan. But it is more important to remark how low a priority Third World aid has been to Tory and Labour governments alike, and to note their paramount concerns even when 'in the humour for giving'. Typically, for example, two-thirds of British aid has been directly tied to the purchase of British goods, and arguably has been primarily of benefit to the donor. Truly it is said, 'It is more blessed to give than to receive.'

As in other spheres, the motives of the Labour leadership in the matter of Third World aid were honourable enough. But Socialist objectives were all too often compromised or confounded (as Bentham would surely have judged) through lack of courage to discriminate in their conscientious calculations between the lesser and the greater good. In a number of more extreme cases the consequences of decisions reached after appropriately agonised appraisals were nothing less than baleful.

Above everything else, the Callaghan interregnum was blighted by the swelling spectre of unemployment. As already indicated, Government ministers were right always to take into account the practical effects of their policies and actions on the principle that had, from the 'forties onwards until the noisome eruption of Thatcherism, been accepted by all parties - the right to a job. They were wrong, however, to let it outweigh every other social and moral consideration. One especially heinous instance of this morally debilitating inclination to do a deal with the devil so long as he was offering employment was the Hoffman La Roche affair. This Swiss pharmaceutical leviathan, which was currently selling world-wide some £750 million worth of drugs at an estimated net profit of £150-200 million (and which, incidentally, was heavily implicated in ethically dubious drug-pushing in the Third World), was induced to build a factory in Scotland for the production of vitamin C by a government contribution of nearly one third of the construction costs. The £45 million grant was justified on the grounds that the site of the plant, Dalry in Ayrshire, was in an area of very high unemployment which was on the point of more than doubling to nearly thirty per cent as a result of the British Steel Corporation's decision to end steel-making in the Garnock Valley. However, the price-tag on the 450 permanent jobs to be created was £100,000 apiece.

Moreover, only a few years earlier the beneficiary of this government handout had been caught out in an act of gross exploitation (even by the shameless standards of pharmaceutical multinationals) of the National Health Service, to which it had been selling two commonly prescribed tranquillisers at forty times the rate it charged the Italians. The Wilson Government had accepted an out-of-court settlement under which Hoffman repaid £3.75 million excess profit out of £24 million netted from British sales - and was then allowed substantial price increases! And this was the company that, with the connivance of the Swiss legislative and judicial authorities, had, in 1973-74, played a part worthy of a despot of Mediaeval or Renaissance times, by causing one of its own executives, Stanley Adams, to be tried in camera and imprisoned for industrial espionage. His 'crime' was that he had alerted the EEC Commission to the company's practice of making 'loyalty' payments to retailers to push its products - a practice which breached EEC laws and the trade treaty between the EEC and Switzerland.

But however reprehensible it may have been for a 'Socialist' government to kow-tow in this way to corporate capitalism (even if it was in their judgement 'in the national interest'), at least in the case instanced above the sales products were intended to be life-enhancing, not, as in the most dubious market of all, nicknamed in a notable study by Anthony Sampson 'the arms bazaar', death-dealing. In May 1978 representatives of 149 States - every single member - of the United Nations met in New York to take part in a five-week-long Special Session on Disarmament. Sadly, since its practical achievements were so marginal, the conference could hardly be said to have marked a turning point in world history. But it was the first world-wide attempt to put a brake on the arms race since the 1932 conference held under the auspices of the League of Nations, and it surely served to make many more people realise that, since the invention of weapons of genocidal magnitude, the greatest threat was not that posed by one nation to another, but that posed by the huge hoards of weapons in every corner of the globe to the future of the whole human race. By now, three-quarters of the way through the UN-declared Disarmament Decade, global expenditure on arms was running at around $400 billions a year, a doubling of the spending rate since 1966. The arsenals of Europe alone contained about 11,000 nuclear weapons; and the destructive power of the world's stock of nuclear weapons was reckoned as equivalent to one million Hiroshima-type bombs. Expenditure on military research and development had passed the $30-billion-a-year mark, and represented, according to one estimate, some 40 per cent of all R & D. Estimates of the deployment of manpower on such work ranged from more than half the world's physical and engineering scientists to a quarter of its total scientific manpower.

In a commentary on the UN Special Session, James Cameron pointed out that the world spent more than sixty times as much on equipping each of its soldiers as it did on educating each of its children. As always, it was, of course, the weakest that went to the wall. As Harford Thomas wrote:

'The arms race has been even more damaging to Third World countries than to the rich. It has distorted and held back development perhaps more than any other single factor. It sets up a cycle of poverty-repression-militarisation. With 95 countries importing major weapons in 1976, the countries of the Third World were spending almost three times as much on arms as they received in development aid.'

Another baleful consequence, as he pointed out, was the undermining of the economic independence of many countries, 'especially of newly independent countries which become the dependent clients of their arms suppliers.'

To whom are we principally to ascribe this lamentable state of affairs? The blessings of representative democracy are not commonly available in Third World countries. On the contrary, tin-pot dictators and their loathsome henchmen tend to spring up like mushrooms on their soil, and their one unfailing need is to arm themselves against rivals for power and against the people at large. This provides the market for the market-led economies of the democracies. If the demand is there, the capitalist's role is to supply it; ergo, the despots are primarily responsible for the arms trade with the Third World. That at least might be an orthodox economist's analysis.

Viewed from the Cold War perspective, the alternative arch-villains were the Communist countries which threatened stability in so many regions of the world by arming client-states, thus obliging the Western democracies to bolster rival powers. But the problem with apportioning blame according to such Cold War criteria is that the United States on its own, without taking into account its NATO allies, was supplying nearly three-fifths by value of the arms shipped to the Third World, almost three times the arms supplies from the Communist States. One might be tempted to conclude from this that it was from the West that this blight on the Third World principally came, if it were not that the weapons from 'the Free World' were obviously for defence, while the Communists were equally obviously busy arming aggressors. Moreover, from a Manichaean and cataclysmic standpoint it had to be appreciated that if the arms supplied for defence against Communist aggression were sometimes also the means of internal repression, that was at worst an unfortunate side-effect - collateral damage, one might call it. The way Uncle Sam in particular saw it, from the moment he pinned the global sheriff's badge on his own breast, has been pithily put as: 'He may be a son of a bitch, but he's our son of a bitch!' - an attitude which gave us a non-stop picture-show of public enemies from Syngman Rhee to Batista, the Somozas, and Ferdinand Marcos.

Furthermore, if stability and peace really were the principal objectives, it was not always clear that gunrunning was the best

172

TRADE WARS AND TRIBALISM

way to secure them. Speaking for Singapore to representatives of 87 member-states of the Non-Aligned Movement, at the Belgrade conference of July 1978, Mr S. Radjaratnam stated that since the end of the Second World War 25 million lives had been lost in 133 wars fought in Third World countries. He charged the superpowers with waging war by proxy under the doctrine: 'Let the Third World fight the Third World War.' Undoubtedly strategic considerations did play an important part in the arms trading of the two great rival power blocs; but in the case of the Western democracies at least it has at times seemed simpler and more honest to explain the gun-running as giving in to an insatiable lust to do a deal. For what it is worth, one might even make a plausible case for maintaining that the motives of the Communist gunrunners were generally purer, at least in the sense that they were less swayed by venal considerations.

But in any case, what was it but the Devil's Trade when the two superpowers and their satellites were supplying poor countries with the means of mutual slaughter? A report released by the International Institute for Strategic Studies in September 1978 noted as 'a new development' that a number of countries were placing orders for arms with both Eastern and Western suppliers 'who are clearly in competition.' Four States forged by Western imperialism to fragment the Arab peoples - Syria, Iraq, Kuwait, and Libya - were named as recipients of these presents from the Pandora's Box of the arms manufacturers, and the report noted that the weapons traded were 'technically very well advanced and comparable to systems now being deployed by NATO and the Warsaw Pact.'

In this Devil's Trade, Britain, then as now, did somewhat better than dabble. Writing in *The Observer*, Anthony Sampson pointed out that as the representatives of the 149 member-states of the United Nations were earnestly deliberating in New York on the problem of how to promote disarmament, at Aldershot the Duke of Kent was ceremonially opening the British Army Equipment Exhibition, a bi-annual trade fair designed to promote the export of British weapons, particularly to Third World countries:

> 'Britain's cross-purposes are well defined. In a carefully
> written speech at the UN two weeks ago, which was
> much praised by other delegates, Mr Callaghan spoke of
> Britain's central role in disarmament, and stressed that
> the suppliers of arms had a special responsibility to

practise restraint. Yet only two weeks later teams of
British salesmen are shouting their wares at an arms
fair, to sell still more guns, tanks and ammunition to
customers abroad. Where exactly does the "special
responsibility" lie?...Among the images of the 1970s
which may look most incomprehensible to our
grandsons could be an arms fair under Royal patronage,
enthusiastically selling weapons to the Third World.'

Weapons were, in fact, amongst Britain's most successful exports,
worth around £1 billion a year to her balance of trade. The
Stockholm Peace Institute computed her share of the global arms
trade in so-called conventional weapons at 9 per cent, ranking her
third equal with France, after the superpowers' slices of 38 per
cent for the USA and 34 per cent for the USSR.

Nor were the Wilson and Callaghan governments of the
'sixties and 'seventies conspicuously more fastidious than the Tories
about the humanitarian credentials of their customers. 'The
beginnings of the British Government's extended role as an arms
salesman were found, oddly enough, under the Labour Government
soon after it came to power in 1964, in the first flush of idealism,'
writes Sampson in a section of *The Arms Bazaar.* Here he chronicles
the way in which a strike-force of Harold Wilson's ministers
demonstrated their marketing skills in a massive three-way arms
deal involving selling to Saudi Arabia British fighters it did not
really want and buying second-choice American fighters with the
proceeds. Every year the Defence Sales Organisation set up by Denis
Healey in 1965 as an agency of the Ministry of Defence organised
a floating bazaar aboard a British warship that sailed half way round
the world to flog weapons to the natives. Ports of call for the three-
month 1978 cruise were in Tunisia, Nigeria, Brazil and Colombia.
This followed the successful 1977 voyage to the Far East which
had secured orders for armoured vehicles from Thailand and the
Philippines and for Hawk training aircraft from Indonesia.

The 'special responsibility' that Jim Callaghan acknowledged
Britain had as a major arms supplier was most conspicuously
displayed in three highly volatile regions of the world - the southern
half of South America, the Persian Gulf, and Indo-China. In South
America two vicious military dictatorships, Chile and Argentina,
had spent 1978 sabre-rattling in a century-old dispute over which

held sovereignty over three small islands at the very tip of the continent, ownership of which also conferred jurisdiction over the adjoining waters and continental shelf. War was averted by a Vatican offer to despatch a special envoy to mediate between the rival powers. But meanwhile both sides indulged in an arms shopping spree, the better to flex their military muscles. France was the market-leader in satisfying these unsavoury customers, but Britain was a keen (not to say crawling) competitor. In July there were disturbing rumours that Argentina was on the point of withdrawing from a very-nearly-clinched £500-million deal to purchase six of Britain's most advanced gas-turbine-powered frigates, each equipped with a helicopter and armed with British Seacat and French Exocet missiles. In high dudgeon after the diplomatic row over its claim to the Falkland Islands, so the story went, Argentina had decided to place the order with the West German firm Blohm and Voss instead. However, ruffled feathers were sufficiently smoothed down again by the end of the year for Whitehall to announce - as Chile's version of 'the Great Dictator', Augusto Pinochet, squared up to Argentina's three-man junta in the Beagle Channel - that one of the triumvirate, the air force commander General Orlando Agosti, was to visit Britain in January as a guest of the Ministry of Defence.

Apart from the obliging policeman who shows Mr Punch how the hangman's noose works by placing it around his own neck, it is difficult to recall a stupidity in the conduct of our affairs of state to match this arming of a hostile, ruthless, and highly unpredictable foreign regime. With one exception. Had it not been for the even greater subsequent lunacy of handing Saddam Hussein the wherewithal to threaten the whole of the Middle East, one might have reasonably assumed that the lesson of this folly would have been branded on the national consciousness for ever, in the months of April, May, and June 1982, by the scorched bodies of British soldiers and sailors on the good ships *Sheffield*, *Sir Galahad*, *Sir Tristram*, and the other British vessels zapped in the South Atlantic conflict by Skyhawks, Mirages, and Exocet-armed Super Etendards sold to the Argies by our American and French allies.

But in any case, such lunacy was outclassed by the callous unconcern over the appalling human rights record of the Argentine regime. In the three years in which the junta had held sway in Argentina by the time Labour lost office in May 1979, its agents rubbed out some 30,000 of their compatriots, men, women and children, about half of whom disappeared without trace. They tortured tens of thousands more and robbed myriads of orphaned children of all knowledge of their parentage. The heart-sickening indifference of the spectator-world to the victims' fate was dramatised by what must surely rank as the supreme triumph of the keep-politics-out-of-sport school of thought, the holding of the World Cup in Buenos Aires in June 1978. As the host-nation's footballing heroes were cheered on to victory in the stadium and the world watched their triumph on its television screens by courtesy of satellite-transmission, other citizens died on the streets and in the cellars in Argentina's 'dirty war'. Such was the progress of civilisation since the days of the Roman circus!

Barely a month later the fans of one of Britain's crack teams, Tottenham Hotspur, could rejoice at the granting of work permits to two Argentinian soccer stars, Osvaldo Ardiles and Ricardo Villa, super-mercenaries bought by their new club for a transfer fee of £750,000. Norman Atkinson, the Labour Party's treasurer and a member of its International Committee, in welcoming the announcement, voiced the widespread concern over the situation of dissidents in Argentina and hoped that political asylum would be facilitated, but added: 'I am convinced, however, that the granting of visas to these two exceptionally gifted footballers will assist that process.'

Experienced political refugees would probably be somewhat puzzled by our Norm's mental processes. Nearer to the mark, surely, were the comments made a few weeks earlier by the Latin America Bureau. It considered that, in dealing with countries in most of which three-fifths of the total income was appropriated by an elite fifth of the population and most of the people were paupers, 'British policy is at sixes and sevens,' and that Labour Party protests about the nature of the regimes, notably in Chile, Brazil and Argentina,' simply could not be squared with Britain's exporting of capital goods, including arms, to a region where 'they not only fail to benefit the vast majority of the population...but actually serve to increase unemployment.' The Bureau characterised the essentially unchanged nature of British policy under Labour with devastating moderation: 'The day-to-day work of the British embassies in Latin America is a difficult and complex one, appearing to stand by civilised values while at the same time doing nothing which would blunt the trade offensiveness of British business.'

CHAPTER 15

The global-stability jigsaw puzzle

> 'The dead do not know how history is made. They have
> fed it with their blood; what comes after, they never
> learn...The dead have never spoken...They have
> forgotten once and for all the precious uses of the voice.
> It is we, then, who must speak in their name. We must
> plead the cause in their absence.'
>
> **Vasilis Vassilikos, Z**

The rationalisations for the even greater lunacy referred to above were rooted in the 1978-79 revolution that drove Mohammed Reza Shah Pahlavi from his 'Peacock Throne'. The Pahlavi dynasty owed its kingdom primarily to the British, who in the aftermath of the First World War helped Reza Khan (a former officer in the Iranian Cossack Brigade which was a contingent of the White Russian forces operating in the southern regions of the Caspian Sea) to seize power in Persia. The object was to establish a buffer-state against the threat of Bolshevik expansionism. However, eventually, in 1941, to counter his friendship with Germany's Nazi regime, the British joined with Soviet Russia in forcing him to abdicate in favour of his 21-year-old son. Mohammed Reza reigned as a puppet shah during the joint occupation of his country by the Red Army and British forces, from 1941-1946, before securing a spurious and inherently unstable form of independent power as the ruler of a key piece of the Truman Doctrine global-stability jigsaw. In 1955, with Britain and Pakistan, Persia acceded to the Baghdad Pact initiated by Turkey and Iraq to maintain security and peace in the Middle East. When Iraq itself withdrew, following the revolution of July 1958 which overthrew its monarchy, Persia remained a member of this loose alliance, henceforth called the Central Treaty Organisation. Within two months of the ousting of the Shah, Iran (as the country, reverting to its more authentic name, now called itself) had withdrawn from the pact and CENTO had collapsed.

The Shah had survived by a whisker the threat to his power posed by the de facto alliance between Mossadeq's National Front and the Communists of the Tudeh Party, turning the country into a virtual autocracy after the engineering, in 1953, of a military coup against his own government. (In one of history's endless ironies, the American colonel who masterminded this coup was the father of the commander-in-chief of the forces launched in the United Nations' authorised Desert Storm campaign against Iraq in January 1991.) With the eager assistance of Western capitalism and NATO gunrunners he had imposed on Persia a high-technology superstructure (with a commensurate standard of living for its elite but only marginal improvements for its impoverished masses) and made it a major Middle Eastern power. Then the sons and grandsons of those 'Persian pipsqueaks' who had so pestered our Herbert in the dying days of his power and glory had struck again, but this time most destructively in the far more virulent form of Shi'ite fundamentalism.

The degree of symbiotic complicity between the 'free world' leaders and the Shah is a measure of their mutual folly and amorality. If the Shah owed his throne to Western imperialism, the leading Western powers became dependent on him for a not insubstantial portion of their prosperity. At the time of the revolution Britain depended on Iran for some 16 per cent of its oil consumption, while Western Europe as a whole received a similar proportion of its needs from the same source. Of America's oil imports, around 10 per cent came from Iran. Israel and South Africa, denied supplies by the Arab states, were highly dependent on Iranian oil, Israel for up to 60 per cent of its consumption, South Africa for no less than 90 per cent. It was a hammer-blow to them when the revolutionary regime joined the Arab boycott against them.

Britain and the United States suffered a serious loss in another respect. Despite Mossadeq's nationalisation of Iran's oil industry, they had retained a strong hold on its products. While the Shah remained on the throne, a consortium led by British Petroleum and including Shell and the five principal American companies continued to market 80 per cent of the country's oil, with the National Iranian Oil Company handling only the remaining fifth. A strike of the country's oil workers, who vowed they would not return to work until the Shah left the country, was not the least of the reasons that persuaded him the game was up. When, after a ten-week break from around Christmas 1978, the taps were turned on again (on the anniversary of Mossadeq's death, a date picked as a symbolic gesture of defiance), it was made clear that the greatly reduced supplies would go to the highest bidders. It was a shaken world market in which, to take an extreme example, Japan, wholly dependent on oil imports for its position as world leader in manufactured exports, was prepared to pay up to 50 per cent more than the official prices set by the Organisation of Petroleum Exporting Countries, while OPEC members were raising their prices by up to 15 per cent. It was anticipated that the total cost to the European Community of oil imports would rise by between 22 and 25 per cent in 1979, and that largely as a consequence of this, EEC growth would be cut by 1 per cent. (In the event, of course, the recession turned out to be much more severe, and for Britain, under the harsh regimen prescribed by the Thatcherites, particularly devastating.) At the beginning of March 1979 the chairman of the International Energy Agency representing most of the world's leading economies issued an alarming warning that the world could not sustain the explosive price rises of recent weeks. Agency members agreed on a 5 per cent reduction in oil consumption, while even in the land of the freedom to guzzle gas President Carter submitted to the Congressional energy committees a standby rationing plan that could limit drivers to little more than a gallon a day if he were to declare an emergency.

For Britain, with its quickening flow from its North Sea assets, the oil crisis would have been the least of its worries had it not been so vulnerable to a downturn in the world economic situation. The almost daily announcements of the cancellation or deferment of lucrative British contracts with Iran had a more direct and immediate impact. *Guardian* economics correspondent Jane McLoughlin described the Shah's downfall as looking like delivering 'a body-blow to British industry.' Around 170,000 jobs in Britain were directly dependent on trade with Iran. Among the Shah's many grandiose schemes was the ambition of making his country the hub of the motor industry in the Middle East, with a production target of a million cars a year by 1985. These were to be built from kits supplied by Western motor manufacturers, including Volkswagen, Renault, the Peugeot-Citroen-owned Chrysler UK, and British Leyland. These schemes, along with export deals involving oil supply facilities, machinery, transport equipment, generating plant, road and building construction, fertiliser production, textiles, and financial services, were all put at hazard by the revolution. And the British taxpayer was seen to be a most audacious gambler, since this vigorous enterprise on the part of British businessmen had been underwritten to the tune of £1 billion by the State-run Export Credits Guarantee Board.

179

That cool billion, however, was only a fraction of the taxpayer's involuntary stake, only accounting for around a third of Britain's export deals with Iran. The most dubious deals, the government-to-government arms contracts, were outside the ECGB's remit. The Shah was the British armaments industry's most important customer outside the NATO alliance, just as he was America's. Between them, Iran and the second biggest purchaser, Saudi Arabia, accounted for 60 per cent of British arms sales. Orders for billions of pounds worth of military facilities and equipment were on the books when the Shah was driven into exile, including 1325 tanks to the value of £500 million to add to the 900 tanks already delivered, 1000 tank-transporters, anti-aircraft missile batteries with a price-tag of £400 million, four naval vessels totalling £50 million in value, and a whole military-support industrial town to be built near Iran's second biggest city, Isfahan, at a cost of around £1 billion.

These colossal military deals were more dubious than the civil transactions on two accounts. For one thing, they raised more manifest and more exigent ethical questions. It is not possible honestly to consider the arms trade in the way commerce in general is treated, as a morally neutral issue *per se*, simply involving a bargain struck between buyer and seller. But even if such questions are pushed aside, for statesmen if not for merchants, there remains the question of sense. It can be argued that civil contracts are just a matter of business judgement, with which the State need not concern itself (even if that is no longer quite true when the normal risks of business enterprise are reduced or removed by government sponsorship). Military deals, on the other hand, concern in some measure the security and perhaps even the survival of the States that enter into them.

If such reflections seem like resounding statements of the obvious, that only highlights the magnitude of the folly we are considering. The Persia of Mohammed Reza Shah Pahlavi may have appeared admirably suited to the exercise of the talents of the *realpolitik* or tribal school of foreign policy pundits, uniting in one regime, as it seemed to each successive government, of whatever colour, in both Britain and the United States, both their strategic and their economic interests. But *realpolitik* depends for its temporal triumphs on the right reading of reality. Apart from the American-manufactured tragedy of Vietnam, in no other instance, in the whole course of the second half of the twentieth century, have the Western imperialists exhibited such unenlightened self-interest. That is, of course, to leave out of this chronicle of imprudence the monstrous misconception and miscalculation of waging the Cold War that subsumes and is the primal cause of most of their other foreign policy mistakes.

As the blood of insurrectionaries stained the city streets in Iran, the American President, Jimmy Carter, sent (on 11th November 1978) his Secretary of State, Cyrus Vance, National Security Assistant Zbigniew Brzezinski, and Admiral Turner, Director of the Central Intelligence Agency, a note of indignant protest at the poor quality of the intelligence reports he had received on the Iranian situation. A top secret CIA assessment of the situation in mid-August, for instance, came to the almost unbelievably complacent conclusions that 'there is dissatisfaction with the Shah's tight control of the political process, but this does not threaten the Government', that 'Iran is not in a revolutionary or even pre-revolutionary situation', and that 'those who are in opposition, both violent and non-violent, do not have the capability to be more than troublesome.' Apart from the irreconcilable fact that many independent observers, including the more perceptive media correspondents, were far from being so sanguine about the outcome of events (as any diligent newspaper reader could have attested), there was the huge irony that, in a country awash with Western agents listening intently for signs of Soviet aggression, the omnipresent clamour of internal revolutionary upheaval went unheard by imperialism's servants and their masters.

After the fall of the Shah, a wrangle ensued between two Yankee black-belts in the art of *realpolitik*. Dr Henry Kissinger attacked the Carter administration for largely causing, through indecisiveness and a mistimed human rights policy, what he saw as an unmitigated catastrophe. The Shah, he charged, had possessed the means to resist rebellion more strenuously but 'chose not to exercise them' because he had been demoralised by 'doubts about our real intentions'. In response to his interviewer's suggestion that faulty CIA reporting was responsible for America's failure to foresee the crisis in Iran, he showed his mettle as a practitioner of US power politics by skilfully blending pure *realpolitik* cynicism with a tenuous hold on reality. He absolved the CIA of blame and said that its 'emasculation' had weakened America's ability to influence events. Five years ago, he claimed, the Shah's opponents might really have feared CIA covert action. 'Now, realistically, they no longer do.'

Kissinger's salvo provoked a withering reply from George Ball, Under Secretary of State in two Democratic administrations and adviser to President Carter at the height of the crisis, who traced its origins back to 1972, when President Nixon, counselled by Kissinger himself, began to pander to the Shah's 'obsession with elegant weapons'. As a quid pro quo for his guaranteeing oil supplies to the Western powers and policing the Gulf on their behalf, Nixon undertook to provide him with arms to put down the Kurdish rebellion, to send him military advisers and technicians, and to sell him whatever non-nuclear weapons he chose. US arms sales to Iran rocketed from a total of $1.2 billion in the 22 years up to this point, to $19.5 billion during the next 7 years; the financial burden this imposed on Iran led to big cuts in construction and high unemployment. Eventually this economic hardship, coupled with widespread corruption in court circles and the Shah's megalomania, united practically the entire country against him. There was no way America could have kept 'a hated monarch' in power, Ball declared, throwing down the challenge: 'What would Kissinger have done? Sent the Sixth Fleet steaming up the Persian Gulf?'

If unintelligence and complacency characterised America's record in shoring up the Shah, the same is true of Britain's record, as is evident from David Owen's reply to questions in the House from Labour back-benchers expressing disquiet at the Government's failure to foresee the debacle. The most he would admit to was that the cohesiveness of the forces against the Shah might have been underestimated. But he saw this as a matter of judgement and rebutted suggestions that it reflected badly on the effectiveness of our intelligence-gathering services. In short, it could be said of this by no means unique instance, that it showed that the good doctor's conduct of foreign affairs was firmly based on wishful thinking.

There is, however, a lesson of much greater import and much wider relevance to be drawn from the comprehensive disaster that this was. The likelihood of such fatal mistakes is inherent in the restricted terms of reference of the *realpolitik* approach itself. It rules out those considerations of humanity that might alert its exponents to the insufferable nature of certain situations, which may in turn upset all their rigorously pragmatic calculations. When catastrophes ensue for the realpolitikers, it is nothing but poetic justice.

Speculating in *The Guardian* on the destiny of Iran after the Ayatollah Khomeini had replaced the Shah as the man at the helm, and setting his thoughts in the context of a Muslim world struggling like the Third World as a whole for change, Altaf Gauhar wrote: 'In the Third world there is a strong feeling of disappointment with Western Governments who never seem to be able to align themselves with the masses or with their movements.' As expectation such words would be unbearably naive; as a *cri de coeur* in commenting on the conduct of a Western government which purported to subscribe to the ideals and values of democratic socialism, they have irresistible force. Just once - and far too late - David Owen spoke for the Labour Movement as he should have spoken and acted all along, when he told the House: 'These last few months have seen a dramatic change in a country of pivotal importance. We will best maintain our interests and influence by being seen to respect the judgement of peoples of the region and by working with them as they shape their own destiny.' The sorry truth is, however, that in this pivotal period in the history of the Middle East and the Muslim world, the vision of the Labour leaders seldom rose much above those preoccupations that are proper in a nation of shopkeepers.

This 'batting for Britain' style of statesmanship that was to be so brazenly promoted in Thatcher's decade put the Labour leadership on a par with the Grub Street scribblers of the popular press, whose venal and insular perceptions were castigated by Altaf Gauhar:

> 'Unfortunately the whole movement in Iran has been seen by the Western media, mainly, in terms of its effects on the political and commercial interests of Britain and the USA. Not in terms of the human beings involved in the struggle. It was not the tyranny of the regime but the 'British billions at stake' which captured the headlines...To enlist the sympathy of the working classes the media obligingly translated each cancelled contract into number of jobs lost, thus strengthening the impression that Muslim agitators were adding to Britain's economic difficulties.'

With such pressing problems as rising unemployment and the balance of trade on their minds, it was not to be expected that much thought would be spared by Jim Callaghan and his team for the fate of the Persian peasantry and proletariat. But what a comment that is on the criteria for the conduct of foreign policy that represents conventional wisdom in all three of Britain's principal political parties! In Iran, throughout 1978, the blood of militant protest scarcely stopped flowing. 'Tanks won't save the tottering Peacock Throne', warned *The Guardian* in mid-August. The answer to the rioters and to the unacceptable demands for an Islamic theocracy, it said, 'lies in the liberalisation that the Shah says he is trying to pursue, together with a real movement toward the social justice that is supposedly the inspiration of the White Revolution. It does not lie with Chieftain tanks, for when you move an armoured column on one of your own cities you make a confession of abject failure that cannot be disguised.' Three weeks later, on 8th September, Iran's 'bloody Friday', upwards of 3,000 people were massacred by the Shah's soldiers and policemen in Jaleh Square, Tehran.

Relatives claiming their dead from the Behesht Zahra cemetery were charged 'bullet money', up to 3,000 rials (£36) for each bullet found in the bodies of the victims, *Guardian* correspondent Liz Thurgood reported in almost the last of a series of brilliant despatches that earned her the accolade of expulsion from the country. The Labour Government's idea of an appropriate response to 'bloody Friday' was a personal message from James Callaghan expressing sadness 'that the disturbances should have occurred just when Iran was moving steadily towards becoming a leading industrialised society' and hope that 'the violence will not interrupt Iran's progress towards democracy and the Shah's programme of liberalisation.' It assured the Shah that 'Iran's stability and prosperity is of key importance to her friends and allies.' In such wise did the Labour Prime Minister measure up to the highest traditions of responsible statesmanship.

His message was reinforced a couple of weeks later by the messenger himself, when Britain's ambassador in Tehran, Sir Anthony Parsons, made an apparently impromptu and certainly gratuitous speech of commendation at an international trade fair. 'My government,' he told the assembled customers, 'has been heartened by the determination which your government has shown to maintain the stability, security, and progress of Iran along the paths mapped out by the present monarchy. Iran is very important for my country. We wish your government well in these tasks.'

For Britain's Foreign Secretary, the Shah was 'our ally and our friend', and when in an interview on Independent Television's

Weekend World, on 22nd October, Brian Walden pointed out that British-built tanks were being used to suppress opposition on the streets of Iran's cities, Dr Owen, quite unabashed, answered: 'Can you simply take their money, sell them tanks, which you do for a strategic interest, sell them cars, persuade them to hold down the oil price in the interests of the world, generally exert influence with them, and then, when they come under attack, just back off? That is the type of political leadership for which I have total contempt.'

Tribune Group MP Russell Kerr, who with an American sociologist and an Italian Christian Democrat MP had formed an International Commission of Inquiry which spent ten days in Iran at the invitation of the Jurists' Committee of Iran, censured the British Government for 'attempting to shore up a bloody and detested regime' that was facing 'a revolutionary upheaval which we ignore at our peril.' Describing Owen as 'profoundly mistaken in his appraisal of what is going on in Iran,' he rebuked him for his remarks on *Weekend World*: 'It is not enough to say, "We stand by our friends in time of need." This is public schoolboy rubbish which does not enhance the reputation of the Foreign Secretary.'

As the Shah imposed military government on Iran, while simultaneously promising his people to banish 'injustice, corruption, and oppression' from his kingdom, the 'public schoolboy' foreign secretary, accepting the Shah's promissory note, assured the House that we now had a guarantee that in future the government would be based on the constitution and on social justice, divorced from tyranny and oppression. Arms shipments would continue, he told left-wing critics, in the interests of stability in the region, particularly in the light of the recent coup in Afghanistan.

Right up to the very bitter end, Owen remained as cocksure as Kissinger, 'neither repentant, nor even wise after the event', in the words of a *Guardian* article by Patrick Keatley charging the Callaghan administration with playing poodle to the American president. 'We will be perfectly content to be judged by history about whether or not we chose wisely in the national interest,' Owen told the House in a statement made after the shattering of the West's strategic jigsaw in the Middle East. He took this opportunity not only to decline Tribunite Stan Newens' invitation to admit that the policies of Britain and America in supporting autocratic and military government in the Gulf and refusing to recognise the democratic forces in the area had proved a complete failure, but to show no contrition at all for Britain's aggressive marketing of homicidal merchandise.

Such as it is, the rationale behind Dr Owen's stance with regard to Britain's strategic interests (a stance which made him not only staunchly resist strong and constant pressure from the Left to stop arms shipments, but even to reject, until less than a fortnight before the Shah threw in the sponge, the calls for him to advise cancellation of the Queen's projected three-day visit to Iran - a February fixture, with Kuwait and Oman as the other targets, in her upmarket promotion of British goods in the Gulf) was his thinking concerning the forces most likely to succeed to power if the Shah fell. When the Tory right-winger Jonathan Aitken invited him to agree with the Shah's allegation that the recent violence had been stirred up by outside Marxist and Communist troublemakers, the Foreign Secretary dismissed it as a simplification. Yet his own assessment given in the *Weekend World* interview was not so different and exhibited the same brain-numbing addiction to Cold War prejudices. 'I believe it would not be in the interests of this country or the West for the Shah to be toppled,' he told Brian Walden. 'He would be toppled initially by a very Right-wing movement that would soon be disrupted by the Left, and the Left is really Communism and the Soviet Union, and some odd terrorist groupings.'

In part this echoed the 'keep firm hold of nurse' admonitions that emanated from Whitehall to counter criticism of Callaghan's letter of support for the Shah - admonitions that highlighted the reactionary and obscurantist nature of much of the Iranian opposition and pointed out that this put in jeopardy the Shah's whole programme of liberalisation. The truth of this assessment of the rebel forces is not to be denied. However, neither approval of the sound of Iran's *vox populi* nor pretensions to prophecy should have become the mainsprings of British foreign policy. With regard to the latter, even such a wise observer as Altaf Gauhar was disastrously wrong about the course of a revolution in which the warnings of the watchers in Whitehall were fulfilled as ayatollahs came to call all the shots.

And as for approval, in a leader published on the morning after Dr Owen, apologising for the imposition of military government in Iran, faced fusillades from his own back benches and more lethal flattery from the Opposition for his 'robust support' for the Shah, *The Guardian* rightly counselled: 'The stock in trade of British political discourse - moderate, democratic, conservative, reactionary - needs adjustment before it is exported to Iran.' Wisdom (even of the limited, pragmatic sort we call 'enlightened self-interest'), as well as humanity - not to mention fidelity to democratic socialism - would have lain in being guided all along by the principle Owen ultimately enunciated: not, with the *hubris* of imperialism, to seek to determine the fate of a foreign people, but honestly to help them shape their own destiny.

It might be argued that the ultimate futility of the *realpolitik* practised in the Gulf by US, British and Soviet administrations in the seventies was only fully demonstrated a decade later. Then the despotic Ba'athist ruler of Iraq, chosen as a substitute for the Shah in the case of the first two global meddlers and seen as an acceptable surrogate for Soviet-style socialism by the third, to keep revolutionary Islamic forces at bay, turned out to be not a mere monster, but a Frankenstein's monster, out of control of the imperialists of both East and West who had created him. We are still asking: 'When will they ever learn?'

CHAPTER 16

Bulldog in the China market

'Don't help on the big chariot.
You will only make yourself dusty.'

Chinese proverb

'"What did you learn in school today,
Dear little boy of mine?"
"I learned that Washington never told a lie;
I learned that soldiers seldom die;
I learned that everybody's free;
And that's what the teacher said to me.
That's what I learned in school today,
That's what I learned in school."

"What did you learn in school today,
Dear little boy of mine?
"I learned our government must be strong;
It's always right and never wrong.
Our leaders are the finest men
And we elect them again and again.
That's what I learned in school today,
That's what I learned in school."'

**From a song by Tom Paxton,
sung by Pete Seeger in the Carnegie Hall, 1963**

The Callaghan Government's third spectacular in the sorcerer's-apprentice school of statecraft - the feverish bid to sell Harrier jump-jets to China - shows just how muddle-headed, illogical, and threadbare of carefully-considered and consistently-pursued long-term objectives its foreign policy was. The soliciting hit the headlines when Britain's Chief of Defence Staff, Sir Neil Cameron, despatched to Beijing to outbid alluring arms sales propositions from the French, discarded diplomatic discretion and civil service protocol in his eagerness to clinch a deal. 'We both have an enemy at our doors whose capital is Moscow,' he told officers of the 6th Tank Division stationed near Beijing. 'Some of our problems are different, but one thing is absolutely clear to us, and that is the growing strength of the Soviet tank force. We must share, I believe, our common experience so that we are in the best position to take on the Soviet tank force if this should ever be necessary.'

His king-sized gaffe, which he self-importantly described as legitimate discussion of ' defence philosophy', provoked calls for his dismissal from the Labour left on the grounds that it damaged the West's objectives of détente and disarmament pacts with the Soviet Union and that it was an intolerable incursion into the Government's province of policy-making. As *The Guardian* pointed out, in an editorial that was curiously cautious over the issue of whether the Government should dispense with Sir Neil's services, considering that it rightly reproved him for his 'melodramatic and over-simplified way of thinking about the way great power relationships work', President Carter had recently sacked a four-star general for publicly disagreeing with official US policy on South Korea. *Pravda's* comment was more caustic: it cast Sir Neil in the role of the Russian folklore character that symbolises folly, the 'drunken hare'.

The fusillade from the Left provided the Opposition with a field-day to wave the flag and scatter-bomb the mutineers with innuendoes of treason. Disregarding the heterogeneous nature of Sir Neil's critics, who were not confined to the Left, let alone to the few who could fairly be-called 'fellow-travellers', and without admitting that no government could allow itself to be seen as letting its servants determine its policies, shadow defence spokesman Sir Ian Gilmour, speaking on the BBC's *World at One* programme, charged the critics in the Government's ranks with providing capital for Soviet propaganda: 'The pro-Soviet lobby in the Labour Party has got off the mark very quickly - as it always does - and they, of course, are not really on our side.' Labour's top brass moved swiftly, if not adroitly, to defuse the incident, the Prime Minister and the Foreign Secretary both assuring the House that nothing had changed with respect to our relations with either China or the Soviet Union, and that policy was as firmly as ever in the hands of Government ministers. Defence Secretary Fred Mulley blandly declared that, although he would have advised the Defence Chief against using the word 'enemy' if he had had the opportunity to do so: 'There is nothing in the impromptu remarks that Sir Neil made that suggests it should diminish my confidence in him as my chief military adviser.'

The show ran and ran throughout the year, with an ever-growing cast and an ever-thickening plot in which it became more and more difficult to decide who was the seducer and who the seduced. During the last quarter of 1978 mandarins popped up in Whitehall like messages in a Chinese box: in October, Foreign Minister Huang Hua (he who, in one sequence of China's stately courtship dance with the West and its allies, had visited the Shah of Persia on the eve of the Jaleh Square massacre - which was *not* a promising omen!); in November, Wang Chen, Vice-Premier in charge of industrial production; in December, Lu Tung, who, as head of China's Third Ministry of Machine Building, was in effect the country's aviation minister.

In February 1979 Britain's Industry Secretary, Eric Varley, returned the visits, with a retinue of high-powered industrialists representing British Aerospace, Rolls-Royce (which was already giving China a helping hand in its efforts to make 'a great leap forward' by signing a contract for the supply of Spey supersonic engines and licensing their local manufacture), British Shipbuilders, the National Coal Board, and engineering groups Acrow and John Brown. The prize had grown ever more alluring, Varley coming home with a two-way trade agreement with a tantalising £7 billion worth of come-ons. It was the French, the Germans, and the Americans, however, who were actually receiving all the favours. And two weeks before the Callaghan Government fell, it was announced that Dr David Owen himself would go to Beijing in the fond hope of a consummation of Britain's courtship.

What makes following these mah-jong manoeuvres more than a trivial leisure pursuit is their deadly serious context, implicating in the final analysis not just company profits nor even just jobs, but the fate of the whole world. It may have simply been par for the course for a businessman like Sir Kenneth Keith, chairman of Rolls-Royce, to maintain (as recorded by Hugh Hebert in a *Guardian* article tellingly entitled 'Can we enjoy both profits and peace?') that the nation's economic self-interest overrode all moral considerations and to tender as if it were sterling coinage the exceedingly droll Chinese claim that 'Never in our long history have we been aggressive,' to which this real life Undershaft added the clinching argument: 'They've always paid on the nail.' But the intellectual calibre of Sir Kenneth's comments no more measured up to the standards required for the successful handling of the country's foreign affairs than had Sir Neil's. Business acumen untrammelled by too many moral scruples might seem like a sound basis for practical politics, but the intelligent practice of *realpolitik* demands something more, as the careers of not a few migrants from commerce to politics attest.

However much they might have shared Sir Kenneth's viewpoint, though, even the most hard-nosed of ministers could not afford to be so dismissive of the moral issues raised by arms sales to China, since for presentational reasons concern for human rights had to be high on the agenda of the Labour Movement. The tragedy is that, for Labour's party and trade union leaders, bread-and-butter and polling considerations have again and again made it difficult in practice to distinguish between the attitudes of Capital and the attitudes of labour and of Labour. Jobs are inescapably hostage to business profits in the kingdom of capitalism. The welfare of the British working class is in every sense a legitimate and primary concern for Labour; but when it is based on relegating human rights for other peoples to the 'isn't it a pity' category of concern, Socialism is shamed and travestied. When the international committee of the Labour Party's NEC passed a motion calling for a review of policy on arms sales and protesting at the Government's decision to sell Harriers to China (with Tony Benn scourging his Cabinet colleagues for their hypocrisy in rightly condemning offences against civil liberties in the Soviet Union and giving them as a reason for the embargo on selling arms to the Russians, while overlooking China's equally unpalatable record on human rights), the Electrical, Electronic, Telecommunications and Plumbing Union denounced the committee for acting in restraint of trade! 'While Britain is trying to establish trade with China, the National Executive Committee seems intent on disrupting relations as much as possible,' thundered the EETPU, one of whose executive committee members, Eric Hammond (later to win renown in the great miners' strike of 1984 and the Wapping print workers' war of 1986) played the part of tribune of the British workers in the Varley delegation to Beijing.

It was not only with regard to China itself that the embarrassing issue of human rights became entangled with more pressing considerations of commerce and geopolitics. In its handling of diplomatic and trade relations in China's backyard (to adopt a term beloved of American imperialists) the Callaghan Government was also successful in sending a series of conflicting signals about the importance it attached to human rights. The Opposition's attacks on its subsidised shipbuilding for Vietnam (a policy which was also criticised when applied to Poland and India) were brushed aside with the argument that it was vital to save British shipbuilding from devastation during a period of world-wide slump in the industry. Yet when, on Christmas Day 1978, Vietnam, after repeated incursions into its territory by Khmer Rouge forces, launched a full-scale invasion of Cambodia and, a fortnight later, Vietnam-backed Khmer rebels overran the capital, Phnom Penh, Britain's Labour leaders joined in the chorus of indignation conducted by the US Government. On 13th February Judith Hart announced in the Commons that, with the exception of the agreements to supply cargo ships and gas turbines, which would be adhered to 'because of the contractual implications', bilateral aid to Vietnam would cease.

Needless to say, the Vietnamese regime was no paragon in the matter of human rights. However, not only did its record, on the worst estimate, compare favourably with China's, but its trespasses in this field paled into insignificance when set against the horrific crimes perpetrated by the Khmer Rouge against their own countrymen. Whatever the motives of the Vietnamese in invading Cambodia - and obviously they were for the most part rooted in what they conceived their national interest to be - to many Cambodians they came as liberators from torment and slavery. By its callous indifference to the terrible fate that had overtaken the Cambodian people, the Callaghan Government set the tone for the Tory governments that followed. The latter, in contradiction to the normal practice of British governments, refused to recognise the *de facto* government that took over in Phnom Penh and continued to treat the delegates of the infamous Khmer Rouge as the legitimate representatives of Kampuchea (as the country was now designated) at the United Nations. In such a contemptible imposture did the world at large collude for the next decade and more, to the very grave detriment of the Khmer people.

It is true that the full horror of the concentration-camp 'utopia' created by the Khmer Rouge in the fervent belief that they were constructing a society of pure communism was only revealed later by 'maverick' journalists like John Pilger (the Western media's general conspiracy of silence, suppression, and distortion in the face of Khmer Rouge 'heart of darkness' barbarism is itself a story that might well engender despair for mankind). But, belated though it was, enough of it came out in the columns of the more reputable

British papers, as the country was liberated from its silent agony, to deprive the Callaghan Government of the excuse of ignorance for its contemptible policy decisions concerning Kampuchea. Even Prince Norodom Sihanouk, that prince of opportunists (formerly king-pin in Phnom Penh, then held under house arrest by the Pol Pot Government until the day before the capital fell to the Vietnamese-backed rebels), now spoke of that 'Hitlerian and bloodstained regime...under which nearly three and a half million citizens had died from hunger, thirst, sickness, and brutality' and vowed he would not co-operate with the Khmer Rouge - though he subsequently sacrificed his finer feelings in the higher interests of his country and the hope of returning to power again. Moreover, in June 1978 the International Federation of Human Rights had issued a damning report, indicting the Khmer Rouge for mass executions, forced labour, and causing famine and disease.

China countered the Vietnamese invasion of Kampuchea, which rapidly drove the Khmer Rouge forces to the borders of Thailand, by a punitive incursion across the northern frontier of Vietnam. The Soviet Union responded by despatching a missile cruiser and other warships to the Gulf of Haiphong as a warning to China that it would not abandon its ally. As a mocking fate would have it, the Chinese attack (involving according to first reports around 150,000 men) came just three days before Varley's caravan of upmarket commercial travellers was due in Beijing. But while this spot of vexation in the Orient generated some worried expressions in Whitehall and an intensified insistence on the essentially 'defensive' character of the formidable Harrier (which, quite apart from the equivocal nature of all such claims, was authoritatively challenged by Anthony Barnett in a *Guardian* article, pointing out how effective jump-jets could be in enforcing China's claims to the Spratly Group of islands, most of which were held by the Vietnamese and lay in an area of the South China Sea where oil had been discovered), it did not dampen the salesmen's spirits as the £7 billion trade target was agreed. No more than its totally alien attitude to civil liberties and human rights, its accumulation of a nuclear arsenal, and its blunt rejection of notions of détente with the other great 'Communist' empire, did China's act of belligerence deter the Labour Government from seeking to sell it the means to enhance and exercise its power. In this respect the record of the Callaghan Government is hardly to be distinguished from that of any other British government before or since.

Apart from the commercial and national economy incentives for its attitude, there were three other reasons for its morally unwarranted discrimination against Vietnam and in favour of China and its Khmer Rouge protégés over these clashes in Indo-China. The most ostensible reason was the importance of upholding international law in a case involving the violation of a country's national sovereignty and interference in its internal affairs. But to take this explanation seriously one would need to drink oneself witless from a large bottle clearly labelled GULLIBILITY. For one thing, as already pointed out, the customary practice with regard to the recognition of foreign governments (which has nothing to do with approval but a great deal to do with common sense) was contradicted in the case of liberated Kampuchea. And for another, this refusal of recognition was wholly inconsistent with the ready acceptance of the overthrow, by an alliance of rebels and foreign troops (Tanzanian), of another monstrous regime, that of Idi Amin in Uganda - to cite but one recent instance in which outside interference had been gladly tolerated.

Of the other two reasons, one was covert and craven, namely, Britain's acquiescence in America's vindictiveness towards Vietnam. Commenting on this shameful vendetta of the world's most powerful nation against the Third World pygmy that, at a devastating cost to itself, had defeated it, *Guardian* correspondent John Gittings pointed out that the Hanoi regime had been driven into signing the 1978 'Treaty of Friendship' with the Soviet Union by Washington's rejection of every overture Vietnam had made since the end of the war in April 1975. Not even Vietnam's dropping of the demand for reparations for the devastation caused by American military might made Washington relent. On the contrary, in the spring of 1978 the United States vetoed a proposal to channel funds for the reconstruction of Vietnam through the Asian Development Bank. Washington and Beijing were on the point of exchanging ambassadors when China attacked Vietnam, and President Carter promptly reassured the Chinese that the invasion would not affect the normalisation of Sino-American relations, which was 'already an accomplished fact'. According to *The Washington Post*, Beijing was even tipped off in advance that US displeasure would be purely formal, so that its unavoidable public condemnation would neither cause loss of face to the Chinese nor make Washington open to charges of collusion in the attack on Vietnam.

The third non-commercial reason for Britain's less than beguiling behaviour in the Far Eastern farrago was the perfectly open geopolitical objective that had lain at the heart of her foreign policy since the start of the Cold War, and that has had such disastrous consequences, most dramatically in the Middle East: the containment of the Soviet Union and her allies. But even if we accept the bunker mentality of the leading Cold War protagonists in the Western camp in order to judge on their own terms the success of their actual conduct of foreign affairs, the verdict that forces itself on one's mind is ineptitude elevated to the level of folly. The Soviet Union was sufficiently exercised by the prospective sale of jump-jets (which were after all not just high-tech aircraft but unique war machines) to China to make a formal protest, followed by two personal letters from President Brezhnev to Prime Minister Callaghan. British pique at being rebuked and squeals of 'Russian propaganda' in no way detracted from the essential truth of the statement put out by the Soviet news agency, Tass: 'To supply arms to a country whose leadership frantically attacks the idea of détente and preaches the inevitability and even desirability of a new world war means, willy nilly, encouraging the militarism of the Maoists.'

Putting in a strong bid to win the competition for authorship of the most fatuous statement ever made by a British foreign secretary, Dr David Owen told the House that while the sale of Harriers to China could affect our policy of a continuation of détente with Russia, 'What is important is how we ourselves view our foreign policy.' Lest this standing of the truth upon its head should not be deemed a sufficiently dazzling feat, he followed it up with a spot of prestidigitation. No doubt to a generally prejudiced audience his sharp asseveration that 'we must not allow any third country to dictate the scope of our foreign policy' seemed eminently reasonable. But we have only to substitute for the word 'dictate' a word more truthfully reflecting the situation, viz. 'influence', to see that to react to the Russian protest in such an affronted manner was not only simply ridiculous but a negation of rational conduct in the handling of foreign affairs. Still not content with his astonishing performance, Dr Owen tossed into the brew the question-begging non sequitur, 'We want a deeper relationship with China and defence must form part of a balanced development of our relations.' When it was announced, in mid-March of 1979, that he was to go to Beijing in the hopes of clinching a deal, he told the

Indian Journalists Association in London: 'We want to improve Sino-British relations, but not at the expense of our relations with the Soviet Union.' Which was a bit like saying: 'We want to be friends with both God and the Devil', since each of the two pseudo-Marxist leviathans viewed itself as the former and its rival as the latter.

Jim Callaghan showed equally alarming signs of believing he could have his cake and eat it. At a summit meeting of Western leaders in Guadeloupe in January 1979 he joined President Carter, President Giscard d'Estaing, and Chancellor Schmidt in pledging their governments to do everything possible to encourage ratification of the new strategic arms limitation treaty (SALT II) being negotiated between the United States and the Soviet Union. But this unequivocal endorsement of détente had no visible effect on his policy *vis-à-vis* China. 'We must reassure the Soviet Union that we do not have a Chinese card to play,' he told reporters. Yet that was exactly what he had been doing and what he continued to do. Ready enough to accuse the Russians of deeds incompatible with their words, he acted as if he gave no credence at all to Russian fears of Western intentions. In this he showed far less wisdom than some of his own left-wingers and, for example, than such a non-partisan pressure group as the Church and Nation Committee of the Church of Scotland. Its report to the Kirk's General Assembly in May 1978, had pleaded for understanding that the military posture of the Western powers was seen by the Warsaw Pact powers as at least as threatening as their own military capability appeared to the West. Furthermore, the committee pointed out that whereas the Communist world seemed to many in the West a threat to their freedom, many people on the other side of the Iron Curtain saw NATO as an integral part of a basically unjust economic system.

CHAPTER 17

No retreat for Cold War warriors

'The confusion between being 'Left' and being 'East' is over. With the end of this confusion the best defence of contemporary capitalism is broken.'
Royden Harrison, Emeritus Professor of Social History, Warwick University (19th December 1989)

Halfway through the Anglo-Chinese courtship dance, in November 1978, Labour's NEC published a discussion document entitled *Cold Peace, Soviet Power and Western Security.* The paper challenged many of the basic assumptions of establishment-thinking in the West about the Cold War, in particular that it was the Soviet Union that had set the pace in the arms race and in the introduction of new weapons systems and that it had overtaken the West in military power. No apology for the Soviet viewpoint, the document conceded that the Soviet build-up had overstepped the legitimate requirements of national security but declared that this was equally true of the West. The authors' primary concern was in fact to show that, as is commonly the case in conflicts between nation-states, the assumptions of those on each side were mirror-images of those on the other, to the serious prejudice of sane thinking. 'There is, of course, the easy assumption in ruling circles in the West that Western purposes are self-evidently peaceful and benign. No doubt the same spirit of self-righteousness informs thinking in the Kremlin.'

In their strictures on what we might call the beam-and-mote syndrome in both camps, the authors were notably restrained. They spoke in the manner of liberal humanitarians and denied themselves the right of those who subscribed (as they did) to a Socialist value-system to denounce the exploitation of Third World countries and peoples by Western capitalism and Western States indulging in economic imperialism, as the following passage on the conflict of Soviet and Western interests in the Third World shows:

'Soviet interference in the Third World is ascribed to a desire to export communism, to incorrigible

expansionism or to the irresistible exploitation of
sensitive situations. Western conduct, in contrast, is
usually described as legitimate efforts to foster their
interests and protect their security and well-being, and
that of the world as a whole. This reasoning is not very
persuasive. It quite conveniently ignores Western,
particularly American, activities in foreign countries
which less partial observers may conclude are at least as
culpable as Soviet ones.'

Even without wholly warranted conviction of the capitalist
'democracies' on the charge of economic gang-rape and robbery
in foreign lands (to leave out of the indictment crimes committed
in their own countries), these arguments are cogent, as the swiftest
of surveys will show. Omitting from the balance sheet the three
regions in which it might be argued US foreign policy has had the
most malign consequences of all, namely, Latin America, the Far
East and the Middle East, let us limit consideration to the two
superpower cockpits of Africa and Afghanistan in which (as Labour
and its dream were wasting away in Britain) the Soviet Union and
its allies were branded by the West as unquestionably the aggressors.
In the explosive Horn of Africa the Americans first intervened on
the side of Ethiopia, in order to counter the arming of Somalia by
the Russians, then on the side of Somalia when it expelled the
Russians, who promptly switched their support to Ethiopia. In short,
unbridled *realpolitik* governed equally the geopolitical manoeuvring
of both superpowers.

In Angola, on the other hand, it was the United States, not
the Soviet powers, which was the first to intervene in an internal
struggle for power that Stephen Ambrose attributes to 'major ethnic
and tribal cleavages' rather than to 'ideological splits over
communism versus capitalism', as the civil war was represented
by establishment-thinking in the West. As a matter of fact, in support
of one or other of the three main contenders for power, no less than
twenty foreign States were happy to trample on the diplomatic
precept of non-interference in another country's internal affairs.
Of the trespassers seven were black African States and one white-
ruled (South Africa), three were NATO members (the USA, France,
and West Germany), and one (Israel) was a US dependant. Of the
eight Communist States that meddled, five (the USSR and its allies)

supported the side that came out on top and three (China, North Korea, and Romania) supported their opponents. That there is precious little cause for self-righteousness and much reason for treating the whole affair as a particularly cynical example of global power politics is underlined in one particular passage of Ambrose's account in *Rise to Globalism*:

> 'American military aid, eventually totalling about $60 million, was sent secretly into Angola by the CIA via Mobuto in Zaire...In addition to [illegally] sending in advisers, the CIA made a de facto alliance with South Africa, which entered the conflict with regular army troops in September 1975. This was the first time South Africa had involved itself in a war in black Africa. It brought about a situation in which Washington, Pretoria, and Peking were fighting side by side, surely a record of some sort for politics making strange bedfellows.'

As for Afghanistan, that thumping headache for the British Raj in earlier times, it provides us with a Spanish-onion-sized opportunity to examine irony after irony as we peel off the concealing skins of moral outrage, clarion calls to defend freedom, and sundry other scraps of puffed-up rhetoric and rationalisation brought to the boil by the Soviet Union's accelerating intervention (so like America's in Vietnam) during 1978-79. But I will restrict myself to mentioning just two of the bigger ironies exposed in this episode. First there was the irony that a resurgent Islam was challenging the economic and strategic interests of both the superpowers, in America's case through revolution in Iran, in Russia's through civil war in Afghanistan. Which, of course, only compounded the irony that Washington, so sensitive to instability in its own so-called 'backyard' of Central America, was either too dumb to appreciate or too dishonest to acknowledge the apprehensions of the Kremlin at the threat posed by Islamic fundamentalism on the march in two big countries with frontiers contiguous to its own mainly Muslim-populated 'Soviet republics'.

The Labour Party discussion document referred to above appeared in a period of heightened Cold War hysteria. There were causes for this on both sides, and as each 'defensive' stratagem was answered by a counter-measure, the rationality of each side's fear was evidently confirmed. Thus misgiving mounted. In the Soviet camp, fear of American hegemony was heightened by the development of the neutron bomb to a stage where it only needed the US President's go-ahead for production to begin. (This bomb was designed in particular to stop tanks in their tracks by wiping out their crews, and thus aimed at counterbalancing the Warsaw Pact's numerical superiority in armour. It was dubbed by some 'the capitalists' bomb' because of its greater respect for property than for people! According to President Brezhnev, the Soviet Union had also invented this weapon, but had renounced its development.) Then the old Bolshevik fear of encirclement was magnified by the rapprochement between the NATO powers and a Communist China stockpiling nuclear weapons, bidding for superpower status, and now hostile to its big brother.

In the West lurid press reports of Soviet Russia's alleged aggressive intentions towards 'the free world' probably did far more to whip up anti-Soviet feelings than did the assiduous (and wholly justified) monitoring of the Soviet States' repression of their own citizens. Surely this must be so, if we are to judge by the fact that public opinion in the 'democracies' did not seem to be excessively exercised by human rights abuses in capitalist dictatorships like Argentina and Chile - except when the victims were European or American citizens. And the captive audience in the West was largely spared the distress it might have been caused had the Western media conscientiously reported the stream of true horror stories about life under Communist China's despotic gerontocracy, Kampuchea's genocidal Pol Pot regime, or the Orwellian Romania of Nicolae Ceausescu. May we never willingly collaborate with those who, like he did, would have us forget and obliterate the past. So let us forever remember that in July 1978 this egomaniacal tyrant was actually accorded by our Queen and her Labour ministers the full honours of a State Visit to Britain.

To cite just three scare stories - circulating during the first quarter of 1978 - as examples of the unflagging campaign to buttress the credibility of Cold War ideology and policies:

1) there were reports (branded by Tass as lies invented to justify the Western military build-up in general and plans to deploy the neutron bomb in particular) that Soviet scientists were

developing new strains of killer virus and microbes for military use;

2) unattributable 'intelligence sources' fed the press an imaginative scenario said to be based on NATO insight into Russian plans for a possible thrust into northern Norway by overwhelmingly superior forces deploying rocket-launched chemical weapons;

3) Swedish intelligence agencies warned that at least thirty-six West European cities could be destroyed by six Russian nuclear submarines that had been moved from the Arctic base of Kola to the Baltic port of Libau in Latvia. (To a populace conditioned to believe that a pre-emptive strike sparking off a third world war was to be feared only from 'the other side', the latter report was more likely to impress than President Carter's statement - designed to disarm critics of his arms control policies! - that just one of America's Poseidon submarines, representing less than two per cent of its total nuclear arsenal, could destroy every large and medium-sized city in the Soviet Union.)

In this climate of paranoia concerning Soviet intentions, it was hardly surprising to learn of the launching by 148 members of Congress, in conjunction with numerous illuminati with academic, military, or intelligence 'qualifications', of a bipartisan 'Coalition of Peace through Strength' campaign designed 'to reverse the unilateral disarmament trend which has made the United States militarily inferior to the Soviet Union.' This was notwithstanding the fact that the second of these assertions was not justified by the evidence available and the first was wholly ludicrous. What was even more alarming was the re-emergence of a school of thought maintaining that it was possible to wage and survive a limited nuclear war between the superpowers; that this was precisely what the Russians were preparing for, through the construction of highly-protected command and communication centres which would ensure continuity of government in such an emergency; and that the United States must follow suit.

The thinking - if we are prepared to call it that - behind this call for an urgent reappraisal of America's defence strategy (which incidentally was echoed in Britain by a Tory think-tank calculation that some fifteen million lives might be saved in the event of an unheralded nuclear engagement if civil defence were taken seriously) was that the younger generation of Soviet generals might believe in and successfully advocate a 'war-fighting' doctrine, since they were not old enough to remember the trauma of the Second World War, with its millions of Soviet dead. Both President Carter's National Security Adviser, Dr Zbigniew Brzezinski, and his Defence Secretary, Harold Brown, evidently found it conceivable that the Russians could calmly contemplate a nuclear engagement with the United States. On 25th January 1979, in his annual report on America's military situation, Brown announced a change of strategy from the 'assured destruction' of large Soviet cities to one aiming to include the targeting of every Soviet missile silo. In most pitiable words, he told Congress: 'It is tempting to believe, I realise, that the US threat to destroy a number of cities - along with their population and industry - will serve as an all-purpose deterrent. Unfortunately, however, a strategy based on assured destruction alone is no longer credible.'

Perhaps one should have expected an ambulance to drive up to Capitol Hill, and men in white coats to take the speaker away; but that would be to dream of a normal world in which sanity reigned outside the asylums. For as long as it lasts the human race should never forget that only by unmerited grace or incredible chance did it survive the forty-year stand-off between the two great nuclear-armed camps which we call the Cold War. During this period of purgatory that blighted the lives of a generation and more the avoidance of direct and catastrophic confrontation between the superpowers was perpetually balanced on the knife-edge of that lunatic 'defence' doctrine of 'mutual assured destruction', so appositely giving us the acronym MAD. (Nor should it be forgotten that this period of so-called peace was a lot more like the post-war world of Orwell's nightmare scenario in *Nineteen Eighty-Four* than Cold War warriors would willingly admit.) And during those long death-row years in which mankind seemed to many to be merely enjoying a stay of execution, *no one*, outside the ranks of the *im*moderates - secular or religious peace campaigners, libertarian socialists, and other out-on-a-limb advocates of alternative societies - seriously questioned the sanity of our nuclear statesmen, who are now so ready to congratulate themselves on having saved the world from destruction through their strength of purpose. With such a cornucopia of 'overkill' facilities still at the disposal of our leaders, we dare not say more than that the threat of Armageddon appears to have receded a little. But at least the MAD doctrine is no longer confidently proclaimed as the rock upon which we should build our hopes of salvation from the annihilation of the human race.

If the Cold War is now over, we owe the thaw which brought it to an end above all to Mikhail Gorbachev, whose essential sanity was shown, for example, by these words, spoken to an International Peace Forum in Moscow in February 1978: 'The nuclear powers must step out from the nuclear shadow, and enter a nuclear-free world, *thus ending the alienation of politics from the general norms of ethics.*' [my emphasis] If only they can hang in there long enough, most politicians are the beneficiaries of the extraordinary amnesia of electorates. The world and his wife are not greatly noted for their long memories, so that the many bad and foolish deeds of their political masters are generally soon forgiven through sheer forgetfulness, while the few good and wise ones are seldom indelibly marked up to their credit. Thus it came about that within two years of the revolutions of 1989 and the collapse of the Iron Curtain, Gorbachev had been ditched by the Russian people in favour of another drunken hare, just as President Carter had been, in November 1980, by the citizens of 'God's own country'.

All the same, it is as clear as daylight where the vision was in those critical years of 1978-79 that might have marked a new beginning for the world. Not for Britain alone were the eighties a lost decade; but looking back on Labour's last chance to pursue, if not a Socialist, at least a positively humanitarian foreign policy, it becomes all too evident that its leaders lacked the vision and the courage to let go of their Cold War certainties. (Indeed, the wry truth is that Brezhnev, the procrustean-seeming potentate of the Soviet Union - whom no one would ever accuse of allowing policy decisions to be unduly influenced by humanitarian considerations - had a clearer insight of where a saner future lay. His foreign minister, that great survivor Andrei Gromyko, even showed, in a speech pleading for significant disarmament made to the UN General Assembly in September 1978, that the Russian leaders fully understood the connection between the arms race and world poverty.) Add the fact that, in the proper Labour tradition, the leaders behaved towards the Party in the manner of managers insisting on their right to manage company and workforce, and no movement out of the mental morass was conceivable. Ironically, it was the Party's dissidents whose thinking on détente was genuinely in tune with that of the leader of the Western alliance, Jimmy Carter.

For example, the authors of the NEC document cited above concluded that the commitment of the Soviet Union to détente was 'firm and deep-seated' and their general stance was more supportive of Carter's central foreign policy objective of securing an arms control agreement with the Soviet Union than the lip-service of the Labour leaders as they sought to play their 'China card'. Just how closely in sympathy Carter and the Labour left was is shown by a marvellously candid concession Carter made to 'the other feller's point of view' in a television interview in November 1978, in the course of which he contended that the Soviet Union was no more expansionist than the United States, and went on:

> 'They want peace and security for their own people, and they undoubtedly exaggerate any apparent threats to themselves. They have to be sure that they protect themselves. At the same time, as is the case with us, they would like to expand their influence among other people in the world, believing that their system of government - their philosophy - is the best.'

In short, both Carter and the Labour left were disposed to believe Brezhnev when he said he was seeking 'irreversible détente' and appealed for peaceful coexistence based on trust and confidence between nations to replace the uneasy truce based on the balance of terror provided by the nuclear arsenals of East and West. There was nothing naive in this disposition to believe. It was not wishful thinking. On the contrary, it was rooted in sanity, reason, imagination, the capacity to empathise, and the courage *not* to believe the worst of one's enemies, however at variance their value-systems might seem. For instance, the very fact adduced by the embattled right in the West as an argument for stepping up the arms race - that the Soviet Union was devoting far more of its productive capacity to manufacturing arms than the United States - was susceptible to less paranoiac and more intelligent interpretations. Reporting from Washington on thinking in the US Arms Control and Disarmament Agency, Jonathan Steele wrote, in April 1978:

> 'The view of senior ACDA officials is that the present Soviet leadership is genuinely anxious for strategic arms control. The Russians spend twice as large a proportion of their gross national product on defence as the US.

The drain is causing increasing consumer problems. Secondly, the present leadership has made a political commitment to the new SALT treaty, and cannot face the alternative of failure. Throughout the 1976 [presidential] election when the Americans were stalling, the Russians continued to push for a treaty. Thirdly - and not necessarily the least important reason - the Russians are afraid that if the arms race goes ahead unchecked, they will lose.'

Even in the case of the USA, 'defence' expenditure, running at 25 per cent of GNP, represented a prodigious waste of the country's resources. For the Soviet Union, trying to keep up was a crippling burden. In Machiavellian minds, indeed, such a calculation may have been considered a conclusive argument for stepping up the arms race, and - mirroring the maxim they pinned on to and professed to despise in their ideological enemies, that 'the end justifies the means' - it may have wholly excused to themselves the lies they told about the military strength of the Warsaw Pact powers.

President Carter's efforts to bring more safety, more sanity, and more humanity into the world have seldom attracted the credit they deserve. That, with the notable exception of the Camp David accord between Israel and Egypt, they were mostly fruitless is arguably more the fault of his 'friends' than of his foes. His sheer perseverance in seeking a new Strategic Arms Limitation Treaty to update SALT I was admirable, even though the bizarre fact must never be overlooked that both SALT I and SALT II (which was signed by Carter and Brezhnev in June 1979 but never ratified by the US Senate!), far from being *dis*armament agreements, were only agreements to limit the multiplication of overkill.

History bears out those who were capable of calmly considering a geopolitical situation in which the 'Communist' powers were if anything even more 'cabin'd, cribb'd, confined' than their 'democratic' enemies. It does not vindicate the more frenzied fears of such Cold War addicts as the astounding Dr Henry Kissinger. In an interview published in *The Economist* in February 1979 Kissinger said that a general nuclear war was unthinkable and would be an 'abdication of moral and political responsibility'. But the main thrust of his argument - that the world 'could be heading into a period of maximum peril' since 'the Soviet Union may perceive a period [of five to seven years]...in which its military power is potentially dominant' and that therefore the United States, instead of increasing its ability to retaliate against a Soviet attack, should strengthen its counter-force capability of destroying military forces targeted against the West - could be taken as supporting the case for a lower nuclear threshold, pre-emptive strikes, and a winnable mini-nuclear war.

Moreover, given his Metternich-like subscription to an often intolerable *status quo* - or, in the modern geopolitical terms he employed, to 'the existing political equilibrium' - and his conviction that the Russians were mainly responsible for upsetting this by their intervention in, for instance, Ethiopia, Angola, Afghanistan, and Cambodia, Kissinger naturally felt that it was a mistake for the Guadeloupe summit to reassure the Soviet Union 'rather than convey the imperative of some acceptable code of conduct.' He believed that behind a facade of unity with President Carter the British, French, and West German leaders shared his view that 'timidity increases our dangers and confuses our policies', and he hoped they would soon speak out. (Kissinger's fear that a new SALT agreement would simply give the West a false sense of security was particularly ironic since he was the chief architect of SALT I, signed in 1972, during Nixon's presidency. His volte-face can be explained, however, by the fact that the two nuclear superpowers were now more nearly equal in military might: Russia had caught up!)

To exude reassurance regardless of the circumstances was the avuncular Jim Callaghan's most conspicuous political talent. Remember his studied air of astonishment, on returning from France's tropical jewel island of Guadeloupe to the bleak winter of a Britain in turmoil, at being greeted by the press gang with demands to know what he thought of the crisis? 'What crisis?' his raised eyebrows, if not his lips, asked. Unhappily, however, heroic imperturbability and soothing sounds proved no substitute for measuring up to reality and taking the appropriate measures, as was soon to be shown at the hustings. While as for his performance on the world stage, how could he expect the Russians to be reassured by mere rhetoric about *not* 'playing the China card' when that was patently his intention.

In his autobiography *Time and Chance*, James Callaghan states that he shared both Carter's conviction that 'both sides possessed far too many nuclear weapons for the purpose of deterrence' and his objective of reaching a SALT II agreement with the Russians. Judging from the way he writes about a memorable meeting in Moscow in 1975 at which President Brezhnev treated Harold Wilson and himself to 'a passionate harangue on the evils of nuclear war', there would also seem to be no doubt at all that he shared Carter's trust in Brezhnev's commitment to 'irreversible détente'. Callaghan says: 'I had no doubt we had listened to the real Brezhnev, and I was convinced of the sincerity of his horror of total war, a sentiment shared by all of us who had experienced the Second World War.' Yet for all the sense and sensibility he shows - such as, for instance, his counsel that 'despite our differences in ideology and philosophy, and notwithstanding the harsh Soviet position on human rights, we should hold a steady course in dealing with the Soviet Union' - he was quite prepared to jeopardise détente with Russia in order to pull off unsavoury deals with China. And for all his expressed conviction that 'it is impossible to believe the security of any one of us was enhanced by the developments of the early 1980s,' the stance taken by him and his lieutenants, most notably David Owen, contributed to the panic over Russia's deployment of SS20s (a temporary advantage which Russia offered to bargain away - an offer which fell on deaf ears) and also helped to lay the groundwork for the West's response with Pershing IIs and cruise missiles, thus heightening not lessening the balance of terror.

In a debate on the defence estimates in March 1979 Labour left-winger Frank Allaun accused Tory MPs and the Tory press of misleading the British people and psychologically preparing them for a war with Russia. There was plenty of substance in the charge when, for example, a Heathite like Peter Walker, who was generally reputed a moderate, could substitute the rhetoric of 'Reds' xenophobia for serious strategic analysis and expect to get away with it, as he had done a year before Allaun's indictment, in a nationally-reported speech to constituency members. In terms reminiscent of the American right, he characterised the West's attitude towards a Russian military build-up which, according to him, would give the Soviet Union the power to 'blackmail' the world within a decade, as 'a perpetual posture of calculated cowardice'. With a fine disregard for historical truth with respect to the age of appeasement, apathy, and general indifference to the fate of foreigners, Jewish or Gentile, not to mention his unrecognisable picture of the current climate of fear and weapon-hoarding, he instructed them:

'Britain's complacency to the Soviet danger is even
more frightening than the disarmament of the 1930s.
Perhaps because Hitler looked nastier and was more
exposed to the media than Mr Brezhnev, perhaps
because his treatment of the Jews and other human
beings was of greater public knowledge, there was at
least some interest in the menace he created.'

(It would have been of greater service to his country - if not to his
party - to repeat the admonition against complacency that the visibly
decaying Brezhnev had made on a visit to West Germany, when he
warned the world: 'It is easy to take peace for granted after thirty
years of it in Europe...' To which he added the poignantly telling
parallel: 'As long as one is not sick, one even becomes complacent
about one's health'.)

Of course, one can consider such onslaughts as Peter
Walker's, along with side-swipes at Labour's Foreign Affairs and
Defence ministers as 'weak and inexperienced', as simply par for
the course in the rough and tumble of British party politics.
Naturally, as the moment for putting to the test that very special
kind of truth that is manifested once every four or five years as the
general will in the polling booths drew close, the Tories played the
patriotic card with ever more shameless abandon. And this despite
the Government's honouring of its pledge to NATO to increase
'defence' spending by three per cent in real terms, in preference to
honouring its 1974 pledge to the British electorate to reduce military
expenditure. But while it might not be quite in order to suggest that
Frank Allaun's charges of conditioning the public for war could
equally have been directed at the leaders of his own party, it is
impossible to avoid the conclusion that, whether for reasons of gross
miscalculation of Russia's intentions or of 'calculated cowardice'
with regard to the verdict of the voters, or both, the Callaghan
Government failed to counteract the long-conditioned fear of a
Soviet attack on the West.

It never was a question of whether there was any reason for
the West to fear the Soviet Union (still less of whether the kind of
society it represented was acceptable) - nor, except in the heads of
absolute pacifists, of massive unilateral *dis*armament - but of calm
consideration of where the greater dangers and disadvantages lay.
Then it should have been a matter of holding (in Jim Callaghan's

own words) 'a steady course' - just so long as it was in a sensible direction and not heading straight for a whirlpool. In fact the Callaghan Government tried to steer in several directions at once, like a pirate ship in the midst of a flotilla of merchantmen unable to make up its mind which was the greatest prize. Did it agree or disagree with Frank Allaun's warning in the March 1978 defence spending debate? 'The threat to humanity is not the possibility of a Russian invasion,' he said. 'It is the arms race itself which is taking us towards a nuclear war.' The fact that we cannot answer this question is a measure of the Government's muddle and its failure.

As has been shown, one of the reasons for this was its determination to treat death-dealing devices as just another kind of commodity to keep the ship of state afloat, an attitude which comes over particularly clearly in Defence Secretary Fred Mulley's remarks during the defence estimates debate of March 1979. He said the Government hoped that sales of British military equipment abroad would amount to £1.1 billion next year, even after allowing for the cancellation of orders from Iran; that these exports were worth 75,000 jobs in Britain; and that they helped to keep down the cost of our own military equipment. And he insisted that the Government would continue to sell such equipment to friendly countries.

Of the difficulty of knowing whether such countries would remain friendly, let alone the question of whether they were the kind of countries we *ought* to be friendly with, he had nothing to say. *The Guardian* did. In a forthright editorial on the fall of the Shah entitled 'Human rights: the best test for the West', it declared:

> 'Certainly a concern for human rights in Iran, and elsewhere, is a much better starting point for Western policy than the narrowly strategic calculations of Carter's predecessors. A human rights foreign policy encourages people to make free choices. Not only is that good in itself: it promotes Western interests too because the Soviet Union can offer no competition. President Carter should not be deflected by the present uncertainties of Iran from making human rights the foundation of his diplomacy in future.'

Unfortunately, however, *The Guardian* offers a somewhat

less than flawless example of consistency on this score. If anything, it appeared to be even less worried than the Government about either strategic or human rights considerations when it came to flogging jump-jets to China, advising the Prime Minister to 'defend his right to do this deal for what it is: part of the normal pattern of defence transactions with *peaceful* and stable governments, and in no way calculated (these are Harriers, not Tornados to enable or encourage less peaceful behaviour in the future.' [my emphasis] While in two editorials commenting on the Vietnamese invasion of Cambodia, that cockpit of almost incredible inhumanity under the Khmer Rouge, *The Guardian* told its readers: 'The present Cambodian regime can hardly be regarded as desirable by Western liberal standards, though there is no certainty or even probability that any other foreseeable regime would be better'; appeared to give some credence to claims that the Khmer Rouge 'pogroms were over and had in any case been exaggerated'; and went on to make comments of such crassness and such callousness that the guardian spirit of the house must still blush with shame to recall them:

> 'But Vietnam's human rights record, if that is how the countries are to be judged, will not bear much scrutiny either. When one dictatorship invades another, there is only the sterility of international law to fall back on, and here it is the Russians' client which is clearly at fault. But it is a low-grade conflict and does not merit much of the attention which China now wants the United Nations to give it. Only if the Soviet Union and China themselves are foolish enough to allow it to assume big-Power proportions, by alarms on their common frontier, need the West differentiate between one misery-making Asian government and another.'

What is still interesting about this puerile piece of opinionising is that it graphically illustrates how extensively and profoundly the Cold War had corrupted Western thought. Even here, in this contemporary voice of a great liberal paper, straight thinking is driven out by specious double-think in which moral judgement is conditioned by considerations of whether other States are allies or 'friends', or, on the contrary, principal powers or protégés of what President Reagan was to dub 'the evil empire'. In this welter of warped thinking on geopolitical problems in establishment circles, now and again a voice rings out as true as a bell, as in this passage from an address by a Government minister to the Royal Institute of International Affairs at the height of the Far Eastern imbroglio:

> 'The Government's concern for human rights does not stop at the Channel. We must relate our concern for human rights abroad to our own belief in the values we as a society stand for...If we condone or explain away behaviour on the part of others which we know and feel instinctively to be wrong, this will rebound on us and harm our own society. If we do not defend what we know to be right, it will damage our own self-respect as a nation, as well as our standing in the international community...We accept the strategic argument that an unequal world is an unstable world...and we cannot ignore blatant violations of fundamental rights in deciding where and how to help.'

It is a matter for infinite regret that with a Labour government in power one has to pronounce such pure judgements and such unequivocal repudiation of *realpolitik* to be so rare. To add to the poignancy, the minister concerned, Minister of State at the Foreign Office, was Frank Judd, whose subsequent career, after losing his seat in the 1979 general election, as Oxfam's director-general suggests that he was always the most *un*political of politicians in Jim Callaghan's Government. But for the most part, in our fixtures with rival nations, a public-school mentality ruled the behaviour of Labour's statesmen no less than it did that of their parliamentary opponents. The rules dictated a bipartisan attitude to the handling of foreign affairs; and a bipartisan foreign policy might be defined as one in which each party, when in opposition, vigorously assails the government for putting the country at risk, and when in office, behaves as blindly, as unintelligently, and as tribalistically as its predecessor.

CHAPTER 18

Our caring society

'The crowning achievements of the Austrian Republic
belonged to the municipality of Vienna. The Austrian
workers proudly called it "Red Vienna"...Vienna, which
had seemed irretrievably doomed in 1919, was ten years
later one of the most remarkable cities of Europe. It had
defied death. It had created new life. It had girdled itself
with beautiful blocks of flats and garden settlements,
with swimming-pools and libraries...Above all it had
transformed the Socialist idea of common property,
social taxation and social welfare into deeds, and had
created among its citizens a new sense of solidarity and
social responsibility...it was, above all, a "red city"
because it succeeded in realising municipal Socialism in
a capitalist country.'
            Julius Braunthal, *The Tragedy of Austria* (1948)

For the British people the early forties are the period when, under the
pressures of the struggle for the nation's survival, the rhetoric claiming
this to be 'the century of the common man' really began to take on
some semblance of reality, at least with regard to common standards
of living. The people's desire for a decisive break with a past in which
suffrage had brought such meagre returns was registered in the general
election of July 1945, though not so resoundingly as political mythology
would have it, since Labour's victory was founded on a little less than
half the total number of votes cast. Nevertheless, history had
handsomely recompensed Labour for its long struggle for a
parliamentary majority, for the bitter trials and tribulations of its schisms
and its long years in the wilderness, by handing it power when it most
mattered. It seemed to be a moment of destiny, when opportunity really
did knock both for the nation and for the world. 'Now Britain has the
chance of leading the democratic revolution,' the Italian revolutionary
Socialist Ignazio Silone enthusiastically pronounced.

Just as throughout the nineteenth and early twentieth
centuries, from the Congress of Vienna to the outbreak of the First
World War, under the pressure of progressive enfranchisement,

Tories and Liberals vied with each other for popular support by proffering the sweetmeats of social reform, so in our time - with the Liberals out of the serious bidding for the contract to run the country - Labour and the Tories have peddled their promises for purchase by vote. Under representative democracy it is necessarily so. Every party, in short, claims to be the party of reform, that is to say, strives to be seen as the party that will most enhance the voters' enjoyment of life. The post-Second World War reforms - reforms for the main part rooted in the wartime coalition's morale-boosting 'land fit for heroes' proposals for a new dawn, and to a large extent resting on consensus - were certainly given a kick-start by Labour's shock victory. That a substantial transformation of what the nineteenth century called 'the condition of the people' took place during the Attlee administrations (which is not, of course, saying was *brought about by* them - a much more debatable opinion) there can be no question. But, in the first place, by the mid eighties - with the Thatcherite counter-revolution fully under way - it should have become obvious to all but the incurably obtuse how narrow the bounds and how fragile the structures of 'the social revolution' of 1945-50 had been. Secondly, social progress in general continued, under Tory as well as Labour governments, in the decades that followed, and more or less in step with the (in twentieth-century terms) fairly rapid and dependable growth of the economy. Thirdly, by the time of the last Wilson/Callaghan governments, the social advance had, on many fronts, stalled.

It may be that a confirmed Labour supporter might reasonably consider a given Labour government - or even each and every known Labour government - preferable to any alternative on offer. But a Socialist must apply stricter criteria, and is obliged to ask not merely: 'Is it better?' but: 'Is it qualitatively different?' And unless he or she can answer: 'Yes', then it does not even begin to measure up to his or her ideals.

In one sense Labour has been the victim of its own success in playing a major role in raising 'the condition of the people' through the development of the Welfare State, and by so doing quietening the clamour for social transformation. In another sense it has been the culprit - by giving way to its fear that its vision of a good society would no longer be attractive to the ordinary voter, cocooned in the new age's material comforts delivered by economic growth and in some measure underpinned by social security provisions, and fearing deprivation through major social change more than through the familiar vicissitudes of the capitalist system. In this manner did Labour, acting under the perceived imperatives of representative democracy, abandon society's 'orphans', the less vocal underclass of the poor and the relatively poor. Whereas they had once formed a majority of the nation (or at any rate a massive minority) they now formed only a negligible fraction of the nation's voters. Lacking solidarity from the general electorate (and such solidarity was never sufficiently fostered by Labour's paternalists), they could be largely neglected without seriously jeopardising - indeed, arguably thereby enhancing - the Labour vote, for to what other party could those disinherited ones turn to look after their interests? Thus have the least privileged been cynically sacrificed to the strategy of consolidating support among the skilled workers and among professionals with tender - but not *that* tender - consciences. (This is roughly the thesis at the core of John Kenneth Galbraith's essay *The Culture of Contentment* (1992), in which he argues that a new development 'in the so-called capitalist countries...is that the controlling contentment and resulting belief is now that of the many, not just of the few...and operates under the compelling power of democracy...[and that] the result is government that is accommodated not to reality or common need, but to the beliefs of the contented, who are now the majority of those who voted'.)

We might measure this massive erosion of Labour's faith and/or its total loss of nerve by contrasting three political pronouncements made by members of the Party's top brass, separated by eighteen years of progressive disillusionment. The first is a clarion call delivered to the Party Conference in 1973, on the eve of Labour's return to power after its fancied drive for a 'white-hot *technological* revolution' [my emphasis] had been so rudely interrupted by Ted Heath's Mark II model Conservatives. The second and third are statements made to *The Guardian* in an interview and a letter by two leading lights of Labour's government-hopefully-in-waiting during the roller-coaster opinion-polling days of the summer of 1991.

In the autumn of 1973, in a belligerent speech in which he promised to wring 'howls of anguish from the 80,000 rich people', Shadow Chancellor Denis Healey won great applause from Conference delegates with these words:

214

'Our aim is to get power, and we join battle armed with
the most radical and comprehensive programme we
have had since 1945. Its aim is, honestly stated, *to bring
about a fundamental and irreversible shift in the
balance of power and wealth in favour of working
people and their families.*' [my emphasis]

Even allowing for what waggish sceptics might characterise as
providing ample scope for possible 'differentials' of opinion under
the baggy formula 'working people', with its perhaps shrewd
avoidance of any class reference, that still has to be one of the most
ambitiously unambiguous statements of Labour's Socialist
objectives ever made. But let us put the clock forward to 1991.

As a student at Oxford, Denis Healey had joined the
Communist Party, but by the time he made the call to arms cited
above no one could have accused him of being too left-wing.
Margaret Beckett, on the other hand, had moved a long way across
the Labour Party's broad political spectrum (from left to right, as is
almost invariably the case) between 1981, when she supported Tony
Benn in his unsuccessful bid to beat Healey in the contest for the
post of deputy leader, and mid-1991, when Melanie Phillips
interviewed her for *The Guardian* because of her high profile as
shadow Treasury minister. Questioned about her drift rightwards,
Mrs Beckett - inasmuch as she was prepared to admit she had moved
a muscle in that direction - responded in wholly predictable terms
of practicalities and priorities. She spoke of having been made aware
when she was shadowing social security of 'such a great well of
justifiable need that it was really hard to see how you could meet it
all', and went on, in words that perhaps subconsciously echoed
Aneurin Bevan's vacuous dictum that 'Socialism is all about
priorities', earnestly to affirm, 'That's where I think having priorities
is the essence.'

One would be hard put to think up any situation in which one
could quarrel with that; but beyond the commendable fact that she
cares about other people and means to do something about it as a
politician, such musings tell us next to nothing about her political
viewpoint. Compassion does not constitute a political philosophy;
nor is it the same thing as a commitment to social justice. In what
respects, if any, for example, does her way of looking at the problem
of the 'great well of justifiable need' differ from the vision of such

noble exemplars of practical compassion as, say, Mother Teresa or Lord Shaftesbury? Or come to that, from the viewpoints of the more humane and social-minded adherents of political parties she never dreamt of joining?

Applauding the great change she feels 'has taken place in the Labour Party,' Margaret Beckett credits Neil Kinnock with having made the Party 'think about where the country was going and where we were going.' Yet a lengthy and sympathetic interview yields no indication of strategy and no goal except that of amelioration. 'You have to establish a system that's reasonably just and fair, and hopefully start to help people out of the trouble they're in. And if that is not possible, try to give them some feeling of human dignity and respect. Now that is immensely difficult, immensely expensive, and probably will take years of work to get right,' she says mournfully, but adds later: 'At least you can do *something* to alleviate their condition and prevent what would otherwise be a continuing deterioration.'

One is tempted to mock such lucubrations, which suggest nothing so much as a private think-tank from which significant thought has been prudently expelled to produce a controversy-free vacuum. (Are we, for instance, being urged to compare favourably the 'reasonably just and fair system' she posits without prescription with ones that are 'unreasonably unjust and unfair'? Humpty Dumpty may not have been a suitable candidate for tutoring a course in semantics, but at least he was a fine tactician when it came to the manipulation of language). But the words quoted above reveal more than their author (presumably) intends: to wit, that paternalism is still alive and well in the political arm of the Labour Movement, as deeply engrained as it is in old-style religious charity. Moreover, surely the Fabians of yesteryear - if not the modernised variety - would agree that such a dispiriting defence of palliation is hardly hopeful enough to be described even as gradualist reformism.

'I have been on the mountain top and I have seen the promised land,' cried Martin Luther King in a famous peroration. Labour once thought it had seen the promised land, but if it did, it went downhill in quite the wrong direction. At least Bevan was offering his pedestrian aphorism in a context of soaring hopes. Beckett serves it up cold forty years later, after Labour has tinkered with a grossly unjust system through an accumulated term in office of over seventeen years.

The long march of Labour from left to right across the stage of British history was to be dramatised by those who played the leading roles in subsequent events in the Party's leadership contests. When John Smith was elected as successor to Neil Kinnock, following Kinnock's second general election defeat and his resignation as Party Leader, Margaret Beckett became the Deputy Leader; then, on John Smith's sudden death, she was for a short time Acting Leader. Challenging for both the post of Leader and that of Deputy Leader in the leadership elections, she lost out in the first contest to Tony Blair and in the second to John Prescott, who, as Blair's deputy dawg, could turn out to be the last politician of working-class origins to get that high in the Party.

As for Blair, who in the Kinnockio times we are considering held the more modest post of shadow employment spokesman, it is fitting that this man who was to rise right to the top should provide our second contrast to Healey's socialistic war-cry of 1973. The minimalist objectives to which Labour had, by 1991, already descended, from the bringing about of equality to which Attlee's Party once professed to aspire, is crystallised in Blair's advocacy - in response to a symposium of contributions to *The Guardian* on Labour's declared intention of establishing a minimum wage if returned to power - of 'a society where there is a minimum threshold of decency below which no-one should fall.' Winston Churchill proposed something very similar nearly half a century before, and although they might differ as to precisely where that threshold lay, one might well assert that all men of any goodwill whatsoever would say amen to that.(By the end of 1995 Blair had taken Labour so far to the right that the Tory MP for Stratford-on-Avon, Alan Howarth, felt he would be more at home in its ranks than amongst the New Tories, and having crossed the floor, he urged all 'one-nation' Tory MPs to 'join the Labour Party, which is now the torchbearer for their beliefs, and is ready to put them into practice in government')

One might seek to excuse such cautious campaigning by an avowedly reforming and radical party (never mind whether it still claimed to be a Socialist party or not) by ruefully reflecting that to be rejected at the polls three times in succession would be enough to take the heart out of any party that had once held power and continued to remain in serious contention for office. But attention has already been drawn to the essentially defensive, pleading nature of Labour's calls for social justice even before the tempest of

217

Thatcherite go-getting individualism swept Labour's brick-by-brick experiment in building a better society off the Monopoly board and into 'the dustbin of history'. After all, notwithstanding his advocacy of public spending as providing 'an important redistribution of income' (a claim that will be considered later) Stan Orme's formula for 'a caring society' (see Chapter 11) was not that much more ambitious, proposing little more than 'moderating [financial] insecurity' resulting from personal misfortune. For all that, Orme's unapologetic countering of demands for tax cuts with a call to reduce inequality and deprivation by increasing the 'social wage' marks a significant difference from the embarrassed negativism now prevailing in the Party whenever the issue of the economic equivalent of positive discrimination in education arises.

Labour does have some claim to be considered as, historically speaking, the principal architect of the Welfare State. If, forty years on, it is content for its achievements to be measured against the very modest claim that it is still the most dependable guarantor of the maintenance of 'a caring society', so be it. An attempt to assess scrupulously the relative performances in 'caring' of Labour and Conservative governments between the Tories' return to power in 1951 and the triumph of Mrs Thatcher in 1979 would be tedious and now unrewarding. I shall just glance at the record in the fields of health, homes, and education. Social security will be looked at in the next chapter, in the context of considering more fully the issue of the distribution of wealth and income, upon which, more than on any other, rests the question of social justice.

The National Health Service - launched, as historical chance would have it, by the legendary Nye Bevan - has always been the flagship of Labour's Welfare State campaigns. During the consensus years there was no wide difference of opinion between the parties over the importance of maintaining and developing the NHS, it being generally agreed that around 4 per cent of the national income should be devoted to this purpose. Although the NHS share of GNP fell steeply between 1950 and 1955, from 4.07 to 3.04 per cent, and thereafter rose only slowly to 3.86 per cent in 1964 (the year in which Labour returned to power) and then continued to rise, the superiority of Labour's record in fact falls well short of undeniable. Under the first Wilson governments the NHS share rose to 4.7 per cent, in 1969; but in his essay on 'Inequalities in Health' in *Labour and Inequality* (published in 1972, when the Tories were again in power, under Ted Heath) Nicholas Bosanquet questions the extent to which this surge in health spending should be credited to Labour, since nearly half the increase had its roots in budgeting planned by the previous administration. 'The real Labour years,' he argues, 'the years over which the [Labour] Government had a full measure of discretion, run from 1966 to 1969,' and 'over this period, the additional real current resources available to the Service fell year by year,' from £38 million in 1966 to £7 million in 1969. This hardly amounted to the record of 'enormous expansion' claimed by Richard Crossman in the House of Commons in July 1969, Bosanquet concludes.

Public spending on the Health Service continued to rise (both in real and in share of GNP terms) throughout the seventies *and* the eighties, reaching 5.4 per cent by 1977 but 6 per cent by the time of Margaret Thatcher's third general election victory ten years later. Its persistence as a burning political issue is partly due to the failure of this growth to keep pace with ever-rising demand (resulting both from demographic changes - in particular the greater longevity of the population - and from higher expectations stimulated by the progress of medicine, and especially of medical technology), and partly from the not ill-founded fear that the long-term goal of a powerful faction in the Tory Party is to degrade the National Health Service into a second-class safety-net service for those entirely dependent for the satisfaction of their health needs on the public purse.

However, in considering the question of whether there was a real qualitative difference distinguishing Labour from its opponents during the years of consensus, it is noteworthy not only that significant progress in consolidating the NHS was made under Conservative governments (hospital development, for example, under Macmillan, with Enoch Powell as Minister of Health, or the major reorganisation of the Service piloted by Keith Joseph during Heath's administration), but that the Tories were in some respects more afraid of being open to the charge of undermining the NHS than were their opponents. It was Sir Stafford Cripps who, near the end of Attlee's first administration, first pressed for charges on patients, and Aneurin Bevan only fended off this assault on 'his baby' by agreeing to the forming of a Cabinet committee to monitor and restrain NHS costs. Less than a year later, as 'defence' spending doubled to meet the costs of Britain's entanglement in the Korean War and its other expanding Cold War commitments, with Hugh

Gaitskell now Chancellor, the imposition of half-price charges on spectacles and dentures for adult NHS patients became a principal factor in the resignations from the Government of Harold Wilson, John Freeman, and, of course, Nye Bevan. He described the saving of £13 million out of a budget of £4 billion as 'the arithmetic of Bedlam'. But Bevan had already been pressurised into conceding in principle the possibility of a shilling charge on prescriptions, which Churchill's Government in fact imposed in 1952.

After 'thirteen years of Tory misrule', with Harold Wilson himself now top dog, the voters were treated to yet another dazzling acrobatic display as Wilson's first Chancellor, Jim Callaghan, redeemed Labour's pledge to scrap prescription charges, and his second, Roy Jenkins, slapped them on again in his 1968 crisis budget. So when Heath's Chancellor, Anthony Barber, raised prescription and dental charges three years later, he was only following in Labour's wake. Writing of a later economic crisis over which Harold Wilson presided, with Denis Healey wielding the Chancellor's axe this time, Bernard Donoghue, who acted as Senior Policy Adviser to both Wilson and his successor in No. 10, makes an astringent observation that highlights the fact that, under Labour no less than under the Tories, the social services are the soft underbelly of government expenditure, the first part of the body politic exposed to the knife in any emergency calling for some slimming down. Healey had proposed a 2 per cent cut in the expenditure planned for 1976-77, expecting all the departments of State to be prepared to make sacrifices. But as Donoghue writes: 'Defence, as was often the case, simply refused to accept or even discuss half of its proposed cuts, whereas the cuts in Education, the National Health Service and public industry investment were imposed in full.'

Big differences of opinion over specific issues will occur in any political party that is not strictly regimented; but the Labour Party has never come close (at least when it matters most, i.e. when in power) to agreeing on those 'priorities' which Bevan and Beckett rabbited on about. From any Socialist perspective, Labour governments have made a habit of getting them wrong. Once upon a time - not all that long ago - Britain had a War Office; now that we live in a more civilised age we have a Ministry of Defence. Call a country's expenditure on its armed forces and their weapons of destruction 'defence spending' and most of its citizens will readily agree that it is the number one priority. And, judging by the history of the post-war world, they will not generally be greatly puzzled to hear that the defence of the nation is apparently being undertaken on the other side of the world in a land they have hardly heard of: Korea, say. But in any case, the danger of becoming the victim of military aggression is only one among a host of problems that face a nation, and the degree of risk involved needs to be assessed, as with every other risk.

Straining to be kind to Labour in office, one would still be hard put to pronounce the degree of priority it has repeatedly given to 'defence' as at all judicious. Ministers more exercised by social priorities (*as long, at least, as these have remained their provinces*) have always had a hard time of it, as Donoghue's comment suggests. In the bright new world of post-war Labour-ruled Britain, housing was viewed by every party as one of these priorities. Back in those earlier days of hope and of promises of 'homes fit for heroes' after the First World War, Christopher Addison (a distinguished anatomist who, having turned his attention to the body politic, had become in 1919, under Lloyd George, the country's first Minister of Health, before switching his allegiance from Liberal to Labour in 1923 and concluding his political career as Labour leader in the Lords), had, in A.J.P. Taylor's words, 'more than any other man established the principle that housing was a social service.' Labour considered the right to a decent home to be of such importance that it had promised to set up a separate Ministry of Housing. In the event Housing remained an appendage to Health, as it had been between the wars, so that it became a second major responsibility for Nye Bevan. Notwithstanding his flippant and foolish jest that he devoted only five minutes a week of his time to it, he fought his corner over housing with his customary ardour. Cripps's devaluation package of autumn 1949 not only threatened the principle of a free health service but slowed down progress in the provision of homes. In a letter to Attlee arguing that the need for greater labour mobility meant that 'a reduction in housing cannot be justified on the basis of the existing national emergency,' Bevan complained bitterly that while the 'already gorged and swollen defence estimates' were to be trimmed by no more than £30 million, housing was to suffer cuts of £40-50 million. As Kenneth O. Morgan says: 'The housing programme, now at the peak of its achievement, bore the brunt of the post-devaluation cuts in public expenditure.'

With around one and a half million units (of which two- thirds were new and one-third conversions or restorations) added to the nation's housing stock during the Attlee administrations, Morgan's verdict is that housing 'deserves its honoured role in the saga of Labour's welfare state.' Nevertheless, the 1951 census revealed that the excess of households over houses (at 1.1 million) remained much the same as it had been in the depths of the Depression, twenty years earlier. Bevan had been forced to abandon his goal of 200,000 completions a year, and it was the Tories who first raised the target (at their 1950 Conference) to 300,000, hitting it in October 1953 and surpassing it by over 50,000 the following year. Harold Macmillan, to whom Churchill had given the responsibility of fulfilling the Tory pledge, proudly told the Party Conference in 1954 that he had made housing 'a national crusade', and T.O. Lloyd remarks: 'The housing problem was nearer to being under control than at any time since 1939.'

After its return to power in 1964, Labour published a White Paper calculating that three million families were in need of housing or re-housing in homes of an acceptable standard and setting up a target of half a million houses a year to be reached by 1970, with the objective of solving the problem within ten to fifteen years. Records of over 400,000 completions were achieved in 1967 and 1968, but the figures fell back thereafter, to below 370,000 in 1969, and (with the June 1970 to February 1974 Heath Government in between) down to around 250,000 by 1974. Denis Healey's 1974 budget provided for an expansion of the local authority housing programme, but his 'rough and tough' budget of the following year cut subsidies for housing, as well as food, with the consequence that fewer houses were built or rehabilitated under the Wilson administration of 1974-76 than under Heath's Government.

And so the dreary tale of high hopes repeatedly dashed dragged on into the premiership of Jim Callaghan. By the last full year of Labour rule (1978) public sector housing, at 107,600 including housing association and new town units, had fallen to its lowest level since the first full post-war year of Labour rule (1946), with council house completions down to little over 75,000. Many local authorities were wilfully underspending because of the hostility of the party in control of the council to the whole concept of public housing, with the total amount of Treasury money not taken up amounting to at least £150 million. But in addition, it turned out that the Department of Environment had itself underspent on its housing budget to the tune of £410 million, 8 per cent of the allocation. At the same time, council house sales, running at the rate of 18,000 a year in 1978, were heading for their highest point since the final year under Ted Heath. This led Shelter to censure the Labour Government for its inconsistency in allowing this to happen at the same time as it promoted a charter to improve tenants' conditions and to provide greater mobility for tenants in public housing, all this in an overall situation of crisis in the provision of homes for the people.

In March 1979 Shelter Scotland published a report estimating that 150,000 houses north of the border (8 per cent of the total stock) were below the officially tolerable standard and that half a million people were in urgent housing need. In April nine housing charities, in a joint protest that, for the first time since the war, a general election was being fought without any debate on the supply of housing, claimed that one in five families in England was either homeless or was living in severely substandard or insecure conditions. In such circumstances the publication of Peter Shore's long-awaited Housing Bill, with the tenants' charter as its core proposal, seemed a trifle superfluous. In any case, Labour's rout in the general election swept the bill into oblivion.

Of course, the Socialists in the Party were by no means content with the Government's record in promoting the provision of homes. In a debate at the 1978 Party Conference at Blackpool, Frank Allaun declared: 'Future generations will think us mad when they see that there was a desperate housing shortage on the one hand, and a quarter of a million building workers unemployed on the other.'

Anyone who is at all disposed to take seriously the claim that Labour's objectives (or at any rate its long-term objectives) are - or at least were until comparatively recently - Socialist in character has to reconcile with this assumption the rather remarkable fact that no Labour government has ever introduced a major bill of educational reform. For all its limitations, the Butler Bill introduced by the wartime coalition government in 1944 unquestionably marked a major social advance on a system that had restricted formal education for the mass of the population to the age of fourteen, and in so-called elementary schools. From a Socialist point of view, however, the limitations of the Butler reform were ominous. By providing a clear framework of free secondary education based on three kinds of school (grammar and technical - both of which were already established, though the latter kind was but sparsely distributed - plus 'secondary modern'), the 1944 Act, as A.J.P. Taylor puts it, 'unwittingly created a new class division between those who were clever enough to get into a grammar school at "eleven plus" and those who were not.'

Apart from a certain unease at his use of the word 'clever' (a shorthand expression, perhaps), the only debatable point about Taylor's judgement is whether the 'new class division' was all that 'unwitting'. James Chuter Ede, a former schoolteacher whom Attlee made his Home Secretary, had been Butler's right-hand man in drafting and promoting his Bill, and thus carried no small share of responsibility for its shortcomings. Furthermore, Attlee's first Minister of Education, Ellen Wilkinson (the celebrated 'Red Ellen' of the Jarrow March, who had by now, however, migrated a long way to the right) rejected the Left's argument that the tripartite division of schools, buttressed by the eleven-plus tests, was socially and educationally divisive. 'Her view,' says Kenneth O. Morgan, 'seems to have been endorsed throughout the Cabinet, where such public-school products as Attlee of Haileybury, Cripps of Winchester, and Dalton of Eton lent their voices to the perpetuation of elitism'; while George Tomlinson, who succeeded Ellen Wilkinson on her death as a result of taking an overdose of drugs in February 1947, 'followed a broadly identical policy.'

That policy was to channel into education such increases in resources as the growth of the economy and the competing claims of other Departments of State allowed, but to develop the system on the lines already laid down by the political consensus, on the complacent assumption that this would in due course provide equality of educational opportunity for all. But secondary schooling in particular provides a notable example of areas (and they are not few) in which it has frequently been difficult to talk of Labour policy without first drawing a careful distinction between leaders and led within the Party - a point that calls for closer consideration in the context of the Party as a representative body. Not until July 1951 did the Labour Party officially commit itself to the policy of changing to comprehensive schools, and even then the conversion of its leadership was far from complete. Writing of the first Labour administration after the Party's thirteen years in opposition, C.J. Bartlett says: 'Harold Wilson, with many others in the Labour party, was a grammar school product. These were not readily persuaded that grammar schools had failed as instruments for social mobility.' Wilson, indeed, in the jockeying for a favourable position during the run up to the 1964 general election, swore that the grammar school would be abolished 'only over my dead body.'

The irony is that, spurred on by the growing acceptance of the case for comprehensive schools amongst teachers and educationists, and even more by growing disenchantment amongst parents (and especially middle-class parents!) over the unfairness and inefficiency of the eleven-plus selection system, grammar school products of a different political persuasion gave comprehensive schools their biggest boost. When Ted Heath came into office in June 1970 and appointed none other than Margaret Thatcher as his Minister of Education, less than a third of secondary school pupils were in comprehensives (which were thus normally skimmed of the greater part of the top ability range in their areas); when they left office in February 1974, more than two-thirds were in comprehensives.

Moreover, it was the Heath Government which, in 1973, raised the school-leaving age from fifteen to sixteen, at last implementing an objective that had been declared Labour policy since the school-leaving age was raised from fourteen to fifteen in April 1947 and had long been accepted by all parties as desirable. In tune with Donoghue's dictum on the distortion of priorities, Wilson's first government had, under the pressure of the economic crisis of 1967-68, postponed its intention of raising the school-leaving age for two years, and lost power before it could redeem its pledge.

In his contribution to the 1972 symposium of Fabian essays, *Labour and Inequality*, Howard Glennerster calls this further delay in keeping what amounted to a twenty-year-old promise to the nation's working class (for it was overwhelmingly the children of manual workers who were affected by it), 'scarcely a disaster'. But taken together with the decision made at the beginning of Labour's return to office not to allocate more resources to going comprehensive, it is indicative of a short-termism that throws into doubt the genuineness of its rhetoric regarding the regeneration of Britain - and that is to put the matter simply in terms of conventional patriotism.

As for Labour's proclaimed commitment to move towards greater equality, Glennerster demonstrates that the expansion of educational provision that did occur under Wilson's first administration (of which he was most proud, boasting that for the first time more was being spent on education than on defence) primarily benefited the middle class, with the families of the 28 per cent of the working population who earned their livelihoods by semi-skilled or unskilled labour benefiting from only 19 per cent of the extra spending on education. This was mainly because most of the extra money was targeted on higher education. Wilson is on record as saying that what he would most like to be remembered for was the establishment of the Open University. Indubitably a notable advance in the provision of educational opportunity, this achievement nevertheless illustrates the low priority Labour perpetually gives (in practice if not in intention) to the least privileged. After all, 80 per cent of the Open University's first student intake came from homes with non-manual breadwinners, making it, in Glennerster's words, 'more middle class than the average university.' Furthermore, in September 1978 it was reported that there had actually been a fall between 1973 and 1977 in the number of children of manual workers who had secured places in universities.

Another contributor to *Labour and Inequality*, Dennis Marsden, does not hesitate to castigate Labour's leaders for their 'failures of perception and will', writing:

> 'The leadership was still quite prepared to live with the grammar and the public schools. And there is evidence of a lack of commitment to the ideal of reducing inequality in society. There was a failure to appreciate that economic and structural changes left to themselves will not reduce and may increase inequality. Labour politicians had apparently developed an overpowering coyness about taking any action which would curb or interfere with the existing maldistribution of power or resources.'

He cites as evidence the Wilson Government's failure to tackle the 'ludicrous' legal fiction that Eton and the other public schools are charities and its pusillanimous waging of its declared campaign to make comprehensives the dominant form of secondary schools, during which the Department of Education issued a circular to the local authorities requesting them but not requiring them to submit plans for the reorganisation of secondary education on comprehensive lines. One might well also include its indulgent disregard of the widespread practice of running comprehensives as if they were grammar schools somewhat hampered by the regrettable obligation of accommodating large numbers of 'secondary modern pupils', a brazen subversion of the whole purpose of going comprehensive.

As for failures of perception and of the need for thinking about fundamentals, it can hardly be without significance that all the major reports on the way forward for the nation's education - Crowther, Robbins, and Newsom - were commissioned and published under Tory administrations. But something even more disturbing than complacency was at work. Perhaps more than in any other field, the ingrained elitism of the leaders of the Labour Party was exposed in their handling of education. It raises the issue of what a Socialist vision implies. Must it encompass a striving for real social equality, or might it mean no more than an affirmation of the desirability of unimpeded social mobility? If it *is* no more than the latter, how *can* we distinguish between its fundamental aims and those of the bourgeois parties in liberal democracies, every one of which claims, in the late twentieth century, to be committed to equality of opportunity for all to prove their worth in a meritocratic society?

Ironically, a measure that might at least have proved an earnest of Labour's serious intention of striving for equality of opportunity - Shirley Williams' draft bill that, besides increasing parental choice and broadening representation on the governing bodies of schools, would have funded a pilot scheme to pay grants to sixteen-eighteen year-old pupils, thereby encouraging children from poorer families to stay on at school and perhaps equip themselves for higher education - was on the stocks when Jim Callaghan's Government was forced into the 1979 general election.

Callaghan had seemed to sense the significance of the issue of education, in relation to his 'what kind of society do we want?' challenge to the Tories, when he spoke of 'the great debate'. Yet three weeks before the Government fell, Shirley Williams was telling a conference in London on future trends in education that they were 'a long way short...of the 'mass' higher education system which we used to foresee.' One of the principal speakers at the conference was Dr Richard Hoggart, 'the hymnist of working-class culture', as *Guardian* correspondent John Fairhall called him in reporting him as saying that:

> 'The educational system perpetuated social and economic
> privilege as much now as it did forty years ago...Hundreds
> of thousands had been rejected by the education system.
> No society was civilised if so large a proportion of its
> population were no more than fillers-in of football coupons
> and haunters of football terraces. We should not be at ease
> when the correlation between attendance at certain schools
> and colleges and many sections of power and influence
> was as tight, or even tighter, than thirty years ago.'

Despite Hoggart's upbeat conclusion that 'a great opportunity' was in our grasp, Fairhall faithfully captures the predominant tone of his speech in calling it 'a requiem for the hopes that educational developments since the Second World War would make Britain a more democratic society.'

227

CHAPTER 19

Labour's crusade for social justice

'O, I have ta'en
Too little care of this. Take physic, pomp;
Expose thyself to feel what wretches feel,
That thou mayst shake the superflux to them,
And show the heavens more just.'

King Lear

'He'd come to believe that human pain could not be
cured by attention to individual cases...When he
compared the number of patients he cured with the
number of human beings the world over who could not
buy even the most ordinary medicines, it was enough to
make him shudder. The same with begging. What was
the good of giving money to the poor? The balance of
poverty on the planet remained unaltered. For the world
to change, the system had to change.'

Vasilis Vassilikos, Z

'The dream I have is of a country in which there is...wealth for everyone,
wealth equally distributed (and I don't mean arithmetically distributed)
and in which we do not have two societies,' James Callaghan told
Llew Gardner in the Thames Television programme, *TV Eye*, a week
before Labour lost power. 'As long as there's a hospital patient who
seeks a bed, as long as there are people living in poverty, as long as
there is a single family that hasn't got a home, then there's a great case
for change,' he went on, reciting a litany of hardship and injustice he
had deployed once before as preface to the ringing declaration: 'Our
purpose as a party is to present a bold creative socialist challenge to all
those forces that perpetuate injustice, class division, racial bigotry,
poverty.' And this spirited affirmation in turn recalled the words he
had used on inheriting Harold Wilson's mantle, when he had summoned
up the blood of his followers with the battle-cries: 'Let's root out
injustice; let's pursue equality.'

Such upbeat exhortations have become as foreign tongues to
the Party leadership. It is an almost incalculable distance between

228

Clement Attlee's quietly confident assertion of 1937: 'No doubt it will be some time before substantial economic equality is achieved, but ultimately it must be...' (which was accompanied by the unequivocal declaration that 'the aim of the socialist State must be equality') and the near-quietist conclusion to a tear-jerking anecdote on chronic poverty from Roy Hattersley's constituency surgery casebook (*Guardian* 4th November 1991): 'If we believe in a more equal society, a more equal society will come.' Equality has been for Labour a quarry forever outdistancing the pursuer. The dream persists but the runner flags, his resolution wilting into mere wish. 'For ever wilt thou love, and she be fair!'

In the opening rally of his first and last general election campaign as Labour's leader, Jim Callaghan, speaking in presciently elegiac tones, told his Glasgow audience: 'We in the Labour Movement may fall short...we make mistakes, but we are still the party of ideals.' Two of the most irreducible of these ideals have to be the first and second of the six characteristics of democratic socialism enumerated by one of his closest Cabinet confidants, Home Secretary Merlyn Rees, in addressing Party members a year earlier, namely the desire to eliminate poverty and the wish to redistribute income and wealth. We are dealing here with men of goodwill, so we ought to be charitable. If their proclaimed goal of equality appeared to be receding into the far future, let us judge Labour's record by the less exacting objectives which most of their political opponents at least purport to share, doing away with poverty and spreading wealth about a bit more.

Taking the second of these aims first, the essential questions are how the distribution of wealth and incomes stood when Rees prescribed redistribution as a principal tenet of democratic socialism, and how distribution had been affected by the fact that Labour had held power for nearly three-quarters of the preceding fourteen years. Rees addressed the subject with admirable candour in pointing out that half the nation's personally-owned wealth was still in the hands of the richest five per cent of its adult population (with the top one per cent of the very wealthy hogging no less than half of that half), and that moreover 'the structure of earnings has remained much the same for ninety years.' As for Labour's influence on this pyramid of economic inequality, his observations were tantamount to an admission that it had been minimal.

Of the contribution of the trade union wing of the Labour

Movement to this close-to-stagnant situation he observed: 'I am bound to say that I doubt the capacity of free collective bargaining to change this structure substantially.' Whether he realised it or not, this effectively sold the pass in the ceaseless conflict within the Movement over calls for wage restraint, in which the Left of the Party as well as numerous trade unionists contended that for the most part the unions were doing little more than struggling to maintain the living standards of their members. Of course, this contention tends to endorse Rees's judgement on the minimal redistributive effects of free collective bargaining. As for the parliamentary wing of the Movement, Rees came perilously close to admitting Labour's complete failure to advance towards its trumpeted objective of a 'fundamental and irreversible shift in the balance of power and wealth' when, in his single concrete proposition, he reasserted 'the Government's commitment to the introduction of a wealth tax.' But we will return to that resurrected weapon later, after looking more closely at the state of the nation with respect to wealth distribution at the time Rees was speaking.

A couple of months earlier, in his Reith Lectures on the changing face of British society, Professor A.H. Halsey had drawn attention to the 'spectacular inequalities' that persisted despite all attempts at redistribution, proffering as one of the most striking illustrations of this socio-economic stagnation a recent estimate that in 1974/75 the richest one per cent of the population got about the same amount in income as the poorest twenty per cent, or, in other words, that they took twenty times as much a head from the common wealth. But focusing on the top and bottom of the ladder is misleading just because the difference is so spectacular and because we are all well-conditioned to the fact that in almost every society there are a few story-book people who are fabulously rich. That they are so exceptional serves as an excuse, and their Olympian state is even portrayed as a kind of blessing in that it lends to the humdrum lives of ordinary people the thrill of watching the wheel of fortune turning, in much the same way that, in his novel *The Power and the Glory* and the travel book, *The Lawless Roads*, which was its source, Graham Greene defends the opulence of the Church in a land of poverty as conferring on the peasantry the gift of forgetting for a while their wretched state. In any case, contend the disingenuous, to share out amongst the many the superfluous wealth of the few would be to attenuate it, *strudel*-like, so much that it would be of no appreciable benefit to the multitude. To see just how specious such arguments are, we need to look at the whole range of income and wealth distribution, not just at the top and the bottom.

As an earnest of Labour's concern about the persistence of gross social and economic inequalities, a Royal Commission on the Distribution of Income and Wealth had been set up in 1975, and in his book based on his Reith Lectures, *Change in British Society*, Halsey used the Commission's findings as a source for tables showing the situation in 1974-75 (the latest year for which figures were available) and for most of the years back to 1959. The 1974-75 figures showed that the income collectively received by the top 10 per cent after the deduction of income tax amounted to just about the same as that collectively received by the bottom 30 per cent; that is to say, on average they got nearly three times more per capita. The top 30 per cent enjoyed more than half (52.2 per cent) the total post-income-tax income, while the share of the bottom 50 per cent was not much above a quarter (27 per cent).

The common contention that the progressive system of income tax had had, over the years, a significant cumulative effect on the distribution of income is quickly dispelled by an examination of the figures. Slight rises (in the order of 0.1 per cent to 0.6 per cent per quantile group) between 1959 and 1974-75 in the share of the total post-income-tax income at the disposal of the lower 60 per cent of income-earners were gained almost entirely at the expense of the top 5 per cent, whose collective share fell from 15.8 per cent to 13.7 per cent, with the top 1 per cent suffering the only dramatic fall, from 5.3 per cent to 4.0 per cent. Despite this, at the end of this period (which covers all but one of Wilson's years in power) the top 1 per cent still had income at their disposal that was nearly a third as much again as the 3.1 per cent of the total available to the bottom 10 per cent. Moreover, the proportionate loss of the top 1 per cent tends to conceal the fact that all the other top quantile groups down to the 40 per cent level actually increased their share of post-income-tax income.

Yet for a number of reasons this still greatly understates the huge disparities in spending power that characterise our society. The single most important reason is that inequalities in the ownership of wealth (and hence in the availability of credit) are even more spectacular than inequalities in personal income. Halsey reproduces from the same Royal Commission report a table showing the percentage shares of estimated personal wealth of given quantile groups between 1960 and 1975. The 1975 figures show that nearly a quarter of the total personal wealth of the UK population was owned by the top 1 per cent, nearly a half by the top 5 per cent, nearly two-thirds by the top 10 per cent, and more than four-fifths by the top 20 per cent, leaving less than one-fifth (18.2 in percentage figures) for the bottom *80* per cent!

It is true that the figures for wealth distribution, in contrast to those for income distribution, appear to show very considerable redistribution from the wealthier sections of the population to the poorer. Between 1960 and 1975 the percentage share of the top 1 per cent fell from 38.2 to 23.2, of the top 5 per cent from 64.3 to 46.5, of the top 10 per cent from 76.7 to 62.4, and of the top 20 per cent from 89.8 to 81.8, while the percentage share of the bottom 80 per cent rose from 10.2 to 18.2. Nevertheless, Halsey finds no convincing evidence to support the contention of 'liberal theorists' that the Welfare State, through its taxation and welfare policies, has substantially reduced 'market inequalities'. On the contrary, he endorses the three principal conclusions of what he calls 'a voluminously and soberly argued empirical account from the Marxist standpoint', *Class in a Capitalist Society* (1975), by John Westergaard and Henrietta Resler: firstly, that the only major shifts in distribution were brought about by the exceptional circumstances of the two world wars; secondly, that such redistribution as has taken place since the Second World War has (in Halsey's words) 'very largely been a spread of wealth to the richest 5 per cent instead of 1 per cent, and much of it reflects arrangements for gifts *inter vivos* - gifts between the living as distinct from those bequeathed at death', whereby 'rich families have passed on their wealth and legally avoided tax'; thirdly, that far from the Welfare State being a 'hugely distributive' force, 'welfare, it would appear, is largely self-financed for the bulk of the population.'

Of the effect of welfare provision, interacting with tax formulae, on the pattern of have-nots, haves and have-lots, the data marshalled by Westergaard and Resler demonstrates that:

'The 'welfare state' does redistribute income. But...this is redistribution between households at different stages of life far more than it is redistribution between households at markedly different levels of income. It is redistribution within classes far more than it is redistribution between classes...The public welfare services are crippled as a means of cutting down class divisions, for two reasons especially. First, because they co-exist with private welfare provisions for the well-off and the wealthy, financed in part from public funds by way of tax concessions. Second, because in general the tax system that feeds them bears down heavily on ordinary wage earners and even the poor.'

The authors show that 'wage earners pay for their 'welfare state' largely out of their own pockets', and that sporadic attempts at 'selectivity' (i.e. targeting through means testing) 'designed to give rather more help to the poorest' have been 'at the expense of the broad masses a little way above them.' And they make a fundamental point about the conspiratorial nature of class power in observing of wage-earners in general: 'They do not have the influence, the proximity to those who make policy and execute it, the sheer self-assurance of privilege, which enable businessmen and high professionals to tap the resources of the state to boost "private" welfare arrangements for themselves and colleagues close to them in the hierarchy.' In fact, as the authors remark elsewhere: 'The public welfare services bear the imprint of [the class] distribution of power' and, like the tax machinery, are geared to 'the needs of a capitalist economy.'

On the wider question of changes in the distribution of income and wealth during the twentieth century, Westergaard and Resler sum up:

'Rising levels of living for every man have gone hand in hand with a marked persistence in economic inequality in relative terms. Exceptional circumstances at times compressed the range of contrasts in income and wealth. Those shifts had lasting effects. But they were confined to the periods around World War II and probably World War I. They formed no part of a continuous trend towards equalization, and they entailed only modest redistribution. Disparities may indeed have widened since the 1950s. They certainly did not narrow significantly, from the early 1950s to the early 1970s, under governments of either political shade.'

There was little difference in the picture by the time Labour lost power in 1979, and it is hardly necessary to add that the following decade brought a distinct darkening of their present and their prospects for the lower ranks of society.

But if the Wilson and Callaghan regimes achieved little in the matter of wealth redistribution, one might be disposed - bearing in mind the severe economic buffeting Britain suffered during the seventies - to plead that, like Rome, Jerusalem could not be built in a day. So let us ask the simpler question: what did Labour do about the more crying needs of the poor, about Margaret Beckett's 'great well of justifiable need'? For is it not reasonable to require of those who speak passionately of social justice that when they are able to act they make the elimination of poverty a high - if not their very top - *priority*?

The first thing to be said about poverty is that it is necessarily a relative concept. It is relative to time, i.e. entailing comparison of the living standards of contemporaries, not of people of different eras stretching back to the Stone Ages. To a large extent it is also relative to place, i.e. primarily a question of comparing the situations of people living within the same or similar societies, like with like, rather than, say, contrasting the living standards of citizens of an advanced technological society with those of Amazonian Indians. This would hardly need saying any more if it were not for the lingering influence of that stony-hearted brood which swarmed through the land while Margaret Thatcher held sway, yapping incessantly that all sections of the population had benefited from rising standards of living generated by the fabulous 'economic miracle' conjured up by 'wealth-creators' such as themselves. Their preferred view appeared to be that poverty referred to some fixed and inerasable line, to be above which was to be properly provided for so long as what was provided was sensibly managed. The attraction of that subsistence-level approach to poverty is that - one way or another! - the problem is eliminated in double-quick time.

Nevertheless when, under the Attlee Government's National Insurance Act of May 1946, Britain's rag-bag of statutory measures and agencies for doling out relief to the financially distressed and destitute was exchanged for a more or less comprehensive social security system, the ultimate yardstick employed was in effect an assessment of subsistence levels. And this assessment was not used to ensure that the non-discretionary entitlements would, on their own, provide subsistence. This was only guaranteed through the discretionary instrument of National Assistance. As the Government acknowledged, in its concern to secure the widest possible consensus both in Parliament and in the country, its Bill was, in the main, Beveridge's proposals in statutory form. In some respects (most notably in its rejection of his recommendation that for actuarial reasons the full implementation of the new pension scheme should be delayed) it improved on Beveridge, but in others it fell well short of his Plan.

As C.J. Bartlett puts it in *A History of Postwar Britain, 1945-74*:

'The choice of flat-rate contributions, determined by
what the poorest of those in employment could afford,
found few critics at the time. But conjoined with the
determination to limit the Exchequer's contribution, the
result was basic pensions in 1948 below the exiguous
Beveridge subsistence level. This meant the defeat of
his hope that in time National Assistance would be
confined to exceptional cases as the bulk of the
population became entitled to full benefits.'

In other words, notwithstanding the Labour Movement's unshakeable opposition to 'means testing', as an affliction visited by an unjust socio-economic system principally upon the working class, by setting the rates for pension and other non-discretionary entitlements at below subsistence level, the first Labour government that was really in command let the means-testing wolf in through the backdoor.

Its successors, Labour as well as Conservative, accepted this system of the doling out of alms to economic casualties by State bureaucrats - the latter-day equivalents of the Poor Law commissioners - apparently without qualms. It was all very well for John Boyd-Carpenter, Macmillan's Minister of Pensions, to tell the House (in June 1959) that no loss of self-respect was entailed in 'exercising the rights which a Christian and civilised society gives of ensuring that no one should fall below the levels that Parliament has laid down'. It was equally fine for Judith Hart, the other Harold's Minister of Social Security, to appeal (in 1967) to people to take up their *rights*, or for Jim Callaghan's Social Services Secretary David Ennals to rebuke (in 1978) certain members on the Opposition benches for referring to supplementary benefits as 'charity'. The fact remained that many people continued to consider it an indignity to have to apply to the State for assistance when in need, and it is not at all clear that re-christening National Assistance 'supplementary benefits' greatly lessened their distaste at the thought of exposing their sores to the purse-holders of State largesse. Though it is true that the mass unemployment manufactured by the Thatcherite miracle-workers has diminished the stigma by making living on the welfare (an opportunity formerly generally reserved for the working class) a way of life for many middle-class people too - the conferment, indeed, of equal shares of misery!

At all events, in July 1978 the Commission responsible for administering the tarted-up alms scheme reported that every year around 900,000 people failed to claim supplementary benefits to which they were entitled. As Maurice Bruce says in *The Coming of the Welfare State*, whatever else the Welfare State is, 'it is...certainly not Socialism', a truth that anyone pondering the use of the term *Wohlfahrstaat* in Bismarck's Germany would surely readily apprehend. Instead of concerning themselves with devising cosmetic cover-ups to conceal the ugly consequences of the gross inequalities inseparable from free-market capitalism, the Labour tribunes would have done better to exhort the people to fight for their *rights*. That would have been in accordance with the Socialist traditions that demanded that the workers be given 'the full fruits of their industry' and taught that social justice lay in the concept of the commonwealth and the principle of contributing and sharing in consonance with the criteria: 'To each according to his needs; from each according to his ability.'

Most commentators outside the circles of the more extreme free-marketeers seem quite convinced that the Attlee Government was on the right lines in laying down the groundwork for the post-war Welfare State. Thus in *Post-War Britain* Sked and Cook contend:

'In its approach to both these measures [the National Insurance Act and the National Health Service Act] the Government displayed a spirit of true egalitarianism by espousing the principle of "universality". This ensured that their legislation bore a distinctive left-wing stamp;

it also ensured that everyone in future would have equal rights to social welfare.'

Implicitly dismissing without answering the objection that 'it would have made much greater sense to have selected the really poor from the mass of the people and to have given them greater benefits' and that the rejection of this approach meant that 'the needs of the poor were being sacrificed to left-wing ideology', the authors, after stressing Labour's overwhelming desire to consign means-testing welfare systems to 'the bad old days' (which, as I have pointed out, they failed to do), go on to speak of the 'canny realism' in the Government's thinking that 'they would only get the best available...if resources were shared with the rich.'

This was unquestionably a cogent practical reason for adopting the 'universality' principle, as the beneficial effect of middle-class pressure for the maintenance and improvement of standards in the comparable case of State schooling attests. Nevertheless, it remains highly debatable whether this blindfolded impartiality in the matter of basic welfare hand-outs was in the best interests of the least privileged in the long-term. 'Positive discrimination', which was later seen as a powerful weapon in the fight against racial inequality, would surely have served them better. Through its obsession with the 'shame' of applying for National Assistance and its crippled perception of equality, Labour deprived itself of the full potential for using the welfare system as a means of making some small restitution to the workers for the rights robbed from them in the marketplace. But if this looks like yet another indication of Labour's lack of serious commitment to Socialist objectives of redistribution and driving down the road to equality, from a non-partisan but humanitarian point of view there is worse to be said. By its rejection of the case for funding social security entirely out of normal tax revenue, setting a decent inflation-proofed standard of living as the basis for benefits - at a time, too, when openly to oppose such proposals would have been to court widespread unpopularity amongst the voters - Labour lost the chance of outlawing poverty in the pioneering Welfare State.

If we accept that poverty is a relative term, inflation-proofing of benefits fixed at a given moment at a rate ensuring a 'decent' standard of living would not on its own end involuntary poverty, of course, since that decent standard would itself be changing all the time. In an epoch of rising standards such as that enjoyed in the fully industrialised countries since the Second World War, those rises need to be truly reflected at the lowest levels. Apologists for Labour's record in the field of social security might be chastened by the reminder that (as already noted in Chapter 11) it was a Tory government - that of Harold Macmillan - that first officially accepted that the poor should share in the growing prosperity of the nation by laying it down in 1959 that the poverty line that triggered extra help from the State should rise with rises in the general standard of living. (A crystal-clear statement to the same effect, explicitly endorsing the concept of relative poverty, was made twenty years later by Lynda Chalker, when she was Under-Secretary of State in Margaret Thatcher's first administration. In a parliamentary written answer she said: 'It is not sufficient to assess poverty by absolute standards: nowadays, it must be judged on relative criteria by comparison with the standard of living of other groups in the community'.)

Without the will to redistribute wealth in favour of the underprivileged, however, acceptance of what might be called this minimal principle of social justice, in an age when medical and other advances were prolonging life and thus constantly enlarging the proportion of the population that was 'non-productive' (for example, between 1948 - the year that the National Insurance Act, the National Assistance Act, *and* the National Health Service Act all came fully into force on the same day - and 1969, the number of pensioners increased by 75 per cent, 3 million people), meant that the elimination of poverty became an ever more distant social objective. Within five years of the Welfare State train departing from the terminus, its founding father was already lamenting the fact that no less than a quarter of all those receiving retirement or widows' pensions had to apply for National Assistance. By 1969, towards the end of Wilson's first stint in power, nearly 3 out of every 10 pensioners were receiving such assistance in the shiny new packaging of supplementary benefits. By 1973, with Ted Heath in office and the State retirement pension a mite more generous than usual, at about one-third of the average manual wage (for most of the time since 1948 it had hovered around 30 per cent, sometimes falling below that figure), some 1¾ million pensioners needed supplementary benefits. Writing (in *Final Term*) of the situation as it was a couple of years later, before the introduction of SERPS, Harold Wilson says that 2 million of our 7 million retirement pensioners

238

and no less than half of the nation's elderly widows were dependent on supplementary benefits. Between 1948 and 1962 the total number of people having recourse to National Assistance nearly doubled to top 2 million. By the following year more than 2½ million people were wholly or partly dependent on National Assistance, with a further million who either did not realise they were entitled to it or shunned the role of supplicant. In *Change in British Society* (1978) Professor Halsey states:

> 'Four and three-quarter million Britons receive money from the Supplementary Benefits Commission. In other words, four and three-quarter million are living at the government's own estimate of the poverty line. And there are more below it who do not claim their due.'

A report published by the Department of Health and Social Security in July 1978 stated that around £2 billion a year was being paid out as supplementary benefits to about one-tenth of the population, that is, to more than 5 million people. The product of a two-year review of the supplementary benefits system, the report was greeted with both bouquets and brickbats - bouquets for the precedent in open government set by the comprehensive publication of the working papers upon which it was based; brickbats for its assumption that no more money would be made available to operate the system and that more rigorous restrictions would have to be imposed on discretionary payments and on the right of appeal against the refusal of assistance, proposals for policy changes which indeed foreshadowed the even harsher tightening up that took place when, in 1988, the Thatcher regime introduced its euphemistically-named Social Fund. The failure of the Attlee Government to measure up to Beveridge's requirements for comprehensive social security in the first place - and of every succeeding government to face up to the problem - was now coming home to roost, as the swelling ranks of poor pensioners and of those thrown out of work began to put an intolerable strain on the supplementary benefits system. In the words of the DHSS report: 'On any realistic assessment, the scheme will have to deal with large numbers of claimants for a long time to come; it is a safety net into which many more people will fall than it was originally intended for.'

This chronic situation drew even gloomier comments from the chairman of the Supplementary Benefits Commission, Professor

David Donnison, when he addressed the annual conference of the British Association of Social Workers a couple of months later. That fewer than half of the unemployed were still able to draw unemployment insurance benefit meant that the insurance scheme designed to keep up the income of those who lost their jobs had collapsed, he told the delegates. Like many one-parent families and families in which the breadwinner was poorly paid, most of the unemployed were now at least partially dependent on supplementary benefit, and in some parts of the country the service was breaking down under the pressure of the demands on it. In an ominous foreshadowing of the evaporation of caring ('compassion fatigue' was the ironic expression later popularised by the media in the analogous case of fading response to calls from charities for donations to help them fight famine in the Third World) that was to characterise the Thatcher help-yourself decade, Donnison observed:

'As the British people have lost confidence in progress, no longer feeling that society can afford to help the poor without holding back the steady advance of everyone else to greater affluence, they have become less tolerant of those who live on incomes provided by the taxpayer. That includes civil servants and social workers along with social security claimants.'

We are unlikely to doubt where Donnison's sympathies lie. All the same, his scrupulously non-partisan, unreproving way of putting an attitude that cannot quite escape the charge of callousness might lead us almost unconsciously to swallow the highly questionable assumption that the nation's economic troubles and the consequential deceleration in growth had deprived it of the resources to cope with poverty or, at the very least, that to find adequate resources would be to demand too great sacrifices of the general population. Paradoxically, the other big danger is that by focusing our attention on the problem of the provision of social security we may lose sight of the sheer dimensions of the poverty we are concerned with - and hence of the kind of society in which we live. For although it is true that in the late twentieth century the severely deprived have come to constitute only a minority of the population of the more advanced nations, they remain so substantial and persistent an element in such countries as ours that we can no longer talk in Crosland's optimistic terms of a merely residual or 'secondary poverty'. On the contrary, it is all too evident that the two-thousand-year-old saying, 'The poor are always with you,' is as true of our times as it was of Jesus Christ's.

In 1975, for example, Help the Aged estimated that around one million of the elderly were living *below* the poverty line, a figure consistent with Age Concern's calculation in October 1978 that poverty persisted for as many as 2½ million out of the 9 million people in retirement. If we raise our definition of deprivation by just twenty per cent, we find that more than half the nation's 'senior citizens' were poor. Such was the second-class citizenship awarded to a large fraction of the people of the Welfare State when their working lives were over. Large numbers of those who had not yet started working for wages but were the nation's future, its children, commonly suffered from the low pay of their parents - to such an extent that by the end of the Thatcher decade it was reckoned that a quarter of British children were growing up in poverty - a dispossessed fraction which by 1995 had been revised upwards to one third. As for the total numbers of the poor, in 1976, at about the mid point of Labour's last inglorious period in office, it was calculated that nearly 10½ million people - around a fifth of the nation - were living on, below, or no more than twenty per cent above the poverty line.

The big change we ('we', that is, in the advanced Western-style societies) have experienced in the last half century is that for the first time poverty has unquestionably become the affliction of a minority. And to that extent capitalism (when harnessed with representative democracy and the Welfare State, neither of which is exactly a natural stable-mate for it) *has*, at long last, delivered the goods. Comparing the purchasing power of male manual workers earning the median income of just over £1 a week in 1905, with that enjoyed by male manual workers with median earnings of just over £60 a week in 1976, Professor Halsey reckons that 'we can safely say that they also represent at least a tripling of real income.' He goes on to remark: 'Nor can there be any doubt that the ordinary manual worker and his wife are very much less the slaves of toil than they were in Edwardian England.' As he says: 'Their market freedoms, whether as earners or spenders, have been transformed.' When, not long after taking over the reins of power from the stricken Sir Anthony Eden, Harold Macmillan told the country, 'Most of our people have never had it so good,' (words which, when recycled by the Grub Street hucksters as 'you've never had it so good', sounded like a Tory taunt to the have-nots or a vulgar come-on to the punters), he was doing no more than telling the truth. That was within a dozen years of the end of the most exhausting and near-mortal combat the country had ever engaged in; and the exponential growth of the advanced economies, whether they had been victors, vanquished, or neutral in the titanic conflict of 1939-45, was to continue more or less unabated into the early seventies, raising general living standards more rapidly than ever before or (so far at least) since.

In February 1978 the Central Statistical Office recorded in its annual supplement on 'Economic Trends' that real incomes had doubled between 1953, when the consumption boom began, and the summer of 1976, when it hit its peak, not long after the great pragmatist Harold Wilson, with that juggler's sense of timing for which he was celebrated, had handed over the golden balls of the State to Sunny Jim. During 1977 living standards fell: only by about one per cent, but the sense of standing on an escalator that would in time carry everyone to prosperity gave way to that gloomier mood to which Donnison alludes - and to a what-we-have-we-hold family-laager frame of mind that left little room for concern for the underclass who never had enjoyed a secure place on the escalator.

A high proportion of this 'submerged fifth' (to adopt a term from history) was naturally composed of some of those who, in a modern civilised society, were considered either too young or too old to be expected to work for wages. They were, in short, dependants by reason and by right of their age. Writing about the problem of the provision of social security at the end of the sixties, Bartlett notes that the ratio of children and pensioners to the working population had risen from 488 to 1000 in 1941, to 655 to 1000 in 1969. Commenting on the fact that 'Britain's overall performance in social welfare ranked below that generally achieved within the EEC', he alludes to the extenuating circumstances of Britain's recurrent economic crises and slow growth, and points out that much of the rise in welfare expenditure during the Wilson ministries was simply absorbed by rising numbers of dependants. 'In these circumstances,' he observes, 'the plight of the poor could only have been relieved by a radical redistribution of wealth.'

But that is precisely what Labour's top brass had set their minds against. As early as April 1949, Attlee's second Chancellor of the Exchequer, Sir Stafford Cripps, laid down the principles which - with the full approval, of course, of their generalissimos - all succeeding Labour chancellors were to follow:

> 'There is not much further immediate possibility of the redistribution of national income by way of taxation in this country; for the future, we must rely rather upon the creation of more distributable wealth than upon...redistribution...Total taxation, local and national, is now more than 40 per cent of the national income, and at that level the redistribution of income entailed in the payment of Social Services already falls, to a considerable extent, upon those who are the recipients of these services. We must, therefore, moderate the speed of our advance in the extended application of the existing Social Services to our progressive ability to pay for them by an increase in our national income. Otherwise, we shall not be able to avoid entrenching, to an intolerable extent, upon the liberty of spending by the private individual for his own purposes.'

That *ex cathedra* pronouncement, made in the context of a budget founded on a TUC-endorsed wage-freeze, is of immeasurably greater significance than all the Healey-style rhetoric of the irreversible-shift-of-power and squeezing-the-rich-till-the-pips-squeak varieties, since it spells out the rules that Labour imposed upon itself in the struggle for social justice. It was as if Samson had bound himself. What scope was left for the pursuit of equality, or even for the abolition of poverty and the guaranteeing of adequate social welfare for all? As for pulling down the pillars of the temples of capitalism, Heavens forbid!

Cripps was voicing his overriding concern for the private individual's 'liberty of spending' (assenting, in effect, to the common proposition that everybody has the right to do what he pleases with 'his own property') as Labour's purported social revolution was still supposedly in full swing. Yet, like any other reputable politician, he put his emphasis not on the problems of sharing fairly wealth produced by common effort, but on the need to increase the size of the cake. 'Let the people eat cake crumbs' - to revamp a celebrated piece of apocrypha. The world created by capitalism was not, at least in its essentials, to be disturbed. Social progress - including whatever creeping steps towards greater equality, if any, were envisaged - was to depend on economic growth steadily increasing the national income. Ruling politicians would play no more than a subsidiary role to capitalism's celebrated 'trickle-down' benevolence by doling out to the most disadvantaged 'the superflux' in the State's coffers.

This always was a fraudulent prospectus for bringing about equality, of course. Even given increasing prosperity for all classes, since when have the more affluent been content to see their differentials diminishing? And no way would they accept that they ought to receive a *smaller* share of the new wealth created than the less affluent! Indeed, to their way of thinking, they were entitled to a share of the new wealth fully proportionate to the hoard they already had! But however devoid of Socialist content such an attitude might have been, it did at least hold out some hope of improvement in the lives of the grossly underprivileged as long as growth kept coming. Throughout the fifties and sixties, notwithstanding the recurrent economic crises and a worrying decline in her trading position in an increasingly competitive world, Britain enjoyed her longest period of sustained growth this century. By the time Wilson lost power in the summer of 1970, however, the prospects already looked gloomier, with Anthony Crosland confessing that he had been too complacent in pinning all his hopes for a more equal society on growth when he wrote *The Future of Socialism*. Six months before the debacle of May 1979, one of the then doughtiest champions of the poor challenged Labour to confirm or deny its presumed identity as a party of radical reform. In an article in *The Guardian*, the director-general of the Child Poverty Action Group and of the Low Pay Unit, Frank Field, who was himself to become a Labour MP by winning Birkenhead in the forthcoming election, wrote:

'If, in the foreseeable future, the economy fails to grow
at a greater rate, Labour will be forced to choose
between ditching its role as the reforming party or
breaking the post-war political consensus...The agent for
lowering the political temperature, while at the same
time removing the stains left by society's grosser forms

of poverty, is a steadily rising national income. The promise to the "haves" was that injustice could be painlessly removed; they would not be required to make real, only accept relative cuts in their living standards. Economic growth would guarantee that the real income of the "haves" rose while only part of the largesse was transferred to the "have nots".'

From Crosland's insistence that 'in a democracy low or zero growth wholly excludes the possibility' of the substantial transference of resources to the poorer sections of society, Field drew the conclusion that in the situation then obtaining - one of low growth with ever-rising numbers of people becoming dependent on State welfare as a consequence of demographic changes and increasing unemployment - 'Labour will not only have to abandon its commitments to creating a more equal society but stand idly by as the poor suffer real cuts in their standards of living.' The gravamen of his case was that Labour's only alternative was to abandon consensus politics in favour of 'a determined policy of redistributing existing resources.'

When the sixth report of the Royal Commission on the Distribution of Income and Wealth was published in the summer of 1978, it had carried an addendum by three of its members who argued that income distribution could be improved by political will. But where was that will to be found? Certainly not among the top Labour leadership, who were wholly engrossed in the struggle against inflation and the concomitant campaign to break-in the trade unions by saddling them with another incomes policy. The project amounted to a straitjacket for working-class aspirations. Not even the most exploited groups of workers got a fair crack of the whip from the Callaghan Government. The poverty lobby, which had bitterly pronounced that the plight of the poor had grown worse under Labour in the sixties, was now only willing to reduce the charge slightly by adding a question mark. On the eve of the 1979 general election Ruth Lister, Frank Field's successor at the Child Poverty Action Group, asked: whatever happened to James Callaghan's pledge of a crusade against poverty? There was nothing for the poor in any of the party manifestos, she protested. Yet again, the cry of the poor was falling on deaf ears. And the callousness was compounded by the fact that 'the people's party' was in power and had ruled for the past five years.

CHAPTER 20

A marriage on the rocks

'The trade unionists...having had their minds so fully occupied with the idea that Parliament is the all-important institution, and never having even hoped to see all workers organised industrially, have failed to realise what enormous power lies in industrial solidarity.'

Tom Mann, *Memoirs* **(1923)**

Moving the address of thanks for the King's Speech in the Commons on 16th August 1945, just after the victory of the Allies over Japan, Major John Freeman told the House that this was 'D-Day in the battle of the new Britain.' In those 'bliss-was-it-to-be-alive' days no one in the triumphant ranks of the 'we-are-the-masters-now' party could have dreamt of the bitterness of the battles that were to come - not those they fully expected to have with their acknowledged political opponents (the 'class enemy', or even the 'vermin', as some Labour members thought of them), but those that were to take place within the ranks of the Labour Movement itself. A third of a century later fratricidal strife threatened to shatter the Movement, as the dominant forces in its parliamentary wing clashed with the trade union battalions that more directly represented the Party's 'working-class' constituency.

Abetted by a press almost wholly hostile to Labour and near-to-universally antipathetic to trade unions, the Tories have been so successful at selling their twopence-coloured broadsheet portrayal of the so-called Winter of Discontent to the electorate at large that it has become - even for many habitual Labour voters - the authorised version of that social upheaval, to be recited by right-wing cheerleaders at election after election as conclusive evidence of Labour's unfitness to govern. The message it punches home is of the gross irresponsibility, greed and intolerable anarchy that prevail whenever law and government fail to keep union power firmly in check. 'What kind of society is this that breeds such selfish callousness?' Margaret Thatcher, with that breath-taking effrontery that comes so easily to her, demanded, lusting after her 'glorious summer'.

The photomontage of rubbish piled high in the streets, the dead denied burial, the sick forsaken by nursing orderlies, and the like, that became imprinted on the mind's-eye of the public, testifies to the easily-won supremacy of image over information and of emotional orgasm over intellectual appraisal. What does on first consideration astonish, though, is that this tabloid travesty of the true story of the Winter of Discontent has gone largely unchallenged by Labour. On first consideration, that is - until one reflects how much more unpalatable for Labour the conclusions of any more carefully-considered analysis must be. For the Winter of Discontent came close to dispelling for ever the illusion that a Labour government has one great and undeniable advantage not enjoyed by its opponents when they are in power - a hotline to the unions that can ensure at least a tolerable measure of industrial peace. The truth is that for many years after the war Labour's leaders were able to make this claim with some credibility. Then, like the lover in Dylan's song, they threw it all away.

The term Labour Movement is, of course, much more than a piece of rhetoric expressing a general sympathy between the purposes of the Party and those of the trade unions. Affiliation to the Party theoretically conferred on the unions enormous - indeed, predominant - power in the formulation of its policy and the election of its leadership. As David Coates says in *Labour in Power?*: 'It is facts like these that give credence to the repeated Conservative claim that the Labour Party in office is the creature of trade union control.' In certain respects the integration of party and affiliated unions is so intimate (Kenneth O. Morgan calls it 'intimate symbiosis') that to talk of the separate wings of one movement and of the dialogue between them may be said to be a tool of analysis rather than a description of reality. Yet by their nature they remain - and cannot but remain - distinct and alternative centres of power; and that natural tension between them which makes of them one structure (a tension inherent in the Party's origins at the beginning of the century as the Labour Representation Committee) may shift so far out of balance as to threaten disintegration. Indeed, considering the potential for conflict between them and the many actual clashes that have occurred (particularly during periods when the Labour Party has been in office), it is a matter for some wonder that - contrary to the view assiduously propagated in the press - the unions have generally behaved with such remarkable restraint that the couple has managed to rub along together for so long.

Time and again (to speak, as is customary, in terms of leaders and elites, not of the common ruck) loyalty to the Party - or to put it more precisely, concern for its prospects at the polls - has overridden trade union interests. This loyalty was, understandably, at its height during the days of hope of Attlee's first administration, when at least it could be claimed that 'the social wage' was being pushed up substantially. A White Paper published in February 1948 in effect called for the freezing of personal incomes except where rises were justified by increased productivity. Despite the fact that there had been no prior consultation with the TUC - let alone union rank and file, this policy was agreed to at a special conference of trade union executive delegates by a majority of 5,421,000 to 2,032,000. It was endorsed by the following TUC Conference, and was not overturned until the autumn 1950 Conference. Then, under the pressures of a rapidly rising cost of living caused principally by the devaluation of sterling in September 1949 and the outbreak of the Korean War in June 1950, wage restraint was voted down by the small majority of 222,000.

Even before a pay pause had become official TUC policy, considerable restraint had been exercised by the unions, as is shown by the fact that the general level of wages was in real terms lower in 1948 than in 1947. Sked and Cook note that: 'From 1948 till August 1950 wage rates rose by only 5 per cent while retail prices rose by 8 per cent. Indeed between 1945 and 1951 average weekly wages rose in real terms by only 6 per cent.' In other words, they say, quoting another's analyst's caustic comment: 'Under six years of socialism the workers had to work a great deal of overtime to improve their standard of living by a tiny 1 per cent a year.'

In his *Years of Recovery: British Economic Policy 1945-51*, Sir Alec Cairncross draws attention to another fact which makes this restraint even more remarkable. In a capitalist economy the price of labour, like that of other commodities, is of course largely determined by supply and demand. Thus periods of labour surplus have always tended to mean hard times for the workers and their families, whilst periods of labour shortages are times of opportunity for increasing their prosperity by militant action or the threat of it. Yet, as Cairncross points out:

'That money wages rose so little when real wages were stationary or falling and unemployment was down to

300,000 is striking testimony to the influence of the trade-union leaders. Hourly wage rates after March 1948 rose no faster than in the mid-1930s, between 1934 and 1938, when unemployment was around two million.'

It is neither coincidence nor perversity which makes periods in opposition, normally speaking, those in which the Labour Movement is most united. In saying this I am not simply making the obvious point which applies to any party defeated at the polls, that, notwithstanding the painfulness of post-mortems and of abrasive debate about how best to adjust their programme and tactics, the will to win next time will tend to draw them together. I am making a point more specific to Labour: that when the Party is out of office it is natural for those in all the echelons of the Labour Movement to feel like comrades in adversity, but when the Party is in power, constitutionally-speaking it represents 'the national interest', while the unions, separately considered and even considered collectively, merely represent sectional interests. (That too might seem blindingly obvious, but far too little account is taken of this fundamental fracture in the Movement in serious analysis, as distinct from partisan squibbery.) So, notwithstanding the fierce debates that took place within the Movement over such momentous issues as 'the bomb' and whether Clause IV should be considered as anything more than an example of junkable antiquarianism, as Hugh Gaitskell hopefully positioned himself for a victory at the polls that never came, Labour's matrimonial difficulties during the 'thirteen wasted years' were as nothing to the turbulent times it experienced after it returned to power under Harold Wilson's leadership.

Wage restraint may not have been an article of faith for Labour governments (as it is, with respect to 'ordinary workers', for what one used to be able to distinguish as 'the bourgeois parties'); but in running a capitalist economy in a situation of slow growth, of a problematic balance of trade, and of recurrent sterling crises, it was no less a practical imperative for them than it was for the Tories. Above all, it was seen by every Chancellor of the Exchequer, of whatever party, as the main means to bind the serpent of inflation. The efforts of Wilson and his Chancellors, James Callaghan and Roy Jenkins, to stem the tide of the trade unions' drive, sometimes to improve but often simply to maintain or recover the position of their members in the pecking order, span Labour's whole period in office between 1964 and 1970.

The details of the four formal stages of wage restraint decreed during those years are of little interest now. What remains significant is the retrogression from the attempt at voluntary co-operation - exemplified by the Joint Statement of Intent on Productivity, Prices and Incomes signed by representatives of the Government, the TUC, and employers' organisations in December 1964, and also by the Prices and Incomes Board set up in April 1965, which had only monitoring and advisory powers - to the Government's mobilisation of powers of compulsory restraint under the 1966 Prices and Incomes Act. Twenty-three Labour back-benchers defied the Government whip when the Bill was pushed through the Commons on the ominous date of August 4th. Nor was this downhill path to division in the Movement taken without protest from trade union leaders as well as the rank and file. Yet it is still significant that it was not until the autumn of 1968 that the Government's wages policy was repudiated by the Movement's two principal annual conferences. Both rejections were by crushing majorities, nearly five to one at the Party Conference and nearly eight to one at the TUC's. And even then, at their conference, the workers' delegates agreed to the TUC's own policy of voluntary restraint, though admittedly only by the tiny margin of 34,000 votes.

The climax of this collision between the two wings of the Labour Movement came a few months later, with the publication in January 1969 of *In Place of Strife*. This White Paper, intended as the basis of legislation designed to pacify industrial relations, had its origin in the disappointment of Wilson and some of his colleagues with the Donovan Report. In February 1965 the Labour Government had announced the appointment, under the chairmanship of Lord Donovan, of a Royal Commission on Trade Unions and Employers' Associations, though as Joe England and Brian Weekes acidly remark in their essay *Trade Unions and the State: A Review of the Crisis* (1981): 'No one doubted that trade unions were intended to be the main target for investigation.' The Commission as a whole, however, was certainly well-disposed towards the trade unions (one of its members, indeed, was the TUC's general secretary, George Woodcock), and its report, published in June 1968, came down decisively against legal coercion as a solution to Britain's industrial relations problems. In taking this view, it showed far more wisdom than Wilson and his Secretary of State for Employment and Productivity, Barbara Castle (the minister principally responsible for the Government's White Paper), who perhaps shared Nye Bevan's incomprehension that workers could strike against 'a workers' government' and were certainly fearful of the electoral consequences of failing to bring the unions to heel.

In *Place of Strife* made twenty-seven specific proposals, including the establishment of a permanent Industrial Relations Commission, a Register of Trade Unions and Employers' Associations, and new kinds of industrial arbitration - ideas to which the Donovan Report had already given currency without arousing much controversy. In his autobiography, James Callaghan cites his own contemporaneous note recording his feeling that '90 per cent of the White Paper is not only acceptable but welcome', and certainly most offence was given by those three proposals (out of the total of twenty-seven) that contained coercive and penal clauses. These chiefly concerned provisions for compulsory arbitration in intractable inter-union disputes, for compulsory ballots before strikes deemed to constitute a serious threat to the public interest, and (mimicking a hamstringing clause in America's notorious anti-labour Taft-Hartley Act), for the imposition of a 28-day cooling-off and conciliation period before a strike could take place. The main thrust of these proposed sanctions was directed against strikes in 'essential services' and unofficial strikes, the latter constituting, according to the Donovan Commission's calculations, no less than 95 per cent of the total number of strikes.

Further testimony to the embarrassing gap between establishment notions of labour discipline and the insubordinate reality was provided by the Prime Minister himself, who appealed for sympathy to an audience of City worthies in a speech at the Guildhall (in so doing, implicitly identifying himself with them and his troubles with theirs, of course), by telling them: 'We face the problem of an assertion of the power of the factory floor.' As Bartlett wryly remarks, with reference to the ascendant influence of shop stewards: 'The government's dismay over the rise of shop floor wage bargaining was a little ironic given its own encouragement of productivity deals, which of course required that type of approach.' He also notes that: 'Incomes policy had been circumvented in other ways, so that the Prices and Incomes Board concluded that its effect between 1965 and 1968 had been to reduce incomes by no more than one per cent a year...'

In any event, in an atmosphere of growing militancy the national leaders of the unions were obliged either to get out in front or be seen as irrelevant by the rank and file. The number of strikes rose from an annual average of 1,181 in the four years before Labour regained power to nearly 1,500 in both 1964 and 1965, and to nearly 2,000 in 1966. It continued to climb steadily through 1967 and 1968, then steeply to well over 3,000 in 1969 and to not far short of 4,000 in 1970, the year in which, in June, the Tories were returned to power under Ted Heath. As for the man-hours lost through strike action, these rose at the rate of around two million strike-days a year between 1967 and 1969, when they reached about 6,800,000 strike-days. It is not easy to calculate the effects of industrial action on the counter-inflation policies of the governments trying to impose them; but despite the common assumption that the effects of such action are devastating, it is a fact that the increase in retail prices was held to an average of below 6 per cent between 1968 and 1970, but rose to 8.6 per cent under Heath.

When Wilson insinuated to his receptive Guildhall audience that the Government had been right in contending that the State needed more statutory powers to control the unions, he had already lost the battle. What is astonishing is that Harold and Barbara ever thought that they could win it (without destroying the Labour Movement in the process, that is). Despite all warnings - including a mutiny in the Commons when the White Paper was debated on 3rd March 1969 in which 55 Labour members voted against it and about as many again abstained, the NEC's decisive rejection by 16 votes to 5 on 26th March, and the strong opposition of the TUC which had been forthrightly expressed from the beginning and never showed signs of wavering - they pressed on with their shackling proposals from January to June, when at last, given pause by a crushing rebuff inflicted by a special TUC conference held at Croydon, they began a face-saving withdrawal. On 17th June, Robert Mellish, the Government's Chief Whip, reported to the Cabinet that more than half the Parliamentary Labour Party was opposed to the penal proposals and that there was no chance of their being pushed through the Commons. The next day the Labour Movement gave birth to the celebrated illusionist Solomon Binding.

Harold Wilson in his memoirs and Barbara Castle by report both claimed that with the threat of penal legislation hanging over them the unions had moved forward farther in a matter of weeks than they had in forty years. (Why 'forty' one can only speculate, but it can hardly be coincidental that that would have taken the scenario back to the despondent aftermath of the near-revolutionary clash between the State and the unions in 1926, in which the leaders of both wings of the Movement had, with few exceptions, played such a pusillanimous part). But the fact was that Labour's would-be statespersons had had their bluff called and had capitulated. Apart from the undertaking given in the trade unions' own counter-proposals (the so-called *Programme for Action* drawn up by the TUC and endorsed by the Croydon conference, which Barbara Castle contemptuously dismissed as a 'pious hope') that they would submit to the rulings of the TUC General Council in inter-union disputes or face suspension, virtually only one additional concession was wrung from them. It was a 'solemn and binding' but not legally enforceable pledge from the General Council that affiliated unions would observe the TUC's own guidelines on the containment of unofficial strikes.

As James Callaghan says: 'This whole episode was a venture bound to end in tears.' Certainly he was a great deal more canny than the Prime Minister and his fiery redhead, whom Callaghan characterises as galloping ahead 'with all the reckless gallantry of the Light Brigade at Balaclava.' In a note he wrote at the time which makes her sound much more like that ultimate conviction (i.e. 'I am always right') politician, Mrs Thatcher, than he perhaps intended, he also distinguishes between those whose unqualified support for the White Paper he considered implicated them in 'the shabby and squalid intellectual dishonesty which pretends that these clauses are going to solve unofficial strikes and, therefore, are vital for our balance of payments problems' and the passionately sincere (but presumably dumb) redhead: 'Barbara is a different case; she believes passionately in any job she is doing at the time...and she is absolutely convinced, but there is no reason why the rest of us should be.'

Callaghan thought the White Paper 'contained excellent ideas' but had a flaw which he clearly considered fatal:

'But the paper was flawed by ineffective proposals for legal sanctions as a solution to the problem of unofficial strikes. Both industrial strikers and unions would be liable to fines, *but it would not be the employers who would take the strikers to court. The Government itself would make an order having legal effect, thereby bringing the state directly into conflict with the men concerned.'* [my emphasis]

Whether or not this dispassionate analysis implies that he saw no objections in principle to such proposals, but only objections, regrettably, on pragmatic grounds, it is undeniably shrewd. Such a conflict between workers and State might be welcome to politicians of other hues (though even then such pugnacity might be deemed rash); but to politically literate Labour politicians it could only spell FOLLY.

Callaghan is equally Olympian in his casual allusion to the fact that, far from being privy to the drafting of the White Paper, as a known opponent of its more draconian measures, he was deliberately kept in the dark. He was, after all, in addition to being Home Secretary, particularly closely associated with the trade unions as Party Treasurer, and was a member of the Cabinet committee on industrial relations, which was vouchsafed no sight of the White Paper prior to its coming before full Cabinet. Yet all we get in his autobiography touching on this 'oversight' (to put the impropriety in diplomatic terms) is the oblique observation that 'the issue had not been considered in the usual manner by Cabinet committee so there were many rough edges and unanswered questions.' A somewhat nicer concern for the workings of inner party democracy and constitutional government might prod a person into voicing some more astringent comment. For example, that this devious and deliberate bypassing of the Cabinet committee most pertinent to the issue under consideration provided just a foretaste of the monstrous-regiment-of-Woman government that was to come in a decade or so.

But however complex and disingenuous or, as he would have us believe, transparent and straightforward Callaghan's motives might have been, his stance served him very well in the long term, winning him widespread union support in the contest for the leadership that took place after Wilson sprung his resignation on the Party in the spring of '76. Indeed, moves were afoot during the crisis provoked by the schismatic proposals of *In Place of Strife* to persuade Jim to challenge Harold for the leadership, and if Harold had not backed down, it seems certain he would have faced a shoot-out. In his contemporaneous note cited above, Callaghan takes pains to refute the allegations being 'put around' that his opposition to the penal proposals in the White Paper was to be explained as a prelude to a bid for the top job. But such a reading of his conduct is not necessarily incompatible with his insistence that his opposition reflected his judgement as to what was prudent and in the best interests of the Party. At any rate, Denis Healey makes no bones about his rival's ambitions in his autobiography: 'Callaghan campaigned publicly against them ["Barbara's proposals"] in the hope of winning enough trade union support to force Wilson out and take his place.'

What may be regarded as of much greater moment than these questions of, on the one hand, conspiracy and vaunting ambition, or on the other, opposition directed solely by disinterested judgement and sense of duty, are the consequences to the Party and to the whole Labour Movement of the internecine strife unleashed by *In Place of Strife*. And here Healey's verdict on what he calls 'six months of civil war throughout the Labour movement', severe though it is, seems fully justified:

> 'The Government had wasted six months on a hopeless
> fight, *which had caused permanent damage to our*
> *relations with the trade unions, without making them any*
> *less necessary to our survival. In Place of Strife* did for
> Wilson what the hopeless attempt to delete Clause Four
> from the Party Constitution had done for Hugh Gaitskell.'
> [my emphasis]

It seems improbable that I can be the first person to observe that periodically the Labour Party seems to exhibit a death-wish. To say this is not to associate oneself with those don't-rock-the-boat chants to which - whether from simplicity or deviousness - many Labour supporters are addicted. Such pleas are nothing more than a sort of obscurantist electoralism. Politics that fail to transcend the pursuit of power and pork barrels are simply squalid and (except for the winners) meaningless. But while meaningful politics necessarily entail the clash of differing viewpoints within every party with any pretensions to being democratic, not simply between the parties, this does not adequately explain why the Labour Party repeatedly tears itself apart in full view of the public eye. Certainly in the case of *In Place of Strife* conflict plunged from a properly combative passion into an abyss of unreason and self-mutilation. One can hardly doubt that, far more than the industrial unrest that engendered the thought of such desperate remedies in the minds of the White Paper's most ardent supporters, the public spectacle of this strife played some part in the defeat of the Party in the general election of June 1970. Certainly the distrust the episode sowed between the two wings of the Movement was still reverberating menacingly in the Winter of Discontent.

Moreover, whenever Labour politicians talk regretfully of the abandonment of the post-war consensus in British politics, they should be brusquely reminded that it was not the Tories but Labour that first reached for the legal truncheon to subdue the unions. It was his adversary's example that Ted Heath emulated in introducing his industrial relations legislation. Indeed, the first thing to be said about the Industrial Relations Bill, which was enacted on 6th August 1971, after no less than 450 hours of debate spread over 60 days (in fact it absorbed one-third of the Government's legislative time during that session of Parliament), is that the Tories were right in maintaining that it was, to use Lord Wedderburn's phrase, 'in line of descent' not only from their own *Fair Deal at Work* but from *In Place of Strife*, and that both were offspring of the Donovan Report. (They might well have gone further than they did in rubbing in the point that their 1968 proposals could reasonably be assumed to have played no small part in prodding Labour into matching their bid for public favour by abandoning the party's traditional dependence on voluntary co-operation between government and unions to maintain acceptable industrial relations 'in the national interest'.)

For despite important differences of emphasis, particularly concerning situations in which individual rights sometimes came into conflict with collective rights, there was more in common than at variance between the Heath-Carr prescriptions and the nostrums so reluctantly withdrawn by Wilson and Castle. Each scheme involved the State registration of trade unions, which was supposed to confer on them the protection of the law, balanced, of course, by legal obligations. In each scheme industrial courts had an important role. Each of them had provisions for secret ballots before industrial action was taken and compulsory cooling-off periods. Each of them, in short, constituted a step down the road to the Corporate State. Additions to the State's coercive armoury under the Industrial Relations Act included powers for the Government to apply to the newly-minted National Industrial

Relations Court for restraining orders under 'national emergency' injunctions, and for Government intervention in cases concerning the disciplining and expulsion of members by the unions to which they belonged. The pretext for assuming this particular power and for the outlawing of the closed shop, which would likewise serve to weaken the solidarity of workers in dispute with their bosses, was the Tories' celebrated concern for 'the right to work' so long as you could find it and could stomach the terms that the 'free contract' of employment imposed upon you.

From the point of view of a party representing the employing classes and prone to thinking of the trade unions as, at best, a bit of a nuisance and, at worst, a threat to 'the spheres in their courses', doubtless this all seemed eminently reasonable. Even supposing that to be the case, however, there remains the problem of tactical consistency. Considering that those who conceived the Industrial Relations Act were not academicians from Lagado but experienced players of the power game, it is a little surprising that they seemed to be gripped by a strange kind of schizophrenia. The muscle-flexing that formed the substance of their strategy in squaring up to the unions could have made some kind of sense if they had had the will to follow far enough in Mussolini's footsteps (although at some hazard even to *parliamentary* democracy). But it was accompanied by the make-believe thinking that it could be seamlessly joined to a let's-all-be-reasonable approach that is best exemplified by two provisions in the Act: one, for the registration of trade unions; two, for collective agreements to be made legally binding if both parties assented. Not only was this agreement-into-contract offer shunned by the unions, but like the outlawing of the closed shop it was not even generally favoured by affected employers. As for union registration, this was not made obligatory, but only those unions that did register were, in effect, to be considered to be unions. But, regrettably, declining to call a lion legally a lion does not make it a lamb. Despite the loss of legal privileges which cost the unions £10 million in taxes and in pension funds, the TUC instructed its affiliates not to register. Only twenty-one unions chose legitimisation by the State in preference to strength through solidarity with the rest of the organised labour movement. One of these cancelled its affiliation to the TUC and the other twenty were expelled.

Like its Labour predecessor, Heath's Government turned from efforts to combat inflation through voluntary co-operation between the Government, the CBI, and the TUC, to statutory control, starting in November 1972 with a 90-day standstill on prices, pay, dividends, and rents, and moving on through two more stages designed to impose strict limits on rises in prices and incomes. The attempt to keep the lid on demands for a better standard of living was challenged again and again by many groups of workers, including gas-workers, power engineers, local authority manual workers, civil servants in their first ever strike, dockers, railwaymen, and above all by the miners, who showed twice that the Government's edicts did not run in the face of workers' militancy.

What the Industrial Relations Act did achieve was a spectacular rise in the number of days lost through strike action. From an average of hardly more than 2 million in the first post-war decade and of well under 4 million between 1955 and 1969, the figure shot up to nearly 11 million in 1970, to over 13½ million in 1971, and to almost 24 million in 1972, the highest total since 1926. The Act designed to put the unions on a leash in fact provoked the rebirth of the political strike in Britain. According to one estimate twice as many workers took part in official and unofficial strikes against the Industrial Relations Act in 1970-71 as were involved in the entire year's more strictly industrial disputes. In keeping with its anti-revolutionary traditions, the TUC refused to call for industrial action against the Act, but for all that, Joe England and Brian Weekes are broadly right in their judgement that: 'Rank-and-file activists joined with the trade union leaders in opposition to the Act, thus bringing about *one of those rare occasions when all levels of union power were operating in the same direction at the same time.*' [my emphasis]

The Tory Government had acted as its own agent-provocateur without ensuring that it could cope with the situation it had provoked (as was most dramatically illustrated by the case of the Pentonville Five, in which a one-day general strike in protest at the imprisonment of five dockers for breaking the industrial relations law was only forestalled by the Law Lords cooking up a pretext for their release from jail). It is true that the same might be said of the authors of *In Place of Strife*, but since the unions were at least nominally their allies, Harold and Barbara, unlike Ted, did at least have some grounds for flattering themselves that they might seduce them into lying down on the procrustean bed of State-regulated industrial action. Since the Tories could hardly share such delusions, theirs must have been engendered by faith in the intimidatory power of the State *per se*. But ''tis the eye of childhood that fears a painted devil.'

Their folly did a singular service to their adversaries, throwing them into each others arms again after the bitter squabbles occasioned by the imprudent attempt of one of the partners to restrict the liberties of the other. The question asked by Ted Heath, however, after the miners' militancy had put industry on a three-day working week and virtually forced him to go to the country - 'Who governs Britain?' - remained unanswered.

CHAPTER 21

A contract dishonoured

'You will eat, bye and bye,
In that glorious land above the sky;
Work and pray, live on hay,
You'll get pie in the sky when you die.'

Chorus from a song by Joe Hill,
The Preacher and the Slave

Following the humiliation of the Tories by the miners, the Labour Movement (to speak mythically) returned to power on 1st March 1974 apparently more purposefully united than at any time since the first Attlee Government. Denis Healey's fighting-talk reference to 'the most radical and comprehensive programme...since 1945' was no exaggeration. Had it 'honestly stated' what the Party's *leaders* were resolved to do, their goal might even have been described as social revolution. According to the manifesto Labour put before the electorate, its aims were:

(a) To bring about a fundamental and irreversible shift in the balance of power and wealth in favour of working people and their families;
(b) To eliminate poverty wherever it exists in Britain and commit ourselves to a substantial contribution to fight poverty abroad;
(c) To make power in industry genuinely accountable to the workers and the community at large;
(d) To achieve far greater economic equality - in income, wealth and living standards;
(e) To increase social equality by giving greater importance to full employment, housing, education and social benefits;
(f) To improve the environment in which our people live and work and spend their leisure.

More specifically, the parliamentary wing of the Movement was committed to what amounted to a 'social contract' with the trade union wing of the Movement, pledging what David Coates justly describes, in *Labour in Power?*, as 'radical and innovatory

260

policy in the fields of industrial relations, housing, prices, social benefits, investment and industrial democracy.' These undertakings stemmed from the *Statement on Economic Policy and the Cost of Living* drawn up by the TUC-Labour Party Liaison Committee and published in February 1973, which embraced (in Coates' summary):

(a) what it termed 'a wide ranging and permanent system of price controls', particularly on food;
(b) a new approach to housing and rent, to include the repeal of the 1972 Housing Finance Act, the long-run municipalisation of private rented property, the public ownership of required building land, and the building of at least 400,000 houses a year;
(c) the strengthening of public transport, and experiments with free public transport in major conurbations;
(d) a large-scale redistribution of income and wealth, by wealth taxes, gift taxes, and steeply progressive direct taxation;
(e) the end of prescription charges, and an immediate rise in pensions, with pensions thereafter to be annually updated in line with average earnings;
(f) the expansion of investment and the control of capital by further public ownership, by the extension of state supervision of private investment, and by new measures of control to prevent excessive investment overseas;
(g) the extension of industrial democracy, by bringing investment policy and closure policy into the scope of collective bargaining.

As Coates comments, the 'contract' was 'significantly quiet on the question of incomes policy'. In joint pursuit of the return to power of a Labour government, neither party to the 'contract' wished to fan the embers of the bitter recriminations provoked by the clash over *In Place of Strife*. None the less, there was undoubtedly an understanding that the union leaders would do their best to moderate wage demands as a quid pro quo for what could fairly be claimed, if the promises were delivered, as a major advance in the social wage.

The second (or should it be called the umpteenth?) honeymoon between the two partners composing the Labour Movement lasted scarcely longer than the seven months between the February and October general elections of 1974, in the second of which Wilson obtained a working majority. Nevertheless, in the opening period of his tenure it really looked as if the Government meant to keep its side of the bargain. In her diary Barbara Castle called Harold Wilson 'custodian of the Manifesto' and spoke of his 'playing it straight down the line of party policy.' Ted Heath's obnoxious Industrial Relations Act was repealed, to be replaced by the much less threatening Trade Union and Labour Relations Act, which was followed up by the positively worker-friendly Employment Protection Act of 1975. Agencies with powers to intervene in the labour market were set up: the Advisory Conciliation and Arbitration Service, the Health and Safety Commission, and the Manpower Services Commission held out real promise of more protection and security for working people. Progress both in the workplace and in wider social fields was made by other legislation, including the Sex Discrimination Act of 1975 and the Race Relations Act of 1976, and by the Government's redeeming of its pledge to repeal Heath's 1972 Housing Finance Act - an act which is a notable example of the tireless ingenuity of the capitalist State in shifting the burden of subsidising the poor from the backs of the well-to-do to those of the hard up. (It was this act that led to the surcharging and disqualification of the twenty-one Clay Cross Labour councillors who refused to implement Government-imposed increases in council housing rents.)

The return of Labour brought an expansion of local authority housing programmes and measures to discourage the sale of council housing. A rent freeze was imposed and the Price Code and Price Commission were retained, with stricter controls applied to price increases, while the Pay Board was abolished and, in July 1974, the compulsory wage restraint imposed by Heath was ended. Pensions and child allowances were raised and there was a substantial increase in the subsidy of basic foods. Thus, despite increases in income tax and in excise duties on cigarettes and alcohol, plus an extension (most notably to petrol) of goods liable to Value Added Tax, the cost of living was broadly contained, with a little redistribution of income to the less advantaged.

But in regaining power when it did, as the global recession really began to gnaw at the economy, Labour had accepted a poisoned chalice. There is no question that it had a harder task to cope with than any previous post-war government in guiding the country to carve out a living in harshly competitive international trading conditions. Engrossed for the first decade and a half since the end of the Second World War in the chimerical project of retaining her great-power status; obsessed with her 'special relationship' with America and her vanishing role as mother country of the Commonwealth; and induced by these illusions of grandeur - reinforced by entrapment in her nightmare of the Soviet threat - to divert far too much of her capital and human resources to the development, production, and deployment of arms, Britain had lost her chance of exercising a decisive influence on the rebuilding of Europe. Meanwhile the six founding members of the European Economic Community (including, of course, another nation, France, which still had many grand illusions to shed) were more prudently laying the foundations for a common prosperity. The Treaty of Rome between the original 'six' was signed in March 1957. Britain's first bid for EEC membership, made during Macmillan's second ministry, was vetoed by De Gaulle in January 1963; and her second bid, under Wilson, was again vetoed by De Gaulle, in November 1967. Not until January 1972 was Britain's application accepted, with Ted Heath, now Prime Minister, succeeding at his second attempt, having led the British negotiating team in the first bid.

Leaving aside the crucial loss of the opportunity to play a major part in determining the structure and thrust of the Community, by this time Britain's chronic under-investment in many of the most rewarding areas for international trade had left her at a grave disadvantage compared with her principal competitors. Britain's relative decline from around the mid-fifties can be roughly measured by a few facts and figures. The growth of her economy was both slower and more unsteady than that of her main competitors. During the fifties Britain's gross national product had risen in real terms by about 30 per cent, compared with an average rise of 80 per cent for EEC members. In 1950 Britain's GNP, at $47 billion, had been worth not far short of two-thirds of the combined GNPs ($75 billion) of the six states which were to forge the EEC; but by 1970 her GNP only equalled a quarter of the EEC's aggregated GNP, $121 billion as against $485 billion. In 1961 Britain ranked 9th out of 25 in the International Growth League of the Organisation of Economic Co-operation and Development, one behind West Germany and one ahead of France. By 1966, a few months before Wilson's bid for EEC membership, Britain's ranking was down to 13th, with France in 7th place and West Germany in 10th. By 1971, with Britain on the point of being allowed to join the club, the relative rankings were Britain 15th, France 9th, and West Germany 5th. By 1976, the year in which (in April) Callaghan took over the reins from Wilson, Britain had fallen to 18th place, while West Germany ranked 7th and France 11th. In per capita terms there was in 1961 near equality between the three countries, at a figure a little more than half that for the then top-ranking country, the United States. By 1976 France and West Germany had narrowed the gap with the US (itself now overtaken by Sweden, Switzerland, and Canada) and both far outstripped Britain. Although her per capita product had doubled in the 1966-76 period, it now stood at less than three-fifths of France's and not much over a half of West Germany's.

Weathering the storm of the recession the world had entered into in the autumn of 1973 was made more difficult by the ill-advised push for growth that had been launched by the Heath Government with Anthony Barber's candy-floss budget of March 1972, along with its massive tax cut of £1.38 billion. The most conspicuous consequences of 'the Barber boom' (in many ways a foreshadowing of the lunatic Lawson boom of 1986-89) were a spectacular increase in investment in property speculation and the sucking in of a spate of imports for consumption. Added to the unavoidable extra imports burden caused by rocketing world commodity prices, the consumer-imports' boom resulted in a record balance of payments deficit of £1.12 billion in 1973. In the following year the deficit shot up to £3.32 billion.

The balance of payments crisis was a major factor in precipitating a sterling crisis, with a flight from the pound in June 1972 and a persistent decline in its exchange rate. In March 1976 it fell below the $2 level for the first time ever, reaching its lowest point of under $1.16 the following October, and not rising to $2 again until the second half of 1978. These crises induced the Wilson Government to take advantage of Britain's Special Drawing Rights with the International Monetary Fund at the end of 1975, and subsequently, in September 1976, to apply for the maximum permitted standby credit of $3.9 billion. During the following two years the pound stabilised, Britain's balance of payments improved, and inflation fell. But naturally the economic crisis was overcome by cutting public spending, and equally naturally, the cuts were largely at the expense of the social wage, affecting the health service, education, housing, land acquisition by local authorities, food subsidies, public transport and roads. And these cuts began with

Denis Healey's first budget after the Wilson Government's tenure had been confirmed in the October 1974 general election.

The interim budget of November 1974, says Coates, 'foreshadowed much that was to come', beginning a retreat from the subsidies and price controls promised in the social contract, and from the tight discipline over private firms anticipated in the debates when Labour was in opposition. Citing the Chancellor's admission to the House that in his view the ever-swelling public sector borrowing requirement had reached 'a disturbingly large figure which one would never accept under normal circumstances', Coates comments: 'The Government was well aware that an immediate and drastic reduction in public sector expenditure could only bring a large fall in output and employment in its wake. But Ministers had at least succumbed to the view that public sector spending had to be curbed, no matter what the Labour Party in opposition had believed, and the November 1974 budget made a series of small beginnings.'

This overriding objective became explicit in the budget of April 1975, which Healey himself called 'rough and tough'. By a combination of higher levies on personal incomes and consumption (income tax was raised 2p to 35p in the pound, VAT on most luxury goods was increased to 25 per cent, duty on tobacco and alcohol went up and duty on private cars was raised from £25 to £40; while corporation tax remained unchanged and capital gains tax was reduced for farmers and small businesses) and planned cuts of £900 million for the fiscal year 1976-77 in subsidies for food and housing and in 'defence' spending, the public deficit was to be brought down to 8 per cent of national output in 1975-76 and to 6 per cent in 1976-77.

As the biggest constituent in public expenditure in a 'welfare state', what can collectively be considered as the 'social wage' is invariably a victim of cuts. Moreover, these cuts were made in the context of rising unemployment (excluding Northern Ireland, more than 450,000 people lost their livelihood during 1975, nearly 150,000 more during 1976, and over 200,000 more during the first nine months of 1977, when the unemployment total peaked at 1,380,000; by the end of Labour's last period in power there were more than twice as many people out of work than when they took office in March 1974) and unremitting government pressure to hold down the wages of ordinary workers. Coates remarks that to a 'shift from control to exhortation in the Labour Government's relationship with the private sector, and to the erosion of the social wage by limits on government spending, the November 1974 budget added a third and later much more significant development in policy: *the beginning of the respecification of the social contract as an agreement pre-eminently concerned with controlling the rate of increase of earnings.'* [my emphasis]

The Government's strategy for countering inflation and coping with the economic crisis was made brutally clear by Healey's 'rough and tough' budget and the drumhead recruitment of trade union leaders to discipline their own troops into accepting a 'voluntary' limit of £6 as a maximum weekly wage rise during the twelve months commencing in August 1975 - the formal Stage One of the Wilson/Callaghan Governments' everlasting incomes policy. The consequence of this keeping-capitalism-on-the-rails strategy was that even for workers who managed to hold on to their jobs, in most cases wage rises barely kept pace with the rising cost of living. Far from stepping confidently along a road that could lead to that promised goal of a 'fundamental and irreversible shift in the balance of power and wealth in favour of working people and their families', the workers, like Alice and the Red Queen, found themselves running hard to stay in the same place.

'Within fifteen months of taking office,' says Coates, 'the Labour Government was back to explicitly cutting the living standards of its electorate by at least 2.5 per cent over the year, on the Government's own figures.' Dennis Kavanagh, in *Thatcherism and British Politics: The End of Consensus?* (1987), notes an 'actual decline in the average citizen's standard of living in 1976 and 1977.' Not until its last year in power, in fact, did those who formed Labour's natural constituents begin to recover from the body blows they had been dealt. The rise in 1978 of 6.3 per cent in real personal disposable incomes reported on the eve of the general election by the Central Statistical Office was the sharpest rise since the 8.6 per cent rise of 1971-72; but it did little more than restore the buying power of the average citizen to that which he had enjoyed when Wilson outmanoeuvred Heath during the election campaigns of 1974.

So much for the Labour leaders' favourite alibi of irresponsible wage demands as a principal cause of the shattering of their last hopes of building Jerusalem. As for the more specific charges against the trade union wing of the Movement, levelled not only by Labour's opponents but by Party members too, before dealing with the final showdown between the Labour Government and the unions, it is necessary to blow away the miasma of misrepresentation spread by a media motivated more by its repressed fear of the potential power of organised labour and an instinctive antipathy to collective action by workers than by concern for keeping the public properly informed. For the record shows that almost without exception the union leaders made extraordinary and exhaustive efforts to accommodate the demands of their political allies. It also shows that, far from being a pre-eminent cause of inflation, as bourgeois propaganda and popular misconception would have it, wage claims during this period were as a rule fuelled by the remorseless rise in the cost of living. Indeed, social history almost invariably shows that widespread popular unrest is a reaction to worsening conditions.

Following the near-terminal marital breakdown during Wilson's previous premiership, the trade union leaders had apparently set their faces firmly against wage restraint policies. The furthest the TUC chiefs would go was to support (in *Collective Bargaining and the Social Contract*, June 1974) sober guidelines for the maintenance of real incomes. Yet within less than fifteen months of Labour's regaining power wage restraint was on the agenda again, with the most influential trade unionist of all as its leading advocate. In May 1975 Jack Jones, general secretary of the Transport and General Workers Union (and according to Barbara Castle's diary, perceived by her officials when she was Employment and Productivity supremo as 'the archetypal trade union villain), proposed to the TUC/Labour Party Liaison Committee of which he was chairman that to safeguard the Social Contract the movement should be asked to agree on a modest flat-rate rise for the next pay round. The figure settled on was £6, representing around ten per cent of average earnings. The policy was endorsed by the General Council of the TUC and Congress accepted it by an overwhelming majority in September.

The policy purported to be voluntary, but Sked and Cook describe it as 'effectively compulsory', since, under the Price Code, sanctions were threatened against any firm which breached the limit in a pay settlement and tried to recoup its higher labour costs by raising prices. Furthermore, Martin Holmes, in *The Labour Government, 1974-79*, implicitly contends that it meant the end of the Social Contract, writing that although the TUC document supporting the £6 policy was entitled *The Development of the Social Contract*, 'the language of the Social Contract had been made redundant, and could not disguise the fact that this was incomes policy on the traditional lines of restricting wages to reduce inflation.'

Moreover, it even failed to fulfil the minimalist objectives of the trade union movement: the maintenance of real incomes. In praising the trade union movement for its 'voluntary agreement', Healey himself admitted that the majority of trade union members would suffer 'some reduction in real take-home pay.' Yet for the most part the agreement stuck, and the Chancellor was able to report to the House in April 1976 that, 'with only a few months of the current wage round left to run, we know of no instance where wages are being paid in breach of the £6 pay limit.'

Stage Two of the pay policy, running from August 1976 to July 1977 inclusive, brought a similar measure of success for official policy. An agreement between the Government and the TUC for a maximum rise of 4.5 per cent was ratified overwhelmingly by a special congress in June 1976, and even though for most workers this meant a rise in money terms of less than half that received in the previous pay round, it was implemented without a single official trade union challenge.

Of the first two stages of the Wilson/Callaghan Government's pay policy David Coates writes:

'These two years of successful pay restraint stand as clear evidence of the loyalty of trade union leaders to this Labour Government, and their willingness to subordinate their wider policy aspirations to Government pressure. They stand too as evidence of the trade union leaders' hold on the loyalty of their own membership and of the weakness of any rank-and-file movement of protest against pay restraint and trade union incorporation. Not even the left-wing union leaders most hostile to what they saw as TUC capitulation to bankrupt Treasury orthodoxy could galvanise mass support against policies which explicitly cut living standards, failed to prevent price rises, and allowed unemployment to grow. By August 1977 the Labour Government could legitimately claim that it had achieved a degree of working class co-operation over a long period that no Conservative Government could match, and had in the process cut back significantly the pressure of wages on industrial costs.'

It is hardly surprising that falling living standards and growing disenchantment at the Cheshire Cat nature of the Social Contract promises led to the withdrawal of co-operation by the unions with the Government's policy of pay restraint. Even so, the withdrawal was itself gradual and, for another year, quite remarkably restrained. Far from kicking over the traces, the TUC continued to accept the policy in principle, while striving to hold on to its mantle of authority by promulgating an 'orderly' return to free collective bargaining. The purchasing power of the pound in the pocket might dwindle day by day, but the customary gap of twelve months between settlements should continue to be observed, it preached, and settlements due before 31st July should not be deferred in order to evade the limits laid down for that stage of the pay policy.

It might be felt that in giving an explanation for its supine attitude that 'the Government is not likely to be deflected from its present course of action', the General Council was abrogating its responsibility to give active leadership to the trade union movement in defence of working-class interests. But while there may be grounds for arguing that counsels of restraint were in the longer-term interests of the Labour Movement as a whole, is the same to be said of the TUC decision that the already trumpeted campaign to increase the target for low-paid workers from a £30 minimum to £50 should be deferred until times were better? Likewise, what is to be said of a government formed by a party purporting to champion the interests of working people that discriminates against its own employees by imposing a ten per cent limit on public sector rises, regardless of wage and price movements in the economy as a whole - especially bearing in mind the high proportion of low-paid workers in the public sector? In undermining Labour's strongholds, such questions were to become as Joshua's trumpets.

The Government made it clear that it would hold the line against breaches of the twelve-month rule, rebuff all attempts to recoup loss of real earnings since 1975, reject spurious (i.e. non-self-financing) productivity agreements, and impose sanctions against private firms agreeing to settlements that exceeded its stipulated maximum of 10 per cent. Even the TUC's guidelines - never mind the Government's stipulations - fell somewhat short of what trade unionists in general, along with their capitalist masters, are pleased to call 'free collective bargaining'. Yet the General Council's decisions were ratified by sizeable majorities (no less than 7.1 million to 4 million in the case of the twelve-month rule) at the September Congress.

Only one union, the firemen's, openly defied the edicts of the Labour establishment by calling an official strike in pursuit of its claim for a 30 per cent rise. The Government's response was to mobilise the Green Goddesses (the antiquated fire-engines used by the army) - neither the first nor the last time a Labour government has deployed soldiers as strike-breakers. After eight weeks out, from mid-November 1977 into the New Year, the firemen were strong-armed into accepting the 10 per cent on offer, on the understanding that they would not be held to the 'norm' fixed for subsequent stages of Labour's pay policy.

Just over half way through Stage Three, in the middle of February 1978, the Department of Employment was able to claim that over 96 per cent of the wage settlements reached in the current pay round had been within the Government's guidelines. Without resorting to more draconian measures to enforce its will, such a high degree of success was not sustainable, but surprisingly, considering the many claims that exceeded 10 per cent and the strength of the rank-and-file pressure for more money that built up, it turned out that even by the end of Stage Three the Government had succeeded in holding the annual rate of increase in earnings to 14.2 per cent. (This figure meant that there had been some *restoration of lost living standards* for some employees, since it was 6.4 per cent above the rate of growth of prices.)

There is no question that the continued collaboration (however reluctant) of the TUC in Stage Three was crucial to the Government's relative success in holding down the incomes of rank-and-file workers, just as it had been the decisive factor in the previous stages of the pay policy. When the firemen called for support in the name of the principle of free collective bargaining which the TUC had just reaffirmed, the General Council rebuffed them, resolving by 20-17 to uphold the policy of wage restraint during Stage Three, and even the Government's strike-breaking measures provoked little more in the way of solidarity from other unions than sighs of regret. The most stunning victory of all for the political overlords was the taming of the miners. Ably abetted by the miners' president, Joe Gormley, the Government persuaded the 232,000-strong National Union of Mineworkers, vanguard of the British working class, to drop its claim for a 90 per cent rise and accept around

10 per cent. Their loyalty to the Labour Government was hailed by the Prime Minister publicly thanking them in the House.

What needs explaining most is not the popular myth of union power (for the persistence of which one would have to anatomise in particular the baleful influence of the media - *and not only the popular media* - in promoting ignorance and prejudice), but the essential subservience of the trade union establishment to the political leaders of the Labour Movement. This perception of a predisposition to acquiesce (to put it at its lowest) lies at the heart of Coates' penetrating analysis of the twilight of Labourism. As he points out, the power of the union leaders was almost wholly negative. When they disagreed with Labour's political leaders, they could argue, haggle, and temporise, but in the end, if the terms fixed upon still remained too unpalatable, they could do little more than decline to co-operate. That at least is how they seemed to see it. And given the nature of the British trade union movement, perhaps that is how it really was. In any case, those union generals who were most powerful on paper lacked the will to shape events. As the Social Contract, which - together with its indispensable underpinning of a heterodox economic strategy - they had played such a large part in forging, disintegrated before their eyes, they looked on as helplessly as small children robbed of their candy by bigger boys. Coates describes the situation lucidly:

> 'Trade union leaders could resist particular details, could block and negotiate, and (where their members' direct co-operation was required) could exercise some kind of veto on particular policy options. But they could not define the agenda of proposals that the Government put before them, nor the context within which policy had to be formulated; and so in the end they proved unable to prevent the transformation of the social contract from its initial character (of a set of concrete and immediate legislative proposals that favoured the working class), into its later form (as a vehicle of wage restraint, buttressed by general statements of aspiration and vague long-term commitments to social change). The drift to incomes policy, the rise in unemployment, and the Government's resistance to the TUC's expansionist policy stand as major pieces of evidence against the thesis of excessive trade union power, and make clear that the visibility of trade union leaders was

less an index of their power than of their subordination. The
story of the relationship between this Labour Government
and the trade union movement after 1974 is one of the
transformation of the national trade union leadership into
vital junior allies of the Cabinet in the implementation of
incomes control - policemen in their own arena of action,
visibly pursuing policies with which they were uneasy
within limits set only by the sporadic degree of rank and file
protest to which they were subject.'

The Wilson/Callaghan Government of 1974-79 presented the
Labour Movement with its most unmistakable moment of truth. Even
if the British Labour Party had been a very different animal (closer in
nature, perhaps, to the dreams of its left-wingers), we would still have
been witnessing, while it lasted, an interlude of collaboration, a passing
period of symbiosis, between two very different creatures, possessing
not the complementary powers of Labour theory, but antithetical kinds
of power: on the one hand, State power - the power to command and
coerce (an arrogated power in essence, notwithstanding all the
paraphernalia of elections and mandates); on the other hand, people
power - the negating power of inertia, withdrawal, resistance, and
outright defiance, whenever the positive power of freely-willed co-
operation was withheld.

It is highly questionable what the workers had really gained by
their reasonableness and restraint. Sympathy perhaps, from a few 'men
of goodwill', but nothing remotely resembling any form of Socialism;
neither with regard to the serious pursuit of social justice, nor even (to
whittle down Socialism to little more than common-sense
Keynesianism) to a credible attempt to manage the economy so as
markedly to mitigate the ravages of capitalism during one of its manic
downswings. In short, it became clear for all with eyes to see that the
so-called Social Contract was what its most far-sighted critics had
always called it, the 'social con-trick'.

It is particularly ironic, in view of the absolutely central position
assumed by the State in Labour (as in Marxist) thinking (before the
'modernisers' had done their work that is), that the two men of power
who dominated the fateful period after Harold Wilson had slipped away
with an *'après moi la deluge'* twinkle in his eye, Callaghan and Healey,
are commonly represented as strong and decisive leaders. And yet both
of them had apparently lost all confidence in the countervailing powers

of the State in its relations with capitalism. With more than a tinge of a fatalism that would have been fitting enough for a faithful free marketeer, one of their Cabinet colleagues, Shirley Williams, confessed to the 'Youth Charter Towards 2000' conference in February 1977: 'We are seeing the increase in unemployment throughout the industrial world, and it is a problem for which we have no real answer.' In fact, by their allegiance to essentially monetarist policies and their refusal to adopt 'New Deal' type strategies, they contributed to unemployment rather than countering it. When, in 1991, Norman Lamont told the Commons that higher unemployment was a price well worth paying to bring down inflation, he was assailed by a storm of protests from the Labour benches. Yet when Healey had been Chancellor, he had cut public spending and sacrificed jobs to counter inflation, in contrast, as Dennis Kavanagh points out, to the Heath Government's reflating of the economy when faced with rising unemployment.

Kavanagh clearly considers Healey's spring 1975 budget a watershed in post-war politics: 'In March 1975 Denis Healey's budget abandoned the commitment to plan for full employment, choosing to cut instead of increase the deficit, a historic breach with one of the main planks of the post-war consensus.' It has been too little remarked that the rejection of Keynesian strategies for dealing with recession began not with the Thatcherite fundamentalists but with the responsible Labour statesmen who preceded them. Absolute confirmation of the new orthodoxy in Labour's economic thinking came in James Callaghan's speech to his first party conference as leader and Prime Minister in 1976:

> 'We used to think that you could spend your way out of
> recession and increase employment by cutting taxes and
> boosting Government spending. I tell you in all candour
> that that option no longer exists, and that insofar as it ever
> did exist, it only worked on each occasion since the war by
> injecting a bigger dose of inflation into the economy,
> followed by a higher level of unemployment as the next
> step.'

An obsession with curbing inflation at any cost and a conviction that it was wage pressure above all that induced that inflation - all part of an essentially monetarist and anti-Keynesian (not to say anti-Socialist) credo that foreshadowed rampant Thatcherism - led Labour's

273

leaders to behave like the legendary Dutch boy who stuck his heroic finger in the hole in the dyke. This not being a tale of derring-do, however, but a gathering storm in real life, Labour's last-chance ministry was, by the time the country shuffled discontentedly into Stage Four of the prices and incomes policy in August 1978, near the point of being swept away by a deluge of demands that it deliver some semblance of what working people had been promised in the Social Contract between the political and the industrial wings of the Labour Movement.

CHAPTER 22

Who does govern Britain?

'Old-fashioned patriotism has become the almost exclusive property of the working class, whose tribal loyalties are kept alive every Saturday on the football terraces. History is ordaining not that the workers of the world unite, but that the executives, bankers, and entrepreneurs erase national differences to advance their own interest.'

Alan Clark (1978)

The problem facing the last Labour government was not simply that faced by all governments, of reconciling - or if not reconciling, then at least of successfully balancing (within the confines imposed by economic exigencies) - demands from the competing vested interests that made up its own constituency, while dishing out minimal portions of appeasement to the electorally most threatening sections of its antagonists. It went far deeper than that, for it was a problem posed by the manifest failure of Labour's political wing to deliver its promise of a new society in which the rules of the game would not be heavily weighted against the interests of 'the common people' - a promise that lay at the very heart of its appeal.

No one had laid down the premises of the Social Contract between government and people more plainly than Harold Wilson did, when he told the 1972 Labour Party Conference: 'There can be no road to national agreement, national unity...except on a basis of social justice.' That at least made it sound as if he had learned the lesson of the bitter strife that had come close to tearing the Labour Movement apart under his administrations in the sixties; and whether through cunning prescience or the devil's own luck, he was to relinquish the burden of office before the times grew tumultuous again. The ironic paradox is that his successor, who had shown much more prudence than Wilson had during Labour's civil war over *In Place of Strife*, now that he held the reins of sovereign power and found himself faced by a restless multitude, displayed arrogant inflexibility, poverty of imagination, and a grossly inadequate concern for the demands of social justice. Hubris had struck again!

Of course, not all the preconditions of a workable accommodation between the Government and the unions were transparently questions of social justice. For example, in the annual round of wage settlements which was propelled in large part by inflation, the issue of differentials posed one of the thorniest problems of all. As commonly represented, as a demand for maintaining the status quo (or for restoring some real or supposed status quo ante) of inequalities, this had at best an oblique and equivocal relationship to the concept of social justice. But for the very reason that Labour was holding office at a critical time in the life of the nation, when the concept of the Welfare State had come to seem to many to be at odds with the demands of national economic prosperity in a fiercely competitive world, the Callaghan Government had a rare opportunity. They could have seized the moral high ground by proclaiming unequivocally that in any pay policy the first call on 'spare' resources must be the claims of the least privileged sections of society. That could only have meant that once the essentials of the economic infrastructure had been provided for, the social wage and more generous remuneration for the low-paid must take priority, and that as far as it lay in the Government's power, there should be no discrimination in this respect between its own employees and workers in the private sector. Then - and only then - would it have had the right to expect the country to heed its exhortations for restraint 'in the national interest'. But instead of acting in accordance with the principles of social justice, the people's government squandered its moral authority by its Janus-faced policies of appeasement towards the strong and intransigence towards the weak. It is true that the official guidelines did allow for more favourable treatment of low-paid workers, but as we shall see, this subtle genuflection in the direction of equity was more honoured in the breach than in the observance.

At all events, at this fateful moment for the British people a sort of stubborn steadfastness masquerading as 'strong government' held sway, revealing yet again that deeply unattractive paternalistic streak that is so characteristic of Labour's tribunes. Notwithstanding ritual obeisances to the doctrine of full consultation, the mind-set of the Labour leaders was more suited to autocracy than to representative government, with Cabinet (or even just *inner* Cabinet) deliberations issuing in what amounted to rule by ukase. Such procedure is anything but foreign to the traditions of British Cabinet government; but it is totally at odds with the proclaimed tenets of the Labour Movement.

In the face of overwhelming opposition, clearly and repeatedly voiced in the democratic forums of the Movement, all the way up to the theoretically sovereign Party Conference, those who held the purse strings decreed a 5 per cent norm for an imposed Stage Four and stuck to it, effectively declining to bargain with their own followers not only over pay but over any other aspect of the Government's economic policy. Yet at the same time, in a White Paper issued in July 1978, the Government called for the reaching of tripartite agreements - between Government, unions and employers - to counter wage-induced inflation. Its contention was that in the absence of such agreements its duty was to fix norms for pay rises. Yet in doing so it took little or no account of considerations of equity, thinking it sufficient to promulgate a percentage-increase figure that in its opinion the economy could afford. Ironically, it did eventually reach some measure of agreement again with the General Council of the TUC (a 'concordat' as it was called by leaders who, it seems, were insensible to the unfortunate Corporate State associations of that term), but only after the storm had broken over the Government's head. It was in any case no more than a fig-leaf donned in the desperate hope of persuading the public that Labour was still the party best able to handle the unions, since in the context of such widespread discontent the union leaders were quite unable to deliver the assent of their rank and file.

Compared with the year in which Callaghan took over from Wilson, 1977 had seen a threefold increase in the number of working days lost through strikes, with the total figure reaching only a little short of ten million. Relatively speaking, 1978 provided a lull. What was ominous, however, was that whereas unofficial stoppages in the motor and engineering industries, together with a considerable contribution from the official firemen's strike at the end of the year, had accounted for a large proportion of the work-time lost in 1977, now that the unions were reasserting their commitment to free collective bargaining, the groups of workers ready to take action to defend their interests or to support their claims practically covered the waterfront of organised employees. Among workers who resorted to some kind of industrial action to supplement the purely verbal persuasive powers of their negotiators were, in the public sector: porters and other ancillary staff in hospitals, including telephonists and laundry workers, ambulance crews, social workers, social security staff, teachers, caretakers in schools and colleges, firemen, refuse workers, traffic wardens, civilian police workers, prison warders, customs officers, industrial civil servants, ministers' drivers, dockyard and other defence industry workers, post office engineers, shipyard workers, dockers, tugmen, pilot ships' officers, airport workers, rail and tube workers, bus crews, steelmen, and miners; and in the private sector: North Sea oilmen, petrol tanker drivers, Channel ferry seamen, construction workers, motor industry workers, lorry drivers, bakers, bottle factory workers, draymen, print-workers, journalists, television broadcasting technicians, stagehands, and bank staff.

That by no means exhausts the list of those who were prepared to use 'industrial muscle' to get their way, and those not listed not only embraced such traditional musclemen as the power workers, but extended to university dons and to such unimpeachably respectable professions as medicine. In April the British Medical Association warned the Government that there would be a mass exodus of medical practitioners from the National Health Service if they failed to negotiate appropriate recompense for their services. Polite society and such pillars of the establishment as the capitalist Press might in such cases refrain from their customary cant of 'blackmail' by strikers, taking refuge, if challenged on the similarity of behaviour between common workers downing tools and doctors and surgeons downing stethoscopes and scalpels, in the contractual relationship of such professional people to public services; but what was it in truth but pressure on the community's most tender spot? And some idea of what the BMA considered to be appropriate rewards for those whose 'vested interests' it represented may be gathered from the claim put in on behalf of consultants for an 80 per cent increase!

Harold Wilson's admonition concerning the conditions for national unity referred to above omits in my citation one crucial phrase: '...on a policy adequate for dealing with inflation and unemployment...' And there was the rub. One fine day in the autumn of 1978, Labour's dauntless double-act, Jim and Denis, yoked together in their three-legged dash for stable sterling undefiled by devaluation, vowed, each in his own way, to stand fast against the inflationary clamour of the multitude. At the annual Mansion House junketing for Chancellor, bankers, and merchants, Denis came right out of the closet by openly admitting his predilection for monetarism, adding with characteristic swagger that the government in which he served was the first for very many years 'which has given monetary policy the importance it deserves.' He made it crystal clear that it would be his main weapon in the struggle to hold down inflation.

Meanwhile, at the Anglo-German summit meeting in Bonn (on the eve of negotiations for a European Monetary System which Britain did not, in the event, join until Margaret Thatcher was badgered into doing so by her Cabinet colleagues more than ten years later), Prime Minister Callaghan told Chancellor Schmidt of his government's determination to meet one of the central preconditions of a durable EMS, no return to high rates of inflation. Making one of the major unintended understatements of the century, he warned: 'There may, as a result of our policies, be some industrial disturbances this winter. But I hope our European friends will not think that the UK has gone down the plug-hole as a result.'

For a fistful of reasons it was the eruption at the Ford Motor Company a month earlier that really breached the dyke, although the full flood did not come for several more months. Among these reasons was, of course, the chance factor of the point at which union agreements at Ford ran out, which happened to be after the transition from Stage Three of Labour's pay policy - for which there had been at least a semblance of voluntary agreement between government and unions - to the diktat of Stage Four, during which sullen acquiescence gave way to defiance. The paramount factor, however, was the Ford workers' undoubted right (speaking in conventional capitalist 'free labour market' terms) as employees of by far the most profitable motor manufacturing firm in Britain (which incidentally turned out the second largest number of vehicles of all Ford's foreign-based factories) to a far higher rise than the 5 per cent limit the Government sought to impose. Thus, as Callaghan puts it in his memoirs, 'the Ford pay claim [became] the bellwether of the flock.'

The 15 unions organising the 57,000 manual workers at Ford (and the involvement of so many unions - itself a consequence of Britain's antiquated craft-based organisation of labour - naturally acted as a green light to great swathes of their members employed elsewhere) had in fact agreed on a rather egalitarian claim of £20 all round, which was equivalent when averaged out to around 25 per cent. (It is worth noting in passing, because of its bearing on the whole question of the responsibility and restraint, or otherwise, of trade unionists under the Wilson/Callaghan regime, that in their previous settlement the Ford workers had agreed to an increase lower than the average Stage Three increase, rejecting the advice of their leaders to push for more.) The Ford strike began on 22nd September, in response to the management's insistence on sticking to the official pay limit, and within three days the whole workforce was out.

The fragility of government when it will not or dare not fall back on brute force to ensure that its edicts are observed was laid bare by a 9-week strike that ended with the acceptance of an offer of 17 per cent, over three times more than the limit, thus exposing the so-called Labour Movement for what it is: an expedient alliance of two separate centres of power with only occasionally coinciding interests - an alliance perpetually threatened by schism. In this withdrawal of co-operation which heralded a wholesale workers' revolt, the social illusions and shibboleths by which we normally live (and on the altars of which, it is true, we sometimes even immolate ourselves) - national identity and national unity, party allegiance, group loyalty, duty to employers or to others in authority over us, and the like, along with such assorted cosy assumptions as that we are all equal before the law; that universal suffrage confers political equality; that, consequentially, a distinction can and should be made between the withdrawal of co-operation for economic reasons (potentially justifiable) and 'political strikes' (*per se* unjustifiable); and that organisations established to promote the interests of particular groups of workers in a market economy should be expected to subordinate their members' economic interests to higher considerations, even to some hypothetical 'national interest' - all were revealed by a lightning flash as the stinking ordurous heap of sanctimonious humbuggery they are.

The right of the trade union wing of the Labour Movement to part company with a Labour government and go its own way was bluntly asserted by Ron Todd, chairman of the union team on Ford's national joint negotiating committee, who was later to become general secretary of the Transport and General Workers' Union:

'We have undergone a great deal of self-sacrifice to help the country overcome inflation. Now we believe is the right time to reintroduce free collective bargaining. This is all we want. *The response of Ford reflects Government policy, and we are reflecting trade union policy. It is getting to the stage when to mention free collective bargaining is to sound revolutionary.*' [my emphasis]

Todd accused Ford of using the Government's pay guidelines as a pretext for refusing to bargain. But while no one could doubt that, like just about every other employer, it would use whatever arguments came to mind to deprive its workers of most of the fruits of their labour, it was certainly not in its interests to provoke a mass walkout by making what *it* must have felt, hardly less than Todd & Brothers, to be 'a derisory offer'. Both sides knew perfectly well that the unions' biggest quarrel was with the Government they had helped to put into power, as Ford's chairman, Sir Terence Beckett, indirectly told them when, in a speech at a conference in London on international planning a couple of days after the walkout, he called it 'a strike against the Government' and added that 'the situation we are in depends on something wider than the Ford Motor Company.' He inadvertently underlined the speciousness of most attempts to distinguish between legitimate industrial action and 'political strikes' by subsequently remarking that the dispute had been 'made into a political rather than an industrial issue.'

In fact a kaleidoscopic rearrangement of forces at once took shape, implying - without, of course, formally bringing into being - new alliances expedient to new circumstances. These were alliances (grotesque, even unholy, if you like) between the two sides we are not to suppose exist in industry and commerce, namely, capital and labour, and more ominously in the long run, between large numbers of ordinary working people who had up till then always instinctively backed Labour and the standard-bearers of so-called 'free enterprise'. The TGWU general secretary, Moss Evans, who, as Ford erupted, had warned the Government that it should expect a similar explosion from more than a million public sector manual workers when their claims were turned down, began to talk of joint union-employer protests if sanctions were imposed on firms to repress free collective bargaining.

A captain of industry and a labour leader did just that at a conference in London organised by the British Institute of Management. They spoke as if with one voice against the inflexibility of a policy that had already imposed crude pay norms for three years and that left little scope for negotiating over problems of differentials and anomalies. Calling for a national body to adjudicate on such matters, the chairman of BIM's economic committee, Sir Fred Catherwood, warned the Government: 'You can do these things for one year and two years and with sanctions and a miracle even three years. But when you go into the fourth year, especially when people didn't expect a fourth year and expected an election, then you are in dead trouble.' While guest speaker Ray Buckton, general secretary of the Associated Society of Locomotive Engineers and Firemen, argued that freedom to bargain over the rate for the job was a prerequisite of efficient and competitive industry. No firebrand, the studied moderation of his position was made very clear by his statement that: 'I hope the 5 per cent policy does not disintegrate, but I hope the rigidity does.'

If the Government would not listen to its friends, in the belief that they were betraying Labour's cause, did it have to be deaf to those who were nominally its foes but who in this case at least shared with it the common purpose of paying as little to the workers as possible? To be deaf even when those 'foes' spoke with the prescience of the London Chamber of Commerce and Industry was to be daft too. Its October report, published a fortnight after the Ford walkout, drew attention to the dilemma faced by companies which 'are able - and willing - to pay more than the norm' and fear a protracted strike more than Government sanctions:

> 'The attitude of the unions suggests that, unlike the first
> three phases of pay policy, the opposition will be both
> vociferous and sustained. Faced with an intransigent
> trade union movement and with no legal powers to bind
> the unions to wage agreements and only ineffectual
> sanctions to reinforce it, the pay policy depends for its
> survival on the goodwill of companies. And the Ford
> experience has severely taxed what goodwill is left.'

The Chamber predicted that sanctions (for which it had earlier in the year actually expressed approval, provided machinery was established for the right of appeal) would be destroyed as a weapon with which to enforce the Government's pay policy by a settlement at Ford that would inevitably exceed the norm, and that this would signal the demise of Stage Four. The only thing wrong with the Chamber's prophecies was that it could not believe that Ford would hold out for as long as it had in 1971, merely to save a pay policy it regarded as totally unrealistic.

As for warnings of the probable dire *political* consequences of the Government simply standing its ground, these came thick and fast from the ranks of those whose allegiance it had to retain in order to survive, and we are at liberty to draw our own conclusions as to whether ignoring them demonstrates strength or stupidity. One day after the stoppage became total, Ford stewards delivered a letter to No. 10 which warned the Prime Minister that the 5 per cent pay limit was seriously jeopardising the chances of the Government winning the forthcoming general election and that 'proposals that we should work for the return of Labour MPs are being openly derided' on the shopfloor. Down at Dagenham, *Guardian* reporter John Andrews sampled some of this derision for himself. 'I don't mind if Mrs Thatcher comes in,' he was told by one young worker who saw himself as 'a slave putting nuts and bolts into engines'. A fellow worker who had been with the company for thirty years and felt he had been reduced from a position of prosperity to the status of a peasant, said the Government should appreciate that they had gone along with it to get the country on its feet, and expressed the view - to which it is hard to take exception without excoriating the kind of society that generated it - that: 'If you work for a firm and they're making money, you're entitled to more.'

The sharply diverging purposes of the two wings of the Labour Movement were summed up by a convenor of shop stewards picketing Ford's tractor plant at Basildon when he pointed out to the man from *The Guardian* that they were acting in accordance with the trade unions' agreed return to free collective bargaining and told him: 'The majority feeling is that we won't keep a Labour Government at any price, and our first job as union officials is to do our best for our members - not to keep the Labour Government in office.'

A more fundamental criticism of this still professedly Socialist government that had rejected as impractical the propositions of the 'alternative economy' strategists for overcoming Britain's economic malaise and was wholly and desperately engrossed in making the late-twentieth-century model of capitalism that it had inherited work, came from the local Labour Party in Southampton, where more than 4,000 Ford workers were on strike. In an emergency resolution tabled for the following week's Party Conference at Blackpool, it declared: 'We reject the idea that trade unionists should be loyal to the Government over their 5 per cent policy because this will only hold down wages to prop up the capitalist system.'

Far from being restricted to rank-and-file dreamers in the constituencies, however, critics of the Government's pay policy within the Party itself included its treasurer, Norman Atkinson, MP for Tottenham, who declared unequivocally on ITV's *News at One* that the Labour Movement could not and would not endorse, nor drift into, statutory wages control. His warning that the Government was 'in grave danger' of being deserted by its traditional supporters was echoed in the motion from Wavertree constituency party on which the debate on pay policy took place at Blackpool on 3rd October. That motion made it clear that wage planning would only be acceptable in the context of a planned economy embracing planned prices, profits, and investment as well.

Since the TUC, at its Congress at Brighton a month earlier, had overwhelmingly rejected (indeed, it might be said, contemptuously dismissed, as a show of hands was all that was needed to put the matter quite beyond doubt) Government policy on pay, with all but four of the forty-one members of the General Council coming out openly against it, and since at the Party Conference the trade union delegates comprised over half the total number of delegates and wielded in aggregate more than 6 million votes out of the total of 6¾ million, the outcome of the battle at Blackpool was never seriously in doubt. The five-per-cent flagship was blown clean out of the water in a two-to-one defeat for the Government, while a motion approving its general economic strategy went down by 3,626,000 to 2,806,000.

The Party's political leaders put the best face they could fashion on the humiliation they had suffered at the hands of the trade union wing of the Movement. That old trouper Sunny Jim turned in a vintage performance. Simulating irrepressible optimism and unshakeable strength, he delivered with comradely bluffness the steely message that the Government's policy would not change come hell or high water, and that if its plea for pay restraint went unheeded, it would be duty bound to resort to further monetary measures to hold down inflation. Redoubled assurances of moderation, trustworthiness and loyalty to Labour came from union leaders, and in response to pow-wow noises from Big Chief Callaghan, David Basnett, general secretary of the General and Municipal Workers' Union, gave tongue on behalf of the TUC to their ever-readiness to take part in further talks on pay and other economic matters. But when Basnett assured Conference: 'Our alliance remains firm', he was papering over a chasm. There was in reality little left for the Party's leaders but the slender hope that the nation's resurgent workforce would refrain from demanding rises greatly in excess of 5 per cent.

The workers at Ford were already fighting for six times as much. With little sense of realism, sundry politicians and political commentators continued to talk of the possibility of a settlement at Ford of as little as 7 or 8 per cent, or at the worst of one just staying within single figures. But within three weeks of the Labour Party Conference Ford's resistance had buckled and it was suing for peace with an offer two and a half times the dictated 'norm'. This was swiftly followed by a 'final offer' of 16½ per cent, which, when it in turn was spurned, was eventually raised to 17 per cent, with some loosening of the work-discipline strings that had been attached to the 'final offer'. It was all very well for the Prime Minister to tell the Commons that the Ford workers would be no better off with a 17 per cent rise after a nine-week stoppage than they would have been if they had accepted 5 per cent in the first place. The dispute had cost Ford £450 million, and, what was for Callaghan more to the point, had comprehensively called his bluff, diminishing the Labour Government's authority not only in the eyes of the trade unions and the employers, but of the general public as well.

The Government could only choose between the unthinkable option of openly conceding defeat, the semi-suicidal option of maximum retaliation against Ford to which being true to its vows would impel it, or the face-saving option of taking whatever measures might serve to veil the fact that it had been utterly routed. Needless to say, it chose the third, or dissembling option. Accordingly, the Ford Motor Company was inscribed on the blacklist of recalcitrant firms which, for whatever reasons, had exceeded the 'norm' laid down for collective agreements.

During Stage Three of its prices and incomes policy the Government had assumed powers, under the Price Code it had conveniently inherited from the Heath Government, to penalise blacklisted employers. It was able to deny them contracts and business with public authorities, discretionary grants and aid, including selective employment subsidies, and export credits. Given the size and purchasing power of a public sector which at that time itself directly employed nearly a third of the nation's workforce, these powers of persuasion were potentially formidable, and conceivably had already served to keep in line many more firms than were ever named. Officially the blacklist was 'confidential', a guilty commercial secret between Government and culprit unless the latter chose to disclose it; but it appears that when Ford's name was added to it, it numbered around sixty firms. (At its peak there were believed to be about 170 names on the blacklist.)

As a major multinational, however, Ford was in a different league from the other blacklisted culprits, and when it came to the crunch the sanctions with which the Government had armed itself proved to be rubber teeth. Healey huffed and puffed in the Commons about how the Government would continue to do its duty to the nation as a whole honestly and courageously; but the 'tim'rous beastie' of substance hiding behind Healey's ballooning sound-bites was his sober observation that, in using their discretionary powers, ministers would take into account such factors as unemployment. On the same day Industry Secretary Eric Varley notified Ford that sanctions would be imposed, and that these would include *recommending* a number of nationalised industries to switch to Leyland when replacing vehicles. In addition, certain investment grants would be withheld, but these would not include the £150 million loan agreed on for the company to develop the new car plant due to open in 1980 at Bridgend in South Wales. The British Government had secured this commitment from Ford in the face of fierce competition from at least two other EEC countries, West Germany and Ireland.

The truth was that it was not Ford but the Government that was over a barrel. The nation's need for economic development and more jobs was too great to really punish Ford. But even if the Government had been hell-bent on imposing sanctions of metal-bashing proportions, the damage it could inflict was very limited. For example, a total public-sector ban on buying from Ford would have cost the company upwards of £80 million; but as we have seen, this was a flea-bite compared with what the strike had cost it. In the event, the penalties imposed were nearer to £8 million than to £80 million. In a passage in his autobiography, Callaghan himself comes near to frankly acknowledging that the whole sanctions policy was based on bluff:

> 'In one respect sanctions resembled the nuclear deterrent, in that they were most effective when they were not used. In another respect they were totally different, for when used would hardly have caused Ford a scratch. They were a gesture of disapproval and as such no one in the Cabinet was enthusiastic about employing them.'

If the Government had been playing a game of bluff because ministers believed that holding down incomes was the key to controlling inflation, the opposition parties and the more sophisticated members of the employing class in general had been perpetrating a double bluff on the workers. On the one hand they volubly protested on grounds of principle against what they considered to be the Government's arrogated, arbitrarily exercised, and unjustified powers of intervening in pay bargaining in the private sector (somehow they did not feel the same indignation about the attack on 'free collective bargaining' when it came to Government interference with statutory pay boards and other nominally autonomous bodies in the public sector). On the other hand they secretly welcomed the weapon Government policy gave them in resisting pay claims. In February the Opposition had divided the House over the practice of blacklisting; but with support from the Liberals the Government had fended off the challenge, despite the abstention of eight Labour left-wingers. When the Tories finally made up their minds to throw down the gauntlet again over the whole issue of sanctions, and it became all-important to rally round their banner all the forces they could drum up, the director general of the Confederation of British Industries, Sir John Methven, in a speech to the Parliamentary Press Gallery, succeeded in reconciling these contradictory feelings and in giving the appearance of speaking up for all those who dissented from the Government's pay policy, irrespective of their particular point of view. The Government was pursuing a legitimate end by unconstitutional means, he argued, while slyly adding, as if it were a consideration that carried weight with him, that the pay policy had no support from the TUC. On the other hand some employers came in for a rebuke for their complaisance over the Government's interference with 'the rights of management', in taking the short-sighted and unprincipled view that the interference helped them in their own pay negotiations. The policy was rigid, he said (making a bid for near-universal approval), yet at the same time pay bargaining in the UK was a 'shambles' that should be replaced by a system (unspecified) in which wages were determined by 'the competitive pressures of the market place', with the private sector setting the pace. Meanwhile the general public should be led to a better understanding of economic cause and effect. Thus spake this quintessential market-place philosopher, fully equipped with state of the art flexible thought-processes.

The most profound lesson to be learned from the Callaghan Government's humiliation at the hands of the Ford Motor Company - that in the global jungle of international capitalism the governments of sovereign states are puny when they come up against the economic power of major transnational corporations - was little remarked on at the time. This was largely because the Government was paradoxically let off the hook by its defeat in the Commons on an Opposition motion condemning sanctions, which allowed ministers to maintain that the other parties were responsible for undermining its ability to control private sector pay. The Government regained its footing on the following day, ten days before Christmas, by calling a confidence vote which it knew would swing the Scottish Nationalists back behind it since they would not wish to jeopardise the holding of the referendum on devolution by bringing about the dissolution of Parliament. But even so the Government only won the vote after the Prime Minister had told the House that sanctions would be abandoned. The curtain was brought down on the final scene of the pantomime after the inherently comical spectacle of a deputation from the CBI visiting Number 10 to thank a Labour government for dropping the threat of sanctions against its members.

Ted Heath's rhetorical question 'Who governs Britain?', to which the general election of February 1974 had appeared to give - from a constitutional point of view - the wrong answer, was being posed again. This time it was in terms of the trade union wing of the Labour Movement challenging a Labour government. But at a deeper, more tectonic level could be detected the rumbling of an even more crucial challenge, that of global capitalism to 'the right to self-determination' of the nation-state.

CHAPTER 23

The winter of discontent

> 'The curse of the British working class is their
> willingness to settle for so little. They are disciples not
> of the politics of envy but the politics of complacency.
> That is why they are so regularly ignored when the
> demands of the middle classes (who suffer from no such
> inhibition) increasingly dominate the policy agenda of
> both major parties.'
>
> **Roy Hattersley (1996)**

As the Ford workers bolted themselves onto the assembly line again for their extra seven or eight quid a week take-home pay, the leaders of the National Union of Miners, bent on restoring differentials internally as well as regaining their overall front-runner position, banged in a claim for between 20 per cent (for the lowest-paid surface worker) and 40 per cent (for coal-face workers) for 232,000 pitmen, plus a four-day working week, with the additional sting of a demand for an eight-month agreement so that settlements should revert from March (the current date for contract changes) to the previous settlement month of November, a strategically much more favourable month for putting pressure on the Coal Board. Rubbing salt into the wound, the Government's Stage Three 'philanthropist', NUM president Joe Gormley, emphasised that his union was bargaining 'in a free collective bargaining situation, not fettered by outside considerations,' and that he expected the Board to do likewise. Perched on his butt in his editorial office, meditating on the happy lot of a coal-face worker already enjoying on average a 'healthy' 20 per cent productivity bonus under the miners' Stage Three settlement, the *Guardian* leader writer had no problem in pronouncing the proposition of paying a pit person a basic wage of £110 a week to be 'blatantly ridiculous'.

The horizon looked distinctly menacing as 1978 - itself dubbed by shadow chancellor Geoffrey Howe, in a catalogue of industrial confrontation, 'the year of the bloody-minded' - drew to a close. As the miners' claim was lodged, half a million civil servants were about to be incited to go for four times the Government's prescribed norm by the Pay Research Unit, the independent body responsible for monitoring their pay. Since the administrator of the Unit was a prime ministerial appointment, this was a major embarrassment for the Government, although it had given no guarantee that it would fully implement the Unit's recommendations. A 40 per cent claim for more than a million local government workers was already on the table, alongside similar claims for over 300,000 health service workers. The gas-workers' Christmas card for the Government was a 20 per cent demand, with the water-works delivering a copycat card. A six-week strike of provincial journalists over a claim for a £20-a-week rise started on 4th December. Threats to Christmas cheer came from television technicians, bottling factory workers, and draymen, though in the event they did not add up to much gloom or excessive abstemiousness. A strike of social workers which had begun in Newcastle and two London boroughs in late August escalated at the end of the year, with some 1,300 (from about a tenth of NALGO's social work branches) out and more set to join them. A five-and-a-half-week strike of bakers responsible for the production of seventy per cent of the nation's daily bread ground to an end twelve days before Christmas in bitter division, with the union settling for little more than half its original claim.

All this, however, was little more than a blustery prelude to the storm that was gathering. The public service unions announced 22nd January as their big Day of Action, and despite the Government's parliamentary reprieve, the political barometer fell in consonance with the weather. The old year slipped away with temperatures diving towards zero and widespread sleet and snow showers. Then 1979 - 'this year of decision and advance', as Prime Minister Callaghan called it, with deaf-and-blind but regrettably not dumb optimism, in his New Year Message - made its entrance as if nature were intent on providing the most apposite possible metaphor for the state of the nation, with Britain (in the *Guardian's* description) 'littered with abandoned cars as thousands of motorists ended their holiday weekend journeys trapped in snowdrifts or trapped behind other vehicles on icy roads.' The exceptionally cold weather continued to grip the country (with brief let-ups) throughout January and for the best part of February, compounding the problems imposed by wilful disruption.

The threat of a strike of petrol tanker drivers had been hanging over the nation's head since the end of November, when they set 3rd January as the deadline for agreement on their claim. As the year ended, troops were put on standby to be ready to take over deliveries to essential services. The deadline was put back a week to give the drivers time to consider eve-of-crisis offers from most of the oil companies, and a nation-wide strike was narrowly averted by a settlement raising the basic wage to £78 without strings, with fringe benefits bringing the total value of the rise for most drivers to between 13 and 15 per cent. Even so, unofficial action hit some parts of Britain, in particular Greater Manchester, where bus services were cut and some schools had to be closed because they ran out of heating oil. In Northern Ireland direct action by tanker drivers rapidly stoked up a crisis, and for seventy-five hours the country was under a state of emergency, with several hundred additional troops despatched from the mainland to drive and escort supplies of oil for vital services. Secretary of State Roy Mason was accused of extending his colonial attitudes into the field of industrial relations by Seamus Mallon of Ulster's Social Democratic and Labour Party, who reminded him that in 1974 a Labour government had stood by as a political strike of right-wing Loyalists toppled the Northern Ireland administration.

The biggest disruption to the life of the nation was caused by the tanker drivers' counterparts in general haulage. A week before Christmas delegates representing 40,000 lorry drivers had also fixed on 3rd January as the date for an all-out strike if their claim for a £65 a week basic (an increase of around 20 per cent) had not been conceded. It was not, and within twenty-four hours they had a stranglehold on the country. 'Lorry strikers cut country's supply lines', cried the front-page headline of *The Guardian* on 5th January. This was above a report that the icy weather, colluding with the strikers, was turning common-or-garden vegetables into luxuries in many parts of Britain, and that anticipated not only that pig and poultry farmers might have to slaughter their stock 'within the next few days as animal feedstuffs supplies fail', but the even direr forewarning that the non-delivery of newsprint might bring the presses to a halt.

When James Callaghan returned from his mini-summit meeting with the leaders of the three other major NATO powers in semi-tropical Guadeloupe (where the Prime Minister had been captured on film strolling across the sands with Audrey) to a bleak Britain, he ran straight into heavy flak. On this occasion his celebrated sangfroid simply provided more ammunition for an overwhelmingly hostile press and opposition politicians. Doubtless there was the malicious intention of misrepresenting him as callous and complacent behind the apocryphal quote 'Crisis? What crisis?' But it was not in fact such an outrageous travesty of what he actually said, in playing that grubby old card brought out by ruling politicians of whatever party when charged with responsibility for the deplorable state of the nation - the one that calls the critics unpatriotic. 'Please don't run down your country by talking about mounting chaos,' admonished Uncle Jim. 'If you look at it from outside, you can see that you are taking a rather parochial view. I do not feel there is mounting chaos.'

But whoever's fault it was, mounting chaos and something awfully like a crisis there manifestly was, even though it was obviously in the interests of capitalists in general and Tories in particular to exaggerate it. On the day of Callaghan's return, John Harvey-Jones, one of the three deputy chairmen of Britain's fourth biggest company, Imperial Chemical Industries, reported that 19,000 of its 90,000 employees were already involuntarily idle, and warned that the company would be forced to close by the end of the following week if the lorry drivers' strike was not called off. 'If we are not careful the whole pack of cards will collapse,' he said. Which is what the CBI began to envisage the next weekend, in predicting that a tenfold multiplication of the current total of 175,000 lay-offs would be caused by the combined effects of the ongoing road haulage dispute and the one-day rail strikes called by the locomen's union for the coming Tuesday and Thursday.

These dire and doubtless disingenuous predictions (which, in the event, were not fulfilled) were eagerly exploited by the leaderene of the Opposition - doubtless motivated by a burning desire to repay in kind the shame the miners had inflicted on a Tory prime minister five years before - in calling for the proclamation of a State of Emergency. From Callaghan's ministers the predictions provoked indignant cries of deliberate exaggeration. Perhaps that well-known mental characteristic of politicians, selective memory syndrome, meant they really had forgotten the even more fearful foreboding of their own Chancellor, voiced three days before the CBI warning, that two million people could have been made idle by the following week if the current and planned industrial action was not called off.

After the road transport disputes were over it was reported that they had caused at the peak point 235,000 lay-offs. The biggest single casualty of the road haulage strike was the massive Sheffield complex of the British Steel Corporation, which was shut down, with the laying-off of its 14,000 workers, through a blockade imposed by picketing lorry drivers. When the official figures were published in March, it transpired that the overall loss of production in January caused by the collusion of strikers and weather amounted to 8.2 per cent, which actually brought January 1979's total production figure to 8 per cent below that achieved during the three-day-working-week period under the unhappy Heath, so perhaps the dishonours were after all about even. The ICI estimated it had lost about £100 million from the road haulage strike, which ended in most areas on the last day of the month, with the general acceptance by the drivers of £64 for a 40-hour week, just £1 short of their original claim.

Of much greater moment than this economic sabotage so far as the formation of the folk memory of the Winter of Discontent is concerned - and thus for its long-term political repercussions - was the revolt of rank-and-file workers in local government services and the NHS. The most obvious reason for the lasting impression of this revolt is that - apart from industrial action in water or fuel supply or in public transport - the services provided by these workers impinged most directly on the lives of ordinary people. The Day of Action and its aftermath might have provided a salutary reminder of just how much was owed by society to the day-after-day dedication of the mostly ill-paid manual workers in these social services. Instead of which, this kicking over of the traces by the menials who customarily kept the machines of civilised living running so unobtrusively, seems to have provoked, more commonly, incomprehension and resentment. That this was the general reaction among ordinary folk may be reasonably inferred from the consideration that, had it not been so, 'superior people' able to command a public hearing could hardly have got away with such outrageous slanders against the public service workers as they did.

To this crucial war of words I will turn presently, after a brief account of the direct action to which the manual workers in local government and the NHS resorted in pursuit of their claims, pausing here only to draw attention to the brinkmanship repeatedly practised by the powers that be in their attempts to buy off trouble at the minimum possible cost. It was public knowledge a week before Christmas that 22nd January was to be a Day of Action involving up to one and a half million members of the four principal unions organising workers in the public services, 'the most co-ordinated industrial action since the General Strike of 1926', as a *Guardian* reporter put it. Alan Fisher, general secretary of the union with the greatest number of public service members, the National Union of Public Employees, had warned at the time: 'The stage is now set for a major confrontation in the public sector unless the Government is prepared to move quickly and decisively to end the low pay of the nation's underpaid workers.'

Yet it was not until four weeks later, just six days before what the Government - if one is to judge from its inertia - hoped would be little more than a jumbo-sized demo, that Callaghan gave another inch on its inflexible five-per-cent formula, by accepting full-time weekly earnings of less than £60, instead of less than £44.50, as providing a case for special treatment under the low-pay criterion. In consequence of this late concession, with its promise of Government funding, two days later, on the Thursday night before the Monday D-Day, the local government employers upped their offer to between 8 and 9 per cent, while at the same time the water authorities raised their offer to 33,000 manual workers to 11.5 per cent. On the same day British Gas and unions representing 40,000 manual workers agreed to set up a working party to examine a 20 per cent claim. The water and sewage workers won themselves a 16 per cent package early in February without having to lace up their bovver boots, with the power and gas workers doing even better by the time their settlement was due. The dispute with the local authority workers was allowed to drag on into March, when they finally settled for 9 per cent plus £1 on account while comparability studies were carried out. (The actual basic rates for a 35-hour working week, under what Environment Secretary Peter Shore imaginatively described as a 'fair - even generous - settlement', were raised by 50 pence a living day to £45.90 for the lowest-paid group and to £51.75 for the highest, as against the £60 target the workers had been aiming at.) It is true that 6.9 per cent of the water workers' package was for a projected increase in productivity, but then productivity was more measurable in the water industry, as in gas and power supply. More to the point, one naturally suspects, is that industrial action in such essential industries has such an immediate, brutal, and comprehensive impact on economic and social life.

But if the Government hoped that the Day of Action would be no more than a passing show, Fisher and his companion commanders leading the host of public sector workers into battle never expected the walls of the five-per-cent citadel to come tumbling down on 22nd January. The Day of Action was intended as an impressive display of solidarity and resolve (which it was), to be followed by such skirmishes and acts of attrition - selective strikes, go-slows, and the like - as turned out to be necessary to ram home the point that they would not be fobbed off with 5 per cent or little more. In some areas council workers moved at once into unofficial strikes of indefinite duration. In others the action was more of a hit-and-run nature. Much depended on local initiative, as in a guerrilla campaign. This was similarly so with ancillary hospital workers, and even in some instances with nurses. Here and there, graves remained undug, icebound roads ungritted, soiled bed linen unwashed.

In a number of areas, schools were closed down from the Day of Action onwards by striking caretakers, and by early February well over a thousand schools in England and Wales were shut. The 37,000 schoolchildren in the Labour-controlled London Borough of Haringey were among those who enjoyed an unexpected holiday, as the council was one of those which had decided not to try to keep its schools open without having caretakers on duty. One Haringey school, Creighton Comprehensive, provided a perfect microcosm of a nation at odds, since its head teacher, Molly Hattersley, was the sister of the Secretary of State for Prices, Roy Hattersley, shortly to be lumbered with the thankless task of smoothing the way to a truce with the public sector workers. Those parents protesting against the closure of the school were confronted by counter-demonstrators composed not only of caretakers, but of teachers (with their own demands in the pipeline), pupils, and other parents who took a more sympathetic view of the caretakers' strike.

In the midst of all this agitation of workers in local government, the civil servants prepared to go into action, fixing 23rd February as the date for a one-day all-out strike, to be followed by selective strikes. These small-scale manoeuvres had quite spectacular results, gumming up the Government's data-processing operations and even stopping its cheques. The unions' campaign was ably abetted by the Government itself. By suspending civil servants taking part in selective strikes, it escalated the action. In Scotland the Government actually succeeded in paralysing itself by suspending thirty-nine civil servants who refused to do work normally undertaken by colleagues. The suspension of thirty-nine people for declining the role of scab labour provoked a walk-out by 30,000.

With indomitable disregard for prudence and the findings of the Pay Research Unit, the Government produced towards the end of March the incendiary offer of 7 per cent, thereby enflaming the normally very moderate Inland Revenue Staff Federation to instruct its members to black all work on the Budget, and the civil service unions jointly to call an all-out strike for the following Monday, 2nd April. Just minutes before the Government was defeated in a vote of confidence in the Commons, on Wednesday 28th March, the First Division Association, representing some 10,000 top civil servants, announced that its members would support the strike. This was surely the very apogee of the Government's achievements. It had succeeded by almost unsurpassable ineptitude in uniting against itself its 600,000 own white-collar employees, divided by their membership of nine different unions, and ranging in rank from office cleaners and all the others constituting the more than fifty per cent who earned less than £65 a week, to senior civil servants with five-figure salaries and the power to bend the ears of ministers. On the last Friday in March the Government tried to retrieve some semblance of being in control of the problem by raising its offer to 9 per cent, with a promise of further rises, based on the recommendations of the Pay Research Unit, to be paid on 1st August and on 31st March 1980. However, its divide-and-rule ploy, masterminded by special agent Roy Hattersley, of seeking to reach a separate accommodation with the smaller unions, failed to avert the unprecedented situation of a government going into a general election campaign while under siege by its own civil servants, with the pitched battle of 2nd April being followed up by ongoing guerrilla warfare.

And yet other bread-and-butter struggles (involving such diverse groups of disaffected workers as tool-men, engineers, printers, stagehands, and Post Office workers) accompanied the Tweedledum-versus-Tweedledee battle of the polls - and in some cases, notably that of teachers in England and Wales (though their Scottish colleagues had already won a famous victory) rumbled on long after the last bit of election litter had been swept up.

One of the longest-running guerrilla campaigns during the Winter of Discontent - and the one that caused the most bitter recriminations - was that of the ambulance crews. So incensed were London's 2,500 ambulancemen by being offered, a week before the public sector workers' Day of Action, an extra 5 per cent (it represented an increase of between 85 pence and £2.50 for drivers and crewmen whose highest wage was £47) that their shop stewards declared, in defiance of union instructions, that no emergency services would be provided during the 24-hour strike due to run from seven a.m. on the 22nd January. The threat was dropped on the night before the strike, but in Birmingham, Coventry, Solihull, Cardiff, Glasgow, Inverness, Fife, and Strathclyde 999 calls went unanswered. By the end of the month emergency-only ambulance services were the general rule, although in some areas cover had to be provided at times by troops or police till towards the end of March.

Hospitals were hard-hit from the beginning. By early in February, as the result of industrial action by ancillary staff, more than half and perhaps as many as two-thirds of the country's 2,300 hospitals were restricting admissions and only providing full treatment to urgent cases. In a few instances some of the nursing staff took part in short strikes, even on one occasion at Great Ormond Street children's hospital.

Fisher's NUPE (with 124,000 members making up nearly half the total of ancillary hospital workers, 12,000 members forming more than two-thirds of the ambulance crews, and over 80,000 nursing members out of the total of some 350,000 nurses and midwives) was in the vanguard of the fight for more generous rewards for health workers, and was the last union to agree to the final offer of 9 per cent plus £1 on account pending comparability agreements, only settling at the end of March after being outvoted by the other unions represented on the national pay bodies. The main still-outstanding grievance of the ambulancemen, many of whom were fully-trained paramedics, was that while, like the local authority manual workers, they had won the principle of comparability, they had not succeeded in securing a guarantee that they would be treated as emergency service workers on a par with firemen and the police.

Alan Fisher himself, who had played such a prominent part in championing the cause of the low-paid, was portrayed by press and politicians as if he were the Grand Demon in a Pandemonium of trade union villains bent on orchestrating what the Prime Minister described at one point - as the disruption of hospitals rose to a crescendo - as 'free collective vandalism'. But before lending an ear to the mouth-to-mouth fighting that resounded from one end of the kingdom to the other in those bitter days, and especially before trying to divine what creeds the clamour really expressed, it might be as well to lay down a few markers by which to measure how exorbitant, or not, were the demands for a larger share of the nation's cake that came thick and fast from just about every quarter.

Figures for the situation in April 1978, released by the Department of Employment at the end of October, recorded the average earnings of men over twenty-one as £86.90, of adult male white-collar workers as just over £100, and of women over eighteen as £55.40. On the Sunday after the public sector workers' Day of Action, league tables based on the latest statistics available from the Department of Employment were published by *The Observer*. They compared the gross average weekly earnings of forty different groups of workers in April 1975 and April 1978, breaking them up into four divisions that helped to show how successful each group had been in playing the snakes-and-ladders wage-bargaining game while their betters got on with their game of Monopoly. With a few exceptions (water workers, gas workers, firemen, miners working on the surface, secondary school teachers, and senior civil servants, for example, had slipped downwards, while draughtsmen, car workers, toolmen, and electricity power engineers had scrambled upwards) their relative positions were much the same in 1978 as they had been in 1975. It is important to bear in mind, of course, that the tables tell us nothing else about the relative rewards of working in different occupations, not even how long it was necessary to work to get the gross earnings indicated.

In the top division, with over £100 a week gross in 1978, were top managers (£149.60) [a somewhat vague category, this: a couple of months earlier the Opinion Research Centre had defined 'top managers' as 'those earning over £12,000 a year, i.e. more than £230 a week], electricity power engineers (£136.10), marketing/sales managers and executives (£131.40), teachers in higher education (£121.30), office managers (£116.10), senior civil servants (£113.70), production and works managers (£110.50), miners working at the coalface (£109.20), accountants (£107.40), and secondary school teachers (£102.70); in the second division, with £84 to £100 gross, were primary school teachers (£99.90), electricians in industry (£95.10), draughtsmen (£92.00), steel workers (£91.70), miners working on the surface (£91.20), policemen (£91.00), car workers (£90.70), toolmakers (£89.80), train drivers (£86.00), plumbers (£85.30), clerical/executives in the Post Office (£84.80), and heavy goods lorry drivers (£84.20); in the third division, with £70 to £84 gross, were gas workers (£81.50), printers outside London (£81.10), food-processing workers (£80.50), firemen (£79.90), bricklayers (£79.20), railway workers (£78.80), electricity supply workers (£78.00), water workers (£74.60), painters and decorators (£73.90), and dustmen (£70.40); and in the bottom division, with less than £70 a week gross, were general clerks (£68.40), nurses (£68.20), clerical officers in the civil service (£62.90), female bank workers (£62.00), caretakers (£61.50), farm workers (£57.70), catering workers (£57.00), bespoke tailors (£43.00), and female retail food workers in England and Wales (£42.20).

Commenting on these pay league tables, and noting among other points that between 1975 and 1978 'the gap between many white-collar, high-income people in the private sector and people in manual labour had widened', Robert Taylor made about as sensible remarks as anyone on the free-for-all situation which had lead to the insurrection of the Winter of Discontent. He called the tables 'the expression of a leap-froggers' system in which workers strive, through fragmented and localised bargaining, to hold their position relative to workers in other work-places and other industries. The most that workers tend to seek...is to climb a rung or two above those whose pay they traditionally compare with their own.' Is not this exactly what we would expect from people conditioned from birth to struggling for a decent livelihood earned in a secure job in a competitive capitalist society? Taylor, who starts his commentary by implicitly rejecting notions - from either left or right - that there was anything revolutionary behind the mass industrial action of the British workers, with the dismissive remark that 'envy of the super rich, or a revival of class warfare, is not the inspiration behind [their] anger and frustration', goes on to make the shrewd observation that 'from some points of view, it may be just as well that most workers do not relate what they earn to incomes throughout the national labour force.'

Whether it is 'just as well' that in general they are not at all well-informed (which is partly what the blessing amounts to!), and that they do not concern themselves overmuch with questions of how society works and whether it gives everybody a fair deal or not, is a matter of opinion, responses to which will vary according to whether the idea of democracy is taken seriously or is just thought of as a useful buzzword. Had 'most workers' made a practice (with the help of the trade union bureaucracies, say) of casting their eyes much higher up the pyramid than where they stood, at the incomes of those who would probably not, except jocularly, regard themselves as members of 'the national labour force', they would have found such fascinating figures as these to compare with the earnings of ordinary workers listed above. The takings of Michael Edwardes, the South African miracle-worker appointed to turn round struggling BL, were estimated at £100,000 per annum (approaching £2,000 a week) and those of dream-child Lord Grade of Associated Television at £150,000 (nearly £3,000 a week). The Chairman of the British National Oil Corporation garnered £50,000 (over £960 a week) and the Chairman of the National Enterprise Board £36,265 (just short of £700 a week). The Prime Minister's salary at that time was £20,000 per annum (£386+ a week) and Cabinet ministers salaries £13,000 (£250 a week). Up till June '78 MPs were paid £6,270 (£120+ a week) and thereafter £6,897 (£132+ a week). The salary of TUC general secretary Len Murray worked out at about £175 a week.

Among the ironies to savour if we include really superior people in our survey of rewards for contributing to the common weal are these. The man with the dazzling name who had been appointed to chair the Royal Commission on the Distribution of Income and Wealth, Lord Diamond, was paid £9,225 per annum for a 2½-day working week, i.e. at a weekly rate equivalent to about £355 - a 'rate for the job' which was to be matched by the salary of the chairman of the Pay Comparability Commission when it was set up in March 1979 (see Chapter 24). A more direct bit of comparability was thrust under the noses of Ford's assembly-line workers, who, as they contemplated an offer of £3.40 pay rise to bring them a sumptuous wage of £72.40 for a forty-hour week, heard that their boss, Sir Terence Beckett, was to get a whacking £459 a week rise, bringing his salary to £54,000 per annum, or around £1,038 a week.

As the clamour from ordinary workers for more money was translated into action, the sympathies of even the fairer sections of the press tended to wane. For instance, Robert Taylor, the 'sensible' observer cited above, began to call the leading campaigning union NUPE 'a four-letter word', while the high-decibel expression 'greedy' was liberally deployed in the media against wage demands. In considering - at least with regard to the lower-paid sections of 'the national workforce' - whether union demands were reasonable or 'irresponsible', one marker is indispensable, namely, the figure alighted on by the Government as the borderline below which earnings would be officially accepted as 'low pay'. This figure was £44.50, and the incomes policy White Paper laid it down that pay increases could be above five per cent if the resulting wage did not exceed that sum. The Government claimed that this was a proper updating of the figure of £30 set by the TUC as a minimum pay target in 1974.

Official acceptance of such pitiful pay (a gross wage of less than one tenth of Sir Terence's *rise*) as adequate invites bitter comment - and direct action! It hardly deserves the reasoned response it got from NUPE's Alan Fisher, who criticised the Government's figure on two scores. In a letter to the Chancellor of the Exchequer of August 1978, he pointed out that, to get as much as he could get on supplementary benefit, a man with two children would have to earn £46.28 gross, and that with three children he would have to earn £53.62. Furthermore, Fisher said, the TUC's unrevised target had been for a minimum basic rate, not for minimum earnings. He maintained that the TUC figure had been calculated as two-thirds of average earnings, and that updating it on this basis would give a minimum basic figure of £60. It is this figure that NUPE and the other unions organising the manual workers in local government and the health service had agreed on as their target.

CHAPTER 24

The battle for Britain

'Never before in the history of human conflict have so
few owed so much to so many.'

Apocryphal

If history is a consideration of why things happened rather than
being merely a chronicle of events (just 'one damned thing after
another,' as Saki memorably put it), if 'the sound and the fury' do
in fact signify something, then we should listen to the voices of *all*
those on its stage, the less as well as the more vocal, the less as
well as the more articulate - and listen even harder to hear the
thoughts that remain unspoken. At times of social upheaval, the
masses break their bonds and, becoming more than the instruments
of others and more than merely a chorus, mock by their actions
Carlyle's dictum that 'the history of the world is but the biography
of great men.' It will not do to talk of the Winter of Discontent as a
kind of collective insanity (though certainly it was a mass getting-
out-of-hand with a vengeance). Nor will it do to treat it primarily
in institutional terms, ending up with the kind of conclusion such
treatises covertly begin with, such as, in this case, that events
demonstrate conclusively that the trade unions had grown too
powerful and/or had failed to adapt so that they could effectively
represent the interests of their members in a changed world.
(Although the latter point is undoubtedly true in ways that little
concern the apologists for capitalism and its warped social
relationships who customarily produce such treatises.) To get to
grips with the Winter of Discontent it is necessary to realise or
recall how ubiquitous and pervasive was the deliberate disruption
of the everyday life of the country.

But beyond that, the point of the account given above of the
course of the Winter of Discontent is simply to serve as a backcloth
to the really significant action: the mental and moral agitation
seething beneath superficially material (and indeed materialistic)
objectives - agitation that challenged the very basis of society. As
had happened to France in 1968, the integrity of British society
was called into question in 1979. And it is a reflection on the
inadequacy of Britain's left-wing intelligentsia in the late seventies

that they failed to rise to the occasion, failed coherently to articulate, cogently to crystallise the common cry of 'it's not fair'. They left the field clear for the self-serving apologists for a society which, however fluid it might appear to have become, remained ineradicably hierarchical in character, to croak loathesomely 'the politics of envy, the politics of envy'.

What did the young Major Freeman intend by his challenge to the elected representatives of the people, during those first elated days of peace after the long struggle against fascism, that this was 'D-Day in the battle of the new Britain'? Surely he meant that, progressively at least, the old social divisions would be demolished, the old injustices done away with, the old inequalities banished from the land by a Labour Movement which had at last won power for the people at a time that gave it a fighting chance of victory in a campaign to construct a good society? The charge against Labour's leaders - and more especially against those who themselves came from a working-class background - is that they allowed themselves to be seduced by 'the sweets of office' into defecting to the ranks of the elite. For however rosy the prospects for Socialism may have appeared in those heady post-war days, by the time of the third round of Labour rule in the mid-seventies, at the latest, the fraudulent nature of the Party's prospectus for transforming society by parliamentary means must have been patently obvious to those who had themselves been transported by the magic boxes of the polling booths to the high seats of power and privilege that representative democracies provide for their really successful politicians.

As the manual workers in hospitals, schools, and local government services took to the streets to support their Day of Action, the Prime Minister was starring in a very different arena, as guest of honour at Granada Television's lunch for 'What the Papers Say' press awards. In addressing the representatives of an 'estate' not greatly distinguished for its record of speaking fair of organised labour, James Callaghan (theoretically chief tribune of the workers) felt impelled by the crisis he did not recognise to acknowledge that 'events in recent days' had been 'a setback, not just for the Government but for the nation as a whole.' He said that what was happening was 'a social, indeed a moral question, much more than a matter of law', hoped 'that these events will make us ask what kind of people and what kind of society we want to be', and concluded with an affirmation of faith that 'the good sense of our people' would prevail. Perhaps the optimistic conclusion was no more than an obligatory obeisance from a politician displaying his democratic credentials and bidding for re-election. Yet once again he could not be faulted for recognising that profound questions were raised by the current social scene. Whether his vision held any answers is another matter. If some of the superficiality in his contemporaneous presentation of the problems posed by the Winter of Discontent can be attributed to the astute manoeuvrings of an active politician at the very centre of the web of so-called 'democratic' politics, the same excuse cannot be made for his retrospective comments. But perhaps one should not expect the passion for self-justification to diminish with loss of power. At all events the judgements he makes in *Time and Chance* on two of his most prominent opponents during the Winter of Discontent, Moss Evans and Alan Fisher, are grossly unjust because his portrayal of the situations in which they found themselves is wholly superficial, either from a natural inability to perceive or from a studied intent to deceive.

Not that penetrating, nor even honest, commentary and analysis was readily to be found amongst the communicators of the time. With rare exceptions, the common purpose of politicians, journalists, and priests alike was rather to clothe the unaccustomed starkness of social division with homily and platitude, however the message might vary according to where the spokesman located the mystic heart of 'the nation'. The trade union tribunes spoke bluntly enough, as was their wont, but were little disposed to dig beneath the surface and expose the treacherous foundations upon which their whole *raison d'être* rested. Inasmuch as a national debate took place, the central issue was (to reduce it to manageable if oversimplified terms) whether it was better for the incomes of employees to be determined by 'free collective bargaining' or through negotiating machinery established by the State, based on national economic targets laid down annually (with the approval of Parliament) by the government of the day. A long-standing exponent of such a policy, Transport Secretary William Rodgers spelt it out a bit at the beginning of 1978:

'I believe that the time has now come to stop thinking of incomes policy as a temporary expedient and to begin to accept it as a necessary - and obvious - component of economic management and social planning...An orderly search for a settled incomes policy would be widely

welcomed. It would be a voluntary policy, reached by
agreement between all those involved, Government,
trade unions, employers, and resting on the broad
approval of public opinion. TUC backing would be
essential.'

Although events could hardly have proved him more wrong
in judging the moment to be propitious for promoting such a policy,
in pointing to the fear of inflation as the spur for those who
advocated it, he could not have been more right. Almost without
exception this was what mainly, if not entirely, motivated them,
and lack of concern for wider and deeper questions raised by the
great wages race condemned their advocacy from the start. On the
same day that Rodgers flew his kite, the Chief Secretary to the
Treasury, Joel Barnett - backing up his bosses, the Chancellor and
the Prime Minister, who were already floating 5 per cent (or little
more) as a suitable figure for the next stage of a pay policy from
which the unions had already made up their minds to withdraw
their co-operation - made it all too clear who was to bear the brunt
of the policy for incomes which he rightly declared the Government
must have:

'In the national interest, and not least in the interest of
maintaining and improving public services, it must be
understood that if public sector wages take a bigger
share of the national cake then - if we are not simply to
finance inflation by printing money, as our predecessors
did - the consequences are clear. And surely, as night
follows day, so excessive public sector wage settlements
must be followed by cuts in public services. The
alternative of financing higher public sector wages from
higher taxation is not an option open to us.'

Barnett's warning contains everything that characterises the
Callaghan Government's surrender of Socialist purposes to the
forces that rule capitalist society. The actual employees of a
supposedly Socialist government - its natural allies - are to be
penalised for contributing their working lives to exemplifying the
proposition that there is another, fairer and more rational, way of
organising society. Not only are public sector workers to be

306

discriminated against in comparison with workers employed to enable individual capitalists to pile up profits (perhaps for the cogent reason that the government has far greater leverage against its own employees than it has against workers in the private sector, though Barnett's intimation that to further increase the proportion of the nation's wealth tied directly to the public sector would be inimical to 'the national interest' powerfully suggests his subjection to orthodox capitalist thinking with regard to the production of wealth). But inasmuch as they succeed in wringing from their State bosses higher rewards for their labour than those superior servants of the State are willing to concede, they are also to be held responsible for whatever cuts the Government decides as a consequence it must impose on public services. That public services must be sacrificed in such circumstances is taken as read.

So much for the Social Contract, the admirable aims of which had to be subordinated to a 'national interest' which, in some mystical, almost Hegelian, sense is thought of as subsuming all personal and sectional interests. Such evasions of the pain of scrupulous thinking are firmly founded on the shallow supposition that there is some measure of justice in the way that that notorious 'national cake' is shared out between the individuals who collectively constitute the nation. Alternatively, the only principle operating is the cynical conviction that the only cause for concern is the relative strengths of those competing for a bigger slice of the cake. What a mouldy state of affairs!

If, on the contrary, it is accepted that justice should come into the equation, a paramount point that Barnett conveniently leaves out is the heavy concentration of low-paid workers in State employment - a concentration persisting through administrations of different political persuasions that tells us much about the 'natural' relationship between leaders and led, bosses and bossed, which overrides all ostensible ideologies. But Barnett was far from being alone amongst ministers in the Callaghan Government in warning public sector workers that unless they accepted the Government's pay policy they would be jeopardising not only the amorphous 'national interest' in general but, in particular, public services and even their own jobs. Besides repeated doses of homily pills from Prime Minister and Chancellor, a series of more specific threats - alternating with or even accompanying nauseous wheedlings - issued from the throats of sundry leaders of 'the people's party'.

For instance, a couple of days after the Ford workers settled for their 17 per cent, the Environment Secretary, Peter Shore, announced that the Treasury's rate support grants for 1979/80 would be maintained at 61 per cent of approved expenditure and that rate increases should not exceed 10 per cent. This ceiling on rate increases, he said, would cause local authorities no problems provided they made wage settlements within the Government's 5 per cent guidelines. Geoffrey Drain, general secretary of the National and Local Government Officers' Association, promptly attacked the Government for failing to provide enough funds to pay their workforces adequately, although in truth it was nothing but normal practice for whatever government happened to be in power to subsidise the Welfare State and the general social wage by, in effect, a levy on the pay packets of public sector workers rather than raising sufficient revenue through general taxation. This is but part of a general principle that, contrary to the common misconception that Welfare States are in the main funded by redistributing wealth from richer citizens to the less affluent, makes the middling sort and even the poor for the most part pay for their own State benefits. Although it was to be further perfected by the Thatcherite counter-revolutionaries, such a principle was, as we have seen, clearly enunciated by Labour's own economic guru, Sir Stafford Cripps, in the early days of the building of Britain's post-war Jerusalem. (See Chapter 19)

In a debate in the Commons while the battle with the local government and health service workers raged in the streets outside, Education Secretary Shirley Williams (later to become one of 'the Gang of Four' who broke away from the Labour Party to set up the Social Democratic Party) told the House that to concede what the local authority employees were still holding out for, 15 per cent, would mean either a rate increase of 20 per cent or the loss of 30,000 teaching and 20,000 other jobs in the education service in England and Wales. Bill Rodgers (who like Williams was to become a founder member of the SDP, along with Roy Jenkins and David Owen) did not scruple to plead with the poorly-paid workers in public transport to moderate their demands for a decent living in favour of the elderly and disabled, warning the busmen that if the settlement they succeeded in exacting was considered to be inflationary the Government would have to abandon its plan to legislate for a national half-fare scheme for those groups.

Time and again the Government lent credence to the Tory capitalistic view that workers in the public sector were featherbedded and that it would be better for the country if many of them were shaken out into the dole queues. A Treasury paper submitted by the Chancellor for Cabinet discussion - just as the leaders of the manual workers in the NHS and local government began to sell to their members the 9-per-cent-plus-£1-on-account settlement of their dispute - asserted that breaching the 5 per cent barrier would have to mean renewed stringency in Government expenditure. Mixing menace with mendacity, it intimated that workers in central and local government had not yet experienced any of the rigours of market forces. Four leaders of white-collar public service workers jointly denounced the absurdity of Government policy which allowed the Treasury to disseminate its view that public sector jobs should be shed at the same time as a special programme to create 50,000 extra jobs was announced. 'It is high time the Treasury were told to adjust the cash limits to provide fair pay settlements in the public sector,' they declared.

Perhaps the most glaring example of a philosophy in which it was thought unexceptionable for ordinary workers and their families to be called on to make disproportionate sacrifices to support a Welfare State that, when everything is taken into account, has always provided bigger benefits for the well-to-do, is to be found in the Government's handling of the problem of funding the nationalised railways. (Though 'handling' is not quite the way to put it, considering its studied determination to keep the problem at arm's length. It has been insufficiently remarked that for Labour governments no less than for Tory administrations the pseudo-constitutional separation of government from the managements appointed to run nationalised industries has been a great blessing to the politicians, especially whenever there was 'trouble at t' mill'.) Higher productivity from a reduced workforce was called for in a report from the Commons Select Committee on Nationalised Industries published at the end of August 1978. The report welcomed the substantial progress made by British Rail during the previous two years towards reaching its target of cutting its deficit by 55 per cent by 1981. However, it noted that this was mainly attributable to a staff reduction of about 6 per cent and a fall in earnings per member of staff of about 4 per cent. In a stunningly perspicacious comment, if they were speaking for the workforce in making it, the Committee doubted that 'a further fall in real average earnings would be considered desirable.'

From the start of municipal and State ownership, public transport in Britain, on both road and rail, has been an industry notorious for maintaining a perpetually precarious fiscal balancing act between expenditure, revenue, and subsidy through the extensive practice of overtime working, operating as an irresistible lure to workers paid at low basic rates. (For example, the bus drivers Rodgers appealed to only hoisted themselves out of the poverty pay basic rate of £34.49 for a 40-hour week by working on average 12 hours a week overtime, frequently including Saturdays and Sundays.) Paradoxically, technological advances, which with the slashing of the country's once-unsurpassed network of services had reduced British Rail's labour force from 446,000 in 1950 to 178,000 by the beginning of 1979, tended to reinforce reliance on overtime (with little concern for the health and safety factors this raised). Yet the financial costs of investment in new technology continued to increase the pressure to cut down on manpower. The railway unions claimed that staff shortages exceeded 12,000, and that if British Rail conceded their claim for a reduction in the basic working week to 35 hours, this would provide 28,000 more jobs. Yet, with exemplary timing, just as last-minute efforts were being made to persuade the locomen's union not to go ahead with its planned series of one-day strikes in support of a bonus claim, BR management released plans for a manpower cut of 20,000. This was raised a month later to between 30,000 and 40,000, the redundancy figures BR said would be necessary if it were to grant an industry-wide bonus scheme.

To make matters worse, there were clear signs that ASLEF's leaders were quite prepared to see a rundown in BR's manpower, provided it was achieved through voluntary 'wastage', in order to get a bonus for the locomen, a stance that was completely unacceptable to NUR general secretary Sid Weighell. He declared that, on the contrary: 'The unions should jointly oppose attempts by management to drastically reduce manning levels.' At the same time, Weighell threatened an overtime ban if BR refused to cut the basic working week and to offer 'realistic' pay rises. In the wake of the 9-per-cent-plus-£1 deal just won by the local authority workers, BR management's notion of realism was, apparently, to offer the railwaymen 6.38 per cent, an offer which only exceeded the 5 per cent 'norm' because the Government had agreed that full-time wages that were still below £70 after a 5 per cent rise could be topped up by up to £3.50. The three rail unions were told that one likely consequence of a settlement that exceeded BR's cash limits would be the raising of fares for the second time that year.

Yet again the State's own employees were being told that they should accept low wages so that the public would not have to pay higher prices, with a Labour government mimicking its political opponents in rejecting the option of raising the living standards of public sector workers by providing more money for public services through general taxation. The dead man's handle operated by Sir Stafford Cripps (that 'superb Christian planner', as one of his biographers dubs him), in ruling out more radical 'redistribution of national income by way of taxation', still stopped the workers in their tracks as they strove for a better standard of living. Yet no consideration of facts which manifestly added up to a serious deterioration in the situation of many people employed in the public sector, precluded Prime Minister Callaghan from pouncing triumphantly on the Leader of the Opposition when, during the first week of that fateful election campaign of spring 1979, she added to her constantly reiterated charge of overmanning in the public sector the warning that if the recommendations of the recently established Pay Comparability Commission exceeded the labour costs allowed for in public sector budgets, it would almost inevitably lead to cuts in services, job losses, or both. 'This is the kind of blunder that can upset industrial peace, which has been so hardly won,' crowed Callaghan, as if he and his ministers were entirely innocent of ever issuing such GBH-type threats.

It was a nice irony that, aside from the few trade union leaders who seriously took up the cudgels on their behalf, the most vigorous defence of the interests of the public sector workers came from the dethroned King of the Tories, Ted Heath, during the course of his personal campaign in support of the principle of an incomes policy - a principle which the Thatcherites were busy denouncing as a heresy from the true path of capitalism. Interviewed on television in a programme which incorporated a film showing him having the poignant experience of being feted in a Lancashire miners' club, he made it crystal clear that he considered it neither fair nor sensible to treat workers in public services or nationalised industries less favourably than those employed in the private sector:

'Let us say that a government tries to hold down the public sector, while on the other hand the private sector gives much higher increases in wages. Those people in the public sector don't accept that. We've learnt that from experience. They say, "Why, because we're in a nationalised industry, because we're public servants in hospitals or elsewhere, because we are nurses or firemen, why should we have worse treatment than those who are working in the private sector?"'

Callaghan may have recognised that there were moral issues underlying the revolt of the public sector workers; but, as with his grudging concession on low pay on the eve of their Day of Action, so it was with his concurrent implicit admission that they never would accept the status of second-class citizens in wage bargaining: only when browbeating had patently failed to intimidate them would he grant the irrefutable justice of their case. He announced that machinery would be established for the continuous review of public sector pay on the basis of comparability with private industry, i.e. of 'the rate for the job'. Seven weeks later, three weeks before the Government fell, Hugh Clegg, Professor of Industrial Relations at Warwick University, was appointed (at what, the Prime Minister made clear, in answer to the doubts expressed by Labour back-bencher Arthur Lewis whether such several-fingers-in-the-pie people were the right sort to consider the pay of the lower-paid, *was* 'the rate for the job' for such posts, i.e. £18,510 for a full year's work) to chair the Standing Commission on Pay Comparability. Its first reports, he told the House, on the pay of local authority manual workers, NHS ancillary workers, ambulancemen, and university workers, would be made on August 1st. The Commission remained standing until it was knocked on the head by Mrs Thatcher in 1980. The VIPs' equivalent of the tribunal set up to see fair play for the PBI of the public sector, the Top Salaries Review Board chaired by Lord Boyle of Handsworth, PC, not only preceded the Clegg Commission by eight years but effortlessly survived its decease.

Like the wages councils (the origins of which lie in the trade boards set up by a bill of 1909 which was introduced, under a Liberal administration, by the man who was to become the century's most considerable Tory statesman, and the final smothering of which was to be engineered in 1993 by the ministry of its least considerable

Tory statesman), the Clegg Commission was, of course, a deviation from the creed of free collective bargaining to which both sides of industry and all parliamentary parties in theory subscribed - or at least had subscribed until relatively recently. In both 1900 and 1979 there were good reasons for this deviation, and strangely one of the most telling reasons was central to both cases, though they sprang from radically different causes. A biblical lifespan before Clegg's collectivist butterfly was broken on the wheel of the first of the Thatcherite kickback anti-combination laws, Winston Churchill had succinctly identified this central reason for the need for State intervention as the absence of 'parity of bargaining' between management and labour to secure 'a decent provision for industrial workers'. Churchill's target was 'the sweated trades' in which workers could be exploited without the restraint of union organisation. The target for Clegg and his colleagues was the biggest boss of all, the government, so that in a sense the State was being enjoined to intervene against itself - or at least against those who, *pro tempore*, held the stewardship of the State and all the powers that went with it.

The trouble with the incomes policy concept which by the seventies had lodged in the minds of more than a few people of varying party allegiances or none at all was that there were two entirely distinct, and indeed antithetical, reasons for the growing disenchantment with the doctrine and practice of free collective bargaining. On the one hand, there was the *weakness* of the workers, in such situations as Churchill had inveighed against or in such cases as public sector workers in the caring services; on the other hand, there was the *strength* of the workers - that is, of those groups of workers who were in a position (to use the smear phrase so liberally applied by the anti-union media) to 'hold the country to ransom'.

Unsurprisingly, the beginning of the wider dispersal of the pay policy proposition coincided with the renascent power of the trade union movement in the post-war years and gathered strength as economic growth weakened. Equally unsurprisingly, many trade unionists and most of the Labour left became totally wedded to a practice that was really a true expression in the labour market of the doctrine of *laissez-faire* capitalism. Thus came the wry consequence that in the great crisis faced by the Labour Movement in the winter of 1978/79 its most ostensibly radical members were

313

in one key respect - that of wage-bargaining - closest in their thinking on industrial relations to the most reactionary of the Tories, who were harking back to the heydays of unfettered capitalism in the nineteenth century. Of course, Labour supporters in the Jim-'ll-fix-it-if-you-let-him-pay-policy bed were equally incompatible. They were all deeply - and rightly - concerned about the effects of inflation on living standards. But while some of them were there primarily to consummate State control over the workers, others had climbed in with the hope of securing fair play for groups of workers who had not done so well out of a free-for-all. However, as we shall see, others just as concerned about workers who failed to get a square deal out of free collective bargaining took a death-before-dishonour stance towards the Government's Stage Four propositioning and to the whole thrust of the Labour leadership's project for a permanent incomes policy.

'Union is strength' and 'united we stand, divided we fall' are the commonest slogans strung across the banners of British trade unions, and the truth of these precepts is in theory well understood by trade unionists and by the Labour Movement as a whole. But every party and every movement, despite the common purposes which bind the members together, has in-built centrifugal forces stemming from the fact that it is actually composed of an alliance of more or less disparate elements. Indeed, to talk of a 'movement' at all may be an indispensable generalisation but is nevertheless a dangerous one, since it tends to obscure or to iron out significant differences and disagreements. The breakdown of Britain's consensus politics under the pressure of faltering economic growth brought increased dissension to the Tory Party as well as to Labour. But the Tory centre held, carrying the Butskellites with it (though perhaps with some heartache and maybe even a twinge of conscience or two - and in the longer term with potentially suicidal consequences for the Party) as it moved markedly to the right. Labour's tragedy is that at this most critical moment it was a movement deeply divided, and no one should be surprised at its rout by the New Tories, whose message seemed more in tune with the spirit of the age. 'Dispirit of the age', perhaps one should say, since its principal characteristics were the loss of optimism in general progress through steady economic growth along with a concomitant switch to an every-man-his-own-enterprise approach to life.

Just how divided the industrial wing of the Labour Movement

314

had become may be gauged by listening to the bitterly discordant voices of some of the trade union leaders. The Brighton Congress of September 1978 may have given the impression of organised labour united against the concept of a national pay policy by its overwhelming backing for a return to free collective bargaining. However, by his very defence of this hallowed principle, in putting the motion composited from all the separate trade union resolutions rejecting the Government's plea for a Stage Four, the miners' general secretary, Laurence Daly, exposed free collective bargaining as a force that fragmented the trade union movement. He insisted that he was not advocating a system in which, in pressing their claims, workers ignored the interests of other workers, or of the community as a whole. Commending it to Congress as an apposite metaphor (evidently he was much pleased with it, since he was recycling it from an address he had made to a Durham miners' gala), Daly likened free collective bargaining to 'free collective motoring, all right unless it turned into free collective suicide, with everyone choosing his own side of the road.' One might take the charitable view that it mattered little what he said, since everyone knew that the motion he was speaking in favour of would be carried overwhelmingly; but to draw attention with such unconscious clarity to the way free collective bargaining worked and to why it never could serve the interests of the community as a whole did seem a little unfortunate.

More pertinent and perceptive comment on the British trade union movement came from the chair, in the opening address by David Basnett, general secretary of the General and Municipal Workers' Union. Mindful of the high probability of a general election being called within a month or so (how was he to guess that three days later Callaghan - in a delirium of hope that, given a little more time, a majority of the electorate would come to see it his way and conclude that his government was after all best fitted 'to carry on with the task of consolidating the present improvement in the country's position' - would announce his Russian roulette decision to soldier on into a fifth session of Parliament?), Basnett was understandably at pains to be conciliatory. (This, indeed, seems to have been a characteristic of his in his dealings with other union leaders and with Government ministers, and for which pains he is dismissed by Denis Healey in his autobiography as 'weak and vacillating in our years of travail'.) So he took care to avoid providing the common enemy with ammunition to fire at the Labour Movement, and urged his fellow trade unionists to work and vote for Labour in the sensibly measured terms of calling it the best of the parties on offer to deal with discrimination and poverty.

To the unions' dispute with the Government over the pay policy issue he only alluded obliquely (and in a way which indicated that he was by no means wholly unsympathetic to the case for a pay policy), in criticising some sections of the Labour Movement for being too often prepared to trade off the social wage for an increase in the pay packet. And gently probing closer to the heart of the problem of worker solidarity in a capitalist society, he reproved the unions for forgetting about the inequalities which still existed in income, housing, and education. Of course, his allusion to making 'the final assault on discrimination, inequality, and poverty' was ludicrously hyperbolic talk from a member of a mountaineering expedition which had hardly trekked as far as the foothills of social injustice. Still, at least his speech suggested that for trade unionists with any vision of a better society there was a great deal more to be thought about than the next pay claim.

Basnett's unreadiness to put his trust in paternalistic politicians was already on record. He clearly saw that government intervention in wage bargaining only further loaded the scales against workers in the public services. Early in May 1978, as Government ministers hoisted their England-expects-every-man-to-tighten-his-belt-again flags, Basnett repeated his call for the TUC to set up a special committee to provide 'better co-ordination and mutual support' for unions in dealing with the Government's 'unilateral policies' of pay control in the public sector. And nearly a year before the Clegg Commission was set up, Basnett called for pay research reviews to draw comparisons between public and private sector earnings. He also suggested that the pay of nurses and the police should be index-linked to that of workers in manufacturing, as had already been conceded to the staff of another emergency service, the fire brigades.

Index-linking, so long as it was honoured, would have the great advantage of guaranteeing that without having to take industrial action themselves, the public service workers to whom it was granted would benefit from the strength and fighting spirit of the private sector workers with whose labour rewards it had been agreed theirs should correspond. By contrast State-sponsored pay review bodies, although conceived (like commissions entrusted with reviewing social security benefits, or more wide-ranging commissions like Diamond's) as independent, were nothing more than advisory bodies - as was made brutally clear by the Callaghan Government's cavalier treatment of the unwelcome findings of both the Burnham Committee on salary scales for teachers in State schools and the Pay Research Unit on Civil Service pay. Furthermore, they were constantly subject to external pressures as well as to internal prejudices. State-sponsored pay review bodies are at best but frail props in the struggle for a fair deal for workers, particularly under such a constitution as Britain's, which not only grossly distorts the representation of the people but, in the absence of any constitutional checks and balances, effectively permits an elective dictatorship to ride roughshod over opposition to its will. The Tory hegemony which followed the rout of Labour in 1979 was all too amply to demonstrate this by - to cite just three examples germane to the present discussion - its severing of index-linking for firemen and its abolition not only of the Burnham Committee but also of the wages councils that had formerly afforded a shabbily minimal protection to the weakest of society's wage-slaves. Nevertheless, such official bodies had proved their value to those sections of workers whose jobs were covered by their reviews, simply by providing the ammunition with which they could fight their own battles. Whatever their philosophical implications, in practice these bodies tended to bolster rather than to undermine free collective bargaining. Propositions for a national pay policy were quite another matter, with disturbing echoes of the Corporate State.

Despite the paucity of its theoretical underpinnings, the British trade union movement has always had a healthy distrust of government, which its experience of operating under Labour rule has, to say the least, done nothing to remove. But no such qualms - nor even the consideration that if a party of a different colour gained power, its leaders would have few scruples in making the most of any convenient precedent set by Labour - sounded in the voices of those who spoke at Brighton in favour of the motion from the National Association of Local Government Officers calling for recognition of the need for government intervention in wage bargaining, particularly in view of the inescapable fact that it would always have a more or less direct influence on the determination of pay in the public sector.

In putting the motion, Glyn Phillips made the cogent criticism of 'free collective bargaining' that in twenty years as a union negotiator he had never seen it operating freely in the public sector. Deploying metaphor more deftly than Daly, he made the caustic comment that he was 'tired of putting empty buckets down the well of free collective bargaining and pulling empty buckets back.' And reason was also on his side when he argued that it was illogical to tell the government to keep out of wage bargaining when concern for every other major aspect of the country's economic life was accepted by the trade unions as part of its remit. Of course he was right to call this opposition to government intervention 'self-interest'. But on what else was the whole competitive economic system in which the Labour Movement had schooled itself to acquiesce, and on which the trade unions had modelled themselves, based but the perpetual clash of conflicting interests?

The two most persistent and most voluble trade union champions of the Government's case were the general secretaries of the National Union of Railwaymen and of the Union of Post Office Workers. In supporting the NALGO motion at Brighton, Sidney Weighell of the NUR focused on the futility of winning big wage settlements only to see them eaten away by higher inflation, while the postal workers' leader, Tom Jackson, arguing that a consensus between government and unions on the amount of money available for wage rises was imperative, made the incontrovertible assertion that free collective bargaining never produced fairness in the distribution of wages. But he spoke as if he knew nothing of those irreducible factors in the equation of wealth distribution that are inseparable from societies operating in accordance with the imperatives of private capitalism.

Tom Jackson succeeded David Basnett as TUC president, so he was in the chair when the General Council rejected by a tied vote the attempt to cobble together a semblance of accord between government and unions ten weeks after the raspberry Congress had blown in Brighton. The pair of linked statements which the General Council was asked to endorse had been drawn up in five weeks of beggars' horse-trading between the Chancellor and the TUC's economic committee. The exasperated Healey calls the statements 'helpful...guidance on pay', and it is true that they were anodyne enough, with neither side giving away anything of substance, unless the sympathetic nod towards low-paid workers in the public sector can be so described. Basnett found their rejection 'incomprehensible', and perhaps he was right, inasmuch as their acceptance would have made little practical difference to union negotiators, while their rejection was bound to highlight the disunity of the Labour Movement. But for anyone with reasons for doubting the Government's good faith, the thrust of the proposed agreement - with its paramount stress on controlling inflation (together, of course, with its implied acceptance of government oversight in wage bargaining) - was bound to have seemed objectionable.

At all events, it was so diplomatically non-committal in its details that it threw the Council into a welter of confusion, so that its members hardly knew why they were voting for it or against it, or at least were doing one or the other from mutually contradictory convictions as to what it meant or did not mean. Jackson, who knew by his very whiskers what he felt, was put in the unhappy position of being obliged by custom to use his casting vote against the proposed accord. This may help to explain why, in attending a House of Commons luncheon for assorted members of the political cognoscenti the following day, he was quite unable to contain himself, laying about him and roundly abusing handfuls of his General Council colleagues by name - which hardly helped matters. His sentiments did him credit, certainly. 'When did the movement march towards Socialism behind the banner of free collective bargaining - a banner saying, "As much as you can get, and to hell with the unemployed?"' he asked belligerently, and presumably with purely rhetorical intent. But unhappily, in asserting that 'what we are going through is an aberration', he only exposed the tenuousness of his hold on reality, as became all too evident a few weeks later, when a delegate conference of his own union agreed to slap in a pay claim of 24.4 per cent.

To cries of derision from those he had abused, he could only retort: 'If there is to be a rat-race, if there is to be a free-for-all, we must be part of the all.' Exactly! That is the standard premise of bargaining - collective or individual, wage or whatever - in capitalist society. Every union in the land was formed, organised, and henceforth operated on that basis, to look after its own members. To use Jackson's scornful words, they were guerrilla groups, each group pursuing its own interests, and inasmuch as his highly emotive talk of 'the rapacious pursuit of self-interest' had validity, it did not represent the *end* of trade unionism (as he would have it), but its whole history, with only intermittent examples of wider solidarity. And little had ever been done either by the trade union movement collectively or the Labour Movement as a whole to amend this situation of working people divided and ruled by capitalists. Certainly the attempts of successive Labour governments to control the proportion of the national wealth that was paid out in wages had nothing whatsoever to do with the fair and judicious distribution of the incomes of working people, whether in or out of trade unions, let alone with the gross inequalities of living standards across the population as a whole.

A particular target of Jackson's animus was the NUPE leader Alan Fisher, who was unable to share Jackson's confidence that the rejected agreement would have ensured at last a square deal for public sector workers. If Fisher believed that Messrs Callaghan, Healey & Co. were only interested in conjuring up a nostrum with which they could convince the country that Labour was the party that could secure national unity through concord with the unions, events were surely about to prove him right, since it took a mass revolt of workers to shift the Government from its 5 per cent formula even for the low-paid. Although it was too late to save the country from vandalisation by the Thatcherites, Denis Healey at least had the grace eventually to admit to the folly of the Government's five-per-cent-fixation. James Callaghan, on the contrary, seems to have regarded standing firm for 5 per cent as an act of faith. In his account in *Time and Chance* of the abortive meeting between himself, the Chancellor, and the Secretaries for Employment and Industry, on the one side, and the General Council of the TUC, on the other, which took place shortly before the September Congress that torpedoed Stage Four, he takes Fisher (the only opponent he names) to task for arguing that 'the whole policy had been unfair. Coming from him,' asserts Callaghan coolly, 'this was singularly wrong-headed for his members, who were among the lowest paid, had benefited more than most other groups as the policy had been deliberately tilted in their favour.'

This particular canard was also given wing, just as the fateful general election campaign got under way, by someone who should perhaps have stuck to duck-shooting. Sports Minister David Howell used a presidential address to his own union, the Association of Professional, Executive, Clerical and Computer Staff (APEX), as a vehicle for a scathing attack on the 'madness' of free collective bargaining. He singled out (though not by name) for the harshest criticism the ingrate public sector trade union leaders whose members, he claimed, had gained most from the Social Contract but had led the revolt against it. Callaghan may have been referring simply to the pay policy in rebuking Fisher, in which case he was just plain wrong, since, during Stage Three at least, pay rises in the public sector had lagged behind those in the private sector. In extending the case for a reprimand to the wider issue of the Social Contract, Howell was guilty of self-deception, if not of the greater crime of conspiring to deceive others - and others who were comrades marching with Tom Jackson, Sid Weighell, and Uncle Tom Cobleigh along what they fondly imagined to be the road to Socialism.

There were plenty of people who, while they were not prepared to accept a Labour government controlling workers' wages simply in order to control inflation, could nevertheless see the point of a trade-off between pay rises and a bigger 'social wage' to jack up the general standard of living. Some of the most telling criticism of the Callaghan Government at the Brighton Congress concerned its failure to deliver its side of the bargain called the Social Contract and its unwillingness to treat organised labour as a partner whose views should at least be given serious consideration. As it happens, it was Fisher who put the composite motion calling on the Government to adopt the economic strategy favoured by the unions (including more public ownership, increased State investment in manufacturing industry and public supervision of investment, more house-building, the use of North Sea oil revenues to boost public service employment, a rapid increase in the overall level of economic growth, and the redistribution of wealth to reduce the massive inequalities in society). And it was another of the Labour leaders' *bêtes noires*, the general secretary of the Association of Scientific, Technical and Managerial Staffs, Clive Jenkins (Healey gratuitously characterises him in *The Time of My Life* as 'the maverick left-wing leader of a professional union whose members mostly voted Tory'), who led the attack on the Government's monetarist policy, moving the composite motion demanding the restoration of cuts in public expenditure and the ending of cash limits which were preventing local authorities from implementing legislation and therefore of fulfilling their mandates. 'The United Kingdom today is a bucket of cash, a reservoir of capitalism,' he piped belligerently. 'Let us use this money to irrigate the public sector.'

A third black bellwether, Moss Evans of the TGWU, led the demand that the Government should make the reduction of unemployment its top priority, the main key to which, most unions had long believed, was a cut in the basic working week, the elimination of 'excessive and systematic levels of overtime', earlier retirement, and more holidays. He said that trade union research indicated that full acceptance of a 35-hour week could create 750,000 new jobs, of which 200,000 could be in the public sector. If the expectation that all this could be achieved 'without loss of pay and without being impeded by any 5 per cent policy' sounded a little hopeful to some, the gravamen of his complaint - that while social security benefits had taken some of the sting out of unemployment 'there is just no adequate compensation for being without a job' and 'we are still as far away from full employment as before the war' and with predictions of far worse times to come - was fully justified.

These three principal opponents of pay policy are not open to the charge of being only concerned with putting more money into the pockets of their members (or to put it in the Chancellor's abusive terms, pandering to 'greedy people'), and the most often vilified of the three, Fisher, made an unanswerable response to Healey's gibes about 'confetti money'. Asked by Peter Jay in a radio interview if it would not be better to have 5 per cent settlements all round, he replied that 'in an ideal situation' that was so. 'But of course the problem that our people have got is that if everybody else this year settles at a higher level, and it looks very much as if that is going to be the case, if they in order to help the Government were to settle at a much lower figure, it would only mean that an already low-paid group would find themselves in an almost desperate situation.' And talking about ideal situations, one might note that Moss Evans went on record as being willing to contemplate an incomes policy, but only in the context of a Socialist society.

The point is, of course, that instead of making a frontal assault on free collective bargaining in the tradition of the World War I donkeys in charge of our lads on the Western Front, Labour should have spent those three years of grace that the trade union movement gave it by its restraint, in conceiving and promoting a fairer system of rewards for work. Seeking to excuse the Party leaders for neglecting to do so, one might surmise that they thought such a project impossibly utopian, to which the reply has to be that it is always for utopia that one must strive. More probably, it never even occurred to them that it was a matter meriting some of their precious time.

Few Labour politicians at that time seem to have succeeded in getting it on record that they were that much bothered even about the plight of the low-paid, never mind the immensely complex issue of fair pay in general and the tangled web of conflicting interests, jostling differentials, and shameful status-squabbling into which capitalist competition has driven all of us workers. But since I take the elimination of poverty-pay as a *sine qua non* for taking a first step along that road to Socialism, let us give one Labour MP who did speak out loudly and clearly the last word here. On the night of the public sector workers' Day of Action, the Tories launched an attack on the Government's handling of the industrial crisis. A 'somnolent Commons debate' was 'lit up' by Jeff Rooker 'with a passionate appeal to the Government to try to see things through the eyes of the low-paid', according to *The Guardian*, who promptly invited him to contribute to its series on 'The Pay Race'. Among the points he made in his speech and his article were the following.

He said that the seeds of the present troubles had been sown over the past three years of an incomes policy that was not directed in substance to the low-paid, and that in fact the Government's own figures showed that they had lost ground in relation to average earnings. They could not be blamed for getting extremely angry and bitter at being forced to take industrial action in order to have their case heard. One reason for the build up to the present troubles was the lack of a co-ordinated government policy for dealing with the public sector. The Prime Minister should appoint Ministers specifically to look after wages and conditions of service in the public sector, and to see that no group, whether it had or had not the muscle to take industrial action, should be allowed to fall behind 'to such an extent that its members have bitterness and anger in their hearts and are prepared to take action which they know damages themselves and their families.'

Rooker made it clear that he had never advocated a free-for-all, 'but I have never yet supported the rigid incomes policies imposed on the workers of this country, in the main by senior civil servants who have never done a real day's work in their lives, aided and abetted by a Cabinet that is so wretchedly lacking in people who have worked in industry.' He ended his article with some words of wisdom for his leaders: 'So long as "incomes policy" operates as "pay restraint" we shall deserve our present difficulties. Preaching by Ministers will not bring about even the minimum changes. A little real leadership might just do it.'

CHAPTER 25

In the national interest

'I am more interested in the Gross National Happiness
of my people than the Gross National Product.'
Jigme Singye Wangechuk, King of Bhutan (1988)

'Where Plenty smiles - alas! she smiles for few -
And those who taste not, yet behold her store,
Are as the slaves who dig the golden ore -
The wealth around them makes them doubly poor.'
George Crabbe, *The Village* (1783)

One of the many early warnings of the wrath to come should the
Government refuse to change course had come from the praetorian
guard of the Labour Movement in the first week of July 1978 - before
the TUC Congress, before the Labour Party Conference, before the
Ford strike, and nearly half a year before the onset of the Winter of
Discontent. At their conference in Torquay the miners' delegates
had carried unanimously a motion demanding the termination of
the Social Contract, which (with either conscious or unconscious
irony) they equated with government intervention in pay bargaining
and stringent controls on public spending. What was needed, they
considered, was an alternative economic strategy designed to reduce
unemployment and raise living standards through stimulation of
the economy. Emlyn Williams from South Wales had a message
for the political leaders of the Movement which they would have
been wise to heed. After chiding his own executive for not always
abiding by conference decisions in the past, he promised that the
miners would negotiate responsibly, 'but not with a government
that is prepared to take cognisance of the dictates of the IMF and
forget its dedication to Socialism.' The miners had remained loyal
to Labour even after their industry had been 'almost completely
massacred' under Wilson's first governments, he pointed out; but,
he admonished the Callaghan Government: 'If we are talking about
loyalty, loyalty must be two-sided. *They* must be loyal to those
who elect them.'

However it might be in feudal contexts, such reciprocal loyalty
is unquestionably indispensable to every functionally efficient

society with any pretensions to being democratic. But precisely therein perhaps - at least in their own conceit - lay the Labour leaders' get-out. Representative government provided them with the constitutional fiction that as ministers of State they represented the interests of every citizen, which in theory at least liberated them from the views of those who had actually voted them into power. In particular, so long as the prime minister can command the support of his own parliamentary party (and for that he possesses formidable powers of patronage, besides almost literally holding in his hand the immediate political fate of the MPs forming it), and provided that party retains a working majority in the House, he is the final arbiter of 'the national interest'. Thus one fiction reinforces the other and vice-versa. All that needs to be added is the arrogance of power - and that comes naturally when others defer to us.

That interests differ, sometimes so greatly as to be irreconcilable even through compromise, makes 'the national interest' a riddle it is impossible to solve. It can only make sense if either the words are construed as meaning 'the greatest good of the greatest number', or 'the nation' is assumed to have a reality independent of the individuals who compose it, thereby making it possible to maintain that 'the national interest' surmounts the interests of any number of particular individuals and the common interests of groups. Holding such a belief would in no way help to determine wherein that greater interest lay. It would remain a matter open to dispute, unless we were prepared to make the further assumption that a particular person or group of persons was peculiarly equipped to perceive that greater interest. Eschewing such metaphysical unrealities and such philosopher-king concepts, we are left with Bentham's formula. Wherein lies the greatest good of the greatest number is still of course subject to argument, but at least it gives us something tangible to argue about. Besides, it is unquestionably the prevailing assumption in representative democracies that this is the proper criterion for decision-making, and furthermore, that it should be at least substantially determined in terms of the material welfare of the general populace. That is why it *should* be reasonable to assume that those parties which have the greatest stake in a hierarchical form of society would have the greatest difficulty in convincing the voters that they were the best fitted to look after 'the national interest'.

The paradox is that despite their obvious preponderant concern for the better-favoured sections of society, who by definition constitute only a minority, the Conservatives (except, arguably, in 1945) have never had much of a problem on this score. Cocooned in their unshakeable conviction that theirs is the patriotic party and that their leaders are thus the natural leaders of the nation (even though they can hardly be said any longer to have patently been born to rule), they generally have little difficulty in persuading themselves - and hardly more in persuading others far beyond their natural constituency - that whatever they do is 'in the national interest'.

Labour's leaders, on the other hand, notwithstanding the great betrayal of 1931 and despite the fact that their natural constituency should provide them with permanent majority support in the country, have remained susceptible to the charge that theirs is a class movement. As one illustration of this hypersensitivity one might cite their near-paranoiac nervousness when faced with criticism of the wing of their movement that - despite the growth of professional unions and the tendency of trade union members to distance themselves from their class origins as they become more affluent - remains firmly rooted in working-class history and culture. It is nothing less than ludicrous that privileged people with easy access to the nation's political commentary box get away with dinning into the heads of the general public the false perception that what the trade unions peculiarly stand for is the promotion of sectional interests (or 'vested interests', to use the more or less meaningless slur most commonly used as a vehicle for this hostile propaganda) inimical to the common good. Instead of deriding such charges as the bogeyman balderdash they are and making a serious effort to enlighten the public regarding the power structures that so affect their lives, the political instinct of the leaders of the Labour Party has almost invariably been to be defensive and apologetic. Such a stance, of course, far from placating the class enemies of the trade union movement, has only served to feed their ineradicable animus and simultaneously to supply them with further 'proof' of its justification. At the same time it has widened the natural fault-line in the Labour Movement and nudged the Party establishment into the arms of the bourgeoisie. At no time did these latent schismatic predispositions become so manifest as during the Winter of Discontent.

Of course, holding a substantial portion of the middle ground is an imperative in the politics of representative democracy. With its natural appeal to present and potential stake-holders and steak-eaters, the Conservative Party has - at least during periods of fair economic growth - done this almost effortlessly. For Labour the problem has been greater, as John Cole (later to become the doyen of the BBC's political commentators) noted in a challenging and perceptive article published in *The Guardian* after the miners had thrown down their challenge to Ted Heath:

> 'The reason for Labour's perpetual pussyfooting over income tax, which goes back at least to Hugh Gaitskell's pledge in the 1959 election, is clear. The classic nightmare of many Labour MPs is of finding themselves standing on the doorstep of a prosperous industrial worker and Labour voter, being rebuked for raising income tax to pay for higher family allowances and better schooling for the inordinately large families of the less well-paid, who, to add political colour and venom, are probably Irish, West Indian, or just feckless. If Britain's main party of the Left, created to foster a social revolution, is not able or willing to carry out the campaign of public education that such attitudes demand, there seems little hope of any turning-point.'

Cole's prescient reflections, five years before the deluge drowned the Labour dream, on the prerequisites for inducing the nation to accept an incomes policy as a normal part of its life are worth returning to. For the moment I shall simply add, for its bearing on Labour's problem with its own identity, Cole's one direct allusion to class, made in the context of comments on the deeply ingrained assumptions about the proper 'pecking order' that prevail in British society. 'Because Marxists talk too much about class others talk too little about it,' he writes. 'Class remains a potent fact in our political attitudes.'

Yet in Denis Healey's memoirs one may read with astonishment his view, expressed in an obituary on Ernest Bevin written for the Norwegian paper *Arbeiderbladet* more than twenty-two years earlier, that 'a policy based on class war cannot have a wide appeal when the difference between classes is so small as Labour has made it.' What can one say, except that this must surely rank among the supreme triumphs of the art of wish-fulfilment?

And, perhaps, that it must have greatly eased the burden of his lucubrations when it came to tinkering with the taxes to know that the class problem had to all intents and purposes already been solved.

Cole is right, of course, in saying that Marxists make too much of class, though a great deal of their over-insistence might be excused as a necessary corrective to the popular and complacent pretence that it has ceased to be of any real significance, culminating in the absurd Foster-Son-of-Thatcher pronouncements that the classless society is now being ushered in. As for many of Labour's leading lights, while they may be anxious to distance themselves from Marxist doctrine, it is difficult to shake off the suspicion that their main problem is that they find the whole subject of class deeply embarrassing. A decreasing minority of them come from working-class backgrounds anyway. Or, like many others in our times, they may feel they have pulled themselves up by their own boot laces, and beyond a residue of sentimentality, this may have left little but a strong belief in equality of opportunity. If they still recognise the realities of social advantage and disadvantage, that might still be enough to make them fight on behalf of what remains their main constituency; but as they themselves get nearer the top, the lure of *national* leadership, with all its illusions of conciliation and unity, becomes too strong to allow them to use their heaviest weapon, that core constituency itself, to batter down the doors of privilege. That can only be done through conflict amounting ideologically speaking (and in some degree if necessary *actually*) to civil war, and real social conflict is what they have come to dread.

On the plane of ideas one can readily accept Healey's statement that 'Socialism emphasises...consensus rather than confrontation'; but where consensus is not attainable and crying injustices persist, the choice becomes one between confrontation and capitulation. This soft reluctance of Labour's leaders to engage the enemy (even to admit there is an enemy, apart, that is, from the mutinous elements in the ranks behind them, and *they* are quite another matter and are not infrequently subjected to drumhead justice by their field commanders) comes out strongly in an illuminating passage in Callaghan's memoirs:

'Society is in a permanent state of flux and I had learned that it is not enough to enforce changes in the fulfilment of ideals. These require changes also in human attitudes and relationships which will only be both permanent and of benefit if they are attained through education, persuasion and understanding, not through coercion. There will be conflicts among such groups and between them and Government. I was not content that these should be resolved by the exercise of muscle alone. We should use rational means to reconcile differences between groups, to persuade them that they are all part of the common weal which determines the quality of our society as a whole.'

This is desperately jejune stuff, and there are few other pauses for thought in the course of the author's pedestrian chronicling of events from which to piece together such semblance of a philosophy as underlay his political career. The paragraph quoted is part of a passage in which he recalls reflecting - on finding himself 'at the head of our national business' (and his citing of Bagehot's description of the prime minister's position is perhaps significant) - on the question 'What did I want my Administration to stand for?' and strongly reaffirming the place of moral judgements in politics and the central purpose of Labour governments to eliminate social wrongs and promote social well-being. Clothing these unexceptionable bare bones with an ounce or two of flesh, he says that 'the class system had grown less rigid during my lifetime but it was still a millstone that hampered progress, as was gross inequality'; and tells us that 'men and women are not born equal in the sense of being equally endowed, but equal opportunity is a basic principle of social justice' and that much working-class talent and creative ability still go to waste. Napoleon Bonaparte might have said as much. Indeed he did, in his famous promotion of the concept of 'la carrière ouverte aux talents.'

So far, then, there is nothing distinctively Socialist about Callaghan's political 'philosophy'; indeed, nothing at which one-nation Tories like Rab Butler, Harold Macmillan, or Ted Heath - nor even the more militant breed of 'new Conservatives' who displaced them - might demur. 'Socialism,' Callaghan continues, 'should concern itself with the weak and underprivileged whoever they are - the poor, ill-educated, disabled, or coloured.' There can be few members of other modern political parties who would not contest the implied claim that Labour has something of a monopoly of such concern; none at all, perhaps, if we remove the word 'coloured' from the list of the disadvantaged.

What is more revealing - especially when considered in the context of Callaghan's constant preoccupation with the power of the trade unions - is the somewhat equivocal observation which follows: 'We were always painfully conscious that the idealism of the Labour Movement could come into conflict with its materialistic aspect - but we claimed it was the aim of socialism to reconcile the two.' It is hard to see why any kind of Socialist whose creed is rooted in egalitarian principles (and however shallowly, Callaghan's kind seems to be so rooted) should be troubled by a supposed antithesis between idealism and materialism, since a concern for the rational stewardship of the means of life is fundamental to every form of Socialism, and equity in sharing supplies the rest. In a very real sense, indeed, surely it is largely in concern for the equitable provision of material 'goods' that the 'idealism' of which he speaks lies.

If there *is* a problem of reconciliation between these supposed opposites for the Labour Movement, it is only because it has in the main continued to accept the mores and the *modus operandi* of individualistic capitalism - a socio-economic system in which idealism (or at any rate idealism of the socialistic sort) and materialism are indeed irreconcilable. As a practising politician leading an uncommonly busy life, it may well be that Callaghan found all too little time for thinking about the theoretical basis of his actions. But this is no rarefied academic point, since it has a crucial bearing on the nature of the Labour Party and on its relations with the Labour Movement as a whole, and in particular on labour organisations condemned tō operate in the context of capitalist society. In the final analysis, the options the trade unions were faced with, from their formation, were to adapt to the capitalist realities - by making themselves, in effect, just another kind of interest group in a highly competitive world - or to react by forging themselves into revolutionary forces. It is hardly to be wondered at that in the history of the world's labour movements, organisations that took the latter course (like America's Industrial Workers of the World and the CNT in Spain) are very much the exception. Even where political awareness has reached a level high enough for the recognition that Socialist ideals are simply irreconcilable with capitalism, trade unionists have usually felt forced to adapt their weapons to the imperatives of the capitalist world in order to survive. By definition, Labour's political wing - and especially its parliamentary echelons - have been relatively free from the exigencies confronting the defence corps of the workers, and the politicians of a movement that gradually abandoned even a gradualistic approach to social revolution have long since forfeited their right to tender a Socialist critique of the unions.

Callaghan's attitude to the unions was highly ambivalent, while being easily understandable and completely rational in terms of the power struggle. Trade union strength was to be welcomed as a subordinate ally of the political leadership of the Labour Movement; as an alternative centre of power, it was intolerable. 'Jim Callaghan belonged to the generation of Labour leaders which had come to depend on the trade union block vote for protection against extremism in the constituencies; moreover, the trade unions had provided his main political base in the previous decade,' writes Denis Healey. 'That base was now crumbling.' Exactly! Though no one not afflicted by Carlyle-like great-men-of-history delusions could have gone on to attribute the crumbling of this base (as Callaghan also does by implication - see *Time and Chance*, Chapter 14) to trade union titans being succeeded by incompetent and untrustworthy dwarfs (who by a remarkable coincidence were generally also markedly more left wing).

What Callaghan is really getting at in his nebulous allusion to the potential for conflict between idealism and materialism in the Labour Movement becomes clear in his next paragraph, in which, following a reference to the nationalisation of the coal mines and the drawing of a hazy and equivocal distinction between ownership and function in the exercise of power, he writes: 'We had limited but by no means removed the power of wealth to exploit [he can say that again!], but whilst we were engaged in doing this, new sources of power had grown up.' Evidently he did not include the trade unions in his 'we', since in the sentence that follows he lists, alongside such overtly capitalist forces as the multinational corporations, 'the post-war strength of the trade unions' as among 'other great sources of power that could and sometimes did exercise their veto against the national interest.' The point is not whether trade union power could be or ever has been used against 'the common weal' (to adopt the less objectionable expression Callaghan himself employs in the paragraph that follows, which I quoted above). Of course it could be and has been. The point is that the generalissimo of the Labour Movement could look upon the workers' organisations which had given birth to it, as enemies to Labour's purposes.

This distrust (to put it at its lowest) comes out more explicitly in his first speech to Labour Conference as Prime Minister and Party leader, the core of which was about the danger of - to use Callaghan's hugely question-begging expression - 'paying ourselves more than the value of what we produce' and pricing ourselves out of our jobs. He went on, in a passage that sounded uncannily reminiscent of the sanctimonious cant about widows' savings and the like commonly to be heard at Tory Party conferences, to say that 'the twin evils of unemployment and inflation have hit hardest those least able to stand them. Not those with the strongest bargaining power, no, it has not hit those. It has hit the poor, the old and the sick.' Pinning onto the organisations formed to defend workers' interests the principal responsibility for the plight of those unfortunates, he continued, in a comment which implied that the principal enemy of Labour's socialistic and humanitarian purposes was not competitive capitalism but militant trade unionism: 'We have struggled, as a Party, to try to maintain their standards, and indeed to improve them, against the strength of the free collective bargaining power that we have seen exerted as some people have tried to maintain their standards against this economic policy.'

Leaving aside the hard facts that the trade union movement did not accept as the way forward the economic strategy adopted by the Government but despite that was for years remarkably co-operative in trying to implement it, the point here is not to do with the dubious merits of so-called 'free collective bargaining', but that the unions had never been offered a fair alternative to fighting their corner. The central theme of John Cole's *Guardian* article cited above was 'our growing awareness of and unease about the inequitable distribution of income, wealth, and privilege...' which raised 'problems which dip deep into our relative valuation of human beings and their contributions to society.' As Heath's Government struggled to make *its* incomes policy stick, Cole pronounced: 'The failure to tackle such issues, the failure often to acknowledge their relevance, makes the search for permanent counter-inflationary policies fruitless.'

However, Cole addressed himself particularly to Labour, since that was the party it was most natural to assume would be concerned about such issues, but with no optimism at all that it would summon up the will to emulate the Swedish social democrats in 'educating its supporters about the relationship between social justice and incomes policy...The Labour movement's leaders - the Shadow Cabinet, National Executive, and TUC General Council - have neither the unanimity nor stomach for any such campaign.'

How right he was! But the principal reason for Labour's failure to grapple with this fundamental but explosive issue (which was to blow the Party into the wilderness five years later) was, for a supposedly Socialist movement, a more discreditable one than natural nervousness about the discord that would arise from stirring the great cauldron of differentials in pay and status. Can one doubt that for many of those who made up Labour's establishment (and who by the same token had done quite nicely, thank you, out of an unjust social system) it was a matter of little concern? 'Socialism is about equality or it is about nothing,' Attlee had once said. Well, equality had long since been laughed out of court in Labour establishment circles as a utopian, and in any case undesirable, objective. 'Social justice', as a far more flexible term, was still acceptable language. However, even among Labour's grassroots' activists, the issues it raised tended to take second place to pushing for policies through which they convinced themselves they were demonstrating their unchallengeable Socialist credentials, as Cole acidly commented:

> 'The Labour Party currently purports to be in a radical mood, measured principally by the length of its public ownership commitment. Personally I prefer to measure its radicalism by the apparent depth of commitment to redistribution of wealth and income.'

This failure to grasp the very prickly nettle of differentials between the rates of remuneration - not simply of workers with differing skills and tasks (a problem of which the political leaders as well as the trade union leaders were all too conscious), but between what amounted, economically speaking, to different classes of citizens: 'professionals' and tradesmen; non-manual and manual workers; 'skilled, semi-skilled, and non-skilled' workers; administrators, executives, clerks and typists; managers and operatives; and so on and so forth; not to mention the great divide between shareholders and units of the labour force - vitiated almost all the calls for sanity from commentators, politicians, and alarmed trade unionists alike. A good example of this fatal flaw in the arguments of the do-let's-be-sensible brigade was provided by Harford Thomas in the 'Alternatives' column of *The Guardian*, precisely because his thinking was profound and prescient yet still lacked the indispensable element of a consideration of distributive justice.

In an article quaintly entitled 'No chance for the meek in today's rip-off society', written as the 1978 season of party conferences moved towards its end with the Tories opening their talking-shop in Brighton, Thomas forcefully propounded the case for a fundamental rethink 'of our political and economic structures' because 'the old order of things is manifestly unsustainable (not only in the UK but throughout the developed world)...we are in a period of transition, possibly to what will later come to be seen as the post-industrial era...' Endorsing the general thrust of thinking in the Ecology Party, and drawing on David Steel's address to the Liberal Assembly in which he declared that 'economic debate was still based on the assumption that standards of living could be doubled every twenty-five or thirty years' and that this assumption was false and profoundly dangerous, Thomas lumped together 'the parties of big business and big unions' as more or less equally culpable 'for the defence of the old order.' While that showed a fine disregard for questions of relative advantage, there was more than a grain of truth in his exceedingly uncomfortable assertion that 'the two big parties are totally committed to the status quo, in the sense that they have no ideas beyond the manipulation of the consumer rat-race to their own particular vested interests.' He claimed that 'in essence they share the same philosophy', that this could be summed up as 'I want what I want and I want it now', and that another way of saying this was 'free collective bargaining'.

If this was putting his whole fist in the scales of judgement, and if it was a mite disingenuous to talk, as he did, of 'a quite *new* [my emphasis] kind of class division between the haves and the have-nots *within the labour movement* [his emphasis], between the strong and the weak, between the ruthless and the well-behaved' (not to mention the use of the word 'today's' in the title of his article), the gaping hole in his thesis - as is so often the case with the prophets calling for a new and sustainable economic system - was the studied avoidance of the issue of the prevailing distribution of wealth. 'Make more, sell more, earn more' ran a *Guardian* leader on the dispute at Ford, taking the orthodox capitalist line on 'wealth creation' and wages. To which, taking that other matter commonly called 'the national interest' into account, one might add 'export more'. But as Thomas' article shows, even those 'green' enough to see the flaws in such prescriptions (which reduce people to economic units and society to a national labour force) tend to be negligent of natural demands for a fair share of what is going. If 'the national interest' means anything, even its purely material aspects can certainly not be adequately defined simply in terms of *general* economic prosperity. It demands facing up to the problems of fair distribution, as Oliver Goldsmith showed an awareness of more than two hundred years ago, advising his readers 'to judge, how wide the limits stand/ Between a splendid and a happy land' and declaring: 'Ill fares the land, to hastening ills a prey,/ Where wealth accumulates, and men decay.'

'Not everyone is convinced by the morals and practices of the market place,' wrote Thomas, citing as dissenting voices the Labour leaders, Callaghan, Healey, and Michael Foot. Which was wry, since in most matters apart from the pay policy (the purpose of which had nothing to do with social justice and almost everything to do with controlling the wages of organised labour in order to restrain inflation) they submitted to market forces rather than grappling with them. Also absolved from his grand remonstrance against the Labour Movement was Sid Weighell, the trade union leader who, in his rage at those in the movement who could not agree that it was in the best interests of the workers to continue to go along with the Government's pay policy, provided everyone who loathed the unions with a singularly damning quotation to bolster their prejudices. 'If you want the call to go out that the new philosophy of the Labour Party is the philosophy of the pig trough and those with the biggest snout get the biggest share, I reject it. My union rejects it,' he told the 1978 Party Conference.

'I am convinced that many of the inequalities and injustices we experience today across the whole of British industry are largely due to so called free collective bargaining,' Weighell had written the previous February, in a *Guardian* article entitled 'Time to halt the mad pay scramble'. He argued that an incomes policy 'is the only way to ensure that some measure of social justice can be inserted into pay bargaining,' declaring it incomprehensible that those 'who want socialist planning to deal with the rest of our resources,' could 'want a free-for-all market system about pay.' And after the Movement had booted out the Government's policy he warned, in another *Guardian* article, of 'a very real danger of social breakdown worse than that which led to the rise of fascism and Nazism.'

Unfortunately, neither jeremiads nor impassioned pleas for 'rational behaviour on all sides' to avoid 'open warfare' were any substitute for the failure of the Movement, through all those years since the Attlee Government had launched British Socialism on its first sea-trials, to work out and agree on a credible strategy for, at the least, a steady advance towards social justice - least of all in the matter of the distribution of wealth and incomes. I reject the pig-trough philosophy and my union rejects it, Weighell had declared. But when the time came for the NUR to put in its next pay claim, in April 1979, it was obliged to submit to the inexorable pressures of capitalism, in order that its members should be able to keep their heads above the swirling waters. It asked for a rise of between 12 and 13 per cent, in line with the miners. A few days later official figures revealed the annual rise in earnings between February 1978 and February 1979 to be 14.9 per cent.

With all these plugged-in communicators putting in their penn'orths on the deplorable state of the nation, it was not to be supposed that the most elect of communicants (whose job, after all, was preaching) would abstain from getting in on the act. In mid-January the Archbishop of Canterbury, Dr Donald Coggan, delivered the first of a series of thunderclap sermons on 'irresponsible strikes' which was to lead to a clash with the NUPE leader Alan Fisher. The debate between them would lead right to the heart of the matter. Stressing everyone's 'duty and responsibility to the community at large,' Coggan declared: 'We need to be more concerned with what is right and less concerned with our rights.' Eleven days later he told his fellow peers of the realm that the right to strike was being used 'far too soon and far too readily and far too irresponsibly', that the strikers had made their point and that he believed 'the average Britisher has the right to say "enough is enough" and look for a return to normal procedures for settling disputes.'

He spoke of 'the sheer pitilessness of much of what is going on,' a charge he reiterated in Folkestone on 11th February. In the course of a sermon in which he acknowledged that there were 'some areas where employees are still badly paid' and that 'some salaries and some salary rises...are out of all proportion to the work done or to the good achieved for the community by those who receive them,' he said that Keir Hardie, who had emphasised the need for brotherhood in the trade union movement, would have had some caustic comments to make on these features of society 'if he were in Britain today'. He went on to suggest that 'he'd have something even more caustic to say about the sheer pitilessness...which injures the old and the very young who can't retaliate even if they wanted to; which leaves the dead unburied and the sick and dying uncared for.'

Coggan might have had a special insight into the cure of souls, but Fisher's 'flock' had wide experience in the care of bodies, and he was not to be deterred from defending his members by the archbishop's accusations that some of them were prey to the 'forces of selfishness' and had abandoned 'pity...mercy...and that sense of brotherhood in the nation'. Inviting the primate to come and meet striking hospital and other public employees to hear at first hand about the problems of the low-paid, Fisher declared: 'Our members are not pitiless. They are caring people. That is why they work in the public sector. That is why up to now they have been prepared to work for such pitiful financial reward. That is why they have been so concerned about the recent spending cuts which, more than they [i.e. his members] are doing now, have closed hospitals and put the sick on to longer waiting lists.'

Into this cockpit in which the archbishop and the trade union leader were engaged in hot disputation about morals and conduct in public life, the Church Commissioners tossed a most embarrassing bundle of propositions, like a bishop's illegitimate baby left at the church door. The Commissioners were already on record as not considering that the Government's incomes policy applied to the clergy. In November 1978 the General Synod had been told by the First Church Estate's Commissioner, Sir Ronald Harris, that the policy was not statutory and did not apply to the self-employed (which technically the clergy were), and that since the greater part of any increases in stipends would come from voluntary donations and would not lead to increases in prices or charges, they would not be inflationary. However dubious this argument was (and dubious it did indeed appear to be, especially when four months later it was learned that the Church had imposed rent increases of 40 to 45 per cent on its 6,000 tenants in Paddington), there was certainly a good case for a substantial rise for the parish clergy. Most vicars and rectors were only being paid between £2,900 and £3,250 a year (although incremental payments in kind were by no means inconsiderable), and the proposed rises, averaging around 13.8 per cent, would in most cases only bring them up to weekly incomes of between £63 and £73, at the bottom end not that much above the £60 minimum demanded by the public sector workers.

The really serious damage to the credibility of the Church's claim to moral leadership of the nation came when, a fortnight after Coggan's most stinging rebuke to the trade union movement, the news broke that the Commissioners had awarded an 18 per cent rise to the bishops and no less than 28 per cent to residentiary canons. The pay of most of the forty-three diocesan bishops was to go up from £5,615 to £6,660, the Archbishop of York's salary from £9,245 to £10,960, and the Primate of All England's salary from £10,590 to £12,555. Opposition led by the Bishop of Liverpool, David Sheppard, who urged that, in view of the national crisis and in solidarity with low-paid workers in the public sector, rises for the clergy should be limited to 8 or 9 per cent, failed to deflect the Commissioners from their munificence. Firm in their faith in the divine right of material differentials for spiritual beings, they argued that whereas average earnings elsewhere had risen by more than 200 per cent between 1970 and 1979, even with the current award, bishops' pay would only have gone up by 79 per cent. Nevertheless, one was talking about *rises* not far short (in the case of the bishops) of half a year's pay for many public sector workers, and as Fisher had remarked in a caustic comment on that perverse but near-universal devotion to percentages in pay bargaining: 'Percentages give least to those who need most, and most to those who need least. At the end of the day, ten per cent of nothing is bugger all.'

Notwithstanding his commendation of Keir Hardie and his reference to Christianity as having inspired the trade union movement, it is difficult not to conclude that there was an element of class-conditioned prejudice behind Coggan's attack on the striking workers. At the very least there was poverty of understanding of their predicament behind his sanctimonious injunctions to trust in 'normal procedures' and Christian prayer to put things right. And without question the picture of 'pitilessness' he painted was too lurid by far - however satisfying it may have been to his taste for histrionic homily. What authenticated cases were there of the old, the young, the sick and the dying callously left to their own devices?

It may be that in his eyes the most heinous sinners were the striking gravediggers. It is almost certainly true that the refusal in certain places to bury the dead and the picketing of graveyards and crematoria caused widespread offence, even though a substantial proportion of the outrage expressed in Parliament and the press may well be accounted for by awareness, on all sides, of the irresistible propaganda opportunity afforded to Labour's opponents by such industrial action. When Environment Secretary Peter Shore made an emergency statement in the Commons in response to a call from his opposite number in the shadow cabinet, Michael Heseltine, only one member of the House stood up for the gravediggers. Accusing his fellow MPs, with few exceptions, of 'indulging in a bout of utter hypocrisy', Dennis Skinner declared: 'There is no one, but no one, in this House who would do the job these people are doing for a take-home pay of £40 a week.' But in urging his comrade to consider what his 'sense of priorities and values' were, Shore's indignant retort was more finely attuned to the popular predisposition to pay greater respect to the dead than to the living. For all that, his appeal to the striking gravediggers for 'some sense of common fellowship and decency between members of the same community' might have been better addressed to all those untroubled by the thought that the relative comfort of their lives rested on the backs of ill-paid fellow citizens.

The question is, what was meant by all these fine words? In real life there may commonly be chasms between the powers and privileges of one brother and another; but we hardly take that as a mark of 'brotherhood'. 'Fellowship', 'common weal' (to go back to the passage in Callaghan's memoirs cited above), and 'community' (except in a purely geographical sense) all carry connotations of common interests. Even 'the nation' commonly does. But apart from tribal-minded confrontations with other more or less artificially circumscribed 'nations', wherein lie the common interests when the stakes held differ so inordinately in size and the individual and sectional interests are commonly so much in conflict?

Skinner's impatient outburst at what he felt to be the intolerable humbuggery of most of his fellow MPs over the gravediggers' strike was a graphic example of a general charge he had made before against the leaders of his party. In the course of a joint meeting of Labour's Home Policy and International Committees held in November 1978 to discuss the economy with the Chancellor, he accused both Healey and Callaghan of not caring about the working classes, declaring that there was all the difference in the world between what *they* called 'the national interest' and the real interests of working people.

We need not get side-tracked into fruitless discussions about who 'the working classes' are, or whether they really exist any more. All we need to do is to remember that it remains essentially true that the great majority of people still have little to sell other than their labour power: they are workers, not capitalists, even if they have been inveigled into buying a fistful of shares in some privatised 'public utility' or other. If we consider how very few people exercise any considerable influence on the political and economic decisions that determine the life of the nation; if we further consider with what shameless cozenry the nation's wealth, to which all contribute, is shared out between a grossly affluent few and the general populace (a broadly unchanging truth encapsulated in the name adopted by the radical theatre company '7:84' to highlight the holding of 84 per cent of the country's wealth by 7 per cent of the population) - and all in the name of 'the national interest' - how can we not conclude that, to realise their trumpery dreams of national leadership, to strut a while upon the stage of history and then to be elevated to the Olympian status of elder statesmen, the leaders of a party which had proclaimed its paramount purpose to be 'to bring about a fundamental and irreversible shift in the balance of power and wealth in favour of working people and their families', had sold out the people?

CHAPTER 26

No love lost for Labour

"'Luk what's happened wi' all his talk. National Gover'ment, an Labour nowhere. 'Tain't no use talkin' socialism to folk. 'Twon't come in our time though Ah allus votes Labour an' allus will."

"Vote for none on 'em, say I. All same once they get i' Parli'ment. It's poor as 'elps poor aaaall world over.'"
**Mrs Bull and Mrs Dorbell in
Walter Greenwood's *Love on the Dole* (1933)**

'In 1979, come to that in 1976, everyone was fed up with the political grandeur of trade unions. Power in few and uncomprehending and above all, sectional hands meant abuse and distortion, high unit costs, a declining currency creating a competitive edge to be wasted in the next round-dance of wage claims. Arthur Scargill with his "bag of crisps" dismissal of a 16.5 per cent increase, was the outward and visible sign of lost grace, of a received idea leeched for blood. The unions were too strong, the workers too strong: policies of full employment had meant anti-economic overmanning. To say that all this had to change was sudden truth.'

Thus *Guardian* opinionator Edward Pearce, in a pendulum-has-swung-too-far-in-the-other-direction polemic, discharged nearly a decade and a half after the Winter of Discontent. As a crystallisation of a fallacy with momentous consequences - embellished with a little *de rigueur* twopence-coloured demonising in the Thomas Carlyle tradition - it could hardly better express the popular perception of the State of the Nation in the final months of Labour's last government. And - notwithstanding its breathtaking political naiveté (or is it disingenuousness?), most fundamentally in its strictures on the concentration of power 'in few...and above all sectional hands', as if, in any hierarchical society, things could possibly be otherwise, its blatant bourgeois prejudice, and its barefaced misrepresentation of the realities of power and privilege in Uncle Jim's Great Britain - by the very act of reflecting popular opinion in a 'representative democracy' it does, of course, go a long way towards explaining the calamity of Labour's loss of power in the only watershed general election since that of 1945.

But besides the desperately ignorant and shallow nature of Pearce's denunciation of the unions, there are two specific objections to the picture he in part sketches and in part insinuates, one concerning the relationship of unions to their members, the other concerning the place of politics in the lives of workers and the related issue of their attitude to the Labour Party. In his zeal for chastising both unions in general and that even bigger body of culprits he calls 'the workers', in particular, Pearce takes no pains to distinguish between the organisations, their officers, and their rank-and-file members. That officials and payers of subs were not infrequently at cross-purposes apparently makes no difference. All were too strong for his cultivated nostrils.

Yet as the rift grew between the trade unions and the Labour Party during 1978, more perceptive observers also noted the general decline in the deference of rank-and-file trade unionists to the views of their own official leaders. Some commentators even went as far as to talk of a new syndicalism. A few days before the end of the harsh month of January 1979, for instance, Peter Jenkins wrote in *The Guardian*: 'In the last few weeks we have seen the coming of age of syndicalism.' This was going a deal too far, since in most cases the insubordination had little intellectual basis or grasp of power structures. However, it does serve to underline the spontaneity and elemental force of the revolt against the establishments (trade union just as much as governmental) of workers with their feet firmly on the shopfloor. Their own official leaders had the option of going along with the revolt - and so in some sense continuing to lead - or being swept aside.

But syndicalism is not just a theory concerning the effective organisation of workers to promote their own interests *vis-à-vis* those of their employers (although it certainly is that). It recognises that those conflicting interests have their roots in a socio-economic structure that extends far beyond the factory gate and is shored up by a legislative political system that arrogates to itself the right to take decisions which profoundly affect the lives of working people, both inside and outside the workplace. At its core is a belief in the primacy of industrial action over political action in furthering the interests of the workers. In their distrust of and disgust with party politicians, whole swathes of workers were in the winter of 1978-79 emotionally poised to accept the syndicalist case; but the means for widely propagating it did not exist. Beyond the passing moment, with its strictly limited issues and possibilities, the people, ideologically purblind, were unable to seize their destiny. From such a state of mental turmoil and disillusionment, with no intellectual creed to foster sustained constructive struggle, the natural outcome is political cynicism, whether its mood be angry or apathetic. In these circumstances it is no cause for wonder that large numbers of workers broke their voting habits and switched to 'the class enemy' or simply abstained. Although they did themselves no service by their polling-booth revolution, what they did do is to teach the Labour Party (or rather those few in it capable of learning) that the Party exists to serve the Labour Movement, not the other way round.

To the consequences of this widespread political disgust I shall return presently, after considering one particular factor in the industrial revolt that gave rise (and lent a little validity) to the notion of the resurgence of syndicalism. But first I am impelled to make a more general reflection on the standard of the debate provoked by the revolt, for its bearing on the fidelity, or otherwise, of prevailing perceptions not only of the 'national crisis' of '78-'79 but, more fundamentally, of the nature of the society which shapes, or at least delimits, our lives.

Perusing contemporary accounts of and comments on the Winter of Discontent, one is struck at least as forcibly by the prevalence of intellectual confusion (at times even of a world-turned-upside-down bewilderment) as by the chaos on the streets. Of course, one has the advantage of hindsight; but the value of contemporary observations (beyond those intrinsic in the faithful recording and graphic portrayal of events) lies in their far-sightedness, and this is gravely impaired whenever - for whatever reason - coherence of viewpoint is lacking. Disingenuousness was only to be expected from those striving for advantage in the cockpit of party politics, and few rose above it. And in greater or lesser measure the same may doubtless be said of many other protagonists in the great debate. But to ascribe to the generality of those contending for public approval some kind of clear-eyed Machiavellianism is at once too cynical and too flattering. What is in question is clarity of vision, not simply of representation. In politics conspiracy is ever present, but purposed deception will not suffice as an explanation of the welter of inconsistent arguments and incompatible postures commonly adopted, on the same or different occasions, by one and the same person in sounding off about this great challenge to the world as he or she knew it. What answering the challenge all too often revealed - making all due allowance for the complexity of the issues raised - was a grievous deficiency of moral and intellectual integrity (i.e. wholeness), a reliance on reach-me-down responses to profoundly unsettling events that could be no substitute for a coherent *Weltanschauung*.

What was hard for any observer to overlook was that 'shopfloor' ferment I alluded to above, with the associated factor of the key role of shop stewards, that gave rise to thoughts (not to say fears) of syndicalism. Implicitly or explicitly, the issue of leaders and led was raised repeatedly (though seldom with reason and honesty reigning over rage) by columnist and politician alike - and better than any other issue it serves as a touchstone for assaying their fundamental social attitudes. What almost all of them shared was a consuming preoccupation with the problems of control of the industrial workforce. Which is not to be wondered at. One may, if one chooses, put this all down to a perfectly natural concern about the serious disruption of the rhythms of the nation's life, with the hardships that caused to many 'innocent' people. That *was* conspicuous or latent in just about every comment made on the crisis. What was near-to-universally *absent* amongst the authorised communicators was any sense that they recognised that they occupied a quite different circle in the matrix of society from those inhabited by the workers on whose conduct they were pronouncing. This gave them (the opinionators who were claiming to speak for the *public* interest) a *vested* interest in stability - which is actually only an undoubted good when everything is at least approximately all right. Irrespective of the particular postures they adopted on the issues of the day, with rare exceptions they acted in essence as 'pillars of the community'. Purporting to speak for it, they had not the honesty to see, the candour to admit, their own thoroughly *un*representative nature - a disability for their spokesman's office they could only counter by a leap of imagination and empathy. Most of them were incapable of making such a leap, since whatever doubts they might have felt about the soundness of the prevailing order were, in the final analysis, really quite superficial.

This comforting - and perhaps partially self-inflicted - blindness is well illustrated by the commentaries of Peter Jenkins. Acclaimed by his peers as 'Journalist of the Year', he certainly exhibited an outstanding propensity for contaminating shrewd and perceptive comment with prejudice and exaggeration. In an article written on the eve of the Prime Minister's visit to the 1978 moment-of-truth TUC congress in Brighton, counselling Callaghan 'to resist too fond an embrace from his union allies' lest a love-in with organised labour should turn off the voters, Jenkins described both the national and the local leaders of the trade union movement as 'finally, and fully, paid-up members of what is in effect the ruling class'. He postulated a bleak scenario of 'diminishing prosperity' in which they served '- as in these last few years - as a sturdy prop to a crumbling establishment'. And he made these extravagant aspersions without giving the slightest indication that he saw himself as anything other than a disinterested social observer. This characteristic missing of his presumed aim of producing really penetrating analysis is, ironically, underlined by his acknowledgement that 'the rank and file haven't done so well' in a period of Labour rule in which (according to him) 'trade unions as institutions have never had it so good.' But then the great constant in his commentary is his liberal bourgeois animus against organised labour and Socialism.

For all that, it is worth citing his testimony on what (from an essentially establishment point of view) had gone wrong, as quite representative of the more sophisticated kind of press comment on the unions. Although his critique is never in danger of seriously challenging his own fundamentally orthodox view of what kind of amendments might bring about a stable and viable socio-economic structure, at least it eschews simplistic or downright dishonest conspiracy theories. He recognises 'the non-revolutionary, even downright conservative character of the British trade union movement' and considers that 'the ultimate threat to the political system in Britain does not stem from the ambitions of trade unions to wield political power...[but] from continuing economic failure,' largely stemming (in his view) from the formidable 'immobilising force of the unions' and the 'inflationary and disorderly travesty' that collective bargaining had become under the halfway 'corporatist' system of the Labour Government's 'trade union connection'. Nor will Jenkins have any truck with the simple-minded or artfully-fashioned fallacy that subversion within the unions is the root of the problem. 'The role of Trotskyists or other troublemakers is real but exaggerated.' On the contrary, Jenkins frankly acknowledges that what was shaking society was 'the militant pursuit of higher wages by *a broad section of the community*' - a pursuit which the national trade union leaders had largely lost control of. 'I have never known them to be more alarmed,' he reveals. 'If the country becomes ungovernable *it is not because of the power of the unions*, it is rather because of their powerlessness to govern their own members.' [my emphases] And in a passage in an earlier article that well illustrates his own proneness to mixing perceptiveness with perversion of realities, he writes:

> 'In office Labour will confer further privileges upon trade unions and, at least to some extent, manage the economy according to their interests or desires, only to discover once more - as now - that a rank-and-file revolt prevents the union leaders from delivering on their side of the bargain for more than a year or two at a stretch.'

Jenkins obviously saw that it posed something of a riddle to expect 'institutions of collective bargaining...which live by the law of competition' (which, with more honesty than many commentators, he admitted to be the trade unions' situation) to exercise 'corporate responsibility'; but he never grappled with it, perhaps because his deepest underlying wish was to see, not reconciliation between the two principal partners in the Labour Movement, but rather divorce. He was clear-eyed about 'the underlying conflict of interest between the industrial and political wings of the Labour movement', sardonically characterising the sentiment and vows that kept them hitched together 'the doctrine of ultimate compatibility', and openly recommended them to call the whole thing off after the government house they intermittently cohabited had been repossessed by the Tories, as he correctly assumed was about to come to pass.

The limits of Jenkins' understanding of radical unionism is highlighted by a passage (in the article from which the quotations in the preceding paragraph are taken) that carries interesting echoes of Denis Healey's strictures on Moss Evans' lack of commitment to the Labour Party. Managing to be both acute and obtuse at one and the same time, Jenkins writes of Moss Evans:

> 'He is an exponent of a trade unionism more akin to aggressive American-style business unionism than to the governmental approach of the British trade union "establishment". His philosophy is of the market place. His job is to do that which is within his power to bargain on behalf of his members...he thinks in terms of firms, not the nation.'

While in one respect the comparison with 'American-style business unionism' may be illuminating, it is profoundly misleading in others, including its intimations of an accommodation with capitalism, which Jenkins reinforces with a subsequent remark that Evans 'in this respect at least [i.e. his market-place approach to his job] is nearer to Mrs Thatcher than to Mr Callaghan.' As Jenkins has himself observed just before the paragraph quoted above, 'upbraided by his General Council colleagues' for 'laying out a welcome carpet for Mrs Thatcher,' Evans responds with 'an attack upon those who would make themselves the slaves of a corporate state.' Having supplied himself with all the pieces necessary to complete the jigsaw, Jenkins fails to see that Moss Evans' position lies not to the right, but decisively to the left of most of his colleagues and of the Labour Party leaders.

In broad terms the same kinds of virtues and the same ultimately crippling limitations are to be found in editorial comment in *The Guardian*, for which at that time Peter Jenkins served as principal political columnist. Like him and in common with the media at large, the paper's overriding concern was with the control of labour and the containment of its economic costs. It did try to peddle the line that the trouble was mainly due to the 'harebrained militancy of stewards', conveniently interpreting the responses to a poorly-designed opinion poll as meaning that 'the silent majority's' claim that they were not properly represented by their union leaders referred not to the national leaders but to local ringleaders. But this was before it became patently obvious that the country was faced with a general (to use Jenkins' phrase) 'peasant revolt in the trade union movement'.

In the longest of all its many hand-wringing leaders on the Winter of Discontent, published two days after the peasants' 'Day of Action', *The Guardian* spoke openly of 'disorganised labour responding to no one's leadership'. Almost sounding as if he was biting back the word 'rabble', the leader writer made it clear that in his view the striking workers had forfeited through their indiscipline the unions' claim to a 'place at the top table'. This was far the most wide-ranging and searching of the paper's leaders on these troubles. Besides dealing in the staple platitudes of union power, law and order, and the overriding rights of the community at large, it raised the issues of 'social justice' and 'national cohesion', the 'hierarchy of needs' which society should recognise, and the 'sense of grievance and...desperation' which had driven (by implication, moderate) trade unionists to join 'the militants' in 'the great pay panic', disregarding the effects of their actions on 'a public against which they have no grievance'. In the final analysis, however, it added up to the standard frugal fare of paternalistic preaching and piety. The promise pregnant in the leader's title, 'How we are and how we might be', never was going to be delivered by a writer who could not understand that the vicarious satisfaction of seeing their tribunes 'at the top table' was no longer enough for plebs who felt they were entitled to a more generous slice of the cake.

To get some sense of the climate of opinion, it can be more rewarding to examine journalistic comment than that of the protagonists. Practising politicians, particularly those at or near the top of the greasy pole, naturally tend to be more inhibited in speaking their minds, for fear of offending one or other section of the voters. One can even see this in the contrast between interventions (at the height of the 'peasant revolt') by the former prime minister - now, blissfully unencumbered, free to vent a Coriolanus-like disdain for the multitude - and the more guarded comments of the incumbent PM. In his new column in the *Financial Weekly* magazine, Sir Harold Wilson maintained, like Peter Jenkins, that the problem was not that the unions were too powerful, but that their leaders were not powerful enough to keep their own members in order. 'My experience suggests,' he wrote, 'that only strong union leadership - not unenforceable legislation - is the way to control the situation.' That was all very well, from an establishment point of view, but strongly suggested *schadenfreude*, especially as it contained no prescription for the reimposition of that order and sense of discipline in the ranks for which his successor in the top job (not to mention many a trade union general) yearned just as much as - and a deal more urgently than - he now did.

Interviewed on Thames Television a week before Wilson's weighty words were exchanged for a more serviceable currency, the beleaguered James Callaghan assumed a tone of judicial detachment, appropriate to the unruffled leader of the nation, towards the heated debate over the behaviour of the unions. 'I am trying to repair relations with the trades unions. We must not treat them as enemies, even though they are not the whole of the community,' he told Llew Gardiner. Instead he directed his 'friendly fire' at the softer target of (to use a favourite expression of his Chancellor's) the 'silly billies' within the unions, chiding the public-service strikers for trying to 'get more out of the bank than there is in it', and reprimanding shop stewards for misleading the rank and file. If there is cause for wry reflection in observing Labour's predominantly union-elected commander-in-chief pleading - in his 'Little Father of the Nation' role - with his fellow countrymen not to judge too harshly the movement which had forged his own party and remained its core power base, his superciliousness towards the authentic functional leaders of the workers is breathtaking. It was only to be expected that one so exalted by fate should endorse the 'officers' mess' view that a major cause of the trouble for which the unions were held to be primarily responsible was the formal devolution of power that they had generally adopted (although a better understanding of the findings of the Donovan Commission would have been enough on its own to scotch such a silly explanation). To go on to assert that the problem lay with shop stewards who did not properly understand the basic tenets of trades unionism was gratuitous insult as well as arrant (and arrogant) nonsense.

But it is only one example of a more general proneness of those busy carving out political careers for themselves not only to scapegoat but to patronise the 'trench-comrade' leaders of mutinous workers. Instance comments made by two purportedly left-wing

349

Labour MPs to Martin Holmes when he was researching for his study of those dismal days. Talking about the salient part played by NUPE in the public sector dispute, Joe Ashton remarked: 'Fisher had taken over a tame union up to 1968 then came great recruitment but the recruits, tea ladies, cleaners and the like, weren't union officials. The officials were got from Ruskin and were militant and wanted to [prove it]. Suddenly ambulance men and hospital porters on strike found they were headline news and were on TV - like the miners.' The second comment is even more intriguing, in view of the subsequent elevation of the man who made it. 'The graduate officials in NUPE thought about the working class as if they had stepped from the pages of a history book. They fitted the working class into economic models which were political science fiction.' It may be true that many a good activist has ended up in some sort of wonderland by becoming too heavily addicted to Marxist (or perhaps pseudo-Marxist) theory, which one assumes to be the target of Neil Kinnock's sarcasm. But the people he is satirising *were* taking part, vigorously, in a struggle that was all too real. It seems inherently improbable that they could out-fantasise any politician (if such there was) who still seriously believed that Labour was on the way to emancipation of the working class (or whatever substitute for that old-fashioned concept they favoured) as long as they could get enough people to vote for them.

In any case, however the balance lay between shrewdness and sneers in these acid comments on extra-parliamentary militants, they tend to conceal one truth of enormous - and perhaps fatal - consequence for the Labour Party and the Labour Movement. Fully-paid-up supporters of Labour probably have more reason to know - and certainly more reason to regret - that the great mass of electors are essentially *a*political. To put it another way, their approach to the political menu on offer, with dishes concocted by the competing parties, is essentially - and perhaps sensibly - *à la carte*. Between meals their appetite for politics is very limited. They prefer to be left alone to get on with their own personal lives, leaving it to others to play political games. If politics were marginal to our lives, there would be nothing to be said against that; but in complex societies it may affect them profoundly. Lack of interest can only mean lack of insight, and in politics no less than in commerce, the ill-informed have no freedom of choice. For a party like Labour, which, if we are to take it seriously, is offering an ongoing prospectus of reform leading to a qualitatively different kind of society (and a party, moreover, which functions, in theory at least, through democratic decision-making processes), such a situation is disastrous.

On the eve of Labour's downfall, Ralph Miliband wrote:

'Regrettably, the idea that the Labour Party is set on the socialist transformation of Britain is dishonest nonsense. A fair number of its members do want such a transformation; but most of its leaders do not and are indeed actively opposed to it. They are also in secure control of the party. Their purpose today is the same as it has always been: to manage Britain's capitalist society somewhat differently than the Tories.'

But paradoxically the case is not greatly altered if we decline to take Labour's 'road to Socialism' (or wherever else the promised land is now to be found) project seriously. It may have been mere rhetoric to Labour's leaders all along; but to supplant the Tories as 'the natural party of government' (as Wilson perhaps once sincerely believed was well within Labour's grasp), it was *necessary* rhetoric, for the Party had to offer more than sound government and low taxes to outbid the parties whose attractions were more obvious to businessmen, professionals, rentiers, and the middle classes in general, along with all those who aspired to the pneumatic lifestyle of such superior people. The Party may never have come within a thousand miles of bringing about that 'fundamental and irreversible shift...' that the real Socialists in its ranks aspired to, but to enthuse the party-workers and to hold the allegiance of an electorally-decisive number of citizens, it had to convince them that the ground gained in their favour could be held and extended. It had to persuade them that this could only be done by continuing to (at the least) nibble away at the powers and privileges of the better-favoured sections of society and by doling these out among the generality of the people. Yet as another Marxist pundit, Eric Hobsbawm, was once again ruefully pointing out, in a plea for a common front against Thatcherism made two years after Mrs Thatcher's second and greater rout of Labour: 'Even at the peak of its forward march (1951) they [British socialists] had failed to convert one third of the British workers, and since then Labour's working class support has plummeted.' With the structural changes in kinds of remunerated employment (in particular the shift from manual to non-manual labour and the shift from production requiring many hands to more automated forms of mass production), even before the decimation of Britain's manufacturing industry by Thatcherite economic policies, occurring alongside the increasing affluence of many workers, Labour always was in danger of suffering a serious haemorrhaging of dependable support.

It is conveniently overlooked by most of those who rightly inveigh against the country's plight (in being in the second decade of the Thatcherites' permafrost grip, contrary to the four-times-expressed choice of a very clear majority of the participating electorate) that since the Second World War neither of the two major contenders for power ever has won majority support in a general election. Moreover, since the resurrection of the Liberals as a serious spoiler of the Box-and-Cox system of taking turns at enjoying the fruits of office, no winning party has secured the endorsement of as much as 44 per cent of those electors who have bothered to cast their votes. As for the government that Callaghan inherited, its mandate rested on a 39.2 per cent share of the votes cast in October 1974 - a lower share than that won by any of its Tory successors. Since Wilson led Labour into its last two general election victories, in February and October 1974, when it took respectively 37.1 per cent (0.8 per cent less than the ousted Tories!) and 39.2 per cent, Labour's percentage share of the vote has been 36.9 per cent (1979), 27.6 per cent (1983), 30.8 per cent (1987), and 34.2 per cent (1992).

In the concluding passage of the section of *Time and Chance* covering his premiership, Callaghan claims that: 'Contrary to the myths which have sprung up since 1979, Labour did not lose support in the general election - our national vote was in fact slightly higher than it had been nearly five years earlier in October 1974, when we had won more seats than the Tories.' He goes on to say: 'It demonstrated how much steady understanding and support existed for what we had tried to do.' There are more ways of deceiving than peddling trays of pork pies. It is quite true that, *in a larger turnout*, Labour did pick up another 50,000-odd votes in 1979. But Callaghan's rosy representation of a deeply gloomy reality is more than economical with the truth: it is positively parsimonious. In his next sentence Callaghan implies that Labour's defeat was mainly due to Tory abstainers returning to the colours. But well over a million voters withdrew their support from the Liberals in 1979, and precious few of them can have redeployed their vote to demonstrate assent to Callaghan's contention that: 'The Labour Government of 1974 to 1979 had no reason to feel ashamed, and much to be proud of.'

Besides which, thirty-four years since Labour had been given its first real chance to show what it could do for the people, with four further chances along the way, it could only rally about the same numerical support it had attracted in 1974, i.e. around 11½ million, while the Tories, back in form again, were pulling in the punters in the old numbers of well above 13½ million. And although it is true (and important to bear in mind) that the country was delivered into the hands of the Thatcherites by only one third of its enfranchised inhabitants, Labour could only manage to retain the allegiance of 28 per cent of the British electorate. If that was not a stinging rebuff for a people's party, what would be?

But there are other figures which in some respects cast an even more sombre light on Labour's decline. Any party whose intentions were really radical should have been deeply disturbed by the evidence that an ever-growing proportion of the electorate did not see a great deal of difference between the parties competing for their support. In polls taken during the general elections, Gallup found that those who felt the parties were 'much of a muchness' rose, in percentage terms, from 20, 20, and 29 in the fifties, to 32 and 37 in the sixties, and up to 41 (as against 54 who were still persuaded there were 'important differences') in 1970, when Heath led the Tories back into power. The last two figures - 41:54 (with 5 per cent 'don't knows') - are what the needle on the gauge of election-year perceptions pointed to throughout the seventies, except for a slight widening (to 38:57) in February 1974. Gallup took a reading about halfway between general elections in 1977 and came up with a figure indicating that hardly more than a third (34 per cent) of the voters saw 'important differences' between the parties, with no less than 60 per cent considering them 'much of a muchness'.

Of course, it may be that the social democrat tendency in the Labour Party would view such a narrowing of perceived differences between the parties as a cause for self-congratulation rather than alarm, as showing that the voters feel at ease with Labour, as a 'moderate' and 'responsible' party. And it is undeniable that in a representative democracy a party intent on taking power must try to occupy the middle ground. But if there was any sense of satisfaction within the Labour Party at this situation (as the striving for respectability since 1983 suggests must have been the case), it was thoroughly misplaced. It could only mean that the Party was contending for supremacy on ground on which its opponents generally had the advantage, for the very tangible reasons already indicated. The forces of inertia, of small-c conservatism, are formidable in every society, and it is these customary modes of perception of the people at large, much more than its avowed opponents, that any radically reformist party must overcome. An intelligent strategy - even for not especially radical leaders of what had to remain (however unfortunate the term might be felt to be) in some sense a 'workers' party' - would have aimed at moving the middle ground decisively (though not too far and not too abruptly, now that the groundwork had been done by the Labour administration of 1945-50) to the left, by implanting the notion that Labour's policies were practicable, reasonable, and really rather moderate. It could have been mooted that the parties which opposed them were essentially elitist and never could properly represent the interests of the ordinary voter. Since this latter charge would have been so demonstrably true (at least in the case of the Tories), it should not have been beyond the bounds of sensible aspiration and steady striving to get the people to see it.

What was needed, in fact, was a sustained campaign (such as Sweden's social democrats had undertaken) to secure a permanent bias in Labour's favour - a campaign incorporating the building up of a mass membership of the Party (not simply of the unions), aiming at genuine and not merely passive or menial participation, and with an ongoing programme of political education conceived (as education always should be) as an all-ways dialogue, not a from-the-top-downwards process. In suchwise it should have been possible to form a critical mass of citizens who identified with Labour, not just at election time and not just from sentiment, but from awareness and comprehension of social structures and social dynamics. Despite certain formidable handicaps (particularly those concerning media control and bias), the Labour Movement did in fact have the means to carry out such a programme through an organic network of working-class institutions which gave it a potentially decisive advantage over its opponents.

Foremost amongst these institutions were, of course, the trade unions themselves. Before it started to decline under the frontal assault of anti-union legislation - and even more through the attrition resulting from the half wanton half wilful regeneration of mass unemployment - union membership had reached a peak of over 13 million, 54 per cent of the national workforce. (Indeed, in March 1979 two researchers, James Curran and John Stanworth, estimated that around 60 per cent of eligible recruits - i.e. remunerated employees excluding top management and the self-employed, as well as the unemployed - had joined up.) Of course, even though the correlation between union membership and voting Labour was once high, there never was any question of the Party being able to take for granted the support of trade unionists in the polling booth, and the spectacular growth of the white-collar unions made the reckoning less and less certain. But that does not alter the fact that, potentially, the trade unions constituted an effective channel to counteract the overwhelmingly anti-Labour bias of the commercial media, and that for the most part that potential was only exploited in a sporadic, tactical, narrow, and thoroughly unimaginative way. As for the course in political economy that could have been a standard part of the package deal of union membership - well, for the vast majority 'could have been' is what it was.

CHAPTER 27

Tory blandishments and Labour hubris

'The antics of Presidents and Senators had been amusing - so amusing that she had nearly been persuaded to take part in them. She had saved herself in time. She had got to the bottom of this business of democratic government, and found out that it was nothing more than government of any other kind. She might have known it by her own common sense, but now that experience had proved it, she was glad to quit the masquerade; to return to the true democracy of life, her paupers and her prisons, her schools and her hospitals.'

Henry Adams, *Democracy* **(1880)**

For anyone who still puts his or her faith in the Labour Movement for the eventual emancipation of the British people, the reasons that come to mind for Labour's long neglect of what was once so important to it - political evangelism - are profoundly dispiriting. Paternalism, vanguardism, leaderism, leave-it-to-me-ism: these are ways of denoting the same psychic inhibition, a political vice of minds conditioned by the mores of a hierarchical society which many no longer even recognise as such - a vice no less anti-democratic in a tribune of the people than in patrician or priest. Add to the prevalence of such frames of mind amongst Labour leaders the structural schizophrenia produced by the yoking together of institutions - those of organised labour and those of The Party - whose purposes are much more often at odds than in harmony, and the wonder is rather that so many people of a Socialist persuasion, through generation after generation, ever could have imagined that Labour was a vehicle adapted to travelling towards the destinations they desired to reach.

   Testimony tainted by its source it may seem - and testimony given with an ulterior motive it most certainly was - but when, shortly after what he described as the 'sustained rally in support of

Labour' at the 1978 TUC Congress, the shadow chancellor, Sir Geoffrey Howe, addressing Kirklees Chamber of Commerce on problems of industrial relations, spoke of 'the myth of a movement whose assumed solidarity on all issues no longer exists', he rather understated the truth. And however tendentious his thesis, there was much substance in his comment on the loss of trust between trade union leaders on the one hand and shop stewards and rank-and-file strikers on the other: 'This steady erosion of traditional union solidarity seems to follow from the increasing politicisation of the union movement, which changes the trade unions themselves from being the servants of their members into their would-be masters.'

Sir Geoffrey's touching concern for the plight of 'ordinary' trade unionists was part of the strategy (by no means new, of course) of weaning enough of them away from Labour to piece together a Tory majority at the polls. The Tory benches are never short of barking dogs when an opportunity arises for verbally savaging the trade unions, but the more ill-trained beasts were now, for the most part, held on a short leash. In view of the almost certainly crucial part played in Labour's defeat in May 1979 by defectors who were union members (and, of course, in view of the decimation that the future held in store for the trade union movement), it is worth underlining the fact that, when still in opposition, the Tories did not indulge their instincts to launch a general offensive against the trade unions. It is true that in the heat of parliamentary battle, when enthusing the troops behind them, even front-benchers did now and then get over-excited. During a Commons debate after the public service workers had followed the lorry drivers into action, John Nott (soon to find himself C-in-C Trade) charged that the nation's economy had been subcontracted to the trade unions and responsibility for law and order to the TGWU, winding himself up to a positive paroxysm of rage with talk of 'workers' soviets', while he who would be Maggie's Chancellor hereafter spluttered on about 'trade union tyranny' and 'collective mugging'. But they were after all speaking in a heady atmosphere of competitive soundbiting in which the Prime Minister himself lashed mutinying unionists with talk of 'collective vandalism'.

Sometimes the Tory Thespians put on a double-act. In response to the assumed majesty of Callaghan's New Year message to the country, with its appeal for a sense of responsibility in wage bargaining, the histrionic Heseltine (soon to be overlord of the Environment) projected fire and lava onto the unfortunate Prime Minister's head. Denouncing him as personally responsible for pulling 'the rug from under his own leader' when Wilson had tried to rein in the unions, he thundered: 'The monster that he unleashed has now turned on him.' Meanwhile, more emolliently in Guildford, the emerging Energy supremo, David Howell, counselled his constituency party to remember the noble history of the British trade union movement, speaking more in sorrow than in anger of its present fall from grace and chiding Callaghan for setting back 'the course of responsible unionism disastrously' by his 'five per cent speeches' and 'strong arm methods'.

For the most part blandishment was the name of the game. Not only did a velvet-gloved fistful of Tory generals (in addition to Howe and Howell, Maggie's faithful Willie Whitelaw, shadow home Secretary; Sir Keith Joseph, shadow industry Secretary; Jim Prior, shadow employment secretary; and the generalissimo herself) very nearly fall to quarrelling amongst themselves for supremacy with regard to the absolute purity of their intentions towards the trade unions (Sir Geoffrey went as far as telling the staff at Smith Square - *on* the record, of course - that if the unions had not existed it would have been necessary to invent them: 'How else to represent the individual and the group interests of those who earn their living in a complex industrial society?' he intoned). Several of them even made proposals, for all the world as if they were a serious part of the Tories' agenda which they had every intention of implementing if they were returned to favour, which amounted to advocating taking a step or two towards industrial democracy - a hallowed Socialist ideal oft hymned in the Labour Movement and shied away from whenever it was in a position to do something practical about it. Sir Geoffrey, for instance, propositioned the unions to accept some reform of industrial relations in return for a pledge of a bigger say for employees through works' councils and/or employee-share schemes. Peter Walker (who had been Secretary of State for Trade and Industry during the miners' assault that knocked out the Heath Government in 1974 and who, as Energy Secretary, was to find himself in a key position for the 1984 replay), scoring a bull's-eye against his opponents with his comment that Labour's 'social contract failed because it was irrelevant to ordinary workers', who 'saw it as a one-sided arrangement allowing TUC barons to strut the corridors of power but reaching down to the shopfloor in the form of nothing but wage controls,' spoke of 'the need for a new social contract to contain wide-ranging proposals for workers' participation and profit-sharing'. He was also shrewd enough in his wooing of the lower orders to observe: 'When, as Mrs Thatcher says, we are trying to get the votes of doubting Labour supporters, we must recognise that individual freedoms are not just the freedoms of the market place.'

Doubtless this lovey-dovey talk sounded like yet more pie-in-the-sky to most workers; but the promise at the heart of the Tory wean-'em-from-Labour campaign, that a Tory government would get off their backs, was appealing enough, and coming from the free-market party, not entirely implausible. As another of Ted Heath's former lieutenants, Jim Prior, put it in a sophisticated party political broadcast 'aimed' (as Ian Aitken reported) 'directly at Labour's traditional supporters in the trade unions' and transmitted as the brothers' talked their way through what was to prove an essentially redundant conference agenda at Blackpool: 'We aim to break out of this damaging cycle [of national incomes' policies] and restore a system of responsible and realistic pay bargaining, free from government interference.'

Early in the first week of the New Year, Margaret Thatcher outlined on London Weekend Television's *Weekend World* what James Prior was to dub 'the Moderates' Charter' to replace 'Labour's Militants' Charter'. Her proposals did not sound so threatening, except perhaps for the call to outlaw strikes in public utilities, and this was quickly remodelled as a proposal to give pay guarantees in exchange for acceptance of a no-strike rule in vital public services. In fact the general thrust of the Tory criticism of the trade unions, with its principal emphasis upon problems connected with picketing, the closed shop, and keeping essential services running, doubtless sounded reasonable enough even to most trade unionists.

By their ceaseless assaults on militant (i.e. forceful) unionism, the Labour leaders manufactured bullets for their political opponents to fire at the trade union wing of their own movement, making it possible, for instance, for Jim Prior provocatively to welcome the Government's recognition of problems over the closed shop, balloting before strikes, picketing, and breach of agreement. As for the Tories' frankly avowed objective of breaking the link between the unions and the Labour Party (an objective, incidentally, which was fully endorsed by the Liberals, on whose indulgence the Government had principally depended for survival from the time they saved it from defeat in March 1977 until they abrogated the Lib-Lab pact in June 1978), what was that to the average apolitical trade union member? Most of them would not have seen the fraudulence of the argument (which erupted most cholerically when a Trade Union Committee for a Labour Victory was set up to second union officials to help Labour candidates in the Party's key 100 marginal constituencies) that trade union power should not be deployed in politics, nor even have felt affronted by Mrs Thatcher's arrogant assertion that 'politics belongs to Parliament'.

Besides which, the Tory critics of trade union affairs (no less than critics from other parts of what, when it comes down to it, is the almost seamless fabric of the establishment-minded) were normally careful to distinguish between the decency of the ordinary union member - matching that of the ordinary British voter - and the subversive activities of 'extremists', or 'industrial terrorists', as Sir Geoffrey dubbed them in an intemperate outburst to his constituency party. The grandees of the quintessential British establishment party might not have cared to put it this way, but they clearly recognised that, at least while Labour was in power, top people in the trade union movement were, however regrettably, part of that establishment. Thus Whitelaw graciously offered organised labour's own establishment a helping hand by promising that a Tory government would legislate to strengthen 'the moderates', telling an audience at Lancaster University: 'We will confront the militant wherever he seeks to undermine traditional standards and the rule of law - and in doing so we will defend the position of respectable workers and trade union leaders.'

On the same day Sir Ian Gilmour, shadow defence secretary, speaking in Liverpool, claimed that a government which acted in accordance with Margaret Thatcher's proposals for trade union reform would have the backing of the vast majority of trade union members, who 'are deeply ashamed of the tiny minority of wreckers.' As the lorry drivers' strike reached its climax, the lady herself used very much the same terms. Amidst the 'mounting chaos' which had been created, according to her, by the 'ruthless determination' of 'a few men', she urged employers to call on the forces of the law to defeat the 'flagrantly unlawful action' of men who 'are wreckers in our midst, not the mass of trade unionists.'

As already indicated, part of the strength of Tory propaganda concerning what had become, as the Winter of Discontent stormed on, a burning issue around every fireside, was its generally temperate and reasoned presentation. Another stemmed from the genuine moderation of the man charged with the principal responsibility for dealing with policy on industrial relations on behalf of the party that was soon to take power. (And it should be marked how central this issue was to the Tories, not just because of their repeated humiliation by union power during Heath's administration - though that supplied highly combustible emotive fuel to their thinking - but because the trade unions were the greatest single obstacle to their project of setting finance free.)

One illustration of Jim Prior's essential fair-mindedness and will to see the point of view of others is provided by the debate on the closed shop, a practice against which both Tories and Liberals were forever fulminating. A particularly emotive issue for those hostile to collectivism, it is not always easy to judge to what extent opposition to this practice stems from genuine scruples of conscience, as distinct from being motivated by a desire - natural enough at least to members of the employing classes - to deprive the workers of their full strength to wrest a good return for their labour. (Similar considerations, incidentally, apply to picketing, not to mention strikes, especially secondary and sympathy strikes.) It may not always be easy to judge, but it is always silly not to be suspicious. Instance the side-swipe delivered by Ian Gow when the Commons agreed to let him introduce a Private Member's Bill on picketing (the second bill on this subject to be allowed to proceed in the space of twenty-four hours, incidentally). Purporting to champion the individual against 'coercion' and the risk of losing his livelihood should his union card be taken away from him by disciplinary action (a risk largely removed in 1988, by the way, by the Thatcher Government's third Employment Act), Gow felt no compunction in invoking 'the founding fathers of the trade union movement, and indeed the founding fathers of the Labour Party,' who 'would be appalled to know that nowadays workers are being conscripted into the unions as a precondition of employment instead of joining it willingly.' In contrast Prior - who would not be suspected by many of conspiring to grant all power to the workers - went out of his way, when commending 'the Moderates' Charter' (see above) to the country, to promise that any amendments a Tory government made to the law affecting the closed shop would meet 'the objections of many trade unionists to so-called free-riders.'

More remarkably, this old-style 'one-nation' Tory made it clear to the 1978 Party Conference at Brighton that he fully accepted what might be described as the post-war settlement of capital with labour:

'It is my passionate belief that the Conservative Party
will never be able to govern effectively, and the country
will never be able to prosper, until we have learned to
understand, learned to work with, and learned to
become part of trade union activity. Trade unions are a
powerful body now present in our institutions and in our
everyday life, and we have to learn to understand this,
and try to come to terms with them.'

That must have stuck in the craw of his lady leader, who in 1981 was to reward Prior for his considerable contribution to her general election victory by shunting him into the politicians' equivalent of the elephants' graveyard, Northern Ireland. Margaret Thatcher's personality was an unpredictable factor in the Tories' campaigning. It is probably largely forgotten now by those who then collectively constituted public opinion that the Tory leader trailed Uncle Jim in terms of personal popularity all the way to the polls, acting as a drag on her party's progress rather than a fillip to it. And this is by no means adequately accounted for by the presumed male chauvinist prejudice against her, which in any case was in the event at least partly counterbalanced by an equally unreasoning female chauvinist prejudice in her favour, as I can personally bear witness.

It may seem like a contradiction in terms to say of one who was to display such sorcery in the acquisition and wielding of political power to call Margaret Thatcher a fantasist, but that is what she was. In the first place, she patently had less understanding of her country - its social structure, its place in the world, and above all its past (her perception of English - and I do mean *English*, other British folk being almost entirely beyond her ken - history had hardly progressed beyond that 'our island's story' stage which an indulgent teacher in her schooldays might have judged adequate

362

in a junior school pupil) - than any other British prime minister, in this century at least. In the second place, her mind had an incurable tendency to run to excess. Talking to Brian Walden, in the *Weekend World* programme referred to above, about the industrial strife, she declared that 'anyone who does not use power responsibly must expect his position to be reconsidered by Parliament', but had preceded this sweetly reasonable remark with the ludicrously inflated assertion that 'unions have been given enormous powers by Parliament', which 'has placed them above the law.' On another occasion she told a fellowship of financiers that the Labour Government had 'left no stone unturned to extend the powers and privileges of the trade unions.'

But perhaps her finest flight of fancy on this subject came in her reply to the Queen's Speech in the final session of Parliament before the downfall of Labour, when she denounced the Prime Minister for buying off the unions in the first three stages of the Government's pay policy by huge increases in public spending, coupled with giant strides towards socialism, brought about by increased nationalisation. Of course, as Oscar Wilde pointed out before Dr Goebbels could copyright the saying: 'Nothing succeeds like excess.' What principally distinguishes Margaret Thatcher from Adolph's Arch-Liar, one may presume, is that she had no idea her mind was bolting. Complexities were really beyond her, qualifications (which disable certainties and are akin to doubts, which are in turn close to treason) foreign to her nature. Her world was black and white, like a B-movie starring one of the few foreign statesmen she did not abhor. This, of course, was the secret of her success as a populist politician. However astonishing it may sometimes seem, she really believed what she was saying.

For one of her impassioned, utterly self-persuaded, wholly adamant nature, it must have taken superhuman effort to rein herself in during those endless months of waiting before the bugle sounded for the last great charge that won the war, but she did just about manage it, though now and again she bared her teeth. When Walden suggested her approach was rather confrontational, she protested: 'Eleven millions - do you think I'm going to be in confrontation with eleven millions?' But a few weeks later, in the more congenial arena of the *Jimmy Young Show*, she momentarily showed her true self, a tomboy spoiling for a fight, declaiming that if the trade unions confronted our essential liberty, 'by God, I will confront them.'

Margaret Thatcher took power in May 1979 as the leader of a team that was still predominantly pre-Thatcherite and paternalist in outlook. Irrespective of the extent to which this was imposed upon her by the realities of the balance of power at that time within the Tory Party (in which, at least so far as people with experience in central government is concerned, 'one-nation' modes of thought still held sway) - as opposed to the part played by political cunning in fielding a team composed principally of moderates - it had certainly worked to her advantage in the campaign to subvert the allegiance of trade unionists to Labour. The half hidden agenda which her mind was busy concocting to deal with the 'collective bullying' of the trade unions (as she once called the process of collective bargaining) is more clearly reflected by a confidential report leaked to the press, almost twelve months before the watershed general election, than in most of her own relatively guarded pronouncements. Drafted by one of the most constant of her political beaus, Nicholas Ridley (who incidentally had been sacked by Heath as Minister of Trade for opposing Heath's U-turn back to consensus politics), and apparently commissioned by the man who came closest to being her guru, Sir Keith Joseph, this report (which, significantly, was never submitted to full shadow cabinet discussion), listed the industries and services in which it was considered a Tory government would be most vulnerable to defeat in the case of a head-on clash with the unions. It made proposals (including certain denationalisation measures, the building up of stocks to lessen the impact of strikes, mobilising special squads of police and non-union drivers, and cutting off State benefits to strikers) for counteracting union power, and frankly recommended paying up when striking unions 'have the nation by the jugular vein.'

The significance of the Ridley report is multiplied by the fact that its leak followed hard on the heels of another leak, of a report in which a senior Tory, Lord Carrington, warned his leader that a future Tory government would be unable to defeat certain powerful unions and recommended that a higher priority be given to emergency planning. Sir Geoffrey Howe might reassure the public, in an authorised press release early in February 1979, that: 'We have no class war to wage.' But who can doubt that the swelling Thatcherite faction was all along planning for the day when it would seem opportune to open hostilities against the unions. When Prior pledged in his 'Moderates' Charter' speech: 'We shall proceed by consent as far as possible,' it carried no sinister overtones of 'and by the rack if necessary'. Doubtless he was doing no more than expressing his belief in trying to reach agreement through negotiation, while registering the Tories right, if returned to power, to legislate as they saw fit after due consultation. His leader's temper was utterly different, as was to be revealed halfway through the 1979 election campaign.

It is seldom easy to gauge the impact on the general public of even widely-disseminated political speeches, and epithets like 'keynote', let alone 'historic', inevitably get overworked. But in one sense at least Margaret Thatcher's remarkable speech of 16th March 1979 (delivered in, of all places, Jim Callaghan's constituency city, Cardiff) is truly historic, since, with the lady poised for a take-over, it marks the end of one era - that of the wartime and post-war consensus - and the beginning of another: the hegemony of the New Conservativism. That she yearned for an end to consensus politics she made clear with characteristic directness, combined with a flattering tribute to the evangelising traditions of Wales, which had taught her that 'if you've got a message, preach it,' she told her audience, before going on to declare:

> 'I am a conviction politician. The Old Testament
> prophets didn't say: "Brothers, I want a consensus."
> They said: "This is my faith. This is what I passionately
> believe. If you believe it too, then come with me."'

The main burden of her message was that 'the bulging Socialist State', falling back on unworkable 'collective alternatives' for free enterprise and stifling 'the natural energy of the people' and 'the elemental human instinct' which drives 'the individual to do the best for himself and his family', was responsible for Britain's economic decline, in which we were caught up in a 'spiral of low productivity and low wages.' Stripped of pejoratives and rhetoric, her wide-ranging speech was a call for a return to capitalist individualism and a minimalist State levying low taxes.

Time was to prove it what a less gullible public would have seen it at once to be - with its easy assurance of national regeneration and prosperity for all willing to work for it - a fraudulent prospectus.

(One quite specific fraud concerns the lady's exploitation of the subject of North Sea oil. 'The windfall of the century' which 'should have been husbanded and deployed in long-term investment' instead of being 'treated like a win on the pools and an invitation to spend, spend, spend,' she admonished, with a side-swipe attributing profligacy particularly to the Labour Left, who as it happens had argued strongly but unavailingly for Britain's increasing revenue from its oil to be used as a nest-egg for exactly that, national investment. (A more canny electorate would promptly have mentally reclassified the lady's withering indictment as a Freudian revelation of what would be most likely to happen to this waxing but transient source of wealth if she got her hands on it, rather than as a fair description of Labour's record on the matter.)

But this is not a speech in which to look for genuine insight or to treat seriously as honest argument; but rather, one to admire for its masterly timing in chiming in with the prevailing mood of a thoroughly disgruntled electorate, and for the sheer impudence of the speaker's claim that her own party in fact represented all that was best in the Labour Movement, without the degeneracy of the conduct (such as 'flying pickets', 'kangaroo courts', 'the merciless use of closed shop power', and sundry other pernicious practices which had turned 'worker against worker, society against itself') into which some of its sections had fallen - epitomised as 'the officious, jargon-filled, intolerant Socialism practised by Labour these last few years.' In the most audacious thrust of all - all the more wounding for its substantial truth - she mocked her enemies for 'the bizarre transformation of the Labour Party which always used to be so proud of its radicalism', charging it in effect with abandoning its ideals:

> 'Labour, the self-proclaimed party of compassion, has
> betrayed those for whom it promised to care. There used
> to be, in this country, a Socialist movement which
> valued people, had dignity and warmth. What a world
> away from the officious, jargon-filled, intolerant
> Socialism...' etc., etc.

For a politician whose essential credo hosannas the inestimable blessings which spring naturally from competitive individualism under a 'free enterprise' capitalist system, and who harbours an inveterate hatred of Socialism (a few years later she was to proclaim from her pinnacle of power that Socialism was totally alien to the character of the British people, and to boast that she had vanquished it both at home and abroad), this was the most infernal humbuggery. But for all that, it may be that her refusal to be reined back any longer by the caution of her counsellors, plus the sheer audacity of her assault on Labour, were decisive in the seizure of the citadel by the caterpillars of New Conservatism.

When, at the first Congress after the rout of Labour, the TUC General Secretary, Len Murray, spoke of trade unionists who had voted Tory, and who subsequently, in the light of the new government's policies, were regretting it, *The Guardian* took issue with his assumption that the Callaghan Government's hard line on pay was the principal reason for the switching of votes. 'It is, to say the least, just as reasonable to argue that his [a hypothetical worker's] defection contained a massive protest vote against union behaviour during the last winter of discontent,' the paper declared. Well, it is certainly true that in looking for the motives which determine where the voter puts his cross in the privacy of the polling booth, it is no use taking it for granted that reason, or at least enlightened self-interest, will prevail over emotion, nor even that the mark will represent some consistency of feeling and conduct on the voter's part. So it seems very likely that disgust over the Winter of Discontent, or at least over some of its manifestations, played some part in Labour's defeat, and that this 'disgusted vote' was swollen by the choices of not a few of those who had themselves behaved militantly enough in the battle with the Labour Government. But it seems even more likely that the decisive factors were disillusionment with apparently unending pay restraint under Labour and the converse conviction in the punters' minds that they would be 'better off' under the Tories, ever ready with the ever seductive message of 'more of the money you've earned left in your pocket to spend as you please'.

Tory propaganda against the level of public expenditure that the Callaghan Government and Labour-controlled councils considered necessary or appropriate, and against the commensurate rates of taxation they levied, and for higher incentives for skill and enterprise, was designed to appeal almost as much to skilled workers as to the entrepreneurial, rentier and professional classes. *In The Conservative Party from Peel to Thatcher*, Robert Blake makes the point that: 'It was, perhaps surprisingly, not true that the highest taxpayers were the only category to favour lower taxation. Those whose incomes were rising from whatever base felt even more strongly about the matter. It was clear too that a large section would be happy to opt out of parts of the Welfare State.'

It should not be forgotten that the labour revolt against the pay policy actually began not with an offensive by the great army of the very low-paid but amongst engineering craftsmen protesting about the shrinking of differentials and mutinying against their own generals. Commenting on the 1983 general election (in which there was admittedly a major complicating factor in the alliance between the Liberals and the breakaway Social Democratic Party), Blake writes of the skilled working class deserting Labour 'in droves'. In fact in 1983 Labour only secured 39 per cent of the trade unionists' vote, with the Tories taking 31 per cent and the Alliance 29 per cent. The Tory share of support from this category of voters was actually down from 40 per cent in 1979, but the defection from Labour was even more massive.

In 1979 Labour gathered in half the organised-labour vote, but the swing to the Tories from this section of the voters was higher, at 7 per cent, than the overall swing of 5.2 per cent. Moreover, Denis Healey points out in his memoirs that it was manual workers in particular who deserted Labour, with the Party's support actually rising by 5 per cent among white-collar workers and by 8 per cent among the professional middle class. In *The Times Guide to the House of Commons, May 1979* Ivor Crewe notes the 'exceptionally high swings [to the Tories] in two types of affluent working class areas', with Labour losing two seats (Birmingham Northfield and Hornchurch) in which car workers formed a significant proportion of the electorate, and suffering big swings against them in two others (Dagenham and Barking) and in New Towns such as Harlow, Basildon, and Hertford and Stevenage. The swings in these constituencies varied from 8.2 to 13.9 per cent. Not till the third general election battle against the Iron Lady, in 1987, did Labour begin to recoup these grievous losses in its natural core constituency, with its share of the organised-labour vote rising to 42 per cent. Even by 1992, with the Tory host led into battle by the incomparably uncharismatic John Major, Labour could not carry with it half the trade union voters, 31 per cent of whom gave their votes to the Tories and 19 per cent to the Liberal Democrats, compared with Labour's share of 46 per cent of the total poll.

In the course of a lengthy conversation with Kenneth Harris covering the whole of his political career, published in *The Observer* in November-December 1978, James Callaghan acknowledged that one factor in the ousting of the Wilson Government in the general election of 1970 was the abstention of trade unionists, who 'did not turn up to vote because of what they thought was the attitude of the Labour Government to them.' As already remarked, he was not prepared to be as candid when it came to their verdict on his own record as a prime minister. But besides the hard facts, we have the testimony of his own Chancellor, whose recognition of the indispensability of the trade unions to Labour has already been noted in the context of Wilson's abortive attempt to shackle them. But before calling Callaghan's principal co-conspirator to give evidence, let us listen to some other witnesses from the Labour camp to supplement those Cassandras from sundry quarters whose voices we have already heard.

First one might cite the general warning of the man who had been the Labour Government's most powerful ally in the launching of its pay policy, and who had 'loyally' (as the follow-my-leader gang - what we might call the O'Grady Says Tendency - like to put it) continued to back the Government through two further stages of pay restraint. On retiring as general secretary of the TGWU, Jack Jones warned the Government that any attempt to introduce a fourth stage, in the teeth of the general opposition of the trade union movement, would be 'counter-productive and bad for unity'. That was in March 1978. In May the general secretary of the Electrical, Electronic, Telecommunication and Plumbing Union, Frank Chapple (who might well have been considered an uncertain friend by some Labour supporters, but who was at any rate admired by the erratically-judging Labour Chancellor) made it crystal clear that the imposition of a Stage Four could do irreparable damage to a labour movement which people had joined to improve their living standards. Four days later, at his union's annual conference at Margate, Alan Fisher threw down his dramatic challenge to the Callaghan Government: 'If they will fight with us on low pay, we will fight with them in a general election.' In July, after it had become as clear as daylight that the Government and the unions were on a collision course, Labour back-bencher Martin Flannery told a Chancellor who was still exuding confidence about the prospects for the economy and for continued co-operation from the trade unions, that the five-per-cent pay limit 'played right into the hands of the Tories electorally and in many other ways.' How right he was!

For a man so little given to admitting his multitudinous mistakes, Denis Healey's subsequent candour concerning the five-per-cent straitjacket is remarkable. Former Labour MP Phillip Whitehead, researching for the Channel 4 television series and book *The Writing on the Wall*, records two of Healey's *mea culpas*. On the general point of the Government's insistence on pushing on with a Stage Four, he says: 'I remember very well in my own area, one of the wisest and most moderate of all trade union leaders, the regional organiser of the Transport and General, Ernie Hayhurst, saying to me, "Denis, it will not work another time; you'll have to find some other way." But we didn't listen to this advice; we were carried away by the degree of success we'd already had.' (Healey harks back to this particular warning in his own memoirs: 'I was warned during a visit to Leeds by his [Moss Evans'] union's regional officer, one of the wisest and most upright men I have known, that it would be simply impossible to operate a national incomes policy for another year.')

And on the ill-chosen five-per-cent figure which, as Harold Wilson was to comment, 'Ministers bravely, but somewhat unrealistically, nailed...to the masthead', Whitehead quotes Healey as saying: 'I'm convinced now that if we had said we want settlements in single figures, we'd have come out with probably something like 12 per cent overall and retained the support of the unions, avoided the Winter of Discontent, and won the election. But hubris tends to affect all governments after a period of success, and by golly it hit us.' 'Hubris' is what he called it too in *The Time of My Life*: 'Our hubris in fixing a pay norm of five per cent without any support from the TUC met its nemesis, as inevitably as in a Greek tragedy...If we had been content with a formula like "single figures", we would have had lower settlements, have avoided the winter of discontent, and probably have won the election too.'

Men (and women!) who have successfully grappled their way up the heights of power (and the summit only just eluded Denis Healey) are not much given to humility, even in retrospect, so there is much merit in Healey's 'hubris' admissions. Regrettably though (for all his many talents, his wide sympathies, and his breadth of mind), he does not appear to have been able to apply the virtue of humility to producing a more searching scrutiny of his own record in office, nor in particular of its sorry conclusion. He writes as he talks, with wit, charm, vivacity, and vividness, but too often like one who cannot spare the time to examine his own convictions and his own judgements, and who therefore frequently fails to carry conviction when criticising others. He seems to think, for example, that the argument of the Labour Left 'that the Callaghan Government had sacrificed the workers for the sake of middle-class votes, and that we could recover our position only by moving left' (an argument which is certainly not immune to serious objections) can be dismissed by a couple of sentences on the manifest disillusionment of working people with Labour, garnished with a sardonic citation of Brecht's incisive poem on the East Berlin workers' rising of 1953 that only serves to illustrate Healey's own aptitude for getting hold of the wrong end of the stick. As ever, he wades into the fight, especially when it is against 'the Left', with enormous zest, but it is all too apt to make little more sense than a John Wayne movie punch-up.

With regard to the particular point at issue - whose fault was the 1979 knockout blow to Labour? - he writes: 'The Winter of Discontent was not caused by the frustration of ordinary workers after a long period of wage restraint. It was caused by institutional pressures from local trade union activists who had found their roles severely limited by three years of incomes policies agreed by their national leaders; they felt, like Othello when he had to give up soldiering, that their occupation was gone.' The unsettling effects of having 'activists' in any institution (from the government downwards) should certainly not be underestimated; but leaving aside the not negligible point that, at least so far as trade union officials - from shop stewards upwards - are concerned, to be active on ordinary members' behalf is precisely what they have been elected or appointed for, Healey's own evidence (as given above) hardly bears out his verdict. He might not like it, but much more in accordance with the realities recorded in these pages is the judgement of NUPE research officer, Reg Race, as transmitted to Phillip Whitehead:

> 'The Labour Government of Harold Wilson and James
> Callaghan was destroyed by its own actions. It was
> destroyed by its action in increasing unemployment. It was
> destroyed by its actions in attacking public expenditure. It
> was destroyed by its relationship with the Labour
> Movement, which deteriorated very markedly...To blame

trade unionists is therefore looking at the symptoms rather than the causes...for what subsequently happened.'

Juxtaposing two more comments on the conflict between the two wings of the Labour Movement, as recorded by Whitehead, makes the ultimate collision seem as inevitable as Thomas Hardy's re-creation of the encounter between the *Titanic* and the iceberg in *The Convergence of the Twain*. The first is again by Reg Race, explaining why his union was prepared to go right up to, but not over, the brink:

> 'We reasoned that it was a good time to do it, first of all because the economy was relatively buoyant at that time...second because we knew that the Government was coming up to a general election and we said to ourselves, "Well, the Government will not risk the possibility of a confrontation with the trade unions over an issue of this kind"...And we therefore went deliberately out of our way to publish in advance documents which described the justice of the claims of the workers concerned.'

The second comment illustrates what has already been detailed, the brinkmanship of James Callaghan. Talking to his aide Tom McNally, the indomitable PM argued:

> 'We'll not get any agreement out of them after a general election. But with a general election imminent we might get them to go along with it...The gun was there, the gun was loaded, and in those circumstances the trade unions surely wouldn't pull the trigger and let in a Tory government.'

An impartial observer might feel that was trying to put all the blame on the other side, i.e. on the rival wing of the Labour Movement, as well as being a teeny weeny bit unbalanced as a statement of the balance of power between the two parties to the quarrel. But as a description of the state of conflict between them, of the confrontation between incompatibles who were nevertheless indispensable to each other in playing the game of 'representative democracy', it is fair enough. If either side can be said to have backed down in the end, it was too late. Labour met its nemesis.

CHAPTER 28

Raising the status of labour

'When you get to No 10, you've climbed there on a
little ladder called "the status quo". And when you're
there, the status quo looks very good.'

Tony Benn (1995)

'The identity of all classes of labour is one thing on
which capitalist and communist doctrine wholly
agree. The president of the corporation is pleased to
think that his handsomely appointed office is the
scene of the same kind of toil as the assembly line
and that only the greater demands in talent and
intensity justify his wage differential. The communist
office-holder cannot afford to have it supposed that
his labour differs in any significant respect from that
of the comrade at the lathe or on the collective farm
with whom he is ideologically one. In both societies
it serves the democratic conscience of the more
favoured groups to identify themselves with those
who do hard physical labour. A lurking sense of guilt
over a more pleasant, agreeable, and remunerative
life can often be assuaged by the observation "I am a
worker too" or, more audaciously, by the statement
that "mental labour is far more taxing than physical
labour"...'

J.K. Galbraith, *The Affluent Society* **(1958)**

Labour's defeat in May 1979 could, at the time, be plausibly
construed as no more than a setback caused, primarily, by temporary
disunity within the Movement. In fact it was a debacle.

Of course, for both Labour politicians and Labour trade
unionists the shared experience of finding themselves out in the
cold was enough for the semblance of a common movement to be
patched together again. But beneath the high-decibel defiance of
the Tory triumph, progressive demoralisation set in, not principally
because of the succession of general election defeats suffered by

Labour or the body-blows delivered to the trade unions by the Thatcher Governments' anti-combination laws, but, more fundamentally, from the Movement's crisis of identity. It was not the shop-around voters alone who became increasingly unsure about what Labour really stood for (beyond the punters' unwavering conviction that it would always want to take more money out of their pockets than would the other parties). Labour members themselves, constantly bombarded by exhortations from the Party illuminati to rethink and modernise, could hardly be expected to know in what direction they were supposed to march, nor why - though they could hardly have failed to get a strong impression of their leaders' impulsion to proceed down whatever path seemed most likely to take them back into power.

'To thine own self be true' and so forth. But how can one be true to oneself if one is not sure who one is? An unmistakable sign of Labour's loss of belief in itself was that the words 'socialism' and 'socialist' accelerated, as it were, out of circulation. The Party establishment, and all those who looked to such blethering bellwethers to lead them out of the mire, had substantially accepted the pejorative connotations so liberally smeared onto Socialism's back by its implacable foes.

Back in the dream-time when Clement Attlee offered his common-sense testament to the common people, he carefully distinguished the character of the Labour Party from that of other national parties promoting social reform. 'They see a form of society in existence which they think to be right although it may require some alterations. Socialists see a society which is wrong and must be replaced by another.' He stressed that 'a Socialist Government must have always very clearly before it its ultimate aims and ideals. It must work throughout with the object of attaining them. It must not rest content with minor successes. It must, even when dealing with immediate problems, keep in mind always the goal to which it is tending.' In those aspiring days Attlee felt pretty clear about whither Labour should be tending. 'Socialism is about equality or it is about nothing,' he declared; and as we have seen in the chapter on 'Labour's crusade for social justice', he did not mean by 'equality' something satisfactorily nebulous like 'in the sight of God', conveniently negotiable like 'before the Law', or pragmatically pointless, as in the American colonies' Declaration of Independence.

A significant feature of Labour's last premiership was Callaghan's cavalier attitude to the concepts of Socialism and equality, which he emphatically endorsed when it suited his purpose and shrugged off when it did not. Instances of his deploying the rhetoric of Socialism at salient campaigning moments have been cited in earlier chapters. At other junctures - as has also been noted - he was at pains to distance himself from such 'extreme' views in order to highlight his claim to being not simply a party leader but the leader of the nation. Some particularly illuminating demonstrations of this chameleon facility were provided by his extended conversation with Kenneth Harris of *The Observer* referred to above.

Towards the end of the interview Harris invited him to comment on the fact that 'some Labour Party members - some people who aren't Labour Party members - say "The Labour Party is no longer Socialist."' Harris asked him: 'What do you think they mean by that?' The gist of Callaghan's 300-word reply, which meandered past signposts to the 'Broad Church' of Labour, scattering along the way reminders that Labour was not a *class* but a *national* political party, containing wholly unexplicated references to 'the principles of democratic socialism', and injunctions to Socialists in the Party to remember that many other members 'are concerned about ethical problems, or about environmental problems, or social problems,' but 'are *not* so interested in a form of society as such' (as though the question of 'the organisation of society' were an esoteric and ritualistic preoccupation) - the gist of his reply was, 'Ask them rather than me.'

So, a third of a century down the road from '1945 and all that', the man who was now Labour's leader seemed to have little idea to where, after all that winding and twisting, it was leading. But then that did not appear greatly to trouble him. And to Harris's related follow-up question - 'You don't think, in fact, that some people have lost faith in the Labour Party because prominent supporters of the Labour Party, not just politicians, seem to have done very well for themselves and have "crossed over to capitalism"?' - Callaghan responded even more dismissively. 'Everybody's standards have gone up,' he said, remarking (in words pre-echoing Kinnock's Conference taunt to his Militant opponents a few years later about miners with holiday homes in Marbella) that pensioners from his constituency city of Cardiff who would once have got no farther than Barry Island for a brief annual break might now take their holidays in Spain. 'That kind of criticism leaves me totally unmoved,' he told Harris.

Not much sign of dedication to the ideal of equality there! Except for a kind of sickly afterglow, even more pallid than Crosland's, amounting to little more than a commitment to social mobility, along with, of course, a decent little life dealt out to all and sundry. A revealing interchange earlier on in *The Observer* interview seems to bear this out. Harris had alluded to talk in inner political circles a few years back that Ted Heath's Chancellor of the Exchequer, Anthony Barber, had thought of putting Callaghan's name forward as the next Managing Director of the International Monetary Fund (now *there* was a commendation for an erstwhile Labour chancellor!) and Callaghan admitted to having seriously considered leaving politics should such an opening arise. 'But you don't regret not having gone?' asked Harris. 'I should say not!' replied Sunny Jim. 'Look how lucky I've been. My life has been very good to me. It ought to be a lesson to everybody who thinks at some time in his life that the door has closed on him,' he added, with log-cabin-to-White-House-style logic. Well now opportunity had knocked for Callaghan's Downing Street gardener, Len Hobbs, too, in the probably unanticipated form of being able to treasure a portrait of himself, nervously fingering his tie, alongside the Labour Prime Minister in a national newspaper publishing the story of 'Callaghan: My Way to the Top'.

Such verbal commerce with journalists is admittedly but small change when weighed in the balance with a politician's actions and inactions. Midway through the April '79 election campaign, on the day after Margaret Thatcher's belligerent anti-consensus speech, with its audacious claim to occupy the territory of radicalism and idealism (even of the old, true Socialism!), Callaghan counterclaimed that 'the centre ground' as well as 'the Left and radical ground' was now held by Labour, who represented co-operation between employers, employees, trade unions, and government, in contrast to the 'reactionary' divisiveness generated by the New Tories. At a press conference in London he attacked 'man and master' class distinctions as damaging for output, living standards, and jobs. 'It is time we ended this status business and had a single status and stopped separation between white-collar workers and blue-collar workers,' he averred, in a ringing Humpty-

Dumpty kind of declaration with which the apostle of a classless Britain who was so miraculously elevated to *primus inter pares* eleven years later would have had no quarrel. (John Major told a gathering of businessmen in St Ives, Cambridgeshire, in February 1994: 'Those artificial distinctions between blue- and white-collar workers are outdated, absurd, damaging, and they should be put in the dustbin immediately and never taken out again.')

It is true that the boy from Brixton would not have wholeheartedly endorsed Callaghan's pledge that the next Labour government would press for voluntary agreements between management and shopfloor - with the deployment of statutory back-up powers if necessary - for the establishment of representative committees to enable companies to discuss with their employees plans for investment, closures, expansion, and other matters affecting them. But leaving aside the question of what such 'consultation' would really amount to, considering that the Labour Government had just dropped a sadly emasculated Bullock, how much faith were authentic advocates of industrial democracy (even those who would settle for colonial-government-style consultative councils) expected to invest in such a pledge anyway?

The truth of the matter is that with all of the parties canvassing for the workers' votes, and even the Tories (Dr Strangelove clones always excepted) fearful that worker-power could derail their agenda if they got back into office, and accordingly operating in their notion of appeasement mode, industrial democracy was the flavour of the moment. Worker co-operatives were not only being promoted by the Liberals, in particular by Jo Grimond and John Pardoe (admittedly the Liberals' advocacy was in some measure motivated by their awareness of the Trojan-horse potential of worker co-ops *vis-à-vis* the power of the Labour Party/trade union bloc; but it was genuine in its way, even enlightened in its conception - not that distant from the vision of some within the Labour Movement itself - of worker co-ops as a more human and more individual-friendly alternative to giant nationalised corporations and socialistic paternalism), but even condescendingly subscribed to by thinking Tories. When the Government bill to set up a Co-operative Development Agency came before the Commons in April 1978, Kenneth Clarke told the House that his party welcomed the kind of co-operative which engaged in commercially-sound exercises and did not rely on subsidies or preferential treatment, and the bill was given an unopposed second reading. And with whatever degree of sincerity or insincerity it might have carried in each case, general endorsement of the concept of industrial democracy was given by a whole string of Tory illuminati, including Prior, Nott, Howe and Walker.

(A sure indicator of just how transformed the scene had become fifteen years later, through the vigorous exercise of Tory mastery, was provided by an easily-overlooked news report of comments made by Employment Secretary David Hunt on the social standing of the battered and depleted trade union movement of the nasty nineties. Speaking after an address to the Industrial Society in which he had gone out of his way to make it gratuitously clear that the trade unions could not expect to be given 'preferential status' - and, as it happens, not long after friendly overtures to the Government from the new TUC general secretary, John Monk, and the first formal invitation since the Tories had returned to power for a government minister to address a TUC conference - he admonished the unions to purge themselves of 'class-war delusions' and to 'recognise their own limitations.' The man with the top job in industrial relations, Cabinet minister in a government which had abolished the National Economic Development Council - the body set up by Macmillan's Government to promote dialogue between the national government and the two sides of industry - bluntly told the unions that they could have no direct role in determining policy. 'The corporate state is wholly discredited. It will not be restored'.)

The trouble was that the bodies representing the employers' interests - the Confederation of British Industries, the Institute of Directors, and, of course, the Tory Party - were naturally implacably opposed to giving the workers a statutory right to representation on company boards. The more reasonable Tories were ready to underwrite - with good grace if not with enthusiasm - a code of practice to foster industrial democracy (or, more accurately, to foster the impression that they were in favour of industrial democracy). Their most substantial shadows on employment and industry, James Prior and John Nott, made this clear to the Party's trade unionists' advisory committee in a letter (written in mid-May 1978, just before, as was known, the Government's subterranean writhings on the issue were about to break surface) which offered workers perhaps the most worthless promise ever made, even if it were to be honoured by the next Tory government: *that company law should be amended to make it incumbent on directors to have as much regard for the interest of employees as for those of shareholders.*

Equally predictably, the Tories were unshakeable in their conviction that workers who were not union members should be at no disadvantage when it came to representation on company boards. This point was also put most forcibly by the director-general of the CBI, Sir John Methven, who in an intervention accusing the Government of 'biased ideology' and obsession with extending trade union power, charged that its proposals would make millions of employees who were not trade unionists 'second-class citizens' - unlike their brother workers enrolled in unions, who were, presumably, 'first-class citizens', just like their capital-wielding bosses and the rentier masses. (It is worth noting, in passing, that in contrast to this display of humbug put on by the boss class there were a few authentic democrats - Eric Heffer for one - who were critical of the unions' insistence that they should be the sole channel of representation for workers on company boards in any scheme that should be set up.)

The great irony is that the unbiased non-ideological mental marsh-ground from which Sir John's explosive gas arose was not so different in character from what lay beneath the Prime Minister's decisive words about Labour's future intentions and his equally decisive present inactivity. While for obvious and inescapable tactical reasons Callaghan could not repudiate the union claim to a dominant role in the worker-representation element of the proposed consultative boards, in fact what real interest he had in the promotion of industrial democracy mirrored that of the bosses. The allegation that he sought an extension of trade union power was frankly risible (indeed, the exact opposite of the truth) and he concurred with his ostensible opponents on the two principal arguments which made some capitalists look not wholly unfavourably on the concept of industrial democracy. The most fundamental of these is succinctly put by Callaghan's Senior Policy Adviser, Bernard Donoghue: 'High hopes were also briefly entertained that British industry might be regenerated by the introduction of greater industrial democracy. The argument was that if British employees became more involved in the decisions affecting their working lives they would work harder and show more commitment to the success of their firms.'

The other, subsidiary, argument for industrial democracy which was naturally shared by all who were complacent about the capitalist system is alluded to in Keith Harper's *Guardian* report on the letter from Prior and Nott to that society for the protection of the curious hybrid species of Tory trade unionists referred to above. 'Mr Callaghan has long been using the carrot of industrial democracy, however far removed from the Bullock principle, as a method of continuing to win union co-operation on further pay restraint.' As a matter of a fact, with his big stick still concealed down his trouser-leg, he had just had the temerity to dangle this chimerical carrot before the noses of the presumed donkeys of APEX (the Association of Professional, Executive, Clerical and Computer Staff) assembled on May Day for their annual delegate conference.

(On the broader field of capitalist societies as a whole, the same considerations are powerful arguments for promoting not only shareholding by a company's own workforce, but the widespread ownership of shares in general, the 'popular capitalism' of Tory - and sometimes of Liberal - rhetoric. The millennium would be reached by this route in the unlikely event of shares ever being spread sufficiently widely and sufficiently evenly to equalise economic power. Perhaps some such dream had possessed the minds of the members of the Labour Party's Home Affairs Committee who in June 1973 endorsed a plan for a take-over of capitalism in Britain through the introduction of legislation obliging employers to issue equity shares to their workers, who would thus be enabled to build up a potentially controlling capital fund. 'A significant move towards workers' control,' according to Ian Aitken in a forty-inch front-page *Guardian* report which incidentally congratulated Left-wing MPs on the committee for their near-unanimity in recognising, like the more sensible comrades to their right, the 'foolishness' of the NEC's attempt to commit the Party to the nationalisation of twenty-five leading companies. No one explained why, if the implacable opposition of the property-owning classes to the latter strategy was certain, they could be expected to accept revolution - or what they would call 'robbery' - by stealth: a flaw transmuting a theoretically brilliant strategy into a 'vain fantasy...as thin of substance as the air.')

These arguments, which seemed cogent to both Callaghan and his official opponents, are not disreputable. Indeed, in an abstract way they are sensible enough for ordinary workers to understand and agree with. However, they are not exactly at the heart of what 'industrial democracy' has to mean if 'democracy' means what Abe Lincoln said it does: 'Government of the people, by the people, for the people.' And of course we all believe in that, don't we?

The Committee of Inquiry on Industrial Democracy appointed in late 1975, with the distinguished historian Alan Bullock as chairman and Jack Jones as its most prominent trade union member, reported to the nation on 26th January 1977, after which, according to Denis Healey: 'The Government spent an inordinate amount of time on this issue.' Whether that is true with respect to its importance is a matter for individual judgement. (Donoghue - hardly an egregiously radical witness - writes that the Bullock Report, for all its shortcomings, might have led to 'a major social advance and contributed to the greater efficiency of British industry'.) What is certainly the case is that, whether or not they were thinking through their bottoms the while, the ministers sat on the report for an inordinate amount of time, not publicly responding until almost the end of May 1978. The main reason for the delay, according to Trade Secretary Edmund Dell (of whom more in a moment), was the problem of how to deal with firms which simply refused to discuss employee-participation on their boards with their staff or with the unions.

Just as the publication of Bullock had been preceded by pre-emptive strikes from the forces whose covert conviction was that the truest expression of industrial democracy - maybe even of democracy itself - was 'one share, one vote' (Nicholas Goodison, chairman of the Stock Exchange, had chimed in on cue with a perfect exposition of Burkeian democracy: that control was inseparable from the rights of property and that it should continue to lie with shareholders who put up risk capital - to which Colin Fowler of Eastleigh Labour Party tellingly retorted that workers often committed to one firm 'the risk capital of their working lives'), so it was when it came to the Government's response to Bullock. The day before the Government White Paper was published, the Institute of Directors went ballistic, its Director General, Jan Hildreth, shooting off missives to the nation's top businessmen urging them to warn their workers that 'their jobs, standards of living and indeed all their happiness, are all in jeopardy.' If the Government were allowed to carry out its presumed intention of imposing trade unionists on boards of directors: 'The board would cease to be an executive *devoted to serving the customer* and would become a committee designed to bicker over the distribution of wealth between shareholders and employees.' [my emphasis] Even codes of practice, according to this high priest of Mammonism, 'will only facilitate destructive meddling', when 'the end we should all be seeking is prosperity.'

The Institute's 30,000 directors, along with all the other worthy wealth-creators, need not have got their knickers in a twist. When the

381

Government at last lobbed its delayed-inaction device to deal with this explosive issue into the public domain, its proposals turned out to be, in the words of Victor Keegan of *The Guardian*, 'a pale reflection of the original Bullock proposals,' and a *Guardian* leader commented approvingly: 'Short of abandoning worker participation altogether...*Mr Callaghan could have done little more to appease the (righteous) wrath of the CBI.*' [my emphasis]

The central recommendation of Bullock was that there should be parity on company boards between representatives of the shareholders and representatives of the workforce, with a third smaller group of independent directors co-opted by joint agreement of the other two groups - the so-called *2X + Y* formula. It was argued that: 'It is unreasonable to expect employee representatives to accept equal responsibility unless...they are able to have equal influence on the decision-making process.' After the report's publication, some critics from the Left pointed out that what Bullock was offering was the appearance, not the actuality, of parity. Amongst these critics was a 33-year-old firebrand named Neil Kinnock, who, writing in *The New Statesman*, called the *2X + Y* formula 'incredible' and said that in practice it would give worker directors 'responsibility without power'. Kinnock, seething with revolutionary indignation, concluded: 'Far from being an assault on either ownership power or on corporatism, Bullock's recommendations provide a democratic face for capitalist hierarchy.'

But since the report was now in the safe hands of a Cabinet committee chaired by Shirley Williams, and with the Prime Minister himself taking a close oversight, it did not matter a whole lot whether or not Bullock was deadly from a capitalist point of view or hopelessly defective from a revolutionary point of view. It was certain to be defused until it was harmless enough for toddlers to handle. The principle of parity, which the majority on the Bullock committee had at least been at pains to underline as a theoretical objective, was simply ignored in the White Paper, which substituted the proposal that the aim should be to give workers in companies employing more than 2,000 people (the same figure as in Bullock) the right to appoint one third of the directors.

Whatever its faults, the Bullock Report argued its case closely and produced a detailed scheme for implementing its proposals, for which it was condemned as 'ill-thought-out, rigid and legalistic' by *The Guardian*, in a leader which proceeded to justify its antipathy by pointing out that: 'Participation, statutory participation, and a lot tougher and more rigid than anything this Government is contemplating, has long been the order of the day in Germany, Scandinavia and the rest of Western Europe. It may not have caused their relative industrial peace and plenty. But it has certainly not subverted it.' Notwithstanding the repeated broadsides *The Guardian* was in the habit of firing at the antediluvian attitudes and practices of both sides of British industry, and the paper's professed attachment to the concept of industrial democracy as a potentially regenerative force, when Change actually knocked at the door, it turned its coat inside out as adroitly as a quick-change artist and became in a twinkling a champion of near-geological evolution. Bullock had tried to rush things, it claimed, attempting 'in one jump to impose in this country a system which had evolved over decades on the Continent.' Much more to its taste was a White Paper which substituted fudge for forceful argument and an almost endless chain of buckets of conciliation for resolution.

The Bullock Committee majority had been anxious to dispel fears that their proposals could lead to worker representatives gaining control of company boards: 'It is no part of our intention to make recommendations which could possibly produce such a result,' their report says reassuringly in one passage. Just how unthreatening to capitalist control the Callaghan Government's White Paper was may be judged by its almost somnolent reception in the Commons from a Leader of the Opposition noted for her stridently combative responses. 'We welcome proposals that will lead to greater involvement by the whole workforce,' the lady purred, going on to comment with a more characteristic caterwaul: 'These proposals seem to be very different from the Bullock version - and rightly so.' Indeed *The Guardian* noted with satisfaction that the plans sketched in by the White Paper 'bear a striking similarity to "minority Bullock" - the counter-proposals produced by the three industrial members of the committee of inquiry.' The paper chided the CBI for its continuing hostility to reform despite the fact that this sober minority composed of three of its leading members appeared to have had the biggest influence on the Government's thinking!

Presumably without intentional irony in its allusion to the most savage of all satires in the English language, *The Guardian* described the White Paper as 'a modest, heartening proposal'. 'Modest' for sure! Not only had it 'discreetly ditched the essential feature of Bullock' now that *enfant terrible* champion of the Bullock approach, Jack Jones, was safely retired. The Government had also made it quite clear that it was its intention to proceed towards its simulation of industrial democracy by voluntary agreements between companies and their employees reached through negotiations so patient that, as *The Guardian's* leader-writer noted, to reach the point of exhaustion when 'the fall-back formula' of arbitration to break absolute deadlocks would come into play 'presupposes two consecutive Labour victories at general elections before a single (compulsory) worker director took office...hardly a recipe for instant revolution.'

If further reassurance was needed that thoughts of the tocsin and of barricades in the boardrooms were out of place in steady heads, it could have been found in the character of the man in charge of the ministry principally responsible for issues concerning company law. Edmund Dell was the very model of a minister specially designed for the use of social democratic governments worried that they might inadvertently make the bourgeoisie bolt. Despite having been one of Denis Healey's CP comrades at Oxford, 'the ultra-cautious Edmund Dell' (as Joel Barnett - not exactly an impetuous soul himself - describes him in *Inside the Treasury*) had developed the perspective of a businessman rather than a politician. By the time he had become 'the ultra-moderate Minister of Trade' (as a *Guardian* leader called him), his attitude was, in the words of the paper's political correspondent Simon Hoggart, 'almost apolitical...scarcely interested in party politics' but 'keen to do a good administrative job.' Just the chap to defuse such a politically-charged issue as industrial democracy, one might feel.

Hoggart was reporting - nearly six months after the publication of the White Paper and shortly after the CBI had bluntly reaffirmed its decision (as Hoggart puts it) 'to have no truck even with a watered-down version of industrial democracy', and with Cabinet ministers still not in accord over the question of whether worker-directors should be directly elected from the shopfloor or only through union channels - on the resignation of Dell, who had decided not to stand for Parliament again in the next general election, but to return to his old firm, the Guinness Peat group, which he was eventually to chair. Dell's replacement as Trade Secretary, and billed as a much tougher proposition for the CBI to tackle, was a forty-year-old newcomer to the Cabinet destined to have to soldier on through four Labour general election defeats before becoming a household name. Who can say whether, granted more than a few meagre months of office, John Smith would have won his spurs in battle with the intransigent CBI over the issue of industrial democracy? As it was, to use the metaphor deployed by both Healey and Donoghue, the whole business 'ran into the sand'.

The extent of Jim Callaghan's disappointment at this trickling away of hopes for some measure of shopfloor suffrage may be gauged from the fact that he has nothing at all to say about the fate of Bullock in his autobiography. The report is simply referred to as a document he was waiting for in the hope that it 'would help create a framework of joint responsibility' in industry. Nowhere else in a detailed chronicle of his political life does industrial democracy get a mention.

Not that he was short of excuses for his government's failure to make any significant progress on this long-standing Labour commitment. for one thing, quite apart from the general hostility of the employers, with no overall majority in the Commons, legislation could not be pushed through without winning some support from MPs in other parties. For another, according to the opinion polls the issue aroused little interest amongst rank-and-file trade unionists in general. And more importantly in terms of getting the Prime Minister off the hook, there was much division of opinion in and some strong opposition from the higher echelons in many trade unions. While the TUC general secretary, Len Murray, went on record as thinking that the debate about industrial democracy was 'of pivotal importance for the 1980s' and that the Bullock Report was 'a signpost for the future', *The Guardian* was not far out in calling Jack Jones 'the one union leader wedded to Bullock'. Among the big unions whose leaders were opposed to the worker-director proposals or who had strong reservations about them were those of the miners (NUM), the electricians (EETPU), the engineers (AUEW) and the construction workers (UCATT), plus the second biggest general union (NUGMW).

Some progress was made in areas of the public sector, where - provided the major unions organising labour were not, like the NUM, hostile - the Government had more elbow for persuading managements to go along with the introduction of some measure of industrial democracy. However, experience in these public sector areas, which included steel-making, the railways, and the Post Office, tended to highlight the incompatibilities between labour organisations in Britain and the concept of industrial democracy. On the railways, for example, it was reported to the annual conference of the NUR just three weeks before the deadline given to British Rail to come up with a full plan for worker participation on the Board, that while the NUR and the white-collar rail union TSSA were in accord, ASLEF was declining to co-operate.

Because of the long association of their union with the campaign for workers' control, the experience of the Post Office workers was particularly poignant. The unions representing Post Office staff had reached agreement with the Board, broadly on the lines of the Bullock recommendations, within a week of the publication of the report. A combination of ironing out residual difficulties and Government stalling delayed the launching of the two-year experimental participation period agreed on until 1st January 1978. Two days after the publication of the Government's White Paper response to Bullock, the annual delegate meeting of the Union of Post Office Workers received the first report-back of their representatives on the PO Board. As the written report they tabled underlined, what they were taking part in was 'certainly not the workers' control envisaged by our forebears when they established the UPW nearly 60 years ago.' Furthermore, it became clear during discussion that the worker-directors felt inhibited from playing a full part on the board through their fear of undermining the bargaining tactics of the union's general secretary and its official negotiators. It turned out that the seven people who were on the board specifically as representatives of the unions and the workforce did not even meet as a group to co-ordinate their interventions to the board's proceedings.

This is but an indication of the genuine and serious problems that worker-participation on company boards posed for the unions. The deepest apprehension of all - that worker-directors could lose the trust of their work-mates by becoming too closely identified with management policy - was deployed with Jesuitical cunning by Tories and others who had no real sympathy with the idea of industrial democracy. Nevertheless, it is hard to avoid the conclusion that opposition in the unions to moves towards greater industrial democracy - moves which long pre-dated Bullock - was generally rooted not in any commitment to the collective power of the workers and the fear of undermining it, but in the awareness of union establishments that it would undercut their own power. After all, shifts in the power of determining the unions' actions from their general staffs to shopstewards in the front-line met with similar sustained hostility in many parts of the trade union movement, not to mention, as we have already seen, in the political wing of the heroic Labour Movement. However, only by looking back from the shadow boxing over Bullock to earlier debates in the Movement can we see how profoundly equivocal has been the attitude of many Labour politicians to the idea of industrial democracy. That is what we shall now do.

CHAPTER 29

Ambiguities of workers' control

'I am not a labor leader. I don't want you to follow me
or anyone else. If you are looking for a Moses to lead
you out of the capitalist wilderness you will stay right
where you are. I would not lead you into this promised
land if I could, because if I could lead you in, someone
else would lead you out.'

**Eugene Debs, quoted by John Dos Passos,
U.S.A. (1938)**

In their compilation of documents published in 1968 as *Industrial
Democracy in Great Britain* and republished in paperback form in
1970 as *Workers' Control*, Ken Coates and Tony Topham in effect
treat the shopsteward movement and the campaign for industrial
democracy as one movement. Despite the dangers of
misunderstanding arising from the fact that some of those associated
with the shopsteward movement have been too closely identified
with movements pursuing political power (most notably the
Communist Party, but in the final analysis the Labour Party too)
with agendas which are ultimately inimical to workers' control,
there are good reasons for doing so. Both the shopsteward movement
and the industrial democracy movement strike (writing in the 1990s
one feels more inclined to say 'struck') at the dominant twin
traditions of political and industrial Labourism: centralism and
paternalism. The never-ending struggle in the Labour Movement
between democrats and autocrats - the struggle, to spell it out, over
who is to be sovereign, the union leaders or the rank-and-file, the
Party or the people - is so central to the question 'what does Labour
really stand for?' that it calls for far more attention than I can afford it.
Besides what has already come out in the course of this narrative and
argument, I must content myself with pointing to a few significant
contributions to the industrial democracy debate prior to Bullock (basing
my references mainly on Coates and Topham), before, in the next
chapter, glancing at the issue of democracy within the Labour Party.

Coates and Topham, the publication of whose book fortuitously
coincided with the widespread ferment of 1968, intended to do more

than make a contribution to the study of labour history. They also aimed, as they say in their preface, 'to provide a practical textbook for *active* students of trade unionism, industrial relations and working-class politics.' [my emphasis] It may be assumed that this was one important factor in their decision to limit the scope of their book to this century. As part of their documentation of what might be called the heroic age of the workers' control movement in Britain - i.e. the years preceding and immediately following the First World War - they include an extract from the autobiography of Tom Bell, the once-upon-a-time Clydesider Wobbly, in which, having remarked that in those 'pioneering days' (to borrow the title of his memoirs) both Fabian guildsmen and syndicalists 'were a source of confusion and distraction for the militant workers; the syndicalists by exorcising all parliamentary action, the Fabians by dragging in their fetish of the State,' he goes on to declare, with wholly unconscious irony: 'With the Russian Revolution most of the problems disturbing both syndicalists and guildsmen were clarified and the best elements from both camps found themselves by 1920 in the Communist Party of Great Britain.'

Whether or not some are born to lead, it often seems that many are born to be misled. It may well be that the common acceptance of the myth that worker-power had triumphed in Soviet Russia was the decisive factor in the outcome of the debate over industrial democracy in Britain in the crucial years between the wars and while Labour was for the first time really in power, from 1945-51. Certainly the 'Workers' State' had, in this as in so many other matters, a most baleful influence on the British Labour Movement. The early extinguishing of the movement for industrial democracy in Soviet Russia itself exposed the 'Workers' State' as fairy-tale rhetoric hiding an ugly reality. (Scarcely a month after the Bolsheviks gained power, they set up a Supreme Economic Council, *Vesenka*, to which all existing economic authorities, including the All-Russian Council of Workers' Control, were subordinated, while the trade unions became mere agents of the so-called Soviet Socialist State. Of the factory committees and other institutions of workers' control which had flourished after the February Revolution, and which had indeed played a major role in the Bolsheviks' ascendancy, Richard Pipes says in *The Russian Revolution, 1899-1919*, 'By 1919, they were only a memory.') But outside the small Anarchist and Anarcho-Syndicalist movement, this was little understood among Socialists or progressive intellectuals in Britain, or indeed in other bourgeois democracies. As Richard Crossman writes in his introduction to *The God that Failed*: 'A very few men can claim to have seen round this particular corner in history correctly...most of those who are now so wise and contemptuous after the event, were either blind, as Edmund Burke in his day was blind, to the meaning of the Russian Revolution, or have merely oscillated with the pendulum - reviling, praising, and then reviling again, according to the dictates of public policy.'

But there is a world of difference between the visions of a good society that led the six intellectuals (Arthur Koestler, Ignazio Silone, André Gide, Louis Fischer, and Stephen Spender) whose self-analyses make up this book first to embrace and then to repudiate the travesty of Communism that was shackled onto the people of Russia and its empire, and later onto Soviet Russia's East European satellites - and between the truly liberating aims of many other people in the decadent bourgeois democracies of the twenties and thirties who, to a greater or lesser extent and for a greater or lesser period of time, became dupes of Soviet Communism - and those like the Webbs for whom the great attraction of the 'new civilisation' was its paternalistic order.

In that appalling apologia for Stalin's nightmare State, *Soviet Communism: A New Civilisation* (first published in November 1935), the Webbs refer to what they call Stalin's 'epoch-making address' of June 1931 to a conference of leaders of industry, in which that titanic thinker made it clear that he had fully absorbed the lessons of that (in the Webbs' words) 'episode of "workers' control"', with its 'leaderless chaos and widespread inefficiency' which had 'led Lenin, in June 1918, to supersede "workers' control" in the direction of industry by one-man management, under the orders either of the State and the municipality...or of the consumers' co-operative movement.' The Webbs explain that 'the extrusion of the profit-making entrepreneur' had led to 'one of the characteristic diseases of non-profit-making enterprises' which 'the Bolsheviks termed "depersonalisation"'. For the benefit of his industrial general staff, Stalin defined this in his speech as 'complete absence of responsibility for the work performed, absence of responsibility for machinery, lathes and tools.'

In the section on the establishment of the Supreme Economic Council, the Webbs write: 'The idea of the "self-governing workshop"; the dream of the anarchist and the syndicalist, which had misled whole generations of socialists, had to be abandoned. Workers' control, though not eliminated for other functions [?!], was definitely deposed from management.' Thus do the Webbs, acting in their capacity as Socialist historians and theoreticians, dispose of the revolutionary force of the factory committees, as their Bolshevik heroes had done in real life.

Elsewhere in their mighty paean to the 'new civilisation', with that patrician disdain which came so naturally to these self-appointed tribunes of the people, they curtly explain what might not have occurred to a more common breed of democrats. 'In any highly evolved industrial society, whatever its economic or political constitution, the citizen as a producer, whether by hand or by brain, in his hours of work, must do what he is, in one or other form, *told* to do...' [*authors'* emphasis] However, anxiety that the interests of the ordinary worker might not, after all, have been properly represented in the Workers' State is quite misplaced. As the Webbs tell us, union 'membership was, by mere majority vote in each factory, made compulsory for all those at work,' with 'trade union dues [being] stopped from wages, and any trade union deficit [being] met by one or other of the forms of government subsidy.' As in any other kind of Corporate State (though the Webbs refrain from drawing attention to such unhappy analogues), this was simply a rational arrangement, because 'the unions became, in substance if not in form, government organs.' The liquidation of that foolish Utopian dream of workers' control was not to be regretted, however, since, the Webbs reassure us, 'the workmen's most effective control over industry was afforded by the fact that the government's boards or commissions had, in their membership, a large proportion of the leaders of the trade unions.' No one reading such words could be in the least surprised to learn that the authors had no time, any more than Joe Stalin himself had, for those 'leftist blockheads' (Stalin's description) who think that Socialism has something to do with equality. But to pursue that point would be to stray too far from our present concern.

The Webbs' approbation for such a totalitarian society, complete with a snugly-fitting straitjacket for the workers, cannot be passed off as an unfortunate consequence of an understandable sense of jubilation that in one great country at least 'capitalism had been overthrown and communism was being constructed in its place,' as the Webbs might have put it. Their problem was that they had a most *un*peculiar, a most unregenerately respectable conception of what representative democracy is. Which is to say, they swallowed - hook, line, and sinker because it all tasted so good to such self-confident candidates for prominent roles as leaders of enlightened opinion - the constitutional myth that representative democracy is, well, some sort of democracy. In *A Constitution for the Socialist Commonwealth of Great Britain*, a verbal panacea offered to an undeserving public in 1920, they labour mightily to distinguish between democracy 'as an "organ of revolt"', deployed 'when people were "subjects" and not themselves the sovereign power', and democracy once that revolt has succeeded, i.e. democracy 'as an "organ of government"', patiently explaining that 'in the completely democratised community' government is carried out by those whom the electors have designated to be 'not their governors, but their agents or servants, chosen for the purpose of carrying out the people's will.'

Applied to the idea of democracy in the workplace, this ripe cerebral wisdom (combined with what the Webbs claim to be - without troubling to substantiate it - the universally unfavourable experience gained from 'innumerable experiments in almost all industries and services, in all civilised countries, during the past hundred years, in every form of "self-governing workshop"') leads inexorably to the irrefutable conclusion that collective criticism by subordinates of those designated to manage is as out of order as is individual criticism. 'The relationship set up between a manager who has to give orders all day to his staff, and the members of that staff who, sitting as a committee of management, criticise his action in the evening, with the power of dismissing him if he fails to conform to their wishes, has been found by experience to be an impossible one.' And no arguing!

Beatrice Webb's detestation of the concept of workers' control was positively virulent. In an entry in her diary for 4th May 1926, forecasting with jubilant confidence the imminent collapse of the General Strike, she predicts: 'Future historians will, I think, regard it as the death gasp of that pernicious doctrine of "workers' control" of public affairs through the trade unions, and by the method of direct action. This absurd doctrine...introduced into British working-class life by Tom Mann and the guild Socialists,' was, in Russia, 'quickly repudiated by Lenin and the Soviets [a politically necessary misrepresentation, the latter reference, since the revolutionary Soviets of workers, peasants and soldiers were an icon to the Socialist movement everywhere], and the trade unions were reduced to complete subordination to the creed-autocracy of the Communist Party.' (What an ally she would have been for Wilson and Callaghan in their struggles to bridle the unions!) Her following remarks - on the Italian fascists (who would not have seized power, she implies, had not the champions of workers' control incited the workers into seizing the factories), make it transparently obvious that she had no objection to subordination (of others, of course) as such, only to the subordination of the workers to private capitalists, against whom they should, presumably, democratically revolt, before, having triumphed at long last, democratically submitting to the 'managers' of their very own State.

Again and again the combination of the sheer glamour that the 'Socialist State' held for the British Labour Movement with the immense ignorance of those in its ranks of what life was actually like under the Bolsheviks (an ignorance that was arguably even greater amongst those who had had the 'benefit' of a guided tour in Soviet Russia - and that applies quite as much to the fellow-travelling intellectuals as to trade unionists), muddied the debates in Britain over workers' control. It may be that the standpoints of the principal protagonists in these debates were essentially determined by their own mind-sets, by where they stood on the real left-to-right political spectrum which reflects degrees of libertarianism shading into higher and higher degrees of authoritarianism. But these were people who had made up their minds. On audiences of workers' delegates composed largely of those with (as the equivocal expression goes) 'open minds' on the issue, arguments deploying - whether disingenuously or not - 'the Russian experience' must have carried great weight.

In his influential book *Socialisation and Transport* (1933) Herbert Morrison, with whatever-suits-my-argument logic, taunted his 'critics in the Labour Party...who so often wrongly persuade themselves that they are on the Left,' and 'find it difficult to believe that the Russian Communist Government can do any wrong,' with yet being (unlike himself) quite out of step with the Soviet Government over workers' control. 'The Russian Soviet mind,' he told them, had evolved 'from the doctrine of workers' control in its crudest form [we have already seen what it became in its most refined form!]...to a position which broadly...corresponds to the general outlook of the Labour Party's Policy Reports on Transport and Electricity.' So there!

Herbert Morrison played a decisive role in shaping the form that public ownership was to take in Britain, since the National Government (formed under the leadership of Ramsay MacDonald after his Labour administration had been shattered, in August 1931, by bitter discord over the budget cuts demanded by Snowden, with the Prime Minister's backing, to cope with the world economic crisis, the last straw being the proposal to slash unemployment benefit, which was rejected by ten of the twenty-one ministers in the Cabinet) substantially adhered to the scheme for a unified London transport system which Morrison, as Minister of Transport in the minority Labour Government, had drawn up after negotiations with the existing undertakings and had been almost ready to implement when the Government fell.

The London Passenger Transport Board, launched in 1933, bore most of the features which were to characterise the public corporations established to implement later nationalisation measures. These features included a very high degree of autonomy and of financial independence, with a management predominantly drawn from business circles and only marginally subject to government or parliamentary interference, a minimum of consumer-interests' input, and the whole issue of employee-participation in management sidelined. Actually, in the case of the LPTB, the green light given by the Labour establishment to capitalists comfortable with a monopoly set-up so long as they were controlling it (and it should not be forgotten that far from distinguishing 'State Socialism' from 'free' capitalism, monopoly - albeit ideally achieved through wheeling, dealing, fixing, and so successfully competing as to wipe out one's competitors, rather than through legislation - is the natural goal of 'free market' capitalists) could not have been clearer. In this case the board was appointed by a body of trustees: not even the chairman was appointed by the Government. And who was the first chairman of the LPTB? Why, the man who was already the biggest cheese in the business of making money out of Londoners' needs for a public transport system, Lord Ashfield. As for a voice for the workers who actually ran the buses, trams, and tube trains, one officer of the TGWU was made a part-time member of the board - after (and this was a point of principle on which the Labour

Movement establishment was thereafter to insist whenever a worker was appointed to the board of a public corporation) relinquishing his trade union duties and responsibilities.

At the Labour Party Conference in 1932, moving an NEC resolution calling for the establishment of a publicly-owned transport industry managed by a National Transport Board, Morrison assaulted the advocates of workers' control with a great windbag of a speech from which banalities and vulgarities tumbled in equal measure. (The quality of Morrison's mind can be gauged by his buffoonish thrust against 'the syndicalist demand of "the mines for the miners"' in *Socialisation and Transport*: 'and presumably,' he chortles, '"the dust for the dustmen"'). Boiled down to its pauper's-fare ingredients, Morrison's message was that people should be appointed, by the appropriate minister, to sit on public boards for their 'individual capacity', not 'to do anybody a good turn', nor because they represent any interest. This was especially so in the case of transport, since everyone, including 'the former shareholders', had an interest in it, and, should the principle of the representation of interests be granted validity, each would be clamouring for a seat on the board.

And to clinch the argument, this model of 'paternalistic Socialism' warned delegates that 'within a year' of being appointed to the board, a workers' representative 'will be regarded by the rank and file as a man who has gone over to the boss class and cannot be trusted any more. You all know that is true. He will become more and more impressed with the work of the Board and the case of the Board. It would be better, if you want a trade union fighting policy, that your officials should not see too much of the other side, but should have a free hand to bargain...' Such was Herbert Morrison's faith in the integrity of his brothers!

Not that his point about the danger of defection to the boss class was not pertinent enough, as anyone who has seen for himself the common effect of granting employees marginal representation on management boards and governing bodies (not to mention anyone with adequate knowledge of the history of the Labour Movement!) can testify. But then the advocates of workers' control were not cap-in-hand supplicants for a seat or two on the boards of industries and utilities which were taken into public ownership. They were calling for the workers to have a statutory right 'to an effective share in the control and direction of the industries which their labour sustains', by which they generally meant that at least '50 per cent of the representation on Managerial Committees shall be accorded to workers' nominees.' (Besides which, for the most part they held firmly to the good old trade union principle of mandating delegates - not 'representatives' - with those who elected them retaining the right of recall if they were not satisfied with their delegates' performance.)

The half-share-in-control claim referred to above is part of a resolution from the General and Municipal Workers' Union put to the Trades Union Congress in 1933, and the resolution ended with the bold Socialistic demand: 'This ultimately requires that the control of industry be taken out of the hands of profit-seeking proprietors, and that "Proprietor control" be replaced by "workers' control" in which the trade unions shall be the recognised nucleus of representation for the whole of the workers - manual, clerical, technical and supervisory.' Not the least interesting thing about this resolution is that - this ultimate, revolutionary aim apart - it broadly foreshadows the central recommendations of the Bullock Committee forty-four years later.

At the Labour Party Conference of 1933, Charles Dukes, who had moved the workers' control resolution at the TUC conference, put on behalf of the GMWU a similar resolution, which, although it was (presumably for tactical reasons) markedly moderated and less specific, still called for a statutory right 'to an effective share in control...' etc. In speaking to it, Dukes tackled head on what he called 'the bogy' of 'interests', roundly declaring that 'a more absurd argument could not be put before a conference of Socialists' than that, for instance, on nationalisation of the mines, the miners were to be denied 'a statutory right to run an industry to which they had given their lives.' He pointed out that 'we have all got our interests,' advising delegates to face up to that fact and secure an adequate share of control over their own industries. 'If I understand the meaning of a socialised industry, it is that it is not merely to be a change of ownership; it is to mean more than the mere creation of a rentier class and leaving the control of industry very largely in their hands.'

At the 1932 Party Conference, in the course of speaking to a TGWU amendment to the NEC resolution on nationalising transport, Harold Clay chided Morrison for talking as if they were already living in a Socialist society. 'This is a class society, whether we like to admit it or not; and whether we say that interests will be represented or not, interests will be there. Every interest except that of the people who are actually doing the job.' While rejecting the syndicalist label ('I went through that movement like many others'), Clay declared: 'I believe in political democracy, but I do not believe that can become complete until you have industrial democracy.' And he commented caustically on the NEC report on this issue: 'One of my difficulties in reading this report is that *it appears to assume the permanency of the commodity status of labour*. That, I think, is a fundamental objection. It assumes that the Board will be a kind, benevolent sort of thing that will give to labour an opportunity to learn more about the job. Good heavens! We can teach them more about the job than they ever knew.' [my emphasis]

At the 1932 TUC conference, John Cliff of the TGWU attacked the General Council's report on the management of socialised industry for offering the workers nothing more than Whitleyism [see below]: discussion but not determination, consultation but not executive powers. While G. M. Hann of the Shop Assistants' Union, demanding 'representative industrial authority on which the workers are in a permanent majority by the simple right that they are the biggest factors in industry,' charged that 'public utility control is not workers' control, and it is bordering on perfidy to put that forward as a substitute for workers' control.'

In this struggle for the hearts and minds of the members of the Labour Movement on this crucial issue, the champions of workers' control had the better of the argument but could not win it against the power of the trade union and Party establishments. Coates and Topham sum up the outcome of the battle, with reference to the anodyne formula agreed between the TUC and the Party and reported to Conference in 1935: 'Much debate, and many votes which appeared to favour the principle of workers' control, were...reduced to the most minimal guarantee of a "statutory right" for trade unions to be represented on the board of socialised industries.'

Just how far the Labour Establishment had moved towards grooming itself for full acceptance in the club of the bourgeois democrats is indicated by a commentator unsympathetic to such democratic extremism as workers' control. In *Nationalization in British Industry* (1966, revised edition 1973), Leonard Tivey writes:

'In the outcome of these arguments it became accepted
that workers' participation would mean that some trade
unionists would be appointed to management boards,
and that the trade unions might suggest who these
should be. But they would nevertheless be chosen by the
Government and would retain no ties with their unions.
They would not act as spokesmen for union policy.
Instead, trade union views would be pressed through
compulsory advisory and consultative machinery.'

Having succinctly summed up a power structure in which the
essentially adversarial and supplicatory relationship of labour to
capital and to management remained unchanged, Tivey goes on to
comment:

'The settlement of this issue after 1935 meant that the
main lines of nationalization methods were decided. In
principle, the Labour movement had accepted the
public-corporation model recommended by the Liberals
and initiated by Conservative Governments. There were
some modifications in practice - such as the rights of
trade unions to consultation, and more explicit powers
of control by the Government - but the main structure of
the new institutions was clear and widely accepted by
all parties. A current of opinion in favour of more direct
representation of workers in management has continued,
but so far it has had little effect.'

Contrast this sidelining of the once vigorous campaign for
workers' control with the enthusiastic response to the call to arms from
the Tailors' and Garment-Workers' Union at the Trades Union
Congress in 1925. The brave little tailors moved:

'This Congress declares that the trade union movement
must organise to prepare the trade unions in conjunction
with the party of the workers to struggle for the overthrow
of capitalism. At the same time Congress warns the
workers against all attempts to introduce capitalist schemes
of co-partnership which in the past have failed to give the
workers any positive rights, but instead have usually served

as fetters retarding the forward movements. Congress further considers that strong well-organised shop committees are indispensable weapons in the struggle to force the capitalists to relinquish their grip on industry, and therefore pledges itself to do all in its power to develop and strengthen workshop organisation.'

Patently a call for the workers to rely on their own direct-action power at the point of production ('in conjunction with the party of the workers' is no more than an aside), this resolution in the spirit of revolutionary syndicalism (its mover, a Mr E. Joseph, made no bones about its 'more or less revolutionary character') was carried on a card vote of 2,456,000 to 1,218,000.

What happened to freeze this revolutionary ardour? Within nine months of this clarion call the TUC leaders had made Britain safe again for bourgeois parliamentary democracy by scuttling the General Strike. In such a fundamentally undemocratic, class-riven power structure, fanciful ideas of workers' control (or anything remotely resembling it) could not be countenanced. Predominant opinion among trade union leaders was at one with that of the Labour Party establishment, and remained so during the critical period of post-war Labour power when the infrastructure industries (coal, civil aviation, public transport, electricity, gas, iron and steel) and the overseer of public finance, the Bank of England, were nationalised.

In her Fabian Tract of January 1951, *Workers' Control?*, the Labour MP Eirene White describes a situation in which the once-strong current running for workers' control has been successfully dammed and diverted by the powers that be:

'At Bridlington in 1949, the TUC General Council restated its attitude in the light of its initial experience of nationalised industries. Substantially this statement reaffirmed the 1944 position [defined in *An Interim Report on Post-War Reconstruction*, a document generated from the liaising of the Economic Committee of the TUC and the Labour Party's NEC, and endorsed almost without debate at the 1944 Trades Union Congress], giving pride of place to the public board, with full consultation, but leaving executive responsibility firmly in the hands of management.

"Consultation does not imply diffusion of authority," said the Council, "nor is direct workers' representation in management acceptable." On the contrary, the General Council underlined the need for a trade unionist taking a full-time appointment on a Board to sever his formal connection with his union. Where part-time trade unionists serve, they must come from unions not directly connected with the industry.'

The TUC has generally been blessed with a talent for seeing all sides of the question and accordingly never coming down so decisively on one side or another as to make it difficult to change its position and still appear to be leading from the front. A 1953 report dismissed advocates of workers' control as a minority (an objection applicable to anyone who puts forward an idea before, as the saying goes, its time has come) unsettling the ranks by propagating 'out-of-date ideas about industrial relations' and 'traditional ideas of what constitutes industrial democracy' which *'lead to criticism of the existing structure of nationalisation'*, [my emphasis] when the instilling of a proper understanding of the purposes of 'joint consultative machinery' would have avoided 'disappointment and frustration' amongst those who had wrongly assumed that it conferred some 'executive power to workers' representatives'. A 1963 report, after preambling upliftingly around the theme that 'one of the purposes of trade unionism is to protect and enlarge the freedom and dignity of the individual worker,' and then proceeding downhill to the difficulties of doing this in the context of 'a complex industrial society' in which decisions are largely 'made by business organisations and by Governments,' has the cheek and duplicity to conclude that the workers and their unions are themselves largely to blame for this unpromising situation because they did not press harder for industrial democracy: 'Past efforts in the direction of securing for working people a greater degree of participation in the decisions which affect them have largely been ineffective, partly because of the low priority that unions have accorded to these activities...'

At bottom, of course, lay Humpty Dumpty's ever-present challenge: 'Who's to be the master?' For those for whom it is unarguable that the wealth of nations is most successfully generated by private capitalism, it can only be the businessmen who so benevolently provide jobs for others and 'create wealth' for all. For State Socialists - politicians and trade unionists alike - the answer, though different, is just as clear: for State Socialists of the purest and simplest sort the answer is equally pure and simple - the State; for those with mixed feelings, i.e. the mixed-economy merchants, the answer is either the State or one of those benevolent private bosses, according to what is on offer. For all these paternalistic people workers' control simply does not figure in the equation, except in the inside-out form of how to control the workers. The overriding problem, in fact, for both free-marketeers and State Socialists (plus all shades of paternalists in between) is how to provide capital with the labour it needs to fulfil its divine purpose, to go forth and multiply.

Certainly the concept of industrial democracy did not much exercise the mind of that ex-worker-firebrand Emmanuel Shinwell when it came to piloting through the Commons that nationalisation measure which more than any other seemed to some at the time to mark the emancipation of the workers. The National Coal Board, appointed by Shinwell, as Minister of Fuel and Power, and composed of 'persons appearing to him to be qualified as having had experience of, and having shown capacity in, industrial, commercial or financial matters, applied science, administration, *or the organisation of workers*' [my emphasis], had the duty of establishing machinery to consult with the trade unions on 'questions relating to the safety, health, or welfare' of employees and 'other [unspecified] matters of mutual interest'; but not only were there to be no worker representatives on the Board, but statutory provision for consultation with the workers actually employed in the industry (as distinct from their union officers) was pronounced by Shinwell to be 'superfluous' to 'the existing conciliation machinery', until the astonishment of MPs *on the opposition benches* prompted him to change his mind.

In more radical times, Labour's policy on taking over the mines (always to the forefront of its programme) had been one of confiscation without compensation ('restitution', its champions might with some justice have called it); but since then hearts - and brains - had softened, at least in leadership circles. In a revealing passage in his autobiography *Conflict without Malice* (1955), Shinwell writes that one of his biggest problems was how to reach agreement with the owners on compensation for pits that in most instances were so run down that without massive investment they would yield little or no profit, and indeed might involve losses to the owners. Not everybody concerned in the matter saw things in quite the same way. 'The miners themselves,' says Shinwell (in a great leap of empathy with the 'caryatids of civilisation', to use Orwell's memorable words), 'did, of course, include many whose bitter experiences precluded any feeling of sympathy for the owners.'

Of course, workers in the industry had rather less reason than their ministerial comrade to be complaisant about the way the nation at last took over the pits; but there were others, too, who did not share the Minister's magnanimity. Putting to the 1948 Labour Party Conference a resolution calling for the immediate nationalisation of the iron and steel industry, without compensation and instituting 'a complete scheme of control by the workers engaged in the industry' (a 'principle...to be applied to all industries nationalised, past and present'), Mr H. Ratner of Salford North District Labour Party commented caustically:

> 'When the workers voted for the Labour Government in
> 1945 they did so in the belief that the nationalisation of
> the basic industries would take the burden of rent,
> interest and profit off the back of the industry, but in the
> nationalisation of the coal industry, the Bank of
> England...and the other industries...the principle adopted
> is that the ex-owners of the industries are guaranteed
> more or less the same amount of money in the form of
> compensation as they were getting before in the form of
> dividends. All that has happened is that the State has
> taken over the running of the industry for the benefit of
> the ex-owners...'

He intemperately demanded that 'the first charge must be not compensation to the ex-owners, but the interests of the working class and the freedom of the country as a whole: the giving to the workers in the industry of a decent standard of living...'

At the behest of the NEC the Conference rejected this motion in favour of an amendment from the Association of Engineering and Shipbuilding Draughtsmen that effectively gutted it of all its radical elements. Truth, however, was on the side of the comrades of Salford North DLP. Who could feel surprised that, despite expeditiously redeeming the relevant pledges in Labour's 1945 manifesto, the Attlee Government's 'nationalisation measures were not accorded great respect by British socialists,' as Sked and Cook put it, with some moderation, in their *Post-War Britain*? And they explain why:

> 'As time went on the defects of the programme became ever more apparent. To start with, it seemed that many of the previous owners had been compensated over-generously; £164,600,000 was paid out, for example, to the mine owners, leaving miners to think that the fruit of their labour was destined even yet - and for some time to come - to find its way into familiar pockets. Moreover, since these former owners were now able to invest this money in much more profitable enterprises, *it seemed as if the Government had really rewarded capital instead of labour*. Thus nationalisation signified no new beginning for labour. No transformation of its relationship with capital occurred. In practice all that happened was that the state bought out the former owners and allowed the former management to remain. Labour was accorded no greater say in industrial decision-making, and since it shared in no profits it gained no economic benefit either.' [my emphasis]

So, in the first place, while nationalisation may have given a wee fillip to the 'dignity' of labour for those who were freed from their former masters to be marshalled instead by the State, without any significant move in the direction of industrial or economic democracy it did nothing to change the essential status of the worker from what pioneer Socialists had had no hesitation in calling him, namely, a 'wage-slave'.

Secondly, Sked and Cook strip away the pretensions of Labour's nationalisation measure to amount to anything more than what might be called techno-socialism:

> 'Finally, there was the criticism of Labour's policy (from the socialist point of view) that in spite of all the fuss the commanding heights had never really been attacked. The 20 per cent of the economy taken over by the government was to a large extent the unprofitable part, while the

profitable sector remained firmly in the hands of private enterprise. *Socialist planning of this type was acceptable even to Conservatives.*' [my emphasis]

Sked and Cook could have added, ' - all the more so since the breaking-even-rather-than-profit-making target generally set by government for nationalised industries meant, in effect, that, whether they were subsidised or not, the way they were run amounted to a concealed subsidy to private industry and commerce.'

Truth, too, came out of the mouths of Tories and Liberals (however ulterior their motives might have been) when the Coal Nationalisation Bill was debated in the Commons. The miners had a proud campaigning tradition not just for nationalisation, but for workers' control. Probably the most celebrated of all the calls for workers' control is that of the Reform Committee of the South Wales Miners, whose pamphlet of 1912, *The Miners' Next Step*, actually warned the workers that State nationalisation would simply benefit society's landlords and capitalists, and calling for industrial democracy, declared: 'Any other form of democracy is a delusion and a snare.' And when the mines came close to being nationalised after the First World War (following the temporary wartime nationalisation) the Miners' Federation of Great Britain was telling the Sankey Commission it wanted fifty per cent representation in management. All such aspirations had melted away by 1945, and for the most part it was not Labour MPs who drew attention to this when at last the pits became public property. Describing the reception of Shinwell's bill in the House in *Labour's First Year*, J.E.D. Hall focuses in particular on three members of the opposition parties:

'It was a Bill, said Anthony Eden, to set up a State monopoly for the production of coal and nothing else. Would the evils disappear once it came under the aegis of the State? Was this the nationalisation the miners wanted - or thought they wanted? The old cry "the mines for the miners" had no place in this Bill. The same men would be managing the mines as before, observed others. Where else could the Minister get them? The miner would go to the same pit and get the same lamp from the same man, said Major Lloyd-

George. He would go into the same cage, be lowered by the same man - and would see the same expression on the face of the pony! Would it make all the difference if the boss was different? One of the complaints under private enterprise was that the boss was so remote. But this one would be even more remote. The boss would be a board composed of nine men - "nine bright shiners" Harold Macmillan called them. They would not be elected by the mining community. The miner would have only one source of employment and he could not change his employer. Surely from the miner's point of view this could not be called a "good swap."'

One Labour back-bencher who, to his credit, did have something to say about the question of bosses, old and new, was the MP for Belper, George Brown, who argued that in the coal mines in particular, 'a very wide measure of industrial democracy is essential.' In the midst of the euphoria of the Labour victors around him, he sounded a decidedly wistful note: 'When I am in my division I frequently stay with mining friends. The last time I was there I was sitting by the fire with two old stalwarts; one of them, who was gently chiding me and pulling my leg, turned to his friends and said, "You know, it will be the same thing under another name."' That is the kind of native wisdom to which George Eliot pays tribute in *Middlemarch*, where an old rural labourer, told that the coming of the railway's 'a good thing', replies, 'Aw! good for the big folks to make money out on,' and says of all the changes he has seen, 'an' it's been all aloike to the poor mon.'

In *Labour in Power*, Kenneth O. Morgan writes of the State take-over of the pits: 'No single measure in the earlier phase of the Attlee government aroused more genuine or spontaneous enthusiasm than did the nationalisation of the coal-mines. On Vesting Day, 1 January 1947, there were mass demonstrations of rejoicing in mining communities from South Wales to Nottingham, Yorkshire, Durham, and Fife, as the flag of the NCB replaced the ensign of the old, discredited private coal-owners.' Had the miners had a better understanding of what they had been fobbed off with, one might have strained one's ears to catch the faintest sound of cheering. But then how many of those Labour politicians who were convinced they were representing the best interests of the vanguard of the Labour Movement understood the point of Macmillan's remark: 'This is not nationalisation; it is State capitalism'?

The kindest comment - still commensurate with the truth - one can make on the tragic failure of the Labour leaders (political and industrial) to proceed towards the genuine 'socialisation' (ironically, that was the term that Herbert Morrison preferred to 'nationalisation', though with democratisation excluded, what he gave the Movement was 'bureaucratisation') of industry when they had the chance is Sked and Cook's: that the question was approached with 'timidity and naiveté' and 'with no imagination whatsoever'. In all too many cases, however, it would probably get nearer the heart of the matter to point the finger at their fundamentally anti-democratic mind-sets and at that ingrained paternalism which hoards power like others accumulate wealth - though perhaps the two kinds of covetousness are simply opposite sides of the same coin. Most of these authoritarians were too fly to oppose the idea of workers' control with quite the aristocratic scorn and candour of Sir Stafford Cripps, whose pronouncement of the present impossibility of 'worker-controlled industry, even if it were on the whole desirable' raised a storm in Conference. (Among those he provoked was the Salford North delegate referred to above, who scathingly remarked that he was 'once a Socialist' but now 'we wonder whether he knows in which party he is'.) But, as the saying goes, there is more than one way to skin a cat, and in the light of the perfidy and pusillanimity that (in those years chronicled by Coates and Topham) repeatedly thwarted comrades struggling to gain for the workers a real voice where it mattered most, in their working lives, the sly slaughtering of Bullock - the last (?final) act in the long campaign for workers' control - was all too predictable.

CHAPTER 30

Labour's leviathan

'Open government is a contradiction in terms. You can be open, or you can have government.'

Sir Humphrey Appleby in BBC Television's
Yes, Minister

'When he asked me if I was hungry, he really forgot for a second or two that he was nothing but a servant of the state. Then he became quite human and showed that he still had some soul left. Nothing strange about that. To be hungry is human. To have papers or not to have papers is inhuman. It is against nature's laws. That's the point. There is a good reason for being the way he is. The state cannot make use of human beings. It would cease to exist. Human beings only make trouble. Men cut out of cardboard do not make trouble. Yessir. Excuse me, I mean: yes, sir.'

Ben Traven, *The Death Ship* (1926)

In opposition Labour can generally be relied on to champion liberty, at home and abroad. [STOP PRESS. This sentence was written before shadow home secretary Jack Straw showed his determination not to be outflanked to the right by the most reactionary Home Secretary since the war on the issue of law and order, by substantially endorsing increased powers for the police and security services to bug and burgle 'in the public interest' contained in Michael Howard's 1997 Police Bill.] In office what it does is quite another matter. This is only partially explicable in ideological terms. Managerialism is only one strand in Labour's ideology. Besides which, though it might be considered an onerous brief to have to defend Labour against the charge that it is the dominant strand, on the other hand Labour rightly argues, in contradiction to the specious claims of Tory 'self-styled libertarians', that in capitalist societies (no less than in feudal ones) the authority of the State can be - and not infrequently has been, both in pre-democratic and in 'democratic' ages - protective of the relatively powerless rather than oppressive. Labour, in short, rightly refutes the charge that it is *more* authoritarian than its Tory opponents, whether these be of either the paternalistic or the self-styled libertarian variety. As a more or less sincere exponent of what we have come to call, with a minimal measure of analysis, 'democratic socialism', it is, all in all, *less* so.

Labour rightly underlines the negative and atomising nature of the traditional 'liberal democratic' attitude to liberty, which largely ignores the dearth of freedom implicit in the gross inequality in the power to choose which is immanent in capitalist society - an in-built situation memorably captured in Anatole France's observation that the millionaire and the tramp are equally at liberty to sleep under bridges. The Socialist realisation that liberty and equality are not rivals but inseparable partners should be Labour's greatest strength. However, as with a number of other fundamental issues, Labour has always been afraid to take the offensive on this score - an irony to which we will return.

Less tainted by moral nannyism so far as social (and particularly sexual) behaviour goes, it is not to be denied that Labour's 'good shepherd' tendencies show that it has more in common with Tory paternalism than it can comfortably admit. What out of office is nothing more than another set of contending opinions is transmuted by the assumption of 'democratic' authority into a prescriptive mandate: exhortation becomes command. This follows ineluctably from the nature of the State and of government as an instrument to implement reforms, especially when these add up to a potentially substantial restructuring of society foreshadowing an attempt to 'remould it nearer to the heart's desire'.

No degree of commitment to the ideal of freedom is proof against the corruption of power, as that quintessential Whig historian Lord Acton, mentor and intimate friend of Gladstone, warned a hundred years ago. 'Power tends to corrupt,' he wrote, 'and absolute power corrupts absolutely. Great men are nearly always bad men.' Nine years after Acton's death the last government formed by that party which believes itself to be peculiarly touched by the grace of truly cherishing civil liberties, laid down the very corner-stone of the institutional dominion wielded by the executive (or to speak more precisely, by the prime minister and a handful of his chosen fellow hierarchs) under the British system of government. On Friday 18th August 1911 an Official Secrets Bill that had been introduced in the Lords and accepted without amendment was presented to the Commons. Within thirty minutes it had been pushed through all its stages, and four days later, having received the Royal Assent, it was law. To those few Members who had still been in the House during that outstandingly inglorious half-hour in the annals of British parliamentary government, the Bill had been represented by the ministerial mountebanks charged with ensuring its passage as an uncontroversial measure designed solely to strengthen the powers of the State to tackle the menace of foreign spies. In fact, nominally at least, it gave (*and gives*) the government in power total control over the dissemination of official information, and with it, draconian sanctions against civil servants, journalists, and the citizenry in general who handle or pass on that information without being authorised to do so.

Labour may not assume that special grace alluded to above, but it does make particular claims to upholding the democratic rights of the people. So it is instructive to contrast the critical assaults launched by Labour on the erosion of liberty and democracy since the State became a tool of the New Tories with the record of Labour in power - particularly during the Wilson/Callaghan period, since that provides the closest parallels in concern and response, while at the same time quite accurately reflecting Labour's whole in-office record. The aspects of governance we shall focus on are those concerning State secrets and government confidentiality, along with the operations of the security services, the police, and the judiciary to safeguard them against the prying eyes of its citizens. The issue which looms over all these matters is the inherent conflict between executive power on the one hand and democratic accountability on the other. Such accountability - to the representatives of the people in Parliament and ultimately to what may be called (in theoretical discussion of representative democracy, at least, though the term is hardly strictly in accord with British constitutional realities) 'the sovereign people' - is dependent on the right to know, together with the actual possibility of finding out. The final years of the Wilson/Callaghan regimes threw up two spectacular examples of the absence of the right to know under Britain's system of parliamentary government, besides numerous lesser ones. One of these two spectaculars, which we shall look at later, concerned the Government's failure to enforce the sanctions it had itself imposed on the rebel regime in Rhodesia. The other pitched the executive into open conflict both with the more independent-minded members of the legislature and with the Fourth Estate (and equally pitched the Labour leadership into conflict with both wings of the Labour Movement) through a secrets trial which surpassed in absurdity the Whitehall 'spycatcher' farce with which, when its turn came, the Thatcher regime was so brilliantly to entertain us.

The ABC trial (as it came to be known from the surnames of the men in the dock) had its source, like so many other noxious emanations of those times, in the Cold War alliance and the supposed 'special relationship' between Britain and the United States. In February 1977 the Home Secretary, Merlyn Rees, told the Commons - to supportive remarks from his shadow, Willie Whitelaw, and from other members of the official Opposition, and outraged cries from the unofficial opposition behind him that he was behaving like the Czech authorities did towards the signatories of Charter 77 - that he was sticking to his decision to deport two American citizens in the interests of national security. One of them, Philip Agee, was a former officer of America's Central Intelligence Agency who had undoubtedly angered his erstwhile masters by his revelations about the CIA, though Rees naturally denied that CIA pressure had anything to do with his decision. The other, Mark Hosenball, was a less street-wise idealist whose dad, Neil, was actually a senior legal adviser to the US space-flight agency, NASA, the National Aeronautics and Space Administration. Mark Hosenball was employed by the London *Evening News*, and according to his editor, Simon Jenkins, he was being victimised by a Labour Home Secretary for being 'a Left-wing investigative journalist'.

Since Rees' original decision, in November 1976, that the presence in Britain of these two men whom he clearly looked on as Cold War subversives was 'not conducive to the public good', both of them had submitted themselves to what Jenkins described as the 'charade' of appealing to the tribunal of 'three wise men' instituted by Heath's Government in 1971 to consider - *in camera* and with no independent powers to detail either charges or evidence, or even to name, let alone to summon for cross-examination, witnesses, and no authority to do more than make *sub rosa* recommendations to the Home Secretary - appeals against such deportation orders. Following Rees's confirmation of his decision, Hosenball applied for and was granted the right to a judicial appeal. This, however, served only to underline the absolutist nature of the Home Secretary's powers. The Lord Chief Justice, Lord Widgery, speaking for all three judges at the hearing in the Queen's Bench Divisional Court, made it clear that under the law the imperatives of natural justice were overruled by those of public security as perceived by the Home Secretary. 'Where matters of public security are in issue and where a minister has certified that certain matters should not be disclosed, they will not be disclosed.' The court did not know what the offence was, but it was only concerned with whether the minister had acted in good faith, which of course was not in question, and whether he had committed any procedural error, which he had not. Accordingly, it refused to quash the deportation order.

In due course the deportations were carried out. But the rumpus the deportation orders had aroused, far from dying down and becoming as stirring as *yesterday's* shock-horror news, was greatly amplified, even before the orders were implemented, by the news that three supporters of the Agee-Hosenball Defence Committee had been arrested by Special Branch officers and charged, after forty-four hours in police custody, under Section Two of the Official Secrets Act. The three accused were John Berry, who had served for four years in the Royal Signals Corps as a Signals Intelligence specialist, Crispin Aubrey, a reporter on *Time Out*, and Duncan Campbell, a freelance journalist and regular contributor to *Time Out*, *Undercurrents*, and *New Scientist*. What had brought these three together, making them, in the eyes of the Special Branch, co-conspirators, was an article in *Time Out* entitled 'The Eavesdroppers', co-authored by Mark Hosenball and Duncan Campbell, on whose researches it was largely based. It was reading this article and relating it to his army service that had prompted Berry to go to the offices of the National Council for Civil Liberties and talk to members of the Agee-Hosenball Defence Committee. Berry told them that he had followed the affair with particular interest because of his SIGINT experience, commenting:

'Both the extent of intelligence activities of this nature and the resources which the British Government deploys in this area are largely unknown to the public. The fact that they remain unknown is due in no small measure to the considerable pressure placed on people who have or have had access to the facts. It appears to me that

410

secrecy is one of the most important keys to power and the existence of an organisation spending vast sums of money in the total absence of public control should do much to dispel any illusions about the democratic nature of our Government.'

The Home Secretary had already demonstrated how to spatter egg all over his own face in this unsavoury imbroglio. Now it was the turn of the Attorney-General, Sam Silkin, to show that he was not to be outdone when it came to clowning. Just as the decision to deport Agee and Hosenball was solely the Home Secretary's, so the decision to apply to the High Court for permission to prosecute the ABC trio, on the basis of the meagre evidence of serious conspiracy unearthed by Detective Superintendent Harry Nicholls and his team of subversion-busters, was the Attorney-General's alone. Labour was committed by its 1974 manifesto to progressing towards more open government, and in particular to reforming the Official Secrets Act. Even more specifically, Merlyn Rees had - only that last November before Sam Silkin had to make up his mind how best to deal with the troublesome trio - announced the Government's decision (in line with the recommendations of the Franks Committee set up by Heath's Government) to replace Section Two of the Official Secrets Act with a less catch-all formula, adding: 'Although the operation of the Act is a matter for the Attorney-General, it will no doubt be open to the Attorney-General to take into account the Government's intention to introduce legislation on the lines I have indicated in considering whether to bring prosecutions under Section 2.' Rees made it clear that the Government accepted that 'mere receipt of official information should no longer be an offence.' Yet as the NCCL predicted at the time of the ABC arrests, when it was still possible for sanity to prevail over a policy of mutton-headed repression of Britain's dissidents: 'In contrast with the Labour Party's manifesto, which promises more open government, Mr Callaghan and Mr Rees have in the last four months made it clear that the Labour Government will harass and intimidate any journalist who attempts to investigate matters which the Government wants hidden.' The Government had already wielded the State cudgel against two American truth-revealers. Now it was about to blunder into a hornet's nest by an assault on British journalists and the freedom of the press, and even, as we shall see shortly, on the hallowed privileges of Parliament.

The ABC affair dragged on damagingly, while the Right Honourable Samuel Silkin chewed his nails and agonised and Harry Nicholls and his team took a crash-course in the anti-democratic nature of British government by rummaging through the thousands of damning documents seized from Duncan Campbell's Brighton flat. Doubtless because of the embarrassment of bringing prosecutions solely dependent on a part of the Official Secrets Act that the Government itself had admitted was untenable, in May further charges were heaped on the heads of the terrible trio. These were brought under Section One of the Act, which was commonly understood to apply only to espionage on behalf of a foreign power. The fishing operations and scissors-and-paste labours of the Special Branch sleuths brought the calendar round to November before committal proceedings could be held. The opening of the trial itself was still nearly a year away, but a cloudburst of protest was about to precipitate copious quantities of indignation, derision, and defiance on the Government's head.

The prosecution's principal witness in persuading the magistrates that those charged had a case to answer was to have been a man who was not even prepared to accept the magistrates' direction that his name should be given to the defence in confidence. So the utterly mysterious Lieutenant-Colonel A (as he was denominated) was replaced by the somewhat less mysterious Colonel B, whose name was revealed in writing to the accuseds' counsels, though not, of course, to the accused themselves. It was, however, no masterly feat of espionage to work out his identity, since he obligingly gave his army number in open court and referred to a specific issue of his own regimental journal, *The Wire*, in which his name and post had been published. Colonel B, who testified in the magistrates' court that his own testimony was damaging to the national interest since 'there should not be any public discussion of Britain's SIGINT activities at all', before making the positively Kafkaesque observation that 'the regulations governing the secret handling of this intelligence are themselves secret', was unmasked by *Peace News* and *The Leveller* as a Colonel Hugh Johnstone - a revelation of great moment, no doubt, to Soviet intelligence!

One could say the colonel then became a household name, since his name was subsequently broadcast on radio and television, batted about in the House of Commons by unruly MPs, launched on red balloons released by dissidents from London's GPO Tower, and even carved in ten-foot-high letters on the beach at Whitley Bay, Northumberland - all of which, according to the prosecuting authorities, made him damaged goods from an intelligence point of view. For prosecutions were now brought against the two campaigning journals and against the National Union of Journalists, whose own publication, *The Journalist*, had given further unwanted publicity to the by now utterly unmysterious colonel in the course of citing motions submitted by branches for debate at the annual delegate meeting of the NUJ, to be held at, yes, Whitley Bay.

In May the three journals were fined for contempt (£200 in the case of *The Journalist*, £500 each for the campaigning journals which had first exposed the unhappy colonel) by the Queen's Bench Divisional Court, again presided over by Lord Widgery. The Court of Appeal upheld the High Court judgement, but on 1st February 1979 the five Law Lords unanimously overturned the ruling and awarded costs against the Crown. (The fines had, in any case, failed to deter *Peace News* from further acts of subversive defiance. To demonstrate 'its opposition to official secrecy, not only in theory but in practice', it published another account of Signals Intelligence work - this time by a former Royal Navy conscript - and revealed the identity of the recently-appointed head of MI6, the first time a British intelligence chief had been publicly named while still in office. And, with maximum provocation in the timing, it committed these criminal acts a week and a half before the ABC trial was to open. Yet they went unpunished.)

Meanwhile the right-to-know row had moved from Whitley Bay to Westminster, the very centre of the constitutional web. The fabled blessings of the British constitution spring from the separation of powers invested in the State between the executive, the legislature, and the judiciary; but the country was about to witness a series of unseemly brawls between the rival arms of the State. When Jo Richardson, followed by three other Labour MPs, provocatively named the once incognito colonel during question time in the House, the Director of Public Prosecutions - at the urging of the Attorney-General, Sam Silkin - promptly warned the Press, through a memorandum to the Press Association, that publishing Colonel B's real name could constitute a contempt of court. This was notwithstanding the fact that it had already reached the ears of millions of people half an hour earlier, through broadcast reports of proceedings in the House.

But there was a much bigger 'notwithstanding' than that, for MPs may say what they please in the House so long as it is within the Rules of Order, and Parliament has an unfettered right to publish its proceedings. The DPP certainly had no powers to gag Hansard. To the credit of the Fourth Estate, not a single newspaper allowed itself to be intimidated by the DPP's warning; but the question remained, 'Did Parliament's right to full publication extend to the Press?' All members of the House are jealous of its privileges, and it was a Tory MP, Graham Page, who described the DPP's action as 'a contempt of Parliament', submitting to the Speaker that it was a prima facie breach of parliamentary privilege, while the most forthright intervention in a subsequent debate on the issue came from the redoubtable right-winger Enoch Powell, who declared: 'I cannot imagine a more direct assault upon the essential privilege of this House.' Unsurprisingly, when this hot potato was passed to the Commons Committee of Privileges, composed of senior members of the House *and including the Attorney-General*, it was far more cautious - not to say mealy-mouthed - in its pronouncements, exonerating the DPP on the grounds that his warning had only been guidance, and failing to grapple with the vital issue of whether the privilege of free speech in Parliament extended to the reporting of it by the media.

Concern for the rights of the Fourth Estate (at least in so far as it constitutes a just-about-indispensable publicity machine for elected politicians!) was not the only cause of conflict between 'the High Court of Parliament' and the judicial arm of the State. Members pressing for a debate in the House on the freedom-of-speech issues arising from the ABC affair unexpectedly won assent from Michael Foot as Leader of the House, only to find themselves gagged by the Speaker's ruling that the matter was now *sub judice*. Then in November the threat of a punch-up between the legislative and judicial arms of the State, following an MP's complaint that the secrets trial judge, Mr Justice Mars-Jones, had shown disrespect for Parliament by neglecting to observe the convention that permission must be sought before referring to ministerial statements published in Hansard, was again only averted by shunting the issue into that misty marshalling yard for mislaying matters which embarrass the establishment, the Commons Committee of Privileges.

All this time the machinery of State justice was grinding on inexorably to crush the menace of the ABC conspirators. Aubrey's alleged offences were the least serious; but when the trial proper at last got under way on 5th September, both Berry and Campbell still faced a charge under Section One of the Official Secrets Act that carried a maximum penalty of fourteen years in prison, since they had turned down plea-bargaining offers from the prosecution. The case had only be running for ten days when the first trial judge, Mr Justice Willis, ordered a retrial because some other pestilential journalist had referred in a broadcast to the presence on the jury of a former member of the Special Air Service (he had, in fact, been chosen by his fellow jurors as their foreman) and of two other jurors who had signed pledges to observe the Official Secrets Act.

Defence counsel had already raised the awkward question of just how impartial the jury could be said to be by protesting that, contrary to accepted practice, the jury panel for the ABC trial had been vetted by the security services. Leading counsel for the Crown, John Leonard QC, admitted the vetting, elucidating the issue with the observation: 'Anyone who is known to have been disloyal would obviously be disqualified.' Which in turn prompted the NCCL to challenge the Attorney-General to make it clear who decided if a person was loyal or not for the purpose of jury selection and on what criteria the decision was made. The clash over jury-vetting in the ABC case led to the official (but secret!) guidelines drawn up in 1975 *for the benefit of prosecuting counsel* being made public, and to the revelation that there had been twenty-five previous occasions during that period when the Crown had weeded out 'unreliable' jurors. Suspected vulnerability to intimidation and/or bribery accounted for about half of these and assumed partisan sympathies in 'terrorist' cases in Northern Ireland to the bulk of the others; but the guidelines made it clear that suspicions of 'disloyalty' could be invoked in cases brought under the Official Secrets Act.

When the stalled trial was restarted, on 3rd October, it was under Mr Justice Mars-Jones, since Mr Justice Willis had had the good fortune to fall sick with tummy trouble. The flimsy nature of the case pieced together against the ABC trio was at once made obvious to the thickest plank on the jurors' bench by the prosecution's announcement that it would be offering no evidence on the most serious charge against Duncan Campbell: that he had collected information about defence communications which was prejudicial to the safety and interests of the State. Mr Leonard (over whom, as Lord Hutchinson QC was to remark in his closing speech as counsel for Campbell, 'an amazing change' had come 'since those early weeks when you first heard him make his original address to you') implicitly admitted that he had been much impressed by the quantity of the material submitted by the defence to prove that the material found in Mr Campbell's possession was already in the public domain. (Not the least droll revelation during this exceedingly droll affair was that this journalist with what Mr Leonard considered an unusual interest in Signals - though Leonard himself described Campbell as 'a qualified and brilliant scientist' - was the co-author of an Open University book on the subject which was about to be published, and that a copy of this book containing much allegedly classified information had been found in his briefcase when he was arrested.)

Mr Leonard's admission showed how badly briefed the distinguished barrister was; but his pretext for the charge having been brought in the first place was truly risible. 'When I opened the case originally, I told the jury that much of the information was no doubt culled from published sources. It was the Crown's contention, nevertheless, that Campbell had committed an offence because much of the information was added to and interpreted with his observations as a skilled scientist, and was built up so as to be likely to be of value to an enemy.'

The real offence, it was thus made clear, was the application of *unauthorised* intelligence to the scrutiny of the State's security operations as published strictly for the attention of its own designated servants; plus the communicating of this information in an accessible form to 'the common people'. Campbell had acted, in fact, as a kind of civic spy, in the spirit of Crispin Aubrey's affirmation to his fellow journalists at their Whitley Bay conference that it was their duty to inform the public about matters they could not find out for themselves, 'not to support those people in positions of power who simply wish to avoid embarrassment.'

Having begun to unravel, the case against the conspirators unwound itself into a virtual nullity at a quite giddy rate considering its constitutional gravitas. After a day and a half of legalistic argy-bargy in its absence, the jury was instructed on 24th October to ignore all four remaining charges under the 'spies'' section of the Official Secrets Act, which left only four Section Two charges, carrying a maximum penalty of two years' imprisonment, to be dealt with. On 6th November the jury was directed to return a 'not guilty' verdict on one Section Two charge against Crispin Aubrey. Now, instead of the formidable nine-count indictment the State had levelled at them in the first place, the three defendants faced only one charge each under the less serious Section Two. On 10th November, motivated perhaps by concern that the prosecution might be utterly discredited and the law appear 'a ass' if all the defendants got off scot-free and he was left with no one to pass sentence on, the judge directed the jury to convict the most vulnerable of them, the ex-corporal John Berry, on the one remaining charge against him. For this direction Mr Justice Mars-Jones earned himself a rebuke from a former Lord of Appeal, Lord Devlin, who pronounced it 'contrary to modern authority' to deprive a jury of the right to acquit.

In the event a vengeful State secured convictions against the upstart journalists as well as against the disloyal ex-soldier, after the jury had agonised over its verdicts for nearly sixty-eight hours and spent three nights in a hotel. And Mars-Jones proved himself a judicious chap after all by the leniency of the sentences he dished out on 17th November: six months suspended for two years for Berry, conditional discharges for three years for Aubrey and Campbell.

But there was no hiding the truth that it had been a State-sledgehammer-to-crack-three-subversive-nuts' affair which had cost the taxpayer a quarter of a million pounds and the Labour Government a great deal more in wasted credit. The very fact that the trial judge had felt constrained to warn both the media and demonstrators showing their solidarity with the defendants that it was 'improper' to try 'to influence the jury's verdict' and dangerous to 'ignore the sub-judice principle and to comment on criminal proceedings during their currency', and then in his summing-up, after flattering the jury by calling it 'the last bastion of freedom', to tell its members they must put out of their heads the campaign to secure the acquittal of the three men, showed how futile it was to try to silence those not prepared to accept that a State describing itself as democratic had the right to keep secret from its citizens whatever it chose.

As this tangled tale of contumacious citizens challenging the authority of the State (Rex v. John Citizen, one might call it) unfolded, the Labour establishment had become increasingly jittery, its rank and file increasingly restless. On the day the ABC trial opened in the Old Bailey, GMWU general secretary David Basnett, chairing the TUC conference at Brighton, postponed debate on an NUJ resolution calling for the prosecutions to be dropped and for the introduction of a Freedom of Information Act. Since pressure from Basnett, TUC general secretary Len Murray, and other members of the General Council failed to persuade the NUJ delegation to remit its motion to the General Council for a quiet interment, it was ruled out of order on the grounds that the matter was now *sub judice*, provoking NUJ president Dennis MacShane to walk out of the conference. Before the decision to impose a gag on the parliament of labour had been confirmed, MacShane acidly remarked: 'We find it highly ironic that a motion about freedom of information should have its debate suppressed by the TUC General Council. He went on to assert that the real problem with his union's motion to the TUC conference was not legal but political. 'A general election is looming and it is clear that the TUC wants no debate which will involve major criticisms of the Government. The Government's track record on official secrets is a shiny black spot in its general record.'

In the ranks of the Labour Party itself, inside as well as outside the PLP, rebelliousness over the Official Secrets brouhaha and the issues of freedom of information and freedom of expression flourished. The attempt by the DPP to gag the press when the ABC affair was aired in Parliament had provoked more than fifty Labour MPs to sign a motion condemning his interference. A similar number of awkward squaddies called for a PLP meeting to discuss the ABC prosecutions. A few Labour MPs publicly - and doubtless many more privately - had urged the Attorney-General to drop the charges against the ABC trio. Now that the trial was over, one of those who had gone public on the matter, Robin Cook, called the 'token' sentences a moral victory for the defendants, suggested the Attorney-General should resign, and declared: 'The Home Secretary must introduce, as a matter of urgency, the long-overdue reform of the Official Secrets Act.'

And in this most ticklish business the Government was quite bereft of that excuse which so often served to extenuate its inaction or backsliding. For nominally at least there was almost universal agreement in the House on the need to reform the Official Secrets Act, and there were enough genuine champions of more open government on the Tory benches to have made it devilishly difficult for the Opposition leaders openly to resist a vigorous push for reform had one been forthcoming. One Tory MP with a particular personal reason for interest in the ABC affair was Jonathan Aitken, who in 1971 had himself been acquitted on a Section Two charge arising from his despatches to *The Sunday Telegraph* on the war in the Nigerian province of Biafra. When the ABC trial was over he commented that the Attorney-General had been 'badly advised by the security services' and had 'made an expensive error of judgement in preferring the Section One charges.'

Outside the party cockpit, striking endorsements of the call for reform came from two pillars of the State whose lives had been spent in the defence of law and order. With the ABC 'conspirators' still in the dock, the former Metropolitan Police Commissioner, Sir Robert Mark, published his memoirs, in which he said he would like to see Section Two of the Official Secrets Act repealed, but that if it remained in the Statute Book he would still hope to see it increasingly ignored. And at almost the same moment a Law Lord, Lord Justice Scarman, addressing the Royal Institute of Public Administration, made a sweeping attack on government obsession with secrecy. He called for a Freedom of Information Act on the lines of those enjoyed - and shown to be workable - in Sweden and the USA, but correctly predicted that the Government would 'totally fail to formulate any general principle governing the right of access to official information.'

Despite its promises the Government showed little inclination seriously to reform this discredited Act and still less to honour Labour's 1974 manifesto commitment to introduce a Freedom of Information Bill. On the contrary, its White Paper on these issues was rightly described at the Blackpool Conference of 1978 as 'a mouse', and when the Liberal MP Clement Freud succeeded in getting a private member's Freedom of Information Bill on to the floor of the House, Government ministers in effect colluded with the Opposition front-bench to water it down and wreck it. Their unholy alliance was superfluous, however, as the Government fell nine days before the bill was due to come up for full debate, and it was thus consigned to the wastepaper bin.

'A story of unrelieved folly on the part of the Crown,' pronounced *The Guardian* on the day the ABC trial ended so humiliatingly for the prosecution. There's nothing uncommon about folly in the history of government, whatever the political colour of the rulers. What was outstanding about this particular specimen of folly was the extent to which the government in question damaged its reputation in the eyes of its own supporters and made itself stink in the nostrils of those not inconsiderable sections of the electorate whose libertarian leanings left them with little or no meaningful choice but to vote for Labour or stay at home. For MacShane was not overstating things all that much in saying after walking out of the Brighton congress to show his disgust at being gagged that the Callaghan Government had 'the worst record of any this century in trying to limit the freedom of expression.'

On the other hand, it was Callaghan's misfortune that it was during his premiership that the noisome evidence of one of the most shameful episodes in the post-war history of the British Commonwealth bubbled to the surface, since it was his predecessor who was chiefly to blame. But as one speaker in the 1978 Labour Conference debate on open government exclaimed, if Labour had legislated earlier for the public's right to know, the country might not have had to wait ten years to hear the truth about the oil sanctions scandal. He was alluding to the fact that when the white-settler government led by Ian Smith resolved on UDI (unilateral declaration of independence), the Wilson Government, having persuaded the United Nations to impose mandatory sanctions on Rhodesia, gave every appearance of actively and wholeheartedly participating in the blockade (even to deploying British warships to patrol the seas off the port of Beira, in the Portuguese colony of Mozambique, over a period of nine years), while secretly conniving at the flouting of the law and the subterfuges by which Western companies (including Shell and British Petroleum, a company in which the British government held a controlling share) conspired to keep the oil flowing which kept the rebel government's war-machine running which prolonged the war which piled the corpses high.

This murky business began to come to light in June 1976, with the publication in the USA by the United Church of Christ of *The Oil Conspiracy*, a report based largely on information leaked to a shadowy anti-apartheid organisation called Okhela, led by the Afrikaans poet Breyten Breytenbach. At about the same time 'Tiny' Rowland, head of Lonrho, a company with major interests in southern Africa, made allegations to the British Government about sanctions-busting operations. The publication in Britain, in March

1978, by the Anti-Apartheid Movement and the Haslemere Group, of another report, concentrating on sanctions-busting by Shell and BP, followed by questions in the House, made it imperative for the Government to act. Thomas Bingham, QC, an obscure London barrister who was destined to become the highest justice in the land, was commissioned to investigate the allegations, and he presented his report to the Foreign Secretary, Dr David Owen, on 22nd August 1978.

Four weeks passed before the report was released, but by then *The Guardian* had published a leaked draft; and although it was at once clear that Bingham had stuck strictly to his brief to investigate the conduct of the British oil companies - as distinct from the conduct of government ministers and civil servants - vaporous intimations of an accusatory finger hovered menacingly over many a venerable head. Rarely outside Lilliput has such nimble footwork, such deft passing of the buck, been seen amongst such eminent men of affairs. Within days of Bingham's findings being delivered to Dr Owen, a pre-emptive strike was launched by the verdantly-styled Lord Greenhill of Harrow, permanent secretary at the Foreign Office between 1969 and 1973, who, as one of the two government-appointed directors on BP's board since leaving the Civil Service, was still in a somewhat sensitive position with regard to this affair.

The principal subterfuge employed by Shell and BP to comply with British law without getting on the wrong side of the white-man's-burden regimes ruling South Africa, Mozambique and Southern Rhodesia was to fix up an oil-swapping arrangement with Total - a French company quite unhampered by scruples about propping up another white-paternalist regime by sanctions-busting - under which it would supply Ian Smith's rebel government with oil and have its own stock replenished by the British companies. (So cynical did this deal eventually become that the swapping degenerated into deliveries from the same Shell Mocambique depot as had been used to supply Rhodesia before the rebellion, with the ownership of the oil being first recorded in the books as transferred to Total.) Greenhill (who curiously enough turned out not to have been interviewed by Bingham) frankly admitted to having known about this swapping scam while he was still at the Foreign Office; then promptly shifted the burden of responsibility to the Commonwealth Relations Office by pointing out that it was the

Commonwealth and Colonial Secretary, George Thomson, who had held the oil-embargo talks with Shell and BP.

Thomson is an interesting figure partly *because* his is not a name which reverberates widely outside the diminishing ranks of Labour's elder statesmen, yet he was just the sort of sound back-up man needed to cement firmly into place the well-earned reputation for responsible politics of the Labour establishment. An old and faithful friend of both James Callaghan and Denis Healey, Thomson began his career appropriately as editor of the comics *Dandy* and *Beano*; rose under Wilson's command to Cabinet rank, becoming Minister without Portfolio and Chancellor of the Duchy of Lancaster, with special responsibility for negotiating with the EEC the terms for Britain's entry (after Labour had been turned out of office by the 1970 general election, along with Labour's new Deputy Leader, Roy Jenkins, and Harold Lever, he resigned from what was now the Shadow Cabinet over Wilson's acceptance of Tony Benn's proposal for a referendum on British membership of the Common Market); accepted the offer of appointment as one of Britain's two EEC Commissioners after Ted Heath had secured British entry; and, to purloin Healey's witticism, 'some would say, completed the circle by ending it as a [life] peer and Chairman of the Independent Broadcasting Authority.'

It was this very model of the great and the good who in each generation shore up our venerable institutions who was now in the telescopic sights. He did the only thing he could: he grassed on his co-conspirators by confessing that he was a mere conduit for communications between the sanctions-busting buccaneers and his own skipper. Less than a week after the putting about of a disclaimer that the Wilson Cabinet had ever been informed of the nose-thumbing smuggling ops, Thomson released a six-page dossier bluntly stating that Cabinet papers 'confirm that I conveyed in writing to the Prime Minister and other Ministers most directly concerned a full account of all that passed at my meetings on behalf of the Government with the oil companies.'

He went on to assert that following UDI 'the most vigorous national and international efforts to bring down the illegal Rhodesian regime by sanctions' had been initiated by the Labour Government, but that they had been 'forced painfully and reluctantly to face the fact that so long as South Africa and Portugal refused to operate the sanctions there was no chance of ending the rebellion' swiftly, since open confrontation with those countries, as well as military intervention in Rhodesia, had been ruled out as unwise and/or quite impracticable. Prosecution of the British oil companies for breaking the sanctions would only have given comfort to the rebels, so we did the best we could, Thomson claimed, which was 'to prevent any further British oil reaching Rhodesia...Of course, the arrangements which began in 1968 were a second best. They did not prevent Rhodesia getting her oil since that was outside our power. But they did mean that the Government was ensuring that British companies under their jurisdiction were observing British law and that was of capital importance in maintaining the pressure on Smith for a negotiated settlement.'

Whether or not it is possible for anybody who has not wholly surrendered to cynicism to consider this apologia as anything better than a tale of pusillanimity and deception, Thomson's account was largely borne out by a vigorous defence of the oil companies' conduct by Shell's chairman, Sir Frank McFadzean, which appeared in *The Times* on the day before Thomson spilled the beans. Sir Frank claimed that the British oil companies had made it clear that oil could only be prevented from reaching Rhodesia by imposing a blockade on South Africa, which the British Government was never prepared to do. 'Once the Government appreciated that the substance of its sanctions' policy was beyond its grasp, all efforts were devoted to trying to keep the companies and their staff within the letter rather than the spirit of the Order.' Hence the oil-swap deal with Total, about which, McFadzean said, there had been several discussions with the Government.

The inescapable implication of George Thomson's statement as to who was in the know was that Roy Jenkins (who was Chancellor of the Exchequer at the time), Michael Stewart (Foreign Secretary 1965-66 and 1968-70), Denis Healey (Defence Secretary 1964-70), probably James Callaghan (who moved in 1967 from the post of Chancellor to that of Home Secretary), and of course Harold Wilson himself, were perfectly well aware of what was going on. While Sir Charles le Quesne, who as head of the Foreign Office's West and Central African Department at the time said that he had been told by the oil companies that they could not prevent their South African subsidiaries from delivering oil to Rhodesia, threw in for good measure the name of the wayward George Brown, who was Foreign Secretary from August 1966 to March 1968, and remained Deputy Leader of the Labour Party (to which post he had been elected in 1960) until he became a life peer in 1970.

To Lord George-Brown, as he whimsically became, we shall return after taking an unsightly squint at the reactions of the others in the frame. Roy Jenkins took refuge behind the self-denying principle of not commenting on matters pertaining to his time in office in Britain since becoming President of the EEC (a post he had conveniently taken up in 1976 and held until January 1981, when he became free to join the 'Gang of Three' and become figurehead of the Social Democratic Party); Messrs Callaghan and Healey kept uncharacteristically quiet and Michael Stewart said as little as possible; while the creature at the centre of the web sent up a circumlocutory smoke-screen which revealed neither qualms of conscience nor any disposition to accept personal responsibility for the total failure of the oil embargo. For such uncomfortable feelings was substituted an exemplary candour in naming others (James Callaghan, Fred Lee, Arthur Bottomley, Michael Stewart) whose almost constant attendance at meetings of the Cabinet or Cabinet committees during the period concerned almost certainly made them privy to whatever his Government could have been said to know. Unfortunately, however, according to him, nobody could remember anything about the reports to the Cabinet to which George Thomson was referring.

As for the parvenu peer who was (like Roy Jenkins) a failed contender for Labour's top job, and in 1976 resigned from the Party, Lord George-Brown washed his hands of the matter, without directly answering the allegations against him, by saying that he was not personally or departmentally involved in the sanctions' supervision; described the debate about who did what and who knew what as 'distasteful and unseemly' and Wilson's call for the publication of all the relevant Cabinet papers 'an insidious, sinister, and malicious attempt which made Cabinet government as we have known it impossible in this country'; attacked David Owen for failing to invite Ian Smith to come to Britain for talks; denounced what had been his own party and the Liberals for feting 'a leader of thugs and murderers' (*viz.* Joshua Nkomo) when 'he came openly to this country'; and announced that he would vote against a renewal of sanctions.

To go back to Bingham, after all the finger-pointing, dodging and weaving which had preceded publication - plus, of course, the leaks about what the worthy man of law was going to say - when the authorised and carefully circumscribed report of this squalid affair was officially released on 20th September, it was naturally a bit of a damp squib as far as new revelations go, though it did add a little to the record and confirmed in a generally no-names-no-pack-drill kind of way the collusion between the British oil companies and both Wilson's and Heath's administrations. One passage in the report referred to a Government note of a meeting, on 21st February 1968, between George Thomson and top executives of Shell and BP, which left no doubt that the Government knew about the massive leaking of British oil to the rebel regime and that the Government's main concern had been to devise a verbal construction which could be deployed in reporting to Parliament on the implementation of sanctions without making any demonstrably false statement or arousing suspicion, while at the same time cloaking the truth, which was that so far as oil supplies went the British blockade was a masquerade. The solution was simple. 'No British company is supplying POL [petrol, oil or lubricants] to Rhodesia' should and did satisfy most supporters of sanctions, since British companies had been responsible for 85 per cent of the country's needs. And the statement diverted attention from the profoundly disturbing fact that while Rhodesia's oil consumption had fallen after UDI, it quite soon returned to its former level and then rose to a figure double the 1965 rate.

This aide-memoire of 21st February 1968 was on its own all but conclusive in answering the question of whether Harold Wilson himself was party to what really amounted to a conspiracy to deceive Parliament and the British electorate, not to mention the international community, since a copy was sent to No 10 Downing Street for the attention of the Prime Minister's private secretary, Michael Palliser (who by the time this came to light in Bingham's report was Sir Michael Palliser, head of the Foreign Office), and no one could believe he would not have drawn his master's attention to such an important matter. In the teeth of ever-inflating implausibility, Wilson persisted in his well-I-didn't-know tactics, even going so far as to scapegoat his civil servants, Palliser and Burke Trend, who was secretary to the Cabinet at the time. It could have been an oversight on Palliser's part, due to pressure of work, was Wilson's line, while Burke Trend was fingered for not bringing the matter before the Cabinet, as he should have done. Among the hosts of people who evidently had difficulty in summoning up sufficient credence in Sir Harold's version of events was his party's International Committee, which declined to nominate him for re-election as Vice President of the Socialist International because of his embroilment in the oil sanctions scandal.

Of course, it was not Labour ministers alone who (to understate the matter) were under suspicion, since the charade of oil-swapping carried on after the Tories took office in 1970 and continued until the reversion to direct sanctions-busting in 1972, and this blatant flouting of British law and UN sanctions went on at least until 1976. 'Nobody knew and everybody knew, because we were collectively determined not to know,' Enoch Powell told his fellow MPs, unfairly, doubtless, to the Labour left and a few but not many others. But the situation was different for the Tories. In the first place they had what was - in terms of the party political cockpit at any rate - the near-perfect excuse that when they came to power they simply (in the words of their foreign affairs spokesman John Davies) 'carried on the policy established by the Labour Party'. And in the second place they did not have the same degree of proclaimed moral commitment as Labour to the defeat of a white-settler oligarchy (indeed, most Tory MPs had a great deal of sympathy for the rebel 'colons' and a sizeable section of their parliamentary party, not to mention the party in the country, was wholly opposed to sanctions), and, by the same token, they were much less susceptible than Labour to political damage from charges of dirty dealings arising from sanctions-busting revelations. The canniest Tories could see clearly enough that their best course was to sit back and enjoy the barney on the Government benches.

The biggest damage to Labour - since, sadly, it would be vain to pretend that this dishonourable affair was of great moment to the great body of the electorate - occurred within its own ranks, with further grave erosion of the faith of many active supporters in their leaders. Two weeks after the Bingham Report was published, an emergency resolution calling for a full public investigation and for prosecution of those implicated in breaking sanctions was passed by Party Conference. Further investigation into the extent to which ministers were in the know was also called for. 'Our reputation and our credibility as a party, as a government, and as a nation, is firmly on the line,' said Ernie Ross of AUEW-TASS in moving the resolution. The 89-year-old anti-colonialist and civil liberties campaigner Lord Fenner Brockway told Conference that, acting on information from Dr Kenneth Kaunda, he had warned the Wilson Government eleven years before that sanctions were being broken and was told that the Zambian President had been duped by a 'fabrication' planted on him. 'I'm not suggesting,' he said, 'that most of the members of our Labour Government at that time, or even of the Tory Government, were aware of what was happening. But some must have been, and even at the cost of some exposure, the integrity of our party demands that a full investigation - with all the Cabinet papers available - be made for our honour.'

West Aberdeenshire delegate Mrs Mary Panko said that it was only to be expected that the Tories, under Heath, were involved in the affair, 'But I'm damned if I will take it from a Labour government.' But like the rest of us, take it she had done, did, and would. When, at the beginning of November, Sir Harold offered to let Parliament see all the Cabinet papers relating to the breaking of the sanctions against Rhodesia, provided the other Prime Ministers concerned (i.e. Ted and Jim) agreed, was it at all Pygmalion likely that he was being serious, man? Or was he laughing up his sleeve, secure in the certainty that his fellow statesmen would see to it that an open and rigorous inquiry would never be up and running? It is true that, from an initial 'nyet' response from both Heath and Callaghan, they did make the political calculation that it would be more prudent to agree that Cabinet papers could be made available to a Special Commission of inquiry composed of members appointed from both Houses; but even that apparent major concession was hedged around with the proviso that the papers should first be scrutinised by the commission chairman, who would then decide whether or not they would be put before the commission!

(Moreover, the inquiry was to be held in private, in order - to quote the Lord Chancellor's subsequent assurance to his fellow peers - 'to limit the risk of public pillorying and limit the damage that might arise from the publication of Cabinet papers and documents.' Perhaps the fellow went in fear of the pillory himself, since his name was Lord Elwyn-Jones, and, as Sir Elwyn Jones, he had been the Attorney-General who, on 17th July 1968 - i.e. four months after the crucial meeting between Thomson and the British oil companies mentioned above - asking for adoption of the full mandatory sanctions ordered by the Security Council, told the

Commons: 'The move to comprehensive sanctions will make it much more difficult for sanctions breakers to carry out illicit deals under the cover of legitimate transactions.' Perhaps it is an earnest of Labour's resolve to stamp out sanctions-busting that, according to Elwyn Jones's successor as Attorney-General, our old friend Sam Silkin, in an answer in the Commons in the first week of November 1978, while the biggest fine for this crime had been £50,000, the smallest - was it for smuggling in chewing gum, or what? - had been a swingeing £10. And since the imposition of sanctions, there had been just 34 prosecutions, which suggests either that the general blockade was remarkably effective, or that it leaked like a sieve, perhaps because the responsible authorities had been turning a blind eye to other criminals besides the executives of the oil companies.)

Besides which, there was the longstop of the Lords, and there was every reason for confidence that the Tory peers would never wear it! (Someone really ought to make a study of how helpful the House of Lords has been to the Labour leadership!) When the proposal was put before the Lords, a week after going through the Commons, Lord Hailsham declared that 'Bingham was enough, perhaps too much', and that the Commons should not ask the House of Lords to 'compromise our own honour, our own integrity, and our fundamental constitutional principles.' His central objection was that full disclosure of what had gone on would break two vital constitutional principles: the confidentiality of advice given to ministers by civil servants and the confidentiality of Cabinet documents and discussions.

A ringing endorsement of his argument came from a former Minister of State at the Home Office. As an official adviser to Michael Stewart and Roy Jenkins in the early years of the oil scam, and at one time secretary to Hugh Gaitskell, Lord Harris of Greenwich (as the homespun John Harris had become in 1974) naturally spoke with strong fellow-feeling. 'I am certain many of my former colleagues must have approached the appointment of this body with a great deal of repugnance, breaking, as it does, virtually all the conventions that attach to the confidentiality of Cabinet and Ministerial discussions.' Lord Harris was one of four Labour peers (the others were Lord Paget of Northampton, the Reginald Paget who had represented that city from 1945 until his elevation in 1974; Lord Gordon-Walker, who as Patrick Gordon-Walker had once held the posts of both Commonwealth Secretary and Foreign Secretary; and Lord Glenamara, who before his transmogrification had been plain Ted Short, Deputy Leader of the Labour Party and Leader of the House of Commons) who joined the Tory peers in kicking out the Special Commission proposal by 102 votes to 58.

When the Commons had debated the matter, on 1st February 1979, it was the shadow leader of the House, Norman St John-Stevas, who made the most revealing remarks. 'We are embarking on a dangerous course - dangerous first of all to the reputation of this country,' he said, adding that the inquiry would be an 'inquisition into the whole process of government, and parliamentary government as we have known it, and into the assumptions on which it is based.' He was absolutely right: telling the people the truth could seriously damage the health of those running the body politic shop. All those who cherished our proud heritage of parliamentary government could breathe a deep sigh of relief at the common sense and steadiness of the Lords, and perhaps at the fact that, as St John-Stevas pointed out, they were at that moment in the midst of one of the gravest crises the country had faced since the war. Who had time, he might have added, to worry about Rhodesia's thirteen-year-old civil war (or what and who had fuelled it) while Britain was in the throes of its own civil war - the Winter of Discontent?

Two months almost to the day after Ian Smith's government plumped (on 11th November 1965) for UDI, Harold Wilson had told the Commonwealth Prime Ministers' meeting in Lagos: 'The cumulative effects of the economic and financial sanctions might well bring the rebellion to an end within a matter of weeks rather than months.' According to Lord Walston (who was Under Secretary of State at the Foreign Office from 1964-67; was identified by Bingham as the Government minister to whom BP and Shell first reported, in April 1966, the massive leakage of oil through the sanctions barrier around Rhodesia; who held informal talks with both the Portuguese foreign minister and the South African Prime Minister, Dr Vorster, to try to bring more pressure on Ian Smith to return to legality; and who claimed to have been a 'hawk' in favour of military intervention to break the rebellion), Wilson's astonishingly optimistic forecast was 'greeted by most of us [presumably behind Harold's back] with derision at the time. It was clearly not according to the facts of the case as known by virtually everyone.'

We have all heard of the man who thought his wife was a hat, so it is perhaps conceivable that Wilson believed his own upbeat rhetoric in Lagos; and it is just about possible that when he met Ian Smith on HMS *Tiger* in December 1966 for talks about terms for a return to legality, Wilson was unaware of the extent to which British oil companies were involved in sanctions-busting. But to ask history to believe that he was still as blissfully ignorant of this scandalous conduct by the time of his second fruitless meeting with Smith, on HMS *Fearless* in October 1968, is to stretch credulity thinner than the dough in *apfelstrudel*. Yet he went on acting out his talking-from-strength charade on the world's stage. Moreover, Britain had signalled, for all the world to see, that the principle from which she would not shift was NIBMAR ('no independence before majority rule'), yet if we are to take the word of Ian Smith's predecessor as Prime Minister of Rhodesia, Sir Edgar Whitehead, if the concessions offered by Wilson in the *Tiger* talks had been accepted by the rebels it would almost certainly have postponed the introduction of colour-blind majority rule 'beyond the end of the century'.

To top up the cup of gall proffered by Labour seigneurs for popular consumption, on the day that Ian Smith was granted a visa to visit the USA to seek support for his plans for progress towards majority rule, and that the Labour Party Conference debated the sanctions-busting scandal, the Deputy Leader of the Party and the Government, Michael Foot, told a Tribune rally, in the course of defending Jim Callaghan's decision to put off going to the country, that one of the reasons this was a good decision was that there had been a real danger that the Rhodesian crisis would have reached its climax during a general election in Britain, or at a time when there was either a Tory government or perhaps no effective government at all. The crowning irony in this tale of perfidy is that it was the Tories under Maggie Thatcher, with Lord Carrington leading the British Government's negotiating team, who, after fourteen years during which Britain (for most of the time under Labour) had, in effect, stood on the sidelines washing its hands in crocodile tears, at last brought the rebellion and civil war to an end, with the Lancaster House Agreement of December 1979, thereby making it possible for the fully-independent nation of Zimbabwe to come into being under majority rule in May 1980.

Like every other historical period, the Wilson-Callaghan years yielded a cornucopia of crimes of State power. Among the subjects which would have to appear in anything like a comprehensive survey, and regarding which the State would have a serious case to answer, would be: legal justice in Northern Ireland, the unaccountability of the security services, phone-tapping, police files, the 'sus' laws, the prison services, immigration law and administration, political asylum, secret treaties, secret 'defence' projects, suppression of the historical record and the related 30-year-rule delaying the release of documents. Instead of attempting such a survey, which in any case could only be tackled here in summary terms, I have chosen to recount two unsavoury stories at some length. Not just because they *are* spectaculars, but because, as the saying goes, the devil is in the detail, and only by looking at the details does one become aware, not simply of the general historical record, but *of the way we are governed.*

Everybody knows that absolute rulers commit crimes against their subjects; but the pretence in constitutional theory is that democratic States do not really have rulers and subjects: they have elected and accountable governments and citizens entitled to hold them to account. The reality is rather different. Lord George-Brown was absolutely right: all government, whatever steps may be taken to make it more open, is founded on secrecy, on keeping the governed in the dark, at least until it is too late for the governed to take over the governing. Only so can it work. Which (as St John-Stevas did not quite say) makes even representative government the enemy of democracy.

CHAPTER 31

Hope deferred

'We've found out in this war how we're all neighbours and we haven't got to forget it...We've been doing some hard thinking lately, and we haven't got-a stop when this job's finished. I mind you saying to me after the last war, this must never happen again. But it has happened. We stopped thinking ourselves and left it to other people...We've made a fine big war effort, and when it's all over we got to see we make a fine big peace effort. We can't go back now we've made a start. There's no two ways about it. Look at that Dunkirk. There wasn't no unemployed there. Every man had a job to do and he done it. And a job's what we got to see they have in peacetime. There mustn't be no more chaps hanging around for work what don't come. There mustn't be no more slums neither; no more dirty filthy backstreets, and no more half-starved kids with no room to play in. We can't go back to the old way of living. Leastways not all of it. That's gone for ever, and the sooner we make up our minds about that the better...We got-a all pull together. That's how I look at it anyway.'

So runs the dialogue between two elderly Home Guards, played by Percy Walsh and Bernard Miles, in *The Dawn Patrol*, a British wartime propaganda film produced by the Ministry of Information. What seems remarkable about it from the perspective of the very different ethos of half a century later is the confidence it exudes that it is expressing not some sectional viewpoint but a national consensus. Healthy scepticism might suggest that showing such a film in the nation's cinemas was just another cynical move in the never-ending game of getting the people to do the bidding of the powers that be, and some acquaintance with State propaganda when the British had their backs to the wall a generation earlier (the promises of making 'a land fit for heroes' and all that jazz) only lends credence to such a sour interpretation. Yet without getting starry-eyed about the Dunkirk spirit or whatever, there are good reasons for thinking that, for the first time ever, the British had indeed reached something like a national consensus.

In its homely way, *The Dawn Patrol* was calling for the slaying of the 'five giants' - Want, Disease, Ignorance, Squalor, and Idleness - named by Beveridge as barring the way 'on the road to reconstruction'. And the whole country was behind him. (This is one of those very rare instances in which such an assertion is almost literally true: The British Institute of Public Opinion reported an astonishing 86 per cent backing for the Beveridge Report, with support from employers and the upper middle classes almost as strong as from manual workers. For once the people had told the politicians in no uncertain manner what was 'in the national interest'.) If the same was less assuredly true of the party which had held sway for so long (and one must avoid the fallacy of giving all the credit to Labour for the establishment of a modern Welfare State in Britain: the Beveridge Committee, after all, was set up under the wartime coalition government; the Education Act of 1944 was primarily down to Rab Butler; the policy of establishing a National Health Service on an every-citizen's-right basis was endorsed by Churchill in March 1944 in a speech which made it clear that the purpose was 'to ensure that everyone in the country, irrespective of means, age, sex, or occupation, shall have equal opportunities to benefit from the best and most up-to-date medical services available'; and perhaps most importantly of all, in a White Paper of May 1944 the Government had pledged itself to maintain 'a high and stable level of employment after the war'), there were 'One-Nation' men in its ranks to remind their ultra-conservative colleagues of the likely consequences of opposing speedy and substantial reform.

'If you do not give the people social reform, they are going to give you social revolution,' Quintin Hogg, echoing Disraeli, had warned, as was noted in the last chapter of the section on the development of the Tory Party. When, to the astonishment of the Tories, an ungrateful country rejected the appeals of its great war-leader and returned Labour to power in July 1945, it looked to many people like the first step in a bloodless 'social revolution' which would at least deliver a markedly more democratic and egalitarian society. What was not easy to see in the euphoria and effulgence of that marvellous summer was that the foundations Attlee's Government was laying down were certainly not those for a classless society. There may have been no more suitable firm available, but Labour was simply the wrong builder for the construction of a Socialist democracy. What the people got from Labour was not so much a new contract - for a contract implies, however misleadingly, at least some measure of equality between the contracting parties) as a new - and admittedly kindlier - dispensation. There was a contract (an implicit one: a kind of 'gentlemen's agreement', in fact!), but it was between the new ringmasters of the political circus and an establishment whose power was not subject to the vicissitudes of electoral politics - the economic ruling class - and it precluded any serious pursuit of social transformation.

The unspoken deal was for Welfare Capitalism (with parliamentary democracy thrown in as a 'free gift', of course): a rockbed of security for the individual citizen, administered by the State, to deliver a basically contented and co-operative workforce to employers, with a dirigiste element not so much greater in scope than had already been seen in America under Roosevelt's New Deal. And ironically, the handling of the issue that had given some of them nightmares, nationalisation, could only reassure the men of property that they had little to fear from the New Order.

Firstly, the old rhetoric of general nationalisation had been dropped from Labour's official pronouncements, so that only basic industries, national transport and communications, and utilities - collectively constituting the nation's material infrastructure - were targeted. Secondly, there never was any question of confiscation, such as had been proposed by some of the more Socialist-minded members of the Party (R.H. Tawney, in his 1921 book *The Acquisitive Society*, for example) in the past. On the contrary, such generous compensation was paid to the dispossessed capitalists that they were frequently better off than they had ever been, considering the commonly rundown state of their former assets, while the 'pensions' they drew from the now State-owned enterprises remained a serious drain on national resources for many years afterwards. Thirdly, those appointed to head these State enterprises, as well as those placed in influential executive and consultative positions, were drawn largely from the ranks of the capitalists themselves.

Most comforting of all was the fact that it was obvious from the start that the new regime accepted that in the 'mixed economy' the private-enterprise sector would massively predominate, and indeed that the Labour junta preferred it that way. Second in importance only to this in putting to rest the fears of the rentier class, was the adoption of the Morrisonian conception of nationalisation (or as Morrison himself preferred to call it, presumably without intending irony, 'socialisation'): giant State corporations aping in most respects their private-sector counterparts. Organised from the top downwards, they displayed no more than a genuflection towards the principles of participatory democracy (with regard either to producers or to consumers) and showed scarcely more concern for accountability to the people through their representatives in Parliament. (With respect to the workforce in the public sector, attention has already been drawn to the large share of blame for acceptance of this undemocratic situation which attaches to the leaders of organised labour. Their failure to demand a bigger say for the workers in State enterprises - especially at the crucial moment of their establishment - may be ascribed in part to timidity or to a naive trust in their political counterparts, the Party leaders, but surely is primarily to be accounted for by the paternalistic and power-seeking attitudes they shared with them.)

Moreover, the State corporations were run primarily as a springboard for successful private enterprise, particularly with regard to international trade. This functional subservience, combined with the need to counter inflationary pressures, made it imperative to hold down wage rates in the public sector to as low a level as possible, and certainly below the 'rate for the job' in the private sector. Thus, as with State education and State provisions for looking after the health and general welfare of the working populace, far from undermining capitalism, nationalisation (as conceived and operated in Britain) shored it up by effectively subsidising the cost of labour.

Almost as baleful in its consequences as the conduct of this Caliban itself was the obsession it induced in the minds of Labourites with the ever-stale-to-putrid but never-quite-dead controversy over the whole issue of nationalisation. Should there be more of it? Should there be less of it? Should 'we' just hold on to what 'we' have? Tory acceptance of some measure of government control of the economy, including a degree of nationalisation, was a *sine qua non* of consensus, since it figured so largely in the minds of their principal adversaries. None the less, Tory instinct (which was not without cogent arguments to back it up) was, of course, to stem the dirigiste tide, and if possible to turn it back. Until the Thatcherite horde swept across the landscape, the Tory counter-offensives to claw back State-acquired enterprises were limited to a few industries like steel, sugar, and shipbuilding. But the battles over nationalisation, denationalisation, and renationalisation diverted attention (and proletarian vigour) from more significant issues, especially ones concerning social justice, to which the whole phoney war was quite irrelevant.

Labour's 'fine frenzy' of reform scarcely outlasted its first post-war period in office. It became obvious soon after it was returned to power in February 1950 that it had run out of steam, and that it was undecided or at odds as to its destination. Within little more than eighteen months Attlee, acting in the spirit of autocracy conferred upon him by Britain's glorious constitution, took an effectively unilateral decision to go to the country. Despite achieving its highest support ever, beating the Tories in its share of the poll by 48.8 to 48 per cent, Labour came out of the general election of October 1951 with 26 fewer seats than the Tories (whose overall majority was 15), largely because of the collapse of the Liberal vote - a lesson in the flaws of first-past-the-post voting systems which it failed to learn then, and perhaps never will learn. It had to wait fully thirteen years for its next chance to show what it could do.

Never mind! As noted at the beginning of this lamentable tale of Labour's downhill 'progress' since World War II, the leader of the Party (since December 1955), Hugh Gaitskell, and the PLP's super-egghead, Anthony Crosland, were satisfied that, while much remained to be done, the decisive battle had already been fought and won in 'this blessed isle': capitalism had been tamed and transformed. If not into a handy tool for fashioning 'the future of socialism' by each new Labour government as it took its turn in office, then at least (it was assumed) 'the people's governments' would have enough leverage to persuade the capitalists to co-operate with them.

At every stage in its life Labour has been excoriated, by assorted pundits basically antipathetic to socialistic and egalitarian objectives, for its reluctance to relinquish 'outmoded traditions' and to change with the times. But Crosland's widely-acclaimed achievement in rethinking Socialism was actually to downsize the

436

dreams - *and the undertakings* - of the Labour Movement almost to vanishing point. Mind you, in one respect his thinking was, *pro tempore*, sound (although naturally this was not a point he was keen to draw attention to). As long as the consensus lasted (and in those days few in establishment circles foresaw its demise), it did not make a great deal of difference which of the contenders was, for the time being, in power: the capitalist tiger would be contained within 'tolerable bounds' by Keynesian economic adjustments and its ravages would be redressed by Welfare State provisions. And so we dreamt and drifted through those 'thirteen wasted years' ('wasted', in particular, for the PLP's ambitious understudies waiting in the wings for their turn to 'strut their stuff'), during which, however much it lagged behind the more royal progress of other nations, Britain's GNP grew steadily and almost everyone's standard of living rose, so that it was simply a matter of fact and a cause for mutual gratification when Harold Macmillan pointed out that: 'Most of our people have never had it so good.'

To the extent that they felt this to be true, most people were naturally little concerned about which party was in power or whether the government and its policies could be described as more or less 'socialistic': if the kind of capitalism that was on offer seemed to be working for them, they were 'not bothered'. That was obvious from the general election results (Macmillan's 1959 victory - the third in a row for his party - was unprecedented, and raised the Tory catch to its highest point ever, 13,749,830 votes); but it was spelt out more explicitly by the public opinion pollsters, who reported a diminishing number of 'loyal voters' as the years went by. In 1951 only about a fifth of those questioned said it made little difference which party was in power; by 1964, assuming the opinion polls accurately reflected the views of the nation, nearly a third of the electorate thought it hardly mattered who won the elections.

That was the year in which Labour's new leader - elected to succeed Gaitskell after his death in January 1963 - just managed to wrest the reins of government from Supermac's successor, Alec Douglas-Home. Harold Wilson was the first Labour leader since the war who had a left-wing reputation. But what he offered the country was not a Socialist but a 'scientific' revolution, a moderate commonsensical Englishman's version of the 'scientific socialism' which had supposedly prevailed in Russia since the Revolution. Just as 'electricity' was a talisman for the Bolsheviks, so 'advanced technology' was to be Labour's Excalibur. The recipe for a regenerated 'land of hope and glory' included a smidgen of the Stalinists' equation of Socialism with State planning and industrialisation and a generous dollop of their obsessive concern with productivity.

Of course, for both geophysical and ideological reasons, a command economy like that of the Soviet Union was (blessedly!) not in the frame in Harold's swinging Britain, though his party continued to invest a deal of faith (though not much else) in a pallid version of State capitalism. However, the reality beneath a rhetoric which lent the appearance of a deep divide between Labour and its opponents was the confirmation of Labour's capitulation to capitalism. The strategy, such as it was, of 'harnessing science to socialism' (see Chapter 12) depended for its success on a formula acceptable to all the parliamentary parties because it threatened none of them: producing more and selling more in a highly competitive global marketplace where the conditions of trade were set by free-enterprise capitalism; and so to creep and crawl towards the millennium of an ubiquitous prosperity (within the bounds of our own 'promised land', that is) which the Party might plausibly represent as the 'virtual reality' of Socialism.

Such at least appeared to be the situation so long as those Party people whose opinions really counted (those who were of Labour's own upper class) were not prepared to grasp the nettle of redistribution. And the premise of the Age of Consensus - of the maintenance of an equilibrium that might, according to personal and party apperceptions of a well-adjusted polity, swing gyroscopically gently out of balance of a focal point subliminally-projected but mutually-apprehended by the chattering classes, without upsetting the basic stability (i.e. without fundamentally disrupting the status quo!) - was that capitalism would deliver ever higher standards of living to everyone. This would happen, whatever the starting points on the magic moving staircase, thereby reducing controversial questions concerning the redistribution of wealth and income to no more than subsidiary, if not quite marginal, problems.

While its acceptance by the Party establishment and its 'loyalist' henchmen betrayed their minimal concern for social justice, the premise did retain a certain air of plausibility throughout the fifties and sixties, despite the somewhat sluggish and erratic performance of the British economy and the sterling crises which partially crippled Wilson's 'scientific revolution'. But the first major oil crisis, of 1973 (see Chapter 21), trashed the illusion that capitalism could be depended on to deliver ever greater national prosperity, and that, with a minimum of fiscal tinkering, 'social justice' would trickle down to everybody. It took another fistful of years for the crunch to come; but the consensus between the parties, which previously only Labour's 'outside left' had seriously challenged, came increasingly to be recognised as no longer viable. No one put the situation more bluntly than anti-poverty campaigner Frank Field: 'The promise to the "haves" was that injustice could be painlessly removed...Economic growth would guarantee that the real income of the "haves" rose while only part of the largesse was transferred to the "have nots"'. And he warned that Labour would be forced to choose between abandoning reform and breaking the consensus. (See Chapter 19)

But the Party leaders - unlike the advance guard of the rampant New Toryism - lacked either the conviction or the courage (or perhaps both) to make a clear choice. Their dilemma was already an old one when Field challenged them. It could be traced through every deflationary and regressive Labour budget measure since 1964. But the embracing of the monetarist doctrines of their supposed political enemies by Healey and Callaghan in 1975/76 (see Chapter 21) should have made it clear to all but the incurably myopic (who would have to await the Winter of Discontent for the scales to be torn from their eyes) that a choice had been made, and that it was a choice in favour of the interests of capital, not of labour - not of working people, and still less of the poor!

Having almost completely abandoned the idea of extending public ownership as a route towards Socialism; having been proved deceived in their faith that capitalism with a light Keynesian touch on the tiller would deliver the goods, so that redistribution to bring about their 'minimum standard of decency' conception of social justice (see Chapter 18) could happen almost unnoticed, without pain and above all without confiscation; and finding themselves economically becalmed, or worse, in choppy seas; in order to sustain their new status as national statesmen, Labour's leaders turned on their own followers, substituting control of the masses for their emancipation. Except in the most extreme circumstances, an amorphous population is little to be feared by its governors; workers organised under their own leaders are quite another matter. So of course controlling the masses took the form, above all, of deploying the machinery of the State to rein in the unions - a task in which they were perfidiously abetted by not a few captains of the workers' battalions. (With due allowance for the constrictions imposed on authority by an established system of parliamentary democracy, it was not so different really from the terrible story of the aftermath of the Russian Revolution, in which the proletariat was enslaved by its 'liberators' partly through the instrument of its own organisations. Different at least principally in degree rather than in principle; and, in the final analysis, in spirit hardly different at all from the Thatcherites' brimstone-and-treacle prescriptions for industrial peace.)

Hence the slanderous attacks by Labour leaders on militant unionism (the Party was hardly back in office after those 'thirteen wasted years' than its reputedly left-wing leader was denouncing, with sublime even-handedness, 'luddites' whether in the boardrooms or the trade unions; while little more than a month after consolidating his power in the spring election of 1966, he was diligently denigrating 'England's' ever-exploited seamen by dubbing them dupes of Communist conspirators who had inveigled them into striking 'against the State, against [note the cunning conflation of quite separate species] the community') which accompanied the never-relinquished claims for Corporate-State-like control of wages and regulation of the unions; hence the abortive attempt to override the disappointingly cautious counsel of the Donovan Commission by imposing the gospel according to Saint Barbara; and hence the ever-rising strife in Callaghan's kingdom which finally drowned Labour's dreams in the Winter of Discontent.

Hence, too, in the decades of disillusionment and desertion which followed the debacle, the substantive endorsement by Her Majesty's Loyal Opposition, of the reforms by which the New Tories hamstrung the organisations which constitute the only effective countervailing force (short of revolution) against capitalism's unrelenting drive for a cheap and pliable workforce to man its machines. Their record in office shows that this accommodation to the agenda of their political opponents was no painful one for most of the Labour Party leaders, nor for a solid core of 'loyal' or simply careerist Labour back-benchers. (Yesteryear's 'beer and sandwiches at No. 10' - the jibe the Press has never grown tired of - only went to show that usually a deal

440

could be done with the union bosses to keep the lads in order, as it had been most momentously in 1926.) But the morale-sapping years of rejection at the polls, with a shocking rout in '83 succeeded by a deeply disappointing defeat in '87 and an absolutely 'gobsmacking' one in '92, induced more shameful accommodations: dishonest concessions to the specious claims of the caterpillar classes that universal welfare - even, perhaps, universal health care, and in the end universal education - has come to cost more than the country can afford and will have to be cut back to a more basic (or if you would rather put it that way, minimally 'decent') level, with everyone having the 'choice' of topping things up for themselves and their families with 'their own money'. In short, that for the satisfaction of desires beyond this basic State-guaranteed level, it has to be left to 'the market' to supply the wherewithal to match what is called in the ludicrous cant of capitalist economics 'demand'. For Labour's leaders, it was anything, anything at all, to exorcise the spectre still crying out for redistributive justice! Until things had reached such a pass that in many matters concerning 'the condition of the people', including the will to wield taxation in such a way as to 'shake the superflux' from the grasp of 'the stinking rich', Labour had ended up markedly to the right of the heirs of the Liberal Party.

This soft-shoe shuffle rightwards provoked, in the dying days of Labour rule and in the early years of the Thatcherite hegemony before Labour morale collapsed, a campaign within the Party and the Movement to reduce the huge deficit between democratic principle and oligarchic (not to say autocratic) practice in Labour's decision-making processes - a campaign which reached its climax in a pyrrhic victory for 'the democrats' at the Special Conference at Wembley in 1981. It had actually taken an eternity for this perennial burning issue to come to the boil. Time and again throughout the whole life of the Labour Party the issue had flared into open conflict. But, to restrict the tale to the post-war years and to put the matter in a most summary fashion, the indictment was that while party activists had indefatigably puffed out their dream signals (about 'capturing the commanding heights of the economy', 'effecting an irreversible shift in the balance of power and wealth in favour of working people', etc., etc., etc.) and diligently drafted resolutions and prospectuses for putting them into practice (an 'Alternative Economic Strategy', a 'Social Contract', a 'Wealth

Tax', and so on and so on, *ad astra*) - *and* succeeded in persuading Conference to support them - the Labour leaders had responded patronisingly by lecturing them on political realities, or simply shrugged their shoulders without bothering to waste their breath, and got on (as one children's story puts the facts of political life) with their 'ruling and fighting'.

The crux of the matter was (and is) the contradiction between the constitutional *fiction* of the sovereignty of Conference (together with the subsidiary fiction of the supreme authority of the NEC between one Conference and the next) and the insurmountable *fact* of the actual autonomy of the PLP. It is insurmountable (except, of course, by insurrection) because it is rooted in the higher authority of the State constitution, which confers on Members of Parliament - as representatives not of political parties but of geographical conglomerates of electors - the right to decide what is best for the national polity. Thus the reality behind the theory of representative government (in which 'the sovereign people' are represented by a 'sovereign parliament' which they have elected, but effective power is in most circumstances in the hands of a caucus called the Cabinet, headed by a Prime Minister with quasi-autocratic powers) is in effect imposed on the political parties competing for parliamentary seats, regardless of what their own constitutions lay down.

The Labour Party's assimilation of and by what must be - of all the national constitutions with any claim at all to being 'democratic' - the most centralised and the most hierarchical of all (so much so that with respect to a party in power the situation approximates to 'democratic centralism'!) has practically guaranteed its inutility as a tool for social transformation. Perhaps no commentator has made this point more forcefully than Gregory Elliott does in his remarkable synoptical history and critique of the Labour Party, *Labourism and the English Genius* (1993). And it is a point which is so fundamental to the issue of radical reform in quest of a more equal society that it reduces (relatively speaking) to little more than academic interest the complex question of the degree of democracy which the Labour Party theoretically offers its members and the long and involved tale of conflict between leaders and led in the Party and the Movement, a story which has often been told in part but, to my knowledge, has never been given the full treatment it merits as a study in the myths and realities of institutional democracy.

One possible objection to the case I have been making is that Labour never has been a Socialist party. It is a point that is made, with varying shades of sincerity, from diametrically-opposed standpoints, by radical left-wing critics (commonly of Marxist or semi-Marxist persuasion) and by 'moderate' apologists intent on fending off left-wing criticism. From the left, Gregory Elliott makes the point with characteristic incisiveness:

> 'Labour is not now - and never has been - a socialist party. Throughout its history it has comprised a coalition of *social reformers* and *reformist socialists*, the latter in a permanent minority, whether among parliamentarians, trade unionists or individual members. As its very name suggests, Labour was founded to advance the interests of the labouring class within capitalism, via reforms, not to create a qualitatively different form of society; to *ameliorate*, not *abolish*, capitalism. At the same time however, the accretions of the 1919 Constitution - in pride of place, Clause 4 section (4) on the 'common ownership of the means of production' - have bred the illusion, stretching far beyond Labour's own ranks, that Labour has been committed to the goal of socialism, its members differing not over the destination, but only as to tactics and timing; or, when this became unsustainable, that a socialist rank and file was pitted against a treacherous leadership from whom the party could be rescued. As recent events have demonstrated, the leadership/ ordinary members dichotomy is a myth, though a beguiling one, inspiring the everlasting project of restoring the Labour Party to a socialist vocation it has never possessed.' [author's emphases]

All of this is true (as well as, incidentally, being uncontaminated by any desire to excuse, or at least to extenuate, Labour's gross historical failure), and it is a most important truth; but paradoxically it is to an extent misleading. Yes, committed Socialists have always been in the minority in the Party, and one might go further and say that they have had a wholly disproportionate influence, at least on its propaganda nexus with the public. But then activists, by definition, always do have a disproportionate influence on whatever group within which they are operating, and in politics activists tend to be more *ideologically* committed than others; or, to put it the other way round, their ideological commitment tends to make them activists. In a sense, they tend to be 'extremists', accentuating the differences between their party and other parties. So it is only to be expected that in the Labour Party commitment has more often than not meant advocating 'more socialism'.

As with the Party proper, so with the larger Movement. So that it is by no means as clear as Elliott's statement suggests that in the political *life* of the Party and the Movement and their constituent parts (i.e. in the expression of their 'democratic will') Socialists have always, or even usually, been in the minority. Without in any way implying the existence of a similar measure of support for each side of the perpetual left-right argument, Labour's story might be better described as a ceaseless contest between activist 'mods' ('moderates' or 'modernisers', it makes little difference) and activist 'rockers' (radicals who, by taking Labour's and their own rhetoric seriously, rock the boat) for the ear and the support of those in the wider Movement and the world outside it, i.e. of the electorate.

(Incidentally, it is pointless, if not disingenuous, to complain that the disproportionate influence of activist minorities usurps the rights of 'silent majorities', since - without getting bogged down in the intractable problem of distinguishing between actual 'public opinion' and its often tendentiously *assumed* varieties - 'mass democracy' only works, inasmuch as it may be considered to work at all, through the agency of those prepared *actively* to participate in its processes. It is the self-evident truth that democracy cannot be *passive* which makes what we call 'representative democracy' a contradiction in terms. All of which highlights the fact that activists who are 'moderates' - i.e. whose attitudes are more or less conservative with a small c - are no less part of the minority who are active than are 'extremist' activists.)

There are also problems - despite their reasonableness and their usefulness as descriptive terms - with Elliott's antithesis between *social reformers* and *reformist socialists*. It is not that the distinction itself is not clear, but that those so distinguished have frequently failed to see that there is such a distinction and that, if they had seen it, they would probably have been even less clear as to which category they belonged. They might even quite reasonably have claimed to belong to both! This is, of course, one of those irresolvable problems in analysis, especially when applied to a subject such as human thought and behaviour, in which inconsistencies are endemic.

One can illustrate the difficulty by pointing out that as late as the mid-nineties, by which time a sober-sided and utterly dependable Party had begun openly courting the middle class, on the pretext that it had been vilely abused by its long-cohabiting Tory partner, the personable New Labour leader would still now and again speak of 'democratic socialism'. Flatulent rhetoric, no doubt, largely attributable to concern for keeping on board the Party's 'other ranks', or at least the old soldiers amongst them. Not altogether, though. In some instances the use of such obsolescent language by Labour politicians and supporters is surely to be ascribed to lack of understanding of what they are saying (as is shown by the growing practice, approved at the highest level, of treating 'democratic socialism' and 'social democracy' as if they were interchangeable terms) - and even of who they are: a cognitive and identity problem compounded and confounded.

Indeed, the emphatic and utterly unequivocal nature of Elliott's analysis raises the problem of just how seriously we are to take the socialistic-sounding pronouncements made on occasion by every Labour leader over the years. For instance, to go back more than half a century, but only two-thirds of the way back through the Party's lifetime on which he comments so confidently, what are we to make of Attlee's unambiguous endorsement of Socialist doctrines and values in *The Labour Party in Perspective*, samples of which have been displayed earlier? Are we to take him at his word - or at least his word in 1937 - or not? It may be that Elliott would be prepared to make such a charge, but what more damning indictment could there be than the assertion that all such pronouncements by Labour leaders never were more than hot air to stoke up the fire in the bellies of their followers?

Indeed, the emphatic and utterly unequivocal nature of Elliott's analysis raises the problem of just how seriously we are to take the socialistic-sounding pronouncements made on occasion by every Labour leader over the years. For instance, to go back more than half a century, but only two-thirds of the way back through the Party's lifetime on which he comments so confidently, what are we to make of Attlee's unambiguous endorsement of Socialist doctrines and values in The Labour Party in Perspective, samples of which have been displayed earlier? Are we to take him at his word - or at least his word in 1937 - or not? It may be that Elliott would be prepared to make such a charge, but what more damning indictment could there be than the assertion that all such pronouncements by Labour leaders never were more than hot air to stoke up the fire in the bellies of their followers?

One of the paradoxes of political thought in Labour circles is that, despite the Party's affiliation to an international movement which coalesces around a body of ideas we recognise as kindred enough to be grouped under the common ideological term Socialism, many Labour politicians are as wary of the very concept of ideology as are most of their Tory opponents. Which does not, of course, mean that there *is* no ideology behind their political projects (indeed, that the truth is quite the reverse has already been demonstrated with respect to Tory thinking in Part One of this essay). It is only that those who do not recognise its presence disable themselves of the possibility of scrutinising it, and thus of explaining it to others, as well as - and even more importantly - of justifying it to themselves or of amending it because they cannot justify it. For Tories this *un*perceiving is in some ways a strength, since it bolsters their self-assurance by hiding from themselves their own prejudices. (Besides, in any context with any claim at all to being democratic, what they really stand for will not stand the light of day for a full five minutes.) For Labourites it is a grave weakness, unless they subconsciously subscribe to pretty much the same tenets as their political rivals.

Distrust of ideological thinking is so prevalent among British and American politicians that it has been identified as an Anglo-Saxon characteristic; but it would be more rational to ascribe it to the more evolutionary development of society and politics in Anglo-Saxon lands than to postulate a predilection for pragmatism peculiar to the progeny of their native soil. At all events, Labour politicians tend to pride themselves on their pragmatic approach to issues, as if to think too deeply about them is to disable oneself when it comes to making practical decisions. (The same is true of union leaders in Britain - as well as in America - and while this may have little effect on their day-to-day activities, since their immediate concerns are of a more practical nature than those of the politicians, the long-term effects of this limitation in modes of thinking are surely of vast if incalculable significance.) For the most part they reject Marxism (or rather, the ersatz condensed concoctions they take to be the bones of the matter) without coming anywhere near to understanding it, and they are temperamentally hostile towards anti-Statist forms of Socialism like Anarchism and Anarcho-Syndicalism, their conceptions of which are even more rudimentary and distorted.

But the point is not that they accept or reject any particular ideology ('ethical socialism' might serve if those who subscribe to it had taken the trouble to work out exactly what it meant to them, so that they could offer us a clear and honest prospectus, instead of fecklessly using the expression as an easy way of distancing themselves from more managerial forms of socialism, including what they benightedly call 'communism'). It is that, by neglecting rigorously to examine the bases of their own thinking and to analyse the structure of society and identify the forces within it which they might harness to haul it towards clearly denoted destinations, they disarm themselves against imposture - inflicted against themselves as well as against others! They suffer from the failing reprehended by J.S. Mill as 'the inability of the unanalytic mind to recognise its own handiwork' - and more to the point, we suffer from the botched handiwork of their inept operations on society! Such food as they offer the intellect on the subject of Socialism and its prescriptions for curing social ills is about as nourishing as the diet in a World War II POW camp run by the Japanese army. For the most part it is insipid, sloppy stuff about 'the brotherhood of man' and the like, samples of which we have already tasted. (See Chapter 25). The prize for the ultimate pronouncement in the 'pragmatic socialism' genre has got to go to Herbert Morrison's definition of Socialism as 'what Labour governments do', but scarcely more illuminating is Nye Bevan's blinding revelation that 'Socialism is about priorities'. All this shows an indifference to, if not a contempt for, serious thinking about Socialist principles - perhaps even of serious thinking about principles, full stop. No wonder the 'socialist' faith of Old Labour could not make a stand against the evangelising fervour of the New Tories!

It is no accident that the only unmistakably socialistic doctrine in the Labour Party's constitution (which is almost entirely concerned with organisational matters) should again and again have become a bone of contention between the Party's leaders and the Movement's rank and file - or at least enough of them to produce some pretty ferocious dogfights. I refer, of course, to the clause introduced into the constitution in 1918 (see the extract above from Gregory Elliott's book) as one of the (ultimately seven) 'Party objects'. As amended, this famous - or as some would have it, infamous - clause reads as follows:

> 'To secure for the workers by hand or by brain the full fruits of their industry and the most equitable distribution thereof that may be possible upon the basis of the common ownership of the means of production, distribution, and exchange, and the best obtainable system of popular administration and control of each industry or service.'

The clause is more famous than familiar. which is to say, more read than understood and more talked about than read, otherwise it could not have given rise to so much accidental (as distinct from deliberate) misrepresentation. Three or four observations are indispensable. Its first *and* primary point echoes the historic demand that workers should enjoy the fruits of their labour and calls for the equitable distribution of the wealth they produce. Outrageous demands indeed! It nowhere mentions nationalisation, which make its references to 'common ownership' etc. and to 'the best obtainable system of popular administration and control' etc. open to wide interpretation - even among the intellectually honest. It is followed by a fifth objective ('generally to promote the political, social and economic emancipation of the people, and more particularly of those who depend directly upon their own exertions by hand or by brain for the means of life') framed in much more general - and thus vaguer - terms, which nevertheless gains strength from the specifics of Clause IV (4). (Incidentally, in his entry on this offensive clause in his *Brewer's Politics*, Nicholas Comfort points to an intriguing parallel in the subversive thinking of the American president who also gave us that dangerous definition of democracy as 'government of the people, by the people, for the people'. Abraham Lincoln concluded his contribution to a discussion of tariff law which took place in 1847 with the remark that to secure 'for each laborer the whole product of his labor, or nearly as possible, is a most worthy object of any good government'.)

Such was Labour's covenant with those dependent 'upon their own exertions...for the means of life' which - within a few years of the Party's brief chapter of glory in leading a nation reforged in fire - faint-hearts had concluded was inimical to the re-election of Labour to power. For timorousness or treachery had set in long before Tony Blair made his successful bid (in 1994-95) for the extinguishing of the clause which 'the lost leader', Neil Kinnock, had contemptuously dismissed as 'tunes of glory'. At the post-mortem conference following Labour's third successive general election defeat in 1959, Hugh Gaitskell, wilfully misrepresenting the offending clause as calling for '100 per cent state ownership' and as implying that that was 'the only precise object we have', called for its deletion from the constitution. He was rebuffed, but (as Comfort puts it) the 'modernisers' continued to see it 'as an albatross' around the Party's neck.

The Labour left saw it quite otherwise. It helped them cling to their hope that the Party might yet prove to be an agency for social transformation. The myths and realities behind the tenacious defence of Clause IV are well expressed by Tony Cliff and Donny Gluckstein in *The Labour Party - A Marxist History* (1988):

'In a body where symbolism frequently outweighs reality, this is the holy of holies. It is the most pious of Labour's many pious resolutions, yet its words are important. They mark *the conversion of the Labour Party into a 'socialist' organisation, or, to be more exact, a mass reformist party* distinct from the two openly capitalist parties...it was drafted by [Sidney] Webb...*as a conscious means of staving off revolution.* It was the fear of mass action which forced them to take this step...There is an important difference between Clause Four in 1918 and Clause Four today. Seventy years ago it registered the high water mark of workers' pressure on the Labour Party. Since then the imminence of revolution has never been so great. But Clause Four remains in the party constitution - a relic of days gone by. In this sense it must now be defended as a sign of Labour's commitment to a minimal anti-capitalist

position which some leaders would like to forget.'
[authors' emphases]

Gregory Elliott, in the paragraph following the passage from *Labourism and the English Genius* quoted above, declares firmly: 'Although the revisionist enterprise of amending the 1918 Constitution faltered, Labour did in fact make the transition from Clause 4 "socialism" to social democracy *in the late 1950s and early 1960s.*' [author's emphasis] At the time few of those on the left can have recognised that - despite their rout of the revisionists - the decisive transition of which Elliott writes had occurred. Paradoxically, perhaps this was just as well, since there was no alternative *parliamentary* channel for propagating Socialist solutions to society's problems (nor will there be as long as Britain's absurd first-past-the-post system of electoral gambling prevails). As for the contentious clause itself, it remained of totemic importance to the Left, and as late as 1983 was overwhelmingly reaffirmed as 'the central aim of the Labour Party', with Conference explicitly demanding 'repossession of all parts of the public sector privatised by the Tories.'

It may be that the Left's staunch attachment to Clause IV was largely to be accounted for by continuing support within the Party for nationalisation. By 1987, however, under the hammer blows of the Thatcherite 'counter-revolution', this particular enthusiasm had waned to such an extent that the NUM resolution to Conference calling for all industries privatised by the Tories to be renationalised was heavily defeated. Doubtless what persuaded delegates to give up their addiction was the pusillanimous argument that to renationalise the industries concerned would entail paying the new private 'owners' something in the region of £15 billion. And given the unfortunate focusing of Labour minds on the secondary issue of public ownership called for in the second part of section (4) of Clause IV, this 'how can we possibly afford to buy back our own property?' defeatism may well explain why the Party's single explicitly Socialist aspiration was eventually consigned to 'the dustbin of history' with relative ease.

For others, however, the question of public or private ownership of 'the means of production, distribution, and exchange' is not, *in itself*, of paramount importance (though the impact which different forms of ownership may have on the kind of society we

450

live in is quite another matter). For such Socialists it is the issue of social justice which is at the heart of the matter. Shortly after Tony Blair's slyly oblique targeting of Clause IV at his first Conference as Party leader, a history research student at Sussex University, Jacqueline Tratt, in a piece written for the 'Face to Faith' column of *The Guardian*, lamented 'the death of Labour's Clause Four' as 'final acknowledgement of the triumph of competition and the market'. She put down the moral impasse we are in to the fact that: 'In the post-Thatcher era, there are not enough votes any more in social justice. The Labour Party has learned the lesson and is adapting its policies and constituency accordingly...'

'And after fifteen years out of office,' she goes on, 'who can blame them?' But that is being altogether too charitable. My own critique is grounded in the conviction that while it may be possible for Labour to abandon all commitment to Socialism without serious damage to its reputation (its moral reputation, that is; its cerebral reputation is another matter), it cannot without dishonour desert the cause of social justice. One can see the logic of the case for ditching the old Clause IV - even if one cannot agree with it and cannot respect the dissembling fashion in which it was foisted on the Party. But healthy scepticism could not but question whether (as was claimed) honesty, with itself and with others (honestly admitting, that is, that bringing about 'the common ownership of the means of production, distribution, and exchange' was not now, if it ever had been, the Party's aim), was the real reason for the determination of the 'modernisers' to amend Labour's constitution. Was it not, rather, the almost antithetical concern for flexibility, for room to manoeuvre, to avoid being pinned down by the mercenaries of a hostile media?

After all, the best safeguard against being charged with failing to deliver on promises is not to make any. But since that is hardly a practicable strategy for winning over the voters, politicians usually fall back on the second-best safeguard, which is to make promises which are so general in character (such as, 'to improve the country's economic performance and raise standards of living', or even, 'to strengthen the position and prestige of the nation in the world') that it is often difficult to disprove their claims to have fulfilled them. Vagueness is the politician's friend, which is why an abstract principle like 'social justice', which needs a lot of defining to mean much at all, is much to be preferred as a declared objective to the old 'full fruits of their industry' promise, while 'fairness' is even better, since it is so flexible as to mean whatever its advocate chooses it to mean. (Nothing illustrates this better than what that pre-eminent precursor of the Blairite 'modernisers', Anthony Crosland, did to the word 'equality' by liberating it from the sordid shackles of being thought of as having some connection at least with considerations of material wealth.)

In Clause IV as refashioned for the dawn of the new millennium (the old millennium of the mind, having signally failed to live up to its promise, could pass away unmourned except by eccentrics) one ancient relic remained, in the astonishingly bold declaration that Labour was 'a democratic socialist party'. But the main engine for its stated aspirations was clearly to be private capitalism, surfing the seas of the 'free market' somehow (unlike the merchants in the Temple) on a wing and a prayer, *in the public interest*. And Labour's new Clause IV passes the acid test for flexibility with flying colours. Although it is true that those parties contending with Labour for 'the trust of the people to govern' (as the final words of the glossy rewrite puts it) would have placed the emphasis on different aspects of the goodies on display, apart from that haunting echo of the bold challenges of a more heroic age just mentioned, there is nothing to which *any* of them could take exception. Or not openly at any rate!

Not that there is anything wrong with what New Labour says it 'believes', it 'is committed to', and it 'will work for'. All, all, are honourable aspirations - if they are more than pious hopes. Which is to say, *if* - despite the unpromising withdrawal from socialistic solutions and the present invisibility of convincing alternative solutions - the words express an underlying and invincible will *for something like a transformation of society*. For nothing short of such a transformation can turn those aspirations into realities.

And the trouble is we have been waiting (and not *just* waiting, either, but working. too) for such promises to be fulfilled for half a century or more, those of us whose lives span the years from the war to stop the tidal wave of conquest unleashed by the great dictators, and perhaps go back to (in J.B. Priestley's words in his trenchant *Letter to a Returning Serviceman*) 'the sickening muddle, darkening to tragedy, of the Twenties and Thirties'. And as it says in *Proverbs*: 'Hope deferred maketh the heart sick.'

In an article written for *The Guardian* four months before

the shock re-endorsement of the Tory hegemony in April 1992, Dennis Kavanagh spoke of the irony that 'Mrs Thatcher changed Labour more than she changed her own party. As her own party discreetly tries to distance itself from her, so Labour has come to terms with much of her work.' Entitled 'The phoney wars', the article makes two further salutary observations for the consideration of those disposed to put their faith, or at least to invest too much hope, in returning Labour to power. The point is not spelt out, but the first and more fundamental observation implicitly warns against expecting too much of changes of government in our kind of society. 'Apart from political careers and party fortunes, do general elections actually make much difference?...The only post-war elections that can be said to have made a difference...were those of 1945 and 1979, and historians may well conclude that even then the new governments confirmed change that was already under way.' The second observation relates to those incredibly enduring illusions about the Labour Party. 'Mrs Thatcher said that she wanted to kill off socialism in Britain, and it is often said that she did so. This is wrong; it died long ago. Under Wilson and Callaghan Labour was concerned above all with gaining and retaining office. Party politics was a battle between the ins and the outs.'

Of course, one can only choose between choices which actually exist (or in exceptional circumstances such as revolutions can perhaps be made to exist), and for anyone with any sense of the fundamentally equal worth of all human beings there is simply no contest between New Labour and the New Tories. Launching a UNICEF report in 1993, the fund's (since deceased) American executive director, Jim Grant, expressed his faith that:

> 'The day will come when the progress of nations will be judged not by their military or economic strength, nor by the splendour of their capital cities and public buildings, but by the well-being of their peoples: by their levels of health, nutrition, and education: by their opportunities to earn a fair reward for their labours: by their ability to participate in the decisions that affect their lives: by the respect that is shown for their civil and political liberties: by the provision that is made for those who are vulnerable and disadvantaged: and by the protection that is afforded to the growing minds and bodies of their children.'

Now that would be worth voting for; and a Labour Party with a real commitment to social justice would be a social reform party worth supporting and working for, even if its new aspirations fell sadly short of its old ones.

But what assurance can we reasonably feel (even if we are sanguine enough to believe that private capitalists in general can somehow be cajoled, cudgelled, or otherwise manoeuvred into a position few of them or their predecessors have ever taken before - a position, that is, of making 'the public interest' their paramount concern) that New Labour will deliver on its (admittedly far more modest) promises where Old Labour for the most part failed? Just over a century ago, in the course of a lecture on the American economist Henry George, whose *Progress and Poverty* was creating such a stir on both sides of the Atlantic, the social philosopher and philanthropist Arnold Toynbee apologised to his working-class audience for the indifference and callousness which had generally characterised the attitude of 'the middle classes...not merely the very rich' towards their hard and not infrequently dire situation. 'Instead of justice we have offered you charity,' he said.

It is difficult (perhaps impossible) for people of a paternalistic turn of mind to recognise the difference. But to my way of thinking Charity was what Labour offered the ordinary people - the real wealth-creators - of post-war Britain. And after it had been chipped away as Britain's relative ranking in the league of nations' wealth listings declined, in order not to jeopardise the privileged life-styles of the seriously rich and those hanging on to their coat-tails, it turned out to be meagre charity at that. Social Justice never was seriously on the agenda.

That is the truth, and we should not hide it from ourselves. Old Labour never came anywhere near to being as good as its word. Maybe, by some miracle of self-transformation, New Labour will shape up to its more modest proposal of ushering in an age of kinder capitalism supervised by 'democratically-elected' paternalists - a proposal not so different really from Plato's ideal of rule by philosopher-kings!

PostScript

Not long after writing this I re-read Michael Young's far-sighted look into the future, *The Rise of the Meritocracy: 1870-2033*, which was first published in 1958. It occurred to me that nothing could provide a more fitting postscript (or should one rather say 'post-mortem'?) for the sorry tale of the Labour Party than the following passage from that scintillating satire:

> 'The Labour Party made the inevitable compromise with the new society it had done so much to create: it ceased to exist. Fewer and fewer electors, however brawny, responded instinctively to the appeal of "labour". Drawn upwards by their aspirations for their children...[they] conceived of themselves as a cut above the labourer at the bottom of the heap. The canny leaders of the...Party...recognised full well the need for change. They scrapped the appeal to working-class solidarity and concentrated on the middle class, partly to capture new sections of the electorate, more to keep pace with their own supporters who had, in their outlook, moved upwards from their point of origin. One of the symptoms of rampant ambition was the upgrading by name alone of occupations which could not be upgraded in any other way...rat-catchers were called "rodent officers", sanitary inspectors "public health inspectors", and lavatory cleaners "amenities attendants". Employers conformed to the changing *mores* by dismissing their "workers" and hiring none but technicians, clothed in white coats instead of dungarees. The Labour Party finally made the same adjustment. "Labour" was a millstone; "worker" was taboo; but "technician", what magic was there! And so the modern Technicians Party was born, catering in the broadest possible manner for technicians by hand and by brain.'

UTOPIA AND REALITY

'A map of the world that does not include Utopia is
not a map that I want to look at.'

Oscar Wilde

Alternative societies

As the dominant personality of British politics in the 1980s, and
acclaimed leader of a capitalist counter-revolution against welfare-
state 'socialism' which reverberated around the world, Margaret
Thatcher attracted a positive cornucopia of colourful nicknames,
adulatory or derisory, and sometimes both at the same time.
Amongst them were 'the Iron Lady', 'Attila the Hen', 'the Great
She-Elephant', 'the Blessed St. Margaret', 'Laura Norder', and
'She-who-must-be-obeyed'. None, however, was more revealing
of the woman's mind-set (nor of the Narnia-like hold it exercised
over the country she ruled for nearly twelve years) than that
deceptively unalarming girl's name, 'Tina'. An acronym of her
relentlessly reiterated assertion, 'There is no alternative', it
epitomises a style of political debate (or rather of the stifling of
such debate) - engendered by tunnel-minded vision and rooted in
dogmatic certitude - which she did not, of course, invent (the great
dictators of her youthful days were consummate practitioners of
the art of what she liked to call 'conviction politics'), but which
she did bring to an exquisite height of perfection in the context of
quasi-democratic politics.

Thatcher and her acolytes never 'won the argument' - as they
were accustomed to boasting they had done - since (with rare
exceptions), togaed in the dignity of first principles and self-evident
truths, they did not deign to treat opposing points of view seriously.
But in a manner quite remarkable for a still nominally pluralistic
society, they did - aided and abetted by a largely like-minded media
and with only a wavering opposition in Parliament - to an
extraordinary extent drown out contrary voices and circumscribe
the agenda for 'sensible' political debate. But perhaps it was not so
remarkable after all. With so many 'socialist' redoubts (including
those engineered by the Liberal economist John Maynard Keynes

to counter unemployment and recession, and which were for a third of a century seen as indispensable to the strategy of Labour governments, and assent to which was, indeed, part of the consensus with their opponents) already surrendered by Labour's establishment even before the Tory triumph of 1979 - and with that triumph soon followed by abject admissions by both Denis Healey and by that once-upon-a-time fiery Welsh radical Neil Kinnock, after his elevation to the Labour leadership following Michael Foot's rout in the 1983 general election, that henceforth market forces would be accepted by Labour as the principal agency of prosperity - it might be felt that the New Tories' hegemony in the field of political thought had not been so hard won.

After all, leading Labour luminary Anthony Crosland had sold the pass as early as 1956 with his absurd contention that capitalism had already passed away; and although it would take another three decades for the concept of 'socialism' to be effectively expunged from Labour's 'authorised version' of the New Jerusalem, no Party leader subsequent to Attlee ever seriously purported to aspire to more than managing capitalism (or non-capitalism, as Crosland would have it) better than its naked but unashamed advocates. Heath's celebrated censure of 'the unpleasant and unacceptable face of capitalism' exhibited by the sleazy Lonrho affair of 1973 provoked no withering retort from Labour regarding the manifest social evils emanating from the grip of private capitalism on the nation's economy, which had once been a general conviction in its ranks. By the 1990s capitalism's shining virtues had become so apparent to the Labour establishment that its leader, whizz-kid Tony Blair, could recycle Ted Heath's disingenuously selective strictures with a silly sally about 'the unacceptable face of privatisation'.

Yet the no-alternative-to-capitalism assumption common to the politicians of all parliamentary parties in Britain (and in every other representative democracy in the world) has given us, in the last two decades of 'the Century of the Common Man', 2-4 million-odd unemployed (with a doleful tally from the European Union countries collectively of upwards of 20 million jobless) and ever-increasing inequality - arguably, indeed, mass poverty. (And that is to say nothing of less blessed realms sustaining - if that is not too mocking a way of putting it - four-fifths of the world's population.) The competitive caterpillars of capitalism have gnawed away at the pillars of the Welfare-State structures built in the aftermath of the great war against fascism, and now threaten to bring the temple down round our ears 'because we cannot afford its upkeep' and to replace it with a more modest, well, poorhouse really. It is truly astonishing that such reactionary and downright dishonest arguments have the remotest chance of prevailing in the counsels of supposedly democratic societies in the late twentieth century! But the truth is that, half a century on from William Beveridge's brave Bunyanesque call to slay the 'Five Giants on the Road to Recovery: Want, Ignorance, Disease, Squalor, and Idleness', they are all alive and kicking back, even if their victims are no longer the majority of our compatriots but only a quarter or so, with the rest of us in the main subject less to hard times than to fear of them.

This is where the practical, down-to-earth, realistic politicians (many of them pleased to call themselves 'radicals') have brought us, with 'revolutionary' redefined in New Labour's *Dictionary for Modernisers* as 'referring to an organisational structure enabling the Party leader to take the decisions necessary for winning power, unhampered by the time-wasting restraints involved in processing them through the Party's democratic machinery' - or something to that effect. (See the leaked report - deliciously entitled 'The Unfinished Revolution' - produced by consultant Philip Gould for Tony Blair and published in *The Guardian*, 12th September 1995.)

As we all know, utopias are, by definition, impossible of realisation, so nothing more needs to be said to shoot down an alternative vision than to call it 'utopian'. Denis Healey's approach to the eradication of social evils, like that of all the Labour leaders he served under, is that of the Fabian inch-worm. He is an admirer of the dissident Polish philosopher Leszek Kolakowski, and in *The Time of My Life* he cites with approval (as 'not an ignoble vision' which 'will do far more to help real people living in the real world today and tomorrow than all the cloudy rhetoric of systematic ideologies') Kolakowski's comment that while it 'does not sell any of the exciting ideological commodities which various totalitarian movements - Communist, Fascist, or Leftist - offer dream-hungry youth', and while 'it has no prescription for the total salvation of mankind', democratic socialism requires, besides 'commitment to a number of basic values, hard knowledge and rational calculation' and also 'an obstinate will to erode by inches the conditions which produce avoidable suffering, oppression, hunger, wars, racial and national hatred, insatiable greed and vindictive envy.'

Silenced in his own country for his unacceptable independence of mind, Kolakowski had ample reason to distrust all-embracing ideologies. But in deploying his words as a kind of apologia for his own record as a politician, Healey was perhaps unaware of Kolakowski's earlier ringing affirmation of the value of utopias. In an essay entitled *The Concept of the Left*, written in the turbulent period following Khrushchev's devastating speech on Stalin's dictatorship to the Twentieth Congress of the Soviet Communist Party, Kolakowski declares that 'the Left cannot do without a utopia', a word he uses ('deliberately and not in the derogatory sense that expresses the absurd notion that all social changes are pipe-dreams') to speak of 'a state of social consciousness, a mental counterpart to the social movement striving for radical change in the world.' His argument is that 'as a conservative force', the Right needs not utopia but 'fraud', since it 'strives to idealise actual conditions, not to change them', unless it be to revert to a former state it considers more desirable; but 'the Left cannot give up utopia because it is a real force even when it is merely a utopia.' To the 'pipe-dreams' jibe he opposes the weight of history:

> 'Much historical experience...tells us that goals unattainable now will never be reached unless they are articulated when they are still unattainable. It may well be that the impossible at a given moment can become possible only by being stated at a time when it is impossible...*The existence of a utopia as a utopia is the necessary prerequisite for its eventually ceasing to be a utopia.*'

And again he writes:

> '*The striving for revolution cannot be born only when the situation is ripe, because among the conditions for this ripeness are the revolutionary demands made of an unripe reality.*' [author's emphases]

It may or may not be that the Kolakowski who wrote the words cited by Healey would stand by his more youthful thoughts on revolution and utopias; but however great may seem the descent in hopes and aspirations from Kolakowski's revolutionary Marxist days to his state of mind when he wrote that tribute to the stoical virtues of democratic socialist politics, the views expressed are not in fact incompatible. However much talk of 'an obstinate will to erode by inches the conditions which produce avoidable suffering' may denote a more pessimistic perception of the obstacles to be overcome and of the time-scale over which they may be surmounted, the need for radical change - as distinct from mere amelioration - remains an imperative for the reformed Kolakowski. And if he now feels that the cost of swift revolution is too great or makes its consolidation too unlikely (though these are not issues he discusses in the passages cited), he can hardly be recommending as a positive good any slower progress towards radical change than it is possible to make by non-violent means.

Revolution through a process of cumulative reform would be another way for stating this attitude. Such is (or at least was) the prescription of Fabian Socialism. Yes, it is 'not an ignoble vision'. But it does demand an apprehended destination and some idea of how to reach it. Furthermore, if more revolutionary routes are rejected, some sense of progress towards that destination must be felt by those who buy tickets in the hope that at least their children or their grandchildren might reach it - a sense which, to say the least, it has been hard to feel after the sidelining of semi-socialist programmes under the Wilson and Callaghan Governments, not to mention the major reversals suffered under the New Tory regimes.

As the twentieth century draws to a close, must we just be grateful that it looks like ending, in Eliot's words, 'not with a bang but a whimper'? What seems most eroded is not those 'conditions which produce avoidable suffering' but the will to change them. Across the length and breadth of Europe and beyond, the 'democratic socialist' parties (or at least their leaders) appear to have no alternative vision to offer the people than the 'free market capitalism' of their ostensible opponents, or at best a customised version of this glorious free-for-all (all with the dosh, that is) alluringly packaged as 'the social market' - an elusive concept pioneered by that once potentially revolutionary force the German Social Democratic Party and eagerly taken up by David Owen in the days when he believed that his SDP was going to 'break the mould' of British politics.

The best part of a century earlier (when abject poverty was

indeed far more widespread even in the industrialised nations) vision was not so wanting among those who called themselves Socialists - and even Labour Party leaders were proud of that label then! Shortly before World War I, writing - in *Socialism and Syndicalism* (1913) - from an avowedly Fabian-gradualist and emphatically anti-syndicalist standpoint, Philip Snowden, observing that 'every political party in the United Kingdom claims to be a party of Social Reform' (to which he could have added that such a claim was indispensable in a representative democracy), proclaimed an essential distinction between 'Social Reformers' and 'Socialists', and that it lay in the Socialists' rejection of the assumption 'that it is possible to abolish social evils...without changing the basis of the economic structure of society.' He maintained that 'there cannot be extremes of wealth without all the moral and social evils which inevitably spring therefrom', and declared: 'No so-called reform touches the problem unless it lessens the power of capitalism to appropriate socially-created wealth.'

And he went on to make an observation which might have served as a warning to all his successors as Chancellors of the Exchequer in Labour administrations, each one of whom half-seriously thought to bring Socialist equality a little nearer through the redistribution of income and wealth, and to effect this with the instrument of taxation. Citing facts and figures for those opening years of 'the Century of the Common Man', Snowden demonstrated that the accumulation of wealth by the wealthy was proceeding far more rapidly than the levying of revenue from that wealth, and that if this were not so, the cry would go up that the taxes were tantamount to confiscation. And as for welfare reforms and rises in the workers' standard of living, although these were obviously to be welcomed, the principal beneficiaries of such advances were (as they always must be under capitalism) those who gained as employers from the workers' higher productivity or as landlords or traders from their greater spending power.

Snowden never was the sort of man one would call a dreamer or a visionary, let alone a revolutionary, yet in those days of hope (eleven years, that is, before he became Labour's first Chancellor of the Exchequer in 1924 and eighteen before he accepted that high office for the third time, when Ramsay MacDonald formed his so-called 'National Government' in 1931, following a general election campaign during which Snowden described the programme of his

461

erstwhile Labour comrades as 'Bolshevism gone mad' - Labour has never been short of turncoats) he looked forward sanguinely to 'the gradual acquisition of political power by the democracy and the gradual transformation of the capitalist system into a co-operative commonwealth'. Eight decades later, New Labour's leaders must surely find such a belief about as utopian as you can get!

Only the present is real: the past is a story and the future a vision. Yet the truth is that there are always *many* alternatives to the tyranny of the present moment - alternatives waiting to be conceived and bounding far beyond the narrow confines of withered imaginations. '*The Left* doesn't accept the reproach of striving for a utopia,' Kolakowski boldly declares in the essay cited. [author's emphasis] And around the turn of the century, when the continuing poverty of the masses in even the wealthiest nations gave ample cause for despair, there was not the present dearth of people bold enough to imagine a just society and to proffer their 'utopias' to others. Such utopias were of two principal kinds, emblematic or analytic. By emblematic I mean presenting a picture of a more desirable society, as Bellamy did in *Looking Backward* (1888) and William Morris did in *News from Nowhere* (1890). By analytical I mean attempting to demonstrate that it is actually possible to change things radically enough to call it creating a new kind of society. These attempts were, in effect, assaults on the 'there-is-no-alternative' mentality in general (a mentality which tends to be prevalent at all times in most places) and, in particular, on the hegemony over the human mind of the capitalist concept, with all its malign offspring: from its Malthuses and Social Darwinists of yesteryear, to its Thatcherites, emasculated Socialists, and obscurantist 'Social Marketeers' of our times. And if we find the case those earlier Socialists made - *something like a hundred years ago* - at all convincing, we must conclude that 'the common man' has been led by the nose through the trials and tribulations of 'his own century'.

The economic system we know as capitalism - a system which, with the fall of The Wall and the effectual capitulation to its sworn ideological enemies of 'Communist' China, more or less holds sway from one end of the earth to the other - depends for its success on the accumulation of wealth to produce yet more wealth. Accumulation is, as it were, the seed corn which must be saved to provide the wherewithal of future consumption. That much is unarguable. How it is saved (whether by individuals or, in some form or other, by the community) is another matter, as is how it is used for the generation of more wealth. And a separate question altogether is how that part of the wealth produced which is not set aside as seed corn but consumed should be distributed. And from the point of view of the people of a country as a whole, however wealthy or otherwise their 'nation' may be, how else should the success of capitalism be judged than by whether it delivers the goods to each and every one of them, or fails to do so?

'Nowhere is the old cliché "Poverty in the midst of Plenty" more easily applicable than in the later years of the nineteenth century in the United States,' writes Peter d'A. Jones in *An Economic History of the United States since 1783*. 'Recurrent economic crises, maldistribution and unintelligent exploitation and wastage of natural resources gave rise to a rich literature of protest and to governmental intervention in economic life - to social criticism and social reform.' Foremost among the critics was the self-taught economist Henry George, whose central idea for remedying the ills of capitalist society, a single tax on that commodity which he believed to be the inalienable right of every human being to use, namely land, winged its way around the world (not only to other English-speaking countries but to realms as far-flung and disparate as China and Denmark), and its force is not yet spent.

This idea was given its fullest development in a book published in March 1879, almost exactly a hundred years before that addle-pated archangel of resurgent capitalism seized that Box-and-Cox State of complacent consensus which its more tradition-minded citizens still most like to call Great Britain. *Progress and Poverty* - dedicated 'To those who seeing the vice and misery that spring from the unequal distribution of wealth and privilege feel the possibility of a higher social state and would strive for its attainment' - is subtitled *'An inquiry into the cause of industrial depressions and of increase of want with increase of wealth'*, and its author devoted the greater part of his fairly short life (1839-1897) to propagating his single-tax remedy for this deplorable state of affairs. Although both his diagnosis and his cure may be highly simplistic, Henry George's one big idea - that the expropriation and exploitation by the few of the land which rightly belonged to the many and which properly constituted the very basis of the *common*wealth was the primary cause of society's ills, and that these ills could be remedied by an appropriate system of taxation - remains a great idea which has been sorely neglected by the Left. That it is a great idea should be obvious from the simple fact that it is patently totally unacceptable to the Right!

More germane to the present polemic, however, is Henry George's passionate indictment of an economic system erected on the expendable lives of the many without whom its triumphs could never have been won, and his equally passionate affirmation that this blighting of lives is not a sacrifice which is necessary for the creation of wealth. Remember, the book which asserts this was written more than a hundred years ago! Yet despite the great elevation in the general standard of living in the most developed countries of the world since then, and despite the welfare safety-nets their societies have strung up to catch those so stricken by ill-fortune of one kind or another that they cannot adequately help themselves, the judgements delivered in *Progress and Poverty* - however dated their forms of expression may make them appear - are in their fundamentals no less just and true today. Consider, for example - in the sombre light of the current condition of the disjointed 'Western' societies, intermittently roughly in step then stumblingly at odds, as they straggle along towards the millennium - the following passages:

> 'The wrong that produces inequality; the wrong that in the midst of abundance tortures men with want or harries them with the fear of want; that stunts them physically, degrades them intellectually, and distorts them morally, is what alone prevents harmonious social development.'

> 'In the very centres of our civilisation today are want and suffering enough to make sick at heart whoever does not close his eyes and steel his nerves.'

> 'Between democratic ideas and the aristocratic adjustments of society there is an irreconcilable conflict. Here in the United States, as there in Europe, it may be seen arising. We cannot go on permitting men to vote and forcing them to tramp. We cannot go on educating

boys and girls in our public [i.e. State] schools and then refusing them the right to earn an honest living. We cannot go on prating of the inalienable rights of man and then denying the inalienable right to the bounty of the Creator. Even now, in old bottles the new wine begins to ferment, and elemental forces gather for the strife!'

As the above passage indicates and the extracts given below make explicit, Henry George is no simpleton, to believe that universal suffrage ushered in 'government of the people, by the people, for the people.' Or to put it another way, he well understood that political democracy is but a bauble without economic democracy.

'All the dull, deadening pain, all the keen, maddening anguish, that to great masses of men are involved in the words "hard times", afflict the world today. This state of things, common to communities differing so widely in situation, in political institutions, in fiscal and financial systems, in density of population and in social organisation, can hardly be accounted for by local causes. There is distress where large standing armies are maintained, but there is also distress where the standing armies are nominal; there is distress where protective tariffs stupidly and wastefully hamper trade, but there is also distress where trade is nearly free; there is distress where autocratic government yet prevails, *but there is also distress where political power is wholly in the hands of the people.*' [my emphasis]

'To educate men who must be condemned to poverty, is but to make them restive; to base on a state of most glaring social inequality political institutions under which men are theoretically equal, is to stand a pyramid on its apex.'

The riddle Henry George set himself to solve was why accelerating economic progress should bring, to so many, not security but poverty. 'The great enigma of our times,' he called it. The book opens with a positively rhapsodic evocation of progress:

'The present century has been marked by a prodigious increase in wealth-producing power. The utilisation of steam and electricity, the introduction of improved processes and labour-saving machinery, the greater sub-division and grander scale of production, the wonderful facilitation of exchanges, have multiplied enormously the effectiveness of labour. At the beginning of this marvellous era it was natural to expect, and it was expected, that labour-saving inventions would lighten the toil and improve the condition of the labourer; that the enormous increase in the power of producing wealth would make real poverty a thing of the past. Could a man of the last century - a Franklin or a Priestley - have seen, in a vision of the future, the steamship taking the place of the sailing vessel, the railroad train of the waggon, the reaping machine of the scythe, the threshing machine of the flail; could he have heard the throb of the engines that in obedience to human will...[and so on, and so on]...could he have conceived of the hundred thousand improvements which these only suggest, what would he have inferred as to the social condition of mankind?...Plainly, in the sight of the imagination, he would have beheld these new forces elevating society from its very foundations, lifting the very poorest above the possibility of want, exempting the very lowest from anxiety for the material needs of life...And out of these bounteous material conditions he would have seen arising, as necessary sequences, moral conditions realising the golden age of which mankind have always dreamed... Foul things fled, fierce things tame; discord turned to harmony! For how could there be greed where all had enough? How could the vice, the crime, the ignorance, the brutality, that spring from poverty and the fear of poverty, exist where poverty had vanished? Who should crouch where all were freemen? Who oppress where all are peers?'

To men and women of goodwill 'at the beginning of this marvellous era' who had such reasonable visions, 'progress' brought bitter disillusionment:

'The march of invention has clothed mankind with
powers of which a century ago the boldest imagination
could not have dreamed. But in factories where labour-
saving machinery has reached its most wonderful
development, little children are at work...large classes
are maintained by charity or live on the verge of
recourse to it; amid the greatest accumulations of
wealth, men die of starvation, and puny infants suckle
dry breasts; while everywhere the greed of gain, the
worship of wealth, shows the force of the fear of want.'

Of course the picture is too stark to portray accurately the advanced
democracies of our times. Yet without casting our eyes any further
afield, into Third World territory, when he goes on, 'The promised
land flies before us like the mirage', we can see clearly enough that
our condition is not so different from the one he is writing about.
And in one passage in particular he speaks of a state which is
common to most of our 'superior' societies today, the tolerating of
the existence of a section of sub-citizens left out of normal
participation in their society ('socially excluded', as the current
cant has it) through that very fact - poverty:

'It is true that wealth has been greatly increased, and
that the average of comfort, leisure, and refinement has
been raised; but these gains are not general. In them the
lowest class do not share. I do not mean that the
condition of the lowest class has nowhere nor in
anything been improved; but that there is nowhere any
improvement which can be credited to increased
productive power. I mean that the tendency of what we
call material progress is in nowise to improve the
condition of the lowest class in the essentials of healthy,
happy human life. Nay, more, that it is to depress still
further the condition of the lowest class. The new
forces, elevating in their nature though they be, do not
act upon the social fabric from underneath, as was for a
long time hoped and believed, but strike it at a point
intermediate between top and bottom. It is as though an
immense wedge were being forced, not underneath
society, but through society. Those who are above the

point of separation are elevated, but those who are below are crushed down.'

Henry George lived and laboured - as seaman, hired hand, printer, journalist, editor, and newspaper proprietor - in the fastest-growing capitalist economy in the world. From Philadelphia and New York in the east to San Francisco in the west, he saw for himself both the marvels and the miseries of that era of exponential increase in the nation's wealth, which is why he could write about them so vividly. From inconspicuous beginnings, he became a man of renown, so that one of his biographers noted that his death 'was followed by one of the greatest demonstrations of popular feeling and respect that ever attended the funeral of any private citizen in American history.'

With regard to lineage, one could not be much farther removed from this American witness against the social system bequeathed to the world by capitalism than was Prince Peter Kropotkin, who was born only three years after Henry George, but lived long enough to see the Bolsheviks seize power in the one country which the prescient French historian Alexis de Tocqueville foretold in 1835 (in his brilliant study *Democracy in America*) might one day come to compete for global supremacy with the lustily-growing young republic in the New World. Paradoxically, however, the mature Kropotkin was in his way no less a self-made man than Henry George. Only so could he have made that almost unimaginable mental journey from his origins as scion of one of Tsarist Russia's most distinguished aristocratic families to a maturity in which his life was dedicated to the realisation of Anarchist-Communism. A member of the Corps of Pages, the most select military academy in Russia, at the age of fifteen; Siberian explorer at the age of twenty-two; acknowledged, when he was barely into his thirties, as an eminent geographer who had transformed understanding of the physical formation of the continent of Asia; he threw away his privileges and his honours to join the International Working Men's Association (the First International) and work for the liberation of labour from enslavement to capital. His activities as a revolutionary propagandist earned him imprisonment both in Russia and in France. From the former he escaped after more than two years in detention; from the latter he was released by the authorities, after more than three years in French prisons, following a sustained campaign involving men and women from the worlds of scholarship and the arts in many countries, united in their indignation that a man of such distinction should be so persecuted for the non-violent propagation of his anti-Statist views.

He took refuge in England, where most of his more substantial works were written. Besides further contributions to geography, these included a book on Russian and French prisons, a history of Russian literature, a history of the French Revolution, and many works more directly promoting his Anarchist philosophy, notably his most famous book, *Mutual Aid* (1902), the subtitle of which was '*A Factor of Evolution*'. Title and subtitle taken together clearly indicate Kropotkin's purpose, which was, by showing the importance of co-operation both in animal societies and in human societies (and even in relationships between different species), to counter the common overemphasis on competition as the driving force of evolution, which in turn served to justify the fiercely competitive nature of contemporary capitalism. In his Anarchist writings as a corpus, Kropotkin shows himself to be in some respects the most fundamental and uncompromising of all the critics of capitalism. Two of his books, *The Conquest of Bread* (1892) and *Fields, Factories and Workshops* (1898), are most pertinent to the present argument: that it would have been perfectly possible to bring economies to the same stage of development as capitalism has done without committing the crimes and incurring the heartaches which every advanced society has suffered in becoming 'advanced', and from which they still suffer today. It is from the first of these two books that most of the following extracts will be taken, but as a preface to crystallise Kropotkin's attitude to the capitalist order and to questions concerning the wealth of nations and the distribution thereof, perhaps one can not do better than quote from the statement of principles which he drew up for himself and his two co-accused for their trial for sedition in Lyons in January 1883.

Contrary to the common assumption of political economists that freedom and equality are naturally at war with each other, the Anarchist-Communist credo of this statement treats them as mutually dependent. Having set out their demand for freedom for every human being and their consequential rejection of 'the governmental idea', the contumacious 'scoundrels' in the dock audaciously brandished a concept which in the context of capitalism is most commonly cant - the concept of 'free contract' - to contrapose to 'the principle of authority' in human relationships. Then they affirmed their adherence to the age-old idea of the commonwealth:

> 'We believe that capital, the common patrimony of humanity, since it is the fruit of the collaboration of past and present generations, should be at the disposal of all, so that none should be excluded from it...We desire equality, actual equality, as a corollary or rather as a primordial condition of freedom. From each according to his abilities, to each according to his needs...Scoundrels that we are, we demand bread for all; for all equally independence and justice.'

The core argument of *The Conquest of Bread* (like that of *Progress and Poverty*) is that, whatever may have been the case in earlier ages, the productive capacity of modern industry and agriculture had rendered deprivation superfluous for *any* section of society, so that were the distribution of wealth equitable, poverty would be but a page in history:

> 'And if in manufactures as in agriculture, and as indeed through our whole social system, the labour, the discoveries, and the inventions of our ancestors profit chiefly the few, it is none the less certain that mankind in general, aided by the creatures of steel and iron which it already possesses, could already procure an existence of wealth and ease for every one of its members. Truly, we are rich - far richer than we think; rich in what we already possess, richer still in the possibilities of production of our actual mechanical outfit; richest of all in what we might win from our soil, from our manufactures, from our science, from our technical knowledge, were they but applied to bringing about the well-being of all. In our civilised societies we are rich. Why then are the many poor? Why this painful drudgery for the masses? Why, even to the best paid workman, this uncertainty for the morrow, in the midst of all the wealth inherited from the past, and in spite of the powerful means of production, which could ensure comfort to all, in return for a few hours of daily toil?'

Kropotkin represented one strand in the rich weave of Socialist ideas contending for the public ear in those days. But he could confidently speak on behalf of all Socialists (revolutionary and gradualist; Marxist, Anarchist, and Social Democratic) concerning their fundamental critique of capitalism. One could not possibly do that today, even on behalf of most of those parties still prepared to admit to a nodding acquaintance with and some sympathy for Socialist ideas, since they have no such critique and little self-knowledge with regard to what they really stand for besides getting into power as quickly as possible. Yet, *mutatis mutandis*, the indictment of capitalism with which Kropotkin answers his own questions is as true of the capitalist dispensation today as it was when he made it. And that is so even of the great liberal democracies. For the masses in what used to be called the Third World (while the illusion lingered that the command economies of the so-called Soviet states offered another way), it is true just about word for word:

> 'It is because all that is necessary for production - the land, the mines, the highways, machinery, food, shelter, education, knowledge - all have been seized by the few in that long story of robbery, enforced migration and wars, of ignorance and oppression, which has been the life of the human race before it had learned to subdue the forces of Nature. It is because, taking advantage of alleged rights acquired in the past, these few appropriate today two-thirds of the products of human labour, and then squander them in the most stupid and shameful way. It is because, having reduced the masses to a point at which they have not the means of subsistence for a month, or even for a week in advance, the few can allow the many to work, only on the condition of themselves receiving the lion's share. It is because these few prevent the remainder of men from producing the things they need, and force them to produce, not the necessaries of life for all, but whatever offers the greatest profits to the monopolists. In this is the substance of all Socialism.'

Moreover, proclaims Kropotkin, human progress is a collective achievement, and everyone has the right to enjoy its fruits:

471

'Millions of human beings have laboured to create this
civilisation on which we pride ourselves today. Other
millions, scattered throughout the globe, labour to
maintain it. Without them nothing would be left in fifty
years but ruins...Science and industry, knowledge and
application, discovery and practical realisation leading
to new discoveries, cunning of brain and of hand, toil of
mind and muscle - all work together. Each discovery,
each advance, each increase in the sum of human riches,
owes its being to the physical and mental travail of the
past and the present...All things for all. Here is an
immense stock of tools and implements; here are all
those iron slaves which we call machines, which saw
and plane, spin and weave for us, unmaking and
remaking, working up raw matter to produce the
marvels of our time. But nobody has the right to seize a
single one of these machines and say: "This is mine; if
you want to use it you must pay me a tax on each of
your products", any more than the feudal lord of
mediaeval times had the right to say to the peasant:
"This hill, this meadow belong to me, and you must pay
me a tax on every sheaf of corn you reap, on every rick
you build". All is for all! If the man and the woman bear
their fair share of work, they have a right to their fair
share of all that is produced by all, and that share is
enough to secure them well-being. No more of such
vague formulas as "The right to work", or "To each the
whole result of his labour". What we proclaim is THE
RIGHT TO WELL-BEING: WELL-BEING FOR ALL!'

And in a passage a little further on in the book - following a bitter
commentary on the fate of French workers whose insistent clamour
for jobs *after* the 'success' of the 1848 revolution was answered
by the new masters of the republic with the threat of being shot
down by the forces of the State - he emphasises the fundamental
difference between reformist calls for full employment and
revolutionary demands for social justice:

'The "right to well-being" means the possibility of
living like human beings, and of bringing up children to

be members of a society better than ours, whilst the
"right to work" only means the right to be always a
wage-slave, a drudge, ruled over and exploited by the
middle class of the future. The right to well-being is the
Social Revolution, the right to work means nothing but
the Treadmill of Commercialism. It is high time for the
worker to assert his right to the common inheritance,
and to enter into possession of it.'

The fraudulent character of 'free market' capitalism is laid
bare in such withering words as these:

'In virtue of this monstrous system, the son of the worker,
on entering life, finds no field which he may till, no
machine which he may tend, no mine in which he may dig,
without accepting to leave a great part of what he will
produce to a master. He must sell his labour for a scant and
uncertain wage. His father and his grandfather have toiled
to drain this field, to build this mill, to perfect this machine.
They gave to the work the full measure of their strength,
and what more could they give? But their heir comes into
the world poorer than the lowest savage...We cry shame on
the feudal baron who forbade the peasant to turn a clod of
earth unless he surrendered to his lord a fourth of his crop.
We call those the barbarous times. But if the forms have
changed, the relations have remained the same, and the
worker is forced, under the name of free contract, to accept
feudal obligations. For, turn where he will, he can find no
better conditions. Everything has become private property,
and he must accept, or die of hunger.'

But while he would never have apologised for giving first
place to ethical considerations in his arguments, Kropotkin was
not simply moralising. He well understood that it was contrary to
the whole character of private-enterprise capitalism to put the
community first - a hard fact which seems to have eluded the subtle
cerebrations of such as Anthony Crosland:

'It is absolutely impossible that mercantile production
should be carried on in the interest of all. To desire it

473

would be to expect the capitalist to go beyond his province and to fulfil duties that he *cannot* fulfil without ceasing to be what he is - a private manufacturer seeking his own enrichment. Capitalist organisation, based on the personal interest of each individual employer of labour, has given to society all that could be expected of it: it has increased the productive force of Labour. The capitalist, profiting by the revolution effected in industry by steam, by the sudden development of chemistry and machinery, and by other inventions of our century, has worked in his own interest to increase the yield of human labour, and in a great measure he has succeeded so far. But to attribute other duties to him would be unreasonable. For example, to expect that he should use this superior yield of labour in the interest of society as a whole, would be to ask philanthropy and charity of him, and a capitalist enterprise cannot be based on charity.'

Of course, the State can oblige capitalists operating within its jurisdiction to pay some tribute; but it is natural to their motivation and *modus operandi* to do so grudgingly and in as mean a measure as possible. And now that the capitalist system is really global (though before our century began Kropotkin wrote, in *Fields, Factories and Workshops*, that 'capital knows no fatherland', observing that it migrated to wherever profits were highest), with international finance and transnational corporations setting the pace, the opportunities to evade, defy - or even to exploit for yet higher profits - the demands of the crumbling Sovereign State are legion, so that even the national bourgeoisies sometimes have cause to regret the boundless powers of capital.

The Conquest of Bread began life as a series of articles for the French-language papers *Le Revolté* and its successor, launched after its suppression, *La Revolte*. *Fields, Factories and Workshops* develops many of the themes of *The Conquest of Bread* - among them the need for the integration of industry and agriculture, of town and country, of schooling and work, of manual and intellectual tasks; and the desirability of counteracting capitalism's tendencies to centralisation, to the division of labour, and to the restless hunt for markets, by fostering a high degree of regional self-sufficiency.

It illustrates them with a wealth of detail and statistical evidence drawn both from study and from direct research during the author's travels in Europe and America. The central theme is again the perfect possibility of supplying all the necessities to all the people of the advanced nations. A more complex and scholarly work than *The Conquest of Bread* (though Kropotkin's ingrained scholarship - his scrupulous concern for evidence, accuracy, and reasoned argument - is ever present in his writings), a sociological treatise rather than a polemic, *Fields, Factories and Workshops* does not lend itself in the same way to excerpting, although it powerfully reinforces the argument of the earlier book. Furthermore, its innate concern for such subjects as (to use modern terminology) 'the conservation of resources', 'sustainable development', and care for 'the global commons' makes its message as resonant today as ever. I shall simply cite from the concluding chapter Kropotkin's heartfelt cry - 'What floods of useless sufferings deluge every so-called civilised land in the world!' - and his appeal to 'the unprejudiced mind':

> 'For centuries science and so-called practical wisdom have said to man: "It is good to be rich, to be able to satisfy, at least, your material needs; but the only means to be rich is to train your mind and capacities as to be able to compel other men - slaves, serfs or wage-earners - to make these riches for you. You have no choice. Either you must stand in the ranks of the peasants and the artisans who, whatsoever economists and moralists may promise them in the future, are now periodically doomed to starve after each bad crop or during their strikes, and to be shot down by their own sons the moment they lose patience. Or you must train your faculties so as to be a military commander of the masses, or to be accepted as one of the wheels of the governing machinery of the State, or to become a manager of men in commerce or industry." For many centuries there was no other choice, and men followed that advice, without finding in it happiness, either for themselves and their own children, or for those whom they pretended to preserve from worse misfortunes.'

But the promised future, insisted Kropotkin one hundred years ago, has arrived:

> 'Modern knowledge...tells thinking men that in order to be rich they need not take the bread from the mouths of others; but that the more rational outcome would be a society in which men, with the work of their own hands and intelligence, and by the aid of the machinery already invented and to be invented, should themselves create all imaginable riches.'

Kropotkin was right. Man had reached a plateau from which he might have struck off towards the promised land - had he had a better sense of direction. The productive capacity of industrially developed societies was such that it could have delivered well-being to all; ceaseless struggle for civic rights had won a general if grudging acknowledgement that the common people had some right to a say in their own governance; and the masses upon whose constant toil, as Kropotkin said, everything depended, had created and were creating self-help and mutual-aid organisations which they could have used to wrest their rightful heritage from their masters, as more and more of the disinherited joined their ranks.

On the plane of intellectual debate Socialist ideas were gaining ground rapidly; but the prospects for seriously challenging the hegemony of capitalism depended on solidarity, and although the Socialists were in essentials at one in their repudiation of capitalism and their reasons for doing so, they were much at odds in their strategies for replacing it and in their blueprints for post-capitalist society. These divisions lay behind the break up of the First International, although the immediate causes had more to do with bad relations between Karl Marx and the foremost champion of Anarchism, Michael Bakunin, the details of which are not pertinent to this discussion.

However, co-operation in the common struggle and many friendships continued across this divide, and it was the outbreak of war which brought about a more decisive rupture in the Socialist movement. Despite the repeated calls from Socialist international congresses for non-collaboration with the State in the event of war, which was firmly pronounced another evil endemic to capitalism, when the nation-states called them to the colours, relatively few

Socialists became war-resisters. International working-class solidarity was easily swept aside by the old nationalistic passions and prejudices that masquerade as patriotism. Ironically, spurred on by his intense hostility for everything that the Kaiser's Germany stood for, Kropotkin himself, whose whole life had been dedicated to the emancipation of humanity, supported the war, even signing, along with fourteen other well-known Anarchists, a manifesto declaring as much. Despite their illustrious names, the signatories, together with the few scores of others who subsequently endorsed the manifesto, were a small minority in the Anarchist movement, whose delegates to the Amsterdam international congress of 1907 had called for war to be met by insurrection, and most of whose leading figures (now that Socialists in one army's trenches were slaughtering Socialists in 'the enemy's' trenches) staunchly continued to urge maximum possible resistance and preparation for revolt. But such unmistakable expressions of the unrelenting opposition of most Anarchists to the war did not inhibit Lenin from exploiting Kropotkin's manifesto to slag off Anarchists in general as 'social-chauvinists'.

Although he had nothing to gain from it, Kropotkin's support for the war was inevitably seen by erstwhile comrades as a terrible betrayal. Of himself as well as of their common cause, since in the final analysis it is impossible to reconcile it with his own life and teachings. Be that as it may, over two other issues pregnant with misfortune for the future of Socialism, he was prescient indeed. These issues concerning possible forms of government in societies considering themselves Socialist, the issues of collectivism and parliamentarianism, are usually associated with two different kinds of Socialism - the former with 'State Socialism' (as in the 'Soviet' system), the latter with 'Social Democracy' - which are thought of as antithetical rather than akin. For Kropotkin, however, they have the same species of worm in the bud, and while they may not be equally undesirable in their effects, are nevertheless simply different methods for an elite to exercise authority over the people. His fears for the future of Socialism were that such authoritarian forms would prevail over the Anarchist-Communist form for which he stood. Unhappily, he lived to see one of these fears fulfilled in his own country, while we have lived to see the other fulfilled in ours.

Since the authoritarian nature of the so-called Marxist States is hardly a matter of debate amongst those who consider themselves democrats, we will take the uncontroversial issue of collectivism first, again using *The Conquest of Bread* to present Kropotkin's opinions. As we have seen, for Kropotkin freedom and equality were interdependent: neither could exist without the other. In the following passage, which incidentally relates to his rejection of the theory of 'surplus value' ('all wages' theories have been invented after the event to justify injustices at present existing,' he says acidly elsewhere) he makes it clear that a collectivist revolution would leave the common people in a position of servitude:

> 'Collectivism, as we know, does not abolish the wage system...It only substitutes the State, that is to say some form of Representative Government...for the individual employer of labour. Under Collectivism it is the representatives of the nation, or of the Commune, and their deputies and officials who are to have the control of industry. It is they who reserve to themselves the right of employing the surplus of production - in the interests of all. Moreover, Collectivism draws a very subtle but very far-reaching distinction between the work of the labourer and of the man who has learned a craft. Unskilled labour in the eyes of the collectivist is *simple* labour, while the work of the craftsman, the mechanic, the engineer, the man of science, etc., is what Marx calls *complex* labour, and is entitled to a higher wage. But labourers and craftsmen, weavers and men of science, are all wage-servants of the State - 'all officials', as was said lately, to gild the pill. Well, then, the coming Revolution could render no greater service to humanity than by making the wage system, in all its forms, an impossibility, and by rendering Communism, which is the negation of wage-slavery, the only possible system.'

He went on to warn that after the revolution the people would be patient no longer and that if food were not forthcoming they would plunder the bakeries. It would end up with the people being shot down and the capitalists lending their support to the so-called revolutionists as 'the champions of *order*'. Thus 'the Revolution itself will become hateful in the eyes of the masses.' One month less one day after Kropotkin's death on 8th February 1921, a devastating realisation of this prophetic warning came to pass when Red Army troops were launched against the naval base of Kronstadt, whose sailors, many of whom had strong Anarchist leanings, had mutinied in defence of the gains made by the revolution. Kropotkin also warned against trying to coerce the peasants to provide food to the cities instead of treating and trading with them fairly, illustrating the folly of coercion from the events of the French Revolution. But the Bolsheviks were deaf to all such warnings, as the terrible story of what almost amounts to the reintroduction of serfdom in Russia shows.

At the beginning of a chapter on possible objections to his kind of Communism, Kropotkin writes:

'It is not for us to answer the objections raised by [i.e. 'against'] authoritarian Communism - we ourselves hold with them. Civilised nations have suffered too much in the long, hard struggle for the emancipation of the individual, to disown their past work and to tolerate a Government that would make itself felt in the smallest details of a citizen's life, even if that Government had no other aim than the good of the community. Should an authoritarian Socialist society ever succeed in establishing itself, it could not last; general discontent would soon force it to break up, or to reorganise itself on principles of liberty.'

Well, such societies did establish themselves, of course, and in the author's native land one such society lasted about as long as a man's allotted span, which may be thought to prove his words far too optimistic, especially as the causes of its demise were a deal more complex than 'general discontent'. For all that, Kropotkin had signposted one of the worst possible deformations of the noble idea of Socialism, a deformation which has so discredited that name that one doubts it ever will fully recover its former good reputation.

As with a woman, there is more than one way of abusing a good idea, and it may be done without ill-intent. Some passages in the chapter on 'The Collectivist Wages System' may be cited as exposing the kinship between the ostensibly mutually antagonistic social systems of collectivism and what would more accurately be called capitalist parliamentarianism. The chapter opens challengingly:

> 'In their plans for the reconstruction of society the collectivists commit, in our opinion, a two-fold error. While speaking of abolishing capitalist rule, they intend nevertheless to retain two institutions which are the very basis of this rule - Representative Government and the Wages' System.'

The Anarchist principle of the proper distribution of responsibilities and rewards in the community are clearly enunciated in the declaration of Kropotkin and his comrades to their judges in the Lyons trial: 'From each according to his abilities, to each according to his needs.' In The Conquest of Bread Kropotkin argues that the collectivists may think they will put right injustices by acting on their principle of remuneration, but in fact they will only perpetuate the evils of capitalist calculation:

> 'The collectivists say, "To each according to his deeds"; or, in other terms, according to his share of services rendered to society. They think it expedient to put this principle into practice, as soon as the Social Revolution will have made all the instruments of production common property...Of course, in a society like ours, in which the more a man works the less he is remunerated, this principle, at first sight, may appear to be a yearning for justice. But in reality it is only the perpetuation of injustice. It was by proclaiming this principle that wagedom began, to end in the glaring inequalities and all the abominations of present society; because, from the moment work done began to be appraised in currency, or in any other form of wage, the day it was agreed upon that man would only receive the wage he should be able to secure for himself, the whole history of a State-aided Capitalist Society was as good as written; it was contained in germ in this principle.'

But Kropotkin does not denounce the wages' system only because of the gross injustices of its consequences. At the heart of his condemnation is his repudiation of the idea that it is possible to weigh and measure a person's worth to the community:

> 'Human society would not exist for more than two
> consecutive generations if everyone did not give
> infinitely more than that for which he is paid in coin, in
> "cheques", or in civic rewards. The race would soon
> become extinct if mothers did not sacrifice their lives to
> take care of their children, if men did not give
> continually, without demanding an equivalent reward, if
> men did not give most precisely when they expect no
> reward.'

The only way out of the 'blind alley' into which 'middle-class'
(i.e. capitalist) society has led us, he says, is to demolish its
institutions:

> 'We have given too much to counting...We have let
> ourselves be influenced into *giving* only to *receive*...We
> have aimed at turning society into a commercial
> company based on *debit* and *credit*.'

If all this sounds like 'primitive Christianity', the comparison would
not have embarrassed Kropotkin, although he was not a believer,
and not just a preacher either, but a revolutionary. After the
revolution, he writes:

> 'We will set to work to demolish the last vestiges of
> middle-class rule: its morality drawn from account-
> books, its "debit and credit" philosophy, its "mine and
> yours" institutions.'

As for the other issue in respect of which Kropotkin draws a
parallel between collectivism and capitalist democracy, that of
'parliamentarianism', it might be felt that he is grossly unfair to
proponents of the latter. After all, it is true that the degree of fraud
in what we call representative democracy is commensurate to the
degree in which citizens may be said to have a say in choosing
their representatives. And it is also true that the quantitative
differences between one-party totalitarian States and multi-party
States with substantial civic rights - free elections, equality before

the law (in theory, at any rate), freedom of the press, and so forth; things we rightly value - may be so great as almost to amount to a qualitative difference. But even taking into account the advances in capitalist democracy (notably votes for women and the development of social welfare systems) since the time he was writing, Kropotkin's radical criticism of 'parliamentary democracy' is still valid. One hundred years ago, he maintained that representative government had already proved its impotence 'to discharge all the functions we have sought to assign to it.' Which was not in the least surprising to him, since he was conscious of 'the absurdity of naming a few men and saying to them, "Make laws regulating all our spheres of activity, although not one of you knows anything about them!"'

Capitalism and parliamentarianism, he considered, enjoy a mutually beneficent symbiosis, and both systems operate in the interests of the middle classes. (Of his time, of course: it is anything but clear what we mean by that term nowadays.) One cannot fault his succinct description of the historical development of representative government; but it is more important to see that in essence the same reality still obtains:

> 'Built up by the middle classes to hold their own
> against royalty, sanctioning, and, at the same time
> strengthening, their sway over the workers,
> parliamentary rule is pre-eminently a middle-class
> rule.'

Similarly, he writes:

> 'A society founded on serfdom is in keeping with
> absolute monarchy; a society based on the wage
> system and the exploitation of the masses by the
> capitalists finds its political expression in
> parliamentarianism.'

Such rhetoric has gone quite out of fashion, of course, particularly in what used to be thought of as the workers' party; but it is none the less true for that. Kropotkin goes on to speak of forms of administration appropriate to the kind of society for which he was campaigning:

'But a free society, regaining possession of the common inheritance, must seek, in free groups and free federations of groups, a new organisation, in harmony with the new economic phase of history.'

Kropotkin's fears that the anti-revolutionary Socialists' project of gaining power through the ballot box would result in the bourgeoisification of the political leaders of the workers have been amply borne out by history. Look where you will, the record shows that whatever the proclaimed intentions of parliament-centred Socialist parties when in opposition, in office they ineluctably act primarily as the agents of the capitalists.

Moreover, 'taking power' in what is, constitutionally speaking, the nation's sovereign institution, invariably induces in the victors the assumption that they have won the right to take the final decisions on behalf of the nation, despite the fact that the capitalist system ensures that, inasmuch as the measures pushed through parliament are anti-pathetic to capitalists, those decision-making powers are largely illusory. Even when in opposition (and perhaps as far from power as Labour was when led by Michael Foot), with respect to their own movement, the leaders of the parliamentary party mentally arrogate all political power to themselves. This has been demonstrated innumerable times in the history of the Labour Party, but never more explicitly than by the spat during Foot's leadership over Peter Tatchell's talk of the need for extra-parliamentary action to defeat Thatcherism. And this ridiculous assumption that a *Socialist* movement can differentiate between *political* power (to be accepted by every supporter as the province of the party politicians) and *industrial labour* power (in which it is conceded that the workers' union leaders have primary - though not ultimate - rights of decision-making) lies behind almost every significant rupture in the solidarity of the Labour Movement. It also means that both wings of the movement have usually been fighting with one hand tied behind their backs. Truly, the case against parliamentarianism from a Socialist (and indeed from a plain democratic) point of view is infinitely more damning than that presented in his 1961 book, *Parliamentary Socialism*, by Ralph Miliband, who naturally failed to see that such radical strictures as those made by Kropotkin applied equally to 'true Marxist' parties.

If Kropotkin's vision was of a more utterly transformed

society than most 'utopias', he was only one of hundreds of nineteenth-century Socialist intelligentsia who dared to dream, who - unlike normal well-to-do people of his time, who (like Julian West's contemporaries in Bellamy's fictional utopia) were capable of going about their business with eyes averted from that nether world which underpinned and indeed made possible their own - were inwardly compelled to contemplate the life of the masses and yearned to make it better. And far from being impractical dreamers, these men and women were, certainly from a sociological point of view, the best-informed people in their society. The 'Tina' sneers of 'utopianism' are turned back on the mockers when Kropotkin writes in *The Conquest of Bread*:

> 'It has always been the middle-class idea to harangue about "great principles" - great lies rather! The idea of the people will be to provide bread for all. And while middle-class citizens, and workmen infested with middle-class ideas admire their own rhetoric in the "Talking Shops", and "practical people" are engaged in endless discussions on forms of government, we, the "Utopian dreamers" - we shall have to consider the question of daily bread...and...with this watchword of *Bread for All* the Revolution will triumph.'

His words carry a mental health warning for constitution-mongers, even those of the more altruistic variety, like Charter 88ists, who look to constitutional formulas for the salvation of society.

And remember those words of Kolakowski's: '*The existence of a utopia as a utopia is the necessary prerequisite for its eventually ceasing to be a utopia.*' All progress starts inside people's heads. And yes, 'bread for all', 'homes for all', 'worthwhile jobs for all' - even such modest demands are 'utopian' whenever and wherever they are not statements of an established social situation, and whenever and wherever it is not universally held to be absolutely unthinkable that it should be otherwise. Or that such things are any more than what we owe to one another - these things and everything else implied by the idea of living together and accepting one another as equals.

Having such utopias in our heads - and being resolved to do whatever we can to manifest them - is not a denial of realities. Of course, it is no good taking the attitude of the proverbial hayseed who upon being asked the way by a stranger replied, 'Well I wouldn't start from here if I were you.' But facing up to reality is not the same thing as surrendering to it. Those who are serious advocates of Socialism cannot do other than work through whatever seem to them the least unsatisfactory organisations or institutions already in being, while exerting what pressure they can to push them in the desired directions and to change them in the desired ways when the opportunity arises, until the time seems ripe to replace them with something better.

Which is why, while organisational forms more serviceable to the furtherance of Socialist objectives are gestating, British Socialists who have not opted out have to use the Labour Movement (both its political and its industrial wings) and the established institutions of so-called 'representative democracy' - but without illusions (which amongst other things means tactical voting to try to keep out the worst candidates up for election, not childish ideas of party loyalty) and without giving up their dreams. Heirs to the noble aspirations of nineteenth-century forerunners, Socialists living in the twilight of the twentieth century bear the burden of having been witness to the repeated rape of Socialist ideals, rape committed most traumatically of all not by strangers or sworn enemies but by family members claiming to subscribe to those ideals.

The twilight Socialists have a choice between three options:

(1) acquiescing in programmes promulgated by party leaders who, at the best, may be genuinely persuaded that all they are doing is sensibly modifying Socialist tenets to match modern times, or, at the worst, may be cynically refashioning their beliefs to maximise electoral support, but who in any case are certainly not propagating Socialism as distinct from social reform;

(2) quiescing, i.e. turning their backs on the struggle;

(3) fighting on to reignite, regenerate, re-propagate those brave ideals dreamed up by the utopian heralds of a new society.

SOURCES AND SELECT BIBLIOGRAPHY

(An asterisk indicates that a work has been cited in the text and that the author's name is to be found in the Index. Newspapers and periodicals cited also appear in the Index. Other works listed here have either been consulted during the writing of this essay or have contributed to it by being in my mind.)

FACT OR FACTION?

Paul Addison, *Churchill on the Home Front 1900-1955* (Cape 1992)

Paul Addison, **The Road to 1945: British Politics and the Second World War* (Cape 1975)

Stephen E. Ambrose, **Rise to Globalism: American Foreign Policy, 1938-1980* (Penguin 1980)

Leopold Amery, **The Conservative Future: An Outline of Policy (Conservative Political Centre* ?1945 - in Buck, q.v.)

Evelyn Anderson, *Hammer of Anvil: The Story of the German Working-Class Movement* (Gollancz 1945)

Anonymous, **How Labour Governed, 1945-1951* (Syndicalist Workers' Federation n.d. ?1957)

Paul Avrich, *Kronstadt 1921* (Princeton 1970)

Paul Avrich, *The Russian Anarchists* (Princeton 1971)

C.R. Attlee, *As It Happened* (Heinemann 1954)

C.R. Attlee, **The Labour Party in Perspective* (Gollancz 1937)

Walter Bagehot, **The English Constitution* (1867, 2nd edn. 1872)

Joel Barnett, **Inside the Treasury* (Deutsch 1982)

C.J. Bartlett, **A History of Postwar Britain, 1945-74* (Longman 1977)

Samuel H. Beer, **Modern British Politics: A Study of Parties and Pressure Groups* (Faber 1965)

Thomas Bell, **Pioneering Days* (Lawrence & Wishart 1941 - extract from Coates and Topham, q.v.)

Tony Benn, *Arguments for Democracy* (Cape 1981)

Tony Benn, *Arguments for Socialism* (Cape 1979)

Tony Benn, five volumes of diaries, 1963-1990

William Beveridge, **Full Employment in a Free Society* (1944)

William Beveridge, **Social Insurance and Allied Services* (1942)

Robert Blake, **The Conservative Party from Peel to Thatcher* (Fontana 1985)

Viscount Bolingbroke, **A Dissertation on Parties* (1773-4 - extracts from this and the next two titles in Buck, q.v.)

Viscount Bolingbroke, *The Idea of a Patriot King (1747-8)

Viscount Bolingbroke, *Origin of Civil Society (1754)

Nicholas Bosanquet, *'Inequalities in Health' (in Townsend and Bosanquet, q.v.)

Julius Braunthal, In Search of the Millennium (Gollancz 1945)

Julius Braunthal, *The Tragedy of Austria (Gollancz 1948)

Gerald Brenan, The Spanish Labyrinth: An Account of the Social and Political Background of the Civil War (Cambridge 1943)

Asa Briggs, *Victorian Cities (Odhams 1963, Penguin ed. 1968)

Asa Briggs, Victorian People (Odhams 1954)

J.A.C. Brown, Techniques of Persuasion: From Propaganda to Brainwashing (Penguin 1963)

Maurice Bruce, *The Coming of the Welfare State (Batsford 1961)

Philip W. Buck, *How Conservatives Think (Penguin 1975)

Tony Bunyan, The History and Practice of the Political Police in Britain (Friedmann 1976, Quartet 1977)

Edmund Burke, *An Appeal from the New to the Old Whigs (1791)

Edmund Burke, *Reflections on the Revolution in France (1790)

Edmund Burke, *Thoughts and Details on Scarcity (1795)

James Burnham, The Managerial Revolution (Penguin 1945)

Sir Alec Cairncross, *Years of Recovery: British Economic Policy 1945-51 (Methuen 1985)

James Callaghan, *Time and Chance (Collins 1987)

John Campbell, Nye Bevan: A Biography (Hodder & Stoughton 1987)

Barbara Castle, *The Castle Diaries, 1964-1976 (Macmillan 1990)

Randolph Churchill, *'Speech to the Organization of the Conservative Party, at Birmingham, 16 April 1884' (from extract in Buck, q.v.)

Tony Cliff and Donny Gluckstein, *The Labour Party: A Marxist History (Bookmarks 1988)

David Coates, *Labour in Power?: A Study of the Labour Government, 1974-9 (Longmans 1980)

Ken Coates and Tony Topham, ed., *Workers' Control (Panther 1970)

William Cobbett, *Rural Rides (1830)

Gabriel and Daniel Cohn-Bendit, Obsolete Communism: The Left-Wing Alternative (Deutsch 1968)

G.D.H. Cole, Self-Government in Industry (Bell 1917)

G.D.H. Cole and Raymond Postgate, *The Common People, 1746-1946 (Methuen 1938-56)

Lord Coleraine, *For Conservatives Only (1970 - from extract in Buck, q.v.)

Nicholas Comfort, *Brewer's Politics (Cassell 1993)

Patrick Cosgrave, *Thatcher: The First Term (Bodley Head 1985)

Ivor Crewe, *The Times Guide to the House of Commons, May 1979 (Times Books 1979)

Anthony Crosland, *The Future of Socialism (Macmillan 1956)

Anthony Crosland, *Socialism Now (Macmillan 1974)

Richard Crossman, The Diaries of a Cabinet Minister, 1964-1970 (Hamish Hamilton and Jonathan Cape 1975-77)

Richard Crossman, ed., *The God that Failed (Harper & Row 1950)

Benjamin Disraeli, *'Speech at the Banquet of the National Union of Conservative and Constitutional Associations at Crystal Palace, 24 June 1872' (from extract in Buck, q.v.)

Benjamin Disraeli, *'Vindication of the English Constitution in a letter to a noble and learned Lord' (1835 - extract from Buck, q.v.)

Milovan Djilas, The New Class: An Analysis of the Communist System (first pub. in English 1957, Allen & Unwin 1966)

Bernard Donoghue, *Prime Minister: The Conduct of Policy under Harold Wilson and James Callaghan (Cape 1987)

A.D. Elliot, *Life of Lord Goschen, 1831-1907 (1911)

Gregory Elliott, *Labourism and the English Genius: The Strange Death of Labour England? (Verso 1993)

Cecil S. Emden, The People and the Constitution (Oxford 1933)

Joe England and Brian Weekes, *'Trade Unions and the State: A Review of the Crisis' (Industrial Relations Journal, 1981 - in McCarthy, q.v.)

R.C.K. Ensor, England 1870-1914 (Oxford 1936)

Eric Estorick, *Stafford Cripps (Heinemann 1949)

Alan Freeman, The Benn Heresy (Pluto 1982)

Milton Friedman and Rose Friedman, Free to Choose: A Personal Statement (Secker & Warburg 1980)

Paul Frolich, Rosa Luxemburg (Gollancz 1940)

John Kenneth Galbraith, *The Affluent Society (Hamish Hamilton 1958)

John Kenneth Galbraith, American Capitalism: The Concept of Countervailing Power (Hamish Hamilton 1957)

John Kenneth Galbraith, *The Culture of Contentment (Sinclair-Stevenson 1992)

Henry George, *Progress and Poverty (1879)

Ian Gilmour, *Dancing with Dogma: Britain under Thatcherism (Simon & Schuster 1992)

William Ewart Gladstone, *'Is the Popular Judgement in Politics more just than that of the Higher Orders? - 2' (in Goodwin, q.v.)

Howard Glennerster, *'Education and Inequality' (in Townsend and Bosanquet, q.v.)

Michael Goodwin, ed., *Nineteenth-Century Opinion: An Anthology of extracts from the first fifty volumes of The Nineteenth Century, 1877-1901 (Penguin 1951)

Philip Guedalla, *Mr Churchill: A Portrait (Hodder & Stoughton 1941)

Marquis of Halifax, *The Character of a Trimmer (1699 - extract from Buck, q.v.)

J.E.D. Hall, *Labour's First Year (Penguin 1947)

A.H. Halsey, *Change in British Society (Oxford 1978)

Michael Harrington, *The Other America: Poverty in the United States* (Macmillan, New York, 1962; Penguin 1963)

Michael Hatfield, *The House the Left Built* (1978)

F.A. Hayek, *The Road to Serfdom* (Routledge 1944)

Denis Healey, *The Time of My Life* (Michael Joseph 1989)

Paddy Hillyard and Janie Percy-Smith, *The Coercive State: The Decline of Democracy in Britain* (Fontana 1988)

Quintin Hogg, *The Case for Conservatism* (Penguin 1947)

Stuart Holland, *The Socialist Challenge* (Quartet 1975)

Martin Holmes, *The Labour Government, 1974-79: Political Aims and Economic Reality* (Macmillan 1985)

Eric Hopkins, *The Rise and Decline of the English Working Classes 1918-1990: A Social History* (Weidenfeld & Nicolson 1991)

Peter d'A. Jones, *The Consumer Society: A History of American Capitalism* (Penguin 1965)

Peter d'A. Jones, *An Economic History of the United States since 1783* (Routledge & Kegan Paul 1956)

James Avery Joyce, *The War Machine* (Quartet 1980, Hamlyn 1981)

Dennis Kavanagh, *Thatcherism and British Politics: The End of Consensus?* (Oxford 1987, 2nd ed. 1990)

J.C. Kincaid, *Poverty and Equality in Britain: A Study of Social Security and Taxation* (Penguin 1973)

Leszek Kolakowski, *Marxism and Beyond: On Historical Understanding and Individual Responsibility* (Pall Mall 1969)

Peter Kropotkin, *The Conquest of Bread* (1892)

Peter Kropotkin, *Fields, Factories and Workshops* (1898)

Peter Kropotkin, *The Great French Revolution* (1909)

Peter Kropotkin, *Memoirs of a Revolutionist* (1899)

Peter Kropotkin, *Mutual Aid: A Factor of Evolution* (1902)

Nigel Lawson, *The New Conservatism* (Centre for Policy Studies 1980)

William Edward Hartpole Lecky, *Democracy and Liberty* (1896 - extract from Buck, q.v.)

Bernard Levin, *The Pendulum Years: Britain and the Sixties* (Cape 1970)

T.O. Lloyd, *Empire to Welfare State: English History 1906-1976* (Oxford 1979)

Anatoly Marchenko, *My Testimony* (Pall Mall 1969; Penguin 1971)

Roy Lewis and Angus Maude, *The English Middle Classes* (Penguin 1953)

W.E.J. McCarthy, ed., *Trade Unions* (Penguin 1972, 2nd ed. 1985)

Harold Macmillan, *The Middle Way* (1938 - extract from Buck, q.v.)

Harold Macmillan, *Winds of Change, 1914-1939* (Macmillan 1966)

Tom Mann, *Memoirs* (1923, Macgibbon & Kee 1967)

Herbert Marcuse, *Soviet Marxism: A Critical Analysis* (Routledge & Kegan Paul 1958)

Herbert Marcuse, *One-Dimensional Man* (Routledge & Kegan Paul 1964)

Dennis Marsden, *'Politicians, Equality and Comprehensives' (in Townsend and Bosanquet, q.v.)

Ralph Miliband, **Parliamentary Socialism: A Study in the Politics of Labour* (Allen & Unwin 1961)

Ralph Miliband, *The State in Capitalist Society* (Weidenfeld & Nicolson 1969)

John Stuart Mill, **Considerations on Representative Government* (1861)

C. Wright Mills, *The Marxists* (Dell, U.S.A., 1962; Penguin 1963)

Kenneth O. Morgan, **Labour in Power* (Oxford 1984)

Kenneth O. Morgan, *Rebirth of a Nation: Wales 1880-1980* (Oxford & University of Wales 1982)

Herbert Morrison, *'Economic Socialisation' (in Tracey, q.v.)

Herbert Morrison, **Socialisation and Transport* (Constable 1933)

Peter Nettl, *Rosa Luxemburg* (Oxford 1966)

A.R. Orage, ed., *National Guilds: An Inquiry into the Wage System and the Way Out* (Bell 1914)

George Orwell, **Down and Out in Paris and London* (Gollancz 1933)

George Orwell, *Homage to Catalonia* (Secker and Warburg 1938)

George Orwell, **The Road to Wigan Pier* (Gollancz 1937)

Thomas Paine, **The Rights of Man* (1791-92)

Jenny Pearce, *Under the Eagle: U.S. Intervention in Central America and the Caribbean* (Latin America Bureau 1981)

Sir Robert Peel, *'Address to the Electors of the Borough of Tamworth' (1834 - extract from Buck, q.v.)

Henry Pelling, **A History of British Trade Unionism* (Penguin (1963)

Henry Pelling, *Origins of the Labour Party, 1880-1900* (Oxford (1965)

Harold Perkin, **The Origins of Modern English Society, 1780-1880* (Routledge & Kegan Paul 1969)

Richard Pipes, **The Russian Revolution, 1899-1919* (Fontana 1992)

K.R. Popper, *The Open Society and Its Enemies* (Routledge & Kegan Paul 1945, revised fifth edition 1966)

J.B. Priestley, **Letter to a Returning Serviceman* (Home & Van Thal 1945)

Joseph G. Rayback, *A History of American Labor* (The Free Press, New York, 1966)

Patrick Renshaw, *The Wobblies: The Story of Syndicalism in the United States* (Eyre & Spottiswoode 1967)

W.G. Runciman, *Relative Deprivation and Social Justice: A Study of Attitudes to Social Inequality in Twentieth-Century England* (Routledge & Kegan Paul 1966; Penguin 1972)

Marquis of Salisbury, *articles from the *Quarterly Review*, 1860-1865 (from extracts in Buck, q.v.)

Anthony Sampson, **The Arms Bazaar* (Hodder & Stoughton 1978)

Victor Serge, *Destiny of a Revolution* (French edition ?1937, English translation published by Hutchinson n.d.)

Victor Serge, *Memoirs of a Revolutionary* 1901-1941 (translated from the French by Peter Sedgwick, Oxford 1963)

Victor Serge, *Year One of the Russian Revolution* (first published in France; Peter Sedgwick translation, Allen Lane 1972)

Emmanuel Shinwell, **Conflict without Malice* (Odhams 1955)

Alan Sked and Chris Cook, **Post-War Britain: A Political History* (Penguin 1979)

Philip Snowden, **Socialism and Syndicalism* (Collins 1913)

I.N. Steinberg, *In the Workshop of the Revolution* (Gollancz 1955)

John Stevenson and Chris Cook, *The Slump: Society and Politics During the Depression* (Cape 1978)

Julian Symons, *The General Strike* (Cresset 1957)

R.H. Tawney, **The Acquisitive Society* (Bell 1921)

R.H. Tawney, *Equality* (Allen & Unwin 1931)

A.J.P. Taylor, **English History, 1914-1945* (Oxford 1965)

E.P. Thompson, **The Making of the English Working Class* (Gollancz 1963, Penguin revised ed. 1968)

Leonard Tivey, **Nationalization in British Industry* (Cape 1966, revised ed. 1973)

Alexis de Tocqueville, **Democracy in America* (1835)

Peter Townsend and Nicholas Bosanquet, ed., **Labour and Inequality* (Fabian Society 1972)

Herbert Tracey, ed., **The British Labour Party* (Caxton 1948)

Beatrice Webb, **Diaries* (ed. M.I. Cole, Longman 1952 and 1956)

Sidney and Beatrice Webb, **A Constitution for the Socialist Commonwealth of Great Britain* (Longman 1920)

Sidney and Beatrice Webb, **Soviet Communism: A New Civilisation* (Longmans 1935, 3rd ed. 1944)

K.W. Wedderburn, **'The New Politics of Labour Law'* (University of Durham Industrial Relations Group, 1983 - in McCarthy, q.v.)

John Westergaard and Henrietta Resler, **Class in a Capitalist Society: A Study of Contemporary Britain* (Heinemann 1975, Penguin 1976)

Eirene White, **Workers' Control?* (Fabian Society Tract 1951 - extract from Coates and Topham, q.v.)

R.J. White, **The Conservative Tradition* (Adam & Charles Black 1950 - from extract in Buck, q.v.)

Phillip Whitehead, **The Writing on the Wall: Britain in the Seventies* (Michael Joseph and Channel 4, 1985)

Harold Wilson, **Final Term: The Labour Government, 1974-6* (Weidenfeld & Nicolson and Michael Joseph 1979)

George Woodcock and Ivan Avakumovic, *The Anarchist Prince: A Biographical Study of Peter Kropotkin* (Boardman 1950)

William Woods, **Poland: Eagle in the East* (Deutsch 1969)

E.L. Woodward, *The Age of Reform 1815-1870* (Oxford 1938)

FICTION?

Henry Adams, *Democracy* (1880)
Lewis Carroll, *Alice's Adventures in Wonderland* (1865)
Lewis Carroll, *Through the Looking-Glass and What Alice Found There* (1871)
Benjamin Disraeli, *Coningsby, or The New Generation* (1844)
Benjamin Disraeli, *Sybil, or The Two Nations* (1845)
Benjamin Disraeli, *Tancred, or The New Crusade* (1847)
John Dos Passos, *U.S.A.* (Constable 1938, Penguin 1966)
George Gissing, *The Nether World* (1889)
Walter Greenwood, *Love on the Dole* (Cape 1933)
John Mortimer, *Paradise Postponed* (Viking 1985)
Ben Traven, *The Death Ship* (1926)
Robert Tressell, *The Ragged Trousered Philanthropists* (abridged edition Grant Richards 1914, first full edition Lawrence & Wishart 1955, Panther 1965)
Anthony Trollope, *The Way We Live Now* (1875)
Vasilis Vassilikos, *Z (Macdonald 1969, Sphere 1970)

UTOPIAS

Robert Ardrey, *World's Beginning* (Hamish Hamilton 1945)
Edward Bellamy, *Looking Backward, 2000-1887* (1888)
Jack London, *The Iron Heel* (1907)
William Morris, *The Dream of John Ball* (1888)
William Morris, *News from Nowhere* (1891)

DYSTOPIAS

Aldous Huxley, *Brave New World* (Chatto & Windus 1932)
George Orwell, *Animal Farm: A Fairy Story* (Secker & Warburg 1945)
George Orwell, *Nineteen Eighty-Four* (Secker & Warburg 1949)
Michael Young, *The Rise of the Meritocracy: An Essay on Education and Equality* (Thames & Hudson 1958)
Yevgeny Zamyatin, *We* (first English language edition 1924; Cape, in translation by Bernard Guilbert Guerney, 1970)

Thanks for the material substance of this lamentation are due to the many people - scholars, social campaigners, journalists, or whatever - who have mined it, and to those Socialists who have striven to keep the faith and to propagate it. Thanks are also due to the politicians who have laboured so hard and so profitably to prove my case. To those who rightly conclude that 'we woz robbed', everything else is due.

INDEX

[Post-World-War-II governments are indexed under the names of their prime ministers, with the page references to matters primarily to do with their administrations following the other references.]

256, 279, 290 *ff.*, 303 *ff.*, 324, 326,
341, 343, 348, 359-52, 367, 370-1,
429, 439-40
Woodcock, George, 250
Woods, William, 104
Woollacott, Martin, 11
workers' control, 380-1, 385-6, 387 *ff.*
  See also industrial democracy
World at One, 189
World Bank, 10
World Development Movement, 15
World Trade Organisation, 14
Wright, Richard, 389
Young, Jimmy, 363
Young, Michael, 455
Young England, 58-9, 71
Zaire, 13, 199
Zambia, 427
Zia ul-Haq, Mohammed, 168
Zimbabwe. *See* Rhodesia